ACCLAIM FOR *IDA: A SWORD AMONG LIONS*

Winner of the John Hope Franklin Research Center Book Award

"*Ida: A Sword Among Lions* is more than brilliant; it is necessary. I can't think of a biography that throws more light on the history of gender, race, and class discord in the United States. Six decades of Ida B. Wells's life constitute a riveting, definitive narrative on a dark and bruising history. In Paula Giddings, this vibrant woman has found a biographer equal to her prowess."

—Toni Morrison

"Historians will profit from the research [Giddings] has compiled."

—*Wall Street Journal*

"Compelling. . . . Ida B. Wells may be the most courageous woman most of us have never heard of."

—*New York Post*

"A groundbreaking biography gives this warrior her due."

—*O Magazine*

"A sweeping and timely biographical narrative about Ida B. Wells . . . a paragon of American history."

—*Ebony*

"A hearty thumbs-up for this powerful retelling of her life."

—*Essence*

"Paula J. Giddings' *Ida: A Sword Among Lions* (Amistad) is a worthy biography of the vibrant crusader who led the nation's first campaign against lynching."

—*Vogue*

"Magisterial."

—*Publishers Weekly*

"With meticulous research, including Wells's own diary, Giddings brings to life one of the most fascinating women in American history, giving readers a real feel for the texture and context of Wells's life."

—*Booklist* (starred review)

"Ida B. Wells was an inspired journalist, an uncompromising civil libertarian, and a woman far ahead of her patriarchal times—a 'difficult' woman. Paula Giddings's monumental achievement restores this extraordinary contrarian to her place as one of the grand pace-setters of American social justice and female empowerment."

—David Levering Lewis,
Pulitzer Prize–winning biographer of W. E. B. Du Bois

"Paula Giddings writes so meticulously. The care and depth of her research became evident only after I finished reading *Ida: A Sword Among Lions*. Paula Giddings has brought another great American out of the mist of history. We are saddened that we did not know Ida B. Wells earlier, but happy to know that she was born here and worked here to make our country a better place for all Americans."

—Maya Angelou

"Paula Giddings's *Ida* is a treasure. Ida B. Wells has waited a century for someone to tell the truth of her life. Giddings sets the record straight about the horrors of lynching and the valiant campaign Wells inspired and led against this American scourge. Surely, with Giddings's exquisitely written, exhaustively investigated, and brilliantly rendered biography, Ida's soul will rest in peace."

—Darlene Clark Hine, editor of *Black Women in America*
and Board of Trustees Professor of African American Studies
and Professor of History, Northwestern University

IDA

A Sword Among Lions

IDA

A Sword Among Lions

IDA B. WELLS AND THE
CAMPAIGN AGAINST LYNCHING

PAULA J. GIDDINGS

Amistad
An Imprint of HarperCollinsPublishers

First Amistad paperback edition published 2009.

Designed by Laura Kaeppel

Library of Congress Cataloging-in-Publication Data has been applied for.

ISBN 978-0-06-079736-2

HB 05.01.2019

To my mother,
Virginia Iola Giddings,
always . . .

and to the late
Alfreda M. Duster,
a daughter who kept the memory
of Ida B. Wells alive

My soul is among lions;
and I lie even among them
that are set on fire,
even the sons of men,
whose teeth are spears and arrows,
and their tongue a sharp sword.

—Psalm 57:4

Contents

Acknowledgments

Like many others who surrounded her, I was deeply inspired by the late Alfreda M. Duster, who encouraged me to write this biography of her mother and assisted my efforts even while she was hospitalized by a stroke. Her children, Benjamin C. Duster, Donald L. Duster, Troy S. Duster, and Alfreda Duster Ferrell, provided invaluable information, support, friendship—and patience—while I worked on this manuscript.

Without the meticulous research of Dr. Otis Maxwell, who is also a descendant of the Wells family, I would not have had access to much of the family's genealogical information and photographs. His support and companionship were also welcome when we explored many dusty archives together in Mississippi and Memphis.

Special thanks to Charles F. Harris, a publisher, and a friend of many years, whose confidence in me and in this project is a major reason it has come to fruition. Writers need good and caring neighbors like Sandra Kelley; and loving friends who keep the faith, tolerate periods of inattention, and who provide consolation and insight. I thank Leon Dash, Jewell Jackson McCabe, David Levering Lewis, and Beverly Guy-Sheftall for being my constant stars.

I have also been fortunate to have had a brilliant array of friends and colleagues who read the manuscript in various stages and/or helped me understand what needed to be done. Toni Morrison—who put me on a particular path when she made the deceptively simple statement, "You know, Ida B. Wells is *important*"—did both. Beverly Guy-Sheftall, Milly Hawk Daniel, David Levering Lewis, John Hope Franklin, Gerda Lerner, Ann Firor Scott, John Bracey, Sidney Offit, Kevin Quashie, and Clay Goss made important contributions at different stages of the manuscript. I also benefited greatly from Joan Benham's editorial guidance. Michael Anderson's expert eye and sage advice were invaluable.

Many people provided important aspects of my research: Mary Helen Washington, Houston Baker, Patricia LaPointe, Hubert McAlexander, Linda Seidman, Charles Cooney, Erik Ludwig, Helen Hwang, Jill Petty, Sara Duckworth, Kenneth Janken, William Greaves, Deborah Willis, Christina Morgan, A'Lelia Bundles, Jewell Jackson McCabe, Wilson Moses, Sherrill Redmon, and Kimberle Crenshaw.

Welcome institutional support for this book includes the National Humanities Center in Research Triangle Park, where I did most of my research; the Guggenheim Foundation; and support in various forms from colleagues and administrators at Rutgers, Duke, and Princeton Universities; and Spelman and Smith Colleges.

Last but not least, I thank my literary agent, Lynn Nesbit; and especially my editor, Dawn Davis, who stood by Ida when she needed it most.

IDA

A Sword Among Lions

INTRODUCTION

Sword Among Lions

Ida B. Wells

(1862–1931)

Ida B. Wells was in New York City when she heard the terrible news. Back home in Memphis, the office of her newspaper, the *Free Speech*, had been gutted; J. L. Fleming, her partner and co-owner, had been run out of the city upon the threat of being hanged and castrated; and a former owner of the paper, Reverend Taylor Nightingale, had been pistol-whipped and forced to recant the words of the May 1892 editorial that had detonated the violent response in Memphis. Ida learned that she herself had been threatened with lynching. She was receiving urgent telegrams telling her that whites were posted at the railway station waiting for her return. Ida did not return. Going home would only mean more bloodshed, she decided, after hearing that black men had vowed to protect her.

The southern city had been in an unsettled state since March, when three black men, including a close friend of Wells's, had been lynched, and she had urged thousands of black Memphians to leave a city that would not give them justice. Her May editorial, published just before a long-planned trip East, was a response to another paper's assertion that the spate of recent lynchings in the South had been triggered by the increasing occurrences of rape perpetrated by black men upon white women. In her riposte,

Wells challenged the charge, and insinuated that cries of rape often followed the discovery of consensual relationships between black men and white women. Wells's short editorial had been written hastily, but not without forethought. Since the Memphis murders, she had begun investigating lynchings by interviewing eyewitnesses and relatives of the victims, and had analyzed the *Chicago Tribune's* annual lynching statistics, which included the putative motives for them.

In June of 1892, Wells, now an exile, wrote a long exposé for the *New York Age,* a black weekly with a substantial white readership. Later published as a pamphlet, *Southern Horrors,* it was the first study of lynching and Wells's initial attempt to show how this particular form of racial violence said more about the cultural failings of the white South than of blacks; how not only race, but attitudes toward women and sexuality, instigated it; and that lynching represented the very heart, the Rosetta Stone, of America's troubled relationship with race. Wells believed that lynching was the central issue that defined blacks as the nation lurched toward the twentieth century, and one that demanded new strategies that included self-defense and civil disobedience. Her determination to follow the logic of lynching into the modern age also demanded that she, in advance of most of her peers, male and female, shed the confines of Victorian attitudes.

The origin of the term "lynching," according to James E. Cutler, author of *Lynch-Law* (1905), the first scholarly text on the subject, is attributed to Charles Lynch, a Virginia justice of the peace (and brother of the founder of Lynchburg). Lynch established informal, extra-legal citizen juries during the Revolutionary War years when official courts were few and traveling to them through British-occupied territories was perilous. The common sentence for those found guilty—mostly horse thieves and Tories—was thirty-nine lashes with a whip. By the 1830s, when southern abolitionism reached its height, lynching was associated more with those who threatened the slave order. Following the Civil War, the practice became more murderous with the bloody struggle for power among northern federalists, Confederates, and newly enfranchised black men.

However, it wasn't until 1886, when increasing numbers of rural blacks migrated to southern cities, that the number of African Americans lynched exceeded that of whites: a trend that continued even as blacks became increasingly disenfranchised; had largely eschewed their political aspirations in favor of building institutions, acquiring wealth, and eliminating ignorance; and ex-Confederates had regained control of their state governments. Both

Wells and Cutler cited what were surely conservative estimates by the *Chicago Tribune*, which reported that 728 persons were lynched between 1882 and 1891, the majority of them African American men. The statistics further showed that less than a third had been accused of rape, much less guilty of it. By the end of 1892, the year of the Memphis lynchings and Wells's forced exile, the annual number of lynchings reached a new peak of 241.

IDA B. WELLS *was a biographer's dream,* I thought when I first began researching her life for my first book, *When and Where I Enter,* a history of black women's activism. Even before it was completed, Wells managed to inhabit my imagination, where she promptly began demanding a book of her own. "Fine," I said with the leisurely naïveté of a first-time biographer, who thought that the task would be demanding but not daunting. In addition to the research I had already done on African American women, I would familiarize myself with the historical contexts that informed Ida Wells's life from her birth in 1862 to slave parents in Holly Springs, Mississippi, to her death sixty-eight years later in Chicago. I would concentrate on the literature concerning lynching, particularly in the New South and seamlessly incorporate it into Wells's articles and her autobiography, *Crusade for Justice.* I knew that I would also benefit from the extraordinary scholarship on black women that has been published during the last several decades. But long before the task was completed, reality set in.

Copies of Wells's newspaper, the *Free Speech,* no longer exist; I would have to rely on quotes that appeared in other papers. Her autobiography, begun in 1928, fewer than three years before her death, was indispensable, yet there are important events missing from it and others are merely alluded to with little explanation. The invaluable text appears hurriedly written, much like her early antilynching editorial, but, in this instance, there was not time to flesh it out. In some ways it was as if Wells was daring someone else to fill in the blanks.

The biggest "blank" was her own persona. Although Wells is a frank writer who leaves things out rather than tell an untruth, there is little to suggest what was at the core of a woman—a college-educated black woman with Victorian values, no less—who had the imprudent courage to stand up to southern lynchers in 1892. Fortunately, there is a fragment of a diary she kept between December of 1885 and April of 1887, when Wells was in her twenties. The journal provides a window into the mind of a highly self-conscious, religious—and highly flirtatious—young woman who constantly struggled with her "besetting sin," as she called the ever-present anger that churned within. Wells had been orphaned at the age of sixteen, when both of her parents succumbed to yellow fever, and throughout the remainder of her life, she struggled to turn the negative emotions of abandonment into a righteous determination to reform herself and the society that had forsaken her race.

The diary also appears to be the only eyewitness account of the everyday lives of southern, reform-minded African American women and men who, one generation removed from slavery, had managed to become schoolteachers, lawyers, newspaper editors, tradesmen, business owners, ministers, missionaries, and an array of political actors unacknowledged by published histories of their time and place. How Wells shaped, and was shaped by, the community she inhabited is important for understanding the full measure of her achievements and failures. It is a dimension largely missing in other excellent studies about her and, indeed, about many African American figures who are primarily viewed through their relationships with white elites.

Completing the picture required researching newspaper accounts from the white daily press and, especially, the black weeklies that, while lacking the documented evidence of scholarly studies, provided visceral evidence of what Wells and her contemporaries were seeing, reading, and, above all, feeling. Wells felt compelled to quote verbatim newspaper passages; I found myself doing the same in this biography, and for the same reason. Without them, her claims about the nature and depth of sentiment toward African Americans seem so far-fetched that they could be easily dismissed.

While informed by the impressive—and prolific—literature on lynching, this biography is not a history of the practice, nor an explication of the conclusions drawn by scholars. Rather, it looks at lynching as Wells saw it within the context of her own life, times, and writings, as it migrated from the rural backwoods to the cities; from lone midnight murders to communal daylight spectacles in which bodies were dismembered and organs kept or sold as souvenirs; from southern cities to northern ones where lynchings took the form of "legal" executions by racist justice systems and mob-led riots that took multiple lives, burned down entire communities, and deprived blacks of their property and livelihoods.

Although Wells's years in the South, climaxed by the dramatic events that led to her exile, could be a book in itself, I soon realized that that period was closer to the beginning of her life as an activist than its end. After being driven from Memphis, she was involved in and/or wrote about national politics and reform issues regarding labor; women (black and white) and

African Americans. Wells traveled, twice, to the British Isles, crisscrossed the country from New York to California, and finally settled in Chicago, where she married a like-minded lawyer and newspaper editor, Ferdinand L. Barnett, bore four children, and balanced motherhood and activism with mixed success. During this period, she was a catalyst for the creation of the first national black women's organization, the National Association of Colored Women (NACW); she founded a black settlement house; she was a member of the NAACP's "founding forty"; and worked with Hull House's Jane Addams. Wells canvassed the state of Illinois to promote women's suffrage and campaigned to elect white women candidates for office. She also founded the first black women's suffrage organization in Chicago, which was instrumental in the election of the city's first black alderman in 1915.

During the World War I years, Wells defied the threats of military intelligence agencies and worked with Marcus Garvey, the Boston editor Monroe Trotter, and the hairdressing magnate and philanthropist Madam C. J. Walker. In the 1920s, Ida, with the help of black women's organizations, including her own Ida B. Wells Club, rallied black Chicagoans to support A. Philip Randolph's Brotherhood of Sleeping Car Porters and Maids when the fledgling union was an anomaly to many blacks who benefited, institutionally and personally, from the largesse of the Chicago-based Pullman Company. In 1930, a year before her death, Wells ran as an independent for an Illinois state senate seat during a time when the gangster Al Capone was filling political machine coffers and candidates were being assassinated.

While I knew that Wells-Barnett's life spanned some of the most tumultuous and defining periods in American history, I was surprised by how much of that history had to be retold because it took on a new meaning and significance when viewed through the eyes of a progressive reformer with Wells-Barnett's passions and concerns. This first became evident when I read a two-line entry in a daybook she kept. In January of 1930, Wells-Barnett wrote that she and her oldest daughter braved Chicago's icy winds to attend a local Negro History Week meeting. The topic for discussion was a book by Carter G. Woodson, the black Harvard-educated "father of African American history" who conceived the idea of setting aside the week every year to focus on the contributions of people of African descent. Wells-Barnett left the meeting, she noted, disappointed that Woodson's book had failed to mention her own contributions to the campaign against lynching.

To exclude Wells from the movement that she had created was a stunning omission, even when taking into consideration the biases concerning women. How could she have been overlooked? Her campaign was amply covered in both the white and black press and was supported, as well as opposed, by whites, blacks, and influential Britons, who had organized the London Anti-Lynching Committee in the wake of Wells's travels abroad. Her movement was instrumental in making lynching a national issue. Several states in both the north and south passed antilynching laws; Congress attempted to pass federal antilynching legislation; and after 1892, the number of lynchings never again reached the threshold that had been recorded that year. Moreover, Woodson knew Wells-Barnett. In 1915, the year he organized the Association for the Study of Negro Life and History while still a student at the University of Chicago, she had invited him to speak before the Negro Fellowship League—the settlement house that she had founded.

The daybook entry led me to look at other books written by those with whom Ida had had meaningful encounters during the course of her life and activism: W. E. B. Du Bois; Booker T. Washington; Mary Church Terrell, the first president of the National Association of Colored Women (NACW) who had known Wells since they had met in Memphis; Jane Addams; and Frances Willard, the president of the Women's Christian Temperance Union (WCTU), headquartered in Chicago, among others. Wells-Barnett's work is not acknowledged in them. Even books about lynching published in the 1920s and 1930s, including Walter White's *Rope and Faggot* and Arthur Raper's *The Tragedy of Lynching*—two widely cited reference texts on the subject—failed to mention Wells. Her name does appear, if cursorily, in James Cutler's *Lynch-Law*. Interestingly, Cutler, an instructor at Wellesley College and Yale University, was also a military intelligence officer during World War I when Wells, characterized as a dangerous and well-known "race agitator," was the subject of War Department surveillance. Finally, several NAACP documents about the history of the antilynching effort, including those published during her lifetime, gave her own role short shrift if any at all.

The oversights could be explained, in part, by her reputation as a "difficult" woman. Wells was certainly that, even when taking into account the double standard applied to assertive, independent women. During the latter period of her life, Wells was more militant than all of the reform figures mentioned above and publicly crossed swords with them. On the other hand, history books are filled with the names of combative and highly individualistic people. And despite her reputation as an isolated—if courageous—crank, there is ample evidence that Wells was not petulant in the sense that she refused to cooperate with those whom she personally disagreed with over matters that benefited the race.

I concluded that Wells's legacy was the victim of those same progressive movements of which she was a part. Predominantly white reform organizations could never subscribe to her views about race; those with race-based agendas, such as the NAACP, the NACW, and to a lesser extent the Urban League, could not accommodate her views regarding leadership and class. The ideological differences were most clear in Wells-Barnett's relationship with the NAACP during the early years after its founding in 1910, when it was struggling to gain legitimacy within the black community. Although later responsible for remarkable achievements, it can be argued that the civil rights organization did not gain that legitimacy until it belatedly made lynching its central issue. Subsequently, the NAACP marginalized Wells-Barnett's contributions, even while it adopted her strategies and perspectives.

DESPITE ALL THAT she had seen, Ida Wells-Barnett, remarkably, never lost her faith in the nation's ability to reform, and she lived to see many victories. But crusades also exact a personal price. She died before her autobiography was completed, and for decades after her death her achievements were largely unheralded. They might have remained so but for the tireless, forty-year effort of Alfreda M. Duster, her daughter, to publish *Crusade for Justice*. It finally appeared in 1970 as one of a series of black autobiographies published under the guidance of the historian John Hope Franklin by the University of Chicago Press. For this writer, the autobiography, the first written by a black woman political activist, was an essential guide to render the full testament of a life, which like a restless ghost, seeks its rightful place in history.

Prologue

Long ago, was I weary of voices
Whose music, my heart could not win,
Long ago, was I weary of noises
That fretted my soul with their din
Long ago, was I weary of places
Where I met but the human—and sin . . .

—Verse from the "Song of the Mystic,"
by Father Abram J. Ryan,
former chaplain of the Confederacy,
quoted in the preface of the diary of Ida B. Wells

On the evening of December 28, 1885, Ida Bell Wells was back in her home of Holly Springs, Mississippi, for the first time since she had left four years before under a cloud of suspicion, grief, and slander.

Ida had arrived at 8:00 P.M. from Memphis, Tennessee, a four-hour train ride away. From the station, she proceeded to the campus of Rust University, her alma mater, founded for former slaves like herself, where she was met by James Hall, identified in the census as a laborer, and his wife, Tilla. The Halls had been assigned guardians for Ida and her five sisters and brothers after the death of her parents in 1878. During Ida's absence, the couple had been keeping an eye on the Wells family home, located near Chulahoma Street, two blocks from the courthouse in the central square.[1]

The next day, the twenty-ninth, Ida began the day early. Accompanied by the Halls, and another family guardian, Bob Miller, also a laborer, she strolled through the town where she saw many of her Holly Springs acquaintances. "How strange everything seems . . ." Ida wrote in the diary she was keeping. There had been many changes since she had left home. A number of the children she knew had grown and she scarcely recognized them. In the last four years Rust, founded in 1866 by the Freedmen's Aid Society of the Methodist Episcopal Church, had added a modern telephone and telegraph service, new laboratory equipment, and the Elizabeth Rust Home for Girls, a model home for young women, operated by the Woman's Home Missionary Society. Later the same day Ida had also gone to the cemetery to find her parents' graves, and that evening a number of old friends and classmates had come to call on her. "The day has been a trying one to me," she recorded in her diary, "seeing old enemies, visiting old scenes, recalling the most painful memories of my life." Now twenty-three, Ida was recalling a web of tragic events that, as her diary revealed, still had a perilous hold on her since she had left Holly Springs.[2]

IDA'S CHILDHOOD HAD been happy. Born in July of 1862, she was the first of eight children (one died soon after childbirth) born to James and Elizabeth Wells. Her parents were slaves at the time of her birth, and during her formative years they had made a remarkable transition as freedpersons. James was a skilled carpenter who established his own business in 1867; and Elizabeth became "a famous cook" who ran the household in which each child had assigned chores and attended Sunday school each week. When Rust was established, Elizabeth attended school alongside her children in order to learn to read and write. But Ida's "light-hearted schoolgirl days," as she later described them in her autobiography, came to a tragic halt soon after she turned sixteen in 1878. In September of that year, both of her parents, as well as her nine-month-old brother, Stanley, died in the yellow fever epidemic that had swept across the Mississippi Valley. When the disease descended on Holly Springs, Ida had been visiting her grandmother's farm some miles outside of the town. Five of her siblings who had remained at home survived.[3]

After the epidemic had subsided, members of the Masons fraternal order—in which Ida's father had attained the position of Master Mason— gathered at the Wells home to discuss caretaking arrangements and assign guardians for the children. At the end of their deliberations, it was decided that the two youngest girls in the family, Annie and Lily, aged five and two, respectively, in 1878, were to be placed with two different Mason-headed families. The boys, Alfred and George, aged twelve and eight, would be apprenticed to work for others and learn the carpentry trade—their father's occupation. One of the men eager to have the boys in his employ was a white man who anticipated that the young men might possess their father's talent. No one wanted Ida's fourteen-year-old sister, Eugenia, who was bent nearly double with what appeared to be spinal meningitis. The group decided that the crippled teenager should be sent to a "paupers" institution that had been in existence in Holly Springs at least since 1868. As for sixteen-year-old Ida, it was agreed that she was old enough to fend for herself.

As she would recall in her autobiography, Ida, who was never consulted during the deliberations, told the assembled group that their decision was unacceptable. Her parents, she said, would "turn over in their graves to have their children scattered like that." It was not as if the family didn't have means. The Wellses owned their small house near Chulahoma Street; and as James Wells, Ida's late father, lay dying he had made provisions to get $300 in cash to the children. Instead of breaking up the family, Ida insisted that her guardians help her secure a teaching position so that she could take care of her sisters and brothers—all of them—herself. The group "scoffed" at the idea of the petite teenager, still in school herself, becoming the independent head of her household—but Ida held firm. Finally, Hall and Miller advised Ida to apply for a position in one of the rural schools. Wells did so, passed the required exam, dropped out of Rust, "lengthened her dresses," and found a teaching position six miles outside of Holly Springs.[4]

But her decision had a number of unintended consequences. She became the subject of vicious gossip after being seen accepting money from a white man in the town square. Wells, still smarting from the imputation of her character more than fifty years after the incident, explained in her autobiography that the man was a visiting physician to whom her dying father had given his savings in order to pass them to the surviving children. "It was easy for that type of mind to deduce and spread the rumor that already, as young as I was, I had been heard asking white men for money and that was the reason I wanted to live . . . by myself with the children," she wrote.[5]

If Ida was burning to face down those "old enemies" whose rumors had been responsible, in part, for what she called the "darkest days" in her life, the latter part of 1885 was an ideal time to do so. In just four years, Wells, despite an education cut short at Rust, had become certified as a teacher in the Memphis public school system and been touted as an "elocutionist" in the *Fisk Herald*, a publication issued by the prestigious black liberal arts university in Nashville.[6] Even now, she was studying the part of Lady Macbeth's "sleepwalking scene" for a public reading to be held shortly in Memphis's Lyceum, a literary salon founded by black teachers. More remarkably, almost exactly a year earlier, Wells had reached celebrity status when she'd successfully sued the Chesapeake, Southwestern & Ohio Railway after it had refused her a seat in the first-class ladies' car. Following the court victory, she had been invited to write for local white dailies in Memphis and black weeklies across the country; by 1885, Ida had gained a formidable reputation as a journalist. Her most recent article, published in December's *New York Freeman*, edited by T. Thomas Fortune, widely regarded as the country's leading black publisher, was an essay on the theme of "true womanhood": the nineteenth-century idea of the ideal woman who possessed the Victorian-era virtues of modesty, piety, purity, submissiveness, and domesticity—virtues denied by the conditions that faced black women during slavery and deemed essential to not only their uplift but that of their families, and the community. Wells's well-received essay had made her an authority on the subject and it was probably what she was referring to in her diary when she noted that she gave an old Holly Springs acquaintance a "paper and a slight sketch of myself for spite's sake."[7]

But if Ida's diary is any indication, whatever successes she had demonstrated to the world, she was still haunted by what had happened in Holly Springs. Despite her fierce determination to be the sole caretaker of her brothers and sisters to keep the family together, she had been unable to do so. Sometime between 1880 and 1881, Ida's sister Eugenia had died, an occurrence never mentioned in her diary or autobiography. Her grandmother, who had cared for the children while Ida was teaching outside of Holly Springs, was befelled by stroke in the same period. In the end, Ida was forced to send her brothers to live with relatives; only her sisters Lily and Annie were now with her in Memphis.

Ida believed that God—her Father as she called Him—had put her through these "trials" in order to "fit her for his Kingdom," as she wrote in her diary.[8] She was trying to be a good Christian, but as she must have confessed to her guardians, the resentment she still felt threatened to overwhelm her efforts. They had urged her to "forget the hateful words," to "cast the dark shadows out and exorcize the spirit," she wrote. But Wells had "clenched her hands darkly and proudly declared [to] never forget! . . . Father, forgive me, forgive me," she continued in her diary. "Humble the pride . . . and make me Thy child."[9]

Wells had left Holly Springs deeply marked by the grief and anger rooted in her abandonment—from the loss of her parents, and later the community. Never successfully repressing her emotions, she would, for the remainder of her life, struggle to reforge them into a cast that transformed her sense of personal injustice into a wider activism, which took on the intensity of a crusade that sought to restore the integrity of not only her own person but that of African American women and the race to which they belonged.

CHAPTER ONE

Holly Springs

I often compare [my mother's] work in training
her children to that of other women who had not
her handicaps.

—*Ida B. Wells*

There was no need to kill here [Holly Springs],
only to deprive . . .

—*Hodding Carter*

Ida Wells remembered being told as a child that her mother, Elizabeth,
called Liza or Lizzie by friends, was born somewhere in Virginia, was
one of ten children, and that her father was part Native American and her
grandfather a "full-blooded" one. The only other detail she recalled about
her mother's early life was that Lizzie was taken from her family when quite
young and, with two of her sisters, was sold by a slave trader into Mississippi, and sold a second time before she was purchased by Spires Boling, an
architect and contractor in Holly Springs. One of her mother's masters had
"seared her flesh and her mind with torturous beatings," and by contrast
Boling, who never used corporal punishment against her, was the "kind-
est" master of all. But Ida did not remember the name of the Virginia family to whom Lizzie "belonged" or the county in which she was born.[1]

However, circumstantial evidence suggests that Lizzie Wells was born to Annie Arrington and George Washington about 1844 on a plantation owned by William Arrington in Appomattox County, Virginia.[2] Lizzie must have been sold when she was seven or eight years old, the average age in most slaveholding states when a child's market value was greater without her mother than with her. Compounding the crime, but softening the blow of separation, the sale also included two of her sisters—Martha, two years younger, and Isabelle or Belle, for whom Ida was named, two years older. The sale was probably handled by George D. Davis and his brother John, merchants reputed to offer the highest prices for slaves in the area, and who had had previous dealings with the extended Arrington family. The two men customarily traveled from estate to estate, picking one, two, or three slaves from each homestead until they gathered a hundred or more to sell on the market.[3]

The Davis brothers purchased most of their slaves during the summer and fall, when they could get them at lower prices and "trim, shave, wash," and "fatten" them until they looked "sleek" and could be sold at a profit. The Arringtons were closest to the Lynchburg slave mart, about twenty miles away, which was then beginning to rival Richmond and Petersburg in its volume of sales. At the height of the buying season, children who had been bought from their owners—like Lizzie, Martha, and Belle—could be seen traveling two by two, their wrists bound by a rope, their pace hastened by an enforcer's whip.[4]

When such children reached Lynchburg, they were taken to a brick building on First and Lynch Street, where slaves were secured before they were sold. The prepubescence of young girls saved them from being intimately scrutinized by potential buyers who routinely examined buttocks and considered breasts. The health of children, by contrast, was determined by making them run in circles, or jump up and down, or skip along in measured distances.[5]

By October of 1858, Lizzie, about thirteen or fourteen, was among the nine slaves owned by Spires Boling; her sisters, Belle and Martha, were settled nearby, in Marshall and DeSoto counties, respectively.[6]

NOW A BOLING, Lizzie's primary responsibility was cooking for the middle-aged contractor; his pregnant wife, Nancy; and the household, which consisted of an older female relative and seven children between the

ages of one and eighteen.[7] Lizzie's development into an excellent cook and
the nonviolent treatment at the hands of her owner were not atypical of the
fourteen hundred slaves in Holly Springs. Although there were laws that
prohibited blacks from assembling, and one published account by a minister noted the death of several women slaves by whipping, the political
economy of the town demanded labor that required more skill than brawn;
and it encouraged paternalism rather than violence.[8]

The white population of Holly Springs had begun to settle in earnest
there in 1837, the year Holly Springs was incorporated and the original
Chickasaw Indian inhabitants had been removed to the Indian Territory
(later Oklahoma). Under the mounting pressure of President Andrew Jackson's land-hungry administration, the Chickasaws signed the Treaty of Pon-
totoc in 1832, which extinguished their title to all of the lands east of the
Mississippi, comprising the entire northern portion of the state. Of the
twelve Mississippi counties jigsawed out of the territory, Marshall County,
in the northwestern part of the state and named after the recently deceased
Chief Justice of the United States, John Marshall, was the largest and the
richest. In a mere twenty years, it would yield more cotton per square acre
than any similar subdivision in the world. Holly Springs—named after a
large, thirty-foot-wide, ten-foot-deep spring in a hollow that watered a thick
grove of holly trees—became Marshall's county seat and administrative center. Soon afterward, the town was embroiled in feverish land speculation
and sales and also became the site of northern Mississippi's first bank.[9]

As such, Holly Springs attracted "Episcopalians, Virginians and
Whigs"—deserting the thinning soil and accumulating debts of the older
cotton states—who brought their "ruffled shirts," "libraries," and "slaves"
with them, as one historian noted.[10] The bustling county seat also attracted
bankers, retail merchants, land speculators, those in the building trades,
and a bevy of lawyers as the town, already cleared of growth by the Chickasaws to facilitate its use as a hunting ground, grew at a dizzying pace. By
1845, the nearly thirty-five hundred residents of Holly Springs had established St. Thomas Hall, a boy's educational academy, and the six-year-old
Holly Springs Collegiate Institute for young women was prepared to award
Mistress of Polite Literature degrees and include subjects such as algebra,
physics, and natural philosophy. "Our object is to impart a sound, substantial, liberal education," announced its president, Thomas Johnson, "not
masculine, but approximating as near to it as the peculiarities of the female
intellect will permit." Less than a decade after its incorporation, Holly Springs

also boasted a land office, six churches, offices for nine doctors, three coach shops, four tailors, as well as several newspaper offices, printing shops, confectionaries, hatteries, and silversmiths. Its early reputation as a retreat with healing spring waters that attracted resort seekers made doggeries, horse-race tracks, bathhouses, theaters, hotels, and gambling houses viable enterprises. By the time Lizzie Boling had arrived, Holly Springs's eight produce houses carried an array of fresh farm products; its town stalls contained turkeys, geese, and quail; and a variety of food shops sold specialities, all of which helped her to make cooking into an art.[11]

IT WAS DURING Holly Springs's exponential growth in the 1840s that the North Carolina–born Spires Boling finally settled there after living for periods in Ohio—where he married his Virginia-born wife, Nancy—and later Arkansas, where two of his children, John and Harriet, were born. In 1850, he was thirty-nine years old and listed in the census as a carpenter who possessed one male slave and no property. But he soon found Holly Springs to be an opportune place for an ambitious house builder. Its forests of hickory, oak, magnolia, and pine provided fine timber; the red clay soil was suitable for brick-making; and the town possessed one of the three foundries in Mississippi that could produce grillwork and other decorative metal fittings found infrequently in other parts of the state. The longing for residences with the neoclassical Greek flourishes that were long out of fashion in Europe also helped assure a plentiful and skilled slave labor force in adjacent Tippah County where a significant proportion of its six thousand blacks were hired out by their masters to contractors and trained in the building trade arts of brick-making, dressing wooden planks by hand, and creating doors, window sashes, and blinds.[12]

Boling, who appeared to be a self-taught designer of houses that reflected the Athenian ideal, became known for a number of signature architectural elements: staircases with longer treads; intricate newel posts with their decorated step ends; cast-iron detailing; large porticos and massive columns and pediments designed to accentuate their monumentality. The contractor's wealth began to rise in the 1850s, and by 1860 he was designated a master builder, had purchased a clock and pleasure carriage—two items that connoted a particular status in the period—possessed nine slaves, and had bought his first parcels of land, which included a spring that provided fresh water and on which he would build his own story-and-a-half house.[13]

Boling's increase in wealth and status coincided with his building, simultaneously, three of Holly Springs's largest and most elaborate homes. Among them was the Walter House, Boling's most lucrative contract to date. Harvey W. Walter was an avid prohibitionist and ebullient lawyer who was the counsel for the town's most important economic achievement in the period: the building of a section of the Mississippi Central Railroad, incorporated in 1852, that extended from Holly Springs to Memphis and New Orleans and that was laid down by slaves loaned out for the task by their owners. In addition to Boling's standard, Greek-style blueprints, Walter wanted two large octagonal turrets on each side of the house to be used as extra bedrooms for the family's ten children. Perhaps in anticipation of the coming war, Walter also requested hollowed tunnels within the columns through which a ladder could be extended from the gabled roof to an underground tunnel. The contracts to build the houses explained the need for Boling to increase his number of slaves from three to nine between 1857 and 1860; among them were Lizzie and a young man by the name of James Wells from Tippah County.[14]

James Wells, called "Jim" by family and friends, was nineteen years old in 1860 and had been apprenticed to Boling by his white father and owner, Morgan Wells, a well-to-do farmer in the part of Tippah known as Hickory Flats. While Jim was perfecting his carpentry skills, he may have been traveling back and forth from Tippah to Holly Springs for several years before meeting, and eventually marrying, Lizzie—with the nuptial occasion being marked, perhaps, by the appearance of a slave cabin on the Boling property in 1860. There are no photographs of her but it is known that she was darker than Jim, and she may have possessed the same high cheekbones and knowing, intense eyes that the pictures of her sister Martha reveal.[15] Whatever Jim's particular features, he probably exuded a kind of confidence that foreshadowed his later acts of political independence.

Jim was the only son of Morgan Wells, who had never laid a hand on him, and he had become, Ida remembered, the "comfort and companion" of the white man's old age. Jim's mother was a slave named Peggy who had lived on the Morgan Wells estate since the 1840s. The later-revealed jealousy of Morgan's wife, Margaret or Polly, indicates that the black woman may have also had a favored place in the household, which included in 1850, James's half-siblings: Alfred, aged six; Henry, four; and Margaret, two—all of whom had a black father.[16]

FOR THE BOLING and Wells families, life and labor proceeded unremarkably through the fall of 1860, when Abraham Lincoln was elected to the White House, and January 1861, when a Holly Springs lawyer, Alexander Clayton, coauthored Mississippi's Ordinance of Secession, severing the state from federal jurisdiction. But the threat of war began to darken the landscape in March of 1861 when fifteen hundred volunteer troops from Marshall County headed for Pensacola under the orders of the Mississippian Jefferson Davis, soon to become the president of the Confederate provisional government, who had resigned from his U.S. Senate seat the month before. By April 1862, Holly Springs's McIlwen Foundry, used to melt metal for Boling's decorative fittings, was sold to the Confederacy and refitted to produce guns. The foundry produced the first cannon in the South, and according to one account, the occasion was consecrated by white townswomen, who, with their children, formed a circle around the foundry's fiery pit of molten metal and one by one, with the "solemnity of a priestess," dipped a ladle into the lavalike mixture and into the newly fitted mold.[17]

For Jim and Lizzie it was a time of heightened concern about their immediate and extended families. That same April, Lizzie was showing her pregnancy of six months, and news came that Jim's father, Morgan, had died at the age of sixty. Whatever grief Jim might have felt was no doubt mitigated by his also learning that the day following his death, Morgan's wife had had his mother, Peggy Wells, "stripped then whipped."[18]

Concern about Jim's family heightened in May when news came of the bitter showdown at nearby Corinth, one of the Civil War's bitterest battles, which claimed nearly five thousand rebel lives, twice the number of Union soldiers who died there. The bloody struggle was soon followed by the fall of Memphis, just forty miles northwest of Holly Springs. By the time Lizzie gave birth to Ida Bell on July 16, 1862, the couple must have wondered what kind of world their first child would be born into. That same month the first Union attack on Vicksburg failed, followed by the Confederate victories of General Robert E. Lee in Virginia and Maryland. It must have been chilling to watch the white Holly Springs residents celebrate the good news with dancing and celebrations with what one observer called "patriotic dissipation."[19]

By November, however, the tables had turned again, leading to the heart-stopping entry of Union general Ulysses S. Grant into Holly Springs, nearly doubling the population of five thousand with his cavalry and the sutlers who served them. Drawn by the Mississippi Central Railroad and the Greek-styled accommodations that were the source of the townspeople's pride, Grant made Holly Springs his personal headquarters from which he planned to supervise a new assault on Vicksburg in a combined land-and-river operation. The general brought his son Jesse and his wife, Julia, with him, and according to one account, Julia, who grew up on a southern-style plantation near St. Louis, also brought her personal slave to accompany them. The Grants chose for their private residence the spacious Walter House, built by Boling and his slaves, with its turrets and strategic tunnels.

On December 20, the most spectacular battle that took place in Holly Springs was led by the Confederate general Earl Van Dorn, who had led his troops to the earlier defeat in Corinth. Under the cover of night, Van Dorn's troops destroyed the Mississippi Railroad poised to aid Grant's transportation to Vicksburg, detonated the piles of ammunition stored by the Union troops, and pierced the predawn darkness by setting the cotton bales and sutlers' supplies afire. In the ensuing chaos, it was reported that "diminutive" Southern belles turned into boisterous night-gowned cheerleaders as they came out of their houses to shout encouragement to the raiders. In the end, both the east and west sides of the central square and three blocks of buildings and the railroad station were destroyed.[20]

Soon after the December raid, Belle Strickland, the nine-year-old niece of Boling's neighbor J. W. C. Watson—a lawyer and state senator during the period of Mississippi's secession—recorded in her diary that she woke to martial music and saw three regiments of blacks passing by. By then, Ida was five months old and Lizzie was pregnant with her second daughter, Eugenia.[21]

The Unionists soon returned "defeated, hungry, and threatening with a torch," noted one observer. In a test of the strategy that would subsequently be used by Union general William T. Sherman in his infamous "March to the Sea," infantry columns subsisted off the food of Holly Springs residents and fanned out to strip a 370-mile swath of the northern Mississippi countryside of its corn, wheat, and livestock before burning plantations to the ground. "The Yankees stole the corn and wheat and drove off the horses and mules and killed the hogs and sheep and took all the chickens," recalled

Callie Gray, who was a slave of Holly Springs resident James Fant. "We are living on corn bread and butter," Strickland wrote on August 18, 1864.[22]

The Wells family must have been worried about Lizzie's sisters and James's mother and siblings, who lived in the outlying counties. Ironically, however, of the extended family members, it was Polly Wells, the wife of Jim's deceased father, who seemed to have gotten the worst of it. She was reduced to near starvation; and in one of those complex ironies of Southern race and family relations, it was Peggy Wells, the victim of Polly's earlier whipping, who aided Polly and saved her life.[23]

Reminiscent of Polly Wells's situation, however, sometimes the tables were turned regarding who emerged intact from the seesaw battles that resulted in Holly Springs changing hands fifty-seven times before the war's end. "We are told," Cora Johnson, a daughter-in-law of J. W. C. Watson, wrote, that "one Southern woman hired an only skillet from a colored woman at one dollar a month."[24] The transaction was one sign of a region turned topsy-turvy by war; another was Strickland's tearful recollection of how her "beloved Mammy" had left the family to join her husband behind the Union lines—an act repeated enough for Mississippi to have provided more fighting men to the Union than it did to the Confederacy![25]

In the wake of the final Union victory, two hundred federal soldiers occupied the town, and Holly Springs became the regional headquarters for the Freedmen's Bureau—a government agency that managed freedmen's labor contracts; kept registers of their marriages; and, in cooperation with other charitable agencies, issued food, clothing, and medical supplies and established schools. Cora Johnson braced for the "ceaseless humiliation [and] oppression worse than slavery by a race whom we already hate and loathe."[26]

HOWEVER, AFRICAN AMERICANS, including the Wells family, devoted their immediate postwar energies to their newly freed families. Less than a year after the war's end, Ida's aunt Martha, Lizzie's sister, married Lewis Howell, a kind-eyed Mississippi-born farmer in 1866; and her other aunt, Belle, married William Gathings, a farmer born in North Carolina. Peggy Wells, Ida's paternal grandmother, married into the prolific Cheers family after the war, and Ida's autobiography described her as owning and tilling many acres. Peggy lived not far from Polly Wells and visited Ida's family each fall when she and her husband brought their cotton and corn to market.[27]

After the war, Ida's father, James, continued to work with Spires Boling, now for wages. Their continued relationship was surely a commentary on Jim's carpentry skills and the relatively satisfactory relations between the two men. Moreover, Boling had emerged from the war with good prospects in contrast to many in Holly Springs whose property and businesses were lost. The architect's own property had remained intact as had the house of Harvey Walter, which was spared, it was alleged, as a reward for the chivalrous treatment of Julia Grant by Van Dorn's troops, who took pains to protect her and her personal property during the attack. Soon after the war, Boling partnered with Walter in several investments, founded his own firm, and bought additional properties.[28]

However, the relationship between Wells and Boling inevitably came to end in 1867, the year when freedmen had their first opportunity to vote under the federal Reconstruction Act. For Confederates the election, scheduled for November, presented a no-win situation. The choice was to remain under military rule, with no congressional representation, or, with the "electorate as then constituted," vote for delegates to a constitutional convention that would reestablish civil authority and restore Mississippi to the Union. For the defeated Southerners, military rule was clearly unacceptable. But the "electorate as then constituted" excluded Southerners who had aided, or held any office in, the Confederacy and included newly enfranchised freedmen in a state where the number of blacks, 437,303, outnumbered the 353, 901 whites. The arithmetic added up to a black majority in thirty-three of Mississippi's sixty counties, including Marshall County, which counted 3,669 black males over twenty years of age and 3,025 whites. In Holly Springs, whites outnumbered blacks by just under one hundred. Since the majority of registered voters had to participate in the election for it to be binding, the strategy left to the Mississippi Confederates was to keep blacks from the polls.[29]

Compared with counties like Tippah, where outright violence against black voters was rampant and where Northerners dared not live, Holly Springs, characteristically, leaned toward more paternalistic methods to disenfranchise blacks. Boling's neighbor J. W. C. Watson, for example (left so destitute by the war that he had to pawn his watch to return to Holly Springs after its end), threatened to take away a former slave's rent-free residence if he voted. But there was always the threat of more violent repercussions. Just the year before in nearby Memphis, a race riot had erupted that took the lives of forty-six blacks and burned ninety-one black homes, four black churches, and twelve black schools to the ground. Additionally, five black women testified to being raped in their own homes by marauding white gangs, often after being robbed.[30]

The specter of similar desecrations hung over Holly Springs, where the "Grand Giant" of Marshall County's Ku Klux Klan resided. In at least one recorded instance, the Giant and another of his compatriots rushed a platform where a Republican was speaking and broke his leg with a brickbat; and a black political leader in Holly Springs, Tyler Williamson, a former slave, was gunned down. And if gang rape was not a threat, sexual assault aimed especially against black and northern-born white women was. In one instance, there was an attempted attack against a Miss Davis, a white schoolteacher who had come South to teach freed men and women. The perpetrator was thwarted, it was reported, but subsequently he abducted a favored black pupil of the woman, forced her at gunpoint to get into a buggy to drive across town, and then raped her. In the aftermath, the young victim was confined to her bed for weeks; the rapist was indicted but ran away before the trial.[31]

Blacks and their Radical Republican allies stood their ground, however, in ways that must have made an indelible impression on the young Ida. A Republican organization, the Loyal League, created in part to protect black voting rights, held mile-long torchlight processions around the Holly Springs square that featured blacks marching in martial formation with horns, drums, and flaming torches. On one remarkable occasion, a Loyal League parade included a float upon which a large black man stood next to a tree stump with dead opossums hanging from its branches. As the float moved down the street, the man sang as loudly as he could: " 'Carve that 'possum, nigger, carve him to the heart.' Then, sharpening his knife, he sang the next chorus, 'Carve that white man, nigger, carve him to the heart.' "[32]

A leader of the Radical Republicans in Holly Springs was Nelson G. Gill, a white, Illinois-born former Union officer who settled in the town after the war. To Confederate sympathizers, Gill was known as Holly Springs's leading carpetbagger (a term derived from the carpetbags Northern settlers used to carry their clothing) and "ugly to boot." But for blacks, Gill was an important figure. In 1866, he cofounded the Asbury Methodist Church, where the Wells family worshiped. The former Union captain also donated seven acres of land for the establishment of a school for the newly freed slaves, which must have been the institution that Ida described in her autobiography as the first school she attended, of which her father was named a trustee. Gill was a particular target of the Ku Klux Klan, and evidence suggests that Jim Wells, a Master Mason and leader in the community, as well as other blacks actively supported him.[33]

After opponents staged mock funeral processions with a coffin bearing his name, Gill was attacked by a mob and stabbed while addressing thousands of blacks at a political rally. A price was put on his head, and the Klan tried unsuccessfully to ambush him one night while he was conducting a Loyal League meeting at his house.[34] The incidents prompted his wife, Mrs. M. E. Gill, to write to the Freedmen's Bureau for protection and support of the 134 pupils at the school. She described to the Bureau how freedmen "of sterling character" participated in all aspects of the school, including "the appointment of school officers." Though "they had no education—*they* were the board of education . . ." she testified. These "noble colored men" were "brave enough to help me . . . through [the] most horrible threatenings," she concluded.[35]

The school was probably the one that diarist Belle Strickland was referring when she wrote, "they [the Negroes] marched all around town with the Yankee flag, and a standard-bearing inscription—The First Colored School in Holly Springs—Most of the girls went to see them, but I would not look at the things for anything."[36] Mrs. Gill, a teacher at the school, appeared to be no less determined than her husband. When there were after-school skirmishes between the mostly Irish white girls attending the Bethlehem Academy and her black female students, she, as described by a witness, "would place herself in the center of her black column of girls who would lock arms so as to form a solid wall across the sidewalk." The white girls would then have to pass around or come into direct contact with the black girls. The report was not dated, but one wonders if at the time little Ida Wells was helping to hold up the black side.[37]

GROWING UP IN this tumultuous period, Ida recalled hearing the words Ku Klux Klan—first organized in 1866 as a social club in Tennessee—long before she knew what they meant. As she would later write, she did glean that the words signified something terrible because they were associated with the nervous way her mother paced the house when her father went to political meetings. Lizzie's anxieties were no doubt heightened by the fact that in 1867 she was pregnant again—with Alfred James, AJ, named for Jim's brother—and there was little reason to feel that she would be immune to any violence. The year before, blacks had formed a posse to hunt down a white man guilty of the cold-blooded murder of a freedwoman.[38]

By the time of the November 1867 election, Jim Wells, then in his late twenties, surely understood the possible consequences when he proceeded to one of the two polls designated for blacks in Holly Springs. He may have even smiled to himself when he took the oath, complying with the Reconstruction Act, that he had never been a member of any Southern legislature, nor held any executive or judicial office or afterward engaged in rebellion against the United States, nor given any aid or comfort to its enemies. After casting his vote, the freedman returned to find his carpentry shop on the Boling property locked. Without a word to anyone, Jim returned to town, bought a new set of tools, and rented a house nearby. Now Jim Wells, born a slave, would work, as well as vote, for himself.[39]

SUFFICIENT NUMBERS OF freedmen followed suit to enable the reestablishment of civil government on terms favorable to the Republicans. By the 1870s, Ida Wells and her family would witness a political transformation of such magnitude that nearly anything seemed possible if blacks and their allies fought for their rights. In that period, Nelson Gill went from heading the local Freedmen's Bureau in 1868 to the position of sheriff, and he was eventually appointed by the Maine-born Mississippi governor, Adelbert Ames, as president of the Marshall County board of supervisors, a position that he would hold until 1872. In that year three blacks were elected to the board. The stunning turn of events was reflected throughout the state. Mississippi's first Reconstruction legislature included forty African Americans, a number of them freedmen. In 1872, a black man was Speaker of the House (John R. Lynch), and in 1873, blacks held the positions of lieutenant governor (A. K. Davis), secretary of state (James Hill), and superintendent of education (T. W. Cordozo). Two black U.S. senators were also elected from Mississippi: Hiram R. Revels, an African Methodist Episcopal (AME) minister and a Holly Springs resident who was elected to fill the unexpired term of Confederate president Jefferson Davis in 1870; and Blanche K. Bruce, a former sheriff of Bolivar County in 1874. For Ida, whose earliest memory was reading a newspaper to her father and his "admiring" friends, the sense of possibility demonstrated by stories in the press and personal relationships with those involved in the developments of the day must have been palpable. James Hill, Mississippi's secretary of state between 1874 and 1878, was a family friend who would continue to watch over Ida as a young adult. Hill, born just two miles outside Holly Springs, was, like Jim Wells, the son of a white father who had once owned him.[40]

THE POLITICAL TRIUMPHS were underlined by developments in Ida's family during the period. On January 28, 1869, a marriage certificate was issued to "Jim" Wells and "Liza" Boling. This, their second vow, as Ida would point out in her memoir, "officially" made Lizzie a Wells. In February of 1869, less than a week after the "official" marriage of Jim and Lizzie, Alfred, Jim's half-brother, by then a working carpenter, married Fanny Butler, described in a Freedmen's Bureau document as brown-skinned with a burn on her neck: an emblem, perhaps, of her occupation as a laundress—or the tyranny of her master or mistress. Alfred and Fanny followed the Mississippi River to Cairo, Illinois, where one of their three children was born, then settled in Memphis. In 1872, they purchased a house on Georgia Street.[41]

The marital record of the entire Wells family is all the more remarkable within the context of the time and place, as, according to a bureau report of the same year, very few freed couples were yet to be "legally" married. No reasons were given for the dearth of marriages, but at least in one instance, a former slave, Belle Myers Caruthers, who had wanted to marry was denied a license from county clerk who had once been her master. Not to be denied, she and her intended hopped a train to Oxford and married there.[42]

Before year's end, another son, George, was born to Jim and Lizzie Wells; and on March 16, 1870, Jim Wells purchased his first lot of land for $130 cash from R. E. Walker, a white man who had enlisted with the "Jeff Davis Rifles"—one of the four Holly Springs military companies that fought in the war. Wells built a three-room single-story frame house near the central square and courthouse with outhouses out back. Three more children were born to Lizzie and Jim during the decade: Annie in 1873, L'il or Lily in 1876, and Stanley in 1877. Another child, Eddie, died either in childbirth or as an infant.[43]

At home, Lizzie Wells, listed as a housekeeper in the 1870 census, ran a disciplined household, as Ida recalled in her autobiography. She even won a prize for the children's Sunday-school attendance. Contemporary observers remarked on the well-attired freed families on their way to worship, and

Ida's later penchant for fashion may have started when she and her siblings—buffed, braided, and beribboned—dressed for their instruction at Asbury Methodist Church.[44]

Asbury included a former slave and minister, Moses Adams, among its founders and would have appealed to the family for reasons beyond its connection to the Radical Republicans. Nineteenth-century Methodists stressed not dogma but "that inward warming of the heart" that believers thought to signify the presence of the Holy Spirit. The church's liturgy was practical and progressive with an evangelical bent. Moreover, the Methodist Episcopal Church (North) had separated from its Southern counterpart in 1844 over the issue of slavery; and the Northern church saw the defeat of the Confederacy in ecclesiastical terms: it was an opportunity to come to the aid of former slaves and reestablish the original church of American Methodism in the South.[45]

In any case, the alternatives were less attractive. The Hopewell Missionary Baptist Church in Holly Springs had a more rural and less sophisticated membership, and the Colored Methodist Episcopal Church (CME) had a broad reputation throughout the South for its preference of light-skinned Negroes—a category that did not include most of the Wells family. While Jim was lighter-skinned, and Annie, the youngest daughter, looked nearly white, Lizzie—deemed "black" in the censuses—did not. Although the children were all noted as "mulatto" in the documents, Ida, Lily, and Eugenia were darker than their brothers.[46] The highest consideration regarding Asbury, however, was its missionary zeal toward the education of freed black men and women.

One of Asbury's cofounders, Albert Collier McDonald, a white, midwestern-born minister who had been establishing mission congregations throughout the state, was instrumental in the 1866 founding of Shaw University (later Rust). The idea for the school originated when McDonald asked for a volunteer to take minutes at a church meeting. Surprised that none of the usually cooperative congregants—which included Ida's parents—responded, he inquired as to the reason. When the minister was told that none of them could write, he announced then and there that he would begin classes in the church building.[47]

The school was taken under the wing of the Methodist-inspired Freedmen's Aid Society, and despite its university designation, only offered elementary-level education in its earliest years. Former slaves were integral to its support from the beginning. "The colored people take a lively interest in the institution," a Freedmen's Aid Society's report stated in 1868, "and have subscribed $2000 toward its erection."[48] Land was purchased for the school that had been the site of Ulysses Grant's campgrounds; another lot purchased had once been owned by Spires Boling. An additional property featured an elegant bell tower. As a tearful freedwoman recounted, it had once rung for slaves to go to work, but now signaled them to go to school. The attendees included African Americans of all ages and backgrounds, some of whom walked miles to attend. As the annals of Shaw's early years attest, freedwomen in particular were an integral part of the school's activities. There were stories of mothers who attended the school alongside their children. Ida's own mother did so to learn how to read the Bible and to learn how to write so she could inquire about her family in Virginia. Many who did not attend made sure that their children did. As one observer wrote, mothers were seen standing over "their washtub and ironing board from four or five o'clock in the morning till eleven or twelve in the evening to make a living and try to educate their children." In her autobiography, Ida recalled that her mother imbued in her and her siblings that their "job" was to go to school, and "learn all we could."[49]

By 1870, the year the school was incorporated, the state took over its normal school; and in 1873, the year that a financial panic gripped the country, a $10,000 appropriation from the Reconstruction legislature allowed Shaw to acquire additional buildings and grounds. One purchase was a former private residence that became the school's main building: a two-story brick structure with fourteen-foot-high ceilings with an elegant veranda on each floor and a fine organ. The five-acre grounds surrounding the building included croquet and baseball fields. The school, under the presidency of the Reverend McDonald, an outspoken advocate of black rights, had to walk an especially fine line to keep the heightened resentment of economically stressed whites at bay when many, such as Spires Boling, saw their wealth and status evaporate during the depression of 1873.[50]

Even before the depression, Boling was reduced to selling illegal liquor made from the springs on his property. His desperation had led to tragedy in 1868 when Boling's nine-year-old son fell into one of the large distilling vats filled with boiling liquid and died. Diarist Belle Strickland demonstrated how contempt for illicit behavior could overwhelm any sense of empathy. "I thinke [*sic*] that ought to be a warning [for] him to stop keeping one [a distillery]," she coldly concluded. The panic of 1873 was the final straw for Boling, who lost his house to indebtedness, and he and his family were forced to occupy it as tenants until his death in 1880.[51]

The economic turns stiffened the political determination of former Confederates to jettison Republican rule. Democratic victories throughout the South in the 1874 midterm elections were accomplished, in large part, by the campaign of violence that kept blacks and their Republican allies from the polls. In Marshall County, the election resulted in Democrats replacing the Radical Republicans and the three blacks who served on the board of supervisors. Nelson Gill, who had previously been elected sheriff, was replaced by the Klansman Henry C. Myers. Two years later, Republican presidential candidate Rutherford B. Hayes promised to withdraw federal troops from the South in a compromise that assured his election.[52]

Nevertheless, in the mid-1870s, Shaw, still under the presidency of McDonald, issued a hopeful report. "However hostile to the education of freed men the whites may be elsewhere in the South, here both teachers and pupils are respected," it said in part. Although the precise year Ida began attending the school is unclear, she was certainly a student by the mid-1870s. Ida had had special affection for the instructors, the "consecrated teachers" from the North, as she described them, a number of whom were devout white women who demonstrated great courage in their determination to teach former slaves in the South even when doing so subjected them to slanderous innuendo and physical threats. Miss Davis, for example, the white northern schoolteacher who was terrorized and whose favorite student was abducted and raped, was the sister-in-law of the Reverend McDonald, and a later congressional investigation of the incident implied that she was a woman of questionable reputation.[53]

Despite Ida's affection for the teachers, she was a rebellious student. She confessed to her diary, for example, that she was jealous of the attention that the president, W. W. Hooper, paid to another student, Annie Talbot, who, in Ida's opinion had the marked advantage of being lighter-skinned. Her jealousy had caused her to "question the white president's authority" in a spirit of "tempestuousness" and "hard-headed wil[l]fullness," Wells wrote.[54]

Although she made no mention of Shaw's curriculum, Ida may well have felt frustrated by the school's philosophy of education, particularly as it applied to young women. Even though the school evolved to include liberal arts, ministerial, and normal (for training teachers) departments, it emphasized the need for its 124 students attending in 1877 to acquire "practical training." As McDonald, its first president, stated, Shaw did not want "to hurry students through a college curriculum . . . sending them into the battle of life only to disgrace themselves and bring reproach upon the cause of education at large." However sincere the conviction regarding industrial education, it was also true that such instruction was more acceptable to whites who took umbrage, as one resident put it, that the "Uncle Neds and Caesars," who used to care for such things as the town's once pristine gardens, were now "perplexing their simple souls with questions of supply and demand and problems of political economy."[55]

For the school's forty-one girls, including Ida, who attended Shaw in 1877, practical training meant that their curriculum also included lessons on how to wash and iron. But Ida, growing up in a town where white female students were exposed to a liberal arts curriculum and delighted in making pupils of their slave charges, was a precocious reader who must have yearned for less practical instruction. She had not only devoured the Shakespeare, Dickens, Oliver Optic stories for boys, and Alcott and Brontë books found in the Shaw and Asbury libraries, but had, as she wrote in her autobiography, "formed her ideals" on them.[56]

Those ideals included challenging the circumscriptions around women's roles and behavior at a time when self-conscious blacks and missionary-prone whites were determined to drive black women into the modest realms of chastity and domesticity. The form of "reproach" that most concerned Shaw authorities concerned sexual behavior. The 1877 report of the Freedmen's Society, which supported Shaw, noted that "no race can be elevated while the wives, mothers, and daughters are the subjects of lust and crime." It concluded, "The women of our Church will aid them to escape from degradation and vice."[57]

Ida had gained her first insight into the "degradation and vice" of slavery through learning about the beating of her grandmother Peggy at the hands of the jealous—and childless—wife of Morgan Wells. Ida had overheard her father talking to his mother about it, and she had apparently gleaned its broader implications—and certainly registered her father's vindictive tone. If it had been up to him, he had told his mother, he would have let Polly "starve to death" during the war crisis.[58] But for Ida, more difficult to understand were the more subtle forms of sexual coercion that black women were increasingly subjected to in a period when the black community, terrorized and left without protection by either federal guns or local ballots, was forced to capitulate to the white South in more ways than one.

In nearby Memphis, for example, the *Memphis Daily Avalanche* reported in 1875 that a "beautiful light-skinned Negro, Miss Lou Lewis," was chosen to offer a bouquet of flowers to the legendary Confederate general Nathan Bedford Forrest. The occasion was sponsored by a black fraternal order whose leader no doubt thought it prudent to demonstrate the community's acquiescent fealty to the victorious former Confederates who may have lost the war but by the mid-1870s had won the peace. Forrest, a founder of the Ku Klux Klan who was notorious for his massacre of three hundred black Union troops at the surrender of Fort Pillow, Tennessee, responded that he appreciated the conciliatory gesture—with its sexually symbolic implications—"particularly since they come from a lady, for if there is any man on God's green earth who loves the ladies, it is myself."[59] It is likely that the content of such newspaper reports was circulated in the black community, but Ida, it appears, only dimly perceived how such a poisonous social environment affected the way in which her own actions and behavior might be seen.

LIKE SHAW, THE Wells family appeared to weather the economic and political crises of the period. Whatever financial problems they experienced, James Wells, unlike his former employer, had managed to keep the house. In 1873, James Wells transferred the deed to his property to Lizzie, apparently to take advantage of a state law, the Women's Property Act, passed in 1839, which allowed husbands to hold on to their assets in their wives' names.[60] But in 1878, neither James nor Lizzie would be able to survive an even greater crisis: an epidemic that, unbeknownst to anyone at the time, was spread by a mosquito-borne viral infection.[61]

Ida was visiting Grandmother Peggy's farm in Tippah County during the summer of that year. She did not explain why she was there without her brothers and sisters, but as Jim and Lizzie's oldest child, she may, as was the custom in many families, have gone to the farm to help with the crops that Peggy and her husband harvested at the end of the season.

By July, yellow fever had seized New Orleans, then traveled to Grenada, Mississippi, and in August to Memphis. Such epidemics were not uncommon, especially in the port cities of New Orleans and Memphis, where the disease had struck in 1867 and 1873. The news of its reappearance did not cause undue alarm to the residents in and around Holly Springs. "Vicksburg Terrified—Holly Springs Not Afraid" ran a headline on a front-page article in the *New*

Orleans Daily Picayune in mid-August. Holly Springs's mayor and board of alderman were quoted as saying that "The place is clean and healthy" and that there was no sign of the disease, and none was apprehended.[62]

Holly Springs, which rested upon a plateau that was a thousand feet above sea level, had historically taken pride in its healthy climate and springs, the latter of which were reputed to have healing properties. Its reputation made the town a favorite destination of resort seekers before the epidemic of 1878, and during the outbreak, a place where those from stricken cities sought refuge. In fact, Holly Springs officials opened the town to such refugees from other parts of the Mississippi Valley.

But then on August 19, one of the out-of-town evacuees fell ill, and by the twenty-fourth he was dead. Soon another exile showed symptoms of the fever, and before the month ended, Holly Springs's mayor became the first local casualty. Others soon followed, including Harvey Walter and three of his sons. A terrifying element of the epidemic was that it often affected an entire household because mosquitoes could easily alight on one family member and then the next in quick succession. When more Holly Springs residents began exhibiting signs of the disease, civic confidence became unhinged—and then slid into terror.

The disease's awful progression made a yellow fever epidemic more dreaded than nearly every other kind of outbreak, including cholera, dengue fever, and smallpox, also known to the region. The symptoms began with flulike symptoms: high fever, chills, a severe headache, and rheumatic pains in the lower back. As it developed, the victim experienced reddening of the tip and edges of the tongue, and foul breath. This was followed by vomiting and the hemorrhaging of gums and blood vessels beneath the skin, making it appear to be deeply bruised. After approximately three days, there was often a remission period of up to twenty-four hours, but the false promise was betrayed by the onset of even more severe symptoms: jaundice—which gave the disease its name—nausea, and increased vomiting. The vomit, made black by the digested blood, was a sign that the disease was reaching its terminal stage. In the following excruciating period, there was more serious hemorrhaging and diffuse oozing from mucous membranes. The virus caused renal damage and in late terminal stages, there was a severe agitated delirium, intractable hiccups, stupor, and then coma.[63]

The only defense known was to burn the clothes of those who had perished, resulting in, as one witness described "a yellow glare [that] lighted the sky and a wind [that] bore a peculiar and horrible odor through the town." More than half of the population of thirty-five hundred fled in panic. Fifteen hundred remained in the town—twelve hundred of whom were black and nearly all of whom showed some symptoms of the fever. Those who remained organized a makeshift hospital in the courthouse and telegrammed the New Orleans–based Howard Association, named after an English philanthropist and organized in 1853 to provide medicines and health workers wherever epidemics appeared.[64]

Still, neither Ida nor her relatives in the country were unduly worried. For one thing, blacks, more apt to possess an immunity to tropic-born diseases, had a history of lower mortality rates during yellow fever epidemics, though they contracted the illness with rates similar to whites. In any case, if the situation in Holly Springs appeared to become too dangerous, Jim and Lizzie could go to the home of her sister Belle and William Gathings in nearby DeSoto County where the Wells family, including Ida's six siblings, frequently visited their eight cousins.

Ida was still at her grandmother's in late September when three men, neighbors of hers from Holly Springs, came to the house. Ida was ill, and in bed, suffering from a malarial-like chill common to the area. Grandmother Peggy, Aunt Margaret, and Uncle Henry were picking the first fall cotton out in the field. The men awakened Ida, but she was happy to see them and anxious to hear news from home at a time when the mail was more irregular than usual because of the epidemic. She greeted the messengers and invited them into the house. Without further explanation, the men handed her a letter and its words "leapt" out at her, she later recalled. "Jim and Lizzie Wells have both died of the fever," it began. "They died within twenty-four hours of each other. The children are all at home and the Howard Association has put a woman there to take care of them. Send word to Ida." That was as far as she read of the letter, Wells wrote, with no further explanation of her reaction to the devastating news. "The next thing I knew grandmother, aunt, and uncle were all in the house and ours indeed became a house of mourning."[65]

Ida wanted to go home at once, but her grandmother forbade it. Three days later, however, Peggy relented after receiving a letter from Dr. D. H. Gray, from Texas, who had come to Holly Springs with the Howard Association. Gray had attended to James and Lizzie and he asked that Ida get home to Holly Springs immediately. Soon after, Ida and Uncle Henry went to the railway depot only to be warned by townspeople against going to

Holly Springs. No local doctor would have asked her to return, they insisted; such advice was easily given by itinerant physicians whose responsibilities ended when they left town. It would be better to wait until the epidemic subsided; only then could she be assured of remaining well enough to take care of her six brothers and sisters—if any of them were left. Again Ida considered waiting, but she was especially worried about her sister Genie, the oldest child remaining in the household. The year before, she had been paralyzed by a fist-sized knot on her spine; now she was bent nearly double.

Passenger trains had ceased running, so on October 10, Ida climbed onto the caboose of a freight train draped in memorial black for two conductors who had perished from the disease. The warnings of the townspeople were reiterated by the trainman, but as he was doing his duty, Ida replied, she was doing hers as the oldest-surviving member of the family. Ida arrived home, still ill herself, to find that with the exception of Genie, all of the children—James, twelve; George, eight; Annie, five; and Lily, two—had had a brush with the disease, and not all of them had yet fully recovered. The youngest, nine-month-old Stanley, had died along with her parents, and Ida would hear that on September 12, her thirty-one-year-old uncle in Memphis, Alfred Wells, had also succumbed, leaving Aunt Fanny in care of their three children.[66]

Upon the news of the first fatality there, half of Memphis's population fled in panic; of the 20,000 or so who stayed in the city—mostly poorer citizens including blacks and the Irish—17,600 had been stricken with the disease; more than 5,000 perished from it. The Ireland-born editor of the *Appeal,* John Keating, was among those who remained through the scourge and continued to publish harrowing eyewitness accounts of a chaotic city in which bodies were piled and putrefying in the streets, male and female corpses entwined in compromising positions, and where "gloom," as he later wrote, settled "thick, black, and hideous, upon every living soul." The mortality rate among whites was 75 percent; among blacks, 7 percent, a figure that included Alfred.[67]

The two Wells families had been close. Jim and Lizzie had named their first son after Alfred; and Alfred and his wife, Fanny, named their oldest daughter after Ida, and another daughter, Eddie, after Jim and Lizzie's deceased child.

Although Ida's brothers and sisters had been fearful about Ida getting the disease if she returned, they were nevertheless relieved that she had come to take care of them as she had in the past. Jim and Lizzie had died on September 26 and 27, respectively; the children had been alone for nearly two weeks. Genie, Ida's oldest sister, had been particularly worried. In addition to the trauma of her parents' and brother's death, she saw a white Howard Association nurse going through her father's pockets after he had fallen ill. The incident prompted Genie to ask Dr. Gray to write Ida to come home to Holly Springs; and for him to be the custodian of the $300 that James had arranged to give the children while he was ill and under the doctor's care.

Before he died, her father, Ida was told, often came to the makeshift hospital in the courthouse to bring food, or try to calm a patient's delirium. His carpentry shop was nearby, and his days became filled with making coffins for the dead. Ida also heard that when Lizzie showed symptoms, a young Irish nurse, who had been sent to the house, took the baby, Stanley, from her and afterward her fever increased and her milk clotted in her breast. Just before she died, Lizzie had despairingly asked what would become of the children. Perhaps she knew that Jim had died the day before.[68]

More than four hundred Holly Springs residents died in the epidemic. Among whites, 200 men, 70 women, and 15 children perished. Among blacks, 70 men, 48 women, and 12 children died. The mortality rates of the 1,440 who were struck by the disease was 71.66 percent among whites and 7.41 percent among blacks. According to the published death announcements, the Wellses appeared to be the only black family to suffer multiple mortalities. James was no doubt one of the blacks who was touted in a rare tribute to the race, published in the local paper, for their "heroism," "devotion," and "earnestness" in "nursing the sick and helping the destitute and needy."[69]

SOMETIME IN MID-OCTOBER Ida went to the town square to meet Dr. Gray, who was scheduled to leave town the following day. The square was crowded. It was commissary day—a day when groceries, clothing, shoes, and other items were donated or sold to surviving citizens. The chaotic scene was made more so by the number of out-of-towners who were now coming to Holly Springs, which was doing a thriving—and startlingly open—business in illegal alcohol sales, even on Sundays. With the breakdown of law and order in the wake of the epidemic,

Holly Springs, long a destination for resort seekers, had a carnival-like atmosphere. Whiskey (provided perhaps by Boling, who survived the scourge only to die of tuberculosis two years later) was being served in the street, and the atmosphere of abandon, including, no doubt, sexual exchanges, was attracting excursion trains from Memphis and other locations.[70]

Such activities were especially flagrant in a section called "Hell's Acre," which long had had a reputation for being notorious and was not far from the Wells home. The entire scene, and indeed the symptoms of yellow fever itself, reflected the worse fears of a Victorian age: the chaos brought on by the loss of control and the attendant excesses of the body and mind. The attitude heightened sexual anxieties in the 1870s, the decade when Congress passed the Comstock Law that forbade the dissemination of contraceptive information and devices—primarily condoms—through the U.S. mails. Physicians were widely perceived as figures who were attempting to wrest authority from the church regarding sexual matters, and the presence of so many out-of-town health professionals must have added to the community's concerns—especially those of blacks.[71]

Judging from the number of African Americans, including her own father, who were listed in the census as "mulatto" and/or carried the name of their previous white owners, Holly Springs, like so many towns in the South, had a history of miscegenation and sexual practices involving white men and black women.

IT WAS IN such an atmosphere that Ida found Dr. Gray and was overheard asking him for the money that her father had entrusted to him. The exchange became the source of the ugly rumors about her motives for wanting to independently support her family against the advice of the Masons, who wanted to split up the children—save Ida and Eugenia—among them.

Wells protested in the passages of her autobiography that recounted the rumors that she was a "young, inexperienced girl who had never had a beau." The statement, of course, does not preclude the possibility of her seeking such a beau at the time, and Ida's diary, written while she was in her twenties, reveals her to be a young woman full of desire and assertive with prospective suitors. Pubescent young women were closely watched in black communities—particularly girls like Ida, who belonged to a proud, successful, and no doubt envied family and was by her own admission a precocious teenager. It is not difficult imagining her chafing under the supervision of a strict mother or being sent to her grandmother's farm as some mode of punishment for a transgression that may have involved some kind of impropriety—if not a physical sexual relationship.

Nevertheless, there is no evidence in the private journal or elsewhere that she was not the sexually "inexperienced" girl that she presented herself to be. And the slander against her was unsettling. "I am quite sure that never in my life have I suffered such a shock as I did when I heard this misconstruction that had been placed on my determination to keep my brothers and sisters together," she wrote in an autobiography that had recorded a great many "shocks" by the time it was written.[72]

To compound matters, the hardship of the teaching position that her guardians had found for her in a school six miles outside of Holly Springs was almost unbearable. There were no passable roads, so she was forced to travel there by mule and remain with local families for the remainder of the week. As Ida later hinted at in a fictional piece she wrote for the *Fisk Herald*, she was shocked by the rural conditions she found there. The essay did not mention specifics, but Ida wrote of the physical and moral "squalor" she found among country folk. On the weekends, she returned home to her brothers and sisters, where she did enough cooking and washing to leave her with a lifelong aversion to housework and to question if she ever wanted to marry and have children of her own.[73]

But the worst was yet to come with the death of her sister Eugenia and the stroke that befell her grandmother, who watched the children during the week. Ida clung to her love of literature to get her through it. "I could forget my troubles in no other way," she wrote, in one of the few published passages that admit despair rather than a public or personal grievance. While in the country during the week, Ida read by firelight on cold winter nights, where she saw in the lives and characters of Brontë, Alcott, and Dickens, the same struggles against life-changing epidemics, of being suddenly orphaned and having to wrest from fate a different outcome, and of contending with the "sins" of pride, envy, and guilt that she herself had faced. Like Ida, Charlotte Brontë was a Methodist, dimunitively build and a social outcast who was devoted to her five brothers and sisters after the premature death of her mother.

After two years of the ordeal, Wells gratefully accepted the invitation from her aunt Fanny, Alfred's widow, for her and her two younger sisters to come to Memphis. Now like the character Jo in Louisa Alcott's *Little Women*, Ida, at the age of eighteen, had the opportunity to recover from her grief and failure in a metropolitan city, where she would have a second chance to do "something heroic and wonderful that won't be forgotten after I'm dead."[74]

CHAPTER TWO

The New City and the Ladies' Car

> There is in every human being, however ignoble,
> some hint of perfection; some one place where as
> we may fancy the veil is thin which hides the di-
> vinity behind it.
>
> —*Quoted in Ida Wells's diary as a Confucian saying*

Memphis, located on the Fourth Chickasaw Bluff that stood like a sentry above the Mississippi River, was only forty miles from Holly Springs, but it was a world away from what Ida had ever known. Its polyglot population of nearly thirty-four thousand was squeezed into 4.6 square miles; and in addition to Anglo- and African Americans, Memphis had a significant foreign-born population. Of the latter, the two largest groups, the Irish and Germans, had begun emigrating to the city in the 1840s—the decade of the great potato famine in Ireland, the liberal nationalist revolution in Germany, and the beginning of the boom commercial years of the Bluff City.[1]

In Memphis, Ida had her first experience in living in an urban black community. By 1880, African Americans made up 44 percent of Memphis's population, and the city's nearly fifteen thousand blacks lived in all ten wards of the city; in seven of them, they were in the majority or at near parity with whites. Aunt Fanny's house, at 62 Georgia Street, was located in

South Memphis's Tenth Ward, which was over 50 percent black. Like four-fifths of the city's African American population, those in her immediate neighborhood were mainly employed in unskilled, semiskilled, or service occupations, including day laborers, domestic servants, seamstresses, and, like Fanny Wells, laundresses.[2]

Memphis's black population had increased significantly after 1862, the year when Union general Ulysses S. Grant captured the city. Even before President Lincoln's Proclamation of Emancipation in 1863, so many blacks who had been slaves on the outlying cotton plantations poured into the city upon the news of Grant's victory that contraband camps had to be erected in and around Memphis to house them. The first wave of the nearly three thousand new refugees were employed in the camps as spies and guides for Union soldiers, as laundresses and cooks, and as laborers to construct Fort Pickering and to load and unload boats on the levee. The black population increased exponentially again after 1863, when Memphis became the collection depot for all able-bodied, draftable "colored men of the west" between the ages of fifteen and fifty to serve with the Union. Unanticipated by the Union command, however, was that the black conscripts were followed to the city by their wives, children, and relatives. From nearly four thousand in 1860, the black population had risen to almost sixteen thousand, or 39 percent of the total population, ten years later.[3]

IDA COULD TRAVERSE the compact city by foot, or by the horse- or mule-drawn trolley cars that cost a nickel a ride. From Fanny's house, Ida could make her way north to one of Memphis's most famous thoroughfares, Beale Street. Wealthy whites owned the imposing homes on Beale's eastern end; on its far western end, near the Mississippi, were a number of the gambling houses, rotgut bars, and houses of prostitution that gave Memphis the reputation as the "toughest town on the River."[4] On Beale, between River and Front streets, was the heart of the black commercial district with its boarding places, barbershops (where Ida got her hair done by the father of a Shaw classmate), saloons, dray owners, undertaking parlors, and dining rooms that ranged from "respectable" eateries to the snack houses that served hog snouts, pig ears, and chitterlings. Beale Street was also the home of Zion Hall, an auditorium that could accommodate mass public meetings; Odd Fellows Hall, belonging to the black fraternal group; and the newspaper offices of the *Living Way,* a black Baptist weekly founded in 1874. Crowning the thoroughfare was the impressive Beale Street Baptist Church: the "first big, fine church" Ida had ever seen.[5]

Intersecting Beale was Front Street, running parallel to the river where Cotton Row—teeming with the manual laborers, clerks, factors, and dockworkers who unloaded, carried, shipped, and traded the staple that made Memphis known as the "city of cotton"—was located. Adjacent to Cotton Row was the "uptown" area of Memphis that included Main Street with its book vendors, department stores with fine clothing, and nationally known entertainment venues such as the Memphis and Leubrie theaters—the first of which was the site of the 1876 public debut of the city's then-leading feminist, Elizabeth Meriwether, who rented the theater in its entirety to speak on the "Spirit of English and American Law as It Relates to Women." Another landmark that might have been of particular interest to Ida was the Greenlaw Opera House, where the black musical prodigy "Blind Tom" had performed and where Radical Republicans had held mass meetings in its sixteen-hundred-seat auditorium after the war. Its owner, W. B. Greenlaw, had sold the lot where the Wells house stood to Ida's uncle Alfred in 1872.[6]

At the time Alfred had purchased his 30-foot by 100-foot lot, only 4 percent of black Memphians owned property in the city. Nevertheless, Fanny and Alfred, like the vast majority of blacks, lived in the least desirable areas of the city. Close to the house were the railway tracks belonging to the Kansas City and Memphis Railroad and a tributary of the festering DeSoto Bayou that snaked across the length of the city. The stagnant water, a fecund breeding place for mosquitoes, may well have been the source of Alfred's demise during the 1878 yellow fever epidemic.[7]

While the Wells family, with its multiple fatalities, suffered more than any other black family in Holly Springs, Memphis had suffered more from the epidemic than any other city in the Mississippi Valley. Already reeling from the depression of the 1870s, the catastrophe was not only measured in fatalities but the loss of an estimated thirty-six million dollars in revenue, and the impact on the future prospects of a city whose social fabric and demographics had been so dramatically affected by the outbreak.

It was the "better" half of the 40,000 panicked population that had fled the city, as one historian sniffed. The fugitives included city officials, many of its policemen and firemen, and much of the business and professional class—those who could afford to leave or pay the black-market fees to escape the "thick, black, and hideous" gloom, described by an eyewitness, that descended on the quarantined city where bodies were piled and putrefying in the streets.[8] Of the approximately 20,000 who remained—including 14,000 blacks and the remainder largely made up of the Irish in the shantytown Pinch District—17,600 were stricken by the disease, and more than 5,000 perished from it.

A milder outbreak of yellow fever in 1879 was the last straw for much of the German merchant and cultural elite, many of whom relocated to St. Louis, taking their philharmonic orchestra, piano factory, and other cosmopolitan features with them. The vacuum of the bankrupted city was quickly filled with migrants from rural Tennessee, Mississippi, and Arkansas seeking to escape peonage and swelling the numbers of poorer Memphians in the city seeking low-skilled work.[9]

By the time Ida reached Memphis, however, the city, like herself, was determined to not only "put off the trappings of mourning and woe," but to prepare for a "bright, prosperous and happy future." The rallying call was issued by John M. Keating, editor of the *Memphis Appeal* and one of the city's most ardent boosters. Keating had remained in the city during the scourge to write harrowing dispatches about the ravaged city, even as eighteen of his staff of forty-one perished and twenty others took ill during the course of the epidemic. Nevertheless, Keating, like other likeminded reformers, had the enduring, progressive faith that Memphis could redeem itself—in every sense of the word—through modern innovation, a diversified economy to wean itself from its atavistic plantation roots, and an industrial spirit that would unleash the city's economic potential.[10]

FROM ITS FOUNDING in 1819—the year after the Chickasaws sold their title to 6,469,800 acres of west Tennessee lands for less than five cents an acre—Memphis had the makings of an important commercial center. It was one of the few sites on the Mississippi River between St. Louis and New Orleans that was above the floodplain. The 1840s saw fervid construction of its railways to take advantage of its location at the crossroads of eastern Arkansas, northern Mississippi, and southwestern Tennessee. By 1850, Memphis had become the largest inland cotton market in the country and the center of the slave trade for the central South.[11] Even the war had not broken its progress. When the city fell to Union troops, Memphians, unlike those in many other defeated cities, were allowed to continue their business practices (upon signing a loyalty oath); trade, along with the influx of Northern speculators and merchants, actually increased during the period. Moreover, supplementing the sanctioned commercial activity, the Bluff City became the center for the lucrative contraband trade of cotton and other items during the war.

In the wake of the hostilities, Confederate and Union loyalists alike looked toward Memphis becoming the "first depot for northern capitalists" who were poised to invest in the rehabilitation of what became called the New South, and the city's preoccupation with business and trade matters continued to drive its politics—and race relations. According to the Memphis feminist Elizabeth Meriwether, the motive for the founding of the city's chapter of the Ku Klux Klan—whose leaders made plans for it in her living room in 1866—had more to do with keeping blacks from voting for a pending bond issue that they feared would bankrupt Memphis than any other issue. Two years later, Keating, a Democrat, affirmed the business-first attitude of many Memphians when he noted in the *Appeal* that he would "rather write one line for the encouragement of trade, commerce, or business . . . than any other of the thousand themes that call for attention of the daily press."[12]

African Americans, too, had been alert to economic necessities in Memphis. Under the occupation, the Union commanders only provided rations, medical help, and aid to blacks who were employed, leaving bereft those who could not work—a number that included many of the women and children who followed the black troops to Memphis and were too old, too young, or too sick to work in the labor force. The increasing number of blacks who had sought freedom in the city came to be perceived, in the words of one historian, as "perennial burdens"; a "huge black army" that had "crept into the city, the women to walk the streets and the men to steal and murder if necessary."[13] But as an analysis of the Freedmen's Bureau showed, the perception did not reflect the facts on the ground. Although the bulk of the bureau's public assistance was given to blacks, the average number of African Americans who actually received aid represented only 3 percent of the black population in Memphis. From May to December of 1865, for example, 521 blacks received aid out of the total of 15,828 blacks in the city.[14] At the same time, the sense of community engendered by African Americans in this period must have been a factor for blacks having a relatively low number of arrests, perceptions about a black crime wave notwithstanding. In a typical pattern of arrests recorded during a two-month period in 1865, blacks constituted only 27 percent of those on the criminal dockets of the recorder's court.[15]

One of the reasons for the low numbers was surely the Herculean efforts of blacks—some of whom had bought themselves and their families out of slavery through hiring themselves out—to establish self-help and benevolent associations, primarily through their religious institutions. The first "fine black church" that Ida had ever seen, the Beale Street Baptist Church, traced its origins to 1865, after its congregants, mostly former slaves, left the basement of a white Baptist church to worship in a brush arbor. In that same year, the worshippers established the female-led Baptist Sewing Society to raise money through a series of fairs. Within a year, the society had raised nearly $500, enough for its minister, Morris Henderson, to put a down payment on an empty lot at the corner of De Soto and Beale Streets. The story of "Mother Beale," as the church became known, might have been exceptional but it wasn't atypical. Although widely perceived as being incapable of meeting the social and economic challenges of emancipation, freedmen and freedwomen did so through forming networks to build churches and schools, help the destitute, care for orphans, aid the sick, and bury the dead. Nevertheless, fearing that its material aid encouraged idleness, the Freedmen's Bureau—which provided for indigent whites as well as blacks—began cutting off its help to former slaves as early as 1865; and black efforts did little to ease racial resentment toward the freedmen and freedwomen—including the black soldiers who had the authority that came with being armed. The latter especially chafed much of the Irish population who competed against blacks for low-wage jobs and housing and made up the majority of the police force.

In May of 1866, the day after a contingent of black soldiers had been mustered out of service, a scuffle ensued when the military men tried to prevent the arrest of a black man in South Memphis. The incident conflagrated into a full-scale, three-day assault on the black community by whites, including firemen and policemen and even municipal officials. Before it was over, forty-eight persons had been killed, forty-six of whom were black; and whites had destroyed four black churches, twelve black schoolhouses, and ninety black homes. One black woman was "roasted alive," according to the press, and at least five black women were raped by marauding whites—a number of whom were the women's neighbors who robbed them of savings and even clothes before they violated them. It was calculated that $110,000 worth of personal property owned by African Americans was destroyed.[16]

Following the riot, federal authorities initiated a campaign to force, with violence when necessary, unemployed blacks to accept labor contracts with the very plantations that had once enslaved them. And yet, amid all of the pathos and loss in the city, blacks remained determined to rebuild their communities. In October of 1866, five months after the riot, the efforts of the Beale Sewing Society resulted in the congregation being able to retire the $5,000 mortgage on the lot, and an additional $1,000 had been collected to erect a temporary building large enough to accommodate a prayer room and Sunday school. The Avery Chapel fund belonging to the AME denomination raised money to rebuild their church that was subsequently valued at $10,000.

According to the Freedmen's Bank records, more than 220 black church and self-help organizations flourished in Memphis between 1866 and 1874, most of them controlled by laboring-class blacks.[17]

But African Americans suffered another blow in 1874 when the Freedmen's Bank failed as a result of the panic of 1873 and questionable business practices. The bank had the accounts of hundreds of black organizations as well as six thousand individuals—including that of Alfred Wells—valued that year at $57,000, an impressive total when the majority of male depositors were fortunate to earn as much as $20 a month and when fully employed women averaged about $12 in monthly income. Nevertheless, African American civic groups, as they had in the past, were meeting the challenge of caring for the orphans and families of the thousand or so blacks who died in the 1878 epidemic.[18]

ONE REASON WHY Memphis did not fare as well during the epidemic as its sister cities, such as New Orleans, was because the debt-laden municipality had failed to institute clean water and sanitation measures. The Bluff City's elite reformers, including Keating, had long complained that the fiscal mismanagement of the city was due, in large part, to the power of the very legislators who represented the poorest constituents, who paid the least taxes and were more prone to corruption and malfeasance.[19]

During the 1870s, Memphis was governed by a mayor and a thirty-member legislature in which officials were elected by wards, a structure that assured broad ethnic, class, and racial representation—including fifteen black city councilmen elected during the decade—but that also led to contentious infighting and inefficiency. But in the wake of the yellow fever devastation, reformers were able to push through a charter that called for Memphis to be run by a taxing district form of government that put fiscal matters in the hands of the state, replaced the old legislature with eight officials, including a number who were appointed by the governor, and provided for at-large instead of ward elections for future elected officials.[20]

Keating, buoyed by the development, began calling Memphis a "New City" and the *Appeal*'s columns sought to prepare its increasingly rural populace for the discipline required to stay abreast of the innovations that accompanied a modern, industrialized economy. Anticipating the near-future electrification of its streetcars, for example, the paper warned its readers that the "rapid and regular time of such vehicles would not permit their waiting for individuals to hold parting conversations with friends on the curb or run back to the house or store for an overlooked article." But if electricity deprived one of the comfort of old habits, it also had the advantage of imposing efficiency and social order. Electric streetcars, Keating predicted, would eliminate the bothersome "street urchins" of both races who customarily tagged onto the back of the animal-drawn vehicles.[21]

Wells, for one, was determined not to be left behind in the New City. She had secured a new teaching position in Woodstock, a small town ten miles north of Memphis in Shelby County, with an eye toward becoming certified to teach in the better-equipped, better-paying Memphis public schools. As a result of a hard-fought interracial political struggle in the 1870s—led by Elizabeth Meriwether and which involved issues of both equal pay for men and women teachers and the right of blacks to teach black children in Memphis's racially separate schools— male and female teachers, as well as blacks and whites, received comparable pay.[22]

NOW THAT IDA had Fanny to help care for her sisters, Annie and L'il, who were seven and four years of age in 1880, she could stay in Woodstock without fear of their being neglected—or lonely. Moving to Memphis meant that they had their cousins, Fanny's own children—Ida, who was eight; Eddie, ten; and King, four—as playmates. There was every indication that the cousins became close to one another and that Fanny cared for her nieces as she did for her own children. Ida must have also felt some satisfaction to know that Fanny benefited from the arrangement, too. As a teacher,

Ida earned $30 a month, and her contribution to household expenses was no doubt welcome. Following Alfred's death, Fanny had been living alone, forced to support herself and her children on a laundress's wage. Her husband had had an account at the Freedmen's Savings Bank but its failure probably left her with little savings. And although Fanny owned the house on Georgia Street, property taxes were high in the city.

Happily, Ida could reach Woodstock by train, a decided advantage over her mule-riding days, though she, like other blacks, ran the risk of being shunted to a filthy smokers' car even after purchasing the fare to ride in the first-class ladies' car. The issue was a sore one with black Tennesseans, especially since the 1875 federal Civil Rights Bill that had given blacks the right to sue in state courts if they were discriminated against because of race in public accommodations. As a countermeasure in that same year, Tennessee's Democratic-dominated state legislature passed the nation's first Jim Crow law, specifying that proprietors had the right to exclude whom they wished from public or private accommodations.[23]

But in 1880, there was a sense of progress, reform, and reconciliation in the air. The memory of blacks forming militias to aid the still heavily Irish police force to keep the city from dissolving into chaos at the height of the epidemic was still fresh. Now there was a broad consensus that such cooperation had to be continued if the city was ever again to rise to its past economic glory. In the spring of the year, Memphis had an unprecented opportunity to show its citizens—and northern investors—that it was indeed a New City when former Union general and two-term U.S. president Ulysses S. Grant put Memphis on his public farewell tour.[24]

Grant's appearance that April could have certainly stirred up unpleasant memories among every member of the "throngs" of persons, including a large number of blacks and "ladies," as the *Memphis Daily Avalanche* pointed out, who came to see the former chief executive and occupier of Memphis. White women, who were often used to smuggle contraband items beneath their voluminous petticoats and skirts during the war, had angrily complained about their treatment at the hands, literally, of Union soldiers who searched them. The indignant women may have been less pleased by the response to their protests: black female former slaves were then employed to frisk them.[25]

For blacks, the withdrawal of Freedmen's Bureau support and the insolvency of the bank had caused much suffering; and though the majority of African Americans voted for Grant after black men were enfranchised in 1867, he had refused the Tennessee governor's request to deploy federal troops against the Ku Klux Klan, which had reared its violent head to keep blacks from exercising their rights. And African Americans had yet to hear the former chief executive utter one word—even in his state of the nation address—regarding the 1875 Civil Rights Bill passed under his administration.[26]

Following the war, Tennessee, under the Radical Unionist governor William C. Brownlow, disenfranchised white Confederates; and Keating's *Appeal* had heavily criticized the 1870 passage of the Fifteenth Amendment, passed under Grant's administration—which stipulated, in part, that the right to vote could not be denied on account of race, color, or condition of previous servitude. As late as 1879, the same paper characterized Grant's scandal-ridden two-term administration a "national stench."[27]

But less than a year later, if Ida and Fanny were among the throngs of well-wishers, they would have seen no evidence of ill will toward Grant or among the Memphians who had come to see him. Instead, they would have seen the three "colored" bands among the others who regaled him upon his arrival. At the beginning of the formal program, David T. Porter—a former vice president of the Chamber of Commerce, and a nonpartisan moderate who had become the city's first executive under the reformed "taxing district" municipal government—welcomed Grant in the name of all of Memphis's citizens "without distinction of races, nationality or party affiliation." Colonel Josiah Patterson, an ex-Confederate officer who fought with the infamous general and Ku Klux Klan grand wizard Nathan Forrest, pointedly included his "fellow citizens of African descent" when he said that the "heroes who wore the blue and the heroes who wore the gray, are embalmed together," signifying a "common history and a common country."[28]

Grant's itinerary also included the Beale Street Church, whose congregation sang a rousing rendition of "Rally Round the Flag Boys" for him. Its minister, Robert N. Countee, said the visit marked "an epoch in the history of our race." The next speaker, Benjamin K. Sampson, the first African American principal assigned to the black Memphis public schools, reminded the former president that African Americans represented "more than a million producers who, by their contributions to home production and mechanical industry, have furnished a measure of the means for the intercourse of all nations."[29]

The presence of the two black men on the same podium was another symbol of rapprochement. In some ways, the Oberlin College–educated Sampson, a native of North Carolina, represented the class of blacks who had been historically alienated from those who attended Beale Street Church founded by former slaves; and it would not have been lost on the audience that he stressed the role of the laboring classes in his speech. The class split among black Memphians was exacerbated after the riot of 1866 by the organized efforts among a small group of prosperous, many of them freeborn, African Americans associated with the Freedman Sanitary Association to aid the federalists in the removal of unemployed blacks from the city! Clearly, the masses of blacks could not depend on black elites or the freedmen's organizations, and many of their benevolent organizations and institutions, including Beale, were built or rebuilt without outside help. For example, when funds were made available to rebuild the northern missionary-staffed Freedmen's schools—which only hired a few elite black teachers—but not the black church schools, grassroots blacks formed their own Educational Association in 1867 to raise funds for private schools, push for reforms, and hire black teachers with the attitude that the elites associated with the bureau need not apply.[30]

After the Freedmen's Bureau turned over its schools to the Memphis Board of Education, the struggle between the factions reached a peak in the 1870s, when the northern-born white superintendent of the black schools tried to fire a black woman teacher. The significance of the political battle deepened when Conservative Democrats, who also did not want white northern teachers, supported the Educational Association. In 1874, Sampson, the candidate supported by the alliance, became the first black principal of the black public schools and by 1875, all the teachers of African American children were black—a change that at once confirmed racial separation, gave blacks control of their schools, and increased the opportunities of Ida and other educated black men and women to teach in the Memphis public education system.

When it was his turn to speak, the former president, demurely noting that his gift of speech could not match that of the black educator, responded to the occasion at Beale with few words. But perhaps anticipating the November 1880 elections in which Republicans had an opportunity to make new gains in the state, Grant did manage to express the hope that blacks would receive full equality in "due time." For African Americans, however, "due time" meant sooner rather than later.[31]

That summer, a well-publicized picnic held at Estival Park was another indication that African Americans were determined to heal the rifts within their community as well as reach across racial lines. The main feature of the social outing was a contest between two black drill companies, the Zouaves and the McClellan Guards. Drill companies, where men could display their martial arts, were popular organizations among both blacks and whites, and the men within them also shared fraternal bonds. White drillmasters were asked to judge the contest, and following the dazzling display of military precision, Anna Wright, a striking, free-born woman of color and called a "southern belle" by the judgmental *Memphis Avalanche,* presented the victorious Captain of the Guards with the first-place prize of a large silver pitcher. Wright, of Chickasaw, African, and English descent, was a graduate of LeMoyne and Antioch College in Yellow Springs, Ohio, and subsequently became principal of the Auction Street School in Memphis.[32]

Other contests that August picnic day featured a well-known black hackman who won a baby carriage for having the "finest child" on the grounds; another "belle of colored society circles" was given a gold watch for being the most popular; and a goblet was taken home by the winner of a walking contest who, by virtue of his years spent carrying soup into the dining room of the well-known Peabody Hotel, had already walked many miles with studied alacrity.

EIGHTEEN-EIGHTY WAS ALSO a propitious time for blacks to heal their differences. In the upcoming November elections, Republicans, for the first time in ten years, had the opportunity to make some inroads against a fractured Democrat party in the state legislature. Among the Republican candidates running to represent heavily black Shelby County were two African Americans from Memphis, Thomas Cassels and Isaac Norris, both of whom Wells knew. Cassels, Oberlin-educated and a former assistant attorney general in the city, attended the Second Congregational Church on Orleans Street, near her Aunt Fanny's house, where Ida took her sacraments; his wife, Emma, was a teacher in the Memphis public schools. Isaac F. Norris, the owner of a coal and wood business, married, some years hence, Ida's cousin, Stella Butler, who was related to Ida on Aunt Fanny's side of the family.[33]

Highest on the reform agenda for blacks was the state measure that allowed discrimination on the trains, and in October, a month before the election, an incident became the harbinger for the political struggles to come in the New City—and for the role that black women, including Ida, would play in them. In that month, a black woman by the name of Jane Brown sued the Charleston & Memphis Railway. After buying a first-class ticket for the ladies' car, Brown complained, she was shunted "with brutal violence" to the "filthy Smokers' Car crowded with mostly immigrants and their children." Because the Charleston & Memphis Railway was an interstate carrier—putting Brown's suit under the jurisdiction of the federal courts—attorneys for the railway argued that Brown was not forced out of the ladies' car because of the color of her skin but because of the content of her character. The ladies' car was reserved, by statute, for "ladies and their gentlemen attendants" deemed "persons of good character, and genteel and modest deportment." Brown, it was alleged, was a "notorious courtesan," who was "addicted to lascivious conversation" and "immodest deportment in public places."[34]

It is not clear what black elites may have felt about Brown, but her case could have rendered Tennessee's state law unconstitutional insofar as it conflicted with the federal laws regarding interstate commerce. In some ways, it was only fitting that it was she who threatened to turn the relationship of rights with class and sexuality on its head. Black women had had a special place in the history of Memphis: they provided a cautionary tale and/or symbolized a disturbing element capable of stirring deep fears, fantasies, and social disorder.[35]

Two of the city's earliest mayors, "around whom the early history of Memphis was woven," in the words of one historian, had enduring, publicly acknowledged relationships with black women. Marcus Winchester, the dashing, aristocratic son of General James Winchester, a founder of the city, was elected mayor after Memphis's incorporation in 1826. Subsequently, he married a free, accomplished quadroon named Mary in Louisiana where such unions were legal. Mary had been introduced to Marcus by a friend, Thomas H. Benton, who had brought Mary to Memphis and who subsequently abandoned her to pursue a long and successful political career out west, where he married a white woman more suitable to his aspirations. After leaving Mary in the care of Winchester, he became a U.S. senator from Missouri in 1820. Winchester, by contrast, was subjected to such reprobation for his decision to marry a woman of color that he lost public favor and set upon a path of drink and ultimate ruin. Before there were "tragic mulattoes," it seemed, there were tragic white men who married them.

Winchester's downfall led to his being replaced in 1829 by Isaac Rawlings, a rough-hewn fur trader who had long been Winchester's political rival. In contrast to the aristocratic Winchester, Rawlings lived openly with his slave housekeeper, Hannah, and had a son by her. However, he never married his housekeeper, and so remained palatable enough to the electorate to have a successful political career.[36]

Before the war, not only were female slaves assumed to be sexual fodder for the white men who owned them, the few free women who lived in and near Memphis (there were 117 in this category in 1860) were assumed to be concubines of white men—an assumption unsupported by the census data of the period, which shows that most were gainfully employed and that a number owned property and lived in female-headed households alone or with other women.[37]

With the coming of the Civil War, the "unruly" behavior of black women became an important element that impacted both the political decisions of the populace and the military prosecution of the occupation. Memphians, who had commercial ties to the North and West as well as the South, had first voted against secession, then subsequently for it. Although they had a host of political and economic reasons to explain their behavior at the polls, one important factor was the fear of a slave rebellion. In 1861, the city was gripped by "insurrection anxiety" when a female slave, calling herself a black Republican, uttered seditious sentiments and was found carrying a loaded weapon. The incident appeared to be a tipping point for the later vote for secession.[38]

During the occupation, it was widely thought that the presence of so many black female dependents made it difficult to discipline black troops. There were also complaints about black women refugees pilfering gardens to feed themselves and their children and anecdotal reports about freedwomen willingly—and without compensation—giving their bodies to Yankee soldiers out of gratitude for emancipating them. To rectify the situation, Union commanders attempted to send the women to nearby President's Island, where there was cotton to be picked. However, the plan was upended when the soldiers and their families resisted the move. Black women protested so vehemently that white troops had to be deployed for the sole purpose of controlling them.[39]

After the war, Memphis, which had been the center of the contraband trade, remained the "toughest town on the river," to the consternation of reformers like John Keating. The Bluff City "supports and harbors a larger number of disreputable women," he wrote in 1865, than any other in proportion to the population. Neither he nor the zealous enumerator who seven years later counted twenty-three houses of prostitution were referring only to black women, but courtesans such as Jane Brown became symbols of a broader concern.[40]

A "New City" needed a new, and chastened, origin myth in a period when it was thought that excessive sexual activity by men depleted the body as well as the soul. The industrial spirit needed for reform required all the energy that the "best white men" could muster. For them to couple with black women—long perceived as hypersexual—much less marry them, was conflated with the lethargy caused, in part, by the Old South's practices of miscegenation. When the *Appeal* talked about the New South needing to be "emancipated from the old traditions which contracted the spirit of enterprise and enfeebled the energies of the people," it was referring to more than verandas and mint juleps.[41]

But such was not the concern of the federal Circuit Court of West Tennessee in October of 1880. It concluded that whatever her reputation, Jane Brown was not acting untoward on the day that she was forced into the smoking car and that the same laws that excluded "unchaste women," from hotels, theaters, and other public places, could not be applied to common carriers. For it was no more possible to put "every woman purchasing a railroad ticket on trial for her virtue" than it was to do so for men, the court found. Brown was awarded a breathtaking sum of $3,000 for damages, and the lessons of the case were far-reaching.[42] If a woman acted like a lady, she had the legal means to enjoy the rights and protections of a lady, regardless of skin color or past reputation—at least in the eyes of the federal courts. This placed the contested status of all black women at the heart of the full-equality struggle, for if someone of the class, sex, race, and reputation of Brown could not be discriminated against, no one could. The damages awarded to Jane Brown had dire implications for railway companies and were sure to make northern investors wary—especially in a city and state where blacks were so politically active.

* * *

INDEED, THE OCTOBER *Brown* decision was followed by a 92 percent turn-out of Tennessee's eligible black voters in the November 1880 election. The heavily pro-Republican support of the state's more than 330,000 African Americans helped win Republicans the governorship and a 37–37 split among Republicans and Democrats in the state assembly. Included on the list of victors were four black assemblymen, including the two Memphians— Thomas Cassels and Isaac Norris—representing Shelby County, which was 56 percent black.[43] The four newly elected black Republican legislators set about to complete the unfinished business of civil rights. Perhaps with the Brown case in mind, one of the earliest bills introduced by Cassels was legislation to repeal the laws that prohibited marriage between blacks and whites. Black resentment about the antimiscegenation law focused on the fact that it allowed black women to be white men's sexual partners but never their wives or women to whom those men had any legal responsibility— even when "illegitimate" children were born out of the unions. Black women in these relationships were marked by a scarlet letter of immorality— a perception that affected black women in general. Cassels's bill sought not only to legalize marriage between persons of different races but also to criminalize interracial "carnal intercourse" outside of marriage.

The ensuing debate in the assembly was characterized by the *Appeal* as "salacious and interesting," mischievously hinting that emotions ran high because it affected a number of legislators personally. Cassels's bill failed, but in its place another was passed that would have wide-ranging implications. It prohibited both interracial marriage *and* cohabitation, but not carnal intercourse.[44]

Black hopes were dashed again when the civil rights bill, proposed by another black assemblyman who won office that year, Thomas Sykes of Nashville, narrowly failed to be passed by the assembly by a vote of 31 to 29, the margin of defeat being five white Republicans who voted against the measure. The black legislators were enraged. After a second effort to pass the bill failed, they called the betrayal a "palpable violation" of "free government." Four hundred thousand citizens of Tennessee, they said, "were entitled to no rights that railroads, hotels, and theaters are bound to respect."[45]

Soon after the vote, in March of 1881, another black woman, Julia Hooks, refused a directive to sit in the "colored gallery" of the downtown

Leubrie Theater after buying a ticket for the orchestra section. Hooks had no doubt sat in the orchestra, also known as the "family circle," before. But because of the popularity of the show, *Hermann the Magician,* as the management later explained, it was decided to reserve the section for whites only. When Hooks determinedly made her way toward the family circle, she was intercepted by two policemen who manhandled her to the extent that the waistband of her dress was torn before they arrested her. "Let go of me, I am a schooteacher," Hooks demanded during the struggle.[46]

In the past, Hooks's appeal might have kept her from being treated no better than a woman like Jane Brown. In Memphis, a certified teacher not only had to pass a written exam, she also had to demonstrate "good moral character" and "the purest and truest of natures" to the satisfaction of a bi-racial board. It was a reason why teaching was one of the few jobs in which "a lady might openly engage without compromising her social status," as one of the flourishing number of ladies' manuals of the period put it.[47]

At the time of the incident, Ida no doubt knew Hooks by reputation, if not personally. The Memphis teacher, whose first husband had died of yellow fever, had recently remarried and lived with her second husband, Charles, on Broadway, not far from Aunt Fanny's house. Hooks was well known in Memphis circles as a musical prodigy who gave classical piano concerts before interracial audiences, and her teaching credentials were impeccable. She was a graduate of interracial Berea College in Kentucky where she also later taught, thus becoming one of the earliest African Americans to teach whites in an institution of higher education.[48] As shocking as her arrest—and the manner of it—was the characterization by the *Avalanche,* the same paper that had described the belles at the Estival picnic. The paper called the light-skinned Hooks "a dusky" woman, "claiming" to be a teacher with the "mistaken" belief that "she had more rights than other people." Hooks filed a complaint against the officers and before a court filled with black Memphians; her suit against the officers was dismissed. Instead, it was Hooks who was fined: five dollars for disorderly conduct. The decision was an ominous sign that the status of black women—prodigies, belles, and teachers included—was not going to rise along with the New City. The week following the incident, the Leubrie Theater featured a play called the *Emigrants,* advertised as a comedy that would feature a character named Aunt Jemima who performed songs and dances.[49]

* * *

DESPITE THE TURN of events, blacks shouldn't be discouraged, was the message of Benjamin A. Imes, Ida's pastor at the Second Congregational Church. He said as much when he addressed students at LeMoyne Institute, a black school founded in 1871 by the American Missionary Association. LeMoyne was associated with the church and best known for its normal school that trained black teachers. Although Imes, a black progressive thinker who believed in the inevitability of progress through reform, did not specifically mention the recent setbacks that had transpired in Memphis, he appeared to have felt the need to counsel the students in light of them. In his speech, published approvingly in the *Memphis Appeal,* Imes reminded the audience that the duty of their generation was to "move beyond their former condition"; that they should not be thwarted by the vestiges of racism and discrimination that belonged to a different era; that they had already gotten through terrible times and awaiting them was the promise of a better future. "Never was another people thrown so suddenly upon their own resources with so many responsibilities, and yet [had] such high inducements to cultivate their energies," he said. Imes reminded his young audience that they "lived in a "Christian Civilization with a Republican form of government"— and that such a nation could only build on the "idea of liberty, intelligence, industry and an equal chance of all in the struggle for manhood."[50]

It was a message that Ida, for one, appeared to take to heart. Second Congregational was in easy walking distance of Fanny's house, and across from LeMoyne, but convenience wasn't the only reason she chose to attend its Sunday services and Wednesday night prayer meetings over those of the other twenty-three black churches in the city. The race-conscious, progressive liturgy by the most educated black minister in Memphis probably came closest to that of her church back in Holly Springs. Born in Pennsylvania of free parents in 1848, Imes had been sent to Congregational by the missionary association in 1880, soon after earning his college and seminary degrees at Oberlin College—the first white institution of higher education to admit blacks. He was Congregational's first black pastor, and the association hoped that he could make the congregation as viable as the black-led AME, Episcopal, and Baptist denominations within the city.[51] Indeed, Imes, a serious, astute minister whose zeal was tempered by reason, appeared to be a man suited for the New City.

But how "new" Memphis really had become was tested again that year. After Hooks's arrest, the *Avalanche* had worried that it would trigger "a new round of civil rights protest," and the paper's concern was soon borne out when the black legislator Isaac Norris focused on the very heart of that struggle when he introduced a bill to specifically prohibit discrimination on the railroads in Tennessee.[52]

If the right to sit in the orchestra section of a downtown theater affected a limited number of blacks, the same was not true regarding common carriers. For African Americans denied mobility in slavery there was no clearer indication of their freedom and social status than their treatment on the railways, which were seen as the "agent and symbol of America's republic civilization," as the legend of a popular Currier & Ives illustration called it.[53]

Norris knew that the time had come when legislators had to confront and resolve the issue. The railways were more important to Memphis than to any other city in the region. They were needed to ship cotton directly to the North where it could be sent overseas to its primary importer, Great Britain, without going through the port of New Orleans, Memphis's primary competitor. The railways, the construction of which had been slowed by the war and the epidemic, were also the key to the city's ability to ship its manufactured goods through the country—a prerequisite for it becoming a modern, diversified economy that was not wholly dependent on the vagaries of cotton prices and unskilled labor. Waiting in the wings was Collis P. Huntington, the California railroad magnate and owner of the Chesapeake, Ohio and Southwestern Railway, who wanted to establish a line in Memphis that ran by way of Paducah to St. Louis and Chicago; and by way of Richmond and Newport News to rail or ship connections to Washington, Baltimore, Philadelphia, New York, and Boston. The plans called for an engineering feat that only the Chesapeake & Ohio was capable of achieving: building a four-thousand-foot trestle over Memphis's Hatchie River Bottoms.[54]

Norris was right in assuming that his colleagues, in both parties, had a sense of urgency about the railroad issue in the wake of the Brown decision. But he was wrong on another count: the intransigence of whites in the New City as well as the old. Norris's bill was ignored in favor of a compromise measure passed with overwhelming support from both white Republicans and Democrats. It provided for separate first-class cars for passengers of each race, with each car to be materially the same and "subject to the same rules governing other first class cars, preventing smoking and obscene language." With the separate-but-equal law, and the matter of first-class black passengers apparently settled, the daily press reported that Huntington had begun including Memphis on his "annual tours of his empire."[55]

But if the white legislators thought that the measure would dull the appetite of protest, or that blacks did not understand the import of Tennessee passing the nation's first law mandating separate-but-equal railroad cars for first-class passengers, they were mistaken. Soon following its passage, blacks in the state capital of Nashville purchased, for three successive days, first-class tickets and then took seats in the "white" first-class ladies' car of the Louisville and Nashville Railways and the Nashville, Chattanooga, and St. Louis Railways. In one of the incidents, whites simply abandoned the ladies' car and locked themselves in another, leaving blacks the abandoned seats. When, the next day, blacks occupied the ladies' car before whites got on the train, the latter went into the car usually reserved for African Americans. When blacks then followed them into the colored car, the whites got up, rushed for the ladies' car, then locked themselves in. The railways on which the bizarre game of tag was being played were cautious, however, and took no action that could materialize into a court challenge. Subsequently, Norris, unable to make Jim Crow disappear, was reduced to trying to make it unfeasible, by offering a bill that raised the penalty for noncompliance to the separate-but-equal law from $100 to $1,000. A compromise whittled it down to $300.[56]

IN THE MEANTIME, blacks, led by the voluble Edward Shaw, who had been a Memphis councilman in the 1870s and one of the leaders of the black and ethnic coalition that had taken city hall in 1874, along with black school principal Benjamin Sampson, were organizing African American political clubs in the counties and Memphis wards—including Aunt Fanny's Tenth Ward—that made up West Tennessee's Tenth Congressional District. The object of the clubs was to foment an insurgency against the Republicans (who had appeared to forget how much they depended on the black vote), to encourage independence among black workers, and to strive for improvements in the black public schools. Their efforts were partially successful in the 1882 elections when Isaac Norris, one of the Republican insurgents, and another black candidate, William Price, broke their alliance with Republicans to run on a fusion ticket with a faction of "low-tax" Democrats who had split with the "state-credit" members of their party over repayment terms regarding the municipal debt. The black fusion candidates lost, but the insurgency reminded the Republicans that blacks, who had had a history of alliances with Democrats, could have an impact on the party. In the gubernatorial election, a Democrat, William B. Bate, who had been supported by Norris and Shaw, won the governorship.[57]

Accompanying the election of the Democrat, one of Ida's closest confidants in Memphis rose to power: Alfred Froman, Sr., Memphis's leading black Democrat, who became one of Bate's leading political operatives and in 1883 was appointed as one of the five commissioners to the newly organized board of education in Memphis. Referring to him as "Dad" in her diary, Ida thought of him as a surrogate father for her and especially her brothers as they got older and began traveling back and forth to Memphis from their aunt and uncle's home in Mississippi.[58] Ida may have met Froman, a former slave who had escaped north before the Civil War and who was the owner of a saddle and harness shop, through Aunt Fanny who—like Froman's wife, Alice, and Ida's cousin Stella Butler—was from Missouri. Froman had also once edited a newspaper with the newly elected Thomas Cassels. Alfred Froman, Jr., his son, also lived in Fannie's neighborhood near Georgia Street.

Froman, Sr., must have been a part of Bate's campaign to secure black support for legislation that would regulate railroad fees by the state. To attract black voters, his faction of the party took up the race issue on the railroads—not by advocating integration but by supporting the right of blacks to enjoy equal accommodations in the cars. Again, women were at the center of the separate-but-equal issue; the question was whether the equality mandated bylaw could be realized if black women were not treated in the same way that white "ladies" were in the first-class cars.

ON THE UNSEASONABLY warm and cloudy afternoon of September 15, 1883, Ida arrived at the spanking new Poplar Street Depot at about 3:30 P.M., for the four o'clock northbound Covington train on the Chesapeake & Ohio Railway line. It was the same train Wells took to her school in Woodstock, and the afternoon hour and the large satchel she was carrying suggested that she was planning to spend the night there. Ida was dressed for the first-class car in which she planned to ride. In addition to the satchel, Ida also carried a parasol—a "lady's" accessory that complemented the customary hat, gloves, and full-length dress corseted and cinched tightly at the waist.[59]

Ida's early arrival at the station afforded her the time to purchase a newspaper to read on the train, and to take in the physical beauty of the depot, completed only that year. The station, with its high square tower of red stone, cobblestone courtyard, and restaurant, was habitually filled with not only passengers, but entire families, dressed in their Sunday best to send off relatives and loved ones. In many ways the station was a worthy portal for the Chesapeake & Ohio, which brought the economic vision of a New City closer to reality by connecting Memphis to Paducah, Kentucky, giving Memphis access to the Kentucky coal mines.[60]

The C & O, unlike some of the other railways that ignored the material parity required by the separate-but-equal law, provided the same beautiful cars, with their mixed mahogany interiors and hand-carved designs, for each race. In fact, the designated first-class "colored" or "accommodation" car used for one leg of the trip became the "ladies' car" on the return passage. The equitable material conditions made the C & O the perfect railway to challenge the idea of whether separate could ever be equal.

For the difference between the accommodations for whites and blacks was a social not a physical one. The colored car, unlike the ladies' car, carried no gender designation and without it, as a black passenger later complained about "Jim Crow" passenger cars in general, the "Negro was not a man nor a woman."[61] Although by law the rules of behavior in the first-class cars were to be the same, the implication that there were no ladies in the colored car who had to be respected or shielded from the coarse behavior of men made the environment of the cars different. While conductors strictly enforced the rules against swearing, drinking, and smoking in the ladies' car, they often failed to do so in the colored car, making it indistinguishable from the smokers' car, where second-class passengers of both races rode together and behavior was unpoliced. In fact, it was common practice for white men to leave their car to smoke and drink in the first-class colored car and then return to the unsullied environment of the ladies' car. Moreover, while black women who bought first-class tickets were confined to the colored car, black nurses and maids accompanying their "missus" customarily rode in the white car.

* * *

WHEN IDA BOARDED the colored car and bought her thirty-cent first-class fare for the trip, she saw an inebriated white man there and telltale curls of smoke. Exercising her rights as a first-class passenger, Ida headed for the ladies' car where she intended to remain for the duration of the trip. Ignoring the stares of fellow passengers, Ida took her seat, opened her newspaper, and commenced to read it. It is not known which paper she had purchased, but if it was the *Appeal,* its front-page story on September 15 would have done nothing to ameliorate her mood. The article was about the "legal hanging" of a black woman in Richmond, Virginia, and the hundreds of citizens who applied for passes to witness the "novel spectacle" of the execution of a woman.

When the train got about a mile outside the station, the conductor, William Murray, came into the ladies' car to collect tickets. Wells handed him hers. He took it, then stopped and looked hard at her, perhaps wincing in recognition. As he would later claim, he had had a confrontation with Wells that summer, when she accompanied Aunt Fanny and another friend, Miss Ragland, to the train at Woodstock. Ida was not traveling herself on that occasion, but she had urged the two women to sit in the ladies' car. When the conductor saw them, he directed Fanny and Miss Ragland to the colored car, and Ida's less battle-ready companions complied. But Ida snapped that she had ridden in the ladies' car before and intended to do so again![62]

On September 15, Murray returned the ticket and told Wells to leave the coach, insisting that it was for whites alone. Wells told him that she was not moving. Murray, saying that he did not want any trouble, told Ida that he wanted to treat her like a lady, but that she would have to go to the colored car. "I replied," Ida recounted, "that if he wished to treat me like a lady, he would leave me alone." When the train paused on the Wolf River trestle, just before its first stop at Frazier's Station, Murray again beseeched Wells to leave the car. Once more, she refused. At that point, the conductor attempted to physically pull her out of the seat, tearing the sleeve off her dress in the process. The ideal of "modest deportment" notwithstanding, Ida, determined not to be taken, hooked her feet under the seat in front of her, began scratching the conductor with her nails, and then bit his hands deeply enough to draw blood. The conductor asked for help from the passengers and they readily complied. Two of them sitting in front of Wells turned the seat around so that she could no longer hold on to it with her feet. Two others helped the conductor pry Ida out of her seat and drag her to the platform between the cars. But Wells refused to be forced into the colored car and chose instead to get off the train. With the cheers of the white passengers echoing in her ears, she disembarked, disheveled but determined.[63] As soon as she got back to Memphis, Wells contacted Thomas Cassels, the black legislator and former assistant attorney general who attended her church.

Since his election in 1880 Cassels had introduced several civil rights bills in the legislature, including an unsuccessful attempt to add an antidiscrimination clause to a bill proposing the creation of a railroad commission. Moreover, Cassels appeared to have a particular empathy for the plight of women. In 1880, he was one of the signers of a woman's suffrage petition, sponsored by an interracial group of citizens and sent to the suffragist Elizabeth Cady Stanton in Washington, D.C. In addition to Cassels's thwarted antimiscegenation bill, he had defended black women in the courts when they were charged with a variety of public offenses.[64] His concerns about women could only have increased in 1883. In January of that year, a Republican-dominated U.S. Supreme Court ruled in *Pace v. Alabama* that state antimiscegenation laws were constitutional when they did not conflict with the equal protection clause of the Fourteenth Amendment. The case passed constitutional muster, it was decided, because both the black man and the white woman who had been convicted of "living together in adultery and fornication" were sentenced equally for the crime: two years' imprisonment in the state penitentiary.[65]

Ida's case was scheduled to come before the Circuit Court of Shelby County in late November; testimony would be heard in January.

IN THE INTERIM, however, Ida's challenge took on an even greater import when in October of 1883, the U.S. Supreme Court decided that the Civil Rights Act of 1875 was unconstitutional. The decision precipitated a national outcry of black leaders about their most recent betrayal at the hands of the Republican Party. The former abolitionist and staunch Republican loyalist Frederick Douglass pronounced that if the party "cannot stand a demand for justice and fair play, it ought to go down." Calvin Chase, editor of the *Washington Bee*, a black newspaper, declared that the Republicans were "little, if any, better than the hidebound slave-holding

Democrats." In Memphis, the news of the decision precipitated a mass meeting at the AME flagship church, Avery Chapel. The papers described its tone as "temperate," but Ida would have certainly been encouraged by the resolution read aloud by her minister, Benjamin Imes. He declared that "we should feel and declare it to be our duty and purpose to agitate and discuss, and in every proper way to contend for these rights and privileges inherent to us as men and citizens, and which have been and are still denied us." Wells, a woman and a citizen, would take Imes's advice to heart by, again, taking a seat in a ladies' car *after* the high court decision—an act that assured her place in the annals of civil rights case law.[66]

On the second important, if less dramatic, occasion, later that fall, Wells had taken a seat in a ladies' car, then momentarily left it. Upon her return, she found it occupied by a white woman. The woman, Allene Kimbrough, a farmer's wife, testified that when Wells saw her, she demanded: "Get up, you have my seat and where is my bag I left on it [sic]." Kimbrough, who had first assumed that Ida was the nurse of another white woman on the car, denied seeing any bag, and told the court that Wells "demanded the seat in very [sic] unladylike manner and finally says if you don't get up and give me my seat I will sit by you and did start to take her seat—when I told her to get away and let me pass as I was not in the habit of sitting on the seat with negroes." The two incidents were tried together and their significance was not lost on the *Avalanche,* which told its readers that "This is, we believe, the first case in the South" in the wake of the Supreme Court decision.[67]

When witnesses to the first train ride were deposed in January, Cassels, a federal-ring Republican who had had ties to the national party, had gotten his people to line up like ducks in a row. C. W. West, a successful painter and a black delegate to the 1880 Shelby County convention, put up the bond for Wells, which he backed by the value of his $1,500 house and a piano worth $500. (The piano alone was worth more than Fanny's house on Georgia Street.) Additionally, the witnesses for his plaintiff were perfectly prepared to testify in a case that would not turn on the legality of race segregation per se, but rather on the question of whether, according to the state law, the colored car fit the criteria of a bona fide first-class car.[68]

Despite conductor Murray's testimony that neither smoking nor drinking was allowed in the colored car, witnesses for Wells testified otherwise. A black man, Silas Kearney, corroborated the presence of an inebriated white man in the car. Another, E. W. Mosely, a Shaw (Rust College) graduate and minister (whom Wells later dated) testified that there was smoking in the car. A second black minister, G. H. Clowers, a Republican operative who had been elected in 1876 as a magistrate in the Thirteenth District, confessed that he himself had smoked in the car that afternoon. Clowers pronounced that the colored car was "very rough," that there was smoking, talking and drinking in it. "It was no fit place for a Lady," he opined. "There were no white ladies in there but there were white men and colored men and women."[69]

With such witnesses there was not much needed from Wells herself. She admitted that she had refused to leave her seat and that she "resisted" the conductor through the whole ordeal; she described, without embellishment, how the conductor and two white passengers carried her out of the car; and she confirmed the fact that there was smoking, drunkenness, and white men in the colored car. But her demeanor was no doubt more important than the words themselves. William Murray, who had since left his conductor's job and was now a saloon keeper, had tried to make the point that Wells's behavior was hardly that of a lady when he said that he had first asked her politely about leaving the car; that in the ensuing struggle that he had gotten "the worst of it"; and that after she bit him, he had "bled freely." But Wells was surely on her best behavior when she came before the judge; she was dressed impeccably, and her petite, barely five-foot frame would make it difficult not to sympathize with her—even when Murray proclaimed that Ida told him that she "would not ride on [the] damned train . . . she would not ride with negroes" (at least without a gender and class distinction).[70]

CLEARLY, THE TRIAL regarding Ida's original refusal to leave the ladies' car was going well, but the adjudication of the all-important second incident, occurring after the U.S. Supreme Court decision, was beset with delays. Ida became suspicious and finally concluded that Cassels had been bought off by the railroad. Bribery was certainly a common enough practice in Tennessee; and the reputation of C & O owner Collis Huntington in this regard was legendary. But it was more likely for a man with Cassels's civil rights record that party politics, rather than anything else, was affecting how he handled the case. In 1884, the election of President Grover Cleveland, a Democrat, and the momentum of the fusionist movement were adding to the further erosion of Republican influence in Tennessee. Moreover,

the state's Democratic governor, with the aid of Ida's "dad," Alfred Froman, was stoking the train discrimination issue in order to get black votes,
and the publicity around Ida's case was probably working against the
Republicans. Perhaps it was the twisting kaleidoscope of political affiliations that had impelled Cassels to take on James Phelan as his cocounsel
for Ida's case. Phelan, who had his own political ambitions, was the owner
of the *Avalanche,* which was no friend of blacks, but like other pro-
industrialist Democrats and Cassels, he was a political opponent of Governor Bate's. The pro-industrialist Democrats were against anything that
made railway proprietors unhappy, including the governor's desire to regulate freight rates through a railroad commission for which he was seeking
black support. On this issue, Bate was looking out for the planter class
whose profits were diminished by the high freight rates to ship their
cotton.

Ida's impatience, as well as Cassels's maneuvering, might have also been
heightened by the spate of articles in the local press about miscegenation in
Memphis. While it is not clear if the articles were spurred by Ida's suit, it
was evident that there was growing determination to keep black women out
of "the family circle" in the New City—and that too many whites were not
cooperating. In February of 1884, for example, the *Appeal* reported about a
black clerk who was sued for knowingly giving a marriage license to a white
man and black woman, the latter of whom, the paper scoffed, had "a complexion so very dark that it shines and her bangs always stay banged." The
paper added that the woman had a mulatto child. An even more publicized
case concerned George Battier, a well-known druggist described in contemporary "Who's Who" accounts as a "sound Democrat," and one of Memphis's "most correct businessmen." Nevertheless, Battier was dragged to court
when he attempted to get a marriage license to marry a black woman, Mary
Burton, with whom he had lived for nine years and had several children. Ida
later referred to the case in her diary, as well as another concerning "a white
man [who] could not get a license to marry a colored girl and he cut open
her three fingers & sucked her blood & then told them he had Negro blood
in his veins & therewith procured a license."[71]

The heightened concern about miscegenation might have also been
spurred by the Supreme Court ruling and the growing alarm on the part of
social scientists about "race-mixing." Modern advances in publishing made
the wide dissemination of scientific discourse in the popular press possible,

and the conclusions of scientists such as Nathanial Southgate Shaler of Harvard were being read more widely. In a November 1884 article in the *Atlantic Monthly,* Shaler wrote that blacks were physiologically incapable of overcoming the "lower passions" required for a new society based on discipline and industry, and, moreover, they had the capacity to enervate any other group that their thick, antediluvian blood intermingled with. Such racist sentiments were not new, but they had particular resonance in a New South and New City at a time when the emergent field of social science provided presumably incontrovertible evidence of racial inferiority and its capacity to thwart progress.[72]

WELLS EVENTUALLY GOT a white lawyer, James Greer, to be the lead attorney for her case. Greer was a candidate for attorney general who, until 1884, had been a judge in the Shelby County Criminal Court and belonged to the same faction of the Democratic Party as Alfred Froman. But there were other important ties to Ida. The judge was from a prominent family in Holly Springs who had provided the town with its first Baptist church in 1837. The Greers lived near Spires Boling, and Ida's family probably knew the Greer slaves.[73]

Whether through legal maneuvering or fortunate circumstance, the case fell into the hands of James O. Pierce, a northern-born conservative Democrat known for his progressive views. In December of 1884, the judge concluded that the colored car, though equal in construction, fell below the standards of a first-class car. He also noted that there was no strict separation of races, since black "nurses" commonly rode in the ladies' car. And finally, Pierce found that Wells was a person of "lady-like appearance and deportment, a school teacher, and one who might be expected to object to traveling in the company of rough or boistrous men." Decision—for the plaintiff.[74]

Not surprisingly, the headline in the *Avalanche* the next day was less than complimentary. "A Darky Damsel Obtains a Verdict for Damages . . . What It Cost to Put a Colored Teacher in a Smoking Car . . . $500," it said. But Ida's case was respectfully written up in the paper, and, most important, no headline could take away from the fact that Ida had won a victory for the race, for black women, and, in light of her damaged reputation, her true-womanhood pride. The triumph was written up by the country's leading black publisher, New York's T. Thomas Fortune, who urged others to follow in Wells's footsteps. And soon after the decision, Wells would no longer have to take the Chesapeake & Ohio Railway to go to Woodstock. She became one of the twenty-two black teachers elected by Froman and other members of the board of education to the Memphis public school system.[75]

CHAPTER THREE

A Breath of Life, A Winter of Discontent

> The [Negro's] ambition is to take position in the
> front rank of progress. And he is catching up . . .
> thirty percent of his illiteracy has been wiped out.
> Twenty-thousand colored teachers are standing
> faithful sentinels over the destinies of the Ameri-
> can Negro. . . . From the university to the semi-
> nary; on down through the common schools, the
> colored people are holding their own.
>
> —*J. Dallas Bowser, 1886*

> It was through journalism that I found the real me.
>
> —*Ida B. Wells*

In January 1885, just days after Ida Wells won her court decision, a group
of black teachers from St. Louis and Kansas City, Missouri, stopped in
Memphis on their way home from the New Orleans World's Industrial and
Cotton Exposition. The fair, especially in the light of the recent Supreme
Court decisions, had been encouraging for progress-minded African Amer-
icans. While the 1876 Philadelphia Centennial had included the work of
only two black artists—*The Death of Cleopatra* by the sculptor Edmonia
Lewis and *Under the Oaks* by the painter Edward Bannister—New Orleans

had dedicated an entire gallery to black inventions and designs that reflected the industrial promise of the new era. "Not only did the colored exhibits compare favorably with other exhibits in skill and art," observed the *Cleveland Gazette,* a black weekly, they were "objects of attraction and admiration." The *Gazette* made special mention of the successful exhibit belonging to the Ohio carriage- and wagon-maker, William H. Dickson. Such a display, the paper added, should be "a stimulus to our young men everywhere."[1]

Women were represented in the exhibits, too. The *Washington Bee,* another black weekly, proudly described their quilts, plush tablecloths, sofa pillows, and the silk embroidery made by Sarah H. Shimm, a Washington, D.C., schoolteacher, which depicted the heroic Toussaint L'Ouverture, who led the successful 1794 revolution in Haiti. The inclusion of so many black exhibits and speakers by the New Orleans organizers was a conscious attempt to show the world that there was a New South spirit of biracial cooperation to meet the growing needs of both foreign and domestic markets.[2] Of course, the equality associated with such a spirit was yet to be perfected. The one major complaint of the fair attendees was that many had been forced to ride in inferior accommodations on the New Orleans–bound trains. The situation had prompted Booker T. Washington, a former slave who had been named president of the Tuskegee Institute in Alabama in 1881, to insist that the train facilities be made the same for blacks and whites. "We can be as separate as the fingers, yet one as the hand for maintaining the right," he had written to a Montgomery newspaper in a phrase that would reverberate across the nation at a future southern exposition.[3]

Still, Wells's recent court victory was evidence that even this vestige of inequality was bound to be short-lived, and it was she, the newest and certainly most famous teacher in the Memphis school system, who was chosen to give the toast at the reception for the out-of-town teachers at the Odd Fellows Hall on Beale and Hernando streets. J. Dallas Bowser, a Kansas City, Missouri, school principal and editor of the respected *Gate City Press,* a black weekly, and the St. Louis teacher Hutchins Inge spoke in response on behalf of the visiting teachers. The festivities that followed included a classical piano selection by a teacher, Julia Hooks, one of the organizers of the gathering; a band selection; and a formal address by Virginia W. Broughton, a leader in black Baptist women's circles and also a Memphis teacher. Broughton, a former slave, had been a member of Fisk University's first graduating class of 1875 and was touted for her facility in the classical languages of Latin and Greek. Other Memphians who gathered for the occasion included the lawyer Thomas Cassels; J. E. Greenfield, a plumber; T. Thomas Turner, a teacher and editor of the newly founded *Memphis Watchman,* a weekly; and Thomas Moss, listed in the city directory as the manager of the New Central House within the Odd Fellows Hall, where the visiting teachers had had coffee and lunch upon their arrival. The young Moss, in his twenties, and a member of the McClellan Guards, was neither a teacher nor a tradesman, but he was also representative of the New South generation of enterprising young men determined to take advantage of the opportunities that came his way. Moss had opened an account in the Freedmen's Bank at the age of thirteen; he subsequently learned the barbering trade and had set his sights on becoming a postal carrier—a position that carried the prestige of a federal appointment, required passing a civil service exam, and whose letter-carrier union was one of the few open to African Americans.[4]

IN THE AGE of scientific observation, blacks had yet to gain access to the new research methods and instruments that measured racial differences beneath the skin, but they believed that their observable achievements in just one generation removed from slavery were evidence that they had, at the least, the same potential as other groups. The most quantifiable mark of their abilities, in a period that translated Darwin's evolutionary idea of the survival of the fittest into social terms, was the accumulation of wealth. Moral and spiritual progress was equated with material progress, and economic success offered a counterclaim to notions of black inferiority. The *Memphis Appeal,* for example, had recently opined that it was the "law of nature" for whites to rule over blacks because of the former's superior wealth, as well as intelligence. Such opinions had impelled the *Washington Bee* to pronounce in 1885 that "We need wealth in order that the race as a whole may move in a solid phalanx against the opposition which threatens our prospects of ultimate equality."[5] Other publications were eager to put on the record the wealth that blacks had managed to achieve. In the same year, 1885, the *Cleveland Gazette,* quoting from the *Chicago Inter-Ocean,* a white liberal daily, proudly noted that "103 colored men in Washington, D.C." were worth over $25,000 each and fifty-two were worth over $10,000. It went on to cite that San Francisco had fifteen colored men assessed above $75,000 each; tailor John X. Lewis of Boston, once "a ragged and barefoot slave," did a business the previous year of $1,600,000; John F. Cook, a Washingtonian who served as tax collector in the city, was said to pay taxes himself on $250,000 worth of income and holdings. John M. Langston, a lawyer who founded and organized the first law department at Howard University, had $75,000; Frederick Douglass, $300,000; and John Jones, a tailor in Chicago whose clientele included the white elite in that city, a half-million dollars. Such men may have proved rare exceptions in the period, but the exception proved the rule of possibility in the postslavery era.[6] As J. D. Bowser wrote the following year in the *AME Church Review*, the most intellectual black journal of the period, "There was no physiological difference between the races, only that of opportunity."[7]

Black Memphians in the mid-1880s had particular reason to believe that their city's new opportunities augured well for their own. Debt was down, investment was up, and the unmistakable scent of progress was in the air. The taxing district's centralized government may have attenuated black political power in the city, but African Americans had token representation on the board of public works, and the taxing district had already achieved unprecedented sanitary reforms through house-to-house inspections, installation of sewers, water closets, more regular garbage collection, and drainage systems.[8] By 1885, local banks and individuals acquired more than $200,000 worth of taxing district bonds to pare down the debt, and an African American, Robert R. Church, was one of the earliest Memphis citizens to purchase the municipal issue. Church, born a slave in Holly Springs, had been a saloon owner after the war, had survived being shot in the head and left for dead during the Memphis riot, and had smartly bought up abandoned properties during the 1878 epidemic. By 1885, the *Appeal,* reporting on Church's second marriage in January of that year to Anna Wright—the freeborn "belle" and teacher who had awarded the prize to the McClellan Guards—called him "honest and punctilious" and estimated his worth at $100,000. His highly publicized purchase of a thousand-dollar city bond had inspired many white Memphians to do the same and, no doubt, had also encouraged the optimistic view of Bluff City blacks.[9]

Indeed, a Memphis correspondent to the *Cleveland Gazette* characterized the New City as the Chicago of the South but opined that blacks had more opportunities in Memphis because there was less competition. "Our colored lawyers and doctors are doing well and still there is room for more," bugled the *Gazette.*[10] Like white Memphians, blacks were engaging in boosterism for their city, but this did not mean they did not anticipate labor struggles ahead. As late as 1877, when a local black bricklayers' union struck for higher wages and was subsequently joined by black longshoremen on the waterfront, they had been attacked by three military units, specially armed policemen, and employers who warned that their services could be easily dispensed with in the future. But the black press and others wrote optimistically about such groups as the Knights of Labor—the first nationwide organization that sought to empower both men and women, blacks and whites, and skilled and unskilled workers. In 1882, the K of L had come to Memphis to organize black washerwomen and cottonseed oil workers, among other groups, and was poised to return in 1886 to launch a new effort.[11]

Black women in Memphis had fewer opportunities to escape unskilled occupations than men did; nevertheless, the *Sholes City Directory* of 1885, which devoted a section to African Americans who headed households, listed the growing number of female seamstresses, nurses, cooks, and midwives among them. For college- and normal-school-educated women, it was the Memphis public school system that symbolized the greatest opportunity, if, in many ways, a limited and contested one. In 1883, Memphis became one of the first cities in the country to adopt a small centralized school board, which, like the new municipal government, eliminated ward-based elections and concentrated power in the hands of the superintendent and a small number of school commissioners. But although taxing district officials, among others, debated the need for public schooling that went beyond the "three R's"—especially for African Americans—the school board, black leaders, and reform-minded newspapers such as the *Appeal* fought for increased expenditures in the belief that education and training was necessary if the city was to reach its full potential. "Negroes Must Be Educated If They are Ever to Be Equal to the Duties of Citizenship," ran a headline of the *Appeal* in the period, "Industrial Education a Particular Necessity."[12]

Black reformers—who in the 1870s had successfully secured the appointment of Benjamin Sampson and the Kortrecht School building, the only brick edifice in the black system and the one school for black children that went beyond the elementary grades—continued to advocate the expansion of educational facilities during the following decade. Most recently, with the help of Ida's surrogate "dad," school board member Alfred Froman, their efforts had resulted in two new schools: the Broadway Street School, in South Memphis, provided after a two-year-long lobbying effort by Tenth

Ward citizens; and the Grant School in North Memphis on Auction Street. In 1885, there were nearly twenty-five hundred black students whose attendance rate—92.3 percent that year—was slightly higher than that of whites. There were twenty-two black instructors, twelve of whom were women, teaching in five overcrowded schools.[13]

Ida had first been assigned to teach first grade at the Saffarans School on the corner of Fourth and Saffarans streets and then at the new Grant Street school, which had an enrollment of 385 students by 1886 and an average of 48 pupils per teacher. Despite the too-large class, Ida now had a better salary—fifty dollars a month, twenty dollars higher than in her previous position—and was moved to congratulate the board in the *Living Way,* a black Baptist weekly published in Memphis, for providing the new facility that she described as a "commodious building of 6 rooms beautifully furnished and arranged."[14]

A NEW WORLD had been opened for Ida. Her love, need really, for literature found expression in an organization the instructors had founded called the Memphis Lyceum. The 1880s saw the growth of black lyceums and literary societies across the country and the Memphis Lyceum, established by black teachers in 1883, typically provided a forum for debates, readings, musical selections, and recitations in which the instructors and other members of the community attended. A highlight of the weekly Friday-night meetings at the Vance Street Church was the reading of the group's publication, the *Evening Star,* which Ida described as a "spicy journal" composed of news items, literary notes, poetry, and social items—and a good venue to publish one's maiden writing efforts. To Wells, whose own creative sensibilities were forged in isolation, the meetings were, as she wrote in her autobiography, a "breath of life."[15]

Ida quickly immersed herself in the lyceum activities. In the spring of 1885, in what may have been her first public performance, she read the part of Mary, Queen of Scots—who was subjected to accusations ranging from political treachery to sexual immorality when she resisted the Protestant Reformation—opposite Virginia Broughton, then editor of the *Star,* who was her "rival," Queen Elizabeth. The reading, replete with costumes, was called "the crowning literary event" of the evening by the Memphis correspondent to the *Cleveland Gazette.* By the summer, Ida's oratorical skills had fashioned her a new identity. The *Fisk Herald* identified her as an "elocutionist" when it noted her presence at Fisk University's commencement exercises that year. For Wells, who was self-conscious about her relatively rudimentary education compared with many of her colleagues', such recognition was a considerable triumph. Fisk was known for its demanding liberal arts curriculum and brilliant students such as Broughton and W. E. B. Du Bois, the latter of whom she may have met there and who became an editor of the *Herald* the following year. Ida confessed to the publication that she had had "a craving" that amounted to a "positive heartache" to attend Fisk—a statement that managed to both praise the Nashville institution and make an implicit gibe at Rust.[16]

Participating in the lyceum activities with the other teachers also helped Ida make friends—an achievement, as she admitted to her diary, that was not easy for her. Wells was sensitive to any perceived slight, and her defensive responses often took the form of haughtiness or indifference. She wrote in her diary, for example, about a Mrs. B., probably the teacher Fannie Bradshaw, that her "studied indifference . . . to 'me royal highness' has piqued me' & I am determined that she shall not succeed in making me show interest in her without a corresponding show on her side." In another instance, she wrote that another teacher, Fanny Thompson, "has been singularly uncommunicative this week & I had not sought to woo her from her silence."[17]

However, Thompson, described as "level-headed," was apparently able to navigate Ida's hypersensitive nature more times than not. Fanny taught with Wells at the Grant Street school and became Ida's closest female friend in the period. The two women attended church and the theater together, and Fanny was one of the few women mentioned in Wells's diary with whom she socialized apart from the group outings and parties that the teachers regularly took part in. Thompson, whose family came to Memphis, apparently from Ohio, where her mother was educated, would have been a good source of information about the history and political ins and outs of the school system. Her mother was the late S. H. Thompson, a Memphis teacher who had been a central figure in the interracial political struggles over black education and equal pay for women in the 1870s. In that period, one of the board members who had been most supportive of the pay issue was J. O. Pierce, the judge who had ruled favorably in Ida's court case. When S. H. Thompson died in 1880, her students were taken over by Virginia Broughton.[18]

Fanny and Ida had also been affected by the loss of their parents and gravitated toward creative expression as a way to grapple with their feelings. A poem dedicated to Fanny that was published in the *Evening Star* exhorted Thompson not to be "sad and weary-hearted," for her parents awaited her in Heaven. It was written by Florence Cooper, a Fisk graduate from Holly Springs. Thompson, who would become a pioneer black woman photographer, was also a songwriter and journalist. It was she who had written the article in the *Cleveland Gazette* that praised Ida's "rival queen" reading.[19]

Others in the lyceum evidently shared Fanny's review of Ida's performance, for when Broughton vacated the editorship of the *Evening Star,* apparently sometime during 1885, Ida was elected to fill it. Wells was surprised by the vote of confidence; she did not feel that she had the "literary graces" demanded by the position. But if she was insecure about her abilities to render the period's florid, classic-inspired phrases, she had confidence in her powers of observation and the kind of writing that the community as a whole both wanted and needed. Ida reported in her autobiography that after she took over the editorship, there was wider interest in the community to hear the *Evening Star* read, and the attendance at the lyceum increased. Among those who came to the meetings was the ebullient Pennsylvania-born Robert N. Countee, former pastor at Beale and by 1885 the minister of the Tabernacle Baptist Church and managing editor of the *Living Way.* He had already published some of Ida's *Evening Star* items in his own paper and invited her to write regularly for his publication.[20]

THE 1880S WAS a propitious time to enter the field. If technological advances that increased printing speed, lowered the cost of paper, and facilitated circulation helped to popularize poisonous perceptions about race, they also facilitated the rise of the black press, which conveyed its own prescriptions for reform regarding race relations, the role of the church, organized labor, higher education for women, home life, and party politics. Nearly two hundred black weeklies were being published throughout the country, and in 1884, the National Correspondents Press Association was founded by Calvin Chase, editor of the *Washington Bee,* which was established in 1882. In addition to Fortune's *New York Freeman* and later *New York Globe,* other important papers founded in the decade included the *Cleveland Gazette, Virginia Richmond Planet,* and the *Indianapolis Freeman.*

Church publications representing the major Baptist, AME, and CME denominations also proliferated.[21]

The confidence and growth of black newspaper owners in the period was driven by the dramatic increase in black literacy. In less than a generation since emancipation, the percentage of blacks who could not read fell from 70 to 57 percent. Further boosted by migration to the cities, black publishers could aspire for the first time toward a readership that could give the kind of support that had been only available through white, mainly Republican, financing. In 1883, T. Thomas Fortune, publisher of the *New York Globe,* boasted that he had six thousand readers and an income derived solely from advertising and subscription—thus "owing no man a cent."[22]

Like their white contemporaries, black editors of both secular and religious papers were inspired by an evangelical faith in reform mixed with the exigencies of capitalism. "We congratulate the country upon the progress and advancement of the colored people," read a resolution of a black journalists' press association in 1884, "and it is with gratitude to God that we renew our pledge as journalists to support and sustain every institution of learning and industry that tends to enlighten and benefit our social, religious, and material interest."[23]

The role of women was key to the realization of social and domestic reform, and women were an integral part of the new age of journalism. By mid-decade, a new, increasingly educated generation of black women journalists were poised to succeed their abolitionist peers such as Frances Ellen Harper and Mary Shadd Carey, the latter of whom's association with the *Provincial Freeman* in the 1850s resulted in her becoming the first black woman editor and publisher in North America. By 1886, white women, including southerners, were also advancing in journalism. Mrs. E. J. Nicholson took over the proprietorship of the *New Orleans Picayune*; and in that year, the *Memphis Daily Appeal* enthusiastically reported the call of newspaperwomen to establish a southern women's press association. The black journalist Gertrude Mossell, reflecting on the rise of white women journalists in the period, pronounced that "There is no question but intelligent colored women of the race should become adept in journalism, as much so as white women." Mossell, a member of the distinguished freeborn Philadelphia Bustill family, framed the new possibilities of journalism as both profession and mission for black women. In her "Women's Column," published in the *New York Freeman,* she even counseled a postponement of

marriage to secure a career in journalism where one could do a "shade better than schoolteaching."[24] By 1891, there were enough major black women
journalists, nineteen, that the landmark publication *The Afro-American
Press and Its Editors* devoted an entire chapter to them.[25]

IF IDA WAS unsure about her literary abilities she was secure in the conviction, drawn from her experiences as a rural teacher and the *Evening Star*
editorship, that it was important to write about the issues that less-educated
blacks faced in a "simple, helpful way." I "wrote in a plain common-sense
way on the things which concerned our people," was the way Wells characterized the weekly letters she sent to the *Living Way*. "I never used a word
of two syllables where one would serve the purpose." She signed her columns, "Iola."[26]

There is no explanation for the selection of her pen name, but it is interesting to note that her handwritten name, as it was listed in the 1880 census
for Holly Springs, looked like "Iola." Since names were often written as
census takers heard them, and Ida was probably away when the census
taker came to the Wells house, it is possible that "Iola" was how her name
was pronounced by her younger siblings. In any case, Iola showed herself to
be a writer of "superb ability," noted I. Garland Penn, a contemporary of
Ida's and a historian of the black press. Within a year of her being assigned
to the Memphis schools, Wells began what would be her lifelong journalistic career—and the discovery, as she put it, of the "real me."[27]

Though unmentioned in her autobiography, Ida's early writings included more than the benevolent, monosyllabic advisories she described.
They also revealed her as a highly judgmental and sharp-tongued critic
whose words could corkscrew into sarcasm or pierce her reservoir of resentment and anger. A theme behind virtually all of her writings was her near-
obsessive concern about the need for protection—a need born of her
personal experiences, and projected upon the larger canvas of the black
community. A particular target was the failure of black male influentials to
provide adequate aid or to protect more vulnerable blacks struggling to
move beyond their former condition, as the Reverend Imes had said several
years earlier. Ida was not the only journalist who wrote such acerbic prose,
but in a period when most female journalists wrote more mundane "woman's columns," she was the only woman to do so with such intensity and
sarcasm.

One group she set her sights upon was the black fraternal orders in Memphis. Local secret societies, such as the Polebearers and the Sons and Daughters of Ham, had been established in Memphis following the war and had had a long history of providing funds for the needy and influencing political affairs during the 1870s. But by the 1880s, the growing popularity of such orders as the Odd Fellows and the Masons were becoming controversial. With growing urbanization, the orders were national in scope, and ministers were becoming increasingly alarmed by the secularization of social life that the lodges represented and the secret order rituals that "bowed to the knees of Baal," as an AME newspaper, the *Christian Recorder*, put it. But of the most immediate concern on the part of the clergy in Memphis was that more and more discretionary income was being diverted from the churches and spent on fraternal social activities and the upkeep of lodges and halls.[28]

Ida appeared most critical of the frivolous pursuits of black fraternity men in Memphis at a time when funds were desperately needed to support the black churches and ministers she was associated with. In 1885, Benjamin Imes was trying to keep his congregation afloat; and W. A. Brinkley, pastor of the Washington Baptist Church and editor of the *Living Way*, was desperately trying to retire a $5,000 loan to rebuild the church after it was damaged by a fire. In that year, Brinkley began expelling secret society members from his congregation, and by August, the names of forty-three church members, including five women, all of whom were either expelled or supported those who were, were listed by the Chancery Court as plaintiffs in a suit against the pastor. The tension between the two groups came to a head on a memorably warm August evening at the lyceum when Imes and the *Living Way* managing editor, R. N. Countee, began to read aloud parts of the secret society rituals. Ida was probably present when the ministers nearly incited a riot by their actions. Later that evening Countee was attacked in his home by a gunman.[29]

Ida was thoroughly disgusted by the episode, which was written about with great derision in the white press, which described Countee's "yellow legs flying wildly" as he was chased from his house in his nightgown and into a nearby bayou. "To the history of an enormous amount of money paid into their treasures with nothing to show for it in the way of real estate, parks or even the multitude of widows and orphans cared for—" Ida wrote, "let us add the union of the mob and we have the history of what societies have done for the elevation of society in general, complete up to today." The article, published in the *Living Way,* and picked up by the *New York Freeman,* was remarkable for Ida's willingness to step into the fray of a potentially violent situation—another assassination attempt on Countee followed that fall— and for her apparent disregard for the consequences it would have on her social life in Memphis.[30]

Ida's most acerbic criticism, however, was reserved for national political leaders, many of them light-skinned, who had risen to power and wealth during the patronage-rich Reconstruction era of the 1860s and 1870s. Responding to a doting article in the *Detroit Plaindealer,* a black weekly that listed a veritable "who's who" of such men, Ida snapped: "I cannot call to mind a single one who has expended or laid out any of his capital for the purpose of opening business establishments . . . for the young colored men and women who have been educated [and cannot] find employment." After "getting wealth for themselves," she continued, the leaders no longer wanted to be identified with "the people to whom they owe their political preferment."[31]

Although she did not name names, Wells's thinly veiled criticism most closely fit former Mississippi U.S. senator Blanche K. Bruce, a former slave born in Virginia and a political rival of James Hill, the Wells family friend from Holly Springs. Bruce, who found his way to Bolivar County, Mississippi, where he held the positions of sheriff and tax assessor before becoming a U.S. senator, had managed, primarily through fees he received as sheriff, to acquire a 640-acre plantation after its previous owner lost it during the Civil War. His tenure as senator between the transitional years of 1875—when Republican Radicals lost their influence—and 1881, had been respectable enough. Bruce had proposed a number of civil rights bills that never gained traction, but his report recommending that Freedman Bank depositors be partially repaid was adopted by Congress and resulted in some restitution to depositors. But after 1881, Bruce had become dependent on presidential patronage for his political survival—and, no doubt, economic wealth. Between 1881 and 1885 he was register of the treasury and the owner of three thousand acres of Delta land.

In Washington, D.C, Bruce and his light-skinned wife, the former Josephine Beall Willson, member of an elite Cleveland black family, belonged to a social circle consisting primarily of whites. Few others were in the position, as Wells complained, to give "entertainments that have but a single representative of their race present." And Ida was understandably peeved when the privileged like Bruce were "able to pay for berths and seats in

Pullman cars" while remaining "unmoved" by the "indignities and insults" that other less fortunate blacks had suffered. "Tell me," Ida demanded, "what benefit is a 'leader' if he does not devote his time, talent, and wealth to the alleviation of the poverty and misery, and elevation of his people?" The article was aptly subtitled, "Iola States Some Facts about Leadership Which May Make Somebody Wince."[32]

Wells was at her journalistic best when she wrote about the treatment of blacks at the hands of political parties. In the wake of the 1883 Supreme Court decisions, blacks were split over how loyal they should remain to the party of Lincoln, which freed the slaves and passed legal protections only subsequently to leave blacks to the vagaries of states' rights and former Confederates.[33] The debate reached a crescendo when the New Jersey–born Grover Cleveland, governor of New York, became the first Democrat to win the White House since the Civil War. Stalwart black Republicans such as the *Washington Bee* editor, Calvin Chase, a freeborn Washingtonian, Howard University graduate, and no stranger to hyperbole, predicted that the election of a Democrat would result in the loss of millions of lives and the murder of helpless colored virgins and babes. Black Democrats such as Alfred Froman, among others, argued that the Republican Party had long ago surrendered its principles and no longer deserved the slavish devotion of African Americans. Still others, such as J. A. Arneaux of the *New York Enterprise,* also known as a Shakespearean actor of some repute, worried about the political purgatory that awaited blacks who became disaffected from both parties. To be "neither Republican nor Democrat," he wrote, "was to be a political infidel and belong to the devil."[34]

The debate, flourishing in the black press and journals, reached a new stage after Cleveland won the election and, in his inaugural address, he promised to protect black rights under the Constitution. Soon after, Cleveland lived up to his word when he resisted his party to appoint (Democratic) African Americans to the traditional patronage posts that they had held under Republicans, namely, the ministers to Haiti and Liberia, and the recorder of deeds in Washington. When Congress rejected the president's nomination of James C. Matthews of Albany, New York, to succeed the aging abolitionist Frederick Douglass for the latter post—an office in which the holder earned $1.50 per transaction during a time when there was a real estate boom in the city—Cleveland gave Matthews a recess appointment. When Congress rejected him a second time, Cleveland successfully pushed through another African American for the position: James Monroe Trotter, a musician, scholar, and Civil War veteran of the famed Fifty-fifth Massachusetts Regiment who had previously worked for the Democratic governor of Massachusetts, Benjamin F. Butler.[35]

Frederick Douglass, the leading black spokesman of the period, counseled political partisans on both sides to have a "wait-and-see attitude" about the Democratic president.[36] Wells agreed. Blacks should give "Caesar his due," she wrote, noting that the president had, thus far, "a splendid record." But she went further to imply that those who continued to lambaste Cleveland were either unreasonable, duplicitous, or dupes of the Republican Party. Cleveland's "promises to us backed as they are by his considerate actions are very hopeful," she wrote, "especially in view of the abuse he got from Negro papers who took the cue from their white leaders." Ida was taking particular aim at Chase, who after his earlier prediction that black lives would be lost if Cleveland was elected, had sought a minor patronage position under the administration only to be thwarted when his earlier editorials against the president were brought to light. "[What] Mr. Chase could have done would have been to have acknowledged his fault and begged forgiveness," Ida concluded.[37] But more to the point for Ida was that blacks should vote according to the needs of the race over those of either Democrats or Republicans.

The view was in line with Thomas Fortune, who had caused consternation in die-hard Republican circles by urging that blacks think about "race first" over party loyalty. His stance had made his Republican partners at the *Globe* so angry that they wrested control of the paper from him. When a determined Fortune responded by seeking funds to establish the *New York Freeman,* Ida stepped in to support him. No one was more "fearless, outspoken, or more worthy of support" than Fortune, she wrote. His race-first position was the "true one," she editorialized, and Ida called those who disagreed with him "sorry shams" without naming Chase, Fortune's primary competitor, who had publicly gloated over the New York editor's loss of the *Globe.* Nevertheless, Ida, demonstrating the independence she would become known for, also subsequently challenged Fortune, a native Floridian, when he went even further to suggest that blacks should cooperate with Democrats in order to gain influence in the southern states. Wells was "puzzled" by the view, she wrote, probably knowing that Fortune's father, a state legislator, had been forced by the Ku Klux Klan to move the family from Marianna to Jacksonville during the Reconstruction years. Did Fortune really think that if blacks "appealed" to the white people of the South, they "could not and would not refuse us justice . . . ?" Her rejection of both parties was summed up in one of the strongest, and clearest, racial statements of the period. "I am not a Democrat," it began, because:

the Democrats considered me a chattel and possibly might have always so considered me, because their record from the beginning has been inimical to my interests; because they had become notorious in their hatred of the Negro as a man, have refused him the ballot, have murdered, beaten and outraged him and refused him his rights. I am not a Republican, because, after they—as a party measure and an inevitable result of the war—had "given the Negro his freedom" and the ballot box following, all through their reign—while advocating the doctrine of the Federal Government's right of protecting her citizens—they suffered the crimes against the Negro, that have made the South notorious, to go unpunished and almost unnoticed, and turned them over to the tender mercies of the South entirely, as a matter of barter in '76, to secure the Presidency; because after securing the Negro vote in full . . . a Republican Supreme Court revoked a law of a Republican Congress and sent the Negro back home for justice to those whom the Republican party had taught the Negro to fear and hate. Because they care no more for the Negro than the Democrats do, and because even now, and since their defeat last November, the Republican head and the New York Republican Convention are giving vent to utterances and passing resolutions recommending State rights, and the taking from the Negro—for the reason his vote is not counted, but represented in the Electoral College, that they claim his gratitude for giving—the ballot.

Even Fortune had to concede that Ida's editorial was a "clear and forcible" statement. He published it in the *Freeman*.[38]

THE FACT THAT Fortune, Countee, and Chase published Ida's political pieces demonstrated, in part, the familiarity they had with women expressing strong opinions about such matters, even when they did not agree with their own. The tradition of black women speaking and writing critically about community matters was a long one. As early as the 1830s, Maria

Stewart—a free black woman and abolitionist from Hartford, Connecticut, and the first American-born woman of any race to lecture before a mixed audience of men and women, blacks and whites—also revealed a sharp tongue when she spoke before Boston's Afric-American Female Intelligence Society and the New England Anti-Slavery Society in 1832. Stewart was a follower of the martyred freedman David Walker, whose 1829 call for armed revolt against slaveholders resulted in several southern states passing laws that made the circulation of insurrectionist literature punishable by death; in Georgia, the fear of Walker's pamphlet, known as *David Walker's Appeal,* caused the legislature to make punishable by fine or jail teaching slaves to read. Like Walker, who died "mysteriously" and was probably murdered in 1830 after a price was put on his head, Stewart proclaimed, "I can but die for expressing my sentiments," before the mixed audience in Boston's Franklin Hall. In addition to her abolitionist sentiments, Stewart's experience as a domestic moved her to criticize both whites and black men who discriminated against and/or refused to aid African American women whose talents—and too often their sexual virtue—were buried in "performing mean, servile, labor." Stewart's black nationalist sentiments were fired by her feminist perspective—and couched within the sanction of biblical scripture. Using the examples of strong, assertive queens and women of wisdom in the Bible, she implored black women to develop their skills, open stores and schools of their own, and not be subservient to men.[39]

After the Civil War, women of strong opinion may have been unable to vote within the general electorate, but they exercised leadership in the political activities within the churches, the schools, and movements of resistance and even in the support of candidates for office. However, by the 1880s, the elites within the black community were beginning to reflect the mainstream idea of separate spheres—where men were delegated the role of political decision makers in public matters, and women were relegated to "private" domestic concerns. Highly differentiated gender roles, behavior, and appearance between the sexes were a marker of social status; and social status, as Ida's court case had demonstrated, could determine if one deserved the civil rights and privileges of first-class citizenship. Black opinion-makers may have argued that there was no inherent difference between the races, but they generally accepted the broad middle-class ideas about class, which separated "true women"—who were pure, pious, and submissive—from their less deserving counterparts. Yet for black women especially, separate spheres meant a loss of political influence in their communities just as they were becoming more educated and prepared for leadership roles. As was true for white female reformers in the period, the challenge for black women in the late nineteenth century was to construct an ideology that would restore their broader authority without bursting through the corsets of true womanhood.[40]

Ida, in her twenties during the 1880s, was, like other women, trying to navigate this social landscape. With her intensity it was exceedingly difficult to find a balance between the feminine ideal and the emotions that roiled within her. Her diary and journalism, for example, extolled women who displayed the true-womanhood virtues of piety, purity, submissiveness, and domesticity. Ida yearned to be like them in the belief that if she could suppress her "unfeminine" anger, she could come closer to the "model woman," the title of an essay she would subsequently write.[41]

For example, Wells, in a *Living Way* article, eulogized the wife of a black Republican politician in Memphis, calling her "a model of noble true womanhood and perfect ladyship . . . [because] of her sublime faith [in her husband] and hope of his ultimate reform." Beneath the Victorian flutter, one can only guess the kind of reform hoped for, but forbearance was obviously thought worthy of praise. In her diary, Ida described the wife of a colleague as "good & kind and soft as a mouse." Ida liked her but couldn't say that the feeling was returned.[42]

Helping Ida to find her way was her exposure to the intellectuals of the black Baptist women's movement of the period. It was logical that churches—where the first critical mass of black women saw challenges to their authority—would be at the forefront in shaping the ideology of womanhood. Female reformers had to contend with religious authorities who, in keeping with the times, saw St. Paul rather than the Old Testament's Judge Deborah or Queen Esther as tantamount models. As Gertrude Mossell noted in 1883, too many ministers were searching "the Scriptures, distorting its truths to prove that all women in all times, whatever their ability to do otherwise, must remain as silent forces in the world."[43]

Baptist women, by virtue of their own contested roles in the church, their access to the denomination's educational institutions, and their employment as journalists on the growing number of Baptist-funded publications, provided much of the intellectual foundation for the reshaping of black women's roles through revisionist interpretations of the scripture. For example, they reminded the brethren that the biblical injunction "Neither bond nor free"—which made slaves equal with others before God—also included "neither male nor female in Jesus Christ"; and that while men were destined to lead the race out of oppression, deliverance required a joint quest for the work of salvation.[44] One of the foremost leaders of the Baptist women's movement was the Memphis teacher Virginia Broughton—Ida's rival queen in the lyceum reading. Others included the Kentucky journalists Mary V. Cook and Lucy Wilmot Smith, who, like Ida, were writing for Baptist publications.

The point of origin for their interpretation of the Bible was the story of Adam and Eve; and in what became Ida's early signature piece on womanhood, "Woman's Mission," published in the *New York Freeman* in December of 1885, she began there, too. In the essay, Wells acknowledged that it was the sin of Eve that put a "curse" on the world, but the Messiah was born to a "Jewish virgin," signifying that women had the capacity to deliver redemption, as well as sin and death. The power of women to do such harm as well as good underlined "the necessity for erecting a standard of earnest, thoughtful, pure, noble womanhood." Such a standard required women to achieve and be educated but they were not to forget that their obligation to be the "civilizing influence" that moved "men's hearts." Thus they were not to wield their considerable power in the manner of "queens," but as "a minister in the home, as daughter, sister, wife and mother." No "other blessing can compensate the loss of a good mother," Wells ruefully concluded.

The spheres of influence belonging to women and men were divined by Adam's awakening to find Eve who was "created alike, yet differently." But different did not mean lower, Ida hastened to add. Eve was not Adam's servant but his "companion," and "helpmeet," a "kindred spirit, to help in doing the same work in the attending and dressing the garden." Work was taken quite literally by the Baptists, who believed in the dignity of labor. Acceptable work for women included poultry raising, dairying, bee culture, lecturing, and journalism—nearly all of which Ida would attempt at one time or another in her life. Enterprise and education prepared women for their duties and burdens and helped them avoid the spiritual dangers of leisure. Yet such achievements shouldn't masculinize women; it was important to remain feminine but in a substantive way. As Ida wrote, women were to be more than "a fashion plate, a frivolous inanity, a soulless doll, a heartless coquette." Ida's exhortations reflected her Baptist colleagues' belief that it was such women whom Paul had silenced in the church. If there was a departure from the Baptists in Wells's worldview, it might have been one of degree over the potential of arts and literature to be a corrupting force. For Ida, the creative process was liberating, both for herself and for society at large. It was Harriet Beecher Stowe's *Uncle Tom's Cabin*, Wells reminded her readers, that was an "indirect cause of the abolition of slavery."[45]

Unlike Ida's secular political pieces, the less transgressive "Woman's Mission" was sanctioned by scripture and it, not the earlier pieces, established Ida's national reputation as a journalist. T. Thomas Fortune told Ida that the December issue that featured her essay sold extremely well; and following its publication, Wells received invitations to write for other periodicals and was the subject of a feature written by Louis M. Browne for the *Washington Bee*. Browne called her one of "the brainiest of our female writers"—a description that did not preclude his observations about her physical characteristics (small in stature and "tolerably well-proportioned"); her ambitions (unusual for a woman); and her pretensions ("we do not advise her to take to the stage").[46]

Browne's tongue-in-cheek, familiar tone, was due, in part, to the fact that he knew Ida. He was a Memphian who had recently left the city for Washington, D.C., where he accepted a position in the Pension and Land Office, earned a law degree at Howard University in 1884, and worked as a city editor for the *Bee*. Browne traveled back and forth between Memphis and Washington, and it is clear from Ida's diary and her flirtatious teasing in her own press pieces that the two of them were attracted to each other. "The *Bee* informs us that His Royal Highness of the 'Browne line of kings' will visit the land of his birth soon," Ida announced in the *Living Way* that previous October. "He no doubt will receive a warm welcome."[47] Browne, despite his own jaunty remarks and apparent vaunted social status, appeared to have genuine respect for the young woman from a small town in Mississippi. From an "insignificant country-bred lass," he concluded in his article, "she has developed into foremost among the female thinkers of the race today."[48]

It was twelve days after "Woman's Mission" was published that Ida headed home to Holly Springs for the first time in four years with a good deal to show those who had disparaged her back home. But before leaving, she had made the conscious effort to reconcile her feelings of resentment. On New Year's Day, Ida went to a watch meeting at a church where members of the community, one by one, testified about their thanks to God. At first, as Ida later wrote in the *Living Way,* she felt like an alien among them, but she forced herself to speak. "I prayed and asked their prayers that the last trace of bitterness be removed from my heart against any one," she wrote. After her own testimony, Ida felt the warmth toward her of those assembled and she came away, she said, "with a lighter and more peaceful heart than I have known for many a day."[49] Typically, however, the feeling was short-lived.

WHEN IDA RETURNED to Memphis from Holly Springs in January of 1886 she found a mound of invitations from the editors of the *Fisk Herald, Detroit Plaindealer,* the *Gate City Press* in Kansas City, and the *AME Church Review,* edited by Bishop Benjamin Tanner (father of the soon-to-be famous painter Henry O. Tanner), among others, to write for them. There was also a letter from the Democratic editor of the newly established *Arkansas Little Rock Sun* that called her a "powfull" writer, as Ida mockingly recalled, and asked if she would start a branch of his paper in Memphis. Her compensation for starting such an enterprise was confined to her earnings from selling the paper, however, and Ida decided that she could not make the scheme pay sufficiently. The offers indicated that the invitations from newspaper publishers were rarely accompanied by adequate—if any—offers of pay for her contributions.[50] The prospects for making journalism a genuine profession where Ida could earn a living that was "a shade better than school-teaching" were dim, and a disappointed Wells publicly complained, at some point, about the lack of adequate pay offered by black newspapers. She also criticized their editing practices. The issue was important to her because she believed she needed such guidance to attain the "literary graces" she yearned for and which she measured against the books she was reading, including *Ivanhoe* by Sir Walter Scott and *Vashti,* a heartthrob romance by Augusta Jane Evans. At this point in her writing career, Ida believed that one's writing was a reflection of one's being. In analyzing Evans's work in her diary, for example, she believed its formulaic plot was "pedantic," but the author's style was "all elegant" and "chaste," revealing the author as an "exquisitely refined creature, passionately devoted to music, art, literature." Wells wanted her own writing to reflect such a feminine, acculturated woman, but in contrast to Evans's smooth transitions and "beautiful" finish, Ida saw her "Woman's Mission" essay as "a little disconnected."[51] As Ida noted in her diary, Bishop Tanner had asked for a contribution from her "brilliant?" pen—the question mark being her own. She might have been thinking more immediately about an unremarkable, strained January piece published in the *Fisk Herald* that touted the virtues of physical exercise as an important corollary to intellectual cultivation.[52]

Ida desired an editor's guidance, but, instead, what she got was a publisher's sharp criticism. In January, the *Bee*'s Calvin Chase showed that he had had just about all he could take of Ida Wells. Her association with Fortune; her knock against him, loyal Republicans, and his friend Blanche Bruce; the hoopla over "Woman's Mission"; and the praise by his editor, Louis Browne, for whom he had a paternal affection, had sent him over the edge. "For several weeks past the *star-eyed goddess* of the *Memphis Living Way*—'Iola' has been pratting to the relative merits of the different colored newspapers which have been 'seen and unseen' by her," Chase began dangerously in the January 23 edition of the paper "Evidently, from her labored efforts, she has offered her effusions to a number of papers, which . . . were inserted without compensation." If she was "getting paid for each of her numerous articles in the *Living Way*," Chase averred, "the resulting financial condition of the paper would demand Ida's retirement." Chase went on to explain that "meagre returns" from papers made it impossible to pay every writer who had "the mania to *scribble for the press* and the desire to see their *maiden efforts* in print." Noting the length of Ida's essays, Chase predicted that "Should 'Iola' *really write* anything worthy of public interest, the *AME Review* will no doubt publish it, and allow her something of compensation, but the space of the average newspaper is too limited and valuable to permit such a practice." As for editing: "Of all the exchanges that come to our office," he informed his readers, Iola's "trenchant pen is the most conspicuous for grammatical and typographical errors." The epigram for the *Bee* was "Honey for Friends, Stings for Enemies." Wells had been properly stung.[53]

Chase was "contemptible & puerile in the extreme," with "fanatical tendencies," and knew little about being an editor, Ida wrote in her diary, and added that she looked forward to one day writing something that would make him "wince." But she perhaps agreed with enough of his rebuke to decide against responding in kind. While "Woman's Mission" was the most sanctioned kind of writing a woman journalist was supposed to publish in the period, it was also the most labored and the least original.

* * *

IN MARCH OF 1886, a lynching in Carrollton, Mississippi, should have made Ida question her own mission as a journalist. The widely publicized incident in the white regional press and black newspapers throughout the country reported that armed whites, in broad daylight, entered the town courthouse where they massacred thirteen blacks who were there as witnesses. The murdered black men had come to testify on behalf of two blacks who had attacked a white lawyer in self-defense after the latter, angry about losing an election in the predominantly black county, had assaulted them.

Violence at the hands of a white mob was familiar to blacks throughout the South who had endured the murderous campaign of the Ku Klux Klan during Reconstruction. But Mississippi's no-holes-barred campaign for Redemption—the term, with all of its religious implications, used to describe the overthrow of northern and carpetbagger influence after Reconstruction—had particular significance. No southern state carried out its violent intentions more openly than Mississippi, whose white supremacists felt little need to mask themselves or their extralegal intentions. In Vicksburg, when whites demanded the resignation of a black sheriff, Peter Crosby, in 1874, Crosby had organized a posse of blacks, which led to better-armed white bands killing perhaps three hundred African Americans. Federal authorities eventually restored Crosby to his position, but a year later, when southern whites slaughtered at least thirty blacks in Hinds County, the massacre received little national attention. Even a leading southern Republican paper opined about the futility of dwelling on the Hinds murders, "for almost no one seemed to care."[54] Mississippi was a bellwether for the fact that the North, and the nation, was tiring of racial strife and that any act of outrage against black citizens, no matter how vagrant, violent, or defiant of law, could be performed with impunity.

Carrollton was a case in point. The massacre took place in a courthouse, of all places, and the murdered African Americans were guilty of nothing more than their willingness to testify in a legal proceeding. Moreover, it had taken place in the shadow of the New Orleans Exposition with its gesture toward interracial cooperation and reconciliation. But still dimly perceived by many was that the Exposition's unfurling of a New South public relations campaign—aimed especially at the North, to counter, in part, the image of a yet-to-be-civilized region incapable of reform and progress—required a new rationale for the continuing violence. The New South would bring on an era of blaming the victims for their crime. The *Cleveland Gazette* noted this when it quoted the *New York Tribune*'s take on Carrollton. Because the northern public was not "so acclimated to such events as to regard them without emotion," the *Tribune* said, "[i]t was declared that the colored people had been the aggressors and it was intimated that the indiscriminate massacre of all the occupants in the Carrollton court room was in some mysterious way necessary to the safety of the perpetrators of the deed, if not to the security of the entire white population." Blacks such as Blanche K. Bruce and John R. Lynch, former speaker of the Mississippi House of Representatives and, in 1873, elected to the U.S. Congress, went to the White House to protest to President Cleveland about Carrollton. There were mass protest meetings about the massacre held by blacks throughout the country, and the Colored Press Association passed a resolution urging migration of blacks from the South to the West. But Mississippi authorities did not even make a pretense to arrest the perpetrators—one of whom was alleged to be the son of Senator George from Mississippi—and white politicians did not condemn the crime. Carrollton revealed that the "solidity of the South [was going to be] strengthened by the cement of innocent blood," concluded the *Gazette*.[55]

The massacre had compelled Texas-born Lucy Parsons, in a publication fittingly called *The Alarm*, to make one of the earliest calls for armed self-defense against lynching. Parsons, a woman of color who identified her heritage as Mexican and Native American, was an anarchist and labor organizer. (Her white husband, Albert, became one of the leaders of the famous Haymarket Square riot in Chicago that took place later that year over the issue of the eight-hour working day, and which resulted in his execution along with three other indicted anarchists.) That Ida would one day be compared with Lucy Parsons, who remained a radical socialist leader and labor organizer for the rest of her life, would have been inconceivable in 1886. Ida did comment about Carrollton in her diary. "Colored men rarely attempt to wreak vengance [*sic*] on a white one unless he has provoked it unduly," she believed. But while Parsons—who was outside of the middle-class black community's formulations about gender—publicly called for armed revenge, Ida, in the secreted pages of her diary, called for her Father: "O God," she beseeched, "when will these massacres stop?"[56]

A MONTH AFTER the Carrollton lynching, Ida published "A Story of 1900" in the *Fisk Herald*. The piece did not address the question of rising violence against blacks, but instead described her coming to terms with her role to uplift the race. The protagonist in her fictional narrative was a young teacher who had awakened to a "true sense of mission" by going to the homes of blacks, "where squalor and moral uncleanness walked hand in hand with poverty." At one time the teacher in Ida's story viewed such conditions with "loathing and disgust," but now realized her purpose was to teach blacks self-respect, a "practical Christianity," and to set an example of "cleanliness and morals for their children." The story provided some insight into Ida's thinking, but the writing again was highly stylized with labored phrases. The teacher's mission, Wells concluded, was one of cultivating "flowers" where the "cruel thorns or rank and poisonous thistles" had once flourished "unmolested."[57]

THE MASSACRE AND perhaps her failure to address it cast a larger shadow over the other dissatisfactions in Wells's life in 1886. The year had gotten off to a bad start with Chase's diatribe and had risen to near-crisis proportion when Ida had to hunt for a boardinghouse after Aunt Fanny had decided to leave Memphis for Visalia, California. Wells did not explain why Fanny had decided to move clear across the country, but California and other points west were attracting both whites and blacks who sought new, unfettered economic opportunities on the expanding frontiers that were becoming more accessible with the development of train travel. Blacks had initially been drawn to California by the gold rush in 1848, and by 1852—two years after it was declared a free state—California's black population numbered two thousand. By 1890, the number reached 11,322 with the largest black communities in Sacramento and San Francisco.[58]

Visalia, the county seat of Tulare County, was about two hundred miles southeast of San Francisco and nestled in the farm-rich San Joaquin Valley. Few blacks lived there among its twenty-five hundred residents in 1886, but the town was enjoying an era of prosperity and there were increasing labor needs for its cotton, trade, and service industries. The cost of living was cheaper in the West than in Memphis, and the California town had another decided advantage: it had never had an epidemic, as its promoters advertised. Expecting that Ida would follow at the end of the school year, Fanny took her sisters L'il and Annie with her. In the meantime, Ida was forced to desperately search for a suitable boardinghouse, which made her life unsettled and, like her essay, disconnected.[59]

Wells thought she had found a place at 39 Ruth Street run by Anna Powell, who was listed in the Memphis directory as a laundress. There is no indication of what the accommodations were like, but the house was located near a trolley line; and in the neighborhood were several of Ida's teaching colleagues and a number of well-established black families. Among the latter was a couple with whom Ida would establish a close friendship: Thomas Moss—who had been one of the hosts receiving the visiting teachers—and his wife, Betty.

But no sooner had she moved in than Mrs. Powell suddenly announced that she was raising the rent. "I cannot do it," Ida wrote in her diary. Despite the raise, she was strapped for funds. One reason for her poor finances was that the spotty support for the public schools often resulted in teachers not being paid on time. Wells did not receive her December salary until late February, and her salary check for January would not be issued until the following April, a circumstance noted in her diary with resignation rather than surprise. Even with a regular paycheck there was not much to spare, considering that boarding fees were $15 a month; streetcar transportation, $6.75; shoes, close to $4 a pair; materials to make just one dress, more than $15; underwear, about 45¢ a pair; elocution lessons, $2; gloves, 20¢. Added to these expenditures was medicine for Ida's frequent chest and head colds, exacerbated by the insufficiently coal-heated classrooms and strict attendance requirements that forced Ida, on one occasion, to tramp through a ten-inch snowdrift with ill-fitting shoes when public transportation had been suspended. In the year, Ida also had to see a white doctor, Dr. Sinclair on Madison Street, to treat a chronic ear infection.

With Fanny's departure Ida was also expected to send money to California to help with her sisters. Her brothers, George and AJ, were always asking for money. Now sixteen and nineteen years of age, respectively, they were perennially under- or unemployed. George, when not working in Millington, outside of Memphis, worked as a hostler and stableman. James, who had spent a good deal of time with their aunt Belle and uncle William Gathins in Mississippi, had recently, to Ida's absolute horror, taken to "gaming" or gambling, and, as she heard from "Dad" Albert Froman, was periodically in trouble over it.

Ida's own spending habits were not abstemious. She may have written that a "true woman" had to be more than "a fashion plate," but Ida, who spent much of her income on clothes, clearly refused to be less than one. In this she was not unusual; female teachers often struggled with low salaries and high expectations regarding their appearance and dress. Certain accessories were expected, such as white gloves and parasols. Then there were the expenses associated with a lady's hair. Though seeming not to use the recent hair-straightening methods imported from France and advertised in the black press, Ida did have her hair shampooed and trimmed in the shop of Mr. Dogan, whose son, Matthew, Ida knew when they were both attending Rust. Ida could justify, to some extent, her paying for elocution and music lessons and splurging on books, all of which she did. The same was true for the ironing and washing she paid someone else to do; the heavy-duty tasks made her hands swell.

Nevertheless, Ida had gone overboard in her spending for clothes. She had succumbed to the siren call of a remarkable, upscale department store where she spent much of her money on clothes: Menken's Palatial Emporium, on Main Street, founded by two liberal German-Jewish brothers, and perhaps one of the few such stores where black women could shop unmolested and pay for items on time. Menken's had risen from bankruptcy in 1883 as another symbol of the city's phoenixlike recovery. The building stood five stories tall, with an interior that flooded the senses with dark mahogany and pure white marble, French plate glass, and shelves filled with fine dresses, rare imported fabrics, and even a floor devoted to wholesale boots and shoes. No less appealing was the store's finely furnished area that featured paper and writing materials, where "a lady may sit and write." In January, Ida had received a whopping bill of seventy-eight dollars from the store, more than her entire month's salary.[60]

Her overspending caused torrents of self-disgust. "I am sorry I did not resist the impulse to buy that cloak," she complained guiltily in one instance, knowing that the fifteen dollars she spent for it could have gone for the promised aid to her aunt in California. She also felt guilty about her landlady, who like a number of less-educated black women was trying to improve her station through the boarding business. But the rent money had gone to Menken's. When Powell told her well-dressed and coiffed tenant that if the rent was not forthcoming, she would be forced to hire herself out in domestic service, Ida again expressed regret about her spending habits. "I am so sorry I bought that sacque [purse] when I could have done without it," Ida wrote in her diary. Ida even avoided her brother George when he came calling one day because she knew he was going to ask her for money. Subsequently Ida started selling encyclopedias to make ends meet.[61]

Ida borrowed money from Froman to give Powell part of the rent, but it was too little, too late, and Wells spent the next few days with Fanny Thompson while she searched for another boarding place. She finally settled in with a Mrs. Hill on Tate Street, though it was far less amenable than Mrs. Powell's. Hill was very "quarrelsome & picayunish," and the contentious household included a willful teenager, Ella, with whom Hill constantly argued and on one occasion beat her with a stick until Ida intervened; on another occasion, Hill locked the young girl out of the house until 1:00 A.M. When Ella was finally let in, Ida noted, she went to bed "cold as ice." Moreover, in February, a little girl by the name of Louise Cage, whose family lived near the Hill place, became ill and subsequently died from scarlet fever. Cage lived "directly across the street," Ida noted in her diary, indicating her concern about her proximity to her new boarding place. Ida herself had been feeling ill. My "system is not in good order," she wrote in her diary, "and I cannot consult a physician till I get some money." Her condition was made only worse when a February snowstorm forced Ida to wade by foot to her school when the streetcars stopped running. When Hill also told Ida that she was going to raise the rent, it precipitated another mad search for lodging and visits to at least six prospective boarding places trying to find a suitable one.[62]

The entire situation made Ida blue. She tried to shake her despondency by going to see in successive weeks during the winter several plays, including the *Mikado*, the new Gilbert and Sullivan comic opera, which she liked, and a play called *Humbug*, which she didn't. It is not clear if she was forced to sit in a segregated section of the theaters, but on another occasion she and Fanny Thompson had decided not to attend a play because the theater was too crowded—an indication, perhaps, that they had decided to avoid the situation that Hooks had encountered at the Leubrie Theater several years before. But Wells did sit in a segregated balcony when she went to hear Dwight Moody, the world-famous evangelist, preach at the Cumberland Presbyterian Church. She had gone to see Moody twice: once at Cumberland and again at AME's Avery Chapel, where he filled its three-thousand-seat auditorium.[63]

IN 1886, DWIGHT Lyman Moody was on a tour through the South, and the large numbers of both blacks and whites who went to hear him preach were a testament to his fame and popularity as the most powerful evangelical leader in the United States. In 1854, when he lived in Boston, Moody had shown his abolitionist stripes when Anthony Burns, a runaway slave from Virginia, was caught and imprisoned in the city under the federal Fugitive Slave Act, which stipulated that whites were compelled to aid in the recapture of slaves who escaped to free states. The law infuriated abolitionists and inspired Harriet Beecher Stowe's *Uncle Tom's Cabin* and the mushrooming of safe havens for fugitives known as the Underground Railroad. When Burns was arrested in Boston, Moody, then a shoe salesmen, was among the angry crowd that had broken into the jail in an abortive attempt to liberate him. (Subsequently, Burns was returned to Virginia but was eventually bought and freed in North Carolina.)[64]

By the Civil War, Moody had become an evangelical minister who became a chaplain for Union troops, and in the 1870s, he went to Great Britain where he held massive revival meetings. The evangelist returned to the United States in 1875, professing he loved the South as much as the North; his "good news" message of regional reunion and reconciliation, interdenominational unity, and the possibility to be born again after yielding to the temptations heightened by urbanization and industrialism spoke to the anxieties of the period.

Ida heard Moody tell his audiences that "both rebel and Yankee" were united in their need to be born again. In the midst of the country's industrial growth and the increasing chasm between rich and poor, Moody also warned that money "availed nothing in the cause of Christ." And citing alcohol and wife-beating among the panoply of common sins, the evangelist noted that nineteen out of every twenty Christians were "unfit for the service of God." If Ida felt that she was not being as good a Christian as she ought to have been, Moody's visit was a reminder that at least she wasn't alone. After his sermon at Cumberland, he invited those who needed saving to join him in the basement of the church. Five hundred (presumably white) "sinners" did so. Ida was impressed by Moody's "plain and natural" style of speaking and his penchant to use well-crafted "charming" narratives rather than religious doctrine to express his views. But she was nonetheless disturbed that Moody subscribed to preaching before segregated

audiences. Wells and other blacks had yet to really grasp that race separation was a consequence rather than a contradiction of the New South reconciliation idea. She intended to write Moody a letter, asking why "ministers
never touched on that phase of sin—the caste distinction—practised [*sic*]
even in the churches ... instead of rectifying it." Eight years later, Ida
would publicly condemn Moody in no uncertain terms, but in 1886, she
was posing questions, not offering answers.[65]

In the same month, February, Wells also went to hear her first "Jewish
discourse," as she put it. It was given by Bavarian-born Max Samfield, the
liberal editor of the *Jewish Spectator,* and Memphis's leading rabbi. Wells
did not indicate the subject of Samfield's talk, though he was well known
for his perorations on Shakespeare and philosophy. But Ida still had to return every day to the benumbing first-grade curriculum she was teaching
in the school that now averaged fifty pupils per instructor. She was not a
patient young woman and felt that because she had never had formal normal instruction, her pedagogy was lacking. Ida complained in her diary
about the students who remained, despite her efforts, uninterested in their
lessons and whose behavior made her temper flare. Moreover, teachers were
closely supervised: their absences and tardiness became a matter of public
record in the board reports, and their behavior was closely watched. "I have
found out that someone tattles to [C. H.] Collier [the white superintendent
of schools] everything I do," Ida wrote in her diary.[66] Just the year before,
Collier had attempted to fire Julia Hooks, Virginia Broughton, and another teacher, James Lott, over a conflict that arose when Collier attempted
to place a new male graduate of LeMoyne, G. P. Hamilton, over Broughton
at Kortrecht. All three liberal-arts-educated teachers had preceded Collier
as superintendent and had a reputation for insubordination and criticizing
the school system at a time when there was a growing preference for home-
grown locally educated LeMoyne teachers. The three recalcitrants, all of
whom were active Baptists, held their jobs—but only after they received
support from key white members of the board; R. N. Countee; Broughton's
husband, Julius, influential in political and Baptist circles; and Fred Savage, a black board member and shoemaker by profession, who had beaten
out Ida's surrogate "dad" (and possible protector) Alfred Froman, Sr., in
the last election. But the frustration Ida wrote about most in her diary, and
the one that challenged all the efforts to contain herself, was the quest to
find an acceptable suitor.[67]

CHAPTER FOUR

Love and Trouble

What kind of creature am I to become?

—*Diary of Ida B. Wells*

Ida may have left Holly Springs inexperienced in affairs of the heart, but she did not remain so in Memphis. Her diary entries written in the nineteen months between January of 1886 and September of 1887 mention a dizzying number of young men who vied for her affection. By then, Ida had grown into an attractive young woman with dark, almond-shaped eyes and a brown complexion burnished by her African and Native American ancestry. She was also smart, ambitious, and, one would guess, more animated than many of her peers who were not wrestling, as Ida was, with such strong, mercurial emotions.

She and her generation of twentysomethings came of age in a period that was alive with notions of emotional fulfillment through romantic love. The era's proliferating fiction and nonfiction on the subject were increasingly viewing sex as an act of pleasure and fulfillment in and of itself, not just as a corollary of reproduction. But at the same time, there were differing views about premarital intercourse itself, and advice manuals about it fell into three categories: some counseled utter restraint; others maintained that unfettered sexual expression was the key to health and happiness; a third opinion approved of sex (including petting and kissing) as long as it was an act of true, sincere love.[1] Nevertheless, the stereotypes regarding black women's sexuality produced a prim public discourse on the part of the black elite, and it is difficult to discern Ida's personal attitudes about sexual relations in her writings. But her diary indicates that like others who aspired to the middle class, she was wary of the predictable perils associated with premarital sex. Still, Ida clearly was a passionate young woman and no shrinking violet as far as finding a suitor was concerned.

In February of 1886, Wells had received a half-dozen Valentine cards, and later that year she counted five men "who with the least encouragement, would make love to me; I have two correspondents in the same predicament."[2] The list did not include the numerous minor contenders, a number of whom lived in other cities, including Washington, D.C.; Nashville; Kansas City, Missouri; and Louisville. It is not clear how Ida met the out-of-towners, but, as her diary and announcements in newspapers indicated, the black urban elite traveled often, if not always comfortably, by train at a time when railways were expanding their routes to various cities where a visitor could find boarding places or homes of friends and acquaintances. Memphis, as indicated by the visiting teachers from St. Louis and Kansas City, was a central depot.

The possibilities of courtship among the educated classes were also enhanced by their ability to write letters to one another. On at least one occasion, Ida corresponded with a prospective suitor with whom she had yet to meet after his name was given to her by a mutual, matchmaking friend. Love-letter writing and reading was not only a means to communicate over distances, it also fostered the highly touted value of exploring one's romantic self: a consciousness of one's authentic emotion, feeling, and identity that existed outside of the rigid social conventions regarding public behavior and outward appearances.[3] Ida yearned for such self-discovery, and the attention of so many suitors was flattering in a city where there were eighty-two men for every hundred women among blacks in Ida's age group. Nevertheless, the middle-class conventions of courtship proved difficult for a woman with her personality and social standing in Memphis.[4]

A successful courtship culminated in finding one true love, above all others, who could be entrusted with one's most intimate self and feelings. The two most important hallmarks of a successful romantic relationship, trust and self-disclosure, meant that courtships went through a number of stages and a series of tests to ascertain a partner's sincerity, mutuality of interest, and worthiness.[5] Wells was more than capable of throwing an array of challenges at her prospective partners, but with her prickly personality and tendency to see grievous insult in any social slight, large or small, she was not adept at fielding them. To complicate matters, after the departure of her aunt, Ida had no family member to play the protective role of chaperone or an experienced adult she could regularly confide in for advice. Finally, as her diary reveals, the social life of single women in such situations was closely surveilled and publicly commented upon by the black elite, perhaps even more so in Ida's case because of her notoriety—and the rumors that had followed her from Holly Springs to Memphis. When she got wind of any gossip that impugned her character, Wells became an angry missile looking for the nearest target and appeared to have particular disdain for suitors who showed any form of weakness—shorthand for a man not having the wherewithal to protect her. In her diary, for example, she wrote about a suitor, identified as BFP, saying, "I don't know what to say to him as I still have the feeling of pity & contempt for the man, who is not strong enough to rise to superior circumstances." And when she got news of the death of one of her former suitors, Harry, who had succumbed to tuberculosis, she wrote in her diary: "My heart smites me to think what a cruel letter I sent in answer to his last declaration of love for me! . . . I always thought a great deal of him, weak and irresolute as he was, for he was the first to help dispel the dark clouds that had settled on my young life, and treated me with the courtesy and delicacy of a true gentleman altho' he knew the whole base slanderous like that which had blackened my life, and offered me his love even while his companions were rehearsing the lie in his ears." Wells, whose circle included men above her social station, was especially subject to slander. As a commentator on southern mores observed, such men were often poised to cast aspersions on a woman's reputation to test her claims to a socially superior husband.[6] Finding a husband, however, was not Ida's intention. The harrowing experience of caring for her siblings in Holly Springs, and, seemingly, her own unrealized ambitions put a damper on any thoughts of matrimony—if not companionship. "I do not wish to be married," Ida pronounced in her diary, but she did "wish for the society of gentlemen."[7]

Of the men Ida mentioned expressing interest in her, three stood out as major contenders, from whom she tried to choose her one true love and confidant: Isaiah J. Graham, a Memphis teacher since 1884; Charles S. Morris, a Howard University divinity student from Louisville; and Louis M. Browne, the *Bee* editor who was shuttling between Washington and Memphis.

Isaiah Graham, the local beau, had both the advantages and disadvantages that came with being in the closest proximity to Ida. She was no shrinking violet toward men who piqued her interest, and she had sent photos of herself to Isaiah, a sign of the period that indicated one was interested in advancing a relationship to a new level after the first phase of casual dating. Isaiah, like all of the men Ida preferred, was attractive, well educated, and upwardly mobile. He was dark-skinned with crinkly hair and had a degree in classical literature from a leading black school, Atlanta University, and a personal library filled with Latin and Greek texts as well as limited editions of Dickens. Graham came from a well-to-do Georgia family. His father, the proprietor of a successful construction business, was a former slave who had been allowed to hire himself out and eventually bought his own freedom and that of his wife with the earnings he made as a carpenter and self-taught architect.[8]

After she sent photographs to him, Ida sent Isaiah a note asking him for a loan—she did not specify the amount—which she promised to repay at 10 percent interest. In her diary, she wrote that her request was one of desperation: she had been "reduced to such dire extremity" that she had asked Graham for the money. But even considering Ida's financial situation, the request was an extraordinary one for someone so sensitive about her reputation. At the least, it indicated that not only had she disclosed her financial situation to Graham, but also that she trusted his discretion and his feelings about her. In the context of the times, Ida's asking for a loan was also no doubt one of her "tests" to see how he would react. Graham failed it miserably.

When he came to visit her after she had sent the photos and the note, he expressed "agreeable surprise" at receiving the pictures but said he knew nothing of the note asking for a loan. Ida suspected that he was not telling the truth about the latter, and Graham compounded the crime—either real or imagined—by trying to get Ida to make the first explicit statement about her own intentions and feelings for him. Such a statement implied a commitment and his asking her to make it was not in keeping with the usual convention in which the man made the first such declaration. Ida concluded that Graham was exploiting her request, and the idea of his trying to take advantage of her set off a slow boil. "I thought it was conceding too much considering he had never told me anything [about his feelings]," she wrote in her diary. "I would like to be friends," she continued, "but shall do nothing more to make us so, nor will I submit to 'conditions' in order to compass it."[9]

Nevertheless, Ida kept seeing Graham, evidently in the hopes that he would be the first to express feelings of affection toward her. She described how he chivalrously piloted her home through the muddy streets when a water main broke and brought her medicine from Isaac Norris's store when she was suffering from a cold. All seemed to be proceeding smoothly until one day Graham made a physical advance toward Ida to which she yielded, in the evident expectation that the sought-after verbal commitment would follow. But when Graham subsequently failed to say anything, Ida swelled with humiliation and anger. "I blush to think I allowed him to caress me, that he would dare take such liberties and yet not make a declaration," she wrote in her diary. Wells thought that Graham sincerely cared for her and attributed his failure to state his feelings to fear and lack of self-confidence. "I believe he loves me, but is certainly enigmatical in his behavior," she wrote in her diary. But for Ida, insecurity was weakness in a man, and her assessment made her lose respect for him. "He seems to not have confidence in my actions and were he to plead with me on his knees now, for no consideration would I consider his proposition. He had his opportunity and lost it thro' fear of being deceived and other timidity and it shall not occur again," she vowed.[10]

No doubt Graham himself was humiliated by the rejection. Wells's rebuffs often became public knowledge and subject to gossip. Moreover, Ida had a reputation for being haughty with potential suitors as well as women. Graham told Ida that he had heard she had told someone else that he, or anyone else for that matter, should feel "honored" for being allowed the "privilege" of going out with her; and that when she was dating someone, all the young men in the town knew about it.[11]

Ida denied ever saying such a thing, but Isaiah's accusation made her think that there might be a conspiracy mounting against her. Louis Browne had already told her that she had alienated the fraternity men with her criticism of the secret societies. Ida had counted on Graham to be her chivalrous protector, but now she began to think that he might indeed be the main provocateur. He was "deliberating setting the men in town against her" she wrote in her diary, through "premeditated" and "deliberate" insults. The sense of betrayal almost unhinged her. "I know it is unchristian-like to burn for revenge as I do," she confessed, "but a demon is tempting me to lead him on and fool him at last. When I think of how I could & can fool [Graham] and of his weak imaginings to the contrary, petty evidences of spite work, and he has been safe hitherto because I would not stoop to deceit—I grow wild almost & determine to pay him back." But Ida, aware that anger was her besetting sin, as she called it, pulled herself back from the brink. "But I . . . will do the right as I know it—because it *is* right," she wrote. Nevertheless, her diary revealed the mix of self-righteousness and deep-seated resentment that would have to be rechanneled if she was to move beyond her own "former condition." She wrote, "I have never stooped to underhand measures to accomplish any end and I will not begin at this late day by doing that that my soul abhors; sugaring men, weak, deceitful creatures, with flattery to retain them as escorts or to gratify a revenge, & I earnestly pray My Father to show me the right & give me the strength to do it because it is right, despite temptations." With her Christian sensibility, Wells could win such battles by imagining herself as an innocent youth, willing to forgive those who unjustly accused her. "I shall pray for Mr. G. & all others who have formed themselves in a league against a defenseless girl, that they may see the light & injustice done me and that I may bear it meekly, patiently."[12]

Wells subsequently made peace with the better angels of her nature by solicitously writing Graham a letter, asking if he was earnest when he had asked Ida if she could love him before he had given his own assurances. Graham replied affirmatively, and the two continued seeing each other. But whether or not Wells knew it herself, her subsequent diary entries reveal that she had not completely been able to summon those angels—especially after Graham appeared to completely surrender to her wiles. He desired to "sip nectar from her lips" he wrote to her on one occasion, and he professed his love for her. But once he had declared himself, Ida began, incrementally, and perhaps unconsciously, to turn a cold shoulder toward him, though she continued to express just enough interest to keep him hooked—and miserable. He began "acting like a mummy" around her, and her conquest brought out Ida's disdain for weakness. Graham became a "poor, thin fellow," in her eyes.[13]

While Ida was contending with Graham, she was also corresponding regularly with Charles S. Morris in Louisville. It is not clear how she first came to know him, but he was attending Howard University in Washington, D.C., and so belonged to the small social circle of black college graduates who either met or were told about one another through mutual friends. Like Graham and Browne, Morris came from a prominent family. His parents and grandparents were freeborn, and his mother was an Oberlin graduate. A biographical sketch of him also included the fact that his maternal great-grandmother was half-sister to Martha Washington.[14]

Morris was good-looking with his brown skin, chiseled features, and slim, oval-shaped, studious face. Unlike the maladroit Graham, Morris had a dazzling way with words—a skill that Ida respected—and it served him well during the early phase of their relationship in which they communicated primarily by writing letters. Her diary recorded more than thirty letters exchanged from December of 1885 to September of 1887, and although no letters from any correspondent are extant, Wells recorded the contents, in part, of those she both sent and received in her diary. Charles's letters were her favorites. The two achieved one of the important measures of success in an epistolary relationship: to communicate ideas, concerns, and confidences in a style that had the informality (and intimacy) of face-to-face conversation. Charles sympathized with Ida's problems with the fraternal men, and when she confessed her own feelings of isolation, Charles admitted that he, too, felt a similar loneliness.[15]

Ida liked to be provocative with her suitors, and Charles Morris alone was up to the task of fielding her taunts without crossing the line of Wells's mercurial temperament. For example, when Ida discovered that he was three years younger than she, she wrote to tell him that she had thought she was corresponding with a "man," but she had discovered that he was a "mere boy." Ida did not record his specific riposte, but she subsequently noted how Morris managed to "deftly" and "skillfully" steer his "epistolary bark clear of [her] shoals and quicksands." Moreover, compared with Graham, Morris also possessed a more expansive, critical mind. He was an "interested, intellectual being who could lead & direct my wavering foot steps in intellectual paths," wrote Ida, impressed by Morris's wide-ranging knowledge of literature, philosophy, and the natural sciences. She felt inadequate about her own development along those lines. She didn't know what books to read, she wrote in her diary, or where to obtain the knowledge. Ida looked to Morris to guide her.[16]

One of those paths, Ida hoped, would lead to her publishing a novel, and the relationship between her and Charles ascended another rung in her mind after she confided to him about her "dream" to do so. That year, 1886, an unsigned letter (perhaps by Gertrude Mossell) to *Lippincott's Monthly Magazine* predicted that the "Great American Novel" would be written by a black woman because of her unique experiences and perspective, and Ida obviously had taken the idea to heart. Morris encouraged the project. If Ida wrote such a "classical" and "representative" book, he told her, she would make herself "loved, honored, & respected." Morris had precisely articulated Ida's aspirations. "I feel my sceptre departing from me before him as before no other . . ." Ida wrote about him in her diary, soon after reading the same classical phrase in Augusta Evans's *Vashti*. She followed the self-revelation with a letter that addressed him, for the first time, by the less formal "Charlie." Addressing him in that manner was a signal that she was prepared to take the next step in their relationship; pet names were the most unambiguous indication of a privileged relationship.[17]

"Mr. Morris," however, did not respond in kind to Ida's gesture. She may have been a bit too "untamed" for the future minister, who, with all his good qualities and sharp intellect, could be very traditional. For example, he complained in his letters of women in general who failed to keep an orderly house; and he was appalled when Ida told him that she was studying for a reading of Lady Macbeth—the murderous Scot who begged the gods to "unsex" her sufficiently to do what she had to. One of the features of intimacy was the ability of partners to reveal desires that might not be in keeping with strict gender roles and Morris's response showed his limitations in that regard. While it eventually became clear that Morris was not on the same page with Ida as far as serious courtship was concerned, she hoped that theirs would be "a lasting friendship, increasing over the years such as I read about, see very rarely and have experienced—never—" she wrote.[18]

In the end, it was Louis Browne who proved to be her most worthy contender. He was much more "a blasé man of the world," as Ida saw him, than Morris. "L.M.B is older, has a more varied experience . . . with no new worlds to conquer or nothing fresh or new to be, for him, learned under the sun," she wrote in her diary. Browne's "varied experience" made him more of a player as far as the dating game was concerned, and he made smug, self-assured pronouncements in the *Washington Bee,* which carried more articles about gender relations than any other black paper in the period. Using the pen name Elembee (a phonetic of his initials), Browne appeared to live by one of his own refrains in the paper: "Some say," he wrote:

> That when you kiss her, do so without force, and you will avoid all
>   scuffles.
> That some say there is no sweetness in a kiss unless force is taken.

That we know there is something sweet in this style of osculation.

That if her ruffles you have rumpled, and put her in a fluster.

That do not mind that, as you can fix it, if you are a re-adjuster.[19]

Browne was evidently fixing a good deal, as his visits to Memphis even-tually resulted in moonlight walks with Ida that, as she noted in her diary, inevitably ended up in their "favorite trysting" place—a phrase that im-plied that the two exchanged unchaperoned intimacies of one sort or another. But Ida was ambivalent about Brown's assertiveness and sexual innuendos. As she recorded in her diary, "he makes use of the following ambiguous statement: 'I could understand you better in another way.'" She continued, "I don't know what construction to put on it," signifying that she knew full well what it meant, "and lest I should be charged with the wrong one I make none."[20]

Wells's agitation with Browne was fomented by his attempts to seduce her when she was still, nominally at least, committed to Graham. One's behavior in romantic relations was thought indicative of one's general integrity and accepting Louis's affections made her feel duplicitous. "I answered his letter Sunday and told him I would certainly cease correspondence if he ever again considered it necessary to let me know the state of his affections . . . ," she wrote about Browne in her diary.[21]

But when Ida rebuked him for his forwardness, Browne smartly re-ceded, and turned the tables by suggesting that they just be friends or by calling Ida his "little sister." He appeared to understand that to sustain Ida's interest, he had to play a complex game of being assertive and showing interest in her while acting nonchalant in the face of her reactions. At one point, Browne even told Ida that he was engaged to another. Wells actually appreciated the forthright declaration because afterward he continued to visit her, and in Ida's eyes this indicated that he cared for her as a friend, not just as a conquest. Additionally, Browne's technical unavailability was, in part, the reason why Ida could be more herself and let her guard down—although she wasn't always happy about it.

There was the time, for instance, when Louis took her to her first base-ball game, played between a Memphis and an Augusta, Georgia, team. It was not decided until the late innings, and toward the end Ida had gotten so angry by the fielder's error that cost Memphis the victory that she pub-licly lost her temper. "I acted in an unladylike way toward those in whose company I was & hardly noticed LMB," she moaned to her diary. On another occasion, she defiantly beat Louis at checkers, a game where victory depended on aggressive moves and penetration of an opponent's line of defense. Her win, she noted with satisfaction, "of course greatly surprised him," but there was no sign that such things really bothered Browne, as they would a more stuffy or less secure companion.[22]

Inevitably, however, Browne's own scepter started slipping. At one point, he told Ida that he was afraid he was falling in love with her; shouldn't he stop coming to Memphis for both of their sakes? Coyly, Ida told him to do neither. At another point, Browne forthrightly asked Ida if she was still "pledged" to Graham. When she did not answer immediately, Browne kissed her. Though his affections were hardly unwelcome, or new, she was upset by it. It "seems even now as if they [Browne's kisses] blistered my lips," Ida wrote in her diary after the episode. Contrary to her own convictions about not being a "soulless flirt," as she had written in "Woman's Mission," she was upset that she could not decisively break with or fully accept either Graham or Browne.[23]

Exacerbating the situation, people in the community began criticizing her behavior. A colleague who empathized with the lovesick Graham accused Ida of being "amiable to men in order to repulse them"; another warned her about playing with a "double-edged" tool. "I feel that I have degraded myself in that I had not the courage to repulse the one or the others. I feel so humiliated at the thought in my own estimation that I cannot look any one straight in the face." Angry at her ambivalence, Browne asked Ida if she could love anyone. Wells confessed to her diary that perhaps she could not.[24]

IT HAD BEEN "a winter of discontent" Wells wrote in one of her common Shakespearean references, and the spring looked no better. In June, the relationships with all three suitors were at the point where she had to make some kind of decision, and she could not. Morris asked her to come to Louisville; she told Browne that she did not love him but wanted to continue seeing him; and she informed Graham that she did not have "an absorbing feeling for him" but thought it would grow. Ida knew that she was stringing Isaiah along because her relationships with both Louis and Charles were shaky and she dreaded feeling as "lonely and isolated" as she had the previous winter. "It seems I can establish no middle ground," she wrote. "It is either love or nothing."[25]

As she took stock of herself, Ida had failed be in control of, or manage, nearly every facet of her life: her finances, her relationships, her nascent journalistic career, her students, or her emotions. "I feel so dissatisfied with my life," she wrote in her diary. "I am an anomaly to myself as well as to others." Overshadowing her general discontent with herself was that she had been unable to make a decision about Aunt Fanny, who expected Ida to join her and her sisters in California at the end of the school year. Ida's aunt had even made arrangements for a teaching position out there. Wells had sent in her application for the position, but since then had gone back and forth about the prospect of relocating to California and leaving Memphis, where, moments of despondency aside, she, as she later wrote, was just "beginning to live" and to take advantage of the opportunities the city offered.[26]

After school let out in June, Ida, as she had six months before, returned to Holly Springs where she appeared to be able to find the means to emulsify her demons and firm up her ideal self. She had received an invitation to the wedding of a former Rust schoolmate, Annie Talbot, who was getting married in Holly Springs and the date of the nuptials coincided with Rust's commencement exercises.

DESPITE HER WORDS the year before about coming to some peace of mind about her experience in Holly Springs, Ida soon realized that she still harbored feelings of resentment. She used the opportunity of returning to Mississippi to work out, again, her anger—specifically concerning her about-to-be-married Rust classmate and the school's president, W. W. Hooper, another figure who she felt had let her down when she most needed someone like him to protect her. Ida had been jealous of Talbot, she admitted in her diary, because she had been a pet student of Hooper's and Wells believed that his favoritism was due to Talbot's being lighter skinned. The issue of color among blacks was a subject of some discussion and tension within the community, not only in regard to how whites viewed it but how blacks saw one another. The *People's Advocate* of Virginia, for example, had criticized the Washington, D.C., elite in 1885 when its editor noticed that "a certain shade of complexion is a qualification for admission to their circle, rather than a certificate or an assurance of good character."[27]

But by the time she saw Annie again in Holly Springs, Ida had shifted the onus of blame to herself. Annie had been "better liked, and thus watched over and shielded," Ida decided, because of her "obedient disposition," which made "her easily controlled and in possession of ladylike refinement." Ida by contrast, had been a "tempestuous, rebellious" student who, with "hard-headed willfulness," had "questioned [Hooper's] authority." "I no longer cherish feelings of resentment," Ida wrote in her diary, "nor blame him that my scholastic career was cut short; my own experience as a teacher enables me to see more clearly and I know that I was to blame." Ida's epiphany was a lesson she would continue to try to abide by, but with her temperament it would not be easy—or wholly successful.[28]

The depth of Ida's feelings and her determination to rectify them rose to the surface when she attended Rust's commencement exercises. "As I witnessed the triumph of the graduates and thought of the lost opportunity a great sob arose in my throat and I yearned with unutterable longing for 'the might have been,'" Ida confessed to her diary. When a Holly Springs acquaintance suggested that she return to Holly Springs to graduate, Ida wrote: "I could not restrain my tears at the sense of injustice I felt and begged him not to ask me why 'I could not.'" But Ida "quickly conquered that feeling and as heartily wished the graduates joy as tho' no bitterness had mingled with my pleasure." During the days she was in Holly Springs, Ida determinedly attended a number of socials, received friends at the home of Mrs. Rachel Rather, the woman who had helped her with her siblings before going to Memphis, and attended church— four times.[29]

IDA RETURNED TO Memphis where she gathered herself to decide what to do about Aunt Fanny and California. Finally, Wells decided that obligations notwithstanding, she could not leave her life in the Bluff City for the "wild West." Hoping to get her aunt's consent to remain in Memphis, Ida decided that the least she could do was go to California to explain her reasons to her aunt, face-to-face.

Wells was yearning to travel in any case, and in July of 1886, a number of Memphis teachers was going to attend the National Education Association meeting taking place in Topeka, Kansas. Black Topekans, who had made an effort to provide inexpensive accommodations for visitors, urged African Americans to attend the meeting where it was anticipated that four thousand to six thousand educators would attend. "We, as colored teachers are usually conspicuous for our absence from educational associations," ran a letter from one of the Kansas organizers to the *Cleveland Gazette*. "Can we not change this and be present in full force at Topeka?" Blacks should not be reluctant to attend interracial meetings as they had in the past, the writer noted in the progressive spirit of the times. For the "way to destroy ignorance and prejudice is for blacks and whites to meet in common council, to cross swords in friendly intellectual combat, to exchange views, to test each other's methods, etc." One of the panels was to be devoted to "The Problem of Race Education" with particular focus on the "Negro, Indian, Mexican, and Mongolian (Asian) races."[30]

Fanny Thompson and Fannie Bradshaw—the latter of whom Ida had become closer to since their earlier meeting—were going, as was Benjamin Sampson, the Kortrecht School principal, and a number of others. There were reduced-rate excursion tickets available for the trip to Kansas, and additional excursion opportunities to take a train from there to California with an itinerary that included stops in a number of western cities along the way. Ida secured an assignment from the *Living Way* to report on some of the famous sites and landmarks. Last but not least the trip was attractive because the first stop was Kansas City, Missouri—the home of J. Dallas Bowser, editor of the Gate City Press, who had responded to her toast to the teachers who had been at the New Orleans Exposition. But most of all, there was a potential new love interest in Kansas City, Paul Jones, a lawyer.

His name had been given to her by a mutual friend and his letters had been more promising of late. Jones's first letters had been awkward—"long homilies about the requirements of the race," Ida called them—but they had warmed up after she chided him for being so "stiff" and suggested to him that she was still available for courtship whatever he had heard about her relationships in Memphis. "I told him," Ida wrote in her diary, that "I had no objection to cultivating the acquaintance of cultured and thinking men of the race."[31] Jones told Ida that he would meet her at the station in Kansas City and make accommodation arrangements for her and Fannie Bradshaw ("level-headed" Thompson appeared to make other arrangements) and at first Ida was worried about the propriety of the bachelor's offer—even though he had told her that a local rector of a church had endorsed the women's accommodations. Wells was advised by Therese Settle, the lady of the house in her boarding place on Lauderdale Street, not to accept Jones's offer. Ida wrote him to this effect, but when Fannie Bradshaw objected to the change in plan, Ida wrote again to agree to the arrangement and for Paul to have a carriage waiting for them at the Kansas City station.

* * *

BEFORE THEIR SUNDAY, July 4, departure, Ida hurriedly made preparations for the trip: she washed and ironed and sewed clothes and, with the back pay she received in June, paid off Menken's in full and paid down some of her other debts. She went to the bank to draw out all of the money in her account, $85, and stopped in the post office where there was a birthday gift sent to her early from Preston Taylor of Nashville, a former slave from Kentucky, who was a minister and up-and-coming businessman and entrepreneur, with whom she had been corresponding.[32] Wells saw Graham at a social on Friday night; Browne, Saturday. Over that weekend she also attended a concert given by Julia Hooks where Ida gave two recitations: "The Letter Reading" and the sleepwalking scene from *Lady Macbeth*. The first "was loudly applauded," Ida noted in her diary, the "last given in My Mother Hubbard was not so effective as I could have wished."[33]

At 4:00 P.M. on Sunday, Ida, the two Fannies, and a number of the other teachers boarded Kansas City, Springfield & Memphis Railroad for the 488-mile trip to Kansas City, Missouri, their first stop. Wells enjoyed her first experience on a "sleeper"—at least until they reached St. Louis, Missouri, where they were all put in a "dingy old car that was very unpleasant." But another in their party, A. S. J Burchette, a dapper, light-skinned, twenty-six-year-old physician (whom Ida had once called a "soft-cake" and was described years later in a biographical reference as a lifelong bachelor) intervened and got them decent accommodations. The incident must have made Ida think about her own court case, due to be heard in April, which was another reason why Ida was reluctant to relocate to California. But like everything else in her life, she was unsure about what was happening with it. Her "dad," Alfred Froman, had told Ida that the lawyer for the railway was trying to quash the case.[34]

ONCE IDA ARRIVED with her party in Kansas City on July 8, she looked for Paul Jones, but he was nowhere to found. Ida and Fannie Bradshaw wandered aimlessly about until she did see *Gate City Press* editor J. Dallas Bowser and his wife at the station who, upon hearing their dilemma, invited them to stay at their house. In the meantime, Ida discovered that the place that Jones had gotten for them was not reputable and that Paul himself was known to be a drinker. Refusing to let the disappointment get her down, Ida was determined to make the best of her stay. She went to "an entertainment" at one of the churches where "hundreds" of Kansas City folks and visitors convened. When Ida saw the friend who had given her Jones's name at the gathering, she expressed her indignation about the situation that he and Paul had put her in. Subsequently, Mrs. Bowser gave a reception where Ida and Fannie were told that Jones, who Ida had yet to see in person, had invited them to go riding the following day. Ida, of course, refused.

In subsequent days she had a good time meeting new acquaintances—she named about nineteen in the diary—with whom she attended a round of socials, went on carriage rides, and accompanied to literary debates and other meetings. When finally Paul Jones showed up for one of the social occasions, Ida, already sour on him, was not impressed. His "physical appearance does not prepossess me," Ida wrote in her diary, "and I perfectly abhor him since later developments." Jones then surreptitiously got one of his friends to invite Ida and Fannie for a carriage ride but when Jones unexpectedly showed up at the appointed time, both women refused to go.[35]

Jones, no doubt, was publicly humiliated by the refusal, and Ida described an "insulting note from the cur" complaining about the rebuff. "I cared nothing for his denouncing our conduct," she wrote in her diary, but then he went further "to say he had heard bad things about me when he was running to Memphis but had believed none of them until now." Ida calmly confided all of this to a sympathetic Bowser, "a good, quiet, sensible" man who made her feel better, but beneath it all the accusation had churned up the bile she had been working so hard to keep under wraps. "I was so angry," she wrote in her diary, "that I foamed at the mouth, bit my lips & then realizing my impotence—ended in a fit of crying." On July 13, the group left for Topeka.[36]

THANKFULLY, THE NEA meeting provided a good many distractions from the disaster in Kansas City. Black Topekans had been rapidly increasing in numbers beginning in 1879 when there was a mass migration of southern blacks to the state capital in search of economic opportunity and freedom from racist oppression. Numbering only 473 in 1870, ten years later the black population of 3,648 had created a black business district on

Kansas Avenue, had published six newspapers, and had an active group of black women's religious, social, and cultural organizations. During the course of Ida's stay, she went to panels and discussions, met more black educators than she had ever seen in one place, and attended a major reception at Music Hall where seventy-five black visiting teachers joined Topekans and heard addresses, music, and readings.[37]

Toward the end of the conference, Ida accompanied a group of teachers to call on the "polished mulatto," as she described him, E. P. McCabe, the state auditor of Kansas. The natty McCabe, acclaimed for having the highest state office of any northern African American, had once worked as a clerk and porter on New York City's Wall Street but had since decided to be "a freeman on the bleak plains of the far west rather than be an underling and political sycophant" in the East, as a contemporary described him. The group might have listened to McCabe's plans to establish all-black towns in the sparsely settled region, an ambition that Wells would promote in some years hence.[38]

Leaving Topeka, Ida took the planned excursion route through Denver, Salt Lake City, and San Francisco. Both the *Living Way* and the *Gate City Press* had assigned her to write for them, and Ida made sure to visit as many attractions en route as she could. She "marveled" at Colorado's Pike's Peak and drank from the Manitou Springs, also known as the Garden of the Gods. In Denver, which had a black population of about two thousand and was the subject of enthusiastic articles to lure more blacks to settle there, Ida saw the famous Tabor Opera House, which was "the finest" she had ever seen. But she might also have been aware of how groups, including the Colored Ladies Legal Rights Association, had fought against the exclusion of blacks from the institution. In fact, Wells, who remained in the city for a number of days, was astonished to find that African Americans were largely excluded from the city's restaurants, hotels, and theaters. There was nearly as much prejudice in Denver as there was in Memphis, Ida observed in her diary. But she also noticed that because the pattern of black settlement was overwhelmingly male in the city, the young men were particularly attentive because of the small numbers of black women who lived there. One man in particular, Edwin H. Hackley, a lawyer and journalist, was one of the "finest young men" Ida had had the "good fortune" to meet. He called on her several times while she was there, and she looked forward to corresponding with him in the future.[39]

* * *

WELLS LEFT DENVER for the forty-one-hour trip to Salt Lake City. The railway route took her through the pastel, crested-ridge canyons that had the triangular shape of a flatiron, and across the Rocky Mountain's Great Continental Divide to reach Utah. In Salt Lake City, Ida visited the Mormon Tabernacle where she heard an impassioned oration and was sorry that her schedule did not permit her to stay there for its conclusion. But her regrets were just beginning. By the time she reached Sacramento, Ida had nearly run out of money and was worried about having enough funds to get back home. In late July, she reached San Francisco, where she visited Chinatown and the office of the historic black newspaper the *Elevator*, begun in 1865 by Philip A. Bell, and whose editor told her harrowing stories about Visalia. His description was "anything but glowing colors," she remarked, making her "almost afraid to go there."[40]

There were not a half-dozen black families in Visalia, she learned, and she was probably told that the white population—smaller than that in Holly Springs—had been prosecessionist and had sided with the Confederacy during the war. Begun as a trading center for gold prospectors and cattle barons, Visalia's development was slowed by its being bypassed as a terminal for Collis Huntington's Southern Pacific Railroad in the 1870s; it was only beginning to grow as an agricultural center later in the decade when citizens financed a feeder line that connected Visalia to the Southern Pacific. Moreover, the school system had little to commend it. The one public school for whites was a two-story wooden structure, in which women of the town held a fund-raising ball to furnish it in 1872. After the festivities, the patrons left the dance only to be greeted by the sight of a man hanging lifelessly from the Court Street Bridge over Mill Creek. No further explanation of the race of the victim or the reason why he was lynched was offered by the historian of the event.[41]

The black school was even more rudimentary. Its origin was dated from 1871, when Daniel Scott, an elderly educated black man, probably from Boston, was employed by Tom Hinds, who lived about three miles away from Visalia, to teach the children in his large family. Soon other children also came to the Hinds residence to be taught by Scott, and in 1873, the tutor had decided to open a private school and purchased a lot for the purpose. Black and Mexican children attended Scott's school and he was able to secure some funds from the Visalia municipality to purchase a lot and erect what was described as a ramshackle building to house a school for his students. However, the teacher left California in 1875, and the city began a search for another teacher to instruct his fifteen students. The description of what was awaiting her in Visalia was disheartening. "I can only pray to the Father of all mercy for guidance and help," Ida wrote.[42]

From San Francisco, Ida arrived in Visalia at daybreak. Its main street was lined by clapboard and brick buildings and an aging sign advertising Mexican saddles. When she got to Fanny's house, Ida was happy to see the family and relieved that all of them seemed to be doing well. Annie and Lily, now aged fourteen and eleven, had matured so much during the year or so she had not seen them. "I look at them in amazement," Ida wrote in her diary, "and find the little sisters of whom I spoke, shooting up in my own world and ripening for similar experiences as my own." Ida's aunt was earning good wages in Visalia and the climate was healthier than in Memphis, but she also saw that Fanny was "careworn" with hard work and "solicitude" for the children and, save for a friend named Lutie Rice, she had little companionship. Rice was probably Lucille Tolbert Rice, who had been born in slavery in Alabama, had come West in the 1850s by wagon train with six other black families, and had married a man named Joe Rice from nearby Farmersville, who was probably deceased by the time Ida met her.[43] Lutie had also written Ida urging her to come to teach in California, and she and Fanny begged Ida to remain there for at least the year whether she was able to get the teaching position or not. Ida reluctantly consented. "I should help her share the responsibility," Ida thought, "and God helping me I will!" Ida sold her return ticket to Memphis.[44]

She regretted doing so almost immediately. Visalia was hot and dusty, and Ida complained about the swelling of her hands and feet that usually accompanied her doing heavy manual labor. There were none of the social and cultural activities that Ida was now accustomed to, and her movements were restricted. Visalia was the kind of place where one did not tarry far from home without an escort—and escorts were hard to come by. "I've no books, no companionship, & even an embargo is laid on my riding out with the only one who can take me," Ida wrote in her diary. She began to feel "lonely" and "far away from anything & everybody."[45]

At least she received lots of letters from friends throughout her stay in California, though they might have made Ida long for home even more. Her landlady, Therese Settle, wrote a "chatty" letter about the goings-on in Memphis. The new friends she had made in Kansas City wrote to tell her how much they missed her. Fanny Thompson wrote to tell Ida that her brother George wanted to get married. Wells hoped that her brother would "get over this season of infatuation safely & do nothing to his own or any one else's discredit." Subsequently, she wrote her brother giving him a "good plain talk on the subject of marriage." She also received some "disjointed" letters from Isaiah Graham and from Louis Browne, who had left Washington with his law degree and "seductively" wrote Ida about his intentions to pass the bar as far west as Denver. Wells, as she had with Graham in another fit of loneliness, did not discourage him. She wrote him that she "commended his determination and told him to do something that called forth admiration and respect and the rest would be easy." Ida even tried to convince herself that if Browne succeeded in his law practice "& in winning my love in the meantime," as she wrote in her diary, "I would help him prove to the world what love in its purity can accomplish."[46]

In the meantime, Ida was still corresponding with Charles Morris about the novel they had hoped to write together. Wells had sent him the outline of a plot and he had responded favorably. When she wrote Morris again, she confided to him that she was "hesitating between marrying and staying [in California] to raise the children." However committed she really was to marrying Browne, Ida got some pleasure in knowing that she had thrown Charles off guard. "I know he will be surprised at the tone of that letter," she wrote. Charles, however, rose to the occasion to offer some advice about marriage, but it was not the kind of reaction she was looking for. It was marred, Ida wrote, by "a preface that reflected somewhat on my common sense . . . and I naturally resent that."[47]

Ida was also trying to do some of her own writing. She sent off an article entitled "Our Young Men" to the *AME Church Review* in late August, but did so, she wrote, not because she thought it worthy of publication but in the hopes that she would get some good editorial feedback. "I never wrote under a greater strain, but kept at it until it was finished," Ida recorded in her diary. In addition to the other pressures she was feeling, Browne had announced that both he and Wells had been asked to write for the prestigious AME publication in the *Washington Bee*. "I think sometimes that I can write a readable article and then again I wonder how I could have been so mistaken in myself. A glance at all my 'brilliant?' productions pall on my understanding; they all savor of dreary sameness, however varied the subject, and the style is monotonous. I find a paucity of ideas that makes it a labor to write freely," she continued, "and yet—what is it that keeps urging me to write notwithstanding all?"[48]

The answer came when Ida read about the August lynching of a black woman, Eliza Woods, in the Memphis papers—although her diary indicated that she had yet to fully realize it. Woods, a black cook in Jackson, Tennessee, was lynched for poisoning the white woman she worked for. The evidence against her was purely circumstantial: the dead woman's stomach contained arsenic and a box of "Rough on Rats" was found in the black woman's house. However, no more proof was needed to condemn a "black creature" with "thick lips," a "female devil," of killing an "esteemed Christian lady," in the words of a white diarist in the town who witnessed the lynching. Woods, noted Ida in her own diary, was "taken from the county jail and stripped naked and hung upon the courthouse yard and her body riddled with bullets and left exposed to view!" The mob was reported in the *Memphis Appeal* to number at least a thousand—a number said to include black men and women among it. The Woods lynching was remarkable not only for the gender of its victim, but for its apparent biracial participation and as a harbinger for the kind of public, communal spectacles that would soon become more common.[49]

Wells did write about the murder of Woods for the *Gate City Press*—"almost advising murder," she wrote in her diary. Wells's emotions had obviously gotten the best of her. But revealing the extraordinary expectations that women in general, and Ida, in particular, had regarding feminine self-restraint, Wells felt the need to justify, and pray over, her unbridled reaction to the lynching of the black woman who shared the skin color, name, and occupation with her deceased mother. "My only plea is the pitch of indignation to which I was carried by reading [the] article," Ida noted in her diary. "It may be unwise to express myself so strongly," Ida wrote anxiously, "but I cannot help it & I know not if capital may not be made of it against me but I trust in God."[50] The article would not be the last she wrote about Eliza Woods.

By September, Ida was becoming desperate about her situation. "I regret more and more every day that I sold my ticket," she wrote in her diary, and finally informed Fanny that she just could not stay in Visalia. "I told my aunt," she recalled in her autobiography, that "[the loneliness] was even worse for me, a young woman, to have nothing to look forward to, as I was just beginning to live and had all my life before me." But the consent that

Ida had hoped for was not forthcoming. Knowing Ida's financial situation, Fanny told her that if she left she would have to take her two sisters with her. "She knew very well," Ida recalled in her autobiography, "that I had no money to do so."[51]

Not to be denied, Ida asked one of her Kansas City friends, a teacher named Robert Coles, about the possibility of finding a position in the schools there. He was enthusiastic about the idea and promised to help Wells in securing one. She wrote the *Elevator* editor in San Francisco, asking the price of a ticket from Visalia to San Francisco. Wells also wrote to Mrs. Turner in Memphis, an older woman who provided dining accommodations for boarders, to ask her to sell some of Ida's personal items. The sale brought four dollars. Finally, Ida asked Alfred Froman to intercede for her to borrow $150 from Robert Church, the wealthy businessman. Ida also wrote Church directly. "I told him the circumstances of my condition," she recalled in her autobiography, and that she was writing him because he "was the only man of my race that I knew who could lend me that much money and wait for me to repay it." Ida promised to repay him with interest, but also asked that he not send the money unless she was reelected as a teacher that year. She had decided that if it was too late to get her Memphis position back, she would not return there. In the meantime, Ida, perhaps with an urgency tinged by guilt, filled her days with sewing a number of garments for her aunt. She completed two dresses for her within the week and started on another.[52]

IN SEPTEMBER, IDA wrote about the earthquakes that were being felt in the Southeast and were especially destructive in Charleston, South Carolina; news of the tremors served as a worthy backdrop to the developing upheaval in the California household. In early September, Ida learned that she had indeed been reelected by the board to teach at the Kortrecht School, and she sent word to Fannie Bradshaw that she would leave California on the fifteenth. Ida's aunt, seeing the writing on the wall, dispatched a representative from the Visalia schools to come to the house with an offer that was hard to refuse: Ida would be paid $80 a month (more than she made in Memphis) to teach eighteen students in the town school. In addition to her aunt's "importunities" for Ida to stay and the sense of obligation that continued to pull at her, the offer brought out Ida's "calmer sober judgment." After all, if she returned to Memphis she wouldn't be paid until

December; but if she stayed in Visalia for a year, she calculated that she could clear $300 for her and her sisters and money to pay her lawyer to continue with the court case. Ida reluctantly accepted the offer. "I shed bitter tears of disappointment," Ida wrote in her diary, at the thought of not returning to Memphis as she had planned. With a heavy heart, Ida wrote Froman to petition the Memphis board for a leave of absence.[53]

But just as she had almost convinced herself to stay in California for the year "at whatever personal cost to myself," Ida received a letter from Louis Browne the day before she was to teach her first class. The letter included a clipping from the *Washington, D.C. Advocate,* which upon hearing of Ida being in the West and Louis's plans to settle and practice in Kansas City, wished that the couple "live long & prosper," with each other.[54] With thoughts of Louis, Ida went to the Visalia school the following Monday and found out that the black families in the town had requested that their children be schooled separately from the Mexican, white, and Native American students. As a result, the black students were assigned to a makeshift one-room building while the white students were given a "commodious" building, as Ida described it in her diary, up on the hill. Wells did not agree with the voluntary separation and, despite feeling that she was helping perpetuate segregation, tried to come to terms with it all. But then Ida received a telegram at the school stating that she had been elected to the Kansas City school system. In addition, J. Dallas Bowser offered Ida a position on the *Gate City Press.*[55]

Ida's aunt had followed close on the messenger's heels to the school and again beseeched Ida not to leave her. Her request was backed by one of the influential black citizens in the town whom Fanny had gotten to accompany her. "My aunt never left [the school] until I had written out and sent a reply telegram thanking my friends but declining the position," Ida wrote in her autobiography. "I know not if I will ever have another chance yet I try not to be rebellious but extract consolation out of the thought that My Heavenly Father will reward and bless me for doing what is right and just," Ida confided in her diary, "and if I did nothing, sacrificed nothing in return for all that has been done for me, I could not expect his blessing and sanction." More lectures on her family obligation and duty to Fanny awaited Ida at home by her aunt, "who cried half the night & all the morning," and from Lutie Rice, making the idea of her debt feel burdensome. It didn't help that Rice showed the signs of a woman who experienced "continuous isolation" as Ida wrote in her diary: a "hard face," an "affected drawl," and an "unconscious tone of superiority and pride in a fact she often repeats; of living within herself and on her own resources."⁵⁶

When a day or so later Ida received a letter from Robert Church with the draft for $150 in it, the remnants of her thinning determination to remain in California dissolved. But she tried to work out a compromise. She would accept the position in Kansas City—if it was still available—where she had made friends, would be closer to the family, be an associate editor of the *Gate City Press*—and not disappoint Louis Browne. Still, Ida knew, the decision meant another "storm" would break at home. When she told her sisters that they were leaving, Annie, the oldest of the two, told Ida point-blank that she would not go back. Annie was near in age to Fanny's daughter, Ida, and was her cousin's only friend. Fanny, of course, supported the decision but if either she or Annie thought that the prospect of leaving a sister behind would deter Ida from leaving, they were wrong. Ida rationalized that taking care of one sister would be easier than having "two half-grown girls on her hands." So after a "promise from my aunt that she would care for Annie as if she were her own daughter," Ida wrote in the autobiography, "I agreed to leave her there" and Ida took L'il with her to Kansas City.⁵⁷

But more tumult awaited Wells in Missouri. She had arrived a day later than expected, and the Kansas City school board had elected a local, recent graduate to take Wells's position. But upon Ida's arrival, the board, preferring a more experienced teacher, dismissed the teacher and gave Wells the assignment to teach the fourth-grade class in Kansas City's Lincoln School. However, the board's decision sparked resentment and a mass protest meeting that condemned the hiring of out-of-town teachers at the exclusion of local ones. Wells was understandably hurt by the demonstration and the hostility directed at her from many of those whose company she had enjoyed just two months before.

Not mentioned in Ida's autobiography but noted in her diary is that she suspected her newest nemesis, Paul Jones, was behind the teachers' protest. Bowser, who had already set in type the announcement that the "brilliant Iola" was to be associate editor of the *Gate City Press,* told her to ignore the outcry. Ida tried to do so but soon told him that she could not. Her "extreme sensitiveness," she told him, made her decide against staying in Kansas City—a statement that was surely true but that, one suspects, helped Ida rationalize her change of mind. Kansas City's segregated school system was more advanced than Visalia's, but it was well behind Memphis's. Bowser, who had probably pulled a number of strings to get Ida the position, was "angry" and "grieved" about Wells's final decision. While Ida regretted that she made Bowser unhappy and did not want to appear ungrateful, she had made up her mind. Her final encounter about the situation was with Louis Browne, who was, understandably, in "high dudgeon" about Ida's decision. He came to where Ida was staying and "remained all the morning pleading but nothing he said moved me," Ida wrote in her diary. "I breathed freer after it was all over, & turned my face to the only home I know."[58]

CHAPTER FIVE

A Race in My Arms

The African race has never had a gleam of light across its dark history and . . . has within itself no promises or possibility of progress. It is a race without history, without ideas, without hope.

—*Edward Carmack, editor of the* Memphis Commercial

. . . within the last ten [years] I have suffered more, learned more, lost more than I ever expect to, again.

—*Ida B. Wells, July 1887*

Ida could not have easily reconciled her decision to leave behind Annie and her aunt in California, Louis in Kansas City, and the sacrifice she believed God was demanding of her. But she had cast her lot with a New City and a New South that had a future grand and supple enough to not only contain her own, but, with the pending court case, that of the race as well.

Indeed, both the Bluff City and the region were on an accelerated track regarding race relations, although they were headed in two directions at once. In the wake of the 1883 Supreme Court decision, there was a vigorous national debate about the status of blacks in the New South. One side of the argument was represented by the southern liberal and popular writer George Washington Cable, who believed that racial friction was inevitable—and regional progress impossible—if African Americans were denied their civil rights. Cable criticized the North for abandoning blacks to the tyranny of the white South, insisted that separate but equal was an oxymoron, and imagined a vast reservoir of liberal sentiment—the "silent South," he called it—which he urged to raise its voice against racial inequities.[1]

Leading the dissent was Henry W. Grady, editor of the *Atlanta Constitution*, who warned that Cable's view would lead to more racial conflict, not less. In 1886, he made a decisive speech before northern businessmen and financiers, including J. P. Morgan and Russell Sage. He argued that the separation of the races was the very thing that would minimize racial strife and that blacks not only enjoyed equal opportunities within their separate spheres (including their white-funded public education), but preferred it that way. Grady concluded with a plea to northerners to let the white South handle the "social relations" between the races without interference. The South's very (and potentially lucrative) existence, he insisted, depended on the domination of the white race, which represented the "assertion of the right of character, intelligence and property to rule."[2]

At the fulcrum of both men's arguments was the unsettling question of race-mixing or miscegenation. Cable was careful to make a distinction between social rights for blacks, and civil ones. No believer in social equality, Cable argued that if blacks were denied civil rights, those who were light-skinned would seek to pass into the white world, making the amalgamation of the races inevitable. Grady, on the other hand believed that the granting of civil rights to African Americans would be the catalyst for miscegenation.[3]

New York editor T. Thomas Fortune entered the debate with his pivotal article, "Civil Rights and Social Privileges." His argument, published in both the mainstream and black press, also made the distinction between civil and social rights, but with a very different rationale. Fortune insisted that while social privileges should be earned through economic and intellectual progress, civil rights were ineluctable and belonged to all the people. He also scoffed at the idea that the southern whites should be left to work out the race problem alone. Blacks, he insisted, would also demand a share in that settlement.[4]

Fortune's perspective was potentially libratory for blacks. After Reconstruction, elite activists had focused primarily on intraracial uplift—"moving beyond their former condition"—with the idea that the race would be granted full citizenship rights once ignorance no longer prevailed among the masses and blacks embraced bourgeois values. This belief made the idea of protest and insistence on political rights appear premature at the least, for blacks assumed that if the race attained the "character, intelligence, and property" that men like Grady were talking about, the very basis for discrimination would disappear. Fortune's perspective—that civil rights should be universal rather than earned, and that neither class, behavior, nor intelligence should confer or take away citizen rights established in the Constitution—had the potential to unleash a new era of black activism.[5]

Wells was aware of Fortune's article, which was published in the *AME Church Review*. She noted in her diary that she asked to borrow the issue from a colleague in order to read it. Ida made no further comment about it, but it was clear that Fortune's potentially revolutionary notion to decouple class standing and behavior from constitutional rights was still beyond Ida's grasp. After all, her own standing and behavior appeared to be the very thing that threatened *her* constitutional rights. Three months after Fortune's article was published, Ida had heard that there was a "conspiracy" afoot to impugn her character before her appeal to the Tennessee Supreme Court was to be heard. Ida did not give any details in her diary. She only mentioned that some well-known figure in the black community had been approached by whites to help undermine her. "It is a painful fact that white men choose men of the race to accomplish the ruin of any young girl," Wells petulantly wrote in her diary. That whites "would deliberately ask a man of reputation to encompass the ruin of one's reputation for the sake of gain is a startling commentary on the estimation in which our race is held," Ida, who saw her own personal fate and that of the race as one, concluded.[6]

The development probably reflected new political developments in Tennessee that especially affected the Democratic Party, a faction of which had supported Ida's first suit in the courts. The successful entrance of the disgruntled, populist Farmer's Alliance into state politics in 1886 made the black vote more important, but it also forced Democratic faction leaders to compete for the newly segmented white vote by accusing one another of being solicitous toward the "ignorant" African American electorate—and, it can be assumed, their civil rights court cases. The dilemma for Democrats was exacerbated by the fact that blacks had a high participation rate as voters, and their support of Republicans made Tennessee one of the most competitive two-party systems in the South.[7]

How the political drama would unfold was unknown at a time when Tennessee, including Memphis, was in the throes of progressive reforms and vibrant economic growth. But Fortune's views notwithstanding, Ida would get her own life in order to prepare herself for a reformed future.

Upon her return to Memphis, Wells threw herself into a self-improvement campaign aimed at remedying her own personal deficiencies—and perhaps at finding some redemption. In October, what she called her "besetting sin"—her eruptive anger—was tested when she learned that the scorned Paul Jones had sent forged documents to the white Memphis superintendent, C. H. Collier; Robert Church; and her principal, Benjamin Sampson, saying that Ida had been fired from the Kansas City schools. Jones was evidently also behind the rumors, circulating in Kansas City, that she and Graham had been dismissed from the Memphis schools because of "immoral conduct." Moreover, Bowser informed her that a friend of Jones's began another round of gossip by insisting that Lily was actually Ida's daughter! As Wells noted in her diary, she was "furiously angry" and wrote to Bowser, demanding to know if Kansas City people "would attempt to blacken the reputation of those who desired to sojourn among them." But after Ida recorded her initial reaction, she appeared to make an extra effort not to dwell in her fury, and determined, instead, to stay positive and "rejoice in good health & fair prospects."[8]

Isaiah Graham, however, was not so amenable. He crossly questioned Wells about Jones's accusations, and the incident appeared to be the final straw as far as he and Ida were concerned. "Mr. G was married very unexpectedly last week," Ida wrote in her diary on October 20. "I wish him joy," she dryly added, apparently relieved that the tumultuous relationship had resolved itself. Wells, in fact, made the effort to reconcile her other relationships as well. She returned the letters of Charles Morris, a gesture of both courtesy and recognition that the journey toward romantic union had ended. But she was still determined to keep Charles as a friend, and subsequently when she heard he was ill, Ida sent him a get-well note and the two continued to correspond. She did the same with the abandoned

Louis Browne. She ignored his more querulous communications, but when she heard that he had become so afflicted by rheumatism that he was virtually paralyzed, Ida hastily sent him flowers to "cheer him in his loneliness."[9]

Ida was determined to "curb herself more" and "not be so indifferent to the young men," as she wrote in her diary: "they feel & resent it." She even forced herself to go to an Odd Fellows dance. She had "a miserable evening," but appeared to keep the opinion to herself. And after her return home, Ida consciously went out of her way to be more sociable and to dwell less on her sense of isolation and loneliness. Her diary entries were filled with her dinner meetings, tea parties, or group outings—sometimes consisting of all women, but more frequently men and women together. Wells also entertained more frequently; in February she hosted a "storm party" for her teacher friends on a rare, snowbound day that closed the schools.[10]

Wells's new determination to be more sociable was helped by the fact that she had finally found suitable living quarters. She and her sister Lily now lived on fashionable Lauderdale Street, the same street where the Hookses, and, for a time, J. O Pierce—the judge in the Chesapeake & Ohio case—lived, though his residence was on its northern end. Lauderdale's most elegant house belonged to Robert Church and his second wife, Anna. Their three-story residence—the first in Memphis to be built in the Queen Anne style—had fourteen rooms, horse stables, and a servant's quarters. The walls of its parlor were covered with hand-painted frescoes by Italian artists, and its floors with carpets from Brussels.[11]

The house where Ida was staying, owned by the lawyer Josiah Settle and his wife, Therese, was less elaborate, but Wells thought her quarters were "splendid." The taciturn, bespectacled Josiah was a graduate of Oberlin and Howard University Law School who had recently moved from Mississippi to Memphis, where he was appointed assistant attorney general of the Shelby County criminal court. Therese came from the prominent Vogelsang family of Maryland and was a teacher at the Broadway School with Julia Hooks. Therese, Ida thought, was the "sweetest, quietest, and most lady like little creature it has been my good fortune to meet." The two attended cultural events together, and Ida went to hear Therese perform at a concert organized by the Liszt-Mullard classical music club where Settle and Julia Hooks were the featured performers. The Settles entertained frequently, and Ida played Parcheesi and other games with their visitors.[12]

It was probably through the Settles that Ida met her favorite escort in the period, Albert Alexander, a teacher and the brother of the better known John H. Alexander, an Oberlin man who had recently graduated from West Point Military Academy. John, square chinned with wavy hair, was described by the *Washington Bee* as being "the first colored cadet who has been successful in coming out [of West Point] without being molested or having his ears cut off," in a reference to Alexander's predecessor, James Webster Smith, who was reportedly beaten, gagged, and had one of his ears slit by fellow cadets. Ida liked Albert "very much," she wrote in her diary, but the comment indicated that he evoked few fireworks, and Ida, for the moment at least, seemed to like it that way.[13]

Ida felt quite sanguine about the flurry of marriages within her social circle during the fall and following winter. In November, her cousin Stella and Isaac Norris were married. Ida was one of Stella's three bridesmaids and remarked with some satisfaction in her diary how "Everybody said we looked 'sweet' & I guess we did." Subsequently, when Wells realized that she was the only female teacher at Kortrecht who was not married, she made the observation in her diary without comment or complaint.[14]

For one thing, neither her standing nor popularity in the community was adversely affected by her remaining unmarried. As the *Cleveland Gazette* noted, she and the similarly single Fanny Thompson had a "host of loving admirers" and were the "two most prominent figures of Memphis's flourishing literary circle." The notice followed Ida's reelection as the editor of the lyceum's *Evening Star*.[15]

Buoyed by the rewards for her self-improvement efforts, she continued them throughout 1887. Ever conscious of her intellectual development, she wrote away for the *Chautaquan,* a journal published by the Methodist Episcopal–inspired educational movement that provided courses and lectures in the humanities, arts, and sciences. Ida also vowed to "find less business up town," she wrote in her diary, "so that I may give no cause whatever for uncharitable remarks." Racial boundaries were congealing in Memphis and just weeks before the entry, Ida had gone uptown with friends to the Stranger's Church, the white counterpart to her own Second Congregational Church. Wells enjoyed the sermon but for them the church was aptly named. Ida mocked how she had witnessed the "practical evidence of 'white folks' Christianity" in the "haste" with which they "passed us when choosing a seat." But the "uncharitable remarks" were issued by blacks who responded to increasing segregation by being more adamant about patronizing black businesses and institutions and about keeping women—especially middle-class ones—within the confines of the community and out of harm's way. Just recently, in the summer of 1885, a black woman visiting a prominent family in Memphis had been manhandled by policemen for unwittingly going into a "white" park; in fact, she had been accosted by the same two police officers who had arrested Hooks some years before.[16]

Uptown was becoming more perilous, but staying away was the most difficult of Ida's resolutions to keep. Of course, there was the larger question of being able to go wherever one pleased, but with Ida it was also difficult to forgo the pleasures of the fancy department stores or an uptown lecture or the ability to go to the physician of one's choice. Above all, there was the question of Ida's love for the theater. Just days after she made the determination to stay within the community, Ida and Albert went to see *The Count of Monte Cristo* in one of the uptown venues. According to Wells's diary, she had been reprimanded about it and later regretted "yielding to the temptation." The situation must have made her even more hopeful about the other direction the city appeared to be headed in: progressive trends that appeared to militate against the kind of racial exclusions that Ida chafed against.[17]

IN THE LATTER months of 1886 and early 1887, Memphis hosted meetings of the Knights of Labor (K of L) and the Women's Christian Temperance Union (WCTU), which were hopeful signs of things to come. Ida attended a large meeting of the Knights in December of 1886, a year when the organization, which represented blacks and whites, men and women, and skilled and unskilled workers, was at the peak of its influence. After its successful 1885 strike to protest pay cuts on railroads owned by the financier and railroad magnate Jay Gould, the membership of the Knights had increased from 104,000 to more than 700,000 in 1886, a year when the organization conducted more than fourteen hundred strikes throughout the country. Now the labor organization was holding large, festive, interracial gatherings throughout the South replete with parades that included black women who rode in carriages and dressed in holiday attire with the Knights' insignias and badges.[18]

Memphis was a particularly fertile ground for organizing against the concentration of capital that allowed tyranny against its workers. The dignity of labor was deemed a necessity to ensure a modern, industrial order by progressive reformers like J. L. Keating, and the *Appeal* railed against such developments as the city's cotton oil trust, which owned Memphis's cottonseed mills and so was able to keep prices—as well as the wages and profits of those who produced the staple—low. Jay Gould was also investing heavily in Memphis, which was in the midst of a railroad building boom that would bring no fewer than seven new lines to the city before the end of the decade. Investments in manufacturing increased almost 300 percent in the period, sharply raising the number of factories and annual trade in local goods. But while factories abounded, so did gray, corrugated neighborhoods filled with workers whose wages were kept low by the plethora of unorganized lower-skilled job seekers migrating to Memphis. The in-migration was largely responsible for both the city's white and black population nearly doubling after the yellow fever epidemic of 1878.[19]

Ida took Albert Alexander to the Memphis gathering and was impressed by the fact that black women were welcomed "with the courtesy usually extended to white ladies," as she wrote in the *Memphis Watchman*, edited by her teaching colleague J. T. Turner. "It was the first assembly of the sort in this town where color was not the criterion to recognition as ladies and gentlemen," she optimistically observed. The demonstration was in stark contrast to what Ida had experienced at the Stranger's Church, an experience that other progressive reformers like Dwight Moody had done little to remedy. "Seeing this," Ida concluded, "I could listen to their [the K of L] enunciation of the principles of truth and justice and accept them with a better grace than the sounding brass and tinkling cymbal of Moody even though expounded in a consecrative house and over the word of God."[20]

No one personified the new progressive spirit more than Lide Smith Meriwether, whom Ida heard address the Knights assemblage. Meriwether, a leading white feminist in Memphis, was the sister-in-law of Elizabeth Meriwether, leader of the equal-pay struggle for teachers in the 1870s. Lide had been instrumental in organizing the Mission Home for prostitutes and their children in 1876, founded on the progressive principle that economic desperation rather than an inherent lack of immorality was responsible for the large numbers of "fallen women" in Memphis.[21]

By the time of the Knights meeting, Meriwether was also the president of the Tennessee chapter of the WCTU, which like the pro-prohibition Knights, was a fast-growing organization—it had two hundred thousand members by the turn of the century—and though neither organization had integrated locals, the WCTU also welcomed black women within its ranks, and even in leadership positions. In 1887, Frances Ellen Harper, the well-known black poet and abolitionist, was appointed the WCTU's national superintendent of work among colored people. Under Meriwether's leadership, Tennessee organized the first black chapters in the South—there were fourteen by 1887—and the 1886 meeting, which established the Memphis chapter, was probably the first interracial gathering among women reformers in the Bluff City. Ida thought the fifty-year-old Meriwether to be a "grand woman."[22]

For reformers, and particularly women, temperance—with all of the word's myriad meanings in the late nineteenth century—was loaded with significance. Liquor's ability to release people's inhibitions and allow them to lose self-control was anathema to Victorian codes of conduct. Alcohol was deemed responsible for a range of illnesses, political corruption at the hands of the large liquor companies, increases in crime (including rape), and the rise of highly organized houses of prostitution and gambling. The vices were burgeoning along with the population, causing social dislocation in the swelling numbers of salaried workers who had the time and the opportunity to seek illicit pleasures. Unless the liquor traffic was stopped, editorialized the *Tennessee Baptist*, a white publication, "it would immolate the fair daughters of Tennessee on the altar of lust." One of the reasons for the WCTU's great success under Frances Willard, its national president since 1879, was Willard's ability to mobilize women who, save for the urgency of "Home Protection" as she called it, would otherwise be reluctant to enter the public sphere and call for women's suffrage. Infidelity, wife-beating, and profligate spending by husbands, who, by law in most states, gained control over their wives' inheritance upon marriage, were also traced to spirits. Black prohibitionists, like Frances Ellen Harper, added another dimension to the dangers of alcohol: she saw it as no less than another form of bondage. Writing in the *AME Church Review* in 1887, she opined that alcohol and slavery were "twin evils," and she believed black women had the same imperative to fight the former as they had the latter.[23]

For blacks, widely assumed to be guilty of a range of promiscuities, temperance was an issue that undermined such stereotypes. For black women reformers, their membership in such organizations as the WCTU was important for another reason. Their public association with elite white women reformers served to affirm their own true womanhood. It was no coincidence that at the time of the Knights meeting and WCTU organizing, Shelby County's attorney general made a rare, if backhanded, declaration of moral equivalency between black and white women. The precise context for the statement is unclear, but according to an article that Ida wrote in response, the attorney general had proclaimed that black women were no longer the "harlots" they had been in the past; they could be as "decent or disgraceful" as white women. Wells, though not unappreciative of the positive sentiment, wrote a mild corrective that was published in the white-owned *Memphis Scimitar,* a Republican paper, as well as in the *New York Freeman.* Black women, she said, were not "consoled by the knowledge that . . . aristocratic circles . . . furnish parallel examples of immorality." The most "disheartening" aspect of race relations was the "wholesale contemptuous defamation" of black women and the "refusal to believe there are among us mothers, wives and maidens who have attained a true, noble, and refining womanhood." Ida added that she only wanted them to be given "equal credit for their virtues."[24]

Such credit, it was hoped, was in the offing. One of the reasons for the WCTU's recent organizing in Tennessee was that in September of 1887, a prohibition referendum was scheduled to extend the state's four-mile law (which forbade dispensing alcoholic beverages within four miles of any chartered educational institution outside of an incorporated town) to make Tennessee completely "dry." The state's sixty thousand black voters, it was widely believed, held the balance of power for its passage.[25]

THROUGHOUT THE EARLY months of 1887, Ida continued her own quest for virtue. She volunteered to teach a Sunday-school class at AME's Avery Chapel for young boys, the group that was thought to be in most need of moral instruction and that Ida, with her own feminine ambivalences, felt more at ease with. In the mid-1880s, the AME denominations were in the forefront of a Sunday-school movement aimed at filling the void brought on by the breakdown of parental and church authority in the growing cities. Urban life provided new opportunities for recreation that included dancing, card-playing, billiards, smoking, theatergoing, and drinking, and young people were rebelling against the traditional idea that amusement was a "peculiar property of the devil," as W. E. B. Du Bois commented in a later article about the issue.[26]

Wells was concerned about her own authority, especially with her brothers, and was worried about them. By her own admission, she habitually
drove George away with her sharp rebukes; and Ida's warnings to her older
brother, AJ, to stop gambling were being ignored. It "takes time to break
up a habit that has been forming for years," he explained, signing his letter
"your wild and reckless brother." Ida largely blamed herself for the situation because of her own inability to communicate with them. "I can get
along well enough with the other boys but am too hasty and impatient
with my own," she wrote in her diary. "God help me be more careful &
watchful over my manners & bearing toward him," she continued. "Let
not my own brother perish while I am laboring to save others![27]

With all of Ida's efforts to better herself, it must have been disheartening to know that her own brothers and sisters were so unsettled and in
disarray. The difficult state of her family affairs was only confirmed when
Ida received the news from her paternal aunt, Margaret, that Grandmother
Peggy had died. The news was shocking because Ida hadn't even realized
that Peggy had been alive during the years she was in Memphis. It all made
Ida determined to try, again, to bring her scattered family beneath one
roof. She was contemplating a number of schemes to make this possible;
she even considered finding a place where the family could pay its way by
raising poultry—a popular moneymaking scheme often advertised in the
press and ladies' manuals. Hopes to be able to attain a place rose in March
when Aunt Fanny, whose taxes on the Memphis house were in arrears,
wrote Ida from California to ask her to find out how much it would cost to
have the house on Georgia Street, valued at $300, "probated to her." Hop-
ing that she would be in a position to provide a homestead for the family,
Ida tried, unsuccessfully, to get a loan, but hoped Fanny could wait for her
to save the money to purchase it.[28]

At the time, Ida did have financial prospects. She anticipated getting
back pay from the school board in April when she could pay off some of her
department store and other debts. She (as well as Isaiah Graham) had
weathered Jones's insinuations; the school superintendent not only dismissed
the fraudulent reports from Kansas City but even suggested that Ida study
for a principal's exam—a position that could earn her a hundred dollars a
month. Ida also anticipated a positive decision in her court case due to be
heard in April. Of course, she relished the idea of a victory in terms of what
it meant for the race and black women in particular, but, with the precedent
of Jane Brown's $3,000 award, Ida also banked on a hefty monetary settle-

ment. Finally, Ida had a bird in the hand as far as her income stream was concerned: Sometime in late 1886 or early 1887, she had become a weekly correspondent for the *American Baptist*.

Ida had been offered the position by William J. Simmons, its publisher, and president of the National Colored Press Association. Simmons, a voluble, thickly built man with a handlebar mustache, was a former slave who had fled to freedom in the North with his mother and two siblings and later graduated from Howard University. He was also the president of the State University at Louisville, a Baptist institution, and of the National Baptist Convention. Through his web of connections, Simmons had been a boon to women entering journalism: mentoring, educating, and employing them as writers and typesetters. Sometime after Ida's return to Memphis, he had come to the city doing some work for the American Baptist Home Missionary Society, and as Ida noted in her autobiography, he told her that he could not resist looking up "the brilliant Iola" while there. Wells was thrilled by his offer for her to write a regular column and to be paid a dollar a week. She had "never dreamed" of receiving money for the work that she "loved" doing—a statement that did not square with her diary, or Calvin Chase's 1885 criticism of her.[29]

Wells's first truly professional assignment in journalism came in a period when the possibilities of racial inclusiveness and the power of unified, collective action were palpable. Rising expectations, however, made Ida impatient with what she saw as the black community's slowness in taking advantage of both. "There had not been a united action since the Haitian Revolution," Wells admonished in the *American Baptist*, and she blamed the "infighting among African peoples" for the situation that resulted in the Europeans being able to capture blacks for the transatlantic slave trade. As a result, the African continent had been "eviscerated" to "the extent that the world had forgotten its great civilization," she wrote. But in the spirit of the age, Ida also believed that blacks did not have to be "entrapped" by history any more than England when it was as "ignorant" and "degraded" as Africa was now. She pointed to the contemporary success of other ethnic groups in Memphis where "an Irishman and a Jew" were editing the city's two dailies, and an Italian was in the state legislature.[30]

In the *Baptist* weekly, Wells also criticized blacks who shunned the mainstream because of their own insecurities. She castigated "the voluntary segregation" of blacks such as those in the fraternal orders, and recalling her experience in Visalia, noted "that there was not a separate school in the state of California until the colored people asked for it." To "say we wish to be to ourselves is a tacit acknowledgment of the inferiority that they take for granted anyway. We are Negroes," Ida concluded, "but we are also Americans."[31]

PERHAPS IT WAS with her Americanness in mind that Ida, despite her past resolutions, regrets, and recriminations, could not resist going uptown to see the renowned Shakespearean actor Edwin Booth perform in both *Hamlet* and *Othello*, at the New Memphis Theater. Ida, along with Fanny Thompson and J. T. Turner, purchased tickets for the plays that were the theatrical and social highlights of the season in Memphis. The audience was made up of "beautiful maidens and gallant beaux, the leaders of society, and men who pay little attention to aught but the demands of business and home life," noted the *Appeal* in a description that managed to combine the chivalric images of the Old South with the industriousness of the New.[32] By 1887, such images, however, were increasingly put into sharp relief by contrasting them with that of blacks. The *Appeal*'s opening-night description was surrounded on each side by stories that carried the headlines: "A Colored Crook," "Colored Robbers Caught," and "A Colored Shooting Scrape."

The decision to see Booth was particularly indiscreet. The actor was the brother of Abraham Lincoln's assassin. And notwithstanding those rare progressive meetings, Ida and her friends probably sat in a segregated section for the performances. The New Memphis Theater had the same manager as had the Leubrie Theater six years before when Julia Hooks had been arrested; and the fact that Booth was playing the part of Iago in *Othello*—a play about miscegenation and the murder of a white woman by a black nobleman—would have done little to make "uptown" more amenable. Compounding the "crime," after the Saturday night performance, Ida and her friends went to Fanny's house on Vance Street where they "stayed up all night in fun and games," Ida wrote in her diary. The next morning, Wells felt "very badly from its effects," she continued, a comment that sounded as if the future teetotaler might have been drinking alcohol.[33]

It is not clear what Ida thought about recreational drinking at the time, although years later she wrote about the predictable perils of overindulgence for impoverished and susceptible blacks whose disorderly conduct cast a bad reflection on the race, and was treated harshly by authorities. Nevertheless, Ida did not appear to share the more extreme views of those, black and white, who believed in the necessity of total abstinence. There is no evidence that she was a member of any WCTU group, and she certainly fraternized with those who were avowed antiprohibitionists. T. Thomas Turner, for example, who joined Ida and Fanny for "fun and games," saw, as he would later write in the *Watchman*, statutory prohibition as a "slave law," a throwback to the preemancipation years when whites could not sell alcohol to slaves and when free blacks were not allowed to sell it. To his mind, and perhaps to Ida's, such laws reflected the stereotype that blacks were naturally docile and kindhearted, but if aroused—by spirits or agitation—could be demons. This stereotype slipped dangerously toward conflating blacks themselves with the evil of alcohol. In 1886, Ida had heard Dwight Moody warn Memphians against "that devil rum," as "black a devil that ever existed."[34]

Ida, though not feeling particularly well after the Saturday-night party, dragged herself to Avery to teach her Sunday-school class the next morning. The boys were rambunctious, Ida was irritable, and after the class she was met by the church's minister, George Dardis, Jr., who gave her a "severe lecture." He told her that his father (also a minister), Professor Thompson (Ida's elocution teacher), Mr. Greenlee, Mr. Selectman, and Dr. Burchette, among others, were complaining that Wells was failing to practice what she preached. Ida had committed multiple indiscretions, but none would have been as serious as drinking at a time when the prohibition campaign was reaching a crescendo just five months before the scheduled prohibition referendum.[35]

By then, the Tennessee black elite, like its white counterpart, was in the throes of a campaign marked by its own combination of religious zeal, secular reform, and the unprecedented opportunity for the race to be viewed as a force against all the "evils" that alcohol represented. Black churches, the state's black higher-education institutions, including LeMoyne, Fisk, Roger Williams College, and Central Tennessee College, were all centers of temperance organizing. Frederick Douglass wrote appeals for the state's prohibition effort, and when J. C. Price, a minister who was instrumental in the founding of North Carolina's Livingstone College, came to Nashville to promote the amendment, four thousand blacks had come out to hear him.[36]

Young women like Ida were needed to set an example, she was told by the minister, and that thought made her contrite and determined to do better. "I had not placed so high an estimate on myself," Ida conceded in her diary, after being reminded of her role-modeling influence on her charges at such a critical juncture. "But [Dardis] certainly gave me food for thought and hereafter when I grow weary and despondent & think my life useless & unprofitable, may I remember this episode, and may it strengthen me to the performance of my duty, for I would not willingly be the cause of one's soul being led astray."[37] If the past is any guide, Wells squirmed beneath her sincere—and circumscribing—obligations as she awaited the court decision that promised to make her a model woman. On the eleventh of April, she heard the news from her lawyer, former judge John Greer.

BY THEN, THE chief justice of the Tennessee Supreme Court was Peter J. Turney, a die-hard secessionist who had raised the first regiment of Confederate soldiers in Tennessee. His associate justices included other Confederate veterans, such as Horace H. Lurton, who had been imprisoned twice by Union forces, and William C. Folkes, who had lost a leg in the war. By 1887, no Democrat, as a faction of the party had in the past, could afford to be associated with a Wells victory in the first legal challenge in a southern state court after the overturning of the 1875 Civil Rights Act.[38] Although Ida's attorney had reiterated the points that had succeeded in the lower court trial, including the fact that there was smoking in the colored car and that in the ladies' car, Ida, a "schoolteacher," was "just as quiet and orderly as anyone else *could* have been [emphasis in original]," the Tennessee Supreme Court chose, unsurprisingly, to view the situation differently.

The judges, against all evidence to the contrary, simply dismissed the testimony by blacks that there was smoking in the colored car; the railway, in the court's view, had no liability because the two cars were in fact equal. Moreover, the justices reconstructed Ida's motives and even her identity. Reflecting upon Ida's recalcitrant behavior on the train, the judges concluded that she was not a "lady" but merely a "mulatto passenger," whose purpose "was to harass with a view to this suit," and whose "persistence was not in good faith to obtain a comfortable seat for the short ride." In any case, the ladies' car, it was further determined, was for whites only, and neither Wells, nor anyone for that matter, had the right to "arbitrarily determine as to the coach in which they take passage." Ida's conduct, therefore, was based on an assumption that was "without the slightest reason."[39]

Ida was devastated. She had hoped that her case would be a beacon, but instead it marked the beginning of a long, lightless tunnel that, with other cases, would eventually lead to legalized segregation. "I felt so disappointed because I had hoped such great things from my suit for my people generally," Ida confided to her diary. "I have firmly believed all along that the law was on our side and would, when we appealed to it, give us justice. I feel shorn of that belief and utterly discouraged," she wrote, "and just now if it were possible I would gather my race in my arms and fly away with them."[40]

IN 1887, IT was becoming painfully evident that the choice had been made about black civil rights in a white South that just could not accommodate standing shoulder to shoulder with its former slaves—even when it was in one's interest to do so. In May, the month after Ida's court decision, she no doubt read in the *Appeal* about a K of L picnic in Birmingham, Alabama, where the whites among the six thousand attendees left in a huff when they realized that blacks outnumbered them two-to-one on the food line. Forced to choose between blacks and whites, the Knights in Birmingham and elsewhere soon abandoned its African American workers.

Although there is no record of the reaction to Ida's court decision by black Memphians, there is evidence that they responded by renewing their efforts to unify themselves—this time for their own protection.[41] Ida applauded the founding of the Mutual Protection Association just weeks following the lost appeal. Its leaders included Isaac Norris, J. Thomas Turner, Thomas Cassels, Edward Shaw, and Benjamin Imes, and represented a new alliance among the once-warring black fraternal, ministerial, and political factions in the city. Ida, accompanied by Albert Alexander, attended its first meeting and was buoyed by what she had seen. "Have just returned from what I consider the best thing out," Ida wrote in her diary. The "Negro," she concluded optimistically, is finding out "that strength for his people and consequently for him is to be found only in unity."[42]

Unity among black Memphians, whose numbers doubled to nearly twenty-nine thousand during the decade (just seven thousand less than the white population), could indeed be a powerful asset. Moreover, there was still some confidence in the fact that Memphis, which was so progressive on other fronts and enjoying an economic boom, would hold the line against the negative trend in the state and in other parts of the South. One of the Mutual Protection Association's resolutions took pains to praise those whites who demonstrated that they were "breaking away from unreasonable prejudice" and appealed to the white elite to help their masses "rise above" race discrimination.[43]

WELLS MIGHT HAVE lost her faith in the law, but not in the white elite or in the ability of blacks to create their own organizations and institutions. After the court decision, Ida redirected her longings for the theater by organizing, with other members of the Memphis Lyceum, their own dramatic club. In May, their fund-raising event for the club was attended by an integrated audience, and according to Well's diary, the affair was a blazing success. It not only raised sixty dollars, but her reading of "Le Marriage de Convenience" gained kudos from one of the most prominent whites in Memphis, Judge Thomas J. Latham, president of the Artesian Water Company and a director of the Union Savings Bank. After the performance, he told her that it was the most artistic piece of elocution he had ever heard.[44]

The lyceum program had also featured former Louisiana lieutenant governor P. B. S. Pinchback, then campaigning to win a place on the Republican National Committee. Ida wrote in her diary that she had been less than impressed by Pinchback's presentation, and it is doubtful that inviting him was her idea. He was the kind of leader Ida had had in mind when she earlier criticized Reconstruction politicians whose considerable material gains were not matched by their efforts to help the next generation. But this was the era of unity, and, moreover, Pinchback was a close friend of her sometime benefactor Robert R. Church. Both men had been saloon keepers who had risen to wealth through their business and political acumen, and Church and his second wife, Anna, had spent part of their honeymoon with the Pinchbacks in New Orleans. Ida, in this instance, used the occasion of Pinchback's appearance to promote local candidates rather than criticize national ones.

Ida's efforts put her in good stead with the circle of Memphians that included Church's daughter, Mary, whom she met in the summer of 1887—the beginning of a relationship that would last nearly sixty years. Mary, or

"Mollie" as she was known, was the daughter of Robert and his first wife, Louisa Ayers, who, before the couple divorced, owned the first fashionable hair salon in Memphis. Mollie had come home after her graduation from Oberlin that summer, and in July, Ida took part in a round-robin of social activities that included attending a concert by Julia Hooks, meeting Albert Alexander's cadet brother, John, whom Mollie was dating, and a brief visit with Mollie herself. Sometime after the visit, Ida got a message that Mollie wished to have a chance to talk to her, and Ida responded immediately. In her diary, Ida wrote of their two-hour get-together with an enthusiasm she rarely expressed regarding women.[45]

Of course, in many ways their experiences could not have been more different. Mollie had had a life of privilege, wealth, private tutors, an elite prep school, and a degree from one of the leading liberal arts colleges in the country. At the same time, they both rebelled against the restrictions of their sex. At Oberlin, Mollie had elected to take what was known as the "Gentlemen's Course," which included an emphasis on the study of Latin and Greek—the specialties of her former teacher in Memphis, Virginia Broughton—brushing off warnings that no man would want to marry a woman so highly educated. And in defiance of her father, who wanted her to stay at home and live a "southern belle" existence, Mollie insisted on taking a position at Wilberforce University—even when her father threatened to cut off support. (He finally relented.) Mollie's advantages, however, did not protect her from discrimination, and, as was true of Ida, such experiences became indelible in their minds and shaped their outlook and activist determination. Mollie later wrote of racist experiences she had at Oberlin that were a painful reminder that one's background or achievement was no protection from awful stereotypes. In one instance, she was selected out of all the Oberlin students in her class to recite a passage in Greek for the visiting Matthew Arnold, the well-known English poet and critic known for his advocacy of maintaining classical standards. Arnold, Mollie recounted, was surprised that a black person could be so facile in Greek; he had thought that the tongues of Africans were so thick that they could not be taught to pronounce the language.[46]

Ida did not mention what the two talked about or why Mollie had asked to see her. No doubt the subject of the Alexander brothers came up, but Ida's comments suggested that they also talked about substantive matters that, in light of the court decision, may well have included Church's experiences on the railways. As she later wrote, two incidents had deeply affected her. The first occurred when Mollie was only six years old and was traveling with her father to Cincinnati. Both were in the ladies' car but when her father left her there to socialize in the smokers' car, the conductor, seeing the little girl of color sitting there alone, tried to force her out of the first-class accommodations. Unlike Ida, Mollie had a protective father. When Robert Church realized what was happening, he returned to the first-class car with his pistol drawn. The conductor relented and Robert and his little girl continued their journey, unmolested, in the first-class car. The second time, when Mollie was sixteen and returning from Oberlin, was even more harrowing. When she had to change trains in Bowling, Kentucky, she was forced by the conductor to sit in the smokers' car. As night fell, she experienced the terror of young women in the smokers' cars who were "at the mercy of the conductor or any man who entered."[47]

For Ida, who could never be the kind of "obedient," "tractable" woman she had written so admiringly about, Mollie must have been a revelation. She managed to be a serious thinker, was tough-minded, and went after what she wanted without sacrificing her womanliness or class standing. "She is the first woman of my age I've met who is similarly inspired with the same desires & ambitions," wrote Ida, who felt that she had "greatly benefited" from their first meeting. "I only wish I had known her long ago."[48]

In fact, Wells may have picked up some pointers about how to successfully conduct and express herself according to the emerging model of late-nineteenth-century women like Church, who were amiable and feminine without sacrificing their star quality or steely intelligence. Comments about Ida in August, when she made her debut among her newspaper colleagues at the National Colored Press Association, held in Louisville, Kentucky, indicated that she had managed to do just that.

THE CONVENTION PROVED to be a watershed for black women journalists, who attended in larger numbers than in the past, and for Ida herself, who had wanted to attend the previous year's conference in Atlantic City but had failed to convince the *Living Way* to pay her way there. In 1887, William Simmons, the publisher of the *American Baptist* and president of the association, offered to pay her travel expenses—but in the wake of the court decision, Ida was less than enthusiastic about attending.

For one thing, she was broke. Instead of the monetary damages she had anticipated with a victory, she had owed court fees in defeat. After getting her salary in April and paying off some of her debts, sending money to Aunt Fanny, and buying some clothes at Menken's, she was in financial arrears again. Her most serious shortfall was her boarding fee with the Settles. Ida had discovered Josiah to be a disagreeable "tightwad"; and she was surprised by the amount of indebtedness that his wife, Therese, said she owed. But Ida did not keep good records and was forced to accept the tally. To make the situation worse, Ida's sister L'il and Josiah did not get along. At least once, he had offered her money for errands, but afterward would not pay the required carfare, leaving L'il none the better for doing the task. Perhaps in retaliation, Ida's sister, on two occasions, was caught stealing. "Had to whip Lily severely this morning for her second peculation," Ida wrote in her diary that June. "I earnestly pray such may never happen again."[49]

With only $35 in the bank, Ida had wanted to find a summer teaching job, but William Simmons, without her consent, had placed her on the program of the press meeting. The Baptist Kentuckian was the host for the conference and was rounding up support to be reelected as president against T. Thomas Fortune.

Simmons had to have been concerned about the better-known Fortune. The New York editor had recently gained a good deal of national publicity as the activist whose challenges to the New South constructions of race relations proposed by Henry Grady and others were published in such leading journals as *Century Magazine* and *Harper's Weekly*. But Fortune was prepared to go beyond fighting words. In May, he had proposed in the *Freeman* the creation of a new organization to press the demands for those rights: the Afro-American League.[50]

Fortune's vision of the league went beyond its predecessors, such as the still extant black convention movement, begun in 1830, in which African Americans—sometimes joined by liberal whites—regularly met in the effort to "devise ways and means for the bettering" of the black condition, particularly through education. By contrast, the Afro-American League presaged the civil rights organizations to come. It was to be a nationally coordinated effort to take on multiple issues, including voting rights, lynch law, unequal distribution of school funds, discrimination in public accommodations, and the penitentiary system, and to have a proactive, militant stance in demanding the civil rights due to blacks as American citizens.[51]

Fortune also eschewed the paternalistic pattern of race relations that depended on alliances with the white elite. Challenging Grady's carefully spun image of the region's aristocratic, cavalier-like figures to whom race relations were to be entrusted, Fortune pointed out that the increasingly frequent outrages against blacks in the South were often perpetrated by the "best people"—the very ones assumed to be above the acts of violence and brutality consigned to the realms of the poor and ignorant. Indeed, the most egregious outrage, lynching—a practice that had origins in the Revolutionary War years—had taken a new turn in the society that Grady and others had proclaimed as undergoing peaceful and mutually agreed-upon racial adjustment. Eighteen eighty-six marked the first year that the documented number of black victims outnumbered that of whites: seventy-five and sixty-two, respectively.[52]

Wells had applauded the League in Simmons's *American Baptist* as a potential means to protect blacks—Ida's chief concern. "Innocent men and women are victims of mob and lynch law; cultured and refined ladies and gentlemen are insulted and proscribed on the railways every day . . . why? Because they have so long done things with impunity," Ida wrote. The League could be the "grandest idea ever originated," if it was "rightly carried out as a means of protection of life, citizenship and property."[53]

Like Wells, many in the black press and elsewhere were supportive of the League idea. Booker T. Washington, head of Tuskegee Institute in Alabama, responded in the *Freeman* with enthusiasm. "Push the battle to the gate," the educator urged. "Let there be no hold-up until a League shall be found in every village. God bless you," he cheered. "God bless the League." But, also like Wells, many voiced their "if rightly carried out" caveats about the organization—or more precisely, about Fortune leading it.[54]

He was a visionary, but for all of his widely acknowledged wisdom on the race question, he was also quixotic, erratic, and often intemperate—all of which was reflected in his physical appearance at a time when appearances were very important. Fortune was of Irish, black, and Native American ancestry, and his "long hair, curling about his forehead and his spectacles . . . made him look more like a dude of the period" than a "strong, sensible, brainy man" Ida once wrote in her diary. To some, Fortune's proposal of the League was marred by his publicly stated willingness to engage in violence, if necessary. While the New York editor had proposed that the organization would stress "peaceful means," including the ballot and the courts to gain rights, he also insisted that "if others use the weapons of violence to combat our peaceful arguments it is not for us to run away from violence." He concluded, "A man's a man, and what is worth having is worth fighting for."[55]

Despite her conservatism on some matters, Wells was never one to fear a fight, and she had more often than not publicly supported Fortune's black nationalist perspective. Even though she supported his idea of the League—and that the election of the association president would be a referendum of sorts regarding it—Ida would go to Louisville as a voting delegate for the more conservative Simmons. She may have well had her doubts about Fortune's leadership, but as her subsequent writings showed, she had yet to grasp his argument that class, behavior, and "intelligence" should neither confer nor take away constitutional rights. Moreover, there is little question that she also acceded to personal—and practical—considerations. Ida was not only a paid contributor to the *American Baptist,* she was also poised to be a writer for another of Simmons's publications in the offing, *Our Women and Children.* Wells, as she later noted in her autobiography, was also grateful for his mentorship at a critical moment in her journalistic career. Her success was "largely due to his encouragement," she wrote.[56]

SO IDA, RELUCTANTLY, planned to go to Louisville, despite Josiah's threats to force her and Lily out of his house and knowing that it would mean spending some of her own less-than-discretionary funds in anticipation of the planned social events in Louisville and Lexington. Before Ida left for the three-week trip to Kentucky, she bought a seersucker suit for the occasion.

Once she arrived, she seemed to greatly enjoy the meeting that was held at Louisville's Fifth Street Baptist Church. In her diary, Ida described the stimulating panels of journalists who had attended, including Alexander Clark of Chicago's *Conservator,* who had invited Ida to write for the paper, the first black weekly established in that city. She served on the resolutions committee and presented a paper entitled "How I Would Edit," all of which impressed her colleagues enough for her to be elected first assistant secretary of the association, becoming (no doubt with the help of Simmons, who was reelected president) the first woman to hold an office in the organization. At the concluding dinner, Ida had been called on, unexpectedly, to talk about the role of women in journalism. She did so, but later, in her diary, chastised herself for not having given men adequate credit for their support of women journalists in general and of herself in particular.[57]

Under the aegis of Simmons, an unprecedented number of women journalists had taken part in the deliberations, including the Kentuckians Mary V. Cook and Lucy Wilmot Smith, two leaders of the Baptist women's movement, who, like Ida, were indebted to the publisher. Both Cook and Smith were graduates of the State University at Louisville over which Simmons presided, and they were also writing for his publications. Cook edited the women's column of the *American Baptist* and would oversee the educational department of *Our Women and Children*. Smith, a former private secretary for Simmons, was made the editor of the children's column of the *American Baptist* while still a college student. She would edit the children's column of *Our Women and Children*.[58]

But it was Ida who stood out. "The noticeable ones in the convention were, first, the brilliant and earnest, I trust, 'Iola,'" observed the reporter from the *New Orleans Weekly Pelican*. In a period known as the age of the publisher in the history of the black press, Ida stood out as "the most prominent correspondent at present connected with the Negro press." But as was so often true of such compliments, especially those directed at Ida, the doting words were followed by an admonition. If Ida "does not suffer her head to become unduly inflated, there is a brilliant and useful future" for her, the reporter concluded.[59]

Fortune's own recounting of Wells at the Louisville conference was less enthusiastic. In the *New York Freeman* he noted how Simmons had stacked the conference with allies and proxies, Ida among them. There is no indication that Wells supported his cause on the resolutions committee or spoke up against *Washington Bee* editor Calvin Chase when he charged that Fortune's national league would only result in a "national Negro mob" that would get "Negroes of the South slaughtered." Nevertheless, the group did pass a resolution that called for local leagues to be established, and Fortune could only hope that it would mark the beginning of a national effort.[60]

In her diary, Ida wrote little about the historic conference. She did not mention her election or Fortune's Afro-American League proposal, an indication, perhaps, of some uneasiness about her role. Instead, she devoted many of her entries to the postconference activities in both Louisville and Lexington, especially her social activities and the people she met in Ken-

tucky. For example, she visited Charles Morris's mother, made friends with
Julia Hooks's sister, Mary E. Britton, a journalist who wrote under the pen
name of "Meb," and continued her serial flirtations and reproaches with a
number of potential suitors.[61]

But Ida's festive mood would end abruptly when she returned to Memphis. In her debt-ridden absence Josiah Settle had locked up her things in
an effort to force her to move because of nonpayment of the boarding fee.
So Ida, again, became preoccupied with finding boarding arrangements
and was forced to place Lily with a woman by the name of Mrs. Hawkins
until she was finally able to find a place at 20 Goslee Street, the address of
the teacher Florence Cooper and her husband, E. E. Cooper.[62] The last
extant entry in her diary, September 18, ended before one of the most pivotal racial developments in Memphis and the state at large: the results of
the September 29 referendum to prohibit the sale of liquor in the state. It
unleashed a storm that would soon sweep away any delusions about Memphis.

BY 1887, AS Fortune had gleaned, it didn't much matter if New South
apostles in Memphis or elsewhere really believed the redemption narratives
they were spinning for northern capitalists and southern romantics. It
didn't much matter if they really believed that the region had risen from its
humiliation upon a parapet of progress without sacrificing its vaunted
southern way of life, heroic personage, or the Golden Rule, which placed
spiritual matters over capital gain. It did not matter because by 1887, the
New South creed had slipped into the realm of myth—and myths only
require half-truths to provide their believers with a fundamental sense of
unity and purpose. Tennessee stepped into the misty vortex when the prohibition referendum lost by the slim margin of 17,000 votes out of 263,000
cast.[63]

Tennesseeans yearned for a sign that—despite all indications to the
contrary—rapid economic growth and capital investment was, as dictated
by the New South creed, bringing the society closer to perfection. The
campaign had become a Manichean struggle of the Christ versus the Anti-Christ, of good versus evil: a movement "directed by the hand of God" to
eliminate the "one great obstacle to man's well-being on earth," averred the
Tennessee Baptist. A vote for prohibition would have been the sign of the
triumph of evangelical zeal over the powerful liquor interests that provided

the state about $222,000 annually in taxes from the sale of alcohol—much of it from Memphis, which was the warehousing and distribution depot for large liquor companies distributing their goods to Arkansas, Mississippi, and Alabama. "Oh, for a state redeemed from drink!" proclaimed Reverend H. A. Jones, minister of the Cumberland Presbyterian Church in Memphis.[64]

But Tennessee was not redeemed on September 29, the date of the vote—and unable to face any other explanation for the defeat, African Americans, whom the prohibitionists had depended upon, were blamed for the loss. "I don't suppose a hundred negroes voted for [the amendment]," wrote a white lawyer and temperance organizer in his diary. Although there were newspaper reports of white politicians receiving bribes from the liquor interests, John MacGowan, editor of the *Chattanooga Times,* spoke for many when he charged that the referendum had been defeated because blacks had been "hired with whiskey and money."[65]

The conclusions discounted the highly publicized efforts of black reformers; the fact that prohibitionists were outspent and less organized than the Tennessee Protective Association, which represented the powerful liquor interests in the state; that pro-growth politicians were against the referendum from the beginning; that leading figures like Civil War hero Jefferson Davis spoke against it; and that even some churches urged its congregants not to mix spiritual matters with politics. Also discounted was the fact that Democrats, led by *Nashville Daily American's* publisher, John J. Vertrees, worried in his editorials that the prohibition movement was a Trojan horse for women's suffrage and the Prohibition Party, both of which were inimical to the Democratic Party. Although it was not possible to get the precise racial breakdown of the vote, it had been defeated in a number of predominantly white wards and counties, and there were more negative votes cast in Democratic strongholds throughout the state than in Republican ones. But the fact that the referendum came up short in counties and urban centers with large populations (including Memphis) was enough to convince white opinion-makers that blacks had overwhelmingly voted against it. In fact, the majority of blacks probably did vote against prohibition; but an objective analysis of the vote revealed that so did the majority of whites![66]

Nevertheless, Bishop Oscar P. Fitzgerald, editor of the *Christian Advocate,* published in Nashville by the Methodist Episcopal Church South, pronounced that there were two "undeniable facts" about the referendum:

"a decided majority of whites voted for prohibition," and "the Negro vote was almost solid against prohibition." Blacks, he deemed, had failed to cross the great divide of civilization; they were, he said, an "obstacle to Christian reform." As such, they were now stamped as incorrigible. Following the vote, southern whites were no longer "sitting up at night . . . devising means to endow schools for the education of the negro [sic]," the *Memphis Avalanche* opined; instead "they are restlessly employed in searching for some means to make him a nonentity in politics."[67]

With God now on the side of "intelligence" (Democrats) versus "ignorance" (blacks and their Republican allies), the deed was done with incredible speed and efficiency. The election of 1888 was marked by wholesale fraud. When the Tenth Congressional District—a Republican stronghold that included Shelby County and whose electorate was 50 percent black—was lost to Democrats that year, the Republican *Knoxville Journal,* among others, charged that the election represented "one of the most flagrant outrages ever perpetuated upon the ballot-box in a free republic."[68]

Protests on the part of blacks evoked calls of an impending "race war" and warnings about "Negro domination" from the *Avalanche*—owned by James Phelan who had earlier been a cocounsel for Wells's 1883 court case and had once supported black suffrage. The *Appeal* dismissed such hyperbolic provocations, but more effective were the *Avalanche*'s charges that blacks were buying Winchester rifles from the Jewish-owned Shuman's Gun store on Main Street and a crude cartoon depicting an angry mob of blacks standing in front of "Republican Headquarters," which was issuing them the weapons.[69]

Republican victories in the national elections of 1888, in which Benjamin Harrison won the presidency and gave the party a majority in the Congress, became the catalyst for the next step, disenfranchisement legislation. Republicans talked of a federal elections bill—spuriously called the "force bill" by opponents—which would provide for federal supervision over elections. In 1888 and 1889, the Tennessee legislature passed three bills calling for new registration procedures, separate polling places for state and federal elections, and a secret ballot that required voters to be literate.[70]

In nearly 50 percent black Memphis (where 2,399 had voted for prohibition and 6,821 had voted against it), the biracial, bipartisan administration of David P. Hadden had become too "riddled" with Republicans and

Negroes (now that reforms and investment were firmly in place). Taxing district officials became a target of a witch hunt to oust corruption within their ranks. In 1888, Hadden himself was indicted for malfeasance, ostensibly for taxing gambling and prostitution establishments instead of closing them. In less than two years after the referendum vote, Tennessee, which had had the most competitive two-party system in the South during the 1880s because of black voters, became a one-party state dominated by the Democrats, newly united on the race issue.[71]

IDA'S FIRST RESPONSE to the events of the late 1880s reflected that of most the black elites in Memphis, which had more reason than ever to eschew electoral politics, withdraw more deeply into the black community, give up on desegregation, and redouble its efforts to establish its own institutions and businesses. The response had its own internal logic, but many African Americans, including Ida, failed to grasp the machinations within the larger framework of white supremacy and political and economic interests. For example, Hadden's most important transgression was probably his standing in the way of land developers and investors who wanted to privatize and electrify the streetcar franchise and extend routes to the suburbs.[72]

The disenfranchising bills were another case in point. The Dortch Bill, for example, called for a secret ballot that carried printed names in lieu of party symbols, prohibited outside assistance to those who could not read, and required a poll tax. Similar legislation had already been passed in several northern states with the purpose of excluding ignorant, gullible, and easily led voters—both black and white—from the electorate. The idea was welcomed by a number of elite blacks, including Frances Ellen Harper and W. E. B. Du Bois, soon to become Harvard's first black to be awarded a PhD. Harper advocated educational and moral requirements for voting, and Du Bois disputed the need for a federal elections bill, noting in the *New York Age*, "When you have the right sort of voters, you will need no election laws."[73]

But "purifying the electorate" as it was called, especially in the South, was calculated to exclude black political power—even if race was not mentioned per se. In Tennessee, for example, at the time the Dortch Bill was passed, 54 percent of blacks and 18 percent of whites could not read. Moreover, to appease white rural voters, the bill applied to *only* those areas with a sizable black vote: Shelby and Davidson counties (which included Nashville) and the cities of Knoxville and Chattanooga. Still, to struggle for political restitution before getting the literacy numbers up appeared to be putting the proverbial cart before the horse. Many black opinion-makers, including Ida, entangled in myths of their own, still saw the voting issue in terms of class rather than race. They, too, were concerned about a black electorate increasingly made up of less-educated, gullible migrants who were inundating the cities. Before the referendum, the pro-temperance (CME) *Christian Index,* out of Jackson, Tennessee, opined that most blacks would vote for prohibition if "left alone," but worried that they would be used as an unwitting "tool" by both parties. With no access to an objective analysis of the vote, the black elite had reason to believe that its worst fears had come true. "The simple irresponsible right to vote does not of itself alone constitute a true citizen," Wells wrote in the *Christian Index* in June of 1889, two months after the Dortch Bill was passed.[74]

Wells's thinking was in line with many black reformers in Memphis who thought that the best remedy for the deteriorating situation was to address poverty, illiteracy, and destructive behavior. Following the referendum vote, new black institutions and businesses emerged to do just that. In 1888, Julia Hooks founded an Orphans and Old Folks Home, largely financed through her concerts, and Virginia Broughton was fervently organizing her Baptist Bible Bands of women, which eventually operated in fifty-seven localities across the state and conducted twenty industrial schools. On the economic front, the number of black businesses rose from 92 in 1880, to 147 by 1890. Among the new proprietors was Thomas Moss, who had helped host the teachers from Kansas City and opened the People's Grocery in 1889, a cooperative venture whose investors included Virginia Broughton's husband, Julius, educator Benjamin K. Sampson, and several other men whose occupations ranged from pastors and carpenters to carpet layers and laborers. Also in 1888, the Howe Baptist Institute, founded by Peter Howe and *Living Way* editors R. N. Countee and W. A. Brinkley, was created to provide "academic, religious and industrial training of Negroes." It prohibited its teachers from affiliating with secret orders, raising money through excursions, or using snuff or tobacco.[75]

IN 1888 AND 1889, Ida Wells was traveling a good deal to places like Indiana, Kentucky, and Ohio on behalf of the CME's *Christian Index,* published in Jackson, Tennessee, and edited by her friend and CME presiding elder E. W. Moseley. The series of articles she wrote for the publication record her lack of optimism about race relations, but mostly her trenchant beatitudes about what the race needed and lacked. While in Richmond, Indiana, Wells, after attending a picnic that included black and white students, wistfully wrote that the South would not see such "harmonious mixing of the races for years to come." In any case, in the wake of the prohibition defeat, the main issue now was development from within the community.[76]

Even before the referendum, Ida had preached in the *American Baptist* about the need for blacks to "use the money spent for tobacco, whisky and snuff" to buy homes and books, and the need to educate and cultivate the minds of their children and teach them "individual, family and race pride." After the referendum, such messages remained the same but they were laced with more vitriol. For example, when the *Avalanche* had criticized black politicians for wanting to "assert themselves in a country where the bulk of their race own nothing, have no interests, and show no disposition to acquire any," Wells, targeting her editorial toward blacks, wrote that the newspaper "gloated over the fact that the white people own and will continue to own the land and, by that reason will always be our masters." She challenged, "Is there not a hint here for us?" The "hint" was that "one wealthy man is worth more to us than 5000 politicians."[77]

She railed against the raucous public behavior of blacks during what she called their "interminable picnics," and the large group excursions on the trains. After the report of train incidents in which boisterous blacks were clubbed by a conductor, and another passenger was killed in Charleston, Ida saw it in terms of African Americans giving the railroad corporations "a stronger stick with which to break our heads." For the sake of pleasure, blacks, she snarled, were willing to be "dragged or kicked out" as if they "were dogs," or even to be "shot down in cold blood."[78]

In a similar vein, Ida scoffed at the breakdown of negotiations between *Memphis Watchman* publisher J. T. Turner and Taylor Nightingale, minister of the Beale Street Church and owner of the *Free Speech* newspaper, to consolidate their publications at a time when there was a particularly urgent need for a strong black publication. In 1889, the *Appeal*'s John Keating—a supporter of Nightingale's onetime ally David Hadden—lost an ugly internecine battle for control of the paper, and with his departure, Negrophobic

Democrats now dominated the Memphis press. Ida, writing in the *Index*, sneered at yet another instance of blacks being unable to rise above their differences even in the light of the "gross injustice," of the now unchallenged Democratic press. "We seem to delight in helping those who spit and spurn us," she had concluded. "Queer isn't it?"[79]

Wells also devoted a series of articles to the role of ministers, who, in her view, had replaced politicians in their importance—and in their own transgressions. Ministers had the "power to wield" the greatest influence over our "church-going and church loving people," she wrote. She accused the Baptist and Methodist denominations of being riddled with "the most corrupt, immoral and incompetent ministry," and called the newly elected bishops W. J. Gaines of Georgia and Abraham Grant of Texas too "uncultivated" for a position that required pastors to be "mild and Christlike, dignified and gentle, wise as serpents and harmless as doves." She also wrote disapprovingly of church leaders sending out vulnerable young girls to collect money from parishioners.[80]

As they had in the past, Ida's articles, focused on uplift, garnered a good deal of praise. A forgiving T. Thomas Fortune had remarked in 1888 that she "handled a goose quill with diamond point as handily as any of us men in newspaper work." Indeed, Wells's *Index* articles showed a substantial improvement since she had published the "Woman's Mission" essay and her contributions to the *Fisk Herald*. Her writing was less self-conscious and labored, her sentences were sharp and clear, and the thesis or argument of her subject was delineated with the smooth transitions she had earlier sought. Ida had clearly gotten in control of the essay form. She had found a feminine voice like the one she wrote about in an essay for Fortune's *New York Freeman* earlier in 1888. Wells had written that the language of the "model woman," the title of the piece, was made elegant through "simplicity and chastity."[81]

Ida was clearly inspired by the example of a new generation of black classical singers who were on the rise, such as the mezzo-soprano Flora Batson, who performed in Memphis in 1888. "It is a two-fold pleasure to listen to her," Ida wrote. "One can enjoy the feast of the mind as well as the senses." This gave Batson the power to "reach the hearts of the people," Ida noted. "That is after all the chief aim and desire of us all," Wells concluded, revealing her own ambition, "to live in the hearts of men and women."[82]

Wells might have been writing as well as any man, but she wasn't writing about the kind of political issues that her male peers were. Her tone and choice of subjects reflected her sincere convictions, but they also provided something that she yearned for: a distinct, largely uncontested role in the national discourse on race. By 1889, she had earned the reputation as the journalist "who struck the hardest blows at the wrongs and weaknesses of the race," observed Lucy Wilmot Smith, writing in the mainstream publication called the *Journalist*. Wilmot's observation was meant as a compliment, for Ida's chastising was widely, and rightly, seen through her maternalist race-in-my-arms concerns, rather than disdain. The formula gained Ida the distinction of being one of the few writers who had the ability to reach men and women, equally, Smith noted, and it was Wells she anointed the "The Princess of the Press"—a title that may have been inspired by the popular new Gilbert and Sullivan opera *Princess Ida*.[83]

IDA CONTINUED TO direct her barbs at the shortcomings of the race in 1889, but the year also brought new perspectives to her thinking. Two events that year made her begin to think more deeply about the issue of lynching, though she was still some years away from the understanding of its implications regarding race, class, and sexuality that marked her later writings.

In March, Ida read the head-snapping news that Eliza Woods, the black cook who had been lynched three years before in Jackson, Tennessee—and about whom Ida had written in her diary—was belatedly discovered to be innocent. The husband of the woman whom Woods had allegedly poisoned was reported to have broken down and confessed to killing his wife. The revelation made Wells furious. In the *Index*, she publicly berated the black men in the community for allowing "white men to outrage all decency and law by stripping one of our women and hanging her merely on suspicion." The whole affair was a disgrace, she said, and Ida exhorted black men everywhere to "rise in their manhood and resent such outrages as white men do."[84]

Her call to act like whites was probably a reference to the recent incident involving Jesse Duke, a black editor from Montgomery, Alabama, who had been run out of town when it was thought that he had insulted a white woman in one of his editorials. In his paper, Duke had questioned a rape charge that had gotten a man lynched the year before. Not only was the relationship between the black man and white woman consensual, Duke implied, but such interracial romances were on the rise. There is a "secret to this thing," Duke had written, "and we greatly suspect it is the growing appreciation of the white Juliet for the colored Romeo, as he becomes more and more intelligent and refined." Reaction to the editorial, fortuitously published when Duke was out of town, was swift and far-reaching. After passing a resolution denouncing the editor, whites went to his house and broke windows while his wife and children were inside. Black leaders of the town were forced to disclaim any association or agreement with the editor. Efforts were even revived to stop the construction of a black college in Montgomery on the basis that it would only produce more "educated Romeos" in the city. "God expects us to defend ourselves," Wells wrote. "When we fail to do so we have only ourselves to blame."[85]

SOON AFTER PUBLISHING the editorial, Ida attended the March 1889 meeting of the National Colored Press Association, held at Washington, D.C.'s, magnificent Metropolitan AME Church, a towering Gothic structure made of red-brick and built by black artisans in 1886. For her, the most powerful presentation was given by Virginia's John R. Mitchell, Jr., vice president of the association and one of the black press's most militant editors; his *Richmond Planet* featured a masthead depicting a muscular black arm with a clenched fist. Mitchell had begun writing editorials on lynching and headed the group's Committee on Outrages. When it was his turn to give a report, he read aloud the names of more than two hundred lynching victims who had been murdered during the preceding two years. The poignant roll call made Ida envision not so much their manner of death as the ignominious shame and terror that accompanied it. "My eyes filled with tears," she later wrote, "as I thought of the *Richmond Planet*'s list of unfortunates." They "had no requiem, save the night wind, no memorial service to bemoan their sad and horrible fate . . . and no record of the time and place of their [death] save this [their names being read], is extant; and like many a brave Union soldier their bodies lie in many an unknown and unhonored spot." Ida ended her observation with the hope that Mitchell's "personal bravery and courage be an incentive to others!" Undoubtedly, the Virginia editor—who in a year would advise blacks to purchase Winchester rifles to defend themselves from "the two-legged animals . . . prowling around your house in the dead of night"—was an incentive to hers.[86]

The association's conference was significant in other ways. Ida was elected secretary of the association (over a male colleague), and this time she made sure to acknowledge the support of women by her male peers. As she wrote in the *Index,* "the men of the race are not troubled with a desire to keep women apart as a separate and inferior force." And, in what appeared to be a sign of détente with the *Washington Bee* editor, Calvin Chase, Ida helped his mother, Lucinda, prepare the reception for the press members.[87]

The press meeting had been held in March to coincide with the inaugural activities of President Benjamin Harrison who narrowly defeated Grover Cleveland on the strength of the black vote, according to John Lynch, former Mississippi congressman and then chair of that state's Republican Committee. Before the conference ended, the journalists prepared an antilynching document to be presented to the president and Wells was among the committee that waited on the shy, five-foot-six Harrison, who subsequently made a mild antilynching pronouncement stating that such violence inhibited economic growth. It may not have been the kind of statement blacks had hoped for, but for Ida it may well have helped her connect the dots between the political economy and antilynching strategies.[88]

The most important development that year was Ida being approached by Taylor Nightingale, pastor of the historic Beale Street Church, to become the editor of the *Memphis Free Speech & Headlight.* Ida was thrilled by the offer, but not too thrilled to make a sober assessment of the paper. It is doubtful that it was making much, if any, profit, but as she noted in her autobiography, the newspaper had good financial prospects. It earned about $200 a month in advertising revenue from white Memphis businessmen. The newspaper was published out of the basement of the Beale Street Church, whose fast-growing congregation numbered about a thousand in 1889, and five hundred copies were sold each Sunday alone to the congregants.

Yes, she would join the paper as editor, Ida told Nightingale, on one condition—that she be made an equal partner with him and J. L. Fleming, the business manager. With her wobbly finances, it is not clear what precise terms Ida was able to negotiate one-third ownership, but she was a master of the layaway and the borrow-from-Peter-to-pay-Paul schools of finance. She also would continue to publish columns in the *Christian Index* and other papers after joining the *Free Speech & Headlight* and would continue with her teaching job. Nightingale accepted Ida's terms, making the one-time country lass the only black woman of record to be an editor in chief and part owner of a major city newspaper.[89] Her taking over the editorship marked the next, most crucial, and most tumultuous phase of her career.

CHAPTER SIX

❧

City of the Three Murdered Men

❧

... even "most superior men ... seeing their late
slave strutting about ... came increasingly to feel
toward him very much as any cracker felt; fell increasingly under the sway of the same hunger to
have their hands on him, and ease the intolerable
agony of anger and fear and shaken pride in his
screams."

—*W. J. Cash*

If Taylor Nightingale had asked Ida to work for his paper three years before, she might well have refused. As a diary entry showed, she hadn't
liked the minister, and worse, had little respect for him. Wells had written
about the pastor during the January 1886 elections, when Nightingale had
run for a position on the board of education against Ida's favored candidate, Fred Savage, Jr., the black incumbent who had gamely defended Virginia Broughton and Julia Hooks against the white superintendent. Both
black men lost to a white candidate, and Ida characterized Nightingale as a
"toady," who allowed himself to be used by whites to split the black vote.
Nightingale, who had run on the ticket headed by taxing district president,
David Hadden, blamed the defeat on a fraudulent return from the predominantly white Fourth Ward. The *Appeal*, a Hadden supporter, sug-

gested a recount, but the tally stood. In her diary, Ida did not mention the controversy about the returns, only that Nightingale had "conducted himself in such an obnoxious manner that it completely disgusted me with him."[1]

Moreover, the voluble Nightingale did not fit Ida's image of the progressive black clergy that she believed, as noted earlier, should be "wise as serpents and gentle as doves." The minister, educated at Roger Williams College and the Meharry Medical School in Nashville, may have been wise, but had the reputation as a blustery tyrant who bullied his Beale Street Church congregation.[2]

But a lot had changed since 1886. No African American had been elected to the school board since that year; the black public schools were suffering from diminished support; and Nightingale's election fraud charge was a harbinger for succeeding elections. Since then, black disenfranchisement had been enshrined in the law and, more alarmingly, justified by Christian doctrine. "Heaven itself would place its seal of disapproval on the political supremacy of the negro in a single Southern state," pronounced the Memphis lawyer and former state legislator Josiah Patterson in 1889. Patterson, like many white Democratic paternalists, once advocated black enfranchisement. But now he believed that excluding African Americans from the electorate would eliminate the need for the fraud and violence, and unleash the "endowments which God and civilization" had bestowed on the superior white race who would lead the region toward "unsurpassed prosperity."[3]

By the late 1880s, blacks were seen not just as morally inert obstacles to "God's plan of progress" but as a race that was devolving on the scale of civilization and becoming increasingly dangerous. Such was the conclusion of Philip Bruce's *The Plantation Negro as Freeman,* published in 1889, which surmised that as blacks became further removed from the "civilizing influence" of slavery, they were increasingly yielding to their "African impulses"—especially sexual ones. Bruce, a University of Virginia and Harvard Law School graduate who grew up on a plantation with five-hundred slaves, specifically blamed the lasciviousness of black women for the "present degradation" of the race. They were so sexually wanton, he wrote, that they failed to check the primitive sexual aggression of their men. Moreover, their stark contrast to prim white women made those southern belles "strangely alluring and seductive" in the eyes of black men. The author, as a later scholar noted, put the case of "black peril" in the South on a firmer foundation than any other book before it.[4]

The times called for more than dovish behavior on the part of black leaders, and Taylor Nightingale fit the bill. In the hotly contested election of 1888, it was Nightingale, reputed to be the only minister in Memphis to possess a repeating rifle, who had stood up to the intimidation and fraud of the Democrats. When he was accused by the *Avalanche* of stirring up "strife" between the races, the pastor insisted that he preferred "quiet methods," but was prepared to use any other "recognized weapon of defense." Colored men "must contend for their rights if they had to die in the ditch up to their necks in blood," he said. "No great race ever succeeded in the world without wading through flame and flood." In the wake of the election, Nightingale made the Beale Street Church a staging area, where he took affidavits from blacks who had been threatened or denied the vote and sent them to Washington as evidence of voting irregularities and the need for the proposed Lodge Elections Bill that called for federal supervision.[5]

Nightingale's partnership with J. L. Fleming to create the *Free Speech & Headlight* was born out of the need for militant action, protection, and the consolidation of the black press—all of which Ida had called for. She knew Fleming, the paper's business manager. He was mentioned in her diary (he appears to have been the informer about Paul Jones's drinking problem), and was a native of nearby Marion, Arkansas, located in predominantly black Crittenden County. As late as 1887, the *Washington Bee* had described Marion as a "mecca for the Colored man," referring to the opportunities there that had created a prominent, if small, African American professional class to which the Fleming family belonged. After attending Le Moyne Institute, Fleming had returned home to found the *Marion Headlight,* a weekly. But in the wake of the pivotal 1888 elections, when four blacks had won offices on a fusion ticket with Democrats, the demand by whites that they vacate their elected positions (the black men were accused of drunkenness) resulted in Fleming and other leaders of the black community being forced into exile. An armed committee of the "best white citizens" had rounded up fifteen blacks—including Fleming, the elected officials, a physician, and a schoolmaster—who were given the "choice" of leaving Marion by train, or being taken by wagon to the Mississippi River for a boat to Memphis. Fleming chose the latter, found Nightingale (who had earlier sought to partner with the *Memphis Watchman*), and consolidated his *Marion Headlight* with the pastor's *Memphis Free Speech.*[6]

Finally, it is doubtful that any other than Nightingale's Beale Street

Church would have hosted a meeting in which white prominent Memphians were openly charged with imperiling the morals of black women—their alleged wantonness not withstanding. In June of 1889, Thomas Cassels, Ida's former lawyer who had earlier tried to get antimiscegenation bills passed in the legislature, led a mass meeting at the church in which he threatened to expose fifty-three white men who "lived indiscriminately" with black women in "defiance of all laws, civil, moral and social." Nearly "one-half of the illegitimate children born of colored mothers in this city betray the shameful fact that they are the children of white fathers . . . ," ran a sentence in a resolution presented by Cassels to the Shelby county criminal judge, Julius DuBose.[7]

IN NIGHTINGALE, IDA had found a man of action and courage whose own Christian certainty matched her own. "The old Southern voice that was once heard and made the Negroes jump and run like rats to their holes is 'shut up,'" the *Free Speech & Headlight* editorialized that same June when Ida joined the paper. "It is no use to be talking now about Negroes ought to be kept at the bottom where God intended them to stay. The Negro of today is not the same as Negroes were thirty years ago," it warned.[8]

If there was a point of agreement between black militants and white supremacists, it was that blacks had changed, and that ideas about sex, God, and evolution had brought the South to the brink. "No country was ever made or can be made for the occupation of two races distinct from one another in color, habits and tradition," pronounced Senator Wade Hampton of South Carolina, an aristocratic paternalist who had once supported black suffrage. "One of the races must migrate, or one of the two must be exterminated, or the two must amalgamate."[9]

Clearly, the quote was a call for race war by the influential Hampton, since "amalgamation" was out of the question and migration, too, was threatened with with reprisal from those who needed black farm labor. "The *Avalanche* will not let the colored brother remain in the South in peace," Ida wrote in September, when the migration question was raised anew with the opening of the Indian reservations for settlement in the Oklahoma Territory, "and the *Appeal* will not let the sons of Africa get away in safety."[10]

A month later, at a time when the growing crisis made blacks across the country, including Ida, look anew at the strategy of militancy, Wells answered an inquiry circulated by the *Detroit Plaindealer* regarding T. Thomas Fortune's Afro-American League. She believed in the organization with "all her heart and soul" she replied, for while "we are resting on our oars, seemingly content with expressing our indignation by resolution at the outrages which daily occur, others are presuming upon this inaction and encroaching more and more upon our rights—nay upon life itself." She demanded, "Agitate and act," "until *something* is done."[11]

Less than a month later, Fortune issued a call for the first National Afro-American League conference to be held. By then he had fine-tuned his proposal to attract a broader spectrum of black representative leaders by stipulating that the League be nonpartisan, expel any member who advocated violence, and establish uplift institutions such as an African American bank. Nevertheless, his own militant vision of the Negro had not changed. In December, his editorial announcing the meeting in Chicago proclaimed the "death knell of the shuffling, cringing creature in black who for two centuries and a half had given the right of way to white men." The new man was "a freeman every inch, standing erect and undaunted, an American from head to foot. What did he look like?" Fortune exhorted. "*He looks like a man.*"[12]

Wells, of course, did not look like a man; and indeed, no woman was among the 135 delegates from twenty-three states (including Tennessee) and territories chosen to write a constitution and form a permanent organization at the conference. The "delegate" organizing principle implied an official spokesperson in public-sphere political matters, a role—especially at times of militant affirmations of manhood and nationalism when men imagined themselves as patriarchal warriors and women their domestic charges—for which women "need not apply."

Following Ida's editorship of the militant *Free Speech* (the name was shortened shortly after she joined it), the *Indianapolis Freeman,* a black weekly, revealed the gender anxieties of her plunging "into politics and other matters of national importance with the vivacity of a full-fledged journalist of the masculine gender."[13] Earlier, Fortune had touted Ida's combination of beauty and brains, but now the assessment was turned into a chiding rebuke that was widely circulated by several black publications, including the *Age.* "Iola makes the mistake of trying to be pretty as well as smart," noted one of her colleagues, who added that female writers like George Eliot, George Sand, and Harriet Beecher Stowe, while brilliant, "were not paragons by any means." Indeed, illustrations of her in the black press began to be less complimentary, moving another commentator to predict that "Iola will never get a husband so long as she lets those editors make her so hideous."[14] As Ida became more militant, she would have to contend with comments regarding her transgressions, but for the moment, she, in a familiar pattern, managed to find a way to be relevant to the historic League conference.

The meeting had at first been scheduled to take place in Nashville, but, to the displeasure of Tennesseans, the site was changed to Chicago after complaints about the accommodations and discriminatory practices in the southern state. Led by the politician Ed Shaw, Tennessee delegates threatened to hold their own meeting rather than go to Chicago, and it was at that point that Ida intervened. "I implore you that as you value your race's general welfare . . . send your delegates to Chicago," Ida pled in a speech before the Tennessee group. "Let it be said that the Memphis League was not in favor of still further dividing the race—but rather that she is willing to do anything that is right to bring together our already much divided people," Ida continued with her familiar theme of unity. Ending her speech with a flourish, she added that "We want to be so banded together as with bands of steel that the race from the Lakes to the Gulf, from the Atlantic to the Pacific, are interested and will contribute to any measure for the relief of the people down south here." The "white man has no fear of us while we quarrel . . ." she warned. "Let us show to the world that the interests of our people are greater than our personal feeling."[15] The Tennesseans did send their two representatives to Chicago, but Ida had to content herself with reading about the meeting from afar.

There was ample newspaper coverage of the unprecedented conference by the white and black press. Never had there been such a meeting, national in scope, where leading black journalists, ministers, and politicians, gathered to boldly assert themselves against white supremacy and defend the race from the mounting and slanderous accusations. The elected chair of the permanent organization was W. A. Pledger, whose address before the conference noted the increasing charges of rape lodged against black men that were used to justify lynching. The "nameless crimes that colored men are alleged to have committed," Pledger charged, were, in many cases, actually carried out by white men in blackface. Pledger, born a slave in Georgia and the son of his master, who had come to prominence in 1880 when he led a black takeover of Georgia's Republican state executive committee to become the state party's first black chairman, knew of what he spoke.

The commanding Georgian had also once led armed blacks to defy a mob intending to lynch two African Americans in Athens. The "nameless crime," rape, was one that Ida would soon identify in no uncertain terms; and the idea that black men were being framed for it would become an important element in her subsequent writings.[16]

Comments in the mainstream press about the conference at which blacks catalogued their rights and wrongs were mixed. The *Nation*, known for its abolitionist sentiments before the war, editorialized that the organization would only strengthen growing white resentment. The *New York Sun* praised Fortune (who often wrote for it), and believed blacks were simply "exercising their rights as American citizens." The *Chicago Tribune*, convinced that Fortune was surreptitiously working for the Democrats, called him "oily" and a "New York coon." *Atlanta Constitution* editor Henry Grady sounded the tocsin of the black militant stance by coining the phrase "Afro-American agitator," no doubt with Fortune in mind.[17]

In the context of the times, "agitator" was becoming less of an opprobrium among Afro-Americans, and although Ida continued to publish "black behavior" columns in the *Christian Index*, she increasingly turned her attention to racial inequities, not just racial inadequacies. Still skeptical of politicians, she nevertheless began to see that politics itself was an arena that needed to be engaged. Wells criticized, for example, the Republicans for "bartering" away the failed federal Lodge Elections Bill to gain votes in the Congress to pass legislation for a higher tariff.[18]

Wells also began to take her cues from the League agenda, which included protests against the convict lease system where prisoners were "leased" for a fee from state penitentiaries to perform labor for large companies and corporations. The Tennessee Coal, Iron, and Railroad Company, which paid the state $101,000 annually to employ prisoners in the mines, was one of the worst offenders of the practice, which not only kept the wages and the labor demands of white workers low, but assured that the pettiest offenses, especially by blacks, were punished with sentences contrived to make them fodder for the system. As a later investigation by the *Washington Evening Star* revealed, Tennessee prisoners had no opportunity to bathe; were fed unclean food and water; and were "fastened to planks by the feet, then bent over a barrel and fastened by the hands on the other side, stripped and beaten with a strap" if they failed to meet their quota of mining between two to four tons of coal a day. "Negroes are sent to the work house, jail and penitentiary for stealing five cents worth of bread or meat," the *Free Speech* charged, "but white men are made honored citizens when they steal thousands." Wells was probably referring to the white Memphis official found guilty of embezzling six thousand dollars from the treasury and given little more than a slap on the wrist. "Such is the administration of justice in Memphis," the editorial quipped.[19]

By 1890, Ida's one-year stint on the *Free Speech* had already made it "a stunningly good paper," T. Thomas Fortune observed, but the achievement had not come without effort. Since joining the paper, Wells had undertaken a grueling schedule. She was still teaching at Kortrecht, taking care of her sister L'il, still writing for the *Christian Index,* and added to her *Free Speech* editorial responsibilities was that of being a coproprietor of a newspaper that had its financial problems and whose progress was closely watched by other editors. The *Free Speech,* as noted by her colleagues, appeared to miss at least one publication date; and one of the issues published a sharply worded reminder to delinquent subscribers to pay their bills. Ida also traveled a good deal that year. Newspapers announced her arrival in Chicago, Milwaukee, and Philadelphia without further comment, but Ida's complaints about there being too many—and too loquacious—Afro-American League meetings where "would-be leaders" seemed to think that "black grievances" could be "talked" out of existence, indicated that she was probably traveling on behalf of the AAL as well as her own paper.[20]

Perhaps it was her criticism of the patriarchal warriors that moved the *Freeman,* in April of 1890, to issue its most provocative gender card to date. It was in the form of a cartoon called "Fortune and His Echo," which depicted an "alpha male" dog (the *Freeman)* with two smaller ones yelping up at it (the *Age* and the *Free Speech*). The head of Ida's dog wore her familiar upswept hairstyle and bun. In the upper left-hand corner was an effigy of Wells, dressed in a man's outfit, saying "I would I were a man."[21]

While such criticism was not unknown to her, for it to come when she was already so extended might have had its effect. By July, both the *New York Age* and the *Indianapolis Freeman* announced that Ida was "recovering" from "an illness superinduced by overwork."[22] The announcement may, or may not, have fully explained her absence at the press association meeting that summer where Josie Heard of Philadelphia, another highly regarded black woman journalist whose clergyman husband was active in the League, was elected to succeed Ida in the secretarial position. And although a full documentation of the *Free Speech* pieces is not available, much of what was republished in other black papers in the wake of the criticism indicates that Ida had again fallen back on her more sanctioned race-in-my-arms pieces, which carried her familiar black behavioral themes: criticism of Blanche K. Bruce for providing a patronage position in Mississippi to a white instead of a black man; of her former landlord, Josiah Settle, for hiring white contractors instead of blacks to perform work on the Lauderdale Street house; and an editorial that frowned on gatherings where "school-teachers," "sporting women," "honored wives and mothers," and "saloon toughs" all socialized and danced together in a much too indiscriminate way.[23]

Ida also returned to castigating wayward ministers—this time at home. In her autobiography, she wrote about her paper's campaign against a Memphis minister (unnamed in Ida's account) for illicit behavior with a married female parishioner. The *Free Speech*'s charges drew the ire of the ministers' alliance in the city and the presiding elder who threatened to boycott the paper—certainly a serious threat to the subscription base. Revealingly, Nightingale did not appear to interfere when Ida responded by publishing the ministers' names in the paper as men who "upheld the immoral conduct of one of their number," and asked the community if they were "willing to support preachers who would sneak into their homes when their backs were turned and debauch their wives." Subsequently, the alliance backed down from their threat and the crisis passed.[24]

Wells had long had her eye on the behavior of ministers, and in 1890 thought she had found an ally in an up-and-coming black educator by the name of Booker T. Washington. In that year, he had railed against untrained black ministers with questionable integrity in his commencement speech at Fisk University. Washington, sounding very much like Ida in her *Christian Index* articles, asserted that too many religious services were full of shouts, groans, and jumping, and that "three-fourths of the Baptist ministers and two-thirds of the Methodists [were] unfit, either mentally or morally, or both, to preach the Gospel to any one or attempt to lead any one." After Washington published the speech in the black press and, in August of 1890, in the influential New York–based mainstream journal, the *Christian Union* published by the Unitarian reformer, Lyman Abbott, the Tuskeegean's words unleashed a debate between black critics and supporters of the view. Ida was among the latter, though, in the *Free Speech*, she criticized his publishing the piece in a white publication. Nevertheless, in November she wrote Washington a congratulatory letter praising his "manly criticism of our corrupt and ignorant ministry," and told him that there was no one more "fitted" to taking on the task of the Protestant reformer Martin Luther to "clean up" the black church. Washington, in turn, invited Ida to attend a black farmers' organization meeting he had arranged in Alabama, but her schedule did not allow her to attend.[25]

When Ida wrote him, she only knew Washington by reputation, a reputation that was growing since he had taken the helm of Alabama's Tuskegee Institute in 1881. Washington, born a slave in Virginia in 1856 to an unknown white man and a slave woman, Jane Burroughs, worked in the mines and as a houseboy before managing to attend the Hampton Normal and Agricultural Institute, where he put himself through school by working as a janitor. The young man's industriousness caught the eye of Hampton's president, General Samuel Chapman Armstrong, and in 1881, when the Alabama legislature authorized the creation of a normal school for blacks, Armstrong suggested that Washington head it. The president's recommendation proved to be the right one. Though the legislature had appropriated $2,000 for teachers' salaries, no provisions had been made for land or buildings, but by 1888, with an initial loan from Hampton Institute, Washington had acquired 540 acres of land for the school, which had an enrollment of four hundred students. Like Hampton, Tuskegee's mission was to teach blacks industrial education, including such trades as carpentry, brick-building, sewing, and cooking. The Alabama school also replicated Armstrong's model of discipline and character-building as major components of education. All Tuskegee students were required to attend chapel on a daily basis and religious services on Sunday.[26]

The *Christian Union* article marked a new phase of Washington's notoriety—and success in gaining support from anxious white philanthropists increasingly concerned about the behavior of the untrained black masses. Soon after it was published, the heiress Olivia E. Phelps-Stokes offered Washington a $2,000 permanent scholarship fund to help in the education of colored men with good character, particularly those bound for the ministry. Subsequently, Phelps-Stokes also contributed money to build Phelps Hall on the campus. The philanthropic gift would be just one among many.[27]

The friendliness of the exchange between Wells and Washington in 1890 would prove to be the last of its kind, but at the time it was indicative of how she, along with both black and white reformers, still believed that the new industrial era required both individual and societal discipline to fulfill the promise of progress. But in a period of such heightened white anxieties and sociological attention to African Americans, the question of publicly criticizing the race became more complex, especially for women. Genuine concerns about the shortcomings of the black community became distorted by both the rewards and castigations heaped on the race in their wake. As Ida, who was on one of her own moralistic crusades in this period, would learn, such criticism now evoked different consequences than it had when she was writing for church publications that few whites saw or cared about.

Around the same time she had criticized Memphis ministers with some success, Wells turned her pen on the Memphis school system and the new crop of black female teachers who were being hired. In her autobiography, she recounted her distress about the "mental and moral character" of the teachers, some of whom "had little to recommend them save an illicit friendship with members of the school board."[28] Feeling that the issue had to be addressed, and that her community had to be protected from such corruption, she set in type a half-column *Free Speech* editorial about the deteriorating conditions of the schools—and the moral behavior of the black female teachers. In her autobiography, Ida went on to explain that the paper's policy was to leave editorials unsigned, but on this occasion she asked Taylor Nightingale to attach his name to it. Ida's rationale, as she wrote, was that the protest would be better heeded if it came from the minister, though she also admitted that she feared losing her teaching position if the editorial was attributed to her. Behind Ida's uncharacteristic request was, in part, the fact that she was still dependent on her teacher's salary and, as usual, she was in a financial bind. Earlier that year, in late January, she had written Robert Church to cash her order from the school board in advance for which she promised to pay him interest. "I find myself in such a push that again ask the favor," she had written to him. Wells's needs notwithstanding, however, Nightingale refused to "father" the editorial, as Ida put it, and since it was too late to substitute another in its place, it ran.[29]

The editorial Ida wrote is not extant, but just as she had predicted, it caused a storm of controversy. As Ida told the story in her autobiography, its publication was soon followed by a comment in another paper, which "openly stated that the charges were true" and went further to exclaim that black women teachers were seen taking "walks and rides" with white board members. Although Ida wrote that she had been careful not to impugn all of the teachers in her editorial, the response in the other paper put her in the untenable situation of demanding that the publication specifically name the women seen with white men in order not to cast aspersions on all of the twenty-nine black female teachers—representing more than half of the instructors then in the public school system. While it is not known if the publication complied, Ida wrote that soon after her rejoinder in the *Free Speech* was published, she saw one of the black woman teachers who was having a "clandestine love affair" with a white lawyer from the school board boldly walking with him on a moonlit evening.[30]

Although Ida does not name her in the autobiography, the teacher she was referring to was Hattie Britton, Julia Hooks's sister, who was living with Julia and Julia's husband, Charles. As the now-named *Appeal-Avalanche* reported, sometime in late May, Britton and Charles got into a heated argument after Hattie had been out all night. He accused her of being "no better than a woman of the street," and following the exchange, Hattie was said to have gone to her room, taken a 38-caliber pistol from a drawer, and, placing it against her right ear, fired. "She fell to the floor, with blood and brains oozing from the wound, and 10 minutes later she was dead," reported the *Appeal-Avalanche*. Wells also included the details of the suicide in her autobiography and added that at the teacher's funeral, the "largest and finest floral arrangement" that adorned the church "had the name of her admirer boldly on it."[31]

Ida's recounting of the tragic incident—both what she said and chose to leave out—was revealing. Although she had left Britton's name out of her autobiography, Ida, according to the *Appeal-Avalanche*, had been accused of identifying Britton and her affair in no uncertain terms in a black scandal sheet published in Memphis. If the report of the *Appeal-Avalanche* was accurate, Ida would have had a role in Britton's suicide, but Wells failed to mention, much less defend herself, against the charges.[32]

Even if Wells was wrongly named by the white paper, her reaction in the wake of such a tragedy revealed her steely moralistic tendencies. She was indeed fired from the school, and afterward sent her attorney to the board to get an explanation. Ida, taking pains to explain that she was not fired because of her conduct or the quality of her teaching, said that her lawyer was told that the editorial was the cause for her termination. Ida, of course, was not surprised, and she thought Josiah Settle, her old landlord whom she had also criticized in the *Free Speech*, was particularly active in a campaign to get her dismissed. Moreover, the passage in her autobiography about the incident showed no remorse, but anger. The worst part of being fired, Ida wrote, was the "lack of appreciation shown by the parents." She complained, "Up to that time I had felt that any fight made in the interest of the race would have its support. I learned that I could not count on that." To her mind, she had struck a "blow" against a "glaring evil" and "did not regret it." Even if Wells herself did not associate her editorial with Britton's suicide, the statements in the light of all that had happened showed not only a certain social obtuseness and a look-no-further sense of right and wrong, but a profound lack of empathy for those who could not get out of the way when the chips, loosed by her righteous indignation, began to fall. They were characteristics that proved to be both a strength and weakness in the career that Wells set out for herself.[33]

But one result of the school controversy and its tragic climax might have been Ida's realization that the unintended consequences of such editorials could do much harm. The *Appeal-Avalanche* subsequently averred in its editorials that there was a "universal immorality" among black women, and that "fact alone would prevent anything like social relations between the two races." While the paper did not make a reference to the school scandal, it was clear that in such a charged environment, even unwitting confirmation of immorality could be forged into a weapon against the very people Ida was so anxious to protect. And despite her stated convictions about the editorial, Wells, after the summer of 1891, was never again so intemperate about charging any individual with moral improprieties.[34]

In any case, the summer of 1891 was an auspicious time for Ida to leave Memphis on an extended travel schedule. She spent the season attending the second national Afro-American League meeting in Knoxville, and subsequently took to the road through parts of Tennessee, Arkansas, and Mississippi to broaden the subscription base of the *Free Speech*.

It is not clear what part Ida had played in getting the invitation to address the AAL meeting. What was evident was that the League would be bolstered by the energy and resources of women whose high attendance, if not formal representation, in Chicago had been noted in the press, and by Fortune himself. "In the League a woman is just as good as a man," he pronounced, "and out of it she is usually much better."[35] In fact, the League needed all the help it could get. Though some leading moderates had shown some early interest in the organization, national figures like Blanche K. Bruce and P. B. S. Pinchback never joined it and, in fact, became involved with a competing organization, the American Civil Rights Association. And, after the first flush of enthusiasm and the early sprouting of local organizations, the League was floundering from lack of any funds to run it. Nearly empty state treasuries was one reason delegates from only seven states traveled to Knoxville; the trepidation caused by the recent passage of a separate streetcar law passed by the Tennessee legislature was another. Ida, T. Thomas Fortune no doubt hoped, would energize the constituency, especially the women. Wells was scheduled to make a major address before the group.[36]

Ida began her address by declaring her fear that she could not make such a speech. The opening statement was one of those conventions to lower expectations and exhibit feminine modesty, but Wells, who had never spoken before such an assembly, was no doubt genuinely anxious about her debut—nevertheless, she clearly rose to the occasion. The press, though not relaying the subject of her speech, noted that Ida "captured the house" with her "clarity," "eloquence," and "earnestness," and created "a bubble of excitement and enthusiasm." It was in Knoxville that Ida may have discovered her charismatic qualities. "She should use the gift of speech God has given her to arouse the women of the race to a full sense of their duty in the work of the Afro-American League," Fortune wrote after hearing Ida's address. Every "woman of the race should rally around such a woman and hold up her hands," he pronounced.[37]

Ida, of course, wanted to "arouse" the entire race to its duty, and her writing about the meeting and her experience in getting there was characteristically critical. In Chattanooga, Wells herself had been forced to ride in a Jim Crow car and was taken aback by the look of "indifference" in the eyes of those she saw in the now all-black waiting room. Yes, "we have to fight," she concluded, but in her view, verbal protest was only half the battle. "So long as the majority [of our own people] are not educated to the point of proper self-respect, so long our condition here will be hopeless."[38]

Ida was most critical of the League when it missed an opportunity to bring an important suit against the discriminatory practices in Tennessee when one of the delegates, the Reverend William Heard of Philadelphia, had been forced out of a Pullman car in violation of the antidiscriminatory statutes of the Interstate Commerce Act. The League's counsel was prepared to go to court and met with Pullman representatives, but because there were no funds to adjudicate the matter, the organization settled for damages being paid to Heard and the dismissal of the offending conductor. Wells, instead of seeing a partial victory, complained that the "right steps were not taken at Knoxville." The meeting "should have never adjourned without adopting [discrimination in public transportation] as its immediate work," she complained. One of the "gravest questions of [the] convention should have been—How do we do it? What steps should be taken to unite our people into a real working force—a unit, powerful and complete?"[39]

To Ida's mind, one of those important steps to be taken was through a vibrant black press like the *Free Speech*, and she left Knoxville to bolster its subscriptions and to apply her theories about the practical side of newspaper distribution.[40] She had, for example, begun having the paper printed on pink sheets to help people quickly distinguish it from other publications. Believing it important to bring newspapers to the people, Ida utilized train passes, available to journalists, to scour the regional area. She was most successful in Mississippi and wrote exuberantly about her being "handed from town to town and treated like a queen."[41]

Ida's Mississippi triumph was largely due to the patronage she received from an unlikely source: Isaiah Montgomery, who had become infamous in many black progressive circles for his role as the lone black delegate at the 1890 Mississippi state convention that met with the primary purpose of disenfranchising black voters. Montgomery publicly supported the convention's suffrage amendment, which—with its poll tax and literacy requirements, exclusion of voters convicted of certain crimes, and an "understanding clause" that gave registration officials the authority to certify whites and disqualify blacks—provided the most effective model to date for disenfranchising blacks while permitting equally unqualified whites to vote without contravening the Fifteenth Amendment. The *New York Age* and the *Free Speech* had "severely" criticized Montgomery for his support of the measure that, in a state with a majority black population, disenfranchised 123,000 blacks as compared to 11,000 whites. Moreover, Montgomery's public acceptance of the amendment had, many believed, blunted criticism about it from the North.[42]

After Wells's *Free Speech* editorial criticizing him, Montgomery had gone to Memphis to explain his position to her. He held the classic conservative view that uplift not politics was the road that would lead to eventual enfranchisement—a view that Wells had once held herself. Now she thought, as she wrote, that it would have been better to go down in defeat rather than acquiesce to the measure, but Ida, as judgmental as she was, also respected those who accomplished tangible benefits for blacks. Montgomery certainly fell into that category. A former slave, he had founded the all-black town of Mound Bayou, south of Vicksburg, in 1888, which was being largely settled by the families of freedmen who had become landowners after the Civil War and would become a thriving center for a colony of eight hundred families with a population of four thousand blacks.[43]

Montgomery's paving the way for Ida was a definite boon for her. In Greenville, she attended a session of the state bar association where she was able to get a subscription from all who were present. In Water Valley, Dr. T. W. Stringer, state grand master of the Masonic lodge and a political ally of James Hill, let her appeal for subscriptions during a meeting. Afterward, Ida wrote, she found herself weighed down with so many silver dollars that she had to proceed directly to the bank. "I was the daughter of Mississippi and my father had been a Master Mason," she explained, "so it was no wonder that I came out of the meeting with paid subscriptions from every delegate."[44]

Ida's hard work, buttressed by the support of men like Montgomery and Hill, resulted in the increase of the *Free Speech*'s circulation from less than fifteen hundred to four thousand in nine months; and Ida was able to derive an income from the paper almost on a par with her teaching salary. Characteristically, however, traveling alone as a single woman was not without the controversy that followed Ida like a bad penny. A stopover in Vicksburg, Mississippi, had again raised questions about her morality.

Ida had stayed at the house of an unidentified northern-born AME minister and his wife, where two other young women were also visiting the family. Their presence attracted a number of "eligible" young men to call on them, and Wells was delighted by the attention and the social opportunities it afforded. But after she left Vicksburg, Hill informed her that the minister was responsible for spreading the vicious gossip that Wells had been fired from the Memphis schools because of her morals. Furthermore, the minister had also impugned southern black women generally. Ida's response showed that she had begun to abandon her own regressive reflex of wide-eyed innocence. No longer "shocked" by the "misconstructions" put on her motives, she waited until her next trip to Vicksburg, where she gathered together the minister and friends with whom he had been talking; she also called Hill to join them. In front of all the witnesses, Ida asked the minister if he had said the things about her and black women that Hill had attributed to him. The surprised minister weakly confessed that he had, but hastened to add that he had only done so among a small circle of friends.

The admission sent Ida into an impassioned tirade about the lack of defense and respect for black women, reminding him that "many a slave woman had fought and died rather than yield to the pressure and temptations to which she was subjected." Wells recalled, "I [also] told him that my good name was all that I had in the world [and] that I was bound to protect it from attack by those who felt that they could do so with impunity because I had no brother or father to protect it for me." By the end of her withering reproach, the minister was forced to promise that he would not only recant his words in front of her friends but also before his entire congregation. The scene demonstrated the lengths Ida was now prepared to go to defend her name—and black women in general. Soon she would be called upon to make others answer to a broader indictment.[45]

WELLS RETURNED TO Memphis in the fall of 1891 when an incident that occurred near Georgetown, Kentucky, resulted in the most provocative editorial in the *Free Speech* to date. She had gotten reports in September that, on August 28, blacks had set fire to the town, including a number of "fine residences" belonging to prominent officials. The act was in retaliation for the lynching of a black man who had killed a white for having "intimate relations" with the black man's wife. The *Memphis Commercial*, a new paper established by Regular Democrats in late 1889, noted that when the black community got news of the lynching, a crowd of black men and women gathered at the site of the murder. Their anger was palpable, especially that of the women, who were heard to say that fires would be set to white residences that night.

As evening fell, Georgetown was uneasy. The white sheriff deputized fifty men to help him stand guard, and the town's leading white citizens met and made arrangements to ring the firebell if any signs of a black uprising was sighted. Then at 11:00 P.M., a "ruby glow" lit the sky in the direction of a judge's residence. The firebell was set off, and whites rushed to the residence to find that the judge's tobacco barn and stripping room were ablaze. The fire was too advanced to save the buildings, and the men who had rushed there later realized that the arsonists had used the barn-burning as a ploy to draw them away from the business section of the town. Indeed, another fire broke out in a dormitory of the Baptist College located there; and soon after, yet another blaze was detected in another judge's house near Hamilton Street, where arsonists had opened a window at the rear of the house and thrown some kind of incendiary device inside. By then, a force of nearly two hundred armed whites had become organized to patrol the town and the agitation appeared to cease, but the incidents were a signal that blacks were increasingly prepared to retaliate against violence.[46]

The *Free Speech* editorial supporting the arsonists in Georgetown was unsigned, but the wording had Ida's "name" all over it. The men showed "the true spark of manhood by their resentment," it said. The Eliza Woods lynching, among others (which recently included the lynching of two men and two women for setting fires to the house of a white man in Alabama), had made the editors wonder if blacks hadn't "the manhood enough in them to wriggle and crawl out of the way, much less protect and defend themselves." One thing was certain, continued the *Free Speech:* "Not until the Negro rises in his might and takes a hand in resenting such cold-blooded murders, if he has to burn down whole towns, will a halt be called in wholesale lynching."[47] The editorial, which linked the eradication of lynching with retaliation rather than uplift—and was reprinted in the *Appeal-Avalanche*—detonated a vein-popping response from the Memphis dailies as well as white-owned papers throughout the region. As the *New York Age* recounted, a paper from Jackson, Mississippi, demanded that Memphians "muzzle" the *Free Speech;* and the *Memphis Commercial* averred that whites should obey the law but could be provoked to "exterminate" blacks if the latter insisted on retaliatory measures. The *Appeal-Avalanche* called the *Free Speech* editorial "remarkably villainous," and though it "deplored" lynching, it also predicted that neither the "unorthodox style of 'Afro-American manhood' reflected in the vengeance of the Kentuckians nor those who advocated it would ever become popular in this country." Assuming that Nightingale had authored the editorial, the *Appeal-Avalanche* concluded by warning the minister "that there are bounds beyond which it is unsafe for him to venture."[48]

The Georgetown editorial, it turned out, was almost as alarming to the congregants of Nightingale's church as it was for white supremacists. The good reverend had already alienated many of his Beale Street flock over a messy, and very public, debate concerning his wife (whom he excommunicated and later reinstated after charging her with adultery) that led to a physical altercation and the excommunication of a number of church members. Several of the offended Baptists (including Ida's old beau, Isaiah Graham) hired Josiah Settle and Thomas Cassels to bring suit against Nightingale, whom they charged with assault as well as illegally using the institution to further his own political gains and "make incendiary and exciting speeches on the race question." Both Ida and Fleming were also named in the suit because of their association with the paper. Subsequently, five hundred Beale Street congregants held a mass meeting at Zion Hall and passed a resolution that the *Free Speech* editors retract the editorial. Nightingale (and presumably Ida and Fleming) refused to do so. The minister was then forced to go before the Shelby County criminal court judge, Julius DuBose, and although Nightingale had gotten two able lawyers to defend him—James Greer (who had defended Ida) and A. H. Douglass (a former Memphis mayor)—he was sentenced to a fine and eighty days in the workhouse. Deciding to take his chances elsewhere, Nightingale fled to the Oklahoma Territory, an increasingly popular destination for southern blacks who sought to escape peonage or persecution.[49]

Wells did not mention the Georgetown editorial or the church episode in her autobiography. She only commented that she did not approve of Nightingale using the paper to lambaste his enemies; and that because the minister had had "trouble" with his congregation (the business over his wife must have made her skin crawl), he left the paper, and Ida and Fleming bought his share in it.[50]

Buying out Nightingale was surely a financial gamble. It is doubtful that white businesses continued to advertise in the paper after the Georgetown editorial; and the alienation of so many in the Beale Street congregation—and perhaps in other churches as well—diminished its subscription base in Memphis. Wells noted that after Nightingale's departure, she became the sales manager for the paper, but in the light of the Georgetown editorial, the Britton suicide, and her diatribes against Memphians like Josiah Settle, her task would be made no easier by the fact that she herself must have been persona non grata among many circles in Memphis.

Not surprisingly, her name was not on the founding list of a new black women's organization, the Coterie Migratory Club, an organization with an agenda of uplift. Its founding president was Julia Hooks. Neither was Ida's name mentioned among the guests at the social occasion of the season: the marriage of Mollie Church and the Harvard- and Howard University–trained lawyer Robert Terrell, in October of 1891, which was performed at the sumptuous Church residence and attended by a "Who's Who" of those with whom Ida had fallen out of favor: former U.S. senator Blanche K. Bruce (whom Ida had recently attacked for having insufficient race love); the Settles; the Casselses; and the Hookses. Surely, Ida was not a favorite among the teachers; she didn't even get along with her brothers and sisters. In her autobiography, she mentioned that two of her best friends in Memphis were Thomas Moss and his wife, Betty; one wonders if, in this period, they were virtually her only friends.[51]

Ida had probably known Thomas Moss, or Tommie, as she called him, at least since 1885, when he had hosted the visiting teachers from the New Orleans World's Fair. Since then Moss had worked hard and had attained a position as a postal carrier; owned his own home; volunteered (as did Ida) at Avery Chapel's Sunday school; and, as noted previously, had saved money to invest in a business enterprise: the People's Grocery. Memphis had emerged as the fifth-largest wholesale grocery market in the country, and Moss's store was a particular source of pride among black Memphians. It was a cooperative enterprise co-owned by ten other blacks in the community and organized along corporate lines. Moss was the president of the grocery; Benjamin Sampson, Ida's onetime principal at Kortrecht, was vice-president.[52]

Wells had probably grown close to the Mosses after she introduced Tommie to a young physician by the name of J. B. Elbert from Indianapolis, who had become one of Moss's closest friends. When Elbert had first arrived in Memphis, he had gone to see Ida in the *Free Speech* office with a letter of introduction from mutual friends in Indianapolis. Ida put him in contact with other Memphians, including Moss, and the physician subsequently met and became engaged to Marinda Cooper, the daughter of Florence Cooper, one of Ida's teacher colleagues (with whom she at one time boarded) and the sister of Moss's wife, Betty. The Mosses made Elbert the godfather of their daughter, Maurine, and Ida, the child's godmother.[53]

The *Free Speech* office, which moved to Beale Street after Nightingale's departure, was on Tommie's mail route and, as Ida noted in her autobiography, whatever "Tommie knew in the way of news we got it first." Moss was popular in Memphis and surely had social news, such as Mollie's recent wedding, where guests were given Piper Heidsick Champagne and Mollie was given a thousand-dollar ring by her father. Moss and Mollie were also close friends. Her father, like Tommie, belonged to the Tennessee Rifles, a fraternal/militia group, and Robert Church was known to use his connections to help blacks attain mail-carrier positions. Tommie and Betty gave the newlyweds a half-dozen silver after-dinner coffee spoons.[54]

The conversations between Tommie Moss and Ida also included politics, for he firmly believed that blacks should focus on practical and business matters rather than the more contentious field of politics and protest. Ida, of course, had been traveling that intellectual road and might have well pointed out how racism was also affecting Moss's aspirations for his own enterprise.

Indeed, there were increasing racial tensions in the neighborhood where the People's Grocery was located, an area known as the "Curve," just outside of Memphis's city limits, in the Fourteenth Civil District, and named for a bend on the streetcar track where Mississippi Avenue merged onto Hernando Road. In fact, Moss himself had been having some trouble from a white competitor, William Barrett, whose own grocery had enjoyed a virtual monopoly of clients until the appearance of the black store. By the 1890s, the area was in transition, as whites were establishing racially exclusive areas within the city and abandoning outlying areas like the Curve to a large number of the poorer African American migrants, who joined the biracial working class already residing there. The latter included blacks, a number of them stockholders in the People's Grocery, who owned property ranging in value from $1,000 to $5,000.[55]

The Curve was experiencing the brunt of the problems that were plaguing Memphis as a whole. By 1890, David Hadden was gone; blacks were largely disenfranchised, and the city had returned to local "Home Rule" dominated by Democrats. Nevertheless, despite the hope that white supremacist rule would bring Memphis closer to Heaven, the deadly sin of greed kept the city grounded. Gambling houses were still bringing thousands of dollars a month in fines and licensing fees, and the liquor business was robust. After Hadden's departure, the city trolley lines were electrified and privately owned by a Chicago investor, but the new lines also facilitated the transportation of illicit activities and their clients. Because the Curve was outside of Memphis proper and had only token police enforcement, the neighborhood had more than its share of businesses that ignored the four-mile liquor law and were often the sites for gamblers and crapshooters. The area had its own resident thugs, a white gang called the "The Dirty Dozen"—one of the many, both black and white, that now roamed the city and suburbs and added to an arrest rate that was nearly equal between the races, and which would make Memphis, in a few years, the murder capitol of the nation.[56]

IDA WELLS MUST have been happy to see the contentious year of 1891 end, but the early months of 1892 were also emotional ones for her. After conducting newspaper business in Natchez, Mississippi, she had stopped in Holly Springs where she received, without comment in her own record, an honorary degree from Rust College. She also contacted her siblings, including Annie, who was still in California, to cosign a deed of sale for her parents' home. In February, she sold it to James Hall, her former guardian and father's friend, for one hundred and fifty dollars.[57]

Wells no doubt sold the family house to invest the money in the *Free Speech*. She was also beginning a new project: she and Jesse Duke—the former *Montgomery Herald* editor who had been run out of Alabama for his "Colored Romeos" editorial—organized a southern press association. Ida was the treasurer of the group and, to the consternation of some of her northern colleagues, had hosted a meeting in which twenty journalists came together to form the organization. Then, while she was still in Natchez on newspaper business in March, Ida heard the news that would direct the course of the remainder of her life. Her friend Tommie Moss had been lynched in Memphis with two other men who worked with him in the People's Grocery: Calvin McDowell, the grocery's manager, and Will (Henry) Stewart, a clerk.[58]

The lynching was the tragic culmination of events that had begun on Wednesday, March 2, at the Curve. On that day, two young boys, Armour Harris, who was black, and Cornelius Hurst, white, initiated a larger drama when they cocked their thumbs, took dead aim behind glass marbles of different colors, and propelled them so that they would collide, then displace those of their opponents, sending them on divergent paths.

The boys had been playing marbles in the yard of Hurst, who lived near the People's Grocery, and they began to argue and then began to fight. Bad sportsmanship rather than race seemed to be at the bottom of the disagreement, but when the black child appeared to get the upper hand in the beating, the white boy's father joined the fray and began to thrash Armour. At that point, Will Stewart and Calvin McDowell came out of the grocery to come to the black boy's defense; they were soon joined by a crowd of blacks and whites who took their respective sides in what became a racially charged mob. During the melee, William Barrett, the white proprietor and competitor who had been giving Moss trouble, got clubbed near the black men's store. He identified Will Stewart, the clerk of the People's Grocery, as his assailant.[59]

The next day, Thursday, March 3, Barrett returned to the People's Grocery accompanied by a police officer. It was Calvin McDowell who came to the door. McDowell, a twenty-one-year-old bachelor who lived with his mother and sister, was light-skinned with curly hair, and he weighed about two-hundred pounds. He was a private in the Tennessee Rifles, the black militia group that Moss belonged to, and often wore his crisp fatigue uniform and a cap with "TR" written across it. No doubt exuding the confidence that came with his youth, good looks, and physique, he told Barrett and the police officer that no one matching Will Stewart's description was within the store. At that point, the frustrated proprietor, muttering that blacks were thieves, struck McDowell hard enough with a revolver to knock him down. When the gun dropped to the ground, the athletic young black man picked it up and shot at Barrett, barely missing him. Barrett and the officer retreated, and in a subsequent interview about the incident, McDowell was reported to have said, in impeccable English, "Being the stronger, I got the best of the scrimmage."[60] It would be yet another mark against him.

McDowell was subsequently arrested but released on Friday under bond. It is not known who helped to get him out, but one of McDowell's sisters was rooming with the lawyer Thomas Cassels and his wife.[61] In the meantime, there was also a warrant issued for the arrest of Will Stewart and Armour Harris—the black marble-player who was later described in the press as a "young viper." The arrests enraged the black Curve residents who purportedly called a meeting where they vowed to clean out the neighborhood's "damned white trash." The threat was an unmistakable reference to Barrett, whose store was characterized as a "low-dive gambling den" by whites and blacks alike. Barrett had been previously cited ten times for violating the liquor law that forbad selling alcoholic spirits within four miles of a church or school.[62]

But the white grocery owner cited the meeting to authorities as evidence that there was a black conspiracy against whites in the making. Julius DuBose, judge of the Shelby County criminal court, son of a wealthy planter, and a former Confederate soldier, responded to the allegation by vowing to protect the whites by forming a posse to get rid of the "high-handed rowdies" in the Curve. On Saturday, March 5, the same day that DuBose's threat was published in the *Appeal-Avalanche*, John Mosby, a black painter, was fatally shot in the leg and stomach by a clerk in another white grocery in the Curve area. As the incident was reported in the paper, Mosby had wanted to buy some items on credit, but was denied by the clerk because he was already in debt to the owner. Mosby cursed at the clerk, and the clerk responded by hitting Mosby with his fist. Mosby left the store, but returned that evening, found the clerk, and hit him with a stick. The clerk then grabbed a pistol and shot him. The black man was said to have participated in the Curve riot some days before and was described as being popular with the "lawless element" in the neighborhood. For the People's Grocery men, the Mosby shooting and DuBose's threat were signs that an attack on them might be imminent, and they consulted a lawyer to determine their course of action in such an event. According to Wells and the *St. Paul Appeal,* a black paper in Minnesota, the men were told that since they were outside of the city limits, they should prepare to defend themselves.[63]

On the evening of the Mosby shooting, six armed white men, including a county sheriff and plainclothes civilians deputized for the occasion, took one of the new electrified trolleys on the Beale Street line to make their way to the People's Grocery. Their intent, the manner in which they carried it out, and how the black men perceived their arrival were matters of contention. The white dailies later claimed that the sole purpose of the sheriff and deputies was to arrest Will Stewart and simply inquire whether he was there or not. However, the first major black account of the incident, written in the *St. Paul Appeal* by five black Memphis ministers, including Ida's minister, Benjamin Imes, and the *Living Way* editors, R. N. Countee and W. A. Brinkley, indicated that the deputized men had a rout of the store in mind, for the whites had first gone to Barrett's place, then divided up, surreptitiously posting themselves both at the front and the back of the grocery. Those inside, the black paper insisted, already anticipating a mob attack that evening, only knew that they were being surrounded by armed whites and did not realize that they were lawmen. The *Memphis Commercial,* however, characterized what happened next as evidence that blacks had been preparing for a race war against whites.[64]

When the white men, led by one of the deputies, Avery Yerger, entered the dimly lit store, they were met by a hail of bullets coming from all directions. Yerger was among the several white men who were hit. The recently released McDowell, who was captured at the scene, was identified as his assailant. When another deputy, Charley Cole, tried to seize a black man—first thought to be Thomas Moss—the black man, using a buckshot-loaded, double-barreled shotgun shot him in the left eye, right cheek, and chest. The shooter, later identified as Nat Trigg, was, like Moss, a postman. Both men were dark-skinned with whiskers that framed their faces. Trigg escaped, leaving the felled Cole with a gaping wound where his left eye had been. Another deputy, Bob Harold, was shot in the neck and face, suffering severe lacerations on his throat. The injured men were taken to Barrett's store where they awaited an ambulance. It was predicted that Deputy Yerger would soon die from his wounds, and Cole, it was thought, would lose his eye. In the meantime, more deputized whites were dispatched to the scene where they eventually arrested a total of thirteen blacks and lifted a cache of weapons and ammunition found in the People's Grocery.[65]

Reports in both the *Commercial* and *Appeal-Avalanche* characterized the shooting incident as a calculated, cold-blooded ambush meant to kill the whites who had come to the store. The article in the *St. Paul Appeal* contended that as soon as the black men realized the intruders were law officers, they dropped their weapons and submitted to arrest—confident that they would be able to explain their case in court.[66]

Following the shootout, hundreds of white civilians were deputized, and as the white-owned Democratic *Nashville Daily American* observed, "Every white man in town is a walking arsenal." The following day, Sunday, the sixth, a large crowd of armed white men and boys, some of them deputized and/or belonging to the three white military companies in the city, congregated at the People's Grocery, where, on the ground in front of its entrance, there was a congealing puddle of Charley Cole's blood. The whites fanned out from the grocery to conduct some one hundred house-to-house searches for blacks suspected of involvement in "the conspiracy." Two women were among the forty blacks eventually arrested, which included Armour Harris, the young marble-player, and his mother; Nat Trigg; and two other black postmen. At about 5:00 P.M., they captured Tommie Moss.[67]

As the *St. Paul Appeal* insisted, Ida's friend had been tending to his books at the back of the store the night of the shooting and could not have seen what was happening at the entrance when the whites had arrived. When Moss heard shots being fired, it was reported that he left the premises. Whether the account of Moss's whereabouts at the time of the shooting was accurate or not, in the eyes of many whites, Moss's position as a postal worker and the president of the cooperative store made him the ringleader of the supposed conspiracy. Moreover, after he was arrested, he was said to boast that his position as a federal employee afforded him federal protection from local authorities. Press reports underlined his insolence by reporting the conversation he had with the deputy who was bringing him in. Moss asked how many whites had been killed in the shootout. When the white man said "three," Moss replied that "they ought to have killed them all," and then applied "a vile name to the posse." The policeman's estimate, however, was incorrect. None of the deputies had died, although the press continued to predict that the wounds of Cole and Harold would eventually prove fatal.[68]

Upon the news of the arrests, armed whites congregated around the fortress-like Shelby County Jail, where they were heard muttering ominously about "lamp posts" and "ropes" in the event of any of the deputies deaths. Members of the Tennessee Rifles also posted themselves outside of the jail, determined to keep watch and guard against a lynching.[69] Inside the jail, the arrested men were forced to stand in ankle-deep mud with wrists bound by irons, but a number of them remained defiant. McDowell, in particular, was reported to have "spit out" an insulting remark at Judge DuBose in the courtroom and was subsequently placed in a "sweat-box"— a near-airless, tightly enclosed chamber, meant to break any prisoner's spirit.

On Monday, March 7, Betty Moss, Tommie's wife, who was five-months pregnant with her second child at the time, went to the jail with food she had prepared for her husband. But DuBose was in no mood to grant visiting rights, and Betty's request to see her husband was denied. However, the judge did tell her to come back again in three days. But it was later believed by Wells and others that DuBose, among others, knew that Moss's life expectancy was only two days.[70]

On Tuesday, March 8, lawyers for several of the black men filed writs of habeas corpus, but DuBose quashed the procedure. Nevertheless, black hopes were buoyed somewhat by the information that the injured deputies were not going to die after all. Tensions outside the jail appeared to have been abated by the news, and on that evening the black militiamen did not think it necessary to guard the jail grounds. The Shelby County Jail, with its Bastille-like walls, massive iron fence, and barred windows was assumed to be impregnable; and despite the events over the last week at the Curve, it was also assumed that legal authorities in Memphis would abide by the law. Of course, they were aware of lynchings in other parts of Tennessee. There had been at least twelve known acts of mob violence in the state between 1880 and 1887; and as early as 1881, Thomas Cassels had gotten an antilynching law passed in the legislature that fined and removed from office any sheriff who "negligently" allowed a prisoner to be taken from custody and put to death by violence. But there was still the wide belief that Memphis was immune from such mob acts of murder. What black Memphians failed to take into account was the rising tide of hatred against them; and, as Ida would write in retrospect, the news that the deputies would survive was actually a catalyst for violence, for the black men could not now be "legally" executed for their "crime."[71]

At about 2:30 A.M. on March 9, seventy-five men wearing black masks surrounded the Shelby County Jail. About nine of them were able to enter the "impregnable" facility. The mob already knew who among the prisoners they wanted. When they found Moss, Stewart, and McDowell, they dragged them out of their cells, then loaded them onto a switch engine that ran on tracks at the back of the jail. Upon reaching their destination—a Chesapeake & Ohio railroad yard, about a mile outside of the city—the three black men were horribly shot to death. The dailies, especially the *Appeal-Avalanche* and the *Memphis Commercial*, wrote up the murders in such harrowing detail that it was clear the reporters had been called in advance to witness the lynching.

After the men reached the railroad yard, it was reported that McDowell "struggled mightily," appearing to have "the strength of ten men." Throughout the whole ordeal, the black man continued to curse his abductors and "gloried in the onslaught" made on the officers Saturday night. At one point during the struggle, McDowell managed to grab one of his abductors' shotguns. After the mob wrested it from him, they shot at his hands and fingers "inch by inch" until they were shot to pieces. What followed was evidence that the mob was bent, quite literally, on eye-for-an-eye vengeance. Replicating the wounds the white deputies had suffered, they shot four holes into McDowell's face and neck, any one of them large enough for a fist to be inserted. Where "his right eye had been there was a big hole," observed the *Commercial,* from "which his brains oozed out." McDowell's left eye was also shot out, and the "ball hung over his cheek in shreds." His jaw was torn out by a "load of buckshot, which gave his face a "grimace horrible to behold." The *Appeal-Avalanche* added that McDowell's injuries were in accord with his "vicious and unyielding nature."[72]

Less was said by Will Stewart, who was described as the most "stoic" of the three: "obdurate and unyielding to the last." He, too, had been shot on the right side of the neck with a shotgun; two pistol shots were also lodged in his body: one in the neck, the other in his left eye. In contrast to the other men, Moss, "the ringleader," was pointedly described in less "manly" terms. He was said to have faced his death with "violent grief and weeping," imploring the mob to spare his life for the sake of his pregnant wife, Betty, and little girl, Maurine. Moss was also shot in the neck, and a point was made to emphasize that his 150-pound body was the smallest of the three lying in the Chesapeake & Ohio railyards, that he had been taken from the cell in his bedclothes and had arrived in the yard with no shoes. Protruding from his pocket was a publication from the Avery Chapel Sunday school. Whatever the accuracy of the portrayal, Moss had managed to say something in his dying breath that would come back to haunt the reporters for publishing it. "Tell my people to go West," were Moss's last words, "there is no justice for them here."[73]

The lynching was "one of the most orderly of its kind ever conducted," was the *Appeal-Avalanche*'s take on the mob murders:

> There was no whooping, not even loud talking, no cursing in fact, nothing boisterous. Every thing was done decently and in order. . . . The vengeance was sharp, swift, and sure but administered with due regard to the fact that people were asleep all around the jail . . . [they] did not know until the morning papers that the avengers swooped down last night and sent the murderous souls of the ring-leaders in the Curve riot to eternity.[74]

But Memphians did know about the murders the following morning. On March 10, the papers reported that blacks, many of them laborers employed in the nearby saw mills, crowded into the coroner's office for the inquest that was conducted that morning. When they saw the mutilated corpses of the three men, they were said to be "sullen," and their subdued expressions but "a foretaste to the wild feeling of indignation and resentment" that became evident later that day when the bodies were transported to the office of the county coroner. Three hundred blacks had been awaiting the arrival of the corpses, and their expressions of grief and anger were anything but subdued. Police had to be summoned to maintain order. Rumors were rife that blacks planned to meet at the People's Grocery and wreak their own vengeance against whites.[75]

The signs of unrest impelled Judge Du Bose to order the sheriff to take possession of the swords and guns belonging to the Tennessee Rifles and store them in the armory where they were headquartered. The judge also ordered that the empathetic Jewish proprietor of Shuman's Gun Store— said to be the source of gun sales to blacks during the 1888 elections—be arrested and his shop closed. DuBose then told the sheriff to dispatch a hundred men to the People's Grocery, where blacks had congregated, and to "shoot down on sight any Negro who appears to be making trouble." When word of the order got out, gangs of white men armed themselves again and rushed out to the Curve, where they began shooting wildly into groups of blacks they encountered. Left to their own designs, the mob then helped themselves to the items in the grocery. They consumed what they could and stole the rest. The money drawer was broken into and its contents taken. A trunk belonging to Calvin McDowell, who had a room in the store, was ransacked. The white men helped themselves to the clothes that were in the trunk; and the rest of the items were dumped on the floor and trampled upon. The only reason that hundreds of blacks were not killed, Wells later explained in her autobiography, was "because of the forbearance of the colored men. They realized their helplessness and had submitted to outrages and insults for the sake of those depending on them." Subsequently, what was left of the People's Grocery was attached by creditors and eventually sold for one-eighth of its cost. The purchaser was William Barrett.[76]

IF BLACK MEMPHIANS had not sufficiently taken into account the new tide of white supremacy that had reached Memphis, whites may well have underestimated the heightened scrutiny of the North regarding the ability of the region in general, and Memphis in particular, to reform its ways and enter an "era of unprecedented prosperity." The Memphis lynching became a front-page story in the New York Times on March 10, and on the following day it noted that the *Associated Press* was asked to forward details about the lynching to businessmen in the North and in Europe who had trade connections with Memphis.[77]

In the wake of the unwanted publicity, the *Memphis Commercial* hustled to secure the city's image, fearing that in light of other recent "lawless acts," the lynching would be "seized upon, especially among a certain class of the North, and made capital for influencing public sentiment against the South." The *Commercial* did not mention which "lawless acts" it was referring to, but recent events made it appear that the white South, new as it was, was on its own downward spiral. The number of lynchings in the region had spiked from 98 in 1890 to 120 in 1891; and two other remarkable mob murders had received attention in the national press. In March of 1891, eleven Italian laborers had been lynched in New Orleans after they were acquitted of conspiracy in the murder of the city's police chief. The grand jury impaneled for the subsequent trial returned a verdict of "death at the hands of persons unknown." The Italian government, however, demanded indemnity, and the U.S. government paid $25,000 in reparations to the Europeans. Then, in January of 1892, a black man, Ed Coy, was lynched in Texarkana, Texas. He was burned to death by a mob for allegedly raping a white woman. Coy's death revealed a new stage of sadism lurking within the vaulted southern way of life. Albion Tourgée, columnist for the *Chicago Daily Inter-Ocean*, promised to investigate.[78]

Memphis itself had gotten unwelcome publicity for a murder in January of 1892, when a young woman by the name of Alice Mitchell, a graduate of Jenny Higbee's elite school for girls, fatally cut her lover's throat in broad daylight. The crime of passion had been described as "very unnatural," not only because of the class and sex of the murderess, but because of the fact that Alice's lover was also a woman—a woman she had openly planned to marry. The Mitchell case, coming soon after reports about the increasing numbers of women filing divorce petitions in the state's circuit court, created not only hand-wringing concerns in Memphis but became a national sensation and the basis for numerous monographs in the emerging field of psychology. In the coverage of the *New York Times* about the lynching of Moss, McDowell, and Stewart, it noted that Alice Mitchell, also in the Shelby County Jail, had watched the masked intruders from her cell on the upper tier of the prison.[79]

The *Appeal-Avalanche*, which had boasted about the conduct of the masked men, subsequently worried that the lynching was "far-reaching in its consequences," and pronounced that it could not be "condoned." Now the "orderly" lynchers were called a "lawless element," and the paper conceded that the store-owner, Barrett, was largely responsible for the entire ordeal. Curve citizens, presumably both black and white, issued a resolution censuring the white man for being the "cause" of the Curve troubles.[80]

Nevertheless, Memphis was unable to quash the criticism. The liberal *Chicago Daily Inter-Ocean*, which featured the "Bystander's Column" by Albion Tourgée—a white northerner who had been a judge in North Carolina after the war and had been forced to leave because of his pro-black sentiments—saw the lynching as evidence that Memphis had not been rehabilitated at all. "The better class of whites," he wrote ". . . are still so bitter . . . that they will not lift their hands to prevent a wholesale murder . . . nor try to bring the offenders against the laws of God." The *Washington Star* said that although it spoke well for Memphis to condemn "the outrageous lynching" in the city, it would have been better if it had held "a public meeting of indignation and protest against all such proceedings." There "are few cities of thickly populated communities in the country, fortunately, where lynch law and other forms of violence are upheld per se by public sentiment," the *Star* concluded, but Memphis, it implied, appeared to be an exception. In response, the *Appeal-Avalanche* riposted, "Every thoughtful citizen, conscious of the fact that the city is orderly, that life and property are safe, and that the moral atmosphere of the community is pure . . . protests bitterly."[81]

But the recapitulations and assurances by the Memphis press were of little solace—or relevance—to blacks. On March 11, the daily papers covered the funeral of the three murdered men, observing that it drew the largest procession that Memphis had ever seen. The site of the funeral was Avery Chapel, which was filled by twenty-five hundred parishioners, with more than an equal number outside of the church. The *Nashville American* estimated that a total of ten thousand blacks had come from outside the city to pay their respects. When the hearses bringing the bodies to the church were first sighted, a low wail rose from the crowd. Moss's casket, the first seen of the three, was particularly handsome. It was metallic, covered with black broadcloth, and garnished with a profusion of elaborate and artistic floral designs done in white. When the coffins, followed by the procession of family and friends, crossed the threshold of the church, the congregation broke into a hymn.

What it took for the pastors, Avery's S. R. Reed and Second Congregational's Benjamin Imes, to control their emotions can only be imagined. But they appeared to take great pains to not incite the crowd. Both men emphasized the virtues of the murdered men's lives in their eulogies; how they had died was not dwelled upon. At the end of the service, "wild sobs and laments," of the mostly female congregation, filled the church. After the funeral, when the recession of the caskets and mourners appeared outside of the church, so many of the waiting crowd pressed forward that the pallbearers had difficulty getting the caskets onto the hearse. Once accomplished, the mourners followed the bodies to Mount Zion cemetery where they were buried. Overcome, Moss's wife, Betty, fainted at the gravesite.[82]

In the wake of the funeral, there were daily reports that Memphis appeared calm. Josiah Settle, Ida's old landlord, was quoted as saying that there was no reason to "apprehend further trouble." He was confident that both "reputable" blacks and "respectable" whites deplored the action of the mob. The newspaper headline that carried Settle's opinions was entitled: "A Sensible Negro Speaks."[83]

Indeed, the reports in the following days after the funeral took note that the Curve and Memphis had quieted. It remained so—until Ida returned to Memphis.

CHAPTER SEVEN

Exodus

> There may be many hardships suffered by those
> who have gone to Oklahoma . . . but there is no
> sacrifice too great for freedom.
>
> —Langston City Herald

> [The Memphis lynching] was our first lesson in
> white supremacy.
>
> —Ida B. Wells

By the time Ida got back to Memphis, Calvin McDowell, Henry Stewart, and Tommie Moss had been buried. Order, the city's dailies assured, had been restored. But as events would soon show, the lull in the black community was more a measure of stunned disbelief than anything else. Yes, there had been bellicose threats; yes, racial hostility had reached disenfranchising heights; yes, there was increasing violence in other parts of the South and the state, but mob violence within Memphis where blacks had held office until just a few years before was not thought possible. As late as 1890, the editor of the Jackson, Tennessee–based *Christian Index* had (perhaps with Ida's encouragement) touted Memphis's advantages to advance the idea of relocating the publication there: its large, industrious black population, municipal reforms, abundant paper mills; and the achievements of the black business class, including a black-owned printing press. Despite the accumulating threats and tensions in Memphis, few had believed that it would come to this: a mob loosed upon the city; the roundup and arrests of dozens of black citizens; and the murder of three men, especially these three men, and especially Tommie Moss. The "shock" of the colored people was "beyond description," Ida wrote in her autobiography.[1]

Sitting at her desk in the *Free Speech* office, where she and Tommie had had so many conversations, Ida struggled to get beyond her own paralyzing sense of disbelief in order to write an editorial about the lynching. At first, she was daunted by her responsibility as a journalist at such a moment, and feared that finding the right words would fail her. But she had to say something and finally the first sentence that led the rest spilled out. "The City of Memphis," Wells wrote,

> has demonstrated that neither character nor standing avails the Negro if he dares to protect himself against the white man or become his rival. There is nothing we can do about the lynching now, as we are outnumbered and without arms. The white mob could help itself to ammunition without pay, but the order was rigidly enforced against the selling of guns to Negroes. There is therefore only one thing left that we can do; save our money and leave a town which will neither protect our lives and property, nor give us a fair trial in the courts, but takes us out and murders us in cold blood when accused by white persons.[2]

The editorial, resonating with the martyred Moss's dying words for blacks to turn their faces to the West, struck an immediate chord. No sooner had it been published than thousands of black Memphians readied themselves to leave Memphis for the newly opened Oklahoma Territory. The nation's first antilynching movement had begun.

WHILE EMIGRATION HAD never been used as a protest against a specific act, leaving the South had a historical and providential meaning for African Americans and for Tennesseans in particular. In the 1870s, the Nashville-born Benjamin "Pap" Singleton, convinced that blacks would never be allowed to acquire farmland in Tennessee, led a movement in which seven thousand black Tennesseans left for Kansas. The same period also saw an estimated twenty thousand blacks from Mississippi, Louisiana, and Texas who left the South. Those who participated in the millenarian movement were called "Exodusters" because of their stated desire to leave the "Egypt" of the South for the "Canaan" of the West.[3]

After the 1886 Carrollton Massacre, the Colored Press Association had urged blacks to leave the South; and T. Thomas Fortune had included aid to emigrants on the agenda of the Afro-American League. By 1889, the question of black emigration had risen anew with the opening of the Oklahoma Territory's Cherokee Cession—made up of portions of the Iowa, Sac, Fox, Comanche, Cheyenne, and Apache reservations—for settlement. African Americans were further encouraged by the establishment of the all-black towns in the Territory, including by 1890, Langston City—located twelve miles outside of the Oklahoma Territory's capital of Gutherie. In April of that year, seventeen hundred blacks from Atlanta left for that destination; subsequently, settlers and scouting parties for groups of blacks from Arkansas and Mississippi began making their way west. By 1891, blacks were reportedly arriving in Oklahoma on "almost every train" to the Territory's seven African American settlements. In the fall of that year—a time when cotton prices were low and the million-member Colored Farmer's Alliance was calling for a strike of black cotton-workers to protest their "starvation wages"—emigration promoters provided cheap, round-trip railway excursions for Tennesseeans to see the Territory firsthand. So many blacks, mainly farmers and sharecroppers from Shelby County, took up the offer that the Memphis dailies speculated nervously about the potential of thousands of blacks leaving the plantations on the edge of the cotton-picking season. Although most appeared to have returned, a new opportunity presented itself in April of 1892, when an additional five-hundred-mile strip of Cheyenne and Arapaho lands were to be opened in Oklahoma's Cimarron Valley.[4]

The scheduled opening made some see the Memphis murders as a sign. The *Indianapolis Freeman* was convinced that just before Moss's death, he had "caught a prophetic glimpse of the future in which the Negro race, weary of proscriptions and barbaric treatment in the South, migrated to the West, where, under kinder and more progressive conditions, it finally rises to the full height of a complete citizenship."[5]

By March 20, so many blacks were leaving Memphis that a hastily called meeting was held on that date at Zion Hall. The meeting was led by the "better element of the colored people," in the words of the *Memphis Commercial,* to protest the exodus. The "better element of colored people" included property-holders and ministers who had a stake in trying to maintain the status quo—or at least some equilibrium in the city. Lymus Wallace, who owned a large dray business, had lost nearly all of his draymen—most of whom were in debt to him from $25 to $50. The furniture dealer Moses Strickland (a friend of Ida's from whom she purchased her own furniture) reported to the group that he had bought out twenty of his competitors who were bound for Oklahoma. Cash Mosby, a railway agent, was reported by the *New York Times* to have sent his family to Cincinnati and was putting his property up for sale—at a loss. Others, including a lawyer and another man employed in government service who were trying to dispense of their properties worth $15,000 and a house worth $500 that earned $30 in monthly rents, were trying to do the same. The *Commercial* added that the black men planned another meeting to "consider the hasty removal of the colored people on account of the late mobbing. Speeches will be made by colored leaders advising calmness, prudence and patience." Signing the call, among others, were Josiah Settle and the Reverends Countee, Imes, Brinkley, and Waters.[6]

"Patience," of course, was the last thing Ida wanted. While representative Negroes were calling for calm, the grand jury was in the process of deciding that the lynching was at the "hands of persons unknown," and had begun indicting the thirty-one blacks suspected of taking part in the shootout that garnered them sentences from five to fifteen years. "The good colored citizens of Memphis, who have been interested in and worked for the prosperity and success of the city; who stood by the white people when the plague of '78 and '79 threatened to sweep the town from the face of the earth," demand "that the murderers of Calvin McDowell, Will Stewart, and Tom Moss be brought to justice," Ida wrote in her next editorial, which stressed a common, not divided, interest among blacks. "We ask this in the name of God and in the name of the law we have always obeyed and upheld and intend to uphold and obey in the future."[7]

Again Wells appeared to tap into and draw out the sentiments of the larger black community in Memphis. The next meeting at Zion Hall, on March 24, reportedly attended by a thousand blacks, adopted a resolution that condemned the lynching and expressed the belief that "no earnest steps were taken by the authorities to apprehend the lynchers." Blacks were also urged to emigrate to Oklahoma because there was no possibility of

getting justice in the Memphis courts. Two days later, on the same day as
Isaiah Johnson was indicted for assault with intent to commit murder of
Deputy Bob Harold, the *Langston City Herald,* a black weekly, added its
own voice of encouragement to would-be migrants. Why invest any money
in a city where their lives were constantly in danger? it asked. Why not
come to Oklahoma, "where you can develop whatever manhood or womanhood you possess. Here you can be all that God intended you to
be . . ."?[8]

On March 27, the *Nashville Daily American* described the three thousand black well-wishers in Memphis who had assembled on the Mississippi
levee to see off 649 men, women, and children in thirty wagons—along
with their dogs, mules, oxen, and all the household and personal goods they
could carry. Ironically, their trip would be made easier by the recent com-
pletion of Memphis's greatest engineering feat to date: the 7,400-foot "Great
Bridge," said to be the longest in the world and built at a cost of three million dollars with steel provided by the Carnegie Steel Company of Pittsburgh. After crossing the bridge that connected Memphis to the Arkansas
banks, the migrants planned to take the steamer *Alice* to Mound City. From
there they would begin a twenty-mile-a-day overland route by wagon and
by foot for the six-week journey to Oklahoma. "This was only the advance
guard," the paper solemnly noted. "Fully 1000 more will leave on Monday
by rail and still others will follow. Arrangements have been made for 1600
to 1800 emigrants, which covers the exodus of to-day and tomorrow."[9]

Ida recalled the scene in her autobiography and captured the drama,
pathos, and humor of it in an anecdote about a tattered old man who had
been trying to get his yellow hound to follow him on the boat. Exasperated, the man finally said, in a voice loud enough for everyone to hear:
"Come on here—what you want to stay back for, you want the white folks
to lynch you too?" There was little question that Memphians had made the
decision to leave, in large part, to demonstrate their solidarity in heeding
the words of protest in the *Free Speech*. While "we think we lost good citizens in that lynching," one of the men on the levee observed, "and that
innocent blood was lawlessly spilled . . . it needed something like that to
bring our people together." This "trouble," offered another, "has accomplished more than all the preaching and teaching could have done in fifty
years."[10]

By then it had become evident that the hegira west had taken on a life
of its own, and that it was supported by blacks across class lines. The black

businessman Robert Church gave $10,000 to the Central Oklahoma Emigration Society, which claimed to have four thousand Memphis blacks organized to go west. The railway agent, Cash Mosby, and Ida's *Free Speech* partner, J. L. Fleming, were appointed to hold funds now being raised by black churches to assist those who needed funds to leave Memphis. Ida recounted the poignant stories about the relief effort. In her autobiography, she told of two women, both visibly pregnant, who had become trapped by the seasonal floods in Arkansas and were urged to return to Memphis. But the women were determined to complete the journey, saying that "they were willing to take their chances in the wilderness rather than come back to Memphis." The emigration fund raised four hundred dollars so that they could take the train west.[11]

The *Free Speech* continued to keep the heat on. It published a story that a deputy said to have died by other means was actually killed by Calvin McDowell during the struggle at the Chesapeake & Ohio railyards. The accusation was an attempt to show that the deputies themselves had been the ringleaders of the mob murder—a suspicion so widely held that even the *Nashville Daily American* noted it. In fact, Ida, as she wrote in her autobiography, was convinced that every prominent white man in the city had known in advance of the plan to kill the men on March 9, and that the criminal court judge, DuBose, had himself been among the lynchers.[12]

THE RESPONSE OF the black press to the Memphis events, which began to appear in late March, was unprecedented. No other event in recent years, including Carrollton, evoked such comment—or fury. The circumstances of the lynching, the rising militance, the consciousness raised by the Afro-American League, and the palpable protest led by Wells with her wide readership and unadulterated race-first position made the Memphis murders reverberate through both religious and secular black publications as no others had before it. The AME's *Star of Zion* warned that if the crime continued to go unpunished, "thoughtful law-abiding, and obedient colored citizens cannot become responsible for the action of the race in the face of such diabolism." The *Christian Index* no longer thought Memphis so progressive and questioned the "orderly" image of the city by calling the lynchers "a frenzied mob" that was "worse than the savage who slays his hundreds and knows no God to call upon for forgiveness." The black

Democrat C. H. J. Taylor, editor of the *Kansas American Citizen,* implored white Memphians to find the responsible "human fiends" and to thus prove that "God is not dead; that religion is not a mockery, and that all of your churches should not be burned to the ground."[13]

The lesson of the Memphis events, raged Ferdinand L. Barnett in the *Chicago Conservator,* was that "the American flag is not a protection to citizens at home, but a dirty, dishonored rag." The crime was an "unspeakable disgrace," he continued. "The people gave us one John Brown," said Barnett, alluding to the white abolitionist who seized the U.S. arsenal at Harper's Ferry and killed six proslavery men. "If we must have another let him be flesh of our flesh and blood of our blood." Barnett's editorial in the *Conservator,* a paper known for its influential readership among blacks and progressive whites, was so alarming that the *Memphis Commercial* republished it as a warning that the black editor was calling for blacks to "take up arms against the government." Surprised that such a man could be considered an important leader, the paper suggested that he should be brought to the attention of the police.[14]

On March 30, a clearly concerned *Appeal-Avalanche* announced that the city's court commissioners had concluded that the lynching had been "ill-advised" and set aside a year's allowance for Betty Moss, Tommie's widow. The decision was an ironic one. When Thomas Cassels had led the passage of Tennessee's antilynching law in 1881, the part in the bill that sought compensation for families and victims of mob violence had failed to pass. But now, the explanation given by the commissioners for their decision was that Moss had owned several pieces of real estate and considerable personal property.

It was an extraordinary concession, but if its purpose was to put the genie back into the bottle, it failed to do so. The *Cleveland Gazette* still thought Memphis a "barbarous" city and emblematic of the "appalling dark and ominous cloud that is hanging over this nation and makes more visible the seething volcano over which the southern people sleep." Blacks kept leaving for Oklahoma, and national protests began to emerge not only in the North but the South as well. In April, the *Indianapolis Freeman* reported that one thousand blacks assembled at the Bethel AME Church in Atlanta to "consider the recent Southern outrages upon their race." When Bishop W. J. Gaines (whom Ida had earlier criticized in the *Christian Index*) asked the audience to join him in singing "America," they refused. Taking up Ferdinand Barnett's call, they sang "John Brown's Body" instead. In the same month, Barnett and Fortune, among others, attended a mass antilynching meeting in New York City. Two thousand blacks met in Cooper Union, the famous hall located in lower Manhattan, to hear speeches and protests about the Memphis lynching as well as other recent atrocities in the South. The *New York Times* called it the largest assemblage of blacks ever held in that city to date. However, Wells, who sat on the dais but did not speak, could not have spent much time in the city. Back home, the Memphis dailies, in anticipation of the April 19 opening of the Cimarron Valley for settlement, began publishing discouraging articles about conditions in Oklahoma. Wells immediately made plans to go to the Territory to see and report on them for herself.[15]

It is conceivable that Ida was somewhat surprised by the depth and spontaneity of the response she had triggered with her editorial. Of course, she was pleased by the show of determination and initiative in the community, but she also had to be concerned about those who had appeared to make a precipitous decision to leave Memphis for the advertised "promised land" in Oklahoma. While the *Langston City Herald* published glowing articles about Oklahoma's fertile tablelands and a dreamed-of life without white oppression, there were also caveats being published in other black papers. Just that February, the *Indianapolis Freeman* had starkly described a group of black migrants who were being forced to return to their homes in Dennison, Texas. "Many of the poor creatures were obliged to walk nearly two hundred miles," said the paper. "They stated that they stood chances for homes, but were crowded out by the white boomers. Great destitution prevails among the colored people . . . in Oklahoma," the dispatch concluded."[16]

Before the lynchings, the *Free Speech* itself might have unwittingly added to a less than happy ending for a group of earlier migrants. In January of 1892, it had been criticized by the *Langston City Herald* for running an ad by Isaac Norris—a former legislator and Ida's cousin-in-law who was now an "emigrationist"—that promised new arrivals free mule teams that migrants could use to help raise a crop. The *Herald* charged Norris with false advertising to collect railway commissions by attracting blacks who might not otherwise come and who often needed aid from the nascent territorial governments. Whether or not Norris was guilty is not known. But the charge reflected the larger issue of unsophisticated blacks being taken advantage of by fee-hungry agents. Earlier that year, the *Herald* reported that a group of seventy-five Memphians paid a railway agent three dollars apiece to attain a piece of paper that fraudulently promised them their train fare would be paid by government officials.[17]

The fact was that objective and full reporting about Oklahoma was virtually nonexistent. Much of the information was anecdotal or came from the emigration or anti-emigration societies that emerged in the period and were driven by competing ideological, racial, and/or economic interests. Even white press reports, as Wells had earlier gleaned, could vary in accordance to the planter or urban interests they represented. On the other side was the well-oiled public relations machine of the Oklahoma Immigration Society that was the force behind the founding of Langston City. Edwin McCabe, the natty former auditor of Kansas whom Ida had seen on her 1886 western trip, was the best-known figure connected with the Society. Since then he had lost reelection for the position in the state and moved to Oklahoma where he unsuccessfully pressed for appointment as territorial governor, but he did gain a position in the Logan County treasurer's office there. The other primary figures behind the Society were William Eagleson, a black newspaper editor, and Charles Robbins, a white land speculator.[18] They had created a sophisticated plan for the city that included a projected university, to be endowed, in part, by wealthy whites, for which the major promoter was John Langston (after whom the city was named)— the former consul general to Haiti and president of Virginia Normal and Collegiate Institute—who in 1890 had been elected to the House of Representatives, representing Virginia.[19] The Oklahoma enterprise, the *New York Age* noted, was directed by "level-headed men, black and white." But however sincere they were in providing the first "systematic effort," as Fortune wrote, "to create a new State where blacks could predominate and hold decisive political power," the Society also desperately needed blacks to settle 320 acres, divided neatly into lots, which had to be sold.[20]

Ida knew, as she wrote, that black Memphians would believe what she told them and that it was incumbent upon her to go to Oklahoma. She secured train passes for herself, Norris, and cousin Stella to go to the Territory where, through the *Free Speech,* she would report back to her community "exactly what I saw and of the chance they had of developing manhood and womanhood in this new territory."[21]

At such a historical moment, Wells, with her influence and readership, could have a tremendous impact on the Oklahoma movement; and by all appearances she was treated accordingly. She arrived to find that appointments had been set up for her with the territorial governor and various state officers. A "gallant young lawyer" was secured to squire her around. Wells also visited the office of the *Langston City Herald,* where the paper's editors took pains to be complimentary. Ida, the editors said, had demonstrated "more real interest in the race than all but C. H. J. Taylor," editor of the *Kansas City American Citizen.* Moreover, she was "affable," "clear-headed" and "prepossessing in her personal appearance."[22]

In all, Ida spent three weeks there where she visited Gutherie, Oklahoma City, and Langston, among other places in the Territory. While no comprehensive record of her weekly reports exists, comments about them by the *Langston City Herald* and other black papers indicate that, true to what she had promised, she told her readers exactly what she saw—both what was good and what was lacking in the developments. With her perspective, she would have shared the sense of pride in Langston City that Edwin McCabe expressed when he pronounced that "Langston City is a Negro City and we are proud of that fact." Ida probably saw what a visitor had described the year before: a thriving town, where "streets were laid out . . . colored carpenters were busy erecting new houses" and where there was "not a white man to be seen anywhere around." In less than two years after it was established, Langston City had more than two hundred residents, a wholesale grocery store and six retail ones, a drug store, a post office, and a public school, as well as lunch counters, meat markets, barbershops, and three hotels. Dwellings were scattered throughout the 320 acres of titled lots for sale—titles stipulating that they could never pass to a white man. Eight months before Wells's visit, Langston City had held its first elections and now had in place three councilmen, a treasurer, and a justice of the peace, a number of whom were probably among the state officers Ida visited in the two-story brick building offices in Gutherie, the territorial capital.[23]

Gutherie itself had between seven hundred and twelve hundred settlers—both blacks and whites—and was a popular destination for Memphians. As a reporter noted, among the new settlers were those who had come without adequate means, "expecting to find Utopia," but he added that "the greater number came prepared to stay, bringing their surplus cash along and depositing the same in the Gutherie banks (which by 1893 had received $15,000 from "colored depositors"). Recent elections in Gutherie had resulted in blacks winning positions on the school board and city council and as justice of the peace and constable. Ida also traveled to Oklahoma City and Kingfisher, the latter of which was close to Langston City and another prime destination for Memphians who were awaiting the April opening of the new territories.[24]

But there was another side to this positive picture. Settlement promoters were clear in their preference for migrants who had skills and means; those who did not have them could fare badly. The latter included black farmers who had sold what they had in livestock, and even tools, to make the journey, only to encounter severe weather that prevented them from growing a crop. Those who had nothing to fall back on were often forced into crowded shelters that were usually unsanitary and insecure. Others lived in tents, or their wagons, or made do with crude log-cabin dugouts, the backs of which were lodged into dirt mounds to protect them from winds unimpeded by the vacant ocean of flat tableland.[25]

As the days grew closer to the April 19 opening, it also became clear that black settlements were not going to be uncontested. Not only whites but Fox Indians were opposed to the idea of "Africanizing Oklahoma," and threats of violence and intimidation tactics were aimed at blacks in both Langston City and Kingfisher. But the situation, as was true with the Oklahoma settlements in general, was emblematic of both the good news and bad about the movement. The good news in this instance was that blacks were free to defend themselves. In Kingfisher, for example, the threats were met by black men who organized a Winchester rifle band and threatened to burn down the whole city if any one of their number was harmed. No one was. "The colored men in Oklahoma mean business," concluded a writer who subsequently visited the town. They had an "exalted idea of their own rights and liberties and they dare to maintain them. . . . I found in nearly every cabin visited a modern Winchester oiled and ready for use."[26] The image left an indelible impression on Ida's mind.

"MISS WELLS WE take it, does not take kindly to Oklahoma," concluded the *Langston City Herald,* indicating that Wells's *Free Speech* columns were less than the unconditional endorsements the paper sought. She "struck us as being a decided exception to the rule of ladies of our race in that she has evidently enjoyed opportunities and has not failed to embrace them," the Oklahoma paper sneered. "We take it that in the effete east, where wealth and luxury obtains among our people, she must be quite a toast, but fear she expects too much of those who inhabit the 'wild and woolly west.'"

"Will the editor of the *Langston City Herald* please soak his head and keep cool?" Ida responded good-naturedly in the *Free Speech*. "As the season gets warmer we'll try to accommodate the *Free Speech* and the country," the Oklahomans responded.[27]

The *Langston Herald* editors were wrong about Ida, and her final assessment about the Territory. Unbeknownst to her hosts and despite her love of Shakespeare and department stores, she had already determined to leave Memphis and seriously considered moving to Oklahoma and bringing the *Free Speech* there. Even before the Moss lynching, the New City had no doubt lost much of its luster; after it, she sensed that she was on borrowed time. In any case, Ida possessed a kind of gritty determination and a black nationalist vision that trumped other considerations. This was evident in an article published in the *AME Church Review* some months later about another emigration movement: this one led by the AME bishop Henry McNeal Turner, who was urging African Americans to settle in Liberia. In the journal, Ida disputed T. Thomas Fortune's view that the "intelligent class" of blacks would never go to Africa. Wells thought Fortune underestimated both the ambition of African Americans and their desire to escape oppression. Why should they not return to the land of the forefathers? Ida asked, noting Africa's fertility and freedom from "Anglo-Saxon" dominance. Was not "the vision of the Puritans just as daunting, their obstacles just as difficult, as those facing African-Americans?"[28]

As Ida wrote in her autobiography, she had approached her partner J. L. Fleming about relocating to the Territory, but Oklahoma might have been a bit too daunting for him. Ida did not have the money to buy out his interest in the paper and began to weigh the possibilities of going to Philadelphia or New York; cities, presumably, that Fleming was willing to consider. But whatever opportunities Ida had seen in Oklahoma for herself and her paper, she appeared to not have soft-pedaled the harsh conditions. She also told her readers to take time to consider the move to Oklahoma and mentioned some alternative places where migrants might settle. As the *Detroit Plaindealer* summed it up, "The *Free Speech* is advertising Afro-Americans to leave Memphis, but also advise people first to get ready, and provide themselves with means to obtain a home elsewhere"—possible destinations like New Mexico, Colorado, Oregon, Washington, and Wyoming. And implicitly warning blacks that they should be aware of propaganda, Wells called for the establishment of a bureau to provide reliable, objective information for migrants. Toward that end, she proposed that representatives from Tennessee, Mississippi, Alabama, Louisiana, Arkansas, Georgia, and North and South Carolina meet in Memphis to further discuss the issue on June 16. It was a date, as future events would show, that must have burned on the minds of white Memphians.[29]

It is evident that Ida's reports were intended to make Memphians think responsibly about leaving the city, not to discourage the migration—and there were no signs that it slowed. "The motto of every Negro living in and around Memphis is: 'Turn your faces to the West,' the last words of poor Tom Moss," observed the *Detroit Plaindealer,* four days before the April 19 opening. "And they are turning there by the hundreds. About 300 left Saturday."[30]

In anticipation of the April 19 opening, thousands of homesteaders were poised to make claims along the five-hundred-mile boundary of the Cheyenne and Arapaho lands, among them black Memphians hoping to take advantage of "the last chance for a free home" as boosters put it. The sandbars of the Cimarron River were filled with families of future homesteaders waiting to see the huge bonfire that signaled the official opening of the land at twelve noon. There was not a mile, a reporter noted, where there were not from one to a dozen camps of prospective settlers who represented all nationalities, races, and sects. "The waiting throng was today augmented by the arrival of 500 negroes from Memphis," observed the *Memphis Commercial,* which had sent a reporter there. "They have gone to the camp at the negro settlement north of Kingfisher and are tonight holding religious services and thanking the Lord for having brought them safely to the promised land." In Gutherie, migrants expressed their gratitude in another way. Three of its streets were named Moss, Stewart, and McDowell.[31]

The Memphis hegira continued through the spring and fall when a number of pastors and their congregations left the city en masse. William F. Morgan of the Union Avenue Baptist Church was the most efficient. He was reported by the *Langston City Herald* to have arrived in Gutherie on a Friday; purchased land on Saturday; and by the following Sunday had erected a church "all finished and paid for" where services were held for three hundred people. Morgan, the *Langston City Herald* added, planned to return to Memphis to arrange the removal of his congregation who "are to come as a colony." Both *Living Way* reverends, R. N. Countee and W. A. Brinkley, who had been at the earlier meeting that had counseled patience evidently lost theirs. Countee moved to Witchita, Kansas; Brinkley sold his Washington Street Baptist Church to the local Jewish community and moved his congregation to Stockton, California. Before his departure, Brinkley had some particular choice words about the city, saying that he was leaving in order to help "depopulate this hell [Memphis] created for colored people." Following his statement, the pastor was attacked by some ruffians, and he himself was threatened with lynching. As reported in the *Detroit Plaindealer,* Brinkley riposted: "This [lynching] may be done easily; you have only to get up some charge against me, whether it be true or not, and put me in jail, and come next morning at 3:30 and get me out. The papers will be ready with the news by morning. But one consoling thing to me, which may be discouraging to the would-be lynchers, is that when I am lynched my soul will not go down to hell, where the souls of the lynchers will soon be." Ida issued her own rejoinder to the minister. "Only those upon whom judgment is passed are sent to hell for punishment," she wrote in the *Free Speech*. "Here we are punished and murdered without judgment."[32]

IDA RETURNED TO Memphis in late April or early May to find that the loss of so many blacks—she later estimated the number as six thousand within the year or nearly 20 percent of the African American population—was having its effect. "Business was at a standstill," Wells wrote gleefully in her autobiography, for the "Negro was famous then, as now, for spending his money for fine clothes, furniture, jewelry, and pianos and other musical instruments, to say nothing of good things to eat." Blacks purchased many items, especially the musical instruments, on installment plans, and so many of them were left unpaid for in the music shops that they could not find storage for them. The number of women who had left was evidenced by the complaints of white housewives who found a "hitherto unknown scarcity of help," Ida further noted. Fearing that any money paid to domestic servants would be used for the trip west, whites "resorted to the expedient of paying their servants only half the wages due them at the end of the week."[33]

Soon after her return, Ida became aware of yet another, and unexpected, weapon in her arsenal when she was visited by the superintendent and treasurer of the City Railway Company in her Beale Street office. She was surprised, she wrote in the autobiography, when the two white men beseeched her to use her influence to get blacks to ride the trolley cars. The men believed that African Americans were not riding them because they were afraid of the electricity, and the resulting loss of revenue endangered the company and their jobs. "So your livelihood depends on black patronage?" Ida asked mischievously, enjoying the rush of red rising to their faces. But she was also biding time with her comment. This was something she hadn't picked up on, though she would never admit it to her visitors. Blacks had been riding the electrified trolleys before the events of March 9; why were they stopping? The white men kept talking. They reminded her that the company had an investment of thousands of dollars in electrifying the cars, that pains had been taken to employ black laborers for the work of relaying and grading the streets used on the trolley lines, and that the company had a policy of treating black riders courteously.[34]

The comment about the treatment of blacks probably reflected the men's awareness of what was happening in other cities, particularly Indianapolis, where blacks felt that they were being mistreated on public transportation. Earlier that year, in February of 1892, African Americans had begun to boycott the trolley cars, protesting that no African Americans were employed to drive them and that black riders, including "respectable" and "aged" colored ladies burdened with bundles," were disrespected by the same whites who were breaking "their necks to assist prostitutes," snarled the *Freeman*. The Indianapolis weekly had made a special appeal to black women to save their money by boycotting the cars—and for good reason. Civic action on city trolleys when black women were mistreated on them had historical precedent. In 1866, the California entrepreneur and former slave Mary Pleasant had sued the San Francisco Trolley Company when she was refused a seat on the vehicle; the abolitionist Sojourner Truth successfully subdued a conductor in Washington, D.C., who tried to physically evict her from a trolley; the newspaper publisher Mary Ann Shadd Carey had reportedly given such a firelike gaze to a conductor determined to pass her by that he found himself mysteriously compelled to stop and pick her up. By the late nineteenth century, the numbers of blacks in the cities gave them additional power to boycott urban transportation, and Indianapolis was the most publicized example of their exercising it.[35]

The men told Ida that if blacks in Memphis encountered any "discourtesy," she should let them know. While they were talking, the explanation for blacks not riding the cars in Memphis suddenly dawned on Wells. Right after the lynching she had told the community to save their "nickels and dimes," to go to Oklahoma. The fare of the trolley was a nickel; a dime, if one needed a transfer. It was a lot of money for the average laborer earning a dollar or a dollar and a half per day. Blacks were saving their money to go to Oklahoma! Ida asked the men if they had noticed that blacks had stopped riding right after the lynching. The question turned what they had thought a fear of electricity into an act of civil disobedience. "But the streetcar company had nothing to do with the lynching," the men protested. "It is owned by northern capitalists." And "run by southern lynchers," Wells retorted. "We have learned that every white man of any standing in town knew of the plan and consented to lynching of our boys," Ida told them, adding she believed that the criminal court judge, Julius DuBose, was one of the murderers. "Tom Moss," Ida continued, "was as fine a man that ever walked the streets of Memphis . . . yet he was murdered with no more consideration than if he had been a dog, because he as a man defended his property from attack." She insisted, "The colored people feel that every white man in Memphis who consented to his death is as guilty as those who fired the guns which took his life, and they want to get away from this town."[36]

Wells wrote up the interview with the two men for the next issue of the *Free Speech,* and on the following Sunday she visited several black churches, encouraging congregants to continue boycotting the trolleys. They did so long enough to set an example that, as the *Cleveland Gazette* observed, "should be patterned after by the race all over the country toward the business interests that refuse to them equal justice." The "answer of the *Free Speech* should be the watchword of every man who cannot claim protection of the law," echoed the *Plaindealer.* "We are saving our money to go where we can have freedom." Although it is not known how long the civil action continued, a full year later the *Cleveland Gazette* observed that "both the Arkansas planters and the Memphis, Tenn. street car superintendent are complaining."[37]

During that year, Ida had kept her editorial guns fully loaded. On the political front, she linked the shortcomings of the Republican administration with the Moss lynching when she castigated President Benjamin Harrison for refusing to meet with a New York delegation about lynching after publicly threatening war with Chile over the death of two American sailors at the hands of a Chilean mob. While "The gunboat Concord . . . was sent post haste to Chile to avenge the taking of the life of a drunken sailor,"

Wells wrote in her searing prose, "three Negroes murdered here March 9th were as loyal American citizens as ever drew the breath of life and were as much entitled to protection. But—they were Negroes." Wells, mindful of the Oklahomans' Winchester rifles, concluded. "Until the Negro learns to protect himself, he may always expect to be without protection."[38]

Wells reiterated the point of protection—or lack of it—from, again, black politicians, particularly in an election year. "Where are our leaders when the race is being burnt, shot and hanged?" the *Free Speech* taunted. "Holding good fat offices and saying not a word—just as they were when the Civil Rights bill was repealed and the Blair Educational and Federal Election bills were defeated . . . however much the Negro is abused and outraged—'our leaders' make no demands on the country to protect us, nor come forward with any practical plan for changing the condition of affairs." No doubt thinking of the likes of John Langston, Blanche K. Bruce, and P. B. S. Pinchback, all maneuvering in a presidential election year, Wells concluded, "A few big offices and the control of a little Federal patronage is not sufficient recompense for the lives lost, the blood shed, and the rights denied the race." As usual, Bruce, the current recorder of deeds, a patronage position in Washington, and now fighting openly with Ida's old friend James Hill over control of Republican election delegates, was a particular target. Wells wrote that word had it that Bruce had been sent south by Republican president Benjamin Harrison, who, like his predecessors, was trying to widen white support, "to pull delegates in line." "They say affairs in the south are alright, save a little dissatisfaction here and there which Bruce will make all right." Wells complained that Bruce "has never uttered a protest, sought to arouse public sentiment against such outrages nor exerted himself for his people at any time save when he wanted their votes to save his job."[39]

Wells emphasized that affairs were not all right in the South, including in Blanche Bruce's home of Mississippi. Ida reprinted in her column a letter she received from a Mrs. Eva P. Green, who lived and owned property with her husband in Mound Bayou, Mississippi, the town that her friend Isaiah Montgomery had founded. After an altercation with a white man, Mr. Green was forced to flee into the woods, his wife wrote, and soon after was followed by other men, women, and children in the community because they did not have "the protection which the law ought to give." Mrs. Green wrote, "I am told Miss editor, that the only way to save our community from destruction is that Mr. Green must make an apology . . . he must now sacrifice his manhood and honor to appease the wrath of the white man." The writer concluded, "we have a nice home, but, alas, we are not free." Mrs. Green had decided like so many others to cast her lot elsewhere. "Please send me the name of a reliable man out west," she asked Ida.[40]

Wells also continued to hammer away at the racist justice system in Memphis. She wrote, for example, of a black man who was sentenced to eight years in the state prison for stealing a box of cigars, four bottles of whiskey, and two steaks, worth about seven dollars. The arithmetic, said Wells, came out to one year for every eighty-seven and a half cents he stole. Criminal court judge Julius DuBose came under fire when Wells learned that his fourteen-year-old son had drowned. "They say the Judge's grief over his loss was terrible," Wells wrote in the *Free speech*. "So was that of the families of the murdered men to whom Judge DuBose refused bond, and left an easy prey to the mob. . . . No sympathy was felt for the orphan sisters of Calvin McDowell, for the wife of Tom Moss who will shortly become a mother; nor for the 18 months old babe who daily hugs and kisses her father's inanimate clothing."[41]

BY 1892, THE year Ida turned thirty, she had taken possession of her power as a journalist and had learned to put it to effective political use. She was trusted and had the ability to inspire her readers. She had brought modern methods of protest to bear in a New South that was so dependent on its extended markets and the civic image that sustained them. Ida had come up with a strategy for a mass movement that crossed class lines in the black community and, in the process, gave courage and purpose to African Americans to take the initiative in finding a better life for themselves and generations to come. She had mastered the art of tapping preexisting sentiment in the black community, then shaping and directing it, to meet the challenges of a new age. Now she had to decide for herself where the next phase of her own life would take her.

Well before the lynching on March 9, Ida had planned to go to Philadelphia in late May. She had been urged by Bishop Henry McNeal Turner to attend the AME general conference that was taking place there; and Frances Ellen Harper, the poet and temperance leader, who had stayed with Ida when she visited Memphis the winter before, invited Wells to stay with her during the confab. The trip would also give Wells the opportunity to assess the possibilities of relocating the *Free Speech* in the city. Afterward, Ida had scheduled a stop in New York to meet with T. Thomas Fortune, who had earlier written Ida in the hopes that she would give New York "a lookover" before finally deciding where to settle.[42]

Just before she left Memphis, Ida wrote one of her shorter editorials, which was to appear in the May 21 edition of the *Free Speech*. It was meant to be a rejoinder to a vicious article in the *Memphis Commercial* written by its editor Edward Ward Carmack. A rabid prohibitionist, who had been writing anti-black vitriol in the *Nashville Daily American*, Carmack had come to Memphis to replace J. L. Keating in early 1892. In May, the *Commercial* had commented on the lynching of "three negro scoundrels," as he called them, accused of raping a white woman in Anniston, Alabama.

His intent, as he admitted in the editorial, was to head off the anticipated criticism by the North about the lynchings as another indication of "southern barbarism." But Carmack, in one of the most extended explanations of the relationship between the rise of lynching and the alleged rise of rape committed by blacks, made the case that African Americans were not only increasingly violating white women, they were doing so in a more pernicious way than in the past. Black men were committing rape not out of sudden "fits of passion," he wrote, but as premeditated attacks in which they waited for the opportunity to attack women when they were left "without a protector." This new phase of sexual violence was terrorizing "thinly settled country communities," averred the paper, where no "man can leave his family at night without the dread that some roving Negro ruffian is watching and waiting for this opportunity." Only the swift retribution of extra-legal violence could check the "horrible and bestial propensities" of black men, Carmack argued; and moreover otherwise rational, law-abiding white men should be excused for the lapse in the rule of law. There "is nothing which so fills the soul with horror, loathing and fury as the outraging of a white woman by a Negro," Carmack opined. Even more alarming was the *Commercial*'s observation that although lynching may have an immediate deterring effect in the communities where they occurred, its long-term impact was questionable, for blacks set aside even the fear of death to consummate their "devilish purpose" and gratify their "bestial desires." "The Negro as a political factor can be controlled," the *Commercial* somberly concluded, "but neither laws nor lynchings can subdue his lusts. Sooner or later it will force a crisis. We do not know what form it will come."[43]

Although Wells did not have the time to write an extended response to the editorial, she felt that she could not leave the city without commenting on it. In the wake of the Memphis murders, she herself had begun to investigate lynchings—or more precisely, the motive of rape which was so often given as the excuse. After all, the Memphis lynching had nothing to do with such charges, and Ida had begun to question the veracity of the charge. She hadn't always done so. As Ida, who in many ways shared the honor codes of the culture—in her diary she had once condoned the murder of a man by a brother of the young woman the victim had slandered—admitted in her autobiography: "Like many another person who had read of lynching in the South, I had accepted the idea meant to be conveyed—that although lynching was irregular and contrary to law and order, unreasoning anger over the terrible crime of rape led to the lynching; that perhaps the brute deserved death anyhow and the mob was justified in taking his life."[44]

But after the Memphis lynching, she began visiting the scenes of lynchings where she interviewed eyewitnesses or families of the victims. In Tunica, Mississippi, for example, she followed up on an Associated Press account of a "big burly brute" who was lynched for purportedly raping the seven-year-old daughter of the sheriff. Wells sought out the girl and discovered that she wasn't seven but seventeen and had been discovered in the black man's cabin. The father, Ida concluded, had led the lynch mob to save the reputation of his daughter. Visiting the scene of another lynching, Wells went so far as to get a sworn statement from the mother of the victim: a young man whom Ida described as a "handsome young mulatto," who had gone so far as to leave his employ in an effort to resist the advances of "the beautiful daughter" of his boss. But he had finally succumbed and when the father discovered the liaison, the mulatto was charged with rape and lynched. "It seemed horrible to me that death in its most terrible form should be meted out to the Negro who was weak enough to take chances when accepting the invitations of these white women," Wells wrote in her autobiography. It occurred to Ida that lynching apologists like Carmack were motivated by both salvaging the white South's image and portraying blacks in a way as to take away any support for the race from the North. "That the entire race should be branded as moral monsters and despoilers of white womanhood and childhood was bound to rob us of all the friends we had," Wells wrote, "and silence any protests that they may make for us."[45]

Hurriedly, with plans to write more when she returned to Memphis, Ida wrote in the *Free Speech:* "Eight Negroes lynched since last issue of the *Free Speech,* one at Little Rock, Ark., last Saturday morning where the citizens broke (?) into the penitentiary and got their man; three near Anniston, Ala., one near New Orleans; and three at Clarksville, Ga., the last three for killing a white man, and five on the same old racket—the new alarm about raping white women. The same programme [*sic*] of hanging, then shooting bullets into the lifeless bodies was carried out to the letter. If Southern white men are not careful," she concluded, "they will overreach themselves and public sentiment will have a reaction; a conclusion will then be reached which will be very damaging to the moral reputation of their women."[46] Her editorial written, she headed for Philadelphia.

WELLS WOULD HAVE been impressed by many features of the eastern city. Philadelphia had a population of about a million persons—nearly forty thousand of whom were black—and a particularly rich history of resistance, business enterprise, publishing, and institution-building among its small African American elite. Black Philadelphians faced similar prejudices—including de facto segregation—social dislocations, and low-wage employment familiar to African Americans throughout the country. But at least the Pennsylvania Supreme Court continued to abide by the antidiscrimination statutes of the 1875 federal Civil Rights Act, and in 1881 forbade discrimination in the assignment of pupils to its public schools. One of the city's schools, the Institute for Colored Youth, founded by the Quakers who had an estimable presence in Philadelphia, was nationally known for its normal department from which graduates were sought to teach throughout the country. The city was also the birthplace of the African Methodist Episcopal Church, established by Richard Allen in 1791, and it was the present home of the AME's *Christian Recorder,* which had been published there since the mid-1850s. In addition to the writers associated with the denomination's paper, there were perhaps a dozen secular journalists who had opportunities to write black religious and social news in local white-owned papers, from which a number went on to write for out-of-town publications or for the most successful black newspaper in the

city, the *Philadelphia Weekly Tribune*, which began publishing in 1884.[47]
Ida knew several of the city's journalists, notably Frances Ellen Harper and
Gertrude Mossell, and had probably gleaned that there was more than
ample room for another publication.

If Wells looked favorably upon the prospects that Philadelphia offered,
she was less impressed by the AME conference itself. Few meetings are
filled with more verbiage than ecclesiastical ones, and Ida was not impressed. "Conventions, and talk and prayer alone are not what are needed
right now," she editorialized about the conference. "An offer of a home for
several families in different localities, a purse to help destitute ones who
wish to go would do more real good than all the conventions in
Christiandom.... The railroad fare of delegates of this convention would
help wonderfully," she quipped.[48]

Nevertheless, Ida did enjoy meeting the "big guns," as she called them,
who were there. Attending were the AME bishops Turner and Daniel A.
Payne, the latter one of the few, besides Turner, whom Ida thought worthy
of the title. Payne was soon to become the first black president of Wilberforce University, the land for which he purchased for $10,000. Wells no
doubt also enjoyed her stay with Frances Ellen Harper, who had first become nationally known in 1854 with the publication of *Poems on Various
Subjects*, which had sold fifty thousand copies by 1878.[49] Harper, in her late
sixties, was much older than Ida, but the two writers had a background in
common. Like Wells, Harper had been orphaned at an early age and forced
to take care of herself as a young teenager. At the time Wells was visiting,
Harper was readying the publication of *Iola Leroy*, one of the earliest novels
published by an African American—and the kind of book Ida had once
dreamed of writing. Whether Harper was in any way inspired by Ida,
whose pen name was the same as the novel's protagonist, is not known. But
Iola Leroy's desire to write "a good, strong book," which could "do something of lasting service to the race," must have resonated with Ida.[50]

Wells met, too, Harper's good friend William Still, now in his seventies,
whose Philadelphia home had been a "stop" on the slave escape route known
as the Underground Railroad. Still had published an important account of
the Railroad, and he and Ida might have compared notes about his own
experience concerning the protest against the segregation of Philadelphia's
streetcars in the 1870s. Ida also "sat at the feet," as she put it in a rare attribution, of the Quaker teacher, missionary, and Oberlin graduate, Fanny
Jackson Coppin. Coppin, then in her late fifties, had been born a slave and

had had her freedom later purchased by an aunt. As a young woman she had worked as a domestic in the home of George Henry Calvert, great-grandson of Lord Baltimore, the founder of Maryland. In 1869, she had been appointed principal of the Institute for Colored Youth in Philadelphia, becoming the first black woman in the nation to head an institution of higher education. In 1881, at the age of forty-four, the puckish-faced teacher had married Levi Coppin, an AME minister (later a bishop) fifteen years her junior, and a "conductor" of the Underground Railroad. At the time Ida saw the couple, Levi was the editor of the *AME Church Review*. On Ida's last morning there, the twenty-sixth, she breakfasted with the Coppins, and afterward, took a train north to meet T. Thomas Fortune.[51]

"Well, we've been a long time getting you to New York," the rumpled New York editor remarked when he greeted her. "But now that you are here I am afraid that you'll have to stay." At first, Ida did not understand what he was talking about. But soon she learned that she would not be able to return to Memphis and that in the bat of an eye, she had become an exile from the city of the three murdered men—and the South—neither of which she would see again for thirty years.[52]

CHAPTER EIGHT

"The Truth About Lynching"

> Having destroyed my paper, had a price put on my
> life, and been made an exile from home for hint-
> ing at the truth, I felt that I owed it to myself and
> to my race to tell the whole truth now that I was
> where I could do so freely.
>
> —*Ida B. Wells*

> Miss Ida B. Wells has added her vigorous pen to
> the pugnacious quill-quivers of the *New York Age.*
> If those sneaking, cowardly, Negro-hating Mem-
> phis copperheads think they have gained anything
> by this arrangement, they are welcome to it.
>
> —*Detroit Plaindealer*

A ll hell had broken out in Memphis, Ida learned from the Associated
Press report shown to her by T. Thomas Fortune. After her May 21
editorial questioning the rape charge and the reputation of white women,
the Memphis dailies had stirred up the city with provocative words of their
own. "Those negroes who are attempting to make the lynching of individuals of their race a means for arousing the worst passions of their kind
are playing with a dangerous sentiment," the *Memphis Commercial* had

warned. The "fact that a black scoundrel is allowed to live and utter such loathsome and repulsive calumnies is evidence as to the wonderful patience of Southern whites." On the same day, the *Memphis Scimitar* (which had also recently fallen into Democratic hands) countered that "patience was not a virtue" under the circumstances. At first, assuming that J. L. Fleming, Ida's partner, had written the editorial, it opined that it was the "duty" of white men to "tie the wretch who utters such calumnies to a stake at the intersection of Main and Madison Streets and brand him in the forehead with a hot iron and perform upon him a surgical operation with a pair of tailor's shears."[1]

The menacing editorials were followed up by a meeting of "leading citizens," as Ida pointedly described them, who gathered at the city's Cotton Exchange Building where "threats of lynching were freely indulged." But the agitated men finally settled on appointing a committee to find Fleming. Ida's partner, fortunately, had been forewarned by an unnamed white Republican and had fled the city with all of his organs intact. However, the men did find Taylor Nightingale, who had chosen a bad time to be back in Memphis. Apparently unaware that he was no longer associated with the *Free Speech,* the white men whipped him with a pistol and then forced the minister at gun point to sign a letter denouncing the editorial as a slander against white women. Ida, upon hearing about the proud minister's capitulation—which also included informing his assailants that *she* owned the paper—was disappointed in Nightingale, but she also admitted that she did not know what she would have done at the point of a pistol.[2]

From New York, Ida telegrammed her attorney, B. F. Booth, to inquire about Fleming's safety and to give him Fortune's home address in Brooklyn where she could be contacted. Fleming was fine, she was told, but furiously angry with her. Ida sympathized with her distraught partner, who, for the second time in four years, was forced to abandon his possessions and livelihood; it was not clear if his hostility was due to more than his having to endure the wrath of white Memphians while she was away back east. Fleming's later comments about her revealed that he was wary of provocative rhetoric, and one wonders if they argued over the editorial. In any case, his remaining in Memphis after May twenty-first indicated that he had not expected such an explosive reaction to the editorial—and neither had Wells.[3]

And yet Ida had not been unaware of the danger. "I had bought a pistol the first thing after Tom Moss was lynched, because I expected some cowardly retaliation from the lynchers," she wrote in her autobiography. "I felt that one had better die fighting against injustice than to die like a dog or a rat in a trap. I had already determined to sell my life as dearly as possible if attacked. I felt if I could take one lyncher with me, this would even up the score a bit." But Ida had expected a confrontation long before May; and, with all that she had written before, she had not anticipated such a reaction to this particular editorial. Of course, she had been aware of what had happened to Jesse Duke in Alabama after he had written about colored Romeos and white Juliets four years before, but Ida had reason to believe that Memphians were more sophisticated about the vagaries of white womanhood.

After all, the "toughest city on the river" had a long history of "fallen" white women, prostitution, and female arrests, among both blacks and whites, for so-called public offenses. There had also been several examples, written up in the white Memphis press, of white women of standing who had absconded with black men without action being taken against them or the black community. As recently as 1888, T. D. Jackson, described by the *Memphis Daily Avalanche* as a "light-skinned" policeman of "stalwart physique" and president of the local black Republican club, was reported to have made a "lecherous" advance toward one white woman; cast verbal "indignities" at another whom he had caught in a "compromising situation"; and was in a relationship with a third who was married but "completely in his power" and a "victim" of his lust. But it was clear that the point of the article, written during the election campaign that year, was not so much to express indignation about white women and black men as to discredit the Republican Party and taxing district president, David Hadden, who had appointed Jackson.[4]

It was not until years after the *Avalanche*'s exposé that Jackson himself felt it incumbent to leave Memphis for Oklahoma, joining Taylor Nightingale (who took up the barber's trade to support himself while awaiting the opportunity to head a church) in another wave of migration after the destruction of the *Free Speech*.[5]

But clearly something had changed. Ida was receiving telegrams from Memphis informing her that her home was being watched, blacks in the community were being asked about her whereabouts, and men were posted at the train station awaiting her return. There was talk of lynching Ida in front of the courthouse and "making her face bleed." Neither Ida nor others had the slightest doubt that her being a woman would inure her from violence. The "brutal instincts of the average Memphis white man would not hesitate to assassinate a woman," Ferdinand Barnett later editorialized in the *Chicago Conservator*. Barnett's advisory also apparently applied to above-average white women. A "leading white lady," Ida learned, was heard to remark that she had been opposed to the lynching of the three men but nevertheless wished that there was some way that Wells could be returned and lynched.[6]

Although her informants were begging her not to come home, Ida did not immediately dismiss the idea of going back to Memphis—if only to save what she could of the *Free Speech*. Every "dollar I had in the world was invested" in the paper, she recalled, and of late, it had, for the first time, begun paying for itself. But Ida finally made the decision to remain in New York after learning that black men were organizing to protect her in the event of her return. The men were probably members of the Tennessee Rifles, the group that both Moss and McDowell had belonged to. The militia group had disbanded after its weapons had been confiscated in the wake of the Curve riot, but it may have reassembled to protect Ida. Wells knew that the prospective face-off "would mean more bloodshed, more widows and orphans," and though she did not mention it in her writings, Ida must have also been concerned about her sister Lily, still in Memphis.[7]

Still in New York on May 27, Ida learned that Memphis's same "leading citizens" had entered the vacated offices of the *Free Speech*, destroyed the type and furnishings, and left a note behind saying that anyone attempting to publish the paper again would be punished by death. What was left was placed in the hands of the sheriff, and the outfit was sold to satisfy creditors. As Ida lamented upon hearing the news, what had taken years to build through "numberless sacrifices" had been destroyed—"as if had never been."[8]

But Ida's words long outlived the printing press of the *Free Speech*. Many black weeklies, including hers, were published on Saturdays, and by the twenty-eighth a number of them had their own response to Ida's editorial. "Sixty colored men were lynched in as many consecutive days by the white South is a disgrace to this nation," opined the *Star of Zion*, which urged that blacks continue to leave Memphis. From Chicago, the home of the Haymarket Riot, Frederick Douglass, who was visiting there and who had recently resigned his diplomatic post as minister resident and consul general to the Republic of Haiti and chargé d'affaires for the Dominican Republic, averred that "If the southern outrages on the colored race continue, the Negro will become a chemist. Other men besides anarchists can be goaded into the throwing and making of bombs."[9]

In the same period, twelve hundred blacks met in Columbus, Ohio, to protest the recent outrages in the South. They called for African Americans across the country to set aside May 31 as a day of prayer, fasting, and resolve to agitate and organize for mutual protection. The published petition was signed by an unprecedented array of more than a hundred leaders who had diverse political views, including Booker T. Washington, Albion Tourgée, Isaiah Montgomery, T. Thomas Fortune, and Frances Ellen Harper. Smaller demonstrations took place as well. A student at Atlanta University, James Weldon Johnson, who later became a noted novelist, successful diplomat, and leading NAACP official, won the prize oration at the school for a speech that advocated that blacks acquire education and wealth but that they not submit to oppression. "Half of the suffering of the race would be eradicated," he averred, if Negroes fought lynching by physical resistance.[10]

White progressives were also becoming more opinionated about lynching. The *Cleveland Gazette* reprinted one of Albion Tourgée's "Bystander" columns from the *Chicago Daily Inter-Ocean,* which noted that among the 121 lynchings the year before, seven colored men had been burned alive in the South; one of them was flayed to death and another had been mutilated, then disjointed and tortured for two hours before his death. The Ohio-born Tourgée had been a Union soldier and later a judge in the North Carolina State Supreme Court during Reconstruction. By the 1890s, he was a well-known writer, the leading representative of progressive whites on the race question, and influential in reform, religious, and Republican circles. In that same pivotal month of May, Tourgée had helped to persuade a general conference of Northern Methodists to call upon the press, the church, and the government to use "all legitimate authority and influence to put an end to the injustice and wrong" committed against blacks, who were being victimized by "violence, mob law, lynching and other outrages against humanity." Soon after the Methodist pronouncement, the Congregationalists and Northern Presbyterians also passed resolutions to condemn lynching. Tourgée also had a hand in persuading the Republican convention in Minneapolis to protest lynching, and President Harrison subsequently resolved to prohibit the practice in the new territories.[11]

The focus on lynching that spring had also affected another bastion of white progressivism, the *Independent,* an influential Congregationalist journal out of New York. The weekly had earlier editorialized that lynchings were decreasing as the education and achievements of blacks in the South had been rising, but now questioned the assumption and opined that blacks could not be expected to "always refrain from protecting themselves. Who would?" The editorial was entitled "Barbarism."[12]

The torrent of criticism put the white southern clergy, in particular, on the defensive. Oscar Fitzgerald, the Southern Methodist bishop who had earlier called blacks an obstacle to Christian reform, responded that he thought it was "notable" that "in all of the spasms of indignation against the Southern people . . . no word of sympathy has been spoken for the women victims." Fitzgerald's charge drew a riposte from the *Independent* that the bishop had relied on the occurrences of rape for his argument, but that according to the *Chicago Tribune,* only a third of the 728 blacks lynched in the last eight years were accused of the crime. Others had been lynched for other offenses, including miscegenation, burglary, quarrels with white men, and murder.[13]

Such protests by white liberal opinion-makers were encouraging, but their criticism tended to hinge on the breakdown of law and order and on questions about the ability of the South to reform itself. Few indicated any regard or defense of the race as a race in a period when spurious assessments of blacks had the imprimatur of elite, northern universities and academic organizations. No lesser an authority than Daniel G. Brinton—a Yale graduate, University of Pennsylvania professor, and the soon-to-be president of both the International Congress of Anthropology and the American Association for the Advancement of Science—had opined in 1890 that African Americans had regressed to being "midway between the Orang-utang and the European white." The "scientific fact" led the Brown University sociologist Lester Ward to conclude that blacks were impelled by the "imperious voice of nature" to rape white women and thus "raise his race to a little higher level." No wonder, as Brinton concluded, white women had no "holier duty" than to maintain the purity of the white race—and men, of course, had no higher duty than to protect them.[14]

African Americans may not have believed the most trenchant conclusions of social scientists, but too many were still convinced that lynching was a class rather than a race issue. As late as 1892, the *Christian Index,* which had condemned lynching and for which Ida had written, was nevertheless convinced that it was the "scum of both races which meet, drink, gamble and propagate corruption . . . the negro is always kindly treated by the intelligent white people but meets his bitterest enemy among the lower classes of the race."[15]

MEMPHIS'S "INTELLIGENT WHITE people" called a meeting in June to stem the new unrest caused by the destruction of Ida's paper. This time both blacks and whites came together for the purpose of restoring interracial "harmony and friendly feeling," according to the *Commercial*. Sixty of the "most prominent citizens in town and nearly an equal number of negroes attended," the paper reported with editor Carmack's penchant for racial insult.[16]

Many of the black Memphians who were at the meeting were men whom Ida knew well. They included the teachers Granville G. Marcus (whom she had once dated) and James Lott, whom she had lived near when she was staying at Mrs. Powell's place; C. A. Thompson, Ida's oration tutor, was also there, as was her former school principal, Benjamin Sampson. Also present were the lawyers who had represented her, Thomas Cassels and B. F. Booth, the latter of whom had arranged the sale of her Holly Springs home and who appeared to be her main source of information while she was in New York.

The spokesman for the group was Ida's once beloved minister, Benjamin Imes, who had earlier written an editorial in the *Langston City Herald* that pled for blacks to condemn lawlessness and rape by both blacks and whites alike, to appeal to justice in language that reflected the "the highest reason, the sense of honor, the love of country," and for blacks to remember that "the white man knows that there is a common welfare of the races." The editorial, entitled "Reason vs Violence," ran in the *Langston City Herald* on May 28, the day after Wells's paper was destroyed.[17]

Imes read a position paper before the attendees of the June meeting in Memphis. In it he applauded the fact that the gathering indicated that the "long and painful silence" of representative white men had come to an end. He assured them that Ida's editorial did not represent the view of the "respectable" Negroes in Memphis who should not be tar-brushed by Ida's provocations. Just as "not all Irishman were responsible for the death of Lord Cavendish" and "not all Germans were anarchists," Imes said in one of his most colorful lines, the black community at large should not be blamed for the "recent offensive utterances of the *Free Speech*." In his reasonable manner, the minister went on to criticize mob law, but also stated his "abhorrence" of that "basest of crimes, so continuously repeated of late: the attack by violence of womanly virtue and safety." But reminding the group of the "unassailable" record of black carriage drivers, house servants, and porters "who are constantly in the service of white ladies and their families," he pointed out that the perpetrators of rape belonged to "the very lowest and most vicious element of the negro race." They should not be confused with the blacks of good character, many of whom were continuing to leave Memphis. The last statement was confirmed by a white participant who grievously recited how "an old negress" in his household, whom his children called "mammy," had recently fled to Oklahoma.[18]

But Reverend J. C. Waters of Collins Chapel, one of Moss's eulogists, offered the less temperate observation that the attacks on black womanhood were also unwarranted. If they continue, he said, "let us go away and take our immoral women with us. Our wives and daughters are as dear to us as those of the white people." Waters continued to make another point that cut to the chase. The "good people of the community might band themselves together in 'a law and order league' for the detection and oppression of criminals of both races. Certainly the colored people cannot always live on the edge of a volcano as they do now," he concluded. The suggestion was dismissed, but it may have been the origins of a subsequent, white-only law-and-order league (which ironically later pushed for Judge DuBose's indictment on corruption charges).

The response of the whites, however, tested the limits of reconciliation by making it clear what was required to maintain harmonious race relations. General Luke Wright, a former Confederate soldier, son of a former state Supreme Court judge, and a corporate lawyer who co-owned the *Commercial*, concurred with Imes's point that each race should condemn its own evildoers, but also reminded black representatives that their people must accept the fact that whites were the dominant race in Memphis, and that "colored people should submit gracefully to the situation." In return, whites would "assume the responsibility to see that no colored shall be ill treated," he generously added.[19]

The infamous Judge DuBose, however, added the caveat that the Curve incident had demonstrated that too many "respectable" blacks refused to cooperate with authorities. "I know that all the people in the community were not implicated in shooting down the officers," he said, "but at the same time I do not want the better element of the colored race to sympathize with those lawless people of their race." DuBose's views reflected that of an earlier June 4 editorial in the *Scimitar* in which he said it was "truly unfortunate" that "well-bred Negroes had to pay . . . the penalty of the offenses committed by the baser sort, but this is the way of the world."[20] Even for Imes, DuBose had gone too far with that one. Blacks were not supporting criminals but were "shocked" when the daily papers upheld the lynchers, he said.

Among the responses recorded that week to the meeting was an obsequious letter written by Benjamin K. Sampson. In it, the black educator expressed the gratitude of the colored people to the whites who "so nobly represented the best people of our Southland." A thousand "grateful hearts will bless you for your own words of encouragement and counsel in directing the spirit of that meeting," he assured. "It has always been my firm belief that the colored people have many warm friends among the intelligent Christian white people in the South," he continued, singling out those especially in Memphis. "We feel the weight of our present responsibility resting upon us to encourage harmony and good will, and to prove ourselves well deserving to our white friends." On June 12—four days before Ida had called for a regional conference in Memphis to discuss emigration—the *Appeal-Avalanche* published a resolution drawn up by the group that called the triple lynching "a flagrant offense" against law, and against "civilization and humanity" that "should not be excused."[21] However, there was no apology given for the destruction of the *Free Speech,* or any promise to prosecute the murderers.

By then, the black weeklies had caught up to the news about the *Free Speech*'s destruction. "Had such a thing happened in absolute Russia," commented the *Indianapolis Freeman,* "where free speech and free opinion are conditions to be dreamed of, very little surprise could be expressed, but in free America, where is the palliation to be found?" The *Detroit Plaindealer* called Ida, "Iola, the dauntless" for standing up for the race; the *American Citizen* said that she was "brave." The *Indianapolis Freeman* cited Ida's devotion to her people—though it worried that too much praise was being heaped on "one single little woman."[22]

Ida, of course, did not see her role in such diminutive or singular terms, and she viewed the resolution, hatched between black and white elites in Memphis, as a travesty against the race that could not remain unchallenged. She couldn't have been happy that the *Independent* commented approvingly about the resolution—though it also noted that whites took great pains to demonstrate their superiority. Benjamin Sampson's servile capitulation must have been especially maddening. But whether Ida knew it or not, the Kortrecht principal was under tremendous pressure. He was being "persecuted" as he wrote in a private memorandum attached to the biographical circulars requested by Oberlin, his alma mater, from its alumnae. "Persecuted because one of my pupils without my consent or knowledge made a speech against lynching . . . Persecuted because I organized the People's Grocery which was destroyed . . . by a mob."[23]

FOLLOWING THE EVENTS from her vantage point in New York, a new thought occurred to Ida. As she explained in her autobiography, when she had first learned about the reactions to her editorial, she had thought that she had underestimated the degree to which white southerners, Memphians included, were willing to go in their "chivalrous defense of white womanhood." But now, she began to see the situation differently. Chivalry, she concluded, was not the spark that had conflagrated into the destruction of her paper. The real provocation, she wrote, was that "For the first time in their lives the white people of Memphis had seen earnest, united action by Negroes which upset economic and business conditions. They had thought the excitement would die down; that Negroes would forget and become, as before, the wealth producers of the South—the hewers of wood and drawers of water, the servants of white men," she continued. "But the excitement kept up, the colored people continued to leave, business remained at a standstill, and there was still a dearth of servants to cook their meals and wash their clothes and keep their homes in order, to nurse their babies and wait on their tables, to build their houses and do all classes of laborious work. . . . In casting about for the cause of all this restlessness and dissatisfaction the leaders concluded that the *Free Speech* was the disturbing factor. They were right," Ida concluded. "They felt that the only way to restore 'harmony between the races' was to get rid of the *Free Speech*. Yet they had to do it in such a way as not to arouse further antagonism in the Negroes themselves who were left in town, whom they wished to placate."[24] In other words, her editorial about white women was merely used as an excuse to put into action what had been long planned. Now Ida prepared to set the record right with an editorial in the *New York Age*.

Because the paper had a significant white as well as black readership, the historical moment dictated that she write not a simple protest but the first comprehensive study of the practice that spoke to its true motives, meaning, and how it reflected not the moral failings of blacks but that of a culture gripped by white supremacy. Moreover, her narrative would have to challenge current race theory and undermine class assumptions in a way that was attentive to the era's emphasis on scientific observation, logic, and documented fact. And if Ida was to succeed in mobilizing both white progressives and blacks to action, her words had to have the power of the classical singers that she so admired: words that appealed to the heart as well as the mind.

As she saw it, there was a core element that had the power to unravel the race analysis of whites and the class analysis of blacks. Both conspired to justify the myth of the black rapist that, as Wells wrote, "closed the heart, stifled the conscience, warped the judgment and hushed the voice of press and pulpit on the subject of lynch law."[25] For Ida, teasing out the implications of the often denied or hidden reality of consensual relationships between black men and white women supplied that element. It at once challenged the "bestiality" of the race, the necessity to chivalrously defend the purity of pure white womanhood against blacks of all classes, and the representation of the New South as articulated by its apologists.

On June 25, the *New York Age* carried a seven-column article on its front page with the banner headline: "The Truth About Lynching." It was signed, "Exiled."[26]

Wells began by throwing down an unmistakable gauntlet. "Mr. [Jesse] Duke, before leaving Montgomery, signed a card disclaiming any intention of slandering Southern white women," Wells wrote, referring to the editor who had written about white Juliets and colored Romeos four years before. "The editor of the *Free Speech* has no disclaimer to enter, but asserts that there are many white women in the South who would marry colored men if such an act would not place them at once beyond the pale of society and within the clutches of the law. The miscegenation laws of the South only operate against the legitimate union of the races; they leave the white man free to seduce all the colored girls he can, but it is death to the colored man who yields to the force and advances of a similar attraction in white women. White men lynch the offending Afro-American, not because he is a despoiler of virtue, but because he succumbs to the smiles of white women."[27]

Wells backed up her assertions by giving specific examples that were widely known and routinely published in the white press. Provocatively beginning with examples from Memphis in a section called "The Black and White of It," she recounted the story about the wife of a leading Memphis physician, who was of "good social standing" and who, in the winter of 1885–86, left her husband and children to run away with her black coachman. More recently, soon after Fleming had been run out of town "by the guardians of the honor of Southern white women," as Ida snarled, a young girl who lived on Poplar Street was discovered to be in love with "a handsome mulatto." The girl stole her father's money to send the young man out of harm's way. The girl had since joined him in Chicago, Wells told her readers.[28]

Wells also included the story about Sarah Clark, who loved a black man and lived openly with him. When she was charged with miscegenation, she avoided the penitentiary by swearing that she was not a white woman and was thus allowed to continue her relationship undisturbed. Who was black and who was white, in other words, was determined by social circumstance, not biology.

A similar conclusion could be reached in Wells's narrative about a Mrs. Marshall of Natchez, Mississippi, who Ida identified as the *creme de la creme* of society." Marshall employed a married black coachman for several years and gave birth to a suspiciously dark child, but one still light enough to attribute the color to a brunette ancestor. But a second child was unmistakably black and upon the "diagnosis," the coachman took his family west, never to return. Mrs. Marshall, too, was sent away in "deep disgrace."[29]

Such women were the Juliets in Ida's editorial, but there also were Delilahs. For example, there was the case of Mrs. Underwood, a minister's wife, who accused a black man of forcing his way into her house and raping her while the husband was away at a Prohibition Party meeting. The black man, who was married and named William Offet, denied the rape charge in court, saying that he had had a reciprocal and long-standing sexual relationship with the woman. But Mrs. Underwood's white female credibility trumped his, and Offet was sent to the penitentiary for fifteen years. Eventually, however, the guilt got the best of the prohibitionist's wife, and she confessed that the black man was telling the truth. When asked why she had lied, she gave no less than three reasons: she was afraid that the neighbors had seen her, that she might have contracted a venereal disease, or that she might have become pregnant. There were thousands of such explanations throughout the South, Wells assured her readers.[30]

Finally, there were the more gruesome scenarios like that of Ed Coy, who was "burned alive" in Texarkana, Texas, in January of 1892—the subject of the investigation by Albion Tourgée and the *Chicago Inter-Ocean*. The white woman who had sealed his fate was discovered to be the wife of a "drunkard," and her own reputation was a dubious one. Moreover, it was publicly known and reported that she had been intimate with the black man for at least a year. Nevertheless, Coy was captured and soon found his oil-soaked body bound to a tree. Just before he was set alight, he asked his lover if she could burn him after they had "been sweethearts" for so long. The answer, evidently, was affirmative.[31]

The story of Coy's immolation also highlighted the fact that lynching was not just a function of the chivalrous protection of southern belles—the scenario often depicted in the southern white press. The circle had come to include the "Honah" of all white women, "the *demi-monde* included," Ida sniffed. And yet, the word of such women still had the power of life and death over men. Wells also told the story of the Memphian and furniture dealer Moses Strickland who was threatened with lynching when he was discovered in the room of a white woman. The only reason he wasn't murdered, Wells explained, was because the white woman told his would-be assassins that he was there to hang curtains in her room.[32]

And who were the men not only permitting but excusing, authorizing, and even participating in these lynchings? They were the South's alleged "best men"—the class deemed by the North and South to be left to their own designs in running the South's business and race relations. Reiterating T. Thomas Fortune's earlier observations, Wells pointed out that the source of the threats to her own life and the destruction of the *Free Speech* had been Memphis's "leading citizens," who had gathered in "their leading business center" not the "lawless element upon which the deviltry of the South is usually saddled." Ida also noted that the chivalrous protectors who had murdered Ed Coy and had been *tut-tutting* about white females were themselves "reputed fathers of mulatto children." Such men were "notorious" for their "preference for Afro-American women," Wells pronounced, and they were not honorable at all; they were violators of black women and, moreover, were no longer content to stand back to let the mob do its work—they were the mob.[33]

Wells made the miscegenation at the hands of whites not simply a complaint but evidence that it was part and parcel of the larger race issue that was also informed by gender and sexuality. As such, it had to be engaged as a "vital phase of the 'race question'" that should instigate an "earnest inquiry as to the best methods by which religion, science, law and political power may be employed to excuse injustice, barbarity, and crime done to people because of race and color." There can be no possible belief," she concluded, "that these people were inspired by a consuming zeal to vindicate God's law against miscegenationists."[34]

Wells made white women and black men more than mere abstractions in her editorial, and she did the same for black women who, in her recital, became full and fully entitled subjects. It was they who were the real victims of lust. Wells wrote about the case of a black woman in Baltimore, who was gang-raped by three white "ruffians" when she was out walking with her black escort. In some ways, the role of black men in this particular incident, as Wells recited it, was emblematic. The escort was held by one of the white men and was presumably forced to helplessly witness the assault of his companion. Nevertheless, the white men, who had had a black attorney defending them, were exonerated.[35]

To further make her point, Wells made a new linkage between lynching and rape by writing of an incident in Nashville where a black man, guilty only of visiting a white woman, was taken out of jail with "the police and militia" standing by and dragged down the street where the mob plunged knives into him at every step. Finally, the man, named Grizzard, was swung out on a bridge, and as he tried to climb up the stanchions his hands were cut to pieces. At the time, when these "civilized whites were announcing their determination 'to protect their wives and daughters,'" Wells wrote, a white man was in the same jail for raping eight-year-old Maggie Reese, a "little Afro-American girl" who suffered injuries that "ruined her for life." The white perpetrator served six months and later became a detective in the city.[36]

Ida also recited cases of the lynching of black women, including that of Eliza Woods, the hanging of a fifteen-year-old girl in Louisiana, and the mob murder of another black woman in Hollendale, Mississippi. Wells, using her own syntax for emphasis, also gave the example of the "legal?" hanging of thirteen-year-old Mildrey Brown of South Carolina. The young girl was convicted, on circumstantial evidence, of poisoning an infant of the family for whom she worked. If Brown had been white, Wells contended, she would not have been so punished—even if it had been proven "unmistakably" that she was guilty. Within this context, Ida took on the southern Methodist bishop Oscar Fitzgerald, who had chided the *Independent* and northern critics for expressing too little sympathy for the [white] female victims of the "unspeakable crime." "What about the black female victims of the crime?" Ida asked, challenging the limit of the bishop's chivalry by leading her readers to assume rather than question the social entitlement of black women.[37]

Two other sections of her editorial, "The Malicious and Untruthful White Press" and "The South's Position," made the point that whites themselves saw through the thick mists of a long-gone chivalry and knew the truth about the goings-on in the South. For one thing, there was on record public admissions about the fear that whites, not blacks, were the ones sinking into "criminal depravity." Wells quoted A. S. Colyar in the *Nashville American* on this point. Coylar was its one-time publisher, the leader of the municipal reform movement in Nashville and the director and general counsel of the Tennessee Coal, Iron and Railroad Company, which leased convicts from the state.[38] Seemingly unaware of his own complicity in the state of affairs in the South, he worried about the ever-more frequent appearance of the mob that goes "into town where everybody knows them [and] sometimes under the gaze of the governor, in the presence of the courts, in the presence of the sheriff and his deputies, in the presence of the entire police force, take out the prisoner, take his life, often with fiendish glee, and often with acts of cruelty and barbarism which impress the reader with a degeneracy rapidly approaching savage life." That "degeneracy," Colyar further complained, was enabled by the fact that the crime was often committed with impunity. "The State, in its majesty, through its organized life, makes but one record, but one note, and that a criminal falsehood, 'was hung by persons to the jury unknown,'" he concluded. Unchecked, Ida confirmed, the "mob spirit" was growing, and it was not confined to the rural backwaters of the South. "It has left the out-of-the-way places where ignorance prevails" and "stakes in broad daylight in large cities, the centers of civilization, and is encouraged by the 'leading citizens' and the press."[39]

Careful not to claim that no black man was guilty of rape, Ida instead was making the case that the South was using the charge against black men to hide its own deficiencies, particularly from the eyes of the suspicious and investor-laden North. In another section of her editorial, entitled the "New Cry," she sought to explain the phenomenon. First, she made an important distinction between what had driven racial violence during the Reconstruction era and what was happening at the turn of the century. Lynching in the New South was not on the same continuum that saw the emergence of the Ku Klux Klan and the racial violence of the earlier post-war years. The latter was a direct response to northern Reconstruction made possible by the enfranchisement of black men. To rectify the Radical Republican domination of the South, even "honest white men," as Wells put it, "conceded" the necessity to intimidate black voters—many of them "ignorant" newly freed slaves. When, in the midst of the struggle, the federal government abandoned blacks to the "tender mercies" of the South, "thoughtful Afro-Americans urged the race to sacrifice political rights for the sake of peace" and in the "honest belief that the race should fit itself for government." But it was the white South, which for all of its external reforms, could not change its hateful, violent ways. "To palliate this record (which grows worse as the Afro-American grows more intelligent) and excuse some of the most heinous crimes that ever stained the history of a country," Wells asserted, "the South is shielding itself behind the plausible screen of defending the honor of its women."[40]

It was a relatively simple point with complex implications about authority, credibility, motive, and the very legitimacy of the New South's cultural representation of both blacks and itself. The sense of chivalry behind the rationales for lynching, Wells was claiming, might have been sincere, but it was inauthentic in a modern age. Moreover, apologists, like Oscar Fitzgerald, and especially the white southern press knew it to be so. In other words, the late-nineteenth-century rise of the "black beast," as later commentators concluded, might have been the product of a tortured imagination and the need to control blacks, served to ease the aching sexual tensions and moral contradictions of the industrial age, kept restless white women too fearful and obedient to their protectors to wander into the public sphere, and helped to bring whites of opposing class interests into a one-party political system. But for Wells, the vicious stereotype in the southern press—the primary publicists for the New South—was largely constructed for the consumption of the North. For, as whites knew, beneath the humming mills, signs of material progress, and insistence about the superiority of Anglo-Saxon civilization, the New South wasn't new at all; it was the Old South, replete with its past promiscuities of thought, action, greed, and hatred.

Wells next looked at lynching from the perspective of logic and documented evidence. Charges of rape, she reasoned, just didn't comport with the statistics, a methodology that belonged to the modern age and that should have plied its way through the misconstructions and lies. Both the *Chicago Tribune* and the *Independent* had published lynching statistics that, as she reiterated, showed the rise in lynching, as well as a breakdown of the 728 lynchings of the last eight years, in which only *"one-third* [of the victims] had even been *charged* with rape, to say nothing of those who were innocent of the charge."[41]

Finally, although much of Ida's own argument was aimed at opinion-makers in the North, some of her most compelling words were directed to the black community. In the final section of her editorial "Self-Help," she added new meaning to the idea that the "Afro-American can only do for himself what no one else can do for him." Ida's purpose here was to challenge the traditional attitudes of blacks who (now unlike her) still believed in the old formula that racial uplift, social harmony, and individual achievement alone would inexorably lead to the restoration of their rights. Their single-minded devotion to "general education and financial strength" were worthy goals, but they were not agents of change. For in the white supremacist world she had described, no good deed went unpunished.[42]

Indeed, the old social contract reached with progressive paternalists with its idea of mutual obligations was dead, she insisted. For the more blacks advanced, the more they were subjected to "legal(?) disenfranchisement, Jim Crow laws, and violence." And despite all that had been achieved, "No other news goes out to the world save that which stamps us as a race of cut-throats, robbers, and lustful wild beasts." Blacks had to work proactively to engender a "healthier public sentiment," and a supported independent black press was the "best instrument" for truth. The "people must know before they can act," Ida wrote, and citing a number of instances in which blacks met their deaths because of flimsy evidence, she called for the race to provide resources for the investigative and fact-finding missions.[43] In other words, what had to be won in the late nineteenth century was a modern-era public relations war, not just a moral one.

Self-help also meant an activist strategy that no longer depended solely on elites, but looked toward an intraclass insurgency in which the laboring class of blacks was central. "To Northern capital and Afro-American labor the South owes its rehabilitation," she continued. "If labor is withdrawn, capital will not remain. The Afro-American is thus the backbone of the South," Ida concluded, and a "thorough knowledge and judicious exercise of this power in lynching localities could many times effect a bloodless revolution." Calling for civil disobedience, Wells went on to demonstrate the effectiveness of the Oklahoma emigration by black Memphians, the Memphis trolley car strike, and a similar action among black Kentuckians who stayed off the trains in the wake of the passage of a separate car law there. Wells estimated that the railway companies in the latter state lost one million dollars in revenue. The "white man's dollar is his god," Ida averred, and the "appeal to the white man's pocket has ever been more effectual than all the appeals ever made to his conscience."[44]

But if civil disobedience was not enough, Wells made no hesitation to call for armed self-defense, for "nothing was to be further gained by sacrifice of manhood and self respect," she wrote. Citing examples from Oklahoma, she noted that the only times blacks avoided scheduled lynchings was when they were armed and prepared to protect themselves. "The lesson this teaches and which every Afro-American should ponder well, is that a Winchester rifle should have a place of honor in every black home," she said, "and it should be used for that protection which the law refuses to give. When the white man who is always the aggressor knows he runs as great a risk biting the dust every time his Afro-American victim does, he will have greater respect for Afro-American life." On the other hand, the "more the Afro-American yields and cringes and begs, the more he has to do so, the more he is insulted, outraged, lynched."[45]

"THE TRUTH ABOUT Lynching" sought to leave the old Victorian beliefs behind, in which the characteristics of race, class, and gender were fixed by immutable laws. In her universe, it was white women who were sexualized, black women victimized; it was white men who were feral and barbaric, black men, successful and sentimental. But her juxtaposition added up to more than a petulant inversion of racial roles and characteristics. When Wells counseled blacks that wealth and social advancement were not agents of change in themselves, she was laying the groundwork for protest movements in a post-Victorian world where conflict had its place, where progress was not inevitable without political protest and action, and where language, not natural law, defined the meaning of race.

In order for Wells to follow the logic of lynching to its ultimate conclusions, she herself had had to take a deliberate flight from the radical innocence that was at the heart of Victorian thought. "It is with no pleasure I have dipped my hands in the corruption here exposed," she told her readers.[46] Ida replaced the language of gentility with reality and dispensed with the "false delicacy" of "the "unspeakable crime." She was one of the few women reformers who actually used the word *rape*, and had learned to do so without apology.

Wells understood the radical implications of her message and was prepared to endure the consequences even if, as she said, "the heavens might fall." But she had made up her mind that her campaign, wherever it took her, was her calling and that she would see it through. It was the determination of a woman who was indeed "dauntless," as the black press characterized her. It was also the determination of a woman whose campaign against lynching fit perfectly with her own leadership aspirations and emotional makeup. As a southerner-in-exile, she possessed an authority that gave her words more weight than those of northern leaders. The "outrage" of lynching matched her inner storm; and the blood-libel horror of the crime gave Wells a wide berth of expression for her moral indignation and anger. Ida's crusade to tell the truth about lynching gave her the means to reorder the world and her and the race's place within it. Once defamed herself, now she would expose the lies that "sullied" the race's name and restore it. Somebody "must show that the Afro-American race is more sinned against than sinning," wrote Wells, who had found the vehicle of her destiny, "and it seems to have fallen on me to do so."[47]

CHAPTER NINE

The Loveliest Lynchee Was Our Lord

"I saw them burn the nigger, didn't I Mamma?"
"Yes, darling, you saw them burn the nigger."

*—Overheard conversation between an eight-year-old
and her mother after the lynching of Henry Smith*

[The white man in the South] had "the repulsive
suspicion . . . that he might be slipping into bestiality."

—W. J. Cash

T. Thomas Fortune had published a special ten-thousand-copy run of "The Truth About Lynching" in the June 25 edition of the *New York Age*. As Ida had hoped, the Bluff City reeled from her editorial, and any armistice that may have been declared quickly wilted. "The colored people have grown indignant," huffed the *Appeal-Avalanche*, reporting on an "indignation meeting" of representative "colored folk," who came together to protest Wells's editorial from exile. Imes and others publicly disapproved Ida's "stirring up, from week to week, this community," and "the spirit of strife" that followed the *New York Age* wherever it was read. There must have been a good deal of strife. One thousand copies were sold in the streets of Memphis alone. Now even moderates like Imes, despite his criticism of Ida, found it difficult to remain in the city. While the actual reason for his leaving for Knoxville before the year ended—or for his subsequent nervous breakdown—is unknown, the events in Memphis probably hastened both.[1]

But in other quarters, Ida was hailed for uncovering "a chapter of southern life which cannot be gainsayed or denied," in the words of the *Topeka Call*, and she was catapulted onto the same stage as other nationally recognized black figures. "Before her audience was a multitude," commented Monroe Majors in his book *Noted Negro Women,* "now it is the nation." In late September, Wells received a hero's welcome at the Afro-American Press Association meeting in Philadelphia. But for Ida, the familiar kudos of her being "unique and inimitable" and "brilliant" wasn't enough. Following up on what she had proposed in her editorial, Ida insisted that the editors put their money where their resolutions were. Funds were needed for a real campaign: for travel, publishing, and on-site investigations by professionals like the Pinkerton detective agency. By the press meeting's end, a resolution was adopted to raise funds for an antilynching campaign. Ida was elected treasurer.[2]

AFTER THE MEETING, Wells returned to her home-in-exile at 395 Gold Street, in Brooklyn, where, cast adrift again, she tried to keep her most despondent emotions at bay. Despite all that had happened in Memphis, Ida felt terribly homesick in a place like Brooklyn. Her new city was a sprawling behemoth with more than 795,000 residents, and yet its black population was only ten thousand—a third of the number back home. Gold Street, located in a section called Vinegar Hill, was at the far northeastern tip of the city. The mostly working-class neighborhood, made up primarily of Irish, Lithuanians, and Italians, with a smattering of blacks, reflected the large foreign-born population in a city where only 28 percent were native-born whites of native-born parents.[3]

But Ida would have also forced herself to see the brighter side of her situation. Her living quarters were in close proximity to those of T. Thomas Fortune and his wife, Carrie; Jerome Peterson, the coeditor and publisher of the *Age;* and T. McCants Steward, Fortune's lawyer. Thanks to the New

York editor—and her own resourcefulness—she was situated as well as one could expect under the circumstances. Ida had managed to get her *Free Speech* subscription list smuggled out of Memphis and she had traded it to the editor for a one-fourth interest in the *Age*. While it is doubtful that the exchange provided much income—the New York paper's poor finances forced Fortune to reduce its pages from eight to four in November—the business arrangement also included Ida's being paid a correspondent's salary for the two *Age* columns she wrote each week under the heading of "Iola's Southern Field."[4]

ONE OF HER earliest articles took special delight in informing her readers about a friend who had managed to escape the lynchers' grasp after the shootout at the People's Grocery. He was the young physician J. B. Elbert, who was the godfather of Moss's daughter, Maurine, and the fiancé of Marinda Cooper, the daughter of Florence Cooper, Betty Moss's sister. Elbert had hidden Isaiah Johnson, the black man who was wounded after shooting one of the deputies and for a time had eluded authorities. When Johnson was caught, however, he confessed that it was Elbert who had aided him. The vigilantes then set out to get Elbert who, as Ida noted, would have been the fourth man lynched but for the fact that he had gotten a heads-up about the situation and had managed to get a late-night train out of Memphis. In the column, Ida triumphantly noted that she had just received a wedding invitation from Elbert and Cooper, who planned to marry in Indianapolis in November; Betty Moss and her children also moved to that city.[5]

In addition to keeping her readers informed about the goings-on below the Mason-Dixon line, Ida wrote articles comparing race relations in the North and South, and occasionally about Brooklyn's cultural activities. As Wells discovered, though she was certainly freer to express her opinions in the North, racial prejudice was alive and well there. In the 1890s, housing discrimination was a big issue in New York City, prompted by fears that property values would decrease once blacks, perceived to be less upwardly mobile and ambitious, moved into a neighborhood. But, at least, two sides of a story were sometimes reported. The discrimination issue prompted a *New York Times* reporter to investigate and he was startled to find African Americans who lived in brownstones, employed white servants, and rode in carriages driven by liveried coachmen in the city. Of course, as in Memphis and elsewhere, such blacks were exceptions, as the overwhelming majority of African American men and women were in low-wage menial and service occupations. But Ida saw a difference in the plight of black southerners and black northerners—the latter of whom were edged out of many forms of work by labor unions that were more active there. As a result, Ida observed, while blacks in the South were restricted in many "individual exertions," they were not excluded from many of the section's "remunerative trades and vocations," as they were in the North.[6]

Ida's ennui must have also been somewhat relieved by the cultural life in New York City and especially Brooklyn (a separate city from New York until 1898). Her celebrity and association with Fortune gave her instant cachet with the activist and literary circles that belonged to a plethora of lyceums that featured lectures, concerts, discussions, and in some instances, lending libraries. The weekly meetings of the Brooklyn Literary Union, the Concord Literary Circle, the Progressive Literary Union, and the Star Lyceum, among others, were so well attended that the white-owned *Brooklyn Daily Eagle* concluded in 1892 that "No other group of people were fonder of literary pursuits than Afro-Americans."[7] Spurring the growth of lyceums in Brooklyn as well as other cities across the country was the heightened racial consciousness of African Americans. At a time when the "plantation-school" of fiction was rising in popularity—replete with "darkies" who spoke dialect rather than dialectically—black lyceums began promoting literature that was deemed valuable for its power to redefine and enlighten African Americans.[8]

Ida had been invited to speak on "Afro-American Literature" at the Concord Literary Circle to open the lyceum season there and drew to its spacious lecture room in the Concord Baptist Church the largest audience that ever attended a literary meeting in that city. She was said to have "completely captivated the large and cultivated audience." Wells also spoke at what was considered the leading lyceum, the Brooklyn Literary Union of the Siloam Presbyterian Church (where Fortune was a member of the board), which had an honorary roster that included Frederick Douglass and Frances Ellen Harper. The Union's president was T. McCants Stewart, who, in addition to being Fortune's lawyer, was the founder of the first black Democratic club in Brooklyn and a member of the Brooklyn Board of Education. Through the Union, Ida met—and in fact debated—Maritcha Remond Lyons, a woman who would have an important impact on her life.[9]

The Brooklyn Literary Union debates followed strict guidelines: four disputants were limited to ten-minute presentations, after which a forty-five-minute discussion took place, followed by a negative or affirmative vote by the members. Lyons, a school principal, and fourteen years Ida's senior, proved to be a formidable opponent. Writing about the encounter, she simply noted that she had received "plaudits" for her performance, but Ida's subsequent actions indicated that the teacher had probably bested her. Wells, never one to be satisfied with past laurels and who missed few opportunities to improve herself, sought Lyons out after the engagement. She wanted the teacher to give her some lessons on public speaking.[10]

Lyons, born to a prosperous freeborn family in New York City whose home was a stop on the Underground Railroad, was the kind of older woman, like Fanny Coppin and Virginia Broughton, whom Ida pursued to learn and, one suspects, seek approval from. Lyons, too, had endured exile. Her father had lost his business in New York City's draft riots of 1863, which had claimed a thousand deaths citywide and where at least one black man was lynched, on Clarkson Street, then subsequently torched while hanging from a tree.[11] The riots, which began with protests against being conscripted into Civil War service, ended, like the Memphis riots of 1866, in the systematic destruction of black homes, institutions, and businesses— including that of the Lyons family. They subsequently moved to Providence, Rhode Island, where Maritcha first came to prominence as a teenager when she successfully sued the sole—and all-white—high school in that city after it refused to admit her.[12] By the time Ida met her, Lyons had been tapped to be the first assistant principal of a formerly all-white school, PS 83, which consolidated its pupils and teachers with the all-black PS 68 in 1893. The education board's decision to consolidate the two schools rather than build a new school for black students was due to the efforts of T. McCants Stewart, supported by the elite members of the Brooklyn Literary Union, and it marked the beginning of a series of successful challenges to board policies that sought separate schools for blacks and whites in Brooklyn.[13]

The first lesson Lyons imparted to her pupil was to "Be so familiar with your discussion that you are literally saturated with it; think, meditate and reflect, to develop all the points in logical sequence." The second rule was to learn how to "manage the voice; if thought is prolific, expression of ideas will become automatic." The tutoring sessions, Lyons recalled, were the beginning of a "valued friendship" between the two.[14]

Their relationship brought Ida into the circle of activist women in New York and Brooklyn. Among them was Sarah Garnet, who was appointed in 1863 as New York's first black public school principal and was the widow of the famous abolitionist, minister, journalist, and U.S. consul general to Liberia, Henry Highland Garnet. Wells attended and wrote up a black art exhibit that Garnet hosted in her home on fashionable De Kalb Avenue, where she was living with her recently widowed sister, Susan Smith McKinney. McKinney was an 1870 graduate of the New York Medical College for Women, the first black woman to practice medicine in New York State and the third black woman to do so in the country. The successful Dr. Susan, as her patients called her, was also an organist and chorister at the Siloam Presbyterian Church, which had one of the finest pipe organs in the city; she also played at the Bridge Street African Wesleyan AME Church, the oldest black church in Brooklyn.[15] The woman who proved to be the most important to Ida was Maritcha's close friend, Victoria Earle Matthews.

Matthews, a year older than Ida, had more in common with her than any of the others. She, too, was a journalist who rose in the profession without virtue of an elite education, and she published frequently in the *Age* as well as other black and mainstream papers. Her mother, Caroline Smith, had also been a slave in Virginia; and Victoria, one of nine children, was born a slave in Fort Valley, Georgia. Matthews's father was white and so cruel that Smith left her children with a nurse and escaped from Georgia to New York. After the war, Smith returned to Georgia to find Victoria and three other of her children in the white man's household. After "considerable legal trouble," Smith was able to regain possession of the children and bring them to New York with her. To help her family, Matthews dropped out of grammar school in the city to work as a domestic, but she continued to read and attend lectures. After marriage at the age of eighteen, Matthews began publishing short stories and newspaper articles. Ida and Victoria had something else in common: both had a prepossessing appearance; Victoria was said to have eyes that seemed to "read the very souls of men."[16]

It was Matthews's suggestion to organize a testimonial for Ida, and Lyons readily agreed. Their idea was not only to show support for Wells and to raise money to publish her *Age* editorial as a pamphlet, but also to use the occasion to bring women activists together from Philadelphia, Boston, New York City, and Brooklyn for a common cause. Very much on the minds of the two organizers was the issue of the less than cordial relations between black women in New York and those in Brooklyn. Wells offered no further insight into the women's concerns, but blacks in the two cities had a long-standing rivalry. The tension between the two groups first appeared after the draft riots of 1863, when more affluent families began abandoning New York City for Brooklyn. The trend continued in the 1890s; as soon as black New Yorkers "amass a considerable fortune, they move across the East River" into Brooklyn, observed the *New York Times*. By the later period, Brooklynites had come to see their city as a cultural mecca and a refuge from the high rents and noisy tenements of vice-ridden New York. New Yorkers in turn, perhaps defensively, had the reputation for being "cold-blooded and selfish in [their] refusal to be interested in anybody or anything who was not to the manner born, whose parents were not known, or who did not belong to their circle," Ida, who was sensitive to such slights, recalled.[17]

Lyons and Matthews had calculated, rightly, that a tribute to Wells would generate enough mutual interest for the women to overcome their differences. In fact, the idea was met with so much enthusiasm, Wells wrote in her autobiography, that soon "no house was large enough to hold those who came." Finally a committee of 250 women was appointed from both Brooklyn and New York to organize a testimonial for Wells on October 5 in Lyric Hall. Ida looked forward to the event, but with some trepidation. She was never at ease with the likes of "Brooklyn's 400" social set or their peers in New York. Morevoer, she had never made the kind of presentation that she thought was demanded.[18] Ida, apparently for the first time in her career, prepared a formal speech.

IDA ARRIVED ON the crisp October evening to find the Lyric Hall stage emblazoned with gas jets that spelled "Iola" across the back of the platform. Her pen name was also sewn onto the silk badges worn by the ushers who passed out programs designed as miniature replicas of the *Free Speech*. Friends, such as her old beau Charles S. Morris, now a minister and married to Annie Sprague, granddaughter of Frederick Douglass, were there. The "brilliant" gathering of women who attended included the Philadelphia journalists Gertrude Mossell and Frances Ellen Harper, and the gray-haired, brisk-stepping grande dame of the group, Boston's Josephine St. Pierre Ruffin. Ruffin, the widow of the Harvard-educated lawyer and former city judge George L. Ruffin, was a journalist and member of both black and interracial women's organizations.

The opening program matched the extraordinary setting with its "beautiful" program of speeches, resolutions, and music. The tribute included Sarah Garnet presenting Wells with a purse of five hundred dollars in gold pieces and a gold brooch in the shape of a pen. After being introduced by Victoria Matthews, Ida made her way to the lectern. Looking out into the audience, Wells was overwhelmed by the scene. It was "the greatest demonstration ever attempted by race women for one of their number," she later wrote. Thirty years old at the time, the realization was enough to make Ida curl up into the child within her—something she often did in situations where she felt herself at the whim of those judging her person. In her mind's eye, she saw a "solid array" of women "behind a lonely, homesick girl who was an exile because she tried to defend the manhood of the race."[19]

Nothing, not even her lessons from Maritcha Lyons, had prepared her for the well of emotion that would rise up when she recounted the lynching of her friend, the "thought of friends who were scattered throughout the country" as well as her own personal experience before an empathetic audience. Ida was astonished—"mortified"—to feel tears beginning to stream down her cheeks. A girl, she was willing to be; an emotional woman, "given to public demonstrations," she was not. "I kept saying to myself that whatever happened I must not break down," she recalled. Finally, she signaled to her hosts sitting in back of her on the platform to bring her a handkerchief. Victoria Matthews came forward with it and Ida wiped her nose and cheeks while continuing to read her speech to the end.[20]

AT THE END of Ida's talk, she received a great ovation and assurances by Charles Morris that her tears, rather than spoiling the presentation, had helped convince "cynical and selfish New York" of the seriousness of the issue.[21] Morris, the future pastor of Harlem's Abyssinian Baptist Church, had gained something of a reputation as a speaker himself. Currently he was a reader on the program of the famous Sissieretta Jones, aka "Black Patti," a singer who had performed at England's famed Covent Garden and at the White House for President Harrison. Indeed, the testimonial appeared successful in every way that its hosts had hoped. It got national coverage in the black press; even the hypercritical *Washington Bee* pronounced it as "one of the finest testimonials ever rendered by an Afro-American"—a statement that surely had blacks in the District buzzing.[22]

The event raised more than four hundred dollars beyond expenses, a sum that was subsequently added to and sufficient to publish Ida's anti-lynching *Age* editorial under the title of *Southern Horrors*. The pamphlet's dedication page acknowledged the "Afro-American women of New York and Brooklyn, whose race love, earnest zeal and unselfish effort . . . made possible its publication." The testimonial also inspired the founding of two of the country's most successful black women's clubs: the Woman's Loyal Union, led by Victoria Matthews, and the Woman's Era Club presided over by Josephine Ruffin in Boston. Ruffin subsequently arranged speaking dates for Ida in New England, and her talks in the region inspired the organization of clubs in Providence, Newport, and New Bedford. The seed planted by Ida's Lyric Hall appearance had become the "the real beginning of the club movement," Ida wrote, referring to the proliferation of clubs that led to the first national organization of African American women.[23]

However, Wells never forgave herself for her tears. At a critical moment she had failed to gain mastery over herself, her voice, and her audience. But Ida was one to learn from her mistakes and she was determined to apply the lessons that Lyons had taught her to good effect. On a subsequent occasion, Ida's mentor wrote of her "extreme satisfaction" in hearing her pupil give a clear, logical speech, without notes, that held the audience "spellbound" during the two-hour presentation.[24] Now Wells was prepared to take full advantage of the future opportunities; and opportunities began to present themselves.

IDA HAD GOTTEN the attention of Frederick Douglass, whom she had first seen at the 1889 press association meeting in Washington, D.C. In

1892, Douglass might not have been at the height of his influence gained in the years when he was a fugitive slave turned abolitionist, newspaper editor, counsel to Abraham Lincoln and subsequent presidents, diplomat, and orator of unsurpassed ability, but he was still a towering national figure, the *éminence gris* among the race men in the country. Now in his mid-seventies, Douglass, the aging but ever-alert lion—a description that reflected his fierce advocacy and long, thick, carefully brushed hair—still had an eye for cutting-edge events and those responsible for them. In the same month of the testimonial, he had written Ida about her *New York Age* editorial. "There has been no word equal to in its convincing power," he wrote. "I have spoken, but my word is feeble in comparison," he continued in his typical self-deprecating manner. "You have given us what we know and testify from actual knowledge. . . . Brave woman! you have done your people and mine a service which can never be weighed nor measured."[25]

The words were an extraordinary tribute, and Ida asked his permission to reprint the letter to serve as an introduction to her *Southern Horrors* pamphlet.[26] He granted it, giving her an imprimatur that would give her the ear of mainstream reformers. The exchange was the beginning of an important, sometimes disappointing, and mostly beneficial relationship. Ida, young enough to be his daughter, was at the beginning of her public career; Douglass, who had the stature to be her paternal guide and protector, was coming to the end of his.

HE HAD RESIGNED from his last public office, minister resident and consul general to the Republic of Haiti, and chargé d'affaires for the Dominican Republic, in June of 1891. As Douglass professed in a September 1892 interview in the *New York Age*, he was enjoying his retirement from the political demands of public life. His typical day consisted of his rising at five in the morning to walk the grounds and extensive gardens of his twenty-four-acre Maryland estate, Cedar Hill, then return to the white frame house with its music room (where he liked to play the violin), parlors, bedrooms for visitors, family, and servants. Douglass took special pride in his spacious library that featured a bas relief of Dante; an engraving of the *Amistad*'s rebel leader, Joseph Cinque; and a picture of the suffragist Elizabeth Cady Stanton, among other items. The remainder of the day was spent answering his voluminous correspondence, writing an occasional article, or reading one of his favorite authors: Shakespeare, Byron, Burns, Whittier, or Longfellow. Douglass seemed to be putting the final punctuation on his life by publishing a revised version of his 1881 autobiography, the *Life and Times of Frederick Douglass* (which carried an introduction by Josephine Ruffin's late husband, George L. Ruffin).[27]

Still, events had conspired against Douglass having the peace of mind of a retired elder statesmen or of his earning the diplomatic equivalent of an honorable discharge with commendation. His appointment to Haiti by President Harrison might have begun with visions of service to the revolutionary land of Toussaint L'Ouverture, but it had ended two years later amid bitterness and controversy. Caught in the crossfire of the controversial policy to establish an American naval base in Haiti, Douglass was made the scapegoat and ended up being criticized by both Haitian nationalists as well as U.S. officials. "Sorry to learn Haiti has made an old man out of you," Fortune wrote to Douglass, referring to not only the criticism but also Douglass's failing health that must have been exacerbated by the ordeal.[28]

As soon as Douglass's resignation was anticipated, support for him was overshadowed by a disheartening scramble to fill one of the few high-status posts that African Americans had access to. "It is generally understood that the Hon. Frederick Douglass will resign . . ." Fortune wrote on a circular he was sending to Republicans. "In the event that he does resign, I desire to succeed him."[29] Even when others reached out to Douglass, it was done in a manner that suggested he no longer had the singular stature to influence public opinion. Ferdinand L. Barnett, the editor of Chicago's *Conservator,* himself on the short list for the diplomatic post, wrote Douglass that he could get space in the *Chicago Inter-Ocean* for him to publish his side of the Haitian affair. Ferdinand was thinking specifically of the "Bystander's Column," belonging to the progressive author Albion Tourgée, whose editorials in the *Inter-Ocean* had criticized the Memphis lynching. Douglass wrote back thanking Barnett, but said that he would defend himself in the *North American Review.*[30]

Douglass had been in the Caribbean during the crucial years when the National Afro-American League was organized (he himself had unsuccessfully advocated the formation of a "National League" in 1849) and had returned home to find a new generation of blacks speaking for the race, and old Republican rivals such as John Langston (whom Douglass refused to support for his reelection to Congress from Virginia) competing for influence in the party. The emergence of Ida Wells and her campaign gave him a new sense of purpose—and perhaps some added cachet. In July, a month after Ida's *Age* editorial, Douglass published his own views on the lynching issue in the prestigious mainstream publication, the *North American Review.* Whether Douglass was asked or pursued the opportunity to write his "Lynch Law in the South," it gave him an opportunity to wax authoritatively on the issue.

Although he did not mention Ida's name in the piece, Douglass, with his usual eloquence, affirmed two of the three most controversial points in Ida's own editorials, and added several perspectives that she would subsequently use. In "Lynch Law," Douglass showed himself to be one of the few willing to stand behind the subversive idea that success (as was true for Jews in Russia and "industrious Chinese in California," he wrote), not antisocial behavior, was warranting deadly violence against blacks, and that the "best white men"—both in the prejudiced North and the violent South—had blood on their hands. The "finger of scorn in the North is correlated to the dagger of the assassin in the South," Douglass insisted.[31]

He also drew a clear correlation, and moral equivalency, between the fight against lynching with that against slavery, giving the issue a broader context and evoking the need to fight against the former with the intensity and moral purpose that the abolitionists had. His framework placed greater emphasis on how lynching, like slavery, was a fundamental wrong and that lynch law threatened the very foundations of government because it flew in the face of due process. Douglass's article also led off with an "all-eyes-were-watching" reference to the 1893 World's Columbian Exposition, due to open in Chicago, where tens of millions of visitors, many of them from abroad, were expected to view exhibits that showed the technological and social progress of the United States. "The frequent and increasing resort to lynch law," he predicted, "will not fail to attract the attention and animadversion" of visitors to the World's Fair.[32]

The biggest difference between Wells's and Douglass's perspectives was that the former abolitionist prescribed no plan of action, though his moral suasion was formidable. There was also a difference in emphasis regarding the "best white men"—whom Ida insisted did not just stoke the mob but were the mob in many cases. Finally, there was Douglass's glaring omission regarding the issue of consensual liaisons between black men and white women.

Even if he agreed with Ida's daring assessment of the latter, there was a good reason why he would rather leave the issue alone. The Haitian controversy had reawakened some sniping about Douglass marrying, in 1886, Helen Pitts—a white woman who had been his secretary when he was recorder of deeds for the District of Columbia—less than two years after the death of his first wife, Anna Murray Douglass. "Blanche Bruce and John Lynch have colored ladies for their wives and ladies of ability at that," gibed the *Washington Bee*. "No common white clerk for them."[33] The marriage also met the disapproval of most of his family, including Douglass's highly opinionated daughter, Rosetta. This period of personal turmoil also included the death of Douglass's son, Frederick, Jr., in July, a recent widower who had had a troubled marriage; problems with his grandson Charley Paul, a habitual runaway; and the precarious health of Douglass's sickly granddaughter, Annie, now married to the itinerant Charles Morris.[34]

Douglass invited Ida to his home at Cedar Hill on a number of occasions, and her visits were no doubt refreshing for the aging abolitionist. As Frederick confided to her, Ida was one of the few black women who treated Helen with respect and courtesy when she came to call. On one occasion, a well-known black woman had, upon her departure, rudely "thanked" Helen for showing her *Anna*'s house! While Ida did not hide the fact that she would have preferred Douglass to marry a woman of color, she nonetheless believed that their interracial union represented the right of choice that she was demanding in her editorials.[35]

IN LATE OCTOBER, Douglass invited Wells to give an address before his home church, Metropolitan AME, in Washington, D.C., where the press association had held its meeting in 1889. The event was well advertised in the *Bee*, which challenged Washingtonians to "outdo the ladies of Brooklyn," and Ida, glowing from her Lyric Hall success and from being sponsored by no lesser figure than Douglass, looked forward to giving her speech in the capital. But to her surprise, and to Douglass's, on the scheduled day she appeared before a near-empty auditorium. Except for Douglass himself and members of his family, few others had come to hear her. Apologizing for the city's "indifference," and no doubt more than a little angry, Douglass promised to bring Wells back to a full house in the future. Ida didn't speculate in her autobiography the reason for the poor showing, but she must have thought hard about it. "Indifference" was possible but not probable. There were other factors that better explained the turnout.[36]

For one thing, her appearance was scheduled just before what promised to be a tough election for the Republicans, and the seasonal jockeying of black politicians in the capital did not augur well for their presence at an engagement where Ida, who habitually pounded on the "Party of Lincoln," was speaking. The District was also the home of a number of black representative women who would have reason to boycott the event, including Josephine Beall Bruce, wife of the former Mississippi senator who was a favorite target of Wells's, and a number of prominent Oberlin almunae, who doubtless had social ties with their peers in Memphis: Settle, Cassels, Imes, and Sampson. The alums included Mollie Church Terrell, who now lived in Washington with her new husband, Robert; and by 1892, Mollie was making her own mark. That year she had become the first woman president of the prestigious Bethel Literary and Historical Association; and before Douglass had taken Ida under his wing, it was Mollie who had received much of the old man's attention. On one occasion he had asked her to accompany him to the White House where they met President Harrison to urge him to act against lynching. Mollie had also been deeply affected by the murder of Thomas Moss, who had been her friend too. Moss was lynched while Mollie was pregnant with her first child, and when she subsequently lost the baby, the two tragedies became linked in her mind. She reconciled the loss by believing if the fetus had survived, it might have been permanently damaged by her state of mind.[37]

BUT WHATEVER PERSONAL or political feelings Washingtonians, especially women, felt about Ida, there was also a larger issue at play. This was a period when a new generation of women was poised to enter the public sphere. As was true with the men, individuals vied for the personal influence and privileges that came with the mantle of representing the race, but there were ideological and organizational issues as well. Though Wells's courageous defense of the race was widely admired, there was less enthusiasm in many quarters about her rhetoric and strategies that challenged traditional notions of women's activism and behavior. In the same year, 1892, the Washingtonian Anna Julia Cooper, who was in the same Oberlin graduating class as Terrell, published *A Voice from the South*, a now-classic black feminist tract that was more in line with the thinking of contemporary elites. Cooper—shaped by many of the same ecclesiastical reformist ideas that Wells had earlier (and less eloquently) expressed in her true-womanhood essays—advocated higher education for women (despite the resistance of men toward it) and a central role for black women in both inter- and intraracial reform. She protested the sexual victimization of the "fatally beautiful class" that black women, including her own mother, had suffered at the hands of white men and the silence of white women. But Wells had since gone beyond Cooper's more Victorian notion that the future of the race depended on, and was inextricably tied to, the "quiet, undisputed dignity of womanhood." Dignity, for the disputatious Wells, came through the authentic voice of militant protest and, sometimes, the barrel of a gun. At such a critical period in representational politics, the question was whose voice was the one to be heard.[38]

The question of representation was made even more urgent by the upcoming World's Columbian Exposition. Its theme was the progress of civilization since Columbus's landfall in 1492, and the exposition was to be the ultimate showcase representing American achievement—including that of women—and its vaunted place in the scheme of world civilization. Unlike the previous New Orleans Exposition, there were to be no separate Negro exhibits in Chicago, and no black representatives had been appointed by President Harrison to the national commission that was to supervise and plan the World's Fair.

Nevertheless, as soon as the commissioners, including a nationwide Board of Lady Managers, were appointed, black women had begun lobbying for inclusion. But they had been held at bay with the rationale that they did not have a broadly representative national organization, such as the predominantly white suffrage groups like the Woman's Christian Temperance Union or the National Council of Women, the latter of which brought an array of white women's organizations under a single administrative umbrella. To bolster their effort to have black women included and to be the representative organization to do so, Hallie Quinn

Brown, the steely dean of women at Tuskegee Institute, urged the formation of the Colored Women's League, established in June of 1892 and headed by Terrell, four months before the Lyric Hall testimonial. The League, as a group, was very protective about their claim as being the first black women's club, and support for Ida could be construed as being contary to their own interests. Frederick Douglass might have unwittingly stepped into the fray when, at the urging of Ferdinand Barnett in Chicago, he had supported Fannie Barrier Williams to be appointed to represent black women on the Board of Lady Managers. Williams was a member of one of the several competing groups of Chicago women for such a position and was the wife of Ferdinand's law partner, S. Laing Williams. Douglass had stayed at the Williams home on his last visit to Chicago. Little wonder that the Washington women were in no mood to rally around Douglass, who apparently did not think he needed to get their approval or help for Ida's visit.[39]

THERE WERE OTHER cities, and Ida must have hoped that what had happened in Washington wasn't going to be a trend. In November of 1892, she was back in Philadelphia for the AME conference; in the same month she traveled to Boston, where she addressed the Women's Department of the Mechanics' Fair, Wesleyan Hall, and the Moral Educational Association, of which Ruffin was a charter member. With the exception of the poor showing in D.C., things were going well, but the first test of how she was to survive the inevitable attacks on her character rose with particular viciousness in December.

On the fifteenth of the month, the *Memphis Commercial,* still boiling over Ida and especially wary of her attention among the "thin-legged scholars" and "glass-eyed" females of Boston, sought to denigrate her character in the strongest words possible. Under the editorship of Edward Carmack, a staunch prohibitionist whose editorial Ida quoted in *Southern Horrors,* the *Commercial* called Wells a "wench," the "mistress of a scoundrel" (allegedly Fleming), and a "black harlot," who was raising money for her own personal use and desired to "marry a white husband." It was just the kind of criticism that black women had feared and that many predicted would be the inevitable consequence of Wells's confrontational—some would say sensationalist—style. And it couldn't have come at a worst time: just when they were striving for public recognition on a national stage.[40]

Fortunately, Ida had the support of not only her black press colleagues (the *Topeka Weekly Call* sniffed that Wells was obviously superior to her critics, and the *Richmond Planet*'s John Mitchell said that "she need feel in no way embarrassed or cast down") but also of Josephine Ruffin, who took the initiative to speak for black women by unconditionally defending Ida. The Bostonian confronted the charges head-on, making it known that her Woman's Era Club believed in Ida Wells's "purity of purpose and character."[41] But Wells, characteristically, wasn't fully satisfied with the passive forms of defense; she was determined to make the paper—which was in the middle of an expensive newspaper war with its Memphis rivals—and Carmack pay. She contacted Albion Tourgée to get the former judge's advice about suing the paper for slander.

It is not clear if Ida had actually met Tourgée, but she, like many other activists, admired his stands for the race in the *Chicago Inter-Ocean* and through his National Citizens Rights Association, an interracial organization established in 1891, to fight racial injustice. Tourgée had written her a letter to congratulate her on the *New York Age* editorial, and in July she, in turn, expressed her appreciation for his role in "awaking the sluggish consciences of the great M.E. Church and the party of great moral ideas."[42] The two might have had previous contact regarding her court case. Tourgée was the co-counsel for Homer Plessy, an octoroon who sued a Louisiana railway after being ejected from a first-class seat in June of 1892. The suit was headed for the U.S. Supreme Court based on the contention that Plessy's being denied the first-class passage was a violation of the Fourteenth Amendment. Ida's appellate case was cited in the legal briefs. In any case, Tourgée was also known as a source of personal and legal advice for blacks and Wells sought him out regarding the *Memphis Commercial*. As Wells told the former judge in her letter, she believed that he would be more objective than the black lawyers she knew.[43]

In response, Tourgée laid out Ida's options—and possible consequences. He told her that the *Commercial*'s attorneys would attempt to prove that she was the mistress of Fleming, and that she had a generally bad character. She could probably win significant damages if she could prove that she had not had any impropriety *"with any man"* (emphasis in original), he told her, reflecting the burden that women had in such circumstances. Tourgée then recommended that she seek out a black lawyer who had the time to tend to the case and whom he knew to be objective, Ferdinand Barnett, who would also keep him informed about the suit.[44]

Wells did contact Barnett, who, after doing some digging on his own, informed Tourgée that he had "the strongest faith that the libelous article is wholly without foundation." Ida had encouraged him to contact people in Memphis, including the "sycophants" Cassels and Settle, as she called them, and the gesture further impressed Ferdinand. "If her record was assailable," he wrote to Tourgée, "she would not send me to her enemies—especially as they are my friends.—I know Cassels." Barnett, who had written favorably about the Memphis legislator's 1881 antimiscegenation legislation in the *Conservator*, noted, "I am sure he will tell me all he knows."[45]

Barnett's views did not change after communicating with his fellow lawyers, and he was prepared to sue the paper in order to give the "scoundrel Carmack" the "scaring he deserves."[46] But in the end, it was decided that the perils of a legal action outweighed the possible gains, and the idea was dropped. In the interim, however, Ida had clearly found a champion who believed and wanted to protect her in the hour when she was immersed in controversy and slander. For a woman like her, there was no better opening for a future courtship.

MORE EVIDENCE OF support came in the form of, as Frederick Douglass had promised, a return engagement in Washington in early February 1893. On this occasion, Washingtonians "filled Metropolitan Church with one of the biggest audiences I had ever seen," Wells wrote. By then several circumstances had changed. In light of the attacks, it would have been seen as churlish for the Washington women to slight Ida. Determined not to be embarrassed again, Douglass himself presided over this meeting, and Mollie Terrell was tapped to provide the introduction. From the podium Mollie touted Wells's "courage, zeal and worthiness of support," although most of the introduction consisted of her own critique of lynching. Recalling the event, Wells pointed out, with just a hint of pique, that the introduction appeared to be Terrell's "maiden" public speech.[47]

Moreover, by February, the election was over, and the Republicans were out of the White House. Also by that date, there had been a compromise resolution, if not a satisfactory one, to the Columbian Exposition issue. Though no black organizations were to be represented, the Board of Lady Managers, under increasing pressure, appointed the Chicagoan Fannie Barrier Williams first as a secretary and later to an unpaid position to supervise the installation of exhibits, which would include a small black one, in the Women's Building. Additionally, a number of black women were scheduled to speak under the auspices of the Congress of Representative Women, one of the auxiliary organizations connected to the exposition. In any case, Wells was satisfied by the showing and the fact that it resulted in a donation of nearly two hundred dollars to aid the antilynching cause. The money, it turned out, would almost immediately be turned over to the Pinkerton detective agency to investigate a lynching that took place in Paris, Texas, while she was in Washington.[48]

"NEVER IN THE history of civilization has any Christian people stooped to such shocking brutality and indescribable barbarism as that which characterized the people of Paris, Texas and adjacent communities," Wells would later write about the brutal death of Henry Smith. Smith, a mentally disturbed "roustabout," had been accused of murdering Myrtle Vance, the four-year-old daughter of the town's sheriff.[49] The sheriff, known for his cruelty, had recently arrested and abused the black man, who appeared to have traits associated with schizophrenia. Several days later, the body of the child was found, and Smith was thought to have killed the sheriff's daughter in revenge. The press reported lurid descriptions of the dead girl's mangled body, provided by the sheriff. No lesser a figure than Atticus G. Haygood, a bishop of the Southern Methodist Church, a former president of Emory College in Georgia, and the first agent for the John F. Slater Fund that gave grants for Negro education in the South, added that the young girl was "first outraged with demonical cruelty and then taken by her heels and torn asunder in the mad wantonness of guerilla ferocity."[50]

The description of little girl's murder—and of Smith—would have made many turn away. But Ida did not. As she had said in her editorial, such charges had to be investigated and Ida arranged for Pinkerton detectives to go to Texas and write up their findings. What she would learn from them and other press sources did not exonerate Smith—but, due in part to the critical eye she had focused on the South with her antilynching editorials, the circumstances of his lynching would condemn the mob-ridden region in no uncertain terms.

THE MADNESS HAD begun with a manhunt in which two thousand men combed the countryside for four days looking for Smith, who had managed to escape after the murder. During the course of their search, they had set upon the black man's stepson and when he wouldn't reveal Smith's whereabouts he was lynched. Finally Smith was caught near Hope, Arkansas, and the news sent the citizens of Paris into a "wild frenzy of excitement," as Wells, deliberately quoting the white-owned *New York Sun,* wrote in her own narrative. "Whiskey shops were closed, schools were dismissed by proclamation from the mayor, and everything was done in a businesslike manner," she emphasized. "Everything" included the actions of a crowd of some ten thousand people who had come from as far away as Dallas, Texas, on a specially chartered excursion train to await Smith's return.[51]

Once Henry Smith got to Paris, he was placed on a chair atop a huge platform wagon, as a "mockery of a king upon his throne," Wells wrote, "so all might see the most inhuman monster known in current history." The platform, with the word *JUSTICE* imprinted upon it, was carried like a float to Main Street and followed by a procession of citizens, including children who had been dismissed from school for the event. As an observer noted, "Fathers, men of social and business standing, took their children to teach them how to dispose of negro criminals. Mothers were there too, even women whose culture entitles them to be among the social and intellectual leaders of the town."[52]

Once the lively procession reached the main square, the sheriff, who was the father of the young victim, conducted the subsequent activities as a demonic maestro might conduct an orchestra. Smith's body was placed on a scaffold. His clothes were torn off, precipitating a struggle by the mob to get possession of the shreds to keep for mementos. Then, for the next fifty minutes, Smith was tortured by red-hot iron brands placed first against his feet, and then inch by inch up his body until they reached his face where his eyes were burned out. Every moan by Smith was met by a cheer from the crowd. Still unsatiated, members of the mob rolled the fiery pokers up and down Smith's stomach and back; finally hot pokers were thrust down his throat. When it appeared that he was dead, kerosene was poured over him and he was set alight. But the poor man somehow found the strength to jump out of the flames, only to be pushed back into the fire again. For days afterward, people returned to scour the ashes for unburned body parts. One man was reported to have made a watch charm from a kneecap. A black man was said to have taken a rib bone to hang over his door for good luck. Lynching, which had evolved first from singular executions to multiple assassinations, had now reached the threshold of bloodcurdling, public spectacle.[53]

The "crime of murder was itself bad enough," Wells wrote, but she discovered from the Pinkerton report that the young girl's body had slight abrasions and discolorations about the neck but no evidence of the kind of brutal assault described by Bishop Haygood. Ida's point was that the crime, horrible as it was, could have been adjudicated in a court of law. There was ample evidence against Smith. But the citizens of Paris, Texas, were so beyond the pale that they had engaged in the bizarre and ritualistic torture. The "shameless" exaggeration about the state of the girl's body by Haygood was consciously construed, wrote Wells, to "bolster the infamous plea that the people of Paris were driven to insanity" by the murder.[54]

Ida also emphasized the fact that Henry Smith was mentally imbalanced and the community knew it to be so. She wrote about a black minister who had known Smith for years and who had previously tried to get him committed to an asylum. Days before the murder of Myrtle Vance, according to the minister, Smith had been "out of his head with delirium" and may well have been thrown into that state by the sheriff's abuse of him. After he was caught and accused of the crime, Smith had said, "Is it true, did I kill her? Oh, my God, my God!'" When the minister tried to stop the lynching by suggesting that Smith be committed, he was threatened with lynching himself and ridden out of Paris on a rail.

Once the full story of Henry Smith's lynching became known, it sent shudders not only through blacks but through the white reformers in the South. "We turn our eyes away from it. It's awful, awful!" wrote E. E. Hoss, the Nashville editor of the Richmond-based *Christian Advocate*, noting that both the crime and the penalty revealed "a demonical side in human nature that startles us." He asked, "Are we savages? Is our civilization only skin deep? Does our religion count for nothing?"[55] The "orgy of torture and festival of agony" was an "unnaturally and incomparably barbarous punishment" read an antilynching resolution prepared by the citizens of Laredo, Texas, led by Edgar Gardner Murphy, a well-known Episcopal priest.[56]

No other lynching had so disturbed the southern clergy or had made the case, as the black Presbyterian minister Francis Grimke charged, that the silence of white northern clergymen made them complicit in the crime. The white southern liberal commentator Lewis Harvie Blair, graphically depicting the crucifix-inspired model of slow, torturous death, went so far as to conclude that lynching was "a distinguishing feature of American Evangelical Christian civilization."[57]

It was also a feature of the commodification of racial violence in an increasingly industrialized economy. For if Smith's ordeal belonged to some premodern past with its collection of human relics, its demand for retributive and vindicatory justice, and its icons of torture, death, and blood sacrifice, its marketing was very much of the present. Railway companies profited from special charters bringing families to the pornographic spectacle. Photographers took pictures of the scene, which subsequently adorned wish-you-were-here postcards. Smith's screams were sold after being recorded by a recent invention, the gramophone. A pamphlet devoted to both the circumstances of the crime and Smith's ordeal—the most detailed account of lynching from the lyncher's point of view—was published, sold, and widely circulated. On the eve of an economic depression—and a World's Fair exposition—the doctrine of white supremacy had found a way to commodify emancipated black bodies without disturbing the wages of white working ones.[58]

IRONICALLY, IT WAS the lynching of Smith, who appeared to be guilty of the crime, that provided the evidence that, despite all of the Christianizing missions by the American Missionary Association and other such entities, the South had descended into a state of barbarism.[59] Although the southern clergy did not abandon their defense of lynching, their own hand-wringing doubts—and the increasing scrutiny of northern elites—began to make their cry about "southern outrages" lose its power to "stifle the conscience" and "hush the press," as Wells had complained just the year before.

Wells's challenge to not only the legitimacy but also the Christianity of the Haygoods of the world—seen as influential arbiters of race relations in the South, who had betrayed earlier condemnation of lynchings—was a harbinger for the next phase of her own antilynching campaign.[60]

CHAPTER TEN

Light from a Human Torch

The fire lighted by this human torch [Henry
Smith] flamed around the world.

—*Ida B. Wells*

There was no better venue for Wells's first speech before a predominantly white audience than Boston's Union Temple Baptist Church on Tremont Street. Established in 1838 by an antislavery man, Timothy Gilbert, when his own Charles Street Baptist Church refused to admit African Americans, Temple historically welcomed both blacks and whites, rich and poor, and was a fount of abolitionism before the war. By the 1890s, the church had a mostly female membership of fifteen hundred, and was one of the nation's leading "people's churches"—so named for its populist culture, public programs, community involvement, and diverse membership.[1]

Ida's appearance there on February 13, 1893, only days after the Smith lynching, was important for several reasons. Reverend Joseph Cook, who had issued the invitation, drew capacity audiences to his twenty-five-hundred-seat auditorium with his Monday lecture series, which focused on the relationship between religion, science, and social reform and was invariably reported in the mainstream press. He himself was the editor of *Our Day,* an influential journal; and most important, Cook was close to

Tourgée, and, like him, he was a leader of what became known as the Social Gospel movement: an extension of the missionary associations of the
antebellum era that would fully emerge during the early years of the twentieth century.[2]

The inequities—as well as the iniquities—of industrial capitalism led
Social Gospelers to believe that improving social conditions, not just saving
individual souls, was key to preparing the way for the Second Coming.
Adherents saw laissez-faire capitalism as inadequate to meet the current
crisis, and replaced the idea that salvation called for separation from a sin-
ful world with a highly developed sense of government reform and activism. Many northern Gospelers, for example, supported the ill-fated Lodge
Election Bill and the Blair Education Bill, which called for federal supervision of elections and expenditures for both black and white educational
systems.

Nevertheless, as had been true of many white abolitionists, the liberal
perspective of the new movement did not necessarily mean that its followers saw blacks as social equals, and they could hold racist views at worst,
and patronizing attitudes at best. In 1890 and 1891, for example, Gospelers
held conferences on the status of the Negro in Mohonk, New York,
without feeling any need to include black leaders. "A patient is not invited
to the consultation of the doctors on his case," said Lyman Abbott, one of
the foremost leaders of the movement, when asked why no African
Americans were asked to attend. T. Thomas Fortune, Booker T. Washington, Tremont's Reverend Cook, and Tourgée protested the exclusion, and
when blacks were not invited to the second conference, Tourgée boycotted
it in protest.[3]

Their impulse toward sectional and ecclesiastical unity also kept the
northern Gospelers conservative on racial issues and relatively silent on
lynching. But, at least, the mostly Anglophile group had not extricated
African Americans from the realms of moral reform, and after the Smith
lynching, they were becoming more sensitive to critics.

Already accomplished by the simple fact of Ida's invitation to speak was
the acknowledgment that she, and blacks in general, had the right to define
race issues. What Ida hoped to do was to recover—and reignite—their
abolitionist spirit as a force against lynching.

Wells, in her now-perfected rhetorical approach, began her talk at
Tremont by addressing the issue of their silence on lynching. "I cannot believe that the apathy and indifference . . . regarding mob rule is other than

the result of ignorance of the true situation," Ida told her audience. Taking a page from Frederick Douglass, she urged her listeners to rise against mob rule "not just from a standpoint of sentiment, not even so much from a standpoint of justice to a weak race, [but] from a desire to preserve our American institutions," which were being imperiled by lynch law.[4] Wells followed the statement with a seamless narrative that wove the passions of her personal experience with that of the more abstract themes of justice.

She poignantly recounted the story of Moss's lynching; the fate of the thirty-one so-called rioters, now serving terms of three, eight, and fifteen years in the Tennessee state penitentiary; the destruction of the *Free Speech,* and explained how these events had changed her own views about lynching. With pathos rather than anger (and no tears), Ida cited the circumstances regarding the lynchings of Ed Coy, Henry Smith, Eliza Woods, and two other black women—a fifteen-year-old accused of poisoning, and another who was accused of being an accomplice in the murder of a man who had raped her. To illustrate the threat of lynching to the government, she spoke about the inability of the federal authorities, indeed, the Constitution itself, to protect the thousand African Americans who had died under mob law within the last ten years. She used the 1891 lynching of the eleven Italians killed by a mob in New Orleans to show how the national government had no power over the "evil-doing" that occurred in the state, and yet was forced to pay $25,000 in reparations. In the name of states' rights, she averred, the "whole country had to pay for the treachery of the South." Aware that the social evils in the cities were becoming the focus of reform, Ida emphasized the fact that lynching had become a modern urban issue that occurred in cities proud of their technological advances.[5]

At the climax of her talk, Ida made the case that the struggle against lynching had the same moral import as the struggle against slavery, for as the Henry Smith lynching showed, both were in "league with death and the covenant with Hell," she said, quoting the abolitionist William Lloyd Garrison. Invoking the apocalyptic visions of Nat Turner and John Brown, Wells challenged the audience to arouse public sentiment against lynch law as "strong, deep, and mighty as that roused against slavery."[6] At a time when mob law had become absolute, she charged the Gospelers to become the new abolitionists in the spirit of Garrison, Douglass, Sumner, Whittier, and Phillips. Ida longed for such voices, "with all the intensity of my soul." She ended with her own formula for reconciliation and reunion.

Only when the nation was aroused to exact justice and put down mob rule "from Greenland's icy mountains to the coral reefs of the Southern seas" would "every member of this great composite nation" be able to join in the singing of America's national hymn . . . "Land of the Pilgrim's pride / From every mountain side / Freedom does ring . . ."[7]

FOR ALMOST ANY reformer other than Ida, the enthusiastic reception to her talk would have been gratifying enough. The black press noted that the audience was impressed by Wells's "heroic," "intelligent," and "reasoned" remarks, and the congregation passed resolutions to condemn lynch law and arouse public sentiment.[8] The lecture in its entirety was published in *Our Day*, and she was written up in the *Boston Transcript and Advertiser*— the first northern white paper, as she noted in her autobiography, to do so. After her Tremont appearance, Wells was invited to speak before a number of other groups. She pointed out in her autobiography that William Lloyd Garrison, Jr., son of the famous abolitionist, was so moved by her depiction of the Moss lynching that he used his influence to get a loan turned down that had been solicited by the Memphis municipality. But to Ida, the impact of her Boston appearances was "meager." Impatiently, she awaited her next opportunity.[9]

While Wells continued to make rounds on the white Social Gospel circuit in Boston and black meetings sponsored by the Afro-American League, Frederick Loudin, best known as a former singer for the famous Fisk Jubilee singers, issued a challenge in the black press. The Smith lynching was such a travesty that if "we are not stirred to some action, then we prove ourselves unfit for the position we seek among the races of the earth," he said. Loudin proposed that blacks make some kind of formal protest at the World's Columbian Exposition and that a committee be formed to pursue the idea. He himself was willing to contribute money to the group, but did not have the time to do much else on its behalf. "I would be glad to see Miss Ida B. Wells on that committee," he urged.[10]

The committee that was subsequently formed for the world's-fair project was made up of two: Wells and Frederick Douglass—though Loudin did add one hundred dollars to Ida's twenty-five-dollar and Douglass's fifty-dollar contributions. As Douglass and Wells informed the press, they settled on the idea of producing a pamphlet to be published in time for the exposition that would set forth "the past and present condition of our people and their relationship to American civilization"; it would be translated into German, French, and Spanish and be freely distributed at the fair. The calculated cost of the publication was $5,000; they asked black newspaper offices to be collection points for contributions.[11]

Involving the black press may have been a necessity for such a project, but it also gave querulous editors a wide berth to comment on the idea— and comment they did. While the *Cleveland Gazette* agreed with the proposal, the *Indianapolis Freeman* thought it a "futile" gesture. The *Washington Bee* said that the race already had "too many pamphlets," and that its money might be better spent in purchasing historian George Washington Williams's *History of the Negro Race in America* or *Men of Mark* by Ida's recently deceased mentor, Willam J. Simmons.[12] In the midst of the flurry of editorials about the pamphlet, a related controversy erupted when a black group in Boston circulated a proposal that blacks raise money in various cities through giving "entertainments" to support a "Jubilee Day" at the World's Columbian Exposition.

The idea of Jubilee Day was to set aside August 25 to feature special events to attract black attendees to the exposition. Fair officials had proposed subsidizing similar days for Germans, Swedes, and other ethnic groups, but the exclusion of formal black participation from the fair made the Boston proposal a controversial one. The black press was mostly critical of a "Colored Day" at the exposition, and some commentators, including Ida, charged that the Boston group were mere schemers who were willing to swallow their race pride in order to make a profit. What Ida either didn't know or care about was the fact that the Bostonians had already secured support for the project from Frederick Douglass. The criticism reached a new crescendo when it was learned that fair officials—without, apparently, any awareness of the offense—had volunteered to provide free watermelons for the Jubilee event. "No Nigger Day, No Pamphlet" was the final appraisal of the *Indianapolis Freeman*.[13]

Ida was furious—at both the Bostonians and the promise of fresh fruit. The "spectacle" of blacks "roaming" the grounds "munching watermelon" showed "lack of dignity, self-respect and judgment, to say nothing of good taste," Ida wrote in a flashback to her "interminable picnic" editorials in the *Christian Index*. She pointed out in the *New York Age* that while little money or support had been given to investigate lynchings, or to publish the pamphlet, black people were being urged, during a depression, to raise money to "defray the expenses" of a "comfortable 'day of praise'" at the same fair that excluded them. The most egregious aspect of the Boston plan was that March 9, the date for the giving of entertainments across the country, was the anniversary of the Memphis lynching of Moss, McDowell, and Stewart. It would be more appropriate to make it "a day of mourning," Ida snapped.[14]

With Wells's *Age* editorial in hand, Boston's Josephine Ruffin marched into the offices of the *Boston Courant*, a black paper, to urge that the publication take a stand against the event. It is not known what position the paper finally took, but Ruffin's visit was reported back to Joseph Adger, a friend of Frederick Douglass, member of a leading black Boston family, and chair of the Boston committee. Wells was greatly influenced by Ruffin, Adger wrote Douglass, and Ruffin had not been asked to serve on the committee because of her "rule or ruin" dictatorial attitude. This was the second letter Douglass had received complaining about Wells. An earlier one, from the Boston committee's secretary, Willietta Johnson, had asked him to write something to rebut Ida's "venomous" attack against the committee to which Douglass himself, she reminded him, had signed on to.[15] The Boston affair was only one of several entanglements involving Ida that Douglass would find bothersome and which he tried, with mixed success, to remain above the fray. As he would soon discover, remaining above the clouds of dust that followed Ida was not going to be easy. However, for the moment, Wells herself got the chance to leave the petty, miss-the-point infighting about the pamphlet and Jubilee Day behind in February 1893, when she received an invitation to depart immediately for the British Isles.

THE INVITATION HAD come from Catherine Impey, an English Quaker and activist whom Wells had met during her November trip to Philadelphia. Ida had been staying at the home of William Still, and Impey had asked to meet Ida to discuss the race question in America. Impey, founding editor of *Anti-Caste*—a journal that focused on the plight of natives of India but also supported movements by other persons of color, including African Americans—belonged to the long tradition of Quaker activists who had, as early as 1783, established the first antislavery society in Britain. The Society of Friends subsequently joined the network of evangelical reformers among Baptists, Methodists, and other denominations, led by William Wilberforce, Member of Parliament, to secure the passage of the Slave Trade Act of 1807 that prohibited British vessels from engaging in the slave trade. Impey first published *Anti-Caste* in 1888, and over the years, she had frequently visited the States, where she befriended Frederick Douglass, Frances Ellen Harper, Thomas Fortune, and Albion Tourgée, among others. Fortune called her "one of the best and most tireless friends of the dark races in the world."[16]

Impey had become interested in the lynching question after Tourgée sent her a photo, taken in 1891, of a black man hanging lifelessly from a tree in Clanton, Alabama. When Impey published the photo on the cover of *Anti-Caste*, she was roundly criticized for what was initially thought a distasteful drawing—until it was realized that it was a photograph. The startling image in her small but influential journal was important in rousing English opinion about the issue of lynching, which was stoked again after the murder of Henry Smith. "Our English press has been getting a hold of some of those Texas lynchings, and our people are beginning to feel that there is something wrong somewhere," Impey had written to Tourgée. ". . . [W]e long from the depths of our heart to set on foot a living effort to remedy the cruel wrongs now suffered and will do our utmost to help you plead the cause."[17] Impey's letter went on to explain that she had read the news about Smith while visiting another activist, Isabella Fyvie Mayo. Mayo, a Scottish writer who had converted her home to an asylum for South Asians, had been sensitized to race issues by the suicide of an escaped American slave who had worked in her childhood home.[18] The two women thought the time was opportune to form a new organization to arouse public opinion against lynching and that Ida would be perfect for the task. Mayo would cover the expenses for the trip.[19]

The Englishwomen's invitation was sent to Ida in Brooklyn and then forwarded to the home of Frederick Douglass, where Wells was visiting. Impey's letter also had a message for Douglass, who had traveled triumphantly through the British Isles as a fugitive slave and abolitionist in the 1840s. She said that she and Mayo knew that he himself was too old for such a trip and, in the event that Ida could not come, to please suggest someone else. According to her autobiography, Douglass told Ida: "You go my child, you are the one to go, for you have the story to tell." The invitation, Ida recalled in her autobiography, was "like an open door in a stone wall."[20]

"WHEN YOU READ this, I will already be three days on the ocean," read Ida's announcement in the black press in mid-April.[21] Wells also expressed her regrets that her sudden departure would interfere with her efforts to raise money for the World's Fair pamphlet and cause her to miss the press association meeting in Richmond, where journalists were prepared to challenge officials at the southern governors' meeting, which was also going to be held in the city. But she explained that her hosts had wanted her to make an impression on the British in advance of the Chicago Columbian Exposition, due to open on May 1, and that if she left right away she would be able to travel with a friend who was also going abroad, Georgia Patton. Patton, the first black woman to earn a degree from Meharry Medical College of Fisk University, and the first licensed to practice surgery in Tennessee, was on her way to Monrovia, Liberia, along with three young Methodist male protégés to establish a school there. Ida had great respect for the medical missionary and for her future husband, David Washington, a respected letter carrier whom Wells described as one of the few "substantial" black citizens who remained in Memphis.[22] Ida could have mentioned a third reason. She loved to travel and could hardly contain her excitement about going on her first trip overseas and having the opportunity to impart her message directly to the British.

Like their American counterparts, British reformers were in the midst of a Christian movement to remedy the disparities and dislocations of rapid industrialism and the failure of traditional ecclesiastical authorities to address them adequately. There was also a broad concern about the coarsening of the culture. What made Great Britain's new ferment of activism so promising was that it had reinvigorated the network of Unitarians, Quakers, Baptists, Congregationalists, and Methodists who had been so effective in Britain's abolitionist campaign. Moreover, the networks extended into a broad liberal movement that sought greater egalitarianism in general and championed issues like women's suffrage, home rule for Ireland, and, in light of Britain's imperialist policy toward Africa and India, a renewed interest in race and pacifism. Wells no doubt anticipated a warm reception in such a political climate, one that could have a significant impact on the antilynching debate back home. On April 5, at about 9:30 A.M., she and Patton boarded the steamship *Teutonic* bound for Liverpool.

WELLS HAD NEVER seen anything like the elegant vessel that belonged to the White Star Line. It was 566 feet long and had a capacity for 1,320 passengers. The ship featured decks with promenades; banqueting halls with Renaissance-style bas-relief figures in gold and ivory; a library with books, writing tables, and stationery; hand-painted Italianesque glass shutters; and sumptuously upholstered couches. Even the spacious second-class cabins, with their beautiful appointments, hot and cold water, and electric appliances, were said to equal first-class accommodations on other ships. Wells and Patton may have traveled in the quarters reserved for unmarried women, where a matron was assigned to keep a protective eye.[23]

However, once the ship left port to plunge into the scowling waves of the Atlantic, much of its beauty was soon lost on the two passengers. "I do not advise anybody to start on a sea voyage with a disordered system," Wells wrote in a travel diary that described six days of escalating sea sickness. After an apparent respite on the second day, by day three both women were hopelessly sick. "We have a stateroom to ourselves and lie in the two lower berths looking at each other. Ugh," Ida wrote. On day four, she was afraid to lift her head; the next day she felt even worse, despite ingesting all of the medicine she could get her hands on. Finally, on the ninth day, the ship docked at its destination, where Ida waited with Patton at the Shaftsbury Hotel until it was time for the physician to make the next phase of her journey. After seeing her off, Ida followed Catherine Impey's directions to go directly to her home in Somerset, located on the northern border of the Bristol Channel.[24]

Ida's first views of England's hills and fertile valleys must have been thrilling—if she was well enough to appreciate them. Once in Somerset, Ida was met by Impey, Impey's mother, and her sister Kate, all of whom worked on the *Anti-Caste*. After a few days of recuperation, Ida and her companions made their way to the home of Isabella Mayo in Aberdeen, Scotland, the "Granite City" on the North Sea known for its extensive gardens and Balmoral Castle, which Queen Victoria had made the royal family's summer residence.

When they reached Mayo's home, they found her and other members of the household—Dr. George Ferdinands, a young dentist and native of Ceylon (now Sri Lanka) who had recently finished his collegiate and medical courses at the University of Aberdeen; one of his relatives; and a German music teacher who had students in the town—all enthusiastically engaged in writing letters, preparing for Ida's meetings, and making press arrangements.[25]

Wells's European debut came on the afternoon of April 21, when she talked about lynching before a group of local VIPs Mayo had invited to her drawing room. Apparently, the event also marked Ida's first success in the British Isles. At the end of her presentation, the group voted to establish The Society for the Recognition of the Brotherhood of Man, whose purpose was to "oppose race separation," which fostered lynchings and "other forms of brutal injustice." Catherine Impey was encouraged enough by the showing to prepare a ten-thousand run of *Anti-Caste* to announce the organization's founding, and went ahead to England to set up speaking dates there.

In the interim, Isabella Mayo had arranged other speaking dates for Ida in Scotland. On April 23, Ida spoke before the men's Pleasant Saturday Evening meeting, with fifteen hundred in attendance; on the same date, she addressed her first public meeting at Aberdeen's Music Hall. From there she went on to give talks in Huntly and Glasgow, and by April 26, she arrived in Edinburgh, Scotland's capital, which was associated with Mary, Queen of Scots, one of the subjects of Ida's lyceum reading in Memphis.[26]

After traveling some two hundred miles in three lecture-filled days, Ida went to Edinburgh where she spoke before more groups, including the Young Men's Christian Association, a chapter of the international organization that had been founded in London nearly a half century earlier. Ida was the guest of Eliza Wigham, a Quaker, veteran suffragist, and temperance leader. Meeting Wigham was especially meaningful for Wells, for she had been a part of Frederick Douglass's antislavery circle in Scotland during the 1840s, and, a half century later, she still maintained a correspondence with him. Douglass's old friend volunteered to head a branch of the Brotherhood in the city. From Edinburgh, Ida went to Glasgow, where she lectured to a Society of Friends meeting before continuing south to Newcastle, Birmingham, and Manchester.[27]

According to Wells, everybody was "jubilant" over the great interest she had aroused in such a short time. The *Edinburgh Evening Gazette* noted that Wells's appearances resulted in the "enrollment of many names [into the Society] and every post is gaining more." Her talks were covered positively in the press, though it paid more attention to Ida's speaking style, which she had revised for her European audience, than to the issue of lynching itself. While Temple was known for its love of exuberant oratory, the Scots and the English were wary of emotive demonstrations, and they were impressed by Ida's unsensational reporting of lynchings in the U.S., her soft voice, and the reputation of her hosts. If it were "not that the facts are spoken to by ladies, whose reputation for truth and carefulness is beyond suspicion, one could fain believe that such things could not be in these days of civilization and freedom," noted the *Peterhead Sentinel and Buchan Journal*.[28] All was going exceedingly well when a bizarre incident happened that threatened the campaign—and ultimately cut short Ida's trip.

IT HAD BEGUN with a letter that the middle-aged Impey had written to George Ferdinands, Mayo's thirty-year-old houseguest. Impey, misconstruing the dentist's attentiveness, had impulsively written him a letter saying that she had the same deep affection for him that he had for her—though she knew he had been too shy to share his feelings because of their color difference. Moreover, Impey told him that she had already written her family, informing them that they should prepare to receive him as her husband, and that the prospective union gave proof to the brotherhood of man. The letter had taken the bewildered Ferdinands by surprise and he immediately turned it over to Mayo. When she read the letter, the high-strung Scot reacted with a whirlwind of rage. She confronted Impey with the letter and demanded that she withdraw from Ida's tour. When Impey refused, Mayo told her that she would no longer work with her; insisted that the current issue of *Anti-Caste* be destroyed because it carried both of their names (and no doubt much of Mayo's considerable largesse); and threatened to spread the word about the incident throughout Edinburgh, London, and even India. Mayo then demanded that Ida have nothing to do with the lovesick Quaker and continue the tour without her. When Ida responded that she didn't understand why such a storm had been created over the issue, as Impey was guilty of nothing more than falling in love, Mayo told Ida that the Quaker was "insane" and the kind of woman who got involved in these causes to meet and romance men of color. This would not be the last time Impey would pull something like this, Mayo insisted, using the term "nymphomaniac," a word Ida heard for the first time.[29]

It is not clear why the object of Impey's affection had felt it necessary to share the letter, or why Mayo reacted so passionately. Whatever the explanation, the development was "staggering," Wells wrote, for she was now forced to choose between Impey, who had become her friend, and the woman who was paying the expenses for the campaign. After a prayer-filled night, Ida finally decided to tell Mayo that she would not abandon a woman who had done so much service for the race. In reaction, Mayo "cast me in outer darkness," Wells said. Neither she nor Impey ever saw her again.[30]

When things fell apart, Impey confessed to Albion Tourgée that she had made a "mortifying blunder" in mistaking Ferdinands's commitment to the campaign for romantic feelings for her. He "was devoting himself to our movement (& to myself as its rather care worn founder,") she wrote. With Mayo out of the picture, Impey continued to make arrangements for Ida to talk at mainly Quaker meetings in Newcastle, Birmingham, and Manchester, but it took much of the air out of the rest of the trip. "We got through as bravely as we could," Impey informed Tourgée, but "with aching hearts and jaded spirits."[31]

Nevertheless, the two women had done as well as could be expected under the circumstances. "We were everywhere well received," Impey told Tourgée. "In some places the meetings were packed—crowded and overflow meetings held." She was referring to the talk in Newcastle, where Ida addressed the Society of Friends on the afternoon of May 9, and where the overflow crowd created the need to hold two meetings. In Manchester, Wells won over a group of key British Unitarians, who vowed to form their own branch of the Society. Like the Quakers, the British Unitarians had a strong abolitionist tradition, and during the Civil War many of its leaders supported the Union at a time when British mercantile interests—especially those dependent on American cotton—were giving aid and comfort to the Confederacy. One of the most enthusiastic supporters of the group was W. E. A. Axon, president of the Manchester and Salford Temperance Union and editor of the (Unitarian-oriented) Manchester Guardian, which gave Ida a splendid write-up that recalled her "brave assertions on behalf of the race." Wells stayed with the Axons while in the city and wrote about her first experience in a vegetarian household where no meat whatsoever was served. (Impey was also vegetarian but provided meat for guests.) Vegetarianism, Ida discovered, along with other social purity movements, was also very much alive in Great Britain.[32]

In another letter to Tourgée, Impey wrote that "Miss Wells has made an impression on the minds of thousands (perhaps ten thousand)." Impey described Ida's approach as that of one bearing witness, speaking with "a cultivated manner—with great simplicity and directness and with a burning intensity of feeling *well controlled*." It was "the *most convincing* kind of speaking," the Quaker continued; "it sounded so intensely genuine & real—There was no attempt at oration—no straining after effects." Newspapers such as the *Newcastle Leader* concurred, calling Wells's delivery "educated and forceful," "quiet but effective," and, in another instance, "refined" and free of "oratorical tricks."[33]

In Birmingham, Ida used another of her rhetorical strategies to good effect. Preceding her appearances, Impey made sure that officials and the press were given antilynching material and protest petitions to sign. This had prompted a city councillor to write a letter to the *Birmingham Daily Post* the week before Ida's scheduled arrival to ask why, with his limited time for public activities, he should extend efforts for a cause over which his country had no jurisdiction, and in which he had no right to interfere. The letter gave Ida the opportunity to emphasize one aspect of her message that she hoped would at once move the English to intervene in the antilynching struggle and shame the United States. On May 16, a day before her arrival in the city, Ida's reply to the councillor was published in the *Post*. "I am in Great Britain today because I believe that the silent indifference with which she has received the charge that human beings are burned alive in Christian (?) Anglo-Saxon communities is born of ignorance of the true situation,"[34] she averred. "It is to the religious and moral sentiment of Great Britain [that] we now turn. America cannot and will not ignore the voice of a nation that is her superior in civilization." Subsequently, Ida spoke at another meeting of Quakers, as well as at the YMCA, the Coventry Road Congregational Church, and other venues, which resulted in recorded condemnations of lynching and the formation of new branches of the Brotherhood. The exchange with the councillor, Wells later recalled, "undoubtedly helped to give us the splendid audience we had in Birmingham. Impey reported to Tourgée that she was sure "America would be sensitive to outside criticism."[35]

BUT GLOWING PRESS accounts from Scotland, Birmingham, Manchester, and the like were one thing; it was London that held the key to the kind of success Ida envisioned. From the beginning, she and her hosts had planned to get to the city in May, when Parliament was in session and when, as Ida noted, every Christian denomination, missionary association, and philanthropic, moral, social, or political movement converged for their annual meetings. However, Impey and Ida were fearful of Mayo's reprisals and they thought it best to let someone else arrange her speaking engagements. Impey found an affable but politically unconnected German woman, and as a result the two of them had to "scour" for meetings, Wells reported. The most important one they could muster up was the British Women's Temperance Association (BWTA) conference, where Ida was promised an opportunity to speak.

As in the United States, temperance was an important political issue in Great Britain. The Liberal Party made it one of the major reforms for which it campaigned. The British organization had had few women until the mid-1870s, but that had changed largely due to the influence of the American movement. The president of the BWTA was Lady Henry Somerset, an aristocrat who was a close friend of the American WCTU president, Frances Willard. The two had met in the States, and in 1892, when Willard was suffering with exhaustion from the American campaign, Somerset invited her to England to recuperate. The two women were still living together at the time of Ida's tour, and both would be in attendance at the BWTA conference.[36]

Ida had been looking forward to confronting Willard since 1890, the year that the *New York Voice* published a scurrilous interview with the temperance leader. Responding to a question about the federal election bill, Willard had made disparaging remarks about black voters, calling them "great dark-faced mobs whose rallying cry is better whiskey, and more of it. . . . The grogshop is their center of power." Willard had added, "The safety of women, of childhood, of the home is menaced in a thousand localities at this moment, so that men dare not go beyond the sight of their own roof-tree."[37]

At the time of the interview, Willard had been attending a WCTU meeting in Atlanta, and two years after the prohibition amendment had been defeated in Tennessee, she was frustrated by other such defeats in the South that were blamed on black voters. Whether calculated or not, Willard's menacing image of African Americans also played into the WCTU's recruitment and women's suffrage efforts, which were increasingly focused on the South. The danger that blacks represented fit perfectly into the WCTU's motto of "Home Protection," which provided a rationale that had convinced women (and some men), wary of more radical suffragists, that they needed the franchise to maintain the integrity of their domestic lives. Ida believed that Willard had "unhesitatingly slandered the entire Negro race in order to gain favor with those who are hanging, shooting, and burning Negroes alive."[38]

What especially irked Wells was that Willard was considered a friend of blacks. Within liberal circles, she often boasted that her parents were abolitionists and that the WCTU membership (unlike many organizations) included black women. In England, Willard's progressive views had accorded her the reputation of being the "Uncrowned Queen of American Democracy," as Wells quoted from a British publication.[39]

During Ida's campaign in the British Isles, Willard's name and reputation had come up again and again with that of the evangelist Dwight Moody, when Ida claimed that the help of the British was needed because of the "silent indifference" of American liberals regarding the issue of lynching. Incredulous that such leaders refused to criticize lynching, Ida had had to convince her audience that Willard and Moody were a part of the problem, not the solution. Wells brought up Moody's well-documented tours before segregated audiences in the South as evidence of her assertion, but Willard (who had once worked for him) had not been so easy to make the case against. Wells had not brought a copy of the *New York Voice* interview to England, and many in her audiences refused to believe Ida's charges against the popular temperance leader. Little wonder that Ida relished the opportunity to finally meet Willard face-to-face.[40]

Ready for battle, Ida entered the BWTA meeting in which Willard sat on the podium. Wells was probably prepared to give her stump antilynching speech augmented by a persuasive critique of Willard, but when she arrived, she was told that she only had a few minutes to speak. What Wells said is unknown, but she would have had to alter her talk to include only the essential points of her message. Although Ida noted that Lady Somerset offered a perfunctory antilynching resolution, Ida was irked by the situation and especially by Willard, who sat silently on the stage during the proceedings. But for now, the temperance leader would have to be another "unfinished business" item in Ida's campaign. After the dissatisfactory stay in London, Wells went back to Southampton, where she met her aggrieved friend Catherine Impey. After calling on Bishop William Wilberforce—

namesake and grandson of the English politician who had successfully campaigned for the abolition of the slave trade in Britain and the 1833 Slavery Abolition Act—Wells embarked on her return voyage.[41]

The trip had not been unsuccessful, though clearly it was not all that Ida had hoped. But she had made a start in mobilizing all-important British opinion, and her trip must have also provided an important psychological lift. On the home-bound ship, Ida found herself in the company of fifteen English passengers on their way to the Columbian Exposition in Chicago, and for the first time, she wrote, she met "members of the white race who saw no reason why they should not extend to me the courtesy they would have offered any lady of their own race." An added pleasure was the shocked expressions on the faces of the American passengers when they saw the gracious attention she received from the Britons.[42]

WHEN IDA ARRIVED home in June, she was met by a whirlwind of praise—and controversy. The crowning compliment came from the usually critical *Indianapolis Freeman,* which went so far as to anoint Ida the "modern Joan of the race," comparing her to the battling saint who saved the throne for France. Ida's campaign abroad had also gotten the attention of the white southern press. The *Memphis Appeal-Avalanche* marked the occasion by calling her a "negro adventuress," who was continuing her "career of triumphant mendacity." But by now, Ida saw such comments as evidence of her success. "I know that the work has done great good," she wrote, "if by no other sign than the abuse it has brought me from the *Memphis Appeal-Avalanche,* the *Atlanta Constitution,* the *Macon Telegraph* and the *Washington City Post.*"[43] Another sign of her good work was that before the year ended, two states, Georgia and North Carolina, passed antilynching laws. No credit (not even by Wells herself) or causal relationship was established between her campaign and the antilynching legislation—and each state had its own political motives—but there was no question that the South was feeling the heat from the attention she was focusing on the region.[44]

There was little time to gloat, however. Ida's immediate concerns upon her return were the state of the proposed World's Fair pamphlet, the fact that the plans for the "Jubilee Day" continued apace, and the role of Douglass in both. As the treasurer of the pamphlet project, he had raised a paltry twenty-five dollars during Ida's absence. And while twenty million visitors, more than half of them from other countries, were making their way to the exposition, and some eight hundred reporters were dispatched to Chicago to cover the fair over its six-month run, blacks were still bickering over the pamphlet—and even getting personal about it. Easily the most insulting was C. H. J. Taylor, editor of the once-supportive *American Citizen,* who predicted that the publication would only arouse an "attack on helpless people." What blacks really needed, he insisted, was "for single women to get husbands and give birth to male children." What had made Taylor turn so viciously is not clear; perhaps he was jealous of the attention Ida was getting, but politics was also a factor. Taylor was a Democrat, and Democrats were back in the White House after Grover Cleveland had reemerged to win the presidency in 1892. Now black Democrats, Taylor included, who were seeking patronage were beginning to circle any prey that put them in good stead with the party. Though Douglass occasionally (as the *Freeman* put it) "spluttered in majestic impatience" against the pamphlet's critics, he was thus far refusing to counter the attacks with the conviction he had displayed with other opponents.[45]

For one thing, the former statesman was preoccupied with his duties as commissioner of the Haitian Pavilion to which he had been appointed by Florvil Hippolyte, president of the Caribbean nation. The Pavilion was a major undertaking. At a time when the failure of the Baring Brothers banking house in England was rippling across the Atlantic to become the Panic of 1893, the Haitian exhibits were constructed at the cost of $20,000; the building that housed them cost $100,000.[46] As the only black American in charge of a pavilion, Douglass also had his hands full in trying to help blacks who had been drawn to Chicago by the fair and were asking if he could help them out with some form of employment. The list of job seekers included a near-starving poet by the name of Paul Laurence Dunbar, a future Chicago newspaper publisher, Robert Abbott, and the soon-to-be-published novelist James Weldon Johnson. As far as participation in the day set aside for blacks, Douglass had put the stamp of credibility on it by deciding to host a program at the Pavilion on that date himself!

INDEED, IDA FOUND that hard-liners like her, some members of the black press, and a small band of black Chicagoans that included Ferdinand

Barnett, were in the minority as far as boycotting the exposition was concerned. It had been hard to resist the pageantry, pride, and patriotism that the fair had taken such pains to display. The exposition grounds spread over 686 acres in Jackson Park—seven miles south of downtown Chicago—and the nation's leading landscapers and architects had created a dreamlike city within a city. Frederick Law Olmsted (designer of New York City's Central Park) oversaw the construction of the fair's spectacular canals, lagoons, and basins. Daniel Burnham, considered by many America's greatest architect, had directed the construction of buildings highlighted by the shimmering "Court of Honor": a cluster of palatial, white plaster-of-paris edifices, rendered in the neoclassical Beaux-Art style, which housed displays devoted to America's technical prowess and innovative engineering. Near the Court of Honor, with its muscular Electricity, Machinery, and Transportation Buildings, was the Woman's Building, designed by architect Sophia Hayden in the softer Renaissance style. Inside were exquisite rooms filled with fine art and craft exhibits by women from all over the world.[47]

The postwar theme of national unity was made even more urgent by the 1893 financial panic, and the fair reflected the impulse with parades in which every racial and ethnic group was represented. There were also spectacles of fealty. The Chicago exposition introduced the idea of a Pledge of Allegiance, which was first performed by masses of schoolchildren lined up in military fashion. And one of the Exposition's most novel attractions was the Ferris Wheel—the "answer" to the 1889 Paris Exposition's Eiffel Tower—which, a later commentator noted, raised fairgoers 260 feet above the grinding realities of the poverty and the race, ethnic, and class conflicts on the ground.[48]

African Americans might have been cast to the margins of the exposition, but they had not been banished from it altogether. Black women, who had fought the planners to be included, had managed to have a token representation in the Woman's Building. In one corner of the New York State room there was a small African American exhibit, comprising, among other objects, ecclesiastically inspired embroideries, gold and silver jewelry from West Africa, and a patented pastry fork invented by Ann Mangin of Woodside, New York, that could be used as both a whipper and flour mixer. In other sections of the fair, there were booths put together by several black universities.[49]

Moreover, in May, while Ida was in London struggling to find meetings to address, black women activists had also gotten the opportunity to participate in a number of exposition-sponsored forums, most notably the Congress of Representative Women. Fannie Barrier Williams, Anna J. Cooper, Hallie Quinn Brown, Frances Harper, and Fannie Jackson Coppin, among others, were invited to give addresses along with white reformers such as the suffragist Susan B. Anthony and Chicago's Hull House founder, Jane Addams.

The appearance of the black women marked a coming-of-age debut for the reformers who were poised to make their mark on American reform—and they had risen to the occasion. All were charged with articulating the progress of black women, and the two most impressive speakers, Fannie Barrier Williams and Anna J. Cooper, did so without sparing the predominantly white audience the harsh realities that faced them. Williams's talk had been fittingly entitled "The Intellectual Progress of the Colored Women of the United States Since the Emancipation Proclamation," and was a tour de force of eloquence.[50] "Less than thirty years ago the term progress as applied to colored women of African descent in the United States would have been an anomaly," she had begun. Conceding that there was still insufficient empirical evidence to document what they had achieved, Williams cited their visible participation in religious, educational, and benevolence institutions, and the evident humanity "borne of their hearts," which were "too warm" and "too large" to engage in "race hatred."[51]

And yet African American women had earned no "general sympathy in the struggle to emancipate themselves"—a struggle that was at once "sorrowful," "wonderfully heroic," and "peculiarly romantic." There was a "touching pathos" in their eagerness "to taste the blessedness of intelligent womanhood"—an eagerness that would inevitably "stamp itself indelibly upon the thought of this country" and its literature and arts.[52]

But these same women were confronted by discrimination in the workplace where their only choices were school teaching or menial work, and Williams wondered aloud why black women garnered respect as servants but contempt when they became women of culture. Her most pointed comments regarded the disparaging stereotypes regarding black women's sexuality.[53] "I regret the necessity of speaking to the question of the moral progress of our women," Williams continued, "because the morality of our home life has been commented upon so disparagingly and meanly that we are placed in the unfortunate position of being defenders of our name." She then talked about the "demoralization" of slavery, adding that "discussion of the moral progress of black women . . . has force and meaning only so far as it tells the story of how once-enslaved women have been struggling for twenty-five years" to emancipate themselves from it. Chivalric black men were giving young women a new sense of protection, she said, but reminded the audience that white men were still preying on black women. "I do not wish to disturb the serenity of this conference by suggesting why this protection is needed and the kind of men against whom it is needed," Williams asserted without specifically mentioning race.[54]

She concluded on a conciliatory note. Williams did not want to overstate the obstacles that black women faced or picture their plight as hopeless. "There is no disposition to take our place at the Congress as faultfinders or supplicants for mercy," Williams averred. "As women of a common country, with common interests, and a destiny that will certainly bring us closer to each other, we come to this altar with our contribution of hopefulness as well as with our complaints."[55]

Anna Julia Cooper, in language no less eloquent, represented herself as speaking for the women of the South. In her brief remarks, the pathos that Williams described came to life in Cooper's rendering of black women whose "unwritten history" included the struggle against overwhelming odds that often "ended in death." Cooper, whose own slave mother was a victim of sexual exploitation, went on to describe "The painful, patient, and silent toil of mothers to gain a fee simple title to the bodies of their daughters, [and] the despairing fight, as of an entrapped tigress, to keep hallowed their own persons . . ." And yet, with faith in a just God, Cooper concluded, "the Afro-American woman maintained ideals of womanhood unshamed by any ever conceived."[56]

After the conclusion of the talks, the audience, obviously impressed, was reported to have asked Frederick Douglass, who was present on the evening that Williams and Cooper spoke, to comment on their presentations. "I have heard tonight what I hardly expected ever to hear," Douglass responded. "I have heard refined, educated, colored ladies addressing—and addressing successfully—one of the most intelligent white audiences that I ever looked upon." He continued, "It is a new thing under the sun, and my heart is too full to speak; my mind is too illuminated with hope and with expectation for the race in seeing this sign."[57]

"HUMPH," ONE CAN almost hear Ida saying to herself when she heard about the program and Douglass's affirmation. Though she must have appreciated the good showing, she would have appreciated it more if one thing had been said about lynching, the projected pamphlet, or some kind of action plan to address the issues that the women had delineated. One thing appeared certain: Wells was going to have a long haul to be considered a "representative woman."

For Ida, the more negative aspects of the exposition would have overshadowed the narrow beams of light that had managed to come through. Like all American fairs, this one was also a paean to America's ability to exploit new commercial markets at home and abroad, but unlike those of the past, African Americans were relegated to a servile, rather than entrepreneurial, place in the economic scheme. Amid the exhibits that promoted an endless array of new products was one that featured a black woman, Nancy Green, a dark-skinned domestic worker with a wide, flashing smile. She was advertising a premade pancake mix for increasingly time-limited housewives. The trademark for the product was Aunt Jemima.[58]

But it was the Midway Plaisance that truly defined the scheme of things as America lurched toward the twentieth century. The Plaisance was a mile-long strip of ethnological exhibits that lifted evolutionary theory off the pages of social science texts and brought it to life. Under the direction of Harvard professor Frederick W. Putnam, and Sol Bloom, a well-known showman, the strip was organized according to the prescribed racial order. At the "top" were folk representations of European villages, followed by Chinese, Turkish, Arabic, Persian, Algerian, and Egyptian villages. Belly dancers were a feature on this part of the strip. On opening day, when President Grover Cleveland's entourage approached the Algerian exhibit (on its way to the Court of Honor), the women, on Sol Bloom's signal, suggestively dropped their veils as the carriage passed.[59]

At the very end of the Midway—and scale of civilization—was a Dahomeyan village where sixty-nine Africans "blacker than buried midnight and as degraded as animals capered numbly to the lascivious pleasings of an unseen tom-tom pounding within," noted a *New York Times* reporter.

They wore brief grass skirts, and the reporter had trouble making a distinction between the men and women. But he had been less confused about their relationship to American blacks. "In these wild people we easily detect many characteristics of the American Negro," he concluded. The spectacle had caused Frederick Douglass to recoil in disgust. The fair planners evidently wanted African Americans to be represented by "African savages brought here to act the monkey," he commented.[60]

Still, Douglass believed that it was incumbent upon blacks to use the opportunity of the fair—and Colored Day—to make a statement and feature the achievements of blacks that militated against the horrific images of the Midway Plaisance. All "we have received has come to us in small concessions, and it is not the part of wisdom to despise the day of small things," he told Ida.[61]

Wells remained unconvinced, but she and Douglass did agree about the importance of publishing the pamphlet. However, as late as July, Ida wrote to Albion Tourgée, who had volunteered to edit the publication, that the outlook for getting it out was "discouraging." Few of the contributors had handed in their manuscripts, and there was still inadequate funding. But she was really writing Albion to ask him to contribute an essay to help foreigners, and especially the English, to understand "how state governments can thus nullify the National constitution." The former judge was the only man who possessed the "data and the ability and the zeal . . . all rolled into one" to write such a chapter for the pamphlet, Wells told him, adding that she needed it by the fifteenth of the month. She promised to pay him "whatever it costs" for the contribution—with the proviso that he could wait until she figured out how to finance the project.[62]

But while Wells was fretting about the pamphlet, a brutal lynching took place in Bardwell, Kentucky. The victim was C. J. Miller, who had been accused of murdering two young white girls, one of whom was raped and found with her throat cut. No doubt at the behest of Tourgée, the *Chicago Inter-Ocean* commissioned Wells to investigate the mob murder. She jumped at the chance to publish her findings in a major newspaper just when the exposition was in full swing. Putting her plans for the pamphlet on hold, Ida made her way to Bardwell.

POSING AS THE dead man's widow, she was able to get a stunning amount of detail about the Miller lynching, and her findings were published in a front-page, six-column article in the *Inter-Ocean*. Wells provided a day-by-day recounting of the search for the alleged perpetrator throughout counties in Kentucky, Illinois, and Missouri, as well as her interviews of law authorities and witnesses.[63] Once Miller was caught and surrounded by a mob, Ida described how he had coolly identified himself and given his wife's address in Springfield, Illinois, as well as a detailed accounting of his travels since the first of the month. On the day of the murder, he insisted, he had not been in Bardwell, the scene of the crime.

According to Wells, after Miller was killed, the fact was verified that Miller was not at the site of the murder of the young girls, and there were also other indications of his innocence. A bloodhound, given the scent of a piece of clothing from the murder scene, had apparently found the real killer. The search animal had lain down accusingly in front of a cottage owned by a white farmer just across the river in Missouri. Additionally, a boatman had identified a passenger embarking for Missouri near the time of the murder as being either white or a fair-skinned mulatto. Miller was brown-skinned. But none of the facts mattered. Miller's body had been mutilated—several fingers and toes were cut off—and a torch had been applied to the body. In "free" America, Ida wrote, "Yet another man had not been given the opportunity to defend himself in court. . . . It is the honest sober belief of many who witnessed the scene, that an innocent man has been barbarously and shockingly put to death in the glare of the nineteenth century civilization by those who profess to believe in Christianity, law, and order."[64] The article was accompanied by an illustration of Miller hanging, from a telegraph pole, by a heavy-linked log chain around his neck while a crowd looked passively on. He had been stripped of all his clothing but what appeared to be a loincloth positioned below his hip. The figure was eerily reminiscent of the image of Christ being crucified on the cross.

The publicity after the July publication of the *Inter-Ocean* investigation that had been entitled the "Brutal Truth" might well have stirred new interest in her pamphlet project, and by the time Ida returned to Chicago, she had come up with a way to help subsidize it. Ida proposed a series of Sunday-afternoon meetings, featuring Douglass as the main speaker, to take place in Chicago's three largest black churches. Douglass agreed, and it turned out to be the right idea at the right time in the right city. The response was immediate; weekly, the pews of Bethel's AME, Quinn Chapel

(AME), and St. Stephen's (Catholic) were filled, and $500 in contributions was collected in a relatively short time. One such program at Bethel alone resulted in the collection of $100 and the endorsement of an unnamed Englishman in the audience who promised to forward a subscription after he returned abroad. News of the success brought about some new sniping in the black press, but Ida answered the skeptical editorials by explaining, again, why the pamphlet was necessary to distribute at the fair where there were so many foreign visitors, especially Britons, who would wonder about the exclusion of African Americans.[65]

In the meantime, Douglass continued to arrange his program at the Haitian Pavilion to take place on Jubilee Day, August 25. As the day unfolded, it appeared that Ida's worst fears would be confirmed. Indeed, watermelon vendors had positioned themselves on the fairgrounds, and when Douglass saw them, he was reported to have left the grounds in disgust. He left Paul Laurence Dunbar in charge of the pavilion and returned to the home of Fannie Barrier Williams and her husband, S. Laing, where he was staying. Early reports suggested that few blacks were coming to the fair, and it appeared that Douglass's program, scheduled for 2:30 P.M., was going to be a bust. But as the time drew nearer a throng of black citizens and a few whites made their way to Festival Hall. Among them were Douglass's honored guests for the occasion: Henry McNeal Turner, the emigrationist, AME bishop, and former president of Atlanta's Morris Brown College; Alexander Walters, the newly elected AME Zion bishop; and Isabel Hooker, a prominent activist and sister of Harriet Beecher Stowe, author of *Uncle Tom's Cabin*. Following their introductions, there was a musical selection from the singer and composer Harry T. Burleigh, who was studying under the Czech composer Antonin Dvořák in New York City, and a poetry reading from Paul Laurence Dunbar (whose appearance was noted by the eminent and career-making *Harper's Magazine* editor William Dean Howells). Douglass, of course, gave the major address of the evening.

Reports about the seventy-five-year-old Douglass's speech remarked how he, seemingly overcome by the moment or the heat of the occasion, began his own oration with a trembling voice, and that he had to cling to the podium with his hands in order to steady them. Encouraged by his apparent fragility, some of the whites in the audience began to heckle him, which, it appeared, was exactly what was needed. Douglass steadied himself, flung his notes aside, and found the sonorous voice that had inspired generations before him. "Men talk of the Negro problem," he thundered. "There is no Negro problem. The problem is whether the American people have . . . honor enough, patriotism enough, to live up to their own Constitution." He continued, now in full control, "We Negroes love our country. We fought for it. We ask only that we be treated as well as those who fought against it." Douglass drowned out the catcalls as "an organ would a pennywhistle," noted a reporter, and Wells, who had boycotted the event, conceded that she had swelled with pride when she read how he had turned such a frugal opportunity into an illustrious moment.[66]

"I went straight out to the fair and begged his pardon for presuming in my youth and inexperience to criticize him for an effort which had done more to bring our cause to the attention of the American people than anything else which had happened during the fair," she wrote.[67] Ida might have been stubborn, but she was also open enough—and committed enough—to weigh the consequences of a strategy she didn't agree with against the results it achieved.

After accepting her amends, Douglass extended the lesson when he picked her up at the Clark Street office of Ferdinand Barnett's *Conservator,* where Wells was now working, to take her to lunch. He suggested Chicago's Boston Oyster House, just across the street, but Ida told Douglass that they did not serve blacks there. Douglass took her arm and said, "Come, let's go there." "Of course I was game," Ida recalled. "We sauntered into [the restaurant] cocked and primed for a fight if necessary." When no waiter came to seat them, Douglass walked to the nearest table, pulled out a chair, seated Ida, then seated himself. In the meantime, the proprietor, who recognized Douglass, came over and addressed him cordially. Soon both of them were getting more attention than they wanted. "Ida," Douglass finally said to her with a "roguish" look in his eye. "I thought you said that they didn't serve us here."[68]

Later that August, miraculously, the pamphlet *The Reason Why the Colored American Is Not in the World's Columbian Exposition: The Afro-American's Contribution to Columbian Literature* appeared and was distributed from Douglass's Haitian Pavilion.

Although the funds for the pamphlet had fallen well short of the $5,000 goal, making it impossible to translate the entire document into other languages, the preface was rendered in French and German, as well as English. "The exhibit of the progress made by the race in 25 years of freedom as against 250 years of slavery, would have been the greatest tribute to the greatness and progressiveness of American institutions which could have been shown to the world," it began.[69]

The preface was followed with Douglass's introduction. "There are many good things concerning our country and countrymen of which we would be glad to tell in this pamphlet, if we could do so, and at the same time tell the truth," he wrote.

> We would like for instance to tell our visitors that the moral progress of the American people has kept even pace with their enterprise and their material civilization . . . that two hundred and sixty years of progress and enlightenment have banished barbarism and race hate from the United States; that the old things of slavery have entirely passed away, and that all things pertaining to the colored people have become new; . . . that the statement of human rights contained in its glorious Declaration of Independence, including the right to life liberty and the pursuit of happiness is not an empty boast nor a mere rhetorical flourish . . . that to the colored people of America, morally speaking, the World's Fair now in progress, in not a whited sepulcher. . . . But unhappily, nothing of all this can be said, without qualification and without flagrant disregard for the truth.[70]

Douglass continued by laying out the history of racial attitudes formed during slavery, the spurious Supreme Court decisions, and the injustice of lynch law and the false cries of rape that drove it. "The Americans are a great and magnimous people and this great exposition adds greatly to their honor and renown," he concluded, but "in the pride of their success they have cause for repentance as well as complaisance, and for shame as well as for glory, and hence we send forth this volume to be read of [by] all men."[71]

The next two chapters traced discriminatory legislation passed by southern states in the wake of Reconstruction and the convict lease system. The latter was characterized as the "twin evil of lynching," which was used to not only net "able-bodied men" but also increasing numbers of young black children—including a ten-year-old in Alabama—and to disenfranchise potential voters. The two chapters had no name attached to them, and the use of terms like "our race" suggest that they had a black author, but there is little question that, as Ida had requested, Albion Tourgée provided the statistics for the chapters—if he didn't write them himself.[72]

In another chapter, Ferdinand Barnett, founding editor of the *Conservator*, wrote movingly about the disappointment that African Americans felt when they learned that the Republican president Harrison had failed to appoint even one black to the exposition's national commission, despite their fervent desire to demonstrate their progress and the fact that blacks represented seven and a half million American citizens. He then recounted a blow-by-blow description of their efforts through official and political channels to remediate the situation. Included were copies of letters—and the unsatisfactory responses to them—that Hallie Quinn Brown and others had written to the Board of Lady Managers.[73]

I. Garland Penn, the black press historian, gave a comprehensive account of black progress in literacy; the number of black teachers employed in education institutions; the numbers in trade, mechanical, medical, dentistry, and legal professions; the gross wealth of blacks broken down by states (Louisiana had the highest figure, more than eighteen million dollars); and achievements in art and literature. Penn also included a list of sixty patented inventions by blacks, which could have easily been included in the industrial pavilions. The inventions included a cornstalk harvester, a locomotive smokestack, a ventilator for railroad cars, a lasting machine for shoes, and a fire escape ladder. Of particular note were the inventions of Granville Woods, who had conceived the apparatus for the transmission of messages by electricity that was assigned to the American Bell Telephone Company, and his patents for a telephone transmitter.[74]

Ida's essay, "Lynch Law," written more than a decade before the first scholarly treatment of lynching, provided a short history of lynching and how it evolved from its Revolutionary War origins. It also included her now-familiar lynching statistics, broken down by years and states, led, like the black wealth statistics, by Louisiana with 29 in 1892, followed closely by Tennessee (28), Alabama (22), and Arkansas (25); she also included the mostly nonrape motives for them. She reiterated, in her matter-of-fact recounting, many of the points she had published in the *New York Age* and her pamphlet *Southern Horrors,* but she added the same photograph that Catherine Impey had used in the *Anti-Caste.* Wells also included vivid, detailed descriptions of several lynchings that had occurred in July since the opening of the World's Fair. In addition to the murder of Miller, she wrote about another lynching that year in Memphis and described how the victim, Lee Walker, had been hung from a telephone pole (a modern innovation that, like Miller's telegraph pole, was fast becoming an urban substitute for tree limbs) in one of the "so-called queen cities of the South."[75]

According to Wells, Walker, driven by hunger, had attacked two white women driving a wagon with the purpose of robbing them. Their screams frightened him away and when the women reported the incident, a ten-day manhunt ensued. Walker was finally caught, jailed, and charged with attempted rape, despite his own protests that he had made no attempts to sexually assault the women. In fact, the women themselves had never accused him of that particular crime. Wells then quoted the *Memphis Commercial*, which described Walker being dragged from the jail by a mob and lynched. His abductors, made up of cursing men and boys, hit him and stabbed him with a knife, "again and again" while the "crowd looked on with complaisance, if not with real pleasure." In the meantime, someone in the crowd stripped off Walker's clothes and mutilated the swinging body. Pistol shots were fired into him while the mob hurled expletives and swung the body so that it was dashed against the pole, kicked the carcass, and continued to cut his hips and lower parts of his legs. After the body was cut down, onlookers eagerly cut and divided up the rope to keep as souvenirs.

But nothing provided more evidence that the mob spirit had completely taken over her former city than what happened next. A policeman gathered up the ghastly corpse and took it to the coroner's office, and after the inquest, plans were announced to convene a jury. At that point, someone among the witnesses to the proceedings screamed, "Burn him, burn him" and others joined the cry. As the crowd lurched toward the body, authorities attempted to stave them off, begging that they not bring additional disgrace to the city—but to no avail. A half-dozen men seized the naked body. A fire was set in the middle of Beale Street and the men who had the body gave it a heave and tossed it into the flames. The "complaisant" onlookers included several white women who, with their escorts, pushed to the front of the crowd where they could get a better look, and a twelve-year-old girl brought to the scene by a man and a woman who were probably her parents. What was left of Walker's charred remains was then tied with a rope and dragged by members of the crowd down Main Street.[76]

The Walker lynching represented no spontaneous outburst of passion, Wells emphasized. Her evidence was that the day before the hanging, she had gotten a telegram by way of the *Chicago Inter-Ocean* from one of the Memphis dailies informing her that Lee would be burned the next night.

Did she want to come to Memphis, the telegram cruelly taunted, so that she could write it up?[77]

In a note on the final page of the pamphlet, dated August 30, Wells apologized for not being able to include all of the data she had wished because of the haste in getting it to press. Nevertheless, she was able to tell her readers that twenty thousand copies of the publication were available for "gratuitous distribution." She also asked that those who wanted a copy to be mailed include three cents for postage and that she would personally fulfill the order.[78]

The return address published in the pamphlet was Clark Street, the address of the *Conservator*. The hope that more subscriptions would come in was surely one reason Ida had decided to remain in Chicago for the remainder of the year; another was the growing affection between her and Ferdinand Barnett. But Wells was also attracted to the Windy City, which, unlike New York and other eastern cities, had yet to organize a black women's club. The closest was the "Ladies' Day" meetings at the Tourgée Club, a black men's club named in honor of Albion's zealous support of the race, but the attendance diminished after the fair closed. According to Wells, interest increased after she decided to speak herself on several Ladies' Day occasions—so much so, that the idea of forming a club became a viable one. However, the real catalyst for its formation, she admitted, was the appearance of W. T. Stead, a British Social Christian minister and editor of *Review of Reviews*, a publication dedicated to promoting the alliance between the reform churches in England. Within a year, Stead would inspire the founding of the Civic Federation of Chicago, a leading reform group, after publishing a well-received, vivid jeremiad called *If Christ Came to Chicago*. It was a reformist exposé of what he called in one chapter "Satan's Invisible World Displayed," delineating the considerable poverty, vice, and government corruption bubbling beneath the city's touted world's-fair triumph. Ida recounted how Stead told the women that protest against racial conditions was meaningless without an effective organization. Inspired, the women made Ida chairman of their group, and they began holding meetings to discuss a formation of a club. Ida suggested that Mary Jones, one of the most prominent women in Chicago, head the movement because of her standing in the community. Mary was the widow of John Jones, who had used his considerable wealth gained in the tailoring business to advance abolition and civil rights. In the 1870s, Jones had been elected the first black to serve on the Cook County Board of Commissioners.[79]

By September of 1893, the black women's organization, later chartered as the Ida B. Wells Club, came into existence as the first such club in Illinois. The club appeared to be immediately successful; by February there were more than three hundred members. But by then, Wells was informed by her English friends in the Society for the Recognition of the Brotherhood of Man that they were prepared to sponsor her second trip to Great Britain.

Actually Ida had also been biding her time until the circumstances were right for her return. After she had left the British Isles, the Society had secured the services of two American men to lead the antilynching campaign with less than satisfactory results, and the organization had continued to roil over the Mayo-Impey split. In November, Mayo wrote Ida asking her to come to England, but the letter also suggested that she was expected to take her side against Impey. When Wells refused to return under such conditions, Mayo retracted the invitation and proclaimed that she would have no more to do with sponsoring the trip.[80]

But in the interim, the Society had hired a new executive secretary, S. J. Celestine Edwards, a black Dominican, to whom Ida wrote asking if the Society agreed with Mayo's directive. The group had split into two opposing factions, she learned; each had wanted Ida to come to England, and the pro-Impey members were prepared to sponsor her tour. Wells, despite the apparently still unsettled state of her prospective hosts, readied herself for her second trip to the British Isles.[81]

So in February of 1894, Ida, presumably, consoled Ferdinand, placed the fast-growing Ida B. Wells Club in the hands of Rosie Moore, the vice president, and found someone to replace her at the Conservator. This time, she wasn't going to let anything get in the way of fully mobilizing British opinion against lynching.

CHAPTER ELEVEN

St. Joan and Old Man Eloquent

I have never met an "agitator" so cautious and impassioned in speech.

—*Reverend Richard A. Armstrong describing Ida B. Wells*

They would have been better satisfied if you had spoken more positively regarding me and my work.

—*Ida B. Wells to Frederick Douglass*

By her second transatlantic voyage, Ida wrote, she had learned not to be seasick—an indication that she had prepared herself in every way that she could to succeed in Great Britain. She had gotten out the World's Fair pamphlet and had written a front-page article about the lynching of C. J. Miller in the *Chicago Inter-Ocean* at a time when many leading Britons were in the States. She had secured two influential allies, Albion Tourgée and Frederick Douglass. The influence of the former judge had undoubtedly helped her to get the assignment to write for the Chicago paper and the results had impressed its editor, William Penn Nixon, who asked Ida to be a paid correspondent for the *Inter-Ocean* with her own "Ida B. Wells Abroad" column. As she wrote in her autobiography, the assignment made her, as far as she knew, the first African American to attain such a position for a daily paper in the United States.[1] Most important, with her own column, she would be in control of at least one facet of the reporting generated by her trip.

Wells had also established a comrade-in-arms relationship with Frederick Douglass, and they had smoothed over their differences regarding Colored Day. Surely she had reason to hope that she could count on him to use his considerable influence on her behalf—especially now that the World's Columbian Exposition, and to some extent his association with her anti-lynching campaign, had rehabilitated his public persona. Douglass was well known among the new generation of English reformers and he still maintained ties with those of his own generation, some of whom were still active and influential in British reform movements.

"Old Man Eloquent," as Douglass was sometimes called, had established his legendary reputation in the British Isles during the 1840s, when he was a strapping young man in his twenties who impressed his overflow audiences with his possessing figure and passionate grandiloquence. He had begun his twenty-one-month stay in 1845, soon after the publication of his bestselling *Narrative of the Life of Frederick Douglass,* an autobiography that brought him the laurels of fame—and its dangers. Douglass had been a fugitive slave at the time, and his decision to go to Great Britain, which had abolished slavery in 1834, was impelled by his need to find a refuge, savor the experience of being in a free land, and aid the ongoing abolitionist movement there to end slavery in the United States and other parts of the world. During his sojourn, he became close to influential reformers such as John Bright, a liberal MP; Eliza Wigham, the temperance leader and former vice president of the British Women's Temperance Association (BWTA) whom Ida had met on her first tour; and Ellen Richardson, a Quaker and abolitionist who lived in Newcastle. They pled for Douglass to settle permanently in Great Britain, but when he announced his intentions to return to America, Richardson, despairing that such a man had to go home a slave, came up with the scheme to liberate him. She raised funds through his friends, including John Bright, and asked the MP to use his influence to negotiate Douglass's purchase and manumission from his owner. Boston lawyers were contacted to make the final deal—for about $1,250—and in 1846, Douglass was a free man. Before he returned to the United States, additional money was raised, $2,175, so that Douglass could found his own newspaper, subsequently known as the *North Star.* By the 1890s, Bright, Wigham, and Richardson were either still active in influential reform circles or had sons and daughters who were. Now Ida was poised to follow in Douglass's footsteps for another campaign to end a horrible wrong. Douglass loaned Wells twenty-five dollars to help with her expenses.[2]

The appointment of S. J. Celestine Edwards promised to be a real boon to Ida's second tour. He was a seasoned temperance activist, a Pan Africanist who supported rebellion against British imperialists, and the first black editor of *Lux,* a Christian anti-imperialist paper. After being hired by the Society for the Recognition of the Brotherhood of Man (SRBM), he had started a new journal for the organization, *Fraternity,* and, despite suffering from a bout of rheumatic fever, he had toured England and Scotland speaking on lynch law at the behest of the SRBM and against the advice of his doctor.[3] The new executive secretary was better known and had better access than Impey to the upper classes of VIP reformers who, like Edwards, were linked to a number of liberal movements.

Finally, Ida was now fully prepared to do battle with the leader of one of those movements, Frances Willard. This time she would bring a copy of the *New York Voice* interview in which the temperance leader had described the "great dark-faced mobs" that were imperiling white women in the South. From the time Wells returned from England in 1893, she had been frantically searching for that interview. She had even gone several times to the Woman's Christian Temperance Union (WCTU) headquarters in Chicago, known as the Temple, to scour back issues of the *Union Signal,* the organization's official organ, in the hopes of finding it. On one occasion, she met Anna Gordon, the WCTU's secretary, and asked her point-blank where the article could be found. Gordon had said that she did not know, but that she would soon be seeing Willard in England and would ask her about it. Ida gave Gordon her address and asked that Willard contact her. Ida, not surprisingly, did not hear from the WCTU president before she left for England. In the meantime, however, she found the interview on her own and sent it to Celestine Edwards to publish in the May issue of *Fraternity.* Another item Wells packed for the trip was the original telegram she had received from the *Memphis Public Ledger* on the day before the Lee Walker lynching. Hopeful, well armed with evidence of American race hatred, and in full possession of her sea legs, Ida crossed the Atlantic.[4]

WHEN SHE REACHED Liverpool in early March, on a Friday, Wells was met by a young Englishwoman from the SRBM who, according to Ida's autobiography, informed her that the organization was still divided but that Edwards was prepared to arrange her speaking dates. What she did not say in her text was that she also learned that Isabella Mayo had quit the organization and withdrawn her financial support, and that the organization could only provide bare minimum expenses for her stay. Moreover, Celestine Edwards had become increasingly frail, the reason, no doubt, he hadn't been there to meet Ida personally. But the promise to arrange speaking dates was immediately fulfilled. The very next Sunday, an appointment had been made for her to have lunch at the home of Charles F. Aked, pastor of Pembroke Chapel.

It would have been difficult to imagine a better person to meet at the start of Ida's second campaign. Aked, a Baptist and Christian Socialist, was a co-founder of the influential Passive Resistance League, a pacifist organization whose concerns included military conflicts in Africa and Armenia.[5] Pembroke Chapel, which he had pastored since 1890, was the largest congregation of Nonconformists outside of London. Nonconformists included a broad range of Protestant dissenters from the Anglican Church and other established churches; many were part of the Christian Socialist movement, which sought to organize Christian Socialist thought across denominations. Wells went to hear Aked preach that day and thought him "young" (he was two years her junior), "eloquent," and "inspired," and that his sermon was "the best" that she had ever heard. They met afterward, and on the same evening Aked invited Ida to his discussion group, which drew about twelve hundred members. The discussion centered around the Henrik Ibsen play An Enemy of the People, and Aked invited those who wanted to stay afterward to hear Ida to do so. Nearly all of the standing-room-only audience remained.[6]

The press coverage of her ninety-minute talk at Pembroke suggested that Wells drew upon familiar themes with her now-familiar mix of personal narrative, commentary, and complaint. She told the story of the Moss lynching, apprised the audience of the Free Speech editorial that got her exiled, rendered graphic descriptions of lynchings, and criticized opinionmakers and the press, including those in the North, who acquiesced to the South's "suppression of the truth." Taking a page from her previous experience in London, Wells also used the tactic of telling Britons that they were in the unique position of being able to influence Americans. Whites in the United States would not listen to black Americans, she told them, but would "unquestionably heed the voice of the British people." Press notices were favorable. Ida's appearance was followed by "a great outburst of cheering which was frequently renewed in the course of her graphic address," noted a reporter, who described her as "young, well-educated, and a capital speaker."[7]

After Ida's well-received debut, Aked invited her to his home to dine with him and his wife, and the three of them got along immediately. The Akeds, Ida wrote, were sensitive enough to realize that she, in her own words, "did not like, or rather had no confidence in, white people," and the couple consciously "set themselves to work to uproot my natural distrust and suspicion."[8] Eventually they exchanged confidences. Aked confessed he had been asked to have Ida speak at Pembroke during her first trip, but had refused, because he did not know her nor did he believe her assertions. But he had since gone to the Chicago Columbian Exposition and had read Ida's account of the C. J. Miller lynching in the *Inter-Ocean*. "I sat under the shadow of the Statue of Liberty in Jackson Park [at the Columbian Exposition] and read these accounts until I was wild," Ida quoted Aked as saying.[9] Ida, in turn, confided to Aked about the problems with the SRBM. Upon learning of the situation, the Akeds immediately took her under their wing. They offered to make their home the headquarters for the tour and proceeded to make contacts with other prominent Britons to aid the cause. According to Ida, Aked also suggested that she write Frederick Douglass immediately, informing him of the problem and asking that he write a strong letter of support on her behalf.[10]

It is not clear how Ida characterized her relationship to Douglass. In early March, Aked had written an article about her in the *Liverpool Daily Post* that said Ida's trip had been sponsored by the former abolitionist. It is unlikely that Ida would have made such a declaration, but she might have created that impression, purposely or not, by innuendo—and there is no evidence that she asked Aked to retract the statement.[11] And in any case, Aked was probably right about Ida needing a letter from Douglass. The unsettled state of the SRBM and the health problems of Celestine Edwards meant that Wells would not have an effective or a well-known Briton to accompany her as she traveled throughout the country. In the absence of a credible sponsor, a letter from Douglass would help to fill the void, and it would be helpful to Aked's own efforts on her behalf. After all, not everyone had gone to the World's Fair or had followed the coverage of lynchings in the United States. And although Ida had honed her speaking skills and message, her claims were, indeed, sensational—some would say prurient—and Aked thought she needed someone who knew her to vouch for her character. Douglass often got such requests. Later that year he would write such a letter for Hallie Quinn Brown, the former lady principal of Tuskegee who was now professor of elocution at Ohio's Wilberforce University. In 1894, she also traveled to the British Isles to raise funds for the school through lectures and recitations. Brown had asked Douglass to write a letter on her behalf and he had done so. "The bearer of this letter . . . is a lady of character and ability," he had written, in part, adding an explanation about the importance of the institution and leaving no doubt that Brown was its legitimate representative.[12]

On March 13, 1894, the day after the Aked piece appeared in the *Daily Post*, Ida wrote Douglass. She began by informing him of the good start her campaign had had in Liverpool and her fortunate meeting with Aked. But she was now finding that she was "compelled to depend on myself somewhat, as there are many places where the Brotherhood is not organized." Isabella Mayo was still "hostile" because of the Impey-Mayo "brouhaha," she confided to him, asking that he keep that information just "between us two." In any case, she was writing, on Aked's suggestion, to ask him to write a letter on her behalf "commending" her to all of his English friends. It had to be done quickly, Ida added, because of the slowness of the mails. She closed with the hope that he would "oblige" her as it was only the "second personal favor" she had ever asked of him (the loan was presumably the first) and that in any case it was not for herself only, but with the "hope" that the "race will benefit hereby." Enclosed also was a note from Aked, who, Ida informed Douglass, had tried unsuccessfully to meet him while he was in Chicago.[13]

While Ida and Aked awaited Douglass's response, the minister arranged ten speaking dates for Ida in Liverpool over the next two weeks, Wells reported, with audiences that averaged a thousand per lecture. Ida addressed fifteen hundred Congregationalists at one stop and, in one of the most important connections she would make, spoke to Unitarians at the Unitarian Hope Street Church. Informed by the idea of the unity of humankind, Unitarians had an activist tradition in the British antislavery and antiracist struggle. After Wells's talk on March 18, the Unitarians passed a resolution that condemned the "barbarities of lynch law" and exhorted Americans, "in the name of our common humanity," to stop the practice. Reverend Richard A. Armstrong repeated the message in a letter to the *Christian Register* of Boston, the chief Unitarian organ in the United States, in which he chastised his American peers, and particularly New Englanders, for allowing a situation in which the "Negro . . . - beneath your national flag" could find no security against the "nameless horrors of the amateur scaffold, the branding iron, and the stake."[14]

Next was the most important event held during Ida's stay in Liverpool, in part because its host, Sir Edward Russell, a good friend of Aked's whom Ida had impressed on her first trip, was its most prominent citizen. Russell was editor of the *Liverpool Daily Post*, a paper that provided some of Wells's most enthusiastic coverage. He was a fervent critic of Britain's imperialist policies in Africa and by 1894, was, according to the *New York Times,* poised to become lord of appeal, the stepping-stone to the lord chief judgeship. Russell's concern about the lynching issue was first sparked by the *Anti-Caste* cover, provided by Albion Tourgée, which featured the photo of the hanging corpse surrounded by complaisant onlookers. Since meeting Ida he had come to believe that there was no "subject upon which the civilized world needs more to be aroused than that of lynching."[15]

Russell said as much in his address before the March 22 meeting at Hope Hall. He also spoke to the issue of Britain's right to come, again, to the aid of blacks as they had during the abolitionist period, and that race prejudice was "inconsistent with Christian character" and "incompatible with civilization." Wells, he said, was "adorned by every grace of womanhood," and her mission was justified by public duty. Ida's own presentation was "cordially received," according to the *Daily Post,* and "narrated in her own quiet and unimpassioned but earnest and forcible way." It was followed by a resolution offered by Charles Aked that couldn't have pleased Ida more. It "confirmed" her pronouncements about the prevalence of lynch law in the United States and said that such unlawful outrages were not only a bad reflection on the administration of justice in America but "upon the honor of its people." The motion was seconded by the ailing Celestine Edwards, who had probably made a great effort to be there, and the resolution was carried with "great enthusiasm."[16]

Wells wrote about all of this in her first two "Ida B. Wells Abroad" columns, due to be published April 2 and April 9. They set the template for subsequent weekly dispatches that, in addition to addressing different aspects of lynching and its American apologists, gave blow-by-blow descriptions of her meetings, the resolutions passed by them, the size of her audiences, a good deal of name-dropping, and long, verbatim quotations from the English press. She also provided her readers with pointed history lessons. She recounted how Liverpool, known as the "Gateway to the British Empire," had swollen in wealth through the Triangular slave trade. Wells pointed out how the same Liverpool, with its expansive cotton market, had built more than "half the slave ships" slated for the Middle Passage, supported the South during the Civil War, and mobbed American abolitionist Henry Ward Beecher when he spoke against slavery there. But the city had since discovered that it did not need the immoral taint of slavery to prosper, she pointed out. Symbolic of the possibilities for reform, she recounted the story of Liverpool's most famous native son, William E. Gladstone, Liberal Party leader and Great Britain's prime minister (most recently from 1892 to 1894). Belonging to a family whose wealth came from the slave trade, Gladstone rose from his conservative origins as a Tory and a supporter of Southern secession to become one of England's great liberals on social and political questions, including the disestablishment of the Anglican Church and home rule for Ireland.

Indeed, Liverpool had lessons to teach America, Ida told her audiences, paralleling their more evolved attitude on the race question with the "superiority" of their civilization. Wells then described how it felt to be in a city where all citizens, regardless of color, were equal before the law. It "is like being born into another world, to be welcomed among persons of the highest order of intellectual and social culture as if one were one of themselves," Ida wrote. "Here, a 'colored' person can ride in any sort of conveyance in any part of the country without being insulted, stop at any hotel, or be accommodated at any restaurant one wishes without being refused with contempt; wander into any picture gallery, lecture room, concert hall, theater, or church and receive the most courteous treatment from officials and fellow sightseers."[17]

Wells's next stop was Manchester, the home of the *Manchester Guardian* and its vegetarian editor, W. E. A. Axon, with whom Wells had stayed on her previous trip. Wells spoke twelve times in ten days there; Axon presided over the largest meeting and no doubt had a hand in arranging the others. As in the past, the *Guardian* wrote an antilynching editorial and reiterated the point that Ida had begun making in her talks about the increasing incidences of lynchings in the North. Ida's *Inter-Ocean* column about her experience there opened with the description of the recent opening of the city's large canal through which ships could pass directly into the city and now could compete directly with Liverpool, its greatest rival in wealth and size. She also wrote about Manchester's vast number of cotton-spinning firms and its support for the Confederacy during the Civil War. But Manchester, like Liverpool, realized the error of its ways, and recent evidence of its change of heart was her reception there. "From the Bishop of Manchester, the Society of Friends, Unitarians, Methodists, and Congregationalists," she wrote, "American lynching has received not only strong words of condemnation but earnest resolutions have been passed in a spirit of Christian love, calling upon the people of the United States to remove the blot upon their good name and put a stop to our 'national crime.' "[18]

BY THE END of March, when Wells prepared to leave Manchester, she should have been pleased with the first month of her trip. Large audiences had come to see her. The press coverage of her appearances had been more than supportive. Strong antilynching resolutions had been passed by important religious bodies and leading figures within them. As a result of her appearances, membership rose in the still reeling SRBM. Most important, her own view about lynching was getting across. Racial violence was about race hatred, not rape; it reflected the immorality of its perpetrators and apologists—not that of African Americans, who were, as anyone who read her world's-fair pamphlet knew, making demonstrable progress; and a civilization that did not have the ability to fully condemn or stop lynchings was sorely lacking. Not only had she brought Britons around to her way of thinking, but in the age when a new generation of blacks were vying to be the representative voice of the race, they saw her as one. "How the [lynching] matter appears to the intelligent and educated Afro-American may be seen by the public utterances of Miss Ida B. Wells," Axon had noted when he introduced Ida in Manchester.[19] Wells's success was also commented on by black women back home. In March, her campaign was mentioned in the *Woman's Era,* established in 1894 and the first monthly magazine published by African American women. Boston's Woman's Era Club, led by Josephine St. Pierre Ruffin, was responsible for the publication, which would provide a valuable record of black women's reform activities, including the effort to create a national entity out of the proliferating numbers of black women's clubs throughout the country. Ida's campaign was a good rallying point to catalyze such an organization, in the opinion of Florida Ruffin Ridley, Josephine Ruffin's daughter.

Wells was creating "so much interest in her crusade against lynching," Ridley wrote in its premiere issue, "that it was a good time to carry out the club's idea."[20]

Their consciousness raised about the situation in the United States, now, as Wells reported, people were coming up to her after her lectures, expressing indignation when they read of an American lynching. She was keeping up with the reports as well, but on one occasion someone told her of a recent incident that she had not yet heard about, and the cruelty and the shock of it unsettled her. A black woman in San Antonio, Texas, Ida was told, had been boxed up in a barrel with nails driven through the sides and then rolled down a hill until she was dead. "I sat there as if turned to stone," Ida recalled, "with the tears rolling down my cheeks at this new evidence of outrage upon my people, and apathy of the American white people." All of this renewed her determination to take to task her favorite targets again: Dwight Moody, Bishop Haygood, and, especially, Frances Willard. In Wells's *Inter-Ocean* column, due to be published on April 23, she spent several paragraphs on the temperance leader, quoting her infamous 1890 interview in the *New York Voice* and noting how her words "encouraged" the South, as she put it, in its "cruelty."[21]

Ida had reason to hope that British reform religious groups might have a greater impact back home than any other, and the movement was gaining momentum. Reverend Armstrong of the Hope Street Church and Reverend S. A. Steinthal, another leading antislavery Unitarian who had been a friend and ally of William Lloyd Garrison and had heard Wells in Manchester, were going to lead an effort to pass a resolution before the national conference of the Unitarian, Liberal Christian, Free Christian, Presbyterian, and other Non-Subscribing Conferences that was meeting in Manchester in April. The conference represented 350 churches.

Nevertheless, although Wells expected a similar reception in Bristol and Newcastle, her final destination, London, was sure to be more of a challenge. She didn't have the same contacts there as she had in Manchester and Liverpool, and the London press was not easily impressed. In addition, a meeting like the big conference scheduled for mid-April also included Americans who were more hostile, if not to lynching, then to Wells's accusations about the role of Frances Willard and other liberal reformers. A good letter from Frederick Douglass would go a long way in helping her and her supporters.

Sometime just before the Manchester conference in April, Ida received Douglass's letter, written on March 27. After the usual niceties of telling Ida that he was glad that she made it safely to England and that she was "fortunate" in securing the aid of a man like Charles Aked, he vented his displeasure. "I see that you are already advertised as accredited to England by me," he wrote, referring to Aked's earlier article in the *Liverpool Daily Post*.[22] Even if he considered this a minor infraction, there were no doubt other reasons for his obvious annoyance. Although unmentioned by Douglass, it didn't help that Aked's article had also quoted Douglass's letter and preface to *Southern Horrors*, replete with the line about the great orator's words being "feeble" compared to Ida's. In the United States, his gracious self-deprecation was understood, but it might be read more literally abroad. Furthermore, Douglass probably read Wells's "being-on-my-own" remark, correctly, as a prelude to a request regarding money. Ida had promised to return the twenty-five dollars he had loaned her once she got overseas, and now she claimed that she would be unable to do so. Douglass, who was living comfortably at a time when there was an economic downturn, was no doubt weary—and wary—of such requests from a growing number of friends, family, and even associates. Editor I. Garland Penn had just written to Douglass about the "urgency" of a hundred-dollar loan from him. Additionally, Douglass's grandson-in-law and Ida's friend, Charles Morris, had requested, and received, an apparently large sum five months previously so that he and his wife, Annie, who was pregnant and ill, could re-settle in Ann Arbor where Morris was studying at the University of Michigan. Annie had died soon after at the age of twenty-eight.[23]

"Will you oblige me by telling me frankly who invited you to spend three months in England and what assurances they gave you of support while on this mission?" Douglass snapped in the letter. "There is nothing new in the story you now tell me of the attitude of Mrs. Mayo," he continued. "[I]f you have not been invited and have gone to England on your own motion and for your own purposes, you should have frankly told me so." Douglass ended the letter on a conciliatory, but admonitory, note. "I am ready to hold up your hands, and want to do so but I wish to do so intelligently and truthfully."[24]

The words must have struck terror in Ida's heart. What was Douglass going to say, or *not* going to say to her newfound supporters? On the same day he had written to Ida, Douglass had also written to Charles Aked; and as Ida had feared, it fell short of the kind of personal endorsement that the English minister and Wells had sought. Reading between the lines, what appeared to really pique Douglass, who obviously read the English press, was that she was being spoken of in the land of his earlier triumph as the "representative" Negro on not only lynching but race relations in the United States. In his letter to Aked, he employed the strategy of faint praise to restore order to the world. "Miss Ida B. Wells, now sojourning in England, known to me by the persecutions she has been subjected on account of her bold exposures and pungent denunciations of Southern outrages upon colored people, has told me of the kindness and help she has received at your hands," Douglass began unpromisingly, as if he had no personal relationship with Ida. "Once an exile in your land, I know of the value of such help you have given Miss Wells." Falling short of accrediting Ida, he nonetheless gave no credit, he said, to the southern papers that "have assailed her as an unworthy person." The "side of the American mob has been told to England by a hundred presses. The side of the Negro has been hushed in death. I have tried to speak for the Negro in this country and, I hope, not entirely in vain, and I am glad that you now have in England, one so competent as Miss Wells, to tell the Negro's side of the story." The word *competent,* Douglass must have known, would have gone over like a deflated balloon. He concluded by telling Aked that if he were a "few years younger," he would have "willingly joined Miss Wells in her work." But in lieu of his being unable to come to England himself, he enclosed in his letter his own pamphlet, which had his picture on the cover.

It was a printed copy of an address he had given the previous January at the Metropolitan AME Church in Washington, D.C. Entitled *Lessons of the Hour,* it was a treatise on white and black relations in the South. Douglass had spoken about the false accusations of rape that led to lynchings, and he explicitly criticized Bishop Haygood and Frances Willard, whom he called a northern woman with southern principles. Although his message echoed that of Wells, Douglass never uttered her name in the speech.[25]

IN 1894, DOUGLASS was especially sensitive about his status. The Democrats were in the White House, and as an elderly Republican, Douglass was struggling to remain relevant in the political scheme of things. At the time, he was actively lobbying to help the black Democrat and *American Citizen* editor C. H. J. Taylor attain the recorder of deeds position that Douglass himself had once held. Taylor, of course, had become one of Ida's most vicious critics. He was the one who had made the remark about the race needing not another pamphlet but for single women to get married and have male children. Subsequently, upon learning that Wells had joined the *Conservator,* he had lashed out again. The *Conservator* was once a "clean paper," he announced, obviously implying that Wells's writings about sexual relationships had sullied the publication's image. The hatefulness of his next remark revealed how deep—and sordid—his particular variation of sexism could be. Taylor suggested that the paper "muzzle" that "animal from Memphis." If "we get after her," Taylor promised, "we will make her wish her mother had changed her mind ten months before she was born." Soon after the editorial appeared in December, Ida had written Douglass about it. "I submit to you if this is not too much to bear," she despaired. It "is very hard to have to withstand such insults from white and black men too." She was "utterly unable" to help herself, she told Douglass, and had asked him to use his influence to punish Taylor, as he had other opponents.[26]

But while Ida was in England, Douglass was writing letters to senators on Taylor's behalf. In addition to Douglass's own political motives, he may have also had reason to believe Taylor when he promised that if he got the position, he would make sure that President Grover Cleveland "in no uncertain words" would address southern governors about lynchings. But whatever Douglass was thinking, it wasn't helping Ida in her time of need.[27]

Writing her reply on April 6, Ida began by taking the not-unfamiliar tack of the wounded martyr who had been misunderstood. She was "hurt cruelly," by Douglass's "tone of distrust," she began. With "all the discouragements I have received and the time and money I have sacrificed to the work, I have never felt so like giving up as since I received your very cool and cautious letter." Wells went on to explain that she was promised funds by the SRBM only to find out about Mayo's resignation after she had already landed in Liverpool. Ida also reminded Douglass that her situation was due to her principled stand regarding Catherine Impey, their mutual friend. "I would never betray a friend," Wells wrote pointedly, "even if it meant that she would have to beg [her] way home." In any case, she did not think that a letter from Douglass, which was Aked's idea, was too much to ask, and she had managed to get significant support without a "single letter of introduction." And now it was probably too late for his letter anyhow.

She planned to attend just a few more speaking dates until the end of the month and return to the States. "My business in Chicago needs me too badly to be giving my time for a work which nobody else will do, and which I cannot afford to do at such cost to myself and suspicion to my friends," she sulked. Finally Ida told Frederick that she did not know Aked was going to accredit her to him, but was anxious to do so because of a wealthy potential American donor who had asked about her. Ida closed the letter like a daughter trying to appease a cross father. She could not return the twenty-five dollars as promised, but hoped to have it in a few weeks, even if she had to borrow it. And if Douglass now put her with that "large class who have imposed on your confidence," Ida concluded, "I still love you as the greatest man our race has produced and because of what you have suffered & endured for the race's sake."[28]

Wells's emotional letter to Douglass rekindled, as she had hoped, his paternal, protective side. He wrote back in May, saying that he had already stood by her in times of trial, and "will for all time to come," and he playfully admonished that he should give her a "whipping" about that twenty-five dollars.[29] Ida may have been relieved by the forgiving tone, but the original request had become moot. Despite the efforts of the Reverends Armstrong and Steinthal, the antilynching resolution had failed to pass at the large conference in Manchester. The *Manchester Guardian* of April 14 described how two American delegates, the Reverend Brooke Herford and Mrs. Ormistan Chant, had, in the discussion preceding the vote, raised questions about Ida's assertions. Herford had said that Wells's charges that the press and pulpit had encouraged lynchings was a "terrible misrepresentation." Chant added that the resolution and the statements made were "unjust to their Unitarian brethren in America."[30]

Wells was not only disappointed but was angered by "the charges of misrepresentation," as she wrote to William Axon. Wells told the *Manchester Guardian* editor that she feared that the campaign could not recover from such a public repudiation by "so large and representative body," and that the precedent would "neutralize & paralyze" further efforts.[31] The good news was that she still had strong Unitarian allies, especially the Reverend Armstrong. He promised to try to pass the resolution again at the larger London Unitarian conference that was to be held in June.

Leaving Manchester, Wells traveled to Southport, Newberry, and Bristol. Her columns in the *Inter-Ocean* about these meetings emphasized the support she was receiving from prominent women. In Southport, after a talk before two thousand persons, an antilynching resolution had been seconded by Mrs. Calendar Moss of the British Woman's Liberal Association, whose first president had been the wife of the former prime minister William Gladstone. In Newberry, Ida had tea with Lady Jeune, wife of Francis Henry Jeune, known for his practice in ecclesiastical courts. That same week, Lady Jeune had hosted Lord Randolph Churchill (father of future prime minister Winston S. Churchill) among other notables. In Bristol, Ida's drawing-room talk was attended by "the wealthiest and most cultured classes of society," she wrote. Amid her other engagements, Ida also inserted yet another criticism of not only the WCTU but also the YMCA. Both organizations, she said, were keen on attracting southern members and in doing so were making negative statements, as in the case of Frances Willard, and excluding blacks from the organization as in the case of the "Y."[32]

In Newcastle, Ida made a point of visiting Ellen Richardson, the octogenarian Quaker who, with the abolitionist lawyer and former MP John Bright, had come up with the scheme to purchase Douglass's freedom when he was in England. Richardson had also been instrumental in the freeing of the fugitive slave and author William Wells Brown, whose *Clotel, or the President's Daughter*, published in London in 1853, was one of the earliest novels written by an African American. As Ida wrote in the *Inter-Ocean*, Miss Richardson, "the benefactress of Fred Douglass," rarely granted interviews, but Wells had managed (after some persistence and using Douglass's name without, apparently, asking him in advance if she could do so) to spend a full morning with the her. Ida's column recounted the inspiring story of how the Quaker, a modest headmistress of a girls' school in the 1840s, initiated a subscription campaign to raise money for Douglass's freedom.[33]

After seeing Richardson, Ida wrote a letter to Helen Douglass, Frederick's wife, about the meeting, in a new effort, no doubt, to soften up the old man. Since Ida had impetuously told Douglass that she no longer needed his letter of commendation, she had begun to think twice about it. The defeat in Manchester had no doubt steeled her determination; and she had also been encouraged by a recent development. While Ida was traveling, the Reverend Aked had called for, and gotten, an antilynching resolution before the National Baptist Union. In light of the former defeat, the victory had been especially welcome because it had been aided by the support of a man who was considered the foremost Baptist in the British Isles, Reverend John Clifford. The fifty-eight-year-old Clifford was a Christian Socialist, Nonconformist president of the Council of Evangelical Free Churches, and a leader of the newly formed Christian Socialist League, an organization that sought to organize Christian Socialist opinion across denominational lines.[34] Clifford had seconded Aked's motion, exhorting the Baptist Union about the duty of the church in the matter and expressing the hope that the American Baptists could be encouraged to speak out against lynching. The passage of the resolution received coverage in the *Christian World, Review of the Churches,* and the *London Daily Chronicle.* Clifford also issued an invitation to Ida to speak before his two-thousand-member Westbourne Park Chapel when she reached London.[35]

Now Ida was looking forward more than ever to the great international city. Not only had she made an important inroad through Clifford's broad connections, she anticipated support at the May Baptist Union meeting in London, representing more than sixty countries as well as other international bodies, including the Congregational Union, the Presbyterian and Protestant Alliance, the Woman's Liberal Association, and the Woman's Liberal Federation.

WELLS TOLD HELEN Douglass that she was writing to her about Richardson because of the Quaker's age and fragility. Taking it upon herself to be a conduit between them, Ida wrote in her letter that she had told Richardson that Helen had longed to come and see her again. (The Douglasses had visited Richardson in 1886 while honeymooning in Great Britain.) Wells also conveyed a message from Richardson to Frederick: she asked that he return two photos he had borrowed and to please send her a copy of the new edition of his autobiography. Wells closed by saying that she would be spending May abroad and would return home in June. She signed off in the epistolary voice of the orphan: "Home did I say?" Ida wrote. "I forgot that I have no home." Ida ended the letter by wishing love to the whole family.[36]

On May 6, Ida wrote again, this time to Douglass directly. She curled into her daughter mode and pulled out every stop. Ida cajoled, ingratiated herself, attempted to incur his sympathy, played to his ego, and called upon his dedication to the race. She began by saying that she had just received his letter of March 27 and had also seen his letter to Charles Aked. "I know from what he and others said that while they did not expect gush, they would have been more satisfied if you had spoken more positively regarding me and my work." Wells went on to reiterate, as Douglass had said in his letter to Aked, about the need to tell the Negro's side of the story, but Ida was encountering persons who had never heard of her and did not know whether to take her word or not. They did know him, Wells emphasized, "and a strong word" from the former abolitionist "would help the race wonderfully." If "there was money and persons sufficient to distribute your magnificent pamphlet [*Lessons of the Hour*] throughout the length and breadth of the kingdom, much would be done," Ida assured him.

Wells also made sure to express her appreciation for his previous letter and her apologies about the loan. She lightheartedly agreed that she deserved the "whipping" about the money and explained why she hadn't sent it. "My sisters in school in California, whom I have been neglecting for the race for some time needed money and I had only 5 [pounds] and sent it to them, I knew you wouldn't mind waiting longer if you knew about about it," Ida told him. On another note, "it lightens my heart wonderfully to have you say at the close of your letter that you have stood by me in every time of trial and will for all time to come. That is spoken like my dear good and grand Old Man Eloquent," Ida wrote, "and I want to beg your forgiveness for my hasty words." Finally Wells recounted the defeat at Manchester at the hands of the Americans and told him that the Reverends Steinthal and Armstrong were going to offer the resolution again in another large meeting on June 14. Ida asked Douglass to write them and this time she explicitly told him what was needed in the letter. "In it you can say whether I speak for my race or not and endorse most strongly the effort to pass the resolution." She also asked that he write Aked and John Clifford to thank them for their efforts on her behalf.[37]

By the date of Ida's letter, Douglass no doubt had surmised that she needed his imprimatur for more reasons than the ones she had given. In late April, the *New York Times* had quoted a prominent New York black Democrat, John S. Durham, who said that Ida's statements about white women did not represent the "intelligent sentiment of the colored people." Durham, who succeeded Douglass as the consul to Haiti and whose forbearers had cofounded the AME Church with Richard Allen, insisted that the "person who is reported as having made the charge against southern women may safely be said to have no representative character," and that England's assistance was not necessary.[38]

Ida's disgruntled former Memphis *Free Speech* partner, J. L. Fleming, now the publisher of the *Free Speech* in Chicago, charged in the *Indianapolis Freeman* that Ida's "fire-eating" speeches were helping no one, in England or the United States. Georgia governor Northen, now a vice president of the Southern Baptist Convention, told the *London Daily Chronicle* that Wells's real agenda was to discourage British immigration to the South and that she was working on behalf of labor agents in the North who were competing for English workers. The same edition of the newspaper carried an article by its London correspondent who described Ida as a "coffee-colored lady," and though not denying there were lynchings in the South, found it difficult to believe Ida's charges that white women were "tempting" black men. "This is just the style of subject which English reformers and busybodies . . . will leap at," he wrote, adding that they were "falling" for Wells's "bait." "The more salacious she can make her revelations the more violently the great Nonconformist conscience of England will be stirred to a response." With a similar sentiment, the May 3 edition of the *Independent* wondered if Wells's campaign was nothing more than a "masterly flank movement.[39]

On May 10, just seven days later, Wells wrote Douglass to ask him for yet another letter that specifically vouched for her character and confirmed that she was speaking for her race, not herself. This one was needed for the lord mayor of London, she claimed, who wanted to host a reception for her at his residence, where Parliament members and other VIPs were to be invited. She was extremely anxious, Wells continued, "that the opportunity shall not be lost, so I come to you again." Wells then informed Douglass that she had gotten Ferdinand Barnett to write the New Hampshire senator and Douglass ally William E. Chandler about her request for support, hoping that he and Douglass could sign a joint letter on her behalf.[40] Ida, as truthful and sincere as she was about the cause, was also prone to committing sins of omission—not a good idea with someone as wily and well connected as Douglass. By the time she wrote this letter, she was also trying to arm herself against the storm of attack about to be released by Frances Willard and Lady Henry Somerset.

DURING THE FIRST week in May, Wells had attended a reception given by the pro-women's suffrage Woman's Liberal Federation in London.[41] Many notable activists were there, including BWTA president Lady Henry

Somerset, and Ormistan Chant, who had criticized the antilynching resolution in Manchester. In the *Inter-Ocean,* Ida noted that she was due to
speak before the BWTA meeting the following day (Wells's article was
datelined May 6) and that the organization was going to pass an antilynching resolution at the meeting. Wells also said that she had talked to Frances
Willard and that the WCTU leader had told her that she now saw "the
subject of lynching as she never saw it before, because she, like others, made
the mistake of judging the negro by what his accusers say of him and without hearing the other side of the story." Willard, as Ida wrote in a later *Inter-Ocean* column, was the "personification of kindness" during their
meeting.[42] Willard may have had a genuine change of heart; but it was
probably also true that she was feeling pressure—or at least getting too
many difficult-to-answer questions about her impolitic remarks in the *New
York Voice* that Ida had so incessantly exposed. As the temperance leader
would later comment, she was particularly shaken by the criticism of Frederick Douglass. Indeed, it was difficult to keep waving abolitionist credentials in the light of his public displeasure. Wells had also spoken to the
other naysayer at Manchester, Brooke Herford, and she reported that he
had come around to her way of thinking after she had spoken to him and
shown him a number of southern newspapers. Herford promised Ida, she
said, that he himself would offer the resolution at the next conference.[43]

Satisfied that she had won over her critics, especially Frances Willard,
Wells entered the Holbert Town Hall to address the BWTA meeting. But
in what appeared to be an almost exact replay from the previous year, Ida,
again, was given only a few minutes to address the 448 delegates and members; and again, Frances Willard sat silently on the stage. For her part,
Wells was as provocative as ever. In her message she condemned southern
white women who did not speak out against the guilt of their husbands
and brothers who perpetrated lynchings against blacks. Nevertheless, before the meeting's end, an antilynching resolution was passed. "I was so
thankful for this crumb of [Willard's] speechless presence that I hurried
off to the editor of Fraternity and added a post-script to my article blazon-
ing forth that fact," Wells, undoubtedly feeling some pressure herself,
wrote. Ida was referring to the soon-to-be published article in the SRBM's
publication that included the *New York Voice* interview and Frederick
Douglass's criticism, which she had sent before she left for England. Of
course, she had already mentioned both in her earlier *Inter-Ocean* columns,
but for the British-based publication to bring it out after the resolution and

after she had gotten an apology of sorts from Willard was untimely, to say the least.[44]

Wells told Florence Balgarnie, a stalwart ally of Ida's and editor of the BWTA journal, *Women's Signal,* about the situation. Balgarnie went into action immediately. She knew that when *Fraternity* hit the streets with the article, it would send Lady Henry Somerset into a rage. Not only were she and Willard "bosom buddies," as Ida pointedly described them, the British temperance leader who had now invited Ida twice before the group was already facing her own political problems within the group. Somerset was attempting to reform the BWTA along the lines that Willard had done with the WCTU—making it more engaged with larger social and political movements—and she was facing resistance.

At first Balgarnie wanted to suppress the May *Fraternity* issue, but monetary considerations precluded that option. At the least, Balgarnie thought, Ida should tell Somerset in advance of its publication and explain the circumstances of the article appearing at that particular time. With Ida (who refused to call Somerset herself) standing by, Balgarnie called Somerset and told her of the situation. As Balgarnie predicted, Somerset did not take the news well. She threatened that if the article saw the light of day, she would use all of her influence to keep Wells from having any further opportunities to be heard in London. Ida, of course, was livid after the exchange, but reported that Balgarnie convinced her to make another attempt to come to some kind of terms with Somerset. When their appeals were ignored, *Fraternity* came out in early May. By the time Ida was writing Douglass, she was bracing for the worst—and it was on its way.[45]

On May 21, the anniversary of Ida's antilynching editorial in the *Memphis Free Speech,* the *Westminster Gazette* published a long interview with Frances Willard conducted by none other than Lady Henry Somerset. It began with Willard lightheartedly noting that Ida's cascade of criticism made her feel like an "eel" who has been "skinned so often" that he learned to like it. Wells's misguided criticisms and assertions about the moral inertness of American Christians were the product of an "exaggeration of mind," she said, which included "race hatred." Willard's evidence of the latter was a remark Ida had earlier made, perhaps in some frustration, to the *Westminster Gazette.* The paper had asked Wells about a southerner's comment that Ida's "tainted" mixed racial heritage was tantamount to her "tainted" allegations about the South. "Taint indeed!" Ida riposted. "I tell you if I have any taint to be ashamed of in myself, it is the taint of white blood."[46]

Willard also was given the opportunity to remind readers of her aboli-tionist background (her parents' Illinois home was a stop on the Under-ground Railroad), her concern for black people in general, and the courtesy and aid she had extended to Ida in particular. She explained that her re-marks published in the infamous interview had nothing to do with lynch-ing, which she believed was contrary to due process of law, but the enfranchisement of illiterate, ignorant blacks, whose threatening behavior had been recounted to her by upstanding citizens in the South. As for Willard's fair-minded and progressive image on race and other questions, she breezily concluded that "British justice may be trusted to guard my reputation in that particular issue as in all others."[47]

The interview had an unmistakably dismissive air, lacked any sense of moral indignation about lynching, and tried to make Ida appear not only half-cocked and wrongheaded but so insignificant that she could be flicked off the scene like a bothersome insect. But the arrogance of the two tem-perance leaders proved, ultimately, to be a terrible miscalculation. As Ida would later write, the public saw that the *Gazette* interview was intended to do Ida harm and it militated against the British sense of fair play. After all, two prominent, powerful white women had "joined hands in the effort to crush an insignificant colored woman who had . . . nothing but the power of the truth with which to fight her battles."[48]

In the short view, Ida, as she could do so skillfully, turned her oppo-nents' own words into a whipping post and her reply to the *Gazette* on the very next day was withering. She pointed out the tone of the interview, in-cluding the "eel" remark being a lame effort at humor. Wells concluded that the temperance leader's words were evidence that Willard's object was not to "determine how best to help the Negro who is being hanged, shot and burned" but "to guard Miss Willard's reputation." "With me," Ida added, "it is not my life or reputation but the life of my people which is at stake." She talked about the segregation of the local branches of the WCTU in the United States, and cited, once again, Frederick Douglass's criticism of Willard in his January speech in Washington, D.C. "The fact is," Ida concluded, "Miss Willard is no better or worse than the great bulk of white Americans on the Negro question. They are all afraid to speak out, and it is only British public opinion which will move them, as I am thankful to see it has already begun to move Miss Willard."[49]

Wells may have won the round on points, but the exchange also stirred deep support for Willard and brought her defenders to bear. The

Christian Commonwealth predicted Ida could "kill her cause" with impudent speeches, and "talking wildly" about Frances Willard. Even the *Inter-Ocean* felt bound to publish a defense of Willard from one of her allies, who castigated Ida for making the temperance leader "a special object of attack."⁵⁰ The pro-Willard, anti-Wells campaign also included an angry cable sent to Douglass from Lady Somerset, who complained that Ida was full of "vituperation," "bitterness," and "unfairness." The aristocrat asked him point-blank what even Ida had not dared to ask directly. Did he endorse Ida Wells?⁵¹

WELLS CALCULATED THAT Douglass would receive her letter by May 22, and that is the date he posted his letters to the Reverends Armstrong and Aked. If either of the men were looking for Douglass to hand them a sword to do battle, all he gave them was a very dull blade. To Armstrong, Douglass wrote that Ida was a "brave and truthful woman," who was "devoted to the cause of her outraged and persecuted people." But he fell well short of personally vouching for her or giving a personal assurance about Wells's right to speak on behalf of blacks. Most of the two-page epistle reiterated his own familiar and highly stylized refrains on the role of British opinion and informed Armstrong, as he had earlier Aked, of his own pamphlet, which he "wished" he had the means to reprint and distribute more widely. He assured the minister that one would be sent to him.

The letter to Aked was even more disappointing. After his opening paragraphs about the "power" of the "moral judgment" of England, he said that Ida was "suitable" to tell the story of the oppressed; that she did not "exaggerate"; that she told the "simple truth" about the situation in the United States. But there was a telling line that said, in so many words, that he was not about to give Ida his personal approval. A cablegram had come to him, he told Aked, asking if "I endorsed Miss Wells. I gave the answer that I endorsed the mission of Miss Wells, I do this entirely."⁵²

Four days after Douglass refused to give his personal opinion regarding Ida's character, the *Memphis Commercial* did. Subheadlined "The Record of This Notorious Courtesan," the Memphis paper began by saying that Wells had been able to influence the British press and public with her "foul and slanderous" tirades because of their ignorance of the true situation in the South: to wit, "a perfect epidemic of outrages perpetrated by negro men upon white women." The *Commercial* asked Englishmen to imagine their "own sisters and daughters violently deflowered by ignorant, unclean men, lower in the scale of morality and intelligence than the basest peasantry in the world." The paper went on to trace the "career" of the "saddle-colored Sapphira," that she came from Holly Springs "where rumors had been rife about her unchastity," and that in Memphis she hooked up with the Reverend Taylor Nightingale of the *Free Speech*, became his "paramour," and had "unpleasant" relationships with his wife. But the most damning commentary came from Memphis blacks, including Ida's former friend, J. Thomas Turner, of the *Memphis Watchman*. "All informed colored people know that the statements which Ida Wells is making in her addresses in England are false and slanderous," the *Commercial* quoted him as saying.[53]

On June 4, the same paper quoted the diplomat and educator John Langston, a onetime U.S. representative from Virginia, as saying that Ida's "cheap notoriety" was doing the race more harm than good. Langston was visiting Memphis at the time, where he stayed with Ida's old nemesis, Josiah Settle. A week later, the *Commercial* published a curious questionnaire that had been filled out by Julia Hooks, the black Memphis schoolteacher who had been arrested in the Leubrie Theater thirteen years before. The questionnaire had been distributed by the Woman's Loyal Union of New York, which had helped to give Ida's 1892 testimonial at Lyric Hall. Although it appeared to be an internal document of the black women's organization headed by Victoria Matthews, the *Commercial* ran it as the "opinion" of "an intelligent and respected colored woman of Memphis," who was "qualified to speak for the best class of colored women" in the community. One of the questions asked was if the respondent believed that the rapes by black men were the cause of lynchings. Hooks's reply was that she wasn't positive, but that "our men do not respect the virtue of their own women as they should."[54]

In June, a last-ditch effort to get Douglass's support came in a letter to him written by Helen Bright Clark, daughter of the abolitionist lawyer and former MP who had purchased Douglass's freedom. Clark, with whom Wells stayed in Somersetshire, wrote Douglass that Wells "will suffer" from the courage of her convictions, and told him that any "testimony" as to her personal character would be of "great value here." Helen wrote the letter in mid-June, Douglass did not reply until July 19, after Wells had already left England for the States. Even so, his response was wanting. He was glad, he wrote Helen, "that the brave little woman found sympathy and shelter under your roof." Adding insult to Ida's injury, he opined that

"Miss Willard is an excellent lady" and attributed her unfortunate remarks to merely not being informed. She had written him, he said, to request an interview, and he had extended her "a welcome to Cedar Hill."[55]

Although Douglass would not give Wells the support she asked, by June others did. The British press circulated the comments, such as that of AME bishop Henry McNeal Turner, from the *Topeka Weekly Call*, who did what Old Man Eloquent had refused to do. Turner "personally" vouched for Ida whom he said he knew and who had been a guest in his home. She was telling the truth about lynchings, he insisted, and her black Democrat critics were motivated by trying to "secure smiles" and attain positions from the very people who were "traducing" her. "Miss Wells is more value to her people than a hundred thousand of them," he concluded, predicting that "Her detractors will be lost in oblivion . . . her name shall blaze upon the pages of the future."

The Woman's Era Club of Boston, led by Ruffin, also weighed in. Speaking "for the coloured women of America," the organization published a letter in the *Manchester Guardian* criticizing Ormiston Chant, one of the Unitarians who had challenged Ida's assertions at the Manchester Unitarian Conference and who had earlier been invited to appear before the organization. "We do not expect that white women shall feel as deeply as we [who] know of good and high-minded women made widows, or sweet and innocent children made fatherless by a mob of unbridled men and boys looking for fun," the letter said. Affirming Wells's assertions that black men were being lynched under false pretenses and that black women were being "horribly assaulted by white men in the South," the letter continued, "we utter our solemn protest. For their sakes we call upon workers of humanity everywhere, if they can do nothing for us, in mercy's name not to raise their voices against us." The letter was "a great help in supporting all of the contentions I had made as to the evils of lynching," Wells recalled in her autobiography. "It was all the more gratifying, because it came from one of the women's clubs which I helped organize."[56]

But just as important, when the English did express their final judgment, most did so in wholehearted support of Wells and the campaign. Clearly, Wells's 102 lectures (as she had estimated) throughout Great Britain were the most telling testimony about her campaign and character. The impression she had made on the English made the heavy-handed accusations by the southern press even more offensive. The *Liverpool Daily Post* called the southern articles "coarse" and "libelous," noting that their own acknowledgment of lynching was "sufficient justification" to pass anti-lynching resolutions. The *Christian Register* took Governor Northen of Georgia to task, saying that he seemed to assume that its editors had not been to the South, but they had, and what Wells was saying was true.[57] The *London Daily News* noted that the southern states were "asking for both labor and capital to develop their magnificent resources and they will get neither till order reigns in their cities." Similarly, as Ida gleefully reported, she had supportive notices or interviews from the *London Daily Chronicle*, which along with the *Daily News* was the most influential daily in London. A cascade of other publications, including the *Christian World*, the *Westminster Gazette*, the *Labour Leader*, and the *Methodist Times*, followed in their wake.[58]

The press support was only the beginning of English affirmation; the British personally embraced her to show their support in time for the June meetings. In London, Ida was invited to stay at the house of Peter William Clayden, a Unitarian and editor of the *London Daily News*. She was befriended by the popular J. Keir Hardie, a Congregationalist and feminist elected to Parliament in 1892, who would, a few years later, found the country's Labour Party. Hardie, who, Ida noted, liked to wear his workman's cap, a dark flannel shirt, and a sack coat in contrast to his "frock-coated" "silk-hatted" colleagues, escorted Wells to attend a Parliament session as his guest. The gesture was a "mark of honor," she observed, although Ida also complained that as a woman, she could only sit in the gallery.[59]

Despite, or perhaps because of the negative coverage, Ida received thirty-five speaking invitations in London, which included those of the Ideal Club led by Lady Jeune, and the Pioneer Club, the first woman's club in England, presided over by the legendary Annie Besant, organizer of the important matchmaker women's strike of 1888 and advocate of Indian nationalism. Wells was invited for dinner by William Woodall, MP and financial secretary to the War Department, along with a number of cabinet ministers in honor of H. H. Kohlsaat, part-owner of the *Inter-Ocean*, who had recently disposed of his interest in the newspaper for a reported $400,000 to Chicago businessman William Penn Nixon. And she was invited to the mayor of London's garden party where being of color was an "agreeable prominence." "Fancy my feeling when I saw the Lady Mayoress taking a leading African prince about at a garden party," Wells noted in her column.[60]

It was clear that the tide had turned fully in Wells's favor. After her speech at the Democratic Club of London—advertised in the *Memphis Commercial* as "A London Democratic Club Harangued by the Wench"— the organization sent an antilynching resolution to the U.S. ambassador.[61] The Unitarians in Manchester, "convinced and ashamed" about their first failure to pass an antilynching resolution, did so on their latest attempt. Antilynching resolutions were passed by the Quakers, the Methodists, the Aborigines Protection Society, and the Congregational Union.[62] As Ida had hoped, such a showing had its impact in the States. Bishop Haygood, in the June issue of the *Independent,* wrote a strong statement against lynching, tying the phenomenon to labor disturbances in the South. South Carolina governor Ben Tillman felt it incumbent to explain that although "southern people weren't blameless" regarding lynchings, the northern press often misrepresented them.[63] John Langston denied the disparaging quotes about Ida in the Memphis press, after other papers (belatedly) took him to task for them. Her old partner, Fleming, denied his critical words as well. The *Indianapolis Freeman,* explaining its prior silence by claiming it always knew that her mission would in time speak for itself, exuberantly embraced Ida, saying that she "is to be made to feel by every means within our power that we are with her . . . That her labors shall be our labors, her trials, ours . . . to hold up her hands, particularly in the face of her Southern enemies, who will stop at nothing to besmirch her as a woman and hinder her as an advocate."[64]

Kudos come and go, Ida must have been thinking, but most important, her work was going to be carried on through the newly formed London Anti-Lynching Committee. In addition to those who had been her most vocal allies during the second British tour were others such as George Douglas Sutherland Campbell, the Duke of Argyll (whose successor and son was married to one of Queen Victoria's daughters, Princess Louise); the Archbishop of Canterbury (Edward White Benson), and the editors of the *London Daily News, Echo, Contemporary Review, Chronicle,* and *Westminster Gazette*—and even Lady Henry Somerset. Ida also made special mention of another member, Ogontula Sapara, who along with six other African students, including two women, had done volunteer work for her in London.[65] The secretary of the committee was Florence Balgarnie; the treasurer was Celestine Edwards of the SRBM. Subsequently there were, as Ida reported, a number of important American signatories to the Committee, including labor leader Samuel Gompers; Carl Schurz, leader of the liberal wing of the Republican Party in the 1880s, and former secretary of the interior under Hayes; Richard Gilder, editor of *Century Magazine*—and, yes, Frances Willard.[66]

"I HAVE BEEN offered engagements which would last through the next three months," Ida reported triumphantly to the *New York Age*. Nevertheless, with her characteristic edge, she explained that she was forced to return to the United States because the SRBM had run out of money—and since she had failed to get any financial support from home, she could no longer stay in Britain to defend the race. But Wells concluded that her four-month tour had been successful. "From one end of the United States to the other, the press and pulpit were stung by the criticism of press and pulpit abroad, and began to turn on the searchlight on lynching as never before." Ida believed that not since *Uncle Tom's Cabin*—the book often cited as the catalyst for the Civil War—had people been so "stirred." When later asked to describe her feelings to the American press, she said it was "like being born again in a new condition."[67]

Before leaving for Liverpool, from where she would board the SS *Parisienne* for home, Ida took a day to visit Cambridge University. From there she headed to the city where her campaign had started and gave a grateful farewell speech in Aked's Pembroke Chapel. She also wrote her final report for the SRBM, making special note of the now terminally ill Celestine Edwards, who, despite his physical condition, had done all he could do to support her tour. "The thanks of myself and my race are due him above all others," she wrote.[68] Wells also wrote a number of stinging articles to the *New York Age*, slamming those who had failed to support her. Then she steadied herself to write a measured but forthright letter to Frederick Douglass.

Ida began by recapitulating the difficult circumstances she had confronted in England, and her own devotion to the cause. She thanked him for the letters he did send, and she affirmed that she "adored" him as a great black leader. Ida also informed Douglass, who had sent his *Lessons of the Hour* pamphlets abroad, that she had distributed them. And then, without any hint of anger or disappointment, Ida let Frederick know that she knew about his response to Lady Somerset's inquiry about endorsing her mission, but not her. The Englishwoman had since made "capital" out of the reply, she said, reminding him that Somerset and Willard "fully meant to harm me." Although she had been "fortunate to win . . . a slight measure" of his regard from "a personal point of view," Ida implied that she had obviously failed to achieve his full confidence in her. But in lieu of his support, she said in so many words, she hadn't needed him. "God had raised up powerful friends for the cause," she told him pointedly. "No other save Divine Strength could have helped me so wonderfully and to God I give all the praise and glory."[69] Her frustration and disappointment partially vented, Wells set sail on July 12 for home, by way of the long route through the Gulf of St. Lawrence, to steal extra time to rest.

CHAPTER TWELVE

Exile No More

> . . . Go on, thou brave woman leader,
>
> Spread our wrongs from shore unto shore;
>
> Until clothed with his rights is the Negro,
>
> And lynchings are no more. . . .
>
> And the wise Afro-American mother,
>
> Who her children of heroine tells,
>
> Shall speak in tones of gratitude,
>
> The name of Ida B. Wells!
>
> —*Katherine Davis Tillman*

An "archway of roses should greet this Joan of Arc on her return from fields of conquest," editorialized the *Christian Recorder,* anticipating Ida's arrival back in the States. But as anyone could see who read her July 12 article in the *New York Age*—published on the day she boarded the SS *Parisienne* for home—Ida was furious. "Are We a Race of Cowards?" was its scornful headline. Ida left England thinking more about the black men who had failed to defend her than the triumphal final days of her campaign. She was particularly upset with J. L. Fleming and Taylor Nightingale for not setting the record straight when Edward Carmack, editor of the *Memphis Commercial Appeal,* accused her of having sexual relations with each of them. (Subsequently, the *Indianapolis Freeman* called them "two tongue-tied niggers.") Fleming had even written her a letter, saying that "Carmack is a man I could kill, but he didn't kill him," Ida sneered. At close second in her low estimation were John M. Langston and J. Thomas Turner, who had "upheld" the *Commercial*'s disparaging words. She did not mention Frederick Douglass, who had disappointed her most. For complicated reasons—affection, his race-man greatness, the fact that she would need his support—he was one man with whom Wells never quarreled publicly. But neither did she mention him as the exception to her disgust with black men in general. "I am indeed placed in a peculiarly unenviable position; for trying to defend the good name of the manhood of my race my business was destroyed in Memphis, my life threatened, and three times since, my good name has been most wantonly assailed by the white people who are lynching the race and blasting its reputation," Ida railed in the *Age*. "For defending the reputation of the manhood of my race I have lost my own good name before the world and only the editor of the *New York Age* and Bishop Turner have uttered a word in my defense." Ida's sense of abandonment prompted as raw an emotion as she would ever put in print.

I am feeling so sorry for myself that the bitter tears have been coursing down my cheeks. I am wondering what a fool am I to sacrifice so much and suffer so much and work so hard for a race which will not defend itself or protect me in defending it. Not for myself alone do I weep. My heart aches for those of my race who are being immolated every day on the altar of the white man's prejudice—hanged, shot, flayed alive and burned; over the widows and orphans made desolate; over the great bulk of the race which reads these things and whose hearts are not stirred to action of some kind on behalf of the victims; over the spirit of envy and jealousy which actuates those who can help to opposition instead of support; lastly and most of all, I weep because the manhood of the race knows itself slandered, its women and children slaughtered, its mothers, wives, sisters and daughters insulted and despoiled and traduced and still fails to assert its strength or extend its protection to those who have the right to claim it. Is mine a race of cowards?[1]

Wells was expressing her personal frustration, but she was also, again, tapping a sentiment that was widely felt. "Negroes, I am sorry to say, are becoming unmanned," wrote John Hope, a Georgia-born Brown University graduate destined to preside over Morehouse College and Atlanta University. The observation was written in a letter to northern friends in which he had remarked on Ida's courage and on the highly publicized refusal of the Georgia Colored Teacher's Convention to endorse Ida's campaign while she was in England. The defeat came at the hands of "colored men in prominent places who are cringing, cowardly, knavish fellows," he wrote. AME bishop Henry Turner, who was touring the South at the time of the failed endorsement, came to the same conclusion: African Americans in the main supported Wells, he wrote in a published article, but were afraid to say so for fear of losing their positions.[2]

Indeed, the obstacles to Wells's support were not only the intimidating specter of violence or the opinion that her confrontational methods created more racial problems than they solved. Her campaign forced blacks of means and influence to face—or face down—the existential quality of their lives. "This is a beautiful country south, society is good and colored people have some wealth and much push," wrote John Hope. "Intelligence is here and hospitality is about as lavish as ever. But my friends don't come down here if you do not want to realize what it is to be made to understand that you are inferior to the most ignorant and the vilest of whites . . . if you want to live in a locality where all the elements that usually go to make a man appreciated and respected tend to make him a target." Hope continued that it was "hard to imagine the 'cussedness,' the dirtiness to which even the best of white people will descend when a Negro is in question." He concluded, "Our advancement appears to stir up their hearts against us. . . . Persecutions ever increasing do not tend to nourish stamina."[3]

And yet, as Hope added, many were bound to the South—and its tyrannies—for fear of losing their economic foothold if they left. Bishop Turner, an advocate of emigration to Africa, warned of the psychological implications for the race. "Whenever a people are so abnormalized by their environment that they are afraid to lift their voices in protest against the murders and exterminators, it is time to leave there or ask for enslavement."[4]

Wells, too, believed in the spiritual peril that faced blacks if they did not stand up to the powers that be, but her criticism was born less out of a sense of futility than the determination to push, scold—shame if necessary—the men of the race to overcome what Hope and Turner described. She ended the article in the *Age* by answering her question about cowardice in the negative. "I do not believe it," she said, "and I spurn indignantly the suggestion from those Englishmen who cannot understand what seems supineness, but I would be willing to suffer all that I have and more, if thereby might be brought about a healthier moral tone, and stronger physical stamina among our men; if they would unite their forces and present a solid front for self defense to the world. Then I could not only love my race with a love which parses my own understanding, but admire and respect it with all the intensity of my nature for its courage, honor and true manhood."[5]

That even a modest but heartfelt acknowledgment of support would sustain her was the message in a subsequent *Age* article, picked up by the *Topeka Weekly Call*. Wells reprinted a letter she received from a poor Mississippi farmer whose name she withheld, she said, so he wouldn't get in trouble. "You must be supported," the farmer wrote. "How you are to carry on the work without the aid of your race passes our understanding. . . . To note that you are a woman (I might say a girl) and I a great big man and you are doing what I ought to do and have not the courage to do it, I think sometimes it's a pity that I am in existence but all this talk won't make you any better off nor does it help you in your work. Enclosed find one dollar." As Wells noted, "a letter of appreciation like this is enough to prevent discouragement."[6]

WHEN IDA REACHED New York by train from Montreal on July 24, 1894, she had further reason to be encouraged, if not altogether forgiving. Upon her arrival, she learned that T. Thomas Fortune had issued a statement calling on the presidents of the local Afro-American Leagues to hold mass meetings on July 16 to show support for her so that the "British public may not be deceived by the avalanche of misrepresentations." It is not clear how effective the rallies were; by 1894, the Afro-American League was nearly defunct. But Ida appreciated the effort, although, as she commented, she wished that it had materialized while she was still in England.[7]

Wells also learned that Victoria Matthews, the Woman's Loyal Union president who had helped organize Wells's triumphant Lyric Hall testimonial two years before, had, along with Fortune, begun to raise funds for Ida to continue her work in the States. So far the effort had raised a modest fifty dollars, but the organizational support of Matthews and the Union was all the more promising because the organization was in the process of establishing affiliated clubs in Charleston, Philadelphia, and Memphis.[8] Matthews and Fortune had also arranged two major speaking engagements for Ida at Brooklyn's Fleet Street AME Zion Church, located near Myrtle Avenue, and in Manhattan's Bethel AME Church on Sullivan Street in Greenwich Village.

Ida's first two stateside appearances in the wake of her British campaign clearly laid out the themes—and her ambition—for the next phase of her work. The "Afro-American has the ear of the civilized world for the first time since Emancipation," she noted in Brooklyn, and blacks should follow up by "entering the wedge which had been driven by our English friends." For her part, she promised to devote a year to carrying the message across the country—if she could get the financial support of "my own people."[9]

The announced undertaking was without precedent among blacks. Taking full advantage of the late-nineteenth-century innovations in communication and train travel, Wells, a single woman, planned to traverse the country to mobilize public opinion against lynching. Moreover, unlike the campaigns for abolition or male suffrage, Ida was determined that blacks provide most of the financing for the undertaking—at a time when the Panic of 1893 was hardening into a teeth-clenching depression. "I thought that it was up to us to show that we could do as much for ourselves as they [the English] had done for us," she recalled in her autobiography.[10] But although she would be loath to admit it, perhaps even to herself, Ida's ambitions went further.

Years before there were professional civil-rights advocates, Ida wanted to be a full-time leader and race woman with the kind of support that legitimized not only her leadership but her authority. There were precedents— among whites. While WCTU president Frances Willard had had to rely on speaking fees early in her tenure with the organization, after 1886 the national WCTU voted to provide Willard a salary of $1,800 in addition to an allowance for clerical help and a salary for her secretary. Ida's stalwart ally, the *Cleveland Gazette,* favored the idea that she should have "a good fat purse" at her disposal, and toward this end, Fortune and a number of other prominent New Yorkers formed a central executive council that would be a publicity arm and clearinghouse for the receipt of funds for her new campaign.[11]

Still, to ask for money in such an explicit un-Victorian way laid Ida's motives open to suspicion. The *New York Times* questioned if Ida's purpose "may plausibly be supposed to have been an income rather than an out-come." The truth was Ida was looking for both but not one without the other. In her autobiography, she noted how an agent from a well-known lecture bureau promised her a lucrative contract with the stipulation that she not speak about lynching! Ida, of course, not only refused the request on principle but was convinced that the bureau representative was wrong when he said that audiences would not pay to hear about such a subject.[12] This conviction was to be sorely tested for the next eleven months.

BY THE TIME Wells was to talk in Manhattan, the New York press corps was fully alert to her presence in the city. The *New York Times* marked the occasion by pointing out that on the very day that Ida was scheduled for an interview with the *New York Sun*, "a negro had made an assault upon a white woman for purposes of lust and plunder" in the city. The "circumstances of this fiendish crime," the *Times* noted, "may serve to convince the mulatress missionary . . . just how her theory of negro outrages is to say the least of it, inopportune."[13] It didn't. In fact, Wells, as was her custom, took the issue, among others, head-on when she spoke on July 29 at Bethel Church.

The pews were filled for Ida's appearance. The audience of about three hundred was made up of mostly women, "many whites," and a contingent of journalists from the *Sun*, the *Times*, and the *New York Tribune*, among others. They witnessed a full program including music and several selections from a choir. Seated on the dais was Fortune; John S. Henderson, the church's minister; Maritcha Lyons; and interestingly, an erstwhile critic, H. C. C. Astwood, a former U.S. consul to San Domingo and president of the black Democratic National League who, just a few months from the midterm national elections, was angling to be named consul to Calais, France.[14]

A "storm of applause" greeted Wells after she was introduced by Fortune. The members of the press, however, seemed to be less concerned with her reception than with her appearance as she took the platform to speak. Wells looked younger than her age of thirty-two; the *Tribune* thought that she was twenty-four, and Ida, as would become her habit, made no efforts to correct the impression. Her outfit was that of a "lady" remarked the *Sun*, consisting of a plain black dress and white straw hat decorated with ostrich feathers. The *Tribune* and the *Times*, respectively, described Ida's voice as "refined" and "musical"; the New York correspondent from the *Chicago Inter-Ocean* noticed that she now possessed a tinge of a British accent. Particular note was taken of her skin color. The *Tribune* said that she had a "light complexion"; the *Times* (which had once described her as "a saddle-colored Sapphira") now insisted that she was "very" light-skinned. Wells, of course, was neither, but her skin tone seemed to vary with her apparent proximity to "ladyhood." It was obvious that Ida had not allowed "the cares and labors of [the crusade] to unsex her," observed the *Indianapolis Freeman* with relief.[15]

Nevertheless, her hour-long talk, delivered without notes (to the pride of her one-time mentor, Lyons), was as trenchant as ever. "Our work is only begun," Ida pronounced in her appeal for support of the movement. The Emancipation Proclamation was a "dead letter," she said and blacks "must strike the blow if they would be free." Wells then cited the need to investigate and document the circumstances of lynching in the most graphic language probably ever heard from a woman wearing ostrich feathers. She told how at the beginning of her campaign, the "British people took with incredulity my statements that colored men were roasted or lynched in broad daylight, very frequently with the sanction of the officers of the law; and looked askance at statements that half-grown boys shot bullets into hanging bodies, and, after cutting off toes and fingers of the dead or dying, carried them about as trophies. They could have easily believed such atrocities of cannibals or heathens, but not of the American people, and in 'the home of the free and the land of the brave.'" She continued, "But when I showed them photographs of such scenes, the newspaper reports, and the reports of searching investigations on the subject, they accepted the evidence of their own senses against their wills. As soon as they were positively convinced, resolutions were passed asking the American people to put away from them such shams and degradation." As for the charges of black rape, Wells, seemingly answering the recent criticism of the *New York Times*, insisted that "black women have had to suffer far more at the hands of white men than white women at the hands of black men. Every single report which is published should be investigated by detectives and let the negro witness ask that her statement be published side by side with that of the lynchers."[16]

Of course, it was her allegations about interracial sex that got the most attention—and not just from whites. When it became known that the *Sun*'s editor, Charles A. Dana, asked for a follow-up interview on the subject, a group of black ministers called upon Wells, begging her to soft-pedal the charges against white women. Wells was frustrated by the fact that they didn't understand that the issue wasn't white women per se but the underlying racism that drove the charges of rape that provided the rationale for lynching. As Wells wrote in her autobiography, she "indignantly" refused the request, explaining that the most difficult part of her ideological task had been disabusing the British of the idea that black men were "wild beasts" who raped white women. She certainly wasn't going to change her approach now. When Dana brought up the issue, she told him that anyone who had read Sir Richard Burton's *Arabian Nights* knew that the idea of white women falling in love with black men was "nothing new under the sun."[17]

The statement created a firestorm. The *New York Times* charged that Wells was a "slanderous and dirty-minded mulatress." One of the ugliest criticisms along these lines came, as usual, from a black Democrat. In this case it was Astwood who called Ida a "fraud" in the *New York Times,* adding that no "decent" colored woman was outraged by a white man, that no "reputable or respectable negro" had ever been lynched. But even a number of Ida's allies looked askance at how Ida framed the issue. The *Freeman* argued that it "weakened her case" if only because it lacked statistical documentation. White Americans, the paper observed, were hard put to believe even one case of such "depravity"; and Ida was making it sound as if it were "common and notorious."[18]

Undeterred, Ida left New York for Philadelphia (with a stopover in Saratoga, New York, where she visited with the Baptist activist from Memphis, Virginia Broughton, no doubt to get her to help with the denominational leaders). Ida had been invited to give a talk for a program hosted by Hiram Bassett, the former minister to Haiti. Frederick Douglass had also been asked to come from Washington, D.C., to join her in the program. Ida gave no indication what their meeting was like after their exchange of letters while she was in England. But if her published writings are any guide, she maintained the same attitude—and affection—for him as a daughter would have toward an exalted father whose occasional behavior was disappointing but who remained high in her esteem. Without revealing their tense relationship while she was abroad, Ida wrote in her autobiography that "nothing had changed her view" that Douglass was the "greatest man that the Negro race has ever produced on the American continent." Nevertheless, she did reveal a bit of residual pique. She recounted in the autobiography that while they were waiting to speak, Douglass confessed that he still got nervous before addressing such large audiences. When he asked her if she shared his anxiety, Ida replied that she did not. She told him that he was nervous because he was an "orator" who was concerned about "the presentation" of his address. "With me it is different," she said. "I am only a mouthpiece through which to tell the story of lynching. . . . I do not have to embellish, it makes its own way."[19] Of course, no one was more conscious of presentation than Ida, but she had made her point.

Wells remained in the city to address white Congregational, Methodist, and Baptist audiences, all of whom passed antilynching resolutions in the wake of her appearances. Ironically, her meeting with a group of AME ministers was the least satisfactory. It seems that after Ida's presentation, one of the black ministers offered a resolution to endorse her work, but it was opposed by a Reverend Embry, who cautioned the body about endorsing someone of whom they knew little when there were more "representative" AME women who could be supported. When others expressed agreement, Ida, after recovering from her "amazement" at the turn of the discussion, gave them one of her sharp-edged lectures, which ended with a proclamation that she didn't need their support. "Under God I have done work without any assistance from my people," she told them.[20]

From Philadelphia she made her way to Chicago, the city where her Ida B. Wells Club was anxious to greet her, where she had worked at the *Conservator,* and where Ferdinand Barnett, who had proposed, awaited. Ida anticipated that the city would provide the warmest reception for her upon her return from Great Britain. She was not disappointed.[21]

"The city made great preparations to receive me," Ida recalled with gratitude and relief. Preceding Ida's arrival, the headline of the *Chicago Inter-Ocean,* noting that she "Speaks for Negroes," unequivocally granted Ida the authority to represent the race.[22] Preceding her scheduled talk on August 7 at Quinn Chapel, a reception was organized by the Ida B. Wells Club, the Payne Literary Congress, the Tourgée Club, and the Bethel, Quinn, Olivet, and Bethesda churches. Supportive articles from the press had also been collected for her perusal. By early August, there was an avalanche of praise and support for Ida to savor. She learned of a mass meeting of blacks on her behalf in St. Paul, Minnesota; and an item in the *London Daily News* contained a letter from blacks in St. Louis who refuted Missouri governor Stone's attack upon her when she was in England. The *Indianapolis Freeman* placed Wells in the pantheon of heretofore all-male "Great Negroes," alongside Frederick Douglass, Booker T. Washington, Blanche K. Bruce, and Martin Delaney (the abolitionist and physician credited with writing the first full-length formulation of black nationalism). Katherine Tillman published a poem about Ida's bravery; Cleveland's Ida B. Wells Ladies' Republican Club was named in her honor. In the *Woman's Era*, the Chicago clubwoman Fannie Barrier Williams, who had spoken so eloquently at the Columbian Exposition, observed that Wells represented an "intellectuality" and "purpose that lifts her into the ranks of reformers." The *Literary Digest* quoted numerous white-owned (mostly Republican) papers on its front page, praising her work abroad and condemning the South's negative response to her assertions. Among them was the *New York Advertiser*, which hoped that the expressions of racial bitterness would not deter her "splendid work."23

On that evening of the seventh, Quinn's large chapel overflowed with two thousand persons. The program began with prayers, after which Ida was led to the platform by the president of the Chicago Woman's Club, the most prestigious white women's reform organization in the city. As she made her way to the front of the church, Ida received an enthusiastic ovation and so many cheers that she had to stop to acknowledge them. As several speakers, including Ferdinand Barnett, gave their introductory addresses, the audience showed their impatience to hear Ida speak. When she finally stood to do so, another cheer arose, and she had to wait for some minutes for it to die down.

In her talk, Wells used the same themes as she had expressed in her New York appearances, although she appeared to put more emphasis on the campaign to come. Ida reminded her audience that the British only provided "their moral force" to help African Americans; the rest of the work had to be done in America. "There remains a part for every man, woman, and child to do in this fight for equality and justice. It must not be said again that [eight million] have left the work of defending the race to one person. I have the same faith I always had in my race, that, when it fully knows its duty, it will perform it."24

By that time, Wells was clear about how the campaign was to be organized and financed. As she wrote in the *Age*, Ida wanted an antilynching committee formed in every city, consisting of not less than seven men and women (later changed to nine) who would have the confidence of the community. Each group was to raise funds to be sent to the Executive Committee that had been formed in Brooklyn, which would make a public report of her expenditures.[25]

Chicago had provided the most substantitive beginning to date. An Anti-Lynching Committee was organized there, replete with a constitution, a nine-member executive committee, and an enrollment of thirty persons, including the city's major black pastors. Barnett was president; and Charles E. Bentley, a political activist and one of the most outstanding dental practitioners in the country, was vice president. Significantly, a prominent white clubwoman and socialist, Mrs. J. C. Plummer, was the secretary of the organization.[26]

AFTER HER CHICAGO appearance, the momentum for Wells's campaign was palpable. She began receiving invitations to speak across the country, including from predominantly white groups in Connecticut, New York, Pennysylvania, and Illinois. Most significantly, in August there was the news that a Republican from New Hampshire, Senator Henry Blair (author of the defeated Blair Educational Bill that sought to distribute federal funds for public education of blacks and whites), was introducing a resolution in the Congress for a $25,000 appropriation to investigate lynchings exactly along the lines that Wells had been proposing. The resolution asked, in part, for the commissioner of labor to document the number, date, location, and attendant circumstances of all alleged assaults by males upon females in the country, as well as investigate occurrences of extralegal violence. Wells, who rightly took indirect credit for Blair's effort, reminded her *Age* readers that it provided an opportunity for them to participate in the upcoming hearings and send petitions to the appropriate congressional committee. At the same time, Ida also reported that the London Anti-Lynching Committee was growing and that it had recently gotten its first outside donation. The benefactors were twelve Africans living in England who had sent the committee fourteen pounds (about $70) "as a testimonial of appreciation," Ida pointedly wrote. If she knew that by contrast the Society for the Recognition of the Brotherhood of Man, as revealed in the September issue of *Fraternity,* had become further polarized by the continuing Impey-Mayo conflict, she did not mention it. Wells added to her good news about the Brits that she now had in hand a petition from leading English clergy asking their U.S. counterparts to give the aid and support to Ida that she needed.[27]

Exhilarated by the positive developments, Ida told her *Age* readers that she would rest for a month and then embark on a cross-country tour in September. Although Ida was still based in Brooklyn, she had already begun to consider Chicago her home—meaning, as can be gleaned from her autobiography, that she had decided to accept Ferdinand Barnett's proposal. But Ida did not want to marry quite yet; there was still a campaign trail before her.[28]

One reason for the month's rest was that she was waiting for the Central Executive Committee's treasury to fill with contributions to finance her travel. But as Wells would discover, while there were those willing to pay her for her lectures and personal expenses, they were less willing to do so when they learned that she wanted the money for activities that were sure to stir up strife: aiding the formation of antilynching committees, hiring detectives, and publishing antilynching literature. Still, she was determined to ask for money for the cause, not for herself. When the *Indianapolis Freeman* suggested that funds be sent directly to her in support, she wrote back asking that the money be sent to the Central Executive Committee in Brooklyn. But Wells soon found that she would have to alter her strategy. She would accept speaking invitations and charge a fee for them; after the engagement, she would remain in town long enough to make a personal appeal aimed particularly at white newspapers and ministers of leading congregations. "For after all," she reasoned, "it was the white people of the country who had to mold the public sentiment necessary to put a stop to lynching." Ida would just have to trust "Providence" she said, for her ultimate success.[29]

PROVIDENCE—AND TRAGEDY—struck on August 31, 1894, when there was a particularly heinous lynching in Kerrville, Tennessee, where six black men were massacred. Kerrville was located in Shelby County near Millington and just outside of Memphis, where Ida had had friends and where her brothers had sometimes worked. She learned of the lynching when a reporter for the *Chicago Herald,* a white daily, rushed in to the *Conservator* office to ask her if she had heard the news.[30]

Kerrville had been the site of land and farming disputes between whites and blacks since the Civil War, and over the course of the last five years, according to the *Commercial Appeal,* there had been a spate of burnings of white-owned barns, residences, and even, the year before, the town's fair-grounds. The immediate tensions that had resulted in the "sextuple lynch-ing" as Ida would characterize it, had begun in April of the previous year when a white farmer's barn was burned to the ground. Nine black men were subsequently arrested for the crime; one of them, Dan Hawkins, was a victim of the current lynching. Hawkins had been convicted of the earlier crime and sentenced to twenty years in the penitentiary, but the evidence was so flimsy that even the unforgiving Tennessee higher courts reversed the decision, and all the men were subsequently freed.[31]

The burnings continued and Hawkins was arrested again, this time with five other men. Clearly, the act was due to frustration about the court reversal rather than any real evidence. The men were all known as upstand-ing citizens in the community, and at the time of the particular barn-burning they were accused of, Hawkins had not yet been released from jail for the first incident. The arresting officer in this case was "notorious as having made a living off of trumped-up charges" against African Americans, Wells wrote in the *Age,* not mentioning that he was himself black. In any case, there was clear evidence of a conspiracy for the lynching. Instead of using a train to transport the prisoners to Memphis, an old uncovered wagon was used. The black men were manacled and a route was chosen that took them through an isolated area. At a particular point in the road, a mob was waiting and gunned the helpless men down. Ida was convinced that that the ambush was arranged by men whose usual pastime, she wrote, was "making negro mincemeat."[32]

The lynching must have rekindled all of her emotions about Thomas Moss. She might have known them or their families. And like Moss they were hardworking, churchgoing men whose economic success was the source of envy among whites who, as the *Cleveland Gazette* noted, "would rather wash their hands in the blood of six innocent and inoffensive Afro-Americans than to longer witness almost daily their success at bread-winning."[33] But as grievous as the murders were, the fact that they took place near Memphis when Wells's celebrity was at its height was bound to aid her campaign. "If Ida B. Wells desired anything to substantiate the charges against the South she has been rehearsing before English and American audiences, nothing more serviceable could have come to hand," was the cool assessment of the *Columbus (OH) Evening Dispatch*.[34]

Indeed, just two years after the Moss lynching, Wells now had, as she had said in her appearances, "the ear of the civilized world." She also had a structure for a stateside antilynching organization and support from some of the leading figures in England. In fact, it was an opportune time to utilize her ace in the hole. In early September, members of the London Anti-Lynching Committee were en route to the States to investigate lynching.

NEWS OF THE imminent arrival of the "English busybodies," as the *Commercial Appeal* called them, in the wake of the Kerrville murders and Wells's publicity caused a flurry of attention in the press. In anticipation of the arrival of the committee—led by Sir John Gorst, an anti-imperialist Tory lawyer who was allied with Lord Randolph Churchill in Parliament—the *New York World* went so far as to canvass thirteen governors about their attitudes toward lynching. Not surprisingly, their answers were defensive on the whole. But of greater significance is that they felt they had little choice but to respond.[35]

Georgia governor Northen's response was typical, saying that the English committee was acting on information from "irresponsible sources"—an unmistakable reference to Wells. Northen continued by reminding the English of their own plunder and wholesale murder of Africans and the fact that Jack the Ripper was still loose on their own streets.[36] The Virginia governor, Charles O'Ferrall, who had earlier criticized Wells's "slanders of the people and the civil authorities in the South," nevertheless condemned lynch law and noted how he had recently called out the state militia, "at heavy expense to the state," to protect three Negroes who were charged with outraging a white woman. "They had fair trials, were convicted and executed," the governor boasted.[37] Governor W. M. Fishback of Arkansas, though questioning the right of the committee to butt into southern affairs, felt nevertheless compelled to explain the recent lynching of three black men by stating their crime (murder), enumerating the number of lynchings in the state during his administration (six), the fact that the mob in some instances included black men, and that a number of lynchers were caught and jailed. North Carolina governor Elias Carr, after a near lynching in his state, defensively explained that he had called a special session of the legislature to criticize mob action.[38] No doubt the Anti-Lynching Committee's own inquiries and their plan to write a report about lynching in the South helped the governors be more forthcoming. The English were well prepared. They were armed with petitions and documentation about specific mob actions in each state. The governor of Alabama, in a letter signed by the committee secretary and Ida's ally, Florence Balgarnie, was asked about the murder of two blacks in his state who were taken off a passenger train by a mob, hanged, and then pummeled with bullets on August 24. "Could we receive assurance from your Honour that the alleged atrocity is unfounded?" their letter asked. "But should it unhappily be true," the letter continued, "we feel constrained to express our horror of this and other outrages of the kind." Despite its own unsympathetic view of the British fact-finders, the *New York Times* predicted that "a good deal of interest will be awakened" when the committee's report was published.[39] Their presence had already done so. If Ida had changed the discourse and attitudes about lynching, it was largely because the South had been exposed in a humiliating fashion before the cotton-importing exemplar of Anglo-Saxon civilization. This was no more evident than in the response to the Kerrville lynching in Memphis.[40]

Peter Turney, Tennessee's governor, promptly called for a full investigation and offered a $5,000 reward for information that resulted in the arrest and conviction of the lynchers. This was the same Peter Turney who had been the chief of the Tennessee Supreme Court where Ida lost the appeal in the Chesapeake & Ohio Railway case. Now, every major Memphis daily unhesitatingly editorialized against the mob action, and the *Commercial Appeal* even had some choice words about violent whites. "We are often shocked by certain crimes to which the negro race is prone," editorialized the paper, "but we must not forget that there is a class of white people, the lowest and most vicious in every community, that seize with avidity upon every pretext to commit outrages against negroes."[41]

The editorial was all the more telling because it was probably written by Edward Carmack, the Negrophobic editor of the paper who had published some of the most vicious antiblack editorials and had slandered Wells before and during her campaign in Britain. However, this time the murdered men were not slandered or criminalized but characterized as "helpless prisoners" for whom a "bloody trap" had been prepared. As had happened just before the *Free Speech* was destroyed, citizens held an indignation meeting at the Cotton Merchants Exchange. Two years later, however, its purpose was to express citizens' "indomitable determination to ferret out the perpetrators of the outrage and have them punished as they deserve." Carmack was among the speakers and was reported to have said that the city must condemn lynching and that it was "time for the soil of

Shelby to be wiped free from the crime and blood which pollute it."[42] Note was taken of the widows and orphans left in their wake. The slain men had twenty-seven children between them. Subsequently, a committee was appointed to solicit money for the families. One thousand dollars was collected at the first meeting and included contributions in a common fund from blacks as well as whites. Carmack himself gave ten dollars to the cause.[43]

Ida watched these developments with decidedly mixed emotions. She must have gained some satisfaction from the evidence of accountability and contrition that she had, single-handedly, wrenched from the South, and Memphis in particular. "Ida B. Wells has licked the Solid South worse than the Union ever did," saluted the black-owned *St. Paul Appeal* in Minnesota. A young Kelly Miller, soon to introduce the study of sociology at Howard University, observed that Wells's "Teutonic pluck had scarcely been displayed by any woman of her generation."[44]

But the law of unintended consequences was also working against her at a time when so many blacks and whites alike yearned for the end of the strife—racial, regional, economic, and otherwise—that gripped the country. To Ida's mind, Americans were too eager to believe that an authentic change had taken place in the South. Albion Tourgée and H. C. Smith of the *Cleveland Gazette* agreed that the behavior of the Memphians was due more to public relations than a sudden concern for justice. And yet the editorial page of the *Inter-Ocean* applauded the "earnest" action of the Memphians. Just months after at least thirty-four persons were killed when federal troops were brought in to quell the Pullman strike of 1894, the paper remarked that the reward offered by Tennessee's governor was more money than had ever been offered for such a crime by the governor of Illinois. There was even a grateful letter written by a black Memphian to the *Commercial Appeal,* thanking the governor for his determination to bring the lynchers to justice.[45]

Wells was most frustrated by blacks. She complained that the black press was too willing to editorialize against such atrocities only to let the matter rest on a pile of angry words. At about the same time, the *New York World* was polling governors, the *Indianapolis Freeman* was doing the same with a number of black leaders (including herself) regarding Kerrville. Ida was appalled with most of the responses. Frederick Douglass said he had not read about it and didn't care to. He had already made his positions on lynching clear, he said, and the "deplorable state of affairs," will "ultimately defeat themselves." Blanche K. Bruce deplored the violence but hoped that it would not erode investment in the state. John Lynch lamented the lawlessness of *both* blacks and whites, implicitly giving equal moral weight to each. All of the leaders "condemned the outrage and all were optimistically of the belief that the South would see the injury to herself and put a stop to these outrages," Ida responded in the *New York Age*. "They forget," she continued, "that no wrong ever rights itself and that whom the gods would destroy they first make mad." The *Age* article ended with another appeal for black churches, newspapers, professionals, and politicians to furnish funds so that independent, firsthand investigations could be done.[46]

Ida certainly was not about to let Memphians off the hook—whatever they were saying at the Cotton Exchange. She told her *Age* readers that Tennessee had offered the reward for the arrest of the lynchers "simply because that town has been made infamous through telling of the evil deeds which have been done there in the name of the law. But now nobody will claim it," she predicted, "and the affair will be forgotten like all the others . . . unless [blacks] keep up the agitation and take the necessary steps to get the facts."[47] Ida remained suspicious of Memphis's motives even as the investigations publicly revealed instances of perjury among witnesses and eventually indicted thirteen individuals with first-degree murder. The action precipitated a mass meeting of the Woman's Loyal Union in Memphis, led by Julia Hooks, which took up a collection for the six Kerrville widows. The group passed resolutions that heaped praise and congratulations on the "worthy governor," "honored judge," "able attorney-general," and "kind editors" for their "sympathetic" actions "in behalf of law and order." Ida must have just shaken her head.[48]

WELLS BEGAN HER nationwide campaign in September, as she had promised, traveling to Des Moines, Iowa, Omaha, Nebraska, and Indianapolis, Indiana. In Des Moines, the secretary of state presided over the meeting, and the dais included the pastors of all of the white churches in the city. Following her hour-and-fifteen-minute talk, a resolution was passed condemning lynching and commending the prompt action of the Memphis authorities regarding the Kerrville murders.[49] In Omaha, Wells spoke before a racially mixed audience in an assembly presided over by the mayor. A white women's club also hosted a reception for her there, and the Episcopal bishop of the diocese made it a point to call on her. In Indianapolis, Ida spoke before another mixed audience that, in anticipation of her arrival, had already formed a local antilynching committee. Her early reception affirmed Ida's conviction that there were heretofore silent but justice-seeking whites who could be moved to support the campaign. "I learned from the lips of these people that which I had always believed," she wrote in the *New York Age,* "that there are many white people in this country who oppose lawlessness and are willing to cooperate once blacks took the initiative themselves."[50]

Wells returned to Chicago in time to keep an appointment at Plymouth Congregational Church, one of the most influential white churches in the city. Its status was largely due to its minister, the dashing, charismatic Frank W. Gunsaulus, and a congregation that included the meatpacking magnate Philip D. Armour. According to one account, after one of the pastor's masterful sermons—"What I Would Do with a Million Dollars," in which he mapped out his views of reforms that were needed in the city—Armour was so impressed that he appointed him the director of the Armour Institute (later the Illinois Institute of Technology), a technical school to help needy, talented boys of both races that was capitalized with an endowment of $1,400,000.[51]

As Wells reported in the *Age,* Gunsaulus was approached by the local antilynching committee to invite Ida to speak at Plymouth. She was told that he was anxious to show that his congregation was as "much interested in stopping lawlessness as the people in England." Ida wrote that on the Sunday she addressed the congregation, the church was full and her address was "received with a silence that was impressive." The description of her reception sounded like she was trying to put the best face on an awkward situation, and the details she added about it in her autobiography confirm the fact. Ida had arrived at the church on the appointed evening, but the entrance was poorly lighted and there was no one to receive her. Finally a young man, who introduced himself as Gunsaulus's son, appeared to tell Ida that his father would not be present, but the service in which she would speak would go on in his absence. Ida absolutely refused to take part in the program without the pastor being present and told the young man so. She waited for a period and then just before she was prepared to leave, Gunsaulus appeared and ushered her into the church. "He made no explanation," Ida wrote, "but his introduction was hearty enough and his denunciation of lynching was all that could be expected." Wells made no attempt to offer her own explanation for the curious behavior in her memoir. But it could be read as a sign for the adopt-the-message-but-not-the-messenger resistance she would find among the more influential white Social Gospel and reformist clergy, as well as black ministers.[52]

Still, September had been a good start, and Wells was able to give her *Age* readers an encouraging report. In addition to the successful meetings in the West, resolutions supporting her condemnation of lynching were passed at the AME conferences in Baltimore and St. Louis; the National Baptist Association meeting in Montgomery, Alabama (representing two million black members); the Alabama Press Association (white); and the Afro-American Press Association. The black journalists, meeting in Richmond, Virginia, issued their strongest statement on behalf of Wells after Governor Charles T. O'Ferrall refused their invitation to address the meeting because it had supported her. "I beg to say I would not think of accepting an invitation to address any convention . . . that endorses . . . the course of Ida Wells in her slanders of the people and civilized authorities of the South," O'Ferrall had said in part. In reply, the group fired back a letter saying that the truth of Wells's assertions was evident in two recent lynchings in Virginia (at Clifton Forge and Richmond) and the lynching near Memphis. "More than this, the fact that Miss Wells is a member of our association and at one time the secretary . . . entitles her to our esteem, respect and sympathy, and her self-sacrificing labors to our hearty commendation." The Association claimed Ida as their own and put her in the same category as the nationalist leaders Charles Stewart Parnell of Ireland and Louis Kossuth of Hungary. The "governor of Virginia himself cannot but admire and respect the association which could issue so manly, dignified yet uncompromising a document," Ida wrote appreciatively.[53]

While still in Chicago, Wells was approached by Mary Krout, women's page editor of the *Inter-Ocean,* to solicit her aid in helping Republican women to elect Lucy L. Coues-Flower as the first female trustee of the University of Illinois. The invitation represented a potential breakthrough for Ida on a number of fronts. It was an entrance into both Chicago and statewide politics and an opportunity to build an alliance with the leading white women reformers. Coues-Flower was one of the city's most important and best-connected activists. She was a founder (along with Frances Willard) of the Woman's League of Chicago, a coalition of fifty-seven organizations, and a prominent figure in the Chicago Woman's Club, whose membership was the crème de la crème of elite female reformers, including Jane Addams, Bertha Palmer (former head of the

Columbia Exposition's Board of Lady Managers), and Frances Willard. The campaign was an especially significant one. Coues-Flower had been serving as a member of the city's board of education, where she had been an effective advocate for raising teacher's salaries and getting concessions for poor students, such as installing bathtubs in the schools for tenement children. But in 1894, the Democratic mayor refused to reappoint her to the board because as he boldly—and rather stupidly—announced, he wanted neither Republicans nor females on the body.

Woman's suffrage organizations in the state had been working for the vote since 1869 and, in 1891, won a highly contested right to vote in school-district elections. The mayor's pronouncement catalyzed Republican activists to engage in one of their earliest campaigns to get a woman elected to a statewide position. Wells's participation in the campaign, which ultimately resulted in Coues-Flower's election, established an important connection to a group of highly motivated suffragists who had their eyes set on extending female suffrage to other offices in the state.[54]

Following the November election, Ida was on the road again—traveling to Pittsburgh, Denver, Topeka, Lawrence, and St. Louis, then Cleveland and back to Brooklyn before she took off to the West Coast. This arm of the trip was written about with little detail in her autobiography, and it was clear that though she met with some success, there was also a good deal of resistance. In Kansas City, she wrote how she eventually prevailed over a contentious black Methodist ministers' alliance she addressed there. A pastor, who was formerly from Memphis, objected not to an antilynching resolution but to Ida, whose aim he believed was to stir up the "very passions she claimed to be anxious to subdue." The comment brought Ida to her feet, asking that her name be taken out of the resolution, and that the alliance merely endorse her work. This threw the group into such dissension that they began singing "The Tie That Binds" and decided to table the discussion. After the group's other business was dispensed with, a minister rose to ask that those who wanted to remain to consider the resolution do so. Forty or so stayed, and they tried to begin where the previous meeting had left off, with a vote on the resolution in support of the antilynching "message," if not the messenger. At that point, however, Ida stood up and told the group that since she was now before a body of men in favor of law and order, she would take it as a "high compliment" if they included her name. The men were nonplussed, but after a minister got up and made an impassioned speech on her behalf, the resolution, with Ida's name attached, passed.[55]

But no effort was going to break St. Louis, Missouri—the state presided over by another of Ida's public critics, Governor W. J. Stone. Wells had one successful meeting there but left concluding that it was "too strongly southern" for her to do more effective work. In fact, she had the chilling experience there of meeting a man who introduced himself as the editor of the *St. Louis Republic* and who admitted to her that he had sent agents throughout the South to find "something that he could publish against me," Wells recalled.[56] Little beknownst to Ida, Missouri would soon be the source of such slander that it would impel an unprecedented movement among the proliferating clubs of black women throughout the country.

Her most eventful—and, predictably, contentious—campaign stop was Cleveland, where she arrived in time for the mid-November national meeting of the WCTU. Frances Willard, her old nemesis, was back from England, and presided over the meeting.

Neither woman could have been in good sorts. Wells must have been tired from all of the traveling and contestation; Willard was suffering from anemia and depression, the latter triggered by the recent loss of her mother. Moreover, both women were frustrated by their organizations. While in England, Willard had become a Fabian Socialist, and her views, like Ida's, were largely out of step with much of her more conservative constituency. As for Ida, despite the publicity, the work of the London Anti-Lynching Committee, antilynching resolutions, and a few stateside committees, there was still no evidence that any movement was really cohering. Certainly no central funds were. Willard's WCTU was having money problems, too. Their magnificent twelve-story, million-dollar-plus building in Chicago, designed by the great architect Daniel Burnham and appropriately called The Temple, materialized in 1892—just in time for the depression. The building cost $450,000 more than first estimated when plans were drawn up in 1887, and efforts to finance it through member-purchased bonds and rent from the offices were being derailed by the financial crisis.[57] The situation caused a great deal of dissension within the organization, which had become less confident without Willard's stateside stewardship for the two years she was in England. Willard hadn't even returned to attend the World's Columbian Exposition, which had proved a boon to leaders such as Susan B. Anthony, whose reception there marked her new status as an exalted veteran to a young generation of reformers. In fact, the exposition marked a subtle shift in predominantly white women's organizations, and

Willard's WCTU was finding itself caught in the middle. Facing competition from the generally more conservative General Federation of Women's Clubs on one hand, and the growing popularity of single-issue organizations such as the National American Women's Suffrage Association (NAWSA) on the other, the WCTU's status as the dominant women's organization was being threatened.

Wells, who attended the WCTU meeting as a delegate of the AME Woman's Mite Society, must have surmised that she now had the upper hand in the tug-of-war with Willard. Whatever shortcomings Ida had in the way of organization, there was increasing pressure for liberal whites to go on record against lynching. This was especially true of Willard, who was fond of flashing her abolitionist-background credentials and whose Cleveland meeting happened to coincide with reports about the six Kerrville widows taking the stand during the trial in Memphis. Their heart-wrenching account, published in the *Commercial Appeal,* was "the most pathetic recital ever heard in any courtroom," Ida later wrote, "and the mute appeal of twenty-seven orphans for justice touched the stoutest hearts."[58]

Finally, in the wake of Ida's British campaign, the British Women's Temperance Association had passed a relatively strong resolution against lynching, one that had been adopted by a number of unions in the States: "We are opposed to lynching as a method of punishment no matter what the crime and irrespective of the race by which the crime is committed, believing that every human being is entitled to be tried by a jury of his peers." But the national WCTU had yet to do so, and Ida was determined to rectify the situation. She thought that Willard was ready to rectify it too. According to Wells, the president had assured her that a resolution would be passed at the meeting.[59] When Ida arrived in Cleveland, Willard also arranged for her to talk to the WCTU's southern caucus. Ida was no doubt anticipating an important triumph.

However, Wells suffered from a chronic case of political myopia, and she failed to take into account three important Willard-WCTU facts of life. The first was that Willard was fighting mightily to regain her declining authority in the organization that she had presided over since 1876. The second was, like other organizations, the WCTU was trying to bolster its membership with the new generation of southern women ready to participate in public life. As was evidenced by recent developments, this was not a generation like that represented by Memphis's Lide

Meriwether, whom Ida had once admired. Just the previous May, the WCTU's annual meeting in Canton, Mississippi, had failed to muster enough votes to graft a woman's suffrage resolution onto its platform. The Mississippians were "indignant" about the resolution, it was reported, as they believed that their "husbands and sons could do their voting and they did not want northern women coming down here and attempting to force such ideas on southern ladies." At the time of the backward-looking vote, Willard was in England, where, with Lady Somerset, she was planning to travel to Italy to present petitions to the kings of Italy and Greece.[60]

The third element that Ida did not take into account was the fidelity of the African American members of the WCTU to the organization, and, indeed, to Willard. As would soon become clear, whatever imperfections the temperance body possessed, there was still no national women's organization that welcomed black women as warmly as the WCTU, and no organization was yet in existence that provided a better infrastructure for reform work in their communities.

On November 17, the *Chicago Inter-Ocean* described the WCTU's opening program. A large banner with the words "For God and Home and Native Land" was draped over the speaker's platform of the large auditorium. The wall behind the platform was decorated with white and yellow bunting, and the upper balconies were intertwined with red, white, and blue ribbons. Willard called the convention to order about 10:00 A.M. with several short raps, symbolizing, she said, love, hope, and gratitude. After the hymn "Rock of Ages" was sung, Willard stepped to the platform and was greeted with applause, followed by the fluttering of handkerchiefs from the delegates. After giving a progress report of what had been accomplished during the year, Willard, to Ida's shock, took on Ida's past assertions directly. Her task was to defend her liberal reputation without alienating her southern caucus, and she did so brilliantly.

First, Willard defended herself against Ida's charges about segregation in the WCTU. "It would be impossible for me to be interested in a movement that made any such distinction," Willard insisted, reminding the audience that her abolitionist family—on both sides—were "devotedly loyal to the colored race." She explained away all-black locals by saying that they were a product of the WCTU's states' rights policies that gave autonomy to each chapter, and in many instances, black women preferred having their own unions. In the western and northern states, "colored women join the same local unions as white women," and the WCTU had black national superintendents among them.

"And now about the lynching controversy," Willard continued, preparing to address the issue of that *New York Voice* interview that Ida had been using as a cudgel. "It is inconceivable that the WCTU will ever condone lynching." Willard explained, again, that her comments were meant to criticize the fact that the uneducated black vote was often manipulated to vote against prohibition legislation. She did not mean to imply "the slightest discrimination against any race." Evidence of this to her mind, was, apparently, her statement that an "average colored man when sober is loyal to the purity of white women; but when under the influence of intoxicating liquors, the tendency in all men is toward a loss of self-control, and the ignorant and vicious, whether white or black, are most dangerous characters." Willard still insisted that the "nameless outrages on white women and little girls were a cause of great anxiety." But she wished she had added the statement that "the immoralities of white men in their relations with colored women" was a source of "intolerable race prejudice and hatred." Further underlining the distinction that white women were raped, while black women had "relations," she went on to explain that the black woman's experience had been shaped by slavery and had since largely ceased.

The conclusion of the fifty-five-year-old president dripped with condescension toward Ida. "The zeal for her race of Miss Ida B. Wells, a bright young colored woman has, it seems to me, clouded her perception as to who were her friends and well-wishers in all high-minded legitimate efforts to banish the abomination of lynching and torture," Willard said. "It is my firm belief that in the statements made by Miss Wells concerning white women having taken an initiative in nameless acts between the races, she has put an imputation upon half the white race in this country that is unjust, and save in the rarest exceptional instances, wholly without foundation." Such was the "unanimous" opinion of the "most disinterested and observant leaders of opinion whom I have consulted," Willard noted, further undermining Ida's authority on the subject.[61] Then came the piece de resistance. According to the *Cleveland Gazette,* at the close of the program, two black WCTU members from Michigan, Madara Preston and Lucy Thurman, presented Frances Willard with a bouquet of flowers.[62]

Ida, blindsided by the personal attack and the symbolic support of black women, was livid. By focusing on Wells's criticism of her and of the organization, Willard had given plenty of ammunition to those who did not want to pass an antilynching resolution that would offend southerners. But the best Wells could do was complain that she had been misrepresented, then to personally confront Willard after the fact, and later make her own protest before black sympathizers in Cleveland.

Fortunately, the city was the home of H. C. Smith's *Cleveland Gazette,* as well as Reverdy Ransom, the militant AME pastor of the influential St. John Church, who became another of Ida's long-standing supporters. A meeting was called at St. John's in which Ida took Willard to task with a performance that rallied the large audience to pass a resolution and form an antilynching committee. At the session, Ransom praised Wells and criticized the women who were "foolish enough" to present Willard the bouquet in the name of "Afro-American ladies" in the "face of [Willard's] adverse comment upon Miss Wells and the race." Despite the efforts of him and his wife, Emma, to get an antilynching resolution passed, they were unable to do so, in part, as implied in the *Cleveland Gazette,* due to the "peculiar conduct and actions of the two colored delegates." They had "forsaken" Wells to "cling to a white woman," Ransom intoned, and "in no sense were they representatives" of the race.[63]

With the battle between Wells and Willard now on again, both gathered their forces. Wells told the story of the Cleveland meeting to Albion Tourgée, who wrote in a subsequent *Inter-Ocean* column that Willard had not been "altogether fair" in her criticism of Wells and that the WCTU had still not taken a firm stand on lynching. On November 27, Wells, from Pittsburgh, wrote Tourgée thanking him for his support. "I feel grateful to you for the only unequivocal expressions in behalf of justice which you alone seemed moved to make," she said. "I feel especially grateful at the word this time in reply to Miss Willard's specious arguments and statements." Willard "could not resist the opportunity to strike at me through her association. She succeeded in doing what she intended," Ida continued. "For the entire organization believes I 'misrepresented' the WCTU while in England. . . . Your words are most opportune in setting the matter clearly before the public."[64]

Albion's public support was no doubt a boost to Ida's reappearance in Brooklyn, where, aided by the Woman's Loyal Union, she made it a point to show that her antilynching committee had the support of prominent whites. Wells spoke in the Association Hall on Fulton Street in a program that was organized by the Woman's Loyal Union and was presided over by

General Stewart L. Woodward, former ambassador to Spain. She also addressed a white Methodist ministers' meeting and appeared at Lyman Abbott's Plymouth Congregational Church. Abbott was the minister who had claimed that black leaders need not be present at the Mohonk Conference on the race situation and was an especially important potential ally. He had succeeded the famous Henry Ward Beecher at Plymouth and was one of the leading proponents of the Social Gospel movement in the States and editor of the influential nondenominational journal *Outlook*. It was quite a coup on her part to be invited to speak to the church congregation, and before such an audience, Ida made it a point to focus on the *Chicago Tribune*'s statistics, which revealed that 159 persons were lynched in 1893. The congregation was stunned by the figures, Ida wrote in the *New York Age*, and after her talk, Abbott promised to publish in *Outlook* any "authentic" information Ida would furnish him on lynching.

The statement could be taken as an insult but again, as in the case with Gunsaulus's church in Chicago, Ida was putting her best face forward. Despite her letters of appeal from leading British clergy, she had not been able to get an appointment to talk with Abbott until the deacon of the church, S. V. White (who, according to the *New York Times*, had spoken at the Association Hall meeting and referred to Ida as "a Moses who had been lifted up to start the great crusade"), intervened on her behalf. As Ida wrote in her autobiography, when she finally got the invitation from Abbott, she was granted only fifteen minutes to talk to the congregation. It was clear that despite her hopes and the denunciations of lynching from American Social Gospelers, she was not going to benefit from the same kind of support that she had gotten from their overseas peers.[65]

Nevertheless, pressure mounted for such support in December when the final verdict regarding the Kerrville lynchers became known. All thirteen of the white men indicted for the mob murder of the six blacks in Tennessee were found not guilty and freed. "I said from the start that I did not believe they would be punished, and they have not been, although the evidence was strong enough to hang them a dozen times over," Wells reminded her *Age* readers. "This . . . makes eleven negroes who have been lynched in and around Memphis since March 1892, and the death of none of them has been avenged, nor will it be." Ida concluded, "If we forget our dead and the injustice to their families nobody will remember them for us. We must continue to organize and agitate."[66]

Ida had written her words about the Kerrville verdict in the same December column in which she excoriated the WCTU meeting and Willard who had "failed to make good her pledge," Wells wrote, because southern women had prevented the passage of a strong antilynching resolution. "I am convinced that we need not hope for anything from the WCTU" were Ida's closing words on the subject.[67]

Ida's column was followed by another criticism of Willard. In late December, the *Indianapolis Freeman* published a long letter from Frederick Douglass. In it, Old Man Eloquent wrote a peroration against lynching—and on this occasion he mentioned Wells by name. He was happy that black newspapers had defended Ida, he said, calling her, again, a "brave little woman." This was followed by the statement that when "Miss Wells was in England, Lady Somerset wired me from across the ocean to know if I endorsed Miss Ida B. Wells. I answered that Lady in the affirmative, and so I answer still," Douglass wrote, with no apparent hesitation to revise history. After expressing additional support for Wells, Douglass fastened on Willard. Although she had "endeavored to set herself right" on the "lynching horror," Douglass chastised her for the "I pity the Southerners" comment in the 1890 *New York Voice* interview. Willard had yet to adequately rectify the characterization of blacks that she had expressed in the piece, he said, and he wished "that Miss Willard could move the impression made upon my mind by this singular sentence."[68]

Being on the wrong side of Ida, who was gathering support in reformist circles, was bad enough, but in Willard's mind, to be criticized by two scions of progressive thought, Tourgée and Douglass, was potentially disastrous. On December 21, she wrote to Tourgée to defend herself. "It is particularly painful to me to be counted on the wrong side in this controversy because I am a dyed-in-the-wool Abolitionist; my father's house was a station on the underground railway (in Oberlin)," she wrote. Alluding to an issue still roiling in Chicago's reform circles, Willard also told Tourgée that she had threatened to leave the Chicago Woman's Club, which is the "largest and the best club in the west," if they succeeded in denying the membership of black clubwoman Fannie Barrier Williams on the basis of her color. Willard went on to explain her "imputation" statement, saying that she thought it "ill-advised" on Ida's part to charge white women with seducing black men and then going "scot free" while the men were lynched for it. As for Wells, she said that Ida "is a bright woman and I have nothing against her except that my study of her character and work leads me to feel that she has not the balance and steadiness that are requisite in a successful reformer. I do not mention this as her fault but her misfortune," Willard added. "I have always treated colored people just as I treated white in every respect," she insisted, "and it is, I think, a downright injustice that I have been made by good Frederick Douglass, by percussive Miss Wells and some others to appear as the enemy of a race that I love and on whose behalf I would do anything that seems to me to be helpful and practicable."[69]

There is no reason to believe that Willard's sentiments were insincere. The blindness about her own racism that stereotyped African Americans as a group while, at the same time, she managed to advocate individual rights for the few would be a perspective that Ida, among others, would have to battle well into the twentieth-century progressive era. Willard would also not be the last to see Wells's "percussiveness" as evidence that Ida was unbalanced.

Of course, what was missing in Willard's letter to Tourgée was any mention of the WCTU's failure to pass an antilynching resolution. This surely weakened her case, and according to Wells, Willard rectified the problem by putting such a resolution on record in the *Union Signal* as if one had actually passed during the convention. As Wells—who might have learned this sometime after the fact—later wrote, a Mrs. Fessenden had offered an unequivocal antilynching resolution at the WCTU meeting but was told that there was already such a resolution in the hands of the resolutions committee. Fessenden yielded and only found later that there was no such resolution and that one would not be passed at the convention. Nevertheless, the *Union Signal* of December 4 not only stated that such a resolution had been passed but also that the resolution itself was spurious. Its wording "prayed" that "the time may speedily come when no human being shall be condemned without due process of law," but added, "and when the unspeakable outrages which have so often provoked such lawlessness shall be banished from the world, and childhood, maidenhood and womanhood shall no more be the victims of atrocities worse than death."[70]

Then by the first of the year, a circular supporting Willard was prepared by Lady Somerset with the object of getting leading liberals to sign it, most of whom were close allies of Wells's, including Frederick Douglass, Bishop Henry Turner, Reverend Joseph R. Cook, and William Lloyd Garrison, Jr.—the last of whom had recently had a letter published in the *London Times* extolling the work of Wells and the London Anti-Lynching

Committee in the States.[71] The circular reiterated some familiar themes: about the WCTU not drawing the color line; the equal treatment given to both black and white women in the WCTU; and the fact that the organization had put itself squarely on record against lynching.[72]

The circular's wording was probably tailored for specific reformers. At least one of the circulars, sent to the Boston philanthropist and former abolitionist Ednah Cheney, also included specific criticisms of Wells. It stated that in Wells's "enthusiasm for her race" she had made "some wild" statements about Willard, and that now a "colored man"—not known to her—was in England and making "outrageous statements as to Miss Willard's position on the subject." The statements, Somerset implied, were not only affecting Willard's work, but that of women throughout England. The letter went on to say that she had spoken to Mr. Garrison on the matter and that he had signed the enclosed document. "Your name would be immense value to us, as your championship of the cause of the colored people is so well known, and I feel quite sure that your sense of justice to women and your personal interest in Miss Willard will make it a pleasure to you to help her by adding your honored signature . . . ," it concluded.[73]

WHILE THE MACHINATIONS of the WCTU were wending their way through reform circles Wells, after leaving Cleveland for Pittsburgh, then Philadelphia, Baltimore, and Washington, D.C, and back to Chicago, made plans to go to California. "I close this Eastern campaign with a heart overflowing with thankfulness at the interest manifested by all our people," Ida told her readers in the *Age* with a rare tribute to black support. Her mood might have been lightened by her learning of a movement among San Francisco blacks to collect funds for the antilynching campaign. She was also surely looking forward to California's milder climes and seeing her sister Annie in time for her graduation, with honors, from Santa Cruz High School. No mention was made in Ida's account of Aunt Fanny or her sister Lily, who appeared to be in California in this period as well.[74]

Wells mentioned in the *Age* that she was prepared to be in California until the spring, but her stay was considerably shorter, about a month, an indication that there was little to remain longer for. In her autobiography, Wells herself mentions only one incident—a contentious one—that took place there. In it she briefly described a ministerial meeting in San

Francisco that "almost came to blows" in arguing over an antilynching resolution. Evidently the situation was saved by Reverend Charles O. Brown, the leading Congregationalist Social Gospel minister in San Francisco, who coaxed a resolution through. The *Indianapolis Freeman* described another incident in which Ida was accused of "passing" for a Methodist when she tried to get their endorsement. This provoked her to write a fiery letter to the *San Francisco Enquirer* in which she declared her Methodist origins, baptism in the faith at the age of twelve, her Methodist-oriented education in Holly Springs, and because of the latter, her "peculiar partiality," as she put it, toward the Methodist Church. But she reminded the naysayers that she had no need to proclaim any denomination, as she already had endorsements from a variety of religious bodies in New York, Brooklyn, Philadelphia, Cleveland, Chicago, Indianapolis, Des Moines, Omaha, and Santa Cruz, as well nearly every Protestant branch in the United States and England.[75]

Believing there was little more to be accomplished, Wells left California, stopping en route in Missouri where she stayed at the home of her old Kansas City acquaintance W. W. Yates and his wife, Josephine Silone Yates, a former educator who had organized the Kansas City Women's League in 1893. Upon Ida's arrival at the Yates home, she was greeted by the news that Frederick Douglass was dead. He had died from a heart attack, at about 7:00 P.M. on the evening of February 20 at his Cedar Hill home. Despite Douglass's age, about seventy-eight, his death was unexpected; earlier that same day he had attended a National Council of Women meeting in Washington, D.C. The Yateses had saved the newspaper issues that announced his death between the heavy black borders of the papers that indicated the passing of a great figure who had been born a slave in Maryland and died a citizen of the world, a figure who had dreamed the dreams of liberty for an imperfect nation. His wife, Helen, would make arrangements for him to be buried in Rochester, Douglass's former home, where, unlike in Washington, he could be buried in a cemetery that did not have a color line.[76]

Once Ida was in Kansas City, requests caught up with her to write something about the fallen abolitionist, diplomat, newspaper editor, and counsel to presidents, but for a long time she was "too overcome with grief" to do so. She had picked up her pen several times, she explained, only to be overwhelmed by her feelings. The news of his death, she finally explained in the *Indianapolis Freeman,* "was the saddest since she had received the notice that she had been orphaned."[77]

With a heavy heart, Wells returned to Chicago "to accept the offer of a home of my own which had been made to me before my last trip to England," she wrote, ready, at last, to end her exile.[78]

CHAPTER THIRTEEN

"Let Us Confer Together"

The public has become so interested in the unique
career of Miss Wells that her determination to
marry a man while still married to a cause will be
a topic of national interest and comment.

—Woman's Era

Memphis had been once characterized as the "Chicago of the South"
by the black press and for good reason. Both had ports that were
indebted to the Mississippi River and had been purchased, with some coercion, from Native Americans. Both had risen with the development of a
network of railroads and had been felled in the 1870s by a tragedy of apocalyptic dimensions. Seven years before Memphis's yellow fever epidemic,
Chicago had been gutted by the Great Fire of 1871 that laid waste to two
thousand acres and eighteen thousand buildings and left ninety thousand
persons homeless. Like Memphis, Chicago—made muscular by its history
of trade, illicit activity, and efforts of social reform—was determined to
reinvent itself as a modern metropolis. The challenge attracted some of the
nation's best architects and engineers, who built a new, vertical city that
included more than twenty of the highest and most brilliantly constructed
buildings in the world, fourteen hundred miles of paved streets, fifteen
hundred miles of sewers, and two thousand acres of landscaped parks.[1]

Of course, there were important differences. Chicago, with more than a million citizens, was the nation's second most populous city—only New York was bigger. Although each had been marked by the early settlement of Irish and German immigrants, by the late nineteenth century, Chicago's foreign-born population had grown while that in Memphis (and generally the South at large) had diminished. In 1890, more than 77 percent of Chicago whites had parents who were foreign-born; and after the 1880s, an influx of Poles, Lithuanians, Czechs, Italians, and eastern European Jews joined the larger numbers of Germans, Irish, and Scandaniavians.[2]

In contrast to Memphis, African Americans made up less than 2 percent of Chicago's population in 1890, although their numbers were rapidly rising. Between 1870 and 1890, the black community grew from less than four thousand to almost fifteen thousand. Like the newest wave of their immigrant peers, most blacks in 1890 were relative newcomers; 80 percent were, like Ida, born outside of Illinois.[3] Still, the black presence in Chicago had been a long-standing one—and no group had a longer history in the city.

Jean Baptiste Pointe Du Sable, a black Haitian fur trapper and businessman who built a cabin at the mouth of the Chicago River in 1790, is widely believed to have been the first permanent settler on the site that became Chicago. The first black community emerged in the 1840s and was made up largely of fugitive slaves (Illinois was bordered by the slave states of Kentucky and Missouri) and free blacks from the East. An important "stop" on the Underground Railroad, a thousand blacks lived in the city by 1860.[4] Chicago, a fount of abolitionism before the Civil War, became a major focal point in the struggle against Illinois's "Black Laws," which prevented African Americans from voting and forbade, in 1853, the entry of any free black into the state. By 1870, blacks gained the franchise and, four years later, the desegregation of the schools. After the nullification of the Civil Rights Act of 1883 (which Ida had challenged in her Memphis court case), blacks successfully pressed the Illinois legislature to prohibit discrimination in public accommodations.

As in Memphis, black Chicagoans, by the 1880s, had established a vibrant community of churches, lyceums, and civic and fraternal groups. As early as 1882, a column of paid society listings in the *Conservator* included twenty-nine chapters or lodges belonging to the fraternal organizations and eleven benevolent societies. In 1885, a black directory listed nine churches and five literary societies and social clubs, and it estimated that five thousand African Americans belonged to fifty organizations and societies of various kinds. Black Chicagoans also had a long tradition of establishing businesses, a number of which catered to an interracial clientele. In 1890, the *Indianapolis Freeman* estimated that the aggregate wealth of blacks in the city was two million dollars.[5]

Chicago's history helped rather than hindered its social reform institutions that strove to cross racial and ethnic differences to relieve inequalities. Two institutions that were gleaming emblems of this spirit were Jane Addams's Hull House, the nation's flagship settlement house founded in 1889, which served impoverished European immigrants, and Provident Hospital, founded two years later, which was the first black-controlled facility of its kind.

If Hull House was the symbol of cross-class fellowship, Provident Hospital and Nurse's Training School represented the city's hallmark of interracial reform. Its founder was the black physician Daniel Hale Williams who, in 1893, had become the first surgeon to successfully perform open heart surgery. Williams had envisioned such an institution since 1888, but it materialized after a black woman, Emma Reynolds, complained to him that she was unable to enroll in a nurses' training school because of her color. Williams intervened on her behalf to no avail, and the episode moved the physician to open a nursing school for black women with an adjoining hospital in 1891.[6]

Provident's board members included prominent black civic leaders: Ferdinand Barnett, the dentist Charles Bentley, and the Williamses— Fannie Barrier and her husband, S. Laing—as well as whites such as George H. Webster, president of the Chicago Savings Bank. The hospital also enjoyed financial support from both blacks and whites, the latter of which included such wealthy donors as Florence Pullman, Marshall Field, Philip Armour, and Henry Herman Kohlsaat, whom Ida had met in London.

Like Tourgée, Kohlsaat, who was co-owner of the race-friendly *Chicago Inter-Ocean* between 1891 and 1894, held a special place in the hearts of the African American community. He was remembered by a trustee of the Bethel Church for providing a financial guarantee when its land was sought by a railway company. The company had initially offered $10,000 but Kohlsaat's guarantee allowed the church members to hold out and negotiate the optimum price for the sale: $41,500. Subsequently, he played a similar role in the purchase of Provident Hospital's property. Kohlsaat had made his wealth through establishing a chain of low-budget (fifteen-cents-a-meal) lunch counters in Chicago for which he hired unionized black waiters. The staff of the *Conservator* frequently ate at one of his nearby restaurants, where they no doubt enjoyed both the meals and the well-furnished reading room that held five hundred volumes for the use of his employees and friends.[7]

OF COURSE, WHAT was truly unique about Chicago was that Ferdinand Barnett was there; and while Wells was on the road, she had not been only thinking and writing about lynching. As evidenced by a short story she published in the *AME Zion Church Quarterly* in early 1894, Ida had also been reminiscing about past relationships and maybe about what might have been in at least one of them. In her "Two Christmas Days: A Holiday Story," Wells's protagonist was Emily Minton, an intelligent, introspective former teacher who had graduated from a missionary college. Emily falls in love and is eventually engaged to a lawyer who seemed to combine the foibles of Paul Jones in Kansas City and Louis M. Browne, the *Washington Bee* editor who had fruitlessly followed her on her first trip west. Emily chides her fiancé to be more ambitious—and to reform his drinking habit—but is devastated when he shows up inebriated at a social gathering she is hosting. She subsequently breaks the engagement and refuses to see him again, until she hears that he is ill and has not had a drink since their separation. In the end, she professes her love for him and the two reunite with the assurance that Emily's influence had saved and made a man of him.

Ferdinand, a graduate of the Chicago College of Law (later Northwestern University), a founder in 1878 of the city's first black newspaper, the *Chicago Conservator*, at the age of twenty-six, and a lawyer with ambition and no apparent weaknesses, seemed to be a perfect match for Ida.[8] He was one of the few who had earlier defended and vouched for her character when such support was hard to come by. Ten years her senior, he had been an outspoken activist since the black convention movement of the 1870s, and the title of one of his speeches before that body, "Race Unity: Its Importance, Necessity, Causes Which Retard Its Development," could have been Ida's own. The *Conservator*, especially in its early years, reflected the same moralistic tone and Victorian sensibility regarding social proprieties and discipline as Ida's columns had in the 1880s. But as the *Conservator*'s call-to-arms antilynching editorials revealed, he, like his intended wife, was capable of militant indignation and believed in self-defense by any means necessary.[9]

Ferdinand was also a feminist. In the *Conservator*, he advocated women's suffrage as early as the 1870s, and, as indicated by his previous marriage to Mary H. Graham—the first black woman to graduate from the University of Michigan at Ann Arbor—he was attracted to bright, capable women. Moreover, Ferdinand was popular and respected and belonged to a social circle that had just the right pitch for Ida. Barnett did not make Chicago's *Blue Book* social register, and although he lived in a respectable neighborhood on Portland Avenue, he was not among the few blacks (i.e., Daniel Hale Williams) whose high social status was marked by living east of State Street, which made up one of the wealthiest sections of the city. Ferdinand did have ties with the black "blue bookers" and fellow Provident board members such as his law partner, S. Laing Williams, founder of the upscale Prudence Crandall Club; Daniel Hale Williams; and the dentist Charles Bentley, professor of oral surgery at Harvey Medical College. But Ferdinand mostly socialized with politicians and up-and-coming young turks such as the future legislator Adelbert Roberts, whom he mentored, and lawyers like John G. "Indignation" Jones, so named for the number of protest meetings he called. Finally, Ida's intended was handsome, liked to wear a silk hat and Prince Edward coat, and was romantic enough to make sure Ida had gotten a letter from him at each stop on her U.S. tour. The virtues of Ferdinand notwithstanding, however, Ida had committed to marry and make her home in Chicago, but not yet to a firm day and time. She postponed the wedding date several times in order to fulfill a number of out-of-town speaking invitations—the most important being Rochester, New York.[10]

IN EARLY 1895, Wells had published her second antilynching pamphlet, *The Red Record*, and probably hoped it would reignite the flagging campaign one more time before she settled into a home of her own. More ambitious but with themes similar to those of *Southern Horrors*, her latest effort included several photographs of lynchings and ten chapters, two of which were devoted to recent lynching statistics, with the victims' names, motives, and dates of their murders that had been published in the *Chicago Tribune.* A total of 159 lynchings occurred in 1893 and 134 (including three women) in the following year. Only fifty-one victims had been even accused of rape in 1893 and twenty-nine in 1894.[11]

Other chapters included narratives of particular lynchings that were selected for their brutality—such as that of Henry Smith in Paris, Texas—and/or because they provided evidence that rape was not the salient factor that was driving the mob. The new pamphlet showed that Ida had not backed down on her critiques, but had refined them. Wells, an increasingly astute student of the social sciences, challenged the pseudoscience of black regression and acknowledged the role of ideology and psychology in the rape charge. "The question must be asked," Wells wrote, "what the white man means when he charges the black man with rape. Does he mean the crime which the statutes of the civilized states describe as such?" "Not by any means," she continued. Because southern white men found it "impossible" to conceive of a voluntary relationship between black men and white women, Ida explained, they always assumed that such liaisons were ones of force.[12]

Wells, with Willard's "imputation" charges ringing in her ears, also felt the need to leaven her criticism of white women. She devoted several paragraphs to the "heroic" northern white women who had come South after the Civil War to teach former slaves. Wells also explicitly stated that it was "not the purpose of this defense to say one word against white women in the South." At the same time, it was their "misfortune," she wrote, that white men, in order to "justify their own barbarism" assumed a "chivalry that they do not possess." Evidence that their claim to honor was a false one was "written in the faces of the million mulattoes in the South," Ida snapped. Another chapter in the *Red Record,* entitled "Miss Willard's Attitude," rehashed the women's dispute in England and in Cleveland and included Ida's exposé of the antilynching resolution antics.[13]

Although Wells's lynching litany had not fundamentally changed since 1892, something important had: the awareness and attitude toward the issue. "The student of American sociology will find the year 1894 marked by a pronounced awakening of the public conscience to a system of anarchy and outlawry," Ida wrote at the beginning of the pamphlet.[14]

Wells should have felt satisfaction from the fact that she was largely responsible for this awakening. In two short years she had made lynching not only a national but an international issue and had demonstrated the potential—if not the full realization—of an interracial reform movement, the likes of which the country had never seen before. As the language of the proposed Blair antilynching bill implied, she had successfully exposed southern duplicity about the rape charge that had so lowered the status of blacks, and by 1895, no official could ignore or explicitly encourage racial violence in his jurisdiction. Antilynching legislation was passed in Georgia and North Carolina in 1893, soon to be followed by South Carolina (in 1895), and other states were in the process of doing so. In 1897, Ohio, Kentucky, and Texas would be added to the list.[15] Although the legislation did not mean that the laws would be effectively implemented, and was largely motivated by political and economic rather than humanitarian concerns, the fact remained that after 1892, the year Wells began her campaign, lynchings continued to decrease in number from their all-time high that year. Nevertheless, if Ida had hoped that the pamphlet, published in January, would kick-start her campaign, she was disappointed.[16]

There was also disparaging news from abroad. In March, John Jacks, president of the Missouri Press Association, had written a public letter to "educate" Balgarnie, the temperance leader and secretary of the London Anti-Lynching Committee, about the race—and the campaign—that she was so ardently defending. Jacks, whose father was a slaveholder, had "lived for years where negroes are plentiful" and the race was "wholly devoid of morality," he informed the Englishwoman. Black men even thought it an "honor" rather than a "disgrace" to go to prison (where they liked to wear the penitentiary-issue striped clothing); and the women "were prostitutes and all are natural liars and thieves." Out of the two hundred blacks who lived in his vicinity, it was "doubtful if there are a dozen virtuous women or that number who are not daily thieving from the white people," he concluded. Jacks did not mention Ida by name in the letter, but it was clear, as she wrote in her autobiography, that he "libeled not only me, but the Negro womanhood of the country through me."[17] Despite the thousands of miles Ida had traveled, she may well have felt that she had been running in place.

By late March 1895, the *Rochester Union and Advertiser*, anticipating what would be one of Ida's last campaign stops, told the world that Ida's tour was a financial failure. Her views are "too radical," it concluded.[18] Wells's April speaking engagement in Rochester would not have disabused her of the feeling. During the course of her lecture before the First Baptist Church, it soon became clear that this was going to be one of those engagements where she would have to endure a rude naysayer in the audience: in this instance, a visiting Texas theological student. When Ida mentioned that more than a thousand blacks were lynched between 1882 and 1892, the Texan interrupted her. Did Wells think that "all Negroes who had been lynched in the South were innocent?" he asked. "I never claimed that," Ida riposted. "I simply claim that they were innocent in the eyes of the law; no man is guilty until found so by trial." When Ida turned to the subject of how the antimiscegenation laws were unjust to black women in the South, the Texan shouted out again, "Do the Negroes want to marry white folks?" The point was, Ida answered, "that if it was illegal for white men to marry colored women, it should also be illegal for them to form alliances with them." When she told the audience that she would herself return to the South if she did not feel the "penalty" for doing so would be the loss of her life, the Texan interjected, "If Negroes are so badly treated in the South why do they not come north or go west or to some more congenial place?" To this Ida patiently explained that many southern blacks were precluded from leaving for economic reasons.

At this point, a white woman, growing increasingly indignant, sprang to her feet. "Blacks did not come North because they are treated no better in the North than they are in the South," she said, citing the recent example of a young colored girl who was told by her teacher that if she tried to attend her integrated school's benefit dance, none of the whites would come. "The outrage on the feelings of that colored girl was the result of the same spirit that inspires the lynchings of the south." The remarks carried a particular significance: they came from the suffragist Susan B. Anthony, who had come to hear Ida speak. Anthony's remarks were picked up by the local press and subsequently by papers in other parts of the country that took up the debate within their pages.[19]

There is no evidence that the two women had met before, but Anthony, who had been accused of being too radical herself on more than one occasion, had apparently admired Wells from afar and, after Wells's appearance at the church, invited her to stay with her and her sister, Mary, for the remainder of the visit. The two activists would have had much to talk about. The seventy-five-year-old suffragist had also been to England, decades before, and had benefited from the same reform circles that Ida had. But their main topic of discussion was undoubtedly their mutual friend, Frederick Douglass. Anthony had had a special relationship with him since 1848, when Douglass had come to the Seneca Falls, New York, meeting that launched the women's rights and suffrage movement in the United States. He was the only man present who publicly supported the franchise for women, and it was Douglass who persuaded Anthony and Elizabeth Cady Stanton that it was not premature to issue their demand at the meeting.

But years of tension and tumult had divided the women's suffrage movement after the passage of the Fourteenth and Fifteenth Amendments, the first of which inserted "male" into the Constitution for the first time, and the second, which enfranchised black men but not women. Douglass was among those who supported the passage of the amendments; and the subsequent women's suffrage campaigns led by Anthony and Elizabeth Cady Stanton had, much as Willard (who had first invited Anthony to address the WCTU in 1881) was now doing, utilized racist and elitist rhetoric that emphasized the need for women to have the ballot in order to protect them from newly enfranchised freedmen and immigrant troglodytes. But by 1890 the major factions of the suffrage movement merged into the National American Women's Suffrage Association (NAWSA), now headed by Anthony, and the new entity was determined to attract white southern women and not run too far afoul of powerful southerners in Congress—who would never grant women the vote if it meant enfranchising black women. With its policy of political expediency, many white suffrage leaders distanced themselves and their movement from blacks in general and black women in particular.[20]

As Anthony told Ida, perhaps guiltily, she had dissuaded Douglass from attending the meeting of the NAWSA, held in Atlanta that January. It was the first annual session of the organization ever held in the South, and as Anthony candidly admitted, she neither wanted Douglass subjected to any humiliation there, nor did she want anything to get in the way of bringing the southern white women into the suffrage association. Moreover, while in Atlanta, Anthony had refused the request from a group of black women to help them establish a black branch of the suffrage organization.[21]

And yet Anthony, a former abolitionist who continued to sustain ties with black reformers, was a woman whom Ida and others knew to disparage racism publicly and privately. During the time Wells was staying at her house, for example, Anthony asked her stenographer to do some work for Ida, but when the young white woman replied that she would not work for a Negro, Anthony fired her on the spot. The suffragist reconciled her beliefs by the ends-justifying-the-means reasoning that anticipated the resolution of race and other issues when women got the vote. Anthony asked Wells her opinion on this and was surprised when Ida, no believer in the moral superiority of women, replied, in the firm if deferential tone she displayed with veteran reformers whom she respected, that she believed that the strategy only confirmed segregationist attitudes. Despite their different views on such an important question, Wells took pride in her relationship with Anthony, and the feeling appeared to be mutual. Some years later, when the white suffragist's biography, *The Life and Work of Susan B. Anthony*, was published—with their meeting in Rochester included—Susan gave Ida a signed copy.[22]

Fortunately, the last time Anthony had seen Douglass, his reception by white women reformers befitted his historic contribution to their cause. On the very day of his death, he had attended a National Council of Women meeting in Washington, D.C., and when Douglass's six-foot figure appeared at the doorway of the room where the conference was held, the proceedings were abruptly halted, the women rose, and Anthony, along with Anna Howard Shaw, then head of the franchise department of the WCTU, went to his side to escort him to the podium amid great applause. Four days later, Anthony had been asked by Douglass's family to speak at his funeral.[23]

WHEN WELLS KNEW she was going to be in Rochester, she wrote to the Tourgées asking if she could visit them in their country home in Mayville, New York. The couple frequently entertained on the estate, which overlooked Lake Chautauqua, and Albion had invited her there when she had last seen him in Chicago. However, Ida was taken aback by the reply from Emma Tourgée, Albion's wife. The letter carried a mild rebuke about Ida's failure to send her husband, as promised, a bound copy of the *The Reason Why . . .* world's fair pamphlet. The complaint was followed by granting Ida "permission," as Wells quoted, "to stop and consult the Judge on matters touching upon the race welfare," and giving train travel directions. The tone of the letter was very different from Albion's earlier, cordial invitation, and Ida decided to skip the visit. She must have been tired and anxious to get to Chicago, and in any case, Wells must have surmised that the Tourgées were out of sorts.[24]

In the spring of 1894, Albion's health wasn't good, and he, like Ida, had dreamed of heading a biracial organization that would attract mass political and financial support, only to be disappointed. His National Citizens Rights Association (NCRA), founded in 1891 to publicize acts of oppression and mobilize its members to push for remedial legislation and attack segregation in the courts, had, like Ida's campaign, been first welcomed with effusive enthusiasm, but had become mired by contestation and failed to materialize substantive support.[25]

Both Tourgée—who was still working on the *Plessy v. Ferguson* case—and Ida now found themselves trying to keep their movements afloat against the swelling wave of accommodationism that would wash over the Atlanta Exposition that fall. His relentless criticism of the Republicans in the *Inter-Ocean,* which was more dependent than ever on the party's patronage, had resulted in a temporary suspension of his "Bystander" column by publisher William Penn Nixon. "Tourgéeism" was also being excoriated by conservative black nationalist critics who believed that no white man could lead or direct blacks, especially one with Tourgée's strategy of agitation and protest.[26]

The trend was even dampening both of their publishing efforts. Despite Tourgée's success as a novelist, he couldn't garner the financial support for a proposed antiracist monthly, the *National Citizen*; and Wells's *Red Record,* selling for twenty-five cents a copy, had failed to pay for itself. The *Freeman*'s observation, "Our noble little heroine is discouraged with the most unappreciative Negro race," could have applied to Tourgée as well.[27]

Despite Wells's oft-expressed admiration for the former judge, she would not have been in the mood to be in the company of a chilly spouse or to be chastised by Albion, who was also prickly about black ingratitude for his efforts. "I have never complained of lack of appreciation from your people because I saw the reasons of their failure to manifest approval, but I have been forced to take note of it by what I saw was its effect on others," he had once written Ferdinand Barnett in a letter that recounted how few blacks attended his public lectures.[28]

But the Tourgées were disappointed when Ida didn't show up; and when Emma wrote Ida telling her so, Wells responded with a long letter that revealed the state of her own emotions. Ida began by apologizing for not sending the pamphlet (she had delegated the responsibility to someone else who had failed to take care of it) and for her "breach of etiquette" for not informing the couple of her change in plans. But then Wells, saying that she wanted to tell Emma the truth rather than evade the reasons for her decision, went on to explain that she had thought Emma's invitation so formal in tone that it had given her second thoughts about coming. Ida feared that she would have been "forcing" herself on them, she wrote, "and I regretted having sent [the request]." But after receiving the reply that expressed regret about not seeing her, Wells felt that she had misread their attitude, adding, "It may be wrong to feel so sensitive, but I seriously doubt if others whose skins are not colored would not feel as keenly the air of social condescension which the Negro generally meets even from his friends among the white people." Wells closed the letter with a note of empathy and deference directed toward the former judge. "I have [also] been made to feel that I, as Ibsen has said, had become the 'enemy of the people' because I desire to help them." It was examples such as Tourgée who "inspired" Ida to "keep up the fight for principle's sake," she wrote. "I know that you do not labor for the applause of the multitude any more than did our Savior who was denied, betrayed and forsaken by his own," she concluded.[29]

A LITTLE OVER a month later, on the evening of June 27, 1895, nine hundred persons filled the pews of Chicago's AME Bethel Church to witness the marriage of Ida Bell Wells and Ferdinand Lee Barnett, Jr. The choice of Bethel was the first social statement that the bride and groom made as a couple. Unlike the AME flagship, Quinn Chapel, located on the well-heeled Wabash Avenue, Bethel, on Dearborn Street, though a magnificent building, was organized in 1862 as a mission church at a time when there were mounting numbers of fugitive slaves in the city, and it was located in a largely black neighborhood already showing signs of neglect. Guests coming to the evening ceremony, some in their elegant carriages, were forced to make their way on a street paved with wooden blocks—many of them displaced—that led them past flimsy frame houses that lined the gaslit streets to the church.

Invitees came from as far away as California, Ohio, New York, and, of course, Tennessee. The Memphians were people Ida had not seen for years: the black businessman and one-time city commissioner Lymus Wallace and his wife, Ida's lawyer James Greer and Mrs. Greer, and Florence Cooper, sister-in-law to Thomas Moss, who now presided over the Coterie Migratory Club, which presented the couple a solid silver water pitcher and goblets. Locally, members of the Women's Republican State Committee were there with their husbands, as well as *Inter-Ocean* publisher William Penn Nixon and his wife. The Tourgées apparently didn't make the wedding but had sent Ida editions of Tourgée's novels and works by George Eliot as nuptial gifts.[30]

The marriage was a major social event in Chicago, as evidenced by the guest list, the announcement in the *New York Times* and the *Chicago Tribune,* and the fact that so many well-wishers had gathered outside of the church that the bridal party had difficulty getting to the church door. The wedding, scheduled for 8:00 P.M., had to be delayed to accommodate their entrance.[31]

Inside the church the anticipation heightened when the organist's soft rendition of "Call Me Thine Own" morphed into the strains of "The Wedding March" from *Lohengrin.* Heads turned to see a young flower girl scatter petals to the right and left of the aisle. The bridesmaids were Ida's sisters, Lily and Annie, reported to be "beautifully attired" in lemon crepe, white ribbons, slippers, and white gloves. The groomsmen were members of the *Conservator* staff, headed by the paper's editor, R. P. Bird. Ida carried a bouquet of roses and wore a dress of white satin *en train,* trimmed with chiffon and orange blossoms.[32]

Although Wells's autobiographical account points with pride to the "hundreds" of friends, including prominent white reformers, who attended the ceremony or sent their good wishes, it also revealed that she was a dour bride. One reason appeared to be that her commitment to wed had awakened Ida's deep emotions about being an orphan and the painful experiences of rearing her siblings. Ida sulked that at first she was not going to marry in a church at all because she had no one to give her away—not even her brothers it seemed, who were not mentioned. Another complaint minimized both the sisterly gesture of the Ida B. Wells Club to "give her away" and the reunion with Lily and Annie, who came from California to take part in the ceremony. As Ida ungraciously explained, she had brought her sisters to Chicago (sourly noting the expense of doing so) to end the bickering among the club members about whose relatives were to be the bridesmaids.

Weighing on Ida's mind was more than the usual distress of coordinating a large wedding. From the moment the marriage plans were announced there had been a "united protest from my people," as Wells put it, who were afraid that she had "deserted" the antilynching cause to marry. They were more outspoken now than during the campaign when she had done all that "one human could do . . . in trying to find the righteous public sentiment which would help put a stop to lynching." Unlike her white peers like Willard or Susan B. Anthony—who had recently been provided a five-thousand-dollar endowment and an eight-hundred-dollar annuity by suffrage supporters—Ida had returned from her tour "physically and financially bankrupt." As much affection and respect as she had for Ferdinand, marriage at this point in her life was also a final admission that hoping for such support was futile.[33]

Ida's resentment and sense of defeat were reflected in the description of the days following the ceremony. The honeymoon was all of a single weekend long, with the bride returning to the *Conservator* office the following Monday. "Having always been busy at some work of my own," Ida explained in her autobiography, "I decided to continue work as a journalist, *for this was my first, and might be said, my only love* [emphasis added]."[34] It was a curious statement for a newlywed, even in light of the circumstances, and may have reflected her pique about another development that she had not counted on. Earlier, Ida wrote of returning to Chicago to "retire to what I thought was the privacy of home." In the context of Ida's life the statement would not have meant that she intended to *stay* at home in lieu of her public work, but rather that she assumed that she would not have any occupational responsibilities that might circumscribe her. However, soon after the marriage, she wrote in her autobiography, she purchased the *Conservator* from her husband and its stockholders, and it is far from clear that the transaction was her idea or even to her liking. Ferdinand was anticipating an appointment as an assistant state's attorney, and it is possible that the requirements of the position made it necessary for him to divest his own financial interest and editorship of the paper. Barnett would be the first African American to hold such a position in Illinois, and its significance outweighed personal considerations—including the fact that the salary that came with it was less than the reported yearly income of $20,000 he earned from his private practice. Ferdinand was prepared to support, financially as well as emotionally, Ida's public career, but as he had confided to a friend, he also wanted a marriage partner who could help him in his own.[35]

Ida, of course, savored having access to the *Conservator,* but she would not have looked forward to taking on the burdens of running a newspaper again—especially in her current frame of mind and fatigue. She was probably expected to take on the same responsibilities as Ferdinand's first wife,

Mary, who had served as the paper's city editor. Mary, a skilled compositor, was also in charge of the mechanical department and had overseen all of the typesetting, reading of proofs, and mailing of the newspaper to subscribers. In addition, if the somewhat murky reports about the *Conservator*'s financing are any guide, Wells-Barnett's gain of majority interest in the paper did not mean that she was able to exercise control over it.[36]

Moreover, it is unclear how much of the editorial duties she shared with R. P. Bird, who was the editor of the paper in 1895 when Ida married. The paper had an active group of investors with their own political interests and who periodically were able to impose their will on the *Conservator*. The internal politics were made more unstable by the precarious nature of the *Conservator*'s finances, which, despite its lofty reputation and a circulation that reached a thousand at its peak, appeared not to yield any more profit than other struggling black papers.[37]

To make the situation even more difficult, Ida's new responsibilities would be another measure of comparison with Ferdinand's stunningly attractive first wife, who had not only been his childhood sweetheart but had been widely admired as an "accomplished scholar, a clever musician, and an agreeable lady"—none of which applied to Ida. Ida's harshest assessment probably came from others in the household. Ferdinand, in 1895, lived with both of his parents, Martha and Ferdinand, Sr., as well as two sons from his previous marriage: Ferdinand III, aged ten, and Albert, aged eight.[38]

The elder Barnett had been a slave in Nashville who purchased his own freedom and that of his wife. The couple fled to Canada (where Ida's husband received his primary schooling) in 1859, in part because Martha's light skin (her mother was Polish and her father Native American and black) subjected them to the hostility reserved for interracial couples. After the war, the Barnetts left for Detroit and eventually Chicago where Ferdinand, Sr., worked as a cook on the steamboats that plied Lake Michigan.[39]

Martha Barnett had a strong will. She had taken over many of the child-rearing responsibilities since Mary's death in 1888, and her and the boys' adjustment to Ida's equally determined presence in the household could have only been complicated by their emotional response to Ferdinand's remarriage. Ida and Martha did not get along, and years of tension lay ahead.[40]

Ida's marriage also meant that she now was faced with the day-to-day responsibility of running a house. The couple employed domestic help but overseeing household tasks was also time-consuming in an age when the family wash required overnight soaking in soda crystals before being scrubbed, wrung, and dried, when gas lamps and hot water boilers had to be watched over, and when the varieties of soot unique to industrial, railway-laden cities had to be dispensed without the later inventions of pre-mixed detergents or electrical appliances. Characteristically, however, Ida was determined not only to meet all of her new challenges both at home and as an activist, but also to forge a new progressive model of marital relations in the process.

Few contemporary female reformers as ardent and travel-minded as Wells were married. They had either remained single all of their lives, as in the case of Susan Anthony, were widowed, like Frances Ellen Harper and Frances Willard, or were living some version of Fanny Coppin's commuter relationship. Ida married at a time when opinions about how to balance one's activist and domestic obligations were sharply divided. For black women, the issue was made more complicated by the fact that both their ability to establish a traditional home life and their achievements in the public sphere were seen as bright markers of racial progress. The "progressive woman of today . . . would not . . . neglect home and husband and children to enter professional life or to further any public cause, however worthy," insisted the Virginia-born educator Josephine Turpin Washington.[41] However, the *Woman's Era,* which provided a forum for different views on the subject, published the opinion of women like Ormistan Chant, the white Unitarian who had voted against Ida in Manchester. The emergence of women's clubs, she said, "will make women think seriously of their future lives and not make girls think that their only future is to marry." The widowed Anna J. Cooper, in her *Voice from the South,* had gone so far as to pronounce that a woman was not "compelled to look to sexual love as the one sensation capable of giving tone and relish, movement and vim to the life she leads." Her "horizon is extended."[42]

There were similar revisionist ideas about having children. Before she accepted the proposal of the twice-widowed Booker T. Washington, Margaret Murray felt obliged to tell him that she did not particularly like children in general (he had three) or Portia—his ten-year-old daughter by his first marriage—in particular. Though she was "annoyed" with herself about her attitude toward "little folks," as she called them, "the feeling

[was] there just the same." On another occasion she wrote Booker that as far as Portia was concerned, she "dreaded" being thrown with her for a lifetime. "I wonder if it is a wise and Christian thing for me to love you feeling as I do? . . . if you feel that you prefer giving me up I should find no fault with you."[43]

Views about marriage and children were also affected by the fact that a number of the new generation of activists married relatively late in life and after their own public careers were established. Margaret Murray Washington, who did marry Booker at the age of thirty-one, was a Fisk graduate and the "lady principal" (dean of women) at Tuskegee before she agreed to become his third wife in 1892 and relinquish the position. Mary Church Terrell married at the age of twenty-eight; Fannie Barrier Williams, like Wells, was thirty-two years of age when she wed.[44]

However, none of the others were so closely associated with the kind of gender- and country-crossing campaign that Wells had undertaken, and her decision to marry, as well as how she was going to manage her competing fidelities, was closely watched. It was Ida's fellow Chicagoan Fannie Barrier Williams who discussed the marriage most fully in the *Woman's Era*—though not without a few barbs. Williams pronounced that Ida's "remarkable zeal for the cause of law and order" was such that in the wake of her campaign, "no one ever reads of a case of lynching without associating with it the indignant protest of our plucky little friend." As a result, Williams continued, Ida's "determination to marry a man while still married to a cause" was sure to be a topic of "national interest and comment." How Ferdinand would respond to this implicit bigamy was also a subject of interest. "Aside from being an attorney of established reputation at the Chicago bar," Williams concluded, "the fortunate groom has manifested a chivalric interest in the cause of his estimable bride."[45] Ida made her own implicit statement about the nature of the partnership she was determined to forge with Ferdinand. Like many of her peers—Terrell, Coppin, Washington, Williams, and others—she would include her maiden name with her married one; but unlike them, she took the idea a step further by hyphenating it. She was now Ida B. Wells-Barnett.

IF WILLIAMS'S REMARKS about Ida's marriage appeared as superficial sniping, the anxieties regarding gender relations and the implications implicit in the kind of zeal that Wells-Barnett demonstrated were substantive ones. There was no greater evidence of this than the John Jacks letter that impugned all black women as prostitutes and thieves. Under the heading "Let Us Confer Together," Boston's Josephine St. Pierre Ruffin had been circulating the diatribe to the growing circles of black clubwomen throughout the country with the advisory that it indicated the "pressing" need for them to formally "band" together, "if only for our protection."[46]

Taking a page from Ida's book, Ruffin tapped a growing sentiment that the time had come for the clubs to come together within a national organization. New York's Victoria Matthews had called for a "congress of colored women's leagues and clubs" in the May 1894 edition of the *Woman's Era*. Earlier, Mollie Terrell and Hallie Quinn Brown had urged a nationwide organization in 1893; in October 1894, an invitation to join the prestigious National Council of Women—an umbrella organization for national professional, educational, cultural, and reform groups—further spurred Washington's Colored Woman's League to call for a national entity. By 1895, the League had affiliates in Baltimore, Cambridge, Newport, Philadelphia, Denver, Norfolk, St. Paul, and Harper's Ferry. And recently, Josephine Silone Yates, with whom Ida had stayed in Kansas City, and Anna Jones had gotten their 150-member group to affiliate with Terrell. Mollie's plea was the most specific one, but it also carried ideological baggage. Ruffin (who belonged to a number of interracial clubs) felt that there was no benefit in joining the white-dominated Council. It is not clear how much the Bostonian's view was affected by her competitiveness with Terrell, but Ruffin and others were also concerned that their movement not be compromised or overshadowed by white organizations. Fannie Barrier Williams stated in the *Era* that black women should "work out, define and pursue a kind of club work that will be original, peculiarly suitable to our peculiar needs and that will distinguish our work essentially from white women's clubs." Terrell, however, was undeterred. She accepted the National Council of Women's invitation on behalf of her newly named National Colored Women's League.[47]

Nevertheless, it was Ruffin's circulation of the Jacks letter and her call to action that "stirred the intelligent colored women of America as nothing ever had done," as Fannie Williams recalled. Ruffin cleverly called for all black women's "clubs, societies, associations, or circles" to meet in Boston to coincide with the conference of the Christian Endeavor Society that anticipated thousands of delegates, including many black women interested in the club movement.

The anticipation for the confab to be held in Berkeley Hall from July 29 through July 31 with the intention of forming a national organization was palpable on the pages of the *Woman's Era*. Its June edition announced that twenty-eight organizations—including both new clubs and traditional black women's temperance, church, and literary groups—were prepared to be represented in Boston to discuss, as Ruffin called for, "our position, our needs and our aims . . . and to provide an object lesson to the world."[48]

Also planning to attend was former abolitionist Henry Blackwell, husband of the recently deceased suffragist Lucy Stone; William Lloyd Garrison, Jr., son of the abolitionist; *New York Age* editor T. Thomas Fortune; Wells's old beau Charles S. Morris; and Booker T. Washington. Ruffin added that the women "will be glad to welcome among them Mrs. Ida B. Wells Barnett [*sic*] who has been invited to attend." Being with them at their formation, and also "being in every sense of the word a club woman," she continued, "the congratulations waiting to be showered upon Mrs. Barnett will be heartfelt indeed."[49]

Ida, however, had no intention of going to Boston. As she explained in her autobiography, she was too "utterly worn out" to attend a meeting called so soon after her cross-country tour and her marriage. In any case her physical presence was hardly necessary, she implied, as the call to action was "a unanimous endorsement of the course I had pursued in my agitation against lynching." However, though not mentioned in the autobiography, there is little doubt that more than fatigue and a sense of fait accompli were keeping her from going to Boston.[50]

For one thing, the air was thick with a new round of contestation between Ida and the WCTU, or more precisely, the black women members of the temperance organization, a number of whom were coming to Boston. In June, the world body of the Christian Temperance Union, meeting in London, had failed to pass a strong antilynching resolution, although one had been offered. This time it was Lady Somerset who sent the convention roiling before the vote by bringing up Wells's "injudicious" charges regarding the organization. At that point, Florence Balgarnie had risen in passionate defense of Ida and added that American women too often apologized for lynching when they should have been denouncing it. The charge against the Americans raised the hackles of, among others, Hallie Quinn Brown, the black former women's dean at Tuskegee and present professor of elocution at

Wilberforce University, who took sides with Somerset against Balgarnie. Upon hearing the news, the *Cleveland Gazette* (which had earlier criticized Lucy Thurman for presenting a bouquet of flowers to Willard after she had chastised Wells in Cleveland) squared off on Brown. Under the headline, "O Shame," it averred that blacks in the city were shocked by her attitude and awaited an explanation from her.[51]

The July issue of the *Era* featured an article in which Libby C. Anthony of Jefferson City, Missouri, who was the WCTU's state superintendent of colored work, denied that Willard was a racist. It was because of Willard's influence, Anthony argued, that many of the state unions had adopted antilynching resolutions. In the same issue, an *Era* editorial, probably by Ruffin, riposted that "Doubtless Miss Willard is a good friend of the colored people, but we have failed to hear from her or the WCTU any honest, flatfooted denunciation of lynching and lynchers."[52]

Most disturbing for Ida was that the circular supporting Willard and the WCTU, which Willard and Lady Somerset had sent to Ida's supporters, had surfaced with the names of the late Frederick Douglass, Bishop Turner, Joseph Cook, and Garrison among the signatories. "We have great respect for the signers of the circular," Ruffin acknowledged, "but it will take more than this and more than Lady Somerset's scoring of Miss Wells to convince us that the WCTU does not hedge."[53]

It is easy to surmise that Ida felt in no condition to go back to the WCTU battlefront, especially now since it had to be fought through black women surrogates. Even more than the decade before, many were invested in the WCTU—segregated branches or not—which was still one of the few nationwide and powerful reform organizations in which they could participate and attain executive positions (albeit in "colored" departments), and did not have to be of the manor born to feel comfortable within. As Fannie Barrier Williams noted, the WCTU "blended rich and poor, intelligence and ignorance, party politics and church creeds."[54]

However, in addition to the WCTU issue itself was a deeper one regarding the politics of representation. To some, Ida's methods were as responsible for the public aspersions cast upon all black women as the beliefs that spawned them. This is what undoubtedly compelled Ruffin to remind the women that Wells-Barnett was in every sense a "club woman" who should be "showered with congratulations." Ida knew that many of those planning to attend the meeting weren't so sure. Although, as they did before the meeting's end, they were bound to pass a resolution against lynching and express admiration for her "noble and truthful advocacy," the "shower," Ida must have suspected, was bound to contain a number of sharp objects. Even Ruffin, her greatest defender among the women, had to subtly acknowledge, in her opening address to the July gathering, that the women represented "an army of organized women standing for purity and mental worth . . . [who] *in themselves* deny the charge [of immorality] . . . not by noisy protestations of what we are not," she stressed, "but by a dignified showing of what we are and hope to become."[55]

While Ida agreed with many of the points eloquently articulated by Ruffin and others, it was clear that their agenda was, relative to her ideas, a conservative one. "Our woman's movement is a woman's movement in that it is led and directed by women for the good of women and men, for the benefit of all humanity," Ruffin pronounced at the confab's opening before one hundred delegates from ten states. The words reflected earlier pronouncements in the *Women's Era* that affirmed the black women's concern for "the oppressed everywhere," including the Chinese, Hawaiians, and Russian Jews—all groups that were struggling in the period. "We are not alienating or withdrawing," Ruffin insisted, "we are only coming to the front." She continued to speak about the practical and "especial" need for black women to provide opportunities and uplift "for the sake of the thousands of self-sacrificing young women teaching and preaching in lonely southern backwoods, for the noble army of mothers who have given birth to these girls, mothers whose intelligence is only limited by their opportunity."[56] The agenda she had set was evident in the meeting's program, which featured discussions about higher education for women, industrial training, temperance, race literature, suffrage, and domestic hygiene.

The conference's emphasis on true womanhood, opportunities, and elevation left little room for the kind of agitation that Wells had come to believe was necessary. Also militating against Ida's strategies were the unmistakable signs of progress among the educated few, and the idea, as Virginia clubwoman Rosa D. Bowser succinctly put it in the pages of the *Woman's Era,* that "Race progress is the direct outgrowth of individual success in life . . . the race rises as the individuals rise . . . and individuals rise with the race."[57]

Even as lynching continued, the great majority of blacks remained impoverished, and South Carolina followed Mississippi in its "legal" disenfranchisement scheme that year, there were unmistakable signs of progress.

As previously noted, organizations such as the National Council of Women were willing to desegregate, and in May 1895, the Chicago Woman's Club, which had bitterly debated Fannie Barrier's membership for fourteen months, finally passed a resolution that stated no woman would be excluded on the basis of race. Women like Ruffin were already in prestigious, predominantly white organizations, and in 1895, Mary Church Terrell—also conspicuously absent from the Boston conference—had been appointed to the District of Columbia's Board of Education, the first black woman to serve in that capacity. In the same year, W. E. B. Du Bois became the first African American to earn a doctorate from Harvard. Even back in Memphis, Wells-Barnett's teaching colleagues—at least those who managed to remain without agitating whites—were doing well. The *Memphis Commercial* in 1894 had reported that Ida's old beau Isaiah Graham (also recently divorced) headed the Intermediate Department of Kortrecht; Granville Marcus, whom Ida had also once dated, was principal of the Virginia Street School. "The race problem seems to be solving itself," a speaker before New York City's Bethel Church had opined. The conclusion was put into the Boston convention minutes.[58]

During the course of the deliberations, little was mentioned about lynching. In the published minutes of the meeting, only two clubs mentioned Ida's name in their reports about their activities and origins: the Belle Phoebe League of the twin cities of Pittsburgh and Allegheny, and the Woman's Club of Jefferson City, Missouri. Not even the Woman's Loyal Union of Brooklyn mentioned her, although it did cite a lecture given by G. F. Richings, who lectured against lynching in the British Isles in the wake of Ida's campaign there. If acknowledgments were scarce, thinly veiled criticism was not. The New York group with the imposing name of the "One Thousand Women of Bethel Church," where Ida had spoken in the past, submitted that,

it would be unwise to permit this convention to be made the sounding board of mere "agitators." We recognize in the "Jacks letter" and other such slanders the natural results of the resentment provoked by the fierce denunciation of "southern white women" that have been injudiciously indulged in by some of the "mercurial persons" of the race. We look with more hope to the conservative workers. . . . The truly representative women of the race can never be enlisted in any movement that is led by the ignorant enthusiasts or the fiery agitators, whose incentive to action is the intoxication of excited sensibilities, full of the chimeras of distempered fancy.[59]

Nevertheless, the conference, sans Ida's presence, was a historic one. The main objective of the meeting—to bring a panoply of activist black women and organizations from across the nation under one umbrella—was accomplished. Before leaving Boston, they had created the National Federation of Afro-American Women (NFAAW), with Victoria Earle Matthews as chair of the executive board and Margaret Murray Washington as president.

THE ELECTION OF Margaret Washington, wife of the Tuskegee educator, marked the beginning of her rise to national power in the new black woman's movement. Born in Macon, Mississippi, to Lucy Murray, a washerwoman, and James Murray, an Irishman, Margaret and two of her ten siblings were taken in by a Quaker family when her father died. Margaret was seven years of old at the time and grew up to become a model student at Fisk University, where she took courses in Latin, Greek, philosophy, science, and literature (specializing in Shakespeare and Hawthorne) and was the associate editor of the *Fisk Herald*. Subsequently, she taught at Tuskegee where Booker T. Washington was so impressed with her that after her first year teaching there he asked her, in 1890, to be the school's lady principal.

Booker was attracted to more than Margaret's pedagogy. She had an enticing combination of an unconventional persona and a western-standard attractiveness—save for one feature. Margaret had "beautiful features, arched eyebrows, blue (?) eyes, a Grecian nose, and a poise of the head like a Gibson girl," as a white settlement worker once described her. She was "lighter than Booker," and "her hands are white as mine and beautifully shaped," the white woman continued, "but her hair is kinky."[60]

After the marriage, Margaret left her formal position at Tuskegee. In March of 1895, she founded the Tuskegee Woman's Club, which soon attracted more than three hundred women every week. Although her achievements were significant in their own right, there was little question that her election to the NFAAW presidency was also due to the rising influence of her husband.

By 1895, Washington, thirty-nine years of age, had gone well beyond being an efficient administrator of a 540-acre campus in Alabama, where blacks learned a trade, discipline, and moral uprightness. At a time when most black schools were run by whites, Tuskegee not only had an all-black teaching and administrative staff, it was at the center of a model black community that Washington created by acquiring surrounding farmlands and selling them at low interest to black landowners.[61]

His philosophy of industrial education, later to become so controversial, reflected a national trend in the mid-1890s, and his view that blacks could dispel the contempt of whites through education and wealth was consistent with the thinking of the Progressive Movement—Ida's views notwithstanding. His traditional view of jettisoning politics and civil rights in favor of community uplift took on new significance in a period when Americans, both black and white, were desperate to end debilitating strife and begin economic recovery. By 1895, militant protest, as Ida could attest to, had exacted few rewards, and had accumulated debts and public denunciation—even among liberals in the North. In the South, it brought death or cowering humiliation in an effort to avoid absolute ruin. Frederick Douglass was dead, the Republicans had been defeated, and there was no one to fill the breach of a leader who could bring the black elite back to the table where philanthropists and leaders of industry were plotting the country's future.

Washington's timing was good; his skills as a master communicator were even better. He had a way of parsing the meaning of his words in such a way that they simultaneously spoke to the anxieties and aspirations of white and blacks. The Tuskegeean would take full advantage of all of his abilities in a major address before the Atlanta Cotton States and International Exposition on September 18, 1895. When Booker, his wife, Margaret, and the three Washington children were escorted to the speaker's stand on that date, a new chapter of American history was about to unfold.[62]

"The wisest among my race understand that the agitation of questions of social equality is the extremest folly," Washington pronounced before the huge crowd that included Georgia's governor, white Southerners, northern industrialists, and black officials. If whites understood the phrase as acceding to the segregation, African Americans could read it as a statement of racial solidarity and pride that they neither wanted nor needed to intermingle with whites. When Washington exhorted that "progress in the enjoyment of all the privileges that will come to us must be the result of severe and constant struggle rather than of artificial forcing," the phrase could also be interpreted in two ways: as an affirmation of an ethic long espoused by blacks that citizenship had to be earned, or as a capitulation to disenfranchisement, segregation, and the loss of civil rights. For many, even the exchange of the latter as a price for constructive biracial cooperation was not such a bad bargain in a region where blacks were unable to exercise those rights in any case.

One of the most famous lines in Washington's speech, "Cast down your bucket where you are," had been used before. In an 1894 essay in the *AME Church Review,* he used the phrase to advise blacks against emigration and to take advantage of the opportunities "that are right before us." In Atlanta, however, the phrase, spoken in the context of how black labor had served the South "without strikes and labour [*sic*] laws" implored whites not to spurn loyal black workers in favor of European immigrants. Washington reached the climax of his speech with another rhetorical device that he had used when he had complained about Jim Crow train travel at the time of the New Orleans fair. "In all things purely social we can be separate as the fingers," he said, spreading his own atop an outstretched arm, "yet as one hand," he continued, clenching his fist, "in all things essential to mutual progress." At that point, the audience, numbering in the thousands, leapt to their feet in wild applause amid a sea of waving handkerchiefs, canes hoisted high into the air, and a rain of flowers pulled from the bosoms of ladies' dresses and tossed onstage.[63]

The national response was no less enthusiastic. Dixie had a "new meaning now," trumpeted the white-owned *New York World.* The *Chicago Inter-Ocean* and the *Boston Transcript* gave good reviews of the speech. President Grover Cleveland wrote a personal letter of congratulations to Washington. "Your words cannot fail to delight and encourage all who wish well for your race," the northern Democrat wrote, "and if our colored fellow-citizens do not from your utterances gather new hope, and form new determinations to gain every valuable advantage offered them by their citizenship, it will be strange indeed."[64]

In fact, Washington's formula for reconciliation was not unreasonable to many blacks. Calming the waters with Booker's bucket would put blacks back to work, build character among the masses (the bane of black bourgeoisie's existence), decrease violence, and preserve the gains of the black elite. "Here might be the basis of real settlement between whites and blacks in the South," wrote the young scholar W. E. B. Du Bois, whose earned degree from Harvard would soon be followed by Booker's honorary one from the same institution. The terms of the "settlement," as Du Bois reiterated in the *New York Age,* was for the South to open to "Negroes the doors of economic opportunity" and "the Negroes [to co-operate] with the white South in political sympathy."[65]

There were black critics of what became known as the "Atlanta Compromise," but they were in the minority. The *Atlanta Advocate* called Washington a "sychophant" whose "hat flies off the moment a small, red headed newsboy is introduced to him in the [Atlanta Exposition's] Negro building." Calvin Chase of the *Washington Bee* thought Washington's words were "death to the Afro-American and elevating to white people"; and Bishop Henry M. Turner predicted that "we will live a long time to undo the harm [Washington] has done to the race."[66]

There is no mention of the Atlanta speech in Ida's autobiography, but according to one source, the *Conservator* went on record mildly praising Washington's "New Negro" approach that took economic development into consideration. It is not clear what Ida's editorial role in the paper was at this juncture. What was clear was that Booker T. Washington, with ideas diametrically opposed to her own concerning the role of black labor and agitation in the South, had been catapulted to national leadership just when she was at her most enervated and distracted.[67]

IN DECEMBER IDA did not attend the Atlanta Congress of Colored Women, where women from twenty-five states were represented. Held under the auspices of the Ladies' Auxiliary to the Negro Department of the Atlanta exposition, it was not formally connected to the NFAAW though a number of women who met there had also been in Boston. However, Ruffin did not attend, and its leaders who did were not Ida's warmest allies. The WCTU's Lucy Thurman, who had presented flowers to Willard in Cleveland, was president of the auxiliary; and Josephine Bruce, wife of former U.S. senator Blanche K. Bruce, was chair. A debate over whether an antilynching resolution should include the condemnation of rape ensued, but it appeared that Victoria Matthews was able to marshall enough support to quell the Willard-inspired wording. A compromise resolution was passed that praised the opportunities the temperance organization afforded black women and, at the same time, insisted it be "less equivocal" in its attitudes toward color prejudice and lynching. The group also called upon southern legislators to protect all women from "outrage" and "insult," chastised southern white women for their "indifference," and criticized black men who had discouraged them in "all attempts at public work" resulting in a lack of "real progressiveness all around." The outcome of the meeting might have made Ida regret not being there, but in addition to the tension she may have anticipated in Atlanta, she had had another reason to stay home: in December of 1895, Ida was five months pregnant.[68]

CHAPTER FOURTEEN

Undivided Duty

I honestly believe that I am the only woman in the
United States who ever traveled throughout the
country with a nursing baby to make political
speeches.

—*Ida B. Wells-Barnett*

For Ida, becoming a mother was even more complicated than being a wife. As she admitted in her autobiography, she did not have a longing for children. "It may be that my early entrance into public life and the turning of my efforts, physical and mental, in that direction had something to do with smothering the mother instinct," she understated. Ida went on to explain that she had also been affected by the fact that as the oldest child in her family she had been expected to help with her younger brothers and sisters and that after her parents died, she had been forced to be their sole provider. "Somehow I felt entitled to the vacation from my days as nurse."[1]

Moreover, by the time Ida was faced with the prospect of having children, progressive ideas about raising them had changed. No longer thought of as little adults, children were seen as a distinct social category believed by the growing class of child experts to have amorphous wills that had to be shaped by knowledgeable mothers and constant surveillance. "If the mother does not have the training and control of her child's early and most plastic years, she will never gain that control," Ida herself believed. Although Ferdinand did not shirk all domestic duties—he had learned to cook from his father and, unlike Ida, enjoyed contributing his culinary skills to the dinner table— there is no indication that he was willing to take on the tasks of child care. In any case, he had been named the first black assistant state's attorney in Cook County in January of 1896 and was more occupied than ever.[2]

In one of the few autobiographical passages that mentioned anything about Ida's private life, she revealed that on the night of her marriage, she had been advised about birth control. Ida did not say who advised her, what method was suggested (rubber prophylactics were popular in the period), or if she had actively sought out the information. In any case, Wells-Barnett decided against any such measures. When she married, Ida was in her thirties, her husband in his forties. If she were to have children at all, time was limited. So Ida determined that if motherhood for her was going to become a profession in itself, it would not be her only profession. While she was pregnant she remained active with the *Conservator,* her Ida B. Wells Club, and speaking engagements. "I was busy," she wrote, but "not too busy to give birth to a male child [on] 25 March 1896." The infant was born nine months—nearly to the day, or night—after her wedding.[3]

Charles Aked Barnett was named for the English minister who had been an ally to Ida during her second British tour. She had seen the reverend the previous November, when he had been invited by the University of Chicago president, William Rainey Harper, to give the Thanksgiving sermon at the school. Ida attended the sermon in which he spoke against lynching, among other issues, and the Barnetts subsequently entertained Aked and his wife at their home. During his stay, the Englishman was invited by Harper to attend a football game and the minister asked Ida to join him. Wells-Barnett loved seeing the surprised reactions when she accompanied Aked to sit in the president's box at the stadium. "It was a more splendid demonstration of the doctrine of actual equality which the English practice than many pages of writing," she wrote. "I am sure that the democratic attitude of our English friends . . . is what determined my husband to name our first-born after this distinguished English preacher." With the naming of their baby, the Barnetts made yet another social statement.[4]

Wells-Barnett spent the immediate postpartum weeks at home, but she was obviously antsy. "Although I tried to do my duty as mother toward my first-born and refused the suggestion not to nurse him, I looked forward to the time when I should have completely discharged my duty in that respect," she confessed. Indeed, 1896 proved a difficult year to remain at home with a newborn.[5]

That May, the U.S. Supreme Court handed down its decision in *Plessy v. Ferguson,* declaring that state laws that provided separate but equal accommodations were constitutional. Ida's own lost appeal in Tennessee was cited as one of the precedents for the decision that, with its twisted logic, jettisoned the equal protection clause of the Fourteenth Amendment and imposed segregation with the police powers of the state. Justice Henry Billings Brown (a native of Massachusetts), who delivered the decision, said that the underlying "fallacy of the plaintiff's argument" was the "assumption that the enforced separation of the two races stamps the colored race with a badge of inferiority." Another statement in Brown's decision eerily codified what Booker T. Washington had implied in his own Atlanta exposition speech. "If the two races are to meet upon terms of social equality, it must be the result of natural affinities, a mutual appreciation of each other's merits and a voluntary consent of individuals," the decision read in part. "If one race be inferior to the other socially, the Constitution . . . cannot put them upon the same plane." Only one Supreme Court justice dissented: John Marshall Harlan, a Kentuckian and former slaveholder.[6] The terrible news got surprisingly little coverage in the national white press, and the black press criticized the decision but few papers appeared to be surprised, or grasp its full significance. After all, southern blacks had already been largely circumscribed in public transportation, and few seemed to envision how the affirmation of separate but equal would seep into every aspect of black life.

News of the judgment prompted Ida to write a sympathetic letter to Albion Tourgée, but she must have also hoped that it would stir a call for renewed action. Following the Court's ruling, the *Washington Bee* called for the reactivation of the Afro-American League, and planned for July of 1896 were two meetings of clubwomen in Washington, D.C. Both the National Federation of Afro-American Women (NFAAW) and the National

League of Colored Women were due in the capital several days apart. They planned to meet in the Nineteenth Street Baptist Church and Francis Grimke's Fifteenth Street Presbyterian Church, respectively. It was a propitious time to create one national entity.[7]

Ida had been asked to be an NFAAW delegate representing the London Anti-Lynching Committee (the Ida B. Wells Club was also represented) at the Washington meeting, and she, evidently, wasn't too tired to attend. In addition to the historical significance of the Washington confab, Wells-Barnett knew that the temperance organizers would have reason to be less pugnacious. Recently, Florence Balgarnie had been fired as editor of the *Women's Signal* and censored by the BWTA executive committee for exposing the fact that the signers of the circular supporting the WCTU had not been accurately informed about the evasive tactics of Somerset and Willard to pass an unconditional antilynching resolution. When William Lloyd Garrison, Jr., a signer of the circular, found out about the manipulation, he was furious and told the temperance leaders so. Helen Douglass, Frederick's widow, also learned of the situation from Balgarnie and wrote her saying that her husband had been unaware of it when he signed the circular. "Any impeachment of his integrity in this or any other matter" was an insult to his memory, Douglass added. Two years before Willard's death in 1898, Wells-Barnett had secured her last moral victory over the temperance leader.[8]

Little Charles was less than five months old, but Ida had decided that if she was going to be the shaper of his will, she would do it on the road. Before the scheduled meeting in Washington, she spoke on "Women Journalists" before the Afro-American Press Association in St. Louis, then made her way to Washington with her baby and a nurse in tow.

THE NFAAW MEETING, with Margaret Murray Washington presiding, began at 9:50 A.M. on July 20. The pastor, Walter H. Brooks, welcomed them, and Rosetta Douglass Sprague, daughter of Frederick Douglass, responded on behalf of black women across the United States. "From the log cabins of the South have come forth some of our most heroic women," she said, "women who have suffered death rather than be robbed of their virtue. Women who have endured untold misery for the betterment of the condition of their brothers and sisters." Sprague continued, "While the white race have chronicled deeds of heroism, so we are pleased to note in the personality of Phyllis [*sic*] Wheatley, Margaret Garner [who had killed her child rather than see it return to slavery], Sojourner Truth and our venerable friend, Harriet Tubman." Of the women mentioned, only Tubman was still alive, and thirty-three years after the end of slavery, the former abolitionist graced the historic meeting with her presence. During one of the sessions, she recounted her own escape from bondage on Maryland's eastern shore, only to return to the South again and again to lead some three hundred slaves to freedom. After the Civil War, Tubman established a home for aged ex-slaves who could no longer perform arduous work or take care of themselves.[9]

During the afternoon session of the NFAAW on July 20, the recitation of the federation's club reports was dramatically halted in order to read a letter signed by Coralie Franklin, corresponding secretary of the National League. The letter expressed her hope that the two organizations would meet each other with the object of forming a union. The very next day, seven delegates from each group met in the Nineteenth Street Baptist Church to draw up articles of agreement. Mary Church Terrell, the president of the League, was elected chair of the joint committee. Although the two groups had more in common than not, there were issues to be resolved, especially the question of a unitary leadership at a time when there were so few opportunities and so much ambition among black women reformers. A prayer was offered. Negotiations began.[10]

From the beginning it was clear that Terrell's group was the most prepared—and the most nimble. The League took the initiative in proposing the major articles for agreement: that the officers of the united entity be chosen in proportion to their respective membership, that a new constitution be drafted, and that the name of the consolidated group be the National Association of Colored Women (NACW). As New York's Victoria Matthews, who headed the NFAAW's committee of seven, observed, she did not have the "final powers of action" as did Terrell for her group, and so was at a disadvantage.[11]

The minutes of the meeting noted two items that received lengthy discussions. One was regarding the proposed new name of the organization. Victoria Matthews argued for retaining "Afro-American" in the title. Matthews, who was light-skinned, "gave the audience to understand that she had African blood in her veins and was of African descent, which entitled her to the name of 'Afro,'" she said. But she was also "an American citizen and entitled to all of the privileges of such. The name 'colored' meant nothing to the Negro race," Matthews concluded.[12]

At that point Wells-Barnett, who no doubt agreed, moved that Matthews be given the power to speak for the NFAAW faction. In response, Terrell, confident that most of the delegates preferred the name "Colored," called for an amendment to Ida's motion, asking that the report of the committee be received first. (For example, the darker-skinned Fanny Jackson Coppin preferred "Colored," believing that "Afro-American" was too lengthy and that the race was known in the census as "Colored.") The amendment was accepted, but Wells-Barnett would not let the matter go. Ida renewed her earlier motion, and although the minutes don't reflect it, the exchange must have been a sharp one. One member, Eliza Sheppard Moore, resigned in the midst of it, stating that she "was too weak and ill to stand such long Committee Sessions" and that she felt "too ignorant of the causes which seem to hinder the general spirit of union." After her resignation was read, the meeting was adjourned with singing, which perhaps provided the needed palliative; Moore survived to give the welcome to the delegates at the next national meeting in Nashville—but so did the name, National Association of Colored Women.[13]

The next major item was who would preside over the national organization that now represented twenty-five states, one district, two territories, fifty cities, and eighty-two clubs. The decision was in the hands of the two committees, and, according to Terrell, whenever a woman from one group was nominated, there would be a seven-to-seven deadlock. The constant ties made Terrell, who was pregnant (with the first of three children that she would lose), "frazzled" until she was nominated a final time, breaking the deadlock. It is not clear how she managed the victory, though Mollie was no doubt the best politician in the group, which also included Matthews and Ruffin. "It was the hardest day's work I have ever done," she recalled. Terrell may have well engineered the vice-presidential structure, which was ungainly but inclusive. There were seven vice presidents: three from the Northeast (including Ruffin as first vice president), two from the Midwest, and two from the South. Victoria Matthews was elected national organizer, Margaret Murray Washington was chair of the executive committee.[14]

Ida didn't figure in the top leadership positions, but, with all of her obligations, she appeared to be content to give a conference paper entitled "Reform," be appointed to represent the women at a forthcoming Prison

Congress of the United States to urge action against the convict lease system, and especially to have a major role in the group's resolution committee. The resolutions, of course, were an important reflection of an organization and, as in the case of the WCTU, could create much internal strife and public turmoil. Joining Ida on the committee were, among others, Mary Church Terrell, Victoria Matthews, and the WCTU 's superintendent of colored work, Lucy Thurman—Willard's flower bearer at the temperance organization's Cleveland conference.[15]

But Ida showed that she, too, was capable of compromise. Though Willard herself was not mentioned in any of the resolutions, the "noble" work of the WCTU and Lucy Thurman was. At the same time, the organization expressed its thanks to Florence Balgarnie for her support and "heartfelt sympathy" for the current "persecution" at the hands of the BWTA because of her "defense of the honored name of Frederick Douglass." Ida's antilynching work was "heartily" endorsed, as were the efforts of Margaret and Booker Washington in their "work for the moral and educational advancement of our people." No mention was made of the Tuskegeean's separation of the fingers; however, Supreme Court Justice John Harlan's dissent condemning legalized separation in *Plessy* was praised, and the majority opinion was condemned.[16]

Those who knew how strong-willed Ida could be, especially about WCTU matters, took note of Ida's willingness to compromise for the sake of the union. The *Washington Bee* anointed Wells-Barnett the "politician" of the meeting, and the *Woman's Era* expressed a particular note of appreciation. "History is made of little things, after all," began its postconvention editorial, written by the NACW's corresponding secretary, Alice Ruth Moore, a poet and short-story writer (who would soon wed the first nationally known black man of letters, Paul Laurence Dunbar):

> It was a pretty little scene in one of the committee rooms that ought to go down in the history of the Afro-American woman—if one could be written. Mrs. Ida Wells-Barnett, whom every one knows, is positive and determined in her opinions, and her expression of them, gracefully and gently, yielded . . . when the question of endorsing in an unqualified manner the work of the WCTU was raised. Considering the difference of opinion between Miss Willard and Mrs. Barnett, and the utterances of the former in regard to the world of the latter, the introduction was somewhat after the fashion a slap in Mrs. Barnett's face.

But she gracefully gave her approval, and thus added another heroic act to the list of self sacrificing acts done at Washington.[17]

"It was a famous gathering of famous women," Wells-Barnett wrote with little further elaboration in her autobiography. Ida specifically named Rosetta Douglass Sprague, who had spoken at the beginning of the session, and Harriet Tubman, who on two occasions during the meeting spontaneously raised her rich voice in song. Certainly the most thrilling highlight for Ida was when Josephine Beall Bruce, wife of the former senator, whom Wells-Barnett had criticized more than once, suggested that as "Mother Tubman" was the oldest member of the group (she was about seventy-five) she introduce Ida's child, Charles Aked, to the audience. Lucy Thurman then moved that little Charles be thereafter known as the "Baby" of the federation. After the motion was carried, Harriet Tubman took Ida's first-born and raised him above her head before the audience. It would be the last time Ida would feel so close to the organization—the first national secular black women's group ever created—that her efforts had been so instrumental in spawning.[18]

TAKING ADVANTAGE OF being in the East for the convention, Ida spent a week in Anacostia, Maryland, with Frederick Douglass's widow, Helen. In addition to paying her respects, it was an opportunity to show off Charles and bring news of the conference and its decision to raise funds to commission a monument for Douglass to replace his modest gravestone in Rochester. Then Wells-Barnett headed back to Chicago just when "the political pot was beginning to boil," as she put it.[19]

Two years before, Ida had been asked to help in the campaign for Lucy Coues-Flower, the first woman to win a statewide position, and in 1896, Wells-Barnett's services were solicited once more by the Republican Women's State Central Committee. Wells-Barnett shared their interest in the party (Ferdinand was a Republican appointee), as well as helping to further the woman's suffrage movement; however, she was hesitant, at first, to travel across the state on their behalf. The budget, she knew, would be low for the campaign, and Ida explained to the women that little Charles would have to accompany her and that she required the services of a nurse. Ida was right about the budget, but the women promised to arrange for volunteers to meet her and take care of Charles at all of her campaign stops.

So, Wells-Barnett took to the road again, traveling to Decatur, Quincy, Springfield, and Bloomington, among other cities. As promised, there was a nurse provided at each stop to take care of the baby while she gave her addresses. There was only one glitch, Ida noted. In one town, the local chairman arranged to bring the baby to the hall where Ida was speaking. When she rose to speak, Charles could no longer see her and "raised his voice in an angry protest," Wells-Barnett wrote. But all in all, things went smoothly and Ida greatly enjoyed the opportunity to "show the women of the state why they should organize their forces and show their appreciation of this crumb which the Republican party offered us," she wrote, referring to the limited franchise of women who could only vote in school-district elections. Ida learned something, too. The tour made her cognizant of how unsophisticated women were in political matters; and she noted that too few black women had come to the meetings. The realization would be the basis of her future activities, but for now she contented herself with having made another important statement. "I honestly believe," she wrote, "that I am the only woman in the United States who ever traveled throughout the country with a nursing baby to make political speeches."[20]

REPUBLICAN WILLIAM MCKINLEY won Illinois—and the White House—in 1896, beating out the free-silver Democrat William Jennings Bryan. Although the new president had a strong interest in regional conciliation between the North and South—a notion that inevitably resulted in a compromise of black civil rights—both Barnetts had reason to welcome his election. Ferdinand had been appointed by a progressive Republican ally of McKinley's, Governor Charles Deneen, and the president's victory augured well for strengthening that faction of the party and lubricating its levers of patronage. More important, as the former governor of Ohio, McKinley had been an outspoken advocate of antilynching legislation. In 1894, Albion Tourgée had been asked by Ida's friend Harry C. Smith, *Cleveland Gazette* editor and a state legislator, to formulate an antilynching law, which Smith proposed before the state legislature. Although the bill had been defeated, Smith had initiated a movement for its passage, and on one occasion rallied five hundred black Ohioans to go to Canton to urge McKinley not to tolerate lynching in the state. The governor had responded by making a clear pronouncement against the practice and had also sent out the state militia on two occasions to back the conviction. In 1896, McKinley, then the outgoing governor, actively supported the antilynching measure and it subsequently passed. Moreover, in McKinley's inaugural address, he explicitly stated that lynching would not be tolerated in the United States.[21]

The Republican platform of 1896 had also taken on another issue that was of particular concern to African Americans. "We watch with deep and abiding interest the heroic battle of the Cuban patriots against cruelty and oppression, and our best hopes go out for the full success of their determined contest for liberty," it said. The words alluded to the Cuban liberation struggle against its colonial ruler, Spain. In 1896, the Spanish crushed a revolt by rebels and afterward turned Cuban cities and towns into "concentration areas," where the populace, including women and children, were driven and "perished like flies," as one historian noted.[22]

In the December after the election, Ida and Ferdinand helped organize a mass meeting at Chicago's Bethel Church to demand freedom for the Cubans and to deplore the killing of the island's Afro-Cuban military hero, Antonio Maceo y Grajales. By then, Bethel was pastored by the tall, willowy Reverdy Ransom, who had come to Chicago from Cleveland, where he had supported Ida in her confrontation against Willard and the black WCTU crowd. Ransom addressed the five hundred Chicagoans who had come to the meeting, and so did Ida. Ferdinand took the responsibility of preparing a resolution and sending it to McKinley's White House.[23]

By the end of the year, Wells-Barnett must have been proud of herself. She had managed to be a wife, a nursing mother, a journalist, and an activist—and to break some social ground in the process. Ferdinand had proved to be more than a husband who tolerated his wife's public career; he supported and even complemented it. As Wells-Barnett noted, she could now look forward to ending her nursing days and tip the balance just a little more toward being better able to travel, write, and be more active with the Ida B. Wells Club—praised by the *Indianapolis Freeman* as a "power in the community"—and the London Anti-Lynching Committee, which was still meeting and sending thousands of antilynching newspaper articles, letters, or resolutions to state officials and newspaper editors.[24] However, just as it felt safe to return to the full range of her activities, Ida, by the early months of 1897, was expecting her second child.

At first, she was again determined to carry on her work as long as possible. Ida was four months pregnant in June when she decided to travel to Urbana, Ohio, where there had been another horrific lynching in which a mob had broken into a jail to murder Charles "Click" Mitchell, a black man who had already been found guilty of assaulting a white woman and sentenced to twenty years in the penitentiary.

The Mitchell case was particularly important for a number of reasons. It came at a time when Booker T. Washington's looming shadow was increasingly being cast beyond the South. In May, his speech before the Chicago Commercial Club had been well received by leading industrialists, including George M. Pullman, Philip Armour, and Cyrus McCormick, among others. But most compellingly, the mob action was the first major test for the antilynching law which held negligent police officials liable for the lynching of prisoners. The legislation also required an indemnity of $5,000 to be paid to the victim's family by the county. Tourgée, after campaigning for McKinley, was back full throttle in the *Inter-Ocean,* and the paper was willing to send Ida to Ohio on a fact-finding mission about the case.[25]

The local white press's portrayal of the Mitchell lynching could have come out of the most virulent corners of the South. As Wells-Barnett recounted it in the *Inter-Ocean,* the victim had been described as a "burly" black man who was a notorious "tough." Mitchell, a milkman who delivered cream to the house of the victim, Mrs. E. M. Gaumer, widow of the publisher of the town's Democratic newspaper, had first been accused of breaking into the house to force her to sign over a check to him. Mitchell was said to have beaten and choked her when she resisted, but Gaumer had managed to escape and later identified him as the assailant. It was not until several days after the incident, Ida discovered, that the charge against Mitchell also included rape.[26]

To Ida, the story had that familiar odor of dissemblance. First she informed her readers that Mitchell was not "burly," but—as seen in a later issue of the *Cleveland Gazette,* which depicted him with an ascot and clean-cut visage—was "genteel" in appearance. The accused was not notorious. He had never been in trouble with the law, and contrary to the impression that he was an unknown outsider in the small town of about six hundred, he had grown up in Urbana and was respected in the community.[27]

Ida noted that when he heard that authorities were looking for him, Mitchell voluntarily turned himself in, although his father, among others, counseled him to leave town. (In the end it was the father who was forced to leave, for Dayton, after being arrested when it was discovered that he had armed himself to protect his son.) But the black man had thought that there was no reason to flee. He and the aunt he lived with insisted that he had been home sleeping at the time of the morning attack—though Mitchell did admit that he had been out drinking heavily the night before.

While Mitchell languished in jail, Gaumer remained out of sight, and rumors began to circulate. One was that Mitchell had bitten the woman's nipple off in the course of the rape and had given Gaumer a "loathsome" disease. When the rumors were found to be false, they were never corrected, Ida noted; the press kept harping on the salacious drama of the affair. When Gaumer kept insisting that she was too ill to face her attacker in court, authorities brought Mitchell to her residence. Gaumer was in bed, and when she saw the black man she lifted herself up and screamed "you brute!" and "hang him," before she fell back exhausted on her pillow. Soon after, Urbana began to swell with mob-bent citizens from adjoining towns; and Mitchell's attorney counseled his client to plead guilty so that he would be taken to Columbus and out of harm's way. The black man did so and was sentenced to twenty years in the penitentiary, but, as Ida complained, he was never moved out of Urbana. A small (too small, according to Ida) contingent of militia was called in, but despite shooting and killing several members of the liquored-up, angry mob of five thousand, they could not keep them at bay after another rumor circulated that Gaumer had died. It wasn't true, but Gaumer's relatives incited the crowd to drag Mitchell out of the jail, beat him, then hang him. While Ida failed to find the underlying motive for the behavior of the Gaumers, there were some indications that the family of the prominent woman was trying to get her to sign checks and legal papers.[28]

Wells-Barnett concluded her report by noting that by the time she arrived in Urbana, several weeks after the June lynching, its citizens were blithely celebrating Independence Day with its decree of the right to life, liberty, and the pursuit of happiness. Ida wondered about the "sociological" reasons why "this city of schools and churches and law courts found it necessary for 5,000 men and women and youths to become barbarians and murderers, because they believed one human being was brutal and criminal."[29]

After writing her account of the murder, Wells-Barnett remained in Ohio to help H. C. Smith raise money for legal expenses and for the intercession of the National Protective Association, a men's organization formed, among other things, to organize election districts across the country. Ferdinand was a vice president. Ida's own intercession might have aided the upholding of the Ohio antilynching law in the lower courts a year later, though the legislation remained mired in court challenges for the next several years.[30]

LESS THAN A week after the publication of Ida's July 17 article about Mitchell, Booker T. Washington received a letter from the Reverend Samuel May, a white former abolitionist and longtime supporter of Hampton Institute, Washington's alma mater. The Tuskegeean, May knew, was scheduled to give a speech in Indianapolis before the Young People's Christian Union, and he thought that Washington should be apprised of the Urbana lynching in case he was asked about it. The minister added that informing the educator was "a duty from which I cannot escape, and to which I seem to be compelled by the power above me." The words were an indication of the profound investment in Washington's success, one that combined spiritual, monied, and racial interests. Enclosed in May's letter was a copy of Ida's *Inter-Ocean* article.[31]

Before the predominantly white group, Washington plied his familiar theme that the training offered by Tuskegee could help blacks alleviate their squalid moral and material condition. He spoke of entire black families, of different sexes, forced to occupy a single room: a situation that "cannot produce a very high state of morality or Christianity." Washington begged the audience to be patient with blacks, "an ignorant" and "childish" race"; and, perhaps in a gibe at the growing discipline of sociology, he exhorted the audience to concentrate not on the causes of the "sickness" among blacks, but on the remedy.[32]

Washington, as Samuel May had surmised, was asked about lynching by the *Indianapolis Freeman* while he was in the state. If the Tuskegeean had read Ida's piece, he either ignored her findings or set out deliberately to undermine them. Using the traditional class-not-race argument, Washington blamed racial violence in general on the lower class of whites and blacks. As far as lynching was concerned, he concluded, "The men that are lynched are invariably vagrants, men without property or standing. . . . With the advancement of the race, the question will settle itself." In response, the *Freeman* predicted that the statement would be resented by "many who lost fathers, sons, husbands and brothers who were not vagrants," but it also acknowledged that Washington's warm reception in Indianapolis was evidence that Washington had "further secured a niche in the times and affairs of this country that cannot easily be wrested from him."[33]

WHILE THE MITCHELL case was being looked after by the Protective Association, Ida left Ohio for the Illinois capital, Springfield, to join the Chicago black attorneys Edward H. Wright and W. G. Anderson in their efforts to save the lives of two black men sentenced to death for killing a Greek peddler. Few details are available about the case, which ended with the men getting life sentences, but Ida's involvement in it foretold the next phase of her career: challenging the northern, specifically, Illinois's, criminal justice system. Crime was rising, particularly in urban centers like Chicago, and as the black sociologist Monroe Work noted in 1897, the proportion of blacks in total arrests in the city was rising faster than the increase of the black population; it was significantly higher than that of New York City, Washington, D.C., Richmond, Virginia, or Charleston, South Carolina.

There was a growing debate about the need for prisons to be reformatory rather than punitive, as well as about prisoner's rights, capital punishment, and the fairness of the justice system when it came to blacks. Wells-Barnett's antilynching campaign had certainly helped shape the debate. In July of 1897, the *Nation,* known for its liberal views, began its editorial on the matter by opining that the prevalence of lynching was evidence of the failure of the criminal justice system in the North as well as the South. However, the editors, convinced that the death sentence was a deterrent, worried about the growing rights of prisoners to issue appeal after appeal, sometimes resulting in a murderer being able to delay a death sentence for a year and sometimes longer.[34]

Later that year, Ida responded to an editorial in the *Chicago Times-Herald* that may have been inspired by the events in Springfield. The newspaper observed that one reason why citizens resorted to lynching was because justice was often delayed through appeals and other legal technicalities. Wells-Barnett countered with a letter to the paper that charged that there was no evidence to back up such a claim, and that mobs used it as an excuse to commit murder. Who benefited from such delays? Ida asked. "Poor men, criminals who are ignorant, penniless and friendless? Certainly not. . . . Appeals cost money, and plenty of it. . . . Let it be confessed with sorrow that many an innocent man has gone to prison or to his death, because his poverty stood between him and substantial justice." Delays, Ida concluded, "operate almost wholly to benefit the rich."[35]

SEVEN MONTHS PREGNANT in September of 1897, Ida decided to skip the NACW meeting in Nashville that month. She would have hardly relished a long train ride south—and to Tennessee in the wake of *Plessy* no less—to attend the gathering. However, she did direct her Ida B. Wells Club delegates to prepare an anti–Jim Crow car resolution for the commissioners of the centennial celebration taking place there. Although Ida missed no great controversy or compelling resolution-making among the sixty-three delegates and twenty-six clubs that attended, she did miss an important development. The decision was made to hold the next biennial meeting in 1899 in Chicago. The proposal led the Chicagoans to form what they called the Woman's Conference, an umbrella organization of seven Illinois clubs (including the Ida B. Wells Club) that would coordinate their efforts to host the meeting. The "Magic Seven," as they called themselves, became the basis of the later formation of the Illinois Federation of Colored Women's Clubs. Fannie Barrier Williams was president of the new group.[36]

In the meantime, Wells-Barnett and the Ida B. Wells Club took on another project: establishing the first black kindergarten in Chicago. A woman who, as Ida noted, had an education degree, approached the club to offer her services if a kindergarten could be organized. The establishment of kindergartens had become a trend, one seen as particularly important for blacks whose families had a high proportion of working mothers. The new NACW president, Mary Church Terrell, advocated that the national group make kindergartens a priority. Under her leadership, black women established one of the first kindergartens in Washington, D.C., and other clubs were following suit.[37]

In Chicago, black parents and their children had to endure long waiting lists for kindergartens such as that run by the Armour Institute, one of the few that accepted blacks, though they attended separate classes. Wells-Barnett contacted Bethel's new minister, Reverdy Ransom, about using the facility for preschoolers and he was enthusiastic about the idea. But to Ida's surprise, the church's trustees balked. They were afraid, Ida explained, that to establish an all-black kindergarten would further diminish the already dim prospects of getting their child into private schools such as the Armour Institute. The community thought it "better to let our children be neglected and do without . . . than to supply the needs of our own," Wells-Barnett complained. Nevertheless, she and Ransom eventually prevailed, and though Ida proclaimed that it was a "happy day" when the first black kindergarten opened in Chicago, the bittersweet experience may have contributed to her determination to retire from public life. Indeed, on the eve of the birth of Herman in November, Ida announced, dramatically, that she was going to give up the editorship of the *Conservator*, vacate the presidency of the Ida B. Wells Club, and remain at home with her children.[38]

The news that Wells-Barnett was bowing out of public life reverberated in the black press. The *Cleveland Gazette* and the *Indianapolis Freeman* memorialized her "fearless pen," and antilynching campaign. The *Charleston Enquirer* and *Michigan Representative*, the *Freeman* noted, also expressed regret about the *Conservator* losing her as an editor. As the *Topeka Weekly Call* had earlier noted, Wells had been responsible for bringing the paper back to "its traditional high standards." (Missing amid the tributes, however, was any explicit encouragement for her to change her mind.) In November, she gave birth to Herman Kohlsaat, named after the former *Inter-Ocean* newspaper publisher and restaurateur who had aided in the purchase of the land for Bethel Church and Provident Hospital.[39]

Wells-Barnett was "quite content to be left within the four walls" of her home, she insisted in her memoir. With a second child, Ida conceded that motherhood was indeed a full-time profession and that she was not at all unhappy about it. In fact, Ida claimed that she had, despite her earlier doubts, discovered the joys of motherhood. "I wonder," she wrote, "if women who shirk their duties in that respect truly realize that they have not only deprived humanity of their contribution to perpetuity, but they have robbed themselves of one of the most glorious advantages in the development of their own womanhood." But Ida's womanhood developed only for the next three months—until February, when there was the news of the lynching of Frazier Baker in Lake City, South Carolina.[40]

EVEN BY RECENT standards, the Frazier Baker lynching was one of the most brutal to gain coverage in the press. "Shame on the South," headlined the *Chicago Tribune*; a "dastardly and damnable act," proclaimed the governor of South Carolina. Baker, a Republican, had been appointed as the first African American postmaster in Lake City, a small town of about one thousand residents in the northeastern section of the state. Described as "burly and black" by white residents, Frazier's presence made the post office "not a respectable place for white gentlemen, much less ladies."[41]

Black appointees in other towns had quit rather than withstand similar threats, but Baker would not budge—not even after the town boycotted him; not even after the post office itself was set ablaze and burned to the ground. Unfazed, Frazier moved the post office to his home, forcing residents to travel outside the corporate limits to what they described as a "shanty" with a partition that divided Frazier's living room from the office. Finally, in the middle of the night on February 21, 1898, a mob of between two hundred and three hundred men surrounded the Frazier house and called him to come out. When he did not appear, the house was set afire, forcing the family to flee outside. Once they emerged, a hail of rifle shots met them. Frazier was shot to death at once; another bullet went through the arm of his wife, who was clutching their one-year-old infant daughter. The bullet exited her arm and killed the baby. Four other children, three daughters and a son, survived but were badly injured. The boy was shot through the abdomen; one of the daughters was shot through the groin, and her right hand was shot off. Another daughter was shot through the left elbow, and it was predicted that she would lose it. The following day, the charred remains of Frazier Baker and his baby were found near what was left of the house.[42]

The crime itself was horrible enough, but the Baker case had additional implications. McKinley's election had resulted in an unprecedented number of blacks being appointed to postmaster and other federal positions, but the murder raised the question of whether the administration was prepared to protect them—especially those who, like Baker, had been so determined to do their duty in a time when blacks were volunteering for the Cuban front. As the *Indianapolis Freeman* put it, Baker died as a "patriot and martyr" to his country. Even papers like the *Charleston News and Courier* unhappily predicted that the South had gone too far with this lynching: federal intervention was inevitable. But blacks knew that they had to demand federal action, and they did so across the country. No group was more vociferous than the Chicagoans.[43]

Two days after the killing, the Reverend Reverdy Ransom's Bethel Church was, again, the scene of a mass meeting; this time Ferdinand Barnett was one of the lead speakers. The government "cannot say again to us: 'This is a matter that concerns only you and the state of South Carolina,'" he said. "Forgetting entirely the fact that the child was cruelly shot in its mother's arms, that another girl had her arm broken by bullets, and that the mother, trying to protect her children, was shot down in cold blood, we come to the fact that the father, who was killed, was a government official and that his office demanded the care of the general government." Ferdinand was followed by the attorney Edward Morris, the sole black member of the Illinois legislature at the time, who compared the Frazier murder to "smoking an animal out of a log, the way boys do in the woods."[44]

Ida rounded out the protest meeting by challenging government officials by name. "If this thing had happened in Cuba, the country would have rung with indignation for weeks," she began. "Senator [William] Mason [Rep., Ill] would have stood up in the Senate of the United States and shouted aloud for vengeance. But you see it is merely the murder of a colored man in our own country, under the Stars and Stripes." Noting that lynching had now gotten to the point where the victim wasn't even accused of a criminal act, Ida snarled that usually the perpetrators "tack a crime onto the man they lynch and make him execrable and justify themselves." But this time, they probably thought that "because of the apathy of the people of this great country of ours that it isn't necessary any longer to worry about excuses. They simply went to the man's house, drove him and his family out, and shot them down. Of course he was a bad man," she sneered, "he held a public office when they told him not to." That the Bethel protest meeting was covered in the same edition of the *Tribune* that depicted the scene of mourners viewing the remains of Frances Willard at WCTU headquarters couldn't have escaped Ida's attention.[45]

President McKinley was reported to be "indignant" about the lynching, which, though not exactly a call to arms, at least did not stymie the intervention of politicians. Chicago's Republican Second District congressman, William Lorimer, whose constituency included the concentration of blacks living in the city's South Side, introduced a resolution to go before the Post Office Committee to initiate "a vigorous investigation." The assistant postmaster general in Washington was quoted as calling the lynching "an offense against the United States" and promised a trial before federal judges in Charleston when the murderers were caught. Rewards were offered for information leading to their apprehension. The attorney general became directly involved in the case.[46]

After another meeting at Bethel, which drew some two thousand persons, Senator Mason himself appeared. He introduced a resolution that called for a joint committee of three senators and U.S. representatives to investigate the Frazier lynching and bring recommendations to Congress. Soon after, a collection was taken at Bethel for Wells-Barnett to join the Illinois officials in Washington to lobby for decisive federal intervention and monetary reparations for Baker's beleaguered family.[47]

IN THE LIGHT of her dramatic announcement to retire to full-time motherhood just a few months before, Ida took pains to explain in her autobiography (and perhaps to herself) that yet another departure from home to do race work was a matter of necessity, not choice. It "seems that the needs of the world were so great that again I had to venture forth," she insisted. Moreover, baby Charles was now old enough, Ida wrote, to stay with Grandmother Barnett, necessitating that she only need take Herman with her on her travels. While it was true that the movement needed her, Ida also needed it, her proclamations and, perhaps, feelings of maternal guilt, notwithstanding.[48]

The day after the collection was taken, the *Tribune* reported that Ida, along with the Illinois congressional delegation and a number of representative ministers, called on President William McKinley. As reported in the *Cleveland Gazette,* when it was time for Wells-Barnett's presentation to the president, she began by expressing her desire, on behalf of American blacks in general and Chicagoans in particular, that he take appropriate action to apprehend and punish Baker's lynchers and urge indemnity for the family. Ida, as she had been saying since 1892 before Boston's Tremont Temple, also told the president that "national legislation" for the "suppression of the national crime of lynching" was needed. For "nearly 20 years of lynching crimes," Ida continued,

> which stand side by side with Armenian and Cuban outrages, have been committed and permitted by this Christian nation. Nowhere in the civilized world save the United States of America do men, possessing all civil and political power, go out in bands of 50 to 5,000 to hunt down, shoot, hang or burn to death a single individual, unarmed and absolutely powerless. Statistics show that nearly 10,000 American citizens have been lynched in the last twenty years. To our appeals for

justice the stereotyped reply has been that the government couldn't interfere in a state matter. Postmaster Baker's case was a federal matter, pure and simple. He died at his post of duty in defense of this country's honor, as truly as did ever a soldier on the field of battle. We refuse to believe this country, so powerful to defend its citizens abroad, is unable to protect its citizens at home. Italy and China have been indemnified by this government for the lynching of its citizens. We ask that the government do as much for its own.[49]

Ida's presentation was characterized in the *Chicago Tribune* as a "clear and able presentation of the case and that the President was very much impressed by what she said." For his part, McKinley promised that the "full power" of government would be used "day and night," further assuring them that he had put the Secret Service on the case.[50]

Wells-Barnett stayed in the capital for five weeks. In addition to speaking to churches, where she drew large crowds and raised money for the case, Ida was spending a good deal of time, according to her autobiography, trying to convince North Carolina's congressman George H. White, who had introduced a bill to provide indemnity for the Baker family, not to reduce the amount asked from $50,000 to $1,000. White, the only African American in the House of Representatives at the time, had explained that he thought the higher amount would never pass muster with the southern congressmen. Wells-Barnett argued that the region's legislators would not agree to any amount, not even five dollars. But Ida really wanted White to withdraw his bill altogether because Illinois Republican congressman William H. Lorimer wanted to offer a bill for a higher amount, but thought that his efforts would be thwarted with White's bill on the floor. Lorimer, known as the "Blond Boss," ruled Chicago's South Side where the majority of blacks lived. One of his protégés had been Charles S. Deneen, the state's attorney who had appointed Ferdinand to his office. Wells-Barnett thought that the Chicagoan's proposal would have a better chance of passing.[51]

Washington D.C.'s *Colored American* asked blacks to support Ida, who "exerted a powerful influence upon the Department of Justice and members of Congress." But not powerful enough, Ida soon found out. Even before she had left for Washington, there were growing demands for a military expedition against Spain; and in February, the U.S. battleship *Maine*, which had been ordered to Havana harbor to protect American life and property, was blown up, resulting in the loss of 250 American lives. The belief that the Spanish were the perpetrators put pressure on a reluctant McKinley to send a war message to Congress in April. The distraction and, as Ida bitterly noted, the lack of funds to support her stay—and resentment on the part of others (whom she did not name) about the publicity she had received—made her decide that remaining in Washington was fruitless. So vowing to return at a later date, she and Herman left the District of Columbia for Chicago, where in May, the Ida B. Wells Club held a big benefit for the Eighth Illinois Volunteer Infantry.[52]

The three-year-old voluntary unit had been created largely through the efforts of John C. Buckner, a black Illinois legislator. At the time, the United States had four regular all-black army units; four additional ones authorized by Congress; and a number of infantries, such as that in Illinois, organized within their respective states and commanded by black officers. Ultimately, the Eighth Regiment hoped to be recognized as a part of the Illinois Militia, with longer-term hopes that they would be made a part of the National Guard. But for the time being, blacks, already anxious to prove their worth as soldiers, were especially inspired by the black-led Cuban rebellion against Spain—and the fact that twenty-two African American sailors had also perished on the battleship *Maine*. Ida went to Springfield that summer to join the lobbying effort to get assurances from Governor John Tanner that he would authorize that the men go to Cuba as a unit. She saw the volunteers entrain for the island in August where they would become the first all-black unit to take up garrison duty there.[53]

WELLS-BARNETT DID NOT attempt to explain or justify in her autobiography her hitting the road the following fall to attend the memorial for Frederick Douglass in Rochester. But she did provide one of those anecdotes, sprinkled throughout the text, that served to show, simultaneously, how much her activism was needed, how dutifully she was committed to being a wife and mother, and how others pressed her to continue her public work.

As Ida had four years earlier, she stayed at the home of Susan B. Anthony in Rochester, who also attended the ceremonies. While in the suffragist's home, Wells-Barnett recounted how Anthony would "bite" out her married name when addressing her; and when it continued over the course of her stay, Ida finally asked her about it. Did Anthony believe that women should marry? she asked her. "Oh yes," the never-married suffragist replied, "but not women like you who had a special call for special work." Anthony went on to say that there was no one in the country "better fitted" to do that work; and since Ida's marriage, agitation had virtually ceased. Ida felt a "divided duty," said the suffragist, whose closest associate, Elizabeth Cady Stanton, was married and the mother of seven. Anthony concluded that Ida was "distracted" by the thought that her children weren't being looked after properly. Wells-Barnett characterized Anthony's words as a "well-merited rebuke," adding that she could not tell the aging suffragist that "I had been unable, like herself, to get the support which was necessary to carry on my work [and] that I had become discouraged in the effort to carry on alone." The exchange, Ida implied, made her decide to fully—and unapologetically—reenter public life, if only to "help unite our people so that there would be a following to help in the arduous work necessary."[54]

Those who had gathered for the Douglass memorial, including Calvin Chase, T. Thomas Fortune, and AME Zion bishop Alexander Walters, discussed the status of the Afro-American League, which, for lack of funds, had become virtually defunct over the previous half-dozen years. The group talked of reviving it and of course they looked to Fortune, the organization's founder and visionary, to lead it. Indeed, he had shown his old prescient self in a presentation before the group, warning, in the wake of the victorious ten-week campaign against Spain, that the United States would extend its racist policies to its growing empire that now included Cuba, Puerto Rico, and the Philippines. But when the time had come to vote for a permanent organization, Fortune, named president, used, as Ida noted, "the bitterest language possible" to denounce the disappointing turnout in Rochester, the infighting during the League's first incarnation, and the unwelcome prospect of leading "any race movement requiring general support." It was evident that Fortune had "lost confidence" in the race, Ida observed, and she halted the proceedings to ask Fortune why, in light of his feelings, he had accepted the presidency. Although Ida had voiced similar complaints, what she had never done—or would ever do, even in her angriest or most dejected moments—was lose confidence in the race. Fortune retorted that, in fact, he would not accept the position, and in a subsequent interview with the *Colored American*, which criticized his "petulance," Fortune added that he "wished not to be burdened with the management of an organization in which people are not interested to the extent of giving proper comfort and support which would eat up my time and earnings and health."[55]

It was clear to Ida and others that Fortune was not the man they had known in earlier years. The "Afro-American agitator" had become riven by the deteriorating racial situation; the confusing combination of Booker Washington's influence, ability, and willingness to compromise sacrosanct rights of citizenship; and the desperation of personal circumstances. By 1898, the thirty-nine-year-old Fortune had sunk into despair over the lingering death of his father in 1896 and his sister soon after, his paper's flagging finances, and the very real prospect of being unable to provide for his wife, Carrie, and their children (only two out of five of whom would reach adulthood). Recently, the editor, after failing to get a patronage appointment in the McKinley administration, had begun lecturing on the road, but the stress, effort, and constant disappointment were threatening his health—and leading him, more and more, to submerge his anxieties in the bottom of a liquor bottle.[56]

The one black leader of influence who appeared to understand his situation and have the wherewithal to provide material assistance was Booker Washington. Although, tellingly, the Tuskegeean had earlier refused Fortune a loan to support the Afro-American League, he did, as early as 1890, pay Thomas for a series of lectures given at Tuskegee, subsequently gave subsidies to the *Age* for publishing items about the school, and paid Fortune as an occasional ghostwriter. In addition to the funds, Washington also periodically invited Fortune to Tuskegee to rest and recuperate from the strain of his situation. Whatever utility each found in the other, they also appeared to have developed a sincere mutual friendship. Washington, uncharacteristically, would remain supportive of Fortune even when doing so imperiled his public image.[57]

In Fortune's stead, AME Zion bishop Alexander Walters, who had supported Fortune's 1889 call for the establishment of the organization and who had urged the present meeting, was elected president of the renamed Afro-American Council. To many, he was an ideal choice for the task ahead. He had been openly critical of Washington's compromise, but he was also known as an eminently reasonable man who had the ability to parse opposing views. Such political skill would be needed in an organization that sought the membership of Booker T. Washington and Margaret, Bishop Turner (who had recently called for blacks to get guns, adding, "May God give you good aim when you shoot" in response to two lynchings in Louisiana), C. H. J. Taylor, Congressman George White, Reverend Francis Gimke, Victoria Matthews, Josephine Ruffin, and Anna Julia Cooper, among others. Wells-Barnett was elected secretary of the Council, and as she wrote in the chapter of her autobiography entitled "Divided Duty," she was again "launched into public movements." However, there is no clear indication that she retook the reins of the *Conservator*—a decision that was, as future events would show, a fateful one.[58]

CHAPTER FIFTEEN

Mobocracy in America

Booker T. Washington made a great mistake in
imagining that black people could gain their rights
merely by making themselves factors in industrial
life.

—*Ida B. Wells-Barnett*

Eighteen ninety-eight promised to be the perfect year for Wells-Barnett to come out of retirement. With the acquisition of Spain's colonies of color—Cuba, the Philippines, and Puerto Rico—America became an imperial power. The war and victory had brought a new sense of patriotism and unity to the country—though with the worrisome idea by leaders such as Connecticut senator Orville Platt that it had been a "righteous" war sanctioned by God in the same manner as that of the work of missionaries in foreign lands.[1]

Nevertheless, the war's most auspicious hero, Theodore "Rough Rider" Roosevelt, soon to be governor of New York, publicly thanked the black troops of the Tenth Calvary for saving his life in Cuba. The men had provided cover for him by steadily firing at the enemy while Roosevelt led his famous charge up San Juan Hill. "It is going to be a delicate thing hereafter to denounce the wrongs of the Negro," noted Reverend F. A. Noble, the white pastor of Chicago's Union Park Congregational Church, recalling

Roosevelt's words. Indeed, President McKinley continued to break records regarding black appointments, which had reached 688 by the count of the *Springfield (IL) Record.* That blacks and whites, and northerners and southerners, had fought together appeared to vaporize lingering regional antagonisms upon the strains of John Philip Sousa's "Stars and Stripes Forever" and the ragtime march "There'll Be a Hot Time in the Old Town Tonight."[2]

In Illinois, old rural towns were becoming new urban ones. By 1900, more than half of the nearly five million persons in the state lived in cities. Meatpacking and the manufacture of foundry, machine-shop, and steel products, among other industries, were the transformative agents. At the same time, the development of new machinery revolutionized farming and the production of grain and livestock. But just below the surface of good feeling and optimism that was hoped to be a feature of the twentieth century were unresolved issues that, if brought to light, painted a very different picture.[3]

Lagging somewhat behind were the state's extractive industries. Bituminous coal was just beginning to be used for coking, and in 1898, the more than thirty thousand employees of the mine industries were locked in a battle with management over wages. When miners working in Pana and Virden struck in that year, mine owners advertised for laborers outside the state to work in their stead. Their labor agents found a contingent of several hundred willing black men from Alabama who headed by train to the mining sites in central Illinois. It is not clear if the men knew that they were to be employed as strikebreakers when they applied for the positions. Many of them brought their families with them, an indication that they were seeking long-term or permanent work in Illinois. It's certainly doubtful that they knew that as soon as the striking miners saw the ad, a number of them gathered at the train stop in Virden, pitched tents, and armed themselves.

The mine owners, learning of the planned confrontation, asked the Republican governor, John R. Tanner, to call the militia in order to provide the black men protection upon their arrival. But the governor, usually a friend to capital interests, refused. According to the *Springfield Record,* a black-owned newspaper, Tanner said that he "did not propose to render military assistance in protecting ex-convicts and scalawags of Alabama," and that "under no circumstances should any negro from another State be allowed to enter Pana." Subsequently, the *Nation,* a liberal journal out of

New York, reported that the governor further threatened to "blow to pieces with Gatling guns" any such body of laborers who might thereafter try to enter Illinois. The mine owners hired their own guards to escort the workers off the train when they arrived in Virden on October 12.[4]

However, the private security men proved to be no match for the angry coal miners who had been awaiting their arrival for weeks. Once the blacks were sighted, the cry "kill the niggers" was heard. While several of the miners tried to dynamite the train, others began firing at the southerners. Amid the shrieks and screams of the black men's wives and children, the exchange of bullets felled several of the miners and guards. The train pulled back out with most of the blacks still on it.[5]

Illinois blacks were enraged by the incident. The Alabamans had merely sought "honest employment where white men refuse to work," said the *Record*. Particular anger was reserved for the governor, whom the *Nation* called a "demagogue" with no respect for law and order. "Colored men all remember that they came to Chicago seeking employment and might have been sent to a St. Louis jail or to starve in some way station if Tanner had been governor when they sought their new homes," said the *Record*. The paper predicted that African Americans would not support Tanner in his upcoming bid for a U.S. Senate seat.[6]

However, the black newspaper was also critical of black Republican politicians who it felt had not expressed adequate indignation about the incident. The list included John "Indignation" Jones—and Ferdinand Barnett, Ida's husband, now serving under the Republican administration of Tanner. "Where is Bro. F. L. Barnett, 'Resoluting Ferd' . . . ?" chided the paper. "Has that $125 per month job closed your mouth too? When I came to Chicago six or eight years ago," continued the columnist, "Bro. Barnett would have a meeting and pass resolutions every week. Now he is Assistant States Attorney and can't afford to speak for his race any longer."[7]

The situation posed a new challenge for the Barnetts—just when they had reached a new phase in their relationship. It was about this time when, following the death of Ferdinand's father and a particularly harsh row between Ida and his mother, Ferdinand bought a new home at 2939 Princeton Avenue where Ida could live apart from the in-laws and stepchildren. Now Ferdinand supported two households, one with his mother and sons by his first wife, and the second with Ida, Herman, and Charles. Virden, no doubt, made for interesting conversation around their dinner table as they weighed their obligations to their work and to each other.

Soon after the shooting, Ida went to Virden with Herman to investigate the matter.[8]

As Ida knew, all of the liberal pronouncements about law and order would amount to little when weighed against the image of convict-leased scabs brought in to keep hardworking whites from making a decent wage. Wells-Barnett soon discovered that the characterization of the black men had originated with the state mine inspector, and that in truth, many of the black men who had answered the ad were skilled miners, blacksmiths, and machine runners. When she confronted the inspector about it, he was forced to publicly retract his statement about the men. Subsequently, Ida went to Governor Tanner to inform him of her findings. She then arranged for several of the black men who had remained to tell their own stories before the Virden community. Ida then brought three of them to appear at an "indignation" meeting in Chicago at Bethel Church where resolutions were passed condemning the governor and supporting the black workers. Ida herself addressed the meeting and was reported to have given Governor Tanner such a "flailing" that her husband started "twitching and pulling his whiskers," reported the *Record,* but Ida continued her assault and the "people were with her." The paper predicted Barnett's imminent removal from his assistant state's attorney position. "Governor Tanner became offended at Mrs. Barnett's activity," the paper explained; moreover, Ferdinand was a member of the resolution committee.[9]

Ferdinand kept his job but now he had to withstand being compared with his independent wife. The *Record* called him "the husband of the brilliant Ida B. Wells-Barnett" and went on to praise only the one spouse. "It is not often that you see a real race leader," piped the *Record,* "but the colored citizens of Chicago are blessed by having identified with them a woman who is a race woman from head to foot and will do and is doing more to advance the interest of her race than any . . . person on this terrestrial sphere." Recounting her investigation and arrangements to have the men speak, the paper concluded, "This is what I call real work. . . . She didn't wait for a big mass meeting, so as to raise money to defray her expenses but went down in her pocket and paid her own way. Oh! that we had more women like Mrs. Barnett."[10]

As for Tanner, the vocal protests from his black constituents and predictions that he might be removed served to make him realize "what a reproach it is to Abraham Lincoln's State that black citizens of the United States are killed for the offence of seeking work at wages that suit them," observed the *Nation*. The journal was responding to the governor's more recent pronouncements in which he promised to bring in the National Guard if necessary to protect blacks and to bring about the arrest and conviction of those who tried to interfere. (Tanner lost the party's nomination for the succeeding term, anyway.)[11]

It is unknown what private role, if any, Ferdinand played in Virden, or how the couple negotiated their own positions with each other. But they had come through a potential marital crisis that helped to prepared them for those to come. Clearly, the Barnetts did not let political issues unravel their domestic life. The same issue of the *Record* that identified Ferdinand through his spouse reported that Ida and her sister Lily gave a surprise whist party for Ferdinand's birthday.[12]

TWO MONTHS AFTER the incident at Virden, Ida was on the road again in her capacity as secretary of the Afro-American Council. In late December, the organization had called an emergency meeting in Washington, D.C. The reason for the urgency was the report of a riot of such magnitude it shocked even veterans of the struggle. In North Carolina, the "Wilmington Massacre" had resulted in dozens, perhaps as many as a hundred lives lost. Much of the black community, called Brooklyn, had been burned to the ground, and thousands of residents were fleeing or preparing to do so from the city. Everything that Ida had been warning about came to pass in Wilmington: the dangerous rhetoric about white women's need for protection, the fact that black achievement was no antidote to race hatred, and that lynching inevitably led to mobocracy.

For many, it was startling that such a thing could occur in that particular port city. Wilmington, with its population of 11,324 African Americans and 8,731 whites, was the most integrated city in the South—and nowhere was the black middle class, many of whom had attended one of the state's fifteen educational institutions available to them, more successful. Like other cities, there was a small professional class that included lawyers and teachers, but Wilmington especially excelled in the number of blacks that had a central place in its business and political sector. Black establishments, many with majority white patronage, had a distinct presence in the city's commercial area. Nine out of the ten restaurants were black owned; twenty of the twenty-two barbers listed in the city directory were African American; and blacks were the majority of boot- and shoemakers. Additionally, half of the tailors, a third of butchers and meat sellers, and a significant number of druggists, bakers, and grocers were African American. Black artisans and craftsmen, including watchmakers, mechanics, and furniture makers, also flourished in the city. In Wilmington, the performance of working-class blacks over the years made them preferred by many employers, and African Americans were well represented in the service industries, cotton presses, lumber mills, warehouses, and shipyards. By 1897, the black community had become one of the few that could support a daily black newspaper, the *Wilmington Daily Record*, edited by Alexander Manly, a graduate of Virginia's Hampton Institute.[13]

One element of the success of blacks in Wilmington was their political strength. By 1898, they held a black voting majority of about fourteen hundred, and in 1894, Democrats (including Wells-Barnett critic Governor Elias Carr) had been defeated by a "Fusion" of Populists and Republicans, many of whom were black. Consequently, in 1896, Congressman George White, who Wells-Barnett had talked to in Washington, was elected to the House of Representatives—the only black to serve in the body at the time. Some fifteen to twenty-five black postmasters had also been appointed in the state, and within the city—where Republicans held the majority on the ten-member board of aldermen that elected the mayor—three of the board members were African American. Until 1897, an African American also served among the five members of the powerful Board of Audit and Finance. There was also a black justice of the peace, and deputy clerk of the superior court, and John Campbell Dancy, a McKinley appointee, was the collector of customs at the Port of Wilmington. His salary of $4,000 a year was more than that of the state's governor. Black women in Wilmington were active in Republican clubs and a wide range of voluntary associations. In no other American city were blacks more integral to its political and economic life.[14]

All of this, however, would change in the bat of an eye. In the fall campaign of 1898, Democrats launched a campaign to recapture the Populists' constituency—including farmers suffering from the low price of cotton and whites whose wives were forced to find jobs. In 1892, fewer than a thousand women worked in the state's cotton mills; eight years later, 13,973 women were employed there. The Democrats' strategy was to shame whites for voting their economic interests over their duties as men to protect women from the inevitable consequences of any alliance with blacks. The campaign symbol was the incubus, a winged demon that had sexual intercourse with women while they slept. The very success of black men in Wilmington made it easy to conflate their power with that of a demon hovering over the courtrooms, political offices, places of business, and workplaces where white women trod and were subject to black authority.[15]

To affirm the message, the white-owned *Wilmington Messenger* reprinted a year-old speech by Rebecca Felton, a white Georgian Populist, member of the WCTU, and wife of a former congressman. Her speech, given at a white farmers' convention in Tybee, Georgia, emphasized the white women's need for protection, especially those on rural, isolated farms. With the economic downturn, white women were not only victims of their husbands' inability to provide for them, Felton charged, but of their men's inability to protect them from assault by marauding, inebriated black men. The rhetoric sounded very much like Frances Willard's infamous interview from which Ida had frequently quoted. In fact, the interview had taken place in Atlanta, Georgia, and one can speculate that Felton, a WCTU member, was one of the sources Willard had referred to when she spoke of how southern white women felt imperiled by blacks. Felton, however, took the need for protection to new heights. If "it requires lynching to protect woman's dearest possession from ravening, drunken human beasts, then I say lynch a thousand a week if necessary," she asserted.[16]

The republished speech was the proverbial final straw for *Daily Record* editor Alex Manly in a campaign season that was characterized by racial smears, inflammatory cartoons, and press stories about black rapists and insolent black "wenches"—all of whom were associated with the Republicans and Populists. In August, Manly wrote an editorial in the *Wilmington Daily Record* entitled "Mrs Felton's Speech," which confirmed, as Ida had done six years before, the reality of consensual relationships between black men and white women. "Every negro lynched is called a Big Burly Black Brute, when, in fact, many of those who have thus been dealt with had white men for their fathers, and were not only not black and burly, but were sufficiently attractive for white girls of culture and refinement to fall in love with them, as is very well known to all." Manly, himself the acknowledged son of former North Carolina governor Charles Manly, even went further. Poor white men were indeed "careless" when it came to protecting their women from men—white and black—he said, and he suggested that Felton tell her men that "it is no worse for a black man to be intimate with a white woman than for a white man to be intimate with a black woman. . . . Don't think ever that your women will remain pure while you are debauching ours. You sow the seed—the harvest will come in due time." The Manly editorial was written in August; but the white-owned newspapers kept their powder dry until October, just weeks before election day.[17]

In that month, the Democratic press reprinted a a hundred thousand copies of Manly's editorial, and it was quoted over and over again at large Democratic rallies. The words fueled the already inflamed white-supremacist campaign, which included terrorist raids throughout the state by the Red Shirts, a Ku Klux Klan–type organization whose members represented every class of white men. Wilmington had its own terrorist band, the Rough Riders, prepared to carry out the open threats to assassinate six prominent Wilmington Republicans and the state's Republican governor, Daniel L. Russell. By late October 1898, North Carolina's Republican senator, Jeter C. Pritchard, was so alarmed that he wrote a confidential letter to President McKinley warning him about the prospect of a race war.[18]

Anticipating a violent election day, the *Indianapolis Freeman* advised blacks to vote "for peace and security and friendlier relations with whites" even if it meant voting themselves out of office—or not at all. In response, Manly's *Daily Record* ran a letter that revealed black women could be just as demanding as their white peers. "Every negro who refuses to register his name next Saturday that he may vote, we shall make it our business to deal with him in a way that will not be pleasant. He shall be branded a white-livered coward who would sell his liberty." The letter was signed: "An Organization of Colored Ladies."[19]

However, with Red Shirts and Rough Riders surrounding the polling place on election day many blacks did stay away on November 8—though there were rumors that some of them were buying weapons. Still, election day ended with little violence, though the governor barely escaped a lynch mob after he cast his vote in Wilmington. But by then, a coterie of Democrats calling themselves the Secret Nine had laid out a plan to forcibly take over the city, the election results notwithstanding. On the ninth, they convened a meeting of between eight hundred and one thousand whites, including businessmen, ministers, laborers, and clerks, who gathered at the Wilmington courthouse to issue what they called the Wilmington Declaration of Independence. It demanded that black officeholders immediately abandon their positions, that white employers fire their black workers and

Ida B. Wells as a young woman. (Sophia Smith Collection, Smith College)

Ida B. Wells's maternal aunt, Martha Arrington Howell; Martha's husband, Lewis Howell; and their grandniece, Isabella Maxwell, c. 1911. (Courtesy of Otis Maxwell)

William Gathings, husband of Ida's maternal aunt, Belle. (Courtesy of Otis Maxwell)

House of Spires Boling, owner of the Wells family, in Holly Springs, Mississippi. (Courtesy of Otis Maxwell)

Left: Beale Street Baptist Church, Memphis, Tennessee. The flagship black Baptist church in Memphis and the first home of the *Memphis Free Speech.* (Library of Congress, Washington, D.C.)

Below left: Robert R. Church, Sr., father of Mary Church Terrell; Memphis's leading black businessman and philanthropist, who loaned Ida B. Wells money on at least one occasion. (Mississippi Valley Collection, Brister Library, Memphis State University)

Above: Charles S. Morris, a former beau of Ida B. Wells who subsequently pastored Harlem's Abyssinian Baptist Church. (Henry Jeter, *Pastor Henry Jeter's 25-Year Experience with the Shiloh Baptist Church and Her History*)

Left: Isaiah J. Graham, a Memphis schoolteacher and former beau of Ida B. Wells in the 1880s. (Courtesy of the Graham Family, Memphis, Tennessee)

Below right: Blanche K. Bruce, U.S. senator from Mississippi from 1875 to 1881 who was a frequent target of Wells's criticism, and his wife, Josephine Beall Bruce *(below left),* who held high offices in the National Association of Colored Women. (Moorland-Spingarn Research Center, Howard University, Washington, D.C.)

Cartoon in the *Indianapolis Freeman,* April 19, 1890, depicting Ida Wells as *New York Age* editor (T. Thomas) Fortune's "Echo."

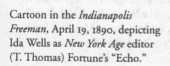

Ida Wells with Betty Moss, widow of Thomas Moss, and Maurine Moss, Ida's goddaughter. (Special Collections Center, University of Chicago Library)

Ida B. Wells with sisters Annie Fitts and Lily Daniels (Special Collections Center, University of Chicago Library)

Maritcha Remond Lyons, circa 1865, a Brooklyn schoolteacher and one of the organizers of the 1892 New York testimonial for Ida B. Wells that raised funds to publish *Southern Horrors*. (Photographs and Prints Division, Schomburg Center for Research in Black Culture, New York Public Library, Astor, Lenox and Tilden Foundations)

Julia Britton Hooks, Memphis musician, clubwoman, and schoolteacher who defied segregated seating in a Memphis theater in 1881. (The Robert R. Church Family Papers, Brister Library, Memphis State University, Memphis, Tennessee)

Frances E. Willard, president of the Woman's Christian Temperance Union and her close friend, Lady Henry Somerset, president of the British Woman's Temperance Association, c. 1892. Both women sought to undermine Wells-Barnett's influence regarding the passage of a strong antilynching resolution by the temperance organizations. (Courtesy of the Frances E. Willard Memorial Library and Archives, Evanston, Illinois)

Albion Tourgée, confident of Wells-Barnett, lead attorney for the *Plessy* v. *Ferguson* Supreme Court case, and a columnist for the *Chicago Inter-Ocean*. (Chautauqua County Historical Society, Westfield, New York)

While in England, Wells met Herman H. Kohlsaat, American restaurateur, philanthropist, and part owner of the *Chicago Inter-Ocean* between 1891 and 1894, who subsequently supported the Negro Fellowship League. The Barnetts named their second son, Herman Kohlsaat, after him. (Library of Congress, LC-USZ62-126772)

James Keir Hardie, circa 1909, founder of Great Britain's Labour Party and, like Charles Aked, a member of the London Anti-Lynching Committee formed during Ida Wells's campaign in Great Britain. Hardie escorted Wells when she attended a session of Parliament in 1894. (Library of Congress, LC-DIG-ggbain-01094)

Reverend Charles F. Aked, Minister of Pembroke Chapel, in Liverpool, England, whose support was instrumental to the success of Wells's 1894 campaign in the British Isles. The Barnetts named their first son, Charles Aked, after him. (Library of Congress, LC-DIG-ggbain-22320W)

Left: Josephine St. Pierre Ruffin, founder of Boston's Women's Era Club, supported Wells's character when it was being assailed by blacks and whites in the United States during the antilynching campaign in England. Ruffin also issued the call for the founding meeting of the National Federation of Afro-American Women in 1895. (Photographs and Prints Division, Schomburg Center for Research in Black Culture, New York Public Library, Astor, Lenox and Tilden Foundations)

The colossal statue *Republic*, overlooking the Court of Honor at Chicago's 1893 World's Columbian Exposition. (Library of Congress, LC-USZ62-102149)

"Darkies Day" at the 1893 World's Columbian Exposition in Chicago that drew criticism from Ida B. Wells and other activists. (Library of Congress, LC-USZC4-2096)

Fannie Barrier Williams, prominent Chicago clubwoman and chronicler of the black woman's club movement. Her address before the World's Columbian Exposition was titled "The Intellectual Progress and Present Status of the Colored Women of the United States Since the Emancipation Proclamation." (Moorland-Spingarn Research Center, Howard University, Washington, D.C.)

Ida B. Wells as one of the race's important leaders as shown in *The College of Life* (1895) by Henry Davenport Northrup. *Clockwise from top*: T. Thomas Fortune, journalist; Booker T. Washington, educator; Ida B. Wells; I. Garland Penn, press historian. *Center*: Frederick Douglass, statesman.

Top left: Margaret Murray Washington, third wife of Booker T. Washington and the first president of the National Federation of Afro-American Women. (Library of Congress, LC-USZ62-119899)

Middle left: Mary Church Terrell, first president of the National Association of Colored Women in 1896. (Library of Congress, LC-USZ62-92821)

Bottom left: Susan B. Anthony, leading suffragist, told Ida Wells that no one was better fitted to do the activist work that she was engaged in, but was distracted by her maternal obligations. (Library of Congress, LC-USZ62-111423)

Ida with firstborn son Charles, soon after he was named "the baby of the federation" in 1896. (Special Collections Center, University of Chicago Library)

The lynching of Charles "Click" Mitchell in Urbana, Ohio, June 4, 1897, about which Wells-Barnett wrote an investigative article for the *Chicago Inter-Ocean*. (Courtesy of the Allen-Littlefield Collection)

Twelve of the twenty-nine founders of the Niagara Movement at its first meeting in 1905. W.E.B. Du Bois is in the center. John Hope, who wrote about Wells's courage in 1894, is third from left on the top row. J. Max Barber, editor of *Voice of the Negro* who fled to Chicago after the Atlanta Riot of 1906, is sitting to the left of Du Bois. (Special Collections and University Archives, W.E.B. Du Bois Library, University of Massachusetts at Amherst)

William Monroe Trotter, editor of the *Boston Guardian,* and a militant ally of Ida Wells-Barnett. (Photographs and Prints Division, Schomburg Center for Research in Black Culture, New York Public Library, Astor, Lenox and Tilden Foundations)

Both Jane Addams, cofounder of Hull House, and Mary McDowell, cofounder of the National Women's Trade Union League, worked with Wells-Barnett for various reforms. (Library of Congress, LC-U5262-50050)

Ida B. Wells in 1909 with her children Charles Aked Barnett, 14, Herman Kohlsaat Barnett, 12, Ida Bell Barnett, 8, and Alfreda Marguerita Barnett, 5. (Special Collections Center, University of Chicago Library)

Real photo postcard, 1909, addressed to Mrs. Jake Petter in Paducah, Kentucky, showing the bridge where Will James was lynched. (Courtesy of the Allen-Littlefield Collection)

Real photo postcard, 1909, addressed to Mrs. Jake Petter in Paducah, Kentucky, showing the ashes of Will James, who was burned after being lynched. (Courtesy of the Allen-Littlefield Collection)

Real photo postcard, 1909, addressed to Mrs. Jake Petter in Paducah, Kentucky, showing lynching victim Will "Froggie" James in Cairo, Illinois. In 1909, Ida B. Wells successfully campaigned against the reinstatement of the sheriff who was removed after the lynching in accordance with the Illinois antilynching law. (Courtesy of the Allen-Littlefield Collection)

Half-burned head of Will James. (Courtesy of the Allen-Littlefield Collection)

Postcard featuring the lynching of Leo Frank, August 17, 1915, in Marietta, Georgia. Leo Frank, a Jew and a northerner, accused of the rape and murder of a white female factory worker in Atlanta, was lynched after his death sentence was upheld by the U.S. Supreme Court and subsequently commuted by the governor. Eight years later, the NAACP, in *Moore v. Dempsey*, successfully argued that a trial dominated by a mob (as in the case of Frank) violated due process of law. In 1985, Frank was posthumously pardoned. (Courtesy of the Allen-Littlefield Collection)

Postcard featuring the lynching of Laura Nelson and her son, Okemah, Oklahoma, May 25, 1911. In her writings, Wells-Barnett cited the mob murder of women as evidence of the falsity of the rape motive for lynching. (Courtesy of the Allen-Littlefield Collection)

Mary White Ovington, a founder and subsequent board chairperson of the NAACP who believed that Ida B. Wells's personality was not "fitted to accept the restraint of organization." (Library of Congress, Washington, D.C.)

In 1913, Suffragist Grace Wilbur Trout, president of the Illinois Equal Suffrage Association, attempted to prevent Ida B. Wells from marching with the Illinois contingent in the 1913 women's suffrage demonstration in Washington, D.C. (Chicago History Museum, Chicago, Illinois)

The Barnett family in 1917, taken before Ferdinand Barnett, Jr., (in uniform) went overseas to serve in World War I. *Standing*: Hulette D. Barnett (wife of Albert G. Barnett), Herman K. Barnett, Ferdinand L. Barnett, Jr., Ida B. Barnett, Charles A. Barnett, Alfreda M. Barnett, and Albert G. Barnett; *seated*: Ferdinand L. Barnett, Sr., Beatrice Barnett, Audrey Barnett, Ida B. Wells-Barnett; *foreground*: Hulette E. Barnett, Florence B. Barnett. The four young girls are the children of Albert and Hulette Barnett. (Special Collections Center, University of Chicago Library)

Irene McCoy Gaines, an eulogist for Wells-Barnett who was a member of the Women's Trade Union League, president of the Illinois Federation of Republican Colored Women's Clubs between 1924 and 1935, and a U.S. congressional campaign coordinator for Ruth Hanna McCormick. (Chicago History Museum, Chicago, Illinois)

Wells-Barnett wearing the controversial "In Memorial MARTYRED NEGRO SOLDIERS" button to commemorate the men of the Twenty-fourth Infantry who were executed in the wake of the Houston Riot of 1917. (Special Collections Center, University of Chicago Library)

CAPT. WALTER H. LOVING
DIRECTOR, PHILIPPINE CONSTABULARY BAND
COPYRIGHT 1909 BY
BARR TARNHAM P.P.C. Co.,
WASHN., D.C.

Capt. Walter H. Loving, Director of the Philippine Constabulary Band, became an officer in the Military Intelligence Division during World War I that conducted investigations of African Americans, including the Barnetts. (The Robert R. Church Family Papers, Brister Library, Memphis State University, Memphis, Tennessee)

The house of Ferdinand and Ida B. Wells-Barnett from 1919 to 1930. Located at 3624 Grand Boulevard (later Martin Luther King, Jr., Drive) it was designated a Chicago landmark on October 2, 1995. (Courtesy Bob Thall Photography)

Alfreda M. Barnett, daughter of Ferdinand and Ida B. Wells-Barnett, at the age of sixteen. (Special Collections Center, University of Chicago Library)

Alfreda M. Barnett Duster (1904–1983). After earning her BS degree from the University of Chicago in 1924, she married Benjamin C. Duster a year later. The couple had five children by 1945, the year of Mr. Duster's death. In addition to making sure that all of her children attended college despite her meager economic circumstances, Mrs. Duster was an active volunteer in the Chicago community, a member of the Ida B. Wells Club—founded by her mother in 1893—a social worker who worked with African American youth, and the editor of *Crusade for Justice, The Autobiography of Ida B. Wells*. (Special Collections Center, University of Chicago Library)

The Duster family (children of Alfreda Barnett Duster and Benjamin Duster) and Paula Giddings (back row). *Center front:* Alfreda Duster Ferrell; second row, from left to right, Charles Duster, Troy Duster, Benjamin Duster. (Courtesy of Otis Maxwell)

Dr. Otis Maxwell, descendent of the Arrington side of the Wells family, photographer and genealogist of the family. (Courtesy of Otis Maxwell)

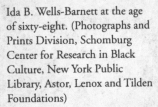

Ida B. Wells-Barnett at the age of sixty-eight. (Photographs and Prints Division, Schomburg Center for Research in Black Culture, New York Public Library, Astor, Lenox and Tilden Foundations)

put whites in their place, and that Alex Manly leave Wilmington posthaste. (Forewarned, he had already escaped the city.) Thirty-two of the city's most prominent blacks were sent for. Their formal compliance was expected by the next morning.[20]

There was no waiting for an answer. On November 10, five hundred whites gathered at the armory of the Wilmington Light Infantry at 8:15 A.M., and commenced to march in military formation down Market Street. By the time they reached Alex Manly's office in Brooklyn's black community, the group had swelled to two thousand. They entered the office, set it afire, and the flames engulfed other buildings in the community. Soon after, the whole city was in chaos. Skirmishes between whites and blacks broke out. Rumors of hundreds of armed blacks prepared to retaliate swelled the number of vigilantes who continued to shoot at any blacks they saw until that afternoon when the state militia was called in by the governor.

But no force was able, or willing, to stop the forcible ousting of the mayor, board of aldermen, the entire police department, and its Populist chief. All the positions were taken over by Democrats; in the case of the police, the ranks were filled with members of the mob, Red Shirts, and Rough Riders. Other positions axed by the Democratic leaders included the health board, superintendent of streets, the lot inspector, and the day janitor and messenger at city hall—all of which were filled by black men. It was the nation's first full-fledged coup d'etat.[21]

BY THE TIME Ida was making her way to Washington, D.C., for the emergency Afro-American Council meeting, fourteen hundred blacks had left Wilmington, many of them escorted by armed guards. Republicans were also escorted out of the city. Special railway cars were rented for the banishments, and each disembarkation was accompanied by cheers and whoops by whites. Even fleeing was no guarantee of safety. In nearby New Bern, whites waited for the refugees from atop a water tower where they could shoot them before they reached their destination. Blacks who did not have the means or opportunity to escape, including a group of more than four hundred women and children, fled into the woods. Abandoned black properties were confiscated.[22]

Ida was determined to force the Council to act decisively. At the least, there should be some censure of the president, who said nothing about Wilmington during his highly publicized goodwill tour through the South, which included a visit to Booker Washington's Tuskegee Institute. In a letter dated November 27, Washington had written to McKinley who had asked his advice about what points he might cover when he arrived on campus. Washington's response to the president, just weeks after the Wilmington Massacre, was that he should encourage "colored people to get education, property, and character, as a basis of their citizenship," and that "both races be moderate, reasonable, self-controlled and live on friendly terms."[23]

But what the Council was obligated to do was clearer to Ida than to many others. The inner wiring of racial protest had become sufficiently crossed to be short-circuited by political partisanship, the fact that many Council members were McKinley administration appointees, and the looming influence of Booker Washington, who had achieved another coup de grace by getting the chief executive to come to the school. Now the Council was a potentially inert mix that included McKinley supporters who were antiaccommodationists, and Bookerites and Democrats who disliked McKinley.

No one's wires were more crossed than Fortune's. He had written a letter of congratulation to Washington for his triumph in hosting McKinley, but the *Age* editor, apparently unaware of Washington's counsel, was also critical of the president's refusal to condemn the "deviltry" in the South that was as "cruel and cold blooded as can be imagined." McKinley was a "thoroughly despicable character," Fortune wrote to Washington on another occasion, "and I despise him." Sensing the editor's emotional fragility, Washington invited him to Tuskegee for a "resuscitive" rest in advance of the December 29 Council meeting. But Fortune declined; he wanted to get to the capital "to do what I can to prevent [the Council] from doing something foolish," he said. Instead it was Fortune, as Washington had surely feared, who did something foolish.[24]

When the *New York Age* editor was invited to speak before a pre-Council meeting of the Racial Protective Association headed by the anti-Bookerite *Bee* editor, Calvin Chase, the charged atmosphere of the assembly, the presence of his old competitor, Chase, and his own alcohol-induced emotions led Fortune to not only accuse the president of "glorifying" mobocracy and the murders of women and children, but to add: "I want the man whom I fought for to fight for me and if he don't I feel like stabbing him." The words were followed by outbursts of "stab him, stab him," from the audience. Warming to his subject, Fortune continued to excoriate the Supreme Court for the recent *Williams v. Mississippi* decision upholding the state's right to impose poll taxes and literacy requirements, accused "chivalrous" white southern men of producing hundreds of thousands of mulattoes through rape, and ended with the charge that the men who had been murdered in Wilmington were probably the sons and grandsons of the white men who killed them. Fortune concluded by insisting that a white man should be killed for every black one murdered in Wilmington. The remarks caused a flurry of vituperation in the press, both black and white, and concerned letters to Booker T. Washington, one of which, ironically, informed the educator that Fortune had been about to land a position in the Republican administration—until that speech.[25]

The Council meeting began its deliberations before the packed Metropolitan Baptist Church, which could accommodate a thousand persons. Despite the tense atmosphere, the initial proceedings went smoothly, largely due to President Alexander Walters's skill in playing the broker role. Both militant and conservative views were heard, observed John Henderson in the *Colored American,* who happened to be pastor of the same Bethel Church in New York whose members had openly criticized Ida in the 1895 club meeting in Boston. With the exception of a chorus of hisses when Ohioan John Green, a McKinley appointee, insisted that the president's silence was at the behest of "certain" black leaders, the meeting was a model of calm—until Ida spoke.[26]

She ascended the platform to the Chautauqua salute, then commenced with her address entitled "Mob Violence and Anarchy, North and South." Called "ringing" by one account, Ida vividly reiterated the violent events concerning Postmaster Baker, the strikebreakers in Virden, and of course, Wilmington. According to reports, the most searing comments were directed toward McKinley, and she was the only one present to explicitly criticize Booker T. Washington. McKinley was "too much interested . . . in the national decoration of confederate graves to pay any attention to the negro's rights," Ida said to great applause. "If this gathering means anything, it means that we have at last come to a point in our race history where we must do something for ourselves and do it now." As for Booker Washington, the events had shown that he "made a great mistake in imagining that black people could gain their rights merely by making themselves factors in industrial life," she pronounced. Ida also outlined a strategy to press northern congressmen to delimit representation of the southern states in light of their disfranchisement policies, and to continue to oppose U.S. racist imperialist expansion. The stirring speech was followed by that of the recorder of deeds, Henry Cheatham, who made it a point to oppose Ida's views and to plead for conservatism and moderation. He was met by groans and hisses.[27]

At the end of the meeting, Ida was elected to the new Council position of financial secretary, and the group passed a resolution, composed by Fortune, criticizing the president's inaction. Nevertheless, Wells-Barnett could only claim a partial victory in an organization where so many influential members had competing interests. While they were in Washington, President McKinley himself consented to seeing a committee of Council members at the White House. Ida, who had earlier seen McKinley with a Chicago delegation about the Frazier Baker murder, was urged not to join her black colleagues for this visit. The unsteady Fortune, founder of the group, was also asked not to be a part of the group for the same reason: they were too bitterly opposed to the administration. Ida put the best face on the situation. The Council did not completely capitulate to Booker Washington's influence, and the "entire country" now knew that the view of the "apologists" for the administration "did not represent the best thought of the race," Ida wrote in her autobiography. Fortune, who, for better or for worse, was the only spokesman to express the full, visceral measure of reaction to Wilmington, also claimed a dubious victory. "It was a terrible fight and I am a shade sick as a result of it and the tremendous victory I won," he wrote to Booker Washington.[28]

FOLLOWING THE MEETING, Wells-Barnett and Fortune, the Council's most willing travelers, went to Boston and other cities where they organized local councils and held forums that in effect were referenda on how blacks should respond to the racial situation, the Republican Party in general, and McKinley in particular. By spring it appeared that the airing of views might be having some effect. For the first time on record, noted the *Cleveland Gazette* in April of 1899, "the federal government has come into the South to take up a lynching trial." Indeed, the intervention of the Justice Department in the Frazier Baker case had resulted in the indictments of fifteen Lake City citizens. The development had added significance because the citizens included the town's best men of standing: a former editor of the local newspaper, a former deputy U.S. marshal, as well as merchants, druggists, and farmers. A hundred and fifty citizens were to be subpoenaed for the upcoming trial.[29]

But in the same month, Georgia, the home of Rebecca Felton, vied for the brutality prize. A strikingly similar array of citizens who were found to be behind the Wilmington Massacre and the Frazier Baker killing hunted down and lynched Samuel Wilkes, aka Sam Hose, who had been accused of killing a prominent farmer and raping his wife in the farming town of Palmetto, Georgia, just southwest of Atlanta. The lynching, as even the Atlanta press observed, was "unsurpassed" in its "sickening sights, harrowing details and bloodcurdling incidents."[30]

The murder was a culmination of racial violence unleashed in Palmetto during March and April of 1899. In March, nine black men, arrested for setting fire to several business blocks, were attacked by a mob who broke into a warehouse where they were being held and shot them. Wells-Barnett later pointed out in her pamphlet *Lynch Law in Georgia* that all nine were "hard-working, law-abiding citizens, men with families."[31]

Soon after, on April 12, the body of the white farmer, Alfred Cranford, whose skull was split in two, was discovered in Palmetto. Hose, a black laborer who worked for Cranford, was accused of killing his employer and raping his wife, Mattie, a young woman in her twenties and formerly known as one of the belles of nearby Newnan. An account of the crime said that Hose had killed Cranford with an axe while he was eating supper. Afterward he allegedly robbed the house, grabbed Mattie Cranford, and raped her—twice—in the very same room where Alfred lay dying. Compounding the sexual violation was the fact that Hose was said to be suffering from syphilis. Before the black man had managed to escape, he was said to have snatched the couple's eight-month-old infant from Mattie's arms and thrown it to the floor. It was reported that the baby would probably die from the injury.[32]

The Hose case would be the first to which Ida dedicated an entire pamphlet. As she had before, she utilized the white press's own accounts, in particular the *Atlanta Journal* and the *Atlanta Constitution,* to reveal to the rest of the world what America had come to. The Hose case marked yet another phase in the sadism that hovered over the country—and a new role that the press played in it. Wells-Barnett collected some five hundred news articles on Hose, and it was clear that lynching narratives had taken on the form of "folk pornography," as one scholar called it. Local and regional papers not only reiterated the prurient details again and again, but as

Wells-Barnett observed, nine-tenths of the clippings she had collected presumed that Hose was guilty of the heinous sex acts just on the say-so of others. Moreover, the *Atlanta Constitution* and other papers went beyond their usual role of slander and stereotype. During the manhunt for the black man, the press took the initiative in promoting and marketing his inevitable death at the hands of the mob. The *Atlanta Constitution* offered a $500 award for the fugitive's capture and did not even consider that the black man might go to trial. He would be lynched, the paper said matter-of-factly, and it speculated on what method of death the public preferred: hanging, burning, or riddling him with bullets. Mattie Cranford, it was said, preferred burning.[33]

On April 23, a Saturday night, Hose was captured. He had been caught, it was alleged, on his way to a "cakewalk" dance near his mother's house in Marshallville, about seventy-five miles away. With echoes of the Texas lynching of Henry Smith, an excursion train was provided for those who wanted to go to Palmetto where the Hose festival of death would take place. Shouts of "Special train to Newnan! All aboard for the burning!" were heard. More than a thousand train tickets were sold; five hundred stowaways also found their way on the transport. On April 24, the *Atlanta Constitution* carried a description of Hose's death at the hands of the mob that the paper proudly noted included "lawyers, doctors, merchant farmers . . . from a half dozen counties."[34]

In broad daylight, about 2:30 P.M., on a warm spring day, Hose was tied to a sapling and made to remove his clothing. Then the mutilation began. His left ear was severed from his body, then his right. Without any sense of irony, he was asked to confess to the crime, which he reportedly did. Then other portions of his body were attended to: his fingers were lopped off and shown to the crowd; his face was skinned; his penis was sliced off; and his genitals were held aloft. Oil was poured over the wood that was placed around his nearly nude body and set aflame. As his body blistered, several of the man's blood vessels burst. When the writhing body fell outside of the flames, the crowd kicked it back into the fire. The spectacle was said to have been accompanied by expressions of unfeigned satisfaction by the two thousand men, women, and children who watched the flames eat away Hose's flesh and his body mutilated by knives.[35]

Although pains had been taken by the press to describe the calm probity that accompanied the "deliberations," it would be hard to reconcile this with the reports of how the crowd was so eager to grab or cut away fingers, bits of bone, and other body parts that some of the trophy seekers cut the hands of others in the crowd competing for them. Then there was the item that noted how one of the lynchers subsequently traveled to Atlanta to deliver a slice of Hose's heart to the governor. Sam Hose's body parts were not only prized by souvenir hunters, there was a lucrative market for them. Bone bits sold for 25¢; thin slices of liver, cooked to a crisp, 10¢. Even the sapling tree was chopped up to sell. The day following the Hose lynching, a minister said to have some vague connection to Hose was also lynched and dissected.[36]

AT THE TIME Hose was lynched, Booker T. Washington was preparing to go to Europe with his wife. This time, he hadn't needed to be forewarned about having to answer questions about lynching. Nevertheless, his response was maladroit, to say the least. In an interview with the *Birmingham Herald*, the educator said that he would have liked to "speak at length" about the Hose lynching, but was "constrained" to do so because of his position and the hopes he had for Tuskegee "and the education of our people." He added that he was opposed to mob violence but that the solution to the "present difficulties" was the "mental, religious and industrial education of both races of the south." He concluded, "It is an encouraging fact that of the hundreds of colored men who have been educated in the higher institutions of the south not one has been guilty of the crime of assaulting a woman."[37]

The reply created such an uproar among blacks that Washington's surrogates were dispatched to reexplain his position—the most bizarre being a statement from T. Thomas Fortune. In an interview with the *New York Times,* Fortune claimed that he had advised Washington against sending a strong letter of protest to Georgia's governor about the killing—and had even torn one up that appeared too incendiary. "I said, Washington, you are the only man that now stands between the whites and the colored man as a bond of sympathy. Don't send that letter."[38]

Among others who responded to the Hose lynching was W. E. B. Du Bois. He was in Atlanta at the time researching his now classic Atlanta University Studies, the first in the field he virtually invented: American urban sociology. As reported by his biographer, Du Bois, "startled" by the gruesome murder, had written a sober antilynching editorial that he was going to give to *Atlanta Constitution*'s Joel Chandler Harris (author of the

"Uncle Remus" stories). With his walking cane and gloves, Du Bois made his way to the newspaper office but was stopped short when he saw, in a shop on Mitchell Street, Hose's charred knuckles on display. It was from that moment that Du Bois realized what Wells-Barnett already knew: "one could not be a calm, cool, and detached scientist while Negroes were lynched, murdered and starved."[39]

But one *could* find out the facts about the Hose lynching, and about the man himself who had been painted as a monster. Soon after hearing about the spectacle, Ida called for a meeting at Ransom's Bethel Church to raise money to hire a Chicago detective, Louis Le Vin, to investigate the lynching. Le Vin, who was white, posed as a seller of hog-cholera medicine, as he gathered information in Georgia to report back to Ida's committee. Upon his return, he presented his findings, which Ida would subsequently publish in her 1899 pamphlet *Lynch Law in Georgia* before another meeting at Bethel.

Sam Hose's real name was Samuel Wilkes and he was far from the monster depicted in the press. Born in Macon, the man had taught himself to read and write and was a hard worker. After the death of his father, he was the mainstay of his family, which included an invalid mother and a retarded brother. Wilkes had worked for Cranford during most of the previous year. Sometime before the incident, the black man had asked the young Cranford, a member of a well-established family in that part of Georgia, for an advance on his wages so that he could go see his mother who had fallen ill. The men argued about this for several days and on one occasion, while Wilkes was chopping wood, Cranford drew a gun on the farmhand. Wilkes reacted by throwing his ax at Cranford, which hit its mark.[40]

Le Vin also stressed that Wilkes had always denied to authorities attacking Mrs. Cranford or her child. Although the detective did not get the opportunity to interview the woman, he discovered that she did not accuse Wilkes of rape following the attack on her husband. At the time that the sexual assault was charged, she was ill to the point of unconsciousness and was recovering in the home of her father-in-law. Le Vin also identified, by name, the citizens who had participated in the lynching, a number of whom he asked about the motive for their conducting such "inhuman" treatment of the black man. "They considered it a useless question," Le Vin reported. "A nigger had killed a white man and that was enough. Some said it was because young niggers did not know their places; others that they were getting too much education, while others declared it was all due to the influence of northern niggers."[41]

As far as the lynching itself, Le Vin added the detail that even in the depths of his anguish, Hose never confessed to harming Mrs. Cranford; and during the entire ordeal, Hose never begged for mercy. "Only once in a particularly fiendish torture," the detective wrote, did he groan, "Oh Lord Jesus," but of begging there was none. Before the crowded church, Le Vin concluded: "With these facts, I made my way home thoroughly convinced that a Negro's life is a very cheap thing in Georgia."[42]

After Virden, after Wilmington, after the lynching of Postmaster Frazier, Sam Hose, and the hundreds of deaths Ida had documented, she somehow found the way to maintain faith in her country. The purpose of her *Lynch Law in Georgia,* as she wrote in the document, was "to give the public the facts, in the belief that there is still a sense of justice in the American people and that it will yet assert itself in the condemnation of outlawry and in defense of oppressed and persecuted humanity."[43] Time would tell.

CHAPTER SIXTEEN

Bull in the China Shop

Miss Wells is fast making herself so ridiculous
that everybody is getting tired of her.

—*Emmett J. Scott, secretary
to Booker T. Washington*

In 1899, the two black organizations with the membership and scope to influence public policy, national politics, and the direction of black reform—the Afro-American Council and the National Association of Colored Women (NACW)—were meeting on Wells-Barnett's home turf of Chicago. The meetings were scheduled within days of each other: the NACW was due in the city on August 14, the Council on August 17. The idea to coordinate the two sessions was Mollie Terrell's. She had convinced "the Lords of Creation," as she described the Council men to a friend, that doing so would assure more press coverage, cheaper excursion rates, and the opportunity for the two groups to attend the other's sessions.[1] Three years after the founding of the first national black women's secular organization, four years after Booker T. Washington's national rise, and just months before a presidential election, black men and women would be the focus of the nation's opinion-makers as never before.

No one was more eager to be in such a position as the woman who had made a career out of publicizing rights and wrongs. Wells-Barnett was the only figure who had played a central role in both the Afro-American Council and the NACW. But in 1899, she was also, "the outsider within" for each.

Ida had missed the 1897 women's meeting in Nashville where Chicagoans had organized a coalition of seven local clubs to make arrangements for the 1899 meeting. Although the Ida B. Wells Club, headed by Agnes Moody, was one of the seven organizations that participated, it is doubtful that Ida's activities and travel over the previous two years had permitted her to be very active in the planning. As future events would show, there was also some friction between Wells-Barnett and local clubwomen, including, it seems, Agnes Moody and Fannie Barrier Williams. The source of the ill feeling is unclear, but as important as any personal pique was the growing ideological divide between Ida and the clubwomen leadership. Williams and her husband, S. Laing (Ferdinand Barnett's former law partner), were growing closer to Booker T. Washington. S. Laing Williams gave the commencement address at Tuskegee in 1895 and would soon become Washington's most enthusiastic operative in Chicago. Fannie was preparing a chapter for the Tuskegeean's upcoming book, *A New Negro for a New Century*.

Moreover, the NACW, under the leadership of Mollie Terrell, was inexorably moving in the opposite direction from Ida and toward the perspective of Washington. This was starkly evident in the different ways that Ida and Mollie responded to the horrific events in Wilmington. In writing about the achievements of the NACW at the end of 1898, Terrell had begun the article: "From the gloom and dismay into which the Wilmington riot and the Illinois outrage have plunged us let us turn away . . . [so] that we may look upon the bright side of our present condition in this country." The "bright side" was the accomplishment of black women who were organizing homes for the elderly, nurses' training schools, kindergartens, sewing classes, and mothers' clubs where women had "heart-to heart" talks about home life and child-rearing.[2]

It wasn't that Terrell and like-minded women weren't fully aware, alarmed, and enraged by recent events, or that Wells-Barnett did not see the importance of uplift. But Terrell and most of the NACW leadership shared the Washingtonian view that Ida had long since abandoned. "The colored people are beginning to realize that their citizenship is secured better by education than legislation," was Fannie Barrier's observation when she spoke at Chicago's All Souls Church just before the

NACW's opening session. Club leaders were determined to live up to the promise of "meaning more to the social order and improvement of the colored race . . . than anything outside of the churches," in the words of the *Indianapolis Freeman*.[3] Although Wells-Barnett was an officer of the Afro-American Council and headed its Chicago branch, her views—and her sex—hardly assured a secure place at the organization's table. Since her December election as the national organization's financial secretary, her fitness for the office had been a subject of debate. Washington, D.C.'s *Colored American* had led the negative campaign. It thought that the position should have gone to someone more capable of considering "all sides" of an issue. But the paper mainly focused on Ida's domestic situation to make its point. The financial secretary was responsible for supervising the affiliates, and the *Colored American* wondered if Ida could undertake the extensive travel required. Wells-Barnett was a capable person, it hastened to add, but she should be using her talents along the lines of "woman's work" that would "not interfere [so] disastrously with her domestic duties." In sum, the secretary position should have gone to the "most active and capable man available," and Ida, the paper mistakenly concluded, "would be more suited to head a woman's auxiliary for the Council where she could be brought into active cooperation with distinguished leaders of her sex, such as Mary Church Terrell, Margaret Murray Washington, and Fannie Barrier Williams." In such a setting, Ida's "surroundings and labors could assuredly be more congenial."[4]

Of course, service in a woman's auxiliary would be voluntary, while the financial secretary was the only paid office in the Council. Funds were recently made available by a five-dollar membership fee—an innovation that Ida had long sought: the ability to earn a regular income for doing race work. Since her election, Ida had been tenaciously digging in her heels. Despite the pressure to give up the position to a man, J. E. Bruce—a journalist with little activist experience but with ties to Booker Washington—Ida had not only refused to do so, but also clung to her original position as secretary, though it, too, was now claimed by another journalist, Robert W. Thompson. All of this would have to be worked out before the end of the meeting, but in the meantime she went about her Council business in Chicago.[5]

Ida was co-chair of the program committee with T. Thomas Fortune and President Alexander Walters. But with Fortune ill and recuperating in Saratoga and Alexander attending to out-of-town duties before the August

17 opening, Wells-Barnett took advantage of her relatively free rein to make the conference arrangements. Working with Ferdinand, she chose the site of the meeting, Reverdy Ransom's Bethel Church, as well as those who would have the most prominent speaking roles. She even selected, no doubt, the flowers and potted plants that graced the dais and were distinctive enough for the press to remark favorably about them.[6]

As was true in 1898, Wells-Barnett wanted the Council to thoroughly condemn the McKinley administration and its apologists—especially Booker Washington. By 1899, there was even more reason to do so. In the wake of Wilmington, the president had not so much as mentioned the mob action in his State of the Union address. The city still simmered without any signs of federal relief, and the Democratic legislature was preparing a disenfranchising constitutional amendment that would require North Carolina voters to pay poll taxes and pass literacy tests. McKinley continued to appoint blacks but refused to go to full lengths to protect them. Despite the indictments in the Frazier Baker case, in the end the administration had yielded to the intransigence of the South. All of the indicted were acquitted. Both McKinley's silence and his presumed support for blacks encouraged a startling spike in the breadth and viciousness of lynchings. Between 1896 and 1900, Wells-Barnett documented 504 lynchings, and evidence was mounting that they were becoming more and more sadistic. In June, the *Chicago Broad Ax* reported that Sam Hose's family had fled to Philadelphia after receiving one of his dismembered fingers in an envelope.[7]

"It is expected that a great fight will result over resolutions . . . denouncing President McKinley for not using the federal authority to prevent lynchings in the South," the *Chicago Tribune* solemnly predicted in regard to the Council meeting. Black officeholders, the paper added, were under pressure to support the president at the confab. Anticipating the showdown, Ida had stacked the program in favor of the militants. She made sure that they had a prominent place in the deliberations and at the all-important opening session that would be attended by the Chicago mayor, Carter H. Harrison, and other politicos. Ida's selection of Bethel Church guaranteed that Reverdy Ransom could set the tone at the beginning of the deliberations. Ida herself prepared to read her report on lynching; and other speakers, besides her husband included Bishop Henry M. Turner, who had recently suggested armed revenge for lynchings; Representative George White of North Carolina, who now employed exiled

Wilmington editor Alex Manly in his office; and the *Cleveland Gazette*'s H. C. Smith, who would talk about the Ohio antilynching bill. Women and moderate Council members were assigned to panels that were not as auspicious as the forums for the individual speakers. Josephine St. Pierre Ruffin, Margaret Murray Washington, Fannie Barrier Williams, and Mollie Terrell were invited to speak about education and moral and home training. Male panel members included Robert Terrell, Mollie's husband and a Booker Washington ally, and W. E. B. Du Bois, who at the time was considering Washington's offer to work at Tuskegee. Du Bois was to present his paper on "Business Enterprises of the Race and How to Foster Them."[8]

Born in 1868, Du Bois was six years younger than Wells-Barnett and by 1899 had completed two years of study at the University of Berlin and had published the *Philadelphia Negro*, the first comprehensive study of a black community in the United States. Ida, though impressed with his scholarly achievements, patronizingly thought of him as a newcomer on the political scene. As she wrote in her autobiography, he was selected to participate in the Council program because he was a "young man just back from his studies in Germany, [and] we thought we should encourage him and give him the opportunity to take hold in the work."[9]

Booker T. Washington was also asked to address the Council, and as Wells-Barnett and other militants knew, the invitation represented a dilemma for the educator. It wasn't that Washington could not hold his own in any debate about his policies. And he knew that even many of those who disagreed with his pronouncements did not doubt his sincerity and understood the delicate position he was in. Moreover, political insiders were aware that while Washington had been criticized for publicly bemoaning the fact that the masses of blacks had been prematurely given the right to vote after the Civil War, he lobbied to stem new antisuffrage measures in South Carolina and Louisiana when they threatened to disenfranchise blacks of all classes. Prohibiting conservative property-owning blacks from voting, Washington argued, would weaken their influence and undermine their incentives to be law-abiding.[10]

Washington's problem was that he had to be perceived as *the* Negro who represented the race. If he was just another contender, there would be no reason to make him the sole surrogate—and repository—for the race just when philanthropic gifts were reaching new heights. In addition to smaller sums, John D. Rockefeller had begun giving Tuskegee $10,000 a year; and in 1899, Collis Huntington, the railroad magnate (whose Chesapeake & Ohio Railway Ida had sued in the 1880s), had bequeathed $50,000 to the Tuskegee Endowment Fund. Between 1895 and 1900, the campus added thirteen buildings, many of which were named after well-known northern benefactors, including Phelps, Slater-Armstrong, Emery, and Parker.[11] But staying away from Chicago where the race's two national organizations were meeting was not an option. It was T. Thomas Fortune who resolved the dilemma.

Washington should come to Chicago, Fortune told him, have a private meeting with Council president Walters, but limit himself to appearing before the NACW, whose priorities reflected his own. In that way, Washington could position himself as being above the anticipated political dissension that appeared gratuitous to many at a time when the race had "real" issues to contend with. Thanks to Du Bois and other black social scientists such as Monroe Work, who was at the University of Chicago, statistics had become available showing that African Americans had considerably higher rates of tuberculosis, syphilis, opium usage, and arrests—including for prostitution—than other groups. Such ills spoke to social decisions that blacks could control themselves. While disenfranchisement, *Plessy v. Ferguson*, racial terrorism, and discrimination within labor unions were legitimate concerns, many thought that they paled against the fact that the race was sinking beneath its own weight. "It is a hopeful sign of the times that the old-time discussion of political equality . . . is giving way to a serious and rational discussion of his industrial future," opined the *Colored American*. The women, it was assumed, would have "honest discussions" where "decorum would reign" and provide practical solutions for the race. As Fannie Barrier Williams had earlier noted, the NACW would "avoid the examples of our colored men, whose innumerable conventions, councils, and conferences during the past 25 years have all begun in talk and ended in talk."[12] Yes, the NACW would be a perfect forum for Washington's presence in Chicago—if, of course, certain agitators, did not roil the proceedings.

Ida was so busy with the Council meeting's arrangements that she did not learn that she was going to be excluded from the NACW program until she happened to overhear a clubwoman's husband gloating about the fact. Ida wasn't even invited to speak on the NACW's panel on lynching;

Fortune's wife, Carrie, was to do the honors. It was a "staggering blow," Ida admitted, all the more so, no doubt, because the meeting was taking place in Chicago; and apparently even the members of the Ida B. Wells Club had not informed her.[13]

Her exclusion must have been orchestrated by Terrell, she reasoned, and Ida confronted her about it. Mollie explained that Ida had not been included because the Chicago women had written her and threatened not to cooperate if Ida was on the program. Ida told Terrell that she was surprised by the information—and disappointed that Terrell, whom she had known since they had been in Memphis together, would go along with the request. What Wells-Barnett actually suspected, however, was that Terrell had used the "narrow-minded" attitudes of Chicago women to thwart Ida's presumed aspirations to become the president of the women's organization. Wells-Barnett neither confirmed nor denied the prospect.[14]

Indeed, there had been press speculation as early as May about who was angling for the position. Ida, Fannie Barrier Williams, Margaret Murray Washington, the recently widowed Josephine Beall Bruce, and Josephine Ruffin were all named as possible candidates. Terrell was not considered because of the bylaw provision that a president could only serve two terms. And in any case, Mollie had been recently feeling the strain of public life and private hardships.[15]

Several months after her election in 1896, Terrell, who had suffered one miscarriage four years before, lost her second child soon after its birth that November. Mollie was so despondent that she checked into a sanitarium to undergo electrical shock treatments. A year later, in 1897, Robert Terrell informed Robert Church, Mollie's father, that Mollie was "losing ground," and that the "Electrical treatments [had] not accomplished any good so far." Since that time both men had pressed her to slow down her public activities, and Mollie was trying her best to comply.[16]

Terrell had publicly endorsed Josephine Bruce for the NACW presidency in 1899. The two women were close. The late senator Blanche Bruce (who had died in 1898) had been a friend of the family, and Mollie's husband, Robert, had stood by his deathbed toward the end of his lingering illness. Mollie publicly praised Josephine as a "well-educated, broad-minded and large-hearted woman with a spotless education," and promised to oppose "any woman who [did] not represent all of this." The remark, it can be surmised, was a dig directed at Ruffin—the only candidate who did not have a postsecondary education. Bruce, in turn, despite being reported as jockeying actively for the position, demurely indicated that Margaret Murray Washington would be a good president.[17]

The three women were called the "triumvirate" by one observer of NACW politics, who crudely characterized the relationship as all three pissing " in the same pot."[18] In addition to their personal friendship, they were also bound by their ties to Booker T. Washington. Bruce had been appointed that year as the lady principal of Tuskegee, and Mollie's husband was seeking Washington's support to replace George F. Cook (brother-in-law of prominent Washington clubwoman Helen A. Cook) as assistant superintendent of the black educational school system in Washington, D.C., with its 350 teachers and thirteen thousand students.[19] Robert Terrell's primary competition for the job was W. E. B. Du Bois.

THE NACW'S FIRST biennial, taking place at Quinn Chapel, began promisingly. On Sunday evening, August 13, there was an elegant, toast-filled reception. The next morning, the opening of the conference began with welcomes from representatives of the city's leading white women's reform organizations: Ellen M. Henrotin of the Chicago Woman's Club, Corrine Brown of the Cook County League of Clubs, and Mary McDowell, director of the University of Chicago Settlement (and later a founder of the Women's Trade Union League). Tuesday's morning sessions included panels on kindergartens, moral standards, the labor question, the convict lease system, and lynch law. That evening, the church was filled to capacity for a formal program in which Booker T. Washington and Bishop Henry Turner, among others, were seated on the dais as honored guests. The minutes of the meeting mention only two speeches given that evening: one by Josephine St. Pierre Ruffin and another by the Reverend Edward Brown of Boston. There is no record of what Ruffin spoke about, but Brown gave a rousing speech about lynch law, followed by the passage of a resolution condemning it.[20]

Wells-Barnett had not attended any of the sessions, but on Wednesday morning there was a discernible stir when she unexpectedly appeared in the hall. As Ida explained in her autobiography, she had a specific reason for being there. Jane Addams, in a brave show of solidarity, had decided to invite the clubwomen to a luncheon at Hull House, and she asked Ida to extend the invitation on her behalf. Ida knew how anxious the women would be to accept it. Addams, who had established the settlement house a decade earlier, was, by many accounts, the most famous woman in the country. She had originated the American settlement movement, the ultimate uplift program, and had been responsible for the passage of child-labor laws and the establishment of the nation's first juvenile court. Additionally, although a number of the leading white women reformers in Chicago had attended and offered official greetings at the NACW's opening session, the invitation to the luncheon meeting had particular significance. As the *Chicago Sunday Times Herald* reported, "it was an exceedingly rare occurrence in Chicago for a colored woman to be received in a purely social way."[21]

When Ida received the word from Addams, she decided to deliver the invitation, personally—and not without her own drama—at the morning session. Once she was spotted in the hall, Terrell had little choice but to formally recognize her and invite Ida to sit on the dais. Ida, however, strategically—and demurely—declined, saying she came only to make two announcements. One was to invite the women to attend the upcoming Afro-American Council meetings, and second, she informed them of the invitation to Hull House. After this, she sat down at the back of the church until, she wrote, the Memphis delegation, which included her good friend (and Thomas Moss's sister-in-law) Florence Cooper from Memphis, made a motion that Ida be seated on the platform. When the motion was seconded, Ida allowed herself to be escorted to the front of the auditorium. Once there, she confined her remarks to details about the luncheon, then turned and quietly left the stage. The convention minutes noted that Ida's "time was limited," and after imparting the information, she "retired on private business."[22]

However diminutive Ida's public role was in the proceedings, she may have been working more intensely behind the scenes. "Our virtuous friend had done all in her evil power to prejudice the Illinois delegates against me," Terrell informed one of her friends in a letter, referring to Ida and the opposition she had received from the Chicago delegation when the predicted "decorum" of the proceedings melted down.[23]

Fannie Barrier Williams, the most insightful commentator on the club movement, once observed that the NACW, with all of the good things it accomplished, was at its worst during the organization's presidential elections. Written sometime after the 1899 meeting, she must have been thinking of the Chicago conference as a case in point. The trouble, recorded by the *Chicago Tribune* as well as the black press, began when an amendment was offered to reelect all of the current officers. After vociferous debate, it failed. But then Mollie Terrell announced her candidacy for president, explaining that she had concluded that it was the 1897 meeting, not the one before it, that marked the beginning of her first two-year term and so she was eligible to run again. The revisionist interpretation was more than Josephine St. Pierre Ruffin could bear. On the floor of the convention, she accused Mollie of "treachery, duplicity and unfaithfulness."[24]

The Bostonian's remarks brought disapproving hisses and "torrents of consuming scorn and chastisement," one black reporter noted; another observed that the ensuing chaos made the women "appear as boisterous and horrid as the men." Five prayers in as many minutes calmed the hostility long enough to read the nominations and prepare for the vote, though Ruffin, not hiding her distrust of the proceeding, asked that each delegate deposit her ballot on the table in front of the convention.[25]

But the die was cast. Terrell won the vote of 106 delegates out of the 144 present, but subsequently found herself having to do some intense politicking to keep the dissension from tearing the group apart. The delegates of Ruffin's Northeastern Federation, which represented a thousand members, had threatened to walk out after she lost a second vote, this time for the first vice presidency, to Josephine Bruce. To add insult to injury, Ruffin's niece, Elizabeth Carter of New Bedford, did not manage to win any of the three recording secretarial positions. Terrell tried to replace a Chicagoan—Connie Curl, first president of the Woman's Civic League—with Carter in one of secretarial posts but had to back down when the fifty-eight-member Illinois delegation threatened to withdraw. Finally, Terrell did enough politicking to keep everyone in place, if not happy, through the ordeal. Curl kept her post, and Carter was also listed as one of the three recording secretaries. Josephine Bruce was first vice president; Lucy Thurman, second vice president; and Margaret Washington was again chair of the executive board. Subsequently, however, Margaret gave Terrell a mild rebuke about the turmoil within the conference. In response, Terrell reminded her that she had "succeeded in placating every body except two ladies in Chicago [Fannie Barrier Williams and Wells-Barnett] and one in Boston [Ruffin] who until she gets the presidency, the Lord himself will not be able to calm."[26]

Despite Terrell's ultimate success, the bitter election had ultimately "killed her influence" in the organization, Ida wrote in her autobiography. "Killed" was probably too strong a word, but it did appear that Terrell never fully recaptured her status in the organization. Nevertheless, Terrell accomplished much of what she had hoped, and the women of the NACW must have been pleased about the final assessment of their conference. The Chicago daily press was obviously enthralled with the NACW meeting. The *Chicago Sunday Times Herald* waved off the internal debate by commenting that "white club women" were not "at all times in perfect control of themselves," either. The paper fluttered about the "continual revelation" of having seen black women who were tastefully attired, cultured, and intelligent, and thus could "hardly be distinguished" from white women.[27]

The *Chicago Tribune* concluded that the four-day convention was a "credit" to the race. "Their efforts are calculated to command public respect," it continued, "and cannot fail to have, in many ways, far reaching influence." The paper also quoted a white clubwoman, who after the convention said: "After watching these capable colored women for three days, I never want to hear another word about there being 'no hope for the Negro.'" The *Inter-Ocean* headlined its editorial "A Meeting That Meant Something," citing the practical topics of the discussions and panels.[28]

African American men also expressed their approval. A beaming Du Bois took especial pride. "Undoubtedly the women assembled at Chicago were rather above the average of their race and represented the aristocracy among the Negroes," he decreed. "Consequently their evident intelligence and air of good breeding served also to impress the onlookers." The *Colored American*, which mirrored the views of much of the black press, concurred: "No one thing in this generation has gone so far to demonstrate her [the Afro-American woman] worth, influence and primacy than the recent convention of the National Association of Colored Women at Chicago."[29]

IRONICALLY, COMPARED WITH the fireworks at the NACW confab, the actual deliberations of the Afro-American Council meeting, which opened on August 17, were anticlimactic. Although the opening session was so crowded that two women fainted in the eighty-plus-degree weather, the number of voting delegates—fifty, with about half coming from Chicago—was paltry, diminishing the significance of any censure vote. In any case, there was no decisive showdown because Washington, after appearing at the NACW session, did not "darken Bethel's door," as one observer put it. His absence was a signal for the McKinley men and the Bookerites to stay away as well.[30]

Bethel minister Reverdy Ransom was so angered by the turn of events that he offered a bitterly worded resolution, which began by scoffing at Washington for being "comfortably situated in apartments at the Palmer House," Chicago's most fashionable hotel, while the Council meetings were debating important issues. "He is a coward and unfriendly to the race," Ransom insisted. "If Booker T. Washington is the leader of the people why is he not here to lead them?"—a point he would sneer several times before he finished. But Ransom made a strategic mistake when, in his frustration, he also suggested that the absent Margaret Murray Washington be expunged from the roll of delegates. The unchivalrous gesture and Ransom's tone about both Washingtons rankled the delegates. Du Bois "promptly repudiated Ransom's unwise attack" and reaffirmed the confidence of the Council in Washington's "integrity, moral worth, and public service."[31]

The scholar's defense seemed to have calmed the waters, and Ransom later apologized for his remarks. The minister no doubt felt additional pressure to do so from the bishop of his district, Benjamin Arnett, an adviser to McKinley, and who was close to Mark Hanna, the manager of the president's 1896 campaign and the man responsible for McKinley's sizable war chest, which had been filled with big-business contributions. Hanna was the point man for Republican patronage and had earlier directed some of the largesse to Ransom when the minister was in Cleveland to help pay off the mortgage of his church. Additionally, the Bethel minister was also preparing to open the Institutional Church in Chicago that would need similar kinds of support. The entire episode was picked up by the Chicago press, which said comparatively little about the Council's resolutions against racism in the trade unions, imperialist expansion, disenfranchisement, and lynching.[32]

But the press did pick up the resolution debate about President McKinley and Booker Washington. President Walters, called on to douse another fire, cobbled together some compromise language to save the situation— and, it was speculated, his own presidency. The Council's resolutions regarding McKinley's failure to protect black lives and property did contain enough animus for the *Cleveland Gazette* to observe that they showed "a deep-seated" antipathy toward the administration, which had added insult to injury when McKinley's vice president, former New York governor Theodore Roosevelt, publicly reversed his earlier laudatory opinion about black soldiers.

At the time of Roosevelt's recent remarks, blacks, citing their exemplary service in the Spanish-American War—including the battle of San Juan Hill where one was killed and three wounded—were demanding that they be given the opportunity to be officers in the regular army. In a seeming effort to undermine their case, the vice president had published an article in *Scribner's Magazine*, in April of 1899, in which he recounted that at San Juan Hill he had had to stop a group of black infantrymen from retreating from the front by drawing a pistol on them. Once he had put a gun to their head, he said, that "was the end of the trouble, for the 'smoked Yankees' . . . flashed their white teeth at one another as they broke into broad grins, and I had no more trouble with them." The article drew much criticism from blacks and the black press. In May, the *New York Age* published a letter from a black veteran of the Cuban campaign in which he explained how Roosevelt had misread the situation. Indeed, the author of the article, Presley Holliday of the Tenth Calvary, admitted that black men moved back and forth from the front, but that was the role that they had been given by regular officers. Positioned at the rear of the Roosevelt's Rough Riders, they traveled to and from the firing lines to carry back wounded men or retrieve ammunition or rations. In some cases, the black men simply wanted to return to their black comrades where they felt more comfortable. But in no instance was their movement toward the rear due to cowardice, noted Holliday, and when his men were on the fighting lines they fought valiantly and aided the Rough Riders' victory. Holliday's letter to the *Age* had ended: "It is unfortunate that we had no colored officers in that campaign, and this thing of white officers for colored troops is exasperating, and I join with The Age in saying our motto for the future must be: 'No officers. No soldiers.' "[33]

Despite the complaints against the McKinley administration, Walters insisted that there was no like-minded resolution regarding the Tuskegeean. The Council, Walters told the press, supported the work of both Booker and Mrs. Washington and understood that the educator was absent from the meeting because his work at Tuskegee precluded his association with partisan political matters. "Negro Leader Is Upheld" was the headline of a *Chicago Tribune* article on the affair."[34]

Soon after the affirmation, Ida hurried off an article criticizing Washington and sent it to the *New York Age*. However, Fortune promptly excised the negative remarks and wrote to Booker about his subsequently receiving from Ida a "sassy letter complaining about the cutting out of her disparaging reference to you." Ida, Fortune concluded, echoing an ever-widening sentiment among organization leaders, is "sort of a bull in a china shop."[35]

Still, even the critical *Colored American* cited Ida's report on lynchings given during the meeting as one of the two highlights of the session. The other was W. E. B. Du Bois, who had "charmed everybody with his dignity and learning." At the end of the conference he was made the head of the Council's business committee.[36]

FOLLOWING THE 1899 meetings, there were adjustments and accommodations among the representatives of the two national organizations. Wells-Barnett maintained her secretarial position but gave up the financial secretaryship. However, she also appeared to get something in return. With the support of Bishop Henry Turner, among others, she headed the new Anti-Lynching Bureau created by the Council, which included an allocation of funds for publicity, travel, and investigations. By September, the *Broad Ax* reported that the bureau had sent out ten thousand antilynching appeals throughout the country.[37]

Ida's new title also made her the de facto authority on lynching and gave her access to mainstream publications and the ability to publish another pamphlet in which she could retake control of discourse about the issue. Contradicting Booker Washington's views, Ida's writings in 1900 and 1901 reasserted that lynching was an endemic part of the national culture, rather than anomalous acts of violence. "Our country's national crime is *lynching*," Ida began her 1900 article, "Lynch Law in America," which appeared in *Arena,* a Boston-based liberal publication. "It is not the creature of the hour, the sudden outburst of uncontrolled fury, or the unspeakable brutality of an insane mob. It represents the cool, calculating deliberation of intelligent people who openly avow that there is an 'unwritten law' that justifies them in putting human beings to death . . . without trial by jury . . . and without right of appeal." Appealing to the logic of progressive reformers, Ida drew an ironic comparison with the current outcry about

Captain Alfred Dreyfus, a French Jewish military officer found guilty of treason. While American citizens were shocked by the evidence of anti-Semitism in France, she wrote, she could "attest to one thousand men, women and children who during the last six years were put to death without trial before any tribunal on earth."[38]

Ida, a few weeks later, published "The Negro's Case in Equity" in the *Independent,* in which she contested the publication's earlier "earnest appeal" to black leaders to "tell their people" to abide by the law and not take it into their own hands. African Americans had been obeying the law, but they had "seen hundreds" of their "race murdered in cold blood by connivance of officers of the law, from the governors of the States down to sheriffs of counties," Ida wrote. Self-defense was the one proven deterrent, she said, giving several examples, and further implying that if whites obeyed the law there would be no problem.[39] Five months later, Ida published a pamphlet that extolled the character of a man who was characterized by the white press as a "desperado," but whom Ida cast in heroic terms.

Mob Rule in New Orleans was a departure from her other writings. This narrative centered on one figure, Robert Charles, who had taken the life of seven of his tormentors before he himself was killed.[40] In addition to revealing another travesty of mob law, Ida took pains to rescue the legacy of Charles, who was pictured on the cover dressed in a suit with an ascot at his neck and a derby on his head.

Ida's well-dressed protagonist had donned dark striped trousers, white shirt, black coat, and brown derby on July 23, when he was sitting with a friend on a stoop awaiting the arrival of his girlfriend, Virginia Banks, and a female friend of hers. The men were approached by a policeman who asked what they were doing there. Charles showed no deference to the officer and when he stood up, the policeman drew his weapon—and the black man drew his. The policeman was shot in the leg. Charles fled the scene.

The black man's friend was taken into custody and "sweated out" until he revealed Charles's address. Police were soon posted outside of the fugitive's door, and when one of them yelled, "Open up," Charles did so, with his rapid-fire Winchester rifle blazing. One bullet pierced the heart of the police captain; another patrolman was hit in the eye. The remaining officers fled and awaited Charles in the alley, only to find that he was waiting for them. Adopting guerilla tactics, he stalked, chased, and cursed his pursuers.

By the next morning, a mob had formed and began attacking any blacks they saw. At least three were killed; fifty were injured badly enough to be hospitalized. Authorities, as they had in the Moss lynching in Memphis, began a wholesale arrest of blacks suspected of being sympathetic to the fugitive. Several days later, the police were informed that Charles was hiding in the home of a friend. When a policeman stumbled upon the closet that was his hiding place, Charles shot him through the stomach and escaped to an upstairs room. Soon the building was surrounded by a thousand men with guns, and the subsequent siege lasted for about an hour while the lone black man picked off targets, one by one. Finally, Charles was forced out and appeared at the doorway with his rifle in hand and his derby set low over his eyes. After a brief escape into another building, Charles was finally shot. His body was dragged out of the house, where he was pummeled with bullets. The son of one of the slain policemen stomped on his face. On the same day, the mob burned down a school building for blacks, killed three African Americans, and beat many others, including women.[41]

Plying beneath the hysterical press accounts of the incident, Ida discovered that Robert Charles, though with little education, was a studious and highly politically conscious man who had been deeply affected by the disenfranchisement of Louisiana blacks in 1898 and the Hose lynching in Georgia. He was a back-to-Africa advocate who was in touch with Bishop Henry Turner and distributed literature on behalf of a local emigration society. Wells-Barnett solicited letters from those who had known him. One respondent noted how hard Charles worked for the emigration society with no remuneration. Another, who had known Charles for six years, said he was a "quiet and peaceful man" who was "frank" in his speaking and had not ever given any trouble to anyone. "So he lived and so he would have died had not he raised his hand to resent unprovoked assault and unlawful arrest that Monday night," Wells-Barnett averred. "The white people of this country may charge that he was a desperado, but to people of his own race Robert Charles will always be regarded as the hero of New Orleans."[42]

IDA'S EXPOSÉS AND Anti-Lynching Bureau activities made it increasingly difficult for Booker Washington to maintain his previous characterizations of lynching. In 1900, he gave an address in Atlanta in which he shared the dais with Georgia's governor. On this occasion, the Tuskegeean stressed that no man should be punished without a legal conviction, and that enforcement of law was in the interest of both blacks and whites. It was no saber-rattler, but it was a departure from his previous pronouncements that had blamed the victim.[43] By then, however, Washington had come up with another strategy that would turn the race discourse toward a direction he could better control.

Just weeks before the next scheduled Council meeting was to take place in Indianapolis in 1900, Booker planned to convene his own meeting in Boston. It was to launch the National Negro Business League, an organization that he would head and that would focus on economic and entrepreneurial enterprise. As could be predicted, it attracted a large number of participants: three hundred black business leaders, including a number of those who made up the leadership class in the Council. It was an effective maneuver, as the Business League represented the aspirations of many of the most successful achievers of the race who would now be under his administrative control. Ida was furious when she heard about it and castigated him in the *Conservator*. Washington had created an organization, she wrote, where he could be "president," "moderator," and "dictator." The move was divisive, she insisted, and nothing less than an opposition meeting to the Council. Moreover, she accused Washington of stealing the idea from Council member W. E. B. Du Bois, who had presented the outline for black business development at the previous year's meeting. Washington had had ample opportunity to present the business idea at the 1899 Council meeting, she said, adding that "Prof. Du Bois, the most scholarly and one of [the] most conservative members of the Council, who is chairman of the Business Bureau would have been glad to receive Mr. Washington's cooperation." As Ida probably knew, Washington used Du Bois's data for his own conference. But Ida appeared to be angrier at Washington than were any of her other colleagues, including Du Bois. "Miss Wells is fast making herself so ridiculous that everybody is getting tired of her," wrote Washington's new, dapper secretary, Emmett J. Scott, referring to the *Conservator* editorial.[44] Again, Booker contested the Council's influence in a way that made his naysayers appear strident and impractical in the face of the urgent need for economic development.

There is no evidence that the Illinois clubwomen were an exception to the "everybody" that Scott mentioned. Wells-Barnett appeared not to be deeply involved with the postconvention developments that included the formation of the statewide Illinois Federation of Colored Women's Clubs (IFCWC) in November of 1900.[45] But they, as well as national NACW leaders, soon realized that despite their acknowledged proximity to elite white women, confrontational tactics were still required.

IN THE SPRING of 1900, both Mary Church Terrell and Josephine St. Pierre Ruffin were barred from the fifth biennial meeting, in Milwaukee, of the predominantly white General Federation of Women's Clubs. By that year, the Federation was ten years old, represented 150,000 women, and Rebecca Lowe, a Georgian, was its president. Terrell had asked Lowe for the opportunity to extend formal greetings to the group in her capacity as the president of the NACW. Mollie was refused on the grounds that such salutations were limited to those who had given them to the body in the past. Ruffin's situation was more complicated. She appeared at the conference as a member of the Massachusetts Federation of Women's Clubs, which included organizations with black members. Ruffin herself belonged to the predominantly white New England Woman's Press Club as well as the Woman's Era Club. When she insisted on getting her delegate credentials as a representative of the black women's group, she was denied on the basis of another vague technicality. Ruffin, however, did not recede quietly. Over the course of the next several days, and with the support of both whites and blacks in her state federation, she challenged her exclusion. Ruffin's allies soon wilted under the barrage of southern dissension, however, that was highlighted by the Georgia delegation's threat to secede if the black woman got her way. Yet it was Ruffin who was seen by whites as the disruptive agent. It would have been better, as she was told by one delegate, if she acted more like Margaret Murray Washington. Finally, when Ruffin was faced with being forcibly removed, she allowed herself to be escorted out of the conference. After the incident, Lowe announced that the race issue would be left up to individual state federations—and counseled for them to select their delegates carefully.[46]

Probably on the invitation of Wells-Barnett, Ruffin came to Chicago where a meeting was held about the incident. The southern women were the "best organized body of women I ever saw," Ruffin told the audience at Quinn Chapel, the site of the recent NACW meeting. She explained how the women's husbands and brothers telegraphed their support and told the women to stand firm. By contrast, her white allies "did not know how to go about" the fight and were "not aggressive."[47]

Wells-Barnett helped stir the pot of protest in Chicago when her complaint about the matter was published in the *Chicago Tribune*. Her letter to the paper was, in part, a response to a feature in the General Federation's newsletter, republished by the daily, about a white clubwoman who invited a light-skinned black woman from a prominent family to join her club. The invitation initiated friendly social relations between the two women and eventually led to the black woman's son marrying the white woman's daughter. When the daughter (by some genetic miracle) subsequently gave birth to a "jet-black" child, the shock was so distressing that after seeing the baby, she turned her head to the wall and died! If southerners were going to bring their sensationalism north, Wells-Barnett would dust off the ripostes she had honed in Dixie. In the *Chicago Tribune*, Wells-Barnett dared reporters to ask her personally about the biracial children whom she and others personally knew of—including one who belonged to a former Chicago mayor! The challenge drew no takers.[48]

But the controversy did not go unnoticed among white women progressives, especially those in the influential Chicago Woman's Club, a member of the General Federation, which had earlier gone through its own struggle with Fannie Barrier Williams's membership application. In January of 1895, the Woman's Club had adopted a resolution that no potential member could be excluded on race or color lines. Ellen Henrotin, a former Chicago Woman's Club president (whose husband was the head of Chicago's stock exchange), who had addressed the Chicago NACW meeting, coordinated the organization's enquiries to the General Federation about the Ruffin incident.[49] After finding their explanations unsatisfactory, the influential Chicago club censured Rebecca Lowe and the General Federation. In the meantime, the black Illinois federation requested membership in the white state federation.[50]

The request and the national federation race issue sent the white Illinois federation into an intense debate. Indicative of the growing influence of the Tuskegeean, several members wrote to Booker and Margaret Washington to clarify their positions on the issue. Alice Bradford Wiles, a past president of the (white) Illinois Federation, addressed her letter to "Mr. or Mrs. Booker Washington" in November of 1900. The "public press has reported you both as saying publicly that in your opinion the time had not come when the admission should be urged of a club of colored women to the General Federation of Women's Clubs," Wiles began. Her purpose was to get them to confirm the press reports so that she could use them as ammunition to argue against including the black federation. Wiles, identifying herself as the daughter of a Boston abolitionist, and a "warm" friend of [William Lloyd] Garrison's, made a point of deploring "the apparent disregard of the feelings of black women" but also made the expedient argument that their admission would be disruptive, as southern women white women had "not yet time to outgrow" their prejudices. A premature attempt to integrate would embitter feelings and perhaps delay a more liberal stance, Wiles reasoned. Nevertheless, she wrote in apparent sincerity that she wanted to be "right" on this question, and "take the side which promises the widest good to our country as a whole." In the same period, Ida and Fannie Barrier Williams were receiving threatening anonymous letters warning them not to try to gain admission into white clubs; and, though there is no explicit evidence of a connection, Wiles was simultaneously being investigated by the Woman's Club for allegedly writing over seventy anonymous letters to club members and newspapers.[51]

Two weeks after Wiles's letter, the Washingtons received another from a white Chicagoan, Clara M. T. Larson, also a former president of the Illinois state federation. She wanted the couple to support the contrary opinion: that there "was no reason for excluding the intelligent colored women from our counsels." In the letter, Larson also cited press reports about the position of Washington, reports that confirmed, she said, her point of view. In the end the white Illinois federation, while not overtly barring black women, utilized a subtle evasive clause that was probably similar to the mechanism that President Lowe had used in keeping Terrell from addressing the General Federation. And though it is not known if Washington replied directly to the Illinois correspondents, he subsequently told other clubwomen who sought his advice that he did not want to be drawn into the controversy. The consequences of his silence would ripple through the next NACW presidential election.[52] But there was no compromise on lynching itself—even (or especially) when it meant challenging the most famous progressive in the world.

During the first part of 1901, Ida published "Lynching and the Excuse for It" in the *Independent* as a direct response to an article by Jane Addams. The fact that such a figure as Addams would seriously engage the issue was significant. No northern white woman reformer had done so, and her attention to the subject had the potential of bringing considerable resources to the antilynching movement. As would be expected, Addams's article, "Respect for Law," came down solidly against lynching. But Ida was compelled to take her to task for a perspective that she believed to be not only flawed, but dangerous. [53]

Addams's article had begun promisingly by decrying the persistence of lynching and mob law. Known for her class analysis, she wrote that violence against blacks—deemed incapable of reason and consequently treated "upon the animal plane"—rose "to unspeakable atrocities when the crimes of the so-called inferior class affect the property and persons of the superior." Many of the most atrocious acts in history were committed by men who had convinced themselves that they were doing right out of "a false theory of conduct" or, even worse, who had "invented a theory of conduct to cover and support their deeds," Addams wrote.[54]

Reading the sentence, Wells-Barnett surely assumed that Addams was referring to the "false theory" of rape as a motive for lynching, but the article took a different turn. While distancing herself from the assumption that black men raped black women, Addams wrote that she would accept the sincerity of the belief for "argument's sake" to prove her point that the "false theory of conduct" was that lynching blacks was not the effective deterrent that whites assumed it to be. "Brutality only begets brutality," Addams warned. "The underdeveloped are never helped by such methods of these, for they learn only by imitation. The child who is managed by a system of bullying and terrorizing is almost sure to be a vicious and stupid child."[55]

"It was eminently befitting that the Independent's first number in the new century should contain a strong protest against lynching," Ida's response began. She appreciated Addams's earnestness and "dispassionate" treatment of the issue. But at the same time, Ida continued, Addams had made an "unfortunate presumption as her basis for her argument," a presumption that did "injury to the memory of thousands of victims of mob law."[56]

Addams had ignored the fact that middle-class blacks were lynched, but Ida made another point in her own class analysis. Of the 147 whites lynched in the previous five years, she noted, not one had been wealthy or "had friends of influence." But, of course, Addams's fundamental error was her failing to take into account the falsity of the rape charge—the point that Wells-Barnett had been asserting for eight years. Warming up to her subject, Wells-Barnett continued by attacking Addams's assumption for argument's sake. It was "absolutely unwarrantable," Ida said, and "vitiates" every suggestion that "inspires Miss Addams to make."[57] For while the large majority "condemn lynching," Ida noted, the presumption allowed the condemnation to be "tempered" with a plea for the lyncher. Ida was clearly exasperated by the fact that despite the motives that accompanied the lynching statistics published year after year—which Ida included in nearly every article—"law-abiding and fair-minded people should so persistently shut their eyes to the facts." Ida continued, "This record, easily within the reach of every one who wants it," made it "inexcusable" for anyone not to debunk the presumption from the beginning. And any conclusion not based on the best evidence is "unworthy of a moment's consideration." Instead of misrepresentations, the "lynching record should be allowed to plead, trumpet-tongued, in defense of the slandered dead," Ida insisted. It was only then that the nation could be summoned "to do its duty to exalt justice and preserve inviolate the sacredness of human life."[58] "Lynching and the Excuse for It" also included lynching statistics in which Ida made special note of the five women who had been lynched during the previous five years.

BY THE SUMMER of 1901, the NACW and Afro-American Council prepared for another round of debate. A presidential election was scheduled for the NACW meeting in Buffalo, New York, but with Terrell acceding to the position of honorary president with voting privileges, and both Josephine Bruce and Margaret Murray Washington as candidates for president, the rule of the "triumvirate" appeared assured. However, Ruffin's experience with the General Federation, the silence of the Washingtons about it, and Wells-Barnett's involvement with the Illinois women's own struggle with exclusion had changed the dynamics of the conference. When, in Buffalo, Washington and Bruce opted to accept an invitation to a white woman's function instead of a black-hosted one on the same night, the rank and file became incensed. A year before, the decision of the leaders to attend a white function might have been seen as politic, but after the experience with the white federation, it was construed differently. "It may be all right from a financial standpoint . . . for Mr. and Mrs. Washington to 'place the white people first,'" sniped the *Cleveland Gazette*, "but it is not alright . . . to stand it, especially whenever there is an opportunity to rebuke such mistreatment." The development surely was a factor in the defeat of both Washington and Bruce (though they retained the offices of chair of the executive board and first vice president, respectively). Josephine Silone Yates of Kansas City, whose nomination had been seconded by the entire Illinois delegation, won the election. Agnes Moody, president of the Ida B. Wells Club, and Elizabeth Lindsey Davis, founder of Chicago's Phyllis [*sic*] Wheatley Club, were elected second vice president and national organizer, respectively. Ida approved of the election of Yates and arranged for Mary Plummer to host a luncheon for her, where black and white clubwomen would meet.[59] The luncheon was a success, according to Ida, but not without her persuasive intervention. Somehow the press had gotten word of the affair (perhaps through Wiles) and began sounding the old alarm of social equality. Plummer tried to back down, but Ida pressed her to honor the invitation. Plummer, no doubt with some trepidation, agreed; but then Wells-Barnett had to convince Yates to accept it after she belatedly discovered through others (not Ida) that Plummer had wanted to rescind the offer.[60]

Ida did not attend the 1901 NACW meeting, nor would she attend the Afro-American Council conference also slated that year. In July, she had given birth to a daughter, Ida, Jr., the third child born in her six-year-old marriage.

CHAPTER SEVENTEEN

Chicago and the Wizard

Both [Ferdinand] Barnett and his wife abused
McKinley shamefully during the first part of his
administration and they did the same thing in regard to President Roosevelt . . . the time has come
when such treachery should be punished as it
ought to be.

—*Booker T. Washington*

The Tuskegee crowd had expressed relief when Ida's pregnancy prevented her from attending the 1901 National Afro-American Council
meeting in Philadelphia. "I am glad Mrs. Barnett was not there to complicate the situation," wrote Emmett Scott to Booker Washington. The "situation" that Washington's secretary was referring to was their continuing
efforts to bring the National Negro Business League and the Council into
closer affiliation. "I found the [Council] convention most sympathetic in
our direction," noted Scott. In deference to Washington's policy of not being openly associated with political matters, for example, he was referred to
in the meeting as "XYZ" rather than by name. "Whenever the initials were
called," the secretary continued, "cheers were given."[1]

By the time of the meeting, Washington's popularity had soared to new
heights, thanks to the publication of his critically acclaimed autobiography,

Up from Slavery, in February. The book had been preceded by a series of articles about his life in *The Outlook,* a publication that had a circulation of more than a hundred thousand and edited by Social Gospeler Lyman Abbott (who had been so parsimonious to Ida when she spoke at his church in Brooklyn). Washington's Horatio-Alger-in-black philosophy, simple, direct, yet eloquent prose, and narrative of his heroic rise from slavery with the help of his self-sacrificing mother and good white folks received near-universal praise from critics and philanthropists. "I have just re-read your book," wrote the camera manufacturer George Eastman, "and have come to the conclusion that I cannot dispose of five thousand dollars to any better advantage than to send it to you for your Institute."[2]

The most notable exception to the critical kudos was the response of W. E. B. Du Bois, who, by the time his review appeared in *Dial,* was no longer considering the invitation to come to Tuskegee and suspected that Washington was not supporting his bid for the assistant superintendency position in Washington. Du Bois applauded the educator's astuteness and achievement but questioned his ridicule of liberal arts education for blacks and his learning "so thoroughly, the speech and thought of triumphant commercialism."[3]

In Ida's stead, Ferdinand had given her Anti-Lynching Bureau report at the Council meeting, which cited the ninety-one lynchings during the previous year and proposed a resolution be sent to the president and the Congress asking for the passage of a federal antilynching bill. The call for such legislation was especially timely. That January, outgoing North Carolina representative George H. White, in one of his last acts as the single black congressman in the House of Representatives, had, in the wake of the Wilmington Massacre and Congressman Henry Blair's legislation to investigate lynchings, proposed the nation's first bill to make lynching a federal crime. The legislation, he no doubt knew, was doomed to fail in the House, but in his valedictory address before the body, he predicted that blacks, "outraged, heart-broken, bruised and bleeding," would one day "rise phoenix-like again."[4]

According to the *Colored American,* the Anti-Lynching Bureau's resolution and report was considered a highlight of the otherwise unremarkable meeting. But as Scott told Washington, Ferdinand Barnett had evidently felt it politic to refer to XYZ as "the matchless orator & wise leader" to cheers from the audience. The praise might have been an attempt to safeguard not just Ferdinand's political interests, but Ida's as well. Leading the lynching fight was no longer a guarantee of being in good stead with the Council. For example, despite George White's congressional heroics, he had been trounced (to the delight of Emmett Scott) by the delegates when he tried to run against Alexander Walters for the Council presidency. Ferdinand's affirmation of Washington might have enabled his absent wife to retain her tenuous hold as head of the Anti-Lynching Bureau at a time when the Tuskegeean appeared to be in firm control of the organization.[5]

His power only increased when, just weeks after the Council meeting, an anarchist's bullet felled William McKinley. The president had been shot point-blank on September 6, while standing on a reception line at the Pan-American Exposition in Buffalo, New York. McKinley's stomach wound became infected, and he clung tenuously to life for the next eight days. On September 14, the very day of McKinley's death, his vice president wrote a letter to Booker Washington. "When are you coming North?" Theodore Roosevelt urgently asked him. "I must see you as soon as possible. I want to talk over the question of possible appointments in the South exactly on the lines of our last conversation together."[6]

The forty-two-year-old vice president was an admirer of Tuskegee—the "salvation of the Negro," he called it. The New York-born Roosevelt was a graduate of Harvard, where he had studied under, and was admittedly influenced by, Nathanial Southgate Shaler, the social scientist whose Negrophobic views, published in *Harper's* and elsewhere, reflected the belief that black atavistic behavior could be chastened by the rod of moral and industrial training. It was not a long stretch for Roosevelt to believe, as he had implied in his *Scribner's* article, that black cowardice would dissipate at the point of a gun. In fact, both of his pro and con positions regarding black soldiers reflected Roosevelt's racial views. Like many Progressives of the period—the heirs of the Social Gospel Movement who sought to reform government, immorality, and the excesses of capitalism—Roosevelt did not think much of blacks as a race. "I entirely agree with you," he wrote to his friend, the novelist Owen Wister, "that as a race in the mass they are altogether inferior to the whites." But Roosevelt also held the Progressive belief in the potential of individuals to transcend their inferior status and in providing them the opportunity to do so.[7] For TR, as he was known, Booker T. Washington fit the bill.

Roosevelt had been especially impressed by Washington's views regarding the political briar patch of the South. Booker had suggested that the president neutralize the Populists, led by William Jennings Bryan who had run twice against McKinley, by steering clear of both Democratic and Populist radical Negrophobes and the "Black and Tan" wing of the Republicans, the latter of which included African Americans with federal appointments and their allies. In their place, Roosevelt should appoint conservative whites, Democrat or Republican, where appropriate, and replace the black career politicians with upright business-oriented men—like those Washington was attracting to his Negro Business League. The new equation fit both men's aspirations, as well as their preferences. Roosevelt thought the race's professional politicians "venal" and was anxious to break the hold of Mark Hanna, who had influence over them. Washington saw the black politicians, many of whom had their own power bases, as potential competitors. Ironically, it was his political advice, coming from a region where the masses of blacks were being steadily disenfranchised, and who had publicly stated that he would steer clear of politics, that consolidated his power at the dawning of the twentieth century.[8]

In October, TR asked the Washingtons to dine with him and his family at the White House. The invitation brought howls of vicious vituperation from white supremacists—and the recognition from blacks that the educator had secured the "final rivet," as his biographer noted, of the Tuskegee machine. In short order, black politicians found themselves not reappointed—or even able to get the president's ear—unless they came through Washington.[9]

Washington's very public alliance with Roosevelt transformed his strategy. The new circumstances dictated that merely dominating black opinion was not enough; now he had to control it. The first order of business was to bring the black press into line. As early as 1901, Washington began buying stock in some publications and subsidizing others in markets where anti-Washington newspapers were published. In October of that year, he dispatched his secretary, Emmett Scott, to the Palmer House, Chicago's swank hotel, where Washington sent him a message: "Without letting them know I have made request wish you to arrange for me to meet separately editors of all chgo colored papers."[10] Chicago's editorial group included the Broad Ax's Julius Taylor, a cantankerous anti-Washington Democrat; the Chicago Appeal's Cyrus Adams, a businessman, National Negro Business League member, and the newly elected president of the Afro-American Press Association; and the current editor and part owner of the Conservator, R. D. Wilkins, a biblical scholar and minister from Kentucky.

Two hours after the first telegram, Washington sent a second: "Conservator has vicious editorial this week want to bring them into harmony if I can do so honorably."[11]

One can only speculate what "honorably" meant in this circumstance, or the subject of the offending editorial. The latter might have been about Washington's daughter, Portia, the recent subject of much comment in the press. With all of Washington's pronouncements about the virtues of industrial education, he had sent his oldest child to Wellesley, an elite women's college in Massachusetts, and the irony was not lost on his detractors. But the "Wizard of Tuskegee," as he became known, was not only courting the press for himself or his daughter or his school alone. He was determined to pull black opinion-makers in line with the Roosevelt administration, and the plan now also included the Afro-American Council. Although Emmett Scott and Thomas Fortune assured the educator that they had things under control for the 1902 meeting in St. Paul, Minnesota, "XYZ" had decided that it was time to come out of the shadows and appear there himself.

By then, Washington had achieved, he thought, a rappaprochement with Du Bois, but a new flank of opposition was mounting in Boston, the home of the voluble Monroe Trotter, editor of the recently established *Boston Guardian* newspaper, which delivered some of the most virulent criticism of the Tuskegeean. The Ohio-born Trotter had grown up in middle-class comfort in Hyde Park, a white suburb of Boston. His mother, Virginia, was, according to family tradition, the great-great-granddaughter of Thomas Jefferson and his slave Sally Hemmings. Monroe's father, James Monroe Trotter, was a Civil War veteran who had been appointed recorder of deeds in Washington under President Grover Cleveland. In 1891, Trotter entered Harvard, making Phi Beta Kappa by his junior year. After graduation, he had worked in real estate, but by 1902 the deteriorating racial situation and his conviction that Booker T. Washington was betraying blacks impelled him to found the *Guardian*.[12] In response, Washington initiated efforts to establish a competing black paper to neutralize the Trotterites.

From July 10 to the morning of July 11, the 1902 Council meeting proceeded predictably with its keynote speeches, welcomes, prayers, and panels—all occurring without Washington. Wells-Barnett's Anti-Lynching Bureau report, which noted 2,658 lynchings since 1885 and 135 lynchings in 1901—numbers that she said indicated two or three lynchings per week during the previous seventeen years—got the most local press attention. But by the afternoon of the eleventh, the behind-the-scenes manipulations of Washington's minions emerged, throwing the Council into chaos. Breaking with the scheduled program, there was an unexpected call for a report from the nominating committee, which recommended that T. Thomas Fortune be president and Bishop Walters become chair of the executive committee. The maneuver brought protests from Monroe Trotter, Wells-Barnett, Fannie Barrier Williams, and W. E. B. Du Bois, among others. But that evening, Washington arrived in St. Paul to mute the complaints sufficiently for the nominating committee recommendation to go forward.

Ida and Nelson Crews, head of the organization's immigration bureau, were the only officers of the Council to resign in protest, but the delegates voted not to accept either resignation. It is not clear what their status was by the end of the meeting, but the episode effectively ended Ida's work with the Afro-American Council. Adding insult to injury, as far as she was concerned, Fannie Barrier Williams replaced her as the one woman with an executive position. She was elected corresponding secretary.[13]

"It was wonderful to see how completely your personality dominated everything," Scott gleefully told Washington after the close of the meeting. "From the moment that you reached there, you were the one center of interest, much to the chagrin and regret of our friends, the Barnetts—especially." The militants, of course, were disgusted. "We might have expected Prof. Du Bois to have stood in the breach here," opined Monroe Trotter, who would later characterize the meeting as calamitous, describe Fortune as Washington's "henchman," and conclude that the coup was for the sole benefit of getting the *Age* editor an appointment in the Roosevelt administration, which the Council had endorsed by the end of the meeting. "Like all the others who are trying to get into the band wagon," Trotter concluded about Du Bois, "he is no longer to be relied on."[14] Unbeknownst to Trotter, however, was that Du Bois was in the process of preparing *The Souls of Black Folk,* which would, in less than a year, mobilize the first major opposition movement to Washington's leadership.

IN THE INTERIM, no one must have felt more glum about recent developments than Ida. The loss of the Afro-American Council to the Tuskegeeans closed the best venue she had had to exercise her leadership and subsidize her antilynching work. By 1902, the Bookerites also prevailed over the Afro-American Press Association, leading the *Broad Ax* to subsequently conclude that the Council, Press Association, and National Negro Business League were "all one and the same thing."[15]

Back home, Wells-Barnett received another blow. She and the *Conservator* had been waging a war against the new Bethel minister, Reverend Abraham Lincoln Murray, who had replaced Reverdy Ransom. Sometime between 1900 and 1901, Murray was accused of sexually harassing the wife of a church board member. The woman in question was said to have a reputation that was beyond reproach and had filed formal charges, but despite Ida's efforts to get the minister removed and the damning editorials in the *Conservator* (republished approvingly by the *Chicago Broad Ax*), the church board refused to investigate the matter. Another minister, Archibald Carey, pastor of the AME's Quinn Chapel, came to the support of Murray, and Ida found herself at odds with the pastors of the two major churches of that denomination in the city. Finally, the bishop of the district, Abraham Grant (whom Ida had once called too "uncultivated" for the position), was summoned to Chicago, and though he had promised Ida that the matter would be adjudicated, no action was taken. As Ida told the bishop, the refusal to censure Murray left her no choice but to leave Bethel. "I had a family of growing children," Ida explained in her autobiography, "and all my teaching would be null and void if I continued in a church with a man who had become so notoriously immoral." With those parting words, Ida left the church where she had married, established the city's first black kindergarten, and helped lead mass protests against injustice for the Grace Presbyterian Church, founded in 1888 by black Presbyterians from Tennessee and Kentucky.[16]

The black women's clubs completed Ida's alienation. Despite Wells-Barnett's hopes, the election of Josephine Silone Yates as president of the NACW did not disturb the power of the organization's "triumvirate"; the offices of the black Illinois federation were dominated by non-Chicagoans; and Ida had even fallen afoul of the president of the Ida B. Wells (IBW) Club, Agnes Moody, who had been elected in 1901 as the second vice president of the NACW. As Ida recounted in her autobiography, the rupture occurred when the IBW Club was invited by Mary V. Plummer, the white reformer who had been secretary of the Chicago Anti-Lynching League, to become a member of the predominantly white League of Cook County Clubs, an organization dedicated to coordinating the work of women's organizations. The invitation also included a spot on the league's board, and Ida, without informing Moody, hastily accepted the offer and the board position. The IBW president was understandably furious and apparently did not accept the explanation that there was a pressing deadline to accept the position and that she was unable to contact Moody (no one in the group had telephones at the time, Ida noted). There is no indication that the rift was healed before Moody, who had a history of heart problems, died in 1903, and it can be reasonably assumed that Wells-Barnett's behavior did little to endear her to other members of the IBW or the other clubs.[17]

In addition to Ida's personal ambitions and her belief that she would be the best representative for black women, another reason she was so adamant about the board position was that with the hegemony of Booker Washington, Ida believed that interracial alliances were the best hope to further the aspirations of blacks. When she was invited in January of 1903 to speak before the Chicago Political Equality League, a woman's suffrage organization founded in 1894 under the auspices of the Chicago Woman's Club, Wells-Barnett insisted that women's clubs were "the new power, the new molder of public sentiment, to accomplish the reforms that the pulpit and the law have failed to do." Of course, the continued prevalence of lynching had to be remedied, but Ida now also focused on the exclusion of black men and women from manufacturing, clerical, and semiprofessional occupations, and the wrongheadedness of Booker T. Washington's philosophy of industrial education at a time when trade unions excluded blacks. Organized women like themselves, Ida continued, were best fitted to move the society forward and provide opportunities for black women who had proven their "dignity, genius, and lack of race hatred." But white women themselves had to be emancipated "from the prejudice which fetters their noblest endeavor and renders inconsistent their most sacred professions," she exhorted. Ida was no doubt willing to help her sisters become unfettered, and she may have truly believed that interracial alliances between women held the best promise for reform, but surely another reason she wanted a prominent role in them was because it offered the one political space where she could exercise any kind of leadership role. This only became more evident in the spring of 1903 when Booker T. Washington and W. E. B. Du Bois parted the sea of race leadership between them.[18]

On April 14, the industrialist Andrew Carnegie, who had recently sold his steel company to the U.S. Steel Corporation for $470 million, made the Washingtons one of the deal's most conspicuous beneficiaries. Carnegie gave Tuskegee $600,000 in U.S. Steel bonds for its endowment and specified that $150,000 be used personally by Washington and his family. But just as the influence of the Wizard appeared to have no bounds, Du Bois published *The Souls of Black Folk* four days later, on April 18.[19]

The fourteen essays in the classic volume of epic-poem economy laid bare the marrow of black history, striving, resistance, culture, and hope for a modern age. *Souls* introduced the idea of the divided self and the concept of "double consciousness," through which African Americans envisioned themselves through the eyes of whites, as well as their own. It prophesied that the "color line" would be the defining inscription of the new century, and it transfigured the disparaged traits of black folk expression into cultural elements of beauty, grace, and, for the world, salvation. But in 1903, the aspect of the publication most talked about was the chapter entitled "Of Booker T. Washington and Others."[20]

The chapter, an extension of Du Bois's *Dial* review of *Up from Slavery*, cut sharply, but with a very fine blade, to expose the contradictions of Washington's educational philosophy and leadership. The "distinct impression left by Mr. Washington's propaganda is first, that the South is justified in its present attitude toward the Negro because of the Negro's degradation; secondly that the prime cause of the Negro's failure to rise more quickly is his wrong education in the past; and thirdly, that his future rise depends primarily on his own efforts." Each point was a dangerous half-truth, Du Bois countered, which encouraged disenfranchisement, "civil inferiority," and the withdrawal of aid from institutions for the higher training of blacks. Tuskegee itself, Du Bois continued, "could [not] remain open a day were it not for teachers trained in Negro colleges, or trained by their graduates."[21]

Insisting that "color-prejudice is more often a cause than a result of the Negro's degradation," Du Bois called for "manly self respect," insisted that voting was necessary to "modern manhood," and concluded that insofar as "Mr. Washington apologizes for injustice, North or South, does not rightly value the privilege and duty of voting, belittles the emasculating effects of caste distinctions, and opposes the higher training and ambition of our brighter minds,—so far as he, the South, or the Nation does this,—we must unceasingly and finally oppose him."[22]

Of course, Ida, among others, had been articulating the core of these ideas for more than a decade, but in addition to the power of his language and analysis, the timing of *Souls* and Du Bois's scholarly, "prodigal son" status made the criticism of Washington an event of seismic proportion in the Windy City and elsewhere. The usually hypercritical *Chicago Broad Ax* called *Souls* the "most remarkable book so far produced by an Afro-American."[23] Soon after its appearance, Celia Parker Woolley, a white Social Gospel Unitarian minister and writer, invited Ida and Ferdinand, among others, to an interracial gathering at her house to discuss the book. Ida and her husband eagerly accepted.

The Ohio-born, fifty-four-year-old minister was highly respected in women's—and especially black women's—circles. A former president of the Chicago Woman's Club, Woolley had nominated Fannie Barrier Williams for membership in that organization and had subsequently written its nondiscriminatory clause regarding future members. In 1894, Woolley had cofounded and was later president of the Chicago Political Equality League.[24]

Williams and her husband, S. Laing, were among the blacks also invited by Woolley for the discussion, as well as the prominent dentist Charles Bentley, also a Unitarian, a friend of Du Bois's, and a former member of Chicago's Anti-Lynching Committee. Florence Bentley, Charles's wife, was also present. She was a former journalist who had written for the *Philadelphia Daily Ledger* and the *Chicago Record-Herald*. Other black attendees included Monroe Work, an ordained minister who was the first African American to obtain a master's degree in sociology and psychology from the University of Chicago, and the prominent businessman Lloyd Wheeler.

As Ida would later recall, Florence Bentley opened the discussion, giving a positive review of *Souls,* but it soon became evident that she, her husband, Woolley, and the Barnetts held the minority opinion about Du Bois's views concerning Washington. The whites revealed their "obsession" with industrial education, and the other black invitees were also pro-Washington. In fact, all had some kind of direct or near-future associations with the Tuskegeean. Fannie Barrier Williams was by then writing speeches for him; Wheeler was a cofounder of the Chicago branch of the National Negro Business League. Both he and Monroe Work would subsequently become employed at Tuskegee.[25]

After the Woolley get-together, Wells-Barnett eagerly wrote to Du Bois, informing him of what had transpired at the gathering and told him that she planned to hold another discussion of his book at her own home in June. She did not mention who her guests would be, only that it would be a meeting of "our best brained"—a reference that seemed to indicate that only blacks would be issued invitations. But Ida's real purpose in writing the scholar was, in effect, to remind him of his manners. Written with the tone of a mentor who was guiding a freshman celebrity in the ways of politesse, she asked Du Bois to acknowledge the just-published autobiography of Woolley (*The Western Slope*), which the minister had sent him, and to get in touch with Jane Addams. Woolley was a friend of the race, Ida explained, who believed that racism was one of the worse ills of society, and she asked that Du Bois send a cordial note about her views in the book and at the interracial meeting. Addams (with whom, she said, she had recently lunched) had both written and called Du Bois in the hopes of meeting with him when she had been in Atlanta, Ida wrote, but had gotten no reply. She suggested that the scholar write and assure her that his lack of response was not intentional. "I don't need to tell you who Miss Addams is," she nudged. Ida signed the letter, uncharacteristically—and perhaps, in Du Bois's eyes, condescendingly—with the informality of using her initials.[26] There is no record of his reply.

The contents of the letter might also be read as a subtle criticism that Du Bois's call-to-protest, with title chapters like "Of the Training of Black Men," "Of the Sons of Master and Man," and "Of the Faith of the Fathers," did not include any intellectual or activist role for women. In fact, *Souls* was very gender specific in urging "black men to judge the South discriminately," and in characterizing the twentieth-century black struggle as one to attain "modern" manhood.[27] Of course, others, including Ida herself used the term "manhood" to point out the socially mandated role of men to protect the race and the necessity for constitutionally enfranchised males to demand full citizenship rights as a prerequisite for the entire race enjoying them. But for Du Bois, it was the singular "longing to attain self-conscious manhood" that had animated the entire history of the black struggle in America, and it was that attainment that, in the end, would "save" the race.[28] If Ida hoped that Du Bois manifesto had provided a catalyst for the formation of new protest organizations in which she and black women could play an integral part, her hopes would only be partially realized.

Du Bois's manifesto did spawn new organizations. In Chicago, five months after the publication of *Souls*, Ferdinand Barnett, Charles Bentley, and Edward Morris, among others, organized the all-male Equal Opportunity League, a civil rights organization in Chicago. Its first public meeting at Bethel Church drew two thousand persons. Soon after, the statewide Equal Rights and Protective League of Illinois was founded.[28] Both groups were dominated by anti-Bookerites of ability and influence, among them Morris, who was chair of the Protective League's executive committee. A former state legislator and a stockholder of the *Conservator,* he was an influential lawyer with considerable connections. Morris was grand master of the Oddfellows, a powerful fraternal group in the city, and his eclectic array of clients included a number of the major black churches, several mainstream corporations, Cook County, and the "Gambler's Trust"—a powerful black gaming syndicate whose influence extended to politics. Morris was one of the most vociferous critics of Washington, who thought, as he would tell the *Chicago Inter-Ocean* in 1903, that the Tuskegeean was "largely responsible for lynchings in this country."[29] Although at times Morris and Barnett had competing political interests, the two men were close. Ferdinand was a regular guest at Morris's elegant whist parities, once winning the first-place prize of a silver cigar cutter.[30]

One of the local issues that had impelled the formation of Chicago's Equal Opportunity League was a discernible trend toward school segregation. Chicagoans had been attending racially mixed schools since 1874; black teachers taught both black and white students; and as late as 1905, only one school had a black enrollment of more than 30 percent.[31] But the increase in the black population, and the racial conflicts between students that followed, alarmed many whites, and the *Chicago Tribune* began publishing articles that, as Ida wrote in her autobiography, tended "to show the benefits of a separate school system for blacks in Chicago."[32] The articles included interviews of school superintendents of other segregated school systems in St. Louis, Baltimore, and Washington, D.C., who touted separate education. The newspaper also published stories of parents who complained of black teachers and canvassed opinions of whites on the issue.[33]

According to Ida's autobiography, Ferdinand had come home one afternoon distraught about the developments and somberly predicted that in five years, the schools would no longer be integrated. "Just what do you all propose to do about it?" Ida asked, probably referring to the Equal Opportunity League. The Leaguers evidently had run out of ideas. Ida hadn't. She was convinced, as she said, that every injustice had a remedy.[34]

First, Wells-Barnett wrote a letter to the *Tribune*, protesting that it had canvassed opinions about the matter from everyone but blacks. She suggested that the editors receive a group of prominent African Americans to discuss the issue. When she got no response, she went in person to see the paper's editor, Robert Patterson, only to be routinely dismissed. As she wrote, the editor thought that she was a church woman who had come to solicit money. After she identified herself and her purpose, the two had "quite a chat," Ida understated. When the conversation extended to general race matters, Patterson told her that his views coincided with whites in the South—he had a winter home in Georgia—adding that he didn't think ignorant Negroes should have the right to vote and rule over whites. Ida replied that she could have the same view about the white men in the First Ward flophouses who were able to vote, but she was not "disposed" to such an unfair opinion. Patterson's parting words were that "he did not have time to listen to a lot of colored people on the subject."[35]

The exchange was a reminder that a new, and new-minded, post–Atlanta Compromise generation now held the reins of newspaper publishing in Chicago. Gone were the iconic Republican reformers like the late Joseph Medill (Patterson was his son-in-law) and Ida's *Inter-Ocean* allies such as H. H. Kohlsaat, William Penn Nixon, and Albion Tourgée, who had been appointed United States consul to Bordeaux, France.[36]

Since blacks did not have the power to make an impact on the Chicago press, Ida turned to someone who did. She called upon Jane Addams to explain the situation, asking her to convene a meeting of leading reformers. Addams agreed and the assembled group at Hull House included editors, ministers, at least one board of education member, and such liberal reformers as the Reverend Jenkin Lloyd Jones, the Unitarian minister of the All Souls United Church; Rabbi Emil Hirsch, who in addition to his pastoral duties was a professor of rabbinical literature and philosophy at the University of Chicago; and Celia Parker Woolley. During the course of the meeting, Ida outlined her own thoughts not only about the school issue, but about the greater need for interracial alliances for a range of race relations issues. Subsequently, Addams led a delegation of the concerned whites to wait upon the editor of the *Tribune*, and from that day forward, Ida recalled, the paper no longer promoted the separation of the city's black and white students.[37]

Soon after the Hull House meeting, Woolley asked Ida what she thought of establishing an interracial center where whites and blacks could meet on a regular basis. It was a groundbreaking concept at a time when institutions like Hull House and other settlement projects subscribed to cultural pluralism but were incapable or unwilling to confront the particular exigencies that race brought to bear.[38] At the time, only two substantive social service institutions existed that catered to African Americans: the Chicago Home for Aged and Infirm Colored People, founded in 1898 by a small group of black women, and the Institutional Church and Social Settlement founded by the AME minister Reverdy Ransom. The idea of the Frederick Douglass Center, as Woolley named it, promised to extend needed social services, as well as provide a unique space where the "best-brained" blacks could engage with their white counterparts about issues of common concern and cultural matters.[39]

Ida's response to Woolley's proposal was recorded in her autobiography: "I told her that she must have had an inspiration on the subject, because her outline was exactly the thing I mentioned in the famous conference at Hull House a few months before."[40] Wells-Barnett's implicit—and sarcastic—claim of originating the idea appeared to go over Woolley's head; after all, she had been one of the few whites to host interracial gatherings in her home, and had been largely responsible for desegregating the Chicago Woman's Club. In any case, Ida agreed to help Woolley with "her" center.

Their first order of business was to find a suitable facility. In the tradition of other settlement workers of the period, Woolley had decided to make the center a residence for her and her husband, as well as the site for the organization's activities. It was decided that Wabash Avenue would be the ideal location. The thoroughfare was located just east of State Street, the unofficial dividing line between the city's white and black communities. As one traveled east of State, neighborhoods became wealthier and more racially exclusive. Traveling west took one into the Black Belt, a thirty-block-long area (and only a few blocks wide) that began south of the downtown Loop area and stretched southward. Wabash was adjacent to the black community (in fact, Quinn AME Church was on South Wabash) and a symbolically appropriate location for the center.

Symbols, however, were just what property owners were afraid of. When they learned what Woolley wanted to do with the property, they refused to sell it to her. Wells-Barnett no doubt kept Woolley from being altogether discouraged. Ida and her family had recently moved east of State, on

Rhodes Avenue, at a time when few blacks had managed to do so. Indeed, Woolley was finally able to purchase a three-story house at 3032 Wabash Avenue for $5,000. However, no sooner had the women gotten over the first hurdle than another loomed—not from whites but from blacks. The ever-territorial black ministers in the area expressed their consternation about having a center in their midst, and it fell on Ida to allay not only their fears but their active resistance. Wells-Barnett's final task was to initiate a fund-raising campaign among black women so that they would have the standing of stakeholders in the center. One hundred fifty dollars was quickly collected, with promises of future contributions.[41]

Sometime in the winter of 1904–1905, the Frederick Douglass Center opened its doors. Its stated object, as member Fannie Barrier Williams noted, was "to promote better race relations, remove discriminatory practices, and encourage equal opportunity."[42] Although it attracted the usual questions—and charges—regarding the propriety of social equality and race mixing, it developed quickly and successfully. Based on the Hull House model, its first year saw an array of classes, programs, and activities, including the establishment of a kindergarten, an adolescent Boys' Club, a Girls' Club, and a gymnasium. Ferdinand himself later conducted sociology classes there and started a boys' athletics club. Black women's clubs, including the Ida B. Wells Club, used the Wabash address for their own meeting place as well.[43]

Ida's activities gave rise to renewed rumors that she might be angling for the presidency of the NACW. "I hear Mrs. Barnett and several others are candidates for the presidency," Josephine Yates wrote Margaret Murray Washington in May of 1904.[44] But Ida did not run for the office, and it is doubtful that she was even a full participant in the Frederick Douglass Center's early formative period. On September 3, she gave birth to her fourth child and second daughter, Alfreda, on the second floor of her Rhodes Avenue home. When the baby was delivered by the Chicago physician George Cleveland Hall, Ida was forty-two years of age; Ferdinand, fifty-two.

AGAIN, IDA HAD been distracted by maternal responsibilities during a period of important political and social developments. During the first three months of 1904, the thirty-one lynchings recorded had renewed the nation's focus on them. In 1903, the Equal Opportunity League protested two lynchings in Illinois—in Danville and Belleville—and the issue subsequently prompted the black legislator Edward Green to propose an anti-lynching bill that held authorities accountable for failing to protect prisoners.[45]

Another lynching, which received national coverage, was so egregious that even Booker Washington was moved to criticize it publicly. The victims were a black man and his wife, the former of whom had fatally shot James Eastland, member of a prominent Mississippi planter family. When the fleeing couple was caught by a mob, the two were tied to trees while a pyre was being prepared. They were forced to hold out their hands so that their fingers could be lopped off, one at a time, and distributed for souvenirs. Their ears were cut off, the man's eye was poked out with a stick, then members of the mob, estimated to be a thousand strong, and which included two of Eastland's brothers, used a large corkscrew to bore spirals of "raw, quivering flesh" out of the couple's arms, legs, and bodies. If the "law is disregarded when a Negro is concerned; it will soon be disregarded when a white man is concerned" was Washington's warning. "And besides" he understated, "the rule of the mob destroys the friendly relations which should exist between the races." The remarks were sent, via the Associated Press to numerous papers, including the *New York Times*.[46]

Uncharacteristically, Ida had written her one major piece that year not about lynching, but about Booker Washington and education. "Booker T. Washington and His Critics," published in the mainstream publication *World Today*, plied themes similar to those in Du Bois's *Souls*, adding specific examples of assertions Du Bois had made and she now repeated. For example, Wells-Barnett told how the railway magnate Collis Huntington had been giving money to Livingston College in Salisbury, North Carolina, until he began believing that Washington was "educating Negroes in the only sensible way, [and] henceforth his money for that purpose would go to Tuskegee." And Ida repeated one of those deprecating stories about blacks that Washington told to elite white audiences—in this case before the Chicago Woman's Club. "Well, John, I am glad to see you are raising your own hogs," began his recitation before the women. "Yes, Mr. Washington, ebber sence you done tole us bout raisin our own hogs, we niggers round her hab resolved to quit stealing hogs and gwinter raise our own."[47]

Ida's choice of subject in a white publication might have been chosen for her. Now that she was no longer the head of the Anti-Lynching Bureau, her authority on the issue was no longer a given and she must have been appalled when the prestigious *North American Review* apparently solicited not hers but Mary Church Terrell's opinion on lynching. In "Lynching from a Negro's Point of View," Terrell, like Ida, cited statistics that questioned the assertion that lynchings occurred in response to rapes, but the difference in the two women's attitudes about class was also evident. Responding to the charge that black aspirations toward social equality inspired sexual assaults, Terrell insisted that "ignorant" Negroes—those most apt to commit the crime—did not even know what the term "social equality" meant. On the other hand, northern-educated blacks, the most likely to be socially ambitious, were the least likely to assault women or commit other crimes, she concluded.[48]

But the most salient development of 1904, a presidential election year in which the Republican Convention was due to be held in Chicago, was the intensified effort of Washington to control the *Conservator* and to remove Ferdinand Barnett from the Negro Bureau position. Both were obstacles to Washington's designs in general and for his desire to dominate Chicago, specifically.

FOR THE TUSKEGEEAN, the Windy City was an important rampart. It was an epicenter of Republican politics in the Middle West, contained wealthy businessmen/philanthropists, and had a growing population of blacks. Between 1890 and 1900, the number of African Americans rose from a little over fourteen thousand to more than thirty thousand—many of them born outside of Illinois and in the South. As Washington might have gleaned from the meeting of his National Negro Business League held in Chicago in 1901, there was a large constituency of the kind of up-from-the-bootstrap business-minded men who were more concerned with the ready-made South Side black market that had been created by Chicago's segregated housing policies than with disruptive racial practices. As black Chicago was becoming more and more a city unto itself, such men were poised to eclipse the integrationist-minded leaders like those in the Equal Opportunity League. For the Wizard, the Windy City was a ripening plum to be plucked, but the fruit was still clinging stubbornly to its vines.[49]

With the formation of the Equal Opportunity League, the city now had an effective "anti-movement" as S. Laing Williams, Washington's most prolific informant in Chicago, had told Emmett Scott in October 1903; and the *Conservator* was the organ through which it spoke.[50] A letter Washington wrote to Theodore Roosevelt in 1903 revealed that he had yet to tame the Chicago paper, which remained critical of the Tuskegeean and unpredictable in its views about the president. "In order that you may be informed as to the attitude of the colored people regarding your administration, I take the liberty of sending you the names and addresses of 178 Negro newspapers published in this country," Washington's letter began. He went on to explain that all but five of the papers "heartily" supported TR. Two newspapers, the *Washington Bee* and the *Boston Guardian* were listed as "opposed" to the administration; the *Conservator, Cleveland Gazette,* and the *Jersey City Appeal* were listed as "uncertain."[51]

Uncertainty was something that Booker T. Washington could not afford—particularly in Chicago, where the Bookerites had revealed themselves to be a poor match against the "anti-movement" men. "Your followers may be equal in number to those arrayed against you," wrote Theodore Jones, a Chicagoan and successful furniture dealer who belonged to Washington's business league, "but they are far out classed by brain, tact, and influence: the opposing faction has the ear of the public and courtesy of the press; while we have neither."[52]

In late 1903, Washington asked Fortune to wire S. Laing Williams to "acquaint himself with the proprietorship of Conservator as it will be helpful."[53] At the time, Washington was feeling especially pressured to line up his ducks. Earlier in the year, *Boston Guardian* editor Monroe Trotter and his "Trotterites" had disrupted a meeting of the Negro Business League in the city; the subsequent row had turned into fisticuffs that required the intervention of police (one of whom was stabbed with a hat pin by Trotter's sister, Maude). Trotter was convicted and sentenced to thirty days in jail, and though few condoned the editor's methods, many saw the heavy-handedness of the Tuskegee machine in the adjudication of the case, the vilification of Trotter in the papers, and subsequent efforts to bankrupt the *Guardian* through a libel suit in which one of the paper's owners was coerced to testify against Trotter and sell his stock in the publication.[54]

One of them was W. E. B. Du Bois, who in January of 1904 was scheduled to lead the anti-Bookerite faction at a meeting in New York's Carnegie Hall. Alarmed by the mounting opposition, Washington had come up with an idea of a summit conference to include twenty-five race leaders (all men) who both opposed and supported his position. But the real purpose of the "unity" conference—and the Wizard's ability to outmaneuver his adversaries—was revealed when, toward its end, Washington's powerful white allies, including Andrew Carnegie, Oswald Garrison Villard, grandson of abolitionist William Lloyd Garrison and owner of the *Nation* and the *New York Post*, and three members of the Southern Education Board, which provided funding for black schools, unexpectedly appeared and expressed their support for him.[55]

In the meantime, S. Laing Williams was providing more than enough information about the *Chicago Conservator*. Du Bois ally Charles Bentley told the scholar that Washington, through S. Laing and Fannie Barrier Williams, had offered the *Conservator*'s editor, R. D. Wilkins, three thousand dollars a year to publish columns that supported the work at Tuskegee.[56] Wilkins told Bentley that he had refused the offer, and in February the *Conservator* charged that Washington had attempted to buy his influence. It is not clear what elapsed between February and May, but correspondence between Wilkins and Washington revealed that they had come to an "understanding."[57]

By then, Allison Sweeney, formerly the editor of the *Indianapolis Freeman* (and a guest at the Barnett wedding), was, with encouragement from Washington, making a bid for the editorship on the basis that he would be able and willing to receive substantial monies from Tuskegee. At the time, the *Conservator* was probably facing financial difficulties, for which Ida might have been partly responsible. In the wake of the *Conservator*'s editorials against Bethel minister Abraham Murray, Archibald Carey of Quinn Chapel, who was also criticized for supporting him, withdrew his own church's business from the paper—a possibly serious blow to its income. Perhaps her asking for a loan of one hundred fifty dollars in 1904 from Robert Church, her onetime benefactor in Memphis (and Mollie Terrell's father), reflected Ida's efforts on the paper's behalf.[58]

Nevertheless, by July of 1904, the *Conservator* die was cast. Sweeney became the paper's editor and received a congratulatory note from Washington. "My dear Mr. Sweeney," wrote Washington in a letter to him on July 16, Ida's birthday, "I want to congratulate you upon the new position which you are occupying as editor of the Conservator." There was no doubt who was now in charge. "It seems to me," Washington continued, "what we need just now more than anything else is a policy of construction, calling the attention of the country to the progress that the race is making and not altogether to the weak points that may exist. . . . Under your wise guidance I am sure that the Conservator will be made a power in this direction."[59] Chicago's banner protest vehicle was now in enemy hands, and the Barnetts must have been distressed to witness Sweeney's subsequent mismanagement of the paper in which publication dates were sometimes missed for weeks at a time. However, the struggle over the Conservator was not mentioned in Ida's writings.[60]

Nor did she mention how Washington was circling Ferdinand Barnett, trying to get him replaced in his position at the Negro Bureau. "Barnett and his wife who had it during the last two campaigns will want it again, but we must defeat Barnett if possible," Washington wrote Charles Anderson, his most important operative in New York. "During the first two years of the Presidential campaign he and his wife spent their time and effort in stirring up the colored people and embittering them against the President, and the last few months of the term they spent their time in trying to prove their loyalty to the powers that be." He concluded, "Both Barnett and his wife abused McKinley shamefully during the first part of his administration and they did the same thing in regard to President Roosevelt, and in both cases at the proper time they laid low, and time has come when such treachery should be punished as it ought to be."[61]

But the task proved to be a difficult one—even for the Wizard. Ferdinand had an excellent record as an assistant state's attorney and had connections with both white progressives and blacks. As Washington no doubt knew, Ferdinand's appointment had come through Edward H. Wright, a black Cook County commissioner. The New York–born Wright was a graduate of City College and arrived in Chicago "penniless and unknown" aboard a train in which he had earned his way by assisting a Pullman porter. Eventually, he landed a job in the registry department of the post office, where he attracted the attention of politicians and effectively worked his way up in the Republican organization; in 1896, he won a position as county commissioner and was admitted to the bar. At the time, Charles Deneen, running for state's attorney, asked for Wright's support, and the commissioner gave it to him in return for a pledge that if Deneen was elected he would appoint Barnett as assistant state's attorney. Deneen won the election but stalled on his part of the bargain, telling an inquiring Wright that he would make the appointment "when he got around to it." Wright bided his time until the county board met to appropriate the funds for Deneen's office, which the commissioner pointedly held up. When an angry Deneen confronted Wright, the black commissioner told him that he would not budge until he fulfilled his promise. "I am the State's Attorney of Cook County," Deneen was said to shout. "You can't dictate to me." As Wright turned to walk out the door, he told Deneen, "Yes, and I am County Commissioner and you can't dictate to me." A few days later, in January of 1896, Charles Deneen announced the appointment of Ferdinand Barnett; soon afterward, Deneen got his appropriation.[62]

Although the fate of many black politicians had been sealed with the demise of McKinley and the loss of influence of his power broker Mark Hanna (who died in 1904), Ferdinand had since established his own ties with Elmer Dover, a former secretary to Hanna and soon-to-be secretary of the Republican National Committee. By August, Washington raised the white flag of defeat in a letter to Emmett Scott. Roosevelt's campaign manager had decided against a separate Negro Bureau, Washington told his secretary, "but it is very probable that Barnett will be a prominent factor owing to the fact the Dover friend, has such a strong position in Chicago."[63]

BARNETT'S WIFE WAS fully ready to emerge in 1905, the year that W. E. B. Du Bois convened the first meeting of the Niagara Movement at Niagara Falls, Canada. Fifty-nine men had answered the scholar's "Call" that promised "organized determination and aggressive action on the part of men who believe in Negro freedom and growth" and opposition to "present methods of strangling honest criticism." No women were among the twenty-nine delegates from fourteen states who came together to implement Du Bois's principles, but the question of their membership was debated at the meeting. Monroe Trotter objected to the inclusion of women; Du Bois proposed a woman's auxiliary. In the end, the Movement's constitution made no gender distinction, and, subsequently, women were named to the position of secretary for women in the South, but there is no indication that they had access to the movement's inner counsels. The development only helped Booker Washington to consolidate his own allies among clubwomen. "Write Mrs. Talbert to keep you closely informed about proceedings and names of people connected to . . . the [Niagara] meeting," Booker Washington wrote his wife. Mary Burnett Talbert was an Oberlin-educated teacher living in Buffalo and was then serving as the president of the NACW-affiliated Empire State Federation of Women's Clubs.[64]

Ida focused her energies on a different endeavor: an interracial women's organization within the Frederick Douglass Center. With the opening of the Frederick Douglass Women's Center on September 13, Woolley had bravely pushed the cause of interracial exchange further. And again, Ida was asked for her advice. This time the minister maladroitly asked her what she thought of a white woman being president of the organization, specifically, Ida's ally, Mary Plummer. "If you plan to place a white woman at the head, Mrs. Plummer would be the best choice," Ida responded, but as her autobiography makes clear, she was insulted by the question. "I saw very clearly that [Woolley] had determined not only that I should not be president but that she had wanted a white woman," she wrote.[65] Nonetheless, Ida agreed to preside over the organizing meeting where Plummer, in absentia, was named president. Once the office was secured, Woolley announced that she thought a colored woman should be vice president and proceeded to nominate Ida for the position. At first Ida declined, but when no one else would volunteer for the office, Ida claimed that she accepted it reluctantly and only until a substitute could be found.[66]

Already disgruntled about the situation, Wells-Barnett became more so by Plummer's frequent and sometimes late-announced absences. On one occasion, Ida had to hastily pull a program together when the president informed her at the last minute that she and the speaker she had arranged for a meeting would be unable to attend. Ida came up with a symposium, "What It Means to Be a Mother." Ida rounded up an artist, a minister, a physician, and a lawyer to talk, presumably, about balancing motherhood with their professions. It was a "glorious meeting," Ida recalled—until the end when Woolley was asked to say a few words. The minister then proceeded to remind the young women in the audience that there were indeed many influential women who were not mothers, among them Jane Addams, Susan B. Anthony, and Mary McDowell, a founder of the Women's Trade Union League. "All of what she said was true," Ida wrote, but it seemed like a dash of cold water on the enthusiasm she had aroused. After the encounter, the relations between Woolley and Ida began to quickly deteriorate. "From that time on Mrs. Woolley never failed to give me the impression that she did not propose to give me much leeway in the affairs of the Center," Ida wrote.[67]

If Wells-Barnett had possessed such "leeway," she would have directed both the Frederick Douglass Center, which, by 1906, had more than three hundred members, and the Women's Center, which numbered seventy, two-thirds of whom were black, to focus more on the growing number of poor blacks, especially southern migrants. The mission of the centers was a subject of debate. A faction, probably the majority, wanted to retain its primary identity as a middle-class, race-relations salon of sorts. Woolley and Fannie Barrier Williams were a part of that group. Willams, correctly, made the point that the center had not been organized to "do slum work," but to "be the center of wholesome influences to the end that well-disposed white people may learn to know and respect the ever-increasing number of colored people who have earned the right to be believed and respected."[68]

Black middle-class Chicagoans had reason to be more sensitive than most about their image. No other city was more adept at thwarting the integration of black middle- and upper-class families into its white neighborhoods, more agile in transforming an all-white neighborhood into an all-black one once a single black family managed to move there, or more efficient in establishing centers of vice in a residential area after whites had fled it. Vice in the Windy City was well organized, well financed, biracial, and, as many knew, could not flourish without the support of the political establishment and law-enforcement authorities. Nevertheless, its appearance and the social anomalies that followed stereotyped all blacks and their residential areas.

The Barnetts were well aware of these patterns. In 1905, amid the tensions of a teamsters strike, a black man who lived only two doors away from their former residence on Princeton Avenue had been shot and killed when he crossed the nearby unofficial boundary that whites had deemed "the Deadline" at Twenty-seventh and Wentworth Avenue.[69] And when Ida's family became one of the first blacks to move east of State Street, on Rhodes Avenue, they were met by the hostility of their neighbors, who showed their displeasure by shaking their rugs or banging their doors shut when Ida appeared on the porch. The Barnett boys found themselves in scrapes with whites in the neighborhood, and once, when a white gang pursued Herman and Charles right up to their doorstep, they were only thwarted when Ida appeared at the doorway and dared them to cross the threshold. Ida, it was known in the neighborhood, possessed a gun.[70]

The presence of the Barnetts had signaled the beginning of the inevitable white flight that would, in less than a decade after their arrival, result in the neighborhood becoming predominantly black, a transformation that also brought with it the appearance of several brothels in the immediate radius of their home. As Fannie Williams observed, the housing situation dictated the "huddling together of the good and the bad" in the Black Belt, and its "corrupting effect" was palpable. Woolley had a less subtle way of putting it. The Unitarian minister wrote of the "hordes" of southern blacks, most of them "ignorant and dissolute," who "lowered the standard of the colored population in our midst."[71]

There are no extant comments from Wells-Barnett regarding the issue, but in 1906, when she was given one of her apparently rare "leeways," she dragged the center, kicking and screaming, toward her own point of view. In that year, she was put in charge of the Frederick Douglass Center's annual charity ball, an assignment that appeared to be immune from Ida's willfulness. Wells-Barnett had attended the center's first charity ball, held the year before and organized by Theodocia B. Hall, wife of Ida's physician George Cleveland Hall. It had been held at the Masonic Temple and attended by the "cream" of the Chicago "Four Hundred," the name given to black Chicago's social registry. The VIPs, dressed in formal attire, led the grand march, set to music, that opened the gala. The lavish gowns worn by the women received special notice by the *Broad Ax*. Theodocia Hall wore a décolleté lavender gown; Ida donned a dress with black silk trimming; Fannie Emmanuel, a chiropodist, was said to have the most expensive outfit, a lace woven dress that cost $500. A long line of carriages stood waiting to convey the "merry dancers to their respective homes" at the end of the evening in which a "fine time" was had by all.[72] One can only imagine the consternation of Ida's colleagues at the center when she informed them that the 1906 charity ball would be held in a converted saloon, located in the heart of the Black Belt and owned by a gangster.

Wells-Barnett's choice of venue, the New Pekin Theater at Twenty-seventh and State Street, owned by Robert T. Motts, showed how far she had come in her attitudes about class. Two decades earlier, she had been critical of social events in which the educated classes hobnobbed with what was commonly called the "sporting types," those involved with gambling, saloons, and the like. But what now distinguished Ida's ideas about class was not her concern about helping the lower economic classes—black women, especially, took the NACW's motto, "Lifting as We Climb," as a sacred trust—but in determining who among the poorer classes deserved to be helped. For understandable reasons, blacks, especially, were concerned about traditional notions of "respectability," whatever one's social class might be. The idea also affected black social institutions that would soon increase in number in Chicago. For example, past work histories were weighed by the Home for Aged and Infirm Colored People before one could be admitted. Wells-Barnett's experience with the ways that lynching victims were criminalized, and her progressive belief in the ability of persons to change for the better, gave her another perspective.[73]

When Ida's committee members balked about the New Pekin, and especially its owner, Ida's response was that she thought it was their duty "to forget the past and help him; that if he was willing to invest the money in something uplifting for the race we all ought to help."[74] Robert Motts certainly had a past. In 1903, amid a crackdown on vice in the city, his saloon license had been revoked for, as the *Broad Ax* noted, "harboring young girls in his place whom it is claimed paid tribute to the police." Said to be worth $300,000, there was little doubt that Motts was one of the leading kingpins of Chicago, whose reach was long. The Equal Opportunity League's Edward Morris, Motts's lawyer, had won a seat in the state legislature due to the saloon owner's influence, then promptly lost it when he supported a measure to legalize the "numbers racket."[75]

Still, the sum of Motts's parts added up to more than his foibles. Born in Iowa, he had arrived penniless to Chicago in 1881 and subsequently established a successful saloon and owned valuable real estate on the South Side. He also worked to improve conditions in the Black Belt. In 1900, Motts had worked with Ida's friend Reverend Reverdy Ransom at Bethel to defeat an unresponsive alderman who had refused to do anything about the poor quality of the roads that surrounded the church. At election time, Motts hired campaign workers whom he paid to register voters and get them to the polls. He was also said to have secured the employment of at least forty black women in the city recorder's office.[76]

But Ida appeared to be most impressed by Motts's intention to turn over a new leaf. He had employed more than a hundred black workers to refurbish his saloon into a lavish, modern, top-of-the-line theater in the heart of the Black Belt. Ida had maintained her interest in the theater and still attended concerts—she had recently heard the black classical pianist Samuel Coleridge Taylor at the Music Hall—and she had heard of Motts's plans from the vaudevillian Bob Cole. The New Pekin had opened in March, and she and Ferdinand were impressed when they went to see it. Motts had remodeled the place to resemble the continental music halls of Europe, which he had seen on one of his trips abroad, where patrons in its twelve-hundred-seat auditorium could enjoy skits, serious drama, music, and variety acts while they ate and drank without worrying about the attitudes of white proprietors or waiters. Motts was the first African American to own such a theater, which had its own stock company of composers and musicians, as well as directors, writers, and singers.[77]

Nevertheless, once the announcement got out that the ball would be held at the New Pekin, there was a storm of controversy. The *Chicago Daily News*, citing the reputation of Mott, refused to run a notice about the affair. Some of the Four Hundred promised to boycott it, and when the Reverend Archibald Carey, whom Ida had earlier castigated for his support of a dissolute minister, heard the news, he howled. From his pulpit Carey denounced Motts as a "would-be race leader and the keeper of a low gambling dive" and subsequently sent a copy of the sermon to local newspapers, including the *Conservator*. Ironically, it was Ferdinand Barnett who got his lawyer, Edward Wright, to serve notice to the paper that publishing Carey's charges would lead to a defamation suit. Carey then took his campaign to the influential Olivet Baptist Church, which was right across the street from the theater. Carey got its minister, Elijah Fisher, so stirred up that he told his congregation that if he ever set foot in the Pekin, "he hoped that his tongue would cleave to the roof of his mouth and his right hand forget its cunning." As a final effort, Carey got the ministerial alliance to wait on Woolley to protest, even saying that they would ask their congregations to give the Frederick Douglass Center a special offering in lieu of holding the affair at the Pekin. To her credit, and remembering their earlier resistance, Woolley reminded them that they had always been against the center, and, in any case, she was not about to get in a snit with Ida about it.[78]

By that time, the controversy had heightened so much interest in the affair that ticket sales became increasingly brisk. Jane Addams, a firm believer in the mutual benefit that both the middle class and the poor derived by direct engagement, assumed the cost of the troupe and musicians for the performance. Flora Batson, a well-known singer from Philadelphia, sang "Little Brown Baby" with lyrics by Paul Laurence Dunbar. At the successful program's end, Ida was escorted to the stage to thank the patrons—and offer a few choice words regarding the behavior of certain ministers she did not name, but whom everyone knew. Although the attendees listed in the newspaper did not include many of the upper echelon, the benefit, according to the local papers was a great success, raising five hundred dollars.[79]

Wells-Barnett was quite pleased with herself. The New Pekin, she noted in her autobiography, went on to great notoriety and became a symbol of pride in the community. Actors like Charles Gilpin, who later originated the title role in Eugene O'Neil's *Emperor Jones,* played there, as well as a young tap dancer by the name of Bill "Bojangles" Robinson. Its stock company musicians included Joe Jordan, who composed the national hit "The Pekin Rag" and popular performers like Scott Joplin and Jelly Roll Morton included the Pekin on their tours.[80]

Following the charity ball, the theater became a quite acceptable venue and was used frequently by prominent black organizations. In fact, the Olivet minister, Elijah Fisher, who had earlier talked about his tongue cleaving to his mouth, even agreed to speak there on one occasion to address a political meeting. When he got up on stage, Ida churlishly reported, he was stricken with a paralysis from which he never fully recovered.[81]

For Ida, the charity ball might have been a part of a larger design. Soon after, the *Broad Ax* published a series of articles that praised Ida and criticized Woolley and blacks at the Center. The object of the paper's complaint was a *Boston Transcript* interview, later circulated as a fund-raising letter, that spoke of Woolley's efforts to benefit the "uncouth," "ill-bred" poor in need of "love and unbound sympathy." Woolley was misrepresenting the Frederick Douglass Center to potential donors, the *Broad Ax* insisted. How she or members of the black bourgeoisie were helping the downtrodden was "shrouded in mystery," the paper sneered, although money was being raised on that basis. Another issue of the *Broad Ax* noted how Woolley "recoiled at being in the company of poorer blacks," and also felt superior to middle-class black women, many of whom, the *Broad Ax* snapped, could "buy and sell her many times in wealth and education." And yet Woolley had been heard to declare that black women "lacked executive ability" regardless of their level of education. The only name besides Woolley mentioned in the articles was that of Wells-Barnett, who the *Broad Ax* claimed had "too much prominence" to be in the position of being "bossed over by a white lady." Ida, the paper averred, "was the only figure at the center who was concerned with the poor in the Black Belt and in its red-light district."[82]

It is not clear where the *Broad Ax* was getting its information; but Mary Plummer was planning to retire from the presidency of the Women's Center, and Ida considered running for the office. As Wells-Barnett explained in her autobiography, she was determined only to do so with Woolley's support. The conviction might have been a recognition of Woolley's influence, or it could have been a power play on Ida's part. In any case, Ida got neither the support nor the position.[83]

By the fall of 1906, Wells-Barnett also reached the breaking point with Plummer, her onetime ally, in the wake of the Atlanta riot, the likes of which hadn't been seen since Wilmington. The ingredients that burst the city into flame were familiar: press accusations of a "torrid wave of black lust and fiendishness," prohibitionist anxieties, and a close gubernatorial race. The final detonator was the opening of the The Clansman, a play by Thomas Dixon, about a Confederate soldier cum Ku Klux Klansman, who returns home after the war to save his South and his girl from the lascivious clutches of enfranchised blacks. The subsequent rampage of burning and murder by the ten-thousand-member mob, and the police who abetted it, did not spare the black middle-class section of Brownsville, where Clark College and Atlanta University were located. Four of the twenty-five blacks killed during the riot included four Brownsville residents.[84]

The horror of the scene moved W. E. B. Du Bois to write his impassioned "A Litany at Atlanta," which petulantly demanded the whereabouts of God on such a day. In it, he condemned, he hoped forever, the philosophy that told a man to "Work and Rise!" at the exclusion of other concerns only to "lieth maimed and murdered, his wife naked to shame, his children to poverty and evil."[85]

Among the approximately one thousand blacks who fled the city was J. Max Barber, editor of the Atlanta-based Voice of the Negro. After protesting the charge that blacks were responsible for the conflagration, he became another of the courageous, exiled editors whose lives were threatened after refusing to be silent. Barber went to Chicago where he found temporary refuge in the home of Charles Bentley; soon after, he was asked to give an eyewitness account of his experience before the Frederick Douglass Center.[86]

If Barber's article published in the Voice of the Negro was any guide, he vividly portrayed the pandemonium in the city, "the agonizing shrieks and wails of hapless men, women and children wounded and dying." Following his presentation, Mary Plummer, according to Wells-Barnett, ignored the "harrowing details" that he had recounted and, in her own subsequent remarks, urged blacks to "drive the criminals out from among you." The comment did not come out of thin air. During the tensions in Atlanta, Booker Washington had actually complied with requests to exhort blacks to be law-abiding and desist from assaulting white women! When Plummer blurted that every white woman she knew in the South was afraid to walk the streets at night, Wells-Barnett was shocked because she had believed that Plummer was one white woman free from that level of prejudice. Wells-Barnett took her to task about the remarks and reminded her of the lynching evidence that she had been documenting for nearly fifteen years. Plummer replied, "My dear, your mouth is no more a prayer book than that of any other of my friends who have talked with me about this subject."[87]

As Wells-Barnett probably suspected, Woolley's sentiments coincided with Plummer's. The riot, Barber's presence in Chicago, Allison Sweeney's anger at not getting the Tuskegee monies promised, as well as Washington's Atlanta comments had resulted in the *Conservator* writing a critical editorial about the Wizard. S. Laing Williams reported the *Conservator*'s misbehavior to Emmett Scott and included the latest box score of who was for Washington and who was against Du Bois. Among those he named was Celia Woolley. "She had become thoroughly sick of Du Bois," Williams wrote. "She calls his 'litany' was [*sic*] simply 'sickening.'"[88]

Ida tried, she said, to take the advice of Ferdinand, who told her that she should not burn her bridges. Although her husband continued to be active in the Frederick Douglass Center, she could not bring herself to have any meaningful association with Plummer or Woolley. She had other things to tend to, Ida noted in her autobiography. In September, her husband had thrown his hat in the ring for a municipal judgeship.

CHAPTER EIGHTEEN

Calls

> Either the spirit of the abolitionists . . . must be
> revived and we must come to treat the negro on a
> plane of absolute political and social equality, or
> Vardaman and Tillman will soon have transferred
> the race war to the North.
>
> —*William English Walling*

Nineteen hundred six appeared to be a prime year for black advancement in the Windy City. With the 1905 election of Edward F. Dunne, Chicago had a "socialist" mayor who appointed his "long-haired friends" and "short-haired women" to an administration dedicated to the working- and middle-classes, municipal ownership of the transit system, tax equity, and education reform. In 1906, Dunne had appointed former *Conservator* editor D. R. Wilkins as a member of a Charter Commission that was to reorganize the public school system.[1]

Wilkins was a representative of the Niagara/Equal Opportunity League movement in the city and hoped to steer the commission toward legislation that would ensure that the schools remained integrated. In the same year, Dunne, a former circuit court judge, had established the municipal court: the first modern metropolitan court system in the country, and the first unified court to incorporate specialized divisions, such as juvenile and domestic relations courts. The new court needed judges, and blacks in Chicago wanted one of their own to be among them.[2]

In June of 1906, a number of black leaders met at Quinn Chapel to decide upon the candidate that they would urge the Republican Party to support for one of the twenty-seven municipal judgeships. Edward Wright, S. Laing Williams, and Edward Morris were all available for the position, but Ferdinand Barnett was the best choice.[3]

His reputation for competence and integrity was superior to the other candidates. As the *Broad Ax* noted, Ferdinand's record as a lawyer and ten-year stint as assistant state's attorney of Cook County had earned him a high rating from the Chicago Bar Association. He had developed the procedures for the newly organized juvenile court, had been in charge of prosecuting antitrust violations against large corporations, and for the past eight years had had charge of extradition and habeas corpus proceedings. The paper added that Ferdinand spoke German and for the past year had been the point man for all office matters requiring the use of that language. Most important was that Barnett had held the line against corruption in a county that was filled with it.[4]

According to the *Broad Ax,* he had successfully argued an Illinois Supreme Court case that overturned a superior court injunction that held over justices of the peace with dubious reputations. On a number of occasions he had also prevented the discharge of criminals who had "friends" among the judges in the lower courts. In one instance, in 1903, when Barnett ordered the rearrest of such a criminal, the judge in the case had cited him for contempt and sentenced him to jail. And despite Ferdinand's tough-minded determination, he had a mild, quiet demeanor that could be mistaken by those who did not know him for softness or even tractability—a quality that helped him get along with blacks and whites. Finally, Barnett's influence was strengthened by the 1904 gubernatorial election of Charles S. Deneen, the former state's attorney who had appointed him.[5]

However, once Barnett announced his candidacy in the countywide election, Chicago soon revealed its own limits of reform—and tolerance. Although African Americans numbered only thirty thousand out of the total population of more than one and a half million, race, particularly against the backdrop of tensions elsewhere, loomed large in the minds of Chicagoans. There was the smoldering specter of the September Atlanta riot and the images of *The Clansman* due to open in Chicago later in the year. More disturbing was the prospect of retaliation by armed blacks. In

August, three companies of the black Twenty-fifth Infantry had been accused of murder and other crimes in Brownsville, Texas, where they were stationed.

The battle-hardened soldiers who had fought in Cuba and the Philippines had been ordered to Fort Brown only to endure from townspeople constant harassment, threats, and charges—including an alleged attempted rape of a white woman. On August 13, a ten-minute shooting spree broke out in an alley near the fort, which killed a white bartender and wounded a policeman. While the soldiers later admitted to War Department investigators that they had armed themselves that day because they had heard of an impending attack from a white mob, they denied leaving their posts, firing their weapons, or knowing who the shooters were. During the fall campaign season, the matter was still under investigation. In the meantime, Democrats were stoking racial unrest in the election year by sending out on tour Ben "Pitchfork" Tillman, the charismatic South Carolina senator and Negrophobe. He was due to come to Chicago at the end of November.[6]

Local Democrats did their part by distributing a poster that pictured Ferdinand with exaggerated Negroid features: a fly-in-the-buttermilk reminder for those who customarily voted straight Republican tickets. The *Chicago Chronicle* (a nominally Republican paper that had been Democratic until 1904) published a crude cartoon depicting a courtroom scene in which a white woman clutching her child stood before a black judge and jury. The caption, reminiscent of the race-baiting in Wilmington, was "Vote the white man's ticket." Now that Barnett was nominated, noted the *Broad Ax,* Republican politicians and ward workers had been heard saying that they would not vote for a colored man for judge. "In other words they are pretending to be friendly to Colored people in the convention," the paper opined, "but reserve their race prejudice at the polls. . . . If all the Republican candidates are elected except Mr. Barnett, the Colored people will know where to place the blame."[7]

The *Chicago Chronicle* predicted that because of Barnett, the Deneen (progressive) machine could lose its newly gained inroads within the heavily black Second Ward (traditionally dominated by Regular Republicans). Still, Barnett's supporters hoped that he would successfully ride the coattails of the party, which was headed for the greatest plurality in an off-year election in history. Indeed, the news of the early returns were assuring.

Although Ferdinand was running twenty thousand votes behind other Republicans, the results, as they were first reported, showed that he had squeaked by, winning by 499 votes out of 200,000 cast. But the drama wasn't over. The *Chicago Chronicle* reported that there were demands that Ferdinand resign. The Democrats demanded a recount, and while the city waited for the results of the new tally, the press campaign against Ferdinand continued.[8]

The *Chronicle* asked the newly elected chief judge and progressive Republican, Harry Olson, what jurisdiction Ferdinand would preside over if the recount went in his favor. To Olson's credit, the chief judge insisted that his would not be a "Jim Crow" court, and Barnett's race would not automatically consign him to the Black Belt. The response, however well-meaning, unleashed a bilious sea of letters sent to the press.[9] One such letter was especially remarkable for its precise delineation of racial attitudes. "The negro is a man, a brother and a citizen, but he belongs to an inferior race," the letter began.

> [W]hile white people are perfectly willing to see him in public offices in which the point of inferiority is not raised they violently resent any effort to place him in a position in which he will exercise authority over them. . . . The present time is particularly unpropitious for the trial of such experiments. The two races are just now particularly antagonistic and lawless outrages by one on the other are of daily occurrence. There never was a time when a negro judge would have been so offensive as the present.
>
> Against Mr. Barnett personally nothing can be said. He is a fair lawyer and an upright and amiable man. He is naturally of a courteous and compliant rather than a firm and obstinate disposition, but while his race would make his obstinacy dangerous to him, his yielding disposition under the urgency of white attorneys would make him dangerous to the public. He should have never been nominated.
>
> The negro is admissible as a policeman, as an attorney and even as a member of the legislature, but his place is not on the bench. . . .
>
> A White Man[10]

When the results of the recount were in, it was announced that Ferdinand Barnett had not won by several hundred votes after all, but had come up a little over three hundred short of his Democratic opponent. It is not clear how accurate the recount was, but by the time it was taken, there were Democrats and Republicans who wished to see Barnett fail. He "could not have been treated much worse in the South," S. Laing Williams informed Booker Washington, who was closely following the election.[11]

In her autobiography, Wells-Barnett did not mention her husband's reaction, nor did she write of the charged racial environment that accompanied his campaign. Instead, she put Ferdinand's defeat squarely on the shoulders of the Reverend Archibald Carey and the Ministerial Alliance. Barnett had appealed to them during the campaign, she wrote, but they were still angry about the charity ball. Ida believed that their lack of support was the ultimate reason for his falling short in the vote. Her statement, in light of all that had transpired, was shortsighted at best and revealed her chronic naïveté about political matters. For even if Carey and company had actively campaigned against Ferdinand, her statement indicated that she took the results of the recount at face value.[12]

Although it would be of little immediate consolation, subsequent events showed that Ferdinand's defeat had a beneficial impact. The loss resulted in heightened black political determination, urged by calls to "Remember Barnett," made clear the limits of the Republican Party, and refocused black political organizing within the wards—which proved to be the best avenue to achieve influence in the city. But neither Ida nor Ferdinand, in terms of their private aspirations, would be the ultimate beneficiaries of the movements they created.[13]

Adding insult to the injury of black Chicagoans, President Theodore Roosevelt waited until the day after the November elections to announce his decision regarding the Brownsville soldiers: one hundred sixty-seven of them were to be dishonorably discharged. The decision was incredibly harsh. The verdict not only carried the ultimate disgrace for the military men—six of whom were Medal of Honor winners—but it left them without any possibility of a pension, of retiring to a soldiers' home, which some had contributed toward for twenty years and more, or of serving the government in uniform or as civilians. More grievously, the president's decision had been made without even giving the men the benefit of a court-martial in a case where the investigation had found no hard evidence against them. The assumption of guilt was primarily based on the vague eyewitness testimony from biased townspeople who insisted that they had seen some of the soldiers but could not identify any of them and War Department investigators who concluded that the black soldiers had formed a conspiracy of silence to protect the guilty among them. However, Roosevelt, with his racial views (he later characterized the black men as "bloody butchers . . . who ought to be hung") and perhaps with his political eye on the white South, did not need any further convincing. What had particularly riled him was that the soldiers, to a man, had refused to name any who might have been involved, despite the threats that all of them would be punished if they didn't do so.[14]

The president's action appalled the nonsouthern press, including the *New York Sun,* the *Washington Post,* and the *New York World,* which called the decision "executive lynch law." African Americans were enraged. "You cannot find a Negro who is not denouncing the President in frightful terms of abuse," S. Laing Williams wrote to Booker Washington. "I have never seen anything like it." Washington himself was taken aback by the decision, and had counseled the Rough Rider against it. But Roosevelt, who had faced down vituperation after inviting the Tuskegeean to dinner at the White House, who had fought Senate opposition to sustain several of Washington's handpicked black appointees, and who had followed the Wizard's political blueprint, had decided to ignore this, the most significant advice of all. As Washington wrote to his New York confidant Charles Anderson, he had told the president that the Brownsville decision was a "great blunder."[15]

The Wizard understood that the Twenty-fifth Infantry, one of only four African American military units authorized by Congress, was a particular source of pride for black Americans. Even those like Ida and Ferdinand, who loathed the imperialist impulses that the soldiers carried out in the rebellious Philippines and elsewhere, took pride in their tenacity and courage and supported them with fund-raising parties, Christmas tidings, and lobbying efforts on their behalf. In a letter to William Howard Taft, the secretary of war, Washington wrote, "I have never in all my experience with the race, experienced a time when the entire people have the feeling that they have now in regard to the Administration."[16]

Washington had also asked Roosevelt to delay the announcement so that it wouldn't appear so close to the election. But again, Roosevelt refused to listen, making the decision all the more onerous. The black vote was decisive in a number of states and had he issued the fiat earlier, observed the *New York Herald*, "it would have caused the Republican majority in the House of Representatives to drop from 59 to 14." Another paper noted that in Ohio, Nicholas Longworth, the president's son-in-law, would have easily been defeated by a switch of one-half of the black votes in Cincinnati. In New York, such a shift would have defeated Charles Evans Hughes in the gubernatorial contest. Ida's one-time beau Charles S. Morris, now the pastor of Harlem's Abyssinian Baptist Church, also condemned Roosevelt's timing. "He shot us when our gun was empty," he said.[17]

Washington was now riding on the back of a tiger. Roosevelt's "blunder" turned into unmitigated disaster when the president alluded to both Brownsville and the Atlanta riot in his annual message to Congress. In it, Roosevelt warned "respectable colored people . . . not to harbor criminals," implying that was what the innocent soldiers had done in regard to their comrades. As for Atlanta, while Roosevelt acknowledged that many lynch victims were innocent, he also opined that "the greatest existing cause of lynching is the perpetration, especially by black men, of the hideous crime of rape." Lynching would be ended once black criminality ceased, he continued, and the best way to achieve that was through the "best type of education for the colored man" offered by Tuskegee, Hampton, and other such schools. Echoing his Tuskegeean adviser at precisely the wrong time, Roosevelt intoned that few of their graduates were guilty of crime, especially of "the form of that brutal violence which invites lynch-law."[18]

The words couldn't have more closely followed Washington's own script. No longer able to dart surreptitiously along the political sideboards as he had with McKinley, the Wizard could never explain that Roosevelt's message and the Brownsville decision did not also have his name written all over them. The fallout, which would fully reveal itself over the coming years, lost Washington allies. Fortune's *New York Age* was critical of the decision; the Afro-American Council censured the president; Mary Church Terrell, whose husband Washington had gotten a municipal judgeship in the District of Columbia, wrote a condemnatory and well-researched article on the decision as a member of the Constitution League, a civil rights organization recently founded by the wealthy white reformer and prominent lawyer John E. Milholland. The League conducted its own investigation of Brownsville, which pointed to the innocence of the men.[19] Milholland, a former supporter of Washington, had already begun to turn away from him over the issue of disenfranchisement. Now he and other former allies, such as news-paper publisher Oswald Garrison Villard, began to question Roosevelt's emotional stability and subsequently the leadership of Washington, who continued to remain loyal to him.[20]

THERE IS NO evidence of Ida's immediate reaction to Brownsville, though in her autobiography she praised Milholland's efforts to lead the "fight against President Roosevelt" with his investigation. Wells-Barnett no doubt welcomed Washington's growing problems, but of greater concern to her was that there was no effective organization to exploit the situation.[21]

The Equal Opportunity League, with all of its talented members, was wracked by dissension. Its efforts to incorporate school antisegregation statutes in the city charter failed, and so in the end did its member, R. D. Wilkins. Abetted, no doubt, by the torturous experience with the *Conservator,* Wilkins had a nervous breakdown. He was institutionalized in 1907 after being discovered walking the streets half-clothed.[22] By the same year, T. Thomas Fortune, who had sold his *Age* interest to Washington surrogates, was on his own downward spiral. After hearing him give a lecture in Chicago, Dr. Daniel Hale Williams wrote to Booker Washington that he discerned cerebral changes taking place. The editor's "once brilliant mind is being gradually obliterated," Williams concluded.[23]

The Niagara Movement, with all of its marvelous resolutions, inspirational drama (it had held a candlelight processional at its 1906 meeting in memory of John Brown), and Talented Tenth membership list, was, according to one observer, a "feeble junta": without funds, influential white supporters, or even internal accord.[24] The NACW was embroiled in a nasty controversy in which the "color question" was raised against the light-skinned Josephine Bruce who ran for president at its 1906 meeting in Detroit. Bruce lost to the darker-skinned temperance organizer and onetime Wells-Barnett adversary, Lucy Thurman of Michigan. Perhaps it was the tensions among club women and the lack of efficiency within the Illinois clubs that inspired Ida to organize the Ideal Woman's Club in 1908. Details of the club's activities are not known, but in addition to charity fund-raising work, it focused on holding reciprocity meetings between the Illinois clubs to help them work more effectively together.

Before that year would end, however, a new phase of race leadership would emerge. The catalyst was a riot—not in the South but in the North.[25]

IN THE SWELTERING heat of August 1908, the citizens of Springfield, Illinois, were preparing for the centennial celebration of the birth of Abraham Lincoln. Born in Kentucky, Lincoln had, at the age of nineteen, moved with his family to New Salem, just a short distance away from the Illinois capital. But pride in the Great Emancipator notwithstanding, there was great racial tension in Springfield. Although blacks constituted only 10 percent of its population of fifty thousand, the increasing numbers of African Americans who were finding their way from the South to the city sharpened the three-way competition for jobs in the factories and coal mines between the black and white migrants from the South and European immigrants. As was true in Chicago, vice followed the ballooning black enclaves in the city, and, combined with the widespread corruption of city officials, Springfield rivaled larger urban areas with the proliferation of saloons, brothels, and narcotics dens.[26]

In July of 1908, Joe James, a black vagrant from Birmingham, Alabama, slashed a white man to death with his razor when the latter caught him allegedly trying to rape his sixteen-year-old daughter. A mob snatched James and beat him to a pulp but authorities managed to wrest him away and put him in custody. A little more than a month later, on Friday, August 14, citizens received the news of a twenty-one-year-old white woman by the name of Nellie Hallam who accused another black man of assault and rape.

Hallam, a married woman who had just lost a child, was reported to have been grabbed by the throat in her own kitchen, raped, and dragged out of the house into the garden where her assailant was finally scared away by Hallam's screams and the arrival of her in-laws. Arrested for the crime was an African American named George Richardson, who was found doing garden work at a residence near the Hallam house. Although Richardson and his wife insisted that he was not the assailant, and Hallam couldn't identify his face, her claim that she recognized his voice was enough to get him arrested and indicted. The black man was described in the press as a felon. Later, it was discovered that he had no criminal record. Authorities spirited both Richardson and Joe James out of town to Bloomington when there were signs that a mob was congealing outside of the jail to lynch both of the men.

When it was discovered that the men were gone, the mob's frustration was stoked by a woman named Kate Howard, a local rooming-house owner who was known for her hatred of blacks. When Howard challenged the men in the crowd to take revenge and protect their women, the mob responded. First, they destroyed the restaurant and car of the white man whose vehicle had been used to take the black prisoners away. Then they attacked any blacks they saw, including porters who were beaten at the railroad depots and black passengers who were dragged off streetcars. Subsequently, the mob, which was reported to have reached twelve thousand, set their sights on the black commercial and residential areas of the city. Property worth $200,000 was looted and destroyed; eighteen fires set off at the eastern end of the city burned down the black section of town. Two blacks were strung by the neck in the public square. Scott Burton, an elderly barber, who had tried to keep the whites at bay with a shotgun, was shot then dragged through the town by a rope before he was hung. The second victim was an eighty-four-year-old black man, William Donegan, targeted because of his thirty-four-year marriage to a white woman. Donegan was taken from his own yard, hung by a tree across from the state house, and while still alive, his throat was cut and his elderly body was hacked with knives. The black men were murdered within a half-mile of the only home Abraham Lincoln ever owned and within two miles of where his grave lay.[27]

An uneasy order in the streets was finally restored by nearly four thousand Illinois Guard militia that Monday, but following the pattern of other riot-torn cities, so many blacks were fleeing Springfield that extra railway coaches were dispatched to carry the exiles. But those who headed for the nearby cities of Peoria and Jacksonville found that their officials refused to let them in. African Americans who remained were boycotted by merchants who refused to sell them food and other necessities. In the meantime, whites scurried to take economic advantage of the chaos. Vendors sold postcards with Hallam's picture; splinters from the trees where the black men were hanged were put up for sale.

Eventually, authorities arrested a hundred fifty suspected mob leaders, though only Kate Howard was found guilty for her role in the Springfield riot. But she escaped her sentence when, on the way to the prison cell, she managed to ingest some poison and subsequently died. Two weeks after the conflagration, Nellie Hallam signed an official statement that said that neither Richardson, nor any other black man, was responsible for her assault. The guilty party, she belatedly confessed, was a white man whose identity she would not disclose.

In the riot's aftermath, Ida was contacted by several papers asking her when and where she was going to hold an indignation meeting about the violence that took place "under the shadow of Abraham Lincoln's tomb."[28] The *Broad Ax* published a letter in which the writer reminded readers that the Barnetts had been agitating about the mob-law question for years, and hoped that now others would be moved to act. But by 1908, Ida doubted if the usual church venues—meaning Quinn and Bethel—would permit her to hold the kind of meetings she had helped lead in the past. She did write a response to the riot, citing the familiar economic and race-hatred issues that impelled the violence, which was picked up by the Associated Press. But the ordeal had made her feel "impotent," she wrote in her autobiography, and she found herself reduced to venting her feelings before the Sunday-school class she was now teaching at Grace Presbyterian. When the pupils asked her what they could do, Ida invited those who were interested in discussing the issue further to come to her house later that afternoon. Three out of the class of thirty came, and Ida, typically, made the most out of it. At the end of the evening, she urged her small band to return the following Sunday and bring at least one other person with them. Soon, a lively group of young men and women were coming to her house to discuss contemporary racial matters and black history. The meetings, Ida noted, led to the formation of the Negro Fellowship League (NFL) in September of 1908, an organization that would grow over the next twelve years.[29]

Ida's hope for a national response to Springfield was buoyed when a group of white progressives, many of them from New York and all fully convinced that the time had come to support a new direction in race relations, issued "The Call" on February 12, 1909, Lincoln's birthday. Written by *New York Evening Post* and *Nation* owner Oswald Garrison Villard, it invited all "believers in democracy to join in a national conference for the discussion of present evils, the voicing of protests, and the renewal of the struggle for civil and political liberty." The conference was scheduled to take place in New York City's Charity Hall and Cooper Union on May 31 and June 1.[30] With the proclamation, it appeared that the neoabolitionist sentiment that Ida had hoped for since 1893—when she had spoken of it in Boston and had moved Villard's uncle, William Lloyd Garrison, Jr.—had finally emerged.

In addition to Villard, the core group included Mary White Ovington, a Brooklyn-born Unitarian social and settlement worker with abolitionist roots who was researching black life for a study of Negroes in New York City; Dr. Henry Moskovitz, a Jewish social worker; Charles Edward Russell, a writer and socialist; and Russell's friend and fellow socialist writer William English Walling, a settlement house worker who was born to a wealthy former slaveholding family in Kentucky. Walling was married to Anna Strunsky, a Russian-born Jew who had once been imprisoned for revolutionary activities in her native country. The Wallings had gone to Springfield to investigate the riot and were alarmed by what they witnessed. The treatment of blacks, they concluded, was worse than Russia's treatment of its Jewish minority. Walling wrote about his findings in the *Independent*. Entitled "Race War in the North," his article intoned that "Either the spirit of the abolitionists . . . must be revived and we must come to treat the negro on a plane of absolute political and social equality, or Vardaman and Tillman will soon have transferred the race war to the North."[31] After reading the article, Ovington responded to Walling immediately and urged him to host the first meetings of the group in Walling's New York City apartment. Soon the numbers grew to the point that meetings were held in the Liberal Club on Nineteenth Street and included such reformers as Rabbi Stephen Wise and Lillian Wald.[32] Determined to create a biracial organization, the reformers invited AME Zion bishop and former Afro-American Council president Alexander Walters, and another black minister, Reverend William Brooks, a friend of Ovington's, to join the group.

Sixty persons throughout the country were listed as respondents to Villard's "Call"; few of them, however, were black.[33] They included Wells-Barnett, Du Bois, Reverend Francis Grimke, Dr. J. Milton Waldron, Bishop Alexander Walters, and E. H. Clement. Ida and Mary Church Terrell were the only black women among the signers; Wells-Barnett was the only black Chicagoan on the list that also included Jane Addams, Rabbi Emil Hirsch, Jenkin Lloyd Jones, and Mary McDowell.[34] One can only imagine Ida's anticipation when she traveled to New York to take part in the first conferences of what would be later known as the National Association for Advancement of Colored People (NAACP).

On Monday, May 31, the mixed audience of about three hundred men and women heard William Hayes Ward, editor of the *Independent*, make the keynote address for a conference that marked a turning point in the discourse concerning race. Liberal anthropologists and other social scientists from Cornell and Columbia Universities challenged the principles of scientific racism and left little doubt, as Du Bois would later write, that the concept of the physiological and biological inferiority of blacks was without any scientific basis.[35]

Other panelists connected issues of race with economic, political, and social considerations. Du Bois spoke about the relationship of black disenfranchisement to cheap surplus labor in the South; Celia Parker Woolley delineated the relationship between race, women's rights, and labor. Wells-Barnett began her talk by enumerating the 3,284 men, women, and children who had been lynched since Reconstruction, and she illustrated the relationship between lynching and the lack of citizenship rights.[36]

Her speech, entitled, "Lynching, Our National Crime," emphasized the failure of the federal government to protect African American citizens.[37] Distilling her experience of nearly two decades of activism and study of the issue, she laid out succinctly, and in deceptively simple terms, the rationale for a strategy that the nascent organization would not adopt until years later. There were three salient facts about lynching, Wells-Barnett exhorted: "First: lynching is color-line murder; Second: Crimes against women is the excuse, not the cause; and Third: It is a national crime and requires a national remedy." Including her familiar statistical analysis, Ida underlined the need to address both race and gender and the necessity for federal legislation. As she noted, voluminous protests, meetings, and resolutions concerning the issue, while helpful, had failed to stop lynching. The practical remedy, she said, was to support antilynching bills such as that drawn up by A. E. Pillsbury, former attorney general of Massachusetts, then under consideration by the Senate and which called for federal prosecution of lynchers when the state failed to protect its citizens. Finally, no doubt thinking about a role she could carve out for herself, she suggested that the organization "establish a bureau for the investigation" of lynchings and for publishing its findings. This would be particularly important, she noted, because the mainstream press was abetting the mob spirit.[38]

Following the first day's triumphant presentations and a luncheon at the Union Square Hotel, a "secret" dinner meeting was held, as Washington was informed by his New York lookout, Charles Anderson.[39] Attend-

ees, according to Anderson, included Ida, Du Bois, former *Voice* editor
J. Max Barber, Nathan Mossell of Philadelphia, Bishop Alexander Walters,
the Constitution League's John Milholland, and J. Milton Waldron, a
militant minister from Washington, D.C. It is not clear what the meeting
was about, but the fact that it included the most adamant anti-Tuskegee
faction of the group was significant. According to Wells-Barnett's autobiography, there was concern that Washington would find a way to exercise
his influence over the group. Oswald Villard, though more wary of the
Tuskegeean than he had been in the past, had a long and supportive relationship with him. At the 1904 Carnegie Hall unity showdown, Villard
had come to show his support for Washington. The two were still on
friendly terms, and Villard had issued a lukewarm invitation to Washington to attend the conference. Washington, no doubt reading the tea leaves
about the direction of the organization, had politely declined, but nonetheless there was still a "Banquo's ghost" kind of anxiety about him, as Ida
characterized it.[40]

Another reason for this feeling was that Mary White Ovington, who
was very involved in the conference planning and who acted as the glue
that held together the group of strong personalities, was concerned that
without Washington's imprimatur, they would not be able to get financial
support from the philanthropist class. As she would write years later about
the founding years of the NAACP, Ovington herself was anti-Washington,
but she and Villard knew that "If you wanted to raise money in New York
for anything relating to the Negro, you must have Washington's endorsement."[41] The secret dinner meeting—taking place just before the upcoming session where resolutions and a list of "Founding Forty" charter
members were to be decided upon—was most likely a strategy session to
make sure Booker would be held at bay.

Wells-Barnett must have been satisfied about what had been decided.
Afterward, she wrote in her autobiography, it was she who allayed the fears
of William Monroe Trotter and Reverdy Ransom, among other anti-
Bookerites, who were worried about Washington. As Ida told them, she
had been privy to the Founding Forty list and she was on it and Washington was not. Moreover, she noted, the fact that Du Bois was chosen to announce the list before the meeting was further evidence that the group was
unalterably opposed to Washington.[42]

Still, the session dedicated to hammering out the resolutions and naming the list of forty was a contentious one, lasting until well after midnight. Thanks in large part to Waldron, Wells-Barnett, and Trotter, proposed resolutions were amended again and again, language was parsed, passion was high. Villard, autocratic and stone-eyed, was especially offended by the displays of "open suspicion," and "ill concealed hostility," of certain blacks who behaved "very badly," as he later wrote to his uncle, Francis Garrison.[43] In Mary White Ovington's account of the session, she mentioned both Trotter and Wells-Barnett as the two personalities who stood out. Both were at the "height of their power" and both had "little belief in our sincerity," she recalled.[44] For both Villard and Ovington, the shock of being confronted by nonobsequious blacks was probably something that they were not used to. To Ovington's credit, she recognized that she had to adjust her thinking and remind herself, as she wrote, that "the Negroes aren't poor people for whom I must kindly do something."[45]

Du Bois, while not identifying Ida by name, described in his account of the meeting how at one point, "A woman leapt to her feet and cried in passionate, almost tearful earnestness—an earnestness born of bitter experience—'They are betraying us again—these white friends of ours.'" It would be hard to imagine that he was describing anyone but Wells-Barnett, who might have been reacting to any suggestion that Washington have a role, or to the group's reluctance to support a federal antilynching bill.[46]

After the hammering out of the resolutions, which called for enfranchisement, equal educational, and job opportunities and condemned violence and prejudice, Du Bois read the names of the Founding Forty. Indeed, the list did not include Washington—but neither did it include Ida or any member of the militant faction. A motion to adopt the Founding Forty list was carried, and the meeting was adjourned—but it wasn't over. As Ida wrote in her autobiography, "bedlam" broke loose over the omissions. The exclusion of Ida was the most egregious not only because of her activist record, but because she had been told—and had told others—that she would be named. Moreover, she had been left out while Mary Church Terrell, Celia Parker Woolley, and Maria Baldwin—an unassuming, if accomplished, school principal in Cambridge, Massachusetts, who had once conducted a reading class that Du Bois attended while at Harvard—had been included on the list.[47]

At the time of the meeting, Ida was forty-six years old, and she appeared to be too enervated to engage in yet another battle to force her inclusion in an organization that was purported to be acting on behalf of the race. Although she must have been stunned by the turn of events, "I put my best face on [the situation] and turned to leave," she wrote in her autobiography.[48] But according to her account, Ida was intercepted on her way out of the room by a distressed John Milholland. He confirmed to her that he had seen the list before Du Bois had read it, and her name "had led the rest." It was "unthinkable" that she, who had fought alone for twenty years while "the rest of us were following our own selfish pursuits," had been left out, he added.[49] Taking the high road, Ida replied that evidently someone didn't want her on the list and that she was just glad that "there was going to be a committee which would try to do something in a united and systematic way, because the work was far too large for any one person." While Ida was still in the hall, she described how Mary White Ovington swept past her "with an air of triumph and a very pleased look on her face."[50]

Before Wells-Barnett could leave the premises, however, she was called back, where Walling, Du Bois, and Charles Edward Russell awaited. Du Bois told Ida that it was he who had taken her off the list, explaining that since she and her husband were members of the Frederick Douglass Center, they would be aptly represented by Celia Woolley, and that he had wanted to add Charles E. Bentley to the list to represent the Niagara movement.[51]

There is no further documentation on this curious episode, which was emblematic of Ida's future relationship with the organization. On its face, there was no rational reason for Du Bois's last-minute switch. Charles Bentley was also a member of the Frederick Douglass Center, and as Ida mentioned to Du Bois, the dentist had not even "thought enough" of the occasion to attend the New York conference. Although he might have been sincere about another Niagaran being on the committee, Du Bois's explanation that he thought Woolley, of all people, could represent her and Ferdinand was either insincere or very misguided (even if he hadn't known that she had called his "A Litany of Atlanta" "sickening"). Even Woolley herself, as Ida later learned, had gone to Villard (as had Milholland) after the meeting to say that leaving Ida off the list was a mistake.[52]

The unanswered question is, did Du Bois act on his own? Milholland certainly hadn't known about Ida's name being dropped, and he was so flustered that he told Wells-Barnett that he had offered to resign in order that her name be put back on. Villard obviously had some authority regarding the list, and he was thoroughly disgusted with the clamorous militants—especially Trotter, whom he had known at Harvard and had never much liked. He wrote his uncle, Francis Garrison, that he and Walling had even considered "withdrawing the whole scheme . . . and doing it ourselves as we saw fit."[53] But he made no mention of Wells-Barnett, and it is unlikely that he would have taken off her name without consulting the others. Ida's observation about the triumphant expression of Mary White Ovington provides a possible key to Du Bois's action.

It was Ovington who appeared to be informally in charge of deciding which blacks would join the early core of those meeting in New York. The social worker had been responsible for inviting the first African Americans to join the group, and she was also an ardent admirer of Du Bois, whom she had gotten to know after covering the Harper's Ferry Niagara meeting at the behest of Villard for the *Evening Post*. As future developments would show, Ovington was an important ally for Du Bois when disagreements broke out in the NAACP meetings. She was also prominent in Unitarian circles and it would not be illogical to assume that putting Woolley on the list—who was also a Unitarian and like Ovington had decided to live among blacks to do her settlement work—was Ovington's idea. It might have been also more than a coincidence that Charles Bentley, too, was a Unitarian.

There are other indications that Ovington believed that Ida would not have been good for the organization. In her later writings about the beginnings of the NAACP, she judged that both Wells-Barnett and Trotter were "fitted for courageous work, but perhaps not fitted to accept the restraint of organization." On another occasion, Ovington wrote that Wells-Barnett "was a great fighter, but *we* knew that she had to play a lone hand. And if you have too many players of lone hands in your organization, you soon have no game."[54]

Du Bois, a lone-hand player himself, might have welcomed the idea not to include Ida and Trotter. Both would have represented the organization's more militant flank and would have not hesitated to criticize the organization or Du Bois himself. There were also other factors deeper below the surface. The nascent organization promised not only a new political configuration but a social one as well: it was the first where both whites and blacks, and men and women, worked side by side on a public level. Sexual tension was only natural under these circumstances, as would be the heightening of both race as well as gender and class self-consciousness. Du Bois's own sensibility and relationship to the white women in the organization were enough for him to prefer to see Ida remain outside of the governing group. The well-documented hauteur of his personality would have made Du Bois chafe under Ida's pat-on-the-head attitude toward him as a junior, if promising, protégé who had only recently come around to breaking decisively with the accommodationist.

Moreover, for Du Bois, who had few social relations, if any, with women like Ida, the specter of being challenged or patronized by someone like her in front of white, attractive, female reformers, like Ovington or Isabel Eaton—a founding member who collaborated with Du Bois on the *Philadelphia Negro*—was enough to make the hairs stand up on his neck. Such women idolized the attractive scholar, who was unfulfilled in his own marriage. Du Bois's relations with them also provided a certain authority for their own professional aspirations at a time when there were efforts to elevate the status of social work through emphasizing social scientific methods and inquiry.[55] Black female migrants to the cities were becoming an important category of analysis for the studies by this group of professionals, and Ida, for one, chafed at the idea that they were becoming authorities on the subject. While the studies took the dire social conditions that such black women faced and were empathetic to them, many also assumed that black women were more promiscuous or prone to prostitution than whites.[56]

THE BROADER CONTEXT of Ida's opinion can be gleaned in an article she wrote in 1910, soon after the New York conference, and published in *Original Rights Magazine*. Entitled "The Northern Negro Woman's Social and Moral Condition," Ida anticipated soon-to-be published studies, such as Jane Addams's "Social Control," which purported to explain why blacks tended not to discipline the moral and sexual behavior of the girls in their families as Italian immigrants did, and "The Colored Woman as a Breadwinner," a chapter in Ovington's *Half a Man,* which delineated the reasons—mainly lack of gainful employment and numerical superiority in the city—why black women were more prone to selling their bodies and playing "havoc with their neighbors' sons, even with their neighbors' husbands."[57]

In her article, Ida, without mentioning any names, critiqued such opinions that made many question if poorer black women in the cities had the "same love for husbands and children, the same ambitions for well-ordered families that white women have." The persistent view of moral inferiority was the reason that, as Ida noted, "Even the Model Lodging House [in Chicago] announces that it will give all women accommodations except drunkards, immoral women and negro women."[58]

Too many whites saw black women as a monolithic undifferentiated class, Ida further complained. But she was making a different point from the more familiar protestations of the black elite; rather, she was commenting on the conflation of morality and class. Many of the "best men and women of the race make their living in menial service," Ida insisted. Finally, she implied that when black women challenged the assertions of white progressives, they were often met by "the frozen stare of the chilly word." As a result, the black woman must be "deaf, dumb and blind to gibe, insult or hostility almost invariably . . . when she accepts public invitations." Ida may have believed in the principle of interracial alliances, but she wasn't going to quietly acquiesce to privileged white liberals, especially women, on race matters, or to their tendency to be condescending and self-congratulatory about their ventures into race relations. Ovington may have been sincere, Ida thought, but her "experience has been confined solely to New York City and Brooklyn, and a few minor incidents along the color line."[59] If Ovington didn't like Ida's confrontational style, Ida had little respect for Ovington's authority. While the white settlement worker "basked" in the "sunlight of the adoration of the few college-bred Negroes who have surrounded her," Ida wrote in her autobiography, she has "made little effort to know the soul of the black woman; and to that extent has fallen far short of helping a race which has suffered as no white woman has ever been called upon to suffer or to understand."[60]

IDA HAD LEFT the New York meeting "steadfast" in her refusal to permit her name being added to the list of forty. But "somehow," she wrote in her autobiography, "before the committee sent out its letterhead they added my name to the list." It is not clear what had transpired in the interim, but Ovington wrote years later that Charles Edward Russell "quite illegally, but wisely, put her on the Committee."[61]

CHAPTER NINETEEN

Smoldering Bridges

> I cannot resist the conclusion that, had I not been
> so hurt over the treatment I had received at the
> hands of the men of my own race and thus blinded
> to the realization that I should have taken the place
> which the white men of the committee felt I should
> have, the NAACP would be a live, active force in
> the lives of our people all over the country.
>
> —Ida B. Wells-Barnett

Wells-Barnett tried not to burn the bridges with the new organization created in New York. Its interracial mix of men and women—many of whom had substantial influence and included journalists, scientists, religious leaders of all faiths, intellectuals, seasoned activists, academics, lawyers, and writers, all committed to civil rights and broader opportunities for black people—was something that she had envisioned since she had begun her antilynching campaign. But for her personally, the experience in New York that began with such promise, only for her to end up in another marginal position, was enervating at best. After returning to Chicago, Ida declined to attend the November meeting of the New York committee and admitted to Ferdinand that month that, for the first time, she was so discouraged, she was prepared to leave much of the important race work to be done by others.[1]

The admission had come in the immediate wake of a November 1909 lynching in Cairo, the port city located on Illinois's southernmost tip at the conjunction of the Ohio and Mississippi rivers. By the early twentieth century, Cairo was a largely integrated city, politically and residentially, with a volatile mix of black upper-class and southern migrants; southern-born whites; predominantly Irish and German ethnics; and Yankees. As was true in many industrial cities, labor competition was fierce and, as evidenced by the clamor of the city's Purity Leagues, so were the concerns about corruption, vice, temperance and crime. "Cairo needed a lynching to purify the town," a resident white minister was quoted as saying after the 1909 mob murder.[2]

The lynching, and the events that led up to it, had been widely covered both in the black and white press. On the ninth of that month, the nude corpse of Anna Pelley, a twenty-six-year-old shop girl, was discovered by townspeople. She had evidently been murdered on her way home from work. There was a gag in the young woman's mouth, and bloodhounds were given its scent to track down her killer. Following the "usual custom," as Wells-Barnett later wrote, "the police immediately looked for a Negro."[3] A black man named Arthur Alexander was arrested for the crime, but released by police. The dogs subsequently led authorities to William "Frog" James, a coal driver, who was said to possess a handkerchief similar to that of the gag found in the victim's mouth. With no other material evidence, James was arrested.

When the familiar strains of the lynch mob were heard, the Illinois National Guard was called in, and authorities removed James from his cell and took him twenty-five miles away to a small town in the county. But a self-appointed posse, refusing to let a second black man out of their clutches, found out where he was, took him out of the jail, and brought him back to Cairo, where a mob of ten thousand awaited their arrival.[4]

Once the posse delivered James, the mob threw a rope around his neck, dragged him off the train, and took him to the center of town. There, they threw one end of the rope over a steel arch that had a double row of electric lights, which, in that period, used blazing carbon rods powered by high voltage. Then, as Wells-Barnett would subsequently write in an article published in *Original Rights Magazine,* "The lights were turned on and the body hauled up in view of the assembled thousands of men, women, and children."[5] The *Chicago Tribune* made particular note of the spectacle of five hundred women taking the lead in pulling the rope over the arch.[6] But because the rope broke before the victim strangled to death, the crowd was impelled to continue the torture by firing hundreds of bullets into James's body. They then dragged the corpse by the rope to where the girl's body had been found. Amid jeering, laughing, and howling, a fire was built; James's body was tossed onto the flames and then pulled back out so that his internal organs could be removed and later sold. Subsequently, James's burnt head was decapitated and stuck high on a public fence post for everyone to see.

Frog James was said to have confessed to the crime and to also have implicated Arthur Alexander. An "elderly gray-haired woman," who was "refined" in appearance, was reported to have then exhorted the men not to let the "black demon escape," which sent the unsatiated mob on another rampage. When Alexander could not be found, the mob then made its way to the jail where a white man, Henry Saltzner, was being held for allegedly killing his wife. The crowd overpowered the sheriff and began to chisel and sledge-hammer the iron bars of the cell for thirty minutes while Saltzer, as described by the *Tribune,* was "reduced to a state of almost idiocy by his terror."[7] Led by a sister of the murdered wife (who Saltzner insisted was the real culprit), the mob finally penetrated the cell, dragged the man out, and hung him from a tree. As in the case of James, the body was then pierced with a fussilade of bullets. The lynching of Saltzner, a citizen later pointed out, was proof that the motive for lynching was not racial. What they were after was to protect their women.[8]

Upon reading what had happened in Cairo, a committee of blacks in Chicago, including Ferdinand Barnett; Ida's physician, George Hall; the lawyer W. G. Anderson; and Reverend Archibald Carey, held an indignation meeting in Chicago's Institutional Church (which Carey now headed.) Ferdinand reminded the assembled that the antilynching bill, passed by the legislature in 1905, had actionable provisions. The law made it "mandatory upon the governor to remove from office forthwith the sheriff of any county in which a man, black or white, has been taken by force from jail or the custody of that sheriff and lynched."[9] However, the sheriff could file a petition for reinstatement, and the governor, upon hearing the evidence, could decide to reinstate the law officer if it was shown that the sheriff had done all in his power to protect the life of the prisoner. According to Ida, it was only after the committee reminded the governor about the mandatory removal clause that he vacated the sheriff's office. But Sheriff Frank E. Davis had petitioned to get his job back and the case would soon come up to weigh the evidence.

Two black eyewitnesses had seen Sheriff Davis give a signal that directed the pursuing mob to James, but Ferdinand was unable to get anyone to appear before the authorities to testify against Davis's reinstatement. Even the eyewitnesses—Frank Dennison, a former Chicago prosecuting attorney who would later be made colonel of the Eighth Regiment, and another man, Robert Taylor—did not want to get involved with such a politically explosive situation. Complicating the situation was that Alexander County, where the crime took place, was an important stronghold for the progressive wing of the party, and the sheriff was an elected official of the faction. The men felt, Ferdinand told Ida, that the whole thing was going to be "white-washed" anyway.[10] Barnett asked his wife to go to Cairo and investigate the matter with hopes that she would find sufficient evidence to prevent the sheriff's reinstatement.

"I objected very strongly because I had already been accused by some of our men of jumping in ahead of them and doing work without giving them a chance" was how Ida responded to her husband. "It was not very convenient for me to be leaving home," she wrote in her autobiography, "and for once I was quite willing to let them attend to the job."[11] Providing a glimpse into their family dynamics, Ferdinand replied that Ida had to know how important the case was, but if she wouldn't go, there was nothing more to be said. At that point he picked up the evening paper and Ida picked up five-year-old Alfreda, whom she sung to sleep each night. She took the child to bed and dozed off beside her. Some hours later, Ida was awakened by her oldest son, Charles, who told her that it was time to get up so that she could take the train to Cairo. When Ida demurred, he remained by her bedside and finally said, "Mother if you don't go, nobody else will." There is little doubt that Ferdinand put Charles up to the persuasion tactic, and the strategy worked. Wells-Barnett, accompanied by Ferdinand and all four children, left for the train that was to take her to Cairo. Revealingly, as Ida observed, it was the first time that the entire family was willing to see her leave home.[12]

Wells-Barnett arrived in the city after nightfall and was driven to the home of a black AME minister. Sitting in his parlor, she asked for his help in providing information to investigate the case, only to be told that he and most of the black community thought Frog James a "worthless fellow" and probably guilty of the crime. Many black citizens had already written letters asking the governor to reinstate the sheriff, the minister added. When Ida heard his words, she sprang to her feet, asking him if he realized that condoning the lynching of a man like James could lead to the lynching of men of all classes. Ida had been invited to spend the night at the minister's home, she explained in her autobiography, but after the conversation, she decided to leave. Since by then it was the middle of the night, the minister's wife accompanied Ida to a house of an unnamed friend in the city, who she hoped could help her identify persons to aid her in her investigation. All in all, Ida found and interviewed twenty-five black citizens about the lynching. She also went to the site where the murdered girl had been found and asked to be taken to the spot where Frog James had been burned. That evening she called a meeting of leading black citizens in Cairo, knowing that if the community wasn't behind her, she had little chance of succeeding. Unfortunately, however, many of the blacks had already signed petitions supporting Sheriff Davis, in part because after he was suspended, his replacement fired the black deputies who had been working with him.[13]

Ida had also learned that a number of blacks felt intimidated by the authorities, and she faced the issue squarely before the assembled group. As she recounted, it became clear that she had come to understand and acknowledge the political issues that blacks confronted—something that she had not always been sensitive to. Ida was willing to be their mouthpiece, she told them, for she understood that it was difficult for those who lived in Cairo to assist in the investigation publicly. She also informed the group during the two-hour meeting that black Chicagoans stood behind them and that they were more than willing to take the lead in the matter, but that she had to know the facts. She reminded the group about her work against lynching for the last fifteen years, and that she could be trusted to do the right thing. Finally, she said that if they did not take a stand on the sheriff, they would be endangering the lives of other blacks in Illinois. At that point, Ida asked several men who had been deputies under Sheriff Davis whether he had taken the appropriate measures to protect the prisoner. Not one of them could honestly say that he had. When Ida asked them to sign a resolution to that effect, the request brought "one single objection by the ubiquitous 'Uncle Tom,'" Ida recalled. In the past, she would have condemned the naysayer, but in Cairo she begged those who couldn't or wouldn't help not to hinder her own efforts.[14]

On her way to the train the next day to go to the Springfield capital, Ida happened to hear that a meeting of Baptists was scheduled to take place in Cairo. She thought it an opportunity to add names to the resolution passed the previous night, and despite being advised that the group was unlikely to cooperate, she delayed her trip to attend the meeting. Ida was permitted to speak and told the group how their letters supporting the reinstatement sent the wrong message to the governor. Although her precise words were not recorded, Ida must have been at her best because the leader of the denomination broke down in tears after her appeal. He confessed to sending such a letter to the governor, and now, understanding its implication, regretted it. Then the minister told Ida to tell the Springfield authorities that he wanted to take back the letter. After he volunteered to sign his name to the resolution, the rest of the group followed.[15]

Now Ida had some ammunition for the Springfield hearing. On her way to the courthouse, she stopped at the post office, where a brief prepared by Ferdinand was waiting. Ida hoped that members of the black community would be at the hearing, but there was only one black face in the room: a lawyer from Springfield named A. M. Williams, who had read of her appearance and came to offer her legal advice. On the opposing side were Sheriff Davis; his lawyer, a well-known former state senator; the state's attorney of Alexander County; a parish priest; and a half-dozen other influential whites who had traveled to support the sheriff. Davis's lawyer proceeded to present the reinstatement petition backed up by letters and telegrams from both Democrats and Republicans, newspaper editors, a panoply of professional leaders, and fraternal and women's clubs. It appeared as if the "whole of the white population of Cairo was . . . behind Frank Davis," Ida noted.[16] Davis's lawyer then began reading the letters and petitions from more than five hundred of Cairo's blacks. Particular emphasis was put on these, Ida wrote, and the lawyer made special note of one of the black petitioners, whom he had known since he was a boy, and had such a reputation for "truth and veracity in the community that if he were to tell me that black was white, I would believe him."[17]

After he had finished, Governor Deneen asked Ida to present her case. She began by reading Ferdinand's brief, which reiterated the antilynching law, and then followed with the results of her own investigation, including her pièce de résistance. She showed those at the hearing the list of black names she had been able to gather who confirmed Davis's negligence in the mob murder. Included were the statements of the deputies, and heading the list was the name of the tearful Baptist minister who happened to be the model of veracity that Davis's lawyer had just referred to. Ida delighted in telling the attorney about the man's recanting of the letter and his new perspective regarding the sheriff. She ended her presentation by exhorting that if Davis were reinstated, the act would encourage the increase of lynchings throughout the state.[18]

The statements by Ida and the deputies must have been convincing, for several days later, Governor Deneen found that "neither the sheriff nor his deputy were disarmed by the mob," and yet they did not resist the mob. The governor then made a strong statement against lynch law before announcing that Sheriff Davis would not be reinstated.[19] On the same day the decision was published in the press, white citizens in Cairo began a movement to make up the loss of the sheriff's salary.[20]

It was quite a victory, one, as Ferdinand knew, Ida needed. The *Springfield Forum* applauded Wells-Barnett as "a lady in whom we are justly proud, her voice is ever heard in no uncertain tones for her people and for right whenever the occasion comes and regardless of how acute the crisis." Adding an observation that gained her as many adversaries as friends, the paper concluded that Ida "towers high above all of her male contemporaries and has more of the aggressive qualities than the average man. It belittles the men to some extent, to have a woman come forward and do the work that is naturally presumed to be that of the men, but Mrs. Barnett never shrinks nor evades she [*sic*] is an heroine of her age and the nation is better off for her having lived in it . . . long live Mrs. Ida Wells Barnett."[21]

The same point was reiterated by the five-year-old *Chicago Defender*, just beginning to make its journalistic mark on the city. "If we only had men with the backbone of Mrs. Barnett, lynching would soon come to a halt," it opined, while reporting on a program attended by three hundred people to hear Ida give her Cairo report before Chicago's Bethel Literary and Historical Club.[22]

Cairo reenergized Ida. For the first five months in 1910, she took part in a dizzying amount of activity. Ida hosted a gala charity ball at the Art Institute and appeared at numerous venues, including the Institutional Church, where she spoke for its annual Frederick Douglass Day, and the Congregational Union, which met at the elegant Palmer House. On the latter occasion she shared a dais with Dr. J. G. K. McClure, the future head of the Chicago Theological Seminary. McClure, whose speech was entitled "The White Man's Burden," preceded Ida and spoke of the rising crime rate among blacks, who, as he noted, made up 3 percent of the population but 10 percent of the crime. Prodded by her host to refute him, Ida said that she had come to speak about lynching, and in any case she could not refute the statistics. When it was time for her to speak, she did talk about lynching, but then added that the crime statistics did not mean that blacks were more criminal-prone, just more neglected by the network of social services.[23]

Ida specifically mentioned the YMCA in this regard. Before the rise of the black population in the 1900s, blacks, at least nominally, were invited to participate in the YMCA on Madison Street, which had a policy not to exclude anyone due to race or color. But after the number of southern migrants began to increase, blacks were no longer welcome at the "Y." The new black migrants might have been wayward but few were hardened criminals, Ida maintained, and they would benefit from such institutions.[24]

Ida's progressive views were formed through her own experience and observations. Her interest in the criminal justice system and its victims had led her to visit Joliet Penitentiary and the Bridewell prison for women on numerous occasions to talk to incarcerated men and women. She had found that most of them were country bumpkins who had made their way to Chicago, sometimes by freight train, where they drifted, wide-eyed and friendless, onto State Street with its cafés, glittering theater shows, and the lure of twenty-four-hour juke joints, gambling houses, saloons, and a lively red-light district. They easily got into trouble and were targeted by a zealous police force known for its "third-degree" questioning to elicit confessions for crimes they were trying to get off the books.[25] In contrast to the immigrant populations of Irish, Italians, Poles, Scandinavians, and Germans, these African Americans had no social agency to help or intercede for them—including, now, the YMCA. No doubt thinking about the role she had decided upon for her Negro Fellowship League (NFL), Wells told the audience that there was not a single uplifting influence along the whole length of State Street for blacks; the saloon was the one social center that welcomed them.

After Ida's talk, Jessie Lawson, the wife of Victor Lawson, publisher of the *Chicago Daily News,* sought her out. She asked Ida if she was sure about the YMCA not admitting blacks, as her husband, a generous contributor to the Christian organization, was unaware of its discriminatory practices. Ida assured Jessie that what she said about the Y was true. After the meeting,

Wells-Barnett did some lobbying. She found out who Lawson's manicurist was and got her to press the case with Jessie about the need for a positive influence on State Street.[26]

In the meantime, Ida spoke about the same subject in other venues. When she spoke before a young men's Bible class in Oak Park, Jesse A. Baldwin, then chief justice of the criminal court, also expressed surprise— and emotion. Tears were in his eyes, Ida remembered, although she wasn't sure she was seeing correctly until her son Charles, who had accompanied her, pointed it out. Subsequently, Baldwin and Victor Lawson vowed not to give any additional money to the Y, and the publisher, with prompting from his wife, agreed to fund Ida's NFL for a year.

Ida and Jessie Lawson found a suitable building at 2830 State Street, in the heart of the Black Belt, and Wells-Barnett also received help from her friend and son's namesake, H. H. Kohlsaat. The restaurateur, who had already established a reading room for his hundreds of black employees, volunteered to help Ida establish one at the new League headquarters in time for its May 1 opening.[27]

IN THE MEANTIME, Wells-Barnett was active on another front when it appeared that calls to "Remember Ferdinand Barnett" finally went beyond wishful thinking. In April of 1910, Edward Wright, the wily former county commissioner who had successfully pressed Deneen to appoint Ferdinand as an assistant state's attorney, made a similar move to force the Republican machine to nominate an African American for alderman in the Second Ward, which by 1910 was 27 percent black and steadily rising.

Aldermen, two of whom represented each of Chicago's thirty-five wards, possessed more power than state legislators or country commissioners. They approved the city's budget, granted franchises, passed local ordinances, recommended and rejected appointments, and supervised the administration of city affairs. When the Republican machine refused to support Wright's request, he called together black leaders in Chicago to support his independent candidacy for the aldermanic position.[28]

Ida supported the idea of black representation on the city council, and in the same month as Wright's bid, she organized the Women's Second Ward Republican Club, whose stated purpose was "to assist the men in getting better laws for the race and having representation in everything which tends to the uplift of the city and government." The group also advocated women's suffrage, and Ida invited both black and white women to its forums. She had evidently seized upon another idea whose time had come. The first meeting drew two hundred women.²⁹ There is little information on the role they played in the aldermanic election in which Wright was trounced, getting only 18 percent of the vote. The Democratic editor of the *Broad Ax,* Julius Taylor (whose Democratic candidate also lost), ridiculed the women's participation, noting that they "should have been at home looking after their untidy and ill-mannered children" instead of "button-holing" men in the Second Ward—"many of them half-drunk"—to vote for Wright. The women may have been "ignorant" in the ways of "practical politics," and wholly outside of their element, as Taylor observed, but they would learn from the experience for another day.³⁰

On May 1, 1910, Wells-Barnett hosted another historic event. Those who came to the open house of Ida's Negro Fellowship League Reading Room and Social Center saw a bright space with a first floor fitted with tables, desks, and chairs, and cases filled with books, magazines, and newspapers. It was clear to those who saw it that the NFL could boast of having one of the finest reading rooms in the city. Spaces were reserved where one could write with the pencils and paper provided, or play checkers on the checkerboards that dotted the room. There was also a Victrola, but in a period when the dance halls pulsed with syncopated music and the cake-walk, the League only had records of "the better class of popular and light classical music." No doubt the piano in the room carried similar rules of usage. Another part of the first floor was the employment center. On the second floor, Ida, fully aware of how many young men got picked up for vagrancy, created a lodging house that provided a clean bed for a small fee. It was the first such venture for blacks on State Street.³¹

Surveying the space and anticipating her work there, Ida recalled that she "was lifted to seventh heaven." Of course, the feeling was far from unanimous. A number of the women who had come to see the place balked at the location, which was much less respectable than the Frederick Douglass Center on Wabash Avenue. In 1909, the *Broad Ax* had counted six "good time" houses, between Thirtieth and Thirty-fifth streets, known for their raucous twenty-four-hour partying.³²

In fact, on the first Sunday afternoon the NFL was open to the public, a program had to be stopped because of the loud voices of at least twelve drunken, disheveled men shooting craps, who had congregated near the open doorway of the building. A bucket of beer stood nearby. The janitor suggested calling the police, but Ida told him no and went outside to invite the men into the meeting. When they demurred, saying that they would return when they were sober, Ida extended her hand and tried to get them to shake on it. Although they said that they were too dirty to touch Ida's white silk gloves, they promised to return. Ida's welcoming gestures quickly paid off. Within the year, the NFL began to register forty to fifty patrons a day, and placed 115 men into jobs.[33]

WELLS-BARNETT WAS FEELING so good about what she had been able to accomplish over the course of the year, she was ready to get back into the ring with her new not-best-friends of the National Negro Committee in New York.

Between November of 1909 and April of 1910, Ida had missed five meetings in which the New York committee continued to grapple with its final list of members, organizational structure, criticisms from Booker Washington's allies, and tensions between its most ego-driven members: Walling and Villard, and Villard and Du Bois.[34] The second annual conference was scheduled for May, and John Milholland, who had investigated Brownsville and had been so aggrieved about the earlier omission of Ida's name from the Founding Forty, beseeched Wells-Barnett to attend the meeting. Ida's achievement in Cairo, he told her, was "the most outstanding thing that had been done for the race that year."[35]

Ida was not about to make the rapprochement easy, however. She told Milholland that she was sorry but that she was very busy in Chicago and, moreover, was financially unable to make the trip. Milholland replied that the organization would pay for her expenses—quite an offer, as the organization had few funds at the time; it had hired its first paid staff member that January. Milholland's response, wrote Wells-Barnett, left her "no choice" but to attend. Frances Blascoer, that newly hired staff member and secretary, characterized Ida's capitulation a little differently. As she wrote Isabel Eaton, the sociologist who had aided Du Bois in his Philadelphia study, "Ida Walls [sic] Barnett has finally calmed down, and has practically accepted an invitation to come on again and speak . . . we to pay her expenses."[36]

The theme of the second conference, held again in New York's Charity Hall and Cooper Union, was disenfranchisement, and Ida was among the principal speakers. In fact, she was given pretty good billing. Her talk was scheduled for the May 12 public evening session at Cooper Union, where she shared the podium with the well-known Chicago lawyer Clarence Darrow, who had famously defended the socialist leaders Eugene Debs and William Haywood; Ray Stannard Baker, the muckraking journalist who had published *Following the Color Line* in 1909; Reverend Reverdy Ransom, now at the Bethel AME Church in New York; and New York congressman William S. Bennett.[37] Ida's thinking about the issue was evident in her subsequent article, "How Enfranchisement Stops Lynching," published in *Original Rights Magazine* in June of 1910. In it she went into detail about the Cairo lynching, making the salient point that the election of a black legislator, Edward Green, who had gotten Illinois's 1905 antilynching bill passed was necessary at a time when few juries convicted lynchers.[38]

Ida also took part in the executive sessions and committee meetings that were dedicated to forming a permanent organization. Her major contribution to the deliberations, she wrote in her autobiography, was her response to the proposal that the organization publish a journal. When Jane Addams, also a founding member and present at the meeting, responded that she thought it more economical for the organization to republish articles in extant publications, Wells-Barnett argued that their independence would only be assured if they had their own organ. Ida, of course, would have loved being the editor of such a publication, but the position, in what became known as *The Crisis,* was subsequently given to the most prominent black insider, W. E. B. Du Bois—a decision that ensured his place in history. By contrast, Ida believed, the leadership made it clear that she would not have any role, "save to be a member."[39]

Again, however, Ida put the best face on the situation and sought to leverage what she could from it. It was probably Ida's idea for her and staff member Frances Blascoer to attend the July 1910 National Association of Colored Women meeting in Louisville to get an endorsement for the newly named National Association for the Advancement of Colored People (NAACP). Trying not to burn bridges, Ida returned to Chicago where she gave a positive report of the meeting before Celia Woolley's Frederick Douglass Center, which had recently added employment services for black women and had secured the admission of blacks to a facility run by the Juvenile Protective Association in racially contested Hyde Park.[40] After the May meeting, Wells-Barnett's NFL also hosted William English Walling and Jane Addams to speak before the group.

But just when she appeared to have passed the point in her life when she no longer reveled in stirring up heated controversies, Wells-Barnett did just that in Louisville. Presiding over the NACW in her second term was her onetime ally Elizabeth Carter, the New Englander who was the niece of Josephine Ruffin and who had threatened to remove her delegation in the wake of the 1899 Chicago elections. Since then Carter had consistently moved up in the NACW, which had grown to forty-five thousand members, and was enjoying growing relationships with other reform organizations such as the YWCA, suffrage groups, and even the General Federation of Women's Clubs, which had excluded Ruffin a decade before.[41] Carter was anxious to heal the old rifts in the organization and had welcomed the return of Wells-Barnett, who had not been to a biennial NACW meeting in a decade. As Ida wrote, her appearance had garnered much applause from the 278 delegates present and she was appointed chair of the resolutions committee.[42]

The proceedings went smoothly until Ione Gibbs, chair of the executive committee, gave a report regarding *National Notes,* the official publication of the NACW. At least since 1899, the publication had been subsidized by Tuskegee and printed by its students under the supervision of Margaret Murray Washington. But for years, there had been complaints about its erratic publication schedule and inefficient distribution.[43] Though unstated, there also may have been political and ideological concerns about the newsletter being controlled by Tuskegee at a time when Booker Washington's image had been tarnished by his unshakable loyalty to President Theodore Roosevelt and his continuing support of Roosevelt's handpicked successor, William Howard Taft, who unabashedly courted the white South. In any case, Gibbs reported that the recommendation of her committee was that the editorship of *Notes* become an elected position.

The recommendation set off a discussion that Ida appeared to heavy-handedly cut off by making a motion that the committee report be adopted. "I reminded [the delegates] that this was the time and place to change the situation by electing an editor who would be responsible to the body," Ida wrote. In her autobiography, Ida added that her subsequent call for a vote showed that her motion prevailed, but, to her surprise, President Elizabeth Carter ruled it out of order because executive board recommendations could not be acted upon until the next biennial. Ida challenged Carter on her ruling, and of course, another row ensued. At one point, former president Lucy Thurman "stepped to the front of the platform to say that the delegates ought to resent action of one . . . who came down there attempting to teach them." Thurman's chastising was followed by hisses aimed at Ida, who became so dispirited by the reaction that afterward she decided not to attend the closing banquet. Instead, Ida wrote, she remained in her room and went to bed.[44]

Typically, Ida's explanation lacked a certain insight. In writing about the incident, she claimed that the culprits behind hissing her off the floor were Margaret Washington's allies, who thought that Ida's real motive was to get the editorship for herself. "Always the personal element," Ida complained. But she did not deny the charge, and especially in light of losing out on the *Crisis* editorship, it was not an unreasonable assumption. Ida also implied that there had been some prior agreement about the issue with Carter. But the NACW president would not have sanctioned such an imperious intervention that made no attempt to finesse the issue and that put her in an awkward position. Furthermore, Wells-Barnett's ten-year absence from the national meetings laid her open to just the kind of criticism that she received and that was later reflected in the coverage of the now unfriendly *New York Age*. Many of the delegates, the paper explained, regarded Ida as an outsider with no relationship to the organization.[45]

Indeed, by the time Ida made her reappearance, the organization would have included a whole new generation of younger women who had little idea of her founding role in Chicago, the formation of the NACW itself, or even that she had been the catalyst responsible for organizing the first club in Louisville. Ida responded in the *Broad Ax*, which, in addition to explaining her side of the story, included her own history with the organization. Wells-Barnett also gave a positive assessment of the NAACP, but the report was given by another clubwoman, Eva Jenifer. The NACW went on record endorsing the organization, "provided it did not interfere with the treasury or divide the working force of the NACW"—a proviso that would have meaningful implications in the future. In August, soon after returning from the confab, Ida and her children went to Wisconsin for a much needed vacation.[46]

IDA RETURNED TO Chicago to find a major crisis unfolding. While she had been away, an illiterate tenant farmer by the name of Steve Green had escaped from certain death in Arkansas to Chicago, where extradition proceedings awaited. Green, who had migrated to Arkansas from Tennessee in the hopes of attaining a better education for his children, left the tenant farm where he had been working after his landlord doubled the rent. Subsequently, when the landlord discovered him farming on another owner's land, he shot Green in the neck, left arm, and right leg. Though wounded, Green had managed to run into his cabin, grab a Winchester rifle, and kill his assailant. The black farmer fled to Mississippi, where friends hid him until they could raise thirty-two dollars to aid his escape to Chicago. By foot and train, Green managed to get to the city on August 12. But in the interim, a black informer told Arkansas authorities of Green's whereabouts and he was subsequently arrested in Chicago on a questionable charge of petty larceny. While Green was in custody, the Chicago police grilled him for four days, denying him adequate food and water. During the period, he heard that a thousand men awaited him in Arkansas to "burn him alive." Green finally broke under the ordeal. He tried to kill himself by ingesting matches and was hospitalized.

Upon learning of the case, Ida arranged (surely with the help of Ferdinand) to get Green a writ of habeas corpus, which requires a person to be brought before a judge or court to investigate a restraint on their liberty. But by the time she found out that the request had been ignored by the Chicago police chief (who would later face contempt charges for his action), authorities had already put Green on a railroad car that was headed south. Not to be outdone, Ida contacted Edward Wright, candidate for alderman who had effectively lobbied for Ferdinand's appointment. She instructed him to get permission from the state's attorney to offer a hundred-dollar reward for Green's re-arrest along the route so that he would be returned to Chicago. Wright hastily contacted a number of people, including Reverend Archibald Carey, Edward Green, and the attorney W. G. Anderson, to raise money so that the reward amount could be increased. Wright then telegraphed every station along the Illinois Central Railroad route with the offer. Ironically, the sheriff in Cairo who had taken the place of the deposed Sheriff Davis was the man who recaptured Green when the train stopped there to be ferried across the Mississippi River.

By the time Green was returned to Chicago, Wright had found an anomaly in the extradition papers. The ensuing trial, with its overflow crowd in the courtroom, rivaled the "old underground [railroad] scenes of a half-century past," noted the *Broad Ax*. Shortly thereafter, when it was learned that determined Arkansas authorities were in the process of amending the request so that Green could be sent south again, Ida turned her NFL into her own underground railroad of sorts. She hid Green there until money could be collected to spirit him to Canada.[47]

The publicity about Steve Green attracted the attention of the NAACP, and Joel E. Spingarn, an independently wealthy professor at Columbia University. As he later recalled, he didn't know why the injustice toward Green appealed to him more than any other, but at some point he said to himself, "I don't care what happens, Steve Green will never be extradited to Arkansas."[48] Spingarn sent a hundred dollars to the new civil rights organization, and subsequently asked Oswald Villard if any more funds were needed. "I have received the following from Mrs. Ida Wells Barnett, the reliable representative of the Association in Chicago of whom I spoke to you over the telephone the other day," Villard replied, informing the professor that Ida had managed to smuggle Green to Canada, but the fact that the farmer could neither read nor write made it difficult to confirm word about his safety. When more about the situation was known, Villard continued, he would tell Spingarn about the need for any additional funds.[49]

At some point, Green was brought back to Chicago where he stayed out of sight by working nights and sleeping days at the NFL. It is not clear how long he remained incognito at Ida's facility, but he did so, Ida wrote, until authorities had given up on having Green extradited. Green was "one Negro," as Ida concluded with an air of satisfaction, "who lives to tell the tale that he was not burned alive according to the program."[50] The *Chicago Defender*, remarking on her role in saving Green, called Ida a "watchdog of human life and liberty," and credited her with bringing the public attention to Green that resulted in successful resolution of the case.[51]

On November 10, "Steve Green's Story" was the prominent headline in the inaugural issue of Du Bois's *Crisis*. In the one-page article, the NAACP took full credit for his rescue but did not mention Ida's role in the affair. In fact, great pains appeared to have been taken to exclude her name, generally. She was not even listed in the historic issue's "What to Read" column, which cited thirty-nine journal and magazine articles by authors writing on racial issues. Although Wells-Barnett had published "The Northern Negro Woman's Social and Moral Condition" in April of the year and "How Enfranchisement Stops Lynching"—detailing the Cairo affair—in June, they were not mentioned on the list that included writings by Ray Stannard Baker, several by Du Bois, three by Mary White Ovington—and even one by Booker T. Washington.[52]

To compound the offense, Chicagoans had formed a Vigilance Committee of which Ida was a part, but as the organization moved toward forming a branch, it became clear that the leadership had decided to minimize Ida's role. Wells-Barnett confided this to Joel Spingarn, whose wariness about the organization's incessant concerns about getting money from philanthropists and his conviction that more blacks should be in NAACP leadership positions made Ida trust him."[53] In April of 1911, Ida wrote Spingarn complaining that Villard had called a meeting of the Chicago branch over at Hull House without her knowledge and while she was out of town. Upon her return, Ida had been unable to find out what had transpired there. "Mr. Villard and Prof. Du Bois gave me the impression that they rather feared some interferance [*sic*] from me in the Chicago arrangements," Ida told Spingarn. "Unfortunately a few of our 'exclusives' have the same idea that Mr. Villard has, that the organization should be kept in the hands of the exclusive 'academic few.' Of course I am not very popular with the academic few, and I can not say that I look with equanimity upon their patronizing assumptions."[54] Ida's temperament and the organization's elitism, however, were not the only issues that kept her outside of the NAACP leadership. Her ideology and militant views were something that the civil rights organization could, literally, not afford.

AT THE TIME, the NAACP was courting Chicago philanthropists and a rapprochement with Booker T. Washington. An incident in March 1911, a month before Ida's letter to Spingarn, had made Washington—already weakened by failing health and lessened political influence under President Taft—more vulnerable than ever before. On March 19, the Tuskegeean had been brutally beaten in a seedy neighborhood near New York City's Tenderloin District. His assailant, a white man named Henry Albert Ulrich, had struck him with his fist, then chased Washington with a cane, finally catching and striking him so forcefully that the educator was subsequently hospitalized; he received sixteen stitches for the wounds on his head and his torn ear. The reason for the assault, Ulrich later explained to police, was that Washington had been loitering around the apartment building where he lived and appeared inebriated. The white man also told police that Washington had addressed a white woman who passed him on the street with "Hello, sweetheart" and at one point was seen peering though a peephole into one of the apartments. The New York press published photos of the educator with his head wrapped in bandages and a sheepish, nervous grin on his face, and prepared to report on the upcoming trial of Ulrich who was charged with assault.[55]

The prestige of those who came to the aid of Washington in the embarrassing affair, in which the usually agile educator was never able to adequately explain why he was in such a notorious neighborhood, was a tribute to the loyalty he still commanded among white supporters. The distinguished New York attorney Paul D. Cravath worked on damage control by negotiating with Ulrich and other eyewitnesses; Andrew Carnegie and Theodore Roosevelt wrote letters of support. Seth Low, the president of Columbia University and chair of the Tuskegee board of trustees, sent out press releases. Villard was reportedly "sick of heart" over the scandal and later wrote to his uncle, Francis Garrison, that Washington had been so overwhelmed by the letters of sympathy (even Du Bois and Monroe Trotter wrote consolate if not exculpatory comments) that he thought it was time to bury the hatchet between the two factions. Villard and Washington discussed sending fraternal delegates to each other's upcoming NAACP and National Negro Business League meetings.[56]

There is no known comment from Wells-Barnett on the matter, but it is doubtful that she would have sympathized with the male leader's indiscretion or sat quietly by while the NAACP negotiated an armistice. However sincere Villard et al. felt about reconciliation being in the race's interests, they, unlike Ida, also calculated the advantage of getting access and support from Washington's circle of philanthropists, and Chicago had one of the most important potential donors in the country: Julius Rosenwald, known as the merchant prince of Sears, Roebuck and Company. Rosenwald, born the same year as Ida, to German-Jewish immigrants who had grown up in poverty, was president of the Associated Jewish Charities of Chicago and also had a demonstrated interest in the plight of black Americans. He donated 25 percent of the annual budget for the black Wendell Phillips Settlement on Chicago's West Side, and in early 1911, Rosenwald had announced that he was earmarking twenty-five thousand dollars for the construction of a black YMCA—a sum that would be matched by two other white businessmen, N. W. Harris and Cyrus McCormick.[57] But Rosenwald, as Villard and the others no doubt knew, was a conservative on race matters. As his secretary, William Graves, once explained, the philanthropist found the southern Negro "who knew his place, more pleasing," because race prejudice "is not on his lips." Rosenwald thought that such obeisance was "a mental attitude to be attained." Under Northern "freedom, a Southern negro *does* change," Rosenwald believed.[58]

In preparation for the formation of the Chicago chapter, the Sears businessman was invited by the NAACP leaders to chair the financial committee of the Chicago branch, and it was calculated, rightly, that Wells-Barnett would not have been an asset toward getting Rosenwald's cooperation.[59] However, Jane Addams would be such an asset. Rosenwald was an admirer and benefactor of Addams who, the NAACP leadership had decided, should be president of the Chicago branch—another development that Ida did not sanction. Wells-Barnett's opposition to Addams wasn't personal; after all, the Hull House reformer had helped her in a number of projects and was one of the city's great egalitarians. But Addams, as Ida wrote in her letter to Spingarn, was simply not appropriate "for the very good reason that Miss Addams whom they desire to mother the movement has not the time nor the strength even if she had the inclination to lead this new crusade."[60]

Indeed, Addams, who was two years older than Ida, described her own temperament as middle of the road when it came to many issues that became enflamed in controversy, and at the time Addams was also serving as president of the National Conference of Charities and Correction and was soon to become the first head of the National Federation of Settlements, as well as first vice president of the National American Woman Suffrage Association (NAWSA).[61] "The same academic few," Ida wrote to Spingarn, "are perfectly willing to be identified with a movement that has Miss Jane Addams as its head in order that they may bask in the light of her reflected glory and at the same time get credit for representing the race that they ignore and withdraw themselves from on every occasion of real need."[62]

Others, of course, saw Addams's temperament and affiliations as a strength rather than a flaw. Often called "St. Jane," she had, as one observer noted, created a bridge between immigrants and old-stock Americans, idealistic reformers and professional politicians, private philanthropy and government. Addams was the key to bringing not only benefactors like Rosenwald to the NAACP, but also those who made up Addams's circle of female devotees. The independently wealthy Louise de Koven Bowen, treasurer of Hull House since 1894, would alone donate more than a million dollars to the settlement.[63] And because of Addams, Anita McCormick Blaine, heiress of the McCormick fortune, legitimated the organization in the eyes of her peers by taking a financial and personal interest in the Chicago NAACP chapter.[64]

But there was an even more fundamental reason to keep Ida on the outer edges of the NAACP. Ironically, but perhaps not uncoincidentally, Ida's exclusion from this phase of the organization's activities came at the precise moment that its leaders had decided to put lynching at the center of its agenda. In 1911, two particularly gruesome murders had gotten the nation's attention. The first was in Livermore, Kentucky, where a black man was taken to an opera house, tied to the stage, and shot by whites who were sold tickets to sit in the orchestra for the privilege. Receipts were to go to the family of the white man who had been allegedly killed by the victim.[65] The Kentucky incident prompted ten members of the NAACP's Washington branch to present a resolution to President Taft, who promptly responded by saying that the federal government had no authority in the matter. The second lynching took place in Coatsville, Pennsylvania, where a black man was seized from a local hospital and, while still chained to his bed, was dragged a half-mile from town. Awaiting him was a mob of four thousand persons who killed him by alternately pushing his body in and out of a roaring bonfire.[66]

In reaction, the NAACP, with a strategy that Ida had used for years, sent board members to Coatsville and employed a detective agency to investigate the matter, pressed for prosecution, and instituted efforts to get an antilynching statute passed in Pennsylvania. If "after all our trouble over the Coatsville matter we could get this antilynching legislation passed, it would be a splendid victory for our National Association," wrote secretary May Childs Nerney to Joel Spingarn.[67]

The meaning of victory had several dimensions in an organization that needed to focus on an issue that was at once important, legitimatized its predominantly white existence in the eyes of blacks, and, largely because of the awareness engendered by Ida's campaign, was capable of attracting funds from not only blacks but whites. Within a year, the NAACP had sponsored an antilynching rally at the Ethical Culture in New York City, published a sixteen-page pamphlet, *Notes on Lynchings in the United States*, and established an antilynching fund that had raised four hundred dollars. The organization had also instituted efforts to get Martha Gruening, a volunteer social worker, to coordinate these and subsequent activities around the lynching issue.

The emphasis on lynching was also evident when the NAACP held its fourth annual conference in Chicago in April of 1912. On the Sunday before the opening, branch members asked Chicago's ministers to preach about the "evils of lynching" in their sermons and to distribute the anti-lynching pamphlet to their congregations.[68]

Although Wells-Barnett was often cited for her take-my-marbles-and-go-home intransigence, both she and Ferdinand cooperated with the planning committee for the three-day Chicago conference, which marked an auspicious beginning for the branch. Present were delegates from Boston, Kansas City, St. Paul, and New York. The first session, held at Rabbi Emil Hirsch's Sinai Temple, was presided over by Jane Addams and attended by a thousand persons despite inclement weather. Villard, Charles Edward Russell, and W. E. B. Du Bois were the principal speakers from the national group, and Woolley, Judge Edward Osgood Brown, and Ida also gave addresses. Although it must have rankled Ida to read Ovington's "expert" views on lynching, earlier published in the *Chicago Defender,* Wells-Barnett invited the NAACP officers and delegates to the second anniversary dinner of the Negro Fellowship League, where Addams and others were given a platform to speak. But for Ida, no good deed would go unpunished. Du Bois's later coverage of the conference in the *Crisis* mentioned every major participant in the conference—except Wells-Barnett.[69]

This oversight further foretold the marginalization of Wells-Barnett not only in terms of the NAACP but also on the lynching issue, which the organization set out to identify itself with. In Ovington's subsequent documentation about the NAACP's early antilynching efforts, published in the *Journal of Negro History,* she said the organization's campaign had begun in 1911, and she credited its activities and investigations for revealing the falsity of the rape charge, and the fact that lynchings led to more general lawlessness. Ovington also documented how in the early years, "much of the best work . . . was done by women." Three were mentioned for special commendation; Ida was not among them.[70]

In the immediate offing, Ida would concentrate her considerable energies into her Fellowship League and transform Chicago's political landscape, which was ripe for dramatic change. In the longer term, Wells-Barnett would challenge the policies of the NAACP, which tried, but could never quite manage, to dismiss her.

CHAPTER TWENTY

The Ladies' Band

We should like to have Mrs. Barnett march with
us, but if the [National American Woman's Suffrage Association] has decided it is unwise to include the colored women, I think we should abide
by its decision.

—*Grace Wilbur Trout, president of the
Illinois Equal Suffrage League*

Ida was all the more frustrated by the NAACP because she had been
struggling against a tide of events to keep her Negro Fellowship League
(NFL) afloat. The opening of its headquarters on State Street in May of
1910 had been made possible by Victor Lawson, publisher of the *Chicago
Daily News,* one of the city's most successful newspapers. He had given Ida
$3,000 and committed another $2,400 to cover the cost of the annual
rent. But Lawson had no interest in funding the NFL activities beyond
keeping up its reading-room facilities, and as Ida quickly learned, even that
bare-bones support was in jeopardy. Almost as soon as she had opened the
doors of the League, she had had to search for a means to keep providing
the array of services that were so desperately needed in the community.[1]

Between May of 1910 and April of 1911 the League, as Ida had written in a letter to Joel Spingarn, had gotten off to a good start. She boasted about its fine reading room and social center, open between 9:00 A.M. and 10:00 P.M., and the NFL's membership, made up of "earnest, sincere, young men and women who realize the need of trying to do something for the race." Ida also pointed out to Spingarn that the NFL was located in the Black Belt, the "heart of that section of the city which has been most neglected hitherto by the religious, social and moral influences."[2] Although she provided no more details in her letter, Ida typically had not waited for the ghetto youths to come to her; she scoured the poolrooms, saloons, and street corners to find and tell young people about the League. The impact, Ida wrote in her autobiography, was discernible. The number of patrol wagons coming into the neighborhood began to decline, and, as she had predicted, the very presence of the League's "moral influence" was making a difference in the community. By way of example, Wells-Barnett recounted the story about a woman who told her that the strains of Sunday music had caused her to feel ashamed to carry her weekly pail of beer past its doors on that day. Another woman, who ran a "good-time" house, moved because her conscience couldn't take it.[3]

The Sunday-afternoon meetings, Ida continued in her letter to Spingarn, were "very inspiring and instructive." Notices in the press revealed that the NFL's Sunday programs were structured along the lines of the Hull House model, which sought to school its patrons about civic and political matters and to expose them to those who achieved in various fields. Early NFL programs had titles like "The Responsibility of Citizenship" and "Christian Education"; speakers included a municipal court judge and the editor Louis Post, who spoke about the Illinois constitution. In September of 1910, Ida, with other clubwomen, hosted a reception for Tina Johnson, mother of the controversial boxing champion Jack Johnson, whose victory over the "great white hope," Jim Jeffries, two months before had sparked racial confrontations and eight racially motivated deaths across the country. The NFL also invited the nervous, if instructive, speaker Henry O. Tanner—the son of *AME Church Review* founder Bishop Benjamin Tanner—and the first African American artist to achieve international renown. At the time of Tanner's appearance, in February of 1911, there was an exhibition of his paintings at Thurber's Gallery in the city. Of course, there was music, too. State Street, where the NFL was located, had a fast-growing number of storefront churches, and the League invited "singing evangelists" on some occasions, as well as soloists of nearly every stripe. Often the meeting notices in the paper simply promised "good music." The NFL's reputation for music grew with the organization's annual Emancipation Day celebrations, which featured talented musicians on its programs.[4]

Particularly fulfilling for Ida was that the Fellowship League gave her the means to protect blacks, something that she had been consistently concerned with. Ida took pleasure in aiding the "friendless," particularly migrants from the South. For example, she told the story of Annabel Jones, who was twenty-three years old when Ida heard about her. Jones had been "given" to a white family in the South at the age of ten. When the family, whose last name was White, moved to Chicago, Annabel was brought with them and virtually treated like a slave. For thirteen years, the young woman, who was never paid for her work, had endured beatings and isolation from the outside world. One day the young girl heard of the NFL from a black man who did odd jobs around the house, and Jones found her way to the State Street headquarters. When Ida heard about her plight, she accompanied Annabel to her employer's house. After identifying herself to Mrs. White, Ida promptly informed her of how many statutes she had broken in the treatment of Annabel, and that she had come to get Annabel's clothes and the compensation due her. One can imagine the look on Mrs. White's face during the confrontation, and in the end, she paid the young woman two years' worth of back wages. With the money, Annabel Jones found housing and employment elsewhere.[5]

"ALREADY IN THIS short time we can see some good results," Ida told Spingarn in her April letter. But her vision for the League was greater than its current budget. "We have no money with which to branch out along the many lines that the work needs," she continued. One of those lines was the pursuit of justice issues through the NFL, the organization, as she reminded Spingarn, where the "Steve Green plan originated." "We take up all matters affecting the civil and legal affairs of the race," Wells-Barnett wrote, "and where we have not been able to start the wheels of justice we have at least affected public sentiment." Ida closed the letter with her characteristic missionary zeal. We know we are on the right track, "and the work is destined to grow because it has the germ of immortality that makes us feel that it can never die."[6]

Wells-Barnett may have had faith in the eternal rightness of what she was doing, but by the time she wrote Spingarn, she already knew that Lawson's support was finite. Ironically, this had become clear with a development that Ida had probably inspired but now was turning against her own interests. She had been complaining about the exclusion of blacks by the Y at the same time that the organization was in the midst of a fund-raising campaign. When, in 1910, its officers approached Julius Rosenwald, he asked if any of the capital campaign funds were earmarked for a Y building for blacks. When told that none were, Rosenwald told them that when they were prepared to undertake such a project, he would contribute $25,000. The YMCA then declared its intentions to raise $100,000 for a Colored YMCA building.

Following Rosenwald's January 1911 announcement that he was heading a fund-raising campaign for a black YMCA, Victor Lawson promptly signed on. As he told Ida, there would be no need to continue supporting the NFL after the Y came into being. This meant that Lawson also had little desire to expand the facilities of the League. Responding to a letter Ida had written him in which she apparently had laid out such plans, he had written that "in view of the purpose of the YMCA . . . there should be no expansion in the way of a boys' gymnasium or employment agency. Be satisfied with the existing work until such time it can be merged into the YMCA undertaking." Wells-Barnett, of course, had no desire to merge with anyone, much less the YMCA. Knowing her time was short, she hastened to implement her own programs. And by March, Lawson had begun complaining about Ida's accounting. His secretary, he told her, couldn't verify her numbers in a "businesslike way."[7]

As Ida may have gleaned, her benefactor was not the kind of man who could be easily swayed. Lawson was the son of a Sabbatarian and refused to print the *Daily News* on Sundays, and he was somber, obstinate, and firm in his convictions. As Ida might have heard, when one of his employees at the (nonunionized) *Daily News* suggested that a pay raise would be more welcome than the annual Christmas turkeys that Lawson handed out, the publisher simply ceased giving his employees the turkeys.[8]

The writing was on the wall in terms of Lawson's financial support. But that was not her only concern. The Y campaign was structured in such a way that it was going to be increasingly difficult for her to get support from Chicago's black entrepreneurial class, which included men like Jesse Binga, who founded the Binga Bank in 1908 from capital largely acquired through his successful real estate business, and Anthony Overton, whose "Brown Face Powder" and cosmetic line for black women was capitalized at nearly $270,000.⁹ Rosenwald had made his offer of $25,000 contingent upon blacks being able to raise $50,000 themselves for the enterprise. The fundraising model drew praise from Governor Charles Deneen, President Taft, and Woodrow Wilson, who would be a candidate for the U.S. presidency in 1912. In the past there would have been more debate among the Chicago black leadership about the propriety of supporting an all-black institution in lieu of demanding that the white-only Y accept African Americans. But by 1912, need, appreciation of the effort by prominent whites, and a growing sense of, and desire for, the black community's emergence as an entity in and of itself resulted in blacks, with few exceptions, supporting the effort. Their subscription campaign was headed by Ida's physician, George C. Hall, of Provident Hospital, who was a member of the NAACP Chicago branch.

Within a mere two weeks, the clarion call for the Y attracted donations large and small from ten thousand black men and women who raised the breathtaking total of nearly $67,000—$17,000 more than the required amount. The campaign was so successful plans were made to replicate it in other major cities, including Atlanta, Washington, D.C., New York, Philadelphia, and St. Louis.¹⁰ "The Chicago Negroes have done something for themselves," declared the *Chicago Evening Post*. "They have taken an important step upward in the estimation of the community in which they live. They can go further," noted the paper with a backhanded slap, "by taking full advantage of the character building machinery that lies in an active YMCA."¹¹

No doubt knowing that her funding days were numbered, Ida feverishly continued her programs and got out an edition of the *Fellowship Herald*—a modest initial effort that contained features on African culture, women's club activities, political news, and an announcement that a special women's edition of the paper was in the offing. The issue came out amid the fanfare of an elaborate reception at the NFL, and Lawson was not pleased. The "$14 for the Fellowship Herald should have been approved" beforehand, he chastised. He also added that he wouldn't approve Wells-Barnett's expenditures for printing, music for a concert, seventy-five dollars for her secretary, and money for the bookkeeper, until he could understand the financial records. "There seems to be an assumption that you are at liberty to incur any expenses," he scolded. "I want this all changed in the future."[12]

One can almost hear Ida's wounded yet defiant response, which recounted all the good work she was doing. Subsequently, Lawson's tone softened, but in a November 1911 letter, it was evident that he remained undeterred. "I understand you are doing good work, and to a good many people," Lawson wrote, responding on this occasion to Ida's request for money to fix up the lodging quarters. But he had "come on board," he wrote, for the reading room only. It wasn't that he didn't appreciate what she was doing, Lawson continued, but the additional expenditures went "beyond the original request and promise."[13]

Soon after the letter, Wells-Barnett went on the offensive—not with Lawson, but implicitly with the idea of the Y. It was to be located at Thirtyeighth and Wabash, which was outside of the "storm-center" of the Black Belt as Ida called it. Moreover, the Y membership fee of twelve dollars was well beyond the reach of those like the people she was seeing at the Fellowship League. In January of 1912, Ida wrote a letter to the *Chicago Record-Herald*:

The sixty thousand negroes [*sic*] in the city . . . shut out of any but the most menial and poorly paid occupations . . . they go hungry but it is said that the color line shuts them out of even Malcolm McDowell's bread line on Madison Street. Most of the trades unions refuse them a chance to make a living at the trades they have learned in Booker Washington's school and elsewhere. Because of lynching and race discrimination in the South they flock to Chicago as the Jews have fled from Russia.

We find, therefore, a great number of idle negro men without money, without homes and without the pale of the civic and social influences which are thrown round every other class of young men who come to this city. . . . Even the Woman's Model Lodging House announces that it will find all women accommodations who need a place to sleep except drunkards, immoral women and Negro women. . . .

Those of us who realize the condition of this great idle, proscribed class and view with pain and shame this increasing criminal record have absolutely no money to use in helping to change these conditions. We do not envy the good fortune of the institutions which have been able to reach the pockets of the philanthropists, but we do wish that somebody could be found to give something to help . . . this neglected and ostracized class.[14]

It is possible that Ida's letter was one of the reasons why representatives of Julius Rosenwald decided to visit the Fellowship League. Rosenwald—who would commemorate his fiftieth birthday in 1912 by giving away $687,000 to various charitable causes—was interested in the class of blacks Ida had written about. He was also a stockholder and financier of the *Record,* now controlled by the Barnetts' friend H. H. Kohlsaat.[15] Rosenwald appeared to stay clear of the ideological divide between blacks, but he was close to Booker T. Washington. The Sears & Roebuck magnate joined the Tuskegee board in 1912, and he was working with Washington on a large project in which Rosenwald was subsidizing the construction of schools in the rural South, to which blacks also contributed. Finally, the two men were personal friends. Rosenwald's home was a refuge where the ailing Wizard could stay for a rest. In March of 1912 Washington was at the Rosenwald residence and Margaret Murray Washington informed Mrs. Rosenwald as to what her husband, in his state of health, could eat. After listing foods like soft-boiled eggs, canned peaches, and broiled steak, Margaret added that "Mr. Washington has given his very life to this work and now when he is only a little over fifty to see him so tired and worn makes my heart ache. I shall feel perfectly happy while he is there with you and Mr. Rosenwald."[16]

Ida, in her autobiography, did not specify the exact date when Rosenwald's representatives came to look at the League, but it is possible that it took place while Washington was at the financier's residence. Anticipating the visit, Ida wrote that she was determined to make a good showing. For her, this not only meant putting the NFL in the best light, but, more challengingly, not offending the sensibilities of visitors who were more accustomed to blacks like Booker Washington. When the committee, headed by a Mr. Sachs, came, all seemed to go well until Sachs decided to retell one of Washington's now familiar "chicken jokes," which he had heard the night before. The story was about "an old man who said his wife had left him [and] did not mind her going so much . . . but she had left the chicken coop door open and all of the chickens had gone too." The teller of the anecdote was "heartily laughing" when he recounted Washington's words, but then suddenly stopped, according to Ida, when he realized that she wasn't sharing the joke. The expression on Ida's face prompted him to ask her if blacks, regardless of their views about his philosophy, accepted Washington as their leader.[17]

Wells-Barnett must have known it was a loaded question, but the fact didn't temper her response. "Rabbi Hirsch is your leading Jew in Chicago," she began, referring to the prominent scholar and activist who was one of the original signers to the NAACP. "He is constantly invited to appear before representative gentile audiences, and because of his wonderful eloquence is a general favorite. But I am wondering," she continued, warming to the subject, "if you Jews would acclaim him so highly if every time he appeared before a gentile audience he would amuse them by telling stories about Jews burning down their stores to get insurance?" The question made Sachs turn "a bright red." Needless to say, she noted, "the conversation ended there." And so, Ida implied, did any chance of her getting financial assistance from Julius Rosenwald.[18]

ON A SUNDAY afternoon in July of 1912, the cornerstone of the Colored YMCA was laid to great fanfare. A parade of twenty-five hundred members of the Masons, Knights of Pythias, the Odd Fellows, and the Eighth Regiment marched down Wabash Avenue where the $180,000 building was to be built by the following year. Speeches were given by Julius Rosenwald, the banker N. W. Harris, and Dr. George C. Hall, among others. Ida, however, remained unconvinced that the Y could be an adequate substitute for the work she was doing, and its imminent reality impelled her to make a last-ditch effort to have the NFL's funding sustained. She got the municipal chief judge Harry Olson, who had been so supportive of her husband's campaign for a judgeship, to intervene with Lawson (who like Ferdinand Barnett, Deneen, and the judge were supporters of the progressive faction of the Republican Party) on her behalf. However, despite the judge's intercession, Lawson stood firm. In addition to his convictions about the matter, his wife, Jessie, who had had the initial interest in the League, became terminally ill and died. Lawson had already contributed nine thousand dollars toward the NFL, and he told Ida that she would have to find another source of income.[19]

No longer able to pay the monthly $175 rent on the spacious building and lodging quarters at 2830 State Street, Ida found a small "cramped" place that had been a store at 3005 State. The rent there was $35 a month.

Announcing the change of address in the *Broad Ax*, Ida, characteristically, put the best face on the development. The League's new location was now in "the more thickly populated section" of the Black Belt, she wrote, and thus the "need of the work" was now "greater than ever." Judge Olson evidently agreed. He had not been able to move Lawson on her behalf, but he did help Ida in another way. He appointed her as the first woman adult probation officer of the municipal court, a position that paid $150 a month.[20]

The position was a natural one for Ida. The League had become known as a place where judges and police officers could send idle males picked up for vagrancy or disorderly conduct, and the empathy of both Barnetts for blacks who got into trouble or were in need went beyond institutional obligations. They were so personally committed to them that they often took young men into their house until they could get on their feet. As Alfreda Barnett, their youngest daughter, later recalled, one such young man, who had been watching an alley "craps" game, had gotten arrested with other spectators when it dissolved into a cutting scrape. The boy was shy and quiet and as a member of the Barnett household he easily fell into a routine of doing chores within the home. He eventually saved up enough money to send to his mother and sister back home, and finally for himself to return. "God bless you all," he wrote in a departing note. "I am going home." Another young man from the South, Elmer, who had hoboed his way to Chicago, was sent to the League after being injured jumping off a train. Elmer's arm had gotten caught under the wheels and was eventually amputated. A cook by profession, the Barnetts took him in until he learned to prepare food with one arm. "I can remember his attempts to steady the egg beater as he prepared his favorite cream pie," Alfreda recalled, "and how he learned to use his chest and side as substitutes for his lost member."[21]

With her appointment as a probation officer, Ida now actually got paid to supervise and guide those in need of her services, and as she wrote in a letter to Joel Spingarn, she enjoyed her position. "The work is most interesting," she wrote, "and the opportunity to be of even greater benefit to my race is most gratifying." She told him that she was on duty at the Harrison Street municipal courtroom from nine to twelve each day, then went out into the field where she looked after no less than eighty-five probationers. The work lasted well into the night most days as Ida dealt with "their woes of adjustment," as she called it.[22]

Despite the workload, Ida still managed to find the time to keep the programs of the NFL going, campaign in the 1912 national, state, and municipal elections, march in the spectacular 1913 woman's suffrage parade in Washington, D.C.—and even found a new organization.

BY THE END of 1913, a seismic shift would shake the political arena affecting all the issues that Ida cared about. The rumblings began with Theodore Roosevelt's announcement that he would be a candidate, once again, for president. Politicos braced for a bruising battle for the Republican nomination against William Howard Taft, the Rough Rider's hand-picked successor in 1909. Governor Charles Deneen, whose political fortunes directly impacted Ferdinand Barnett's assistant state's attorney position, was also up for a grueling reelection. Moreover, the gubernatorial and statehouse races were bound to affect Illinois's women suffragists. Since 1893, two years after women had gotten the right to vote in school-district elections, Catharine Waugh McCulloch, a lawyer and legislative chair of the Illinois Equal Suffrage Association (IESA), had aggressively lobbied in Springfield for a partial suffrage bill that extended the women's right to vote for presidential electors, mayors, aldermen, municipal court judges, and township and other officials (but not governors, other state officers, members of the legislature, or congressmen). Wells-Barnett and McCulloch were friends; both exhibited a bulldog determination and did not suffer fools lightly. While the lawyer had made some headway over the years in Springfield, her efforts had come up short. But by 1912, suffragists in Illinois and elsewhere were benefiting from the rising progressive winds at their backs. Enfranchised women, as activists had stressed, would sweep away corruption as surely as they had ridden their own homes of smudge and smut.[23]

In 1912, Grace Wilbur Trout was elected president of the IESA. Trout had been the president of the Chicago Political Equality League (once headed by Celia Parker Woolley and more recently, McCulloch) and was a skilled organizer who had coordinated over one hundred suffrage organizations across the state. Active with the Daughters of the American Revolution and a number of civic associations, the stylishly dressed Trout was more acceptable than McCulloch to conservative women, and her non-combative, placating style changed the tone of the organization's lobbying efforts. By 1912, other organizations, including the Women's Trade Union League and Hull House, mobilized immigrant women and formed special interest organizations such as the Wage-Earners Suffrage League. Suffragists were poised in 1912 to lobby the newly elected legislature with more influence and numbers than ever before.[24]

At the same time, black Republicans across the nation were trying to cope with the fact that they had less influence than in the past. For them, the choice between Taft and Roosevelt was one between the lesser of two evils. Under the guidance of Booker T. Washington, TR had stood behind black appointments such as that of South Carolinian physician William D. Crum as collector of customs at the Port of Charleston, despite Senate opposition by southern Negrophobes. And when Minnie Cox, a Fisk graduate, was forced at the hands of a mob to resign from her position as postmistress in Indianola, Mississippi, Roosevelt closed down the post office. But Roosevelt's unforgivable decision regarding the Twenty-fifth Infantry at Brownsville more than offset any political-capital gained by the president's support of individual blacks.

Taft was not only the secretary of war who had actually implemented the Brownsville decision, he had appointed three former Confederates to the U.S. Supreme Court—one of whom became chief justice—and his platform in 1912 made, for the first time in the history of the Republican Party, no reference to the Fourteenth and Fifteenth Amendments. Moreover, Taft had instituted a policy that was determined not to provoke the white South's ire by making or even sustaining black appointments in the region. Soon after his election, the president forced William Crum to resign from the customs position. Washington, who had unsuccessfully lobbied for retaining his appointee, was at least able to convince the administration that it would be politic to give Crum another position. The South Carolinian was finally appointed to the traditionally black post of minister to Liberia, where, in 1912, he succumbed to a tropical fever and died.[25]

As predicted, the Republican convention, held in Chicago in June of 1912, was bitterly contested. The party was split between Roosevelt and Taft supporters, but Taft's control of the party machinery—including its black southern delegates—gave him the victory. When chagrined Roosevelt delegates subsequently met and decided to form a new Progressive Party, which nominated Roosevelt to be its leader, Republicans split into oppositional fragments.

Reform leadership was also riven by events. Du Bois, fully aware of TR's past transgressions, nevertheless abhorred Taft and believed that Roosevelt's advocacy of women's suffrage, workers' rights, and insurance for the unemployed and elderly, among other policies, made him the superior candidate. The *Crisis* editor drafted a pro-civil-rights plank for the Progressive Party convention held in Chicago in August, but not only was Du Bois's offering ignored, insult was added to injury when Roosevelt instructed his lieutenants not to seat black southern delegates at the convention whom he suspected of being placed there by Taft. Du Bois subsequently switched his allegiance to the Democrat, Woodrow Wilson, who openly sought black votes and made campaign promises accordingly; Boston's Monroe Trotter did the same. Jane Addams, head of the Chicago's NAACP branch, stuck with TR.[26]

Addams had tried to persuade Roosevelt to be attentive to civil rights and not to unseat the black delegates. But her failure to do so did not prevent the NAACP Chicago branch president from accepting Roosevelt's invitation to become the first woman to second a nomination for a major presidential candidate. Addams's decision caused consternation within NAACP circles. "Is Jane Addams going into the convention after her stalwart attitude on the negro question . . ." wrote Francis Garrison to Oswald Garrison Villard. "Is she so blind & stupid as to take any stock whatsoever in [Roosevelt]?"[27] The Progressive Party was the only one to support the enfranchisement of women but Monroe Trotter, after hearing what Addams had done, fired off an angry telegram warning her that "woman suffrage will be stained with blood unless women refuse alliance with Roosevelt."[28]

Under a barrage of criticism, Addams defended herself in the *Crisis*. In the unconvincing and vaguely argued piece in which she reminded readers of her abolitionist ancestry, she concluded that the reform principles of the Progressive Party were bound to lift all questions, including that of race, toward social justice. The argument sounded a good deal like the expediency argument that Susan B. Anthony had earlier expressed to Ida—and would soon reemerge during the suffrage battle.[29]

In 1912, Ida showed that she was not beyond political expediency herself. Governor Charles Deneen's already tough gubernatorial race against the Democrat Edward Dunne, the progressive former mayor of Chicago, became more so when the Progressive Party also fielded a candidate, Fred Funk. Deneen no doubt directed the party faithful, including Ida and Ferdinand, to campaign for the Republican ticket, which meant campaigning for Taft. Ida, the founder of the Women's Second Ward Republican Club, gave a speech in October before the Woman's Party of Cook County, where she praised the Republicans for giving the country Abraham Lincoln and condemned Roosevelt's Brownsville decision. According to the coverage of the talk in the _Chicago Defender,_ however, Ida managed to cover the points without once mentioning Taft by name.[30]

The Republican split assured the election of the progressive Democrat Woodrow Wilson, who had served as governor of New Jersey and president of Princeton University. Wilson also won a plurality in Illinois, and the Democrats succeeded in making significant gains in the legislature and electing Edward Dunne as governor, the first chief executive of that party in twenty years. The election had both personal and political import for the Barnetts. With the Republican loss, Ferdinand thought it prudent to resign from the state's attorney office. With the new makeup of the legislature, which included two pro-suffrage Progressive Party state senators and twenty-five representatives in the House, women suffragists pressed their effort to extend their franchise in Illinois.[31]

Ida seized the moment by founding, on January 30, 1913, the Alpha Suffrage Club (ASC), the first black women's suffrage club in Chicago. "When I saw that we were likely to have restricted suffrage and the white women were working like beavers to bring it about, I made another effort to get our women interested," Wells-Barnett wrote in her autobiography. She was assisted in the effort by two white suffragists, Virginia Brooks, a young member of the Illinois Equal Suffrage Association (IESA), and Belle Squire, president of the No Vote, No Tax League, an organization advocating that women who could not vote should not have to pay taxes.[32]

Unlike the Women's Second Ward Republican Club, the new suffrage organization was focused on mobilizing black women throughout the city, and it was nonpartisan. One of the ASC's first orders of business was to raise money for Ida to represent them at the huge suffrage rally in Washington, D.C., on March 3—the eve of Woodrow Wilson's inauguration.[33]

The 1913 suffrage parade in Washington, D.C., was the brain child of Alice Paul, a Quaker and militant in the burgeoning British suffrage movement. Paul, and another activist, Lucy Burns, had convinced the National American Women's Suffrage Association (NAWSA) to undertake what became a parade of unprecedented scale and spectacle. Five thousand suffragists converged on the capital from across the country and prepared for their white-attired procession down Pennsylvania Avenue, replete with banners and pageant-inspired floats that invoked the history of the suffrage struggle for women at home and abroad. Leading them would be the stunning figure of Inez Milholland, daughter of the NAACP's John Milholland, riding majestically on a white horse. "Helen of Troy was not more upsetting," the suffragist Harriet Stanton Blatch later observed.[34] An allegorical tableaux, staged on the steps of the Treasury Building, was constructed that would feature six women figures, representing Columbia—donned with plumed helmet—and costumed artists symbolizing Justice, Charity, Liberty, Peace, and Hope, who would perform the various roles through music and dance.

Ida arrived in Washington with the sixty-two-member contingent of Illinois suffragists who promptly began going over the logistics of their walking four abreast down Pennsylvania Avenue. According to the *Chicago Tribune,* which sent a reporter to cover the delegation, their practice session at the drill hall of parade headquarters was interrupted when Grace Trout, IESA president, rushed in from another room to make an announcement: "Mrs. [Alice] Stone [Blackwell] of the National Suffrage Association [NAWSA] and the woman in charge of the entire parade has advised us to keep our delegation entirely white." The stunning words caused a "murmur of excitement . . . around the room," the reporter noted, "and those standing near the colored woman kept an embarrassed silence." Trout went on to explain that many eastern and southern women had expressed resentment about black women marching side by side with whites rather than with the all-black contingent that was also scheduled to participate in the parade. "A number of women had even gone so far as say that they would refuse to march with blacks," Trout added.[35]

NAWSA was concerned that the resentment of whites would jeopardize congressional support for a federal women's suffrage amendment—especially, if not exclusively, in the South. Negrophobes like South Carolina senator Ben Tillman worried, as he would write, that the enfranchisement of black women would reinvigorate the resistance against white supremacy. Black women, he felt, were more aggressive in asserting the "rights of race" and had always "urged the negro men on" in racial conflicts.[36]

"We should like to have Mrs. Barnett march with us," Trout concluded, but "if the national association has decided it is unwise to include the colored women, I think we should abide by its decision." At that point, the *Tribune* reporter noted, Trout looked around the room for approval, and one of the delegates, who was Georgia-born and lived in Oak Park, expressed her agreement. "You are right," said the delegate, "it will prejudice southern people against suffrage if we take colored women into our ranks." The words infuriated Virginia Brooks, who with Belle Squire had helped Ida organize the Alpha Suffrage Club. "We have come down here to march for equal rights," Brooks insisted, adding that to exclude Wells-Barnett on the basis of race would be undemocratic. "If the women of other states lack moral courage," she continued, "we should show them that we are not afraid of public opinion. If the women didn't stand by their principles, the parade will be a farce."[37]

Finally, Wells-Barnett—who had been a member of Illinois suffrage organizations longer than many of the women there, and who knew that her exclusion would cause untold damage to the black women's suffrage movement—spoke. Her voice trembled with emotion, noted the *Tribune* reporter, and two large tears coursed down her cheeks before she could raise her veil and wipe them away. "If the Illinois women do not take a stand now in this great democratic parade then the colored women are lost," Ida insisted. Indeed, the history of white suffragists who had repeatedly sacrificed principles of race equality was already an obstacle that Ida faced in mobilizing blacks for women's suffrage. Already, black papers like the *Chicago Defender* were speculating that if "women got the vote in America, the colored race will suffer further ills in legislation."[38]

Ida's statement appeared to change Trout's mind. "It is time for Illinois to recognize the colored women as a political equal," she agreed, and stated that Wells-Barnett would march with the delegation. But then, after being taken aside by another woman in the group, Trout amended her declaration, saying that she would have to confer again with Stone before making a final determination. While the women waited for Trout's return, they kept discussing the issue, and Belle Squire patted Ida's hand assuring her that "everything will be alright." She was wrong. When Trout came back into the room, she said that despite her personal preference, she would abide by the wishes of the national association. Ida, she said, would have to march with the black delegation. At that point, according to the reporter, Ida's face became set with grim determination. "When I was asked to come down here," she said, "I was asked to march with the other women of our state, and I intend to do so or not take part in the parade at all." At that point, Belle Squire and Virginia Brooks volunteered to walk by Ida's side if she marched in another section of the parade. Ida was said to consent to the offer. The meeting adjourned, and the Illinois delegation left the drill hall to take their places in the procession.[39]

Like the other delegations, the Illinois women had to contend with the jeering mob that lined Pennsylvania Avenue, but there was another concern as well. Missing from the contingent were Belle Squire and Virginia Brooks, and Ida was nowhere to be seen. Brooks did finally show up, asking the whereabouts of the other two. When she was told that Squire had taken ill, Brooks announced her intention to march with Wells-Barnett, alone. This drew charges from a member of the delegation that she was simply trying to seek publicity by her action. "Let anyone say anything they please," sneered Brooks. "I cannot prevent that, but I can prevent having one of our delegation left to march alone, almost as if she were in disgrace." With that, Brooks left the line and found Squire but could not locate Ida. The two women feared that their friend had elected to just stay away from the march entirely and took their places with the delegation.

However, the *Tribune* reporter saw Ida. As he described it, when the Illinois delegation started to march, "Suddenly from the crowd on the sidewalk Mrs. Barnett walked calmly out to the delegation and assumed her place at the side of Mrs. Squire." However, as the reporter observed, "There was no question raised . . . and she finished the parade."[40] And whether the three suffragists—Squire, Brooks, and Wells-Barnett—wanted publicity or not, the *Tribune* of March 5 carried a large photo of them, standing together, with a broad suffrage sash across their dresses. Each had a satisfied expression on her face.

Ida remained in Washington for two weeks after the march and took the opportunity to write her friend Catharine Waugh McCulloch, author of the women's suffrage bill set to go before the legislature. Catharine, who did not get along with Grace Trout, had written Virginia Brooks, "condemn[ing] the weakness of those who acceded to the discriminatory demands" in Washington. McCulloch evidently also sent a similar letter to Ida, assuring her that if she had been in Washington, Ida would have had her full support. Ida responded by thanking Catharine, adding, "Our women should be as firm in standing up for their principles as the southern women are for their prejudices." She closed by accepting an invitation from McCulloch to speak before the Current Events Club on the twenty-third, and for Ida and Ferdinand to come to her house for dinner.[41]

The coverage of the march and the incident with the Illinois delegation must have reflected some of Wells-Barnett's highest hopes—as well as her worst fears. She was probably pleasantly surprised by the *Tribune*'s coverage, which, though depicting some of the delegation's tensions with poke-in-the-ribs semi-seriousness, gave the racial matter the weight it deserved and presented Ida, Belle Squire, and Virginia Brooks in a positive light. The *Broad Ax* and the *Chicago Defender* treated the suffrage parade in general, and the "incident" regarding Ida in particular, with ambivalence. The *Broad Ax*, which had chided black women for their participation in Ed Wright's 1910 campaign, admiringly described the march as a "spectacle without parallel" but could not help itself when it came to commenting on the women themselves: "Some of 'em pretty, but most of 'em ugly—hideous, like sin, but without any of sin's allurements . . ." However, it did praise the Howard University students who were members of Delta Sigma Theta, a sorority founded earlier that year, who also marched in the suffrage parade. The group members had decided to make their participation in the event their first public act as a sorority and had asked Mary Church Terrell, an honorary member, to escort them. They were "a pleasing bevy of Colored girls," the paper said, "all looking quite nifty in caps and gowns" and "greeted with hearty applause all along down the line." But the paper was more serious about Ida's role in the march. She "proudly marched with the . . . head Ladies of the Illinois delegation showing that no Color line existed in . . . the first national parade of the noble women who are in favor of equal suffrage," it proclaimed.[42]

The *Chicago Defender* also praised Ida's actions. "The race has no greater leader among the feminine sex than Mrs. Ida B. Wells-Barnett," said the paper, noting Ida's "firm stand," but also said that if NAWSA officials did not issue a public apology for "drawing the color line, we shall not have much respect for colored women who can be used as tools or flattered into helping the cause of votes for women."[43]

Upon her return to Chicago, Ida hastened to pay public tribute to her suffragist friends and to generate some positive publicity. She announced in late March that the Alpha Suffrage Club would hold its first public entertainment in April at Quinn Chapel. Music would be provided by the Emancipation Chorus, a hundred-member choir that Ida had introduced at her January 1913 NFL Emancipation Day Program. Belle Squire and Virginia Brooks, described by the *Broad Ax* as the "two white women who stood so loyally by Mrs. Barnett," were scheduled to be the featured speakers. By time the affair was held, the suffrage lobby in Springfield was going full tilt—and so was Ida.[44]

Documentation about Ida's Springfield activity regarding suffrage is scarce, but there is information about what she and black women activists from the Illinois clubs were doing on another front. In the early months of the year, the black press was following the status of three discriminatory bills proposed in the legislature—bills that reflected a national trend. Democrats riding on the coattails of Woodrow Wilson had made gains in states like Illinois (where Democrats had become the legislative majority) as well as in the Congress, and the president, a Virginian by birth, did nothing to stem the tide of the party's Negrophobes. The first U.S. congressional session under his presidency received the greatest number of discriminatory bills that had ever been introduced.[45] At least twenty pieces of such legislation were offered that advocated measures like the exclusion of blacks from army and navy commissions, prohibition of intermarriage and the immigration of persons of African descent, and segregation of public transportation in the capital.

The new Illinois legislature had also introduced discriminatory bills: a Jim Crow transportation bill regarding streetcars and Pullman cars; a Full Crew Bill, which would allow white transportation unions to replace nonunion blacks in positions such as train flagmen, brakemen, switchmen, and porters; and several antimiscegenation bills.[46] All of them were being debated at the same time that the women's suffrage bill was on the agenda in the capital.

The introduction of the bills brought members of Chicago's Appomatox Club (founded in 1900 by Edward Wright as a center for black politicians) to Springfield where they began lobbying legislators. Accompanying them were Wells-Barnett and black club members from throughout the state who, as Ida noted, were very much "aroused" by the bills.⁴⁷ In her autobiography, Ida made special mention of the antimiscegenation legislation. Attention to the issue had been kick-started by the boxing champion Jack Johnson. Known as a womanizer, he had made national headlines when his despairing first wife, who was white, shot herself in 1912, allegedly because of his philandering, and when, soon after, he married a second white woman—a teenager. In May of 1913, Johnson was found guilty of violating the Mann Act—also known as the "white slavery law"—which made it a crime to transport women across state lines for unlawful purposes. In June, the boxing champion was sentenced to the penitentiary, but fled first to Canada, then to France with his wife, Lucille Cameron. Wells-Barnett, as she wrote in her autobiography, had criticized Johnson in the *Fellowship Herald* for squandering his largesse on the Café de Champion, his club that was known for its interracial "entertainments" and that was located near the Fellowship League. Wells-Barnett believed that he should have used it to provide a gymnasium for young black boys, which would have helped so many youth in the community. However, she was more critical of the antimiscegenation legislation that the Congress did indeed pass and that Illinois legislators were attempting to do.⁴⁸

The black women who came to Springfield were joined by local residents, and Ida wrote about the dramatic impression that the presence of several hundred black women winding through the halls of the state capitol made on the legislators. White suffragists were also impressed, according to the *Defender*. "The Suffragists are coming out boldly and declaring that colored women are welcome in their organizations, the only opposition to them coming from the southern contingent," stated the paper, which also praised the demeanor and determination of black women. "It looks as though our enemies were beginning to see the light," the *Defender* concluded.⁴⁹

All of the discriminatory bills were eventually defeated. In April, the *Defender* chronicled the death of the Jim Crow transportation bill, reporting how "its author declared that he had never met so many brilliant persons of color before" and that he was sorry that he had ever proposed it. The newspaper published an honor roll of fourteen persons who were most responsible for the defeat. Ida had been the spokeswoman for the black women lobbyists, and her name led the rest and was the only one written in all capital letters. "The name of Mrs. Barnett stands alone," the *Defender* explained, "because that constant and fearless champion of equal rights was on the firing line all the time. Her eloquent pleas in private conferences with the legislators and in open session were eloquent and forcible. Ida B. Wells-Barnett has again endeared herself to the world."[50]

It would have been logical for Ida and the rest of the women also to lobby for the suffrage legislation, and perhaps their doing so was a factor behind the *Defender*'s report about the suffragists being so impressed. In any case, on May 7 the IESA bill passed the Senate and was headed toward the rough-and-tumble House, whose majority antiprohibitionist Democrats were traditionally the women's most vehement opposition. Indeed, the debates in the chamber were highly emotional ones. As one legislator described it, when each man's name was called, he "got up and fought out his position in shrieking oratory."[51]

However, Trout and her four IESA lieutenants had lined up allies in each of the three parties that were instrumental in managing the bill and bringing it to a successful vote. The suffragists were also aided by the unexpected and impassioned testimony of a former Republican opponent about the need for women to have the vote in order to stem the rising tide of vice in the state. The lone black in the House, Robert L. Jackson, a Republican elected in 1912, also spoke and voted for the bill.

On June 26, Governor Dunne signed the historic legislation, which extended the right of women to vote in Illinois. The partial suffrage bill made Illinois the first state east of the Mississippi River to give women such voting rights and as NAWSA's Carrie Chapman Catt observed, after the victory, "suffrage sentiment doubled over night."[52]

Following the bill's passage, Chicago women celebrated with a spectacular automobile parade. Amid the more than one hundred "gaily decorated" vehicles winding their way along Michigan Avenue were five large touring cars bearing the members and friends of the Alpha Suffrage Club. Wells-Barnett was the parade marshal, and her nine-year-old daughter, Alfreda, was pressed into service alongside her.[53] Subsequently, the legislator Robert L. Jackson, who was commended by the IESA for his support, was feted by the ASC, where the speakers included McCulloch; Antoinette Funk, described as Trout's second lieutenant; and Medill

McCormick (of the *Tribune* McCormicks), a Progressive Party stalwart who had been an active supporter of the bill and the husband of Ruth Hanna McCormick, daughter of the late Republican kingmaker Mark Hanna, who also worked closely with Trout.[54] After the speeches, noted the press, the group heard music played by an all-ladies' band.[55]

The Alpha Suffrage Club

The men have made several attempts to elect an alderman. They failed, but we [women] will succeed.

—*Quoted in the* Chicago Defender

Now that Ida, at the age of fifty-one, had the vote, she saw a new world
of political possibilities. Again she would be a catalyst to put historic
events in motion; and again she would find herself entangled in controversy and struggling to stay at the center of the very developments she had
been instrumental in creating.

No sooner had Governor Dunne signed the bill that enfranchised
women than Ida found herself in a new round of contestation. According
to her autobiography, a man named Thomas Swann, a black Democrat,
approached her about leading black women in a new lobbying effort in
Springfield. Under way were plans for a month-long commemoration of
the fiftieth anniversary of black freedom, and Swann hoped that the women
could help convince the legislature to appropriate $25,000 toward the pro-
gram. Scheduled to open in Chicago in August of 1915, twelve years after
the World Columbian Exposition excluded blacks, the Illinois National
Half-Century Exposition was conceived as an event to engender a spirit
of brotherhood between the races and demonstrate the progress of African Americans since Emancipation. Governors from seventeen states

were named as honorary vice presidents, and the event received endorsements from William Howard Taft, Theodore Roosevelt, and President Woodrow Wilson.[1]

The first lobbying effort by black women had been Swann's idea, Ida noted in her autobiography, and he urged her to agree to lead another effort to get the appropriation. The money would be under the jurisdiction of a commission appointed by the governor and made up of civic leaders to administer the exposition's exhibits and programs. "I refused on the ground that a matter of such importance should be deliberated upon by our organization," Wells-Barnett wrote, referring to the Illinois Federation of Colored Women's Clubs (IFCWC).[2]

Wells-Barnett did not offer an opinion about the exposition, but she was clearly wary of Swann's motives. In her autobiography, she characterized him as a "shrewd soldier of fortune" who had his eye on becoming the executive secretary of the commission, an influential office from which he could dispense considerable patronage jobs and direct activities. Ida may have also known that Reverend Archibald Carey, who was the minister of the Institutional Church (and had been a rival of her friend Reverdy Ransom), was also involved in trying to attain the appropriation. Carey had supported the sitting Democratic mayor, Carter Harrison II, as well as Governor Dunne. He also had some financial control over the moribund *Conservator* and was reported to be planning to revive it in order to get printing contracts from the commission.[3]

Unsatisfied with Ida's response, Swann simply circumvented her. He got one of the leading downstate federation members, Sarah Sheppard of Peoria, who held the office of organizer for the IFCWC, to lead the lobbying effort. The legislature subsequently appropriated the $25,000, Swann attained his secretarial position, and black women were appointed to various administrative positions in the departments of industry and education, among others.[4]

Ida, assuredly unhappy that she had been outflanked, seized, quite rightly, on the fact that although black women had some minor positions, none were named among the nine supervisory commission members. Governor Dunne appointed eight men—three whites and five blacks, including Carey and Swann—and a white woman, Susan Lawrence Joergen-Dahl. A white bishop who served on the board of Carey's church, Samuel Fallows of the Reformed Episcopal Church, was named to head the commission.[5]

Joergen-Dahl was appointed to represent all women on the body. She came from a wealthy Republican family in Springfield, and her charitable work included support for the Lincoln Colored Home, an orphanage for black girls in Springfield. Another institution in that city, the Mary A. Lawrence Industrial School for Girls, was named after Joergen-Dahl's mother and was run by a black clubwoman, Eva Monroe.[6]

On the day the commission appointments were announced, Ida had already been scheduled to address Chicago's City Federation of Colored Women's Clubs, which represented nearly seventy black women's organizations. As Ida wrote in her autobiography, instead of giving her scheduled address, she used the opportunity to complain about how "Negro women, who were the only organized force in the state for civic work," had been ignored on the commission. For Ida, the idea that a white woman—from the bloody battlefield of Springfield, no less—was deemed appropriate to represent blacks because of her charity work was doubly infuriating. Though not mentioned in the autobiography, the *Broad Ax* noted that someone during the course of the meeting—probably Ida, who was not named in the piece—also provided much more provocative rhetoric about Joergen-Dahl. The question was asked, noted the reporter, where Joergen-Dahl had been while blacks were being slaughtered during the Springfield riot, and why she hadn't gotten "White Christian men and women" to refrain from "shooting down in cold blood innocent and law abiding Colored men, women and children, setting fire to their humble homes, destroying their personal property and driving the best and the oldest Colored families from that cursed city like so many wild beasts or criminals." No wonder, as Ida wrote in her autobiography, at the end of the meeting the "women had been aroused to such a fever heat that they immediately drafted a protest to Governor Dunne."[7]

After receiving the women's complaint that pointed to the fact that "one-half of the Negro race" had been ignored in the exposition commission appointments, the governor, according to Ida, dispatched Bishop Fallows to "see and placate the women"—her in particular. Fallows had been told that the real source of Ida's discontent was that she was not named to the commission. After the exchange of some unpleasantries, he informed her that he had consulted with women in both the state federation (where a number supported Joergen-Dahl) and the National Association of Colored Women. With their names in hand, Fallows told Ida that the women were perfectly willing to work with the commission as it had been appointed. Adding insult to injury, when the IFCWC subsequently met in Springfield, they accepted Joergen-Dahl's invitation to come to her sumptuous mansion for a reception. Afterward, they passed a resolution endorsing the commission. When Ida later asked the City Federation president why she did not raise any protest about the meeting, she replied, "Well, Mrs. Barnett, you weren't there and I did not know what to do." At that point, Ida wrote, "I realized the hopelessness of the situation, and in a figurative sense I made up my mind 'to go way back and sit down.'"[8]

Of course, Ida wouldn't sit forever, and her protest was not in vain. Word came from the governor that although he could not make any additions to the commission, the women should contact him in the event of a vacancy. In the interim, Wells-Barnett bided her time, and as future events would show, she also drew some important lessons from the episode. In the meantime, Ida planned her trip to Washington, D.C., where she and the *Boston Guardian* editor, Monroe Trotter, would lead a delegation to see Woodrow Wilson.

WHILE THE PROGRESSIVE Democratic governor of Illinois was trying to develop better race relations and cooperation through the symbolic commemoration of fifty years of black freedom, his counterpart in the White House was, quite literally, reversing a half-century tradition of a desegregated civil service.

Within a month after Woodrow Wilson's inauguration, Albert G. Burleson, a Texan who was Wilson's postmaster general, complained in a cabinet meeting about the racial friction in the railway mail office, and that he thought it best to "segregate white and negro employees in all Departments of the Government." According to Navy Secretary Josephus Daniels, no one objected to the idea, and another southerner, Treasury Secretary William Gibbs McAdoo, agreed with the suggestion. At the same meeting, the question of black appointments came up. The consensus was that the president did not wish to decrease the number of Negro appointments, but "he wished the matter adjusted in a way to make the least friction."[9]

Following the meeting, Burleson and McAdoo, whose two departments had the highest number of blacks, began to systematically segregate workers in the offices, shops, rest rooms, and dining areas in the Post Office, the Treasury Department, and the Bureau of Engraving. McAdoo, with the president's approval, went so far as to attempt to make the Registry Division of the Treasury Department an all-black bureau, and the administration nominated Adam E. Patterson, a black Democrat from Oklahoma, as registrar.[10]

The "avoid-friction" rationale of the segregationists had, of course, multiple dimensions and one of them was the bugaboo about white women associating with blacks in general and black men in particular. "Deserving white girls in this City have appealed to us from nearly every Government Department where they are compelled to work alongside of a greasy, ill-smelling negro man or woman," read a broadside from a powerful lobby group called the National Democratic Fair Play Association, which promoted mass meetings to support discriminatory legislation and segregation within the federal government. In addition to the lobby and the shrieks of the resident southern Negrophobes in the Congress, Wilson also heard from others outside of Washington. "I am heartsick over the announcement that you have appointed a negro to boss white girls as Register of the Treasury," wrote *Clansman* author Thomas Dixon to Wilson in June of 1913. "Please let me as one of your best friends utter my passionate protest," added the author who had known Wilson since they were classmates at Johns Hopkins University. Dixon need not have worried. The Senate refused to confirm the black registrar, thus undermining any viability of creating a black department, or, in the administration's view, of making new black appointments or sustaining previous ones that came under assault.[11]

Soon, anecdotal stories about the treatment of blacks began being published in the black press. The *Chicago Defender*, for example, wrote about Ebert A. Hall from Des Moines, Iowa, who had placed second out of the large group that had taken the civil service exam for stenographers. Not knowing that Hall was black, the U.S. Patent Office offered him a job in Washington. When his race was discovered upon his arrival, however, Hall was not given the job for which he had been certified, but an inferior position that consisted of filing documents in an isolated office near the roof of the office building. Hall soon discovered that his plight was similar to that of other blacks and though he sought to rectify the situation, it was to no avail. He returned to Iowa.[12] Eventually, the Wilson administration required photographs to accompany applications to avoid such mistakes in the future; and soon blacks suspected that the test scores themselves were manipulated for all civil service positions. Such was the reason, the *Chicago*

Defender speculated, for the untraditionally low number of African Americans who passed the post office exam in the city: six out of a total of two hundred sixty.[13]

Although the status of blacks had been steadily declining under Wilson's two Republican predecessors, the raw evidence of systematic segregation was a particular blow to black leaders who had supported the president. If the five hundred thousand black male voters had been wary of the Virginia-born Wilson's southern roots, or the fact that Princeton University, under his presidency between 1902 and 1910, remained the only Ivy League institution that did not admit blacks, Booker Washington and W. E. B. Du Bois, among others, helped to allay their fears. "Mr. Wilson is in favor of things which tend toward the uplift, improvement and advancement of my people," Booker T. Washington had assured. Woodrow Wilson "will not advance the cause of oligarchy in the South, he will not seek further means of 'Jim Crow' insult, he will not dismiss black men wholesale from office," bugled Du Bois in the *Crisis*, who was counting on the fact that Wilson, with his degree from the University of Virginia and Ph.D. from Johns Hopkins, was a "cultivated scholar" with "farsighted fairness" and large ideas of a "New Freedom."[14] In 1912, Wilson tallied the largest number of African American votes ever given to a Democratic candidate, only for the black electorate to be betrayed by the president's segregation policies. "I have never seen the colored people so discouraged and bitter as they are at the present time," Washington wrote to Oswald Garrison Villard in August of 1913.[15]

No one was more bitter than Monroe Trotter. He and his National Independent Political League (NIPL) had campaigned hard for Wilson after the candidate had assured AME Zion bishop Alexander Walters in an open letter that if he became president it was his "earnest wish" that Negroes receive "not mere grudging justice, but justice executed with liberality and cordial good feeling." Now Trotter, who had published a friendly interview with Wilson in the *Boston Guardian* during the campaign, had to fend off charges that he had betrayed the race to gain favor in the administration. No doubt a number of Trotter's critics remembered that his father, James Monroe Trotter, had also campaigned for Democrats and had been appointed in 1887 as recorder of deeds by the Democratic president at the time, Grover Cleveland. In the fall of 1913, Trotter responded by circulating a petition protesting Wilson's policies; by November, he had collected twenty thousand signatures in thirty-six states. Trotter informed the administration of the petition before he and Ida were due to see the president.[16]

The two activists, were, in many ways, unlikely partners. Trotter was ten years younger than Ida, had spoken against the membership of women in the Niagara Movement, and his background and education at Harvard—where he had become the institution's first black Phi Beta Kappa inductee—put him solidly in the Talented Tenth coterie. But like Ida, he had been offended by the Founding Forty fiasco, and both activists had lost confidence in the NAACP. Neither Trotter nor Ida got along with the leaders of their local chapter. The Boston branch, where Francis Garrison was an officer, had an ambivalent policy regarding Booker T. Washington. The Chicago branch, as Ida had predicted, was flagging under the leadership of Jane Addams, who stepped down from the presidency soon after her performance at Roosevelt's convention. The chapter was showing no improvement under Illinois appellate court judge Edward Osgood Brown, its new president, who would remain in the position for the next decade.[17]

More important, both Trotter and Wells-Barnett, by temperament and ideology, were believers in direct action and the need for black-led protest organizations to mobilize the kind of mass sentiment that made the NAACP's "social-control" progressives nervous. With such views, neither would have felt that the letter of protest to Wilson from the NAACP national office or its investigation concluding that there was a systematic enforcement of segregation in the civil service was a sufficient response.[18]

When they met with Wilson on November 6, Trotter and Wells-Barnett were the designated spokespersons for the delegation that included five other members of the NIPL.[19] But on this occasion, Ida (the only woman in the group) was decidedly the second fiddle. Much of the thirty-five-minute meeting appeared to be taken up by a long and eloquent statement by Trotter, which noted that segregation, in addition to being "hostile" in itself, constituted a declaration of innate inferiority and compelled "resistance forever." He also reminded the president of his former promises about affording blacks justice and pointed out that African Americans had served in an unsegregated federal civil service for the past fifty years under both Democrats and Republicans. Trotter ended by appealing to Wilson's "personal integrity," concluding: "We cannot believe that you would stain your own honor or the record of your administration in history to satisfy a sectional prejudice."[20]

After Trotter's testament, Ida added only that the group had felt obligated to bring the matter to Wilson's direct attention. Wilson, who remained standing during the meeting, told them that Trotter's petition was "impressive" but he sidestepped the question about segregation, saying only that his administration did not have any hostile intent toward blacks or harbor "any spirit of discrimination." There probably had been some mistakes made, Wilson admitted, but he insisted that there was "no policy on the part of the administration looking to segregation."[21]

When Trotter then asked him about the Registry Department, Wilson said that he had thought at the time that the idea of making it all black was in the best interests of everyone, that the subsequent withdrawal of the proposed registrar's name from Senate consideration was not his doing; and that the pressure from the party's southern flank was making things difficult. In any case, Wilson promised to investigate the segregation matter further. "I assure you," the president told his visitors, "it will be worked out."[22]

Ida thought that the president had paid "careful attention" to the appeal. Trotter, encouraged, reported the meeting positively in the *Guardian*.[23] Whatever the meeting lacked in substance, the fact that the activists directly confronted the president was an important symbolic act that made the NAACP look timid in comparison. The idea of this set Du Bois's teeth on edge. The *Crisis* editor (who had not acknowledged Ida's heroics at the Washington suffrage demonstration) failed to mention the visit of Trotter and Wells-Barnett to the White House in either the December or January issues of the publication. Instead, Du Bois published a snide commentary about "individual sharpshooters" whose "guerrilla warfare" might be effective in the short run, but that the "flat fact remains: There is in the United States but one organization with permanent headquarters, paid officials, active nation-wide membership, live local branches . . . prepared to make a front forward fight on racial prejudice in this land," he wrote. "Join or die!"[24]

Du Bois was correct, of course, in citing the NAACP's resources in comparison to those of the NIPL or the Negro Fellowship League. Between 1911 and 1917, the NAACP's annual budget ranged between $11,000 and $15,000. Moreover, by 1914 the *Crisis*, under Du Bois's brilliant editorship, had a circulation of more than thirty thousand and had become the most influential race publication in the country's history. But the editor's petulant refusal to give Trotter and Wells-Barnett a modicum of praise might have also revealed his own insecurities about the NAACP. The organization was still dependent on a small group of contributors, had been incapable of accommodating respected militants, and was still looked upon with suspicion by blacks. All "of the old, strong forces have either been put out of Villard's organization, or have withdrawn," Booker Washington wrote to his secretary, Emmett Scott, soon after Ida and Trotter had met with the president. "Dr. Mossell has withdrawn or been put out. The same is true of Ida Wells Barnett, and Trotter of course." Villard and Du Bois "do not speak to each other. They have been at daggers points for a good many weeks. There are a good many colored people who resent the idea of a white man assuming to lead and control the colored people," he explained. While assistance and advice from whites were welcome, Washington concluded, "we are not ready to be taken charge of bag and baggage by any white man."[25] The Tuskegeean's observation proved to be especially prescient in Wells-Barnett's Chicago.

IDA RETURNED FROM Washington to get her Alpha Suffrage Club ready for Chicago's February 1914 primaries. For her, the election was doubly significant: it would be the first held since the Presidential and Municipal Suffrage Bill gave women the vote; and the first in which there was a real possibility of electing a black alderman. It was up to Wells-Barnett to make palpable the connection between the aspirations of black women and those of the race in the political arena—a connection bound to make history in twentieth-century Chicago.

Indeed, the stars were aligned for such a historic breakthrough. When Edward Wright first ran for alderman in 1910, the Second Ward was about 27 percent black; by 1914–1915 African Americans probably constituted the majority. Moreover, the demographics were changing at the very time when there was growing disaffection toward the Wilson administration, dissatisfaction with the deteriorating conditions in the Second Ward, and rising expectations of Chicago's black women—all developments that were now indisputably documented.[26]

Fannie Barrier Williams (who had apologized to her audience at the World's Columbian Exposition for not having such statistics) enumerated the increasing number of black women moving into Chicago's professional and semiprofessional occupations, including public school teachers (fifty), physicians (six), dentists (three), and growing numbers of nurses, stenographers, clerks, manicurists, chiropodists, and meat inspectors.[27]

Investigations by Alzada P. Comstock—a social-work student of one of the NAACP's "academic few," Sophonisba P. Breckenridge—revealed that both the rent and the degree of residential disrepair were higher in the black ghetto than in the poorest immigrant slums inhabited by Poles, Bohemians, and Jews. Added to residential segregation was the powerlessness of blacks to keep vice out of their communities. Prostitution had been outlawed in 1912, but, as studies showed, whites could push bordellos out of their neighborhood or—as in the case of the predominantly white First Ward's thousand brothels (that generated sixty million dollars annually)—confine them to a certain area. By contrast, city authorities continued to allow prostitution to flourish indiscriminately in black neighborhoods, a pattern that Wells-Barnett could personally attest to. Her once respectable neighborhood now had a brothel at Thirty-third and Rhodes Avenue, near the Barnett residence, and four more within three blocks.[28] While the presence of brothels attracted a motley mix of both races, the *Chicago Defender* was particularly offended by the "countless numbers" of white men who "infested" black neighborhoods at night and assumed that any "woman of color may be approached and degraded at their wish and will."[29]

Despite the dissatisfaction with the white aldermen in the Second Ward, dethroning the (Regular) Republican machine in the jurisdiction wasn't going to be easy. Virtually all of Illinois's black state representatives, political appointees, and beneficiaries of political patronage were indebted to the political organization and, especially, to its chieftain, Martin B. Madden. The English-born Madden, a U.S. congressman representing the First Congressional District that included the Second Ward, had an impressive record. He had helped defeat Democrat-inspired discrimination and anti-miscegenation bills that had accompanied Wilson's first term; he had interceded, with some success, to get blacks federal patronage positions; and as a member of the House's Post Office Committee, Madden had been responsible for the employment of hundreds of blacks as postal workers whose organization, the Phalanx Forum, was a major political and social force in the city. Ed Wright had thrown down the first gauntlet when he ran as an independent in the 1910 and 1912 aldermanic contests, but his own dubious connections with the machine did not inspire confidence in the electorate. In 1913, however, when he announced that he would back another candidate for the position, he fomented the needed change in the political dynamics of the ward.[30]

Wright supported William Randolph Cowan to run against the machine candidate and incumbent, Hugh Norris, in the February 1914 primary.

Cowan, a prominent real estate broker who had lived in the city since 1880, would be, as Wright knew, particularly appealing to women as well as progressive reformers. He was good-looking, articulate, and a political newcomer who was untainted by the murk of Chicago politics. The purity-seeking Municipal Voter's League, Victor Lawson's *Daily News,* and the *Chicago Defender,* supported Cowan's candidacy.[31]

Wright's announcement gave direction to Wells-Barnett's mobilization efforts. For her, Cowan was the obvious choice. But Ida had finally learned that her leadership style of imperious impatience caused more problems than it solved. If the Alpha Suffrage Club was to achieve what she envisioned, she would have to make sure that not only men but women themselves became invested in the importance of the female franchise.

As evidenced by the 1912 issue of the *Crisis* that devoted a special section to women's suffrage, there was a consensus among leading reformers about the necessity of women in general, and black women in particular, to exercise the vote. The publication featured a "Woman's Suffrage Symposium" that included articles by leading blacks and whites, men and women, all stressing the importance of the franchise. Du Bois's editorial delineated the issue from a broad human-rights perspective and its relationship to the exigencies of the race. Votes for women "mean votes for black women," he wrote. There were more than three million women of African descent in the country, and, as the recent biennial of the NACW had demonstrated, women were "moving quietly but forcibly toward the intellectual leadership of the race," the editor conceded. Du Bois also expressed the oft-heard rationale that the inclusion of women in the electorate would "dethrone" the political "heelers" and "grafters" and make for better politics and race betterment.[32]

But well-argued articles published before the great majority of women could actually cast their votes was one thing; working on the operational ground level in a city where, in addition to the usual concerns, the political status quo provided men with employment, patronage, and social mobility, was another. Chicago's two major black newspapers may not have been against African American women voting per se, but neither did they see any particular value in the exercise. Black women did not have to "leave home to rule the nation" was the advice of the *Chicago Defender.* Indeed, few encouraging words were heard from black ministers, politicians, and other civic leaders on the eve of Illinois women exercising the franchise.[33]

Ida's earliest press announcements concerning the Alpha Suffrage Club indicated that she knew that she would have to make the case for mobilizing the electoral power of black women—even to the women themselves. In the past, she had been especially disappointed by the lack of interest among clubwomen, though it is not clear how much of their enthusiasm was dampened by the racism among white suffragists or by Wells-Barnett's own leadership style. In any case, her press announcements were written in pragmatic rather than ideological terms. "If the colored women do not take advantage of the franchise they may only blame themselves when they are left out of everything," ran a notice about an upcoming ASC meeting that brought to mind the recent issue regarding the exposition commission issue. "All other nationalities are studying how to vote. . . . Clubs are being organized among foreign women, even those who don't know the English language. Why should not the colored women who are natural born Americans not be interested in our own welfare?"[34]

Another of Wells-Barnett's tasks was to undermine as much opposition as she could. One of her chronic difficulties was that her dominating style often resulted in her being the issue rather than the principle she was trying to impart. Although Ida was listed as president of the ASC over the course of the next few election cycles, she had learned to delegate authority. Meeting notices showed that a number of them were presided over by other officers of the ASC, including recording secretary (and later vice president) Sadie Adams, a future president of the City Federation and member of the Gaudemus Charity Club, among other numerous black women's organizations, and ASC treasurer Laura Beasley, who taught domestic science at the Frederick Douglass Center. Ida even delegated the editorship of the *Alpha Suffrage Herald,* the ASC's newsletter, to another member of the organization, K. J. Bills.[35]

On a broader level, Ida also made it clear that women did not want to usurp male-held political offices. The object of the ASC, she told the *Defender,* was to make women "strong enough to help elect some conscientious race man as alderman."[36] Wells-Barnett also emphasized that the ASC was nonpartisan. The principle was underlined by the content of the early meetings, held weekly on Wednesdays at 8:00 P.M. at the Negro Fellowship League, which stressed practical matters. Many of the ASC meetings were devoted to educating women about election laws, the use of voting machines, and the political universe of the alderman.

Chicago's seventy aldermen, in addition to being members of the city council and responsible for quality-of-life issues like sanitation and recreational areas, also controlled an intricate network of committeepersons, precinct captains, and their functionaries within the ward. Committeepersons were responsible for delivering the vote in precincts of four hundred to six hundred voters—an area that might be only two city blocks in some instances—and for appointing the precinct captains. The Second Ward, with its population of more than sixty-three thousand, had fifty precincts, and its precinct captains headed their own organization, which consisted of a president, vice president, secretary, treasurer, and block workers—the latter of whom were expected to know each area's constituents and centers of influences, such as churches and fraternal lodges. Ida also understood from her previous campaigns across the state that such lessons were important for women who, by and large, were unsophisticated about the political process, for this ignorance could lead to insecurity, apathy, or downright hostility. The ASC went so far as to train fifteen women to work as precinct judges and clerks who had the specific responsibility of verifying those who had registered to vote.[37]

The most practical—and difficult—thing that women had to learn was the kind of nuts-and-bolts, door-to-door canvassing that white suffragists and machine politicians had perfected. The idea was for the ASC members to go to people's homes and explain why it was important for them to register and make a good showing at the polls. This could be a daunting task in the Second Ward; the *Defender,* for one, was appalled at the prospect of women having to visit rundown rooms, basements, and garrets where all kinds of activity might be going on.[38] But it was not the conditions of the homes or what was going on inside of them that presented the greatest challenge. The women's worst encounters were with the men.

Canvassers returned to ASC headquarters with terrible stories about men telling them that they should be home taking care of babies or that they were trying to take the place of men and "wear their trousers." The sexist barrage was the one thing that appeared to have the power to discourage the ASC members, and it was incumbent on Ida to neutralize the blow. Adjusting her earlier words about the object of the organization, she told the women to go back into the field and tell the naysayers that they were asking blacks to register "so that they could help put a colored man in the city council."[39]

This "line of argument appealed very strongly to them," Ida recalled, and it reenergized the women's efforts. Still, it would take some time for them to be taken seriously and sometimes they were hoisted on their own petards. At the registration centers, women, many of them no doubt for the first time, were obliged to reveal their ages. But a number took advantage of the fact that the law only required them to be twenty-one or older in order to vote. A *Chicago Defender* reporter wrote than when he overheard the wife of a prominent politician tell officials that she was twenty-seven, he "fell to the floor in a fit of laughter." The *Defender* went so far as to list the names of some of the most well-known women with the age they told the registrars in one column and the paper's own estimate next to it. Ida was listed as *admitting* that she was thirty-two; the *Defender* thought her actual age to be forty-one. Evidently, Ida was still looking younger than her fifty-one years.[40]

Once the women's registration numbers were posted, however, the comments about them became more serious. By the registration deadline 7,290 women had been registered in the Second Ward. The work of the women was so effective, Ida wrote in her autobiography, that the number of registrants in the Second Ward (which also included 16,327 men) became the sixth highest among the thirty-five wards of the city.[41]

Politicians were stunned. Suddenly they realized that they had no idea about the impact of "so many ladies who have been hurled headlong into the swirling pool of politics," noted the *Broad Ax*. The *Defender*, which had been advocating the need for a black alderman since Edward Wright's first campaign, now saw the women's entrance into the political arena as the long-sought constituency that put race over patronage and could break the hold of the Second Ward machine. When the paper published its headline "Women To Show Loyalty By Casting First Ballot for Cowan," it was referring to race loyalty. Women were "anxiously" awaiting election day to vote for the black candidate, the paper informed its readers, to "see their first vote make race history in Chicago."[42]

The "first vote," however, came up short. The machine had been able to hold on to enough voters—including a number of black women—for its candidate, Hugh Norris, to prevail in the primary. But he did so by such a slim margin that the political calculus was forever changed in the Second Ward. Norris received 3,056 votes and Cowan, 2,704. The black candidate had lost by a mere 352 votes and had garnered twice as many votes in the overwhelmingly black precincts around State Street. A reason for the impressive showing was Cowan's support by the majority of women. They had cast 1,089 votes of his total, or nearly 45 percent. As the *Broad Ax*, commented, if only 300 black votes had been transferred to Cowan "nothing could have prevented him from breaking into the city council."[43]

The closeness of the election only encouraged the ASC and the *Defender*. They urged Cowan to run again in the April general election. With headlines like "Is the Second Ward a Plantation?" the paper kept drumming up the theme of loyalty, not only to the race but to the women as well. It challenged black men to "shake off the raiment of greed and graft," and to "stand by the women" who had more "race pride" for the "protection of the race."[44]

Following the election, shaken Second Ward bosses dispatched Oscar De Priest, a black politician who had come up through the ward organization, and Samuel Ettleson, a state senator and president of the ward organization, to appear at one of the ASC's weekly Wednesday-night meetings. De Priest, a former county commissioner with a commanding six-foot figure, erect carriage, and a shock of white hair, did most of the talking. He first congratulated the women on their efforts, then told them that their wishes for a black alderman had been heard loud and clear by the organization. He went on to tell the suffragists that George F. Harding was going to run for a state senate seat in the next election and that a black candidate would be named to take his place in time for the 1915 primaries. Consequently, it was no longer necessary to look outside of the ward organization for a black alderman, De Priest assured them; moreover, their continuing to do so would split the Republican vote in the general election and allow a Democrat to win the seat.[45]

Not easily convinced, the women asked how they could be reassured that the organization would keep its promise. De Priest responded by suggesting that the group form a committee to maintain pressure on the ward organization. According to Wells-Barnett's autobiography, the women did organize the committee and were subsequently satisfied by the assurances of the ward politicians.[46]

The visit by De Priest was a brilliant move on the machine's part. The promise to put up a black candidate changed the terms of the political debate from black versus white to that of who would be the best "race man" to represent the Second Ward. The usually astute (but now disgruntled) Edward Wright did little to further an independent candidacy when, in the April election, he supported a less impressive candidate, Charles Griffin, a real estate and insurance broker, who was rumored to be supported by Democrats to split the black vote. Griffin lost decisively to the machine incumbent, Hugh Norris, in the April election.[47]

Apparently, Wells-Barnett and the ASC had decided to hold their powder for the 1915 round of elections and were unaware, as a later historian of Chicago politics observed, that one of the objectives of De Priest and the machine was to counter Wells-Barnett's growing influence.[48]

WHILE WAITING FOR developments in the 1915 elections, Ida remained, as usual, incredibly busy. In May of 1914, she, representing the ASC, was the only "Afro-American commandant" in a large suffrage parade that featured some three hundred women from various suffrage organizations. After the march, Ida spoke at a banquet at the downtown Hotel La Salle that also featured Medill McCormick and Grace Wilbur Trout. The nervousness of black men notwithstanding, Ida and the ASC reached out to white suffragists and candidates. Judge Mary M. Bartelme, the city's only circuit court woman jurist; Marion Drake, who ran for alderman in the First Ward in April; and Mary Dowell and Harriet Vittum, candidates to become county commissioners, all appeared at ASC meetings. The "Alpha Suffrage Club especially insists that every woman voter should register," stated the ASC notice, "so they can vote for the two women candidates and also for Negro candidates on the County Commissioner Board."[49]

Ida also remained busy with her charges from the municipal court and with the struggling Negro Fellowship League. A 1914 *Defender* article, written by a visiting citizen from Denmark, observed that the NFL was doing good work by catering to the "down and outs: the man who gets in conflict with the law not because he is criminal but because he is a fool." The writer called Wells-Barnett the "Jane Addams among Negroes" and lauded the *Fellowship Herald,* which he said had five hundred subscribers, as the "best" Negro paper because it wasn't filled with "nonsense" as were other publications. Little is known about the NFL's economic state in these years, but the writer noted that Ida was "struggling to keep it alive" and expressed surprise that it was so poorly patronized.[50]

It was under the name of the NFL that Ida kept up her fight against racism in Chicago. As the president of the organization, she wrote a public letter to the *Chicago Herald Tribune* when, in eulogizing one of its newspaper sellers—a seventy-year-old black Civil War veteran—the man was referred to as a "boy" and a "darkey." Ida lambasted the paper and noted that such lack of respect was also at the bottom of vicious acts such as a recent lynching in Oklahoma. In June, she was written up when she created a commotion at the Marshall Field's department store after a saleswoman refused to serve her and called Ida a nigger. A crowd gathered around the scene, and Ida, who later said that she never "bandied with hirelings," called for the manager. The manager, probably recognizing her, apologized and promptly fired the saleswoman.

In July, Wells-Barnett wrote a letter to the *Defender* to publicize a number of incidents in which blacks were beaten, shot, and in at least two instances, killed by Greek restaurant owners whose establishments were located near the Fellowship League on State Street. The black victims had either been in quarrels with the owners over the bad quality of food they were served, or were accused of trying to steal it. Wells-Barnett was peeved at the attitude of some black officials who would not criticize the restaurateurs because they thought doing so was tantamount to encouraging blacks to secure food without paying for it. "The league does not believe that Negroes can afford to concede that the Greeks have the right to whip out revolvers and shoot men down in cold blood for alleged offenses," Wells-Barnett wrote. "Our point is that it is time we made a righteous protest against the deadly practice."[51]

Then sometime before the National Association of Colored Women biennial meeting in August of 1914, Susan Joergen-Dahl announced her resignation from the exposition commission due to illness. The governor, it should be recalled, had told black women that in the case of a vacancy, they should revisit the matter with him. Ida, who had not planned to attend the NACW meeting that was to be held in Wilberforce, Ohio, changed her mind when she read of the resignation. She saw the opportunity to get a black woman appointed to the commission if the NACW and the Illinois women could put their support behind a single candidate.

Ida took the train to Wilberforce, and this time she made sure not to have her intentions misunderstood. When the matter came up before the group, she told them that she had come for the sole purpose of informing them about the vacancy on the commission; and that the organization could not be true to its motto ("Lifting as we climb") if it did not send back a demand for a black woman to fill it. "They say that I am interested because I want to be that Negro woman," Ida continued. "That is not my reason. I do not care who is appointed so long as it is a woman of character and ability; but I do not see how colored women can be true to themselves unless they demand recognition for themselves and those they represent." The women agreed and Ida drafted the resolution that was sent to the

Illinois governor. As the group prepared to depart, Ida had one more piece of advice: "I said to the Illinois women, 'Now don't half a dozen of you apply to the governor for appointment. If you do he will be confused and will have a good excuse for not choosing among you.'"[52]

Wells-Barnett did not attend the following state federation meeting in which the women would select a single nominee for the commission spot. As she explained in her autobiography, she had no more leave time from her court job, and in any case, Ida wrote, she did not think that the Illinois clubwomen would choose her to represent them. They didn't. Mary Fitzbutler Waring, a Chicago physician, was chosen. Nevertheless, Waring was obviously a woman of "character and ability," as Ida noted. She was the chair of the NACW's Health and Hygiene Committee; a member of Chicago's Phyllis [*sic*] Wheatley Club, corresponding secretary of the IFCWC, and was already serving as the vice chair of the exposition commission's Education Committee. Her father, Henry Fitzbutler, was also a physician who earned his medical degree from the University of Michigan and later established the Louisville Medical College in Kentucky to train young physicians, one of whom was Mary's mother, Sarah Fitzbutler.[53]

Ida's thinly veiled disappointment did not keep her from continuing to work with the clubwomen in the IFCWC and the NACW to support the hiring of a black woman to become superintendent of nursing for Provident Hospital. The founding of the institution had been inspired by the need for a facility to train black nurses, but black women had been consistently overlooked when it came to filling such high-ranking positions. When a black woman was finally named in September of 1914, Ida sardonically stated that she was glad for the "sake of the hospital that at last the board has decided to do justice to the Colored women who graduate there and give them a chance in their own institution to get the experience and to develop the executive ability which has been denied them all these years."[54]

BY THE FALL, the "denial" of a black alderman for the Second Ward was coming to a dramatic end. As the Republican machine had promised, Alderman George Harding vacated his seat to run for the state senate, and the Madden organization announced that they would support Oscar De

Priest. But the genie of insurgency that the ASC had helped to release was still outside of the Second Ward bottle. Charles Griffin threw his hat in the ring once more, as did a forty-two-year-old lawyer by the name of Louis B. Anderson.

Anderson was by far De Priest's most formidable opponent. Born in Virginia, he was a former newspaper reporter who had come to Chicago from Washington, D.C., to cover the World's Columbian Exposition. Anderson had subsequently served as assistant county attorney between 1898 and 1914, was a former president of the black Republican Appomattox Club (founded by Wright), and was active in a number of important fraternal orders. The lawyer had neither "raiments of graft" nor political enemies to cast a shadow over his reputation. He also had the adamant support of Robert Abbott, publisher of the *Defender* and a reformer who had known Anderson from his earliest days in Chicago when the lawyer got him a printing job at a time when he was making his way in the city.[55]

The *Defender*'s strategy was to insist that Anderson was the "People's Choice." The paper sent a reporter to canvass opinions among blacks and whites in the Second Ward and claimed that nine out of every ten voters preferred Anderson over De Priest, the ward bosses' candidate. The *Defender* also featured testimonies of pro-Anderson constituents and supported the candidate's call for a preprimary straw poll to determine which of the three candidates voters believed to be the best race man for the job. Neither De Priest nor Griffin rose to the bait.[56]

Predictably, the campaign was filled with charges and countercharges, driven, in large part, by the black press's criticism of the past behavior of black politicians in general and of De Priest in particular. De Priest had never supported the Second Ward insurgency. He had always backed whomever was most favorable to his interests, Republicans or Democrats.[57] His preference for expediency over principle was also evident in his business dealings. De Priest, who had risen from a semi-employed house painter in Chicago to become a successful real estate agent, exploited Chicago's residential racism instead of challenging it. He managed his properties by taking a long lease on apartment buildings that were occupied by whites but located on the periphery of the ever-expanding black community. He would then encourage blacks to move in and thus begin the cycle of white flight, which culminated in full black residency and the higher rental rates he could charge once the complexion of the neighborhood changed.

At the same time, De Priest was no political hack and had earned the ward organization's support the hard way—by working assiduously through the precinct levels to become a county commissioner in 1904.[58] From the time he had first spoken to the women of the Alpha Suffrage Club, De Priest had begun accruing the support of the grassroots political and working-class community. By 1915, he had gotten the support of thirty-eight of the ward's fifty-three precinct captains as well as of such groups as the Hotel Waiter's Association, the Colored Barbers Association, Baptist and Methodist ministers, and, of course, women—including, it appeared, Wells-Barnett.[59]

Ida admired De Priest's work ethic, and as her support of the late saloon owner Bob Motts revealed, she forgave past sins if she believed that the person was bound to make an important contribution to the race. Moreover, she would have liked De Priest, a native of Florence, Alabama. Much of his life had paralleled Ida's own. De Priest's father, a farmer, was an independent man who, like James Wells, had defied orders to vote for the Democratic ticket during Reconstruction. Subsequently, he defied a lynch mob by hiding a well-known black politician in the family home. De Priest was himself combative, and after the family migrated to Salinas, Kansas, he used his fighting skills to protect his five siblings, who were the only blacks in the town. He carried no airs and made up for his comparative lack of education and polish with dogged determination and shrewdness.[60]

As the February primary drew near, the Second Ward appeared to be heading for a split vote between the three black candidates, but just days before the election, the Alpha Suffrage Club again became a deciding factor. A testament to its influence was the fact that it was the only organization in which all three candidates came to present themselves. Each gave a campaign talk before the clubwomen at their State Street headquarters and remained to answer their questions. By then, the ASC had about two hundred members, and to assure against any last-minute treachery, it had passed a resolution that any member thought to be working for a white aldermanic candidate would be expelled. After hearing all three men, the women discussed the aspirants with the objective (as Ida had insisted in the case of the commission appointment) of coming to a consensus about the single candidate that the organization would support.[61]

There is no information about the deliberations of the club, but as noted in the *Alpha Suffrage Record*, De Priest won the backing of Ida's organization, and it is likely that Ida had an important hand in the selection. In addition to the personal qualities of De Priest, there was another reason why Ida would favor him. As she freely admitted in her autobiography, De Priest "had asked my support and I had told him that I would give it to him with the understanding that if he won he would use his influence to see that Mr. Barnett realized the dream of his life and was elected judge." De Priest, it seemed, agreed. Unstated in her autobiography was that De Priest had probably also promised Ida help with her Negro Fellowship League; in 1914, the NFL's letterhead listed De Priest as chairman of the board.[62]

The black politician wasn't the only one who would ask for Ida's endorsement. Running in the Republican mayoralty primary was a former Second Ward alderman, William Hale Thompson, who invited both Barnetts to one of his political meetings to aid his candidacy. "Big Bill," as he was known, was a rakish, affable WASP. He was a yachtsman who was no stranger to a barroom brawl and was fond of wearing the Stetson cowboy hats he had donned as a child growing up in Wyoming and Nebraska. Thompson understood the political math in a period when Democrats had secured their first- and second-generation ethnic niches; middle-class native-born whites were hurling themselves headlong to the suburbs, and blacks were showing their muscle. He had calculated that he needed the two latter constituencies to win and knew how to appeal to progressive-minded whites, black reformers, and—with his glad-handing, folksy, populist appeal—"unreformed" African Americans as well. "I'll give you people jobs," he told one black audience during the campaign. "And any of you who want to shoot craps go ahead and do it."[63]

He may not have been the kind of politician that the Barnetts preferred, but Ida must have been flattered to be told that Thompson had inquired as to who the "masses accepted as their leader" in the Second Ward, and that her name had been given to him. When she and Ferdinand went to Thompson's political meeting, Ida was asked to speak and took the opportunity to demand where the candidate stood on a number of issues and to express her disdain for white politicians who came to the Second Ward on election day to buy votes and thereafter were not seen again. Ida told him that blacks needed more opportunities for employment in city work and that "representation be given us commensurate with our voting strength." At the end of the meeting, Thompson publicly addressed Ida's concerns, convinced her of his sincerity, and offered Ida the deal clincher. If Thompson won the mayoralty, he would make the NFL reading room and social center an auxiliary of the city, thereby assuring its financial stability. He also promised to give city jobs to blacks who came through the NFL's employment agency. At last, Ida thought, she had "a friend in court who believed in working for the benefit of our people." Soon after her meeting with Thompson, the Alpha Suffrage Club became the first black organization to endorse him for mayor.[64]

Ida "threw her heart and soul" into his campaign. She appealed to every woman's club, civic organization head, and others, to get more than twenty thousand pledges in the Second Ward on Thompson's behalf. Ida also created a hundred-member committee of the ASC to work for De Priest. She organized programs and gave a reception for ward chieftain Martin Madden. In the *Alpha Suffrage Record*, she praised Madden's votes in the last Congress and reiterated the club's enthusiastic endorsement for "our young giant, Oscar De Priest," and William Hale Thompson.[65]

Ida's hopes must have been high as she found herself becoming a player in the complicated politics of Chicago. But as happens to most amateurs in the professional ranks, Ida just as assuredly found herself on the wrong side of the field. Late in the primary race, Governor Deneen's progressive faction of the party decided to put up their own candidate for mayor: one of the Barnetts' most stalwart supporters, chief municipal court judge Harry Olson. Olson had stood by Ferdinand during his 1906 race for the judgeship, and he had gotten Ida the probation job that had helped keep the Fellowship League afloat. As Ida knew, the judge didn't stand a chance against the charismatic Thompson. Even Deneen, said to have the charisma of a mud turtle, looked exciting compared to Olson. As the *Chicago Tribune* observed, a "certain sort of laboratory exactness and chill efficiency" characterized the jurist's campaign.[66]

Nevertheless, Ida could not betray her friend. "All my life I have been the victim of ingrates," she explained, noting that she agreed with the Spartan philosophy of putting those who fit the description to death. She and Ferdinand concurred that she had to leave the Thompson campaign; and together they decided to recommend that Ed Wright, who had also been collecting pledge cards for Thompson, take her place.[67]

In February, black women excitedly arrived early at the polls. The papers noted how "club women and church women" vied with each other to make the best showing" and described how the candidates' wives walked briskly through hundreds of well-wishers (and a few women loiterers leaning against saloon doors) to cast their votes at the polls. The results reflected the women's enthusiasm. De Priest polled 3,194 votes against Anderson's 2,632 and Griffin's 1,432. Women cast a total of 2,355 votes, with 1,093 of them going to De Priest and the rest split between the two other candidates. Clearly, women and, it can be argued, the ASC, provided De Priest his victory.[68]

Big Bill Thompson won his primary as well, by 2,500 votes, and the margin of victory had been secured by the "Colored voters down in the Second Ward [who] swung the decision in favor of William Hale Thompson," the *Chicago Daily News* concluded. As one biographer of Thompson noted, the Second Ward vote was not as much the doing of "Big Bill" as it was the (Regular) Republican ward organization's decision to support a black candidate in 1915. Thompson's victory was merely an extension of that decision; and that decision had been made largely as a result of the race-first attitude of black women in general, and of Ida and the ASC in particular.[69]

After the primary results, Ida doused another potential split when the ever-restless Edward Wright announced that he was going to back William Cowan, the women's previous favorite, to run in the April general election. Wright announced his intention at a meeting of his Political Equality League to which Ida also belonged. When Ida tried to cut off the discussion by offering a motion for the group to support De Priest, Wright ruled her out of order, precipitating one of Ida's spirited denunciations. She scolded Wright, saying that his support of Cowan at this point would surely split the vote and diminish the chances to elect the first black alderman. When her plea came to no avail, it was probably Ida who stirred the subsequent uproar among black women who began demanding the names of all those who planned to support Cowan so that they would know "who the traitors are." It is not known how much Wright was influenced by the promise of a backlash for his candidate, but before the April general election, he came around, as all of the other black candidates did, to support De Priest.[70]

In the general election both Thompson and De Priest were victorious. "Big Bill" received 80 percent of the Second Ward vote; De Priest, the sole black candidate in a field of four, won with less than a three-thousand-vote plurality. Again, women had proved to be the difference. They cast 3,899 votes for De Priest, and he would not have won without their support.[71]

De Priest's victory was cause for much celebration in the Second Ward and provided many poignant moments for blacks. The *Defender* recounted the first city council meeting in which the new aldermen were present and De Priest's mother smiled with "tears of joy trickling down her cheeks" when her son rose to make a motion. De Priest, before the crowded chamber, moved to declare August 23, 1915, a legal holiday in Chicago to celebrate the memory of the freedom of blacks to coincide with the scheduled opening of the Lincoln Jubilee and National Half-Century Exposition. The resolution was approved and became the first ordinance signed by Mayor Thompson.[72]

Ida should have been feeling a great deal of satisfaction to know that her hard work and her vision had been so instrumental in making history. After she founded the city's first black women's suffrage club in 1913, Chicago soon became the home of the greatest number and largest black women's suffrage clubs in the nation. Ironically, however, in the end, she would gain less and lose more than any other political figure connected to the campaign.[73]

After the election, Ida was informed by Thompson's men that the mayor owed nothing to her because she did not "go with him to the end." At the same time, Ed Wright, who had tried to rout the Republicans before he had replaced her in the Thompson campaign, was appointed as an assistant corporation counsel with a salary that was higher than that of any other black appointee. Losing candidate Louis Anderson was also appointed to the same office by the mayor. Mary Waring was indeed appointed by Governor Dunne as a commissioner for the exposition, which De Priest had further enshrined at his first city council meeting. However, the new appointee evidently had accepted the laurel with no acknowledgment of how she got it. "The fact that she did not show me any recognition of the work I had done did not destroy the force of what had been done in her behalf," Ida wrote in her autobiography in an apparent attempt to find the better angels of her nature.[74]

But the biggest slight was from De Priest. When he was interviewed for the *Crisis* and asked about the role of women in his campaign, he responded that he had found that the women's vote was as "intelligent" as that of the men, and that women "seemed to realize fully what was expected of them, and with the men, rolled up a very large and significant vote for the colored candidates." De Priest did add that the women were "consistent" and "contributed to the plurality" for the "colored candidates," but relative to the work of Chicago's black women and to Ida—who was not mentioned by name—the words were faint praise indeed.[75]

Faint praise was also a good way to describe words about Wells-Barnett in the September 1915 issue of the *Crisis*. Her name was mentioned in a feature entitled "Some Chicagoans of Note," a six-page article with no byline, in which the first mention of any woman was found on the lower half of page five. After claiming that it was difficult to find women of note because "of their natural desire to avoid publicity," the writer called Ida "one of the best known colored women in America." The article went on to recount the Memphis lynching that was responsible for her subsequent "crusade," and concluded that "not before or since has the world been so aroused over the disgrace of American mob murders." The description sounded more like an obituary than the description of a woman who had just helped change the political dynamics of one of the largest cities in the United States.[76]

But the oversights paled against the worst cut of all. Wells-Barnett's costly political about-face resulted in her losing her job as a probation officer, the salary of which was helping her keep the NFL alive. Even if De Priest had been willing to help, he soon ran into his own difficulties. A year after his election, he was indicted by the state's attorney, Maclay Hoyne, a Democrat whom De Priest had once supported but abandoned in the last election for the Republican candidate. Defended by Clarence Darrow, De Priest was eventually acquitted of influence peddling for a "notorious saloon and cabaret" in the ward, but the Republican organization asked him not to run in the next election. Louis B. Anderson, whom Ida had campaigned against, succeeded De Priest as the next black alderman. The campaign season, which had begun with such promise, had ended in utter disappointment. A weaker woman would have thrown up her hands in despair.

CHAPTER TWENTY-TWO

Unsafe for Democracy

If we don't work in the South we are jailed; if we
do work in the North we are mobbed.

—Atlanta Independent

In June of 1915, Ida, as was her custom, was scouring the newspapers before sitting down to dinner with her family, when an item caught her eye. It was a story about a black man named Joe Campbell, who was being held in solitary confinement in Joliet Penitentiary. Campbell, already doing time for killing a labor goon, had been accused of murdering the prison warden's wife.[1]

Both Barnetts had long been interested in prisoners' rights. Ida's Alpha Suffrage Club had recently visited incarcerated women at the Bridewell prison to conduct civic classes; and just the month before, she, along with other committee members from the City Federation of Colored Women's Clubs, had gone to one of the county jail facilities to assess its condition, and its treatment of black inmates and to thwart any attempt to segregate blacks in a new facility that was planned. Governor Edward Dunne, a former judge, made penal reform one of the hallmarks of his administration, but as the Barnetts knew, vigilance was necessary to ensure that such reforms did not occur at the expense of blacks.[2]

In 1913, Dunne had appointed Edmund M. Allen as warden of Joliet to reform the overcrowded facility, which had a history of disciplinary problems and inmates who contracted tuberculosis and other lung diseases caused by the smoke belched out daily by the nearby steel mills. A new facility in a better location was under construction, and Allen had already begun to implement his progressive views about how prisoners should be treated. He believed, as he had written in a 1914 report, that the "barbarous exactions and ruthless discipline" traditionally aimed at inmates should be replaced with policies that brought out their human potential. "There is some good in every man," he wrote, "and there exists some influence which will appeal to his heart and reason." Acting on this principle, the warden instituted an "honor system" for inmates wherein good conduct was rewarded with certain privileges and better job assignments.[3]

Joe Campbell's conduct had earned him the status of a trusty, who was assigned to be the personal servant of Odette Allen, the warden's wife. Campbell was due, in a little more than a week, to go before the Board of Pardons and Parole, and Mrs. Allen had promised to testify on his behalf. But on June 20, while Edmund Allen was out of town, a fire broke out in the second-floor bedroom of the warden's house. When prison guards and convicts from the volunteer fire department rushed to the residence, they found the lifeless body of Mrs. Allen. A later investigation found that alcohol had been spread over the bedding and that Mrs. Allen's skull had been fractured. The coroner concluded that she had been knocked unconscious before succumbing to smoke inhalation and the flames. The Allens' physician, who also had access to the warden's living quarters and was himself a convict in the prison for killing his wife, claimed that Odette Allen had also been strangled and sexually assaulted—though he had not made a thorough examination and no secretions were analyzed.[4]

Campbell was immediately arrested for the crime and put into solitary confinement—an ordeal that included being put in a lightless cell with his hands manacled, being subjected to third-degree questioning at any time of day or night, and being fed only bread and water. After forty hours of such treatment, Campbell confessed to the crime. But when he testified at the inquest, he insisted on his innocence and did so with such earnestness that he gave the impression, as the *Chicago Defender* reported, that he was telling the truth.[5]

Impressions aside, Ida understood where Campbell was headed: to a guilty verdict and a death sentence. "Here we are," Ida thought, after reading the account at the dinner table, "seventy thousand Negroes sitting up here in Chicago enjoying ourselves and giving no concern whatever to his plight."[6] Unable to eat, Ida excused herself and went upstairs to her room. As she lay across her bed, she turned the situation over in her mind, wondering where she could turn for help. Clearly she had little faith that politicians, gearing up for national and state elections, would come to Campbell's aid, and she had little faith in the NAACP's Chicago branch. Ida was still fuming over the fact that the civil rights organization had been utterly unprepared for the court case that successfully challenged the city's injunction against the showing of *Birth of the Nation*. The film—a cinematic masterpiece based on *The Clansman*, Thomas Dixon's toxic novel depicting black corruption and rapacity during Reconstruction—debuted at the White House, where President Wilson was heard to comment that it was "all so terribly true."[7]

While Ida was still mulling over the Campbell problem, two friends rang her doorbell. It was about 10:30 at night, and they had just seen the racist film and were complaining about what an outrage it was. "I am not worrying about that anymore," Ida told them. "I am worrying about that man down in Joliet." By that time, Ida had decided to go and see the new editor of the *Chicago Record-Herald*, James Keeley, and Ida invited the women to accompany her that same evening to the newspaper office.[8]

Keeley was empathetic, even relieved, Ida noted, that she had come to him about Campbell. He proposed that she write something then and there that would appear in the next edition of the paper. "All shudder to think so terrible a crime could be committed within the prison walls, but I write to ask if one more terrible is not now taking place there in the name of justice," Ida's appeal began. Campbell was "sweated and tortured to make him confess to a crime that he may not have committed. Is this justice?" she demanded. "Is it humanity? Would we stand to see a dog treated in such a fashion without protest?" Ida added that the Negro Fellowship League was going to provide a lawyer to represent the accused man. As Keeley had promised, the appeal was displayed prominently in the paper, and according to Wells-Barnett, it persuaded Governor Dunne to move Campbell from the penitentiary into the nearby county jail.[9]

The lawyer that the NFL had promised to provide was, of course, Ferdinand, who was now in private practice. He went to Joliet only to be told by authorities that Campbell already had an attorney, so Barnett returned to Chicago without seeing him. Subsequently, Ferdinand met the man who was said to be Campbell's attorney, but he denied that he was. He had just happened to be at Joliet at the time of the hearing and had advised Campbell to plead guilty. At that point, Ida wrote a letter to Campbell himself. In the meantime, a number of black Joliet citizens who had read Ida's article asked her to address a meeting in the city. When she arrived, she discovered that they had been told that they could not see Campbell. Refusing to accept the prohibition, she led the group to the jail and demanded access to the prisoner.[10]

Like the *Defender*, Ida was impressed by Joe Campbell, and she believed him when he told her he was innocent. He had no relatives, no money, no standing in the community, and he said that Wells-Barnett was the first person of his race who had written or visited him. "I know that if I am given a chance I can prove that I am innocent of this crime," he said.[11] After their meeting, Ida was determined to raise money to pay for an attorney and court expenses. It was estimated that three hundred dollars was needed for the cost of court reporters, witness fees, and other contingencies. Ida began the campaign by speaking before a Baptist church in Joliet, and after returning to Chicago, she sent a representative of the NFL into the field to solicit funds. Meanwhile, prosecutors had solicited the county board to provide a fund to help their own case. With the little the NFL had raised, Ferdinand took on the case of Campbell with a commitment no less intense than his wife's.

For the next six weeks, he left for Joliet at seven in the morning and returned home at seven or eight each night. The case demanded all of his attention and soon he was forced to turn over other clients—and their fees—to his colleagues. Wells-Barnett kept up her own fund-raising campaign, aided by her Alpha Suffrage Club and the *Defender*, which promised to publish the names of the contributors. Subscriptions began to trickle in from members of church groups and other "common folk," but she was frustrated that politicians and other prominent persons remained unmoved. Ida, of course, kept haranguing influential blacks, and in July, the NFL hosted a conference with representatives from ten black organizations, including women's groups and male-led political groups. The pressure finally began to bear fruit. By the fall, just before the trial date, Louis Anderson, Ed Wright, and S. A. T. Watkins—an old acquaintance and a Democrat who had apprenticed with her former Memphis lawyer, T. F. Cassels, and was an assistant city prosecutor—lent their names to appeals for Campbell. The Chicago NAACP's Robert McCurdy and another lawyer, A. M. Cowings, also agreed to help Ferdinand in the case.[12]

In November, the *Defender* carried a story about the trial. Campbell made a good witness and Ferdinand skillfully challenged a number of claims by the prosecution and provided a time line of Campbell's movements on the day of the fire to show that he had not been near the residence when it had been set. While the case was proceeding, another major story broke, one that would have an impact on the Barnetts and on the plights of all the Joe Campbells in Chicago and beyond.[13]

ON THE TENTH of November, the *New York Tribune* reported that Booker T. Washington was in St. Luke's Hospital, suffering from a nervous breakdown and hovering near death. The news came as a surprise. Washington had been active over the previous several months on a number of issues that found common cause with those whom he had once opposed. In January, he was decidedly at the helm of an intense and extensive lobbying effort regarding the bill to bar all immigrants of African descent from entering the country. The Senate had already incorporated the measure, and the bill was set to be voted upon in the House. Washington, with less than a week to accomplish the task, put his famed machine to work, using the black press and mobilizing various organizations in the effort, as well as his Business League lieutenants across the country who were assigned to buttonhole various congressman about the bill. The NAACP, Monroe Trotter, and Ida also had fought the proposal, but there is little doubt that Washington's effort and standing was instrumental in getting Chicago congressman Martin Madden to throttle the legislation in the House, and thus assure its defeat. In the last year of his life, Washington also wrote daily press articles against the inequality of separate facilities on southern railroads and streetcars, and he discreetly tried to thwart the rising tide toward residential segregation in the nation's cities.[14]

He had entered St. Luke's on November 8, following a busy schedule of meetings and lectures in New Haven, Connecticut. Upon his arrival in New York, Washington went to the hospital for a prearranged series of exams by a team of physicians. His health had been precarious for some years, but only a few intimates knew of his condition. One of those was Provident Hospital physician George Cleveland Hall, who had once been Ida's doctor and was the president of the Chicago branch of the National

Negro Business League and the Chicago branch of the NAACP. In late October, Hall had written a concerned letter to Julius Rosenwald in which he described three severe kidney attacks in a space of fifteen days he had recently spent with the educator. Washington, Hall also told the philanthropist, had dangerously high blood pressure.[15]

Indeed, the doctors at St. Luke's confirmed that Washington was critically ill. The attending physician, Walter A. Bastedo, told reporters that Washington was "aging rapidly," that there was "noticeable hardening of the arteries," and that he was extremely nervous. It is not clear what possessed Bastedo to make public what Washington had made such effort to keep so private for the last several years—or why the physician volunteered an additional statement about the Tuskegeean: "Racial characteristics are, I think, in part responsible for Dr. Washington's breakdown."[16]

When Hall read the comments, he wrote an anguished letter to Rosenwald's secretary, William Graves, complaining that the "racial characteristics" comment was commonly construed as syphilis, and that Washington had had no indication of the sexually transmitted disease, nor had he ever been tested for it. It is unclear if the doctor's diagnosis was influenced more by stereotype than science. But the breach of ethics on so many fronts might have been an ironic demonstration of the kind of low racial regard that Washington himself had encouraged. Graves suggested that a more temperate version of the Chicago physician's remarks be sent to Tuskegee's trustees.[17]

Bastedo also intimated to the press that Washington was near death. Soon after the pronouncement, the educator summoned his wife, Margaret, to come to New York. When she arrived, Washington requested that he be released from the hospital so that he could return home to Tuskegee. His doctors advised against it; they did not think he could survive the trip. But Washington insisted. He told the physicians that he had been born in the South, had lived and labored in the South, and that "I expect to die and be buried in the South." Refusing the wheelchair provided by the hospital, Booker T. Washington leaned on the arm of his wife to exit the building for the car that took them to the Pennsylvania Railroad Station. He reached the Tuskegee campus at 12:30 Sunday morning, November 14—and died at 4:45 A.M. the same day.[18]

The man who had held the power to interpret and define the aspirations—and inadequacies—of African Americans like none other before or after him was gone. The cloud over the diagnosis did little to diminish the high-sounding memorials from former presidents, students, friends, industrialists, and civic and religious leaders reflecting his unique stature in American culture. If Ida commented publicly about Washington's death, there is no extant record of her words. Du Bois, however, did sound a dissonant note about Washington's role in hastening the decline of Negro colleges and the "firmer establishment of color caste. "Gravely and with bowed head let us receive what this great figure gave of good," he eulogized in the *Crisis*, "while silently rejecting all else."[19]

Chosen to continue Washington's legacy was Robert Russa Moton, a Hampton graduate and president of the National Negro Business League. Before being selected to take over the reins of Tuskegee, Moton had been a long-time associate of Washington. He often accompanied the educator on his fund-raising trips, where he preceded Booker's appeals by leading the audiences in singing "Negro melodies." Theodore Roosevelt, a member of the Tuskegee board, had preferred Moton over the other candidates. He was "absolutely free from the bumptiousness or self-assertiveness which at once [would] ensure failure in his position," TR informed his fellow Tuskegee board member Julius Rosenwald. The Chicago philanthropist replied that he was happy to hear that Moton was free from the "assertiveness which is so likely to be a disagreeable trait in one of his race."[20]

IN THE WAKE of Washington's death, Joel Spingarn, who replaced Oswald Garrison Villard as chair of the NAACP board in 1914, convened what he called a "unity" meeting at his wooded estate in Amenia, New York. Among the black attendees in 1916 were Du Bois, Emmett Scott, Fred Moore of the *Age*, Atlanta University's John Hope, Howard University's Kelly Miller, and clubwomen Mary Church Terrell, Nannie Burroughs (a founder of the Woman's Convention of the National Baptist Convention, U.S.A., and founder of the National Training School for Women and Girls in Washington, D.C.), and NACW president Mary Talbert. Terrell, appraising the lineup, chirped that it was "the first time that so many colored people who differed so widely . . . had come together since the Emancipation Proclamation."[21] Nevertheless, the two persons who differed most widely from any in the assembled group were absent: Ida Wells-Barnett and Monroe Trotter.

The *Guardian* editor had declined Spingarn's invitation. From his two letters to the NAACP official, it was obvious that Trotter sensed that the meeting's real purpose was to get the others to fall in step with the NAACP. But Trotter believed that the "welfare of the race as well as harmony" would be "best promoted by the positive recognition of the need for racially autonomous organizations . . . that will enable all to abide by their convictions." As for the NAACP, specifically, Trotter hoped that it would "do its good without doing harm, and therefore encourage and not discourage national self-organization and self-leadership."[22]

There is no record of Ida's explanation for not joining the group. She still wrote occasionally to Spingarn, and it is likely that she, too, was invited. Ida, of course, would have shared Trotter's sentiments. In fact, in January of 1915, she had been elected vice president of his National Equal Rights League (NERL). In the same month, Ida had invited Trotter to be the keynote speaker for the NFL's Fifth Annual New Year's Eve Celebration of the Emancipation Proclamation at Orchestra Hall, and she had later arranged a speaking tour for him across a number of states as far west as Nebraska, where he organized new branches of the NERL. The gesture on Ida's part was more than an act of solidarity; it was also a show of public support at a time when he, again, was coming under public criticism—this time for his behavior during his second visit to President Wilson two months before.[23]

IDA HAD NOT accompanied Trotter on his second visit to the White House. On that occasion, the NERL president had very specific information about particular departments and floors where black employees were being cordoned off in isolated alcoves and "herded" to separate tables, eating facilities, and most "humiliating" of all, lavatories. Trotter again reminded the president of his promises regarding racial justice and asked in his opening statement if Wilson meant to have a "new freedom" for whites, and a "new slavery" for blacks.[24]

In response, Wilson again talked about avoiding "friction," spoke of the "intrinsic" equality between the races ("because we all have human souls"), and said, in so many words, that separating the races wasn't a humiliation unless Trotter and blacks of his ilk believed it to be so. The exchange got sharper when Trotter began interjecting questions while Wilson was speaking. How did the common use of toilets create friction? Exasperated, Wilson finally told the *Guardian* editor that he was the only American who had ever spoken to him in such a tone, and that if representatives of the NERL wanted to meet with him again, they would have to find another spokesman.

A transcript of the meeting showed that Trotter was insistent but never disrespectful or intemperate. In fact, as Wilson later admitted to an aide, it was he who had lost his temper. He had been distraught since the recent loss of his wife, Ellen; and affairs of state were weighing on his mind. That August, three months before Trotter's visit, the world's first global conflict had broken out, pitting Germany, Austria, Hungary, and Turkey against Britain, France, and Russia (soon to be joined by Italy).[25]

The confrontation between Wilson and Trotter made national headlines and brought mixed reactions. Liberal mainstream newspapers, as well as a good number of black publications, faulted both Trotter's behavior and Wilson's segregation policies. Robert Moton informed the president that blacks, generally, did not approve of Trotter's conduct; Charles Anderson, Booker Washington's one-time aide-de-camp, boasted to Wilson aide Joseph Tumulty that he was responsible for the cancellation of a New York meeting where Trotter was to speak. Anderson added that he hoped he would not be dismissed from his job as collector of internal revenue in New York. (He was dismissed, anyway.) Joel Spingarn wrote the NAACP's official response to the president, saying that while the Association did not "excuse any rudeness or lack of courtesy," it did agree with Trotter's views about segregation.[26]

This time Du Bois was more generous. He gave ample space in the *Crisis* to what he called the "curious incident" and praised Trotter's "fearlessness" and "unselfish devotion to the higher interests of the Negro race."[27] The editor's turnabout might have reflected a change of heart, but the NAACP was also cognizant that Trotter had won the hearts and minds of the "common folk," as Ida called them. After the Wilson episode, the *Guardian* editor's appearances drew large crowds who were hungry for leaders willing to stand up to the powers-that-be, rules of etiquette notwithstanding. "Afro-Americans Do Not Cringe: President of the U.S. Becomes Incensed," was the congratulatory headline of the *Chicago Defender.*[28]

Monroe Trotter "accomplished more by insulting the President . . . than all the polite words ever uttered on segregation could or will accomplish," opined Albert Pillsbury, a former Massachusetts attorney general who was a member of the NAACP's Boston branch. NAACP staffer May Childs Nerney was concerned about "what Mr. Trotter's next coup may be. He mustn't make us appear to the country as having done nothing on the segregation issue."[29] Trotter was on the rise when he spurned Spingarn's unity meeting in 1916. At the time, the drift—and the volume—of black public opinion was such that the NAACP needed him more than he needed them.

A year after Booker T. Washington's death, a tectonic shift was beginning to be felt in the country. Beginning in 1916, the migration of southern black men and women to the North was reaching the proportions of a mass movement. Cotton-killing boll weevils and distastrous floods in the South colluded with the diminishing number of immigrants from war-torn Europe to create a perfect storm of reasons for some half-million African Americans to find their way North, where eager employers awaited to hire them.[30]

The rapid demographic change created a new challenge for prim NAACP liberal progressives, black and white. In the past, black leaders and northern intellectuals could claim to speak on behalf of the race— the vast majority of whom lived at a metaphorical and geographical distance away in the South. But now the southern working classes were trooping into northern cities where they could vote for, judge, and choose those who best represented their interests and the strategies to employ.[31] Wells-Barnett and others could now envision amassing "our political strength," as she told the delegates of the NERL, so that "no president again would ever dare to offer us such insults as we [have] suffered . . . and thus teach them to fear our vote as they do now the labor vote." Run out of the South for her direct-action techniques against lynching, Ida was now in the position to effectively use the strategy again—particularly after the death of Booker T. Washington, lynching's most effective black arbiter.

Particularly horrific murders in 1915 and 1916 had turned the nation's attention again toward lynching. In 1915, a Jewish businessman, Leo Frank, was falsely accused of raping and killing a young white girl in Marietta, Georgia. Frank was hung by a mob in the town square after his sentence was commuted by the governor. In 1916, the fifty-five lynchings of blacks included the mob murder of Jesse Washington, a retarded adolescent, who was tortured and burned alive before fifteen thousand onlookers in Waco,

Texas; and in Newberry, Florida, five blacks, including two women, were hung in a row from a single oak tree.[32]

In 1916, Boston philanthropist Philip G. Peabody informed the NAACP that he would give the organization $10,000 if it could come up with a viable antilynching strategy. Roy Nash, the white NAACP executive secretary, was charged with writing a report to the philanthropist about the organization's conclusions.[33]

Only two names were mentioned in the final thirty-five-page document, which included statistics, the history of lynching, and antilynching legislation. One was that of James Cutler, author of the first scholarly text on lynching, *Lynch-Law* (1905), which Nash used for the historical section. The second name was Ida's. Nash detailed how her campaign in the United States and abroad resulted in antilynching laws in Texas, Virginia, Georgia, Tennessee, Kentucky, Ohio, and Maryland. However, he also noted that few states had such statutes, and while demanding damages from counties in which lynching occurred appeared to pass constitutional muster, he was less sure about the clauses that called for the removal of sheriffs. Nash then referred Peabody to the article "A Federal Remedy for Lynching," written by Albert Pillsbury and published in the *Harvard Law Review*. The former Massachusetts attorney general had designed an antilynching bill that Ida had supported in her presentation before the NAACP's first national conference in 1909. Though Pillsbury remained unconvinced about the constitutionality of a federal law that superseded states' rights, he believed that the legal issue could be resolved in the federal courts once Congress acted.[34]

However, what was clear from the report was that the NAACP had no new ideas about combating lynching. Its focus on three areas of activity— information gathering, investigation, and influencing southern business and political leaders to speak out against lynching—borrowed from Wells-Barnett, but did not include the kind of direct action that was the key to her strategies.[35] The Joe Campbell case was the most recent example of the need to mobilize opinion as well as to seek legal remedies. Despite the legalistic errors that Ferdinand and the defense team had uncovered in the case, Campbell was found guilty and sentenced to be executed in April of 1916. But thanks in large part to Ida and the *Defender,* who kept up the campaign in the increasingly politically potent black community, Governor Dunne and his Republican successor, Frank Lowden, felt obliged to give the prisoner reprieves while Ferdinand continued his appeals. It could be argued that Campbell was still alive because of the clamor of the increasing number of black voters who were making their new homes in Chicago.[36]

Peabody remained unconvinced by the NAACP report. He withdrew the initial offer, but said he would give the organization a thousand dollars if it could raise another nine thousand from people who thought his assessment was wrong. Villard headed the fund-raising committee, and by the fall of the year, the group had raised ten thousand dollars. The exercise had convinced the NAACP that it should create its own anti-lynching fund, and William English Walling headed a special committee for that purpose. The development set the stage for the competition for resources and popular appeal as the country headed toward some of the worst violence ever recorded—violence that followed the black migrants to the cities of the North, cities like East St. Louis, Illinois.

EAST ST. LOUIS had all the makings for a major race riot in 1917. Known as the "Pittsburgh of the West," it was an industrial center with large meatpacking and manufacturing houses, thousands of unskilled laborers and immigrants, and, following the outbreak of World War I, an influx of black migrants. In 1917, the blacks who made up 10 percent of the city's population of fifty-nine thousand were joined by thousands of African American strikebreakers brought in from the South by the Armour, Swift, and Morris meatpacking plants. The inevitable labor tensions seethed against a backdrop of a tough port city, inefficiently governed and known for political corruption. A close election in 1916, in which Woodrow Wilson and his party struggled to hold on to power, prompted Democrats to charge that the Republicans were "importing" blacks to the city, and "colonizing" them there to cast illegal votes for the G.O.P.[37] A black Republican leader, Le Roy Bundy, was briefly incarcerated for allegedly accepting money to further the scheme but was released for lack of evidence.

During the campaign, the "colonization" angle was whipped to a froth in the press, which spouted familiar slanders about the dangerous element of corrupt, crime-prone blacks who were getting large sums of money to buy arms and lure southern migrants to East St. Louis. Speculation for the source of funds ranged from the Industrial Workers of the World (IWW), a militant socialist labor organization, to large manufacturers who sought to undermine striking white workers, to the German government, which sought black conscripts in the city that was also a site of a number of munitions factories. Wells-Barnett later asserted in the *Chicago Record-Herald* that blacks and law-abiding whites were victims of a well-financed conspiracy perpetuated by the labor unions, southern manufacturers, and planters to force blacks back to the South.[38]

But it was the German angle that would prove especially troubling. According to one scholar of the period, the rumors that blacks could fall sway to German agents was an important subtext for the inflated fears regarding German subversion in the coming years. President Wilson added fuel to the madness by warning about vote fraud at the hands of "conscienceless agents of sinister forces" and had his assistant attorney general investigate the colonization charges.[39]

In the end, Wilson lost woefully in Illinois, by two hundred thousand votes to former Supreme Court Justice Charles Evans Hughes, but the president won reelection by carrying the western states. Democrats also prevailed in East St. Louis where the residue of race-baiting continued to fester. In May of 1917 a raucous union meeting—that had opened with the parading of white women from the waitress and laundry workers unions to emphasize the need for their protection from black men—proved to be the precursor of a larger tragedy when it disintegrated into the formation of a mob that spilled onto the downtown streets, beating every black man and woman in sight.[40]

Tensions were still high two months later when, on the evening of July 1, 1917, a Ford automobile occupied by four white men drove at high speed through a middle-class black neighborhood in the city. The men in the car were reportedly yelling and cursing and brandishing revolvers, which were fired into dwellings and a church. When the car returned again, waiting blacks shot at it, and the car sped off. Police, informed that armed Negroes were on a rampage, were dispatched to the scene. The police car was also a Ford. In the front seat were two white detectives in civilian clothes and the driver; uniformed officers sat in the back. When the car appeared in the neighborhood, shots rang out. The two white detectives were killed.[41]

By the next morning, July 2, an enraged mob that had heard of the shooting marched in military formation down one of the city's main streets to a major intersection for a streetcar line. An excited crowd gathered at the site in anticipation of what surely was to come. They were in good humor, an observer recalled, who likened them to a group waiting for a circus parade.[42] When the first African American victim unwittingly appeared at the intersection, he was murdered in full view of the bystanders. By nightfall, a full-scale attack was unleashed in the same half-mile area. Streetcars were stopped; men, women, and children were pulled off to be clubbed, kicked, and stoned. Witnesses saw whites who came across beaten black bodies lying unconscious in the street calmly stop and shoot them. As the mob fanned into the black community, terrorized citizens fled homes set afire, only to be routinely mowed down, tossed back into the flames, or left to burn on the street. Even the bringing in of the Illinois militia offered little respite. A number of witnesses and newspaper reports pointed out that instead of protecting blacks, they disarmed, jailed, taunted, and even killed them. The *Chicago Defender* reported that Illinois troops stood around and laughed as children and men were killed and women were stripped of their clothing. Another reporter saw a member of the Illinois Guard strike a black woman and young boy and toss them back into a burning shack. *Crisis* investigator Martha Gruening, who was white, relayed that she had come upon some militiamen who grinningly boasted about their killing "seven niggers" and dumping them into the Cahokia Creek.[43]

Before the two-day riot subsided, two hundred homes had been burned down, most in the sixteen-block African American Black Valley district. Some five thousand blacks fled the city. It was impossible to accurately calculate the death toll. The official total was thirty-nine; other estimates were at least double the figure. However, the bodies that continued to find their way to the surface of Cahokia Creek, and the belated discoveries of piles of charred bones, attested to an even higher death count. Ida put the figure at one hundred and fifty.[44]

"Never at one time in the south were so many black men and women deliberately murdered in cold blood," observed the *Chicago Daily News*. What had happened in East St. Louis was "more than a race riot," the paper concluded.[45] Oscar Leonard, a Jewish civic leader in St. Louis, likened the violence to the pogroms against Jews in Eastern Europe—with one difference. At least the Russians "gave the Jews a chance to run while they were trying to murder them," Leonard observed. Russians could learn a lot about "pogrom making from East St. Louis whites," he insisted.[46] In the *Crisis* article on East St. Louis, Du Bois added another distinction. "In all the accounts given of German atrocities, no one, we believe, has accused

the Germans of taking pleasure in the suffering of their victims." A letter
to the *New York Tribune* predicted that East St. Louis represented the "first
shot of a worldwide racial struggle." Its author was a then little-known Jamaican who had just arrived in America: Marcus Garvey.[47]

On July 3, 1917, the Negro Fellowship League called a meeting at its
State Street headquarters. "I presided," Ida wrote in her autobiography,
"and suggested to the audience that while we were waiting for our speakers, they might sing 'America' or the 'Star-Spangled Banner.'" The "suggestion" was no doubt a provocative wartime gesture. In April of 1917,
Wilson had called upon the nation to support the Allied war effort in
order to "Make the world safe for Democracy." The overflow crowd not
only refused to take up Ida's invitation, they railed against the bitter irony
of it.[48]

Adelbert H. Roberts, a protégé of Ferdinand's who was a deputy clerk of
the municipal court, hoped that God would take revenge against white
Americans on the battlefield for every black life that had been lost at home.
Roberts loved his race better than he loved his country, he proclaimed. But
it was Ferdinand Barnett, no longer hamstrung by his position as a state's
attorney, who was the most insurrectionist. "Arm yourselves now with
guns and pistols," he told the audience, adding that Chicagoans should not
let police come into their homes and confiscate their weapons, as they had
in East St. Louis. Many of the same sentiments were festering in Chicago
and blacks should be prepared for the worst. When "trouble starts, don't
hesitate to call upon our Negro militiamen to defend us," he concluded,
referring to the all-black Illinois Eighth Regiment—which had, since 1898,
distinguished itself fighting in Cuba and Mexico.[49]

At the end of the meeting, a Citizens' Committee was formed and a
resolution was passed to send to Governor Frank Lowden, a Regular Republican, that complained about the "reckless indifference of public officials."
Money—eight dollars and sixty-five cents—was also raised to send Ida to
East St. Louis to investigate and then present the facts to the state executive.[50]

IDA TOOK THE sleeper to East St. Louis the following day. The conductor, she said, was incredulous that she would dare to set foot in the still-
smoldering city that had erupted just forty-eight hours before. Ida got off
the train and began to walk toward city hall. She saw no blacks on the

street until she reached the city hall building. A young guardsman was posted in front and she asked him about the situation. "Bad," he replied; blacks had killed seven whites the day before and three that morning. Wells-Barnett thought that he was lying but kept the opinion to herself and asked to be directed to the adjutant general's office in the city hall. Her interview with the officer confirmed that the militia had been ordered not to shoot white men and women and that many had stood by as blacks were being savaged.[51]

Before she left the office, Ida saw a number of black women come into the waiting room. Their clothes were dirty, she recalled, and their heads were bare. Ida went over to talk to them and learned that they had just returned from St. Louis, across the river, and the city's municipal housing lodge where thousands of dazed and battered men, women, and children had found refuge. The women were waiting for a military escort—motor trucks with soldiers on the front and back with thirty rounds of ammunition each—to take them back to their homes. Ida asked if she could go along with them.[52]

When they arrived at the site where the homes had once stood, the women found that those that had not been burned had been looted. The women recounted their experiences, and Ida wrote them up in a pamphlet, *The East St. Louis Massacre: The Greatest Outrage of the Century*. If the title skirted hyperbole, it also signaled that "outrages" not only had taken on a new form, and in another region of the country, but also had reached a new scale of violence.

Much as she had done in her antilynching pamphlets, Ida—in addition to her recounting the political and racial origins of the riot, the resolutions of the Citizens' Committee, and her interview with the city's mayor—wrote short narratives about the victims. *The East St. Louis Massacre* opened with the stories of the four women she had followed back to their homes. Ida wrote briefly about their backgrounds, how long they had lived in the city, the material possessions they had lost (one woman saw a white neighbor wearing some of her finer clothes), and their eyewitness accounts of seeing blacks beaten and killed.[53]

Ida interviewed some fifty persons; she also included in her report damning descriptions from the white press about the "best classes" being involved and the participation of white women in the violence. She quoted the *St. Louis Post-Dispatch*, for example, which described how white women pounced on a young black girl. "Please, please, I ain't done nothing," the girl protested before she was silenced by a "blow in the mouth with a broomstick" swung like a bat. Another woman seized the young black girl's hands, and others clawed her with their fingernails while she was being continually hit with the broomstick. Finally, sleeves were torn from her waist, and some male onlookers shouted, "Now let her see how fast she can run."[54]

IDA RETURNED TO Chicago on July 8, only to find out that electoral politics had reared its self-interested head. Another group of black Chicagoans, calling themselves the "Real Citizens Committee," had already called on Governor Lowden. Led by Ed Wright, Oscar De Priest, Louis Anderson, and Robert Jackson, they assuaged Lowden, according to Ida, by telling him that they did not agree with the Barnetts and that both she and Ferdinand were considered "radicals" and outside the mainstream of black attitudes.[55]

Anderson was the Second Ward alderman, and Jackson and De Priest were preparing to square off to run for the second alderman seat in April of 1918. All three politicians were no doubt taking account of the fact that Lowden, the son-in-law of the late sleeping-car magnate George Pullman, was angling for a presidential nomination and could not afford to be found negligent.

Ida convened an overflow meeting at the Fellowship League, which selected a group to travel to Springfield to demand courts-martial for the offending militia. The meeting was followed by a larger one at Bethel AME Church, to raise money for the delegates to go to the capital. Bethel was now pastored by W. D. Cook, a North Carolina–born Howard University graduate, who joined the Citizens' Committee with the Barnetts, Adelbert Roberts, and Ida's brother-in-law, Bernard Fitts, among others. As Wells-Barnett pointedly noted, when De Priest, Anderson, and Wright were mentioned at the meeting, their names were "hissed."[56] Once in Springfield, the governor, according to the *Broad Ax* (whose editor, Julius Taylor, was also a member of Ida's group) promised aid to the victims and to punish the offending militiamen.[57]

Ida also characterized the meeting with Governor Lowden as "very satisfactory," with the exception of his advising the group against "incendiary talk." At that point, Ida responded that if he had "seen women whose husbands had been beaten to death, whose children had been thrown into the flames and the river, whose women had been burned to death, he would not say it was incendiary talk to denounce such outrages."[58]

Ida, in the company of Delores Farrow, a nurse from Provident Hospital, subsequently returned to East St. Louis and to the St. Louis municipal lodging house where many of the refugees had been staying. Ida hoped to get more testimonies about the militiamen; Farrow had come because, as she explained, the Red Cross, which helped to escort East St. Louis refugees to the municipal lodging house, did not accept black nurses, and so she was particularly anxious to provide any needed assistance.[59]

Ida had expected to see hundreds of blacks at the municipal facility, but by the time they got there, many had either left during the day to return to work in East St. Louis (returning to St. Louis each night) or had left for good. Nevertheless, she was able to get some of the needed information. One witness, John Avant, told her how soldiers had fired into a group of blacks standing near a restaurant, shooting off a woman's arm in the process. Another victim, William Bass, told Ida that soldiers had entered his home and, before driving him, his wife, and nine children out, had asked how much money he had in the house.[60]

After getting these and other statements, Ida prepared to leave for East St. Louis, only to be stopped by officials. Smallpox had broken out in the lodging house, and Ida was told that she had to be vaccinated before she could leave the station. Although angry that officials seemed to only be vaccinating blacks who wanted to leave the city, she nonetheless acquiesced. The policeman, she said, looked as if he would like nothing better than to arrest some "obstreperous Negro."[61]

Ida was taken by patrol wagon all the way to the other side of town to get her shots, but she was nonetheless able to find a way to avoid the long lines and slip out the door. At that point she saw her friend Annie Turbo Malone—the well-known manufacturer of Poro hair preparations and cosmetics—and her husband, James. They spirited her away to their house, where Ida stayed for the remainder of her visit.

Before she left the city, an inquest had already begun. The first group of witnesses testified that Le Roy Bundy, a black dentist, was the leader of the group that fired the first shots at the white-driven automobile and that the provocation was part of a massive conspiracy to kill whites in the city. Bundy, who had earlier been arrested in connection with the colonization scheme, was a member of a prominent family from Cleveland. He was an outspoken, militant political figure who had been a member of the East St. Louis County Board of Supervisors and a founder of the St. Clair County (Negro) Republican League. His stands had made him particularly anathema to labor and to Democrats.[62]

In the meantime, W. E. B. Du Bois visited the city to publish a firsthand report. The subsequent coverage in the *Crisis* used Ida's familiar blueprint: graphic details, excerpts from white press accounts, and vivid testimonies of eyewitnesses, though Gruening's access to white soldiers and witnesses—including one of the latter who had seen a black man beheaded with a butcher knife—added another dimension to the account. The dramatic *Crisis* article was the first comprehensive investigation of the massacre to be published and it proved to be a boon to the NAACP's fund-raising efforts. One thousand dollars was donated toward its campaign to aid in providing legal assistance to blacks charged with taking part in the conspiracy. Mary White Ovington was especially pleased to get contributions from black fraternal orders; it indicated, she said, that the NAACP's reputation was growing among the black rank and file.[63] With its resources, the civil rights organization also conducted the most effective public protest against the violence. On July 28, nearly ten thousand demonstrators marched in silence to the sound of muffled drums down New York's Fifth Avenue.

DU BOIS'S REPORTAGE of the East St. Louis riot moved the black soldiers of the Twenty-fourth United States Infantry, Third Battalion, to organize a relief committee on behalf of the Illinois city's refugees. The men had arrived at Camp Logan in Houston, Texas, on the very day of the Fifth Avenue parade. The committee collected nearly $150 and sent it to the NAACP along with expressions of praise for Du Bois's "fearless" stand and also informed the national office that the soldiers desired to form a chapter of the NAACP among themselves.[64]

There was a good deal of pride in the Twenty-fourth. Its origins hailed back to the Civil War when the infantrymen had shown their valor and courage in battles at Milliken's Bend, Fort Wagner, and Port Hudson. During the first three decades of its existence, the Twenty-fourth had the lowest rate of desertion in the army and fewer courts-martial than most white units. During the Spanish-American War, the infantrymen had been at San Juan Hill with Theodore Roosevelt, and they later volunteered to nurse soldiers stricken with yellow fever at Siboney, Cuba, after eight other units had refused to do so. Subsequently, they served honorably in the Philippines.[65]

With the outbreak of World War I, the Twenty-fourth had fully expected to be sent overseas but instead were ordered to Texas, where they were consigned to the relatively menial tasks of guarding government property. Also stationed at the camp were the Eighth Infantry and National Guardsmen from West Texas and Illinois. The presence of the black soldiers created racial tension, both on the base, between black military guards and white laborers doing construction work, as well as in the city. Black soldiers refused to abide by the segregated seating in the city's trolley cars and on one occasion a scuffle ensued with police when a soldier ripped off a "colored only" sign in a segregated restaurant.[66]

However, it was in August 1917 when a series of incidents occurred that later resulted in the largest court-martial ever held within the United States. On the 23rd, a black soldier was beaten and incarcerated for coming to the aid of a black woman, Sara Travers, a housewife and mother of five, who was being abused by two policemen. The two police officers had earlier burst into the woman's home in pursuit of several black teenage crapsshooters, and when she objected to the intrusion, they dragged her out of the house to take her to the police station. The black soldier had come upon the scene and was jailed after challenging the policemen about their treatment of Travers.

Upon hearing about the incident, Corporal Charles Baltimore, a black provost guard, sought out the white police officers, who had returned to their station in the San Felipe district. According to the lawmen, Baltimore appeared threatening. The Houston officers attacked the soldier and then shot at him when he tried to escape. Subsequently, they arrested him. Word about the shooting got back to Camp Logan, where a rumor (proven to be false) spread that Baltimore had been killed.[67]

The soldiers were overheard throughout much of the day threatening reprisals—not only against Houstonians but members of the white Illinois Guardsmen who had been in East St. Louis during the massacre. By that evening, the determination to do so superseded orders to remain in their quarters or the fact that some had learned that Corporal Baltimore was alive and that one of the offending policemen had been suspended. The final catalyst was a cry that a white mob was coming for them. Under the direction of Sergeant Vida Henry, a thirty-five-year-old Kentuckian and thirteen-year veteran, about one hundred soldiers made their way to the police headquarters in San Felipe. By then a mob of one thousand whites was waiting. Henry gave orders to fire; and before the confrontation ended, fifteen whites—including five police officers, two soldiers, and two civilians working with the police—were killed. Two black civilians lost their lives, as did four of the black soldiers. The latter included their leader, Vida Henry, who, rather than surrender to authorities, discharged his rifle into his mouth.[68]

Upon hearing about the mutiny, the NAACP arranged for a white attorney, A. J. Houston, son of the famous Sam Houston, to aid in the soldiers' defense. Among others who offered support was the Illinois Federation of Colored Women's Clubs. The women demanded that "justice be meted out to those prepared to shed blood for the preservation of the flag" and sent the resolution to President Wilson, Congressman Martin Madden, and Secretary of War Newton D. Baker. Wells-Barnett was chair of the resolutions committee.[69]

WHILE MILITARY AUTHORITIES investigated the mutiny, Illinois was furiously bringing indictments against blacks in East St. Louis. By the end of the process, the *Chicago Defender* concluded that blacks "received decidedly the worst of it." In October, eleven black men, nearly all of whom were considered "citizens of good repute" and active in lodges and their churches, were sentenced to fourteen years in the penitentiary for conspiracy in the killing of the two police officers.[70] In shameful contrast, four whites were convicted of homicide, and forty-one, under plea-bargain arrangements, were found guilty of only misdemeanors. Two policemen who shot unarmed blacks, and who were accused of doing so by a white militiaman, received fines of one hundred and fifty dollars. A number of whites, complicit in the violence, simply fled the jurisdiction with impunity.[71] Enraged blacks demanded a congressional investigation, and U.S. Congressman Leonidas C. Dyer, who represented a large African American constituency in St. Louis, called for hearings.

During the course of the trials, it became clear that one black man above others would be made the scapegoat to justify the travesty of the riot and the legal proceedings: Le Roy Bundy. If found guilty of murder and conspiracy, he could receive no fewer than fourteen years in the penitentiary;

but, there was an expectation that as the alleged leader of the conspiracy, he would be given a life—or death—sentence.

Bundy had fled to Cleveland where he engaged the NAACP to fight extradition proceedings, but by October he was in an Illinois jail, and, as he claimed, he did not have adequate funds to pay for a lawyer. "The Race as a whole must stand by this man," insisted the *Chicago Defender,* for his "was not the fight of one man, but a fight of the entire Race." Letters started pouring into the newspaper office containing contributions for Bundy. The *Defender* promised to publish the names of contributors and forward the money to Mrs. Bundy.[72]

Wells-Barnett, too, urged the community on. By "our parades and protests, and prayers the Negro has succeeded in securing the congressional hearings," Ida pronounced in the *Broad Ax.* But "we are now entering upon the second stage when dollars will win the battle." We "must strike in our own defense," she emphasized. It was time to work in the "trenches."[73]

Soon after she was quoted in the press, Ida got word that Bundy himself wanted to see her. Assigned by the *Defender* to interview him, Ida, on a Wednesday afternoon in late October, took the train to Granite, Illinois, where she was met by a friend of Bundy's, Dr. Earle Williams, who drove her the twenty-two miles to the Belleville County jail. As Ida described in her autobiography, when Bundy saw her, his face lit up while he explained why seeing her was the first ray of hope he had had in many a day.[74]

Ida hadn't realized it, but Bundy, whose father was a presiding elder of the AME Church, had been the manager for Reverend Archibald Carey's efforts to become a bishop of the church the year before. Carey had had the support of De Priest, Louis Anderson, and Robert Jackson—the same trio who had undermined her report to Governor Lowden. It was believed that the minister had the position in hand until Ida intervened. She had discovered that Carey was greasing the palms of the AME electorate with money given by Mayor Thompson and other politicians. Ida sent a letter to the black Methodists saying that Carey had been buying votes and that it was enough "to make Richard Allen [a founder of the denomination] turn over in his grave." There may have been any number of factors that Carey failed to get the bishopric that year, but Bundy told Ida that her letter had "turned the trick."[75]

Now he wanted her to help him. As he explained, his father had given the NAACP two thousand dollars for his defense, but no attorney had yet seen him about his case since his return to Illinois. According to the dentist, the local defense attorney who had adjudicated the earlier cases was still owed money for those trials and refused to take on Bundy until he was adequately compensated. Bundy asked Ida to see NAACP officials in St. Louis about the matter. (The Missouri chapter was in charge of the Bundy case.) Ida told Bundy she would do what she could. "I wish the Defender staff could have seen the look of gratitude and hope on his face when he understood that he had new help coming to his defense," Ida wrote in the November 3 edition of the paper.[76] After leaving the prisoner, Ida went to see the chair of the chapter's executive committee, Charles A. Pitman.

Pitman, Ida reported, was annoyed by her inquiries. Everything had been arranged, he said, informing her that the NAACP had been able to get the services of Charles Nagle, a lawyer of national prominence who had served in the Taft administration as secretary of commerce. Nagle, it appeared, had agreed to defend Bundy pro bono, but the strategy was that local lawyers would continue to defend a number of the accused, including Bundy, and that Nagle would come in later to sum up the dentist's defense. "But," Ida insisted, "unless you have somebody to prepare the case and get the evidence in shape, there won't be anything to sum up, and that is what somebody ought to be doing right now and that is what is making Dr. Bundy so anxious."[77]

Dissatisfied with the St. Louis branch's plans for Bundy, Ida contacted two lawyers whom the dentist had recommended. One of them asked for a fee of three thousand dollars in cash; the other told her that the defense would require an extraordinary effort. Recently, he had attended a dinner where he had overheard Governor Lowden tell Attorney General Brundage that the full power of the state would support his prosecution. At that point, Ida thought that the thing to do was to raise money for a retainer fee. She formed a finance committee that included Dr. Williams and was under the auspices of the Fellowship League and Trotter's Equal Rights League. Pledges for funds, she announced, should be made through the *Defender.* Ida was indeed in the trenches.[78]

Wells-Barnett did not identify the lawyers by name, and though the chronology of events is not clear, it appeared that sometime after her visit to Bundy and Pitman, Thomas Webb of the prestigious law firm Webb and Zerwick was retained by the NAACP for Bundy's defense. In any case, in

November, Bundy's lawyers had managed to get a change of venue and the NAACP was satisfied about the progress of their case. Bundy, however, was not. As Ida had earlier implied, his fate, he believed, rested more with politics than good lawyering. In November, Bundy, in what appeared to be a plea-bargain deal, pled guilty to accepting three hundred dollars in a voter-fraud case.[79]

The confession enraged—and embarrassed—the NAACP, which had determined that the organization's support should be confined to those believed to be innocent of any crime. "Imagine our situation," Du Bois later wrote. "We were making a hero of Bundy. We were holding him up as a brave and persecuted man. . . . In the midst of all this Mr. Bundy comes out and confesses that he is hand and glove with the men and is part of the system which made East St. Louis a city of corruption and made it possible for such a horrible riot to go on without interference by authorities."[80] But as Ida and many others knew, immaculate heroes are rare indeed, personal ledgers were filled with deficits, and the ultimate corruption that got blacks killed was race hatred. What mattered was the final balance regarding racial justice. The NAACP would eventually sever ties with Bundy while Wells-Barnett, the *Defender*, and much of Chicago's black political community continued to support and raise money for him.

The difference in perspective became clear regarding the Houston soldiers. The NAACP had had trouble unfurling its pristine banner about the mutiny. Staffer Martha Gruening's investigation had revealed that in addition to the brutal treatment of black Houston residents by the police and policies prohibiting black military police to carry arms, another underlying reason for the rebellion was the lax discipline at the camp where excessive drinking, partying, and promiscuous behavior took place.[81] Moreover, the timing of the mutiny had also dampened plans for the establishment of a black officers' training camp, and it had even been responsible for a temporary halt in all black recruitment while the government debated whether blacks should be in combat at all.

In October of 1917, Du Bois had written a gut-wrenching editorial in the *Crisis* that bemoaned the "wells crimsoned with the blood of black martyrs." Always "WE pay; always WE die," he wrote. It was obvious that his empathy was deep for the soldiers of the Twenty-fourth, who had reacted to the raw injustices of race, but in the final analysis they had broken the law and Du Bois pronounced, as his final word: We ask "no mitigation of their punishment."[82] None was given.

In the predawn hours of December 11, 1917, thirteen of the sixty-three soldiers who had been charged with disobedience, mutiny, assault, and murder were taken from their cells to an isolated spot where a hastily constructed gallows awaited them. With their hands tied behind their backs, and their feet secured, the men were lifted from army vans and placed on a row of folding chairs on the gallows' platform. To the man, they refused blindfolds. While the hangman's knots were being adjusted, they softly sung a hymn in which the words "I'm coming home" could be distinguished. As the nooses went around their necks, they appeared relaxed, they did not struggle. Trapdoors on the scaffold finally opened, and soon after, the bodies were placed in unpainted coffins, and lowered into thirteen predug graves. The execution had been carried out before the verdicts had been announced to the public and without the customary right of appeal to the president. Not even their requests to be shot by firing squad instead of the degrading death by noose were honored.[83]

Of the remaining soldiers, forty-one were given life sentences; four long prison terms. Five additional men were also condemned to death. In a second court-martial, eleven were also given a death sentence. Du Bois, distraught by the raw reality of the hangings, offered a stinging criticism of the administration's failure to allow the men the opportunity for appeal. His January 1918 editorial in the *Crisis* ranted against the double standard that allowed "hundreds of thousands of white murderers, rapists, and scoundrels" to walk "scot-free" and "unrebuked by the President of the United States." The editorial's lack of restraint earned the reprobation of, among other members, Mary White Ovington, whom the editor supported to replace Joel Spingarn as chair of the board.[84]

When Ida learned of the execution, she attempted to hold a protest rally in one of the major churches. Despite her claims that she wanted to conduct a "solemn" and "dignified" protest, no one was about to take a chance on the Barnetts so soon after the passage of the Espionage Act in June of 1917. The vaguely worded legislation carried a fine of $10,000 and a prison term of up to twenty-six years for any person judged to interfere with the conduct of the war, inciting mutiny or disloyalty, or making false or malicious statements intended to hinder the military effort. In charge of the new powers regarding the press was Postmaster General Albert Burleson, architect of the federal segregation policies in the Wilson Administration. Unable to hold a protest, Ida did the next best thing. She traveled to Leavenworth for the *Defender* to interview the soldiers of the Twenty-fourth who were incarcerated there.[85]

In the piece she characterized them as "stalwart young chaps," "with a quiet reserve," whom other prisoners saluted to show their respect. She expressed their hopes that others would take interest in their plight and try to get them a new trial. The article also included a testimonial to Vida Henry, the leader of the mutiny. She pointed out that it was Henry who had led his men in collecting funds for the East St. Louis refugees. In contrast to the anguished assessment of Du Bois, Ida concluded that whatever "the motive and however wrong the action, his bravery and daring will make his memory live forever in the hearts of those who knew his story." He was a lover of the race, and that was what in the end mattered.[86]

Ida returned to Chicago determined to formally recognize the fallen soldiers in some way. "It seemed to me a terrible thing that our government would take the lives of men who had bared their breasts fighting for the defense of the country," she wrote in her autobiography. Later that month, January of 1918, five additional soldiers of the Twenty-Fourth were sentenced to hang. Ida believed that if the Negro Fellowship League did nothing, no one else would, so she came up with the idea to have buttons made that memorialized the martyrs of the Twenty-fourth. Soon after, a reporter from the *Chicago Herald Examiner* came in to ask about the buttons. Ida gave him one of them, explaining their purpose while keeping to herself why she was forced to make them in the first place. "I didn't want the white people to know that we were so spineless as not to realize our duty to make a protest in the name of the black boy who had been sacrificed to race hatred," she wrote.[87]

Predictably, Ida was soon visited by two intelligence officers who warned her that if she continued to distribute the buttons, she would be arrested. "On what charge?" Ida demanded. "Treason," riposted the smaller of the two men. She was not guilty of treason, she said, but "if you think I am, you know your duty." Somewhat taken aback, the agents then said that they were going to confiscate the buttons because they were critical of the government. The government deserved to be criticized, Ida told them, for hanging soldiers as if they were criminals. When reminded that few took the stand that she did, she said that she'd rather go down in "history as one lone Negro who dared tell the government that it had done a dastardly thing," than save her neck by being quiet. It would be an "honor" she added, to go to prison under such circumstances.[88] Ida was dauntless, but not imprudent. Despite the government's intimidations regarding subversion, criminal guilt, she must have known, was difficult to prove in court.

Nevertheless, the intelligence file describing the same meeting indicates that the account written in her autobiography was, if anything, understated. Although much of the report is smudged and hardly legible, the agents' description of Ida going "into a great deal of detail concerning her protest" about the soldiers being hung without the benefit of an appeal to the president is discernible. The report continued to say that she would not promise to stop distributing the buttons and that she would consult a lawyer about her next course of action. Although it was hard to make out the full text, the words "she would die for . . . if she had to" can be discerned. Unable to get Ida to comply, one of the agents in the case, Frank G. Clark, instead warned the manufacturer of the buttons to neither accept more orders nor distribute those that remained.[89]

The intelligence report was at least the third that concerned the Barnett family. Ida's East St. Louis Massacre pamphlet was also on file, appended by a note that said it was being used "to stir up a great deal of inter-racial antagonism." Additionally, soon after Ferdinand's "arm yourself" speech, a report to the chief of the Bureau of Investigation, probably aware of his German constituency when he was a prosecutor, described him as "rabidly pro-German," and fluent in the language. The dossier went on to note that Illinois law allowed any number of firearms and ammunition in one's residence, that "several thousand negroes are believed to have bought rifles from Department Stores," and that most of the large black population in Chicago was armed. "Men like Barnett," the report grimly concluded, "can very easily cause a good deal of trouble if they are not careful."[90] On that matter, the investigators turned out to be right.

CHAPTER TWENTY-THREE

Known Race Agitator

> It is reported to this office that Ida B. Wells-
> Barnett is considered a far more dangerous agita-
> tor than Marcus Garvey.
>
> —*Military Intelligence Division*

D uring 1917 and 1918, the fear of German sabotage and its effect on African Americans thrust the issue of black patriotism high on the agenda of the Wilson administration. The new premium put on black loyalty provided African American leaders with a new leverage to demand their rights at home; it also raised their level of risk—and surveillance by the government.

By 1918, the Wilson administration had put in place the nation's first modern political intelligence apparatus. Information gathering, once the purview of scattered civilian and military agencies, was coordinated and centralized; new laws were passed to facilitate the prosecution of offenders; and new agencies had been created to monitor Americans. The latter included the Military Intelligence Branch (MIB) of the War College Division headed by Lieutenant Colonel Ralph Van Deman. Following the East St. Louis riot, Van Deman became convinced that an MIB subsection on "Negro Subversion" was warranted.[1]

National security concerns were especially high during the first months of 1918 when the war was at a critical juncture. By then, the newly created Unified Allied Command, after reversals the year before, was winning bloody victories against the Central Powers; Bulgaria, Turkey, and the Austria-Hungary Empire were on the verge of surrender; Russia had had a Bolshevik Revolution; Germany was planning a spring offensive—and after a good deal of hand-wringing, the United States was finally prepared to send black troops to the European front.

Making democracy safe for Negroes was a common concern of race activists, who were nonetheless divided over the best means to proceed. For some, a display of loyalty was the key to gaining citizenship rights, which, it was believed, would inevitably be conferred if blacks demonstrated their patriotic mettle. That patriotism rather than protest was the key to black progress was the wartime version of a philosophy that Ida had militated against since the beginning of her antilynching campaign, when she had exhorted that compliant behavior on the part of blacks was not an agent of change. While she put her organizations to work to aid the U.S. war effort through selling Liberty Bonds and preparing Christmas packages for Illinois's Eighth Regiment (which included her stepson, Ferdinand Barnett, Jr.), Ida still saw no value in muffling dissent. The familiar debate over the efficacy of protest versus that of accommodation took on a new dimension in the period—and new protagonists. The conservatives were led by Du Bois and the NAACP, and the militants, by Wells-Barnett and Monroe Trotter.

The NAACP had tried, unsuccessfully, to get an appointment with the president following the East St. Louis riot, but by February of 1918, the morale of black troops was an important concern, and Wilson thought it politic to receive a delegation from the organization. The group had come to lobby the president about commuting the sentence of sixteen additional Twenty-fourth Infantry soldiers who were slated for execution in the wake of a second court-martial. Additionally, in the light of forty-eight lynchings that occurred in 1917, and several at the beginning of 1918, they also expressed their hope that Wilson would make a statement that condemned the practice.[2]

Heading the delegation was James Weldon Johnson, soon to become the NAACP's first black executive secretary. He cut a very different figure from Wilson's former black petitioners, Trotter and Wells-Barnett. Johnson, a novelist, musician, and the lyricist of "Lift Every Voice and Sing"— known as the Negro national anthem—had served (with the support of

Booker T. Washington) as a U.S. consul at Puerto Cabello, Venezuela, then at Corinto, Nicaragua. If he still possessed the militant passions that had inspired him as an Atlanta University student in 1892 to advocate violent resistance to lynching in the wake of Ida's early editorials, he had learned to express them with the reserve of a diplomat. Johnson's temperament served him well in his negotiations with the president who, at least on one occasion, regaled the former consul with stories about his "old black mammy" back home. At the end of the half-hour meeting, Wilson told the group that he would review the decision of the court-martial and "seek an opportunity" to say something about lynching. Shortly after the visit, the federal government commuted the sentences of ten of the sixteen soldiers to life imprisonment. The remaining six were executed as planned.[3]

The government's decision reflected, in part, its carrot-and-stick approach, which included compromise, punishment, and persuasion. The most convincing agent for the last was Major Walter H. Loving, one of the half-dozen or so black operatives in the MIB. Loving, who had served in the Philippines constabulary, where he had founded and conducted the Manila Band, fervently believed that if blacks proved their unswerving loyalty during the war, first-class citizenship would be the inevitable reward.[4] His power of persuasion had been evident when, in March, he convinced the mother of one member of the first group of executed soldiers, Corporal Larmon Brown, not to fall sway to "certain organizations" that were planning to exploit her son's funeral in order to spread "discontentment" among colored people. Mrs. Brown "was so touched at the way I approached her," the intelligence agent boasted to his superiors, "that she not only consented to have a quiet funeral, but would have the body taken to her home in Maryland for interment."[5] The major's reports contained the most insightful observations of blacks in the period, and he was the government's most valuable "Negro Subversion" operative.

If the promise of progress was the carrot for blacks, there was also a stick to keep them and other putative subversives in line. In May of 1918, Congress passed the Sedition Act, an even more draconian amendment to the Espionage Act. The law made it a crime to say or publish anything "disloyal, profane, scurrilous or abusive" about the government, the flag, the armed forces or to bring "contempt, scorn, contumely or disrepute on them."[6]

The legislation's vague wording allowed an administration filled with segregationist southerners to interpret virtually any published protest as treason. In the same month that the Sedition Act was passed, military intelligence launched an investigation of the Georgia-born Robert Abbott, publisher of the *Chicago Defender*. By 1918, the paper—begun with a total capital of twenty-five cents in 1905—had a circulation of 120,000, with two-thirds of its readers from outside of Chicago. The *Defender* was not considered the most influential of all of the black publications; that attribution belonged to the *Crisis*. But the Chicago weekly was, in many ways, considered the most dangerous because of its combination of popular appeal, race advocacy, and stories calculated to spur black migration. Abbott consistently compared the terrors of the South with the opportunities and cabaret pleasures in the North—especially in Chicago. Its ads flaunted some of the city's more than 731 black business establishments; and its sports pages touted Chicago's all-black baseball team. The *Defender* painted State Street in colors that could brighten any tedious life. The "Stroll," between Twenty-sixth and Thirty-ninth streets, not only included churches, the Negro Fellowship League, Provident Hospital, and offices, it also featured the dance halls of the Pekin Theater and the Palace Garden, which offered live jazz and all-night dancing. Most important to authorities, the *Defender* carried news of lynchings and black exploitation throughout the South, which was in stark contrast to the stories that showed that African Americans snared by Chicago's justice system had tireless—if not always successful—advocates. A number of those stories involved the Barnetts.[7]

In April of 1918, the paper announced that Joe Campbell would not be executed. After losing his appeal in the Illinois Supreme Court, his sentence was commuted by the governor. Campbell was not freed; he was sentenced to life in prison, sparing him from what appeared to be an inevitable death sentence. The *Defender* also published a story about Ferdinand's defense of Emile Mixon, a Mississippi migrant who had been a sharecropper and was employed as a fireman for the Illinois Central Railroad. When Mixon filed a grievance against the company, his supervisors tried to get him extradited to Mississippi where he had allegedly committed a crime. Although the *Defender* did not detail the nature of the infraction, it noted how Barnett was able to quash the extradition order after he traveled to Mixon's home to investigate and brought evidence that his only crime was asserting his "manly rights" in resisting the southern peonage system.

Both Barnetts also worked with the Board of Pardons by testifying on behalf of prisoners. According to the *Broad Ax,* Ferdinand, by 1917, had managed to attain freedom for seven parolees from the Illinois State Penitentiary and more than fifty from the state reformatory. Ida, as the *Defender* noted, continued to work for prisoners' rights through the Negro Fellowship League. In April of 1918, she appeared before the parole board at Joliet on behalf of William Smith, who had been found guilty of kidnapping a child and sentenced to ten years. Smith, who was without funds, appealed to Wells-Barnett to investigate the case. Subsequently, he was released when Ida discovered that the child had been found and was living with his parents.[8]

Wells-Barnett's work on behalf of John Cloures, who was imprisoned in Joliet for killing a policeman, was the subject of several articles. Cloures had claimed self-defense in the shooting, and while in the penitentiary, he was convicted of murdering a fellow prisoner after the latter made a sexual advance. Although Cloures had wanted to plead guilty in exchange for a plea bargain, the judge in the case forced a jury trial in which the black man was sentenced to be hanged in June of 1918. His appointed attorney, a white man, failed in a last-minute appeal to get the Illinois Supreme Court to review the case, and as the time drew closer to the execution date, Cloures wrote to both Ida and the philanthropist Julius Rosenwald for help. Two days before the execution date, the lawyer waited upon Governor Lowden to ask for a reprieve. At that point, according to the *Defender,* Lowden told him that he had already done so, explaining that he had acted after receiving a letter from Wells-Barnett. Unmentioned in the article was the fact that Rosenwald had agreed to donate two hundred dollars toward the cost of a Supreme Court appeal. However, after months of Ida working on the man's behalf through the Fellowship League, the Supreme Court again refused to hear the case in July, and in September, Cloures was executed.[9]

A VISIT TO Robert Abbott by Major Loving that May was only one of many by Justice Department and intelligence officials, who may not have gotten Abbott to betray his deepest principles but whose threats made him and other editors begin to temper their tone.[10] In June, the government, through its newly created Committee on Public Information (CPI) headed by George Creel, called for an editors' conference of forty-one prominent African Americans in Washington, D.C. What was significant about the meeting, which included Du Bois and Robert Abbott,

Calvin Chase, John Mitchell, and Robert Vann (of the *Pittsburgh Courier*), as well as Tuskegee's Robert Moton, and Robert and Mary Church Terrell, among others, was that the mission of the CPI, founded at the beginning of the war, was to encourage "voluntary" self-censorship of the press.[11]

Prominent in the planning of the conference were Emmett Scott—the former secretary of Booker T. Washington who now served as special assistant to the secretary of war in charge of Negro affairs—and Joel E. Spingarn, who had recently resigned from the board chairmanship of the NAACP to join the war effort. Like Loving, Spingarn held the status of major, was assigned to the MIB, had a Svengali-like power of influence over others, and was deeply concerned about black patriotism. Spingarn's particular take was, according to his biographer, that as an insider in the intelligence agency, he could be in the position to convince the government that redressing black grievances was the best way to assure black loyalty.[12]

After hearing speeches by the War Secretary, Newton Baker; Joel Spingarn; and the assistant secretary of the navy, Franklin Delano Roosevelt, among others, the black invitees, were encouraged to cite the grievances that caused black unrest and to write up a statement that summed up their position. Written by Du Bois, the fourteen-point resolution cited lynching as the most egregious issue that aroused black Americans. Others included the execution of the Houston soldiers and various exclusions such as that of black nurses from serving in the Red Cross. But its summation sounded more like an early armistice than protest. "The Negro is not disposed to catalogue, in this tremendous crisis, all his complaints and disabilities," Du Bois wrote in part, and "he is more than willing to do his full share in helping to win the war for democracy." But "he is today compelled to ask for that minimum of consideration which will enable him to be an efficient fighter for VICTORY."[13]

However, in Du Bois's July editorial in the *Crisis,* entitled "Close Ranks," even the minimum was reduced. "Let us, while this war lasts, forget our special grievances and close ranks shoulder to shoulder with our white fellow citizens and the allied nations that are fighting for democracy," the editor wrote. "We make no ordinary sacrifice, but we make it gladly and willingly with our eyes lifted to the hills."[14] As the figure who, for many, had embodied the very meaning of militance while Booker Washington acted as his foil, the editors' placating words stirred a good deal of controversy. "The learned Dr. Du Bois has seldom packed more error into a single sentence," noted the *Pittsburgh Courier* with a typical black sentiment about the "Close Ranks" editorial. Other assessments were even more harsh. The *New York News* charged Du Bois with "crass moral cowardice."[15]

Charles Pitman, chairman of the executive board of the St. Louis NAACP branch (with whom Ida had tangled with over Bundy), expressed his concern to John Shillady, the recently named secretary of the national office. Fearing that the editorial reflected badly on the organization, he reminded him that already "a large element of the Colored People of this country do not especially care for the NAACP . . . because [of its preference] to proceed along the lines of least resistance."[16]

Pitman was probably referring to the fact that the NAACP was already being criticized for formally—and publicly—severing its connections with Le Roy Bundy, ostensibly over an accounting dispute with the organization that arose after the dentist was able to raise bond and went on a personal speaking tour to raise monies for his defense. The *Cleveland Gazette* was so angry about the NAACP's withdrawal that it advised its readers to resign from a "white-men controlled" association that stood for the persecution rather than the advancement of colored people. Subsequently, the *Defender* editorialized that because Bundy's case was important to the race as a whole, the NAACP should have continued to defend him "in spite of any personal matters which it does not approve. That is exactly what the people are paying their money into it for."[17]

Moreover, insiders like Pitman probably knew that the NAACP president, Moorfield Storey, had demurred in May from testifying in Congress on behalf of an antilynching bill, which had been introduced in April by Merrill Moores (R-Indiana) and the same representative, Leonidas Dyer (R-Missouri), who had earlier called for an investigation of the East St. Louis riot. Dyer had asked Storey to testify to the constitutionality of the legislation, which was based on the equal protection clause of the Fourteenth Amendment. Though Storey refused ostensibly because the legislator had not given him enough time to prepare, the real issue was the NAACP's cautiousness and a view that its fate was tied to legality rather than politics. In 1918, the NAACP's lawyers had still not resolved the issue of the constitutionality of a law that gave the federal government jurisdiction over a state crime. While passage was questionable under any circumstances, the NAACP's support of the bill would have garnered leverage and publicity at a time when lynching was perceived as a problem in terms of the war effort.[18]

Caution, no doubt, also played a role in Du Bois's "Close Ranks" editorial. The ubiquitous monitors of black opinion had not only visited Robert Abbott in May, but the Justice Department had also warned Du Bois and the NAACP board about the *Crisis*. Soon afterward, Du Bois had cited the warning when he refused to publish a provocative poem by the Washington, D.C., branch president, Archibald Grimke.[19] But the editorial found an even more controversial context when it was discovered that at the time Du Bois had written it, he was pursuing a commission to be made a captain in the MIB—and moreover had planned to continue the editorship of the *Crisis* while serving the intelligence agency.

To monitor and investigate black folks would have been a nutty idea on its face, but to think about doing it on behalf of an administration like Wilson's while editing the nation's most influential black publication was a travesty. The NAACP board as well as the MIB rejected the commission plan, and when chapter members like Neval H. Thomas of Washington heard about it, the latter went so far as to write Oswald Villard to ask him to take over the editorship of *Crisis*. Du Bois had "reversed his whole life, and is no more good to us," wrote Thomas, a longtime Du Bois adversary. "You don't know how chagrinned [*sic*] we are . . . at the miserable showing our so-called leader made." The general sentiment of chapter members was noted in the *Chicago Defender* when it observed that many were claiming that Du Bois had abandoned the race.[20]

The idea for the commission had been Spingarn's, who, as Du Bois's biographer wrote, had painted a "glowing picture" of what the two of them could accomplish together. There is no question that they envisioned the work as being beneficial to blacks and that their judgment was clouded by contemporary events and the fact that Spingarn, a Jew, and Du Bois, an African American, both shared, if differently, a sense of outsiderness that they longed to remedy. Later Du Bois, who had anguished about his sense of "twoness" as an American and a Negro, noted that Spingarn's suggestion had made him feel "nearer to [being] a real and full American than ever before or since."[21]

It was also true that expressions of caution and patriotism had eased President Wilson's task to finally make a pronouncement about lynching at a time when he was receiving urgent reports from government officials that black unrest was increasing. In July, he issued an open letter that said, in part, "Under the current conditions," any person who took part in mob violence is "no true son of this democracy, but its betrayer" because he has "adopted the standards of the enemies of his country." The phrase "current conditions" at a time when the end of the war was in sight was worrisome, but it was a step in the right direction. Further effort to keep the racial situation unruffled was the opening of the all-black officers' camp in Des Moines, Iowa, commissioning six hundred men.[22]

Characteristically, Monroe Trotter remained unimpressed by the concessions, and his public criticism of Du Bois's "Close Ranks" sentiment was the most denunciatory. The *Guardian* editor railed that at the very time "when the greatest opportunity is at hand during the war for democracy for others," Du Bois had "finally weakened, compromised, deserted the fight, betrayed the cause of the race." While there is little extant documentation of Ida's views of these developments, her opinion was evidenced by her activities in the period and her continued partnership with Trotter.[23]

Neither activist had attended the June editors' meeting in Washington. By then, the National Equal Rights League had allied with another militant organization, the New York–based Liberty League, headed by the writer and intellectual Hubert H. Harrison, a native of the Virgin Islands. At its inaugural meeting in June of 1917, the organization had featured Marcus Garvey as one of its speakers—an event that helped to launch the career of the Jamaican Pan-Africanist who would soon lead the largest mass movement of persons of African descent in American history. Together, the NERL and the Liberty League planned to hold national liberty race congresses whose purpose was to demand that black Americans be extended the rights of the worldwide democracy for which America was allegedly fighting, and to make lynching a federal crime.[24]

Such developments were grist for the government's monitoring mill, and Trotter, unsurprisingly, had also been contacted by a northeastern department military intelligence officer in the summer of 1918 who warned him that bitter expressions by the race congress could aid the German cause. Trotter questioned the idea that protesting against lynching and demanding democracy for the black troops fighting in France was aiding the Germans, but he added a tongue-in-cheek promise that if he heard of any enemy propaganda, he would be sure to let the MIB known about it.[25]

In September of 1918, Wells-Barnett organized a meeting of the NERL in Chicago where its ninety delegates from twenty-two states represented "by far the most largely attended and truly representative convention" in the group's history, according to the *Defender*. Anticipating the peace conference at Versailles, where interest groups from all over the world would converge, the NERL voted to send a delegation to France, to be selected at the December congress meeting.[26]

Woodrow Wilson was preparing to make his own mark. In the wake of some ten million dead and twenty-one million wounded, he prepared to offer the nations of the earth his Fourteen Points, a formula that included a proposed League of Nations (forerunner of the United Nations) and a set of principles that he believed would sustain world peace. Among the latter was "self-determination," an idea with which Trotter and Wells-Barnett would certainly agree (and to which Wilson's secretary of state, Robert Lansing, warned would be "dangerous in the minds of certain races"). The NERL determined to add a Fifteenth Point: "the elimination of civil, political, and judicial distinctions based on race or color in all nations for the new era of freedom everywhere."[27]

THE MONTHS FOLLOWING the September NERL meeting were busy ones for Wells-Barnett. In November, Marcus Garvey had invited her to address a meeting of his United Negro Improvement Association (UNIA) in Harlem. Ida had probably met Garvey in 1917 when the Jamaican leader made his first visit to Chicago. He had been traveling around the country to meet black leaders and on the list in Chicago was Ferdinand, whom he met at his law office. Like the Barnetts, Garvey, who was the editor of the *Negro World* newspaper, had been involved with the newspaper business for much of his life. He had early been a printer's apprentice and had worked on publications in Costa Rica, Panama, and London. In England, he met African nationalists who sharpened his perspective on the exploitation of people of African descent throughout the Continent and the Diaspora.

After their meeting at Ferdinand's office, Barnett invited him home to have dinner with Ida and the family. As Ida recalled in her autobiography, Garvey talked about the exploitation of blacks in Jamaica by the minority white population. Believing that education would change the situation, Garvey's UNIA sought to develop a school in Jamaica modeled on the Tuskegee Institute. He had written Booker T. Washington about his plans and had hoped to visit the Alabama school. But he did not arrive in the States until 1916, the year after Washington's death. Garvey finally settled in New York City where he and his future wife, Amy Ashwood, developed his organization and where Garvey's electrifying race-first, race-pride, race-solidarity speeches moved black masses, Ida noted in her autobiography, as no other black leader's had. Garvey admired Ida, who invited him to speak before the Negro Fellowship League. In a 1917 article, he praised her, among others, as being "conscientious workers . . . whose fight for the uplift of the race is one of life and death."[28]

In November 1918, Garvey met Ida at the train station in New York to personally accompany her to the UNIA's capacious Palace Casino Hall in Harlem where she was to speak on Sunday, November 10—the eve of the armistice. Also on the bill were Garvey and A. Philip Randolph. Randolph, nearly thirty years Ida's junior, was a graduate of Cookman Institute and a socialist, pacifist, and an editor of the radical *Messenger* newspaper. Of all the black editors, Randolph was the most contemptuous of the sedition threats. The *Messenger* published statistical evidence that blacks were opposed to conscription, and it blatantly editorialized that it would be better to make "Georgia safe for the Negro" than die for the country in France. The paper was eventually throttled by the postmaster general, and in August of 1918, Randolph and his co-editor, Chandler Owen, had been arrested and charged under the Espionage Act, which carried a penalty of a twenty-year prison term. The charges were eventually dismissed, but the publication was suppressed until the following year.[29]

Randolph's defiance had made him a hero to the UNIA crowd, but on this occasion, Ida was the draw. Her advertised presence, as a Garvey biographer pointed out, was responsible for the large crowd of three thousand to five thousand persons who filled the hall to hear her demands for justice and an end to lynching. Garvey called another meeting to be held on December 1 to determine delegates to represent them in Versailles. Again, thousands showed up, and Randolph, Ida, and a Haitian, Eliezer Cadet, who was to act as translator for the group, were chosen to represent the organization in France.[30]

The November 10 program had been one of the first UNIA meetings to attract such a sizable crowd. The numbers, Garvey's association with Ida, and his proclamations at the meeting—"No nation is safe with twelve million dissatisfied people within its borders" and "For every black lynched in the South a white should be lynched in the North"—alerted authorities who began putting him under close surveillance. Reports were compiled by the Bureau of Investigation and military intelligence, letters from Eliezer Cadet were intercepted by New York Postal Censorship authorities, and copies were sent to the Justice and State Departments, and naval and military intelligence, as well as to the British and French liaisons in New York. Emmett Scott beckoned Garvey to his Washington office in December, complaining about the provocative editorials in the *Negro World*.[31]

AFTER ADDRESSING THE UNIA, Ida remained in New York for the NERL meeting that had been planned in Chicago some months before. By then, however, she, as others, must have wondered if Trotter would be able to attend. After leaving Chicago he had returned home to find his wife, Geraldine, ill from influenza. In 1918, the flu had reached pandemic proportions that claimed a half-million Americans before it subsided. Geraldine died on October 8 at the age of forty-six. Friends of the childless couple knew of their devotion. Geraldine had dedicated much of her energy to keep alive the struggling *Guardian*, for which Monroe refused liquor and skin-lightening ads that would have alleviated much of its debt. By December, Trotter had decided that the best tribute to her was to rededicate himself to "perpetuating the Guardian and the Equal Rights cause . . . for which she made such noble, and total sacrifice." What he would do next for the civil rights cause, he would do for her.[32]

The *Guardian* editor was very much in evidence at the December National Race Conference in Washington, D.C., where 250 persons from thirty-nine states convened to vote for representatives to attend the peace conference at Versailles. Also present was an agent from the Justice Department's Bureau of Investigation, who had little to say about it except that Ida presided over the meeting, criticized the execution of the Houston soldiers, and "abused white people generally throughout."[33] The committee that met to decide upon the delegates was a querulous one. Although Trotter should have been an obvious choice, a number of the delegates, citing his earlier controversy with Woodrow Wilson, questioned whether the Bostonian should be one of their representatives. Ida was incensed at the suggestion. "I asked the committee," she wrote, "if they were going to allow President Wilson to select our delegate."[34]

Her argument won the day for Trotter, but not for herself and Madam

C. J. Walker, both of whom also expected to be chosen as delegates. Walker (née Sarah Breedlove), the hair-product magnate and the first woman in the country to become a self-made millionaire, was, in addition to being an activist in her own right, a generous benefactor to black organizations, including the NAACP, NERL, National Association of Colored Women (NACW), and UNIA—for which Walker had contributed funds for the publication of Garvey's *Negro World*. Both Walker and Ida were voted as alternate delegates, a designation that did not carry any financial support from the organization. Writing about the decision in her autobiography, Ida simply stated that she declined the offer, saying that her years in "fighting the race's battles" had made her "financially unable" to make the trip.[35]

Walker, who also wrote about the meeting in a letter to her business manager, had a more unvarnished description of the proceedings. It had been attended by a number of "ignoramus preachers," all of whom wanted to be sent to Paris or have their friends sent there. As a result, the nominating committee, appointed to winnow the names down to five, had decided that no women be sent except as alternates. "Mrs B[arnett] registered a strong protest," Walker noted, "and declined the empty honors." Ida had undoubtedly given the men one of her withering harangues, which resulted in both of them "being elected from the floor as full and legal delegates."[36]

Ida and Walker may have first met at the 1914 NACW meeting in Ohio, which Walker attended and which had selected Mary Waring to represent Illinois women on the exposition commission. In September of 1917, Ida had attended the NERL's tenth annual convention in New York, and on that occasion, she had stayed at Walker's Harlem town house at 108-110 West 136th Street. (At the time, Walker had yet to move into her Italian-style thirty-room mansion in Irvington-on-the-Hudson.) Wells-Barnett recalled the dinner Walker had served the NERL officers, and how she sat regally at the head of the dining room table in her décolleté gown with her butler serving dinner under her directions.

Wells-Barnett was a great admirer of the businesswoman, who had risen from a poor washerwoman in Louisiana to become a wealthy entrepreneur, employing three thousand persons, mostly women, in her various salons and product plants. In addition to her contributions to civil rights enterprises, she also provided scholarships for young women, supported orphanages and old-folks homes, and established a trust fund for a mission school in West Africa. In a rare tribute, Ida wrote that Walker's accomplishments had made her "take pride anew in Negro womanhood." Their meeting in New York would be their last. In a year, Walker would die from uremia; her condition turned for the worst, it was reported by the *Defender,* when she learned that her friend James Reese Europe, the famed musician whose band had played before troops in France, was murdered soon after his return to New York.[37]

IDA LEFT WASHINGTON, D. C., for Baltimore where she and Garvey were scheduled to address another UNIA meeting in the city's Bethel AME Church. By then, there were heightened concerns in the government about both Garvey and Wells-Barnett. The black operative Walter Loving, recommended that the delegates chosen in Washington be checked carefully before being issued passports.

Before 1918, American citizens did not need passports to travel outside of the country, but by May of that year, the Passport Act placed control of traveling abroad in the hands of the State Department, which worked hand in glove with the War Department, Bureau of Investigation, and other agencies. Loving was especially concerned about Wells-Barnett. She was a "a known race agitator," he reported to his superiors.[38] Driving the heightened concern was that Japan's leading negotiator for the conference, Baron Makino, had been instructed by his government—which was sensitive to the treatment of Japanese immigrants on America's West Coast—to obtain guarantees from other participants against racial discrimination. The American government feared that black "agitators" would exploit Japanese intentions and embarrass the U.S. president, and few black delegates chosen by a number of black organizations in the period got its imprimatur. An exception was W. E. B. Du Bois. He had written Secretary Robert Lansing that it would be "a calamity at the time of the transformation of the world to have two million of human beings absolutely without voice." The *Crisis* editor promised to be discreet in selecting delegates and that he would consult with Robert Moton, Emmett Scott, and the white philanthropist George Peabody in doing so. What Du Bois, smartly, had failed to make clear was that in Paris he would convene the first of six Pan-African congresses, which fifty-seven delegates from the Caribbean, Africa, and the United States attended, to call for greater autonomy, government participation, and land ownership among colonized peoples of African descent. By

December, Du Bois, further aided by Emmett Scott, had gotten his passport.[39]

In the meantime, when Loving heard that Ida was to address another UNIA meeting in Baltimore on December 17, he dispatched a agent to cover it; but this time, the group got wind that they were being watched. On that date, when the UNIA's Madre Marshall introduced Ida to speak, she made a pointed reference to the fact that it was known that a black spy was in their midst. There "are always traitors among the race," Marshall began. "When it was known that [Wells-Barnett] was coming to Baltimore, it was tipped off to us that there was going to be sent a spy to report her speech." Such information, of course, provided a great foil for Ida's still unblemished reputation for defying the powers that be. "You know nothing would intimidate Ida B. Wells-Barnett," Marshall said, followed by cries of "hear, hear" from the audience. "When only a girl of nineteen years old she had the courage to write a protest against lynching, for which she had to leave her home to avoid being lynched," she continued, evidently unaware that Ida had actually been thirty at the time. (Characteristically, Ida did not appear to correct the error.) "Nothing but a girl," she repeated for emphasis. Not then or since, Marshall noted, had Wells-Barnett "held her mouth." She couldn't be "bought off"; she "is the most fearless and outspoken speaker or champion that the race has produced." Nevertheless, Marshall told the audience that on this occasion Ida could not be her usual provocative self because the UNIA did not want anything to stand in the way of her being issued a passport to go to Versailles. "What I want to ask of you is, if there is a person near you who attempts to report this speech, make it known to us," Marshall said, adding that in times of war "we usually shoot spies." She continued, "Not that [Wells-Barnett] is afraid of anything . . . there will be no buying her off when she gets to the other side, or on this side for that matter."[40]

Nevertheless, it was conceded that discretion was the better part of valor. Ida's speech contained "nothing of interest," according to intelligence files, but after receiving reports on Ida's activities in Washington and Baltimore, Colonel John Dunn, acting director of military intelligence, made it clear to Emmett Scott that even in the absence of clear evidence of sedition, the government would not be happy if Wells-Barnett made it across the Atlantic to the peace conference.[41]

Indeed, both Garvey and Wells-Barnett were seen as potential threats in this regard, but Ida, with her longer track record, was deemed especially worrisome. "Both of these people are being carefully watched," noted an MID report, which added: "It is reported to this office that Ida B. Wells-Barnett is considered a far more dangerous agitator than Marcus Garvey."[42]

Predictably, passports were denied to Ida, Walker, and Trotter. Nevertheless, the newly widowed Bostonian would not be denied. Posing as a cook, Trotter managed to stow away on the European-bound ship, *Yarmouth*. Upon his arrival, he began churning out petitions and news releases, which were picked up by the French press, that detailed the discriminatory treatment accorded black soldiers and the brutality African Americans faced at home. Trotter also sent word to Woodrow Wilson asking for an audience and must have enjoyed imagining the look on the president's face when he received the request. In the end, however, Trotter's late arrival and catch-as-catch-can campaign got little recognition from the delegates at Versailles. However, as he wrote a friend, he had gotten great satisfaction for getting to the seat of the world conference at all. "May it do honor to Mrs. Trotter's memory," he wrote.[43]

THE AMERICAN PRESIDENT did not appreciate how important Trotter, Wells-Barnett, and other antiracist petitioners were to his dream of world peace. Others, however, had a clearer perspective. While Wilson was negotiating the Treaty of Versailles, a story circulated in Paris about a conversation he had with France's prime minister, Georges Clemenceau. The Frenchman told Wilson that nothing could prevent a future war unless they could agree on three fundamental principles: to declare and enforce racial equality, to ensure freedom of immigration, and to advocate a policy of free trade throughout the world.

Wilson rejected all three. The race question, he reportedly said, was a very sensitive topic in the United States and neither southern nor West Coast senators would ratify a treaty with such a stipulation. Free immigration was not acceptable because the United States was determined to exclude "Orientals" and was in the process of considering restrictions on European immigrants. And though he was for free trade, and his administration had already lowered tariffs, he did not believe that the Congress would agree to a customs union with Europe, Asia, and Africa. After hearing Wilson's response, Clemenceau replied that the only other means of maintaining peace was to "remain strong ourselves and keep our past and potential enemies weak." That this view prevailed was evident in the Allied policies toward Germany, especially, which, indeed, kept the defeated nation weak—at least for a while.[44]

In the United States, peace broke down even sooner. While Ida must have been disappointed that she did not make it to Europe, there was plenty to do at home.

Prisoners of War

The Negro cannot understand why it was a brave thing to kill the Germans and not equally brave to kill white Huns in his own country, who take his life, destroy his home, and insult his manhood every step of the way in free America.

—*Ida B. Wells-Barnett*

The fallacy in the statement that Negroes, by insisting upon their rights and *fighting* for them will break down race prejudice, seems to be entirely overlooked at this time, even by most of the more thoughtful and better informed Negroes.

—*Major J. E. Cutler,*
Military Intelligence Division, 1919

In February of 1919, Illinois's 370th Infantry (formerly the Eighth Illinois Infantry) marched triumphantly down Chicago's Michigan Avenue. The returning soldiers, among them presumably Ferdinand Barnett, Jr., hoisted flags that "never touched the ground," according to the *Chicago Defender,* and many of them donned the military decorations that attested to their heroic contribution to the Allied victory. The 370th had fought the last battle in Belgium and the *Defender* described how the fighting men had smashed across the Hindenburg Line to drive back the elite Third Prussian Guard, and had emerged victorious after hand-to-hand combat with the enemy. The 370th had gone to France with 2,500 men and returned with 1,260. Twenty-one men had earned Distinguished Service Crosses. Sixty-eight had been given the Croix de Guerre by the French. "France will write the names of this regiment and its bravery and heroism in their history," the *Defender* observed. "What will America do?"[1]

The answer became painfully evident during the course of the year. In April of 1919, Le Roy Bundy was found guilty and sentenced to a life term in the penitentiary. The country shuddered with twenty-five major race riots in 1919. While President Wilson was negotiating the articles of the League of Nations abroad, the number of lynchings at home rose from sixty in 1918 to seventy-six the following year. Ten of the victims were army veterans, several of them lynched while still in uniform.[2] American attitudes might not have changed, but African Americans—more worldly and less patient with racism at home—had. After dying for their country, the bitter irony of dying within it was too much to bear. More and more recognized, as Ida had decades before, that accommodation did not bring change, that citizenship rights had to be achieved through determined protest. "We return. We return from fighting. We return fighting," wrote a somewhat discredited but prescient W. E. B. Du Bois in the May 1919 issue of the *Crisis* (which postal authorities withheld from the mails for seven days). "We saved [Democracy] in France," said Du Bois, "and by the Great Jehovah, we will save it in the United States of America, or know the reason why."[3]

NO CITY TO which the fighting men returned was more rife with postwar tension than Chicago. The population bulged with returning veterans, immigrants, and southern migrants. Long-held tensions between Chicago's white ethnic groups, now proxies of the global conflict, rose.[4] The war-time production of Chicago's industries slowed, causing massive layoffs at a time when the cost of living in the city had risen a staggering 75 percent since 1914. In 1919, Chicago would witness more labor strikes than any other city in the nation. Simmering beneath the postwar pressure cooker was the predictable racial tension in a city where shortages were accompanied by the presence of fifty thousand more blacks than it had had the decade before.[5]

It was the struggle over housing that overwhelmed the other issues in postwar Chicago. Of course, the city had long experienced friction between whites in the heavily Polish and Irish meatpacking district and blacks in the contingent and ever-expanding Black Belt. Familiar, too, was the pattern of white flight following the "incursion" of a black family into a once racially exclusive neighborhood. But the lack of residential construction during the war years added a new dimension to old frictions: "fight" rather than "flight" became the byword of newly created housing associations determined to maintain all-white reserves.

Established in 1918 explicitly "to make Hyde Park white," the Hyde-Park-Kenwood Property Owners' Association led the effort to establish a "united front" to keep blacks out of Grand Boulevard, from Twenty-ninth to Thirtieth streets, and Michigan Boulevard, from Thirty-ninth south to Sixty-third Street. In the same year, eleven bombings greeted black residents who moved to or who already lived in the contested areas.[6]

Nevertheless, by 1919, "Most of the beautiful homes . . . on Grand boulevard and on South Park, Calumet and Prairie avenues are now occupied by colored people, where two years ago there were none," observed the *Chicago Post*, which called for both martial law to protect black residents and for the legislature and city council to create a racial zoning law to thwart further encroachment. One of those homes belonged to the Barnetts who, in 1919, purchased a house for $8,000 at 3624 Grand Boulevard. The Queen Anne–style residence was three stories high and had fourteen rooms (including four baths), Italian parquet floors, Italian marble fixtures, and a ballroom.[7]

"Something has to be done," the *Chicago Post* demanded, and something was. During the first six months of 1919, fourteen bombings were aimed at black residents or realtors (black and white) who sold property to them. One bombing took the life of a little girl on Indiana Avenue. Jesse Binga, a black man who owned a bank and a real estate business that controlled a half million dollars' worth of property, was the victim of no fewer than six bombings, aimed at both his residence and office.[8]

In May, the bombing of Richard and Gertrude Harrison's home at 4408 Grand Boulevard took no lives and damage was minimal, but it became significant in the minds of Chicagoans because of the prominence of Richard Harrison, a Shakespearean actor (subsequently known for his role as "De Lawd" in *The Green Pastures*); the fact that the Harrisons were the first blacks to move in the previously "white" section on Grand Boulevard; and the circumstances that surrounded the crime. On May 16, a black janitor warned the Harrisons that their neighbors were planning to bomb the house, and Gertrude Harrison, alone at the time, subsequently called the police. A policeman came to the home and promised to keep an eye out, but on the following night, the house was bombed by a man who had jumped out of a yellow cab to place the incendiary device on the porch. Although a police detail was dispatched to guard the residence, a second bomb was tossed into the house from an adjoining apartment building on May 18. That the culprits were never found followed a familiar pattern. With all of the bombing incidents, law officials only made two arrests. The number of indictments was zero.[9]

Soon after the incident, Wells-Barnett, Mrs. Head, the mother of the slain little girl, and several other concerned citizens attempted to call on Mayor William Thompson, who had been reelected in April with only 38 percent of the vote, but with an office-saving plurality delivered by blacks in the Second Ward. Ida's group had wanted to demand that he speak out against the violence, but they were directed to the Chicago chief of police, John J. Garrity, who told them that "he could not put all of the police in Chicago on the South side to protect the homes of colored people."[10]

The Chicago police were not only indifferent—at best—to the bombings, but as spring warmed into a sweltering summer, clashes between white officers and blacks in the streets, fatal confrontations between white gangs and blacks in the parks, and the rising tide of industrial tensions—particularly in the stockyards, which employed more blacks than any other industry—set the scene for one of the worst conflagrations of what James Weldon Johnson called the "Red Summer" of 1919.[11]

In early July, Ida, concerned about the rising violence, made a plea in the *Chicago Tribune*. "With one Negro dead as the result of a race riot last week, another one very badly injured in the county hospital; with a half-dozen attacks upon Negro children, and one on the Thirty-fifth street car Tuesday, in which four white men beat one colored man, it looks very much like Chicago is trying to rival the south in its race hatred against the Negro," she wrote in the paper's "Voice of the People" column. "Will the legal, moral, and civic forces of this town stand idly by and take no notice of these preliminary outbreaks? . . . [I]n all earnestness, I implore Chicago to set the wheels of justice in motion before it is too late: and Chicago be disgraced by some of the bloody outrages that have disgraced East St. Louis."[12]

Soon after the column was published, Washington, D.C., was "disgraced" by a white mob that rampaged through the city for four successive days in the city's worst riot in history. However, unlike many of the mob actions that had preceded the conflict in the capital, armed blacks struck back. While whites had done most of the beatings, blacks had done most of the shooting. Of the twenty-one who died, fourteen were white. Less than a week after an uneasy order was restored in Washington, Chicago burst into flame.[13]

ON A SULTRY Sunday, July 27, 1919, five Chicago black teenagers chose not to swim at the Twenty-fifth Street "black" beach, or the "white" beach at Twenty-ninth Street. The friends had found their own spot, located between the two, where they kept a homemade raft made from railroad ties. The boys took the raft into the water and jockeying around as they usually did, they, unwittingly, drifted toward the Twenty-ninth Street beach, which was already embroiled in a rock-throwing racial dispute between white and black bathers. A white man, who saw the raft, hurled a rock at the boys, hitting one of them in the head and causing him to fall into the water. Despite the efforts of his companions to save him, the young man, Eugene Williams, drowned. Subsequently, when the white offender was pointed out to a white policeman, the officer not only refused to arrest the man, he refused to let a black policeman arrest him. The exact sequence of events from that point varies, but soon word about the incident spread to the black community. Enraged, a group of African Americans started running toward the Twenty-ninth Street beach, where they pummeled the white policeman and chased him into a drugstore. It was then that the white street gang, the Irish-led Ragen Colts, came to the officer's aid, beating, stabbing, or shooting twenty-seven blacks between 9:00 that evening and 3:00 the next morning. The seven-day race war had begun.[14]

It is not clear why Mayor Bill Thompson did not bring in the state militia at that point. What is known is that he considered Governor Frank Lowden a rival and calling for the state guards would have been tantamount to admitting that he had lost control of the city. In any case, an uneasy quiet reigned Monday morning, one that could have thrown officials off guard. But on Monday afternoon, white gangs pounced on black workers leaving the stockyards, beating and stabbing them. When a number of the blacks were able to escape the scene by jumping onto a passing trolley, whites forced the streetcar to stop and dragged the blacks off. At least four died in the melee and there might have been more but for the heroics of Oscar De Priest. Taking advantage of his six-foot-plus frame and eerily penetrating blue eyes, he donned a policeman's cap and uniform and drove a patrol wagon into the stockyards and brought out black men who were trapped by the whites brutalizing them there. He did this again and again, fighting whites when he had to, until all of them were carried to safety from the mob.[15]

On Tuesday morning, amid a trolley-car strike, the battles raged once more, rising to a high pitch when a young black man was killed by a policeman. By that evening, it was heard that the Ragen Colts, who had already set a series of fires under black homes in the area near Wentworth Avenue in the meatpacking district—Chicago's "Hindenburg line" as Ida called it—were amassing to cross State Street to invade the black community. A black woman who later described the scene for the *Baltimore Afro-American* explained how blacks, both men and women, lined up along State between Twenty-sixth and Sixty-first streets and prevented the whites from "coming over to annihilate Negro citizens." The blacks "told the mob-bent whites to come on," the woman told the paper. Whites, she said, "did not think the colored people had any ammunition, but they had enough to blow up all Chicago."[16]

Blacks not only defended themselves but went on the attack, sometimes killing innocent victims. When Casmero Lazeroni, a sixty-year-old banana peddler, unwittingly drove his horse-drawn carriage into a black mob on Thirty-sixth Street, near State, he was dragged from his cart and stabbed to death by teenagers. Blacks also murdered a white laundryman and a white shoemaker who appeared to only be guilty of being in the wrong place at the wrong time.[17]

The *Defender* described how trolleys were stopped in the vicinity of Thirty-fifth and State streets "and every white face was taken from the cars and severely beaten." As the "fever of race antagonism gained ground, more fuel was added to the flame when workers from the stock yards came with stories of horrible attacks made by the whites upon Colored women," the paper noted. This seemed to transform a collection of individual rioters into a swarm of fifteen hundred blacks that crossed Wabash Avenue, breaking windows and firing on whites. Confronted by at least a hundred police, a number on horseback, one of the blacks threw a brick at the officers. The authorities responded with gunfire, killing four blacks.[18]

Sixty-five encounters between whites and blacks took place throughout the city—including in Ida's Grand Boulevard neighborhood. If more evidence was needed that self-defense in all neighborhoods was necessary, it was provided when the home of Mary Byron Clarke, at 4406 Grand Boulevard, was threatened by a mob. When she called the police, the officers, at the demand of the whites, battered down her doors and arrested her and her husband. Mrs. Clarke also owned a property at 4404 Grand Boulevard that she rented out to A. Clement MacNeal, a newcomer to Chicago and a Yale graduate who had directed the opening of a new Chicago NAACP branch office that spring. When a mob of whites attempted to storm the residence, MacNeal did not call the police; rather, when one of the whites managed to break through the door, the intruder was shot to death.[19]

Before the mayhem was ended by the belated intervention of sixty-two hundred members of the state militia, thirty-eight Chicagoans had lost their lives—twenty-three blacks and fifteen whites. Five hundred thirty-seven more were wounded, a hundred thousand dollars' worth of property was destroyed, and at least a thousand people were left homeless.[20]

For many, the Chicago uprising was the clearest example of what writers were calling the "New Negro"—the likes of which had "come home fighting." As the socialist A. Philip Randolph's *Messenger* observed, a unique characteristic of the Chicago uprising was that the black middle classes were engaged in the fighting, though their activities were largely confined to protecting their own homes.[21] The willingness to fight back in the wake of the war was quite logical, Ida told the *Chicago Daily News*. For the "Negro cannot understand why it was a brave thing to kill the Germans and not equally brave to kill white Huns in his own country, who take his life, destroy his home, and insult his manhood every step of the way in free America."[22] Even the MID's most patriotic black informer, Major W. H. Loving, was "inclined," as was written in an intelligence report after the riot, to feel that government failure to safeguard the interests of blacks had left them little recourse.[23]

In light of New Negro attitudes, Chicago had little recourse but to attempt to come to terms with the city's race problem, a problem that had a fuse at both ends of the racial divide. But the remedy depended on one's view of the fundamental causes of the conflict. The Bureau of Investigation's General Intelligence Division (GID)—then headed by a young J. Edgar Hoover, and founded in response to the "red scare" to keep an eye on radicals—looked in vain for Bolshevik influences. The bureau officer's report finally concluded that the *Chicago Tribune,* the *Messenger,* the local black press, former Colonel Franklin A. Denison of the 370th Infantry, and Ida Wells-Barnett—"considered by the black population of Chicago to be some kind of superwoman"—were the main culprits responsible for the bad race relations that produced the riot. Before the uprising, intelligence reports had noted that Ida and Monroe Trotter were publishing articles in the black press "to the effect that France will welcome American negroes as citizens," and encouraged African American workers to emigrate there where they "will be treated without discrimination." After the riot, another intelligence report stated that both Ida and Oscar De Priest were stockpiling bombs and hand grenades.[24]

The apparently unsubstantiated charge was unlikely, although Ida believed, as she noted in the *Chicago Tribune,* that blacks had that right to bear arms and that the police had acted unjustly when they searched only black homes for guns during the conflict and its immediate aftermath.[25] From her point of view, at the heart of the trouble was racial prejudice that had imperiled blacks and reduced the city to the level of the mob. "Free Chicago stands today humble before the world," the *Chicago Daily Journal* quoted Ida as saying in the wake of the riot. "Notwithstanding our boasted democracy, lynch law is king."[26]

Responding to Wells-Barnett's words, a letter to the *Chicago Daily News* reflected the boundaries of race tolerance. "She appears to have no sympathy whatever with the viewpoint of the northern white man suddenly shoved out of his environment by an influx of a race alien to him and in a large majority of cases hostile. She fails to understand the psychology of the people of the north . . . willing to give [blacks] every opportunity . . . and still resent the fact that we must eat, sleep, and bathe with them . . . we feel we have a right to live in communities of white people only. Until the millennium comes," the writer concluded, "we cannot expect to be perfect."[27]

Not banking on the millennium, blacks organized the Peace and Protective Association (PPA) in the wake of the riot. It began as an initiative of church leaders and was headed by Dr. Lacey Kirk Williams of the New

Olivet Baptist Church. Williams had succeeded the stroke-fallen Elijah Fisher in 1916, and had astutely led his flock through the surge of the black migration years. Under his leadership, the Olivet congregation doubled in number to eight thousand members to become the largest in the city. Williams was lauded for his social service mission, which clothed, housed, and found employment for black migrants. In 1918, he had offered his church to the National Equal Rights League (NERL) for its large and successful September meeting, which Ida had organized. Wells-Barnett, representing the NERL and the Negro Fellowship League (NFL), was a member of the PPA, which met in late July.[28]

After the meeting, both Williams and Wells-Barnett were asked by the press to state their views about the next steps that needed to be taken. Both of their replies stressed the need for a commission to investigate the causes of the riot. Wells-Barnett called for an interracial committee that included both men and women whose purpose would be to "devise ways and means for protecting the defenseless within our doors, whether they be black or white." Williams called for a group of "strong men" from both races to come together to discuss and try to resolve the city's problems.[29]

Their difference over the inclusion of women was not the only one. Williams, as the head of the PPA, called for Republican attorney general Edward Brundage to be brought in personally to direct the prosecutions, despite Ida's objections. As she later complained to the *Chicago Defender*, Brundage's handling of the East St. Louis indictments had been a travesty. As Ida reminded her readers, 150 African Americans had been massacred in that city, and yet twice as many blacks as whites had been convicted of crimes. She also recounted in the paper that when she had confronted the attorney general about the disparity, he had shrugged her off, saying that she did not "represent any organized public body of people," and that he had brought sixty-five indictments against whites. However, as Ida pointed out, what he could not justify was that only five whites had been sent to the penitentiary with substantial sentences. Bringing Brundage in for the Chicago trials, she believed, was tantamount to accepting the judgments that had been rendered in East St. Louis.[30]

Reverend Williams and the PPA maintained their preference for Bundage, who was a rivet in the Regular Republican machinery that dispensed a good deal of patronage and needed support for churches such as Olivet that aided their social programs. But the strongest argument for retaining the attorney general was Maclay Hoyne, the progressive Democratic state's attorney. Hoyne was avidly anti-vice and was responsible for the earlier indictment of Oscar De Priest (who was now back in the Regular Republican fold). Hoyne had run for mayor in 1919 against Bill Thompson and the Democratic machine candidate, Robert Sweitzer. Nothing in Hoyne's biography would have offended Ida, and like a number of black progressives, she shared his abhorrence of vice in the Second Ward. With the reelection of Thompson and the passage in 1919 of the Eighteenth (prohibition) Amendment, the vats of corruption, already spilling over, were on the verge of gushing at full force.

When Reverend Williams told Ida that the PPA would continue to support Brundage, Wells-Barnett wrote: "I rose and laid my membership card on the table and told the men that I would be guilty of belonging to an organization that would do such a treacherous thing as to ask the white man who had put fifteen of our people in prison to take hold and do the same thing here." Williams simply responded, "Good-bye." Another minister added, "Good riddance." Ida left the meeting, she reported, with tears in her eyes.[31]

While Ida never accepted Brundage, she subsequently had to also denounce Hoyne when he began piling up indictments against blacks but not whites. The Democrat believed that the fundamental cause of the riot was the corruption in the Second Ward where criminals, aided by Thompson-enabled black politicians, were allowed to run rampant with impunity. With this view, he assumed that many of the black rioters had escaped arrest through the favoritism of those same politicians—and he acted accordingly.[32]

Hoyne brought fifty-two cases before the grand jury involving black rioters before the first white face was seen. Among those brought before the jury were several women and the NAACP's A. Clement MacNeal, who was indicted for the murder of the white man who had forced his way into his Grand Boulevard home. Hoyne was so obviously racist—and so impolitic in a city full of tension and black influence—that the all-white, all-male jury (whose photos, names, and addresses were carried in the *Tribune*) declared that they would hear no more cases until whites were also brought before them. Hoyne finally relented and began bringing cases against whites before the jury, but saw "the hand of vicious black belt politics" behind the walkout. When he subsequently ordered storm-trooper-like raids into the Second Ward gambling houses and homes to attain evidence, Ida condemned the action in no uncertain terms.[33]

"Unable to use the grand jury to voice his discovery, [Hoyne] sends his hand-picked confederates to raid gambling houses and homes, then rushes into print with a 'discovery' which he will not dare to submit to any grand jury in Cook County," Ida charged. The state's attorney, she concluded, was "either woefully incapable or criminally derelict in his duty" when he "refused to arrest white rioters and murderers, and insisted on indicting and imprisoning colored victims of the mob." She also denounced Hoyne's publicly stated view that blacks were responsible for the riot as "malicious" when it was blacks who had been the "victims of a premeditated orgy of assaults, bloodshed, and murder." Ida called for a special prosecutor. Her complaint—and appeal—was echoed by the *Chicago Defender* and a subsequent mass meeting of ten thousand blacks who gathered at the old Eighth Illinois Regiment Armory to protest Hoyne. However, the special prosecutor asked for at the meeting was Brundage.[34]

Again, launched onto an independent course, Ida took matters into her own hands. One reason for the small number of white indictments was that blacks who could identify white rioters were often fearful of coming forward. Ida herself testified before the grand jury, and she also patrolled the streets for other black witnesses. When she found them, she invited them to come to her house at night to tell her what they had seen and then accompanied them to the state's attorney's office where they gave their statements. Ida also initiated a fund-raising campaign through the Negro Fellowship League to aid black defendants.[35]

In the meantime, the national office of the NAACP got involved in the post-riot legal actions. It had been urged to do so by Walter White, a twenty-six-year-old graduate of Atlanta University who had been appointed assistant national secretary in 1918. White was convinced, as he wrote in August of 1919 to Mary Ovington (made chairman of the board and director of branches in January of the year), that the "whole future of the Association in Chicago depends on our work in the crisis, as we are supposed to be a militant, aggressive organization."[36] Unsaid, but surely understood, was that the Chicago branch was still inert, and intervention by the national office was needed. By August, fifty blacks (compared to seventeen whites) had been indicted, and it was essential to augment and coordinate legal defense efforts. Funds were direly needed and the NAACP had the wherewithal to raise them through its connection with Chicago philanthropists like Julius Rosenwald.[37]

Upon his arrival to the city in August of 1919, White—blond and blue-eyed and able to pass for white—reconnoitered the stockyards, searched for eyewitnesses, appeared undercover at Hyde-Kenwood association meetings, and interviewed Chicago civic leaders. Among those White made an appointment to see was Ferdinand Barnett. What White did not know was that Ida was Ferdinand's spouse, and that she would also be at his meeting with Barnett in August. By then, Ida was thoroughly frustrated by the post-riot developments and vented her anger. "She launched into a tirade against every organization in Chicago because they have not come into her organization and allowed her to dictate to them," White reported to Ovington. "She is a troublemaker and is causing complications by starting a fund of her own to defend riot victims."[38]

Wells-Barnett was a "troublemaker" because White's plans included subsuming other organizations under the NAACP's leadership in Chicago. The "complications" White referred to reflected, in part, the fact that Rosenwald, as he had done in the black YMCA campaign, was willing to donate money, but on a matching basis. This meant that the ultimate success of the NAACP depended on funds it could raise, and account for, within the black community—funds that Ida threatened to siphon off through her independent efforts.[39]

Nevertheless, in the short run, Wells-Barnett's opportunities to make trouble in Chicago became increasingly few. She was isolated from the organizations that had the most resources and her voice was marginalized in the debate on the remedies concerning racial tension in Chicago. When Governor Lowden announced in August the establishment of what became later known as the Chicago Commission on Race Relations—a philanthropist-funded study to examine the causes of the riot and make recommendations to avert such future conflicts—it was a foregone conclusion that Ida would not be one of its twelve commissioners. As the Reverend Kirk Lacey Williams had suggested, the commission was made up of men (including himself) who were evenly divided between blacks and whites.[40]

By October, however, a new development put Ida into the scheme of things once more—not in Chicago, but in Phillips County, Arkansas.

WHILE PRESIDENT WOODROW Wilson was stumping the country in a vain attempt to rally support for his League of Nations (that had met Senate opposition), there were press reports that a black conspiracy to massacre whites in Phillips County—located in east-central Arkansas across the Mississippi River from the state of Mississippi—had been thwarted. The "conspirators" were from the towns of Elaine and Hoop Spur; the white counterattack had come at the hands of members of the American Legion, deputized posses, and a collection of armed whites from surrounding towns in Mississippi, Tennessee, and Arkansas. Five whites and somewhere between twenty-five and several hundred blacks had died in the confrontation. The governor, Charles Brough, requested federal troops from Camp Pike to restore order. One hundred forty-three blacks were eventually arrested. By October 7, the camp commander and county officials agreed that the "trouble" had been "settled" and told blacks to go back to work in the cotton fields and saw mills where most were employed.[41]

Walter White was first to investigate what became known as the Elaine Riot. His plan was to pose as a white newspaper reporter (Charles Bentley had arranged to get press credentials for him from the *Chicago Daily News*) to find out what he could. In October, White first traveled to Memphis, where he conferred with Robert Church, Jr., the son of the late Memphis businessman and one of the founders of the NAACP's Memphis chapter, which had been organized in 1917. The NAACP assistant secretary then made his way to Helena, where the prisoners were being held.

For a week, White's undercover identity worked spectacularly. He was able to get interviews with white witnesses and officials, the latter including Governor Brough himself, who led White on a guided tour of Phillips County and later pronounced him one of the smartest reporters he had ever met. Soon after meeting with Brough, the assistant secretary was on his way to the county jail to interview the prisoners. But he never got there. A black man, whom White did not know, pulled him aside to tell him that his true identity had been discovered and that people were looking to lynch him. White hurriedly boarded the next train out of Helena.

Surely weighing on his mind was the increasing dangers that NAACP officials were facing since the Chicago and Washington upheavals. Exacerbated fears of additional black reprisals against whites had resulted in, among other repressive activities, efforts to shutdown the organization's chapters in the South. When a Texas chapter of the NAACP faced such action, John Shillady, the association's secretary, went to Austin in August of 1919 for the specific purpose of conferring with Governor William P. Hobby and other officials to explain that the NAACP's purpose was not to incite insurrections against whites. Following the meeting, Shillady, who was white, was attacked by a group of thugs (including a judge and a constable) who beat him to the point of unconsciousness. When the national office subsequently demanded that the governor punish the assailants, Hobby replied that there was only one assailant—Shillady—and he had already been punished.[42]

As Walter White later recalled, while he was riding on the outbound train from Arkansas, the conductor mentioned to him that it was a shame that he (White) was leaving town "just as the fun is going to start." When White asked him what he meant, the trainman said that there was "a damned yellow nigger . . . passing for white" in town, and when the "boys get him, he won't pass for white no more."[43]

Once he got safely back to the North, the assistant secretary published his findings in October and November in the *Chicago Daily News* and the *Chicago Defender*, respectively. The trouble had begun, he wrote, when two whites, including a deputy sheriff, had been fired upon by blacks outside of a church in Hoop Spur. One of the white men was killed, the other was seriously wounded. Whether blacks had taken the initiative or were defending themselves was unclear at that point, but White revealed the origin of the conflict. The whites had come upon a meeting of the Progressive Farmers and Household Union of America that was taking place in the church. The union, made up largely of black tenant farmers, was planning a united effort to force white proprietors to pay them their fair share of the money from the cotton they had picked. Included in the group was a white lawyer, O. S. Bratton, son of U. S. Bratton, a former assistant U.S. attorney who had successfully prosecuted several eastern Arkansas planters for holding blacks in peonage. The black farmers had retained the young Bratton to represent them against the planters in time for the fall harvest. The information led White to further explain the exploitive practices of the peonage system by using Wells-Barnett's perfected technique of giving names and specific examples of what the Arkansas farmers were subjected to.[44]

Unmentioned by White was another element that had undoubtedly provoked the white response. In Elaine, black sawmill workers had been prohibiting black women to pick cotton or work for white men at any price. A letter to the *Topeka Plaindealer* about the situation revealed the sexual tension in Elaine where there were many instances "of white men living in open adultery with colored women and rearing families by them."[45]

Although White's exposé was subsequently picked up by the Associated Press, and although it evoked expressions of indignation about the plight of the black men, Arkansas authorities remained unmoved. They sentenced thirty-seven blacks to prison terms ranging from five to twenty-one years. One man was acquitted. Twelve black farmers were convicted of first-degree murder and sentenced to death. Execution, by electric chair, was slated for six of the men in late December; for the remaining six, early January. The black men had been represented by court-appointed local white attorneys. No jury had taken more than eight minutes to render guilty verdicts.[46]

By November, when it still appeared that nothing was being done to save the Arkansas men, Ida marshaled her forces: the Negro Fellowship League, the National Equal Rights League (which was still basking in the afterglow of Monroe Trotter's dramatic stowaway voyage to Paris), and Oscar De Priest's People's Movement, which had gained stature through the politician's heroic exploits during the riot and the growing disaffection among blacks with the elite-led organizations in Chicago.[47]

The Chicago NERL's president was N. S. Taylor, a lawyer who had been driven from his home in Greenville, Mississippi, after whites found out about his being elected to the position the previous year. According to Ida's autobiography, when she tried to interest him in acting on behalf of the Arkansas prisoners, he expressed concern about them but said that he did not think anything could be done. After insisting that the NERL should at least send resolutions about the case to the president, governor, and Illinois officials, the organization did so. In the meantime, Ida got De Priest to telegram Illinois congressman Martin Madden about the situation. U.S. senator Medill McCormick was also contacted. Madden was the first to respond; he asked De Priest to give him more details about the Arkansas case. De Priest referred him to Ida.[48]

While Taylor was still temporizing over any further action by the NERL, Ida was invited to speak before a huge meeting of the People's Movement. She read the resolution before the thousand-member group that had been sent to Brough and others. "Hundreds of Negroes have left

Arkansas because of unjust treatment, and we pledge ourselves to use our influence to bring thousands away if those twelve men die in the electric chair," it read, in part. "Arkansas needs our labor but we will never rest till every Negro leaves the state unless those men are given justice."[49]

In mid-November, Brough responded to the NERL's demand—a tactical mistake as he may have realized in hindsight. In any case, the governor gave a lengthy explanation to the *Arkansas Gazette* as to *why* he was ignoring the request of the organizion. The Equal Rights League was not in a position to "judge the merits of the case," he said, but he also added that he had always been against lynch law, that he was "deeply concerned" about the "negro race," and, perhaps following the model in Chicago, that he would consult with black and white civic leaders and appoint an interracial commission to study race relations in the state. Subsequently, however, Brough stayed the executions. Of all the protests that Brough received, Ida concluded, hers was the only one he "heeded."[50]

The claim is difficult to prove. At the time, Wilson, still feeling the reverberations of the Houston military hangings, made it known that he did not want the December death sentences carried out—at least not before they were reviewed by the higher Arkansas court. Local blacks were making their voices heard on the matter; and the NAACP, with its long reach into white and black communities alike, was also working behind the scenes. Yet, as Wells-Barnett knew from experience, the threat to extract black labor from the South was one that generally elicited a response when others failed. In any case, when Brough's interracial committee recommended that the sentences should not be carried out before a review by the higher court, it gave him political cover to postpone the executions in the face of mounting pressure.[51]

Ida, buoyed by the developments, attended a local NERL meeting only to find that the group was angry with her because she had presented the resolution before the People's Movement without consulting them—an act that under the bylaws of the organization called for suspension. Ida explained that the next NERL meeting was scheduled two weeks after Oscar De Priest had invited her to address the People's Movement and that time was of the essence. Moreover, she thought that the NERL should have taken pride in the fact that "one of our largest organizations [the People's Movement] had acted on the result of our work." Ida also reminded the NERL members that they had initially believed that nothing could be done about the Arkansas issue. Nevertheless, a motion was entertained to suspend her. Ida did not wait for the vote. "I walked out of the meeting and never again attempted to do any work through the medium of the Equal Rights League," she wrote in her autobiography. If Ida was dismayed by her divorce from yet another organization that she had worked so hard for, she also took advantage of the fact that she now had free rein to act according to her own convictions.[52]

On December 13, both Ida and Walter White had articles published about the Arkansas men. White's piece in the mainstream *Survey* focused on debunking the Associated Press items that continued to frame the Arkansas incident in terms of a black plan to massacre whites. He reported the findings of the NAACP's investigation that found that the two white men killed outside of the Hoop Spur church had initiated the shooting, and he provided examples from court records that showed how black Arkansas farmers were being defrauded by whites.

Wells-Barnett's article in the *Defender* was a call for black grassroots support and vigilance. "We are thanking God for this reprieve," but "let us not sit down to idleness, believing all is well," wrote Ida, who had seen favorable developments turn sour in the cases of Frazier Baker in South Carolina and the Millington murders in Tennessee once pressure ceased. "The Arkansas Supreme Court may affirm the [guilty] decision," she prophesied, adding that if this was done, blacks should be willing to take the case to the U.S. Supreme Court. To do so required funds to retain legal representation, and she asked her readers to support the effort. "Let me hear from individuals, churches, secret societies, business men's leagues and women's clubs at once . . . furnish me with the sinews of war and I will fight your battles just as I have done for the last twenty-five years—only this time," she pointedly concluded, "you will be helping. Will you do it?"[53]

By 1919, the *Defender* had a circulation of 130,000, and according to Ida, her article had gotten a widespread response that included a plaintive letter written by one of the imprisoned men. "I thank God that thro [*sic*] you our Negroes are looking into this truble [*sic*] and thank the city of Chicago, for what it did to start things," it read. As Ida commented after receiving the letter, "During all that two months of terrible treatment"— which had included electric torture being used on the men—"no word of help had come from their own people until a copy of the *Chicago Defender*, December 13th fell into their hands." Soon letters and contributions came pouring in from blacks throughout the country, Ida reported. Her article appeared to have also inspired Arkansas black leaders, a number of whom had served on Brough's interracial commission, to organize, in December, a legal defense fund themselves.[54]

The NAACP must have been beside itself. Wells-Barnett's call for funds threatened the organization's efforts to raise money in the case, which they estimated would cost fifty thousand dollars. Julius Rosenwald had offered five hundred dollars to every forty-five hundred dollars raised up to twenty-five thousand dollars. Along with the requests for the remittances, the philanthropist required that the NAACP submit names and the amount collected from each, with a certificate that the forty-five-hundred-dollar increments had been collected.[55]

The NAACP was already having difficulty with the matching business. As late as April 1920, the Chicago branch had been forced to report to Rosenwald that it was able to raise less than two thousand dollars for that city's defense fund. A. Clement MacNeal (who was exonerated due to lack of evidence in his Chicago riot case) tried to explain that the paltry sum was not a reflection of black interest in the matter, for "Nearly $7000 have [*sic*] been given by colored people to this cause thru [*sic*] other agencies working for the same end." The only other agency cited in the letter was the PPA, but White had earlier mentioned Ida by name in these efforts.[56]

Moreover, Ida was taking credit for the Arkansas movement at a time when the NAACP was working furiously on behalf of the defendants. The organization was actively attaining information, consulting congressmen, and had retained a leading white Arkansas lawyer, Colonel G. W. Murphy, a former Confederate soldier who had been the attorney general of Arkansas from 1901 to 1905. However, the NAACP had decided to do all of this as surreptitiously as possible. Board chairwoman Mary Ovington, in soliciting NAACP branches for funds in November, cautioned that a general appeal not be made regarding Arkansas. "*Our name for obvious reasons must not be used in connection with the defense of the prisoners*" (emphasis in original), she wrote. Again, the strategies of behind-the-scene caution and open confrontation were pitted against each other. While the NAACP was acting under the assumption that, as James Weldon Johnson wrote, "publicity now will not help us and will only hurt them [the prisoners], Wells-Barnett began assembling her protest campaign in the belief that more publicity, not less, was needed in the situation.[57]

Soon after Ida's appeal, however, the NAACP decided to make its own defense-fund efforts known. Wells-Barnett discovered as much when she approached the *Defender* about publishing the names of those who had sent her contributions. The managing editor denied her request, explaining that the NAACP had objected to the paper permitting her to start a prescription list because the organization was "doing all that was necessary for the Arkansas case and that monies already collected should be turned over to them."[58]

Of course, Ida was not about to comply. Instead, she prepared a circular letter that she sent to those on the contribution list to apprise them of the situation and ask permission to use the money they had sent to go to Arkansas to investigate the matter for herself. Exactly how the authorization was acquired is unclear, but Ida noted in her autobiography that "consent" had been given, and in January of 1920, the same month that the NAACP became engaged in blocking the extradition of union leader Robert Hill, who had fled to Kansas, Ida, at the age of fifty-seven, was on her way to Elaine, Arkansas.[59] It would be her first trip south since she had been banished nearly three decades before.

To GAIN INFORMATION about the case, Walter White and other members of the NAACP had conferred with black leaders, mostly outside of Arkansas, like Robert Church; the empathetic and knowledgeable Arkansas lawyer U. S. Bratton; Justice Department officials; and members of Congress, but no one had yet spoken to the prisoners themselves. Ida was determined to be the first to do so.

When she alighted from the train in Little Rock, she went directly to the home address on the letter sent to her from one of the twelve prisoners. When she arrived there, she found the wives and mothers of the defendants who had gathered to visit the prisoners in the penitentiary. Accompanying them to the prison, Ida put a scarf on her head to make herself look as inconspicuous as possible. When the guard looked up, she wrote, "he saw only a group of insignificant looking colored women who had been there many times before." Once the women got close to the men's cells, Mrs. Frank Moore, wife of one of the men who had been scheduled for execution, identified Ida, and the men, according to the autobiography, responded with an "expression of joy spread over their faces."[60]

After Wells-Barnett interviewed the men, she recounted in her autobiography that at the end of the visit, the prisoners began singing in plaintive tones. While in prison, they had written songs that gave "testimony from their overburdened hearts," with verses like "My heart is overwhelmed with sorrow / My eyes are melted down with tears / But I have called to the God of Heaven / And I know he always hears." The women would take up the refrain, and by the end of the song, they were all in tears. Wells-Barnett, however, became impatient. "Finally I got up," she wrote, "walked close to the bars and said to them in a low tone, 'I have been listening to you for nearly two hours. You have talked and sung and prayed about dying, and forgiving your enemies, and of feeling sure that you are going to be received in the New Jerusalem because your God knows that you are innocent of the offense for which you expect to be electrocuted. But why don't you pray to live and ask to be freed? The God you serve is the God of Paul and Silas who opened their prison gates, and if you have all the faith you say you have, you ought to believe that he [*sic*] will open your prison doors too.'"[61]

During the remainder of Wells-Barnett's two-week stay in Arkansas, she gathered information that would be the basis of her later self-published pamphlet, *The Arkansas Race Riot*. Ida also made it a point to meet the state's leading black lawyer, who had the formidable name of Scipio Africanus Jones. Jones, a former slave, had been admitted to the bar in 1889. Because the University of Arkansas did not admit blacks, he had attained his legal education by reading law under the supervision of white attorneys. Jones, whose clients included a number of black secret societies and fraternal groups, was the founder of the Citizens Defense Fund Commission (CDFC), an outgrowth of the local black committee that had formed in December to defend the Arkansas farmers. By the time Ida met him, he had been selected by Colonel Murphy (whom the NAACP had secretly retained) to work on the defense case.[62]

Jones received Ida warmly. He credited her "for starting this whole movement," she wrote. Jones explained that when the case began, he hadn't thought that there was a chance of winning it, but since the publicity, "a new trial has been granted, colored people of the state themselves are organized, and they are raising money all over the United States to help in the case." Money was also being raised by the CFDC, which for the next several years, raised more money ($10,000) than did the NAACP ($8,000).[63]

In February, Ida reported about her Arkansas trip in the *Chicago Defender*. She wrote about her visit with the accused men and how much they had appreciated the support of the people of Chicago and how the *Defender* had come to their aid. Mentioning Jones and Murphy by name, Wells-Barnett informed her readers that the defense of the men was now in able hands and that the next task was to "educate public sentiment by publishing the inside facts of this whole story." Ida then announced that she would begin a campaign to raise money to publish her pamphlet. "I truly believe," she concluded, "when these facts are laid before the world it will so open the eyes of the country and make for public sympathy for these men that the whole country will say let those men go free!"[64]

THE EYE-OPENING DOCUMENT to which she was referring was *The Arkansas Race Riot*, a fifty-eight-page pamphlet that was the most ambitious and comprehensive tract she had published to date. It contained many of her classic features: facts she uncovered with her investigation that refuted biased press accounts, the true motives and meaning of the alleged "crime" (black assertiveness against white economic interests), a day-by-day account of the riot, replete with the names of those killed, including women and children, and the precise circumstances in which they were murdered, a history of the Progressive Farmers and Household Union (that had its origins in 1865), and biographical details about the men on death row.

As she had done in her East St. Louis pamphlet, Wells-Barnett wrote about the plight of the women during the Elaine riot, which had been overlooked by other accounts. She wrote how the wife of Frank Moore had escaped the mob with her children only to return to a house in which all of her furniture and clothes had been taken by the landlord while her husband was in jail awaiting execution. The landlord not only refused to return the possessions and pay her for the crop that represented a year's work, but threatened to kill her if she did not leave the premises. A wife of another leader of the union, Ed Ware, was arrested and put in jail to do hard labor for four weeks. Yet another spouse, Lula Black, was beaten, kicked, pistol-whipped and incarcerated after she was asked if she belonged to the union and defiantly responded in the affirmative. A housekeeper who worked in another union member's house that was raided by the mob was killed and thrown onto a public road where her body lay exposed with her clothes pulled up over her head.[65]

The distinguishing characteristic of the pamphlet was Wells-Barnett's economic analysis coupled with the personal narratives that she was able to attain through her interviews of ten of the twelve men slated for execution. She provided a summary that included the names of nearly all of the farmers who had been incarcerated during the riot, alongside how many bales of cotton each had picked, and the amount of money they should have received if they had successfully gotten the planters to pay them the market price for cotton: 45 cents per pound. The twelve men facing the death penalty would have earned $86,050—enough for most of them to no longer be in debt and to purchase their own land. As Ida noted, the figure did not include the one hundred acres of corn raised by the men or the stock, cattle, chickens, mules, and hogs that the men had owned and that had been stolen from them after they were imprisoned. A statement from each man was also featured in the pamphlet in which they spoke of what they had witnessed during the riot, the acreage they had worked, who they worked for, and the possessions lost—including farming tools and, in one man's case, all of the clothes that his wife had possessed. Finally, Ida included depositions that recounted the torture, including electric shocks and mock hangings, that many of the blacks endured to get them to testify against others or confess to certain crimes.[66]

Carrying a copyright date of May 1920, the pamphlet was published about the same time that the convictions of six of the men were upheld in a new trial, prompting the *Arkansas Gazette* to editorialize that the court's action had again brought tranquility to Phillips County and that the plantations were once more "alive with busy workers and there are no longer secret meetings of armed negroes at midnight."[67] Wells-Barnett was determined to disturb the pastoral scene. She had raised enough money to print a thousand copies of *The Arkansas Race Riot* to circulate throughout the state.[68]

This "booklet goes into the greatest court in the world and before the bar of public opinion," Ida wrote. "Every reader a member of that bar and the white people of Arkansas—the honest, law-abiding Christian men and women of that state—are the judges and jury to whom this appeal is made. They are urged for the honor of the state and its material welfare to investigate the facts given in this book in an unprejudiced and impartial manner," Ida exhorted.[69]

Wells-Barnett returned to Arkansas in September of 1920, while the complex case in which the two sets of six prisoners were tried and defended separately was still going through appeals. From Arkansas, Ida, though not mentioning it in her autobiography, went to Memphis that month, the city that had made her an exile thirty years before.

CHAPTER TWENTY-FIVE

Unfriendly Takeovers

> The Woman's Forum has only commendation for
> the NAACP's work on the Dyer Anti-Lynching
> bill, but they should have their own National and
> local organizations and should do their own work,
> and our women [of the National Association of
> Colored Women] should be left to do theirs.
>
> —*Ida B. Wells-Barnett*

In 1920, Wells-Barnett reentered Memphis with no less fire than when she had left it in 1892. She gave at least two speeches in the city: one at Metropolitan Baptist Church and another at Avery Chapel, the church where she had once taught Sunday school with her slain friend Thomas Moss. Although the *Bluff City News* of September 4 did not specify the subject of her talk, it reported that she "stirred audiences to a high pitch of enthusiasm with a persuasive eloquence rarely ever excelled."

Ida left no record of how she felt about returning to the city that had set her on a life-altering path. Memphis itself had seen many changes. It now had a prominent skyline punctuated by office buildings. Automobiles whirred by on the same streets that Ida had once traversed by mule-drawn trolleys. In 1909, Tennessee had finally passed a statewide prohibition law—thanks in part to her nemesis, Edward Ward Carmack, who had once slandered her in the *Memphis Commercial.* In the wake of Ida's exile, Carmack had served in Congress, and in 1908 had run unsuccessfully for the Tennessee governorship. After losing the gubernatorial primary race, he lambasted his antiprohibitionist rival, Malcolm Patterson, with his trademark vitriol in the *Nashville Tennessean,* the newspaper he then edited. When Carmack subsequently saw two of Patterson's supporters on a Nashville street in November of 1908, the editor drew his gun on them, wounding one. The other, a man named Robin Cooper, shot back, killing Carmack instantly. Prohibitionists made a martyr of the editor, and his death turned the tide of opinion in Tennessee to vote for prohibition.[1]

Clearly Memphis, in many ways, had also remained the same. The city struggled with its continuing purity campaigns, which drove saloons and houses of pleasure underground—and mayhem above it. By 1916, the Bluff City had the highest murder rate of any city in the country. In 1917, the vicious mob lynching of a black man, Ell Persons, accused of raping a white woman, prompted the establishment of the Memphis branch of the NAACP, headed by Robert Church, Jr.[2]

Church, named after his father, who had been so supportive of Ida, was the most powerful black political figure in Memphis and one of the most influential black Republicans in the country. His Lincoln League, founded in 1916 to mobilize black voter registration, had grown from being a statewide force to a national one. By 1920, Church was a member of the national GOP's Advisory Committee on Policies and Platform and one of three blacks who were appointed as national directors of the Division of Colored Voters for the upcoming presidential campaign.[3]

The November national election that year would be the first in the wake of the Nineteenth Amendment, which gave women throughout the country the right to vote. After a furious debate in August of 1920, Tennessee, with prodding from Woodrow Wilson, had become the decisive thirty-sixth state to ratify the Susan B. Anthony suffrage amendment. Church, cognizant of the potential of the female franchise, encouraged the participation of women in the Lincoln League, and probably met with Wells-Barnett while she was in Memphis. When Church held his Lincoln League convention in February of 1920, Ida was listed as one of the women delegates.[4] After her stopover in Memphis, Ida headed home. Weighing on her mind was the future of her struggling Negro Fellowship League.

* * *

IN 1920, CHICAGO was in the midst of a severe recession. Unemployment, rife throughout the city, hit African Americans especially hard. Gains that had been made in the war years, when black workers and wages were at a premium, had disappeared. Black women were the first to be added to the black unemployment rolls, which reached twenty thousand by the end of the year.[5]

The economic situation had made it particularly difficult to sustain the NFL, which had been teetering since the loss of Wells-Barnett's adult probation job, the withdrawal of Victor Lawson's support, and more recently, the founding of the Chicago branch of the National Urban League (NUL) in 1916. The mission of the NUL, founded in New York City in 1911, was to "improve the industrial, economic, social and spiritual conditions among Negroes." Built upon a foundation of philanthropic support and professional social and settlement workers, it, like the NAACP, also attracted what Ida called the "academic few" of progressive social scientists and black civic leaders. In fact, the Chicago Urban League (CUL) and the NAACP shared many of the same members: Jane Addams, Edward O. Brown, Drs. George Cleveland Hall and Charles Bentley, Julius Rosenwald, and Sophonisba Breckinridge, among others.[6]

In its early years, the CUL's first president, Robert E. Park, a white University of Chicago sociologist (who had been one of Booker T. Washington's ghostwriters between 1905 and 1914), focused the organization's efforts on research. Park's stated objective of increasing the effectiveness of Chicago's many "rather primitive Negro organizations" by providing them with a "body of authentic fact,"[7] had, at first, made many look upon the CUL with wariness. But the tide of support turned when it won the acceptance of the *Chicago Defender* and most importantly the black women's clubs.[8]

There was little question that the "primitive" category included the NFL, whose secretary was an elevator man, the treasurer, a Red Cap at the Illinois Central Station, and the Bible-class instructor, a ragpicker whom Ida often saw when she went downtown, carrying a large bag of dirty rags on his back. Ida had earlier gone to early CUL meetings and had pledged cooperation. But she soon began to suspect that the Urban League did not intend to help the NFL but to "supplant it."[9]

Wells-Barnett gave no further explanation as to why she thought that the NFL was targeted for extinction. But perhaps her seeking out the Chicago diocese of the Methodist Episcopal Church in 1918 to underwrite the

NFL was, in part, an effort to stave off the inevitable. Moreover, as Ida wrote in her autobiography, she had long dreamed of making the NFL an alternative institution to train others in the field of social work. For the Methodists to aid in such a project offered some poetic justice. It was the same denomination that had supported her alma mater, Rust College.

Encouraged when the church showed interest in her plan, her hopes soured when she was told that one of the conditions of their support was that Ida would have to step aside as president so that one of their young ministers could run its day-to-day operations. Ida was "heartbroken" by the realization that the church failed to appreciate her decade's-worth of work at the NFL. Though never well-funded (the NFL's membership fee was twenty-five cents a month; there was no charge for use of its reading room) or supported by some of the same groups who had become active with the well-financed Urban League, the NFL, according to a 1916 report, had provided aid, advice, and job placement assistance to ten thousand men, women, and children, had provided the "home" for the Alpha Suffrage Club and Ida B. Wells Club, and had taken up numerous causes. In addition to providing the base for Ida's political activities, the NFL had hosted literary contests and readings of Paul Laurence Dunbar's poetry, had led discussions about the dispensation of the German colonies (present-day Tanzania, Namibia, Togo, and the Cameroons) in Africa, and had featured lectures by persons who ranged from the anarchist Lucy Parsons (one of the first to advocate armed self-defense against lynching) to members of the NAACP, and Carter G. Woodson, the second black to earn a Ph.D. from Harvard who was in the process of establishing (with George Cleveland Hall) the Association for the Study of Negro Life and History.[10]

Ida, after a sleepless, prayer-filled night, had decided (she thought) to accede to the church's wishes and step aside. But on the very day that she was to turn over the reins of the NFL, she abruptly changed her mind. As she explained in her autobiography, when the church representative showed up with the check that was to seal the deal, he told her that he did not want to give it to her, but hand it directly to the building's proprietor (a saloon keeper). Insulted that she had been deemed untrustworthy, Ida nixed the deal there and then.[11]

The NFL's situation only worsened in 1919 when the Urban League took over the operations of the U.S. Employment Services in the Black Belt and attained a virtual lock on the occupational services upon which the NFL had become so dependent. There is no question that the Urban

League, which found jobs for some twenty thousand black men and women between 1917 and 1919, was a necessity at a time when the migration overwhelmed small organizations like the NFL. But Ida would have also worried that the Urban League's dependence on large employers, and its neo-Tuskegeean philosophy of weeding out blacks who were deemed undesirable or incapable of assimilating into industrial life, meant that Ida's "down-and-outs" were still largely left behind.[12]

Wells-Barnett had not been able to come up with the rent for NFL headquarters at 3005 State Street since the Chicago riot of July 1919, an indication that whatever discretionary personal income she and Ferdinand had used to subsidize the organization had run out. The NFL and the recession had no doubt weighed heavily on the Barnetts and their four children. Although Ferdinand's law practice must have been affected by the economic downturn, he continued to defend needy, unpopular, or controversial clients. For example, Ferdinand had provided his services to the NAACP-dominated Committee to Secure Equal Justice for Colored Riot Defendants, which despite achieving extraordinary success in the courts (only three cases, involving seventeen blacks, were brought to trial, and of that number three were convicted) was slow to pay its lawyers.[13] One document from April of 1920 showed that Barnett had litigated $500 worth of services but had only received $100 to date.[14]

Moreover, Ferdinand took on at least one of the most difficult cases that more image-conscious attorneys might have refused. He was the lawyer for sixteen-year-old Walter Colvin, one of the teenagers accused of stabbing to death the Italian banana peddler who had been surrounded by a black mob on State Street. Colvin and another boy were found guilty but avoided the death penalty by being sentenced to life in the penitentiary. After the December 1919 verdict, Barnett did not give up on the case and filed for an appeal to the Illinois Supreme Court, which refused to review the case. It is not known if the defense committee had supported the appeal.[15]

After the guilty verdict of East St. Louis's Le Roy Bundy, Barnett joined his defense team in order to get an appeal before the Illinois Supreme Court. He also defended another controversial figure, Marcus Garvey. Now fully within sight of the intelligence services in both the United States and Great Britain, Garvey in mid-1919 had set upon the scheme of selling stock, at five dollars a share, to underwrite the purchase of a fleet of vessels to be used to transport his followers back to Africa. As Ida had earlier noted, the Back-to-Africa movement had helped to fire the imagination of blacks; in August of 1919, Garvey's first international conference in New York attracted several thousand delegates from all forty-eight states and three continents. Ida, who approved of Garvey's ability, as she wrote in her autobiography, to endow the "the masses of our people . . . with racial consciousness and racial solidarity," nevertheless advised Garvey against the Black Star Line stock scheme, which, she understated, was "a much more complicated program than he had helpers to carry out."[16]

Garvey had begun having sharp exchanges with a number of leaders who had become alarmed by his popularity, separatist ideology, and/or suspicion that the stock scheme was laden with fraud. One of those he tangled with was the *Defender*'s Robert Abbott, who sued Garvey for libel. Garvey retained Ferdinand Barnett for one hundred dollars in the case, which was prolonged when the UNIA leader left the States for a trip to Central America and the Caribbean in 1921 and was denied an entry visa for five months when he attempted to return. During that period, a default judgment against Garvey was rendered for five thousand dollars.[17]

Ida, now listed in the 1920 census as a "lecturer," tried to augment the family's income by speaking. But she did not have a reputation as an "elocutionist" who recited popular poems or theatrical readings for established fees. Many of those who asked her to speak had few resources or were unfamiliar with making arrangements that guaranteed their speakers would leave with more money than they had when they arrived. In October of 1920, for example, Ida, addressing her letter "Dear Folks," wrote home to explain such a situation that prevented her from returning in time for the family's traditional Halloween festivities. Wells-Barnett had been asked by the Conference on Charities and Corrections to speak at the state school for the blind and deaf. "I told them that if they wd arrange to cover expenses, I wd be glad to speak," she wrote in the letter. "They had a good house for a short notice & only raised ten dollars in collection! That just paid the fare one way," she explained, "so as they want me to stay over & make another speech and possibly get the rest of my expenses." Electing to remain, Ida apologized for not being able to get home in time for the planned Monday-night dinner. "As it is," she wrote in closing the letter, "you will have to do the very best you can without me."[18]

In late November, Ida looked forward to spending Thanksgiving with the family. A week before the holiday, she, as was her custom, arrived at the

Fellowship League early in the morning—only to open its doors to an empty shell. The landlord, in the middle of the night, had removed the desks, chairs, stove, and most of the equipment. Surveying the tiny empty refuge that had been the center of so much activity over the decade, Ida knew that it was over. On December 8, she turned over the keys to the owner, never to return.[19]

FROM THE TIME she was a young woman, Ida had reacted physically to certain kinds of setbacks. The closing of the NFL appeared to be one of them. A week later, on December 15, she was taken to Provident Hospital. The diagnosis was gallstones; however, there were complications. Ida was sick enough that not even her family was allowed to visit her until Christmas Day. She remained in the hospital for five weeks and was brought home, but then had a relapse and was confined to her bed for another eight weeks. Ida did not fully recover, she said, for a year. Emotionally, the term was probably longer.[20]

The one thing that Wells-Barnett, now fifty-eight years old, dreaded—besides Ferdinand dying before she did—was a prolonged illness that left her physically helpless or dependent. "All at once the realization came to me that I had nothing to show for all those years of toil and labor," she wrote. "It seemed to me that I should now be making some preparation of a personal nature for the future, and this I set about to accomplish."[21]

Being bedridden also allowed Ida to dwell on the accumulating deaths and disabilities of so many she had known. In March of 1918, Celia Parker Woolley had died. Following her death, the Frederick Douglass Center had closed and Woolley's husband donated the Wabash Avenue building, which Ida had helped her find, to the Urban League. In 1921, while Ida was in the hospital, the *Washington Bee* editor, Calvin Chase, died of a heart attack while he was sitting at his desk. In October, she must have read the long, gushing elegy in the *Defender* devoted to the death of publisher Allison Sweeney, who had edited the *Conservator* and been a guest at her wedding; in December, Ferdinand's former law partner, and Fannie Barrier's husband, S. Laing Williams, died after collapsing on the street a short time before.[22]

Early in 1921, Ida's brother-in-law, Bernard Fitts, a one-time precinct captain, the publisher of a small paper called the *Chicago Searchlight,* and an officer of the Chicago Equal Rights League, had finally retired from his Crystal

Printing Company after years of fighting asthma and the severe injury to his arm he had sustained while operating an electrical press. Now it fell on Annie, who had also learned the printing business, to keep it going.[23]

But mostly, the closing of the Fellowship League might have prompted Wells-Barnett to assess what her public life had cost her family. For example, Ida had thought herself to be responsible, in part, for the fact that her husband never attained his dream of becoming the city's first black municipal judge. That honor, due again to Edward Wright's intervention, would go to Albert George, a graduate of Northwestern Law School.[24]

From the incomplete information available about Ida's brothers and sisters, her relations with them seemed spotty, at best. After her baby sister, L'il, had married William L. Daniels in Chicago in 1901, her "little" sister had moved to California. L'il, who had a son, William, Jr., visited on occasion, but the Barnetts actually saw more of her husband, who was a railman and frequently came to Chicago. Ida's one-time troubled brother, Alfred or AJ, also settled in California, and had two sons, Emory and Stanley. Ida did not see much of AJ, though her nephews did come to visit on occasion. Ida's aunt Fanny married William Tipton in California. She died in Sacramento in August of 1908, and it is far from clear if Ida was ever forgiven for leaving her and her sister out West. Ida's younger brother, George, who married Ophelia Smith and moved to Kansas, was another infrequent visitor, though she was closer to his son, Jack. Jack was so impressed about what he had heard about Ida that as a teenager, he had hitchhiked from Kansas determined to meet her. Jack hadn't told anyone that he was headed for Chicago and did not know the address of the Barnetts. As Alfreda recalled, one evening Ida received a telephone call from the police, who told her that her nephew was searching for her. Ferdinand, Jr., was sent to the station to bring Jack to the house. Ida was closest to her sister Annie and must have been proud of the fact that in 1916, Annie had become one of the first three black women to pass a civil service exam for the police force—though she never pursued it further. The Barnett brood often visited Annie on Sundays. But, as in the past, relations with her sister could be stormy—especially about Ida borrowing money from her. Family members recalled periods when the two weren't on speaking terms.[25]

Ida had worked hard to be a good mother to her children: Herman, Charles, Ida, Jr., and Alfreda. Birthday parties given for them were often written up in the *Defender*. Ida also hosted a large reception to celebrate the marriage of Herman and his bride, Fione Davis, in 1918. Occasionally, Ida turned her husband's birthday parties into large social gatherings that also became family reunions. On at least one occasion, the celebration included Ferdinand's son by his first wife, Albert G. Barnett—a graduate of De Paul University's Law School who went into newspaper work—and his wife, Hulette, as well as many out-of-town guests and friends. Ferdinand regularly visited Albert and Hulette on Sundays and brought Alfreda along with him. But Ida's children were never close to their half-brothers, a situation that developed, in part, because of Ida's early desire to live apart from them.[26]

One could guess that none of Ida's own children fully lived up to her high standards. Her favorite son appeared to be Herman, who graduated from the University of Illinois and for a time practiced law with his father. He and his wife lived with the family on Grand Boulevard after their marriage and gave Ida and Ferdinand their first grandchild, Herman, Jr., in 1921. But Herman also had the ability to "pull the wool over mother's eyes," as Alfreda later recalled, and he had a predilection for hanging around "the big shots," like the aldermen Louis Anderson and Robert Jackson, who played high-stakes poker games. Herman also loved betting on the horses, and Ida must have felt a sense of déjà vu when she remembered her brother AJ's gaming habit.[27]

Her son Charles never exhibited much ambition and seemed unable to show up to work on time, even when given the opportunity by "Uncle Fitts" to employ his talents as a commercial artist and layout specialist in his Crystal Printing Company. Charles, once given the title of "Baby of the Federation" at the historic National Association of Colored Women meeting in 1896, had dropped out of high school after an altercation with a teacher for which he refused to apologize. He had been pretty rudderless since then, and much like Ida's brother Jim, was restless. "Of course mother lectured him but he had too many ideas of traveling about," Alfreda recalled. Charles did eventually marry, had a daughter, and, listed as a mechanic in the census, also worked, at some point, as a chauffeur in Milwaukee.[28]

Perhaps Ida's sons made her put more stock in her daughters. In the October 1920 letter explaining why she could not get home in time for Halloween, she closed with a loving, but in its way, demanding, sentiment: "Whenever I think of my dear girls, which is all the time, such a feeling of confidence comes over me. I know my girls are true to me, themselves, and their God wherever they are, and my heart is content. I have had many troubles and much disappointment in life, but I feel in you I have an abiding joy. I feel that whatever others may do, my girls are now and will be shining examples of noble true womanhood. And so mother's heart is glad & happy when she thinks of her daughters, for she knows that wherever they are & whatever they are doing they are striving to please her and reach the ideal of true womanhood." The letter was signed, "With all the love in the world [,] Mother."[29]

Ida's affection was evident—but so was the tremendous pressure put on them, pressure that her two daughters would react to in different ways. The more passive Ida, Jr., became her father's secretary in his law office, never married, and remained in the household. The implied caveat in the letter was probably directed at the more rebellious Alfreda, who graduated from Wendell Phillips High School (where her mother often made surprise visits) and entered the University of Chicago in 1921. Alfreda was restless to experience life—and love—outside of her watchful household. In 1921, a year belonging to the Jazz Age, an indicative and very old-fashioned announcement was published in the *Defender*. "Mrs. Ida B. Wells-Barnett and her daughters . . . will be at home to their gentlemen friends who are to honor the beautiful custom, New Year's day, January 1, 1922 from 8 to 10 pm."[30]

Ida had grand plans for Alfreda, who had been a particularly bright student. She wanted her daughter to complete law school. But what also may have made Ida so conscious of having nothing to show for all that she had done was the reflection of her life in Alfreda's eyes. As her youngest daughter later explained, she had seen her parents stand "almost alone" in many of their causes and suffer because of it. "I've seen my mother shed tears after she'd come from some organization where she worked so hard to try to get change . . . and had met with just obstinate antagonism. All of these things had an impact on my life," Alfreda continued. "I was determined I would never have anything to do in public life, that I was going to marry and have six children and stay home and enjoy my life at home."[31]

But if Ida's earlier diary writings were any guide to her state of mind after the closing of the Fellowship League, she dug deeply into herself and into her Christian beliefs. By doing so Wells-Barnett had always been able to see a purpose behind the tribulations that God threw in her path. They were a test of sorts, a challenge to reach for the "better angels of her nature" in order to qualify for the destiny that her Father had planned for her.

IN APRIL OF 1921, five months after the closing of the Negro Fellowship League, U.S. Representative Leonidas Dyer reintroduced an antilynching bill (H.R. 13) before the Sixty-seventh Congress of the United States. Prospects for its passage were brighter than ever. President Wilson, broken by ill health, and obstreperous to the last, failed to get the Treaty of Versailles ratified by the Senate and Democrats had failed to win the White House in 1920. Republicans now held majorities in both chambers of Congress. The new president, Warren G. Harding, pressed by the NAACP's James Weldon Johnson, had declared in his inaugural address that Congress "ought to wipe the stain of barbaric lynching from the banners of a free and orderly representative democracy." There were even signs that the South might mend its ways. Soon after Harding's statement, Governor Hugh Dorsey of Georgia released *The Negro in Georgia,* an antilynching pamphlet that cited 135 lynchings that had taken place in state and that only two had involved the question of rape.[32]

By 1921, Mary White Ovington; the NAACP's new secretary, Johnson; and the assistant secretary, Walter White, had pushed the NAACP past its paralyzing timidity concerning the constitutionality of an antilynching measure. The change in leadership was important to its change in direction, but it was also true that the NAACP was, in significant ways, a different organization. By the end of 1919, it had grown to 310 branches with 91,203 members—a growth spurred by the activity of black women who had, on a voluntary basis, done most of the nuts-and-bolts fieldwork and community organizing to plant the flag of the civil rights organization in communities across the country. The NAACP "would be a mere National Negro Committee but for the organized work of the women in the branches," observed Ovington, assessing the work of field workers like Kathryn Johnson, Mary Wilson, and, especially, Mary B. Talbert. Talbert, president of the National Association of Colored Women (NACW) from 1916 to 1920, traveled more than seven thousand miles in 1918 and 1919 for the organization through the hostile states of Louisiana and Texas to organize nine new branches.[33] The significance of black women's participation went beyond numbers: their access to an array of social networks and their standing in the community had done much to make the organization more reflective of black concerns and had allayed much of the distrust of the NAACP among African Americans.[34] Moreover, the clubwomen's very origins were deeply connected to the issue of lynching.

Talbert had worked with Dyer as early as 1918, before the NAACP had publicly supported the bill. In the same year, the NACW's Northeastern Federation of Colored Women's Clubs had also endorsed the antilynching legislation. A year later, the Empire State Federation of Women's Clubs, with its two thousand New York members, urged the passage of a federal antilynching law at its annual convention in Harlem.[35] At the 1920 NACW biennial meeting in Tuskegee, Alabama, memorials for the departed Booker T. Washington had been accompanied by criticism of the Republican Party's antilynching plank, which had been characterized by president Hallie Quinn Brown as "only a splinter." A subsequent motion to endorse the Republicans was defeated.[36]

Wells-Barnett, whose antilynching campaign had focused women's concerns on lynching since 1892; who had pressed the NAACP to support an antilynching bill at its first annual conference in 1910; and who had honed her skills in leveraging the political power of the women's electorate, must have looked at these developments with some satisfaction and a good deal of anticipation.

By 1921, Wells-Barnett had also found a church that suited her "better angels"—and that provided her a means to make her presence felt amid so many important developments: the nondenominational People's Community Church of Christ and Metropolitan Community Center. It was pastored by W. D. Cook, who founded Metropolitan after the AME district bishop ordered him transferred from Bethel AME Church. Many believed that his removal was precipitated by Reverend Archibald Carey—finally made a bishop in 1920, and an ally of Mayor Bill Thompson—because Cook refused to "open" his church to politicians. The transfer order caused a rebellion in the five-thousand-member congregation, more than half of whom followed Cook to the Metropolitan Church.[37]

As a member of Metropolitan, Ida organized a group called the Woman's Forum. Little is known about its specific activities, but they probably corresponded with Ida's long-held concerns. Sometime near the beginning of the decade, Ida also founded a journal with the same name. The connection between the Woman's Forum organization and the publication is unclear, as is how the journal became the official organ of Illinois's Northern District Federation of Women's Clubs—which, through a reorganization in 1919 and 1920, now represented only Chicago women.[38] Again, Ida had found a means and a constituency to legitimate her voice.

FROM APRIL OF 1921 through January of 1922, Dyer's antilynching bill was making its tortured way through the House of Representatives. Despite the favorable pronouncements and the Republican majority, the GOP, never eager to be perceived as a close ally of blacks, had to be pressed, cajoled, and threatened before it exerted its will to push the legislation past the parliamentary maneuverings and recalcitrance of those who outright opposed the legislation and others who saw it as a low priority. Fortunately, James Weldon Johnson was up to the task. In addition to pulling out all of the stops in his arsenal of quiet diplomacy and persuasion, Johnson, with the new mood of blacks in the wake of the Red Summer, also warned legislators that African Americans were "no longer in a temper to be played with." The antilynching bill got to the floor on January 25, 1922, nine months after it was first introduced.[39]

During the subsequent debates, there was no hiding place for House Republicans who supported the measure in public, only to become indifferent or obstructionist behind closed doors. According to one paper, more than seven hundred blacks filled the congressional galleries, and they displayed no reluctance to cheer or shout down congressmen as they spoke in favor or against the bill. On January 26, there was cause for a particularly vociferous celebration. The Dyer antilynching bill passed the House of Representatives by a vote of 231 to 119.[40] Unfortunately, however, there was a hiding place for senators, fifty-nine of whom were Republicans. Another Herculean effort by the NAACP, a demonstration of some five thousand black persons who picketed the White House, and the focused lobbying by the NERL's Monroe Trotter on Republican Massachusetts senator and majority leader Henry Cabot Lodge got the bill endorsed by the Senate Judiciary Committee in June of 1922, but it languished thereafter.[41]

The status of the bill in the Senate was very much on the minds of the five hundred delegates representing thirty-seven states who attended the NACW's Thirteenth Biennial in Richmond, Virginia, during August of 1922. James Weldon Johnson was slated to speak on the antilynching bill, and as Ida had probably heard, at the NAACP's June annual meeting, Helen Curtis, a New Jersey club leader, had proposed that women, working with the NAACP, manage a "short, sharp campaign" (from October 1,

1922, to December 31, 1923) in support of the Dyer Bill. The civil rights organization had welcomed the idea. Former NACW president Mary B. Talbert, an NAACP board member whose fieldwork had yielded nine new chapters, was to be the national director of what became known as the Anti-Lynching Crusaders. With her new *Woman's Forum* pulpit, and her youngest daughter, Alfreda, who was slated to speak about the publication on one of the programs, Ida made her way to Richmond.[42]

In the publication, Ida reported on each day of the NACW's meeting held from August 6 to 12. The era's "New Negro" and "New Negro Woman" were very much on display in the star-studded gathering. Ida praised the "clever" maneuver of Ora Brown Stokes, chair of the local committee of arrangements, when she introduced the white state officials in the opening program as "not the type of men who regaled Negro audiences with stories of black mammies for they knew that while we cherished the memories of our black mammies, they knew this was the progressive type of Negro womanhood and would talk of that type." The white officials made "a poor showing" in their addresses, Ida wrote, surmising that they were befuddled by the prospect of excluding their timeworn mammy anecdotes, or addressing "a colored audience of brainy women and men as 'ladies and gentleman' and the presiding officer as 'Madam Chairman.'"[43]

Ida praised the eloquence of NACW president Hallie Q. Brown (whom she had once sparred with over Frances Willard and the WCTU) and mentioned the "brainy" participants who took part in the program. Adelaide Hayford, wife of the Sierra Leonean Pan-Africanist and nationalist Casely Hayford, spoke on "West African Womanhood and Its Needs." Jessie Fauset, soon to have her first novel published and to emerge as a major figure of the Harlem Renaissance, brought greetings from W. E. B. Du Bois and reported on the Second Pan-African Congress he had organized in London. Mary B. Talbert told the three thousand gathered at Richmond's City Auditorium about the activities of the International Council of Women in Christiana, Norway, for which she was the first black woman to attend as a delegate. Maggie Lena Walker spoke to the women on "The Colored Women in the Business World." Among her other accomplishments, Walker, a former slave, rose to become president, in 1903, of Richmond's St. Luke Penny Savings Bank, making her arguably the first woman to hold such a position in the United States.[44]

However, Wells-Barnett surely began to sour on the meeting when

James Weldon Johnson was introduced by Virginia clubwoman Addie Hunton, a field organizer for the NAACP who was also active with the YWCA. With Ida sitting in the audience, Hunton credited John Mitchell, Jr., editor of the *Richmond Planet*—who had written some of the earliest editorials against lynching—with starting the "agitation" against the practice. According to Ida, Hunton went on to attribute subsequent work against lynching solely to the efforts of the NAACP.[45]

Johnson, Ida wryly commented, "was gracious enough to say that one of the national association's number in the person of Mrs. Ida Wells Barnett had done some work against lynching," but his talk did nothing to remove the impression that the civil rights organization had done all of the effective antilynching work. Of course, Ida smarted over the personal oversight, but she was also critical of the NACW ceding so much credit and so much of its program to the NAACP in a way that undermined the women's own contributions. The NACW seemed "bent" on making itself "a tail to the kite" of the NAACP, Ida commented in the *Woman's Forum*. However, Ida, never one not to give credit where credit was due, wrote that Johnson had given an "excellent" talk on the issue.[46]

But Wells-Barnett criticized the fact that Representative Dyer hadn't been invited to address the women (they would have "given him heart to go on with the fight," she wrote) nor had key senators been present. Since they had not come to the NACW, Ida proposed that the NACW go to them and "let the Senators see that our women, who had the vote, were going to use those votes against the men who did not work and vote for the bill." The motion was carried and Ida then telegrammed Illinois senator Medill McCormick to make the arrangements for them at the Capital. Wells-Barnett, no doubt remembering the lobbying experience in Illinois, had wanted the women to go en masse to the Capital, but Johnson and Hallie Q. Brown preferred sending only members from states with key senators, a number of whom were up for election in November. Ida, made chair of the delegation, deferred to the suggestion, but one wonders if the group would have had a greater impact if they had followed Ida's wishes. As she described it, their visits to the senators and President Harding, all of whom reiterated their support for the bill, appeared rather perfunctory.[47]

Ida saved her most trenchant criticism in the *Woman's Forum* for the Anti-Lynching Crusaders. Mary B. Talbert had structured the campaign along the lines of the NACW. There was a national board, state directors, "key women" in charge of organizing and fund-raising in towns, and the identification of individuals who could help with the effort. The campaign was conceived as an interracial one with the object of uniting a million women who, if they contributed a dollar, could raise a million dollars for the NAACP's antilynching fund.[48]

It is not clear how much Wells-Barnett knew about the proposed campaign, to begin in October, when she was in Richmond. But at some point, probably after she had returned to Chicago, she received a form letter from Talbert, asking her to be one of the "key women" for the campaign. Even if Ida minimized the insult of her not being appointed to a higher position, the details of what Talbert asked of women sent her into a tailspin. The campaign was to begin with a sunrise prayer meeting followed by a noonday prayer and special sermons between October 1 and November 5. To raise the one dollar, buttons would be sold and worn daily. All were to find as many women to get involved as possible and send their names to Talbert and the money to the designated state director.

When Ida was particularly enraged, she responded in print by beginning with words of praise followed by a cascading litany of complaint that ended with a note of withering denunciation. Indeed, there was much to praise about Talbert. She had been remarkably successful in a number of endeavors. In addition to her NAACP fieldwork, she had raised $5 million dollars among black clubwomen as the leader of the Third Liberty Bond Drive during the war. And it was under her NACW administration that Frederick Douglass's Anacostia home, threatened with foreclosure, had been purchased by the organization and made into a shrine.[49]

"Mrs. Talbert is a very able, energetic woman and did a splendid piece of work in raising the money for the Douglass Home," Ida began, "but this editor cannot be a 'key woman' for this new organization which has sprung full-fledged overnight." Following the opening paragraph, Ida listed, numerically, the reasons why she would not be a part of the effort. The work could have been done within the NACW itself, which had raised $10,000 for the Douglass Home—money, Ida added, that would have been better used to employ legal talent in defense of the race. There was no clear explanation of how the money raised from the Crusader campaign was going to be used; and in any case, Talbert's appeal had failed to show how "Prayer meetings . . . and wearing buttons are going to make the Dyer Bill a law." "If you had started a crusade to get every voting woman out to the polls this month and next to work and vote against those congressmen and senators who are up for election who are known to be against [the bill]—then indeed you would have been doing something," Ida insisted. By the end of her editorial, Ida's temper flared. "The whole scheme is utterly unworthy of you, Mrs. Talbert, and a direct insult to the intelligence of Negro woman-hood of the land."[50]

Ida might have thought so, but plenty of others did not. Many on Tal-bert's list of more than a thousand women whom she had deemed the cream of the activist crop immediately went into gear, organizing their ju-risdictions, selling buttons, soliciting contributions, distributing ten thou-sand pamphlets given to them by the NAACP, attending prayer meetings, and traveling for the crusade. All of the women were volunteers; state di-rectors were responsible for raising money for their own travel and other expenses; and all funds raised by selling the buttons and donations for the campaign were to be given to the NAACP, whose only contribution to the effort was a *loan* of $500.[51]

Even if most did not find themselves in the situation that Talbert wrote about to Walter White, the sacrifice called for was a tall order. Early in the campaign, she had spent $600 of her own income (to her husband's dis-may), which didn't include her having to hire a cook and housekeeper because she had not time in her early-morning to late-night campaign schedule to deal with domestic responsibilities. Subsequent letters revealed Talbert's growing exhaustion and stress, the latter of which increased when the black press and even the NAACP membership, which had never been officially informed about the contractual relationship with the Crusaders, began to question the legitimacy of their solicitations.[52]

In the end, as Ida had surely gleaned, Talbert felt betrayed by the NAACP. In November, when the Senate vote on the Dyer Bill was in the offing, the association asked Talbert to turn over collected Crusader funds to be used by the national office to place an ad, "The Shame of Lynching," in publications and on billboards. Talbert balked. Women were told that they were raising money specifically for "legislation" work, not an ad. Moreover, the NAACP was asking for the money that these women had raised dollar by dollar and often through great personal sacrifice to merely satisfy a matching grant from a white philanthropic organization that had offered $2,500 to the orga-nization if it could raise the same amount. But Talbert was forced to relent when Ovington threatened to ask local Crusade campaigns directly for the money. Talbert's request to preserve the new network by establishing a chapter-at-large for them, or to keep the raised funds to continue the work, was also denied.[53]

However, by the last month of 1922, neither the ad, nor the campaign, nor the NAACP could keep Republican senators from abandoning the Dyer Bill fight. Three weeks after the defeat, Mary Talbert confessed in a letter: "I'm all in—nervous breakdown," she wrote. "Have canceled everything . . . It's awful to be an invalid after 22 years of active life. *But I'm all in*—" In 1922, Mary Talbert was the first woman to be awarded the NAACP's prestigious Spingarn medal. She died in October of 1923 at the age of fifty-seven.[54]

There is no indication as to what Wells-Barnett thought about the failure of the Dyer Bill and the women's crusade. It certainly confirmed her belief that the proper strategy would have been a greater focus on women's political leverage. Whether Ida's jeremiad in the *Woman's Forum* had had any impact on a parallel strategy to defeat opponents of the Dyer Bill, it had produced some notable, if limited, results. In three states—Delaware, New Jersey, and Wisconsin—opponents of the Dyer Bill were defeated in November. Delaware was a clear example of how the work of black women activists made a difference in the 1922 November elections. Alice Dunbar-Nelson, head of the Delaware Crusaders, led African American women in the Anti-Layton League, made up of men and women voters whose purpose was to defeat Congressman Caleb R. Layton, an opponent of the Dyer Bill. The group registered more than twelve thousand black voters; Layton lost by seven thousand votes, a number equal to the black ballots cast for his Democratic rival. The state's senator T. Coleman Du Pont also voted against the bill. His defeat was attributed to the loss of six hundred key black votes.[55]

TO IDA'S MIND, the NACW had shown its great potential, its wrongheadedness, and its too-short memory regarding her own antilynching role. Her hopes to right the foundering, if powerful, organization would explain her actions when the organization met for its 1924 biennial meeting.

The NACW conference was held in Ida's home city of Chicago, the site of the momentous—and fractious—association meeting twenty-five years before when Mary Church Terrell was reelected to the presidency. There had been rumors during that 1899 meeting that Ida had wanted to run for the presidency herself. In 1924, there was no need for such speculation. Ida announced that she was a candidate for the NACW's highest office.

What was she thinking? Certainly it wasn't the prospect that she could actually win. Wells-Barnett had no more support from ranking top officers than she had had in previous years. Then there was the fact of Ida's competition. Also running for president that year was the vice-president-at-large, Mary McLeod Bethune, past president of the Southeastern Federation of Colored Women's Clubs and founder of the Daytona Normal and Industrial Institute for Girls (which merged with the Cookman Institute in 1923 and later became Bethune-Cookman College). The story of Daytona, begun in 1904 with a vision and a dollar and a half in hand, had already given the educator iconic status. By 1920, forty-seven girls had completed a full high school course, and ten taught in Florida's public schools. Three years later, three hundred students were attending the college and the school's debt-free physical plant was valued at $250,000. Bethune would have run unopposed if it were not for Ida's tepidly supported candidacy. Minutes from the meeting reveal that Wells-Barnett's nomination had been endorsed by five delegates among the seven hundred assembled.[56]

Bethune, known for her rousing, "silver tongued" oratory, was given the opportunity to deliver a major address before the group. The talk drew a standing ovation, remarked the *Baltimore Afro-American,* which called her one of the "greatest women in America" whose achievements rivaled that of Booker T. Washington.[57] By contrast, Wells-Barnett's role in the proceedings was a minor one. When she did have a chance to speak, she talked about the necessity to register, and vote, and to do so according to one's convictions over loyalty to any one party.[58] The Ida B. Wells Club, of which she was president again, invited delegates to a reception at her Grand Boulevard home. At the convention itself, she was a member of the committee that memorialized those who had died, including Talbert, and Ida's pioneering ally, Josephine St. Pierre Ruffin, who had passed away earlier that year at the age of eighty-one.

Predictably, Wells-Barnett lost the NACW presidential election by a landslide. Of the 700 delegate votes, Bethune received 658. After the tally, Ida moved to make Bethune's election unanimous. Nevertheless, Ida's visibility at the conference and her nonpartisan talk might have been a factor in her being selected for a position in a new political organization founded hours after the end of the biennial, the National League of Republican Colored Women (NLRCW). Led by Mamie Williams and Mary Booze, both members of the NACW and Republican national committeewomen from Georgia and Mississippi, respectively, the organization was, in part, a response to the Republican Party's Colored Women's Department, headed by Hallie Q. Brown. Booze and Williams criticized the fact that the NACW, through Brown, was taking such a partisan stance. Ida was selected as one of five NLRCW's publicity committeewomen.[59] The position was but one signal that Ida was ready to embark on a new campaign.

CHAPTER TWENTY-SIX

The Price of Liberty

I pledge myself to work as hard for the benefit of
my Race and my district as I have done for the
past 37 years I have lived in Chicago.

—*1930 Campaign pledge, Ida B. Wells-Barnett*

In September of 1926, Ida received a letter from Milton P. Webster, the large-framed, cigar-smoking organizer of the Chicago division of the Brotherhood of Sleeping Car Porters and Maids (BSCPM). "At the special request of Mr. A. Philip Randolph, I herewith extend to you an invitation to both yourself and the members of your Club to attend our next Mass Meeting," Webster wrote. Randolph, who headed the new union, organized in August of 1925, had known Ida at least since 1918, when both had been elected to represent Marcus Garvey's Universal Negro Improvement Association in Versailles. The BSCPM meeting was to take place at the Pilgrim Baptist Church (which happened to be Ferdinand's church) on Sunday, October 3, and Webster and Randolph understood that the fledgling union needed Ida's help. Webster told her that she would render a "valuable service" if she could put them in touch with other interested women and requested permission to see the Ida B. Wells Club's membership list so that he could send notices to them directly.[1]

Webster, a former porter who was active in Chicago's ward politics, might have known that Ida had actively supported the Pullman porter's cause as early as 1915. In that year, the Negro Fellowship League had had a program that featured R. W. Bell, a Pullman conductor who had been fired because of his efforts to organize Pullman porters. "The public is urged to be present to discuss if it would be better for the porter to content himself with the small wages which the company pays him and depend on tips from the public or to be paid a better wage," ran the NFL's notice.[2]

More than a decade later, the Pullman Company, one of the nation's most successful corporations, was the largest employer of blacks in the country. Yet the current wages for Pullman porters, $72.50 a month, had fallen even further behind that of many other black workers, including unskilled meatpackers who made $22 a week. Pullman conductors, the vast majority of whom were white and who lorded over the porters, earned $150 a month. The situation was bad enough on its face, but what also chafed was the fact that the pay structure reflected the Pullman Company's determination to maintain its long tradition of paternalism among black workers.[3]

When company founder George M. Pullman created the opulent overnight Pullman Palace Car after the Civil War, he exclusively hired blacks, many of them former slaves, to cater to his passengers. Important to the continued success of the Pullman Car—first made famous by its use in transporting the body of Abraham Lincoln from Chicago to Springfield—was the personal beck-and-call service of black porters that epitomized the height of luxury for its clientele. In an era that had featured militancy and talk of a New Negro, each of the country's over twelve thousand Pullman porters continued to depend heavily on tips and was still addressed as "George," the first name of the company's founder.[4]

Still, convincing porters (who had a company union within Pullman) that the Brotherhood should be their sole representative was not going to be easy. Tips could be more than generous, and porters were also compensated by their status as worldly "traveling men" who served the rich and famous. Unlike many other occupations, Pullman employees could count on steady employment, health insurance, a pension, and access to education and other benefits. But like all paternalists, the Pullman Company could be as punitive as it was giving. Company spies reported on porters' activities, and the fledgling efforts of the Brotherhood was already being met by Pullman's carrot-and-stick countercampaign of concessions, reprisals, and subsidies. "Every attempt made by porters to organize has met with an avalanche of Pullman funds to thwart their efforts," noted New York congressman Emmanuel Cellar, who was investigating the employment conditions of the porters. "Negro publications have been subsidized; Negro pulpits have been bought."[5] Apart from Pullman's chicanery, many national opinion-makers were wary of unions in general and Randolph's socialist ties in particular. The labor leader's great debating ability and the support of the NAACP's W. E. B. Du Bois and James Weldon Johnson had been helpful in other cities, but as Webster wrote to Ida, Chicago had given the Brotherhood its most "strenuous opposition."[6]

And yet no city was more important to the Brotherhood than Chicago: the home of the Pullman Company, the center of the country's rail system, and the city where four thousand porters and one hundred maids lived.[7] Milton Webster's first hint that there would be problems was in October of 1925, when he had asked about fifty prominent blacks to come to a meeting in the hopes of getting their support. Only five of the leaders consented to come; of that number only one actually showed up: the Reverend William D. Cook of Metropolitan Community Church—the church where the meeting was held and which Ida attended. The attendance reflected the number of "prominent blacks" who were more beholden to the family-run company than to the fledgling movement.[8]

The Pullmans had been a primary benefactor of Provident Hospital and its nursing school, Chicago's premier black institution. The company had helped Archibald Carey keep Quinn Chapel from foreclosure, thus enhancing his reputation as an efficient church executive. Pullman had been instrumental in the capitalization of the black Wabash Avenue YMCA, where activities and classes for Pullman porters were held. The Chicago Urban League and the black Binga Bank benefited directly from Pullman's largesse. Over the years, the company had also nurtured relationships with the city's black elite. The Appomattox Club, the civic organization founded by Edward Wright, whose 450 members represented the black business and political leadership in the city, featured a life-size portrait of George M. Pullman that hung in its parlor.[9]

Beyond the historic relationship to the company, the Chicago of 1926 was not the Chicago of 1919 that Randolph had written about in the *Messenger*. By the mid-twenties, industry was booming again and blacks were enjoying the most prosperous years that they had ever experienced in the Windy City. Racial strife had largely abated, and there was a reluctance to support any movement that could ignite the sporadic Ku

Klux Klan meetings, bombings, and labor tensions into a full-fledged explosion.[10]

Chicago elites, reflecting the decade's national trend toward interracial cooperation (a trend institutionalized by philanthropist-subsidized organizations such as the Council of Interracial Cooperation) had come to a consensus about a progressive prescription to maintain social order. Future racial conflict was to be avoided, in part, by maintaining racial boundaries while developing better (not open) housing and social institutions within the black and white communities. In 1922, the biracial Commission on Race Relations, which had been appointed by Governor Frank Lowden in the wake of the riot, said as much and also cautioned against provocations, race-baiting, and expressions of racial chauvinism. The caveat was particularly aimed at both the black and white press, but also was more generally applicable. For example, the commission also condemned "self-seeking agitators, Negro or white," who use race sentiment to establish separate trade unions to replace existing biracial ones.[11]

Randolph had understood that success depended on a larger social movement that "possessed the spirit of Harriet Tubman and Nat Turner," and defined Pullman's policies as nothing more than "peon slavery." Webster concluded his letter to Ida: "You may rest assured that in the Brotherhood of Sleeping Car Porters the Race has a staunch, progressive, militant movement, which will ever be on the alert to wield its power whenever the interests of the race demands."[12]

The sentence would have been music to Ida's ears. She had never conflated the absence of agitation with justice or racial well-being; and in her view, racism in Chicago only increased after the issuance of the report. This was no time to accept the status quo, and she envisioned a similar task as to what she had done with the Alpha Suffrage Club (seemingly a lifetime ago) when she had been determined to ply open the grip of the Republican machine to give blacks the opportunity to represent themselves.

Webster had been desperate after the no-show October 1925 meeting, but just when the pivotal year of 1925 looked as if it would end without any progress, the Chicago and Northern District Association of Colored Women, a member of the Illinois Federation of Colored Women's Clubs (IFCWC), invited A. Philip Randolph to speak in December. The precise circumstances of the invitation are unknown, but Webster's later letter to Ida (whose Ida B. Wells Club was a member of the federation) might have indicated that she had been behind it. In any case, the Chicago women were the first major group to respond to the Brotherhood, and their doing so was significant.[13]

By 1926, the Illinois Federation represented ninety-two clubs with more than two thousand members who were active in both black and interracial civic organizations. Moreover, in the wake of the black migration, the new generation of leadership was sensitive to labor issues. The federation's president (and past president of the Chicago City Federation), Irene Goins, a onetime owner of a millinery shop, had been in the forefront of organizing black women in the stockyards after the war. She had also served on the executive council of the Chicago Women's Trade Union League (CWTUL) where she worked with Mary McDowell (a founder of the WTUL) and Agnes Nestor (a founder of the International Glove Workers' Union of America and president of the CWTUL). Like many of the black activists, she was also active in politics. Goins served as an executive board member of the Illinois League of Women Voters, and was the founder of the Douglass League of Woman Voters, a black unit of the League.[14]

Wells-Barnett had followed up the meeting by attempting to get Randolph a hearing before the Appomattox Club, but was told that his appearance would "embarrass" them with the Pullman Company. Ida then took matters into her own hands. Two weeks after his appearance before the Federation, she invited Randolph to her house to speak before twenty-five members of her Woman's Forum. She told the group that it was important to hear his side of the story because they had not found "anything in our press favorable to this movement," and she criticized the "narrow and selfish" views of black leaders. Ida's comment was directed at Robert Abbott and the *Chicago Defender,* seen by the organizers as their most formidable opponent. By 1925, the *Defender* had a national circulation of two hundred thousand, and when it wasn't publishing pro-Pullman articles or ignoring the Brotherhood completely, the paper charged that the union aimed to perpetuate a racial monopoly among porters—a criticism that only made sense within the context of the race-relations commission findings.[15]

While there is no way to measure the impact of the invitation at a time when the BCSPM was both under attack and being largely ignored by the Chicago black political and civic establishment, there is little doubt that, as in the case of the NAACP, the women's support carried the weight of not only their own standing in the community but of the vast array of networks that they had engendered. "We are grateful to you, and other women in Chicago, who rendered us such noble assistance when we were passing though our most critical period," Webster had written to Ida in September of 1926. Now, he was calling upon her and women to assist with the all-important October 3 mass meeting at the Pilgrim Baptist Church.[16]

In response to Webster's appeal, the clubwomen went into gear, producing and distributing BSCPM broadsides and urging women to use their contacts to mobilize all of the forces at their command. By 1926, the union had also organized the Chicago Colored Women's Economic Council, made up of wives and relatives of the porters who helped to raise money, educate the porters' families about the importance of the union, aid those who suffered reprisals for their activities, and inform porters and maids about meetings—often surreptiously and beyond the eyes and ears of Pullman informants.[17]

Randolph and women's union leader Mary McDowell (who helped organize the meeting) were to be the main speakers for the October event. McDowell, whose relationship with Irene Goins might have been instrumental in her initial interest in the BSCPM, became a loyal advocate and the only white Chicagoan who publicly supported the union and criticized Pullman's paternalistic policies. On the meeting day at the overflowing Pilgrim Church, McDowell told the crowd that the year before when she had asked the Pullman porter who was assigned to her about his union status he did not want to talk about it. But on a recent trip, when she asked her black attendant the same question, he proudly told her he was a member of the BSCPM. The anecdote drew great applause and reflected the growing determination and defiance of the Pullman porters, which black newspapers like the *Pittsburgh Courier* had begun to notice by 1926.[18]

The mass meeting exceeded expectations. It was "conceded by all as being the best and most successful one ever held by the Brotherhood," Webster wrote Randolph. "I don't think we could have bought the same publicity in Chicago with the expenditure of a thousand dollars . . . and it created a vast amount of enthusiasm [not] only among our own men but among the general public here in Chicago." Webster concluded, "From the interest that it created, I am satisfied that we have at last broken down the bulk of the opposition and have convinced the most skeptic that the Brotherhood is an organization that will have to be dealt with."[19] If there was one disappointment, it was the lack of coverage in the mainstream press—and the silent treatment still being given by the *Chicago Defender*.

However, Webster turned out to be right about the opposition. A year later, in October of 1927, a mass meeting was held in Reverend Cook's Metropolitan Community Church, which drew two thousand persons who heard Randolph demolish a black Pullman representative and challenge the *Defender*'s race loyalty—a ploy the paper had used on occasion against others. Randolph accused Abbott of betraying blacks because of the financial connection between Pullman and Binga Bank, of which the publisher was a director. Abbott, stung by the charges, had already been humiliated earlier that year when Wells-Barnett had exposed (to Abbott's embarrassed dismay) how he had been shunned by the American Citizenship Foundation, an organization whose purpose was to break down the color line and to which, according to Ida, Abbott had contributed $10,000. After learning that the organization had withdrawn his invitation to a lunch in a downtown hotel purportedly because of fears that the waiters would not serve him, Ida brought the matter up at a meeting of the foundation, which was attended by the women of the City Federation. The women, of course, displayed their displeasure, and the controversy ultimately upended the foundation's two-million-dollar fund-raising drive to which they had been asked to contribute. Abbott, already having a difficult year, was finally broken by mid-November, after receiving waves of mail asking why he did not support the Brotherhood, and when his circulation began to decline, in part, because porters had started to refuse carrying the *Defender* on their routes.[20]

By 1927, Pullman let it be known that porters were no longer to be addressed as "George"; the Brotherhood's membership reached a thousand; and, capitalizing on the momentum, the BSCPM formed a support organization called the Chicago Citizens' Committee, which included middle-class black Chicagoans who represented a wide array of organizations and interests. When Provident Hospital's George C. Hall (a former member of the Commission on Race Relations and a board member of the Chicago Urban League) lent his active support to the committee, it was a signal that most of the black male elite was prepared to sign on to the BSCPM's cause. Predictably, black women were particularly active in the committee, among them Irene McCoy Gaines, one of its founding members. A graduate of Fisk University, she had honed her speaking and leadership skills in the annual oratorical essay contests conducted by Bernard Fitts, Ida's late brother-in-law, at the Bethel Literary Society, emerging the winner in three of them between 1910 and 1914. Subsequently, she became the industrial secretary of the Young Women's Christian Association in Chicago and helped organize and was president of the Illinois Federation of Republican Woman's Clubs. Her husband, Harris Gaines, was serving in the Illinois legislature.[21]

In 1927, Webster, Randolph, and the BSCPM were still years away from becoming the sole representative of the Pullman porters, and periods of pessimism and retrenchment lay ahead. But with the widening circle of support in Chicago, they had, thanks to women, gotten their social movement, which allied men and women, and the black middle and working classes—an alliance that Ida had long dreamed of and that became a model for the civil rights struggles to come.[22]

IN THE SPRING of 1927, Ida was several months short of her sixty-fifth birthday; her husband, Ferdinand, had already turned seventy-five on February 13. Both Barnetts were beginning to show the frailties of age, and Chicagoans began hosting testimonials for them. In May, the Ida B. Wells Club honored Ida at the Wabash YMCA to celebrate the "Mother of all clubs." The event was followed later in the month by a large dinner at the Appomattox Club where the two hundred attendees heard testimonials to both Ida and Ferdinand, the guests of honor. One of the tributes indicated that Chicago owed more to the Barnetts than to any other couple for "the betterment of racial conditions."[23]

But if anyone thought that the salutary words signaled a retirement of sorts, they were mistaken. Ferdinand, who had taken cases from that of the teenager accused of murder in the 1919 riot to that of Le Roy Bundy—released in 1923 when the Illinois Supreme Court concluded that the involvement of the East St. Louis dentist in the riot was not proven—would continue to defend the down-and-out and the controversial. And Wells-Barnett, though less apt to travel outside of Illinois to investigate or publicize some travesty, found that the victims of them were coming to her.[24]

One of them, Ida recalled in her autobiography, was a well-dressed young man who came to the Barnett residence one evening. Ida opened the door and did not recognize him until he identified himself as one of the former prisoners in Elaine, Arkansas. The last of the black men had been freed in 1925, following numerous appeals that finally reached the U.S. Supreme Court, where the NAACP's Moorfield Storey won the landmark

Moore v. Dempsey decision that invalidated the men's guilty verdicts. When Ida introduced him to the family, he told them how she had insisted that the prisoners stop talking about dying. After that, the young man said, "we never talked about dying any more, but did as she told us, and now every last one of us is out and enjoying his freedom."[25]

In the summer of 1927, another visitor was a reminder that while the BSCPM was ending peon slavery in the Pullman Company, the floods in the Mississippi Valley that year revealed that oppressive labor was still alive and well in the South. The waters had surged past broken levees that spring, plunging over twenty thousand square miles of land under water. At least five hundred were known to be dead, and a half million were left homeless. The *Chicago Defender,* among other papers, had reported the horrid scenes of bodies being hastily buried by railroad tracks; and corpses cut open and filled with sand until they could be disposed of. Large numbers of the refugees were black, many of them sharecroppers who were prohibited from leaving their plantations by their employers and forced to huddle in tents or in abandoned railway boxcars with no ventilation and little to eat. Hastily constructed camps had such unsanitary conditions that measles, mumps, and typhoid broke out in them.[26]

The issue hit home, literally, when a wounded man found his way to the Barnett residence from Greenville, Mississippi, where he had been in one of the distribution camps for refugees. While the conditions and lack of adequate relief (including unequal rations being doled out by the Red Cross to white and black victims) were largely known, what Ida heard from the Mississippian who came to see her was even more egregious. He told her how authorities had rounded up the black men into work gangs and forced them at gunpoint to shore up the levees when they were at their breaking point. After the waters subsided, black men were forced into doing the filthy cleanup work and to endure inoculations that made them sick. At least twenty-five men had died in his camp after being injected, according to Ida's Greenville informant. He had been shot in the leg when he had made his attempt to escape.[27]

As Ida later wrote in the *Defender,* she was also told of the "devilish practice," of refusing "to issue rations to black women and children unless there is a man in the family whose presence had to be certified to by a white person." In "other words," Ida wrote, "our women and children must suffer, starve, and die, because there is no man in the family to work on the levee for $1 a day"—the maximum allowed if his family was to receive aid.

"So it is now left for us who still have a measure of freedom to act for our Race and demand an investigation," she exhorted.[28]

Typically, Ida was prepared to blast anyone, white or black, who was victimizing African Americans. While much of the black coverage of the postflood conditions focused on the behavior of white officials and planters, Ida also discovered that black ministers in Greenville were being paid off to ensure investigators and the public that the refugees weren't being ill-treated. "Better that no information be given out at all than that people in the North should learn from the mouths of subsidized preachers that they are happy and contented," Ida wrote in the *Defender.* "Ignore such leaders."[29]

The Ida B. Wells Club, now headed by Ida's widowed sister, Annie, in alliance with the Baptists Ministerial Alliance, sent a protest letter to the Secretary of Commerce Herbert Hoover. The act drew the familiar charges that Ida was merely a crank whose politics put her outside of the mainstream. Wells-Barnett answered the criticism: "Some of our people have told secretary Hoover and others who can correct these evils that . . . 'Mrs. Barnett is a radical and that nobody pays any attention to her, as she is seeking notoriety.' "[30] There is no indication that Hoover, who would be a candidate for president in 1928, responded to or even received the protest, but Ida later praised him for his subsequent supervision of the Flood Relief Commission, which, as she noted, "brought order out of chaos."[31] Now Wells-Barnett wanted to do the same for Chicago's political landscape.

Three decades before, Ida had traveled throughout the state for the Republicans with her nursing baby Charles to find that few women and even fewer black women knew much about politics. She had become a model to others, first, by her involvement with biracial suffrage organizations, then with her founding of the Alpha Suffrage Club (ASC) in 1913, the first such black women's organization in Chicago. Through it, Ida had led women to understand their lobbying power and their ability to change the face of Chicago politics by helping to elect Oscar De Priest as the city's first black alderman. By the 1920s, black Chicagoans had both the greatest number and the largest all-women suffrage clubs in the country and were increasingly involved in the grassroots work of machine politics. By the later years of the decade, black women made up about one-fourth of the Second and Third Ward precinct captains—who headed the informal support networks for the ward organization.[32]

African American women had also established suffrage organizations throughout the country and continued to create ever more efficient nation-wide networks. Most dramatically, they had shown their political potential when the Anti-Lynching Crusaders had been instrumental in defeating candidates who did not support the Dyer Anti-Lynching Bill in 1921. But there was still much to achieve—and there were frustrations. On the national level, black women, aided by Mary White Ovington and Walter White of the NAACP, went head-to-head with the predominantly white National Woman's Party and the League of Women Voters (formerly the National American Women's Suffrage Association), which were reluctant to go on record and push for antidisenfranchisement measures that plagued black women voters, especially in the South.[33] In Illinois, the *Chicago Defender* indignantly reported about the refusal of the Illinois Republican Club, a white organization, to ally with the Illinois Division of the National League of Republican Colored Women's Clubs, allegedly because the black women were paid workers of the Republican Party.[34] By 1927, Wells-Barnett, characteristically, was determined to impose her more independent vision on Chicago politics. In that year, she founded the Third Ward Women's Political Club.

Her new organization, she determined, could affect developments in the black community that couldn't have been to her liking. The monster she had helped to create, Mayor "Big" Bill Thompson, after an all too short four-year hiatus from the mayoralty, ran and won the spring primary for the mayoralty in 1927 with the help of the usual suspects. These included the voters in the Second Ward, which gave Thompson 94 percent of the Republican primary vote. He also received more than 83 percent in the Third Ward, which after lines were redrawn in 1921, included a portion of the old Second Ward and became majority black.[35]

By 1927, Thompson also had a new ally who was making hay from, among other activities, selling alcoholic spirits during the Prohibition era: gangster Al Capone, who was reported to have contributed somewhere between $100,000 to $260,000 to the mayor's campaign chest. For Ida, as well as other black progressives, vice was only second to race prejudice in its damaging impact on the community. "Chicago colored people are held fast in the damning grip of our vice lords," she had written as early as 1922 in the *Woman's Forum*. Five years later corruption was poised to reach new heights, and Ida believed that women, as she wrote, were the ones needed to "crusade against this oligarchy of vice."[36]

The reappearance of Thompson also signaled the phoenix-like rise of

Oscar De Priest, who had lost a number of closely contested races in recent years but was on the rebound by virtue of his support for Thompson. Ida had worked with De Priest and his People's Movement organization in the wake of the Chicago, Arkansas, and East St. Louis riots, but he worked too closely with the city's "vice-lords" for her taste. De Priest and his People's Movement headquarters were, after the redrawn ward lines, now located in the Third Ward, which was poised to follow the same corrupt-ridden path as the Second.

Another political development had also risen with the demographic changes of the new decade. Similar to the circumstances that had precipitated Ida's earlier quest to mobilize support for a black alderman in the Second Ward, the mid-1920s offered the possibility of electing the first black U.S. representative to Congress since House member George White of North Carolina was forced out of his seat in the wake of the 1898 Wilmington massacre. By the late twenties, the more than ninety thousand black adults who resided in the First Congressional District, long represented by the now ailing South Side boss Martin B. Madden, were in the racial majority. Again Wells-Barnett envisioned a political breakthrough for African Americans.[37]

Mobilizing black women in the electorate was, largely thanks to Ida's past efforts, not going to be as difficult as it had been in the past. There were ten black women's suffrage organizations in Chicago in the late twenties, according to the activist Irene McCoy Gaines. Another contemporary observer, I. Marie Johnson, named four particularly significant ones: the Women's Colored Republican National organization, the Chicago Woman's Republican Club, the Independent Woman's Republican Club, and Ida's Third Ward Women's Political Club. All were led by women with a good deal of political experience, according to Johnson. But in some ways, the very presence of so many groups provided another challenge for Wells-Barnett. As the names of the other organizations implied, they were tied to the Republican Party, a circumstance that obfuscated the independent role she saw women as playing. Indeed, Johnson also noted that despite their numbers and political acumen, the black women seemed to be "floundering" because they were not "quite sure whether their interests could best be served by allying themselves with men or by maintaining separate organizations." As a "political factor," the writer concluded, "our women have not yet advanced beyond the stage of the ward heeler."[38]

Wells-Barnett was clear about where she thought those interests lay. The platform of the club, Ida announced in November of 1927 at the first annual reception held at the Appomattox Club, was "For Women, Of Women, and By Women."[39]

Taking enfranchised women to the next rung, the Third Ward Women's Political Club was established not merely to support candidates but to train women to run for office themselves. It was an aspiration that again pushed the envelope in the black community, which (largely thanks to her) had gotten used to black women as facilitators in the political process but not as candidates themselves. Surely on Ida's mind was the fact, as had happened at the previous critical juncture of women's political empowerment, that those from other groups had already broken down barriers, and again Ida indicated her openness to an alliance with white suffragists. One of the honorees at the Club's reception was Lottie Holman O'Neill, who in 1922 had become the first Illinois woman to win a seat in the state legislature.[40]

Ida's new suffrage organization was founded in time for the 1928 elections. For the upcoming congressional contest, the group approached a young politician by the name of William Dawson—a relative newcomer to Chicago who was born in Georgia, graduated from Fisk, and was a Northwestern University–trained lawyer who was an admirer of Ferdinand. Dawson soon proved to be an effective campaigner who harped on Ida's theme that it was time an African American with his training represent the First Congressional District and that Madden, who did not even live in the jurisdiction, could "hardly voice the hopes, ideals, and sentiment of the majority of the district."[41]

Nineteen twenty-eight was also a presidential election year, and Ida put her own toe into the political waters by running as a delegate to the Republican National Convention from the First Congressional District. Two delegates were to be chosen out of a field of five, and to say that Wells-Barnett, an independent and the only woman on the ticket, was an underdog understates the case. For starters, two of her opponents were Oscar De Priest and Daniel M. Jackson, and both were endorsed by the *Chicago Defender*.[42]

De Priest not only had the support of Madden and the Regular Republicans but his People's Movement also had a formidable female presence. There was, for example, the group known as the "Flying Squadron," an all-women's group that acted as an auxiliary support organization.[43] In addition,

De Priest had developed a large female constituency through the ever increasing numbers of women working on the ward levels as well as his Oscar De Priest Charity Club, organized to raise money to create a home for convalescents. His top lieutenant and organizer was Jennie Lawrence, a North Carolinian and a trained social worker who had served as superintendent of the Phyllis [*sic*] Wheatley Home before heading the People's Movement Employment Bureau. Lawrence's success in finding jobs and advising young people was touted in the local newspapers.[44]

Daniel Jackson, also an ally of Thompson's, was a Lincoln University graduate, a mortician, and the vice king of the Second Ward. After the death of the Pekin Theater's Robert Motts, Jackson married Motts's sister and inherited his estate. By the late 1920s, Jackson headed the syndicate that controlled vice, bootlegging, cabarets, and gambling on the South Side. Both Jackson and De Priest had a particular investment in the delegate election, because they were also running for committeemen of their wards. The committeeman was the chief patronage dispenser of the ward political apparatus who formulated party policy, nominated judges for the superior and circuit court, filled vacancies, and placed constituents in city jobs—the number of which could reach in the thousands. Jackson, in particular, was engaged in a bitter power struggle to replace Ed Wright, who refused to support Thompson, in the Second Ward position.[45]

Indeed, by the late 1920s, the political stakes were high and, as the candidacy of Jackson and the support of Capone attested to, Chicago politics was not for the fainthearted. In 1927, Thompson opponents conducted raids into the Second Ward, arresting more than a thousand men and women potential voters.[46] For the following two years, when Ida was at her most politically active, two black ward political candidates were assassinated, as was a white precinct captain. The homes of two Thompson aides were also bombed, and two political operatives of Senator Charles Deneen were shot to death. The homes of Deneen and his candidate for state's attorney were also bombed.[47]

The time was also not propitious for those outside of the political patronage structure. Dawson predictably lost to Madden in the 1928 election, and Wells-Barnett to De Priest and Jackson, both of whom also became committeemen in their wards. Ida received fewer than eight thousand votes in her run, but Dawson's showing—which launched the political career of the future U.S. congressman—did inspire hope. He won 29 percent of the Republican primary vote, a signal that black Chicagoans were indeed becoming restless to send an African American congressman to Washington.[48] And as future development would show, Ida did not give up the idea of attaining political office for herself or other black women whom the Third Ward Women's Political Club supported.

However, it would be De Priest, once again, who benefited from the development when, soon after the April primary, Congressman Martin Madden succumbed to his long-term illness and died. De Priest immediately contacted ward committeemen and Thompson and got their support for the nomination to run for the U.S. Congress in Madden's place. If successful, De Priest would represent the second major political breakthrough in Illinois in the period.[49] Also in April, Ruth Hanna McCormick, long an influence in Republican women's political circles, handily won her election for Illinois congressperson-at-large. McCormick was the daughter of the late Republican kingpin Mark Hanna and was the widow of Medill McCormick.[50]

In the meantime, Wells-Barnett was working hard for the Republican National Committee (RNC) in Illinois—though she had to elbow her way into the position that she wanted. The RNC had a Colored Voters Division (CVD) with a Colored Women's Organization (CWO). The western division of the CWO was headed by Lethia Fleming, a prominent Cleveland clubwoman and a close friend of Mary Terrell, who directed the eastern division. It is not clear who made the decision to bring Myrtle Foster Cook, the Missourian who edited the NACW's *National Notes,* to Chicago to be a primary organizer of Illinois women, but the idea did not sit well with the Chicago locals—and particularly Ida. "You know how Mrs. Barnett would act," noted one of the RNC men, describing Ida's reaction about the decision at one of its early meetings. "She and her cohorts held a meeting of protest . . . against bringing up [Cook] when she [Wells-Barnett] is here . . . and could do so much better." Soon after the meeting, Ida was sending out campaign literature announcing that she (not Cook) had been appointed "National Organizer of Negro Women for Illinois."[51]

Ida, of course, never lacked confidence in her abilities or in the importance of every campaign she signed on to. As she confirmed to Claude Barnett, secretary of publicity for the CVD and founder of the Associated Negro Press (a news service that supplied items to black papers), "I believe a large number who are today indifferent or hostile will listen to an expression by me and be guided by it." Less than 25 percent of the black women throughout the state had yet to vote in a presidential election, she informed him, and as she pointed out in her own campaign letter, "if we neglect to intelligently use [the franchise], this power can be taken from us, just as it has been taken from our people in the South."[52]

Her conviction impelled her to dive headlong into the work—and to complain that the higher powers that be were coming up short in support. In September, Ida wrote Barnett that she had held a mass meeting for the ticket at Wendell Phillips High School, which drew a thousand persons. It was the only meeting of "national character" held in Chicago, she said, and yet she was forced to pay for the publicity handouts out of her own pocket. By October, she was canvassing the southern part of the state as far as Springfield. "I have just returned from ten counties where our people are in the largest numbers," she wrote Barnett, and "I am happy to say I left active women's organizations at work for [Herbert] Hoover . . . in every one of those counties." With the aid of three assistants, Ida continued, she had been able to "raise the colored woman's registration in this campaign nearly 50 per cent over what it has ever been in Illinois."[53]

Wells-Barnett wrote her own campaign literature, and her "Why I Am for Hoover" broadside lavishly praised the Republican presidential candidate's progressive views, humanitarian record (he was able to raise the Allied blockade of Germany to send food to its starving citizens), engineering skill, and efficiency regarding the Mississippi flood relief, among other accomplishments. She, mistakenly it turned out, believed that Hoover's record for "standing up for the weak," and "the oppressed" and his can-do attitude, as she wrote to Barnett, would translate into his will and ability to solve "our racial problems with justice for all."[54]

But Ida's advocacy was also driven by the perils she saw in returning a Democrat, in general, and their presidential candidate, Alfred E. Smith, particular, to the White House. "You ask for specific instances of inimical legislation or mistreatment of our group by the Democratic Party," Ida noted in her letter to Barnett. "Why the Democratic Party has never passed any other kind of legislation but the sort which segregates, disenfranchises, or discriminates against our progress." Ida was also disturbed about Smith's anti-prohibitionism, fearing that it could lead to the annulment of the Eighteenth Amendment to the Constitution, which made the sale of alcoholic beverages illegal. Her main concern was that the precedent of such a constitutional action could lead to the overturning of the Fourteenth and Fifteenth

Amendments, which, as she wrote, "gave our race liberty and citizen-ship."[55]

DURING THE HEAVY campaign season, Wells-Barnett wasn't only stumping for candidates. While she was working on the political front, she was also doing what she had always done: publicizing and protesting injustice. Although instances of lynchings in the country were at a low—eleven were recorded in 1928—Ida commented in her autobiography that race prejudice was unabated. One difference in her activist work, however, was that after the war and the organizing through the Brotherhood of Sleeping Car Porters and Maids, clubwomen, with whom she now worked on justice issues, were more apt to support blacks whom Wells-Barnett had helped in her Negro Fellowship League.[56]

In 1928, for example, Ida, acting in her capacity as the chair of the civics committee of the Chicago Federation, forced the state's attorney and the coroner to investigate the shooting death, by policemen, of a sixteen-year-old black boy, Ernest Whitehurst, who had been sought by authorities for allegedly breaking a glass window. When at first he refused to come out of his apartment, police shot into the residence. Gunfire was returned from the apartment, wounding several officers. Subsequently, the police left the premises and then returned with enough artillery to conduct a small war. Whitehurst was promised that if he surrendered he would not be harmed, but when the young boy appeared at the doorway, the police rushed in and fired thirty-five shots into his body while his horrified family looked on. It is not known what the outcome of the investigation was; what is known is that without vigilance, what happened to Whitehurst and others like him would only escalate if police could in such a way with impunity.[57]

While Ida was campaigning, she also continued to go before parole boards and seek stays of execution; protested the stoning of a black Girl Scouts Troop at Jackson Park Beach; and intervened to keep a young black girl from the dreaded Geneva school, a facility for female delinquents known for the discriminatory treatment of its black charges.[58]

AS IDA HAD earlier written to Claude Barnett, she anticipated that the election of Hoover would have an ameliorating effect on the racial prejudice she was confronting. But if she and other African Americans celebrated Herbert Hoover's victory by more than four hundred thousand votes in Illinois and polling about 75 percent of the black vote in Chicago, the party was short-lived. Hoover promptly acceded to the strategy of creating "Lily White" Republican organizations in the South, prompting Alderman Louis B. Anderson to advise that "The Republican Party has shown us the gate. Now let all the colored people walk out of this gate"—and African Americans soon would make a tectonic shift toward the Democratic Party. Another victor in November of 1928 was Oscar De Priest, who made history by winning his congressional seat, representing the First District. The triumph, however, was complicated by the fact that soon after, he was slapped with an indictment (later dismissed) for abetting South Side racketeers to operate gambling houses.[59]

Wells-Barnett was in no mood to abide by politics as usual in 1929, the year that the ever-ambitious congresswoman Ruth Hanna McCormick announced she would run for United States senator just two months after winning the House seat. Wells-Barnett would have been wary of the congresswoman despite the fact that her late husband had been popular with African Americans and she herself associated easily with black women activists—a number of whom saw her as a pathbreaking symbol for all women's aspirations.[60]

Nevertheless, McCormick, who also supported the Regular Republican De Priest, was preparing to run against the progressive-wing candidate, Senator Charles Deneen (who had appointed Ferdinand as assistant state's attorney), and was a candidate who wobbled on such issues as prohibition.[61] Moreover, although McCormick had benefited from her ability to organize thousands of Republican women into political clubs, she made it a point to declare in her campaign that she was not "a feminist or a suffragette" but a "politician."[62]

Whatever Ida's opinion of McCormick, the congresswoman added insult to injury when she announced that she would bring in Mary Church Terrell, a friend whom she had known in Washington circles, to manage the black women's vote for her senatorial campaign. As events would show, the selection of Terrell was perceived as a poke in the eye to black Chicago women who had a good deal of experience and broad political networks such as the Women's Republican Council. Founded in 1927 by Susie Meyers, one of the most prominent leaders among the women, the council was an umbrella organization of the numerous political groups in Illinois.

At a time when a number of black women, such as Mary C. Clarke (who would run for the legislature) and Ida herself, were candidates, bypassing their organization could be seen as a commentary that they were deemed inadequate to the task. Moreover, at the head of the council was the very capable Irene McCoy Gaines, who was also the president that year of the Illinois Federation of Republican Colored Women's Clubs and the logical choice to work in McCormick's well-financed campaign.[63]

"Illinois women are up in arms," wrote Elizabeth Lindsey Davis to NACW president Sallie Stewart, "and many letters of protest have gone into Mrs. McCormick's office." It was not that they objected to Terrell coming in as a volunteer, Davis explained, but "they are indignant that Mrs. McCormick has put her over . . . Gaines."[64] Although the objection to Terrell was a broad one, it was Ida, chair of the Women's Republican Council's resolution committee, whose name headed the signers of the protest that officially gave notice of the "slight" that the appointment of an "outsider" represented to the "Negro Women of Illinois." The resolution noted that black women had supported McCormick "every time she has come to us asking our vote, and who thus had the right to expect political recognition which they have not received at her hands, for themselves and their daughters, regret that she could find no Negro woman in the state which must elect her, to her campaign."[65]

As a result of the protest, McCormick was forced to limit Terrell's activities to outside of Chicago. Terrell "did not like it," Davis reported, "but the Chicago women made such a strong protest that there was nothing else for Mrs. McCormick to do. Irene Gaines is heading up the state and Terrell is subject to her orders."[66]

There is no evidence as to what difference Gaines made, but in April of 1929, McCormick handily beat Deneen in the Illinois primary, though she subsequently lost the election for the Senate seat in November. The political season, however, would not be as welcoming to Wells-Barnett in 1930 when she became the first black woman to throw her hat in the ring for a state senate seat in the Third Senatorial District.

The district was a large one, made up of Wards One, Two, Three, Eleven, and Thirteen. Its total population of approximately a hundred thousand was 55.1 percent black. Ida was running against two political veterans: Warren B. Douglas, a lawyer, who was supported by the Deneen faction; and the incumbent, Adelbert H. Roberts, a former member of the Illinois House and clerk for the municipal court, who had stood beside Ferdinand when he issued his 1917 call to arms after the East St. Louis riots. Roberts was backed by De Priest and the Regular Republican machine.[67] Seeking a state senate seat was ambitious for any African American—the first black was not elected to the position until 1924—much less a black woman. At some point, Ida must have sought some help from Edward Wright, but as Ida later noted in a daybook she kept, he was "still stubborn about helping women."[68]

Wells-Barnett wasn't the only black woman to run for office that year. The Third Ward Women's Political Club endorsed Mary C. Clarke, who headed the Illinois Women's Political League, to run for a vacated seat in the legislature from the Fifth District. However, the club's proud announcement that it was the first to put a black woman in the race lost some of its significance when another black woman, the attorney Georgia Jones-Ellis, ran for the same seat. Although the *Chicago Defender* remarked on the controversy that pitted the two women against each other, it paid little attention to any of their campaigns—even to that of Ida's, who had had such a long relationship with the paper.[69]

Wells-Barnett was forced to rely on the thin reed of independent organizations like the Abraham Lincoln Republican Club, the hub of the Independents that proved to be unreliable and quixotic. Ida's campaign also ran headlong into the Depression, which hit Chicago harder than any other of the ten largest cities in the nation; it threw more than a third of the city's black population on relief and bankrupted Chicago's black businesses, most notably the Binga Bank.[70] It was less than the most opportune time to initiate an independent, patronage-free political campaign, especially as the Barnetts themselves appeared to be in some financial difficulty.

There is little indication that the couple had much savings in this era that predated Social Security funds. Ferdinand did have life insurance, but most of it was already cashed out.[71] Soon after the 1929 stock market crash, the Barnetts moved from their copious Queen Anne–style house to a small apartment on Garfield Avenue, though it appears they rented out their former residence. Ida's daybook, where she tersely recorded events in the period, revealed that she could not afford a coat for her daughter Ida during a blizzard-filled Chicago January. She wondered, as she wrote, why the family managed never to have any money.[72]

The worst blow to the family in the early part of the year was the news that her lawyer son, Herman, had fled Chicago after it was discovered that he had fraudulently appropriated money to satisfy gambling debts. Ida had not learned of this before she announced her candidacy, and by the time it was discovered, "it was too late to withdraw," she told herself. "Have been thro hell over revelations of Herman's actions," Ida wrote in the journal. "He used people's money right & left and went away leaving us the bag to hold." Herman's case was due before the bar association "& there seems nothing in sight save expulsion and disgrace," Ida feared. The news certainly could not have helped her candidacy. As she had in the past, Ida had to read to keep from thinking about her troubles, in this instance a book about Catherine the Great and another written by Mary Baker Eddy.[73]

Nevertheless, she put the same manic energy into the campaign as she did into her other endeavors. In a relatively short period of time, Ida visited churches and attended YMCA, YWCA, and Urban League meetings where she sought to get petitions signed for her candidacy. She made a deal with a local printer to give her a discount for printing up a thousand cards, a thousand letters, and six hundred window cards. Ferdinand helped her to establish headquarters at 3449 Indiana Street and paid for two thousand additional copies of what she called the *New Deal Paper,* at his own expense.[74]

But the final count in the April primary was typical of an independent candidate with with more vision than hard-core support. Ida received 752 votes; Roberts, 4,502; Douglas, 3,715.[75]

ONE OF THE most remarkable things about Ida Wells-Barnett, who had seen her share of victories, was how she took defeat. After the election, she predictably complained about the weakness of the independent political organizations, but immediately planned to convene a meeting of her supporters, so, as she wrote in her daybook, "we may profit by lessons of the campaign."[76]

The words indicated that Wells-Barnett, as always, was still looking toward and had faith in the future. Her refusal to sink into bitterness or to become cynical, or to lose hope in the idea of racial reconciliation on equitable terms, was in some ways a self-conscious and self-taught art. But she also had the mind-set to live fully in the present while judging both her achievements and failures in terms of what they would mean for the generations that came after her. True, her highest ideals had yet to be realized, but she had lived long enough to see the world begin to catch up to them. Lynching had not been eradicated but her relentless campaign against it, beginning with her *New York Age* editorial-from-exile in 1892, had diminished its numbers and, just as important, had been the first to lay bare the myths about race and gender that surrounded it. She had forced many to see how lynching threatened the deepest values of a modern democracy, and how central the issue was to the aspirations of black men and women, and white women as well. In November of 1930, the Association of Southern Women for the Prevention of Lynching was founded in Atlanta by white activists determined to expose the relationship between the tradition of chivalry and mob murder. Ida's faith in women did not falter, even as she alternately berated, dismissed, organized, and moved them to realize their power in a modern age. Wells-Barnett had also demonstrated that ideals had to be fought for and that the race could never rise above how the least of them was treated.

SOON AFTER IDA'S electoral defeat, she threw herself into the campaign to prevent the North Carolina judge John J. Parker from being appointed to the United States Supreme Court. President Herbert Hoover had nominated the jurist, despite Parker's public statements that he opposed the idea of African Americans not only holding political office, but also voting at all. Upon the announcement of the nomination, Irene McCoy Gaines orchestrated the Women's Republican Clubs and the Citizens' Committee of the Brotherhood of Sleeping Car Porters and Maids to rally against the nomination. Ida worked with her, representing the Douglass Civic League, which Gaines had also organized, anxious, as Ida stated, to show "Hoover a lesson." Twenty-five thousand signatures were attained for a petition against the nomination, and Ida's May *Defender* article (which also credited the NAACP effort and Walter White for Parker's final defeat) highlighted the fact that before Senator Charles Deneen had left the Senate he had cast the deciding vote, which upended the nomination. The campaign probably encouraged Ida to plan a new venture: a publication called the *Chicago Review,* which would sell for five cents a copy. Despite the Depression, Ida, characteristically, was optimistic about its success. "Watch it grow," she exhorted her prospective readers.[77] In the meantime, Ida was trying to finish her autobiography, *Crusade for Justice.*

She had begun writing the first full-length autobiography written by a black woman activist in 1928. Her daughter Alfreda, then married for three years, recalled the image of her mother writing it in longhand, perched at a table with its leaves fully extended and its surface covered with papers.

Wells-Barnett's groundbreaking act of writing about her life, begun seven years before the publication of W. E. B. Du Bois's *Black Reconstruction in America*, was surely inspired, as the introduction noted, to inform young people of a history, especially that of the post–Civil War period, that they could not have known. But undoubtedly, Wells-Barnett also had her own legacy in mind.

Although she was one of the relatively few black women mentioned in the six-volume classic *History of Woman Suffrage*, co-edited by her old associate Susan B. Anthony, she was overlooked by many contemporary chroniclers. When, in 1930, the *Chicago Defender* announced a list of fifty prominent leaders, put together by the muckraking journalist Ida Tarbell, whose exposés succeeded those of Wells-Barnett, Mary McLeod Bethune was mentioned, but not Ida.[78] Her name was also missing from *Who's Who in Colored America*, a 499-page biographical dictionary, which covered the years 1930 to 1932. Walter White's 1928 publication, *Rope and Faggot*, which became a classic text on lynching, also left Ida's name out.

The most disturbing evidence that the substance of her accomplishments was forgotten was when she and her daughter Ida attended a local Negro history club meeting to discuss a book written by black historian Carter G. Woodson, the "father of Negro History." As she ruefully noted in her daybook, there was "no mention of my anti-lynching contribution.[79] As previously noted, Ida had hosted Woodson at the Negro Fellowship League at the very time he was launching the Association of Negro Life and History.

Ida must have sensed she was dying—made more acute, perhaps, by the deaths in 1930 of others whose passing seemed to mark an end of the era to which she had belonged. In that year, Irene Goins, George Cleveland Hall, the Reverend W. D. Cook of Ida's Metropolitan Community Church, and Edward Wright passed away. As her daughter Alfreda recalled, Ida, directing her life to the end, said that she wanted a modest, dignified funeral; that she hated the idea of "weeping and wailing and lavishing of flowers around the bier"; and that one of her favorite verses was Tennyson's "And may there be no moaning of the bar / When I put out to sea."[80]

"I've Done My Work"

In March of 1931, Ida was looking forward to the African American book fair she had planned to benefit the Wabash YMCA. She was going to donate many of her own books written by black authors and asked women in Chicago's clubs to do the same. The formal appeal to the black women's organizations was her last.

On Saturday, March 21, 1931, Ida returned from her shopping in the downtown Loop area earlier than her family had expected. She wasn't feeling well, she explained, and decided to turn in early. Sunday mornings were usually spent in church and followed by a visit with her sister Annie. But Ida still did not feel well and remained in bed for the day. On Monday, Ferdinand, as he did each morning, stopped by her bedside to kiss her good-bye before leaving for his law office. He noticed then that Ida's forehead was terribly hot and that her eyes were unnaturally bright and unseeing. Ferdinand called Alfreda, who immediately got someone to watch her two children and dashed to the apartment. She found her mother "tossing, and muttering, and not rational." They got Ida to the small hospital of the noted surgeon U. G. Dailey, but she never regained consciousness. She "slipped away quietly," Alfreda recalled, at 1:00 A.M. on Wednesday, March 25, 1931, four months before her sixty-ninth birthday. The cause of death was uremic poisoning.[81]

"With simple dignity and a solemnity befitting the occasion of the passing of a great woman, last rites were said over Ida B. Wells-Barnett on Monday afternoon," began the coverage of Ida's final testimonial by the *Chicago Defender*. The service, like Wells-Barnett herself, was straightforward and direct and had few flourishes. "No fanfare of trumpets, no undue shouting, no flowery oratory—just plain earnest, sincere words" were spoken on her behalf, noted the paper, which that weekend also covered the more lavish funeral of Bishop Archibald Carey. Ida's last rites "were in keeping with the simple lives led by members of the Barnett family since it became a force in Chicago public life nearly 38 years ago," the *Defender* concluded.

The Metropolitan Church, where the service was held, was overflowing. Many more stood outside in the biting March wind, waiting for the opportunity to pay their last respects. Ida's pallbearers were the men of her family: sons Herman and Charles; stepsons Ferdinand, Jr., and Albert; and nephews Jack Wells and Emory Wells, the sons of her brothers George and Alfred James, respectively.[82]

Ida's minister, Joseph M. Evans of the Metropolitan Community Church, spoke for only thirty minutes. His brief eulogy recounted "her fight for political emancipation of her people, her international battle to wipe out lynchings . . . her untiring but almost hopeless war against civic oppression . . . [and] . . . her ceaseless war on ignorance within the folds of her own race. . . . Tomorrow is the new moon; and thou shalt be missed, because thy seat will be empty," concluded Evans, quoting from the Bible's 1 Samuel 20:4. When the minister repeated, "She will be missed," noted the *Defender,* "the throng in the pews, the throng lining the walls, the throng high up in the balcony, the throngs packed in the vestibules answered with nods of their heads—She will be missed."

As the family had requested, only one resolution was read, and that was from the Ida B. Wells Club, which told of Ida's pioneering efforts. It was followed by a representative of the National Association of Colored Women, Elizabeth Carter Brooks, who told of her acquaintance with Ida since the days when she was writing antilynching editorials for the *New York Age.* Ida Clark, a member of the Alpha Suffrage Club, spoke of Ida's "efforts to gain political recognition for the race, out of which effort grew the Illinois Women's Republican Club." At the end of the service, Ida's lifelong love of music and theater was personified by her longtime friend and well-known soprano Anita Patti Brown, who sang "Come Unto Me." Another singer, George G. Garner, sang "I've Done my Work."[83]

THE *CHICAGO WHIP* had the most extensive obituary. Describing Wells-Barnett as a "militant organizer," it recounted her life in Holly Springs, Mississippi; her newspaper career in Memphis and at the *New York Age*; and the lynching of Thomas Moss, Calvin McDowell, and Will Stewart, which had set her upon her campaign against lynching. The newspaper also wrote about her coming to Chicago where she protested the exclusion of blacks at the world's fair, her association with Frederick Douglass, her founding of the Ida B. Wells Club and the city's first black kindergarten.[84]

Nevertheless, as Wells-Barnett would have surely predicted, most of the obituaries written about her were far from comprehensive; none captured the essence of her work and life, and others took the opportunity to marginalize her contributions. In the *Crisis,* W. E. B. Du Bois called her "the pioneer of the anti-lynching crusade," who "began the awakening of the conscience of the nation." But churlish to the last, he added that the crusade had been easily forgotten because "it was afterward taken up on a much larger scale by the NAACP and carried to greater success."[85]

Outside of the public view, Chicago clubwoman Elizabeth Lindsey Davis hinted in a letter to the NACW president, Sallie Stewart, that many would be unable to reconcile themselves to Ida's sharp-edged persona. "A strong forceful woman has gone," Davis wrote, "in spite of all that might be said."[86] The same theme was picked up in the memoriam published in the NACW's *National Notes.* Touting her courage, the eulogy also noted that "She was often criticized, misjudged and misunderstood because she fought for justice and civil righteousness both in American and Europe as God gave her vision to see the RIGHT."[87]

But there was one eulogy, by Irene McCoy Gaines, that insightfully captured Ida's lifework with the understanding that perhaps required the distance of a younger generation whom Ida always saw in her mind's eye. "It was her special mission to interpret and express the wrongs and sufferings of an oppressed race," it began. "She knew how white publicists & statesmen had denied [the] Negro's courage & valor & how white historians had sustained the denial. She was a profound student of sociology. She not only knew the white race, but she knew her own. . . . She knew that there were many who were doubtful of the natural equality of their race; that many were ashamed. . . . She knew that only a few people knew the Negro's part in world history and culture and there is a destiny [to] complete freedom & emancipation."[88]

Ida Wells-Barnett's sense of destiny drove her to write her own story in *Crusade for Justice.* The last chapter had begun with the Revolutionary War's inspired phrase "Eternal vigilance is the price of liberty." Characteristically, Ida must have been writing it until the moment that she could no longer lift her hand. The chapter ended in midsentence.

Notes

Author's note on statistics: Lynching statistics, due to the difficulty of getting accurate records, are inconsistent and, as most scholars agree, underrepresented; additionally, they do not represent the number of "legal" executions or the deaths in the wake of major race riots in the period. Annual tabulations of lynchings began being recorded in 1882 by the *Chicago Tribune* and Tuskegee Institute.

James Cutler, in *Lynch Law,* the first scholarly study of lynching, Table IV, notes that 1886 was the first year that more blacks than whites were lynched; and that the number of lynchings peaked in 1892. E. M. Beck and Stewart E. Tolnay, "When Race Didn't Matter: Black and White Mob Violence Against Their Own Color," in W. Fitzhugh Brundage, ed., *Under Sentence of Death: Lynching in the South,* p. 133, notes that the lynching peak was 1893. The figure of 241 in 1892 was given by Ida B. Wells, "Lynch Law in America," pp. 239–240, in Mildred I. Thompson, *Ida B. Wells-Barnett.* The article was originally published in *Arena,* 24 (January, 1900): 15–24. Wells's source was the *Chicago Tribune,* but her figure differs slightly from that of Cutler, *Lynch Law,* p. 160, citing the same source. Arthur Raper, *The Tragedy of Lynching,* Appendix C, noted that 100 whites and 155 blacks were lynched that year. His source was Monroe N. Work, ed., *The Negro Year Book and Annual Encyclopedia of the Negro, 1931–1932* (Tuskegee: Negro Yearbook Publishing Company, 1931), p. 293.

Many scholars reference the sociologist and Tuskegee director of records, Monroe N. Work, for lynching totals. Between 1882 and 1944, Work calculated that 1,291 whites and 3,417 blacks were lynched. Walter White's appendix in *Rope and Faggot* has one of the most detailed and comprehensive tabulations of lynchings between 1882 and 1927, calculated from the work of Cutler and NAACP documents, the latter including *Thirty Years of Lynchings in the United States, 1889–1918.* White counted a total of 4,951 lynchings, of which 3,513 were black and 1,438, white. He also noted that 92 lynching victims were women, 16 of them white, and 76 who were black. The state of Mississippi, with 16 women victims, led the rest in this statistic. Beck and Tolnay's *A Festival of Violence,* pp. 269–270, enumerated 2,805 lynchings between 1882 and 1930 in ten southern states, excluding Virginia and Texas.

Bibliographical Notes

I found Daniel Joseph Singal's concept of "radical innocence" in *The War Within: From Victorian to Modernist Thought in the South, 1919–1945* very useful regarding Victorian culture. Full-length studies on Wells include: Linda O. McMurry, *To Keep the Waters Troubled*; Patricia A. Schechter, *Ida B. Wells-Barnett and American Reform*; and Mildred I. Thompson, *Ida B. Wells-Barnett*. On lynching, oft-cited texts include: Edward L. Ayers, *Vengeance and Justice*; George C. Wright, *Racial Violence in Kentucky*; E. M. Beck and Stewart E. Tolnay, *A Festival of Violence*; W. Fitzhugh Brundage, *Lynching in the New South*; Trudier Harris, *Exorcising Blackness*; Jacquelyn Dowd Hall, *Revolt Against Chivalry;* and Philip Dray, *At the Hands of Persons Unknown*. For an examination of the NAACP's antilynching campaigns, see Charles Flint Kellogg, *The NAACP* and, especially, Robert L. Zangrando, *The NAACP Crusade Against Lynching, 1909–1950*.

Marvin Eisentadt et al., in *Parental Loss and Achievement*, delineate the emotional development of orphans who are able to transform their bereavement and rage into what the authors call "creative mourning"—the compulsion to restore what was lost through a creative enterprise—and accomplishment. Such persons are able to assume increased responsibility for their families, compensate for feelings of unworthiness by becoming a more worthwhile person; consciously try to master changed and changeable environments, thus leading to striving, achievement, and a sense of independence. Such individuals are particularly attracted to politics and religion as the most effective means to modify, create, re-create, or even revolutionize a social order that will conform to their conception of the world and their efforts to "wrest" from fate a different outcome. Such persons commonly have the capacity to endure a self-punishing regimen to pursue their goals; a capacity for suffering and dissatisfaction, and unhappiness with current circumstances; can be aggressive and domineering vis-à-vis society and ruthless in their dealings with others; and can experience problematic personal relationships. Their poor ego defenses make them exceedingly sensitive, and they can easily regress into childlike behavior. Additionally, such persons often become imbued with an extraordinary sense of morality and conscience that develops into a heightened sensitivity toward injustice.

Allison Davis, *Love, Leadership and Aggression* (San Diego: Harcourt, Brace, Jovanovich, 1983), explores a similar dynamic regarding the transformation of anger into more constructive activism in case studies of several black leaders. Texts with similar perspectives that were useful include: Erik H. Erikson, *Identity and the Life Cycle* (New York: Norton, 1980); Alice Miller, *The Untouched Key: Tracing Childhood Trauma in Creativity and Destructiveness* (New York: Doubleday, 1988); Melanie Klein and Joan Riviere, *Love, Hate and Aggression* (New York: Norton, 1964); and John Bowlby, *Loss: Sadness and Depression* (New York: Basic Books, 1980). For an interdisciplinary and insightful reading of psychoanalytic theory as posited in African American literature, see Claudia Tate, *Psychoanalysis and Black Novels: Desire and Protocols of Race* (New York: Oxford University Press, 1998).

Prologue

1. Diary of Ida B. Wells, 29 December 1885, Ida B. Wells Papers (hereafter Wells, Diary). For a published edition of the diary, see DeCosta-Willis, *The Memphis Diary of Ida B. Wells: An Intimate Portrait of the Activist as a Young Woman*. James Hall was listed as a twenty-four-year-old laborer in the Ninth Census of the United States (1870) for Marshall County, Holly Springs, Mississippi (hereafter 1870 Census). He was a mulatto, born in Virginia. His wife, Tilla, also a mulatto and nineteen in 1870, was born in Mississippi. Deed Record Book, Marshall County, Marshall County Court House,

Holly Springs, 8 February 1892, p. 150, shows Ida Wells and her siblings as owner of the house.

Rust College was established in 1866 by the Freedmen's Aid Society of the Methodist Episcopal Church. In 1870, the school was chartered as Shaw University (in honor of Reverend S. O. Shaw, who made a gift of $10,000 to the institution). In 1882, the name of the school was changed to Rust University (named for Richard S. Rust, secretary of the Freedmen's Aid Society). In 1915, the school was renamed Rust College. The Rust Home for Girls is mentioned in Jay S. Stowell, *Methodist Adventures in Negro Education* (New York: The Methodist Book Concern, 1922), p. 123.

2. Wells, Diary, 29 December 1885.
3. Duster, ed., *Crusade for Justice*, pp. 7, 16–17 (hereafter Wells, *Crusade*).
4. Wells, *Crusade*, p. 17.
5. Ibid., p. 17.
6. "Personals Column," *Fisk Herald*, June 1885, p. 7.
7. *New York Freeman*, 26 December 1885. For details on the idea of "true womanhood," see Barbara Welter, "The Cult of True Womanhood: 1820–1860," *American Quarterly* 18 (1966): 151–174, and Linda M. Perkins, "The Impact of the 'Cult of True Womanhood' on the Education of Black Women"; Wells, Diary, ibid.
8. Ibid.
9. Ibid.

Chapter One: Holly Springs

1. Duster, ed., *Crusade for Justice*, p. 8 (hereafter Wells, *Crusade*); Duster, "Ida B. Wells, Her Life and Work," chap. 1, p. 2.
2. The circumstantial evidence regarding Lizzie Wells is derived from the following: Records from the Chancery Court of DeSoto County, Mississippi (William Gathings Deceased *vs* No. 4235, Order Appointing Guardian Ad Litem Decree Settling Rights of Heirs, 26 March 1919) indicate the family surname was formerly Airington [Arrington] rather than Warrenton as cited in *Crusade for Justice*, p. 8. Also the death certificate for Lizzie's sister Martha (Certificate of Death, Martha Howell, State of Tennessee, 11 December 1924) states that her father's name was George Washington, and her mother's Anna Airington. The author is indebted to Otis Maxwell for this information.

   There were seventy-two Ar[r]ington/Errington heads of household listed on the 1850 Virginia Population Schedule. As no index exists for the corresponding slave census, it was necessary to read the slave schedule for each of the twenty-two counties where Airingtons resided to determine if the resident family owned slaves. Of the seventy-two, only one was found to have three slave females of the appropriate age to be Lizzie and her two sisters. "Report to Paula Giddings from Donna Rachal Mills, M.A. Genealogist, re: Arringtons of 1850 Virginia," December, 1994.
3. Bancroft, *Slave-Trading in the Old South*, p. 197.
4. Ibid., pp. 90–94.
5. Ibid., p. 93.
6. Thomas Smith, "Personal Property Tax Roll, Marshall County," Marshall County Courthouse, Holly Springs, MS, p. 18. A marriage certificate, issued in DeSoto County, 20 October 1866, shows that Martha was married there; the 1870 Census for DeSoto County, p. 28, shows Martha living there that year; the 1870 Census for Marshall County, p. 65, shows Bell residing in that county that year.
7. Eighth Census of the Federal Population Schedule, 1860, Marshall County, Mississippi, p. 147 (hereafter 1860 Census).

8. Reverend John H. Aughey, *Tupelo* (Chicago: Rhodes and McClure Publishing Company, 1905), p. 419; Hamilton, *Holly Springs, Mississippi to the Year 1878*, pp. 30–31.

9. Rowland, *Mississippi: The Heart of the South,* pp. 673–677; Carter, "A Proud Struggle for Grace," p. 57; Stone, "Economic Development of Holly Springs During the 1840s," *Journal of Mississippi History* 32 (November 1970): 356.

10. Carter, ibid., p. 2; "Looking Backward: The First Ten Years." Typescript, n.p., n.d. Marshall County Public Library, Holly Springs, Mississippi.

11. *Marshall County Republican* (Holly Springs), 1 June 1839; quote in Hamilton, ibid., p. 71; Hamilton, ibid., pp. 13–14.

12. Seventh Census of Federal Population Schedule, Marshall County, Mississippi, 1850, p. 369; 1850 Slave Schedule, Marshall County, Mississippi, p. 119; Smith, "Personal Property Tax Roll," ibid; Marshall County Deed Book, Y: 44–45, 2 April 1860. In 1860, Tippah had an aggregate population of 22,550, and a slave population of 6,331. Brown, *History of Tippah County*, p. 32.

13. The most comprehensive information regarding architecture in Holly Springs, including Boling's architectural style, is found in Crocker, "The Greek Revival Architecture of Holly Springs," especially pp. 29, 43–44, 85–86; 1860 Census, Marshall County, Mississippi, p. 147. There were no slave deeds found for the acquisition of Boling's slaves. They may not have been recorded, especially since a number of slaves, including James Wells, were acquired through apprenticeship cum indenture agreements with their owners. Characteristically, there are some inconsistencies regarding dates and name spellings, but the information given in this text appears to be the most reliable. The author is indebted to Hubert H. McAlexander (a distant relative of Boling) for additional information on the Boling family.

14. Crocker, ibid., p. 45. The other two houses Crocker ascribes to Boling are the Oakleigh and Montrose Houses; Robert Mottley, "Southern Grace," *Colonial Homes* 20 (April 1994): 88–93. The Walter, Oakleigh, and Montrose Houses still stand in Holly Springs. Additional information on Walter and the Mississippi Central Railroad is found in Hamilton, pp. 54–66, 118–119.

15. See a photograph of Martha Howell in this volume.

16. Wells, *Crusade*, p. 8. The 1860 Census, Slave Schedule, Tippah County, Mississippi, shows six slaves in Morgan Wells's household, including one mulatto slave, aged nineteen, who is certainly James Wells. Morgan Wells is the only Wells in the county who had a male slave of the age described by Ida Wells in *Crusade* and was shown with his wife, Margaret (Polly), to have had no other children. Additionally, the ages of other slaves in the household correspond to those of James's half-siblings in the household. James's mother, Peggy Wells, and his half-siblings are all listed as "black." Alfred Wells, James's half-brother, named his father as Ed Neighbors in the Signature Books of the Freedmen's Bank, Record no. 3855, 20 April 1872, Memphis (Tennessee) Branch, 1866–1874 (hereafter Freedmen's Bank Record).

17. Hamilton, ibid., pp. 90–91; Bonner, "From '60 to '65," *Lippincott's Magazine*, 17 (October 1876): 502. In modern parlance, Bonner's description would be called a "factional" account of Holly Springs. The Holly Springs–born Bonner (Katherine Sherwood McDowell) is credited with creating the Mammy character in fiction. Cathy N. Davidson and Linda Wagner-Martin, eds., *The Oxford Companion to Women's Writing in the United States* (New York: Oxford University Press 1995), pp. 800, 829. Also see Hubert H. McAlexander's *The Prodigal Daughter: A Biography of Sherwood Bonner* (Baton Rouge: Louisiana University Press, 1981)

18. Wells, *Crusade*, p. 10.

19. McLemore, *A History of Mississippi*, p. 459; *Holly Springs South Reporter*, 11 November 1930.

20. Deupree, "The Capture of Holly Springs, Mississippi, Dec. 20, 1862," p. 58; Hamilton, ibid., p. 40.

21. "Belle Strickland Diary," 9 August 1864, p. 4.

22. Rawick, *The American Slave*, p. 867; "Belle Strickland Diary," 18 August 1964, p. 6.

23. Wells, *Crusade*, p. 10.

24. Johnson, "Life Within the Confederate Lines," p. 56, n. 4.

25. "Belle Strickland Diary," ibid., p. 4; Garner, *Reconstruction in Mississippi*, p. 19.

26. The Bureau of Refugees, Freedmen, and Abandoned Lands, often referred to as the Freedmen's Bureau, was established under the War Department by an act of March 3, 1865. Congress assigned to the bureau responsibilities that previously had been shared by military commanders and agents of the Treasury Department; Johnson, ibid., p. 54.

27. Wells, *Crusade*, p. 9; 1870 Census, Tippah County, Mississippi, p. 26.

28. Hamilton, ibid., pp. 40, 45, 46. Boling became a stockholder in the Marshall Manufacturing Company, incorporated to deal in lumber and iron castings among other items. *Laws of Mississippi*, 1866, p. 172. In 1870, Boling also joined eight other prominent Holly Springs residents, including Harvey W. Walter, in incorporating the Holly Springs Hotel Company. *Laws of Mississippi*, 1870, pp. 384–385. The author thanks Hubert H. McAlexander for providing this information. The 1870 Census, Marshall County, Mississippi, p. 333b, shows Boling listed as an architect with $11,000 in real property and $2,000 in personal property, sums which represent a good recovery so shortly after the close of the war.

29. Wharton, *The Negro in Mississippi*, p. 13; Watkins, "Reconstruction in Marshall County," p. 160.

30. Hamilton, ibid., pp. 120–121; Testimony of G. Wiley Wells (U.S. district attorney for the northern district of Mississippi), "Affairs in the Late Insurrectionary States, Condition of Affairs in Mississippi," 2nd Session, 42nd Congress, 1871, p. 1146; Testimony of J.W.C. Watson, "Affairs in the Late Insurrectionary States," ibid., p. 292. For details on the Memphis riot, see "Majority Report," *Memphis Riots and Massacres: The Reports of the Committees of the House of Representatives made during the First Session, Thirty-Ninth Congress, 1865–1866* (New York: Reprinted without comment by Arno Press, 1969); Ryan, "The Memphis Riots of 1866"; Waller, "Community, Class and Race in the Memphis Riot of 1866"; Holmes, "The Effects of the Memphis Race Riot of 1866."

31. Hamilton, ibid., p. 44; Testimony of G. Wiley Wells, ibid., p. 1165.

32. Watkins, ibid., pp. 185–186; Wharton, ibid., p. 166.

33. Hamilton, ibid., pp. 41–42; Oral Book Review Committee, comp., "The History of Rust College," n.d., p. 2, Rust College Library, Holly Springs, Mississippi (hereafter *History of Rust College*); Wells, *Crusade*, p. 9.

34. Watkins, ibid., pp. 186–187; Hamilton, ibid., pp. 43–44.

35. M. E. Gill to J. M. Langston, Inspector General of Schools, B.R.F. 15 July 1867, Registers of Letters Received, vol. 3 (Jan. 1867–Aug. 1867). Records of the Assistant Commissioner for the State of Mississippi, Bureau of Refugees, Freedmen, and Abandoned Lands, 1865–1869 (hereafter Freedmen's Bureau Records).

36. "Belle Strickland Diary," 22 May 1868, p. 43.

37. Watkins, ibid., p. 199.

38. Wells, *Crusade*, p. 9; Foner, *Reconstruction*, p. 121.

39. The vote was 76,016 to 69,739 in favor of the constitution. Garner, *Reconstruction in Mississippi*, p. 181; Wells, *Crusade*, pp. 8–9.

40. Wells, *Crusade*, p. 9. For a biographical sketch of James Hill, see Wharton, ibid., p. 163.

41. Marriage Certificate, James Wells and Liza Boling, 28 January 1869. Probate Court Records,

Marshall County Courthouse, Holly Springs, Mississippi. Marriage Certificate, Alfred Wells and Fanny Lucas, 4 February, 1869, ibid. The description of Fanny is found in Alfred Wells, Freedmen's Bank Record, ibid.

42. Captain John Power to Office, Sub-Commissioner, Bureau of Refugees, Freedmen, and Abandoned Lands 4 January 1868, Narrative Reports from Subordinate Officers Jan–June 1868, Freedmen's Bureau Records. Belle Myers Carruthers testified that in 1868, "I married Caruthers . . . Captain Myers [was the] clerk in the Court House and wouldn't let us have a license so we went to Oxford and married there." Rawick, ibid., p. 367. The testimony is corroborated in Belle Strickland's diary, which noted that Belle "was very much disappointed" that she could not marry the day she intended because she couldn't get a license, and took the 5 o'clock train to Oxford. "Belle Strickland Diary," 7 April 1868.

43. Sectional Index, City of Holly Springs, Lots 201-400 Section 6 T4R2, 16 March 1870, Book 30, p. 222, Marshall County Courthouse, Holly Springs, Mississippi. Information on Walker is found in Hamilton, ibid., p. 147.

44. Wells, *Crusade*, p. 9.

45. Edwards, "History of Rust College, 1866–1967," pp. 42, 56.

46. Unpublished Interview, Alfreda Duster, recorded by Donald Duster (1964). The author is indebted to Donald Duster for providing this interview.

47. Edwards, "History of Rust College," p. 2.

48. Ibid., pp. 47–48.

49. *History,* ibid., p. 5; Wells, *Crusade*, pp. 8–9.

50. Mayes, *History of Education in Mississippi* (Washington: United States Bureau of Education, 1899), p. 269.

51. The author is indebted to Hubert McAlexander, who consulted Deed Books (DB 36:24) for the information regarding Boling's distillery. "Belle Strickland Diary," 10 June 1868, p. 47. Boling died of consumption in February of 1880, according to the Mississippi Mortality Schedule of that year.

52. Watkins, ibid., pp. 182–183.

53. *Ninth Annual Report of the Freedmen's Aid Society of the Methodist Episcopal Church* (Cincinnati: Western Methodist Book Concern, 1877), p. 9. Quoted in Edwards, "History of Rust College," p. 48; Testimony of G. Wiley Wells, ibid.

54. Diary of Ida B. Wells, 12 June 1886, Ida B. Wells Papers. For a published edition of the diary, see DeCosta-Willis, *The Memphis Diary of Ida B. Wells: An Intimate Portrait of the Activist as a Young Woman.*

55. Edwards, "History of Rust College," p. 63; Bonner, ibid., p. 50.

56. Wells, *Crusade,* pp. 21–22.

57. Quoted in Edwards, "History of Rust College," p. 48.

58. Wells, *Crusade,* p. 10.

59. *Memphis Daily Avalanche,* 6 July 1875, quoted in Tucker, *Black Pastors and Leaders,* p. 32.

60. General Index to Deeds, Marshall County, 1869–1873, vol. 3, p. 446, no. 188, Marshall County Courthouse. The Married Women's Property Act is mentioned in Clinton, *The Other Civil War,* p. 75.

61. In 1900, the physician Walter Reed discovered that yellow fever was transmitted by the *Aedes aegypti* mosquito that thrived in tropically warm areas and perished upon the first frost. Before that date, it was assumed to be transmitted by germs and thus was associated with poor sanitation in urban areas. Although sanitation was not a factor, standing water, often found in bayous, gullies, and cisterns, was a breeding place for the insect.

62. *New Orleans Daily Picayune,* 13 August 1878.

63. The pathology of the disease is quoted from a letter from Dr. James E. Hamner, Professor, Department of Pathology, College of Medicine, University of Tennessee, to Patricia

LaPointe, 16 July 1986. The author is indebted to Ms. LaPointe of the Memphis Public Library for sharing the letter.

64. Accounts of the epidemic in Holly Springs are included in: Olga Reed Pruitt, *It Happened Here: True Stories of Holly Springs* (Holly Springs, South Reporter Printing Company, 1950); W. A. Anderson, "A Chapter in the History of the Epidemic of 1878 from Private Memoranda, Holly Springs" (McComb, MS: Press of the McComb Weekly Intelligencer, 1879); Hamilton, ibid.; *South Reporter*, 20 November 1930 and 26 November 1931; *Memphis Commercial Appeal*, 6 October 1878. See Margaret Humphreys, *Yellow Fever and the South*, for the clinical as well as social implications of the history of the disease.

65. Wells, *Crusade*, p. 11.

66. The listed death of Alfred Wells, 62 Georgia Street, is found in J. M. Keating, *A History of the Yellow Fever.* (Memphis: Howard Association, 1879), p. 237; *Holly Springs Reporter*, 13 September 1878.

67. Keating, *A History of Yellow Fever*, p. 110; Capers, *The Biography of a River Town*, p. 198. There was also an additional milder outbreak of yellow fever in Memphis in 1879.

68. Wells, *Crusade*, pp. 10–15.

69. Statistics compiled from various sources. See *Memphis Daily Avalanche*, 6 November 1878, for a comprehensive list of Holly Springs residents who perished in the epidemic; *Holly Springs Reporter*, ibid.

70. Hamilton, ibid., p. 51.

71. D'Emilio and Freedman, *Intimate Matters*, p. 60.

72. Wells, *Crusade*, p. 17.

73. For a "fictional" account of Wells's experiences as a country teacher, see Wells, "A Story of 1900," *Fisk Herald*, 8 April 1886, p. 3; Wells, *Crusade*, p. 21.

74. *Memphis Appeal*, 21 August 1880, quoted in Baker, *The Memphis Commercial Appeal*, p. 136; quote in Abel et al., eds., *The Voyage In*, p. 121.

Chapter Two: The New City and the Ladies' Car

1. Capers, *The Biography of a River Town*, pp. 107–108.

2. Davis, "Against the Odds," pp. 55, 123–124.

3. Berkeley, "Like a Plague of Locust," pp. 144–146; Capers, *The Biography of a River Town* pp. 164, 183.

4. Sigafoos, *Cotton Row to Beale Street*, pp. 68–70; Taylor, *The Negro in Tennessee*, p. 40; Capers, *The Biography of a River Town* p. 183; *Daily Memphis Appeal*, 22 April 1872 (hereafter *Appeal*).

5. Hutchins, *What Happened in Memphis*, p. 96; Duster, ed., *Crusade for Justice*, p. 22 (hereafter Wells, *Crusade*.)

6. For a description of Meriwether's lecture, see Wedell, *Elite Women and the Reform Impulse in Memphis*, pp. 24–25. For more details on Meriwether, see Kathleen Berkeley, "Elizabeth Avery Meriwether, 'An Advocate for Her Sex': Feminism and Conservatism in the Post-Civil War South," *Tennessee Historical Society* 43 (Winter 1984): 390–406. Elizabeth Avery Meriwether, *Recollections of 92 Years*, p. v.

   Alfred Wells purchased the 30' × 100' lot 21 February 1872 for $300 from W. B. Greenlaw, a well-known white Memphis businessman, Radical Republican, and proprietor of the Greenlaw Opera House. Memphis Chancery Bill no. 7252, Deed Record Book, 84, p. 510; Wrenn, *Crisis and Commission Government in Memphis*, p. 12.

7. Wrenn, ibid.

8. Keating, *The History of the Yellow Fever*, p. 636; See Capers, *The Biography of a River Town* chap. 8, pp. 187–209, for a general description of the 1878 outbreak and its immediate consequences; Keating, ibid., p. 110.

9. Capers, ibid., pp. 198, 208.

10. *Appeal,* 8 June, 21 August 1880, quoted in Baker, *The Memphis Commercial Appeal,* p. 136. For more on Southern progressive thought, see Cobb, *Redefining Southern Culture,* and *Industrialization and Southern Society*; Grantham, *Southern Progressivism*; and Belissary, "The Rise of Industry and the Industrial Spirit of Tennessee."

11. Roper, *The Founding of Memphis,* p. 51; Wrenn, ibid., p. 1; for a history of the early Memphis years, see Capers, ibid., chap. 1 and 2, pp. 3–43.

12. Meriwether, ibid. *Appeal,* 10 October 1868, quoted in Baker, ibid., p. 122.

13. Capers, ibid., pp. 163, 176.

14. Robinson, "Plans Dat Come'd from God," p. 81. Robinson provided the model for studying the leadership role of laboring-class blacks in institution-building through the Freedmen's Bank and other records. Also see Berkeley, ibid., chap. 4, pp. 165–223, for a detailed study of black self-help and organizational efforts in Memphis between 1865 and 1880.

15. Robinson, ibid.

16. Berkeley, ibid., pp. 177–178; Taylor, *The Negro in Tennessee,* p. 87; *Nashville Dispatch,* 5 May 1866. On the Memphis riot, see "Majority Report," *Memphis Riots and Massacres: The Reports of the Committees of the House of Representatives made during the First Session, Thirty-Ninth Congress, 1865–1866* (New York: Reprinted without comment by Arno Press, 1969); James Ryan, "The Memphis Riots of 1866"; Altina Waller, "Community, Class and Race in the Memphis Riot of 1866; Jack Holmes, "The Effects of the Memphis Race Riot of 1866"; and Jack Holmes, "Underlying Causes of the Memphis Race Riot."

17. Berkeley, ibid., pp. 165–166, 180; Tucker, *Black Pastors and Leaders,* pp. 8–9; Robinson, ibid.

18. Davis, ibid., p. 63. The Freedmen's Bank, officially known as the Freedman's Savings and Trust Company, was chartered in 1865 as a private corporation but it often shared offices with Freedmen's Bureaus and used army officers to solicit customers. Some individual depositors received compensation that averaged about three-fifths of the value of their accounts after it went into receivership. Foner, *Reconstruction,* pp. 531–532. For additional analysis of the impact of the bank's failure on the black community, see Davis, ibid., pp. 61–65; Signature Books of the Freedmen's Bank, Record no. 3835 for Alfred Wells, 20 April 1872 (hereafter Freedmen's Bank Record); Berkeley, ibid., p. 180; Davis, ibid., pp. 61–65.

19. Baker, ibid., p. 133.

20. Joe Walk, "Memphis's Unknown African-American Councilmen: 15 Served in the 1870s." Typescript, provided to the author by Joe Walk. The "taxing district" replaced the office of mayor and a bicameral legislature of thirty aldermen and councilmen elected by wards. The new form of government was made up of a three-member board of fire and police commissioners (two appointed by the governor) and a five-member board of public works (one appointed by the governor, one chosen by the county court, three elected at large). The president of the board of police and fire commissioners was appointed by the governor and functioned as the chief executive officer of the city. The state collected taxes, drew up an annual budget, and specified how the monies were to be spent. While the new structure appealed to the white elite municipal reformers who were critical of the political power of blacks and poor whites under the old ward system, the taxing district effectively diminished their political power in the city. See Wrenn, ibid., chap. 3, pp. 28–40, for the most thorough discussion of Memphis's municipal government in this period.

21. *Appeal,* 1 August 1882.

22. All teacher's salaries were scaled according to administrative rank, experience, and/or the grade level one taught. For example in the 1884–85 school year, the principal of the Kortrecht School, Benjamin K. Sampson, earned $100 a month, as did a white counterpart, Miss

Cora H. Ashe, principal of the Jefferson School. Ida Wells, teaching first grade that year, earned $50 a month, the same as a white first-grade teacher, Mary Shallue. In other instances, black teachers who had more experience actually earned a higher salary than whites teaching the same grade. But there were inequities based on the fact that only one black school, Kortrecht, had grades above the primary level, as compared to four such schools attended by whites. In addition, there were fewer black schools (five) than those for whites (six) and the former had larger teacher-student ratios than the latter. *Report of the Board of Education of the City of Memphis*, 1883–84 and 1884–85, Memphis: S. C. Toof Co., 1885, pp. 3–4.

For the most comprehensive description of the political struggle regarding the Memphis public school system, see Berkeley, ibid., chap. 5, pp. 224–274. For a greater focus on the role of black women teachers in the struggle, see Bond, "'Till Fair Aurora Rise," chap. 5, pp. 132–167. Also see Hilliard, "The Development of Public Education in Memphis," pp. 36–49.

23. Franklin, *From Slavery to Freedom*, p. 262. For an analysis of the 1875 Civil Rights Act and its enforcement, see John Hope Franklin, "The Enforcement of the Civil Rights Act of 1875." The Civil Rights Act, also known as the Civil Rights Bill, was introduced by U.S. senator Charles Sumner (R-MA) in 1870. It became law on March 1, 1875, stating that "all persons within the jurisdiction of the United States shall be entitled to the full and equal enjoyment of the accommodations, advantages, facilities, and privileges of inns, public conveyances on land or water, theaters, and other places of public amusement" and that such enjoyment should be subject "only to conditions and limitations established by law and applicable to alike to citizens of every race and color, regardless of any previous condition of servitude." Fines of $500 and/or imprisonment were levied against those who violated the law, and against district attorneys who failed to prosecute the required proceedings.

After the passage of the Civil Rights Act, Tennessee lawmakers contravened the federal statute by abolishing the common-law right of "any person excluded from any hotel or public means of transportation, or place of amusement" to bring legal action. Instead it allowed proprietors to "control the admission or exclusion of persons regarding public venues as perfect and complete as that of any private person over his private house, carriage or private theater, or places of amusement for his family." See *Acts of the General Assembly of the State of Tennessee*, 1875, pp. 216–17. For a discussion of the Tennessee legislature's countermeasure, see Joseph Cartwright, *The Triumph of Jim Crow*, p. 102; Taylor, *The Negro in Tennessee*, pp. 101, 103, 227, 230.

24. Wrenn, ibid., p. 23; Belissary, ibid., p. 206.

25. Berkeley, ibid., pp. 144–146.

26. In 1867, Tennessee became the second state outside of New England (Wisconsin was the first) to extend the franchise to blacks. Cartwright, *The Triumph of Jim Crow*, p. 11. For a comprehensive study on the struggle for black enfranchisement, including the activist role of blacks in securing their political rights, see Taylor, *The Negro in Tennessee*, Chapter 1. On Grant and the Civil Rights Act of 1875, see Franklin, "The Enforcement of the Civil Rights Act of 1875."

27. *Appeal*, 22 March 1871, quoted in Baker, ibid., p. 128; *Appeal*, 19 November 1879, quoted in Baker, ibid., p. 148.

28. *Memphis Daily Avalanche*, 14 April 1880 (hereafter *Avalanche*).

29. Ibid.

30. Berkeley, ibid., pp. 172–178, 233–235; Goings, "Duty of the Hour," p. 135.

31. *Avalanche*.

32. Ibid., 28 July 1880; Church and Church, *The Robert Churches of Memphis*, pp. 27–32.

33. *Avalanche*, 22, 24 September, 6 October 1880; *Appeal*, 14 September, 5 October 1880. The other black elected officials were Thomas A. Sykes (Davidson County) and John W. Boyd (Tipton County); Cartwright, ibid., pp. 27, 72.

34. *"Brown v Memphis & C.R. Co."* 6 August 1880. Peyton Boyle, ed., *The Federal Reporter*, 4 Oct.–Dec. 1880 (St. Paul: West Publishing, 1881), p. 39; *"Brown v Memphis & C.R. Co."* 30 October 1880; Peyton Boyle, ed., *The Federal Reporter*, 5 Dec. 1880–March 1881 (St. Paul, West Publishing, 1881), p. 500.

35. Folmsbee, "The Origin of the First Jim Crow Law," p. 237.

36. Capers, ibid., pp. 51–53; Roper, ibid;, p. 46; Bond, ibid., p. 22.

37. In 1860 there were 276 free blacks in Memphis and Shelby county, 117 of whom were women. Bond., ibid., p. 23. See Bond, chap. 2, pp. 33–68, for the most comprehensive study of free black women in Memphis and Shelby county.

38. Berkeley, ibid., p. 96.

39. Capers, ibid., p. 159; Berkeley, ibid., p. 151.

40. *Appeal*, 14 November 1865; 22 April 1872, quoted in Taylor, ibid., p. 40. For one of the best discussions about the relationship of race, class, sexual exertion, and industry, see Bederman, "Civilization and the Decline of Middle-Class Manliness."

41. *Appeal*, 8 June 1882, quoted in Baker, ibid., p. 136.

42. *"Brown v. Memphis & C.R. Co.,"* 30 October 1880, ibid. For further discussion of the significance of the Brown case, see Minter, "Freedom: Personal Liberty and Private Law," p. 6.

43. Kousser, *The Shaping of Southern Politics*, pp. 105, 121; Cartwright, ibid., pp. 26–27.

44. *Appeal*, 17 March 1881, quoted in Cartwright, ibid., p. 115.

45. Cartwright, ibid., p. 103.

46. *Avalanche*, 13 March 1881.

47. *Report of the Board of Education of the City of Memphis for the Sessions of 1883–4, and 1884–5* (Memphis: Toof & Co, 1885), pp. 11, 84; Ella Rodman Church, *Money-Making for Ladies* (New York, Harper Brothers, 1882), p. 75.

48. For more biographical information on Julia Hooks, see Hine, ed., *Black Women in America*, vol. 1, pp. 572–573.

49. *Avalanche*, 13, 15–16 March 1881. After the incident, Hooks was the subject of a board of education meeting, but it is not clear what was decided. Two years later, however, she was reassigned from the prestigious Kortrecht School—the only black school that went beyond the elementary grades—to the Broadway School, the latter of which had inferior facilities. However, at the time of her reassignment, Hooks had had a series of conflicts with the white superintendent of schools over other issues. *Report of the Board of Education*, ibid., p. 31.

50. *Appeal*, 6 April 1881.

51. Tucker, *Black Pastors and Leaders*, p. 41. Also see pp. 41–53 for more details on Imes and the Second Congregational Church.

52. *Appeal*, 6 April 1881; *Avalanche*, 16 March 1881; Cartwright, ibid., p. 104.

53. Quoted in Kasson, *Civilizing the Machine*, p. 179.

54. Coppock, *Memphis Sketches*, p. 115.

55. The bill required railroad companies to provide a separate, equal facility or to partition off a section of the first-class car "which all colored passengers who pay first-class passenger rates or fare, may have the privilege to enter and occupy." Cartwright, ibid., p. 104; Minter, ibid., p. 7. Also see Folmsbee, "The Origin of the First 'Jim Crow' Law," and Cartwright, "Black Legislators in Tennessee in the 1800s," pp. 268–271, for their differing views as to the degree white lawmakers were trying to appease blacks with the law. The *Memphis Commercial*, 21 March 1892, describes Huntington's visits to Memphis beginning in 1881.

56. *Nashville Daily American* , 1–3 October, 1881; Cartwright, ibid., pp. 105, 184.

57. Cartwight, ibid., p. 27. A state-credit faction wanted to scale down the debt on terms acceptable to the bondholders while a low-tax wing wanted outright repudiation or a sharp reduction of the debt and submission to the voters of any agreement between the state and the bondholders; Carwright, ibid., p. 23.

58. Wells, Diary, 23 March 1886, is one of the entries that refers to Froman as "Dad." See Wrenn, "The Taxing District of Shelby County," especially pp. 272–274, for more on the Memphis board of education. It was reorganized in 1883 through the Lynn Bill, making Memphis one of the first cities in the United States to adopt a small, centralized school board. The bill authorized the governor to appoint five new commissioners immediately, but in the future, commissioners would be elected at large for staggered four-year terms. Alfred Froman, Sr., who had served on the board in 1878, was one of the appointees in 1883. More information on Froman can be found in Cartwright, ibid., pp. 31, 58–59.

59. *Ida B. Wells v. Chesapeake, Ohio & South Western Railroad Company,* Circuit Court of Shelby County, manuscript court record, 16 February 1885, Tennessee State Library and Archives, Nashville, Tennessee, p. 22 (hereafter Transcript).

60. Coppock, ibid. pp. 114–115.

61. Quoted in the *Cleveland Gazette,* 24 March 1893.

62. Transcript, p. 29. The author gratefully acknowledges the especial efforts of the library to make these handwritten transcripts available.

63. Transcript, pp. 20–22, 30–33; Wells, *Crusade,* pp. 18–19.

64. Cartwright, ibid., p. 105; "Petition with Signatures," Martha McWilliam of Memphis, Tennessee, to Elizabeth Cady Stanton, 21 May 1880. National Woman Suffrage Association Collection, Collections Department, Manuscript Division, Library of Congress, Washington, D.C.

65. *Pace v. Alabama,* 106 U.S. 583 (1883). The decision that basically sustained the illegality of interracial marriages remained in effect for the next eighty years.

66. Quoted in Meier, *Negro Thought in America,* pp. 29–30; for more context, see Vincent P. DeSantis, "Negro Dissatisfaction with the Republican Party in the South, 1882–1884," *Journal of Negro History* 36 (April 1951); 148–159; *Avalanche,* 3 November 1883. Wells's court case: *Railroad Co. v. Wells* 85 Tenn. 613, 4 S.W. 5 was cited in the 1896 *Plessy v. Ferguson* (163 U.S. 537) decision, which upheld the constitutionality of state-imposed racial segregation and, until overturned in the *Brown v. Board of Education* decision in 1954, was the legal foundation for the separation of races; Wells, *Crusade,* p. 20.

67. Transcript, pp. 50, 52; *Avalanche,* 25 December 1884.

68. Ibid., p. 2.

69. Ibid., pp. 25, 23, 24.

70. Ibid., p. 33.

71. *Appeal,* 17 February 1884. For a biographical sketch of Battier, see *Goodspeed's History of Hamilton, Knox and Shelby Counties of Tennessee* (Nashville, 1974), p. 925 (reprinted from Goodspeed's History 1887); also, the *Avalanche,* 5 August 1885, recounts the black Republican activist Ed Shaw being indicted for perjury in the case of Battier and Burton. The couple was arrested and indicted, partly, it appeared, because of Shaw's testimony in court that Burton's father was white but her mother was a mulatto. Subsequently Shaw testified in another court hearing that Burton's father was Mexican and her mother an Indian, and the couple was acquitted. Shaw was indicted after it was realized that he had provided contradictory testimony to the court. It is not clear how the case was resolved, but an 1887 biographical sketch of Battier mentions his marriage to Mary and the fact that they had three children without making reference to Mary's race; Wells, Diary, 18 February 1886.

72. N. S. Shaler, "The Negro Problem," *Atlantic Monthly,* November 1884, pp. 696–709.

73. Hamilton, *Holly Springs, Mississippi, to the Year 1878*, p. 4.

74. Transcript, pp. 61–62.

75. *Avalanche*, 25 December 1884; *New York Globe*, 24 May 1884; *New York Freeman*, 10 January 1885. T. Thomas Fortune was the publisher for both New York newspapers; "Report of the Board of Education,1884–1885," ibid., p. 4.

Chapter Three: A Breath of Life, A Winter of Discontent

1. *Cleveland Gazette*, 27 June 1885; also see ibid., 23 August, 8 November, 13 December 1884, for more descriptions of the New Orleans Exposition.

2. *Washington Bee*, 28 March 1885; Rydell, *All the World's a Fair*, p. 82; *Cleveland Gazette*, 17 January 1885.

3. Quoted in Rydell, ibid., p. 83.

4. For more on Broughton, see Hine, et al., eds., *Black Women in America*, p. 86; Higginbotham, *Righteous Discontent*; and Bond, "'Till Fair Aurora Rise,'" pp. 149, 150, 163–165. *Cleveland Gazette*, 17 January 1885; Thomas Moss, Memphis Freedmen's Bank Bureau Records, No. 4065, 11 July 1872. The record states that Moss was thirteen when he opened the account on that date. Kate Born, "Organized Labor in Memphis, Tennessee, pp. 60–79.

5. *Memphis Daily Appeal*, 10 August 1882 (hereafter *Appeal*); *Washington Bee*, 1 August 1885.

6. *Cleveland Gazette*, 14 March 1885.

7. *AME Church Review* 3 (July 1886): 65.

8. Lymus Wallace, a black businessman who owned a substantial draying business, was elected in 1882 to the board of public works. Ironically, Wallace, whose business depended on the patronage of cotton merchants, beat out the independently wealthy Robert Church for the position in the at-large election. Wallace was reelected in 1884. Wrenn, "The Taxing District of Shelby County," pp. 47–48; Ellis, "Memphis's Sanitary Revolution," pp. 65–67.

9. *Appeal*, 2 January 1885; Wrenn, *Crisis and Commission Government in Memphis*, p. 77. For more on Robert R. Church, see Logan and Winston, *Dictionary of Negro American Biography*, pp. 109–110, and Church and Church, *The Robert R. Churches of Memphis*.

10. *Cleveland Gazette*, 14 November 1884.

11. Born, ibid., pp. 77–78; Wrenn, ibid., p. 14.

12. Wrenn, ibid., p. 98. The reform eliminated the board's broad social and ethnic representation by replacing the twenty-member board of school visitors, elected by wards, with a board of five school commissioners who were appointed by the governor in 1884 and subsequently elected at-large; *Appeal*, 10 November 1882; Belissary, "The Rise of Industry and the Industrial Spirit in Tennessee," pp. 212–213.

13. *Appeal*, 10 October 1882; *Report of the Board of Education of the City of Memphis* (1883–4 and 1884–5) Memphis: SC Toof & Co., 1885, p. 18; "Memphis Board of Education Reports," 1885, p. 4, Memphis Room, Memphis Public Library; *Appeal*, 14 August 1883, 1 September 1885.

14. *Appeal*, 9 November 1886; Quote from Duster, "Ida B. Wells, Her Life and Work," chap. 2, p. 4, unpublished manuscript, Ida B. Wells Papers (hereafter IBW Papers).

15. Duster, ed., *Crusade for Justice*, p. 23 (hereafter Wells, *Crusade*).

16. *Cleveland Gazette*, 4 April 1885; *Fisk Herald*, 3 January 1886, p. 5.

17. Diary of Ida B. Wells, 21 January 1886 (hereafter, Wells, Diary), IBW Papers (hereafter IBW Papers). For a published version of the diary, see DeCosta-Willis, *The Memphis Diary of Ida B. Wells*; ibid., 28 January 1886.

18. For more on the Thompsons, see Bond, "'Till Fair Aurora Rise,'" pp. 153–163.

19. Quoted in the *Cleveland Gazette*, 4 April 1885.

20. Wells, *Crusade*, p. 23. The dates and chronology of Wells's election, followed by the invitation from Countee and her writings in the *Living Way*, are not clear in her text and may, as is true in other instances, be slightly out of order. Wells was writing for the *Living Way* at least as early as February 1885.

21. Dicken-Garcia, *Journalistic Standards in Nineteenth-Century America*, p. 65; La Brie, "Black Newspapers," p. 111.

22. Detweiler, *The Negro Press in the United States*, p. 61; Thornbrough, *T. Thomas Fortune*, p. 57.

23. Quoted in the *Christian Recorder*, 24 July 1884.

24. *Indianapolis Freeman*, 6 May 1886, and 5 January, 23 February 1889.

25. *Appeal*, 5 December 1886; *Washington Bee*, 2, 16, 23 April 1887; Penn, *The Afro-American Press*, chap. 21, listed nineteen major black women journalists.

26. Wells, *Crusade*, pp. 23–24.

27. Penn, ibid., p. 407; Wells, *Crusade*, p. 31.

28. Hamilton, *The Bright Side of Memphis*, pp. 82–84; *Christian Recorder*, 12 April 1883; Tucker, *Black Pastors and Leaders*, pp. 25–40.

29. *Appeal.*, 1 August 1885.

30. Ibid., 5, 7, 11 August 1885; *New York Freeman*, 12 September 1885 (excerpt from the *Living Way*, n.d.); *Cleveland Gazette*, 14 November 1885.

31. *New York Freeman*, ibid.

32. Logan and Winston, *Dictionary of American Negro Biography*, pp. 74–76; Gatewood, *Aristocrats of Color*, pp. 3–6.

33. For more on the black political debate over Cleveland and Republican Party loyalty, see the *Appeal*, 15 January, 19 November 1884; *Christian Recorder*, 4 December 1884; *The Nation*, 23 July 1885, p. 67; Vincent DeSantis, "Negro Dissatisfaction with Republican Policy in the South, 1882–1884," *Journal of Negro History* 36 (April 1951): 148–159. *The AME Church Review*, 1 January 1884, pp. 213–250, devoted a roundtable to the issue.

34. *Washington Bee*, 9 May 1885; *Cleveland Gazette*, 3 January 1885; *Washington Bee*, 7 August 1886; Penn, ibid., p. 290.

35. Logan, *The Betrayal of the Negro*, p. 50; Logan and Winston, ibid., pp. 75, 602–603.

36. *Cleveland Gazette*, 24 January 1885.

37. *Washington Bee*, 9 May 1885, picked up from the *Living Way*, n.d.

38. *New York Freeman*, 7 February 1885 (excerpt from the *Living Way*).

39. Joanne M. Braxton calls this critical discourse the tradition of the "outraged mother," which she traces to women's slave narratives. Braxton, *Black Women Writing Autobiography*, p. 82. Stewart is quoted in Sheftall, *Words of Fire*, p. 31. This important text also includes a biographical sketch and two of Stewart's speeches. Stewart's speech before the Afric-American Female Intelligence Society, "Religion and the Pure Principles of Morality, the Sure Foundation on Which We Must Build," was previously reprinted in abolitionist William Lloyd Garrison's *Liberator* newspaper and in Maria Stewart, *Productions of Mrs. Maria W. Stewart* (Boston: W. Lloyd Garrison & Knapp, 1832). Also see Marilyn Richardson, ed., *Maria Stewart: America's First Black Woman Political Writer: Essays and Speeches* (Bloomington: Indiana University Press, 1987).

40. See Brown, "Negotiating and Transforming the Public Sphere," for an insightful discussion of political activity of black women during Reconstruction and the changing modalities of their decision-making authority in the public sphere, beginning in the 1880s.

41. Wells, "The Model Woman: A Pen Picture of the Typical Southern Girl," published in T. Thomas Fortune's *New York Age*, 18 February 1888, included the characteristics of refinement, modesty, sweetness of disposition, and being "far above mean, petty acts and

venomous, slanderous gossip of her own sex . . ." Another Wells article of this ilk was "Our Women," published in the *New York Freeman*, 1 January 1887.

42. *Living Way*, 5 October 1885, quoted in Duster, ibid., chap. 2, p. 4: Wells, Diary, 30 January 1886.

43. *Christian Recorder*, 12 March 1883.

44. The definitive text on the black Baptist women's movement is Higginbotham, *Righteous Discontent*, from which this author's conclusions were drawn. For an analysis of the relationship between Christian thought and true womanhood among black women, including specific references to Wells's religious, moral, and social ethics, see Townes, *Womanist Justice, Womanist Hope*. Broughton's contribution to the movement included her establishment of women's Bible Bands for studying scripture throughout Tennessee, and the publication of *Women's Work, As Gleaned from Women of the Bible* (1904).

45. "Woman's Mission: A Beautiful Christmas Essay on the Duty of Woman in the World's Economy," *New York Freeman*, 26 December 1885.

46. *Washington Bee*, 12 December 1885.

47. *Living Way*, 5 October 1886, quoted in Duster, ibid., chap. 2, p. 4.

48. *Washington Bee*, 20 March 1886.

49. *Living Way*, ibid.

50. Wells, Diary, 5 January 1886.

51. Ibid., 29 December 1885.

52. Ibid., 2 January 1886; 15 June 1886; *Fisk Herald*, 5 January 1886, p. 5.

53. *Washington Bee*, 23 January 1886.

54. Quoted in Blum, *Reforging the White Republic*, p. 126.

55. *Cleveland Gazette*, 17 April 1886; *Washington Bee*, 27 March, 3 April, 28 August 1886; *Indianapolis Freeman*, 10 April 1886.

56. Lucy Parsons identified herself as Native American and Chicana to cover up her black heritage, according to her biographer. Ashbaugh, *Lucy Parsons*, p. 267, n. 4, also pp. 65–66, 268; Wells, Diary, 18 March 1886.

57. *Fisk Herald*, 8 April 1886, p. 4.

58. Taylor, *In Search of the Racial Frontier*, pp. 84, 135.

59. *Tulare Times*, 25 March 1886.

60. *Appeal*, 18 September 1883; Wells, Diary, 29 December 1885.

61. Wells, Diary, 5 January 1886.

62. Ibid., 21 January, 14 February, 24 January, 2 February 1886.

63. Ibid., 8 February 1886.

64. Blum, ibid., pp. 120–145.

65. *Appeal*, 6, 7, 9, February 1886; Wells, Diary, 8 February 1886.

66. See *Memphis Avalanche*, 3 November 1883, for coverage of a Samfield discourse entitled "The World of Truth"; Wells, Diary, 1 March 1886.

67. Wells, Diary, 29 April 1886. Broughton was subsequently moved from Kortrecht to the Monroe School, and eventually left the school system altogether to work in a Baptist private school, Howe Institute. *Appeal*, 27 March, 14 July, 20 August, 29 December 1885; Wrenn, "The Taxing District of Shelby County," pp. 274–276.

Chapter Four: Love and Trouble

1. Lystra, *Searching the Heart*, p. 102.

2. Diary of Ida B. Wells, 15 June 1886 (hereafter Wells, Diary); Ida B. Wells Papers (hereafter IBW Papers) For a published version of the diary, see DeCosta-Willis, *The Memphis Diary of Ida B. Wells*.

3. Lystra, *Searching the Heart*, pp. 27, 30.

4. Davis, "Against the Odds," p. 120.

5. Lystra, *Searching the Heart*, pp. 7, 38, 10, 86, 59.

6. Wells, Diary, 18 August 1886; Erikson, *Identity and the Life Cycle*, p. 36.

7. Wells, Diary, 21 January, 28 June 1886.

8. Hamilton, *Bright Side of Memphis*, pp. 363–364. The author is grateful to the Graham family for allowing the author to see his library and photo album and for additional information regarding the family.

9. Wells, Diary, 13 January 1886.

10. Ibid., 30 January, 6 May 1886.

11. Ibid., 30 January 1886.

12. Ibid., 1 March, 30 January 1886.

13. Ibid., 30 January, 6 May, 12 June 1886.

14. Charles S. Morris attended Howard University between 1886 and 1891. LaVerne M. Hill Flanagan, Assistant Registrar, Office of Enrollment Management to Paula J. Giddings, 20 October 1994. Morris's biographical information is found in *Pastor Henry N. Jeter's Twenty-Five Years Experience with the Shiloh Baptist Church and Her History* (Providence: Remington Printing Co., 1901), p. 61.

15. Lystra, *Searching the Heart*, p. 4; Wells, Diary, 8 February 1886.

16. Wells, Diary, 21 January, 11 March, 28 January 1886; Jeter, ibid., p. 60; Wells, Diary, 11 March, 21 January, 1886.

17. Quoted in "Forward," p. xviii, Henry Louis Gates, Jr., *Selected Works of Ida B. Wells-Barnett,* compiled with an introduction by Trudier Harris; Wells, Diary, 28 January 1886; Lystra, *Searching the Heart*, p. 19.

18. Wells, Diary, 21 January, 8 February 1886.

19. *Washington Bee*, 9 May 1885.

20. Wells, Diary, 1 March 1886.

21. Ibid.

22. Ibid., 19 May, 20 April 1886.

23. Ibid., 28 June 1886.

24. Ibid.

25. Ibid., 28 and 3 June 1886.

26. Ibid., 15 June 1886; 16 July 1887.

27. *The Washington Bee*, 28 March 1885.

28. Wells, Diary, 12 June 1886.

29. Ibid.

30. The National Education Association was organized in 1857 in Philadelphia under the name of the National Teacher's Association. The name was changed in 1870. Its membership was open to "any person in any way connected to the work of education." *Bulletin of the National Educational Association*, p. 1 (Second Edition, Annual Meeting at Topeka, Kan," July 9–16, 1886); *Cleveland Gazette*, 24 April 1886; "Program of the National Education Association, Bulletin," p. 2.

31. Wells, Diary, 11 March 1886.

32. Lamon, *Black Tennesseeans*, p. 26.

33. Wells, Diary, 4 July 1886.

34. Ibid., 8 July 1886; 21 December 1887; Church, Walter, and Crawford, *Nineteenth Century Memphis Families of Color*, p. 8.

35. Wells, Diary, 13 July 1886.

36. Ibid., 16 July 1886.

37. Taylor, *In Search of the Racial Frontier*, pp. 212–213; *Topeka Daily Capital*, 16 July 1886.

38. Simmons, *Men of Mark*, p. 1057.

39. Taylor, ibid., pp. 202–204; Wells, Diary, 20 July 1886; *Washington Bee,* 19 September 1885.

40. Wells, Diary, 29 July 1886.

41. Joseph E. Doctor "Rebels of Old Visalia," *Quarterly Bulletin of the Tulare County Historical Society* (June 1961): 1–3; K. E. Small, *History of Tulare County* (Chicago: F. J. Clarke Publishing Co., 1926), vol. 1, p. 426.

42. "A Centennial Featurette" (reprinted from the 25 March, 1885 issue of the *Tulare Times*), 19, 21 July 1952; Mervyn G. Shippey, "A Short History of the Visalia Colored School" (San Francisco: R and E Research Associates), typescript, pp. 1–17; Tulare County Historical Library, Farmersville, CA; Wells, Diary, 29 July 1886.

43. Regarding Lutie Rice: Letter, 14 July 1951, signed by Joe Doctor, The Tulare County Historical Library, ibid.

44. Wells, Diary, 2 August 1886.

45. Ibid., 4 August 1886.

46. Ibid., 7, 12 September, 29 July, 26 August 1886. Browne earned his LLB degree in 1884. Laverne-Hill Flanagan, Assistant Registrar, Office of Enrollment Management to Paula J. Giddings, 20 October 1994.

47. Wells, Diary, 4 September 1886.

48. Ibid., 26 August 1886.

49. For a statement about biracial participation in lynchings, see Brundage, *Lynching in the New South,* pp. 31–32.

50. Wells, Diary, 4 September 1886.

51. Wells, *Crusade,* p. 24.

52. Ibid., p. 25; Wells, Diary, 1 September 1886.

53. Wells, Diary, 9 September 1886.

54. Ibid., 12 September 1886.

55. Wells, *Crusade,* pp. 25–26.

56. Wells, Diary, 14 September 1886.

57. Wells, *Crusade,* pp. 25–27; Wells, Diary, 7, 12 September 1886.

58. Wells, *Crusade,* pp. 26–31; Wells, Diary, 2 October 1886.

Chapter Five: A Race in My Arms

1. George Washington Cable, "The Silent South," *Century Magazine,* 30 September 1885, pp. 674–691; Cable, "The Freedman's Case in Equity," *Century Magazine,* 29 January 1885, pp. 409–418.

2. Quoted in Thornbrough, *T. Thomas Fortune,* pp. 82–83. For W. E. B. Du Bois's analysis of Grady's perspective as an anachronistic one that flew against the principles of industrial growth, see Lewis, *W. E. B. Du Bois, Biography of a Race,* p. 113. Also see the *Cleveland Gazette,* 4 April 1885, for an editorial on the Grady-Cable debate.

3. See this interpretation in Williamson, *The Crucible of Race,* p. 101. Also see, Logan, *The Betrayal of the Negro,* pp. 259–261.

4. T. Thomas Fortune, "Civil Rights and Social Privileges," *AME Church Review* (January 1886), pp. 125–131; *New York Freeman,* 16 January 1886. Thornbrough, ibid., p. 83

5. For a comprehensive study of black thought in this period, see Meier, *Negro Thought in America.*

6. Diary of Ida B. Wells, 3 April, 21 January 1886 (hereafter Wells, Diary); Ida B. Wells Papers (hereafter IBW Papers). For a published version of the diary, see DeCosta-Willis, *The Memphis Diary of Ida B. Wells.*

7. Cartwright, *The Triumph of Jim Crow,* pp. 212–213.

8. Wells, Diary, 12 October, 28 December 1886.

9. Ibid., 28 December 1886; 20 October 1886; 24 April 1887.

10. Ibid., 14, 20 February 1887.

11. Church and Church, *The Robert Churches of Memphis*, pp. 33–34.

12. Smith, *Emancipation*, p. 340; Gatewood, *Aristocrats of Color*, p. 21; Wells, Diary, 18 March 1886.

13. *Washington Bee*, 25 June 1887; Wells, Diary, 28 December 1886.

14. Wells, Diary, 28 November 1886; 1 February 1887.

15. *Cleveland Gazette*, 26 March 1887; Wells, Diary, 20 March 1887.

16. Wells, Diary, 28 December, 28 November 1886; *Cleveland Gazette*, 8 August 1885.

17. Wells, Diary, 18 January 1887.

18. Painter, *Standing at Armageddon*, pp. 39–42; *Memphis Appeal*, 12 October 1886 (hereafter *Appeal*).

19. *Cleveland Gazette*, 26 March 1887; Baker, *The Memphis Appeal*, pp. 141–142; Davis, "Against the Odds," p. 209. In the 1880s, the white population had increased from 18,696 to 35,789; the black population had risen from 14,896 to 28,706. Davis, ibid., p. 107.

20. *New York Freeman* (picked up from the *Memphis Watchman*), 15 January 1887;

21. Wedell, *Elite Women and the Reform Impulse in Memphis*, pp. 37–44.

22. Ibid., p. 68; *New York Freeman*, ibid. The Memphis WCTU chapter was headed by Mrs. C. H. Phillips, wife of the pastor of CME's Collins Chapel, the most refined black congregation in the city, according to Wells.

23. Quoted in Isaac, *Prohibition and Politics*, p. 39; Harper, "The Woman's Christian Temperance Union and the Colored Woman," p. 313.

24. *The Memphis Scimitar*, n.d., picked up in *New York Freeman*, 1 January 1887.

25. Walton and Taylor, "Blacks, Prohibition and Disenfranchisement," p. 68.

26. Boylan, *Sunday School*, pp. 22–27; Du Bois, "The Problem of Amusement," p. 181.

27. Wells, Diary, 18 January 1887.

28. Ibid., 18 April, 20 March, 9 September 1887.

29. Logan and Winston, *Dictionary of American Negro Biography*, pp. 556–557; Wells, *Crusade*, pp. 31–32.

30. *American Baptist*, 25 February 1887 (reprinted in the *St. Paul (MN) Appeal*, 5 March 1887).

31. *New York Freeman*, 15 January 1887 (from the *American Baptist*, n.d.).

32. *Appeal*, 12 February 1887.

33. Wells, Diary, 14 February 1887.

34. Wells et al., "Symposium—Temperance," *AME Church Review* (April 1891), pp. 375–381. In Tennessee, laws passed in 1813 and 1830 had made it illegal for slaves to purchase alcohol, and by 1836 free blacks were prohibited from selling liquor. Walton, "Another Force for Disenfranchisement," pp. 729–730. Wells, Diary, 4 February 1887. The *Memphis Watchman* editorialized that "prohibition is a slave law, as it puts some in bondage and leaves others to do as they please." Quoted in Walton, "Another Force for Disenfranchisement," p. 732. *Appeal*, 6 February 1886; *Memphis Daily Avalanche*, 2 November, 4 April 1888.

35. Wells, Diary, 20 February 1887.

36. Isaacs, ibid., p. 36.

37. Wells, Diary, 20 February 1887.

38. *Memphis Appeal–Avalanche*, 4 June 1893.

39. "Cases Argued and Determined in the Supreme Court of Tennessee for the Western Division. Jackson, April Term, 1887. *Chesapeake, Ohio & Southwestern Railroad Company v. Wells*, April 5 1887, pp. 613–615.

40. Wells, Diary, 11 April 1887.

41. *Appeal*, 31 May 1887; Foner, *Organized Labor and the Black Worker*, pp. 60–62.

42. Wells, Diary, 18 April 1887.

43. *Appeal*, 19 April 1887.

44. Wells, Diary, 24 April, 2, 3, 5 May 1887.

45. Ibid., 13 July 1887.

46. Jones, *Quest for Equality*, p. 11, p. 95, n. 29.

47. Terrell, *Colored Woman in a White World*, p. 16; Jones, *Quest for Equality*, p. 10; quote in Minter, "Freedom, Personal Liberty, and Private Law," p. 5, n. 29.

48. Wells, Diary, 3 July 1887.

49. Ibid., 17 June 1887.

50. *Harper's Weekly*, 31 (21 June, 1887), p. 450; quoted in Thornbrough, ibid., p. 109; *New York Freeman*, 28 May 1887.

51. Franklin, *From Slavery to Freedom*, p. 166.

52. Quoted in Thornbrough, ibid., 106; Cutler, *Lynch Law*, graph opposite p. 171.

53. *Indianapolis Freeman*, 9 July 1887, quoting the *American Baptist* (n.d.). The author is grateful to Mary Helen Washington for providing this citation.

54. *New York Freeman*, 25 June 1887.

55. However, Wells, writing to Charles Morris about Fortune, also noted that one should not judge a person by the "cut" or rather "uncut" of his hair. Wells, Diary, 11 March 1886. Fortune quote in Thornbrough, ibid., p. 107.

56. Higginbotham, *Righteous Discontent*, p. 78; Wells, *Crusade*, p. 32.

57. Wells, Diary, 12 August 1887.

58. Hine et al., eds., *Black Women in America*, vol. I, pp. 84–88; Penn, *The Afro-American Press*, pp. 367–374, 376–381.

59. *New Orleans Weekly Pelican*, 13 August 1887.

60. *New York Freeman*, 13, 20 August 1887; *Washington Bee*, 3 September 1887.

61. Wells, Diary, 3–24 August 1887; *New York Freeman*, 20 August 1887; *Washington Bee*, 20 August 1887; *Christian Index*, 20 August 1887; *New Orleans Weekly Pelican*, 13 August 1887.

62. Wells, Diary, 18 September 1887; DeCosta-Willis, *The Memphis Diary of Ida B. Wells*, p. 158.

63. Singal, *The War Within*, pp. 17, 24. The final vote was 145,000 against the amendment and 118,000 for it. Isaac, ibid., p. 55.

64. *Tennessee Baptist*, 20 (25 June 1887); p. 3, quoted in Isaac, ibid., pp. 39, 48; *Appeal*, 5 September 1887, quoted in Isaac, ibid., p. 39.

65. Quoted in Cartwright, *The Triumph of Jim Crow*, p. 205; quoted in Isaac, *Prohibition and Politics*, p. 39.

66. Cartwright, ibid., p. 207; Walton, ibid., pp. 732–734; Isaac, ibid., pp. 55–60.

67. Cartwright, ibid., pp. 214, 205; quoted in Cartwright, ibid., p. 204. The consequences of the defeat is also analyzed in Walton, ibid., pp. 734–736.

68. Federal election supervisors also found unmistakable fraud in Shelby, Fayette, and Haywood counties. Kousser, *The Shaping of Southern Politics*, p. 108; quoted in Kousser, ibid.

69. *Memphis Avalanche* (hereafter *Avalanche*), 2 November, 4 April, 1888;

70. The Myers Bill called for new registration procedures requiring voters in districts or towns that cast five hundred or more votes in 1888 to register at least twenty days before every election. The Lea Bill provided for separate polling places for federal and state elections. See Cartwright, ibid., pp. 223–224, 227, 229. For a full analysis of the Dortch Law, see Kousser, ibid., pp. 104–138.

71. Cartwright, ibid., p. 140; Wedell, ibid., p. 70; Kousser, *The Shaping of Southern Politics*, p. 104.

72. Cartwright, ibid.

73. Quoted in Meier, *Negro Thought in America*, p. 192; Harper, "Woman's Political Future," p. 42.

74. Cartwright, ibid., pp. 223–225; *Christian Index*, 2, 16 April 1887, 21 June 1889.

75. Fuller, *History of Negro Baptists in Tennessee*, pp. 118–122; Higginbotham, *Righteous Discontent*, p. 70. The number of black businesses increased to 196 by 1900. Davis, "Against the Odds," p. 211. Others listed as People's Grocery cooperators included M. L. Copeland, the pastor of Macedonea Church; John Brownlee, a carpenter; Harry Bell, carpet layer at Menken's; H. S. Jordan, a shoemaker; J. H. Norrell, a porter; Samuel Martin and S. J. Walton, laborers; and John Greenfield, a plumber. Corporate Record Book, 1889, no. 4, p. 354. Tennessee State Library and Archives.

76. Hamilton, *Bright Side of Memphis*, p. 251; *Christian Index*, 1 September 1888.

77. *Memphis Daily Avalanche*, 24 February 1889; *Christian Index*, 30 June 1889.

78. *Christian Index*, 12 May, 1 June, 11 May 1889.

79. Ibid., 23 February 1889.

80. Ibid., 30 June, 10 March, 21 April, 12 May, 9 June 1888.

81. *New York Age*, 11 August 1888; *New York Freeman*, 18 February 1888.

82. *Christian Index*, 21 July 1888.

83. *The Journalist*, 26 January 1889, p. 158.

84. *Christian Index*, 2 March 1889.

85. *Montgomery Herald*, 13 August 1887; *Washington Bee*, 10 September 1887. For more details on the Duke episode, see Hodes, *White Women, Black Men*, pp. 188–190; *Christian Index*, ibid.

86. Quoted in Penn, *The Afro-American Press*, p. 186; Logan and Winston, *American Negro Biography*, p. 444; for more on Mitchell's antilynching campaign, see Brundage, "To Howl Loudly."

87. Lynch, *Reminiscences of an Active Life*, p. 135; *Christian Index*, 30 March 1889; *Washington Bee*, 21 September 1889.

88. Logan, *The Betrayal of the Negro*, pp. 50–51; Dray, *At the Hands of Persons Unknown*, p. 113.

89. Wells, *Crusade*, p. 35.

Chapter Six: City of the Three Murdered Men

1. *Memphis Daily Appeal*, 8 January 1886 (hereafter *Appeal*); Diary of Ida B. Wells, 13 January 1886 (hereafter Wells, Diary). Ida B. Wells Papers (hereafter IBW Papers). For a published edition of the diary, see DeCosta-Willis, *The Memphis Diary of Ida B. Wells*.

2. Hamilton, *Bright Side of Memphis*, pp. 138–139.

3. *Appeal*, 12 September 1889, quoted in Cartwright, *The Triumph of Jim Crow*, pp. 201–202.

4. *Nashville Daily American*, 29 July 1890, quoted in Cartwright, *The Triumph of Jim Crow*, p. 215; Philip A. Bruce, *The Plantation Negro as Freeman* (New York: Putnam, 1889), quotes from Gutman, *The Black Family in Slavery and Freedom*, pp. 534, 536. For a more extensive commentary on Philip Bruce, see George Frederickson, *Black Image in the White Mind*, pp. 244–282.

5. *Memphis Daily Avalanche*, 2 November, 4 April 1888 (hereafter *Avalanche*); Tucker, *Black Pastors and Leaders*, p. 44; *Appeal*, 15 January 1889.

6. Wells, Diary, 8 July 1886; *Washington Bee*, 12 March 1887; *Cleveland Gazette*, 4 August 1888; *Appeal*, 11 October 1888; *Anti-Caste* (April 1889): 1, 3–4.

7. *Knoxville Daily Journal*, 27 June 1889; *Memphis Public Ledger*, 27 June 1889.

8. *Free Speech* reprinted in the *Avalanche*, 13 July 1889. Unfortunately, no copies are extant of the *Free Speech* (whose name was shortened soon after Ida joined it), but its unsigned

editorials, as well as Ida Wells's signed editorials, some of which did not mention the *Free Speech* as its origin, were quoted in other papers.

9. *Avalanche,* 5 September 1889.

10. *New York Age,* 21 September 1889.

11. *Detroit Plaindealer,* 18 October 1889.

12. *New York Age,* 21 December 1889, quoted in Thornbrough, *T. Thomas Fortune,* pp. 110–111.

13. *Indianapolis Freeman,* 20 July 1889.

14. *Cleveland Gazette,* 31 August 1889; *New York Age,* 24 August 1889.

15. *Christian Index,* 11 January 1890.

16. Logan and Winston, *Dictionary of American Negro Biography,* pp. 496–497; Thornbrough, ibid., p. 114; *Cleveland Gazette,* 25 January 1890; *New York Age,* 14, 21 December 1889; 25 January 1890.

17. *Nation* 50 (February 13, 1890): 123; *New York Age,* 8 February 1890, quoted in Thornbrough, ibid., p. 116.

18. *Christian Index,* 7 June, 11 January 1890.

19. The prisoners were also used to prevent strikes of company workers, which led to a series of violent confrontations in 1891. Woodward, *Origins of the New South,* pp. 4, 233; Washington, D.C., *Evening Star,* 27 September 1892, quoted in "The Reason Why the Colored American Is Not in the World's Columbian Exposition," reprinted in Harris, *The Selected Works of Ida B. Wells Barnett,* p. 71. Also see the *Cleveland Gazette,* 19 April 1890, for a vivid description of the vermin-infested conditions of the Arkansas prisons where convicts were used to work the mines, slept in damp clothing, and were routinely whipped. *Free Speech,* quoted in the *Indianapolis Freeman,* 21 June 1890.

20. *New York Age,* 29 December, 1 February 1890; *Indianapolis Freeman,* 17 May, 12 July 1890; *New York Age,* 29 December 1890; *Indianapolis Freeman,* 5 April 1890. Wells wrote, "If the meetings continued at such a rate, the grievances of blacks, which some would-be leaders seem to think can be talked down, will become ridiculous as well as monotonous." *New York Age,* 1 February 1890.

21. *New York Age,* 24 August, 1889; *Cleveland Gazette,* 31 August 1889; *Indianapolis Freeman,* 19 April 1890.

22. *New York Age,* 5 July 1890; *Indianapolis Freeman,* 21, 12 July 1890.

23. *Indianapolis Freeman,* 7 June 1890; *Detroit Plaindealer* 9 May 1890; *New York Age,* 8 August 1891; *Washington Bee,* 4 October 1890.

24. Duster, ed. *Crusade for Justice,* p. 40 (hereafter Wells, *Crusade*).

25. See, for example, the *Christian Index,* 10 March, 21 April, 12 May, 9, 30 June 1888. Wells, *Crusade,* p. 41. Ida B. Wells to Booker T. Washington, 30 November 1890, reprinted in Harlan, *The Booker T. Washington Papers,* vol. 3, p. 108; *Washington Bee,* 29 November 1890; Wells, ibid., pp. 40–41. For a discussion of Washington's speech and publication entitled "The Colored Ministry: Its Defects and Needs," see Harlan, *Booker T. Washington, The Making of a Black Leader,* pp. 194–196.

26. Logan and Winston, ibid., pp. 633–644.

27. Harlan, ibid., pp. 196–197.

28. Wells, *Crusade,* p. 36.

29. Ida B. Wells to Robert R. Church, Sr., 29 January 1891. Church Collection, Memphis State Library; Wells, ibid.

30. Wells, ibid.

31. *Appeal-Avalanche,* 1 June 1891; *Detroit Plaindealer,* 12 June 1891; Wells, ibid., p.37.

32. *Appeal-Avalanche,* ibid.; *Cleveland Gazette,* 5 September 1891; *Huntsville Gazette,* 26 September 1891; *Indianapolis Freeman,* 19 September 1891. The exact date of the *Free Speech*

editorial is unclear, and so it can only be surmised that Britton's June 1891 suicide occurred during the controversy it stirred up.

33. Wells accuses Settle in a letter: Ida B. Wells to Albion Tourgée, 22 February 1893, Albion Tourgée Papers; Wells, *Crusade*, p. 37.

34. *Appeal-Avalanche*, 15 September, 29 November 1891.

35. *New York Age,* 23 November 1889, 30 May 1891.

36. Bruce and Pinchback became subsequently involved with the American Citizens Civil Rights Association, which called a conference, apparently to compete with that of the League, in Washington, D.C. One of the leading moderates to give a tentative endorsement of the organization was John M. Langston, former consul general to Haiti and president of Virginia Normal and Collegiate Institute. However, Langston never became an integral part of the League. Thornbrough, ibid., pp. 116–117

37. *New York Age,* 25 July 1891; *Detroit Plaindealer,* 24 July 1891; *New York Age,* 25 July 1891; *New York Age,* 23 November 1889, 30 May 1891.

38. *Detroit Plaindealer,* 10 July 1891, specifically notes that the Tennessee Railways violated the antidiscriminatory statutes in the Interstate Commerce Act. The act, passed in 1887, was in response to a complex of motives, including protection of the public and saving the railways from rate wars and rebates individual states imposed without national regulation. Applications of racial discrimination required additional adjudication to make it stand. *New York Age,* 8 August 1891.

39. *New York Age*, 8 August 1891.

40. Wells, *Southern Horrors*, p. 18. Wells had discussed such ideas about publishing with Gertrude Mossell, who also wrote on the topic. *Christian Index,* 9 March 1889.

41. Wells, *Crusade,* p. 42.

42. The Fifteenth Amendment prevented "the States or the United States . . . from giving preference . . . to one citizen of the United States over another on account of race, color, or previous condition of servitude." Franklin, *From Slavery to Freedom,* p.259; *New York Age,* 27 September, 8 November 1890. For more on Montgomery, see Logan and Winston, *Dictionary of American Negro Biography,* pp. 445–446.

43. Logan and Winston, ibid., p. 446; Wells, *Crusade,* pp. 38–39.

44. Wells, *Crusade,* p. 42.

45. Ibid., pp. 41, 44.

46. *Memphis Commercial,* 30 August 1891 (hereafter *Commercial*).

47. Quoted in *Appeal-Avalanche,* 6 September 1891; *Cleveland Gazette,* 26 September 1891.

48. *New York Age,* 19 September 1891, quoted in *Jackson, MS Tribune and Sun; Commercial; Appeal-Avalanche,* 6 September 1891.

49. *Appeal-Avalanche,* 13 September 1891; Tucker, "Miss Ida B. Wells and Memphis Lynching," p. 115. The details of the months-long feud between Nightingale and Beale Street members were gleefully covered in the Memphis daily press. See *Public Ledger* 2, 15 May; 28, 29, 30 October; 2 November 1891; *Appeal-Avalanche* 14 May; 9, 10, 11, 13 September 1891.

50. Wells, *Crusade,* p. 39.

51. Ibid., p. 37.

52. Davis, "Against the Odds," p. 209.

53. *New York Age,* 12 November 1892; Wells, *Crusade,* p. 47.

54. *New York Age,* 8 August, 12 September 1891 and 7 November, 26 December 1891. Wells, ibid., p. 48.

55. By 1900 when the area became Ward Eleven, its population was 4,719 blacks, 1,847 whites. Davis, "Against the Odds," pp. 130, 137–142; *Memphis Commercial Appeal,* 6, 7 March 1892.

56. *Memphis Commercial Appeal*, 26 September 1894. Of the 4,360 arrests of men in 1892, 51 percent were African American; 49 percent were white. Of the 817 arrests of women, more than 77 percent were African Americans, mostly for public order offenses. Duggan, "The Trials of Alice Michell," p. 116. From 1900–1910. Memphis had the highest homicide rate in the country—47.1 per hundred thousand population. By 1916, Memphis's homicide rate was twice as high as its nearest competitor. Miller, *Memphis During the Progressive Era*, p. 92.

57. *Indianapolis Freeman*, 5 February 1892; *Cleveland Gazette*, 5 February 1892; Ida B. Wells et al. to James T. Hall, Indenture made 8 February 1892 in consideration of $150. Sectional Index, City of Holly Springs, Marshall County, p. 150.

58. *Detroit Plaindealer*, 8 January 1892; *Indianapolis Freeman*, 9 January 1892.

59. Wells, *Crusade*, p. 48; *St. Paul Appeal*, 26 March 1892.

60. *Appeal-Avalanche*, 6 March 1892.

61. *Appeal-Avalanche* , 10 March 1892; *Commercial*, 10 March 1892.

62. *Appeal-Avalanche*, 10 March 1892; *Memphis Commercial*, 11 March 1892; Tucker, "Miss Ida Wells and the Memphis Lynching," p. 115; *Nashville Daily American*, 7 March 1892. The *Nashville Daily American*, a Democratic paper, characterized the People's Grocery as a rendezvous where drinking and gambling took place. However, neither Wells nor any of the white Memphis dailies so characterized the People's Grocery.

63. *Appeal-Avalanche*, 6 March 1892; *Commercial* 6, 7 March 1892. Wells, *Crusade*, p. 48; *St. Paul Appeal*, 26 March 1892.

64. *St. Paul Appeal*, ibid., *Commercial*, 6 March 1892.

65. *Commercial*, 6 March 1892; *Appeal-Avalanche*, 6 March 1892; *Nashville Daily American*, 7 March 1892.

66. *Appeal-Avalanche*, 6 March 1892; *Commercial*, 6 March 1892; *St. Paul Appeal*, 26 March 1892.

67. *Nashville Daily American*, 7 March 1892.

68. *Commercial*, 6, 7, 1892; *St. Paul Appeal*, 26 March 1892.

69. *Commercial*, 10 March 1892; *Appeal-Avalanche*, 9 March 1892.

70. *Commercial*, 7, 10 March 1892; Wells, "Lynch Law in All Its Phases," p. 174.

71. Cartwright, *The Triumph of Jim Crow*, pp. 115–116; *Appeal-Avalanche*, 8 March 1892; Wells, ibid.

72. *Commercial*, 10 March 1892; *Appeal-Avalanche*, 10 March 1892.

73. *Commercial*, 10 March 1892; *Appeal-Avalanche*, 10 March 1892; Wells, *Crusade*, p. 51.

74. *Appeal-Avalanche*, 9 March, 1892.

75. *Appeal-Avalanche*, 10 March 1892.

76. Wells, *Crusade*, p. 51; Wells, "Lynch Law in All Its Phases," p. 174.

77. *New York Times*, 10, 11 March 1892.

78. *Memphis Commercial*, 10 March 1892; Cutler, *Lynch Law*, p. 183; Hale, *Making Whiteness*, p. 207. For a book on the Italian lynching, see Richard Gambino, *Vendetta: A True Story of the Worst Lynching in America: The Mass Murder of Italian-Americans in New Orleans in 1891, the Vicious Motivations Behind It, and the Tragic Repercussions That Still Linger to This Date* (Garden City: Doubleday, 1977); Wells, *Southern Horrors* (reprinted in Wells-Barnett, *On Lynchings*, p. 10; hereafter Wells, *Southern Horrors*); *Appeal-Avalanche*, 30 August, 11 September 1891.

79. For a book on the Mitchell case, see Duggan, *Sapphic Slashers*; *New York Times*, 10 March 1892.

80. *Appeal-Avalanche*, 10 March 1892.

81. *The Washington Star*, quoted in *Appeal-Avalanche*, 16 March 1892; *Chicago Daily Inter-*

Ocean, quoted in the *Detroit Plaindealer,* 18 March 1892; *Appeal-Avalanche,* 10 March 1892; *Commercial,* 10 March 1892.

82. *Appeal-Avalanche,* 11 March 1892; *Nashville Daily American,* 11 March 1892.
83. *Appeal-Avalanche,* ibid.

Chapter Seven: Exodus

1. *Christian Index,* 3 May 1890; Duster, ed., *Crusade for Justice,* p. 51 (hereafter Wells, *Crusade*).
2. Wells, *Crusade,* p. 52.
3. Logan and Winston, *American Negro Biography,* pp. 557–558. For a comprehensive study of the movement, see Nell Irvin Painter's text, *Exodusters.*
4. *Memphis Appeal-Avalanche,* 7, 16 September 1891 (hereafter *Appeal-Avalanche*).
5. *Washington Bee,* 8 April, 28 August 1886; *Indianapolis Freeman,* 26 March 1892.
6. *Memphis Commercial,* 20 March 1892 (hereafter *Commercial*); *New York Times,* 11 March 1892.
7. *Free Speech* quoted in the *Kansas City (Mo.* and *Kan.) American Citizen,* 1 April 1892. Because copies of the *Free Speech* are not extant, the events and the dates of the editorials picked up by other publications do not always follow chronologically.
8. *Nashville Daily American,* 24 March 1892; *Appeal-Avalanche,* 12, 18, 26 March 1892; *Langston City Herald,* 26 March 1892.
9. *Nashville Daily American,* 27 March 1892; *Appeal-Avalanche,* 30 August, 11 September 1891.
10. Wells, *Crusade,* p. 56.
11. *Commercial,* 27 March 1892; Wells, *Crusade,* ibid.
12. Wells, *Crusade,* pp. 54–55; *Nashville Daily American,* 11 March 1892.
13. *Star of Zion,* 31 March 1892; *Christian Index,* 19 March 1892; Kansas City *American Citizen,* 25 March 1892.
14. *Commercial,* 29 March 1892.
15. *Appeal-Avalanche,* 30 March 1892; Cartwright, *The Triumph of Jim Crow,* p. 116; *Cleveland Gazette,* 28 May 1892; *Indianapolis Freeman,* 16 April 1892; *New York Times,* 5 April 1892.
16. *Indianapolis Freeman,* 6 February 1892.
17. *Langston City Herald,* 27 February, 16 January 1892.
18. See Taylor, *In Search of the Racial Frontier,* pp. 143–151, for details about the Society and the black settlements in the West, including Oklahoma. Logan and Winston, ibid., pp. 410–412.
19. In 1897, the year that John Langston died, the Colored Agricultural and Normal University (later renamed Langston University) was founded in Langston City. The land for the co-ed institution was purchased by 1898, after a series of fund-raising activities led by black settlers. The school officially opened on September 3, 1898. "Langston University" website.
20. *New York Age,* 15 March 1890.
21. Wells, *Crusade,* pp. 57–58.
22. Ibid., p. 57; *Langston City Herald,* 16 April 1892; *Kansas City (Mo.* and *Kan.) American Citizen,* 20 December 1889.
23. *Langston City Herald,* 11 June 1892, quoted in Taylor, *In Search of the Racial Frontier,* p. 146; *Cleveland Gazette,* 9 May 1891.
24. *Langston City Herald,* 12 January 1893.
25. Ibid., 5 March 1892; *Indianapolis Freeman,* 6 April 1889; *Washington Bee,* 8 March 1890; *Cleveland Gazette,* 9 May 1891. Quotes from *Indianapolis Freeman,* 6 February 1892.

26. Taylor, ibid., p. 147; *Cleveland Gazette*, 9 May 1891; *Langston City Herald*, 9 May 1892.

27. *Langston City Herald*, 16 April 1892.

28. Wells, "Afro-Americans and Africa," pp. 41, 42.

29. Wells, *Crusade*, p. 58; *Detroit Plaindealer*, 29 April, 17 June 1892.

30. *Detroit Plaindealer*, 15 April 1892.

31. *Commercial*, 14 April 1892; *Indianapolis Freeman*, 7 May 1892.

32. *Langston City Herald*, 1 October 1892; *Detroit Plaindealer*, 15 April 1892; *Indianapolis Freeman*, 30 April 1892.

33. Wells, "Lynch Law in All Its Phases" (reprinted in Thompson, *Ida B. Wells-Barnett*), p. 177; Wells, *Crusade*, p. 53.

34. Wells, *Crusade*, p. 54.

35. *Indianapolis Freeman*, 27 February, 5 March 1892; Wells, *Crusade*, p. 54; Giddings, *When and Where I Enter*, p. 262.

36. Wells, ibid.

37. *Detroit Plaindealer*, 13 May 1892; *Cleveland Gazette*, 6 May 1892; 15 May 1893.

38. *Free Speech*, quoted in the *Cleveland Gazette*, 28 May 1892.

39. *Indianapolis Freeman*, 19 March 1892; *Free Speech*, reprinted in the *Cleveland Gazette*, 28 May 1892. Note: The papers carrying Wells's editorial comments are inconsistent in attributing them to the *Free Speech*.

40. *Detroit Plaindealer*, 27 May 1892.

41. *Cleveland Gazette*, 28 May 1892; Wells, *Crusade*, pp. 54–55; *Afro-American Advocate* (Coffeyville, Kansas), 6 May 1892.

42. Wells, ibid., pp. 58–59.

43. *Commercial*, 17 May 1892, quoted in Wells, *Southern Horrors* (reprinted in Wells-Barnett, *On Lynchings*, pp. 16–17 (hereafter Wells, *Southern Horrors*).

44. Wells had written in her diary: "It seems awful to take a human life but hardly more so than to take a woman's reputation and make it the jest and byword of the street; in view of these things, if he really did them, one is strongly tempted to say this killing was justifiable. Diary of Ida B. Wells, 8 February 1887 (hereafter Wells, *Diary*); Wells, *Crusade*, p. 64.

45. Wells, *Crusade*, pp. 65, 71.

46. Quoted in Wells, *Southern Horrors*, p. 4.

47. Lane, *The Roots of Violence in Black Philadelphia*, pp. 17, 33, 34. The classic study of the city in the late nineteenth century is W. E. B. Du Bois's *The Philadelphia Negro* (1899). Also see Gatewood, *Aristocrats of Color*, pp. 96–103, for an analysis of the origins of Philadelphia's black upper class; Penn, *The Afro-American Press*, pp. 145–148.

48. *Cleveland Gazette*, 28 May 1892.

49. Logan and Winston, *Dictionary of American Negro Biography*, pp. 485, 289.

50. Quoted in the introduction by Frances Foster for *Iola LeRoy or Shadows Uplifted*, p. xxxi. (New York: Oxford University Press, 1988). (Originally published 1893.)

51. Logan and Winston, ibid., pp. 130–132.

52. Wells, *Crusade*, p. 61.

Chapter Eight: "The Truth About Lynching"

1. *Memphis Commercial*, 25 May 1892 (hereafter, *Commercial*); *Memphis Scimitar*, 25 May 1892; quoted in Wells, *Southern Horrors* (reprinted in Wells-Barnett, *On Lynchings*, pp. 4–5; hereafter, Wells, *Southern Horrors*).

2. Wells, "Lynch Law in All Its Phases" (reprinted in Thompson, *Ida B. Wells-Barnett*, p. 179; hereafter Wells, "Lynch Law").

3. Duster, ed., *Crusade for Justice*, p. 67 (hereafter Wells, *Crusade*).

4. Wells, *Crusade*, p. 62; *Memphis Daily Avalanche*, 4 April 1888.

5. Wells, "Lynch Law," ibid.; *Langston City Herald*, 5 January 1893.

6. Wells, "Lynch Law," ibid.; *Conservator*, quoted in the *Washington Bee*, 11 June 1892.

7. Wells, *Crusade*, p. 62.

8. *Kansas City (Mo.* and *Kan.) American Citizen*, 1 July 1892. Wells, "Lynch Law" p. 179; Wells, *Southern Horrors*, p. 5; Wells, *Crusade*, pp. 61–62. Wells's chronology which pairs days of the week with their dates is inconsistent in the autobiography, her pamphlet, *Southern Horrors*, and "Lynch Law in All Its Phases." I have corrected the dates.

9. Quotes in the *Cleveland Gazette*, 28 May 1892.

10. *Langston City Herald*, 13 May 1892. Ida Wells's name was not listed among the signatories. She may have been traveling, or less than enthusiastic about the relatively passive demonstration; quoted in August Meier, *Negro Thought in America*, p. 79.

11. *Cleveland Gazette*, ibid; quote from Luker, *The Social Gospel in Black and White*, p. 90; Wells, *Southern Horrors*, p.21.

12. *The Independent*, 26 May 1892, p. 11.

13. *The Independent*, 2 June 1892, p. 13.

14. Thomas Gossett, *Race: The History of an Idea* (New York: Oxford University Press, 1997), p. 166; quoted in Dray, *At the Hands of Persons Unknown*, p. 100; Daniel G. Brinton, *Races and Peoples: Lectures on the Science of Ethnography* (New York: Hodges, 1890); Baker, *From Savage to Negro*, p. 35.

15. *Christian Index*, 30 July 1892.

16. *Memphis Commercial*, 8 June, 1892.

17. *Langston City Herald*, 28 May 1892; Tucker, *Black Pastors and Leaders*, p. 47.

18. *Memphis Appeal-Avalanche*, 8 June 1892 (hereafter, *Appeal-Avalanche*).

19. Ibid.

20. Quoted in Wells, *Southern Horrors*, p. 18.

21. Quotes in *Memphis Appeal-Avalanche*, 12 June 1892.

22. *Indianapolis Freeman*, 11 June 1892; *Detroit Plaindealer*, 17 June 1892; *Indianapolis Freeman*, 16 July 1892.

23. *The Independent*, 23 June 1892, p. 12. "Benjamin K. Sampson," 20 February 1895. Alumni File, Oberlin College Archives, Oberlin, Ohio. Before the year ended, Sampson was removed from the Memphis Public Schools. He went to Paris, Tennessee, where, after serving as principal of the Colored High School there for twelve years, returned to Memphis where he died on August 10, 1906, of malarial fever. Obituary Record, Alumni Oberlin College, 1906–1907.

24. Wells, *Crusade*, pp. 63–64, 69.

25. Wells, *Southern Horrors*, p. 14.

26. The issue of the *Age* does not appear to be extant, but in her preface to *Southern Horrors*, Wells states that "the greater part of what is contained in these pages was published in the *New York Age*, June 25, 1892."

27. Wells, *Southern Horrors*, p. 6.

28. Ibid., p. 8.

29. Ibid., p. 10.

30. Ibid., pp. 7–8.

31. Ibid., pp. 11–12.

32. Ibid., p. 9.

33. Ibid., pp. 5, 10, 11.

34. Ibid., p. 10.

35. Ibid., p. 11.

36. Ibid., p. 12.

37. Ibid., pp. 13–14, 24, 11.

38. Ibid., p. 21; Woodward, *Origins of the New South*, p. 4; Wells, ibid., p. 20.

39. Wells, ibid., p. 15.

40. Quoted in ibid, pp. 21, 14.

41. Wells, *Southern Horrors*, p. 14.

42. Ibid., pp. 22, 15.

43. Ibid., pp. 13, 24.

44. Ibid., pp. 22, 23.

45. Ibid., p. 23.

46. Ibid., p. 1.

47. Ibid.

Chapter Nine: The Loveliest Lynchee Was Our Lord

1. The chapter title comes from a poem about a lynching by Gwendolyn Brooks; *Memphis Appeal-Avalanche*, 30 June 1892; Duster, ed., *Crusade for Justice*, p. 69 (hereafter Wells, *Crusade*, p. 69); "Benjamin A. Imes," biographical record, Alumni File, Oberlin College Archives, Oberlin, Ohio, 20 August 1908.

2. *Indianapolis Freeman*, 8 October 1892 (hereafter *Freeman*); *Washington Bee*, 29 October 1892 (hereafter *Bee*).

3. Connolly, *A Ghetto Grows in Brooklyn*, pp. 21, 45. The statistics for both cities are for the year 1890.

4. Wells, *Crusade*, p. 63. See *New York Age*, 19 November 1892, for Fortune's statement that "It almost breaks my heart to have to go back to the four page *Age*. . . . I have for so long been proud of the eight page, and confident in the belief that the people would support it."

5. *New York Age*, 12 November 1892.

6. *New York Times*, 14 August 1895; *Topeka Weekly Call*, 22 April 1893. Note: There are many missing issues of the *Age* for the year 1892, so many of Wells's *Age* writings are quoted from other papers that reprinted them.

7. *Brooklyn Daily Eagle*, 18 December 1892, quoted in Connolly, ibid., p. 32.

8. McHenry, *Forgotten Readers*, p. 188; Taylor, *The Black Churches of Brooklyn*, p. 30.

9. *Bee*, 29 October 1892.

10. Taylor, ibid., p. 29; Maritcha Remond Lyons, "Memories of Yesterdays: All of Which I Saw and Part of Which I Was: An Autobiography," p. 33. For more on Lyons, see Howard Dodson, *Jubilee: The Emergence of African-American Culture by the Schomburg Center for Research in Black Culture of the New York Public Library* (National Geographic Books, 2003); and Tonya Bolden, *Maritcha: A Nineteenth-Century American Girl* (New York: Abrams, 2003), a children's book.

11. Burroughs and Wallace, *Gotham*, p. 892.

12. Lyons, ibid.

13. PS 83 opened in 1893 with one thousand white and two hundred black students, black and white teachers, a white principal, and Lyons as assistant principal and head of the black department. Connolly, ibid., p. 28.

14. Lyons, ibid.

15. *Detroit Plaindealer*, 28 April 1893. For more biographical information on Garnet and McKinney (Steward), see Hine, ed., *Black Women in America*, p. 479, vol. 1; and pp. 1109–1111, vol. 2, respectively.

16. Davis, *Lifting As They Climb*, p. 21; for more on Matthews, see Hine, ed., ibid., vol. 2, pp. 759–761.

17. Gatewood, *Aristocrats of Color*, p. 106; *New York Times*, 14 July 1895; Connolly, ibid., pp. 32–33; Wells, *Crusade*, p. 78.

18. Wells, *Crusade*, p. 78.

19. *Detroit Plaindealer*, 21 October, 16 December 1892; Wells, ibid., p. 79.

20. Wells, ibid., pp. 80, 78–79.

21. Ibid., p. 80.

22. Wells, *Crusade*, p. 78; *Kansas City (Mo. and Kan.) American Citizen*, 21 October 1892; *Bee*, 29 October 1892; *Detroit Plaindealer*, 23 September 1892; McFeely, *Frederick Douglass*, pp. 372–373.

23. Ida B. Wells, *Southern Horrors* (reprinted in Wells-Barnett, *On Lynchings*, p. 2 (hereafter, Wells, *Southern Horrors*); Wells, *Crusade*, p. 81.

24. Lyons, ibid.; *Bee*, 22 October 1892.

25. Frederick Douglass to Ida B. Wells, 25 October 1892, Ida B. Wells Papers. Reprinted in Wells, *Southern Horrors*, p. 3.

26. Ida B. Wells to Frederick Douglass, 17 October 1892, Frederick Douglass Papers (hereafter FD Papers).

27. McFeely, ibid., p. 296; *New York Age*, quoted in the *Cleveland Gazette*, 10 September 1892.

28. T. Thomas Fortune to Frederick Douglass, 21 May 1891, FD Papers.

29. Ibid., 15 May 1891, FD Papers.

30. Ferdinand L. Barnett to Frederick Douglass, 10 August 1891; Frederick Douglass to Ferdinand L. Barnett, 13 August 1891, FD Papers.

31. Frederick Douglass, "Lynch Law in the South," pp. 21, 24. Also see McFeely, ibid., p. 361, for additional commentary on the Douglass article. David Blight's *Race and Reunion* provides an insightful study of Douglass's views and rhetoric regarding the exigency of both regions to live up to its values of liberty and democracy.

32. Douglass, ibid., p. 17.

33. *Bee*, 15 August 1891.

34. *New York Sun*, 5 June 1887; E. M. Hewlett to Frederick Douglass, 22 February 1893, FD Papers. See McFeely, ibid., especially pp. 366–367, for information on Douglass's domestic life. Also see Maria Diedrich, *Love Across Color Lines*, for the most comprehensive discussion of Douglass's previous romantic relationships with two white women, Julia Griffiths and Ottilie Assing, while he was still married to Anna Douglass. Assing's relationship with Douglass extended over twenty-five years. Soon after learning of his intention to marry Helen Pitts, Assing, suffering from cancer, committed suicide. She left Douglass a trust fund in her will.

35. Wells, *Crusade*, p. 73.

36. *Bee*, 22, 29 October 1892; McFeely, ibid., p. 362; Wells, ibid., p. 82.

37. The Oberlin Washingtonians included Anna Julia Cooper, who was in Terrell's graduating class; and Mary Jane Patterson, whose graduation from Oberlin in the 1860s made her the first black woman to receive a BA degree from a predominantly white American college. The three women were among the group that established the Colored Women's League, which also included Helen A. Cook, member of one of the most distinguished families in Washington; Terrell, "I Remember Frederick Douglass," *Ebony Magazine*, October 1953. Reprinted in Jones, *Quest for Equality*, p. 338; Terrell, *Colored Woman in a White World*, pp. 107–108.

38. Anna Julia Cooper, *A Voice from the South*, pp. 31, 32. For further discussion of the text in the context of Wells's writings, see Hazel Carby, *Reconstructing Black Womanhood*, especially chap. 5; and Patricia A. Schecter, *Ida B. Wells and American Reform*, pp. 34–35.

39. For discussion of the issues around black exclusion from the fair, see Jeanne Weimann,

The Fair Women, pp. 103–124; Ann Massa, "Black Women in the 'White City'"; Elliott Rudwick and August Meier, "Black Man in the 'White City'"; Ferdinand Barnett to Mrs. Potter Palmer, 20 December 1891, Board of Lady Managers Papers, Chicago Historical Society.

40. *Memphis Commercial*, 15 December 1892.

41. *Topeka Weekly Call*, 8 January 1893; quote in Majors, *Noted Negro Women*, p. 192; *Freeman*, 25 February 1893; *Cleveland Gazette*, 11 February 1893.

42. Ida B. Wells to Albion Tourgée, 2 July 1892, Albion W. Tourgée Papers (hereafter AT Papers).

43. Ida B. Wells to Albion W. Tourgée, 10, 22 February 1893, AT Papers.

44. Albion W. Tourgée to Ida B. Wells, 4 March 1893, AT Papers.

45. Ferdinand L. Barnett to Albion W. Tourgée, 23 February, 4 March 1893, AT Papers.

46. Ibid., 4 March 1893, AT Papers.

47. Mary Church Terrell, "Introducing Ida Wells Barnett—To deliver an Address on Lynching ca. 1893," holograph mss. Mary Church Terrell Papers; Wells, *Crusade*, p. 83.

48. Massa, ibid., pp. 134, 334; Wells, *Crusade*, p. 83.

49. Ida B. Wells, *A Red Record*, p. 25.

50. Quoted in Wells, ibid., pp. 25–26.

51. Ibid., p. 27.

52. Williamson, *The Crucible of Race*, p. 186.

53. See Luker, *The Social Gospel in Black and White*, pp. 94–95; Williamson, *The Crucible of Race*, pp. 185–186; Dray, *At the Hands of Persons Unknown*, pp. 77–79; and Hale, *Making Whiteness*, pp. 207–209, for descriptions of the Henry Smith lynching. Hale emphasizes the "spectacle" and "commodity" aspects of the lynching.

54. Wells, *A Red Record*, pp. 26–27.

55. Quoted in Luker, ibid., pp. 98–99.

56. Luker, ibid., p. 95.

57. Francis J. Grimke, "The Anglo-American Pulpit and Southern Outrages," *Independent* 45 (22 June 1893): 844–845. Articles on the lynching debate included: Atticus Greene Haygood, "The Black Shadow in the South," *Forum* 16 (October 1893): 167–175; "Are We a Nation of Barbarians?" *Independent* 45 (28 September 1893): 1306; Benjamin Arnold Flower, "The Burning of Negroes in the South: A Protest and a Warning," *Arena* 7 (April 1893): 634–635; Joseph Cook, "New Black Codes at the South," *Our Day* 12 (July 1893): 14; the *Independent* 46 (1 February 1894) devoted a special issue to lynching; Lewis Harvie Blair, "Lynching as a Fine Art," *Our Day* 13 (July/August 1894): 307.

58. See Hale's *Making Whiteness*, chap. 5, for a discussion about the commodification of lynching in the late nineteenth century.

59. Ralph Luker, ibid., p. 88.

60. For more on Haygood, see Ralph Luker, ibid., especially pp. 20–24.

Chapter Ten: Light from a Human Torch

1. Bendroth, *Fundamentalists in the City*, pp. 104, 101, 20, 107.

2. Luker, *The Social Gospel in Black and White*, p. 1. The term, according to Luker, came into wide usage about 1899.

3. Ibid., pp. 2, 24–28. Quote from ibid, p. 25.

4. Wells, "Lynch Law in All Its Phases," p. 171, reprinted in Mildred Thompson, *Ida B. Wells-Barnett*.

5. Ibid., p. 181.

6. Ibid., p. 185.

7. Ibid., p. 187.

8. *Kansas City,* (*Mo.* and *Kan.*) *American Citizen,* 24 February 1893; *Indianapolis Freeman,* 25 February 1893.

9. Duster, ed. *Crusade for Justice,* p. 86 (hereafter, Wells, *Crusade*).

10. *Detroit Plaindealer,* 24 February 1893. *Washington Bee,* 29 April 1893; F. J. Loudin to Frederick Douglass, 6 March 1893. Frederick Douglass Papers, (hereafter, FD Papers).

11. *Atchison (KS) Blade,* 25 March 1893; *Topeka (KS) Weekly Call,* 26 March 1893.

12. *Cleveland Gazette,* 22 April 1893; *Indianapolis Freeman,* 25 March 1893; *Washington Bee,* 15 April 1893.

13. *Indianapolis Freeman,* 25 March 1893.

14. *New York Age,* 18 February 1893.

15. Joseph Banneker Adger to Frederick Douglass, 24 February 1893; Willietta Johnson to Frederick Douglass, 20 February 1893. FD Papers.

16. *New York Age,* 5 July 1890.

17. Ware, *Beyond the Pale,* p. 174; Catherine Impey to Albion W. Tourgée, 3 January 1893; 2 February 1893. Albion W. Tourgée Papers (hereafter AT Papers).

18. Isabella Fyvie Mayo, *Recollections of What I Saw, What I Lived Through, and What I Learned* (London: n.p., 1910), p. 18. Ms. Mayo wrote under the pen name of Edward Garrett.

19. Wells, *Crusade,* p. 85.

20. Ibid., p. 86.

21. Quoted in *Topeka Weekly Call,* 15 April 1893.

22. Wells, *Crusade,* p. 89.

23. For the description of the *Teutonic,* see *The Engineer* (August 2, 1889): 121–124.

24. Wells, *Crusade,* pp. 87, 88.

25. Ibid., pp. 89–90.

26. Ibid., pp. 90–91.

27. Ibid., pp. 92–93.

28. Ibid., pp. 92, 91; *Edinburgh Evening Gazette,* 1 May 1893; *Peterhead Sentinel and Buchan Journal,* 2 May 1893. Wells quotes much of these and other press accounts from overseas verbatim in her autobiography; Wells, *Crusade,* pp. 92–93.

29. Ibid, p. 104.

30. Ibid., pp. 104–105.

31. Catherine Impey to Albion W. Tourgée, 23 June 1893, AT Papers.

32. Wells, *Crusade,* p. 102; *Manchester Guardian,* 9 May 1893.

33. Catherine Impey to Albion W. Tourgée, 24 June 1893, AT Papers; Wells, *Crusade,* pp. 95–96; *The Newcastle Leader,* 10 May 1893; *Birmingham Daily Gazette,* 18 May 1893; *Birmingham Daily Post,* 19 May 1893.

34. Wells, *Crusade,* pp. 99–101.

35. Ibid., pp. 98, 101; Catherine Impey to Albion Tourgée, ibid.

36. Bordin, *Women and Temperance,* p. 159.

37. *New York Voice,* 23 October 1890; Wells, *Crusade,* pp.151–152. The Willard interview excerpts are quoted in this section of the autobiography.

38. Wells, *Crusade,* p. 151.

39. Ibid., p. 202. The journal Wells was referring to was the influential publication *Review of Reviews,* edited by W. T. Stead.

40. Wells, *Crusade,* pp. 111–112.

41. Ibid., p. 109–110.

42. Ibid., p. 113.

43. *Indianapolis Freeman*, 8 June 1893; *Memphis Appeal-Avalanche*, 23 April 1893 (hereafter, *Appeal-Avalanche*).

44. The 1893 antilynching laws, as others that would follow in the South, were not in response to protecting blacks but measures of political or economic expediency. In Georgia's case, the law, rarely enforced, was an effort by Democratic governor William Northen to neutralize the Populists who were gaining black votes by denouncing lynching. North Carolina's law was enforced once in 1918. Grant, "The Anti-Lynching Movement," pp. 68, 70.

45. *Kansas City (Mo.* and *Kan.)American Citizen*, 5 August 1893; *Indianapolis Freeman*, 5 August 1893.

46. John J. Finn, comp., *The Official Guide to the World's Columbian Exposition* (Chicago: The Columbia Guide Company, 1893), p. 137.

47. For more descriptions of the exposition, see Weimann, *The Fair Women*; Carr and Gurney, *Revisiting the White City*; and Miller, *City of the Century*.

48. Rydell, *All the World's a Fair*, p. 20.

49. Weimann, *The Fair Women* p. 269. For the origins of the exhibit, see Ann Massa, "Black Women in the White City," p. 335.

50. Loewenberg and Bogin, eds., *Black Women in Nineteenth-Century America*, p. 275. For fuller texts of the all of the speeches at the Congress of Representative Women, see May Wright Sewell, ed. *The World's Congress of Representative Women*.

51. Loewenberg and Bogin, ibid., pp. 270, 274.

52. Ibid., pp. 271, 270–271, 273.

53. Ibid., pp. 275–276.

54. Ibid., p. 274.

55. Ibid., p. 278.

56. Ibid., p. 329.

57. Ibid., p. 279.

58. Hale, *Making Whiteness*, pp. 151–152, 160–162.

59. Larson, *The Devil in the White City*, p. 236.

60. *New York Times*, 19 June 1893, quoted in Bederman, "'Civilization,' the Decline of Middle-Class Manliness," p. 11. Bederman's text is especially insightful regarding the race and gender implications of the Exposition and its relationship to Ida Wells's campaign in the British Isles. Also see Rydell's, *All the World's a Fair*, and his essay in *Revisiting the White City*, pp. 19–61, for comprehensive bibliographical sources, illustrations, and the best analysis of the myriad cultural implications of the exposition. Douglass, quoted in Rudwick and Meier, "Black Man in the 'White City,'" p. 359.

61. *Indianapolis Freeman*, 15 April 1893; quote in Rudwick and Meier, ibid., p. 360.

62. Ida B. Wells to Albion W. Tourgée, 1 July 1893, AT Papers.

63. *Chicago Daily Inter-Ocean*, 19 July 1893; Aked, "A Blot on a Free Republic," *Christian Literature and Review of the Churches*, p. 98.

64. *Chicago Daily Inter-Ocean*, 19 July 1893.

65. *Cleveland Gazette*, 15, 22, July 1893; *Indianapolis Freeman*, 29 July, 5 August 1893; *Atchison (KS) Blade*, 24 June 1893.

66. Quoted in McFeely, *Frederick Douglass*, pp. 370–371.

67. Wells, *Crusade*, pp. 118–119.

68. Ibid., p. 120.

69. *The Reason Why the Colored American Is Not in the World's Columbian Exposition*, p. 49 (reprinted in Trudier Harris, comp., *Selected Works of Ida B. Wells-Barnett*.)

70. Ibid., pp. 50–51.
71. Ibid., p. 61.
72. Ibid., pp. 73–74.
73. Ibid., pp. 116–137.
74. Ibid., pp. 92–116.
75. Ibid., pp. 78–79.
76. Ibid., pp. 80–85 (includes a word-by-word description of the lynching by the *Memphis Commercial*, 23 July 1893).
77. Ibid., p. 85.
78. Ibid., p. 137.
79. Wells, *Crusade*, pp. 121–124.
80. Isabella Fyvie Mayo to Ida B. Wells, 12 September 1893, Ida B. Wells Papers.
81. Ida B. Wells to Frederick Douglass, 6 April 1894, FD Papers; Wells, *Crusade*, p. 124.

Chapter Eleven : St. Joan and Old Man Eloquent

1. Duster, ed., *Crusade for Justice*, p. 125 (hereafter Wells, *Crusade*).
2. Douglass, *The Life and Times of Frederick Douglass*, p. 259; McFeely, *Frederick Douglass,* pp. 137–144; Logan and Winston, *American Negro Biography,* pp. 182–183; Ida B. Wells to Frederick Douglass, 6 April 1894, Frederick Douglass Papers (hereafter FD Papers).
3. Ware, *Beyond the Pale*, pp. 192–194; Fryer, *Staying Power*, pp. 277–279.
4. *Chicago Daily Inter-Ocean*, 13 August 1894 (hereafter *Inter-Ocean*).
5. On Aked, see *Los Angeles Times*, 15 August 1941 (obituary); Phillips, *A Kingdom on Earth*, p. 14.
6. Wells, *Crusade*, pp. 126–130; *Fraternity* (August 1894): 4; *Christian World* 38 (March 15, 1894): 187, quoted in Hutton, "The Rhetoric of Ida B. Wells," p. 65.
7. *Christian World*, ibid.
8. Wells, *Crusade*, pp. 126–127.
9. Ibid., p. 129; *Inter-Ocean*, 2 April 1894.
10. Wells, *Crusade*, p. 129.
11. *Liverpool Daily Post*, 12 March 1894.
12. Frederick Douglass to My British Friends, 6 October 1894, FD Papers.
13. Ida B. Wells to Frederick Douglass, 13 March 1894, FD Papers.
14. *Christian Register* 73 (April 12, 1894): 227; quoted in Crawford, "Ida B. Wells: Her Anti-Lynching Crusades in Britain and Repercussions from them in the United States," p. 10. Wells, *Crusade*, pp. 146–147; Hutton, ibid., p. 67.
15. Porter, *Critics of Empire*, p. 90, n. 3; *New York Times*, 29 April 1894; *Inter-Ocean*, 2 April 1894; Wells, *Crusade*, p. 130.
16. Quoted in the *Inter-Ocean*, 9 April 1894; Wells, *Crusade*, pp. 139–141.
17. *Inter-Ocean*, 9 April 1894; Wells, ibid., pp. 133–136.
18. *Manchester Guardian*, 30 March 1894; *Inter-Ocean*, 23 April 1894; Wells, ibid., pp. 143–146.
19. *Manchester Guardian*, 30 March 1894; quoted in *Inter-Ocean*, 23 April 1894; Wells, ibid., p. 150.
20. *Woman's Era* (March 1894): 4.
21. Wells, ibid., p. 149.
22. Frederick Douglass to Ida B. Wells, 27 March 1894, FD Papers; *Liverpool Daily Post*, 12 March 1894.
23. Charles S. Morris to Frederick Douglass, 3 October 1893, FD Papers.
24. Frederick Douglass to Ida B. Wells, ibid.

25. Frederick Douglass to C. F. Aked, 27 March 1894; Douglass, *Lessons of the Hour*, 1894, FD Papers.

26. *Kansas City (Mo.* and *Kan.) American Citizen*, 15 December 1893; Ida B. Wells to Frederick Douglass, 20 December 1893. Ida was hoping that Douglass would punish Taylor, as she thought he had H. C. C. Astwood, a black Democrat who accused Douglass of derailing his efforts to attain a diplomatic post. Charles Douglass, Frederick's son, publicly accused Astwood of bigamy, among other charges. See clipping "The Case of Mr. Astwood," in the FD Papers in which Douglass denies having a hand in the exposure of Astwood. The clipping carries no precise citation, but Douglass's letter to the editor is dated 15 September 1893. FD Papers.

27. See, for example, U.S. Senator George F. Hoar to Frederick Douglass, 16 May 1894, affirmatively answering Douglass's inquiry that he was supporting Taylor for the position; C. H. J. Taylor to Frederick Douglass, 16 April 1894, thanks Douglass for his supportive words in commending him to the U.S. Senate; regarding the support of President Cleveland, see C. H. J. Taylor to Frederick Douglass, 2 May 1894; C. H. J. Taylor to Frederick Douglass, 24 May 1894, thanks Douglass for his help in getting the nomination. FD Papers.

28. Ida B. Wells to Frederick Douglass, 6 April 1894, FD Papers.

29. Douglass's words are recounted in a letter Wells wrote to him. Ida B.Wells to Frederick Douglass, 6 May 1894, FD Papers.

30. Wells, *Crusade*, pp. 192–193.

31. Ida B. Wells to Mr. Axon [April 1894] William E. Axon Papers, John Rylands Library, Manchester, England, quoted in Patricia Schechter, *Ida B. Wells-Barnett & American Reform*, p. 100.

32. *Inter-Ocean*, 19 May 1894.

33. Ibid., 28 May 1894; Wells, ibid., pp. 161–164; Ellen Richardson to Frederick Douglass, 22 April 1894, FD Papers.

34. *Dictionary of National Biography*, 1922–1930, pp. 188–190. Wells actually called John Clifford the country's leading *living* Baptist as Charles Haddon Spurgeon (1834–1892) had held that mantle before his death. Wells, *Crusade*, p. 166, n. 2; *Inter-Ocean*, 28 May, 4 June 1894; Jones, *The Christian Socialist Revival*, pp. 330–331.

35. Wells, ibid., p. 167; *Inter-Ocean*, 28 May 1894.

36. Ida B. Wells to Mrs. Frederick Douglass, 26 April 1894, FD Papers.

37. Ida B. Wells to Frederick Douglass, ibid.; *London Daily Chronicle*, 28 April 1894.

38. *New York Times*, 30 April 1894; *Indianapolis Freeman*, 28 April 1894.

39. *London Daily Chronicle*, 28 April 1894; *Independent*, 3 May 1894, p. 560.

40. Ida B. Wells to Frederick Douglass, 10 May 1894, FD Papers; F. L. Barnett to Sen. Willam E. Chandler, 8 May 1894, William Eaton Chandler Papers, Library of Congress.

41. The pro-woman-suffrage Woman's Liberal Federation was an organization that had broken off from the Woman's Liberal Association over the issue of securing the vote for women. Wells recounted the history of the two organizations and added that both had been helpful to her campaign. However, describing a reception hosted by the more conservative association, which included such society luminaries as the Countess of Carlisle, she characterized it as "a splendid school from which to graduate into the stronger, more vigorous, and active federation." *Inter-Ocean*, 4 June 1894.

42. Ibid., 13 August 1894.

43. Ibid., 4 June 1894.

44. *London Daily Chronicle*, 10 May 1894. Quoted in Hutton, "The Rhetoric of Ida B. Wells," p. 69; Wells, *Crusade*, p. 209.

45. Wells, ibid., p. 203.

46. *Indianapolis Freeman*, 28 April 1894; *New York Times*, 30 April 1894; *Westminster Gazette*, 10 May 1894.

47. Quoted in Wells, ibid., p. 208.

48. Ibid., p. 210.

49. Ibid., p. 209.

50. *Christian Commonwealth*, 24 May 1894; *Inter-Ocean*, 23 June 1894.

51. Lady Henry Somerset to Frederick Douglass, 22 May 1894, FD Papers.

52. Frederick Douglass to R.A. Armstrong, 22 May 1894; Frederick Douglass to C. F. Aked, 22 May 1894, FD Papers.

53. *Memphis Commercial*, 26 May 1894.

54. Ibid., 6 May, 4, 11 June 1894.

55. Helen Bright Clark to Frederick Douglass, 15 June 1894; Frederick Douglass to Helen Bright Clark, 19 July 1894, FD Papers.

56. *Topeka Weekly Call*, 5 June 1894; *Manchester Guardian*, 19 June 1894; Wells, *Crusade*, pp. 199–200.

57. Quoted in Wells, ibid., p. 184, and *Inter-Ocean*, 7 July 1894; *Christian Register*, 10 May 1894.

58. Quoted in *New York Age*, 21 June 1894; Wells, ibid., pp. 179–180.

59. *Inter-Ocean*, 25 June 1894; Wells, ibid., pp. 174–175.

60. *Inter-Ocean*, ibid.; Wells, ibid., pp. 174–180. Information about William Penn Nixon in *Memphis Appeal-Avalanche*, 4 May 1894.

61. *Memphis Commercial*, 1 June 1894; *New York Times*, 1 June 1894.

62. *New York Age*, 19 June 1894.

63. *Indianapolis Freeman*, 28 June 1894; quoted in *Cleveland Gazette*, 9 June 1894.

64. *Indianapolis Freeman*, 24 June, 14 July 1894.

65. Wells, ibid., p. 214.

66. Ibid., pp. 215–217.

67. *New York Age*, 21 June 1894; Wells, ibid, p. 214; *Inter-Ocean*, 4 August 1894.

68. *Fraternity*, 4 August 1894, p. 6.

69. Ida B. Wells to Frederick Douglass, 3 June 1894, FD Papers.

Chapter Twelve: Exile No More

1. *Christian Recorder*, 2 August 1894; *New York Age*, 12 July 1894; *Indianapolis Freeman*, 21 July 1894.

2. John Hope to the Tolliver Sisters & Miss Mary E. Jackson, 14 September 1894, John Hope Papers, Atlanta University; *Topeka Weekly Call*, 4 August, 1894.

3. Hope, ibid.

4. *Topeka Weekly Call*, ibid.

5. *New York Age*, ibid.

6. *Topeka Weekly Call*, 15 July 1894.

7. Ibid., 21 July 1894; *New York Age*, 26 July 1894.

8. *New York Age*, 16 August 1894.

9. Duster, ed., *Crusade for Justice*, p. 218 (hereafter, Wells, *Crusade*).

10. Ibid., p. 219.

11. Earhart, *Frances Willard*, p. 351; *Cleveland Gazette*, 28 July 1894.

12. *New York Times*, 2 August 1894; Wells, *Crusade*, pp. 226–227.

13. *New York Times*, 27 July 1894.

14. *Christian Recorder*, 9 August 1894.

15. *New York Daily Tribune*, 30 July 1894; *New York Sun*, 30 July 1894; *New York Times*, 30

July 1894; *Chicago Daily Inter-Ocean*, 4 August 1894 (hereafter *Inter-Ocean*); *Indianapolis Freeman*, 25 August 1894.

16. *New York Daily Tribune*, 30 July 1894.

17. Wells, *Crusade*, pp. 220–221. Wells mistakenly identifies Charles A. Dana as Richard Henry Dana.

18. *New York Times*, 2, 4 August 1894; *Indianapolis Freeman*, 1 September 1894.

19. Wells, *Crusade*, pp. 232, 231. Wells states that the joint appearance occurred in November, in Providence, Rhode Island, but it is more likely that their meeting was earlier and in Philadelphia. Wells, who mentions in the autobiography that her own source of clippings was destroyed, is on occasion incorrect with her chronology of lectures and travel dates. Wells also wrote to Douglass asking to see him on July 24. Ida B. Wells to Frederick Douglass, 23 July 1894, Frederick Douglass Papers.

20. *New York Age*, 16 August 1894; Wells, *Crusade*, p. 222.

21. Wells, *Crusade*, p. 238.

22. Ibid., p. 225; *Inter-Ocean*, 8 August 1894.

23. "Ida B. Wells in England: An Address Adopted by a Mass Meeting of Afro-American Citizens of St. Paul, Minnesota, June 11, 1894, Under Auspices of Ladies' Home Circle," Albion Tourgée Papers; *Indianapolis Freeman*, 4 August 1894; *Christian Recorder*, 2 August 1894. The formulation of Martin Delany's *The Condition, Emigration and Destiny of the Colored People of the United States, Politically Considered* (1852) included seeing African-Americans as a "nation within a nation." Tillman poem in *Christian Recorder*, 5 July 1894; *Topeka Weekly Call*, 22 September 1894; *The Woman's Era* 1 (August 1894): 1; *The Literary Digest* IX (11 August 1894): 1.

24. *Inter-Ocean*, 8 August 1894.

25. *New York Age*, 16 August 1894.

26. Ibid.

27. *New York Times*, 11 September 1894, *Congressional Record*, 53rd Congress, 2nd Session, XXVI, pt. 8 (3 August 1894): 8188, 8206; *New York Age*, 16, 23 August, 1894; *Fraternity* (September 1894): 5.

28. Wells, *Crusade*, pp. 227, 238.

29. *New York Age*, 13 September 1894; *Indianapolis Freeman*, 1 September 1894; Wells, *Crusade*, p. 219.

30. *New York Age*, 11 September 1894.

31. *Commercial Appeal*, 2, 4 September 1894. The paper first appeared under that name on July 1, 1894, after the courts forced the *Appeal-Avalanche* to be sold because of indebtedness. The owner of the *Commercial* purchased it and called it the *Commercial Appeal*.

32. *Commercial Appeal*, 4 September 1894. The names of the other slain men were Warner Williams, John Hays, Graham White, Robert Haynes, and Ed Hall. In the *Commercial Appeal*, 8 September 1894, Hawkins's white lawyer called the arresting officer a "nigger" who was bribed to do the deed; *New York Age*, 11 September 1894.

33. Ibid., 22 September 1894.

34. Quoted in the *Cleveland Gazette*, 8 September 1894.

35. *Commercial Appeal*, quoted in the *New York Times*, 23 November 1894; *New York World*, quoted in the *Washington Star*, 11 September 1894.

36. *New York Times*, 11 September 1894.

37. *Topeka Weekly Call*, 22 September 1894; *National Baptist World*, 28 September 1894.

38. *New York Times*, 23 November 1894; *Norfolk Landmark*, 9 September 1894.

39. Quoted in the *London Times*, 6 October 1894; *Norfolk Weekly Landmark*, 11 September 1894; *New York Times*, 10 September 1894.

40. For example, see Ferdinand Barnett's letter, dated September 22, to Florence Balgarnie,

telling her that the committee's work was largely responsible for the attitude expressed by Memphis officials regarding the Kerrville lynching. Letter reprinted in the *London Times*, 7 October 1894.

41. *Commercial Appeal*, 6 September 1894.

42. Ibid., 8 September 1894.

43. Ibid., 9, 17 September 1894.

44. *St. Paul Appeal*, 29 September 1894; *Washington Post*, 12 September 1894.

45. Editorial, *Cleveland Gazette*, 15 September 1894, quoting Albion Tourgée's "Bystander's Column"; Miller, *City of the Century*, p. 545; *Inter-Ocean*, 8 September 1894; *Commercial Appeal*, 5 September 1894.

46. *Indianapolis Freeman*, 8 September 1894; *New York Age*, 11 September 1894.

47. *New York Age,* 11 September 1894.

48. Ibid., 13 September 1894; *Indianapolis Freeman;* 8 September 1894; *Commercial Appeal*, 22 September 1894.

49. *New York Age*, 4 October 1894; *(Witchita, Kan.) People's Friend*, 28 September 1894.

50. *New York Age*, 4 October 1894.

51. James C. Peebles, "A History of Armour Institute of Technology," p. 7. Unpublished manuscript, The Carl F. Shepard Memorial Library, Illinois College of Optometry, Chicago, Illinois.

52. *New York Age,* 4 October 1894; Wells, *Crusade*, pp. 233–234.

53. *Norfolk Weekly Landmark*, 13 September 1894; *National Baptist World*, 28 September 1894; *New York Age*, 4 October 1894.

54. James, ed., *Notable American Women*, pp. 635–636; Schulz and Hast, eds., *Women Building Chicago*, pp. 273–276; also, Wheeler, "Conflict in Illinois," pp. 96–97.

55. Wells, *Crusade*, pp. 235–238.

56. Wells, ibid., pp. 234–236; *New York Age*, 20 December 1894.

57. Earhart, *Frances Willard*, pp. 348–349.

58. *Commercial Appeal*, 16 November 1894; Wells, *The Red Record*, pp. 86–87.

59. Wells, *A Red Record*, p. 87.

60. Bordin, *Woman and Temperance*, pp. 140–144; *Commercial*, 8 May 1894; *Inter-Ocean*, 5 June 1894.

61. *Inter-Ocean*, 17 November 1894.

62. *Cleveland Gazette*, 24 November 1894.

63. Ibid.

64. *Inter-Ocean*, 24 November 1894; Ida B. Wells to Judge A. W. Tourgée, 27 November 1894, Albion Tourgée Papers (hereafter AT Papers).

65. *New York Age*, 20 December 1894; *New York Times*, 11 December 1894; statistics quoted in Wells, *The Red Record*, p. 19; Wells, *Crusade*, p. 220; Luker, *Social Gospel in Black and White*, p. 108.

66. *Commercial Appeal*, 15 December 1894; *New York Age*, 20 December 1894.

67. *New York Age,* ibid.

68. *Indianapolis Freeman*, 22 December 1894.

69. Frances Willard to Albion Tourgée, 21 December 1894, AT Papers.

70. Wells, *A Red Record,* pp. 87–88.

71. *London Times*, 9 November 1894.

72. Ware, *Beyond the Pale*, p. 210.

73. Isabel Somerset to Mrs. Cheney, 9 February 1895, Sophia Smith Collection, Anti-Lynching File.

74. Ida's aunt Fanny died in Sacramento, California, on August 1, 1908. The information was provided by Mr. Phil Reader, a historical and genealogical researcher specializing in

the central coast of California. *New York Age*, 22 November, 20 December 1894; *Indianapolis Freeman*, 7 July 1894.

75. Wells, *Crusade*, p. 238; quote in the *Indianapolis Freeman*, 27 April 1895.
76. *Washington Star*, 21 February 1895.
77. *Indianapolis Freeman*, 30 March 1895; Wells, *Crusade*, p. 232.
78. Wells, *Crusade*, p. 238.

Chapter Thirteen: "Let Us Confer Together"

1. Pierce, *History of Chicago*, II, p. 6; Miller, *City of the Century*, p. 177.
2. Pierce, ibid., p. 22; Spear, *Black Chicago*, p. 4.
3. Spear, *Black Chicago*, pp. 6, 11.
4. Spear, ibid., pp. 5, 6. The spelling of Du Sable's name varies; I have used the spelling cited in Logan and Winston, *Dictionary of Negro American Biography*, p. 207.
5. *Colored Men's Professional and Business Directory*, quoted from Kreiling, "The Making of Racial Identities in the Black Press," p. 110; *Indianapolis Freeman*, 30 August 1890.
6. For the history of Provident Hospital and the biography of Williams, see Buckler, *Daniel Hale Williams*, and Harry Lemat, "Provident Hospital and Training School," *The Voice* (December 1906): 559–561. For the history of black women in the nursing profession, see Hine, *Black Women in White*. For information on Reynolds, see the *Chicago Daily News*, 21 January 1961.
7. Harlan, *The Booker T. Washington Papers*, vol. 6, p. 275; *Memphis Appeal-Avalanche*, 4 May 1894; *Cleveland Gazette*, 31 May 1890; R. E. Moore, *History of Bethel A.M.E. Church* (Chicago: Fraternal Press, 1919), pp. 39–43.
8. Wells, "Two Christmas Days: A Holiday Story," *AME Zion Church Quarterly* (January 1894): 129–140, reprinted in Thompson, *Ida B. Wells-Barnett*, pp. 225–234. Some of the biographical information concerning Ferdinand Lee Barnett, Jr., including his birth date is contradictory. He was born February 18, 1852, according to the date on his headstone, in Nashville, Tennessee, and he attended Chicago Central High School, graduating in 1874; taught for two years; and received his law degree in 1878. Albert Nelson Marquis, *The Book of Chicagoans*, p. 37.
9. *National Conference of Colored Men of the United States Proceedings*, Nashville, Tennessee, May 6–9, 1879 (Washington: Rufus H. Darby, 1879), p. 83.
10. See Drake and Cayton, *Black Metropolis*, pp. 48–49, for samples of *Conservator* editorials bemoaning young Chicago blacks on "the road to ruin" and wearing "gaudy" attire. The author is indebted to Donald Duster for sharing undated copies of 1870s clippings from the *Conservator*, which include Barnett's pro-suffrage views.
11. Wells, *A Red Record*, pp. 19, 95.
12. Ibid., p. 11.
13. Ibid., pp. 12–13, pp. 80–90.
14. Ibid., p. 7.
15. Grant, "The Anti-Lynching Movement," pp. 66–69.
16. For Wells's recounting of the threat to southern investment, see *The Red Record*, pp. 76–79. For a statement on how lynchings were negatively impacting immigration, see the statement of the *Richmond (VA) Planet*, quoted in the *(Witchita, Kan.) People's Friend*, 7 September 1894. See Cutler, *Lynch Law*, p. 171, for yearly statistics of lynchings between 1882 and 1903.
17. John Jacks to Florence Balgarnie, 19 March 1895. The author is grateful to Wilson J. Moses for sharing this letter. Wells, *Crusade*, p. 242.
18. *Rochester Union and Advertiser*, 29 March 1895.

19. Wells, *Crusade*, pp. 227–228; *Rochester Herald*, 8, 22 April 1895. The event was also described in Harper, who noted the subsequent national coverage in *The Life and Work of Susan B. Anthony*, vol. 2, p. 815.

20. Wells, ibid., p. 229. For discussions of the suffrage debate, see Terborg-Penn, *African-American Women in the Struggle for the Vote*, pp. 8–10; Giddings, *When and Where I Enter*, pp. 64–68; Ellen Carol DuBois, *Elizabeth Cady Stanton, Susan B. Anthony: Correspondence, Writings, Speeches* (New York: Schocken Books, 1981), pp. 90–94.

21. Wells, ibid., pp. 229–230.

22. Ibid., p. 230. The signed book is in the possession of Donald Duster, grandson of Ida B. Wells-Barnett.

23. McFeely, *Frederick Douglass*, pp. 381–382.

24. Ida B. Wells to Emma Tourgée, 19 May 1895, Albion Tourgée Papers (hereafter AT Papers).

25. Olsen, *Carpetbagger's Crusade*, pp. 312–313.

26. Ibid., pp. 322, 318.

27. Ibid., p. 318; *Indianapolis Freeman*, 8 June 1895.

28. Albion Tourgée to Ferdinand Barnett, 16 September 1891, AT Papers.

29. Ida B. Wells to Mrs. Tourgée, 19 May 1895, AT Papers.

30. Ida thanks the Tourgées for the gift in a letter. Ida B. Wells to Mrs. Tourgée, 26 August 1895, AT Papers.

31. *New York Times*, 25 June 1895; *Chicago Tribune*, 28 July 1895.

32. Wells, *Crusade*, pp. 239–240; *Indianapolis Freeman*, 7 July 1895.

33. Wells, *Crusade*, p. 241; Harper, ibid., p. 813.

34. Wells, ibid., p. 242.

35. Wells, ibid., p. 238; *Indianapolis Freeman*, 11 June 1892. The friend of Ferdinand's was Stella Reed Garnett, who worked in the *Conservator* office with Ferdinand. When she asked him about his intentions to marry a younger woman he had been dating, Barnett replied that though the woman was a "dear sweet child," he had not forgotten his first wife and added: "When I do think of marriage it will be to a woman—one who can help me in my career." Stella Reed Garnett, "A Chapter in the Life of Ida B. Wells," 23 April 1951, in a letter: Stella Reed Garnett to Alfreda Duster, 26 April 1951, Ida B. Wells Papers.

36. Records about the financial state of the paper, or even Ferdinand's Barnett's financial relationship to it, are difficult to glean. Ferdinand was the main inspiration and had a financial interest in the *Conservator* when it first appeared on January 5, 1878. At that point James E. Henderson, a physician, and Abram Hall, a newspaperman, were also associated with the paper. In 1881, Barnett broke his association with the paper and founded the *Right Way* in Evanston, Illinois. By 1882, Barnett again had an interest in the *Conservator*. This time his partners were Alexander Clark, and his son Alexander C. Clark, the former of whom remained with the paper when Ferdinand, due to the demands of his law office, left the paper again in the mid-1880s. In March 1887, the elder Clark sold the *Conservator* to the Conservator Company, which probably also included Barnett. Clark died in 1891, while serving as the U.S. minister to Liberia. Unlike most black papers of the period—which had their own print shops and made extra income by doing job printing on the side—the *Conservator* did not have its own press. Kreiling, "The Making of Racial Identities in the Black Press," pp. 125, 129, 131; *New York Age*, 27 June 1891. On the *Conservator* not having a press, see the comments of Stella Garnett, ibid.

37. *Indianapolis Freeman*, 19 January 1889; Kreiling, "The Making of Racial Identities," pp. 129, 131, 132.

38. *Conservator,* 18 November 1882.

39. Unpublished interview, Alfreda Duster, 1964, pp. 19–21, conducted by Donald Duster. I am grateful to Mr. Duster for sharing this interview; interview, Alfreda Duster, 8, 9 March 1978, p. 119, Black Women Oral History Project. The Barnetts appeared to have returned to Chicago in 1869, according to Marquis, ibid. p. 17, although there are less standard references that give other years as the date they returned. The elder Barnetts' marriage date of 1847 is cited in an invitation to their fiftieth wedding anniversary, 1847–1897, found in vertical files of the Amistad Research Center, Tulane University, New Orleans. It appears that Ferdinand, Sr., died sometime soon after 1897; Martha, according to Alfreda Duster, died about 1909.

40. Unpublished interview, Alfreda Duster, conducted by Dorothy Sterling, 22–25 March 1976. The author is grateful to Mary Helen Washington for sharing this interview.

41. Quoted in Scruggs, *Women of Distinction,* p. xi.

42. *Woman's Era,* 24 March 1894. p. 4; Cooper, *A Voice from the South,* pp. 68–69.

43. Quoted in Harlan, *Booker T. Washington, The Making of a Black Leader,* p. 183; Margaret James Murray to Booker T. Washington, Oct–Nov 1 1891, in Harlan, *The Booker T. Washington Papers,* vol. 3, pp. 177–178.

44. There is a slight discrepancy in terms of Margaret Murray Washington's age. See Harlan, ibid., pp. 180–181.

45. *Woman's Era,* July 1895 , p. 5.

46. *A History of the Club Movement Among the Colored Women of the United States of America, as contained in the Minutes of the Conventions, held in Boston, July 29, 30, 31, 1895, and of the National Federation of Afro-American Women, held in Washington, D.C., July 20, 21, 22, 1896 (1902)* (hereafter *History*), pp. 4–5. A copy of this document is found in the Ida B. Wells Papers.

47. Jones, *Quest for Equality,* p. 320; Salem, *To Better Our World,* pp. 18–20; *Woman's Era,* June 1894, p. 5; Williams, "The Club Movement Among Colored Women in America," p. 397; *History,* p. 4.

48. Ibid.

49. Ibid.; *Woman's Era,* July 1895, p. 1.

50. Wells, ibid., p. 242.

51. *Anti-Caste,* June–July 1895, p. 6; *Cleveland Gazette,* 29 June 1895.

52. *Woman's Era,* July 1895, p. 6; ibid., p. 12.

53. Ibid.

54. *Chicago Evening Journal,* 1 November 1895.

55. *History,* ibid., pp. 12, 32.

56. *Woman's Era,* March 1894 p. 9; *History,* ibid., pp. 32–33; Salem, ibid., p. 22.

57. *Woman's Era,* April 1895, p. 14.

58. *Memphis Commercial,* 11 September 1894; *History,* ibid., p. 14.

59. *History,* ibid., pp. 13–14T, 15, 19.

60. Quoted in Harlan, *Booker T. Washington, The Making of a Black Leader,* pp. 180, 188.

61. Logan and Winston, *American Negro Biography,* p. 634; Harlan, ibid, p.161.

62. Harlan, ibid, p.161.

63. Harlan, ibid., pp. 213, 218–219. The speech is quoted in full in Washington, *Up From Slavery,* pp. 218–225.

64. Fortune quoted in Thornbrough, *T. Thomas Fortune,* p.162; *New York World* quoted in Harlan, *The Booker T. Washington Papers,* vol. 4, p. 3; Harlan, *Booker T. Washington, The Making of a Black Leader,* p. 210; Grover Cleveland to Booker T. Washington, 6 October 1895, in Harlan, *Booker T. Washintgton Papers,* vol. 4, p. 30.

65. Quotes in Harlan, *Booker T. Washington, The Making of a Leader*, p. 225.

66. Ibid., pp. 225–227.

67. Ibid., p. 226.

68. *Woman's Era*, January 1896, pp. 2–7; February 1896, pp. 2–5, 9; Moses, *The Golden Age of Black Nationalism*, pp. 122–124.

Chapter Fourteen: Undivided Duty

1. Duster, ed., *Crusade for Justice*, p. 251 (hereafter, Wells, *Crusade*).

2. Ibid., p. 250; Interview, Alfreda Duster, 8, 9 March 1978, p. 119, Black Women Oral History Project.

3. Ibid., pp. 252, 243. There were differing views about the issue of marital sex for the purpose of pleasure as well as procreation in the period. At least one African American arbiter of moral thought, Henry D. Northrup, averred that intercourse for the sole purpose of having children put a woman's love "on the pure." For increasingly independent women, such ideas produced responses like "voluntary motherhood," which proposed that wives were obligated to have sex with their husbands only when they wished to become pregnant. Penile withdrawal before orgasm was another method. Wells-Barnett consulted at least one Catholic priest, and one of Ida's colleagues at the *Conservator*, Lincoln Charles Valle, an editor of the paper for a period in the late nineties, was a prominent black Catholic who organized the first Colored Catholic Congress and assisted in establishing several churches. Northrup, *The College of Life*, p. 133; Kreiling, "The Making of Racial Identities in the Black Press," p. 132.

4. Ibid., p. 248.

5. Ibid., pp. 248–249.

6. *Plessy v. Ferguson*, 163 U.S., p. 537, quoted in Logan, *The Betrayal of the Negro*, p. 112. For a succinct analysis of Albion Tourgée's reaction, see Olsen, *Carpetbagger's Crusade*, pp. 329–331. Also see additional commentary from Logan, ibid., pp. 83–84, 111–113.

7. *Washington Bee*, 14 November 1896.

8. Ware, *Beyond the Pale*, pp. 210–211.

9. Hine et al., eds. *Black Women in America*, II, pp. 1176–1180.

10. *Records*, p. 38.

11. *Records*, pp. 38, 44.

12. Ibid., p. 45.

13. Ibid, pp. 44–45.

14. Terrell, *Colored Woman in a White World*, p. 151; Salem, ibid., p. 27; *Woman's Era*, July 1896, p. 8; January 1897, p. 2.

15. *Records*, ibid., pp. 55, 39.

16. Ibid., pp. 47, 51, 53.

17. *Washington Bee*, 25 July 1896; *Woman's Era*, August–September 1896, p. 10.

18. Wells, *Crusade*, p. 243; *Records*, ibid., p. 54.

19. Ibid.

20. Wells, ibid., pp. 244, 245.

21. Olsen, ibid., pp. 325–326; *Cleveland Gazette*, 29 August 1896; Logan, ibid., p. 88.

22. Quotes from Logan, ibid., p. 87; Allen Nevins and Henry Steele Commager, *A Short History of the United States* (New York: Random House, Modern Library Edition, 1969), p. 412.

23. *Indianapolis Freeman*, 2 January 1897; 19 December 1896.

24. *Indianapolis Freeman*, 30 May, 4 January 1896.

25. *Indianapolis Freeman*, 29 February 1896; *Cleveland Gazette*, 12, 19 June, 3 July 1897; 22, 29 October 1898; Olsen, *Carpetbagger's Crusade*, pp. 325–326.

26. *Chicago Daily Inter-Ocean*, 27 July 1897.

27. *Cleveland Gazette*, 23 October 1897.

28. Ibid.

29. Ibid.

30. *Star of Zion*, 24 June 1897; *Cleveland Gazette*, 12 December 1899. The county commissioners appealed, and in 1899, it was reported that the court upheld the commissioners and that Mitchell's attorneys would appeal. *Cleveland Gazette*, 4 February 1899.

31. Samuel May to Booker T. Washington, 22 July 1897, Harlan, *Booker T. Washington Papers*, vol. 4, pp. 314–315 (hereafter Harlan, *BTWP*).

32. "Extracts from an Address in Indianapolis," Harlan, ibid., pp. 322–323.

33. *Indianapolis Freeman*, 27 August 1897.

34. Ibid., 31 July 1897. In 1872 the ratio of black arrests to total arrests (1 to 33) was two and a half times as great as the ratio of the black population to the total population; in 1896 the ratio of black arrests to total arrests (1 to 10) was seven times as great as the ratio of the Negro population to the total population. The ratio in Chicago was two to seven times higher than the other cities in the study. Work, "Crime Among Negroes of Chicago," *Journal of American Sociology* 6 (September 1900): 204–223; *The Nation*, 1 July 1897, pp. 6–7.

35. *Chicago Times Herald*, 21 November 1897.

36. *Indianapolis Freeman*, 30 January 1897; Davis, *The Story of the Illinois Federation of Colored Women's Clubs*, p. 2. The seven black women's clubs were: the Ida B. Wells Club; Phyllis [*sic*] Wheatley Club; Civic League; Progressive Circle of King's Daughters; Ideal Women's Club; G.O.P Elephant Club; and the Julia Gaston Club.

37. Jones, *Quest for Equality*, pp. 24–25; Mary Church Terrell, "The Duty of the National Association of Colored Women to the Race," *AME Church Review* (January 1900): 340–354, reprinted in Jones, ibid., pp. 139–150. For articles in black publications about the issue, see Annie E. Tucker, "Formation of Child Character," *Colored American Magazine* (February 1901): 258–261; Mrs. J. W. E. Bowen, "The Nation's Nursery," *Voice of the Negro* (March 1904): 113–115.

38. Wells, *Crusade*, p. 249.

39. *Cleveland Gazette*, 23 October 1897; *Indianapolis Freeman*, 16, 31 October 1897; *Topeka Weekly Call*, 2 September 1895. Few issues of the *Conservator* during the period of Wells-Barnett's editorship appear to exist. Excerpts in other papers include an article about the killing of a young boy by a white woman who accused the boy of stealing pears from her father's garden (*Indianapolis Freeman*, 7 March 1896); a killing of a black school teacher by a white teacher after a quarrel about admission of black students to the school (*Indianapolis Freeman*, 11 July 1896); an item about AME bishop Benjamin Arnett's losing his home in a fire (*Indianapolis Freeman*, 8 August 1896); and a defense of the Reverends H. T. Johnson and D. A. Graham who were libeled by Monroe Majors (*Indianapolis Freeman*, 8 May 1897).

40. Wells, *Crusade*, pp. 251, 252.

41. *Chicago Tribune*, 23, 24 February 1898.

42. Ibid., 23, 24 February 1898; *Indianapolis Freeman*, 5 March 1898.

43. *Indianapolis Freeman*, 5 March 1898; *Chicago Tribune*, 26 February 1898.

44. *Chicago Tribune*, 24 February 1898.

45. Ibid.

46. Ibid., 21, 24, 26 February 1898.

47. Ibid., 21 March 1898; *Indianapolis Freeman*, 26 March 1898.

48. Wells, *Crusade*, p. 252.

49. *Cleveland Gazette*, 9 April 1898.

50. *Chicago Tribune*, 22, 21 March 1898.

51. *Washington, D.C. Colored American*, 26 March, 19 April 1898 (hereafter *Colored American*); Wells, *Crusade*, p. 253.

52. *Indianapolis Freeman*, 15 May 1897.

53. Gatewood, *Smoked Yankees*, pp. 181–182; Franklin, *From Slavery to Freedom*, p. 299; Wells, *Crusade*, p. 254.

54. Wells, *Crusade*, p. 255.

55. Ibid., pp. 255–256; Thornbrough, *T. Thomas Fortune*, p. 180; ibid., n. 4; *Indianapolis Freeman*, 1 October 1898.

56. Thornbrough, ibid., pp. 172–175.

57. Ibid., p. 171.

58. *Indianapolis Freeman*, 1 October 1898; *Salt Lake City* (later *Chicago*), *Broad Ax*, 27 March 1897; Wells, ibid., p. 256.

Chapter Fifteen: Mobocracy in America

1. Senator Orville Platt of Connecticut told his colleagues that "Among Christian, thoughtful people," the war and the control of the islands was "akin to that which has maintained the missionary work of the last century in foreign lands." Quoted in Blum, *Reforging the White Republic*, p. 233.

2. Dalton, *Theodore Roosevelt*, p. 174; quote in the *Springfield (IL) Record*, 26 November 1898 (hereafter *Illinois Record*).

3. Tingley, *The Structuring of a State*, pp. 3–7.

4. *Illinois Record*, 22 October 1898. *The Nation*, 21 September 1899, p. 216.

5. *Illinois Record*, ibid.; *St. Paul Appeal*, 15 October 1898.

6. *Illinois Record*, ibid, In 1901, Tanner lost the nomination to sitting Senator Shelby Cullom; *The Nation*, 21 September 1899, p. 216.

7. *Illinois Record*, ibid.

8. Unpublished interview of Alfreda Duster, conducted by Dorothy Sterling, 22 March 1976, p. 4. The author is grateful to Mary Helen Washington who provided her with this interview.

9. *Illinois Record*, 26 November, 3 December 1898.

10. Ibid., 25 February 1899; 29 October 1898.

11. *The Nation*, ibid.

12. *Illinois Record*, 25 February, 1899.

13. Prather, *We Have Taken a City*, pp. 24–26, 31, 68–69.

14. Prather, ibid., pp. 31, 22–23. See also, Edmonds, *The Negro and Fusion Politics in North Carolina*, for an analysis of fusion politics in the state; and Gilmore, *Gender and Jim Crow*, for information on the activities of North Carolina black women in this period.

15. Gilmore, ibid., pp. 95, 99. This text provides the most comprehensive analysis of gender politics and its intersection with race in the North Carolina campaign.

16. Ibid., p. 105; Prather, ibid., p. 71. For more on Felton's discourse on protection, see Lee-Ann Whites, "Rebecca Latimer Felton and the Problem of 'Protection' in the New South," pp. 41–61.

17. Hodes, *White Women Black Men*, pp. 195–195; *Wilmington Daily Record*, 18 August 1898, quoted in Prather, ibid., pp. 72–73; Gilmore, ibid., pp. 105–108.

18. Hodes, ibid.; Prather, ibid., p. 87.

19. *Indianapolis Freeman*, 5 November 1898, quoted in Gilmore, ibid., p. 107.

20. Prather, ibid., pp. 101, 103–104, 111.

21. Ibid., p. 112. See chap. 4 of the book for the most detailed description of the riot. The text also has the most comprehensive analysis of the political events that led up to the massacre.

22. Gilmore, ibid., pp. 113–114.

23. Booker T. Washington to William McKinley, 27 November 1898, in Harlan, *Booker T. Washington Papers*, vol. 4, p. 521.

24. T. Thomas Fortune to Booker T. Washington, 16 December 1898 in Harlan, ibid., p. 532; T. Thomas Fortune to Booker T. Washington, 17 December 1898 in Harlan, ibid., pp. 535–536; T. Thomas Fortune to Booker T. Washington, 14 December 1898 in Harlan, ibid., pp. 530–531.

25. Quoted in Thornbrough, *T. Thomas Fortune*, pp. 182–184; J. M. Holland to Booker T. Washington, 21 December 1898, in Harlan, ibid., pp. 543–544.

26. *Washington, D.C., Colored American*, 7 January 1899. In 1898, Green, who had formerly served in Ohio's House of Representatives and the Senate, was appointed agent of postage stamps in the U.S. Post Office Department. Harlan, ibid., p. 446, n. 2.

27. *Washington, D.C., Colored American*, 7 January 1899; *Washington Evening Star*, 30 December 1899; *Cleveland Gazette*, 7 January 1899; *Indianapolis Freeman*, 21 January 1899; (Omaha) *Afro American Sentinel*, 28 January 28, 1899.

28. Wells, *Crusade*, p. 258; T. Thomas Fortune to Booker T. Washington, 1 January 1899, in Harlan, ibid., vol. 5, p. 3.

29. *Cleveland Gazette*, 8, 16 April 1899; 18 January 1899.

30. Quoted in Hodes, ibid., p. 207. For coverage of the Hose lynching, see *Atlanta Constitution*, 14, 24, 25 April 1899; *Atlanta Journal*, 15, 24 April 1899; *Macon Telegraph*, 24, 25 April 1899.

31. Wells-Barnett, *Lynch Law in Georgia*, pp. 1–6.

32. Brundage, *Lynching in the New South*, p. 83; Dray, *At the Hands of Persons Unknown*, p. 4.

33. Wells-Barnett, "Lynch Law in America," in Thompson, *Ida B. Wells-Barnett*, p. 241. The article originally was published in *Arena*, January 1900, pp. 15–24; Hale, *Making Whiteness*, pp. 210–212; Dowd-Hall, "The Mind That Burns in Each Body," p. 335.

34. Hale, ibid., p. 210.

35. Accounts of the lynching can be found in Dray, *At the Hands of Persons Unknown*, pp. 13–14; Hale, ibid., pp. 212–215; Wells-Barnett, *Lynch Law in Georgia* (taken directly from newspaper accounts), pp. 9–10.

36. Williamson, *The Crucible of Race*, p. 205; Harlan, *Booker T. Washington, The Making of a Black Leader*, p. 262; Hale, ibid. Hale's thesis in *Making Whiteness* is that lynching evolved into a modernized, standardized spectacle, whose features became commodified in a way to suit a segregated consumer culture. See, especially, chap. 5.

37. "A Statement on Lynching in the Birmingham *Age-Herald*," 25 April 1899, in Harlan, *The Booker T. Washington Papers*, vol. 5, pp. 90–91.

38. *New York Times*, 11 May 1899; quoted in Harlan, ibid., p. 117, n. 2.

39. Quoted in Lewis, *W. E. B. Du Bois, Biography of a Race*, p. 226.

40. Wells-Barnett, *Lynch Law in Georgia*, p. 15.

41. Ibid., p. 14.

42. *Cleveland Gazette*, 17 June 1899; *Chicago Daily Inter-Ocean*, 5 June 1899, p. 6; Wells-Barnett, *Lynch Law in Georgia*, pp. 16, 18.

43. Wells-Barnett, ibid., p. 1.

Chapter Sixteen: Bull in the China Shop

1. Mary Church Terrell to Frances Settle, 5 September 1899, Mary Church Terrell Papers.

2. *Indianapolis Freeman*, 24 December 1899.

3. *Chicago Tribune*, 14 August 1899; *Indianapolis Freeman*, 19 December, 1896.

4. *Washington, D.C., Colored American*, 14 January 1899 (hereafter *Colored American*).

5. *Colored American*, 21 January 1899.

6. *Chicago Broad Ax*, 29 July 1899; Duster, ed., *Crusade for Justice*, pp. 258, 261 (hereafter Wells, *Crusade*). Thornbrough, *T. Thomas Fortune*, p. 212.

7. Gilmore, *Gender and Jim Crow*, p. 120; *Boston Evening Transcript*, 3 January 1899; Wells-Barnett, "Lynching and the Excuse for It," reprinted in Thompson, *Ida B. Wells-Barnett*, p. 253. This number is slightly higher than the 489 figure found in Cutler, *Lynch Law*, p. 185; *Chicago Broad Ax*, 6 June 1899.

8. *Chicago Tribune*, 14 August 1899; *Chicago Broad Ax*, 29 July 1899; Logan and Winston, *American Negro Biography*, p. 645; W. E. B. Du Bois to Booker T. Washington, 12 July 1899, in Harlan, *The Booker T. Washington Papers*, vol. 5, pp. 152–153 (hereafter Harlan, *BTWP*).

9. Wells, *Crusade*, p. 262.

10. See, for example, the letter of Nathan F. Mossell (a militant Philadelphia physician and husband of journalist Gertrude Mossell) addressed to Booker T. Washington in which Mossell begins: "I have read with regret and chagrin in the public press, statements purported to have come from your lips. I feel sure of your sincere friendship for the race, and I appreciate also that these are trying times and that you occupy a peculiar position." Harlan, *BTWP*, vol. 4, p. 520; *Cleveland Gazette*, 21 January 1899; *Boston Evening Transcript*, 3 January 1898. The bill was the Hardwick Bill. See Lewis, *W. E. B. Du Bois, Biography of a Race*, pp. 231–232; and Harlan, *Booker T. Washington, The Making of a Leader*, pp. 290–292, for more details on the campaign.

11. Harlan, *Booker T. Washington: The Wizard of Tuskegee*, p. 130; Harlan, *BTWP*, vol. 5, p. 286; Lewis, *W. E. B. Du Bois, Biography of a Race*, p. 233.

12. *Colored American*, 5, 26 August 1899; Harlan, *Booker T. Washington, The Making of a Black Leader*, p. 264; *Woman's Era*, 24 March 1894, p. 5.

13. Wells, *Crusade*, p. 258; Wesley, *The History of the National Association of Colored Women's Clubs*, p. 45; "Minutes of the Second Convention of the National Association of Colored Women, August 14th, 15th, and 16th 1899," p. 3, African-American Perspectives: Pamphlets from the Daniel A. P. Murray Collection, 1818–1907. American Memory, http://memory.loc.gov. (hereafter "Minutes"). The members of the Chicago NACW planning committee included: Mrs. Agnes Moody, Mrs. Rosa Moore, Mrs. Albert Hall, Miss Anna Douglass, Miss Birdie Evans, and Mrs. Mary Davenport; *Chicago Broad Ax*, 12 August 1899.

14. Wells, *Crusade*, pp. 258–259, 260.

15. *Colored American*, 27 May, 24 June 1899.

16. Robert Terrell to Robert Church, 17 May 1897, Robert R. Church Family of Memphis Papers.

17. *Colored American*, 27 May 1899, 24 June 1899. Josephine Ruffin attended primary common schools in Salem, Massachusetts, and had two years of private tutoring. At the age of sixteen, she married George L. Ruffin. Jenkins, "She Issued the Call . . ." p. 74.

18. Quoted in Gatewood, *Aristocrats of Color*, p. 244.

19. Logan and Winston, *Dictionary of American Negro Biography*, p. 123.

20. *Washington, D.C. Evening Star*, 2 September 1899; "Minutes," p. 9.

21. *Chicago Sunday Times Herald*, 21 August 1899, quoted in "Press Comments, The Second Convention of the National Association of Colored Women," p. 9, Chicago, Illinois. Mary Church Terrell Papers, Container 23. See the *Washington Evening Star*, 2 September 1899, where Mary Church Terrell, in an interview, mentions the role of white women

at the NACW meeting. Official greetings were to be offered by the predominantly white League of Cook County Women's Clubs. Another who would address the NACW was Mary McDowell, the future cofounder of the Women's Trade Union League, who had established kindergartens through Hull House and was the director of the University of Chicago Settlement. Also giving greetings was Ellen Henrotin, the well-to-do former president of the General Federation of Women's Clubs (GFWC) and future president of the Chicago Woman's Club.

22. Wells, *Crusade,* p. 259; "Minutes," p. 9.

23. Mary Church Terrell to Frances Settle, 5 September 1899, Mary Church Terrell Papers; Wells, *Crusade,* p. 260.

24. Williams, "The Club Movement Among Colored Women," p. 229; *Colored American,* 26 August 1899; *Chicago Tribune,* 16 August 1899; "Minutes," p. 10.

25. *Chicago Broad Ax,* 26 August 1899; "Minutes," ibid.

26. *Chicago Tribune,* 17, 18 August 1899; *Chicago Daily Inter-Ocean,* 18 August 1899; Mary Church Terrell to Margaret Murray Washington, 3 May 1900, Mary Church Terrell Papers; Davis, *Lifting As We Climb,* p. 33.

27. Wells, *Crusade,* p. 260; *Chicago Sunday Times Herald,* 21 August 1899, quoted in "Press Comments, The Second Convention of the National Association of Colored Women," p. 6. Mary Church Terrell Papers, the Library of Congress, Container 23; Wesley, *The History of the National Association of Colored Women's Clubs,* p. 45.

28. *Chicago Tribune,* 16 August 1899; *Chicago Sunday Times Herald,* 21 August 1899. *Chicago Daily Inter-Ocean,* 18 August 1899.

29. Quoted in Wesley, *The History of the National Association of Colored Women's Clubs,* p. 48; *Colored American,* 30 September 1899.

30. *Colored American,* 26 August 1899. For example, Robert Terrell, P. B. S. Pinchback, Bishop Benjamin Arnett, and W. A. Pledger did not attend.

31. *Cleveland Gazette,* 26 August 1899; *Chicago Journal,* 19 August 1899; *Chicago Tribune,* 20 August 1899.

32. *Chicago Daily Inter-Ocean,* 25 August 1899; *Chicago Journal,* 19 August 1899.

33. Roosevelt, "The Rough Riders," *Scribner's Magazine,* 25 April 1899, quoted in Baker, *From Savage to Negro,* p. 85; *New York Age* letter quoted in Gatewood, *Smoked Yankees,* pp. 92–97.

34. *Cleveland Gazette,* 20 August 1899; *Chicago Tribune,* 19, 20 August 1899; *Chicago Journal,* 19 August 1899. Washington later clarified his position in an interview with the *New York Times,* 21 August 1899. He said that the leading Council members agreed that he could do the best service to the race by devoting himself to its "moral, educational, and industrial development. . . . Some of my race think I ought to participate in political activity," the educator concluded. "I have not entertained this view."

35. T. Thomas Fortune to Booker T. Washington, 25 September 1899, in Harlan, *BTWP,* vol. 5, p. 220.

36. *Colored American,* 26 August 1899.

37. *Chicago Broad Ax,* 30 September 1899.

38. Wells-Barnett, "Lynch Law in America," in Thompson, *Ida B. Wells-Barnett,* pp. 235, 243. Originally published in *Arena,* January 1900, pp. 15–24.

39. Wells-Barnett, "The Negro's Case in Equity," in Thompson, ibid., pp. 245, 246–248. Originally published in the *Independent,* 26 April 1900, pp. 1010–1011.

40. Wells-Barnett, *Mob Rule in New Orleans: Robert Charles and His Fight to the Death,* reprinted in Harris, ed., *The Selected Writings of Ida B. Wells-Barnett,* pp. 253–322. The pamphlet also included lynching statistics and brief mentions of the lynchings of Henry Smith, Sam Hose, and Frazier Baker, among others, pp. 320–322; Williamson, *The Crucible of Race,* p. 208.

41. Wells-Barnett, ibid., pp. 256–301; Williamson, ibid., pp. 201–209. Also see Hair, *Carnival of Fury*, for a full text on Robert Charles and the New Orleans riot.

42. Wells-Barnett, ibid, pp. 312–314.

43. Williamson, ibid., p. 205; "An Address in Atlanta," 25 September 1899, in Harlan, *BTWP*, vol. 5, pp. 215–220.

44. *Chicago Conservator*, 7 July 1900, clipping in the Booker T. Washington Papers, Container 1032, Library of Congress, also cited in Harlan, *BTWP*, vol. 5, p. 589, n. 1; also quoted in the *Indianapolis Freeman*, 15 July 1900; Harlan, *Booker T. Washington, The Making of a Black Leader*, pp. 266–267; Lewis, ibid., pp. 220–221; Emmett Jay Scott to Booker T. Washington, 21 July 1900, in Harlan, ibid., *BTWP*.

45. Several Chicago clubs, including the Ida B. Wells Club whose president was Agnes Moody, began holding meetings to bring together the officers of the Illinois clubs, including the Civic League, the Woman's Conference, the Julia Gaston Club, the Girls Friendly Club, the Lyceum, and the Phyllis [*sic*] Wheatley Club, to exchange ideas and coordinate their work. *Chicago Broad Ax*, 10 February 1900. On 21 November 1900, Illinois women officially agreed on the mission statement, constitution, and elected officers of the Illinois Federation of Colored Women's Clubs (IFCWC). Hendricks, *Gender, Race, and Politics in the Midwest*, pp. 23–25. As Hendricks notes, there appears to be little documentation regarding the early deliberations of this body. The first president of the organization, Mary Jane Jackson, of Jacksonville, Illinois, was the wife of a minister and active in a number of black women's organizations.

46. Logan, *The Betrayal of the Negro*, p. 236; Salem, *To Better Our World*, pp. 42–43.

47. *Chicago Tribune*, 11 June 1900.

48. Wells, *Crusade*, pp. 270–271; Salem, ibid., p. 272, n. 61.

49. Frank and Jerome, comp., *Annals of the Chicago Woman's Club*, p. 145; Ellen M. Henrotin to Madame Secretary, 23 January 1901, Chicago Woman's Club, Correspondence Files, 1898–1902.

50. See, for example, Rebecca Lowe to Emily Keith, 16 November 1900, Chicago Woman's Club, Correspondence Files, 1898–1902; Wells, *Crusade*, p. 269.

51. Alice Bradford Wiles to Mr. or Mrs. Booker Washington, 23 November 1900, quoted in Harlan, *BTWP*, ibid, p. 679.

52. Clara M. T. Larson to Booker T. Washington, 6 December 1900, in Harlan, ibid., p. 680, n. 2.

53. Wells, *Crusade*, pp. 263–264.

54. Addams, "Respect for Law," quoted in Aptheker, "Lynching and Rape," pp. 23, 25. Originally published in the *Independent*, 53 (3 January 1901): 18–20.

55. Ibid., p. 55.

56. Wells-Barnett, "Lynching and the Excuse for It," quoted in Aptheker, ibid., p. 29. Originally published in the *Independent*, 53 (16 May 1901): 1133–1336.

57. Ibid.

58. Ibid, pp. 30, 33, 34.

59. *Cleveland Gazette*, 20 July 1901; Neverdon-Morton, *Afro-American Women of the South and the Advancement of the Race*, p. 193.

60. Wells, *Crusade*, p. 268.

Chapter Seventeen: Chicago and the Wizard

1. Emmet Scott to Booker T. Washington, 15 August 1901, in Harlan, *The Booker T. Washington Papers*, vol. 6, p. 186 (hereafter Harlan, *BTWP*).

2. Harlan, *Booker T. Washington, The Making of a Black Leader*, pp. 248–253; quoted in Harlan, *Booker T. Washington, The Wizard of Tuskegee*, p. 130.

3. Lewis, *W. E. B. Du Bois, Biography of a Race*, pp. 232–237; Du Bois, "The Evolution of Negro Leadership," *Dial* 31 (16 July 1901): 53–55. Also see Lewis, ibid., pp. 262–264, for further comment on Du Bois's review and Washington's text.

4. After being forcibly driven from the state Republican conference in 1904, White helped found the all-black town of Whitesboro, New Jersey, practiced law in Philadelphia, and became a member of the executive committee of the NAACP in that city. Logan and Winston, *American Negro Biography*, pp. 645–646; Grant, "The Antilynching Movement," p. 66.

5. *Washington, D.C. Colored American*, 17 August 1901; Emmett Scott to Booker T. Washington, ibid.

6. Theodore Roosevelt to Booker T. Washington, 14 September 1901, in Harlan, *BTWP*, vol. 6, p. 206.

7. Baker, *From Savage to Negro*, pp. 84–87; Theodore Roosevelt to Owen Wister, 27 July 1906, quoted in Seth M. Scheiner, "Theodore Roosevelt and the Negro," p. 171.

8. Harlan, *Booker T. Washington, The Making of a Black Leader*, pp. 306–307.

9. Harlan, *Booker T. Washington, The Wizard of Tuskegee*, p. 5. For a full discussion of the relationship between Washington and Roosevelt and the reaction to the October dinner by blacks and whites, see Harlan, ibid., pp. 3–31.

10. Meier, "Booker T. Washington and the Negro Press," p. 67; Booker T. Washington to Emmett Scott, 7 October 1901, in Harlan, *BTWP*, vol. 6, p. 233.

11. Biographical information on Wilkins is found in Kreiling, "Making of Racial Identities," p. 300; Booker T. Washington to Emmett Scott, 7 October 1901, published in Harlan, *BTWP*, vol. 6, p. 234.

12. Lewis, ibid., pp. 265–277; Harlan, *Booker T. Washington, The Wizard of Tuskegee*, pp. 39–40; Logan and Winston, ibid., pp. 602–605.

13. *Pioneer Press*, 11 July 1902, quoted in Nelson, *Frederick L. McGhee*, p. 101; Nelson, ibid., p. 104. Alexander Walters was elected chair of the executive committee; and the vice presidents were George H. White, E. A. Deas, and Willam H. Pledger, political men who might not have agreed entirely with Washington but by 1902 depended on him. Thornbrough, *T. Thomas Fortune*, p. 227.

14. Emmett Scott to Booker T. Washington, 17 July 1902, published in Harlan, *BTWP*, vol. 6, p. 497; *Guardian* editorial republished in the *Chicago Broad Ax*, 26 July 1902 (hereafter *Broad Ax*). The Chicago paper added that Fortune had been so drunk at the 1901 business league meeting that he had staggered on the podium and afterward had to be helped by Washington to an awaiting car. This "is the creature whom Prof. Washington chose for President of the Afro-American Council," editor Julius Taylor charged; Trotter quote published in Thornbrough, *T. Thomas Fortune*, p. 229.

15. *Broad Ax*, 11 July 1903.

16. *Broad Ax*, 6 December 1902, 17 January 1903; Duster, ed., *Crusade for Justice*, pp. 297–298 (hereafter Wells, *Crusade*). It is not known what Carey's motives were, but since the Atlantan had come to Chicago from his pastorate in Florida in 1897, he had been competitive with Ransom and had made several attempts to undermine him. Carey, no doubt, had welcomed Ransom's replacement by Murray. Ransom, *The Pilgrimage of Harriet Ransom's Son*, p. 88. Grace Presbyterian Church celebrated its twenty-fifth anniversary in 1913. *Chicago Defender*, 4 October 1913; Spear, *Black Chicago*, p. 94.

17. Wells, *Crusade*, pp. 272–274; *Broad Ax*, 10 April 1903.

18. *Baltimore Ledger*, 17 January 1903; *Cleveland Gazette*, 17 January 1903.

19. Harlan, *Booker T. Washington, The Wizard of Tuskegee*, p. 136. Fearing that news of the personal sum would tarnish his image, Washington requested a change in the stipulation

and the money was used to endow his salary at Tuskegee, relieving the Institute of having to pay it.

20. For discussion of *Souls*, see Lewis, *W. E. B. Du Bois, Biography of a Race*, pp. 265–296; Rampersad, *The Art and Imagination of W. E. B. Du Bois*; and Carby, *Race Men*.

21. Du Bois, *The Souls of Black Folk*, pp. 93, 88–89.

22. Ibid., pp. 90, 94.

23. *Broad Ax*, 2 May 1903.

24. For biographical information on Woolley, see Schultz, *Women Building Chicago*, pp. 993–995.

25. Ida B. Wells to Professor Du Bois, 30 May 1903, in Aptheker, *The Correspondence of W. E. B. Du Bois*, vol. 1, pp. 55–56; Wells, *Crusade*, p. 280.

26. Ida B. Wells to Prof. Du Bois, ibid.

27. Du Bois, *The Souls of Black Folk*, pp. 91, 92, 45.

28. *Chicago Tribune*, 19 October 1903; *Broad Ax*, 17 October 1903; Homel, *Down from Equality*, p. 9.

29. Spear, ibid., p. 6; *Broad Ax*, 21 June 1903, 12 November 1903; Logan and Winston, ibid., pp. 453–454.

30. *Springfield (IL) Record*, 7 January 1899.

31. Chicago public schools saw various periods of exclusion, however. In 1849 and 1851, local ordinances abrogated previous segregation policies in the schools. In 1863, a short-lived law that called for racially separate schools was rescinded after black protests; and in 1874, Illinois passed a law forbidding segregation in the schools. Spear, ibid., p. 6; Homel, ibid., pp. 6–9.

32. Between 1900 and 1910, the black pupil population rose from 2,694 to 4,160, but still represented only 1.2 percent of the population. Homel, ibid., p. 6; Wells, *Crusade*, p. 274; Spear, ibid., p. 85; Homel, ibid., p. 9.

33. Diner, "Chicago Social Workers and Blacks in the Progressive Era," p. 395; *Chicago Tribune*, 3 October 1903.

34. Wells, ibid., pp. 274–275.

35. Wells, ibid., p. 276.

36. *Centennial History*, chap. 16, "Chicago's Newspapers," pp. 78–85.

37. Wells, ibid., pp. 276–278.

38. Diner, ibid., p. 402. For extensive analyses on race and the settlements in Chicago, see Philpott, *The Slum and the Ghetto*, and Lasch-Quinn, *Black Neighbors*.

39. Jackson, "Black Charity in Progressive Era Chicago," pp. 404, 411. There was also the Trinity Mission, which closed soon after founder Richard R. Wright left Chicago in 1905.

40. Wells, ibid., pp. 279–280.

41. Ibid., p. 280.

42. Williams, "The Frederick Douglass Centre," (1904), p. 602.

43. Williams, "The Frederick Douglass Centre," (1906), p. 334. Williams, "A New Method for Dealing with the Race Problem," p. 502; *Broad Ax*, 20 January 1906.

44. J. Silone Yates to Margaret Murray Washington, 9 May 1904, *Records of the National Association of Colored Women's Clubs*, Correspondence File.

45. Tingley, *The Structuring of a State*, p. 291; Wells, ibid., p. 310.

46. *Vicksburg (Mississippi) Evening Post*, 8 February 1904; Booker T. Washington, "A Protest Against Lynching," in Harlan, *BTWP*, vol. 7, pp. 447–448.

47. Wells-Barnett, "Booker T. Washington and His Critics," reprinted in Thompson, *Ida B. Wells-Barnett*, pp. 257, 256.

48. Terrell, "Lynching from a Negro's Point of View," pp. 855–856.

49. Spear, ibid., pp. 71–72.

50. S. Laing Williams to Emmett J. Scott, 14 October 1903, Booker T. Washington Papers, Special Correspondence, Library of Congress.

51. Booker T. Washington to Theodore Roosevelt, 20 October 1903, published in Harlan, *BTWP*, vol. 7, p. 297.

52. Theodore Jones to Booker T. Washington, 28 January 1904, published in Harlan, *BTWP*, vol. 7, pp. 416–417.

53. Booker T. Washington to T. Thomas Fortune, 27 December 1903, in Harlan, *BTWP*, vol. 7, p 380.

54. Harlan, *Booker T. Washington, The Wizard of Tuskegee*, pp. 46, 48–50; Lewis, ibid., p. 301.

55. Harlan, ibid., p. 71; Lewis, ibid., pp. 302, 305–310.

56. W. E. B. Du Bois to Oswald Garrison Villard, 24 March 1905, in Harlan, *BTWP*, vol. 8, p. 224.

57. Booker T. Washington to John Asbury, 22 February 1904, in Harlan, *BTWP*, vol. 7, p. 445; D. R. Wilkins to Booker T. Washington, 5 May 1904, in Harlan, ibid., p. 495; Booker T. Washington to D. R. Wilkins, 19 May 1904, in Harlan, ibid., p. 508.

58. *Broad Ax*, 28 March 1903, 22 September 1906; Ida B. Wells-Barnett to Robert Church, 22 February 1904, Robert R. Church Family Papers.

59. Booker T. Washington to Allison Sweeney, 16 July 1904, published in Harlan, *BTWP*, vol. 8, p. 19.

60. *Broad Ax*, 4, 11 February 1905.

61. Booker T. Washington to Charles Anderson, 16 June 1904, published in Harlan, *BTWP*, vol. 7, p. 533.

62. Brahnam, "Transformation of Black Political Leadership in Chicago," pp. 53–56; Gosnell, *Negro Politicians*, pp. 154–155.

63. Booker T. Washington to Emmett Jay Scott, 15 August 1904 in Harlan, *BTWP*, vol. 8, p. 49. Dover became secretary of the RNC in 1904. Harlan, ibid., vol. 7, p. 477.

64. In 1908, Mrs. Ida B. Bailey, one of the incorporators of Washington, D.C.'s Colored Women's League, was the organization's secretary for women in the South; and upon her death, Mrs. Carrie Clifford, a former president of the Ohio State Federation, took her place. Wesley, *The History of the National Association of Colored Women*, p. 57; Lewis, *W. E. B. Du Bois, Biography of a Race*, pp. 316, 328; Booker T. Washington to Margaret Murray Washington, 8 July 1905, in Harlan, *BTWP*, vol. 8, p. 321; Salem, *To Better Our World*, p. 47.

65. *Broad Ax*, 13 September, 1905; Wells, ibid., pp. 281–282.

66. Wells, *Crusade*, p. 282.

67. *Broad Ax*, 20 January 1906; Wells, ibid. p. 283.

68. Williams, "The Frederick Douglass Centre" (1906), p. 334.

69. *Broad Ax*, 27 May 1905.

70. Unpublished Interview, "Alfreda Duster," 22 March 1976, p. 8. Conducted by Dorothy Sterling.

71. Less than a decade after the Barnetts became the first blacks to move to Rhodes Avenue, three hundred blacks moved into the neighborhood. In another decade, there would be thirteen hundred. Philpott, *The Slum and The Ghetto*, p. 153; see the Chicago Commission on Race Relations, *Negro in Chicago*, map denoting houses of prostitution, facing p. 342; Williams, "Social Bonds in the 'Black Belt,'" p. 40; Wooley, "The Frederick Douglass Centre, Chicago," *The Commons*, pp. 328–329, quoted in Philpott, *The Slum and the Ghetto*, p. 317.

72. *Broad Ax*, 13 May 1905.

73. Jackson, "Black Charity in Progressive Chicago," p. 407.

74. Wells, ibid., p. 290.

75. *Broad Ax*, 7 November 1903. Brahnam, "The Transformation of Black Political Leadership in Chicago," p. 24.

76. *Broad Ax*, 14 July 1911; for additional biographical details on Motts, see Gosnell, *Negro Politicians*, pp.127–131.

77. For some reviews of the Pekin's diverse entertainments, see *Broad Ax*, 15, 22 May; 25 September; 16 October 1909; 10 August 1912.

78. Wells, ibid., pp. 291–292.

79. *Broad Ax*, 5, 12 May 1906.

80. Bontemps and Conroy, *They Seek a City*, pp. 96–97. Motts died in 1911, and though the theater continued for a number of subsequent years, it did not retain its high quality after his death.

81. Wells, ibid., p. 295.

82. *Broad Ax*, 23, 30, June; 7 July, 1906.

83. Wells, ibid., pp. 286–288.

84. For the details of the Atlanta riot, see Crowe, "Racial Violence and Social Reform Origins of the Atlanta Riot of 1906."

85. "Litany of Atlanta" is reprinted in Lewis, ed., *W. E. B. Du Bois: A Reader*, pp. 441–444.

86. *Broad Ax*, 6 October 1906.

87. Barber, "The Atlanta Tragedy," p. 273; Wells, *Crusade*, pp. 284–285.

88. S. Laing Williams to Emmett Scott, 22 October 1906, published in Harlan, *BTWP*, vol. 9, p. 102.

Chapter Eighteen: Calls

1. John D. Buenker, "Edward F. Dunne: The Limits of Municipal Reform," p. 33, in Green and Holli, eds., *The Mayors; Chicago Broad Ax*, 18 November 1905 (hereafter *Broad Ax*).

2. Barbara Welke, "City of Courts: Socializing Justice in he Progressive Era." *Journal of Interdisciplinary History* 36 (Autumn 2005): 292–293; *Broad Ax*, 23 June 1906.

3. *Broad Ax*, ibid.; see Phil Waters to Emmett Scott, 28 December 1905, Booker T. Washington Papers, Special Correspondence File, Library of Congress, regarding Barnett being up for consideration for the Registership of the Treasury Department.

4. *Broad Ax*, 10 November 1906; Branham, "The Transformation of Black Political Leadership," p. 56.

5. *Broad Ax*, 3 September 1903.

6. For a full account of the Brownsville incident, see Weaver, *The Brownsville Raid*; *Broad Ax*, 24 November 1906; 1, 8, 15 December 1906.

7. *Centennial History of the City of Chicago*, p. 81; *Chicago Chronicle*, 6 November 1906; *Broad Ax*, 27 October 1906.

8. *Chicago Chronicle*, 9 November 1906.

9. Ibid., 9 November 1906.

10. Ibid., 10 November 1906.

11. Gosnell, *Negro Politicians*, p. 85; S. Laing Williams to Booker T. Washington, 16 November 1906, Special Correspondence File, Booker T. Washington Papers, Library of Congress.

12. Duster, ed., *Crusade for Justice*, p. 294 (hereafter Wells, *Crusade*).

13. Branham, ibid., pp. 80–81.

14. Tinsley, "The Brownsville Affray," pp. 44, 46; Terrell, "The Disbanding of the Colored Soldiers," p. 554; quote in Dalton, *Theodore Roosevelt*, p. 322; Wells, *Crusade*, p. 324.

15. Tinsley, ibid.; Harlan, *Booker T. Washington, The Wizard of Tuskegee*, pp. 310–311; S. Laing

Williams to Booker T. Washington, 26 November 1906, Booker T. Washington Papers, Special Correspondence File, Library of Congress; Harlan, ibid., p. 310.

16. Booker T. Washington to William Howard Taft, 20 Nov 1906, in Harlan, ibid., vol. 9, p. 141.

17. Papers such as the *Broad Ax* pointed out that Republicans would have lost recent elections, especially in the key states of New Jersey, Maryland, Ohio, and New York, but for the black vote. *Broad Ax*, 25 June 1904; quotes from Tinsley, ibid., p. 47.

18. Quoted in Harlan, *Booker T. Washington, The Wizard of Tuskegee*, pp. 319–320.

19. Tinsley, ibid., p. 46; Storey, "Athens and Brownsville," cites an earlier incident when more than fifty white soldiers killed a guard in their attempt to break one of their comrades out of jail in Athens, Ohio. Only one of the soldiers was sentenced to the penitentiary; another was fined. Also see Terrell, "The Disbanding of the Colored Soldiers"; Du Bois, "The President and the Soldiers"; *Broad Ax*, 16 February 1907.

20. Oswald Garrison Villard to Booker T. Washington, 16 November 1906, in Harlan, *BTWP*, vol. 9, p. 129.

21. Milholland's Constitution League sent investigators to Brownsville who wrote up a report exonerating the men and criticizing the inadequate evidence of their guilt. The report, which included a finding that the spent bullet shells did not come from the men's weapons, prompted Senator Robert Foraker (R-Ohio), who was seeking the presidential nomination, to call for a resolution in December of 1906 for the Senate to investigate the matter. The findings were released on March 11, 1908, with a majority opinion that upheld the president. However, Foraker led the Senate in a passage of a subsequent bill to establish a Court of Military Inquiry on Brownsville. In its findings, released April 6, 1910, it echoed the previous investigative results: that a small group of the black soldiers were responsible for the shoot-out, but that there was no way to separate the guilty from the innocent. The court, however, qualified fourteen men for reenlistment; eleven did so. Tinsley, ibid., pp. 50–61. In 1972, President Richard M. Nixon rescinded the dishonorable discharge; Wells, *Crusade*, pp. 324, 299.

22. Kellogg, *NAACP*, p. 23; *Broad Ax*, 27 July 1907.

23. Daniel Hale Williams to Booker T. Washington, 4 November 1907, published in Harlan, *BTWP*, vol. 9, p. 395.

24. Crouthamel, "The Springfield Race Riot," p. 180.

25. *Washington Bee*, 28 July 1906; *Broad Ax*, 21 July 1906. Reflecting on the NACW controversy, the disgusted outgoing president commented: "It hurt me that people . . . could do things so basely. What is the question of color to a race like ours?" J. Silone Yates to Margaret Murray Washington, 30 September 1906. Records of the National Association of Colored Women's Clubs, Correspondence File; Davis, *The Story of the Illinois Federation of Colored Women's Clubs*, p. 15; Kellogg, ibid., p. 23; Davis, *The Story of the Illinois Federation of Colored Women's Clubs*, p. 15; *Chicago Defender*, 19 February 1910.

26. Crouthamel, "The Springfield Riot of 1908," pp. 164–165. My account of the riot owes mostly to this text. See also *Broad Ax*, 22, 29 August 1908; *Springfield (IL) Forum*, 5 September 1908.

27. Crouthamel, ibid., pp. 168, 172–173; Franklin, *From Slavery to Freedom*, p. 317.

28. Wells, *Crusade*, p. 299.

29. *Broad Ax*, 22 Aug 1908; "A Crusader Tells the Story of the Crime," Clipping, n.d., NAACP File, Schomburg Center for Research in Black Culture; Wells, ibid., p. 300.

30. Kellogg, *NAACP*, p. 14. For details of the earliest meetings and participants, see pp. 9–30; other accounts include Ovington, "The National Association for the Advancement of Colored People" (1924); "The Beginnings of the NAACP" (1926); *Black and White Sat Down Together*, pp. 56–65; *The Walls Came Tumbling Down*, pp. 100–146; Wedin, *In-*

heritors of the Spirit, pp. 105–135. For the best study, see Lewis, *W. E. B. Du Bois*, vol. 1, pp. 386–407.

31. Kellogg, ibid., p. 10; Walling, "Race War in the North," p. 534.

32. Wedin, *Inheritors of the Spirit*, p. 106; Lewis, *W. E. B. Du Bois, Biography of a Race*, p. 389.

33. Kellogg, ibid., pp. 15, 298–299; Reed, *The Chicago NAACP*, pp. 17–18.

34. Regarding Terrell, whose husband, Robert, was appointed a municipal judge through Washington's influence, the Tuskegeean wrote Robert Terrell that Mary's name on the list was an embarrassment, and added, "To have Mrs Terrell's name appear on a program where the opposition is in charge naturally makes it harder for your friends to help you when the time comes." Booker T. Washington to Robert Terrell, 27 April 1910, in Harlan, *BTWP*, vol. 10, p. 323. Subsequently, however, Mary Terrell's insider status proved valuable to Washington, who wrote: "I had a long talk with her [Mary Terrell] and she told me many things of interest. . . . She gets on the inside of things and is always capable of stirring up trouble in any organization that she has a part in. . . . I can keep in close touch with her if her name is not quoted." Booker T. Washington to Emmett Scott, 12 December 1910, published in Harlan, ibid., vol. 10, p. 594.

35. Kellogg, ibid., 20; Du Bois, "National Committee on the Negro," *The Survey*, 22 (June 12, 1909), reprinted in Aptheker, *A Documentary History*, p. 925.

36. Kellogg, ibid.

37. Wells-Barnett, "Lynching: Our National Crime," reprinted in Thompson, *Ida B. Wells-Barnett*, p. 261. Between 1901 and 1920, fifteen measures relating to the lynching of foreign nationals were passed by the U.S. Congress. Almost one million dollars was paid to the dependents of the victims. Grant, "The Anti-Lynching Movement," p. 67.

38. Wells-Barnett, "Lynching Our National Crime," p. 264.

39. Charles W. Anderson to Booker T. Washington, 31 May 1909, in Harlan, *BTWP*, vol. 10, p. 127.

40. Wells, *Crusade*, p. 322.

41. Ovington, *The Walls Came Tumbling Down*, p. 105.

42. Wells, ibid., p. 324.

43. Oswald Garrison Villard to Francis Garrison, 4 June 1909, Villard Papers.

44. Ovington, "Beginnings of the NAACP," p. 77.

45. Quoted in Wedin, ibid., pp. 110–111.

46. Du Bois, ibid., p. 927; also see his statement regarding the resolutions, pp. 926–927.

47. Kellogg, ibid., pp. 302–303; see ibid., p. 300 for the final list.

48. Wells, *Crusade*, p. 324.

49. Ibid.

50. Ibid., p. 325.

51. Ibid.

52. Ibid., p. 326.

53. Oswald Garrison Villard to Francis Garrison, 4 June 1909, Villard Papers.

54. Ovington, *The Walls Came Tumbling Down*, p. 106; Ovington, *Black and White Sat Down Together*, p. 60.

55. Muncy, *Creating a Female Dominion in American Reform*, p. 74.

56. Carby, "Policing the Black Woman's Body in an Urban Context"; Lasch-Quinn, *Black Neighbors* (especially chap. 1); Diner, "Chicago Social Workers and Blacks in the Progressive Era"; Philpott, *The Slum and the Ghetto*.

57. Addams, "Social Control"; Ovington, quoted in Wedin, ibid., p. 30.

58. Wells-Barnett, "The Northern Negro Woman's Social and Moral Condition," p. 35.

59. Wells, *Crusade*, p. 327.

60. Ibid., p. 328.
61. Ibid., p. 326; Ovington, *The Walls Came Tumbling Down*, p. 106.

Chapter Nineteen: Smoldering Bridges

1. Duster, ed., *Crusade for Justice*, p. 311 (hereafter Wells, *Crusade*).
2. For a study of Cairo, see Herman R. Lanz, *A Community in Search of Itself: A Case History of Cairo, Illinois* (Carbondale: Southern Illinois University Press, 1972); quote in the *New York Age*, 25 November 1909.
3. Wells, *Crusade*, p. 309.
4. *Chicago Tribune*, 12 November 1909.
5. Wells-Barnett, "How Enfranchisement Stops Lynching," reprinted in Thompson, *Ida B. Wells-Barnett*, p. 271.
6. *Chicago Tribune*, 13 November 1909. Also see the *New York Times*, 18 November 1909.
7. *Chicago Tribune*, 12 November 1909.
8. Ibid., 13 November 1909.
9. *New York Age*, 25 November 1909.
10. Wells-Barnett, ibid., p. 270; Wells, *Crusade*, p. 311.
11. Wells, ibid.
12. Ibid., pp. 311–312.
13. Ibid., pp. 312–313.
14. Ibid., pp. 313–314.
15. Ibid., p. 314.
16. Ibid., pp. 314–315.
17. Ibid., p. 315.
18. Ibid., pp. 315–317.
19. Quoted in the *Illinois State Register*, 10 December 1909.
20. Ibid., 10 December 1909.
21. *Springfield (IL) Forum*, 11 December 1909.
22. *Chicago Defender*, 1 January 1910.
23. Wells, ibid. pp. 301–302.
24. Spear, *Black Chicago*, p. 100.
25. Duster, "Ida B. Wells, Her Life and Work," chap. 9, p. 10.
26. Wells, ibid., pp. 302–303.
27. Ibid., pp. 306–307.
28. Gosnell, *Negro Politicians*, pp. 73–74.
29. *Chicago Defender*, 19 February, 2 April 1910; *Chicago Broad Ax*, 9 April 1910.
30. *Chicago Broad Ax*, 16 April 1910; Gosnell, ibid., p. 74.
31. Duster, ibid., chap. 9, pp. 8–9.
32. *Chicago Broad Ax*, 11 September 1909.
33. Wells, ibid., p. 306.
34. Kellogg, *NAACP*, pp. 31–33; Lewis, *W. E. B. Du Bois, The Biography of a Race*, pp. 397–405.
35. Wells, *Crusade*, p. 326.
36. Ibid., p. 327; Frances Blascoer to Isabel Eaton, 26 March 1910, W. E. B. Du Bois Papers, ms. 312.
37. Others scheduled to speak during the course of the conference included Mary Church Terell, Kelly Miller, Charles Chesnutt, Albert Pillsbury, John Dewey, Franz Boas, Jacob Schiff, and W. E. B. Du Bois. Kellogg, ibid., p. 45.
38. Wells-Barnett, ibid., p. 271.

39. Wells, *Crusade*, p. 327; Ida B. Wells-Barnett to Joel E. Spingarn, 21 April 1911, Spingarn Papers.

40. *Chicago Defender* 4, 25 June 1910; *Chicago Broad Ax*, 1 October 1910; *Chicago Defender*, 27 January 1912.

41. Salem, *To Better Our World*, p. 105.

42. Wells, ibid., p. 328.

43. See J. Silone Yates to Margaret Murray Washington, 16 May 1904, for example, noting the complaints about the publication and Yates's defense of both it and Washington. Records of the National Association of Colored Women, Correspondence Files.

44. Wells, ibid., pp. 328–329.

45. *New York Age*, 29 July 1910.

46. *Chicago Broad Ax*, 6, 27 August 1910; Davis, *Lifting As We Climb*, p. 52.

47. *Chicago Broad Ax*, 24 September 1910, quoted in Reed, *The Chicago NAACP*, p. 37; Wells, *Crusade*, pp. 335–337; *Chicago Defender*, 27 August, 24 September 1910; *Chicago Broad Ax*, 1, 15 October 1910; *The Crisis* 1 (November 1910): 14.

48. Ross, *J. E. Spingarn and the Rise of the NAACP*, p. 21.

49. No doubt, Ida was seen as particularly "reliable" after she alerted Villard to the possibility that Wright, whom Spingarn had also written to ask if more money was needed, was seeking to make notoriety as well as money out of the case. She explained that Wright's response to Spingarn, saying that more money was needed, had come after Green was safely out of Chicago and Ida herself had already given Wright some funds. Oswald Garrison Villard to J. E. Spingarn, 19 October 1910, Oswald Garrison Villard Papers.

50. Wells, *Crusade*, p. 337.

51. *Chicago Defender*, 24 September 1910.

52. *The Crisis* (November 1910): 14, 15.

53. Lewis, ibid., p. 485.

54. Ida B. Wells-Barnett to Joel E. Spingarn, 21 April 1911, Spingarn Papers.

55. Harlan, *Booker T. Washington, The Wizard of Tuskegee*, pp. 379–384.

56. Ibid., p. 392.

57. Jackson, "Black Charity in Progressive Chicago," p. 412; C. H. Tobias, "The Colored YMCA," *The Crisis* 9 (November 1914): 33.

58. W. C. Graves to Clement MacNeal, 26 December 1919, Rosenwald Papers.

59. Rosenwald did not accept the chair position but gave five hundred dollars toward the expenses for the fourth annual conference to be held in the city in April of 1912, and subsequently promised to contribute a yearly sum equal to 25 percent of the branch's budget. Julius Rosenwald to Oswald Garrison Villard, 27 January 1912; Julius Rosenwald to Edward Osgood Brown, 16 April 1914, Julius Rosenwald Papers.

60. Ida B. Wells to Joel E. Spingarn, ibid.

61. Davis, *American Heroine*, p. 134.

62. Ida B. Wells-Barnett to Joel E. Spingarn, ibid.

63. Diner, "Chicago Social Workers in the Progressive Era," p. 396.

64. The description of Addams by Henry Steele Commanger is found in Buechler, *The Transformation of the Woman Suffrage Movement*, p. 158; Reed, *The Chicago NAACP*, p. 23.

65. Kellogg, ibid., p. 210.

66. Zangrando, *The NAACP Crusade Against Lynching*, p. 26.

67. Ibid., p. 27.

68. Ibid., pp. 26–27; *Chicago Defender*, 20 April 1912.

69. *Chicago Defender*, 13, 20 January, 30 March 1912; *The Crisis* (May 1912): 89.

70. Ovington, "The National Association for the Advancement of Colored People" (1924),

p. 113. Ida's name was mentioned as an early "revolter" though not in context with the antilynching movement.

Chapter Twenty: The Ladies' Band

1. Victor Lawson to Ida B. Wells, 9 January 1911, Victor Lawson Papers.
2. Ida B. Wells to Joel E. Spingarn, 21 April 1911, Joel E. Spingarn Papers.
3. Duster, ed., *Crusade for Justice*, p. 330 (hereafter Wells, *Crusade*).
4. *Chicago Broad Ax*, 22 October 1910; 21 January 1911; 24 September 1910; 15 April 1911; 17 September, 11 February 1911 (hereafter *BA*).
5. Duster, "Ida B. Wells, Her Life and Work," chap. 9, pp. 12–13.
6. Ida B. Wells to Joel E. Spingarns, ibid.
7. Booker T. Washington, "A Remarkable Triple Alliance: How a Jew Is Helping the Negro Through the Y.M.C.A.," *Outlook*, 28 October 1914, summarized in the Julius Rosenwald Papers, Folder, "YMCA," SB/13/37; Victor Lawson to Ida B. Wells-Barnett, 9 January, 4 March 1911, Victor Lawson Papers.
8. Bukowski, *Big Bill Thompson*, p. 18.
9. Spear, *Black Chicago*, p. 113.
10. Ibid., p. 100; *BA*, 21 January 1911; *Chicago Defender*, 21 January 1911 (hereafter *CD*).
11. The *Chicago Evening Post*, quoted in the *CD*, 21 January 1911.
12. *The Fellowship Herald*, 22 June 1911; Victor Lawson to Ida B. Wells-Barnett, 16 August 1911, Victor Lawson Papers.
13. Victor Lawson to Ida B. Wells-Barnett, 18 November 1911, Victor Lawson Papers.
14. *Chicago Record-Herald*, 26 January 1912.
15. "Julius Rosenwald and the Negro," *The Crisis* 24 (September 1922): 208; H. H. Kohlsaat to Julius Rosenwald, 9, 16 May, 30 September 1912; 22 May 1913, Julius Rosenwald Papers.
16. Harlan, *Booker T. Washington, The Wizard of Tuskegee*, p. 197; Margaret Murray Washington to Mrs. Rosenwald, 4 March 1912, Julius Rosenwald Papers.
17. Wells, *Crusade*, p. 331.
18. Ibid.
19. "I was sure," Wells-Barnett wrote in her autobiography, "that the YMCA would never take over the work that we were doing" and "that the need for continuing our work was greater than ever." Wells, ibid., p. 332; *BA*, 3 August 1912; "Julius Rosenwald and the Negro," ibid., p. 203; Victor Lawson to Ida B. Wells-Barnett, 18 November 1911, Victor Lawson Papers.
20. *BA*, 20 September 1913; Wells, ibid., Gosnell, *Negro Politicians*, p. 204.
21. Duster, ibid. p. 11.
22. Ida B. Wells-Barnett to J. E. Spingarn, 29 July 1913, Joel E. Spingarn Papers.
23. In 1891, the Illinois Supreme Court had ruled that the legislature could extend suffrage for any offices not established by the state constitution. Wheeler, "Conflict in Illinois," p. 97; "The Suffrage Conquest of Illinois," *Literary Digest*, 28 June 1913, p. 1.
24. Buechler, *The Transformation of the Woman Suffrage Movement*, pp. 175–177.
25. Harlan, *Booker T. Washington, The Wizard of Tuskegee*, pp. 349–350, 353, 338–441. The notable exceptions were the appointments of Nashville's J. C. Napier to the office of register of the Treasury and Bostonian William Lewis as assistant attorney general. Robert Terrell, who received a municipal judgeship in 1910, had technically been appointed by Theodore Roosevelt.
26. Lewis, *W. E. B. Du Bois, The Biography of a Race*, pp. 421–422.
27. Francis J. Garrison to Oswald Garrison Villard, 6 August 1912, Oswald Garrison Villard Papers.

28. Quoted in Fox, *The Guardian of Boston*, p. 166.

29. Addams, "The Progressive Party and the Negro," *The Crisis* 5 (November 1912): 30–33.

30. *CD*, 19 October 1912.

31. Wheeler, ibid., p. 105.

32. Wells, *Crusade*, p. 345; *Alpha Suffrage Record*, 18 March 1914. For more on the Alpha Suffrage Club, see Hendricks, "Ida B. Wells-Barnett and the Alpha Suffrage Club of Chicago," and Williams, "The Alpha Suffrage Club," *Half-Century Magazine* (September 1916): 12.

33. Williams, ibid.

34. Quoted in Moore, "Making a Spectacle of Suffrage," p. 92.

35. *Chicago Tribune*, 4 March 1913.

36. "A Personal Letter from Senator Tillman to the Editor of the Maryland Suffrage News," 27 November 1914. NAACP Suffrage Files, Mss. Division, Library of Congress. For the most comprehensive study of African American women and women's suffrage, see Terborg-Penn, *African American Women in the Struggle for the Vote*.

37. *Chicago Tribune*, ibid.

38. Ibid.; *CD*, 8 March 1913.

39. *Chicago Tribune*, 4 March 1913.

40. Ibid.

41. Catharine McCulloch to Virginia Brooks, 5 March 1913; Ida B. Wells Barnett to Catharine McCulloch, 15 March 1913. Catharine Waugh McColloch Series, Schlesinger Library.

42. *BA*, 8 March 1913.

43. *CD*, 8 March 1913. Curiously, neither the suffrage march episode, nor the reactions to it, were recounted in Wells-Barnett's autobiography and it is not clear if the exclusion was merely an oversight. However, due perhaps to the fact that she became increasingly ill as she was writing the latter chapters of the book, other events were also severely truncated or not included.

44. *BA*, 29 March 1913.

45. Franklin, *From Slavery to Freedom*, p. 324.

46. *CD*, 19 April 1913; *BA*, 17 May 1913.

47. Wells, *Crusade*, p. 360.

48. Logan and Winston, *American Negro Biography*, pp. 352–353; Wells, ibid., pp. 358–360.

49. *CD*, 26 April 1913.

50. *CD*, 5, 19 April 1913.

51. Wheeler, ibid., p. 110.

52. Quoted in Wheeler, ibid., p. 95.

53. *CD*, 5 July 1913.

54. *BA*, 19 July 1913.

55. *CD*, 12 July 1912; *BA*, 19 July 1913.

Chapter Twenty-One: The Alpha Suffrage Club

1. Hendricks, *Gender, Race, and Politics in the Midwest*, pp. 83–86.

2. Duster, ed., *Crusade for Justice*, p. 361 (hereafter Wells, *Crusade*).

3. Logsden, "The Reverend Archibald Carey," p. 24; *Chicago Broad-Ax*, 19 July, 23 August, 1 November, 1913 (hereafter *BA*).

4. Hendricks, ibid., p. 84.

5. Other commission members included Medill McCormick, Robert Jackson, John Daley, W. Duff Piercy, and George W. Ford.

6. Hendricks, ibid., p. 85.

7. The City Federation was organized in 1906 and represented seventy clubs by 1916. Hendricks, ibid., p. 29; *BA*, 12 July 1913; Wells, ibid., p. 362.

8. Wells, ibid., p. 363.

9. Link, *Wilson: The New Freedom*, pp. 246–247; quote in Weiss, "The Negro and the New Freedom," p. 64.

10. Link, ibid., p. 247. For a detailed description of the administration's segregation in the departments, see Lunardini, "Standing Firm," p. 251, n. 1. For a study of the pattern of segregation, see Meier and Rudwick, "The Rise of Segregation in the Federal Bureaucracy."

11. Link, ibid., p. 246; Thomas Dixon to Woodrow Wilson, 27 June 1913, quoted in Fox, *The Guardian of Boston*, p. 170. A lengthy biographical sketch of Dixon, including his friendship with Wilson, is found in Williamson, *The Crucible of Race*, pp. 140–179.

12. *Chicago Defender*, 22 February 1913 (hereafter *CD*).

13. *CD*, 30 May 1914.

14. Washington quoted in Link, ibid., p. 244; Du Bois's quote in Lewis, *W. E. B. Du Bois, Biography of a Race*, p. 424.

15. Link, ibid., p. 244; Booker T. Washington to Oswald Garrison Villard, 10 August 1913, in Harlan, *The Booker T. Washington Papers*, vol. 12, pp. 248–249 (hereafter Harlan, *BTWP*).

16. Fox, ibid., pp. 137–138, 168, 173.

17. Judge Osgood Brown became president of NAACP's Chicago chapter and in the next three years, Celia Parker Woolley; the banker N. W. Harris; Willoughby Walling, brother of William English Walling; and Charles T. Hallinan—editor of the *Chicago Evening Post*—all left the chapter, a number of whom cited Brown's ineffectiveness. S. Laing Williams, still reporting to Booker Washington, was the branch's vice president in 1912 and was soon to become its first legal counsel. Reed, *The Chicago NAACP*, pp. 33–37, 39–43.

18. See, for example, Du Bois's "Another Open Letter to Woodrow Wilson," *The Crisis* 7 (1913–1914): 1144–1147; May Childs Nerney's investigation for the NAACP found that segregation had been given a "tremendous impetus" under Wilson and that it was being systematically enforced by the administration. May Childs Nerney to O. G. Villard, 30 September 1913, Oswald Garrison Villard Papers, quoted in Link, ibid., p. 247.

19. Wells, *Crusade*, p. 376. The other members of the delegation were William Sinclair, Byron Gunner, Thomas Walker, Maurice Spencer, and Freeman H. M. Murray. Fox, ibid., p. 175. Wells-Barnett mistakenly records the year of the White House meeting as 1915 and identifies the NIPL by its later name, the National Equal Rights League.

20. Lunardini, ibid., p. 249. This text includes a transcript of the meeting.

21. Ibid.

22. Ibid., pp. 250–251.

23. Fox, ibid., p. 175; Wells, ibid., p. 376.

24. *The Crisis* 7 (1913–1914): 133–134; quoted in Fox, ibid. p. 176.

25. Kellogg, The *NAACP*, pp. 106–107; Lewis, ibid., p. 474; Booker T. Washington to Emmet Jay Scott, 16 January 1914, in Harlan, *BTWP*, ibid., p. 417.

26. Gosnell, *Negro Politicians*, p. 74.

27. *CD*, 10 October 1914.

28. Alzada P. Comstock, "Chicago Housing Conditions, VI: The Problem of the Negro," *American Journal of Sociology* 18 (September 1912): 253–255; Philpott, *The Slum and the Ghetto*, pp. 157–158; *The Negro in Chicago*, "Houses of Prostitution" map 1, facing p. 342; Kantowicz, Edward R. "Carter H. Harrison II: the Politics of Balance," in Green and Holli, *The Mayors*, p. 29. For further comment on the situation in the Black Belt, see

Williams, "Social Bonds in the 'Black Belt.'" Another study in the period was Sophonisba P. Breckenridge, "The Color Line in the Housing Problem," *Survey* 29 (1 February 1913): 575–576.

29. *CD*, 3 October 1914.

30. The other major Second Ward political leader was its senior alderman, George Harding, a wealthy real estate agent who was reputed to be particularly lenient with his delinquent tenants come election time. Both Harding and Madden were known to lavishly entertain their important constituents. Spear, *Black Chicago*, p. 36; Bullard, "From Businessman to Congressman," pp. 208–210; Gosnell, ibid., p. 142.

31. Branham, "The Transformation of Black Political Leadership," p. 86; *CD*, 29 January, 2 April, 12 March 1910.

32. Editorial, *The Crisis* 4 (September 1912): 234. For an overview of black attitudes toward women's suffrage, see Terborg-Penn, *African American Women in the Struggle for the Vote*, chap. 4, passim; and Giddings, *When and Where I Enter*, chap. 7, passim. Also see Terborg-Penn, ibid., chap. 6, for an overview of "anti-black woman's suffrage tactics" on the part of both whites and blacks.

33. *CD*, 29 November 1913; Wells, *Crusade*, p. 346.

34. Wells, ibid., p. 345; Katherine E. Williams, "The Alpha Suffrage Club," p. 12; *CD*, 23 August 1913.

35. Knupfer, *Toward a Tenderer Humanity*, p. 145. Sadie Adams, a native of Staunton, Virginia, became president of the City Federation in 1921. Knupfer, ibid., p. 144; Davis, *The Story of the Illinois Federation of Colored Women's Clubs*, pp. 80–81. The ASC's first officers also included Mary Jackson, first vice president; Viola Hill, second vice president; and Vera Wesley Green, recording secretary. Subsequent officers included Mrs. E. D. Wyatt, secretary; Mrs. W. N. Mills, corresponding secretary; and Mrs. J. E. Hughes, assistant secretary. Williams, "The Alpha Suffrage Club," p. 12; *Alpha Suffrage Record*, 18 March 1914 [1915]; Hendricks, ibid., p. 90.

36. *CD*, 23 August 1913.

37. Williams, ibid.

38. *CD*, 21 February 1914.

39. Wells, *Crusade*, p. 346.

40. *CD*, 7 March 1914.

41. Wells, ibid.; Hendricks, "Ida B. Wells and the Alpha Suffrage Club of Chicago," p. 270; Hendricks, "Vote for the Advantage of Ourselves," p. 177. It is not clear how many registrants the ASC was directly responsible for. Another black women's suffrage organization, the Aloha Political Club, was founded some time around 1914. But the ASC appeared to be the only woman's organization that conducted house-to-house canvassing, and did so with the specific object of electing a black alderman.

42. *CD*, 21 February 1914.

43. *BA*, 28 February 1914; *CD*, 28 February 1914; Branham, ibid., p. 86; Hendricks, ibid., p. 180. It is unclear how divided the black women's vote was. The *Broad Ax*, which supported Norris, reported about a Republican rally, presided over by Marie Mitchell, a black clubwoman. According to the paper, when Edward Wright attempted to disrupt the rally by speaking on behalf of his independent candidate, William Cowan, Mitchell took Wright to task and the showdown, which Wright lost, was said to reinforce the decision of many present to vote for Hugh Norris. *BA*, 21 February 1914; Hendricks, ibid.

44. *CD*, 28 February, 4 April 1914.

45. Wells, *Crusade*, pp. 346–347.

46. Ibid., p. 347.

47. Griffin was also supported by Reverend Archibald Carey who had purportedly believed

that the time wasn't right for a black alderman and had supported the sitting Democratic mayor, Carter Harrison II, and the Democratic governor, Dunne. According to the *Broad Ax,* a Democratic paper that supported the campaign for a black alderman, Griffin was a Trojan horse who was put up by Democrats to split the black Republican vote. *BA,* 18, 11 April 1914. Norris received the votes of 4, 690 men and 2, 221 women; Griffin, 2007 men and 1,182 women. *BA,* 11 April 1914.

48. Branham, ibid., p. 88.
49. *CD,* 30, 9 May, 3 October, 27 June 1914.
50. *CD,* 18 April 1914.
51. *CD,* 9 May, 20 June, 25 July 1914; *BA,* 25 July 1914.
52. Wells, *Crusade,* p. 365.
53. Wells, ibid., pp. 364–365; Schultz and Hast, eds., *Women Building Chicago,* pp. 936–938; Hendricks, *Gender, Race, and Politics,* p. 84.
54. *CD,* 12 September 1914.
55. Branham, ibid., pp. 90–91.
56. *CD,* 12 December 1914; 9 January 1915.
57. *BA,* 7 March 1914; *CD,* 12 December 1914; 6, 30 January 1915.
58. Branham, ibid., p. 89–90.
59. Gosnell, ibid., 170; Wells, *Crusade,* pp. 347–348.
60. Gosnell, ibid., pp. 165–166.
61. *BA,* 6 February 1915; Thompson, *Ida B. Wells-Barnett,* p. 105.
62. Wells, ibid., p. 348.
63. Bukowski, *Big Bill Thompson,* pp. 21–22.; quote in Spear, *Black Chicago,* p. 187.
64. Wells, *Crusade,* pp. 350–351.
65. Ibid., p. 350; *Alpha Suffrage Record,* 18 March 1914 [1915].
66. Quote in Bukowski, ibid., p. 22.
67. Wells, ibid., p. 352.
68. *CD,* 27 February 1915.
69. Quote in Bukowski, ibid, p. 22; ibid., p. 23. Thompson won 8,633 votes in the ward; Olson, 1,870. Gosnell, ibid., p. 41, n. 10.
70. Wells, ibid., p. 348; *BA,* 13 March 1915; *CD,* 13 March 1915.
71. The vote results were De Priest, 10,599; Al Russell, 6,893; Simon P. Gary, 3,697; Samuel Block, 433. Hendricks, "Vote for the Advantage," p. 184.
72. *CD,* 1 May 1915.
73. Hendricks, *Gender, Race, and Politics in the Midwest,* p. 89. Also see Knupfer, *Toward a Tenderer Humanity,* pp. 53–56, for more on the suffrage groups as well as suffrage activities of other black women's organizations; Gosnell, ibid., p. 157; *CD,* 10 July, 18 September 1915.
74. Wells, ibid., p. 365.
75. De Priest, "Chicago and Woman's Suffrage," *The Crisis* (August 1915): 179.
76. "Some Chicagoans of Note," *The Crisis* (September 1915): 242.

Chapter Twenty-Two: Unsafe for Democracy

1. Alfreda Duster, ed., *Crusade for Justice,* p. 337 (hereafter Wells, *Crusade*); Duster, "Ida B. Wells, Her Life and Work," chap. 9, p. 16; *Chicago Defender,* 26 June 1915 (hereafter *CD*).
2. *CD,* 29 May 1915.
3. Edmund M. Allen, Warden, *Report of the Commissioners of the Illinois State Penitentiary at Joliet For the Two Years Ending Sept. 30, 1914* (Springfield: State of Illinois, 1915), pp. 7–10, quoted in Richard Lawson, *The Joliet Prison Photographs, 1890–1930* (Champaign, IL: Andromeda Printing, 1981), p. 5.

4. Duster, "Ida B. Wells, Her Life and Work," Chap. 9, p. 16; Lawson, ibid., p. 7; Wells, *Crusade*, p. 341.

5. *CD*, 26 June 1915.

6. Wells, ibid., p. 338.

7. Ibid., pp. 342–344; *CD*, 1, 22 May 1915; quote in Williamson, *The Crucible of Race*, p. 176. The NFL held a meeting, which included the Chicago NAACP president, Judge Edward O. Brown, about what could be done about the showing of the film. *CD*, 12 June 1915. Blacks in other cities, including Philadelphia and Boston, attempted, with mixed success, to prevent the film from being shown. As had happened in Chicago, D. W. Griffith sometimes appeared personally to challenge injunctions against the film.

8. Wells, ibid., p. 338.

9. *Chicago Record-Herald*, reprinted in *CD*, 26 June 1915; Wells, ibid., pp. 338–339.

10. Wells, ibid., p. 340.

11. *CD*, 17 July 1915; *BA*, 17 July 1915.

12. *CD*, 3 July, 23 October 1915; 20 May 1916.

13. *CD*, 27 November 1915.

14. Harlan, *Booker T. Washington, The Wizard of Tuskegee*, pp.451, 413–415.

15. Harlan, ibid., pp. 446–450; George C. Hall to Julius Rosenwald, 25 October 1915, Julius Rosenwald Papers, quoted in Harlan, ibid., p. 447.

16. Quotes in Harlan, ibid., pp. 451–452.

17. Harlan, ibid., p. 452.

18. Quote in Harlan, ibid., p. 454; ibid., pp. 454–455.

19. Harlan, ibid., pp. 413–415; *The Crisis* 11 (December 1915): 82, quoted in Lewis, *W. E. B. Du Bois, Biography of a Race*, p. 502.

20. Logan and Winston, *American Negro Biography*, p. 459; Theodore Roosevelt to Julius Rosenwald, 18 December 1915, Julius Rosenwald Papers; Julius Rosenwald to Theodore Roosevelt, 18 December 1915, Julius Rosenwald Papers.

21. Quoted in Fox, *The Guardian of Boston*, p. 203.

22. William Trotter to Joel Spingarn, 16 and 23 August 1916, Joel E. Spingarn Papers.

23. After Trotter's meeting with Wilson, Ida had invited him to be the keynote speaker for the Fellowship League's event. However, the date conflicted with the New Year church services and the turnout was so poor that Ida was unable to pay him the promised $100 speaking fee. But she was able to arrange other speaking engagements for him and a western tour that took him as far as Nebraska. George W. Ellis, a prominent lawyer, was voted NERL president; and Ida's brother-in-law Bernard Fitts, secretary. *CD*, 9 January 1915; Wells, ibid., pp. 376–377.

24. Lunardine, "Standing Firm," p. 258.

25. Ibid., p. 260. The text provides a transcript of the conversation. For other discussions of the Wilson-Trotter confrontations, see Weiss, "The Negro and the New Freedom." Fox, ibid., pp. 180–182.

26. See Fox, ibid., p. 183 for commentary from the *Boston Evening Transcript*, the *Independent*, the *New Republic*, the *New York World*, the *Cleveland Gazette*, the *Indianapolis Freeman*, and the *New York Age*; quote in Fox, ibid, p. 185.

27. *The Crisis* 9 (1914–1915): 82.

28. *CD*, 21 November 1914.

29. Albert E. Pillsbury to Archibald Grimke, 21 December 1914, quoted in Fox, ibid., p. 186; May Childs Nerney to Archibald Grimke, 7 December 1914, quoted in Fox, ibid., p. 187.

30. The number of immigrants dropped from 1,218,480 in 1914 to 326,700 in 1915, and 110,1,218,480 618 by 1918. Spear, *Black Chicago*, pp. 131, 141.

31. This point is eloquently made in Carby, "It Jus Be's Dat Way Sometime," p. 10.

32. *CD*, 14 October 1916; Kellogg, *NAACP*, pp. 218–219. See Dray, *At the Hands of Persons Unknown*, for more detailed accounts of the Frank and Washington lynchings, pp. 207–214 and 215–218, respectively. Dray's conclusion that the coverage of the Washington lynching in the *Crisis* was the first carefully written analysis of a lynching death ignores Wells-Barnett's earlier analyses. For a particularly insightful analysis of the Leo Frank lynching, which also pays close attention to its gender implications, see Nancy MacLean, "The Leo Frank Case Revisited," pp. 158–189, in Brundage, ed., *Under the Sentence of Lynching.*

33. Kellogg, ibid., p. 216.

34. Roy Nash, "Memorandum for Mr. Philip G. Peabody on Lynch-Law and the Practicability of a Successful Attack Thereon," May 26, 1916, Moorfield Storey Papers, Subject File, Anti-Lynching Correspondence, 1910–1918, Box 8.

35. Kellogg, ibid., p. 217.

36. *CD*, 14, 25 December 1915; 11 March, 15 April, 10 June 1916; 20 April 1918; *BA*, 13 April 1918. Transcript, *The People of Illinois vs. Joseph Campbell*, no. 11574. Supreme Court of Illinois, February 20, 1918, p. 7 (Lexis-Nexis document).

37. Elliott Rudwick, *Race Riot at East St. Louis*, pp. 5, 8.

38. *Chicago Record-Herald*, 6 July 1917.

39. Kornweibel, *Investigate Everything*, p. 8; *Chicago Daily Tribune*, 6 November 1916, quoted in Rudwick, ibid., p. 13.

40. Tingley, *The Structuring of a State*, pp. 188–189; Rudwick, ibid., p. 27.

41. Rudwick, ibid., p. 18.

42. Ibid., p. 44.

43. See ibid., pp. 41–57 for the details of the violent acts during the riot; "The Massacre of East St. Louis," *The Crisis* (September 1917): 225; *CD*, 7 July 1917.

44. Wells, ibid., p. 383.

45. *Chicago Daily News*, 5 July 1917.

46. Leonard, "The East St. Louis Pogrom," *The Survey* 38 (July 14, 1917): 329.

47. *The Crisis*, ibid., p. 220; *New York Tribune*, 11 July 1917, quoted in Stein, *The World of Marcus Garvey*, p. 41.

48. Wells, ibid., p. 383.

49. *Chicago Tribune*, 4 July 1917.

50. Wells-Barnett, *The East St. Louis Massacre*, p. 3.

51. Ibid., pp. 3–4; Wells, *Crusade*, p. 386; Wells-Barnett, ibid., p. 9.

52. Wells-Barnett, *The East St. Louis Massacre*, ibid., p. 4.

53. Ibid., pp. 4–7.

54. Ibid., p. 12.

55. Wells, *Crusade*, p. 388; *BA*, 21 July 17.

56. Wells-Barnett, *The East St. Louis Massacre*, p. 3; *CD*, 12 July 1930); Wells, *Crusade*, p. 388.

57. *BA*, 21 July 1917.

58. Wells-Barnett, *The East St. Louis Massacre*, pp. 13–14.

59. *CD*, 28 July 1917.

60. Wells-Barnett, ibid., pp. 14–15, 16.

61. Wells, *Crusade*, p. 387.

62. Rudwick, ibid., p. 186.

63. "The Massacre of East St. Louis," *The Crisis*, ibid., p. 226; Zangrando, *The NAACP Crusade Against Lynching*, p. 37.

64. Haynes, *A Night of Violence*, p. 59.

65. Ibid., pp. 8–10; Buckley, *American Patriots*, p. 145.

66. Haynes, ibid., p. 66.

67. Ibid., pp. 94–100. Another account of these events is found in Edgar Schuyler, "The Houston Race Riot, 1917," pp. 321–333.

68. Haynes, ibid., pp. 160, 167–169. See Haynes, ibid., chap. 6, passim, for a detailed description of the confrontation. *BA*, 17 November 1917; *Houston Chronicle*, 28 August 1917; *Chicago Tribune*, 26 August 1917.

69. *CD*, 1 September 1917.

70. Rudwick, ibid., pp. 116–118.

71. Ibid., pp. 98–99.

72. *CD*, 27 October 1917.

73. *BA*, 27 October 1917.

74. Wells, *Crusade*, p. 392; *CD*, 3 November 1917.

75. Wells, ibid., p. 393.

76. *CD*, 3 November 1917.

77. Wells, *Crusade*, p. 394.

78. Ibid.

79. *CD*, 1 December 1917; *BA*, 8 December 1917; *St. Louis Globe Democrat*, 27 November 1917; *East St. Louis Star*, 27 November 1917; *Chicago Record-Herald*, 26 November 1917.

80. *CD*, 1 December 1917; W. E. B. Du Bois, "Leroy Bundy," *The Crisis* (November 1922): 17, 19.

81. Kellogg, ibid. p. 261.

82. W. E. B. Du Bois, "Editorial," *The Crisis* 14 (October 1917): 284.

83. Haynes, ibid., pp. 2–7. Forty-one of the remaining soldiers were given life sentences; four were sentenced to two and a half years or less, and five were acquitted.

84. Du Bois, "Thirteen," *The Crisis*, 15 (January 1918): 114; Lewis, *W. E. B. Du Bois, Biography of a Race*, p. 545.

85. Under the act, postal authorities could also refuse second-class items, such as newspapers, advocating such any of the above. Kornweibel, ibid., pp. 17–18.

86. *CD*, 26 January 1918.

87. Wells, *Crusade*, p. 369.

88. Ibid., pp. 369–370.

89. Agent Frank G. Clark to Bureau, 2 January 1918, and Division Superintendent Hinton Clabaugh to A. Bruce Bielaski, 16 January 1918, Old German Case File (OG) 123754, Record Group (RG) 65, Bureau of Investigation (BI) 1908–23, National Archives and Record Administration (NARA); "Memorandum to the Inspector General," 24 November 1917, 10218–60 RG 165, Military Intelligence Division (MID), NARA.

90. Clabaugh to Bielaski, 5 July 1917, and Agent J. C. Brantzburg to Bureau, 14 September 1917, OG 37586, RG 65, BI, NARA.

Chapter Twenty-Three: Known Race Agitator

1. Kornweibel, *Investigate Everything*, p. 10; Ellis, "'Negro Subversion,'" pp. 69–71.

2. Zangrando, *The NAACP Crusade Against Lynching*; p. 39; National Association for the Advancement of Colored People, *Thirty Years of Lynching*, p. 29.

3. Logan and Winston, *American Negro Biography*, pp. 353–357; Meier, *Negro Thought in America*, p. 79; Zangrando, ibid., pp. 39–40; Kellogg, *NAACP*, p. 227. Johnson relayed the "Mammy" story to, among others, Alice Dunbar-Nelson. Hull, ed. *Give Us This Day* p. 85.

4. Kornweibel, ibid., p. 124.

5. Major W. H. Loving to Chief, Military Intelligence Branch (MIB) Executive Division,

Subject: "Negro Subversion," 5 March 1918, File 10218 102, Record Group (RG) 165, National Archives and Record Administration (NARA).

6. Kornweibel, ibid., p.121.

7. Grossman, "Blowing the Trumpet," p. 85; Grossman, *Land of Hope*, p. 84.

8. *Chicago Defender*, 6 October, 15 September 1917; 20 March 1920 (hereafter *CD*); *Chicago Sun Tribune* 17, 18 August 1919; *Chicago Broad Ax* (hereafter *BA*), 27 July 1917; *CD*, 27 April 1918.

9. *CD*, 4 May 1918; 22 June 1918; Folder, John Cloures, Julius Rosenwald Papers.

10. Kornweibel, ibid., pp. 124–126; Logan and Winston, ibid., pp.1–2; ibid., p. 129. See Kornweibel, ibid., chap. 4, passim, for a detailed analysis of the attitude of the government toward the *Defender*.

11. Kornweibel, ibid., p. 19; *CD*, 6 July, 3 August 1918.

12. Ross, *J. E. Spingarn and the Rise of the NAACP*, p. 98.

13. For a complete listing of the fourteen points, see Jordan, *Black Newspapers and America's War for Democracy*, p. 126; *CD*, 6 July 1918.

14. Du Bois, "Close Ranks," *The Crisis* 16 (July 1918): 111.

15. *Pittsburgh Courier*, 20 July 1918; quotes in Lewis, *W. E. B. Du Bois, Biography of a Race*, p. 556.

16. Charles A. Pitman to John R. Shillady, 25 July 1918, NAACP (Branch) Files, St. Louis.

17. Du Bois, "LeRoy Bundy," *The Crisis* 25 (November 1922): 16–21; *Cleveland Gazette*, 27 July 1918, quoted in Rudwick, *Race Riot at East St. Louis*, p. 123; *CD*, 14 September 1918.

18. Zangrando, ibid., pp. 43–44. The Dyer Bill, H.R. 11279, defined a mob as three or more persons acting without authority of law and held them liable to prosecution in a federal court for a capital crime. It also stipulated that officials who allowed lynching to occur were to be subject to fines and imprisonment for up to five years; and that the county in which the lynching took place was also to be assessed fines from five to ten thousand dollars to be paid to the victim's heirs.

19. W. E. B. Du Bois to A. H. Grimke, 4 May 1918, Papers of A. H. Grimke, Moorland-Spingarn Collection, Howard University; Ellis, ibid., pp. 150–151.

20. Neval H. Thomas to Oswald Garrison Villard, 13 September 1918, Oswald Garrison Villard Papers; Lewis, ibid., p. 557; *CD*, 20 July 1918.

21. Du Bois, *Dusk of Dawn*, pp. 256–257, quoted in Lewis, ibid., p. 555.

22. Sheiber and Sheiber, "The Wilson Adminstration and the Wartime Mobilization of Black Americans," *Labor History* 10 (Summer 1969): 457; *New York Times*, 27 July 1918.

23. *Cleveland Gazette*, 27 July 1918; quoted in Fox, *Guardian of Boston*, p. 219.

24. Ellis, ibid., pp. 170–171; Fox, ibid., pp. 221–222.

25. Ellis, ibid., p. 173.

26. *CD*, 28 September 1918.

27. "'Self-Determination' and the Dangers," 20 December 1918, Robert Lansing Papers, Private Memoranda, 1915–22, Container 63, Reel II, Manuscript Division, Library of Congress. "What a calamity that the phrase was ever uttered!" the memorandum said in part. "Think of the feelings of the author when he counts the dead who died because he coined a phrase! A man, who is a leader of public thought, should beware of intemperate or undigested declarations"; Fox, ibid., pp. 180–181.

28. Duster, ed., *Crusade for Justice*, pp. 380–381 (hereafter Wells, *Crusade*); Logan and Winston, ibid., pp. 254–255; Garvey, "West Indies in the Mirror of Truth," *Champion Magazine* 1 (January 1917): 167–168. Reprinted in Hill, ed., *The Marcus Garvey UNIA Papers*, vol. I, p. 197. Garvey had written to Booker Washington of his admiration for the Tuskegeean's "good work" although "there is a difference of opinion on the lines on which the Negro should develop himself." Marcus Mosiah Garvey to Booker T. Washington, 8

September 1914, in Harlan, *Booker T. Washington Papers*, vol. 13, pp. 126–127. For an extensive bibliography of biographical studies on Garvey, see Hill and Bair, eds., *Marcus Garvey, Life and Lessons.*

29. Jordan, *Black Newspapers & America's War for Democracy*, pp. 112–113. For a biography of A. Philip Randolph, see Anderson, *A. Philip Randolph: A Biographical Portrait.*

30. Stein, *The World of Marcus Garvey*, p. 188.

31. Ellis, ibid., pp. 433–434, 374, 438.

32. Fox, ibid., p. 213.

33. Ellis, ibid., p. 371.

34. Wells, ibid., p. 379.

35. Ibid., p. 380.

36. Madam C. J. Walker to Mr. Ransom, 19 December 1918. The author is grateful to A'Lelia Bundles for providing this letter.

37. Logan and Winston, ibid., p. 621; Hine et al., *Black Women in America*, vol. 2, pp. 1209–1213; Wells, ibid., p. 378. For a full-length biography of Walker, see Bundles, *Madam C.J. Walker*; *CD*, 31 June 1919.

38. Major W. H. Loving to the Director, MID, Subject: Marcus Garvey, Editor of the "Negro World," and Mrs. Ida B. Wells-Barnett of Chicago, 20 December 1918, File 10218–3023, RG 165, NARA, also published in Hill, ed., ibid., vol. 1, pp. 328, 329.

39. W. E. B. Du Bois to The Honorable Robert Lansing, 27 November 1918, W. E. B. Du Bois Papers (microfilm) Series I, Correspondence, Reel 1, Frame 87. For details on the Pan-African Congress, see Lewis, ibid., pp. 561–562, 563, 567–569, 574–578.

40. "Meeting of the Baltimore Branch of the Universal Negro Improvement Association and African Communities League," 18 December 1918, File 10218–261–33, RG 165, pp. 4–6.

41. Dunn to Scott, 21 December 1918. MID File 10218–261, RG 165, NA; Ellis, ibid., p. 375.

42. Major Wrisley Brown to Lt. Col. H. A. Pakenham, "Memorandum," Subject: United Negro Improvement Association and African Communities League, and Marcus Garvey, 21 December 1918, File 10218–26121, RG 165, MID, NARA.

43. Quoted in Fox, ibid., p. 231.

44. Samuel Eliot Morison, *The Oxford History of the American People*, vol. 3 (New York: Meridian, 1994), pp. 209–210.

Chapter Twenty-Four: Prisoners of War

1. *Chicago Defender*, 22 February 1919 (hereafter *CD*); Buckley, *American Patriots*, p. 189.

2. Zangrando, *The NAACP Crusade Against Lynching*, p. 54; Tuttle, *Race Riot*, p. 22.

3. Du Bois, "Returning Soldiers," *The Crisis* 17 (May 1919): 14.

4. For example, throughout June of 1919, Jews charged that Polish youths were harassing them in Douglas Park, a West Side facility that the two groups had informally divided before the war. On June 8, rumors of a Polish invasion in the park resulted in eight thousand residents of the Jewish West Side gathering to defend themselves. An extra detail of police sent to the park appeared to minimize the confrontation. Forty-two youths were later arraigned for their attacks in the park. Bukowski, *Big Bill Thompson*, p. 96.

5. Tuttle, *Race Riot*, p. 182. By the census of 1920, blacks in Chicago numbered 109,458, nearly fifty thousand more than the 65,355 in 1910. Spear, *Black Chicago*, p. 141.

6. Philpott, *The Slum and the Ghetto*, p. 164; Tuttle, ibid., p. 175.

7. *Chicago Post*, 31 July 1919; Interview, "Alfreda M. Barnett Duster," in Travis, *An Autobiography of Black Chicago*, p. 213. Mrs. Duster indicates that the Barnetts bought the residence of the Richard B. Harrisons, but this appears to be inaccurate.

9. Tuttle, ibid., pp. 175–176; Chicago Commission on Race Relations, *The Negro in Chicago*, pp. 125, 126 (hereafter *The Negro in Chicago*); *CD*, 24, 31 May; 21 June 1919.

10. Gosnell, *Negro Politicians*, p. 43; *Broad Ax*, 7 June 1919 (hereafter *BA*).

11. Tuttle, ibid., p. 237; for details on the tense black and white labor relations, especially within the stockyards after the war, see Tuttle, ibid., chap. 4, passim.

12. *Chicago Tribune*, 7 July 1919.

13. The Washington riot followed two months of reports in the press about a black crime wave that was largely victimizing white women. An alleged robbery attempt of a white woman by two black men on July 18, 1919, set off an all-too-familiar rampage by a white mob, many of them servicemen, who moved about the city attacking blacks for four successive days before the militia was brought in to quell the violence. Ellis, "Negro Subversion," p. 467.

14. The riot continued intermittently for thirteen days from July 27 to August 8, the day that the troops were withdrawn. Of this period, seven days involved active rioting. *The Negro in Chicago*, ibid., p. 7. For the most detailed explanation of the riot, see Tuttle, ibid., chap. 2, passim.

15. Tuttle, ibid., pp. 204–207; Branham, "The Transformation of Black Leadership," p. 133.

16. Duster, ed. *Crusade for Justice*, p. 406 (hereafter Wells, *Crusade*); *Baltimore Afro-American*, 8 August 1919.

17. Tuttle, ibid. p. 40.

18. Ibid., pp. 40–41; *CD*, 21 August 1919.

19. *Chicago Tribune*, 13 August 1919; *The Negro in Chicago*, ibid., p. 126.

20. Tuttle, ibid., p. 64.

21. "A Report on the Chicago Riot by an Eye-Witness," *The Messenger* 2 (September 19, 1919): 712.

22. *Chicago Daily News*, 27 July 1919.

23. Major J. E. Cutler, "Memorandum for the Director of Military Intelligence," Subject: The Negro Situation, 15 August 1919, File 10210–361, RG 165, MIB, NARA.

24. Rpt Mills Kitchin, Chicago, August 2, 1919, Bureau File no. OG 369914, RG 65, NA, quoted in Ellis, "Negro Subversion," p. 480; "Negro Agitation," 29 August 1919, Old German Files (OG) 3057, RG 65, Bureau of Investigation (BI); Thomas B. Crocket to Director of Military Intelligence, 20 October 1919, MID File 10218–377.

25. *Chicago Tribune*, 1 August 1919.

26. *Chicago Daily Journal*, 29 July 1919.

27. *Chicago Daily News*, 1 August 1919.

28. Sernett, *Bound for the Promised Land*, pp. 143–144, 119.

29. *Chicago Daily News*, 29 July 1919.

30. *CD*, 16 August 1919 ; Wells, *Crusade*, p. 408.

31. Wells, *Crusade*, p. 408.

32. *Chicago Daily News*, 31 July 1919.

33. *Chicago Tribune*, 5 August 1919; *CD*, 7 August 1919.

34. *Chicago Tribune*, 7, 13, 25 August 1919; *CD*, 6 September 1919; *Chicago Post*, 13 August 1919.

35. Wells, *Crusade*, pp. 406–407.

36. Walter White to Mary White Ovington, 7 August 1919, NAACP Papers (microfilm) Part I, Reel 24, Frame 475. The author thanks Dr. Kenneth Janken who provided this letter and the additional correspondence between White and Ovington below.

37. Waskow, *From Race Riot to Sit In*, p. 46.

38. Walter White to Mary White Ovington, 11 August 1919, NAACP Papers (microfilm), Part I, Reel 24, Frame 475.

39. In August of 1919, the Joint Emergency Committee (JEC) made up of the NAACP, the Negro YMCA, the Urban League, the Peace and Protection Association, and the Cook County Bar Association, was established to protect black interests. The JEC was headed by the president of the Urban League, Robert E. Park, a white sociologist whom Walter White criticized as doing little and being hostile to White's suggestions. The NAACP also had conflicts with the Peace and Protection Association, which eventually withdrew from the JEC. By October, the JEC reconstituted itself into the Committee to Secure Equal Justice for Colored Riot Defendants and was dominated by the NAACP. Waskow, ibid., pp. 46–48; Walter White to Mary White Ovington, 13 August 1919, NAACP Papers (microfilm), Part 1, Reel 24, Frame 476. See, for example, W.C. Graves (Rosenwald's secretary) to Clement MacNeal, 26 December 1919, which said, in part, ". . . you may count on us for $500. if [*sic*] the Colored people show sufficient interest in the matter to make it plain that they really are in earnest in helping these defendants . . . Mr. Rosenwald might help again later," Julius Rosenwald Papers, Folder, Nat'l Asso'n Adv. Colored People; Chicago Race Riots.

40. The other more well-known members included Robert Abbott, Edward Osgood Brown, George Cleveland Hall, Victor F. Lawson, Julius Rosenwald, and Edward Morris. Waskow, ibid., pp. 64–65.

41. Ibid. pp. 128, 135, 137.

42. Shillady never fully recovered psychologically from the beating. He became disillusioned about the efficacy of the NAACP's program and resigned from the secretary position in 1920. One of the most disturbing aspects of the incident was the discovery that it had been a prominent black minister who had provoked the attack by informing a Texas Ranger that the NAACP was trying to incite insurrection among blacks. Kellogg, *NAACP*, pp. 239–240.

43. Walter White, *A Man Called White*, pp. 49–51; Cortner, *A Mob Intent on Death*, p. 26; Janken, *Walter White*, pp. 51–52.

44. Cortner, ibid., p. 27; *Chicago Daily News,* 18 October 1919; *CD,* 1 November 1919.

45. Rogers, "The Elaine Race Riots of 1919," *Arkansas Historical Quarterly* (Summer 1960): 144; *Topeka Plaindealer,* 28 November 1919.

46. Waskow, ibid, pp. 138–139.

47. Branham, ibid., pp. 117, 122, 132.

48. Wells, *Crusade,* pp. 397–398.

49. Wells-Barnett, *The Arkansas Race Riot*, p. 3; the NERL protest sent to Brough in early November, and the resolution endorsed by the People's Movement on December 7, "had the same subject matter but was worded differently." Wells, *Crusade*, p. 400.

50. Wells, *Crusade,* pp. 397–398, 399; *Arkansas Gazette,* 16 November 1919.

51. Cortner, ibid., p. 48; *Montgomery (Al) Advertiser*, 28 November 1919.

52. Wells, *Crusade,* p. 400.

53. White, *The Survey,* "Race Conflict in Arkansas," 13 December 1919, pp. 233–234; *CD,* 13 December 1919.

54. Wells, ibid, p. 398; Wells-Barnett, ibid., p. 5; Grossman, "Blowing the Trumpet" p. 88.

55. W. C. Graves to James Weldon Johnson, 9 January 1920, Folder, NAACP, Julius Rosenwald Papers.

56. A. Clement MacNeal to W. C. Graves, 3 April 1920, Folder, NAACP, Julius Rosenwald Papers.

57. Cortner, ibid., p. 43; Mary White Ovington, "Appeal," 26 November 1919, Robert R. Church Family Papers; Kellogg, *NAACP,* p. 240.

58. Wells, *Crusade,* p. 401.

59. Wells-Barnett mistakenly gives the date of her Arkansas trip as 1922. Wells, ibid., p. 401.

60. Ibid.
61. Ibid., pp. 402–403; Wells-Barnett, ibid., p. 6.
62. Cortner, ibid., pp. 48–49, 51–52.
63. Wells, *Crusade*, pp. 404–405; Cortner, ibid., pp. 106–107.
64. *CD*, 28 February 1920.
65. Wells-Barnett, ibid., pp. 20–21.
66. Ibid., pp. 22–24, 14.
67. Quoted in Cortner, ibid., p.93.
68. *CD*, 28 February 1920.
69. Wells-Barnett, ibid., pp. 57–58.

Chapter Twenty-Five: Unfriendly Takeovers

1. See http://tennesseeencyclopedia.net, "Edward Ward Carmack."
2. Miller, *Memphis During the Progressive Era*, pp. 193–194.
3. Tucker, *Memphis Since Crump*, p. 18; Church and Church, *The Robert R.Churches of Memphis*, p. 108.
4. Church and Church, ibid., pp. 106, 124–125.
5. Strickland, *History of the Chicago Urban League*, p. 70.
6. Ibid., pp. 13, 32–33.
7. Ibid., pp. 28, 36.
8. Harlan, *The Booker T. Washington Papers*, vol. 6. p. 203; Strickland, ibid., pp. 40–41.
9. Duster, ed., *Crusade for Justice*, p. 358 (hereafter Wells, *Crusade*).
10. *Chicago Defender*, 17 February 1919; 23 November 1918; 6 March 1915; 24 July 1915; 15 January 1916 (hereafter *CD*).
11. Ibid., p. 355–358.
12. Branham, "The Transformation of Black Political Leadership in Chicago," p. 180; Strickland, ibid., p. 48.
13. The Chicago Commission on Race Relations, *The Negro in Chicago*, p. 48 (hereafter, *The Negro in Chicago*).
14. A. Clement MacNeal to William C. Graves, 3 April 1920, Julius Rosenwald Papers.
15. "The People of the State of Illinois, Defendant in Error, *vs* Walter Colvin et al., Plaintiffs in Error," No. 13367, Supreme Court of Illinois, June 16, 1920. It was ruled on this occasion that there was insufficient grounds for granting a new trial: *The Negro in Chicago*, p. 664.
16. *CD*, 25 April, 3 May 1919. A committee was formed for the appeal that also included Oscar De Priest and A. Clement MacNeal. Logan and Winston, eds., *American Negro Biography*, p. 255; Wells, *Crusade*, pp. 380–382.
17. Garvey expressed some unhappiness about Barnett's defense in the case, complaining that Ferdinand had not informed him about the case going to court. Abbott's subsequent warrant against him prevented Garvey from returning to Chicago before his eventual imprisonment in 1925 and deportation two years later. Marcus Garvey, "Why I Have Not Spoken in Chicago," pp. 321–323, in Jacques-Garvey, comp., *Philosophy and Opinions of Marcus Garvey*; Stein, *The World of Marcus Garvey*, p. 79. Logan and Winston, ibid., pp. 254–256. For a discussion regarding the relationship between Garvey and Du Bois as well as the talented tenth leadership, see Lewis, *W. E. B. Du Bois, The Fight for Equality in the American Century*, chapter 2 passim.
18. Ida B. Wells-Barnett to My Dear Folks, 30 October 1920, Ida B. Wells Papers.
19. Wells, *Crusade*, p. 414.
20. Ibid.; *CD*, 1 January 1921.
21. Duster, "Ida B. Wells, Her Life and Work," chap. 11, p. 20; Wells, *Crusade*, p. 414.

22. Schultz and Hast, *Women Building Chicago*, pp. 994–995; Logan and Winston, ibid., p. 101; *CD*, 29 October, 31 December 1921.

23. *CD*, 19 February 1921; 7 September 1918.

24. Albert George was elected in 1924, a year when Edward Wright had gained control of the Second Ward organization. Gosnell, *Negro Politicians*, p. 86.

25. Interview, Alfreda Duster, 8, 9 March 1978, p. 135, Black Women Oral History Project (hereafter Duster, Project); Unpublished Interview, Alfreda Duster, conducted by Dorothy Sterling, 22 March 1976 (hereafter Interview, Sterling). The author is grateful to Mary Helen Washington for sharing this interview. Unpublished Interview with Donald L. Duster, Alfreda Duster Ferrell, and Benjamin C. Duster, 15 July 1993, Chicago, Illinois (hereafter Author's Interview); information on Fanny Wells was provided by Phil Reader, a genealogical researcher specializing in the central coast of California.

26. *CD*, 17 August, 20 July, 27 July 1918; 22 February 1919; Duster, Project, pp. 129–130; Unpublished Interview, Alfreda Duster, 1964, conducted by Donald Duster and Maxine Duster. The author thanks Donald Duster for the tape of this interview; and thanks Dr. Otis Maxwell who provided many genealogical notes and research.

27. Duster, Project, p. 131.

28. Interview, Sterling; Duster, Project, p. 131.

29. Ida B. Wells-Barnett to My Dear Folks, 20 October 1920, Wells Papers.

30. *CD*, 31 December 1921.

31. Duster, Project, p. 153.

32. Quote in Zangrando, *The NAACP and Crusade Against Lynching*, p. 57.

33. Kellogg, *NAACP*, 137; quote in Salem, *To Better Our World*, p. 158; Salem, ibid., p. 177. Kathryn Johnson, the "first field worker" began as an agent for the *Crisis* in Kansas City, Kansas, and proceeded to do field work in the South and West. Mary Wilson helped organize branches in Pittsburgh, Pennsylvania; and in Springfield, Dayton, Toledo, and Cincinnati, Ohio. Salem, ibid., pp. 159–160.

34. This point is made in Salem, ibid., p. 159. For an excellent study of black women and the NAACP, see Salem, ibid., chap. 5, passim.

35. Terborg-Penn, "African American Women's Networks in the Anti-lynching Crusade," p. 154, in Frankel et al., eds., *Gender, Class, Race, and Reform in the Progressive Era*.

36. *Afro-American Ledger*, 23 July 1920.

37. Sernett, *Bound for the Promised Land*, p. 165.

38. Davis, *The Story of the Illinois Federation of Colored Women's Clubs*, p. 3.

39. For a discussion of the history of the bill in Congress, see Zangrando, chap. 3, passim; quote, ibid., p. 62.

40. Ibid., p. 64.

41. Ibid., p. 66.

42. *Woman's Forum* 1, no. 2 (September–October 1922): 3, Mary Church Terrell Papers, Library of Congress.

43. Ibid.

44. During the decade, St. Luke absorbed other black financial institutions until it became the sole black bank in the city by 1929; Hine et al., eds., *Black Women in America*, pp. 1214–1219; Wesley, *The History of the National Association of Colored Women's Clubs*, pp. 90–91.

45. *Woman's Forum*, ibid., p. 4.

46. Ibid.

47. Ibid., pp. 2, 4, 6.

48. "The Ninth Crusade," *The Crisis* (March 1923): 213; "The Anti-Lynching Crusaders," *The Crisis* (November 1922): 8.

49. Hine et al., eds., ibid., vol. 2, pp. 1137–1139.

50. "The Anti-Lynching Crusaders," *Woman's Forum*, ibid., n.p.

51. To "Dear State Directors" from Mary B. Talbert, W. E. B Du Bois Papers (microfilm) 4877, Reel 10, Frame 0962; "Agreement Between the Anti Lynching Crusaders and the NAACP," undated. W. E. B Du Bois Papers (Microfilm) 4877, Reel 9, Frame 0969.

52. Mary B. Talbert to Walter White, 4, 9 October, 1 November, 11 December 1922. Papers of the National Association for the Advancement of Colored People, Part 1, Series C: Subject File 1910–1940, "Anti-Lynching Measures—Crusade" (hereafter ALM-C); *Pittsburgh Courier*, 28 October 1922.

53. The NAACP had received a matching grant of $5,000, to be paid in two installments of $2,500, from the American Fund for Public Service, a private philanthropy to fund the ad. Appeals to the usual philanthropists to match the fund had not been successful. Zangrando, ibid., pp. 81–82. The Crusaders donated two thousand dollars to the NAACP. Talbert to Ovington, 4 November 1922; Ovington to Talbert, 6 November 1922; ALM-C; Talbert to Ovington, 6 November 1922. The "Shame of America" ad itself was quite striking—and taken right from Ida's own publicity methods. The bold headline was "The Shame of America." The next line asked: "Do you know that the United States is the Only Land on Earth where human beings are BURNED AT THE STAKE?" The next line notified its readers that 3,436 people had been lynched between 1889 and 1921. The following line noted that only 17 percent of the victims had been accused of rape and was followed by the statistic that 83 women had been lynched in the United States. See for example, the ad in the *New York Times*, 23 November 1922. Although the Anti-Lynching Crusaders had raised less than $14,000, the NAACP's total budget was less than $58,000, and it used the Crusader money to shore up its general fund. Board Minutes, 12 March 1923, NAACP Papers, Part 1, Series A, 2; Zangrando, ibid., p. 98.

54. Mary B. Talbert to Mary McLeod Bethune, 30 December 1922, Records of the National Association of Colored Women's Clubs, Correspondence File.

55. Terborg-Penn, ibid., pp. 155–156.

56. Hine et al., eds., ibid., pp. 113–127; *CD*, 9 August 1924.

57. Hine et al., eds., ibid., pp. 113–126; *Baltimore Afro-American*, 3 August 1924.

58. Minutes, Fourteenth Biennial Convention of the National Association of Colored Women, August 3–8, 1924, p. 39.

59. Ibid., p. 40; *CD*, 16 August 1924; Higginbotham, "In Politics to Stay: Black Women Leaders and Party Politics in the 1920s," p. 209.

Chapter Twenty-Six: The Price of Liberty

1. Milton Webster to Mrs. Barnett, 15 September 1926, Box 1, Folder 10, Brotherhood of Sleeping Car Porters Papers (hereafter BSCPP). Randolph had since broken with Garvey over his separatist stance, and Ida's unheeded warning to the nationalist leader about his Black Star Line had by 1925 come to fruition. Garvey was convicted of mail fraud and served time in the Atlanta Penitentiary until 1927, when his sentence was commuted and he was deported to Jamaica. Logan and Winston, *American Negro Biography*, p. 255.

2. *Chicago Broad Ax*, 24 April 1915.

3. Bates, *Pullman Porters*, pp. 26, 31.

4. Ibid., pp. 20–23, 50–52.

5. *Pittsburgh Courier*, 1 May 1926.

6. For a discussion of opposition and support for the union, see Harris, *Keeping the Faith*, pp. 39–49; Milton Webster to Mrs. Barnett, ibid.

7. Bates, ibid., p. 42.

8. Ibid., p. 65.

9. Ibid. pp. 42–45.

10. Drake and Cayton, *Black Metropolis*, p. 77.

11. Philpott, *The Slum and the Ghetto*, p. 225. The Chicago Commission on Race Relations, *The Negro in Chicago*, p. 649. For an analysis of the commission report, see Waskow, *From Race Riot to Sit-In*, chap. 5, passim.

12. Bates, ibid., p. 89; Milton Webster to Mrs. Barnett, ibid.

13. *Chicago Defender*, 19 December 1925 (hereafter *CD*); Bates, ibid., p. 72.

14. Between 1910 and 1920, Illinois's black female population grew from over 56,000 to nearly 89,000. Hendricks, *Gender, Race, and Politics in the Midwest*, p. 113; Bates, ibid., pp. 78–79; Higginbotham, "In Politics to Stay," p. 215.

15. S.W.O. 193 Report on the Woman's Forum, 21 December 1925, File: History of the Brotherhood of Sleeping Car Porters, Box 10, A. Philip Randolph Papers.

16. Milton Webster to Mrs. Barnett, ibid.

17. Bates, ibid., pp. 79, 82. For a study of the BSCPM's women's councils, see Chateauvert, *Marching Together: Women of the Brotherhood of Sleeping Car Porters*.

18. Bates, ibid., pp. 79–80; *Pittsburgh Courier*, 2 January, 5 May 1926. Quoted in Harris, ibid., p. 66.

19. Milton Webster to Brother [A. Philip] Randolph, 9 October 1926, BSCPP, Box 1, Folder 11.

20. Randolph charged that Abbott's opposition was motivated by Pullman's placing the account, to the tune of $10,000, of the Pullman Porter's Benefit Association with the Binga Bank. Bates, ibid., pp. 80–81; *CD*, 19 March 1927; 14 January 1928. Duster, ed., *Crusade for Justice*, pp. 415–418 (hereafter Wells, *Crusade*).

21. Bates, ibid., pp. 81–82. In 1952, Gaines became the president of the National Association of Colored Women's Clubs. Schultz and Hast, eds., *Women Building Chicago*, pp. 294–296.

22. *CD*, 20 April 1929. For problems, including an unsuccessful call for a strike in 1928, see Harris, ibid., pp. 117–132. In 1935, the Pullman Company recognized the BSCPM as the bargaining agent for its porters and maids.

23. *CD*, 8, 14 May 1927.

24. Rudwick, *Race Riot at East St. Louis*, p. 131.

25. Wells, *Crusade*, p. 404. *Moore v. Dempsey* ruled that a trial in a mob-dominated court resulting in a miscarriage of justice constituted a failure to provide due process of law. Kellogg, *NAACP*, p. 244; Zangrando, *NAACP Crusade Against Lynching*, pp. 85–86.

26. *CD*, 28 May 1927.

27. *CD*, 16 August 1927.

28. *CD*, 11 June 1927.

29. *CD*, 23 August 1927.

30. *CD*, 16 July 1927.

31. *CD*, 11 June 1927; Ida B. Wells-Barnett, "Why I Am for Hoover," 20 September 1928, Leaflet, Claude A. Barnett Papers.

32. Hendricks, ibid., p. 89. Precinct captains were the eyes, ears, and legs of an organization. They had direct contact with residents and performed minor services such as fixing traffic tickets or arranging bail of a neighbor arrested for a minor offense. It was precinct captains who canvassed the neighborhoods and were the first to greet new residents to them. Women were especially effective as precinct captains, as residents were more apt to answer the door and invite them in to discuss candidates. Branham, "Transformation of Black Political Leadership," p. 212; Gosnell, ibid., p. 139.

33. Terborg-Penn, *African American Women in the Struggle for the Vote*, pp. 151–158. Giddings, *When and Where I Enter*, pp. 159–170; William Pickens, "The Woman Voter Hits the Color Line," *The Nation* (October 6, 1920): 372–373.

34. *CD*, 7 July 1929.
35. Gosnell, *Negro Politicians*, p. 41; Branham, "The Transformation of Black Leadership," pp. 214, 196.
36. Bukowski, "Big Bill Thompson," in Green and Holli, eds., *The Mayors*, p. 77; *Woman's Forum* (September and October 1922): 11.
37. By the census of 1930, the adult citizens in the First District numbered 94,000, which included more than 54,000 African Americans. Gosnell, ibid., p. 80.
38. Irene McCoy Gaines, "The Negro Woman in Politics," in Robb, *The Book of Achievement*, p. 88; I. Marie Johnson, "Women in Chicago Politics," *America's News Magazine*, 19 November 1927, p. 5.
39. *CD*, 26 November, 10 December 1927.
40. Ibid., 26 November 1927; Schultz and Hast, eds., ibid., p. 647.
41. Duster, "Ida B. Wells, Her Life and Work," chap. 10, p. 7; quote in Gosnell, ibid., p. 79.
42. *CD*, 14 April 1928.
43. Brahnam, ibid., p. 256.
44. Ibid., pp. 244–245.
45. Ibid., p. 213.
46. *CD* 12 March 1927, 10 March 1928.
47. Ibid., 12 March 1927; Bukowski, *Big Bill Thompson*, p. 203; Gosnell, ibid., p. 146.
48. Gaines, ibid, p. 206; Gosnell, ibid., p. 79; *CD*, 14 April 1928; Branham, ibid., p. 236; Gosnell, ibid., p. 160. William Dawson climbed up the political ladder in the Second Ward, winning an aldermanic seat in 1932 and was elected to the U. S. Congress in 1942 where he held his seat until he retired in 1970.
49. Gosnell, ibid., pp. 181–182.
50. *CD*, 7 April 1928.
51. See, for example, Lethia Fleming to Mary Church Terrell, 16 October 1920, in which Fleming points out a "mean article" Ida wrote, presumably about their political efforts. Terrell, addressing Fleming as "Lady-Bug," responded on October 19, stating that she was not surprised. "I did everything I could for that lady [Wells-Barnett] years ago when she had very few friends." Both letters found in the Mary Church Terrell Collection, Correspondence, Container 6, Reel 5, Library of Congress; P. L. Prattis to Claude Barnett, 8 August 1928, Claude Barnett Papers (CBP), Box 333, Folder 4. Dear Friend from Ida B. Wells-Barnett (Campaign Letter), 11 September 1928, CBP, ibid.
52. Ida B. Wells-Barnett to Claude Barnett, 19 October 1928, CBP, Box 333, Folder 5.
53. Ibid., 21 October 1928.
54. Ibid.
55. Ibid.
56. Wells, *Crusade*, p. 408.
57. *CD*, 22 December 1928.
58. *CD*, 16 February 1929; 10 August 1929, pp. 1, 15. The girl's name was Frances Jordan, who was reported to have struck a school official. The young girl was arrested, threatened with physical harm by police, examined for venereal disease, and held in confinement for several days before her parents were notified and able to raise bail. In too many cases, as Ida noted, such young girls were sent to the State Training School for Girls, a dangerously overcrowded facility for youthful female offenders, located in Geneva, Illinois, sixteen miles outside of Chicago. The school was known for practicing discrimination against black girls who lived separately from whites and were given the menial tasks and treated poorly. The intervention of the Barnetts made a difference in the case, which was subsequently adjudicated by juvenile court judge Mary Barteleme, an ally whom Ida had featured to speak before the Alpha Suffrage Club more than two decades earlier. Subse-

quently, Ida, the judge, and a delegation of citizens from the Illinois Federation, the Urban League, the NAACP, and others waited on Governor Len Small to protest the poor conditions and segregation practices of the school. *CD*, 1 March, 15 March 1930; 7 April 1928; *CD*, 10 August 1929.

59. Tingley, *The Structuring of a State*, p. 389; quoted in Gosnell, ibid., pp. 30, 182.

60. See, for example, a letter expounding this view from Elizabeth Lindsey Davis to Sallie Stewart, 10 April 1930, NACW Papers.

61. In 1929, while still a congresswoman, McCormick had gotten the Speaker of the House to alter the swearing-in ceremony, traditionally given to each member individually, to save the newly elected Oscar De Priest from possible embarrassment. Although he had been exonerated from the recent fraud charges, there was anxiety that racist members of the House might challenge his credentials when it was his turn to be sworn in. McCormick had convinced the Speaker to swear in the new members as a collective group, a procedure that took his naysayers by surprise and who did not recover in time to voice any objection. In return, De Priest supported McCormick's Senate bid, despite the fact that she was opposed by Mayor Thompson. His defiance, rather politically calculated or not, marked a beginning of Thompson losing his stranglehold on Chicago blacks. Gosnell, ibid., pp. 183–184; James et al., eds., *Notable American Women*, p. 294.

62. James et al., eds., ibid., p. 294.

63. *CD*, 4 May 1929; 1 October 1929.

64. Elizabeth Lindsay Davis to Sallie Stewart, undated, Reel 7, Frames 796–799; Elizabeth Lindsay Davis to Sallie Stewart, 24 December 1929, NACW Papers.

65. *CD*, 19 October 1929.

66. *CD*, 12 October 1929; Elizabeth Lindsay Davis to Sallie Stewart, 24 November 1929, NACW Papers.

67. Gosnell, ibid., p. 69.

68. Ida B. Wells-Barnett, "Day-Book," 27 January 1930, IBW Papers; DeCosta-Willis, *The Memphis Diary of Ida B. Wells*, p. 170. The day book was apparently kept between January 1 and May 19, 1930. The truncated entries in the palm-sized calendar book don't always appear to coincide with the printed dates on the pages. Citations will correspond to dates when appropriate and page numbers in DeCosta-Willis's text, which includes these entries.

69. *CD*, 8 March 1929; 9, 16 November 1930.

70. "Day-Book," Ida B. Wells-Barnett, 19 May 1930; Gosnell, *Machine Politics*, p. 3; Elmer Henderson, "Political Changes Among Negroes in Chicago During the Depression," *Social Forces* 17 (October–May 1941): 539.

71. "Afterword," DeCosta-Willis, ibid., pp. 198–199.

72. Wells-Barnett, ibid., January 1930; DeCosta-Willis, ibid., p. 167.

73. "Day-Book," ibid; DeCosta-Willis, ibid., p. 174.

74. Wells-Barnett, ibid.

75. *CD*, 12 April 1930.

76. Wells-Barnett, ibid., date unclear; DeCosta-Willis, ibid., p. 173.

77. For more on the Association of Southern Women for the Prevention of Lynching, see Hall, *The Revolt Against Chivalry. CD*, 30 April 1930; 10 May 1930.

78. *CD*, 20 September 1930.

79. Wells-Barnett, ibid., 13 January 1930; DeCosta-Willis, ibid., p. 168.

80. Duster, "Ida B. Wells, Her Life and Work," chap. 11, p. 19, IBW Papers, University of Chicago.

81. Duster, "Introduction," pp. xxx–xxxi, in Wells, *Crusade*.

82. *CD*, 4 April 1931.

83. Ibid.

84. *Chicago Whip,* 28 March 1931.

85. *Chicago Tribune,* 25 March 1931; "Ida B. Wells-Barnett: Postscript," by W. E. B. Du Bois, *The Crisis* (June 1931): 207.

86. Elizabeth Lindsay Davis to Sallie Stewart, 7 April 193, Correspondence File. Records of the National Association of Colored Women's Clubs, Correspondence File.

87. "In Memoriam: Ida B. Wells-Barnett," *National Notes* (May 1931), p. 17.

88. Irene McCoy Gaines, "Tribute" (handwritten manuscript), 30 March 1931, Irene McCoy Gaines Papers. It was Gaines, who with the Ida B. Wells Club, led the campaign to get the Chicago Housing Authority (of whom Ferdinand's son Albert was a field representative) to change the name of the South Parkway Gardens housing development to the Ida B. Wells Homes in 1940.

Selected Bibliography

Primary Sources

Atlanta University Center, Atlanta, GA
   The papers of John and Lugenia Hope
Bethune Museum and Archives
   National Council of Negro Women Records
   Washington, D.C.
Boston Public Library, Boston, MA
Brooklyn Historical Society, Brooklyn, NY
Carter G. Woodson Public Library, Chicago, IL
   Vivian G. Harsh Collection
Chautauqua Historical Society, Mayville, NY
   Albion Tourgée Papers
Chicago Historical Society, Chicago, IL
   Brotherhood of Sleeping Car Porters Papers
   Claude A. Barnett Papers
   Chicago Woman's Club Papers
   Chicago World's Columbian Exposition Papers
   George Washington Ellis Papers
   Illinois League of Women Voters Papers
   Irene McCoy Gaines Papers
   Municipal Court Papers
Holly Springs Public Library, Holly Springs, MS
Houghton Library, Harvard University, Cambridge, MA
   Oswald Garrison Villard Papers
Illinois Historical Society
Library of Congress, Washington, DC
   William E. Chandler Papers
   Frederick Douglass Papers
   Ruth Hanna McCormick Papers

National Association for the Advancement of Colored People Papers
Mary Church Terrell Papers
Booker T. Washington Papers
National Woman Suffrage Association Collection
Moorfield Storey Papers
A. Philip Randolph Papers
Marshall County Courthouse, Holly Springs, MS
Marshall County Historical Museum, Holly Springs, MS
Marshall County Library, Holly Springs, MS
Memphis and Shelby County Library and Information Center, Memphis, TN
Mississippi Valley Historical Collection, Memphis State University,
    Memphis, TN
Robert R. Church Family Papers
Moorland-Spingarn Research Center, Howard University, Washington, DC
Joel E. Spingarn Papers
Mary Church Terrell Papers
Anna Julia Cooper Papers
Walter F. Loving Papers
National Archives, Washington, DC
Records of the Bureau of Refugees, Freedmen, and Abandoned Lands
National Archives and Records Administration, College Park, MD
Investigation Case Files of the Bureau of Investigation
Newberry Library, Chicago, IL
Victor F. Lawson Papers
Oberlin College Archives, Oberlin, OH
Regenstein Library, University of Chicago, Chicago, IL
Julius Rosenwald Papers
Ida B. Wells Papers
Ripley Public Library, Tippah County, MS
Rust College Library, Holly Springs, MS
Schlesinger Library, Radcliffe Institute for Advanced Study, Harvard University, Cambridge, MA
Black Women Oral History Project Interviews, Alfreda M. Duster
Catherine Waugh McCulloch Series, Mary Earhart Dillon Collection
Schomburg Center for Research in Black Culture, New York, NY
Sophia Smith Collection, Smith College, Northampton, MA
Southern Historical Collection, University of North Carolina, Chapel Hill
Tennessee State Library and Archives, Nashville, TN
Tulare County Library, Visalia, CA
University of Massachusetts Library, W. E. B. Du Bois Papers, Special Collections and University Archives, Amherst, MA
University of Michigan Ann Arbor, MI
Bentley Historical Library, Necrology Files

Collections on Microfilm

National Archives and Records Administration, College Park, MD
Investigation Case Files of the Bureau of Investigation
Papers of the National Association for the Advancement of Colored People

Records of the National Association of Colored Women's Clubs, 1891–1992. Bethesda, MD: University Publications of America, 1994.

Temperance and Prohibition Papers, 1977 microform edition. Ohio Historical Society, Columbus, OH

Tuskegee Institute News Clippings File, Series z, 1899–1966. Tuskegee Institute, Tuskegee, AL

Selected U.S. Newspapers and Periodicals

ALABAMA

Huntsville Weekly Gazette
Montgomery Herald
National Notes

DISTRICT OF COLUMBIA

Colored American Magazine
People's Advocate
Washington Bee
Washington Colored American
Washington Evening Star
Washington National Intelligencer
Washington Post

GEORGIA

Atlanta Constitution
The Voice of the Negro

ILLINOIS

The Alpha Suffrage Record
The Champion Magazine
The Chicago Broad Ax
Chicago Chronicle
Chicago Conservator
Chicago Daily Inter-Ocean
Chicago Daily News
Chicago Defender
Chicago Evening Journal
Chicago Record-Herald
Chicago Times Herald
Chicago Tribune
Chicago Whip
The Fellowship Herald
Half-Century Magazine
Illinois State Register
Springfield Illinois Forum
Springfield Illinois Record

INDIANA

Indianapolis Freeman

KANSAS

Afro-American Advocate
Atchison Blade
Leavenworth Herald
Kansas City American Citizen
Parsons Weekly Blade
Topeka Weekly Call
Witchita People's Friend

KENTUCKY

American Baptist

LOUISIANA

New Orleans Weekly Pelican

MARYLAND

Baltimore Afro-American
Baltimore Colored American

MASSACHUSETTS

The Arena
Boston Evening Transcript
Boston Guardian
North American Review
Springfield Republican
The Woman's Era

MICHIGAN

Detroit Plaindealer

MINNESOTA

St. Paul Appeal

MISSISSIPPI

Holly Springs South Reporter
Marshall County Republican

MISSOURI

Kansas City American Citizen
St. Louis Post-Dispatch

NEBRASKA

Afro-American Sentinel
Omaha Enterprise

NEW YORK

Brooklyn Daily Eagle
The Crisis
The Independent
The Literary Digest

The Nation
Negro World
New York Age
New York Daily Tribune
New York Evening Post
New York Freeman
New York Globe
New York Sun
New York Times
New York World
The Outlook
Public Opinion
Rochester Herald
Rochester Union and Advertiser
The Survey
The Voice
World Today

North Carolina

AME Zion Church Quarterly
Star of Zion
Wilmington Daily Record

Ohio

Cleveland Gazette

Oklahoma

Langston City Herald

Pennsylvania

AME Church Review
The Christian Recorder
Pittsburgh Courier

Tennessee

Christian Index
Fisk Herald
Memphis Appeal or *Memphis Daily Appeal*
Memphis Appeal-Avalanche
Memphis Commercial or *Daily Commercial*
Memphis Commercial Appeal
Memphis Daily Avalanche
Memphis Free Speech
Memphis Living Way
Memphis Public Ledger
Memphis Scimitar
Memphis Watchman
Memphis Weekly Avalanche
Memphis Weekly Commercial
Nashville Daily American

Virginia

Norfolk Weekly Landmark
Richmond Planet

British Isle Newspapers

Aberdeen Evening Gazette
Anti-Caste (Street, Somersetshire, England)
Birmingham Daily Post
Christian Register (London)
The Christian Commonwealth (London)
The Christian World (London)
The Daily Chronicle (London)
The Edinburgh Evening Gazette Echo (London)
Fraternity (London)
The Inquirer (London)
Labour Leader (London)
Liverpool Daily Post
The Liverpool Review
London Daily News
Manchester Guardian
Newcastle Leader
Review of the Churches
The Sun (London)
The Times (London)
Westminster Gazette

Theses and Dissertations

Bates, Beth Tompkins, "The Unfinished Task of Emancipation: Protest Politics Come of Age in Chicago." PhD diss. Columbia Univ., 1997.

Baum, Jack. "Holly Springs: The Architecture of a Small Town." MA thesis, Univ. of Tennessee, 1978.

Berkeley, Kathleen Christine. "Like a Plague of Locust: Immigration and Social Change in Memphis, Tennessee, 1850–1880." PhD diss., Univ. of California, Los Angeles, 1980.

Bond, Beverly Greene. "'Till Fair Aurora Rise': African-American Women in Memphis, Tennessee, 1840–1915." PhD diss., Univ. of Memphis, 1996.

Branham, Charles Russell. "The Transformation of Black Political Leadership in Chicago, 1864–1942." PhD diss., Univ. of Chicago, 1981.

Bullard, Thomas Robert. "From Businessman to Congressman: The Careers of Martin B. Madden." PhD diss., Univ. of Illinois at Chicago Circle, 1973.

Cash, Floris Loretta Barnett. "Womanhood and Protest: The Club Movement Among Black Women, 1892–1922." PhD diss., State Univ. of New York, Stony Brook, 1986.

Chase, Hal Scripps. "Honey for Friends, Sting for Enemies: William Calvin Chase and the Washington Bee, 1882–1921." PhD diss., Univ. of Pennsylvania, 1973.

Crocker, Leslie Frank. "The Greek Revival Architecture of Holly Springs, Mississippi, 1837–1867." MA thesis, Univ. of Missouri, 1967.

Davis, Dernoral. "Against the Odds: Postbellum Growth and Development in a Southern Black Urban Community, 1865–1900." PhD diss., State Univ. of New York, Binghamton, 1987.

Davis, Ralph Nelson. "The Negro Newspaper in Chicago." MA thesis, Univ. of Chicago, 1939.

Duggan, Elizabeth A. "The Trials of Alice Mitchell: Sensationalism, Sexology and the Lesbian Subject in Turn-of-the-Century America." PhD diss., Univ. of Pennsylvania, 1992.

Edwards, Ishmell Hendrex. "History of Rust College." PhD diss., Univ. of Mississippi, 1993.

Ellis, C. M. D. " 'Negro Subversion': The Investigation of Black Unrest and Radicalism by Agencies of the United States Government, 1917–1920." PhD diss., Univ. of Aberdeen, 1984.

Grant, Donald L. "The Anti-Lynching Movement, 1883–1932." PhD diss., Univ. of Missouri, 1972.

Hamilton, Tulia Kay Brown. "The National Association of Colored Women, 1896–1920." PhD diss., Emory Univ., 1978.

Hamilton, William Baskerville. "The History of Holly Springs, Mississippi." MA thesis, Univ. of Mississippi, 1931.

Hart, Roger Louis. "Bourbonism and Populism in Tennessee, 1875–1896." PhD diss., Princeton Univ., 1970.

Hendricks, Wanda. "The Politics of Race: Black Women in Illinois, 1890–1920." PhD diss., Purdue Univ., *1990*.

Hilliard, David Moss. "The Development of Public Education in Memphis, Tennessee, 1848–1945." PhD diss., Univ. of Chicago, 1946.

Hooper, Ernest Walter. "Memphis, Tennessee: Federal Occupation and Reconstruction, 1862–1870." PhD diss., Univ. of North Carolina, Chapel Hill, 1957.

Hutton, Mary Magdelene Boone. "The Rhetoric of Ida B. Wells: The Genesis of the Anti-Lynch Movement." PhD diss., Indiana Univ., 1975.

Johnson, Cary. "Life Within the Confederate Lines as Depicted in the War-Time Journal of a Mississippi Girl." MA thesis, Louisiana State Univ. and Agricultural and Mechanical College, 1929.

Krieling, Albert Lee. "The Making of Racial Identities in the Black Press: A Cultural Analysis of Race Journalism in Chicago, 1878–1929." PhD diss., University of Illinois, Urbana-Champaign, 1973.

Logsdon, Joseph A. "The Reverend Archibald J. Carey and the Negro in Chicago Politics." MA thesis, Univ. of Chicago, 1961.

Melton, Gloria Brown. "Blacks in Memphis, Tennessee, 1920–1955: A Historical Study." PhD diss., Washington State Univ., 1984.

Roitman, Joel M. "Race Relations in Memphis, Tennessee, 1880–1905" MA thesis, Memphis State University, 1964.

Russell, Mattie. "Land Speculation in Tippah County, 1836–61." MA thesis, Univ. of Mississippi, 1940.

Walker, Eunice Rivers. "Ida B. Wells-Barnett, Her Contribution to the Field of Social Welfare." MSW thesis, Loyola Univ., 1941.

Walter, Robert Lee. "Equality or Inequality: A Comparative Study of Segregated Public Education in Memphis, Tennessee, 1862 to 1954." PhD diss., Western Colorado Univ., 1974.

Wrenn, Lynette B. "The Taxing District of Shelby County: A Political and Administrative History of Memphis, Tennessee, 1879–1893." PhD diss., Memphis State Univ., 1983.

Unpublished

Crawford, Floyd. "Ida B. Wells: Her Anti-Lynching Crusades in Britain and Repercussions from Them in the United States: 1958." Ida B. Wells Papers, Univ. of Chicago.

———. "Ida B. Wells: Some Reactions to Her Anti-Lynching Crusades in Britain." 1963. Ida B. Wells Papers, Univ. of Chicago.

Duster, Alfreda M. "Ida B. Wells: Her Life and Work." Ida B. Wells Papers, Univ. of Chicago.

"History of Rust College," pamphlet in the Rust College Library, Holly Springs, MS.

Lyons, Maritcha Remond, "Memories of Yesterdays, All of Which I Saw and Part of Which I Was: An Autobiography." (n.d.) Henry Albro Williamson Papers, Schomburg Center for Research on Black Culture.

Strickland, Belle. "Belle Strickland Diary, July 25, 1864–July 29, 1887." Marshall County Public Library, Holly Springs, MS.

Selected Articles, Pamphlets, and Documents

"A Brave Little Woman." *AME Zion Church Quarterly* 4 (July 1894): 406.

Addams, Jane. "Has the Emancipation Act Been Nullified by National Indifference?" *The Survey* (1 February 1913): 565–566.

Aked, C. F. "A Blot on a Free Republic." *Christian Literature and Review of the Churches* 9 (May–October 1894): 96–98.

———. *Eternal Punishment: Two Lectures.* London: Clarke & Co., 1891.

———. "The Race Problem in America." *The Contemporary Review* 65 (June 1894): 818–827.

Baker, Ray Stannard. "Lynching in the South." *McClure's* 25 (February 1905): 422–430.

———. "What Is a Lynching?" *McClure's* 25 (January 1905): 299–313.

Barber, J. Max. "The Niagara Movement." *Voice of the Negro* (September 1906): 671.

———. "The Niagara Movement at Harper's Ferry." *Voice of the Negro* (October 1906): 405.

———. "The Atlanta Tragedy," *The Voice* (November 1906): 473–479.

Bartelmae, Mary M. "Opportunity for Women in Court Administration." *Annals of the American Academy* 52 (March 1914): 188–190.

Bethune, Mary McLeod. "Faith That Moved a Dump Heap." In *Black Women in White America: A Documentary History,* edited by Gerda Lerner, pp. 134–143. New York: Vintage, 1974.

Bowen, Cornelia. "Woman's Part in the Uplift of Our Race." *Colored American Magazine* 12, no. 3 (1907): 222–223.

Bowen, Louise DeKoven. *The Colored People of Chicago: An Investigation Made for the Juvenile Protective Association.* Chicago, 1913.

Brief of Greer and Adams, "Chesapeake, Ohio & Southwestern Railroad Company v. Ida Wells, April 1885," Tennessee State Library and Archives.

Brown, L. J. "Philosophy of Lynching." *Voice of the Negro* (November 1904): 554–559.

Bruce, Mrs. Josephine B. "The Afterglow of the Women's Convention." *Voice of the Negro* (November 1904): 541–543.

Burroughs, Nannie Helen. "Not Color But Character." *Voice of the Negro* (July 1904): 283–287.

"Chicago's Liberality." *Voice of the Negro* (November 1906): 467.

"Chesapeake, Ohio & Southwestern Railroad Company v. Ida Wells, 5 April 1887." *Tennessee Reports,* 85 (1887): 613–615.

Congressional Record, 53rd Congress, 2nd session, XXVI, Pt. 8 (3 August 1894); 53rd Congress, 3rd session, XXVII, Pt. 1 (9 December 1894).

Deupree, J. G. "The Capture of Holly Springs, Mississippi." *Publications of the Mississippi Historical Society* 4 (1901): 49–61.

Douglass, Frederick. "Lynch Law in the South." *North American Review* 155 (5 July 1892): 17–24.

———. *The Lessons of the Hour.* Boston: Thomas & Evans, 1984.

Du Bois, W. E. B. "The President and the Soldiers." *The Voice* (December 1906): 552–553.

———. "The Litany of Atlanta." *The Independent* 51 (October 11, 1906): 856–858.

———. "The Problem of Amusement." *The Southern Workman* 27 (September 1897): 181–184.

————. "The Evolution of Negro Leadership." *Dial* 31 (18 July 1901): 53–55.

————. "National Committee on the Negro." *Survey* 23 (June 12, 1909): 407–409.

Fortune, T. Thomas. "Ida B. Wells, A.M." In *Women of Distinction: Remarkable in Works and Invincible in Character,* edited by Lawson V Scruggs, pp. 33–39. Raleigh, NC: Lawson V. Scruggs, 1893.

————. "Civil Rights and Social Privileges." *AME Church Review* (January 1886): 125–131.

Garvey, Marcus. "West Indies in the Mirror of Truth," *Champion Magazine* 1 (January 1917): 167–168, reprinted in Cary D. Wintz ed., *African American Political Thought, 1890–1930: Washington, Du Bois, Garvey and Randolph.* New York: M. E. Sharpe, 1966.

Harper, Frances Ellen. "The Woman's Christian Temperance Union and the Colored Woman." *AME Church Review* 4 (1887): 313–316.

————. Mrs. F. E. W, Ida B. Wells, et al. "Symposium-Temperance." *AME Church Review* (April 1891): 375–381.

————. "Woman's Political Future," reprinted in World's Congress of Representative Women, edited by Mary Wright Sewell, pp. 33–37. Chicago: Rand McNally & Company, 1894.

Historical Records of the Conventions of 1895–96 of the Colored Women of America, N.p. 1902.

Hunton, Mrs. Addie W. "A Deeper Reverence for Home Ties." *Colored American Magazine* 12 (1907): 58–59.

————. "The National Association of Colored Women: Its Real Significance." *Colored American Magazine* 14 (1908): 417.

————. "Negro Womanhood Defended." *Voice of the Negro* (July 1904): 280–282.

Ida B. Wells v. Chesapeake, Ohio & Southwestern Railroad Company, 4 November 1884, manuscript court record, Tennessee State Library and Archives.

Illinois Youth Commission. *Illinois State Training School for Girls, Geneva, Illinois.* N.p., 1963.

Leonard, Oscar. "The East St. Louis Pogrom." *The Survey* 38 (July 14, 1917): 331–333.

Mitchell, John, Jr. "Shall the Wheels of Race Agitation Be Stopped?" *Colored American Magazine* 5 (1903): 386.

"The NACW" (editorial). *Voice of the Negro* (July 1904): 310–311.

National Association for the Advancement of Colored People (NAACP). *Burning at the Stake in the U.S.* New York, 1919.

————. *The Fight Against Lynching.* New York, 1919.

————. *Notes on Lynching in the United States.* New York, 1912.

————. *Thirty Years of Lynching in the United States, 1889–1918.* New York, 1919.

————. *National Negro Conference: Proceedings.* New York, 1909.

National Conference of Colored Men of the United States, *Proceedings,* Nashville, Tennessee, 6–9 May 1879. Washington: Rufus H. Darby, 1879.

Phelps, Howard A. "Negro Life in Chicago." *Half-Century Magazine,* May 1919, p. 12.

"Report of the Memorial Service." *Unity Magazine,* 18 April 1918, pp. 115–122.

Report of the Select Committee on *the Memphis Riots and Massacres.* Washington, DC: Government Printing Office, 1866 [reprint by Johnson Reprint Corporation, New York, 1970].

"Respect for Law," *The Independent* 53 (January 3, 1901): 18–20.

Roosevelt, Theodore. "Lynching and the Miscarriage of Justice." *The Outlook* (25 November 1911): 706–707.

"Social Control." *The Crisis* 1, 3 (January 1911): 22–23

Stemmons, James Samuel. "The Unmentionable Crime." *Colored American Magazine* 6 (1903): 636–641.

Storey, Moorfield. "Athens and Brownsville," *The Crisis* 1 (November 1910): 13.

"The Suffrage Conquest of Illinois," *Literary Digest* 46 (28 June 1913): 1409–1411.

Terrell, Mary Church. "The Duty of the NACW to the Race." *AME Church Review* (July 1896): 219–225.

———. "Lynching from a Negro's Point of View." *North American Review* 178 (June 1904): 853–868.

———. "The Disbanding of the Colored Soldiers." *The Voice* (December 1906): 554–558.

Tillman, K. D. "Afro-American Women and Their Work." *AME Church Review* (October 1894): 477–499.

Tyler, Ralph W. "Does Lynching Thrive Under Democracy?" *Colored American Magazine* 14 (1908): 477–479.

Walling, William English. "The Race War in the North." *Independent* 65 (3 September 1908): 529–534.

Washington, Booker T. *An Open Letter by Booker T. Washington of Tuskegee Alabama upon Lynchings in the South*. Tuskegee, Ala., 1901.

———. "The Tuskegee Idea." *World Today* 6 (1904): 511–514.

Washington, Margaret Murray. "The Advancement of Colored Women." *Colored American Magazine* 8 (1904): 183–189.

———. "Club Work as a Factor in the Advance of Colored Women." *Colored American Magazine* 2 (1906): 83–90.

———. "The Social Improvement of the Plantation Woman." *Voice of the Negro* (July 1904): 288–290.

Wells, Ida B. "Afro-Americans and Africa." *AME Church Review* 9 (July 1892): 40–45. Reprinted in *Ida B. Wells-Barnett: An Exploratory Study of an American Black Woman, 1893–1930*, by Mildred I. Thompson, pp. 165–169. Brooklyn, NY: Carlson, 1990.

———. "Liverpool Slave Traditions and Present Practices." *The Independent* 46 (19 May 1894): 617.

———. "Lynch Law in All Its Phases." *Our Day* 11 (May 1893): 333–337. Reprinted in *Ida B. Wells-Barnett: An Exploratory Study of an American Black Woman, 1893–1930*, by Mildred I. Thompson, pp. 171–187. Brooklyn, NY: Carlson, 1990.

———. *The Reason Why the Colored American Is Not in the World's Columbian Exposition* (1893). Reprinted in *Selected Works of Ida B. Wells-Barnett*, compiled by Trudier Harris, pp. 46–137. New York: Oxford University Press, 1991.

———. "The Requirements of Southern Journalism." *AME Zion Church Quarterly* (April 1892): 189–196.

———. "A Story of 1900." *Fisk Herald* 3 (April 4 1886): 12. Reprinted in *The Memphis Diary of Ida B. Wells*, edited by Miriam DeCosta-Willis, pp. 182–184. Boston: Beacon, 1995.

———. "Two Christmas Days: A Holiday Story." *AME Zion Church Quarterly* 4 (January 1894): 129–140. Reprinted in *Ida B. Wells-Barnett: An Exploratory Study of an American Black Woman, 1893–1930*, by Mildred I. Thompson, pp. 225–234. Brooklyn, NY: Carlson, 1990.

———. *United States Atrocities: Lynch Law*. London: Lux Publishing, 1894.

Wells-Barnett, Ida B. *On Lynchings: Southern Horrors, A Red Record, Mob Rule in New Orleans*. New York: Arno Press, 1969.

———. *A Red Record: Tabulated Statistics and Alleged Causes of Lynchings in the United States, 1892–3–4*. Reprinted in *Selected Works of Ida B. Wells-Barnett*, compiled by Trudier Harris, pp. 138–252. New York: Oxford University Press, 1991.

———. *Southern Horrors: Lynch Law in All Its Phases* (1892). Reprinted in *Selected Works of Ida B. Wells-Barnett*, compiled by Trudier Harris, pp. 14–45. New York: Oxford University Press, 1991.

———. *Mob Rule in New Orleans: Robert Charles and His Fight to the Death*. September

1, 1900. Reprinted in *Selected Works of Ida B. Wells-Barnett*, compiled by Trudier Harris, pp. 253–322. New York: Oxford University Press, 1991.

———. *The Arkansas Race Riot*. Chicago: Ida B. Wells-Barnett, 1920.

———. "Lynch Law in America." *Arena* 23 (January 1900): 15–24. Reprinted in *Ida B. Wells-Barnett: An Exploratory Study of an American Black Woman, 1893–1930*, edited by Mildred I. Thompson, pp. 235–243. Brooklyn, NY: Carlson, 1990.

———. "Booker T. Washington and His Critics." *World Today* 6 (April 1904): 518–521. Reprinted in *Ida B. Wells-Barnett: An Exploratory Study of an American Black Woman, 1893–1930*, by Mildred I. Thompson, pp. 255–260. Brooklyn, NY: Carlson, 1990.

———. *The East St. Louis Massacre: The Greatest Outrage of the Century*. Chicago: The Negro Fellowship Herald Press, 1917.

———. "How Enfranchisement Stops Lynching." *Original Rights Magazine* 1 (June 1910): 42–53. Reprinted in *Ida B. Wells-Barnett: An Exploratory Study of an American Black Woman, 1893–1930*, by Mildred I. Thompson, pp. 267–280. Brooklyn, NY: Carlson, 1990.

———. *Lynch Law in Georgia*. Chicago: Ida B. Wells-Barnett, 1899.

———. "Lynching and the Excuse for It." *The Independent* 53 (May 1901): 1133–1136. Reprinted in *Ida B. Wells-Barnett: An Exploratory Study of an American Black Woman, 1893–1930*, by Mildred I. Thompson, pp. 249–254. Brooklyn, NY: Carlson, 1990.

———. "Lynching: Our National Crime." In National Negro Conference: *Proceedings*, 174–179. New York, 1909. Reprinted in *Ida B. Wells-Barnett: An Exploratory Study of an American Black Woman, 1893–1930*, by Mildred I. Thompson, pp. 261–265. Brooklyn, NY: Carlson, 1990.

———. "The National Afro-American Council." *Howard's American Magazine* 6, (1901): 413–416.

———. "The Negro's Case in Equity." *The Independent* 52 (April 26, 1900): 1010–1011. Reprinted in *Ida B. Wells-Barnett: An Exploratory Study of an American Black Woman*, by Mildred I. Thompson, pp. 245–246. Brooklyn, NY: Carlson, 1990.

———. "The Northern Negro Woman's Social and Moral Condition." *Original Rights Magazine*, (April 1910): 33–37.

———. "Our Country's Lynching Record." *The Survey* 29 (1 February 1913): 573–574. Reprinted in *Ida B. Wells-Barnett: An Exploratory Study of an American Black Woman*, by Mildred I. Thompson, pp. 277–280. Brooklyn, NY: Carlson, 1990,

———. "Bishop Turner's Ray of Light. *The Independent* 44 (July 28 1892): 5–6.

White, Walter. "The Race Conflict in Arkansas." *The Survey* (13 December 1919): 233–234.

Williams, Fannie Barrier. "The Awakening of Women." *AME Church Review* (April 1897): 392–398.

———. "The Club Movement among the Colored Women of America." In *A New Negro for a New Century*, edited by Booker T. Washington, N. B. Wood, and Fannie Barrier Williams, pp. 378–428. Chicago: American Publishing House, 1900.

———. "The Colored Girl." *Voice of the Negro* (June 1905): 400–403.

———. "Do We Need Another Name?" *Southern Workman* (January 1904): 33–36.

———. "An Extension of the Conference Spirit." *Voice of the Negro* (July 1904): 300–303.

———. "The Frederick Douglass Centre." *Southern Workman* (June 1906): 334–336.

———. "The Frederick Douglass Centre: A Question of Social Betterment, and Not of Social Equality." *Voice of the Negro* (December 1904): 601–604.

———. "The Intellectual Progress of the Colored Women of the United States since the Emancipation Proclamation." In *The World's Congress of Representative Women*, edited by May Wright Sewell, pp. 696–729. Chicago: Rand McNally, 1894.

————. "A New Method for Dealing with the Race Problem." *Voice of the Negro* (July 1906): 502–505.

————. "Religious Duty to the Negro." In *Black Women in Nineteenth-Century American Life: Their Words, Their Thoughts, Their Feelings,* edited by Burt Loewenberg and Ruth Bogin, pp. 265–270. Philadelphia: Pennsylvania State University Press, 1976.

————. "The Smaller Economies." *Voice of the Negro* (May 1904): 184–185.

————. "The Woman's Part in a Man's Business." *Voice of the Negro* (November 1904): 543–547.

————. "Work Attempted and Missed in Organized Club Work." *Colored American Magazine* 14 (1908): 281–285.

————. "Social Bonds in the 'Black Belt' of Chicago." *Charities* 15 (October 7, 1905): 40–44.

————. "Colored Women of Chicago." *Southern Workman* 63 (October 1914): 566–568.

Williams, Katherine E. "The Alpha Suffrage Club." *Half Century Magazine,* September 1916, p. 12.

Woolley, Celia Parker. "The Frederick Douglass Center, Chicago." *The Commons* 5 (July 1904): 328–329.

Work, Monroe N. "Crime Among Negroes in Chicago." *Journal of American Sociology* 9 (September 1900): 204–223.

Yates, Josephine Silone. "Kindergartens and Mothers' Clubs." *Colored American Magazine* 12 (1904): 304–311.

————. "The National Association of Colored Women." *Voice of the Negro* (July 1904): 283–287.

Selected Books

Addams, Jane, *Democracy and Social Ethics.* Cambridge: Harvard University Press, 1964. Originally published 1902.

————. *Twenty Years at Hull House.* New York: Signet, 1981. Originally published 1910.

Baker, Ray Stannard. *Following the Color Line: The State of the Negro Citizen in the American Democracy.* New York: Harper Torchbooks, 1964. Originally published 1908.

Broughton, V. W. *Twenty Year's Experience of a Missionary.* Chicago: Pony Press Publishers, 1907.

————. *Women's Work, As Gleaned from Women of the Bible, and Bible Women of Modern Times.* Nashville Baptist Publishing Board, 1904.

Brown, Hallie Q. *Homespun Heroines and Other Women of Distinction.* New York: Oxford University Press, 1988. Originally published 1926.

Bruce, Philip A. *The Plantation Negro as Freeman.* New York: G. P. Putnam's and Sons, 1889.

Catalogue of the Le Moyne Normal Institute, Memphis, Tennessee for Years 1901–1902. Memphis: LeMoyne Institute Press, 1901.

Centennial History of the City of Chicago: Its Men and Institutions. Chicago: Chicago Inter-Ocean Press, 1905.

Chicago Commission on Race Relations. *The Negro in Chicago: A Study of Race Relations and a Race Riot in 1919.* New York: Arno, 1968. Originally published 1922.

The Chicago Daily News Almanac and Year-Book. Chicago: The Chicago Daily News Company, 1914–1930.

Cooper, Anna Julia. *A Voice from the South.* Edited by Mary Helen Washington. New York: Oxford University Press, 1988. Originally published 1892.

Cutler, James Elbert. *Lynch-Law: An Investigation into the History of Lynching in the United States.* New York: New Universities Press, 1905.

Davis, Elizabeth Lindsay. *Lifting as They Climb.* New York: G. K. Hall, 1996. Originally published 1933.

————. *The Story of the Illinois Federation of Colored Women's Clubs.* New York: G. K. Hall, 1997. Originally published 1922.

Detweiler, Frederick G. *The Negro Press in the United States.* Chicago: University of Chicago Press, 1922.

Douglass, Frederick. *Life and Times of Fredrick Douglass, Written by Himself: His Early Life as a Slave, His Escape from Bondage, and His Complete History to the Present Time.* New reverend edition. Boston: De Wolf, Fisk, Co. (1892).

Du Bois, W. E. B. *Darkwater: Voices from Within the Veil.* New York: Schocken, 1969. Originally published 1920.

————. *The Philadelphia Negro.* New York: Schocken, 1967. Originally published 1899.

————. *The Souls of Black Folk.* New York: Signet, 1982. Originally published 1903.

————. *Dusk of Dawn: An Essay Toward An Autobiography of a Race Concept.* New York: Harcourt Brace, 1940.

Duster, Alfreda M., ed., *Crusade for Justice: The Autobiography of Ida B. Wells.* Chicago: University of Chicago Press, 1970.

Eaton, John. *Grant, Lincoln and the Freedmen.* New York: Longmans, Green & Co., 1907.

Franklin, John Hope, ed. *Reminiscences of an Active Life: The Autobiography of John Roy Lynch.* Chicago: University of Chicago Press, 1970.

Garvey, Amy-Jacques, comp. *The Philosophy and Opinions of Marcus Garvey,* Volume II. New York: Universal Publishing House, 1925.

Gilbert, Hiram T. *The Municipal Court of Chicago.* Chicago: Hiram T. Gilbert, 1928.

Greenbaum, Frances Henrietta, and Amalie Hofer-Jerome. *Annals of the Chicago Woman's Club for the First Forty Years of Its Organization, 1876–1916.* Chicago: Chicago Woman's Club, 1916.

Grimke, Reverend Francis J. *The Lynching of Negroes in the South: Three Sermons.* Washington, DC: 1899.

Hamilton, Green Polonius. *Beacon Lights of the Race.* Memphis: F. H. Clark, 1911.

————. *Booker T. Washington High School, Retrospective Prospective from 1889–1927.* Memphis: Henderson Business College. Reprinted 1985 by Printing Services, Division of Instruction Materials and Technology, Memphis City Schools.

————. *The Bright Side of Memphis.* Memphis: 1908. Reprinted by Burke's Book Store, n.d. Memphis, Tennessee.

Harper, Frances Ellen. *Iola, or Shadows Uplifted.* New York: Oxford, 1988. Originally published 1893.

Harper, Ida Husted. *The Life and Work of Susan B. Anthony.* 2 vols. Indianapolis: Bowen-Merrill, 1910.

Keating, John M. *History of the City of Memphis and Shelby County, Tennessee, vol. I.* Syracuse, NY: D. Mason & Co., 1888.

————. *A History of the Yellow Fever: The Yellow Fever Epidemic of 1878 in Memphis, Tennessee.* Memphis: Howard Association, 1879.

Kletzing, H. E., and W. H. Crogman. *Progress of a Race; or, the Remarkable Advancement of the Afro American.* New York: Arno, 1969. Originally published 1897.

Lowry, Robert, and Thomas W. Henderson, *A History of Mississippi.* Spartanburg: The Reprint Co., 1978. Originally published 1891.

Majors, Monroe A. *Noted Negro Women: Their Triumphs and Activities.* Chicago: Donohue & Henneberry, 1893.

Marquis, Albert Nelson, ed., *The Book of Chicagoans: A Biographical Directory of Leading Living Men and Women of the City of Chicago, 1917.* Chicago: A. N. Marquis Co., 1917.

Meriwether, Elizabeth A. *Recollections of 92 Years, 1824–1916.* Nashville: Tennessee Historical Commission, 1958.

Mossell, Mrs. N. E. [Gertrude]. *The Work of the Afro-American Woman.* New York: Oxford University Press, 1988. Originally published 1894.

Northrop, Henry Davenport. *The College of Life; or Practical Self-Educator: A Manual of Self-Improvement of the Colored Race.* Chicago: Publication & Lithograph, 1895.

Penn, I. Garland. *The Afro-American Press and Its Editors.* New York: Arno, 1969. Originally published 1891.

Pickens, William. *Lynching and Debt Slavery.* New York: American Civil Liberties Union, 1921.

Ransom, Reverend Reverdy C. *The Pilgrimage of Harriet Ransom's Son.* Nashville, TN: Sunday School Union, 1949.

Riley, E. L. *School History of Mississippi.* Richmond: B. F. Johnson Publishing Co., 1900.

Scruggs, Lawson V. *Women of Distinction; Remarkable in Works and Invincible in Character.* Raleigh, NC: Lawson V. Scruggs, 1893.

Sewell, May Wright, ed. *The World's Congress of Representative Women.* Chicago: Rand McNally, 1894.

Shannon, Robert T. *Reports of Cases Argued and Determined in the Supreme Court of Tennessee, Vol. 8.* Louisville: Fetter Law Book Co., 1902.

Simmons, William. J. *Men of Mark: Eminent, Progressive and Rising.* New York: Arno Reprints, 1968. Originally published 1887.

Smith, Mrs. Amanda. *An Autobiography: The Story of the Lord's Dealings with Mrs. Amanda Smith, the Colored Evangelist.* Edited by Jualynne E. Dodson. New York: Oxford University Press, 1988. Originally published 1893.

Stanton, Elizabeth Cady. *Eighty Years and More: Reminiscences, 1811–1897.* New York: Schocken, 1971.

Terrell, Mary Church. *A Colored Woman in a White World.* Washington, DC: Ransdell, 1940.

Washington, Booker T. *Booker T Washington Gives Facts and Condemns Lynchings in a Statement Telegraphed to the New York World.* Baltimore, MD, 1908.

———. *Up from Slavery.* New York: Penguin, 1986. Originally published 1901.

Washington, Booker T., N. B. Wood, and Fannie Barrier Williams. *A New Negro for a New Century.* Chicago: American Publishing House, 1900.

Weatherford, W. D. *Lynching: Removing Its Causes.* New Orleans, LA: 1916.

Willard, Frances E. *Woman and Temperance, or The Work and Workers of the Woman's Christian Temperance Union.* Hartford, CT: Park Publishing Co., 1883.

Wood. J. B. *The Negro in Chicago.* Chicago: Chicago Daily News, 1916.

Young, J. P. *Standard History of Memphis, Tennessee.* Knoxville, TN: H. W Crew & Co., 1912.

Selected Secondary Sources: Journal Articles, Books

Alexander, Elizabeth. "'We Must Be about Our Father's Business': Anna Julia Cooper and the In-Corporation of the Nineteenth-Century African American Woman Intellectual." *Signs* 90 (Winter 1995): 330–342.

Allen, Robert. *Reluctant Reformers: Racism and Social Reform Movements in the United States.* Washington, DC: Howard University Press, 1974.

Alpern, Sara, Joyce Antler, Ingrid Scobie, and Elizabeth Israels Perry, eds. *The Challenge of Feminist Biography: Writing the Lives of Modern American Women.* Urbana: University of Illinois Press, 1992.

Anderson, James D. *The Education of Blacks in the South, 1860–1935.* Chapel Hill: University of North Carolina Press, 1988.

Anderson, Jervis. *A. Philip Randolph: A Biographical Portrait.* New York: Harcourt Brace Jovanovich, 1973.

Anderson, Kathryn. "Practicing Feminist Politics: Emily Newell Blair and U.S. Women's Political Choices in the Early Twentieth Century." *Journal of Women's History* 9 (Autumn 1997): 50–72.

Anderson, Kristi. *After Suffrage: Women in Partisan and Electoral Politics Before the New Deal.* Chicago: University of Chicago Press, 1996.

Angell, Stephen Ward. *Bishop Henry McNeal Turner and African American Religion in the South.* Knoxville: Tennessee University Press, 1992.

———. "The Controversy Over Women's Ministry in the African Methodist Episcopal Church in the 1880s: The Case of Sarah Ann Hughes." In *This Far by Faith: Readings in African American Women's Religious Biography,* edited by Judith Weisenfeld and Richard Newman, pp. 94–109. New York: Routledge, 1996.

Applebaum, Stanley. *The Chicago World's Fair of 1893: A Photographic Record.* New York: Dover Publications, 1980.

Aptheker, Bettina. "Lynching and Rape: An Exchange of Views." Occasional Paper No. 25. San Jose, CA: American Institute for Marxist Studies, 1977.

———. *Woman's Legacy: Essays on Race, Sex, and Class in American History.* Amherst: University of Massachusetts Press, 1982.

———. "W. E. B. Du Bois and the Struggle for Women's Rights: 1910–1920." *San Jose Studies* 1 (May 1975): 7–16.

Aptheker, Herbert. *The Correspondence of W. E. B. Du Bois,* vol. 1. Amherst: University of Massachusetts, 1973.

———, ed. *A Documentary History of the Negro People in the United States: From Reconstruction to the Founding of the NAACP.* New York: Citadel Press, 1951.

Asbaugh, Carolyn. *Lucy Parsons: American Revolutionary.* Chicago: Charles H. Kerr, 1976.

Ayers, Edward L. *The Promise of the New South: Life After Reconstruction.* New York: Oxford University Press, 1992.

———. *Vengeance and Justice: Crime and Punishment in the 19th-Century South.* New York: Oxford University Press, 1984.

Bair, Barbara. "True Women, Real Men: Gender, Ideology and Social Roles in the Garvey Movement." In *Gendered Domains: Rethinking Public and Private in Women's History,* edited by Dorothy O. Helly and Susan M. Reverby, pp. 154–166. Ithaca, NY: Cornell University Press, 1992.

Baker, Houston. *Turning South Again: Re-thinking Modernism/Re-reading Booker T.* Durham: Duke University Press, 2001.

Baker, Lee D. *From Savage to Negro: Anthropology and the Construction of Race, 1896–1954.* Berkeley: University of California Press, 1998.

Baker, Thomas Harrison. *The Memphis Commercial Appeal: The History of a Southern Newspaper.* Baton Rouge: Louisiana State University Press, 1971.

Bancroft, Frederic. *Slave-Trading in the Old South.* Baltimore: J. H. Furst Company, 1931.

Barbeau, Arthur Edward, and Florette Henri. *The Unknown Soldiers: Black American Troops in World War I.* Philadelphia: Temple University Press, 1974.

Barry, John M. *Rising Tide: The Great Mississippi Flood of 1927 and How It Changed America.* New York: Simon and Schuster, 1997.

Bates, Beth Tomkins. *Pullman Porters and the Rise of Protest Politics in Black America 1925–1945.* Chapel Hill: University of North Carolina Press, 2001.

Bearss, Edwin C. *Decision in Mississippi.* Little Rock: Pioneer Press, 1962.

———. "The Armed Conflict 1861–1865." In *A History of Mississippi,* vol. 1, edited by Richard A. McLemore. Hattisburg: University and College Press of Mississippi, 1973.

Beck, E. M., and Stewart E. Tolnay, *A Festival of Violence: An Analysis of Lynchings 1882–1930*. Urbana: University of Illinois Press, 1995.

Bederman, Gail. "'Civilization,' the Decline of Middle-Class Manliness, and Ida B. Wells's Anti-lynching Campaign (1892–4)." *Radical History Review 52* (Winter 1992): 1–31.

———. *Manliness and Civilization: A Cultural History of Gender and Race in the United States, 1892–4*. Chicago: University of Chicago Press, 1996.

Belissary, Constantine G. "The Rise of Industry and the Industrial Spirit in Tennessee, 1865–1885." *Journal of Southern History* 19 (May 1953): 192–215.

Bendroth, Margaret. *Fundamentalists in the City: Conflict and Division in Boston's Churches, 1885–1950*. New York: Oxford University Press, 2005.

Berkeley, Kathleen C. "'Colored Ladies Also Contributed': Black Women's Activities from Benevolence to Social Welfare." In *Black Women in United States History: From Colonial Times to the Nineteenth Century*, edited by Darlene Clark Hine, vol. 1, pp. 61–83. Brooklyn, NY: Carlson, 1990.

———. "The Politics of Black Education in Memphis, Tennessee, 1868–1881." In *Southern Cities, Southern Schools: Public Education in the Urban South*, edited by Rick Ginsberg and David N. Plank, pp. 199–231. Westport, CT: Greenwood, 1990.

———. "Elizabeth Avery Meriwether, An Advocate of Her Sex: Feminism and Conservatism in the Post–Civil War South." *Tennessee Historical Quarterly* 4 (Winter 1984): 390–409.

Blight, David. *Race and Reunion: The Civil War in American Memory*. Cambridge: Harvard University Press, 2001.

Blum, Edward J. *Reforging the White Republic: Race, Religion and American Nationalism, 1865–1898*. Baton Rouge: Louisiana State University Press, 2005.

Bontemps, Arna, and Jack Conroy. *They Seek a City*. Garden City: Doubleday, Doran and Co., 1945.

Bordin, Ruth. *Frances Willard: A Biography*. Chapel Hill: University of North Carolina Press, 1986.

———. *Woman and Temperance: The Quest for Power and Liberty*. New Brunswick: Rutgers University Press, 1990.

Born, Kate. "Organized Labor in Memphis, Tennessee, 1826–1901." *West Tennessee Historical Society Papers* 21 (1967): 60–69.

Boyer, Paul. *Urban Masses and Moral Order in America, 1820–1920*. Cambridge: Harvard University Press, 1978.

Boylan, Anne E. *Sunday School: The Formation of an American Institution, 1709–1880*. New Haven: Yale University Press, 1988.

Braxton, Joanne M. *Black Women Writing Autobiography: A Tradition within a Tradition*. Philadelphia: Temple University Press, 1989.

Brown, Andrew. *History of Tippah County, Mississippi: The First Century*. Ripley, MS: Tippah County Historical and Genealogical Society, Inc., 1976.

Brown, Elsa Barkley. "Imaging Lynching: African American Women: Communities of Struggle, and Collective Memory." In *African American Women Speak Out on Anita Hill–Clarence Thomas*, edited by Geneva Smitherman, pp. 100–124. Detroit, MI: Wayne State University Press, 1995.

———. "Negotiating and Transforming the Public Sphere: African American Political Life in the Transition from Slavery to Freedom." *Public Culture* 7 (Fall 1994): 107–46.

———. "To Catch the Vision of Freedom: African American Women's Political History, 1865–1880." In *African American Women and the Vote, 1837–1965*, edited by Ann D. Gordon,

Bettye Collier-Thomas, John H. Bracey, Arlene Voski Avakian, and Joyce Avrech Berkman, pp. 66–99. Amherst: University of Massachusetts Press, 1997.

———. "'What Has Happened Here': The Politics of Difference in Women's and Feminist Politics." *Feminist Studies* 18 (Summer 1992): 295–313

———. "Womanist Consciousness: Maggie Lena Walker and the Independent Order of Saint Luke." *Signs* 14 (1989): 610–633.

Brown, Victoria Bissell. "Jane Addams, Progressivism, and Woman Suffrage: An Introduction to 'Why Women Should Vote.'" In *One Woman, One Vote: Rediscovering the Woman Suffrage Movement,* edited by Marjorie Spruill Wheeler, pp. 179–202. Troutdale, OR: New Sage, 1995.

Brownell, Blaine A., and David R. Goldfield, eds. *The City in Southern History: The Growth of Urban Civilization in the South.* Port Washington, NY: Kennikat Press, 1977.

Brundage, W Fitzhugh. *Lynching in the New South: Georgia and Virginia, 1880–1930.* Urbana: University of Illinois, 1993.

———. "'To Howl Loudly': John Mitchell, Jr., and His Campaign Against Lynching in Virginia." *Canadian Review of American Studies* 22 (Winter 1991): 325–341.

———, ed. *Under Sentence of Death: Lynching in the South.* Chapel Hill: University of North Carolina Press, 1997.

Buckler, Helen. *Daniel Hale Williams, Negro Surgeon.* New York: Pitman, 1970.

Buckley, Gail. *American Patriots: The Story of Blacks in the Military from the Revolution to Desert Storm.* New York: Random House, 2001.

Buechler, Steven M. *The Transformation of the Woman Suffrage Movement: The Case of Illinois, 1850–1920.* New Brunswick, NJ: Rutgers University Press, 1986.

Buenker, John D. "The Urban Political Machine and Woman Suffrage: A Study in Political Adaptability." *Historian* 33 (February 1971): 267–268.

———. "Edward F. Dunne: The Limits of Municipal Reform." In *The Mayors, The Chicago Political Tradition,* edited by Paul M. Green and Melvin G. Holli, pp. 33–49. Carbondale: Southern Illinois University Press, 1995.

Bukowski, Douglas. *Big Bill Thompson, Chicago and the Politics of Change.* Urbana: University of Illinois Press, 1998.

Bundles, A'Lelia. *On Her Own Ground, The Life and Times of Madame C. J. Walker.* New York: Scribner, 2001.

Burrows, Edwin G., and Mike Wallace. *Gotham: A History of New York City to 1898.* New York: Oxford University Press, 1999.

Capers, Gerald M., Jr. *The Biography of a River Town, Memphis: Its Heroic Age.* Chapel Hill: University of North Carolina Press, 1939.

Carby, Hazel V. *Reconstructing Womanhood: The Emergence of the Afro American Woman Novelist.* Cambridge: Harvard University Press, 1987.

———. *Race Men.* Cambridge: Harvard University Press, 1998.

———. "'On the Threshold of the Woman's Era': Lynching, Empire, and Sexuality in Black Feminist Theory." *Critical Inquiry* 12 (Autumn 1985): 262–277.

———. "'It Jus' Be's Dat Way Sometime': The Sexual Politics of Black Women's Blues." *Radical America* 20 (1986): 9–22.

———. "Policing the Black Woman's Body in an Urban Context." *Critical Inquiry* 18 (Summer 1992): 738–755.

Carlson, Shirley J. "Black Ideals of Womanhood in the Late Victorian Era." *Journal of Negro History* 77 (Spring 1992): 61–71.

Carnes, Mark C., and Clyde Griffen, eds. *Meanings for Manhood Constructions of Masculinity in Victorian America.* Chicago: University of Chicago Press, 1990.

Carr, Carolyn Kinder and George Gurney. *Revisiting the White City: American Art at the 1893 World's Fair*. Washington, D.C.: National Museum of Art and National Portrait Gallery, Smithsonian Institution, 1993.

Carson, Mina. *Settlement Folk: Social Thought and the American Settlement Movement, 1885– 1930*. Chicago: University of Chicago Press, 1990.

Carter, Hodding. "A Proud Struggle for Grace, Holly Springs, Mississippi." In *A Vanishing America, The Life and Times of the Small Town*, edited by Thomas C. Wheeler, pp. 56–60. New York: Holt, Rinehart & Winston, 1964.

Cartwright, Joseph H. *The Triumph Of Jim Crow: Race Relations in Tennessee, 1869–1880*. Knoxville: University of Tennessee Press, 1985.

———. "Black Legislators in Tennessee in the 1800s: A Case in Black Political Leadership." *Tennessee Historical Quarterly* 32 (Fall 1973): 265–284.

Centennial History of the City of Chicago: Its Men, Institutions, Biographical Sketches of Leading Citizens. Chicago: Inter-Ocean, 1905.

Chadbourn, James Harmon. *Lynching and the Law*. Chapel Hill: University of North Carolina Press, 1933.

Chateauvert, Melinda. *Marching Together: The Women of the Brotherhood of Sleeping Car Porters*. Urbana: University of Illinois Press, 1998.

The Chicago Blue Book of Selected Names. Chicago: Chicago Directory Co., 1890–1919.

Chicago Commission on Race Relations: The Negro in Chicago, A Study of Race Relations and a Race Riot. Chicago: University of Chicago Press, 1923.

Church, Annette E., and Roberta Church. *The Robert R. Churches of Memphis. The Father and Son Who Achieved in Spite of Race*. Ann Arbor, MI: Edwards Brothers, 1974.

Church, Robert A., and Ronald Walter. *Nineteenth-Century Memphis Families of Color: 1850– 1900*. Memphis, TN: Church-Walter, 1987.

Clinton, Catherine. *The Other Civil War: American Women in the Nineteenth Century*. New York: Hill & Wang, 1984.

Cobb, James C. *Industrialization and Southern Society, 1877–1984*. Lexington: University of Kentucky, 1984.

———. *Redefining Southern Culture: Mind and Identity in the Modern South*. Athens: University of Georgia Press, 1999.

Coleman, Willi. "Black Women and Segregated Public Transportation: Ninety Years of Resistance." In *Black Women in United States History: The Twentieth Century*, edited by Darlene Clark Hine, vol. 1, pp. 295–302. Brooklyn, NY: Carlson, 1990.

Collins, Patricia Hill. *Fighting Words: Black Women and the Search for Justice*. Minneapolis: University of Minnesota Press, 1998.

Connolly, Harold X. *A Ghetto Grows in Brooklyn*. New York: New York University Press, 1977.

Coppock, Paul R. *Memphis Sketches*. Memphis: Friends of Memphis and Shelby County Libraries, 1976.

Corlew, Robert E. *Tennessee, A Short History*. Knoxville: University of Tennessee Press, 1981.

Cortner, Richard C. *A Mob Intent on Death: The NAACP and the Arkansas Riot Cases*. Middletown, CT: Wesleyan University Press, 1988.

Cronon, Edmund David. *Black Moses: The Story of Marcus Garvey and the Universal Negro Improvement Association*. Madison: University of Wisconsin Press, 1966.

Crouthamel, James L. "The Springfield Race Riot of 1908." *Journal of Negro History* 45 (July 1960): 164–181.

Crowe, Charles. "Racial Violence and Social Reform: The Origins of the Atlanta Riot of 1906." *Journal of Negro History* 53 (July 1968): 234–256.

Culley, Margo, ed. *One Day at a Time: The Literature of American Women from 1764 to the present*. Old Westbery, NY: Feminist Press, 1985.

Dalton, Kathleen. *Theodore Roosevelt: A Strenuous Life*. New York: Vintage Books, 2002.

Dann, Martin E. *The Black Press, 1827–1890: The Quest for National Identity*. New York: G. P. Putnam's Sons, 1971.

Davis, Allen E. *American Heroine: The Life and Legend of Jane Addams*. New York: Oxford University Press, 1973.

Davis, Allison. *Love, Leadership and Aggression*. San Diego: Harcourt Brace Jovanovich, 1983.

Davis, Simone. "The 'Weak Race' and the Winchester: Political Voices in the Pamphlets of Ida B. Wells-Barnett." *Legacy* 1 (1995): 77–97.

Davis, Thadious. "Separating Self from Self-Created Fiction." In *The Challenge of Writing Black Biography*. New York: Hatch-Billops Collection, 1986.

DeCosta-Willis, Miriam, ed. *The Memphis Diary of Ida B. Wells: An Intimate Portrait of the Activist as a Young Woman*. Boston: Beacon, 1995.

D'Emilio, John, and Estelle B. Freedman. *Intimate Matters: A History of Sexuality in America*. New York: Harper & Row, 1988.

Dennis, Charles H. *Victor Lawson: His Time and His Work*. N.p., 1935.

Dicken-Garcia, Hazel. *Journalistic Standards in Nineteenth-Century America*. Madison: University of Wisconsin Press, 1989.

Diedrich, Maria. *Love Across Color Lines: Ottile Assing and Frederick Douglass*. New York: Hill and Wang, 1999.

Diggins, John Patrick. *The Promise of Pragmatism: Modernism and the Crisis of Knowledge and Authority*. Chicago: University of Chicago Press, 1994.

Diner, Steven J. "Chicago Social Workers and Blacks in the Progressive Era." *Social Service Review* 44 (December 1970): 393–410.

Dodson, Howard. *Jubilee: The Emergence of African American Culture by the Schomberg Center for Research in Black Culture of the New York Public Library*. New York: National Geographic Books, 2002.

Drake, St. Clair. *Churches and Voluntary Associations in the Chicago Negro Community* (report of official project). Chicago: Works Project Administration, 1940.

Drake, St. Clair, and Horace R. Cayton. *Black Metropolis: A Study of Negro Life in a Northern City*. New York: Harcourt Brace, 1945.

Dray, Philip. *At the Hands of Persons Unknown: The Lynching of Black America*. New York: Random House, 2002.

DuBois, Ellen Carol, and Linda Gordon. "Seeking Ecstasy on the Battlefield: Danger and Pleasure in Nineteenth-Century Feminist Sexual Thought." In *Pleasure and Danger: Exploring Female Sexuality*, edited by Carol Vance, pp. 31–49. New York: Pandora's Books, HarperCollins, 1989.

Duggan, Lisa. *Sapphic Slashers: Sex, Violence, and American Modernity*. Durham: Duke University Press, 2000.

Dummett, Clifton O., and Lois Doyle Dummett. *Charles Edwin Bentley: A Model for All Times*. St. Paul: North Central Publishing Company, 1990.

Earhart, Mary. *Frances Willard, From Prayers to Politics*. Chicago: Chicago University Press, 1944.

Edmonds, Helen G. *The Negro and Fusion Politics in North Carolina, 1894–1901*. Chapel Hill: University of North Carolina Press, 1951.

Edwards, Laura F. *Gendered Strife and Confusion: The Political Culture of Reconstruction*. Urbana: University of Illinois Press, 1997.

———. "Sexual Violence, Gender, Reconstruction and the Extension of Patriarchy in Granville, N.C." *North Carolina Historical Review* 68 (July 1991): 237–260.

Edwards, Rebecca. *Angels in the Machinery: Gender in American Party Politics from the Civil War to the Progressive Era.* New York: Oxford University Press, 1997.

Eisenstadt, Marvin, Andre Haynal, Pierre Rentchniock, and Pierre de Senarclens. *Parental Loss and Achievement.* Madison: International Universities Press, 1989.

Ellis, John H. "Disease and the Destiny of a City: The 1878 Yellow Fever Epidemic in Memphis." *West Tennessee Historical Society Papers* 28 (1974): 75–89.

———. "Memphis' Sanitary Revolution." *Tennessee Historical Quarterly* 23 (March 1964): 59–72.

Epstein, Barbara Leslie. *The Politics of Domesticity: Women, Evangelism, and Temperance in Nineteenth-Century America.* Middletown, CT: Wesleyan University Press, 1981.

Erikson, Erik H. *Identity and the Life Cycle.* New York: W. W. Norton, 1980.

Faust, Drew Gilpin. *Mothers of Invention: Women of the Slaveholding South in the American Civil War.* Chapel Hill: University of North Carolina Press, 1996.

———. *The Creation of Confederate Nationalism: Ideology and Identity in the Civil War South.* Baton Rouge: Louisiana State University Press, 1988.

Ferrell, Claudine. *Nightmare and Dream: Antilynching in Congress.* New York: Garland, 1986.

Filler, Louis. *The Muckrakers.* Stanford: Stanford University Press, 1968.

Findlay, James F., Jr. *Dwight L. Moody: American Evangelist, 1837–1899.* Chicago: University of Chicago Press, 1969.

Fitzpatrick, Ellen F., ed. *Muckraking: Three Landmark Articles.* New York: St. Martin's Press, 1994.

Flanagan, Maureen A. "Gender and Urban Political Reform: The City Club and the Woman's City Club of Chicago in the Progressive Era." *Journal of American History* 95 (October 1990): 1032–1050.

Folmsbee, Stanley J. "The Origins of the First Jim Crow Law." *Journal of Southern History* 15 (May 1949): 235–247.

Foner, Eric. *Reconstruction: America's Unfinished Revolution, 1863–1877.* New York: Harper and Row, 1988.

Foner, Philip S. *Organized Labor and the Black Worker, 1619–1973.* New York: Praeger, 1974.

Foster, Frances Smith, ed. *A Brighter Coming Day: A Frances Ellen Watkins Harper Reader.* New York: Feminist Press, 1990.

Fox, Richard Wightman. "The Culture of Liberal Protestant Progressivism, 1875–1925." *Journal of Interdiscplinary History* 23 (Winter 1993): 639–660.

Fox, Stephen R. *The Guardian of Boston: William Monroe Trotter.* New York: Atheneum, 1971.

Frankel, Noralee, and Nancy S. Dye, eds. *Gender, Class, Race, and Reform in the Progressive Era.* Lexington: University Press of Kentucky, 1991.

Frankenberg, Ruth. *White Women, Race Matters: The Social Construction of Whiteness.* Minneapolis: University of Minnesota Press, 1993.

Franklin, John Hope. "The Enforcement of the Civil Rights Act of 1875." *Prologue* 6 (Winter 1974): 225–235.

Franklin, John Hope, and Alfred A. Moss. *From Slavery to Freedom: A History of African-Americans.* New York: McGraw-Hill, 1994.

Frazier, E. Franklin. "Chicago: A Cross Section of Negro Life." *Opportunity* 7 (March 1929): 70–73.

———. *The Negro Family in Chicago.* Chicago: University of Chicago Press, 1932.

Frederickson, George M. *The Black Image in the White Mind: The Debate on Afro-American Character and Destiny, 1817–1914.* Middletown, CT: Wesleyan University Press, 1971.

Freedman, Estelle B. "Separatism as Strategy: Female Institution Building and American Feminism, 1870–1930." *Feminist Studies* 5 (Fall 1979): 512–529.

———. *Their Sisters' Keepers: Women's Prison Reform in America, 1880–1930*. Ann Arbor: University of Michigan Press, 1981.

Fryer, Peter. *Staying Power: The History of Black People in Britain*. London: Pluto Press, 1984.

Fuller, T. O. *History of the Negro Baptists of Tennessee*. Memphis, TN: Roger Williams-Howe College, 1936.

Gaines, Kevin K. *Uplifting the Race: Black Leadership, Politics, and Culture in the Twentieth Century*. Chapel Hill: University of North Carolina Press, 1996.

Gaither, Gerald H. "The Negro Alliance Movement in Tennessee, 1888–1891." *West Tennessee Historical Society Papers* 27 (1973): 50–62.

Garner, James W. *Reconstruction in Mississippi*. New York: Macmillan, 1901, 1964.

Gatewood, Willard B. *Aristocrats of Color: The Black Elite, 1880–1920*. Bloomington: Indiana University Press, 1971.

———. *"Smoked Yankees" and the Struggle for Empire: Letters from Negro Soldiers, 1898–1902*. Urbana: The University of Illinois Press, 1971.

Giddings, Paula. *When and Where I Enter: The Impact of Black Women on Race and Sex in America*. New York: William Morrow, 1984.

———. "Ida Wells-Barnett." In *Portraits of American Women from the Civil War to the Present*, vol. 2, edited by G. J. Barker-Benfield and Catherine Clinton, pp. 367–385. New York: St. Martin's Press, 1991.

———. *In Search of Sisterhood: Delta Sigma Theta and the Challenge of the Black Sorority Movement*. New York: William Morrow, 1988.

Giddens, Anthony. *The Consequences of Modernity*. Stanford: Stanford University Press, 1990.

Gilkes, Cheryl Townsend. "The Politics of 'Silence': Dual-Sex Political Systems and Women's Tradition of Conflict in African-American Religion." In *African American Christianity*, edited by Paul Johnson, pp. 80–110. Berkeley: University of California Press, 1994.

Gilmore, Glenda Elizabeth. *Gender and Jim Crow: Women and the Politics of White Supremacy in North Carolina, 1896–1920*. Chapel Hill: University of North Carolina Press, 1996.

Glass, Kathy L. "Tending to the Roots: Anna Julia Cooper's Sociopolitical Thought and Activism. *Meridians, Feminism, Race, Transnationalism* 4 (Autumn 2005): 23–55.

Goings, Kenneth W., and Gerald L. Smith. "'Unhidden' Transcripts: Memphis and African American Agency, 1862–1920." *Journal of Urban History* 21 (March 1995): 372–394.

———. "'Duty of the Hour': African-American Communities in Memphis, Tennessee, 1862–1923." *Tennessee Historical Quarterly* 57 (Summer 1996): 132–143.

Gonzales, John Edward. "Flush Times, Depression, War and Compromise." In *History of Mississippi*, vol. 1, edited by Richard Aubrey McLemore. Hattiesburg: University and College Press of Mississippi, 1973.

Gordon, Ann D., Bettye Collier-Thomas, John H. Bracey, Arlene Voski Avakian, and Joyce Avrech Berkman, eds. *African American Women and the Vote, 1837–1961*. Amherst: University of Massachusetts Press, 1997.

Gosnell, Harold E. *Negro Politicians*. Chicago: University of Chicago Press, 1935.

———. *Machine Politics*. Chicago: University of Chicago Press, 1937.

Gould, Stephen Jay. *The Mismeasure of Man*. New York: W. W. Norton, 1996.

Grantham, Dewey. *Southern Progressivism: The Reconciliation of Progress and Tradition*. Knoxville: University of Tennessee Press, 1983.

Green, Paul M., and Melvin G. Holli, eds. *The Mayors: The Chicago Political Tradition*. Carbondale: Southern Illinois University Press, 1995.

Griffin, Farah Jasmine. *"Who Set You Flowin'?: The African American Migration Narrative*. New York: Oxford University Press, 1995.

Grossman, James R. *Land of Hope: Chicago, Black Southerners, and the Great Migration*. Chicago: University of Chicago Press, 1989.

————. "'Blowing the Trumpet': The Chicago Defender and Black Migration During World War I." *Illinois Historical Journal* 78 (Summer 1985): 224–232.

Gutman, Herbert G. *The Black Family in Slavery and Freedom, 1750–1925.* New York: Pantheon, 1976.

Guy-Sheftall, Beverly. *Daughters of Sorrow: Attitudes toward Black Women, 1880–1920.* Brooklyn: Carlson, 1990.

————, ed. *Words of Fire: An Anthology of African-American Feminist Thought.* New York: The New Press, 1995.

Hair, William Ivy. *Carnival of Fury: Robert Charles and the New Orleans Race Riot of 1900.* Baton Rouge: Louisiana State University Press, 1976.

Hale, Grace Elizabeth. *Making Whiteness: The Culture of Segregation in the South, 1890–1940.* New York: Vintage, 1999.

Hall, Jacquelyn Dowd. "'The Mind That Burns in Each Body': Women, Rape, and Racial Violence." In *Powers of Desire: The Politics of Sexuality,* edited by Sharon Thompson, Anne Snitow, and Christine Stansell, pp. 328–349. New York: Monthly Review Press, 1983.

————. "O. Delight Smith's Progressive Era: Labor, Feminism, and Reform in the Urban South." In *Visible Women: New Essays in American Activism,* edited by Nancy A. Hewitt and Suzanne Lebsock, pp. 166–198 Urbana: University of Illinois Press, 1993.

————. *The Revolt Against Chivalry: Jessie Daniel Ames and the Women's Campaign Against Lynching.* New York: Columbia University Press, 1992.

Hamilton, William Baskerville. *Holly Springs, Mississippi to the Year 1878.* Holly Springs: The Marshall County Historical Society, 1984.

Harlan, Louis R. *Booker T. Washington: The Making of a Black Leader, 1856–1901.* New York: Oxford University Press, 1975.

————. *Booker T. Washington: The Wizard of Tuskegee, 1901–1919.* New York: Oxford University Press, 1983.

————. "Booker T. Washington and the Politics of Accommodation." In *Black Leaders of the Twentieth Century,* edited by John Hope Franklin and August Meier, pp. 1–18. Urbana: University of Illinois Press, 1982.

————, ed. *The Booker T. Washington Papers.* 14 vols. Urbana: University of Illinois Press, 1972–1989.

Harley, Sharon. "For the Good of Family and Race: Gender, Work and Domestic Roles in the Black Community, 1880–1930." *Signs* 15 (Winter 1990): 336–349.

————. *The Timetables of African-American History: A Chronology of the Most Important People and Events in African-American History.* New York: Simon and Schuster, 1995.

Harris, Trudier. *Exorcising Blackness: Historical and Literary Lynching and Burning Rituals.* Bloomington: Indiana University Press, 1984.

————, comp. *Selected Works of Ida B. Wells-Barnett.* New York: Oxford University Press, 1991.

Harris, William H. *A Philip Randolph, Milton P. Webster, and the Brotherhood of Sleeping Car Porters, 1925–1937.* Urbana: University of Illinois Press, 1991.

Hart, Roger L. *Redeemers, Bourbons and Populists: Tennessee, 1870–1896.* Baton Rouge: Louisiana State University Press, 1975.

Haynes, Robert V. *A Night of Violence: The Houston Riot of 1919.* Baton Rouge: Louisiana State University Press, 1976.

Hendricks, Wanda A. *Gender, Race, and Politics in the Midwest: Black Club Women in Illinois.* Bloomington: Indiana University Press, 1998.

————. "Ida B. Wells-Barnett and the Alpha Suffrage Club of Chicago." In *One Woman, One Vote: Rediscovering the Woman Suffrage Movement,* edited by Marjorie Spruill Wheeler, pp. 263–276. Troutdale, OR: New Sage, 1995.

———. "'Vote for the Advantage of Ourselves and Our Race': The Election of the First Black Alderman in Chicago." *Illinois Historical Journal* 87 (Autumn 1994): 171–184.

Hewitt, Nancy A., and Suzanne Lebsock, eds. *Visible Women: New Essays in American Activism.* Urbana: University of Illinois Press, 1993.

Higginbotham, Evelyn Brooks. "African American Women's History and the Metalanguage of Race." *Signs* 17 (Winter 1992): 251–276.

———. "Club Women and Electoral Politics in the 1920s." In *African American Women and the Vote, 1837–1965,* edited by Ann D. Gordon, Bettye Collier Thomas, John H. Bracey, Arlene Voski Avakian, and Joyce Avrech Berkman, pp. 134–155. Amherst: University of Massachusetts Press, 1997.

———. "In Politics to Stay: Black Women Leaders and Party Politics in the 1920s." In *Women, Politics, and Change,* edited by Louisa A. Tilly and Patricia Gurin, pp. 199–220. New York: Russell Sage, 1990.

———. *Righteous Discontent: The Women's Movement in the Black Baptist Church, 1880–1920.* Cambridge: Harvard University Press, 1993.

Hill, Robert A., ed. *The Marcus Garvey and Universal Negro Improvement Association Papers.* 10 vols. Berkeley: University of California Press, 1983.

Hill, Robert A., and Barbara Bair, eds. *Marcus Garvey, Life and Lessons.* Berkeley: University of California Press, 1987.

Hine, Darlene Clark. *Black Women in White: Racial Conflict and Cooperation in the Nursing Profession, 1890–1956.* Bloomington: Indiana University Press, 1989.

———. "Rape and the Inner Lives of Black Women in the Middle West: Preliminary Notes on the Culture of Dissemblance." *Signs* 14 (Summer 1989): 912–920.

———, ed. *Black Women in America: An Historical Encyclopedia.* 2 vols. Brooklyn: Carlson Publishers, 1993.

Hine, Darlene Clark, and Kathleen Thompson. *A Shining Thread of Hope: The History of Black Women in America.* New York: Broadway, 1998.

Hodes, Martha. *White Women, Black Men: Illicit Sex in the Nineteenth-Century South.* New Haven, CT: Yale University Press, 1997.

Hofstader, Richard. *The Age of Reform: From Bryan to F.D.R.* New York: Vintage, 1956.

———. *Social Darwinism in American Thought.* Reverend ed. Boston: Beacon, 1955.

Holloway, Karla F. C. *Passed On: African American Mourning Stories: A Memorial.* Durham: Duke University Press, 2002.

Holmes, Jack D. L. "Underlying Causes of the Memphis Race Riot of 1866," *Tennessee Historical Quarterly* 17 (September 1958): 195–225.

———. "The Effects of the Memphis Race Riot of 1866." *West Tennessee Historical Society Papers* 12 (1958): 58–79.

Holt, Rackham. *Mary McLeod Bethune: A Biography.* Garden City, NY: Doubleday, 1964.

Holt, Thomas. "The Lonely Warrior: Ida B. Wells-Barnett and the Struggle for Black Leadership." In *Black Leaders of the Twentieth Century,* edited by John Hope Franklin and August Meier, pp. 39–61. Urbana: University of Illinois Press, 1987.

Homel, Michael. *Down from Equality: The Segregation of Chicago Public Schools 1920–1940.* Urbana: University of Illinois Press, 1984.

Horton, Oliver James. "Freedom's Yoke: Gender Conventions Among Antebellum Free Blacks." *Feminist Studies* 12 (September 1986): 51–76.

Hull, Gloria, ed. *Give Us Each Day: The Diary of Alice Dunbar Nelson.* New York: Norton, 1984.

Humphreys, Margaret. *Yellow Fever and the South.* New Brunswick, NJ: Rutgers University Press, 1992.

Hutchins, Fred L. "Beale Street As It Was." *West Tennessee Historical Society Papers* 26 (1972): 56–59.

———. *What Happened in Memphis.* Kingsport, Tenn.: Kingsport Press, 1965.

Isaac, Paul. *Prohibition and Politics: Turbulent Decades in Tennessee, 1885–1920.* Knoxville: University of Tennessee, 1965.

Jackson, Kenneth T. *The Ku Klux Klan and the City, 1915–1930.* New York : Oxford University Press, 1967.

Jackson, Philip. "Black Charity in Progressive Era Chicago." *Social Service Review* 53 (September 1978): 400–417.

Jacques-Garvey, Amy, comp. *The Philosophy and Opinions of Marcus Garvey or Africa for the Africans,* vol. II. New York: Universal Publishing House, 1925.

James, Edward, et al., eds. *Notable American Women: A Biographical Dictionary.* 4 vols. Cambridge: Harvard University Press, 1971.

Janiewski, Dolores E. *Sisterhood Denied: Race, Gender and Class in a New South Community.* Philadelphia: Temple University Press, 1985.

Janken, Kenneth Robert. *White: The Biography of Walter White, Mr. NAACP.* New York: The New Press, 2003.

Jenkins, Maude T. "She Issued the Call: Josephine St. Pierre Ruffin, 1824–1924." *Sage,* 2 (Fall 1988): 74–75.

Jones, Beverly W. *Quest for Equality: The Life and Writings of Mary Eliza Church Terrell, 1863–1954.* Brooklyn, NY: Carlson, 1990.

Jones, Jacqueline. *Labor of Love, Labor of Sorrow: Black Women, Work, and the Family.* New York: Vintage, 1985.

Jones, James, Jr. "Municipal Vice: The Management of Prostitution in Tennessee's Urban Experience: The Experience of Nashville and Memphis, 1845–1917." Part I. *Tennessee Historical Society* (Spring 1991): 32–41.

Jones, Peter D'A. *The Christian Socialist Revival, 1877–1914: Religion, Class and Social Conscience in Late-Victorian England.* Princeton: Princeton University Press, 1968.

Jordan, William G. *Black Newspapers & America's War for Democracy, 1914–1920.* Chapel Hill: University of North Carolina Press, 2001.

Kasson, John F. *Civilizing the Machine: Technology and Republican Values in America, 1776–1900.* New York: Penguin Books, 1976.

Kellogg, Charles Flint. *NAACP: A History of the National Association for the Advancement of Colored People.* Baltimore, MD: Johns Hopkins University Press, 1967.

Kerber, Linda K., Alice Kessler-Harris, and Kathryn Kish Sklar, eds. *U.S. History as Women's History: New Feminist Essays.* Chapel Hill: University of North Carolina Press, 1995.

Kilson, Martin. "Political Change in the Negro Ghetto, 1900–1940." In *Key Issues in the Afro-American Experience,* edited by Nathan Huggins, Martin Kilson, and Daniel M. Fox. pp. 167–192. New York: Harcourt Brace Jovanovich, 1971.

Kluger, Richard. *Simple Justice.* New York: Knopf, 1976.

Knupfer, Anne Meis. *Toward a Tenderer Humanity and a Nobler Womanhood: African American Women's Clubs in Turn-of-the-Century Chicago.* New York: New York University Press, 1996.

Kornweibel, Theodore, Jr. *Investigate Everything: Federal Efforts to Compel Black Loyalty During World War I.* Bloomington: Indiana University Press, 2002.

Kousser, J. Morgan. *The Shaping of Southern Politics: Suffrage Restriction and the Establishment of the One-Party South, 1880–1910.* New Haven: Yale University Press, 1974.

———. "Post Reconstruction Suffrage Restrictions in Tennessee: A New Look at the V. O. Key Thesis." *Political Science Quarterly* 4 (December 1973): 655–683.

Kraditor, Aileen S. *The Ideas of the Woman Suffrage Movement.* New York: Columbia University Press, 1965.

Kreiling, Albert Lee. "The Rise of the Black Press in Chicago." *Journalism History* 4 (Winter 1977–78): 132–136.

Kusmer, Kenneth L. "The Functions of Organized Charity in the Progressive Era: Chicago as a Case Study." *Journal of American History* 60 (1972): 657–678.

LaBrie, Henri K., III, "Black Newspapers: The Roots Are Deep." *Journalism History* 4 (Winter 1977–78): 111–113.

Lamon, Lester C. *Black Tennesseans, 1900–1930.* Knoxville: University of Tennessee Press, 1977.

Lane, Roger. *Roots of Violence in Philadelphia, 1860–1900.* Cambridge: Harvard University Press, 1986.

LaPointe, Patricia M. *From Saddlebags to Science: A Century of Health Care in Memphis, 1830–1930.* Memphis: Health Sciences Museum Foundation of the Memphis and Shelby County Medical Society Auxiliary, 1984.

Larson, Erik. *The Devil in the White City.* New York: Crown, 2003.

Lasch-Quinn, Elisabeth. *Black Neighbors: Race and the Limits of Reform in the American Settlement House Movement 1890–1945.* Chapel Hill: University of North Carolina Press, 1993.

Lee, George C. *Beale Street, Where the Blues Began.* College Park, MD: McGrath Publishing Co., 1969.

Lerner, Gerda. "Early Community Work of Black Club Women." *Journal of Negro History* 59 (April 1974): 158–167.

Lewis, David Levering. *W. E. B. Du Bois: Biography of a Race, 1868–1919.* New York: Henry Holt, 1993.

———. *W. E. B. Du Bois: The Fight for Equality and the American Century, 1919–1963.* New York: Henry Holt, 2000.

———, ed. *W. E. B. Du Bois: A Reader.* New York: Henry Holt, 1995.

Link, Arthur S. *Wilson: The New Freedom.* Princeton: Princeton University Press, 1956.

Lisio, Donald J. *Hoover, Blacks, and Lily-Whites.* Chapel Hill: University of North Carolina Press, 1985.

Loewenberg, Burt, and Ruth Bogin, eds. *Black Women in Nineteenth-Century American Life: Their Words, Their Thoughts, Their Feelings.* University Park: Pennsylvania University Press, 1976.

Logan, Rayford W. *The Betrayal of the Negro: From Rutherford B. Hayes to Woodrow Wilson.* New York: Collier, 1964.

Logan, Rayford W., and Michael R. Winston, eds. *Dictionary of American Negro Biography.* New York: Norton, 1982.

Logan, Shirley W. "Rhetorical Strategies in Ida B. Wells's *Southern Horrors: Lynch Law in All Its Phases.*" *Sage* 8 (Summer 1991): 3–9.

Lorimer, Douglass A. *Colour, Class and the Victorians: English Attitudes to the Negro in the Mid-Nineteenth Century.* Leicester, England: Leicester University Press, 1978.

Lovett, Bobby L. "Memphis Riots: White Reaction to Blacks in Memphis, May 1865–July 1866." *Tennessee Historical Quarterly* 38 (Spring 1979): 9–33.

Luker, Ralph E. *The Social Gospel in Black and White: American Racial Reform, 1889–1912.* Chapel Hill: University of North Carolina Press, 1991.

Lunardini, Christine A. "Standing Firm: William Monroe Trotter's Meetings with Woodrow Wilson, 1913–1914." *Journal of Negro History* 64 (Summer 1979): 244–264.

Lystra, Karen. *Searching the Heart: Women, Men, and Romantic Love in Nineteenth-Century America.* New York: Oxford University Press, 1989.

Mack, Kenneth W. "Law, Society, Identity and the Making of the Jim Crow South: Travel and Segregation on Tennessee Railroads, 1875–1905." *Law and Social Inquiry* 24 (Spring 1999): 377–409.

McAlexander, Hubert Horton. *The Prodigal Daughter: A Biography of Sherwood Bonner.* Baton Rouge: Louisiana State University Press, 1981.

———. "Flush Times in Holly Springs." *Journal of Mississippi History* 48 (February 1986): 1–13.

McCarthy, Kathleen D. *Noblesse Oblige: Charity and Cultural Philanthropy in Chicago, 1849–1929.* Chicago: University of Chicago Press, 1982.

McFeely, William S. *Frederick Douglass: A Biography.* New York: W. W. Norton, 1991.

McHenry, Elizabeth. *Forgotten Readers: Recovering the Lost History of African American Literary Societies.* Durham: Duke University Press, 2002.

MacLean, Nancy. *Behind the Mask of Chivalry: The Making of the Second Ku Klux Klan.* New York: Oxford University Press, 1994.

———. "The Leo Frank Case Reconsidered: Gender and Sexual Politics in the Making of Reactionary Populism." *Journal of American History* 78 (December 1991): 917–948.

McLemore, Richard Aubrey, ed. *A History of Mississippi*, Vol 1. Hattiesburg: University and College Press of Mississippi, 1993.

McMurry, Linda O. *To Keep the Waters Troubled: The Life of Ida B. Wells.* New York: Oxford University Press, 1999.

Mangan J. A., and James Walvin, eds. *Manliness and Morality in Britain and America, 1800–1940.* New York: St. Martin's Press, 1987.

Marilley, Suzanna M. "Frances Willard and the Feminism of Fear." *Feminist Studies* 19 (Spring 1993): 123–146.

Marks, George P., III, ed. *The Black Press Views American Imperialism, 1898–2000.* New York: Arno, 1971.

Massa, Ann. "Black Women in the 'White City.'" *American Studies* 8, no. 3 (1974): 319–337.

Meier, August. *Negro Thought in America, 1880–1919: Racial Ideology in the Age of Booker T. Washington.* Ann Arbor: University of Michigan Press, 1966.

———. "Booker T. Washington and the Rise of the NAACP." *The Crisis* 59 (February 1954): 69–76, 117–123.

———. "Booker T. Washington and the Negro Press." *Journal of Negro History* 38 (January 1953): 67–90.

Meier, August, and Elliott Rudwick, "The Rise of Segregation in the Federal Bureaucracy, 1900–1930." *Phylon* 28 (Summer 1967): 178–184.

———, and John H. Bracey, Jr., "The NAACP as a Reform Movement, 1900–1965: 'To Reach the Conscience of America,'" *Journal of Southern History* 49 (February 1993): 3–30.

Meyerowitz, Joanne J. *Women Adrift: Independent Wage Earners in Chicago, 1880–1930.* Chicago: University of Chicago Press, 1988.

Miller, Donald. *City of the Century: The Epic of Chicago and the Making of America.* New York: Simon & Schuster, 1996.

Miller, Kristie. *Ruth Hanna McCormick: A Life in Politics, 1880–1944.* Albuquerque: University of New Mexico Press, 1992.

Miller, William D. *Memphis During the Progressive Era.* Memphis: Memphis State University Press, 1957.

Mink, Gwendolyn. *The Wages of Motherhood: Inequality in the Welfare State, 1917–1924.* Ithaca, NY: Cornell University Press, 1996.

Minter, Patricia Hagler. "Freedom, Personal Liberty, and Private Law: Class, Gender and the Evolution of Segregated Transit Law in the Nineteenth-Century South." *Chicago Kent Law Review* (1995): 1–19 (Lexus-Nexus).

Moore, Sarah J. "Making a Spectacle of Suffrage: The National Woman Suffrage Parade, 1913." *Journal of American Culture* 20 (1997): 89–103.

Morrison, Toni. *Playing in the Dark, Whiteness and the Literary Imagination.* Cambridge: Harvard University Press, 1992.

———. *Paradise.* New York: Knopf, 1998.

Moses, Wilson Jeremiah. "Domestic Feminism, Conservatism, Sex Roles, and Black Women's Clubs, 1893–1896," *Journal of Social and Behavioral Sciences* 24 (Fall 1978): 166–177.

———. *The Golden Age of Black Nationalism, 1850–1925.* New York: Oxford University Press, 1978.

Moss, Alfred A., Jr. *The American Negro Academy: Voice of the Talented Tenth.* Baton Rouge: Louisiana State University Press, 1982.

Mottley, Robert. "Southern Grace." *Colonial Homes,* April 1994, pp. 86–95.

Muncy, Robyn. *Creating a Female Dominion in American Reform, 1890–1935.* New York: Oxford University Press, 1991.

Nelson, Paul D. *Frederick L. McGhee: A Life on the Color Line, 1861–1912.* St. Paul: Minnesota Historical Society, 2002.

Neumann, Caryn E. "The End of Gender Solidarity: The History of the Women's Organization for National Prohibition Reform in the United States, 1929–1933." *Journal of Women's History* 9 (Summer 1997): 31–52.

Neverdon-Morton, Cynthia. *Afro-American Women of the South and the Advancement of the Race, 1899–1929.* Knoxville: University of Tennessee Press, 1989.

Ochiai, Akiko. "Ida B. Wells and Her Crusade for Justice: An African American Woman's Testimonial Autobiography." *Soundings* 75 (Summer/Fall 1992): 365–382.

Olsen, Otto H. *Carpetbagger's Crusade: The Life of Albion Winegar Tourgée.* Baltimore: Johns Hopkins Press, 1965.

Ottley, Roi. *The Lonely Warrior: The Life and Times of Robert S. Abbott.* Chicago: Henry Regnery, 1955.

Ovington, Mary White. *Black and White Sat Down Together: The Reminiscences of an NAACP Founder.* New York: Feminist Press, 1995.

———. *The Walls Came Tumbling Down.* New York: Schocken, 1970.

———. "The National Association for the Advancement of Colored People." *Journal of Negro History* 92 (April 1924): 107–116.

———. "The Beginnings of the NAACP." *The Crisis* 32 (June 1926): 76–77.

Painter, Nell. *Southern History Across the Color Line.* Chapel Hill: University of North Carolina Press, 2002.

———. *The Exodusters: Black Migration in Kansas after Reconstruction.* New York: Knopf, 1977.

———. *Standing at Armageddon: The United States, 1877–1919.* New York: W. W. Norton, 1987.

———. "'Social Equality,' Miscegenation, and the Maintenance of Power." In *The Evolution of Southern Culture,* edited by Numan V. Bartley, pp. 47–67. Athens: University of Georgia Press, 1988.

Patterson, Orlando. *Rituals of Blood: Consequences of Slavery in Two American Centuries.* Washington, DC: Civitas/Counterpoint, 1968.

Peiss, Kathy. "'Charity Girls' and City Pleasures: Historical Notes on WorkingClass Sexuality, 1880–1920." In *Powers of Desire: The Politics of Sexuality,* edited by Ann Snitow, Christine Stansell, and Sharon Thompson, pp. 74–87. New York: Monthly Review Press, 1983.

———. *Hope in a Jar: The Making of America's Beauty Culture.* New York: Henry Holt, 1998.

Perkins, Linda M. "The Impact of the 'Cult of True Womanhood' on the Education of Black Women." *Journal of Social Issues* 39, no. 3 (1983): 17–28.

Phillips, Paul T. *A Kingdom on Earth: Anglo-American Social Christianity, 1880–1940.* University Park: Pennsylvania State University Press, 1986.

Philpott, Thomas Lee. *The Slum and the Ghetto: Neighborhood Deterioration and Middle-Class Reform in Chicago, 1880–1930.* New York: Oxford University Press, 1978.

Pierce, Bessie Louise. *A History of Chicago: Rise of a Modern City, Vol. III, 1871–1893.* New York: Knopf, 1957.

Pinderhughes, Dianne M. *Race and Ethnicity in Chicago Politics: A Reexamination of Pluralist Theory.* Urbana: University of Illinois, 1987.

Porter, Bernard. *Critics of Empire: British Radical Attitudes Toward Colonialism in Africa, 1895–1914.* New York: St. Martin's Press, 1968.

Prather, H. Leon. *We Have Taken a City: The Wilmington Racial Massacre and the Coup of 1898.* Rutherford, N. J.: Fairleigh Dickinson University Press, 1984.

Prescott, Grace Elizabeth. "The Woman Suffrage Movement in Memphis: Its Place in the State, Sectional, and National Movements." *West Tennessee Historical Society Papers* 18 (1964): 87–106.

Pruitt, Olga Reed. *It Happened Here: True Stories of Holly Springs.* Holly Springs, MS: South Reporter Printing Co., 1950.

Qualls, J. Winfield. "The Beginnings and Early History of the Le Moyne School at Memphis, 1871–74." *West Tennessee Historical Society Papers* 7 (1953): 5–37.

Rabinowitz, Howard N. "Continuity and Change: Southern Urban Development, 1860–1900." In *The City in Southern History: The Growth of Urban Civilization in the South,* edited by Blaine A. Brownell and David R. Goldfield, pp. 92–122. Port Washington, NY: Kennikat, 1977.

———. "From Exclusion to Segregation: Southern Race Relations, 1865–1880." *Journal of American History* 63, no. 2 (1976): 325–350.

———. *Race Relations in the Urban South, 1869–1890.* New York: Oxford University Press, 1978.

———. "Half a Loaf: The Shift from White to Black Teachers in the Negro Schools of the Urban South, 1865–1890." *Journal of Southern History* 40 (November 1974): 565–594.

Raper, Arthur F. *The Tragedy of Lynching.* Chapel Hill: University of North Carolina Press, 1933.

Rawick, George P. *The American Slave: A Composite Autobiography.* Westport, CT: Greenwood Press, 1977.

Reed, Christopher Robert. *The Chicago NAACP and the Rise of Black Professional Leadership 1910–1966.* Bloomington: Indiana University Press, 1997.

———. "Organized Racial Reform in Chicago during the Progressive Era: The Chicago N.A.A.C.P., 1910–1920." *Michigan Historical Review* 14 (Spring 1988): 75–99.

Robb, Frederick H. H., ed. *The Book of Achievement: The Negro in Chicago, 1779–1929.* 2 vols. Chicago: Washington Intercollegiate Club of Chicago, 1929.

Robinson, Armstead L. "'Plans Dat Come'd from God': Institution Building and the Emergence of Black Leadership in Reconstruction Memphis." In *Toward a New South: Studies in Post-Civil War Southern Communities,* edited by Orville Vernon Burton and Robert C. McMath, Jr., pp. 71–102. Westport, CT: Greenwood, 1982.

Rogers, O. A. "The Elaine Race Riots of 1919." *Arkansas Historical Quarterly* 19 (Summer 1960): 142–150.

Roper, James. *The Founding of Memphis, 1818–1820.* Memphis: Memphis Sesquicentennial Inc., 1970.

Ross, B. Joyce. "Mary McLeod Bethune, and the National Youth Administration: A Case Study of Power Relationships in the Black Cabinet of Franklin D. Roosevelt." In *Black Leaders of the Twentieth Centuy,* edited by John Hope Franklin and August Meier, pp. 191–220. Urbana: University of Illinois Press, 1982.

———. *J. E. Spingarn and the Rise of the NAACP, 1911–1939.* New York: Atheneum, 1972.

Rouse, Jacqueline Anne. *Lugenia Burns Hope: Black Southern Reformer.* Athens: University of Georgia Press, 1989.

Rowland, Dunbar. *Mississippi: The Heart of the South.* Chicago: Jackson S. J. Clarke Publishing, 1925.

Royster, Jacquelyn Jones. "'To Call a Thing by Its Name': The Rhetoric of Ida B. Wells." In *Reclaiming Rhetorica: Women in the Rhetorical Tradition,* edited by Andrea A. Lunsford, pp. 167–184. Pittsburgh: University of Pittsburgh Press, 1995.

———, ed. *Southern Horrors and Other Writings: The Anti-Lynching Campaign of Ida B. Wells, 1892–1900.* Boston: Bedford, 1997.

Rudwick, Elliott. "The Niagara Movement." *Journal of Negro History* 3 (July 1957): 177–200.

———. *Race Riot at East St. Louis, July 2, 1917.* Carbondale: Southern Illinois University Press, 1964.

———. "W. E. B. Du Bois: Protagonist of the Afro-American Protest." In *Black Leaders in the Twentieth Century,* edited by John Hope Franklin and August Meier, pp.63–84. Urbana: University of Illinois Press, 1982.

Rudwick, Elliott, and August Meier. "Black Man in the 'White City': Negroes and the Columbian Exposition, 1893." *Phylon* 26 (Winter 1965): 354–361.

Ryan, James Gilbert. "The Memphis Riots of 1866: Terror in a Black Community During Reconstruction." *Journal of Negro History* 62 (July 1977): 243–253.

Ryan, Mary P. *Women in Public: Between Banners and Ballots, 1825–1880.* Baltimore, MD: Johns Hopkins University Press, 1990.

Rydell, Robert W. *All the World's a Fair: Visions of Empire at American International Expositions, 1876–1916.* Chicago: University of Chicago Press, 1984.

Salem, Dorothy. *To Better Our World: Black Women in Organized Reform.* Brooklyn, NY: Carlson, 1990.

Sandburg, Carl. *The Chicago Race Riots, July 1919.* New York: Harcourt Brace and Howe, 1919.

Sawyers, June Skinner. *Chicago Portraits: Biographies of 250 Famous Chicagoans.* Chicago: Loyola University Press, 1991.

Saxton, Alexander. *The Rise and Fall of the White Republic: Class Politics and Mass Culture in Nineteenth-Century America.* New York: Verso, 1990.

Schechter, Patricia A. *Ida B. Wells-Barnett and American Reform, 1880–1930.* Chapel Hill: University of North Carolina Press, 2001.

———. "'All the Intensity of My Nature': Ida B. Wells, Anger, and Politics." *Radical History Review* 70 (Winter 1998): 48–77.

———. "Unsettled Business: Ida B. Wells against Lynching, or, How Antilynching Got Its Gender." In *Under Sentence of Death: Lynching in the South,* edited by W. Fitzhugh Brundage, pp. 292–317. Chapel Hill: University of North Carolina Press, 1997.

Scheiber, Jane L., and Henry N. Scheiber. "The Wilson Administration and the Wartime Mobilization of Black Americans, 1917–18." *Labor History* 10 (Summer 1969): 433–458.

Scheiner, Seth. "President Theodore Roosevelt and the Negro, 1901–1908." *Journal of Negro History* 47 (July 1962): 169–182.

Schirmer, Sherry Lamb. *A City Divided: The Racial Landscape of Kansas City, 1900–1960.* Columbia: University of Missouri Press, 2002.

Schuler, Edgar A. "The Houston Race Riot, 1917." *Journal of Negro History* 3 (July 1944): 251–338.

Schultz, Rima Lunin, and Adele Hast, eds. *Women Building Chicago, 1790–1990: A Biographical Dictionary.* Bloomington: Indiana University Press, 2001.

Scott, Anne Firor. *The Southern Lady: From Pedestal to Politics, 1830–1930.* Chicago: University of Chicago Press, 1970.

———. "Most Invisible of All: Black Women's Voluntary Associations." *Journal of Southern History* 56 (February 1990): 3–22.

Sernett, Milton C. *Bound for the Promised Land: African American Religion and the Great Migration.* Durham: Duke University Press, 1997.

Shapiro, Herbert. "The Muckrakers and Negroes." *Phylon* 31 (Spring 1970): 76–88.

————. *White Violence and Black Response: From Reconstruction to Montgomery*. Amherst: University of Massachusetts Press, 1988.

Shaw, Marian. *World's Fair Notes: A Woman Journalist Views Chicago's 1893 Columbian Exposition*. Chicago: Pogo Press, 1992.

Shaw, Stephanie J. "Black Club Women and the Creation of the National Association of Colored Women." *Journal of Women's History* 3 (Fall 1991): 10–25.

————. *What a Woman Ought to Be and to Do: Black Professional Women Workers during the Jim Crow Era*. Chicago: University of Chicago Press, 1996.

Shay Frank. *Judge Lynch: His First Hundred Years*. New York: Biblio and Tannen, 1968. Originally published 1938.

Sherman, Richard B. *The Republican Party and Black America: From McKinley to Hoover, 1896–1933*. Charlottesville: University Press of Virginia, 1973.

Sigafoos, Robert. *Cotton Row to Beale Street: A Business History of Memphis*. Memphis: Memphis State University Press, 1979.

Singal, Daniel Joseph. *The War Within: From Victorian to Modernist Thought in the South, 1919–1945*. Chapel Hill: University of North Carolina Press, 1982.

Sklar, Kathryn Kish. *Florence Kelly and the Nation's Work: The Rise of Women's Political Culture, 1830–1900*. New Haven, CT: Yale University Press, 1995.

————. "Hull-House Maps and Papers: Social Science as Women's Work in the 1890s." In *The Social Survey in Historical Perspective, 1880–1940*, edited by Martin Bulmer, Kevin Bales, and Kathryn Kish Sklar, pp.111–147. Cambridge, England: Cambridge University Press, 1991.

————. "Hull-House in the 1890s: A Community of Women Reformers." *Signs* 10 (1985): 655–677.

————. "Who Founded Hull-House?" In *Lady Bountiful Revisited: Women, Philanthropy, and Power*, edited by Kathleen D. McCarthy, pp.105–110. New Brunswick, NJ: Rutgers University Press, 1990.

Smith, J. Clay. *Emancipation: The Making of the Black Lawyer 1844–1944*. Philadelphia: University of Pennsylvania, 1993.

Smith, J. Frazier. *White Pillars: Early Life and Architecture of the Lower Mississippi Valley Country*. New York: Bramhall House, 1941.

Snorgrass, J. William. "Pioneer Black Women Journalists from the 1850s to the 1950s." *Western Journal of Black Studies* 6 (Fall 1982): 150–158.

Spear, Allan H. *Black Chicago: The Making of a Negro Ghetto, 1890–1920*. Chicago: University of Chicago Press, 1967.

Spelman, Elizabeth V. *Inessential Woman: Problems of Exclusion in Feminist Thought*. Boston: Beacon, 1988.

Spillers, Hortense V. "Mama's Baby, Papa's Maybe: An American Grammar Book." *Diacritics* 17 (Summer 1987): 64–81.

Stange, Douglas Charles. *British Unitarians Against American Slavery, 1833–1861*. Rutherford, NJ: Fairleigh Dickinson University Press, 1984.

————. *Patterns of Antislavery amongAmerican Unitarians, 1831–1860*. Rutherford, NJ: Fairleigh Dickinson University Press, 1977.

Stearns, Peter N., and Carol Z. Stearns. *Anger: The Struggle for Emotional Control in American History*. Chicago: University of Chicago Press, 1986.

Stehno, Sandra M. "Public Responsibility for Dependent Black Children: The Advocacy of Edith Abbott and Sophonisba Breckinridge." *Social Service Review* 62 (September 1988): 485–503.

Stein, Judith. *The World of Marcus Garvey: Race and Class in Modern Society*. Baton Rouge: Louisiana State University Press, 1986.

Sterling, Dorothy, ed. *We Are Your Sisters: Black Women in the Nineteenth Century.* New York: W. W. Norton, 1984.

Stone, James. "The Economic Development of Holly Springs during the 1840s." *Journal of Mississippi History* 32 (November 1970): 341–361.

Stovall, Mary E. "The *Chicago Defender* in the Progressive Era." *Illinois Historical Journal* 83 (Autumn 1990): 159–172.

Stowe, Steven E. *Intimacy and Power in the Old South: Ritual in the Lives of Planters.* Baltimore: Johns Hopkins University Press, 1987.

Streitmatter, Rodger. "African American Women Journalists and Their Male Editors: A Tradition of Support." *Journalism Quarterly* 17 (Summer 1993): 276–286.

———. "Economic Conditions Surrounding Nineteenth-Century African American Women Journalists: Two Case Studies." *Journalism History* 18 (1992): 33–40.

———. *Raising Her Voice: African American Women Journalists Who Changed History.* Lexington: University Press of Kentucky, 1994.

Strickland, Arvarh E. *History of the Chicago Urban League.* Urbana: University of Illinois Press, 1966.

Suggs, Henry Lewis, ed. *The Black Press in the South, 1865–1979.* Westport, CT: Greenwood, 1983.

Syndor, Charles. *Slavery in Mississippi.* New York: Appleton-Century Co., 1933.

Tate, Claudia. *Domestic Allegories of Political Desire: The Black Heroine's Text at the Turn of the Century.* New York: Oxford University Press, 1992.

Tax, Meredith. *The Rising of the Women: Feminist Solidarity and Class Conflict, 1880–1917.* New York: Monthly Review Press, 1980.

Taylor, Alrutheus Ambush. *The Negro in Tennessee, 1861–1880.* Washington, DC: Associated Publishers, 1941.

Taylor, Clarence. *The Black Churches of Brooklyn.* New York: Columbia University Press, 1994.

Taylor, Quintard. *In Search of the Racial Frontier: African-Americans in the American West, 1528–1990.* New York: W. W. Norton, 1998.

Terborg-Penn, Rosalyn. *African American Women in the Struggle for the Vote, 1850–1920.* Bloomington: Indiana University Press, 1998.

———. "African American Women's Networks in the Anti-Lynching Crusade." In *Gender, Class, Race and Reform in the Progressive Era,* edited by Noralee Frankel and Nancy S. Dye, pp. 148–161. Lexington: University Press of Kentucky, 1991.

———. "Discontented Black Feminists: Prelude and Postscript to the Passage of the Nineteenth Amendment." In *We Specialize in the Wholly Impossible: A Reader in Black Women's History,* edited by Darlene Clark Hine, Wilma King, and Linda Reed, pp. 487–504. Brooklyn, NY: Carlson, 1995.

Thompson, Mildred I. *Ida B. Wells-Barnett: An Exploratory Study of an American Black Woman, 1893–1930.* Brooklyn, NY: Carlson, 1990.

Thornbrough, Emma Lou. *T. Thomas Fortune: Militant Journalist.* Chicago: University of Chicago Press, 1972.

———. "The National Afro-American League, 1887–1908." *Journal of Southern History* 27 (February 1961): 494–512.

———. "The Brownsville Episode and the Negro Vote." *Mississippi Valley Historical Review* 44 (1957–1958): 469–493.

Tingley, Donald F. *The Structuring of a State: The History of Illinois, 1899–1928.* Chicago: University of Chicago Press, 1980.

Tinsley, James A. "Roosevelt, Foraker, and the Brownsville Affair." *Journal of Negro History* 41 (January 1956): 43–65.

Tolnay, Stewart E., and E. M. Beck. *A Festival of Violence: An Analysis of Southern Lynching, 1882–1930*. Urbana: University of Illinois Press, 1995.

Townes, Emilie M. *Womanist Justice, Womanist Hope*. Atlanta, GA: Scholars Press, 1993.

Travis, Dempsey J. *An Autobiography of Black Chicago*. Chicago: Urban Research Press, 1987.

Trimiew, Darryl M. *Voices of the Silenced: The Responsible Self in a Marginalized Community*. Cleveland: Pilgrim Press, 1994.

Tucker, David M. *Black Pastors and Leaders: Memphis, 1819–1972*. Memphis, TN: Memphis State University Press, 1975.

———. "Black Politics in Memphis, 1865–1875." *West Tennessee Historical Society Papers* 26 (1972): 13–19.

———. "Miss Ida B. Wells and Memphis Lynching." *Phylon* 32 (Summer 1971): 112–122.

———. *Memphis Since Crump: Bossism, Blacks and Civic Reformers, 1948–1968*. Knoxville: University of Tennessee Press, 1980.

Tuttle, William M., Jr. *Race Riot: Chicago in the Red Summer of 1919*. New York: Atheneum, 1970.

———. "Contested Neighborhoods and Racial Violence: Prelude to the Chicago Riot of 1919." *Journal of Negro History* 55 (October 1970): 266–288.

———. "Labor Conflict and Racial Violence: The Black Worker in Chicago 1894–1919." *Labor History* 10 (Summer 1969): 408–432.

Tyrrell, Ian. *Woman's World/Woman's Empire: The Women's Christian Temperance Union in International Perspective*. Chapel Hill: University of North Carolina Press, 1991.

Wade-Gayles, Gloria. "Black Women Journalists in the South, 1880–1905: An Approach to the Study of Black Women's History." In *Black Women in United States History: From Colonial Times to the Nineteenth Century*, edited by Darlene Clark Hine, vol. 4, pp. 1409–1423. Brooklyn, NY: Carlson, 1990.

Walker, Clarence. *A Rock in a Weary Land: The African Methodist Episcopal Church during the Civil War and Reconstruction*. Baton Rouge: Louisiana State University Press, 1982.

Walkowitz, Daniel J. "The Making of a Feminine Professional Identity: Social Workers in the 1920s." *American Historical Review* 94 (1990): 1051–1075.

Wall, Cheryl A. *Women of the Harlem Renaissance*. Bloomington: Indiana University Press, 1995.

Waller, Altina. "Community, Class and Race in the Memphis Riot of 1866." *Journal of Social History* 18 (1984): 233–246.

Walton, Hanes, Jr. "Another Force for Disenfranchisement: Blacks and Prohibitionists in Tennessee." *Journal of Human Relations* 18 (1970): 728–738.

———, and James Taylor. "Blacks, the Prohibitionists and Disfranchisement." *Quarterly Review of Higher Education Among Negroes* (April 1969): 68–79.

Ware, Vron. *Beyond the Pale: White Women, Race, and History*. New York: Verso, 1992.

Waskow, Arthur I. *From Race Riot to Sit-in, 1919 and the 1960s: A study in the connection between Conflict and Violence*. Garden City, NY: Doubleday, 1966.

Watkins, Ruth. "Reconstruction in Marshall County." *Publications of the Mississippi Historical Society* 12 (1912): 155–215.

Weaver, John D. *The Brownsville Raid*. New York: W. W. Norton, 1970.

Wedell, Marsha. *Elite Women and the Reform Impulse in Memphis, 1875–1915*. Knoxville: University of Tennessee Press, 1991.

Wedin, Carolyn. *Inheritors of the Spirit: Mary White Ovington and the Founding of the NAACP*. New York: John Wiley & Sons, 1998.

Weibe, Robert H. *The Search for Order, 1877–1920*. New York: Hill and Wang, 1977.

Weimann, Jeanne Madeline. *The Fair Women: The Story of the Woman's Building, World's Columbian Exposition, Chicago, 1893*. Chicago: Academy, 1981.

Weiss, Nancy J. "The Negro and the New Freedom: Fighting Wilsonian Segregation." *Political Science Quarterly* 84 (March 1969): 61–79.

Welke, Barbara. "When All the Women Were White, and All the Blacks Were Men: Gender, Class, Race, and the Road to Plessy, 1855–1914." *Law and History Review* 13 (1995): 261–316.

Welter, Barbara. "The Cult of True Womanhood, 1820–1860." *American Quarterly* 18 (Summer, 1966): 151–174.

Wesley, Charles Harris. *The History of the National Association of Colored Women's Clubs, A Legacy of Service.* Washington, DC: NACW, 1984.

Wharton, Vernon L. *The Negro in Mississippi, 1865–1890.* Westport, CT: Greenwood, 1984.

Wheeler, Adade Mitchell. "Conflict in Illinois: The Woman Suffrage Movement of 1913." *Journal of the Illinois State Historical Society* 76 (Summer 1983): 95–114.

———, and Marlene Stein Wortman. *The Roads They Made: Women in Illinois History.* Chicago: Charles H. Kerr, 1977.

White, Deborah Gray. "The Cost of Club Work, the Price of Black Feminism." In *Visible Women: New Essays on American Activism,* edited by Nancy Hewitt and Suzanne Lebsock, pp. 247–269. Urbana: University of Illinois Press, 1993.

———. *Too Heavy a Load: Black Women in Defense of Themselves, 1894–1994.* New York: W. W. Norton, 1999.

White, E. Frances. "Africa on My Mind: Gender, Counter Discourse, and African American Nationalism." *Journal of Women's History* 2 (Spring 1990): 73–97.

White, Walter. *Rope and Faggot: A Biography of Judge Lynch.* New York: Knopf Publishers, 1929.

———. *A Man Called White: The Autobiography of Walter White.* New York: Viking, 1948.

Whites, Lee Ann. "Rebecca Latimer Felton and the Problem of 'Protection' in the New South." In *Visible Women: New Essays in American Activism,* edited by Nancy A. Hewitt and Suzanne Lebsock, pp. 41–61. Urbana: University of Illinois Press, 1993.

Wiegman, Robyn. *American Anatomies: Theorizing Race and Gender.* Durham, NC: Duke University Press, 1995.

Williamson, Joel. *The Crucible of Race: Black-White Relations in the American South Since Emancipation.* New York: Oxford University Press, 1984.

Wolcott, Victoria W. "'Bible, Bath and Broom': Nannie Helen Burrough's National Training School and African-American Racial Uplift." *Journal of Women's History* 9 (Spring 1997): 88–110.

Woodson, Carter G., and Charles H. Wesley. *The Negro in Our History.* Washington, D.C.: Associated Publishers, 1966.

Woodward, C. Vann. *Tom Watson: Agrarian Rebel.* New York: Oxford University Press, 1938.

———. *Origins of the New South, 1877–1913.* Baton Rouge: Louisiana University Press, 1951.

———. *The Strange Career of Jim Crow.* New York: Oxford University Press, 1974.

Wrenn, Lynette B. "Commission Government in the Gilded Age: The Memphis Plan." *Tennessee Historical Quarterly* 47 (Winter 1988): 216–226.

———. "Politics of Memphis School Reform, 1883–1927." In *Southern Cities, Southern Schools: Public Education in the Urban South,* edited by Rick Ginsberg and David N. Plank, pp.81–107. Westport, CT: Greenwood, 1990.

———. "School Board Reorganization in Memphis, 1883." *Tennessee Historical Quarterly* 4 (Winter 1986): 329–341.

———. *Crisis and Commission Government in Memphis: Elite Rule in a Guilded Age City.* Knoxville: University of Tennessee Press, 1998.

Wright, George C. *Racial Violence in Kentucky, 1865–1940: Lynchings, Mob Rule, and "Legal Lynchings."* Baton Rouge: Louisiana State University Press, 1990.

Wyatt-Brown, Bertram. *Southern Honor: Ethics and Behavior in the Old South.* New York: Oxford University Press, 1982.

Yarborough, Richard. "Race, Violence, and Manhood: The Masculine Ideal in Frederick Douglass's 'The Heroic Slave.'" In *Frederick Douglass: New Literary and Historical Essays,* edited by Eric J. Sundquist, pp. 166–188. Cambridge, England: Cambridge University Press, 1990.

Young, J. F. *Standard History of Memphis, Tennessee.* Knoxville: H. W. Crew & Co., 1912.

Zangrando, Robert L. *The NAACP Crusade Against Lynching, 1909–1950.* Philadelphia: Temple University Press, 1980.

Zollinger, Janet Giele. *Two Paths to Women's Equality: Temperance, Suffrage and the Origins of Modern Feminism.* New York: Twayne Publishers, 1995.

Index